DATE DUE

Ronald F. Abler, Geography De

which
are located
appear in th

specific trib

500

0

500

Miles at 40° N.

110

CREEK
NATCHEZ
KIOWA
NAVAHO
WALAPAI ZUNI
MOHAVE
LUISEÑO
G
F.1
C.2
C.3

NATIVE A
AR
A.1 Arctic
A.2 Wester
B. Northw
C.1 Plateau
C.2 Great B
C.3 Califor
D. Greate
E. Plains
F.1 Northe
(Easter
F.2 Easter
G. Ultra-Mississippi:
     Southeast
H. Mesoamerica

The Native Americans

Second Edition

THE NATIVE

Ethnology and Backgrounds of the North American Indians

AMERICANS

Robert F. Spencer,   Jesse D. Jennings,   et al.

JESSE D. JENNINGS
Professor of Anthropology, University of Utah

ELDEN JOHNSON
Associate Professor of Anthropology, University of Minnesota

ARDEN R. KING
Professor of Anthropology, Middle American Research Institute, Tulane University

ROBERT F. SPENCER
Professor of Anthropology, University of Minnesota

THEODORE STERN
Professor of Anthropology, University of Oregon

KENNETH M. STEWART
Professor of Anthropology, Arizona State University

WILLIAM J. WALLACE
Professor Emeritus, Department of Anthropology, Long Beach State College

HARPER & ROW, PUBLISHERS ● *New York, Hagerstown, San Francisco, London*

Sponsoring Editor: Marlene Ellin
Project Editor: Renée E. Beach
Designer: Gayle Jaeger
Production Supervisor: Stefania J. Taflinska
Photo Researcher: Myra Schachne
Compositor: P & M Typesetting Incorporated
Art Studio: J & R Technical Services, Inc.

THE NATIVE AMERICANS: Ethnology and Backgrounds of the North American Indians, Second Edition

Library of Congress Cataloging in Publication Data

Spencer, Robert F
   The native Americans.

   Bibliography: p.
   Includes index.
   1. Indians of North America. 2. North America—
Antiquities. I. Jennings, Jesse David, 1909—
joint author. II. Title.
E77.S747 1977   970'.004'97   76-46940
ISBN 0-06-046371-6

Contents

X

Mesoamerica 445

XI

American Indian Heritage: Retrospect and Prospect 501

XII

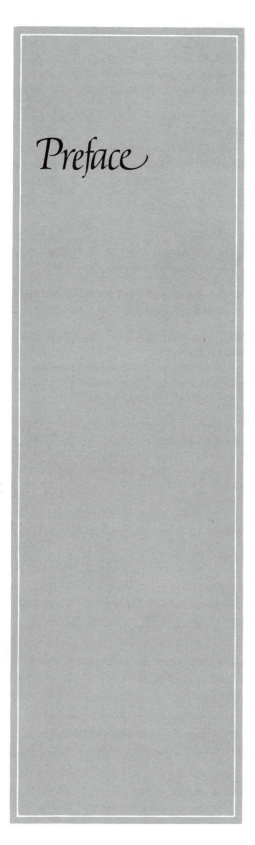

Preface

Perhaps it is impossible to write a wholly adequate book about the American Indian, one which can both meet the needs of serious students of anthropology and inform the layperson of the rich past of his or her country and continent. Not that successful and informative books on the native peoples of the New World do not exist; but in the opinion of the present authors, those that do are either too detailed or not detailed enough. This book represents what we could agree upon as desirable either as a textbook at the college or university level or as an introduction to the American Indian for the general reader.

Because of the complexity of the subject and its vast literature, very few people could be considered expert in the general area; team action seemed to be the best solution. We have tried to follow a direct, critically selective, and generally restrictive plan. Undoubtedly, our selections and our arrangement of topics will be questioned. Our hope, however, is that the defects are not fundamental, and that the omissions are not critical. Regional specialists may be offended by some of the choices we have made and some of the emphases we have assigned. Limitations of space and the need for a fairly rigorous selection have precluded wholly adequate coverage of every New World people and the citation of every competent scholar.

The plan of the book is first to provide perspective in time with the archeological background, followed by general data on an areal scale, and then by detailed contrasting treatment of selected tribes within each culture province. The presentation is in essentially straightforward, ethnological terms. Every attempt is made to avoid highly specialized terminology, but where it is necessary to employ a technical vocabulary, we do not go beyond the scope of definition presented by any of the standard textbooks in general anthropology. Our goal, in summary, is to offer the reader a sense of living cultures in a series of geographic areas and to convey a sense of historical background.

The bibliographic listings are fairly representative, although we do not pretend that they are complete. At the same time, references in the text have been kept fairly minimal. Major references from which materials were drawn are quoted in the essentially standardized way which most anthropological publications employ. These appear in parentheses, with the author's name followed by date and pagination;

the reference is to the dated item under each author's name in the complete bibliography. In addition, because it is difficult to weigh the individual items in an extensive listing, we have offered in each chapter some of the more important source materials relevant to the contents of the chapter.

There is literally no end to the creation of books, monographs, articles, and summaries about the American Indian. In the ten years between the initial publication of this book and the appearance of a second edition, new discoveries have been made and new syntheses suggested. The process is continuous, so that it simply has not been possible to incorporate all of the newest discoveries and the latest data. Some say that the heyday of ethnography is over, that it is no longer possible to follow the primary aim of this book and to lay bare the native cultures as they were. But some Native American cultures are still active and new problems are constantly being raised for solution. In addition, one can go back to the ethnographers who saw the native cultures as they were, and as the techniques of the social sciences expand, find new meanings in old data. The field of archeology especially continues to develop new methods and techniques. New dates and awareness of new relationships come to the fore. Similarly, in linguistics, modern methods permit the recognition of new issues and relationships. We had to be selective and we could not be wholly up to date, but we have taken cognizance of these new elements in the changing picture of the Native Americans.

This book is not a symposium. It has been written with an essentially uniform goal in mind: to describe some important phases in the history and development of the various groups of American Indians and to convey as well some sense of the nature of their cultural systems.

Although we have attempted to bring a scientific approach, interest, and detachment to the subject of American Indians, recognizing that in their many and diverse cultural manifestations they have provided a veritable "living laboratory" for study, we cannot feel uncommitted and uninvolved. Our long-term acquaintance with our subject has evoked great respect and affection. Although we seek to remain objective, it is with some regret that we note the departure of the native cultures, the

assimilation of the Indian into the social stream of Euro-American life. Over the past decade, however, many Native Americans have been rediscovering themselves. They live in the greater society, but Indians they remain. They seem to be building a new self-awareness, and ultimately a new Native American culture may evolve.

We all agree that the dedication of this book is to the North American Indians themselves.

The chapters and other components of this book were written by:

Introduction:
Robert F. Spencer, Professor of Anthropology, University of Minnesota, Minneapolis, Minnesota
Jesse D. Jennings, Professor of Anthropology, University of Utah, Salt Lake City, Utah

Perspectives: (Prehistory and Archeology)
Jesse D. Jennings
    Prehistoric and archeological sections in each area chapter were written by Jesse D. Jennings or in consultation with him.

Language:
Robert F. Spencer

Arctic and Sub-Arctic, Northwest Coast, Plateau, Basin:
Robert F. Spencer

California:
William J. Wallace, Professor Emeritus, Long Beach State College, Long Beach, California

Southwest:
Kenneth M. Stewart, Professor of Anthropology, Arizona State University, Tempe, Arizona

Plains:
Elden Johnson, Professor of Anthropology, University of Minnesota, Minneapolis, Minnesota

Eastern Woodlands:
Elden Johnson—Iroquois and Ojibwa
Robert F. Spencer—Micmac and Huron

Southeast:
Theodore Stern, Professor of Anthropology, University of Oregon, Eugene, Oregon

Mesoamerica:

Arden R. King, Professor of Anthropology, Middle American Research Institute, Tulane University, New Orleans, Louisiana

Retrospect and Prospect: (Heritage)
Kenneth M. Stewart

The Urban Native Americans:
Kenneth M. Stewart

Illustrations:

Archeological illustrations were prepared by Rulon Nielson and Gail Hammond, University of Utah. David G. Crompton photographed the original art and prepared his excellent photographs for transmittal to the publishers. Much appreciation to Herbert L. Jennings for the figures he prepared. Ethnological dioramas and specimens were drawn by Charles Johnston, State of Minnesota, Department of Natural Resources.

We are greatly indebted to the McGraw-Hill Publishing Company for their permission to use the original art work, where appropriate, from Jesse D. Jennings, *Prehistory of North America*, 2nd edition, 1974.

Several museums and state historical societies have given permission to reproduce photographs from their collections. Their assistance and suggestions are much appreciated. Sources of the various photographs are indicated in the captions.

Acknowledgements:

For typing, editorial assistance, bibliographic verification and many other chores, we express our appreciation to Edith Lamb, Ginny Austin, Mary Lukaska, Betty Williams, and Geri Hockfield. Appreciation for a critical reading is extended to Mrs. Jane Jennings.

Robert F. Spencer
Jesse D. Jennings
and Associates

The Native Americans

Introduction

This book is concerned with the most interesting and diverse human population on earth—the American Indian. At that, the book considers only half of the New World and gives attention solely to the Indians of North America. A fascinating story might also be told of the dwellers of the tropic forests, the Andean highlands, and the pampas of the far south in the neighboring continent of South America. Still, the North American account, even if closer to home, is no less striking. The pages which follow attempt a portrayal of the now virtually extinct lifeways of the Native Americans from the Arctic to the southern reaches of Mexico. The authors have asked an essentially simple question: If one lived in one of the societies of native North America before the arrival of things mechanical, of Christianity, of conquest and paternalism, what would one's life have been like? How would one make one's living, what values would one have, what solutions to the problems of living with other men would one have found?

The North American Indian, from the days of Columbus to the present, has been the butt of speculation, he has been misunderstood and misrepresented, he has been simultaneously ill-treated and exploited. One day he has been protected from himself, the next he has been cast off. He has been the object of charity while being robbed of his cultural heritage. Yet out of a plethora of interests, over four centuries of time, there has arisen an enormous literature, one which reflects every view, every bias, every conceivable degree of ignorance and lack of understanding, every degree of hate, fear, distrust, or indeed, of love. The Indian has been reviled and glamorized at the same time. He has been romanticized in poetry, song, and novel, he has inspired clubs and children's play, and has left an indelible mark on the culture of every American, if not of every European as well. But in spite of all the myth and misconception, it is possible to put the Indian into the perspective of history and to arrive at an objective sense of his nature and being. G. P. Murdock's exhaustive list (1975) of scientific materials on the Indian contains some 15,000 entries. These sources, founded in the anthropological and ethnological disciplines, provide the starting point.

The problems are numerous. An initial consideration has been to find some common ground for discussing American Indian life. In addition to the first question posed—what was it like to be an Indian?—there is also the important issue of how the various New World cultures developed. The latter point marks the start of this book. It leads from the ancient record of the Paleo-Indian, the first comers to the New World, to the description of what went before the native cultures as recorded history knew them. These archeological records grow daily more complete as current research fills in the gaps, answers old questions, and poses new ones. From the prehistoric arises the question of what might be called the ethnographic present, a description of the native societies as they were in their heyday before the encroachment of alien forces of change. Except for the suggestions of the final two chapters as to what has happened to the Indian in North America as a result of contact with the outsider, that is, with the "American" of European background, the major concern has been with the untrammeled past. But even in the remote past of prehistory or in the so-called ethnographic present, there was an interplay of forces shaped by the Indians themselves. The processes of culture, of change over time, of invention, of diffusion, of the impact of the natural environment, of bursts of creative energy and periods of stagnation, operated in the Indian past as one native group laid its mark on another or was in turn affected by another. What is suggested as a result is the remarkable diversity of culture across the native New World.

It is this diversity which makes the task of description difficult. The Indian, whatever his origins, was not one single people. It can be said that the beginnings lie in a twofold ecological adaptation—a sub-Arctic and Arctic hunting pattern, and a temperate, tropical and subtropical seed-gathering adjustment. There are those groups which retained the hunting base and there were those seed-gatherers who found their way into agriculture, controlling nature instead of being controlled by it. Indeed, the resulting diversity in culture and way of life keeps alive the keen interest in the American Indian. One need only look at language, for example, considering the great number of separate languages, not "dialects" as they are frequently and erroneously called. The Navaho sheepherder of the Southwest can no more communicate with a Blackfoot warrior than a monolingual English speaker with a monolingual Chinese. And just as languages differ, so also do cultures. One is struck by the military and governmental development of the pre-

Columbian Aztec state in Mexico and yet at the same time must consider that the Indians of the Great Basin, in what is today Nevada and Utah, who by any standard possessed the simplest brand of North American culture, spoke a related tongue. It is legitimate to ask why there should be such a range of languages and cultures, why some tribes are more nearly related, or why some stand out as unique. Diversity exists; it requires definition and description.

Clearly, if the concern were only for difference—ecological, cultural, social, linguistic—bases of classification would be difficult to find. It is obvious that tribes A and B living in different areas, making their living in different ways, speaking different languages, permit explanation in terms of divergent historical factors. Yet tribes B and C speak the same language, have the same kinds of material objects, social structure, values, and live in the same kind of terrain. On this basis one can assume a common history for B and C; but there is still a problem. B and C are not alike in the ways in which they have put together the component elements of their respective cultures, however much these may be dependent on a common history; there are subtle shadings of difference. It seems axiomatic that no two groups of people are wholly alike; an emphasis here, a rephrased and specially interpreted element of culture there, suggest that to do justice to so varied a series of groups as are represented in the American Indian requires detailed treatment of group by group, tribe by tribe, or community by community. This is obviously impossible. Nor is it necessary since somewhat broader and more meaningful classifications can be made.

The concern of this summary of Native American life lies both in ethnology and ethnography. Essentially sides of the same coin, branches of anthropology, the study of human beings, both imply a historical perspective. In ethnology, there is a comparison of the manifestations of human cultures, with an attempt to infer the circumstances of cultural growth and development. One can take, for example, types of housing, compare them in form and structure, note their distribution, and thereby reach some conclusions as to their origins and spread. Such comparisons of these or any other elements of culture, whether in the New World or elsewhere, lead to modes of classification and contain historical suggestions. In ethnography, the task generally involves the description of a single functioning society, and in the case of the American Indians, of the social systems as they were among the many single tribes. A history is also suggested here. Ethnology leads to classification (Driver, 1969). Once the relation of a group of people to others with whom they share a common history is understood, description reasonably follows.

Yet the description varies through time. Comparative ethnology may permit, by the use of an inductive method, conclusions about time and temporal sequences. But there is yet another set of methods made available with the spade of the archeologist. It is axiomatic that cultures change. Over time—considering the introduction of new ideas and cultural patterns, the movement of peoples, new developments, achievements of peaks of growth and subsequent decline—no human group remains unmodified. With archeology, one may obtain some sense of sequence, some awareness of the changes which have led to a conceptual present. It is not always possible to resolve accurately a sequence of temporal development. Yet for each major area of the Native New World it is possible to move down the corridors of time and to obtain some sense of sequence. It is for this reason that the present book, classifying Native America into major geographic, ecologic, and cultural areas, gives attention to prehistory and seeks to resolve the issues of time and space together. If the concern here is primarily with ethnographic description, it is also with the chain of events which have led to the conceptual present. The problem is thus one of classification.

There are several acceptable ways of classifying the complex variety of the cultures of the American Indian. One can, for example, take a general topical approach. This has been successfully done by several eminent students of the native peoples of the Americas. The late Clark Wissler, in his overall summary of American Indian cultures, gave preponderant emphasis to items of material culture, considering the variations among the native tribes of stonework, weaving, work in skins, clothing, house types, and similar material inventions and activities (1938, etc.). He attempted to make some generalizations and to apply essentially the same methodology to nonmaterial elements, considering marriage, ritual behavior, or government. Implicit in Wissler's thinking was the question of historical relationships. He sought to place these various and varying native devel-

opments in a temporal sequential pattern, as some of his researches into specific areas attest. Much the same approach is employed by Professor Harold E. Driver in a strikingly detailed and exhaustive book (1969). Driver's work far outstrips Wissler's earlier effort in its scope and depth. While both writers stress the importance of ecology, the ways in which the American Indian have utilized the resources provided by the natural environment, Driver demonstrates how, given the various areas of American Indian habitation, ecology and material culture can affect and become interrelated with all features of native life, social and political organization, trade, war, or religion. Driver's classifications are not only sound but contain a good measure of carefully weighed theoretical points. One can, through Driver, see the precise distribution of various elements and complexes of culture and at the same time note how the various American Indian groups have responded to the challenge of environment and historic circumstance.

The work of both Wissler and Driver is aimed at specialization. There is another consideration which a purely historical orientation precludes. Again the issue of diversity obtrudes. While it is unquestionably useful to take such a topic as pottery making, or again, of dart and arrow point chipping, and to note variations in materials, techniques, and styles, the conclusions reached by such analyses are somewhat different from those attempted by the present book. While it is true that the archeologist has employed his methods of research to define the origins of the various areas of culture, raising questions about beginnings and prehistoric development and answering them insofar as the data permit, the ethnologist has sought to deal with the living socio-cultural systems of the historic present. Contemporary anthropology has tended to inquire as to the workings of a given culture, viewing the socio-cultural system as a holistic entity in which the parts are definably constellated. Rather than ask where a system has its origins, although this remains most important, the tendency has more recently been to note how the system works.

In the ethnographic sections of this volume, attention has been directed to the latter issue. A selection has been made of representative American Indian groups, each reflective either of a total or of an especially typical segment of it. An attempt has been made to depict the kind of culture characteristic of that area. Where pertinent, parallel groups have been either mentioned or contrasted, the hope being that some sense of total culture area might be forthcoming. It is obvious that while the goal of the authors can to some degree be achieved, there is room for argument as to why this tribe is chosen to represent an area rather than that one. It must be admitted that the criteria for what is "typical" must to some extent depend on accident. The authors have chosen tribes for description which they know either from firsthand experience, that is, actual ethnographic field investigations, or those about which there is an extensive literature. Fellow anthropologists, it is believed, will in the main agree with the choices made.

It is also true that in keeping with the wish to capture the sense of the native culture, its atmosphere, its "feeling-tone," its ethos, some sacrifice has been made. A topical treatment of individual culture elements and complexes is superior in the amount of detail it can provide, even if, by its very treatment, it cannot portray a total cultural system. Here and there, throughout this text, reference is made to a specific item of material or social culture. No attempt has been made to systematize this, however. It might have been useful to go into full detail on such matters as house construction, the nature of weapons, containers, or clothing. Or similarly, kinship nomenclature might have been included in the description of each group. It is not, as will be evident, that these points have been omitted; it is simply that in the attempt to show how the cultural system functioned, these features and many more like them could be viewed only in the perspective of the total array of material and nonmaterial goods.

The problem of selection of ethnic groups to be described, recalling that the present goal is to provide a sense of the native culture of all of North America, has suggested that the description given should relate to a wider area. Several considerations emerge at once. Perhaps the most important is the one to which the present authors are agreed and committed—that of culture area. The concept of the culture area can be viewed as a device for cataloging. Driver makes the point succinctly: "A culture area is a geographical area occupied by a number of peoples whose cultures show a significant degree of similarity with each other and at the same time a significant degree of dissimilarity with the cultures of the peoples of other such

areas." (Driver, 1969:17.) Implied for each culture area is of course a common history. One may assume, too, that for each area there must be a wholly typical group, one possessing the greatest number of traits diagnostic and characteristic of that area. While the ethnologist of today is by no means indifferent to the theoretical issues posed by the culture-area concept, it may suffice to note that for present purposes the culture area can be used as a peg on which to hang some ordered data.

Wissler and Professor A. L. Kroeber (1939) saw culture area in the light of ecology. Wissler, in fact, employs the concept "food area" as a point of departure for the delineation of his culture areas. Kroeber, too, considers that the resources made available through the natural environment put limits on potential human achievement. Hunting-gathering types of culture do contrast with those based on agriculture. The Eskimo exploited sea mammals, the peoples of the Northwest Coast made extensive use of the salmon, the native Californian of the acorn, while the agricultural dependence reached out from Middle America to the Southwest on the one hand and the Mississippi River system on the other. The result in each instance was a distinctive kind of adaptation, one which points up the importance of the human relation to the land and which has implications for the growth of culture. Environment limits, but it does not determine. Land, climate, and natural resources can explain a good deal of why certain groups behaved as they did, but they do not explain the special "bent" of a given culture. They do not explain why the Eskimo chose all but to ignore the not inconsiderable vegetable resources of their region, or why, in the Plains area, some groups chose to remain sedentary farmers while others abandoned the hoe to become hunters of bison on an intensive scale. Here the historic processes of culture building must be taken into account. A culture area is a product of many factors.

The classification of North America into culture areas presents some difficulties. Chief of these is the question of boundary. There are few areas of sudden transition. The result is that a group on the margin of two areas is assigned to one or the other with difficulty. For example, an area frequently defined as the Plateau and generally defined as eastern Oregon, Washington, and British Columbia, bears on its western fringes the unmistakable stamp of the Northwest Coast. Its eastern sections, however, show the imprint of the Plains. A still more revealing example is that of the Yurok, Karok, and Hupa, tribes of northwestern California. Native California had small, separatistic settlements or hamlets which depended on acorns as a basis of subsistence. The Northwest Coast thrived on salmon and developed strong village organization in which rank and wealth become dominant concerns. The Yurok lived in small settlements, used both acorns and salmon, and developed a strong wealth complex. To assign the Yurok and their neighbors to a culture area requires a consideration of the nature of their culture, raising such questions as what they did with their idea of wealth, one seemingly suggesting the Northwest Coast influence. Actually, because the Yurok viewed wealth somewhat differently than did their neighbors to the north, because they seem to have created a special phrasing of the concept, one quite out of keeping with that of the Northwest Coast, it may be suggested that there was basically a Californian type tribe with a diffused overlay of a Northwest Coast concept. The overlay was given a phrasing or twist which created a special and local brand of culture.

Once the particularized focus of a culture area is understood, such questions as the above can be answered without too marked a variation in interpretation. It is evident that there were strong and weak culture centers and it was to this problem that Kroeber addressed himself when he sought to consider the climactic focus of a given area. Ecological and culture-historical forces shape a given area and it follows that a high point of development is reached, a center from which strong, productive influences may radiate. In the chapters that follow, this climax is implicit. Reference is made to the specific tribe serving as an example of an area in its entirety at the point in time when the area seems most adequately typified. The ethnographic present is not therefore always the same. It can be recalled that when Cortez conquered the Aztec nation, the people who were to become representatives of the particular areal constellation of the Great Plains were either semiskilled farmers or gatherers not unlike those of the Basin. Nor was the distribution of the Plains tribes the same as it was after 1750, roughly the time when the horse, so vital to bison hunting and the Plains configuration of war, began to become an integral part of Plains culture. If the concern is with culture area, it

has to be remembered that at some points in time groups of peoples in one area developed a good deal of push, of cultural vigor, markedly influencing their neighbors with their inventive drive and their institutions. Other areas, less strategically situated, less subject to influences from without, retained a marginal character. In terms of the ethnographic present, the Northwest Coast, the Plains, the Southwest, and to a more marked degree at a point further in the past, Mexico, were all vital cultures whose influences go far beyond the definable boundaries of culture area. On the other hand, the native Californians, the northeastern Algonkins, or the Canadian Athabascans, among others, seem never to have possessed the same degree of vitality and vigor.

The problem is an open one but it may be elucidated further by noting how the three anthropologists mentioned have chosen to make cultural subdivisions of the North American continent.

Culture Area Classification
Wissler (1938)
Areas 1. Eskimo, and 2. Yukon-Mackenzie, are linked with Wissler's caribou food area, implying that Eskimo sea mammal hunting is a later specilization. Areas 3. Northwest Coast, and 4. Plateau, are conceptualized as the salmon food area. Wild seed gathering characterizes area 5. California-Basin. Area 6. Plains, is identical with the bison food area. The modified agriculture of the eastern United States from the Mississippi eastward and from the Great Lakes to the Gulf creates areas 7. Eastern Woodlands (Northeast) and 8. Southeast. This, in Wissler's view, is set against the area of intensive agriculture as seen in areas 9. the Southwest, and 10. the Nahua or Aztec (Valley of Mexico) configuration. Wissler then classifies South America, adding five more areas, including the Antilles.

Kroeber (1939)
Kroeber's major areas number seven, with subdivision into eighty-four subareas. The major areas, together with some of the subareas, include 1. Arctic Coast, 2. North, consisting of an Eastern sub-Arctic (Algonkin) area and a Western (Athabascan), 3. Northwest Coast, 4. Intermediate and Intermontane Areas, including the Plateau, Great Basin, and California. For the east, Kroeber sees a total configuration of which the Plains forms a part. The area, 5. East, in-

cludes Plains, Prairie, Great Lakes, Ohio Valley, Atlantic Coast Southeast. Area 6 is the Southwest, while area 7 is represented by Mexico and Central America. Kroeber's subareas are quite detailed, offering great precision and being more indicative of the manifold variation of native American cultures.

Driver (1969)

Driver's classification is a modification of Kroeber's. He lists seventeen major areas: 1. Arctic, western, 2. Arctic, central and eastern, 3. Yukon sub-Arctic, 4. Mackenzie sub-Arctic, 5. Eastern sub-Arctic, 6. Northwest Coast, 7. Plains, 8. Prairie, 9. East (Great Lakes and St. Lawrence to the Gulf, inclusive of the Atlantic Coast), 10. California, 11. Great Basin, 12. Baja California, 13. Oasis (Southwest), 14. Plateau, 15. Northeast Mexico, 16. Meso-America, 17. Circum-Caribbean.

All three classifications have their merits. Wissler's, first conceived in 1917, was a pioneer effort, much refined by Kroeber. For historical and ecological analysis, Kroeber's divisions remain classic. Driver suggests the diversity rather than temporal depth and employs, as this volume does, the culture-area concept as a device for initiating discussion rather than as a classificatory end in itself. The present book, in line with its stated aims, has chosen to let single cultures stand for the greater areas. Implicit, however, is the following culture area division: 1. Arctic and Sub-Arctic, 2. Northwest Coast, 3. West, consisting of Plateau, Basin, and California, 4. Southwest, 5. Plains, 6. Ultra-Mississippi, or East, consisting of Plains-Prairie, Eastern Woodlands, Southeast, 7. Mexico or Mesoamerica.

This classification has its advantages and its faults. While the advantages may lie in giving a fuller account of the social structure and cultural orientations of a particular tribe, some detail on historical perspectives, especially as suggested by a more rigorous culture-area classification, must inevitably be lost. The Antillean or Circum-Caribbean area, one legitimately assignable to South America, has been omitted. The result is to sacrifice for this area, for example, the sense of historical relationships between it and the Southeast, especially as the latter shows some imprint, through the Antilles, of the cultures of the tropical forests of South America. The same point may be made with regard to a number of discernible relationships between other areas. Recognizing that the problem exists, and in some measure to

avoid complete disregard of historical points, attention is called in the text to some of the more significant aspects of interrelationship.

Within an area of essentially common culture, whether a subarea or a major geographic region, lived the various peoples of the American Indian. Convention has designated these as "tribes," although the term has little actual meaning. It must be understood at the outset that the cultures of the American Indian permitted little or no generalization as to what made up a group, a "tribe." Although real property, in the sense of precise land ownership, never assumed too great an importance anywhere in North America, there were some groups with a strong national sense who did identify the group with a defined territory. Some groups were tribes in the political sense, while others saw themselves united with their fellow tribesmen only informally, on the basis of language and community of culture rather than because of any precise unifying institutions. There is a considerable range between the simple socio-economic band and the elaborated political federation. The circumstances of the locality and of the culture area must obviously be taken into account. Tribes existed because of common language, common culture and social organization, common territory and in some instances, common residence in town or village. All such factors are variously operative.

A related feature is the issue of tribal names. Designations vary considerably, partly because of the confusion in defining just what a tribe is, partly through time and historic contact. The names of Indian tribes have depended pretty much on convention; a designation has crept into the literature because a trader, a missionary, an Indian agent, or even an anthropologist found the term definitive and useful. Sometimes the name is that used by the group in referring to itself, sometimes it is the designation, not always complimentary, applied to a group by its neighbors. As is frequently the case among nonliterate peoples, the tribal name can mean merely "man," "human being," and it can be assumed that if we of the in-group are men, those of our neighbors who speak differently and do things differently fail to measure up to a wholly human standard. Tribal names, those stemming from a native language, have been anglicized, gallicized, hispanicized. The result is a fair convention, but by no means a sacred tradition.

The problem of mapping, even if there is agreement on tribal designation and the appropriate orthography, is also difficult. It is made so by the issue of the ethnographic present, the fact that groups moved, as for example, in the Plains, following the advent of the horse, and because in viewing the climactic development of a given area, there must be recognized the time disparity. A map such as that of tribal distribution which is used here is a construct. The most recent and carefully prepared North American ethnographic map is that of Driver and associates (1953). This, with some simplified modifications, has provided the essential source materials for maps appearing in this volume. Boundaries can only apply generally. They are a compromise between legend, history, tradition, and actual observation, not to mention theory. The maps aim at showing tribal territory as it was when the tribe was first observed. Hence, maps do not represent literal truth but rather a compromise and a composite story which has actually taken one to four centuries to unfold.

When several contributors come together, as in the present case, to define and describe an area, they are at once confronted with their special interests, their own research specialties, and their individual biases. While each author entrusted with the task of areal description has been allowed to select his own style and manner of presentation, an attempt was made to strike a common set of topics in essentially the same order. Each section devoted to the description of the individual tribe has aimed at the following:

1. The tribe in question and its neighbors; the place of the tribe in relation to culture area.
2. Its geographical location; its relations to the local terrain, to climate, land form, faunal and floral resources.
3. Historic and prehistoric data. Archeology.
4. Language and linguistic relations.
5. Ecological adaptations; subsistence and material culture.
6. Tribal social organization, including family and kinship, socio-political groupings, socio-economic structure, including trade, types of associations (i.e., non-kin groupings), ceremonial and religious life, world view, and general cultural orientations.

It is the hope of the writers that an overall picture of the major configurations of North American culture, both in the prehistoric past and the ethnographic present, will emerge.

I

Perspective

Objectives

This volume opens with a partial summary of North American archeology in order to provide time depth or perspective. The story of man in North America is not a series of separate episodic and unrelated events but is, instead, a series of interconnected developments occurring on this continent with rare influence from Eurasia. The later tribes or cultures show their origin in relation to, and elaboration upon the earlier, simpler cultures that we know only through archeology. There is, in brief, a long history of cultural evolution upon the American continent readily seen in the archeological evidence. The story is told here in order that the historically observed peoples we call American Indians (a homogeneous variety of *Homo sapiens* restricted to the two Americas) may be understood in historical depth.

The establishment of perspective, which is another purpose of this introductory chapter, requires that history itself be given consideration. Through archeology a culture history is slowly constructed. Such a history lacks specific dates, just as it lacks the names of great men and the details of important crisis events, yet limited as its data are, archeology provides the evidence on which can be built a systematic account of the ebb and flow of human movements across a continent and over a long period of time. In some ways the archeological record may be more revealing than a history based upon documents. In the absence of writing or any other technique for preserving a record of names, dates, places, and actions, which might prove distracting, archeology can make more apparent the broad movements, or interrelationships and blendings, of cultures as they come into contact, either hostile or peaceful, with each other.

It is hoped that this first chapter will serve also to establish the great cultural vitality, as well as the depth in time, of several important historic tribes. The Pueblo, for example, have a known history of perhaps 1800 years. We believe that archeology and linguistics together can demonstrate the presence of the Shoshone in parts of the Great Basin for a comparable span of years. The Woodland tribes of the East are apparently little different today from the way they have been for the past 3000 years; this is particularly true of those tribes in the extreme Northeast, on the East Coast, or in central Canada.

CHRONOLOGY

For history, a chronology must be established; if archeology is history of a special kind, the matter of telling time is crucial. Much archeological work is, and has been, devoted to learning the sequence of culture succession in a given area, either by studying the evidence from one site or by combining the evidence from several sites in a given region or, perhaps, along a river system. By comparison of local sequences, regional sequences may be built. Sometimes the full regional sequence can be observed at one place, for example, in the Plains where the Blackwater Draw #1 site, near Clovis, New Mexico, was discovered in 1937. This was a stratified site, which showed that the Clovis or Llano culture was succeeded by the Folsom culture and that both were overlain by a third stratum containing more recent specimens belonging to what was called the Portales (a Plano type) culture by Sellards (1952). Later, this basic stratigraphy, or portions of it, was observed in other places in the Plains. What is now recognized as the whole regional sequence is essentially the one observed at Blackwater Draw (T. R. Hester, 1973). Another example of a regional chronology can be seen in New York State where many years' work was needed to identify the following culture succession: Earliest is the Lamoka, upon it is the Laurentian, followed in turn by the Middlesex, Hopewellian, Point Peninsula, and Owasco cultures. The latest two cultures in the sequence are the historic Iroquois and Algonquin known to us from numerous sites and from ethnology.

Since neither of these regional chronologies tells us anything about exact time, we are faced with the questions of how time's passage can be measured in the absence of written records, and how a regional sequence can be put together. Of course, there are two *kinds* of time that can be established: (1) *Relative* time—the two sequences above are examples—simply establishes that some phenomenon, culture, or object is earlier, or later, than some other phenomenon, object, or culture. (2) But in an *absolute* chronology, fixed dates in the Gregorian calendar are assigned to archeological specimens or layers. If they can be learned, absolute dates are final. Sometimes, absolute dates can be assigned to part of a sequence. For example, if a historic Natchez village were excavated, the upper layer would be likely to contain French metal and objects of china. From evidence in historic documents, a fairly positive date span of A.D. 1699 to 1731 could be assigned to this layer. If there were very similar collections below this upper layer, which lacked only metal or other evidence of European trade, it would be reasonable to assign a date slightly earlier than 1699 to these second, deeper deposits. If, underlying the second deposit, there were still a third complex of artifacts differing from the first two, it would be assigned to the lowest and first place in the local site stratigraphy, but about its actual age, all that could be said is that the deepest layer is older than the other two. How much older must be deduced from, or arrived at, on grounds other than simple stratigraphy.

Until recently, most regional sequences were entirely of the relative sort. Although the full cultural succession of a large region is rarely demonstrated at a single site, as it was at Blackwater Draw in Mexico, a reliable and accurate relative chronology can be built on the basis of artifact likeness from site to site. Obviously it is possible to synthesize a regional stratigraphy from the evidence of a series of stratified sites which have no fixed or absolute dates. The cultural succession can be known, but the length of time required to achieve this cultural shift or build this sequence cannot be established by such comparisons.

In addition to this basic, relative chronology, which can be derived from stratigraphy, fixed dates can sometimes be assigned; two powerful chronometric methods for doing so are available to archeologists (Michels, 1973). Both are well known. The one most widely used is the measurement of radioactive decay in radiocarbon, a method that works with organic materials of many kinds—wood and plants, bone, antler, and shell for example.

Radiocarbon. Introduced in 1951, the technique involves measuring radioactive carbon, or carbon 14. Cosmic ray bombardment of the upper atmosphere results in the conversion of nitrogen 14 into radioactive carbon. The carbon atoms thus formed unite with oxygen in the atmosphere to form radioactive carbon dioxide molecules which circulate uniformly throughout the biosphere. Living plants take up both inert and radioactive carbon dioxide and utilize both in the manufacture of carbohydrates needed for growth. When the plant tissue is eaten by animals radioactive and inert carbon are incorporated in the animal tissue. Human beings, who

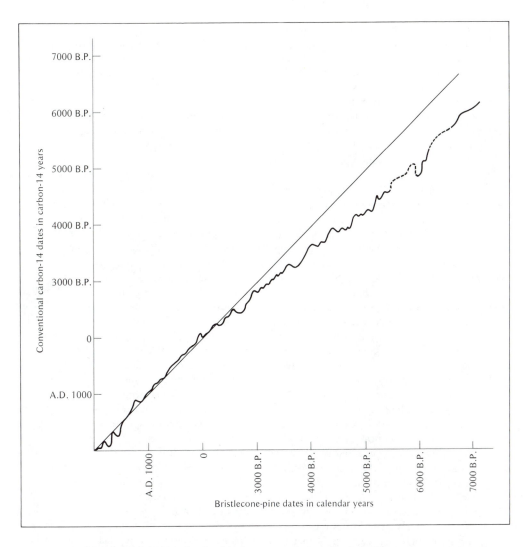

Figure 1 ● Radiocarbon lag behind calendrical time. (After Renfrew, 1971; Jennings, 1974:17)

eat both plants and animals, take in radioactive, as well as inert, carbohydrates. Hence, all organic specimens have within them an amount of radioactive carbon comparable to, or in balance with, that in the biosphere. When a plant or animal dies, the intake of carbon ceases, but decay continues. It has been established that the carbon 14 atom has a half-life of 5568, plus or minus 30 years. After the rate of decay per minute was calculated for carbon in newly dead modern organic material, it became possible to determine the age of any given archeological specimen by measuring its present radiations to discover how much radiocarbon remained. After the assumptions and tech-

niques involved in the process were tested, radiocarbon dates were first released in 1951. Since that time several thousand such dates have been derived for old organic material from all parts of the world.

Although a carbon sample can be contaminated in a variety of ways, either with inert carbon or with fresher radiocarbon, and many precautions must be observed against field contamination, it is apparently possible to derive very accurate absolute dates from such organic material as wood, charcoal, bone, horn, and shell. Soft body tissues, where preserved, may also yield sufficient carbon to make radiocarbon tests possible.

Several radiocarbon laboratories, now operating in various parts of the world, are utilized for many research purposes. Incidental to their other research objectives, these laboratories have dated many archeological sites, as well as geological locations and events. Even though there are hazards to reliance on their complete accuracy, including various kinds of sample contamination in the ground before discovery, during the recovery, and in the laboratory, selected radiocarbon dates are regarded as valid for purposes of this account because they are often the best clue to antiquity and chronologic relationships available.

Dendrochronology. The most accurate dating technique is dendrochronology or tree-ring dating, which was first developed in the American Southwest and then found to be applicable in other areas of the world. In concept, the dendrochronological or tree-ring calandar is really very simple. It is based on the well-established fact that in areas of limited rainfall, certain species of plants deposit annual growths, differing in width in direct relation to moisture available. (Winter precipitation is believed to be more important to tree growth than summer rain.) Yellow Pine, a southwestern tree of wide distribution, will lay down very broad growth rings in good, or wetter-than-average, years and will lay down little or no growth in extremely dry years. "Normal" years have growth rings of essentially identical size. The key to utilization of the tree-ring calandar is the alteration of very broad and very narrow rings. Because most droughts and most good seasons are regionwide, all trees living at the same time will put down similar rings; wide ones in good years and very narrow, sometimes microscopic, ones for exceedingly dry years. It is therefore possible to date trees from various places by matching the very wide and the very narrow marker rings. Archeological specimens can be matched against the master regional chart, which has been established for the span from 2000 B.P. (before the present) to the twentieth century: a tree matched to the chart is absolutely dated.

Although several other techniques for dating are available to archeologists, they are not listed here because the basic methods, in addition to stratigraphy, are radiocarbon assays and dendrochronology, which are the most precise of all for those limited areas where it is applicable.

HISTORY OF AMERICAN ARCHEOLOGY

Although Indians have been a source of interest, study, and speculation since the discovery of the continents, for a long time the study of the prehistory of North America was somehow not regarded as a study of the American Indians. The prehistoric monuments, such as burial mounds, cemeteries, ruined cliff dwellings, and midden areas were not considered to be related to Indian history; instead, they were thought to be relics of some ancient vanished race. Indeed the application of scientific methods to the study of antiquities in America is only about 150 years old. Scientific interest (or indeed any interest) in the history of the two American continents before their settlement by Europeans is little more than a corollary of the development of science and of a general scholarly concern with the long adventure of human beings on the earth. Curiosity about the Indians, their origins, language, and behavior began in 1492, long before the viewpoint that we call science existed in its modern form. It is not surprising that the new bronze race, called Indian, was explained within the limits of informed thought of the period when they were first encountered. At that time the tendency to explain natural phenomena in religious terms can be understood when one considers that knowledge of the exotic was vested in the churchmen, who alone were learned.

The hardiest, most popular explanations, and the one for which no shred of evidence exists, is that the red Americans were descended from Hebrew migrants. This myth remains healthy even today (Wauchope, 1962; Huddleston, 1967), and some have even invoked vast fleets of ships and feats of daring in sailing them to bolster the conviction that Palestinian, or other migrants from the Near East, settled the two American continents. But the Hebrews, as revealed in the Bible, are well known to have been herders, vineyard tenders, and small-scale farmers as far back as Biblical history goes. Such a background would make it not only remarkable but incredible that their seamanship could be so advanced that they could sail into uncharted waters thousands of years ahead of Columbus. And, of course, neither scientific archeology nor linguistics nor botany nor biology offer any support for this old and hardy but nonsensical legend.

Not nearly so farfetched, but equally unsupported so far by evidence, are the notions that the Welsh, Scandinavians, or Phoenicians, famous mariners of the centuries after and before Christ, fathered the various tribes in America. Other theories about the peopling of the Americans also have very hardy and deep roots. One belief is that mythological continents, especially those called Atlantis and Mu, existed in the vast stretches of the Atlantic and Pacific and that these now sunken continents once provided land bridges by means of which the Americans were peopled from the Old World.

The simpler view first offered in 1589 by Joseph de Acosta (see Jarco, 1959; Huddleston, 1967), who based it on what are now considered all the right reasons, is that a migration into this country from Eurasia happened early and that many of the developments in the two Americas are indigenous ones; this explanation has more archeologic and logical support than any of the others. Without a detailed proof, it can be stated that the assumption of ingress via a land bridge between Eurasia and North America is the theory generally accepted today.

Certain ideas having their origin in religion led to interpretations that there could be no connection between any group alive in historic time and the thousands of mounds, burial grounds, ancient villages, which stud the river valleys of the East, or the mud and stone castles of the great Southwest. Lacking a scientific approach to the facts of human history and wishing to remain inside the bonds of religious orthodoxy, some people (as recently as 75 years ago) believed that the prehistoric remains on the continent belonged to a mythical golden age before man was vile and sinful.

The effect of such myths is that Indians today can still be denied the universal biological right to local ancestors, a condition difficult to believe when one considers the work of the many dedicated scholars who have contributed to replace myth with evidence. Thomas's (1894) researches and Powell's (1894) well-known examination of the myths of Indian origins, which were held by the American white populations of the late nineteenth century, cleared the way for the modern archeologist. These men can be credited with scientific breakthrough, for the scientific study of prehistory could proceed only when the unfounded notion of a time break, between those cultures represented in the prehistoric monuments and those Indian cultures alive during the past four centuries, could be eradicated.

Although Powell and Thomas, a Bureau of American Ethnology scientist, wrote in the late 1800s, it was not until 1930 that American archeology finally abandoned antiquarianism, an approach which had neither problems nor

perspective. There was one exception in the fifty years of intensive but disorganized work by romantic scholars in the restricted and specialized area of the American Southwest. Before 1920, A. V. Kidder and A. L. Kroeber had developed a sense of problem and were making a systematic attack upon the problems. Refinement of the disorganized work in the Southwest resulted by 1950 from the efforts of E. H. Morris, F. H. H. Roberts, Jr., Harold Gladwin, Emil Haury, and Erik Reed, among others.

Much earlier, study of the earthworks of the eastern half of the continent had begun, for example, Thomas Jefferson himself excavated an earthen mound and reported his findings. In the early stages of mound exploration between 1820 and 1920 the important figures were such men as E. G. Squier, E. H. Davis, Cyrus Thomas and W. Powell (already mentioned), and Henry C. Shetrone. Despite the quantity of work until 1930 most Anglo-American archeological data were chaotic and discrete. Writing was general, descriptive, and romantic. The technique of comparison with other sites (whether distant or adjacent) was not yet in common or systematic use. Stratigraphy, upon which all relative chronology is ultimately based, was not often observed; even if artifacts from the various strata were kept separate, these divisions were almost ignored in interpretation. Field techniques were far from adequate. Until Cyrus Thomas wrote, the reports often concerned vanished races of giants, lost tribes, or lost arts rather than cultural connections or time/space relationships. In the 1930s, however, a classification system called the Midwest taxonomic was devised. William C. McKern (1939) is credited with the major work on the scheme, which operated just as biological classification does; its objective was the establishment of degrees of similarity between collections of data. Although time/space problems were explicitly ignored, the similarities that were discovered through comparisons made time and space inferences immediately possible. The system was espoused by all leaders in the fields of eastern and middle western archeological study, with the result that tremendous progress could be made in the organizing of archeological material.

Scientific progress after 1930 was, however, not limited to classification. Under the leadership of Fay-Cooper Cole, Alfred Guthe, and others, the techniques of digging and recording were greatly improved. Excavators became conscious of the need for exact and painstaking records. Stratigraphic evidence was noted; the segregation of specimens by precise provenience was kept constantly in mind. More maps, sketches, photographs, and written observations were made routine in excavation technique. One result of this technical improvement was that Cole and Deuel (1937), in an epoch-making study of Fulton County, Illinois, established the basic chronological sequence of Middle Western cultures as discovered in the area. Although the work of Cole and Deuel has been modified, it has not been challenged to date. Obviously, greater technical care resulted in more, and more exact, information: more precision in analysis was, therefore, possible. By 1950 it was possible to say that archeological technique was more advanced than archeological interpretation.

Beginning with the 1950s, theory has become increasingly important in archeology. A small but vocal group are convinced that archeological data can be understood and interpreted to provide explanations of culture process that would be as powerful and useful as the explanations generated in the physical sciences. Some of their claims are overoptimistic, but their self-conscious aim to contribute to anthropological theory can only be applauded. Their interest lies in discovering and explaining process (culture change) and in extending in other ways the usefulness of recorded culture history.

It can be seen that Anglo-American archeology has moved through four distinct phases. First, one that can be characterized as antiquarian or romantic, with a flat prehistoric landscape and disorganized data, lasted until about 1920. Next, systematic and improved techniques began to interest scholars by 1930. Since that date, classification of data and the development of regional chronology went on very rapidly alongside increased recognition and improved description of prehistoric cultures. Then, in the 1940s it became possible to undertake syntheses of regional data, and this concern with synthesis marks the third phase—the beginning of maturity for Anglo-American archeology—and makes possible an attempt, such as this, to tell a connected, coherent story which can rightly be called culture history. In the middle 1950s a phase developed, which continues to attract students; its prime objective is the gathering and statistical analysis of new information.

Several valuable studies of North American prehistory can be recommended for those who desire more detail: These are Fitting (1973), Hallowell (1960), Jennings (1974), Schuyler (1971), Willey (1968), and Willey and Sabloff (1974).

IN THE BEGINNING

Because one purpose of this chapter is to provide a brief account of the beginnings of the American Indian experience in the New World/Western Hemisphere, we must look to a time more than 25,000 years ago when Asia and North America were joined by a broad land bridge which formed part of a province called Beringia (Fig. 2). A broad flat plain, now under the shallow waters of the Bering Sea, was exposed every time the glacial ice masses reached their maximum extent during the Pleistocene or Ice Ages (See Fig. 3), utilizing more of the available water and causing a consequent lowering of sea level. When fully exposed, this portion of Beringia was over 1000 miles wide. It is presumed to have supported a tundra vegetation where Arctic fauna, particularly the caribou, flourished. Across this tundra, the forbears of the Native Americans moved in pursuit of the game animals, or following the beaches for their rich marine fauna, or deriving sustenance from both.

Nearly all of Alaska was also open at this time, for the glacial ice was restricted to the northern and southern mountain ranges. Thus, most of interior Alaska, and even parts of western Yukon Territory, were included in Beringia. The Alaskan Refuge, as the ice-free area (Fig. 4) was called, was a cul-de-sac, blocked on the east by the Cordilleran ice mass, which extended from the Canadian Rockies eastward toward central Canada. Perhaps the Refuge was never completely blocked off from the rest of North America; geologists are not certain because they have not established the timing of the contraction and expansion of the central Canadian (or Laurentian) ice sheet with respect

Figure 2 ● (top) Three comparative chronologies and the exposure of Beringia during oscillations of the ice mass. (Modified from Haynes, 1969; Hopkins, 1959; Hough, 1958; Jennings, 1974:65)

Figure 3 ● (bottom) Extension of North American shorelines resulting from lowered seas during the second major Wisconsin glaciations. Note land "bridge" across the Bering Strait. (Modified from Haag, 1962; Jennings, 1974:49)

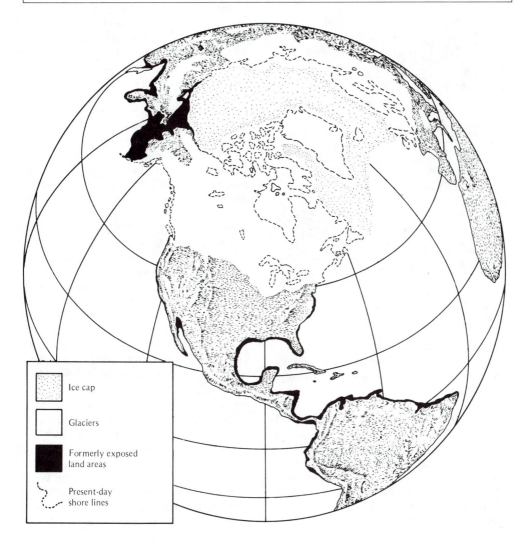

Years ago	Hopkins chronology	Hough chronology	Haynes chronology
8,000	7.	Cochrane	
	6. Valders	Valders	Valders
10,500	5. Mankato	Two Creeks interval Port Huron (Mankato)	Two Creeks interval
	4. Cary	Cary	Woodford
20,000	3. Tazewell	Bloomington (late Tazewell)	
	2. Iowan	Shelbyville-Iowan (early Tazewell)	
25,000	1. Farmdale	Farmdale	Farmdale

Ice cap

Glaciers

Formerly exposed land areas

Present-day shore lines

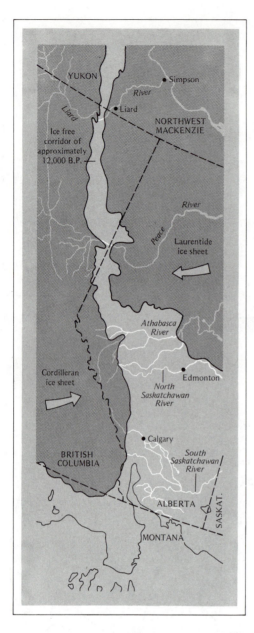

Figure 4 ● Ice masses at 12,000 B.P. showing ice-free corridor. It is believed that the corridor never again closed. (After Prest, 1969; Jennings, 1974:101)

to the waning and waxing of the separate Cordilleran ice mass. If both ice masses expanded simultaneously, their edges surely overlapped and closed all pathways to the south. If the spreading movements were not synchronized, it is possible that a narrow ice-free corridor (Fig. 4) existed often, if not all the time, from about 27,000 or 28,000 years ago until 12,000

B.P. (before the present) when both ice sheets began their final retreat.

The geographic description of a land bridge open for a span of years, across which migration occurred, is supported by the general agreement among thoughtful scientists that the American Indian comprises a distinctive population, closer in physical type to the Mongoloid Asiatic populations than to any other. To state flatly that the American Indian is a Mongoloid variant is more conclusive than the evidence warrants. More accurately one can say that the "founders"—the first Asiatic migrants to enter the Refuge—were of the same *Homo sapiens* stock that evolved into the modern Mongoloid strain. Thus, although the Mongoloids of Asia and the American Indians are genetically related, the genetic drift, mutations, isolation, and environmental selection processes, operated differently in the two hemispheres to produce two quite different populations. Among other things, the American Indian physical type is more homogeneous than the Asian one (except for the Eskimo and Aleut who migrated much later). Greater homogeneity on the American continent probably results from the small number of original settlers, who provided a "founding" gene pool. Moreover, when water from the melting ice raised world sea level to the height which it maintains at present, the sea reclaimed the Bering land bridge and further contact or infusion of other genetic material dwindled or ceased altogether. This was not the case for the Mongoloid population in Asia, where intrusion or addition to the gene pool was still possible from the rest of the continent.

Because there is a lack of human skeletal evidence from earliest times, no description of the physical attributes of the Americans of 25,000 years ago can be offered. Their descendants, today's native Americans, however, can be described in general terms. The description, paraphrased from Stewart (1960) and Hulse (1963), as described by Jennings (1974), must be taken as *general*; there are variations as there are in any population which is spread over such an enormous expanse of land that segments are effectively isolated from each other. Generally, then, the American Indian of both sexes is of stocky rather than gracile build regardless of overall stature, which may be either short or tall. The degree of skin pigmentation is less than can be seen in the Old World, but the ability to tan is exceptionally high. The eyes are dark, the hair is coarse and straight, and body

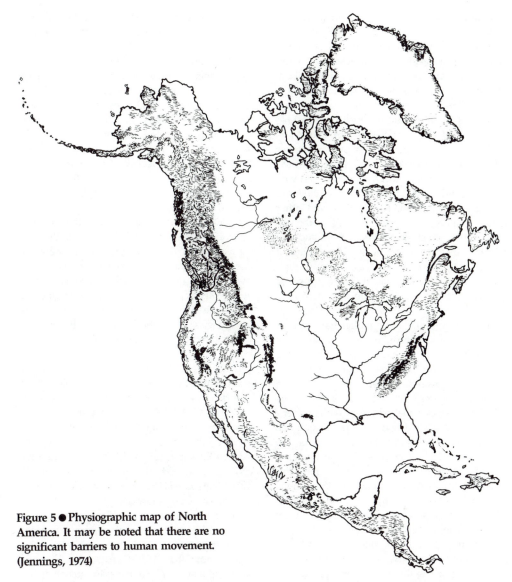

Figure 5 ● Physiographic map of North America. It may be noted that there are no significant barriers to human movement. (Jennings, 1974)

hair is scant in both sexes. Females often have the Mongoloid fold; incisor teeth are distinctive in the frequency of the shovel shape. Blood types A^2, B, D , and r are lacking. The sickle-cell anomaly is not found in Indian blood. The Indian male is rarely bald and rarely becomes gray in old age. Certain hair-whorl patterns and distinctive fingerprint patterns are known.

This description is not thought, however, to depict accurately the first Americans because the modern Indians it does describe represent the end product of, perhaps, 25,000 years of evolution from a parent stock, not the parent stock itself. Nothing entirely trustworthy can be said about the physical type of the very earliest arrivals because there have been no skeletal

finds. Several theories of what the earliest settlers were like have been offered by thoughtful scholars who have examined the possibilities; their conclusions remain conjectural, even though they are logical/persuasive. Birdsell (1951) thinks the modern evidence justifies the conclusion that the migration took place at a period when the Mongoloid population was just beginning to evolve from a generalized, primitive, vaguely Caucasoid stock which characterized eastern Asia at the time. To a degree, the enclaved Ainu of northern Japan exemplify the physical type he envisions as the original. Neumann (1952), working with skeletal remains of American populations of the past 5000 or 6000 years, also recognized that the earliest individuals would not closely resemble today's Indians.

Two American skeletal fragments recovered from archeological situations at least 9000 years old are fully credible and have been described. Claims of antiquity have been made for perhaps a dozen others, but there are serious doubts of their validity. The two credible finds—the Marmes in Washington and Midland in Texas—are both skulls only; no other bones survive. Marmes "man" is represented by fragments of the skulls from two individuals; Midland "man" consists of one skull cap from a young woman. Radiocarbon and other tests give a date of at least 9000 B.P. to the deposits from which they were taken and the Midland may be even older. The skulls, of course, are modern *Homo sapiens* in form, high vaulted, long narrow skulls. It is not surprising that distinctive American Indian osteological traits are noted, because only the skull caps remained and the diagnostic Indian traits appear in the facial and postcranial bones. To speculate further about the physical appearance of the first Americans on so little evidence would be fruitless. The reasonable assumption is that a scanty population of strong, vigorous, and fertile pioneer stock survived the rigorous screening of the arctic cold and embarked upon the conquest of the rich, virgin landmass of the New World. The adventures of these pioneers, in so far as they are known, and the more detailed account of their descendants, the American Indians who occupied North America when it was discovered by Europeans nearly 500 years ago, make up this book.

Even though we lack the osteological evidence that would give us a picture of the people themselves, there are other kinds of evidence that tell us they were here. Evidence of human handiwork exists in the tools, fireplaces, living sites, and butchering sites, which lie buried in the earth; sometimes discarded tools, fireplaces or hearths, and the broken bones of food animals occur in combination at one site. Such evidence of human presence is incontestable when the location is sealed by undisturbed sediments, or can be dated through radiocarbon assays of organic materials (charcoal, bone, shell, or uncharred vegetable debris). Thus, we can speak confidently of human adaptation to varied environments and resources, despite that human remains are normally missing from the most ancient sites. It is also possible to speak confidently of changing environ-ments during the 25,000 years (or longer) that human beings have been in the Western Hemisphere.

The earliest evidence of human presence on the continent is found on the very eastern edge of the Alaskan Refuge, at a location called Old Crow Flats on the Old Crow River in Yukon Territory. Here, Irving and Harrington (1973) discovered a caribou foreleg bone, carefully shaped into a toothed hide scraper or "flesher." It was with a large deposit of cracked/split caribou bone; the scrap bones and the flesher were equally discolored from long burial. The scraper itself was radiocarbon dated at 27,000 (?) years ago. Although no stone tools or other artifacts were found there, the Old Crow site is the oldest recorded American location where the presence of human beings seems to be documented. The timing is credible because it falls at the very beginning of the 10,000 year period when the Bering land bridge was above sea level (Fig. 4); that the location of the find is *within* the limits of the Refuge also lends credibility.

Until the discovery at Old Crow, abundant and unchallenged evidence existed which could establish the human presence only back to about 12,000 B.P. Although that time span is now more than doubled, there are still only one or two credible locations for the period between Old Crow (27,000 [?] B.P.) and the several well-controlled locations dated at 12,000 B.P. This hiatus is real, but probably reflects only a temporary lack of knowledge.

The antiquity of the Old Crow site leads to the speculation that migration from the Arctic scene spreading toward the south may have began more than 20,000 years ago. There is *some* evidence (not universally accepted) for dates earlier than 12,000 B.P. for locations in Central and South America, at Tlacopaya and Valsequillo in Mexico, and in the Ayacucho Valley high in the Andes. The dates claimed for Tlacopaya are 22,000 to 23,000 B.P., but not all scholars accept the findings. At Flea Cave in the Ayacucho Basin, a quite acceptable association of extinct animals and flaked tools is dated at about 14,000 B.P. Below this deposit are earlier layers dating at 19,000 B.P., but there is doubt that the associated stone specimens are actually artifacts (i.e., are the work of human beings). At many other locations in South America, tool complexes are reliably dated at 10,000 B.P. or earlier, supporting the idea that there was a rapid spread of human beings over

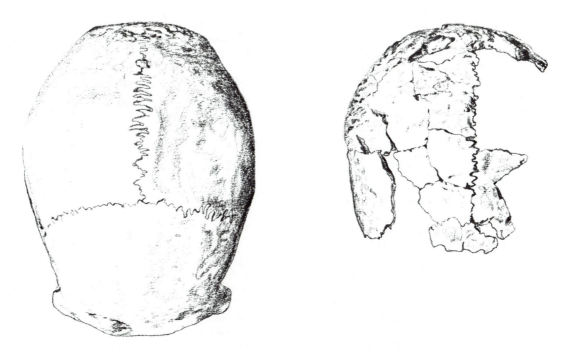

Figure 6 ● Marmes skull fragment. (After Fryxell, et al., 1968; Jennings, 1974: 63)

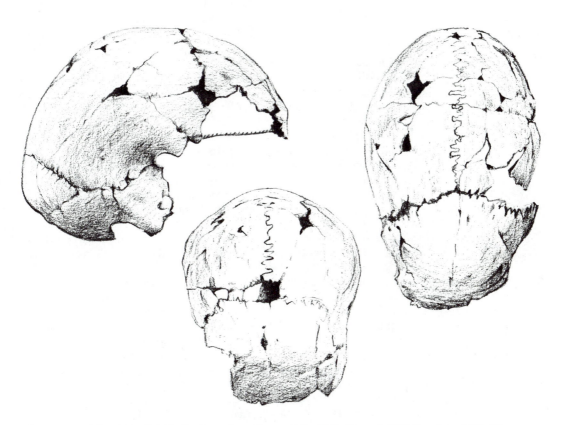

Figure 7 ● Midland Skull. Side, back, and top views. (After T.D. Stewart, 1955; Jennings, 1974: 61)

the hemisphere after 12,000 B.P. A particularly convincing location is Cueva 3 de Los Toldos in Patagonia where an abundant basalar flake industry is dated at 12,600 B.P. (see Cardich et al., 1973).

Evidently human beings were in the Alaskan area by 25,000 B. P. or earlier. South of the Arctic, 15,000 B. P. may be ascribed to one or two sites (Meadowcroft is one), and cultural remains later than 12,000 B. P. are known—even common—in North and South America. However, a shelter location discovered in Pennsylvania in 1974 yielded dates of 15,000 B.P., in firm context with prismatic flakes, cores (from which the flakes were made), and many fine small tools made from the prismatic flakes. This site (Adovasio et al., 1975) is the best evidence we have yet for human presence south of the ice masses during late Pleistocene times. Although this site lends credibility to the central and South American finds, the period from 25,000 to 15,000 or 14,000 B.P. is still not documented by dated locations which would fill in this gap in the sequence. Discoveries of locations from this period are eagerly awaited.

THE PALEO-INDIANS
Modern readers will find it hard to believe that as recently as 1930 professional anthropologists, because of the vigorous dogmatism of a few leaders, rejected any and all evidence that there had been human occupation of the American continent for longer than perhaps 3000 years.

In the Plains, at Folsom, New Mexico, the bonds of this dogma were broken. Here, in a fruitful collaboration that lasted from 1926 to 1928, J. D. Figgins, a paleontologist from the Denver Museum of Natural History; H. J. Cook, a paleontologist; Frank H. H. Roberts, Jr., an archeologist from the Bureau of American Ethnology; Alfred V. Kidder, an archeologist and Director of the Division of History of the Carnegie Institution of Washington; and other scholars demonstrated to the scientific world that distinctive man-made weapons, the fluted Folsom dart (or lance) points or knives, were in undeniable association with 23 deeply buried skeletons of a now extinct long-horned bison (*Bison antiquus*), which validated human presence on the continent back to the terminal phases of the Wisconsin glaciation. One of the most exciting discoveries ever made in American anthropological research, the Folsom find

captured the romantic interest of the public as well as the attention of specialists. More important, scientifically, was the validation (in probability at least) it provided for the many earlier reports of artifacts found in association with extinct mammals; most important was that it raised research interest in ancient Americans to a plane of respectability. Most of the research and most of the finds of early American man have been, until quite recently, in the Plains. Hence the special niche the Great Plains occupied in the history of American scholarship.

The Big Game Hunters or Paleo-Indians
The best evidence of the early Americans after 12,000 B.P. is found in western North America; the cultures represented by the finds there can be divided into three distinctive ones. The earliest, dated between 12,000 and 11,000 B.P., is characterized by a fluted projectile point or knife called Clovis Fluted (Fig. 9). There is an accompanying complex of flint tools; the locations are more or less similar; and the main game hunted was evidently the mammoth. This culture has also been called the Llano (Sellards, 1952).

Next youngest, at roughly 11,000 to 10,000 B.P. is the Folsom, usually associated with extinct bison. It is marked by a fluted flint knife or point called the Folsom point and an extensive tool kit. The Folsom Fluted point is smaller and finer than the Clovis point (Fig. 10).

After 10,000 or 9,500 B.P., there is a plethora of very similar projectile points, unfluted but carefully and expertly chipped, which have been described as generally lanceolate or leaf shaped in form (Figs. 11, 12, 13). Most often these are found at locations where modern, rather than extinct, fauna have been taken by aboriginal hunters. Even so, these remains are often ascribed to Paleo-Indians, and the cultures they represent called the Plano. These cultures tend to fade out, either disappearing or perhaps blending with the later archaic cultures by 8,000 B.P. or later. The several named point or knife types appear in a fairly well established succession ending about 8,000 B.P. (see Irwin, 1971; Jennings, 1974). The entire Western Plains sequence, much simplified (and ignoring known overlaps), is given in Figure 14.

The tabulation in Figure 14 is based on a very important location in eastern Wyoming called Hell Gap. There, in a neatly stratified situation, was a record of occupancy from Llano to terminal Plano covering some 4,000 years

Figure 8 ● Reconstruction of the Folsom Kill
site (After Museum display at Mesa Verde
National Park)

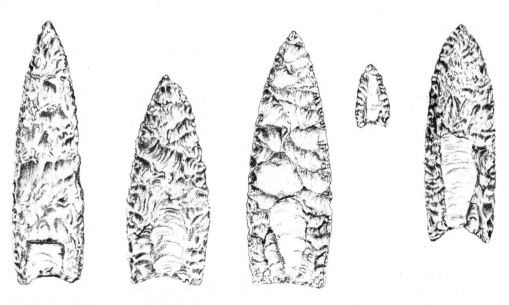

Figure 9 ● Typical Clovis Fluted Points, 3/4
size. (Drawn from J. A. Eichenberger casts.
This and succeeding credits to the Eichenberger
casts refer to a collection well known to
American archeologists. Reproductions may be
purchased from the Denver Museum of
Natural History; Jennings, 1974:84–85)

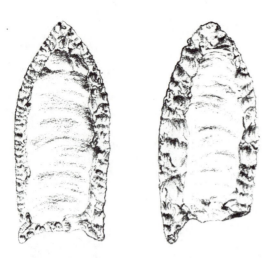

Figure 10 ● Folsom fluted points. (Drawn from J. A. Eichenberger casts; Jennings, 1974:85)

from 12,000 to 8,000 B.P. Although the deposits were thin, there were enough diagnostic point types found to validate the sequence. Although the dates for the same cultures at other Plains locations might be slightly different (older or younger by a few hundred years) the sequence can be accepted, even though some scholars think (as I do) that the Plainview types come after Folsom and are contemporary with the Midland type in the southern Plains. The Hell Gap site is of considerable importance because of the long, well-documented Plano culture sequence it provides for the High Plains.

Although the cluster of early cultures are here discussed separately—Llano, Folsom and Plano—they are very often lumped under the term Paleo-Indian. A term, which has no precise definition, but is merely a loose designation for those cultures once believed to have been the earliest in the Americas, with a subsistence pattern apparently focused on megafauna, both extinct (mammoth, long-horned bison, etc.) and modern.

Llano Culture

After the Folsom location, which provided a "breakthrough" in thinking, the most important site so far discovered is the Clovis site (New Mexico), or Blackwater Draw, locality #1. Discovered in 1932, it firmly associated Clovis points with mammoth kills. Moreover, it showed that the Llano culture was earlier than Folsom; both were represented in separate strata at Blackwater Draw. Above the Folsom layer was a local Plano culture called the Portales. Thus, at one location, the basic strati-

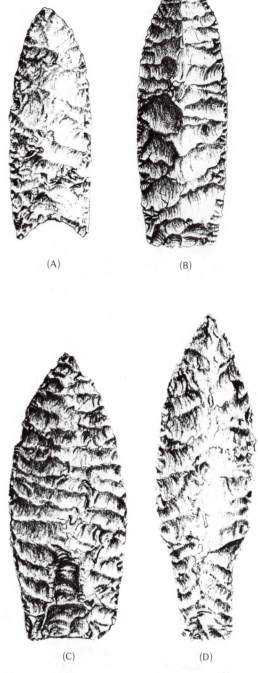

(A)

(B)

(C)

(D)

Figure 11 ● Plano points, 1 to 1/4 size. A, Plainview; B, Milnesand; C, Browns Valley; D, Hell Gap. (A, C, D drawn from J. A. Eichenberger casts; B after Sellards, 1955; Jennings, 1974:112)

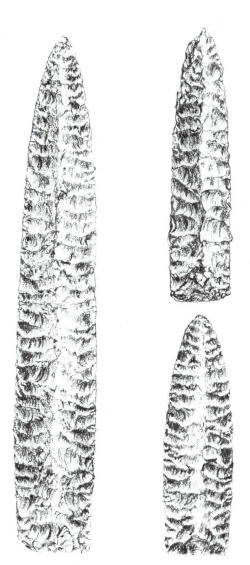

Figure 12 ● Eden points. Actual size. (Drawn from J. A. Eichenberger casts; Jennings, 1974:113)

graphy/succession of the Paleo-Indian cultures of the Plains was delineated. The location has been called the "yardstick" against which other less lengthy sequences at other sites were compared and evaluated. It therefore provided, some 25 years earlier, the same type of control the Hell Gap site does for the High Plains.

Important as the site was, and is, Blackwater Draw suffered shameful neglect from a host of scientific investigators. Only in 1972 did a dedicated scholar, James J. Hester (1972), publish the record for other students; he salvaged the scattered notes, maps, and records of over 20 excavation programs at the site, correlating them

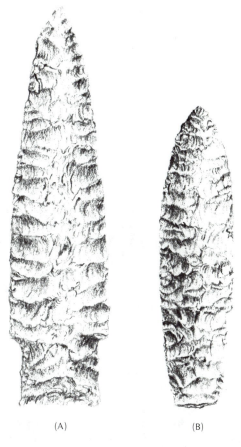

(A)   (B)

Figure 13 ● Other Plano points. Actual size. A, Scottsbluff, B, Agate Basin. (Drawn from J. A. Eichenberger casts; Jennings, 1974:113)

masterfully into a summary of knowledge about Locality #1. Although the site has since been destroyed by the operations of a commercial gravel pit, Hester records that Blackwater Draw was once a large, oval, spring-fed pond. The bog along its west bank was the scene of dozens of mammoth kills, which were ambushed as singles by the Llano hunters. Later Folsom and Plano spearmen killed the extinct long-horned and modern short-horned bison, also along the west bank. Knives and other tools that were lost or discarded during the kill and subsequent butchery had been sealed in sediment and form the evidence on which the record is constructed. The pond later dried up completely, and the Archaic peoples dug wells in the center of the pond for the ever scarcer water as they continued to use the old campsites.

Some 220 Clovis and 534 Folsom points were

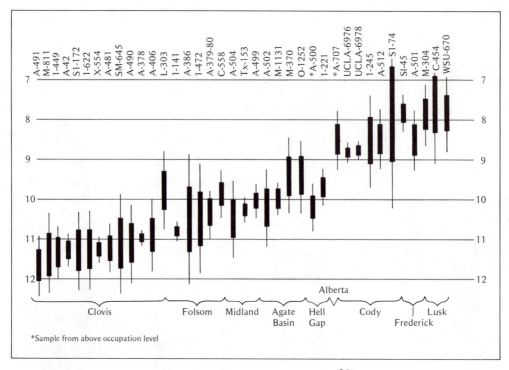

Figure 14 ● Radiocarbon dates associated with Paleo-Indian finds. (Jennings, 1974:106)

recovered during the years the site was worked. Other stone tools studied and tabulated by Hester were unifacial knives (flakes with chipping on only one surface), scrapers, burins, and hammerstones. The Clovis points were all made of Alibates chert, quarried 100 miles to the northwest of the pond; the Folsom pieces were of Edwards chert from a quarry 150 miles to the southeast. Rarely mentioned, but emphasized by Hester, is the heavy use of bone that characterized Clovis hunting. Long, slender, carefully shaped points, scrapers, perforators, and many other tools of dense heavy bone are reported from the Blackwater Draw collections.

As was true at Blackwater Draw, the Clovis Fluted points are normally found in association with extinct mammoth bones. They have been found under good scientific control at Dent (Colorado), Clovis (New Mexico), Miami (Texas), Lindenmeier (Colorado), and Naco and Lehner (Arizona) among others. Hundreds of specimens very similar to Clovis Fluted points are reported from many eastern sites (and from the far West at Borax Lake in California) but are not found in association with extinct animals; often, indeed, they are surface finds, subject to no provenience control.

Figure 15 ● Chopper-scraper sites and complexes in North America. (Modified from Krieger, 1964; Jennings, 1974:77)

In the Plains, such remains are most often found (e.g., Clovis and Lindenmeier) in deposits of muck or sand under, and earlier than, deposits containing Folsom culture artifacts. Frequently, too, the sites (as exemplified at Blackwater Draw) appear to have been marshes, bogs, or shallow mucky ponds. That no such ponds now exist there indicates that there was a different climate; the very presence of elephant argues for a coarse and abundant vegetation. The actual causes of the disappearance of the mammoth are not known. Probably the onset of somewhat drier times, the depredations of humans on the herds, and even perhaps disease can all be offered in partial explanation.

Since most of the open sites were once swamps or bogs, it is reasoned by some that the mammoth were killed and butchered while they were mired and immobile. Whether these beasts were accidentally trapped in the sticky bottom, and hunters merely made an opportune kill while the animal was helpless, or whether the animals were driven into the bog by organized hunt is, of course, unknown. In view of the popularity of the surround-and-kill techniques throughout Plains history, the odds seem to favor the organized hunt over the casual slaughter of an occasional mired individual.

The Lehner Site

At Lehner, for example, there had been nine separate mammoths entrapped or surprised in the sharp bend of an ancient sandy creek bed or on a sandbar. With their bones, were fragments of tapir, horse, and bison bone, showing that these animals had also been sought as food. The site, thoroughly worked and well reported, assumes great importance because there was a hearth area that yielded charcoal, from which a series of radiocarbon dates were derived. The site is important also in revealing—through the presence of oak, pine, and ash charcoal—species still found in the general vicinity. Hence, although the presence of mammoth argues more precipitation and a lusher growth of vegetation, the full biotic range would be likely to have included all the modern species still to be found there. A year-round climate not widely divergent from today's, save for the amount and distribution of the rainfall, can be argued. The present aridity and restricted growth of the area is, in fact, known to be a very recent development. One hundred years ago, the creek was a marshy grass-lined slough where the grasses which constituted the mammoth's preferred food grew in abundance. The artifact-hearth layer of the Lehner site is dated by radiocarbon at about 11,000 B.P.; it may well be older. Later finds near Lehner include mammoth kills at Murray Springs and Escapule. The Murray Springs location is of particular interest because it is also a camp or living site as well as a kill, and among the tools was a unique (so far as Amer-

Figure 16 ● Mammoth-bone shaft "wrench" from Murray Springs, southeastern Arizona. (Haynes and Hemmings, 1968)

ica is concerned) "wrench" of mammoth bone (Fig. 16), which resembles one found at the famous Ukrainian site, dated at about 13,000 B.P., of Molodova V (see Klein, 1973), where mammoth appears to have been the major food source.

Fluted points very like the Clovis occur at two well-controlled locations in the Northeast—one is at Bull Brook in Massachusetts and the other is at Debert in Nova Scotia. Debert is dated at 10,600 B.P., with Bull Brook later at 9,000 B.P. Both are campsites with hearth areas and possible house or shelter areas, where artifacts and the debris from manufacture of flint tools were concentrated. At neither site had bone scrap been preserved so the preferred prey is not known.

Of the two, Debert is the better understood. Excavated by MacDonald (1968), it consisted of eleven "living" areas where some 4000 artifacts were collected. Knives, drills, awls, scrapers, gravers, and other tools used for butchery, food preparation, or for the making of other tools were identified. Because the occupancy occurred when glacial ice was no more than 50 miles away, the assumption that the environment was essentially tundra, with caribou the chief game, is reasonable. Bull Brook, although dug by amateurs (and since also destroyed by

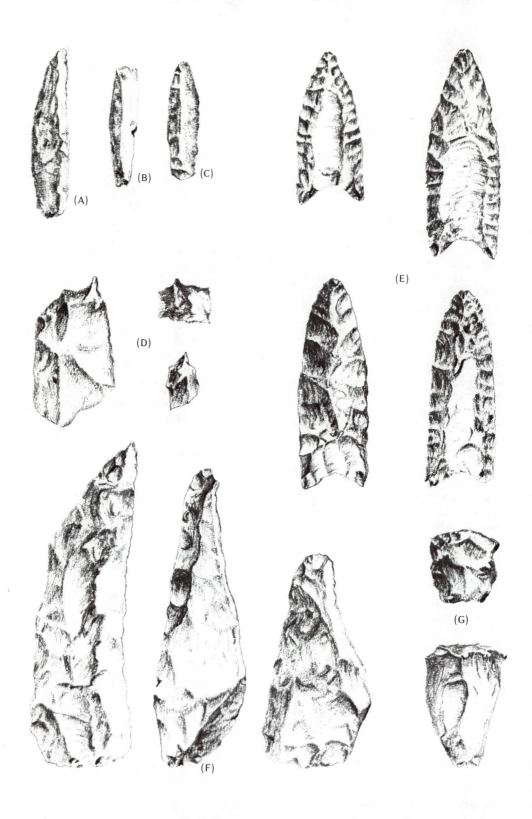

Figure 17 ● Tool assemblage from Bull Brook. A, B, retouched blades; C, "twist drill"; D, uniface gravers; E, fluted projectile points; F, side scrapers, G, end scrapers with graver spur at edge of blade. (After Byers, 1954; Jennings, 1974:97)

gravel pit operations) is an equally important site. The chipped flint resembles Clovis materials very closely and the tool kit is about the same.

Argument whether the Debert–Bull Brook complex should be called Llano/Clovis tends to be a waste of time. The complex does resemble the western Clovis finds. It falls, more or less, coeval with Folsom and, so far, is not in association with extinct fauna. The more important point is that fluted points are found in buried context in the ice-free areas in both the western and the extreme northeastern parts of the continent, attesting to a rapid spread of what is assumed to have been a thin population.

Folsom Culture

Next in time after the Llano culture and best known to the public are the Folsom remains, first found at, and named after, the location near Folsom, New Mexico. As reported by Steen (1955) the find was made accidentally; that it came to scientific notice was also accidental. Indeed, many important buried sites have been discovered through lucky accidents and chains of circumstance, rather than through deliberate search. In the case of Folsom, a cow-puncher named George McJunken noticed in a newly deepened arroyo some bones which had been deeply buried; he mentioned these many times to a friend, Mr. Carl Schwachheim, of Raton, New Mexico. For several years McJunken tried to get Mr. Schwachheim to visit the Crowfoot Ranch where the deposit was located. McJunken died in 1923 before the Raton man could visit the site. Later, in 1925, Mr. Schwachheim got out to the ranch, found the deposit, and brought the material to the attention of paleontologists from the Denver Museum of Natural History who began a purely routine investigation of the fossil bones. During the three-year excavation program (1926, 1927, and 1928–1929) chipped flint tools of distinctive form were recovered. These were unquestionably associated with bones of 23 extinct giant bison—*Bison antiquus*—at the site of an ancient trap or surround kill in a small gulch. American archeology entered a new phase! At that time the presence of extinct big-horned bison in a new association with human beings was very important. Llano specimens occur with elephant, but evidently elephant did not survive into Folsom times.

Although no skeletal remains of Folsom people have yet been identified, we do know: they hunted the giant bison of the day; they often camped along the shores of the shallow, marshy lakes or beaver meadows that dotted the country during the glacial ages. It is believed that the chief weapon in use was, as during Llano times, a light spear, lance, or dart. It may have been propelled by a clever tool called the spear thrower, still in use today by the Eskimo and Australians. The throwing board or *atlatl* is a short board or stick with a hook or knob at one end (the other end is the handle or grip), into which the notched end of a spear is fitted. The spear is thrown with an overhand motion. The spear thrower, for practical purposes, lengthens the arm and increases the leverage normally provided by the arc of arm movement.

From the many stone implements left in these camp grounds beside the marshes, we have learned that Folsom man was a skillful stoneworker. In fact, the diagnostic trait of the culture is the finest of fluted points, apparently made only by this group and never subsequently manufactured in the Plains. This point was formed by the careful removal of a single lengthwise flake on each side of the flat blade, which left a long concave groove or trough extending from the base almost to the tip; the troughlike scar is called a "flute" and gives the point its name. The excellence of this style of point and its characteristic form have led most students to ignore the fact that the Folsom culture contains many other stone artifacts. For example, a thin sharp knife was made from the flakes removed from the fine point that identifies the culture. Other implements found in Folsom sites include various kinds of scrapers, knives, and blades of rougher form. Flakes with small sharp points (for scoring or engraving), choppers, drills, sandstone smoothers or abraders (used to smooth down stone, bone, and wood objects), and small sandstone palettes for paints are known. Although these tools are common in Folsom sites, similar or identical types occur in later cultures. These latter Folsom pieces are not distinctive enough to allow their use as evidence in drawing cultural distinctions. Usually the Folsom culture, assuming adequate geological and palentological controls, is identified by the presence of a certain type of arrow or dart point.

There are several important sites or locations where Folsom remains have been found. Folsom (New Mexico), Lindenmeier (Colorado), and Blackwater Draw (New Mexico) are the earlier authenticated finds. From sites in Nebraska, Canada, Montana, Texas, and Wyoming, artifacts of characteristic Folsom form have been reported, but full studies of these later discoveries have not yet been made. Although the lingering glamor of scientific breakthrough gives the Folsom site a special value for everyone, the more solid information about Folsom culture comes from the Lindenmeier site.

About 30 miles north of Fort Collins, Colorado the Lindenmeier site lies buried under many feet of recent sediment in what was once one of a series of narrow parallel valleys separated by conglomerate topped ridges. In several spots along the narrow Pleistocene valley, debris is found in both campsite and midden circumstances. Later the valley filled level with sediment, covering the evidence of human occupancy. Then, in very recent years, the erosion of the terrace edge was accelerated by the down-cutting of an arroyo. In the sides of this narrow cut in a deeply buried black stratum were found animal bones, flint, and charcoal. Sediment in depths up to 17 feet effectively sealed the artifact layer. The site has so far not been surpassed in richness and constitutes the most important single source of information about the Folsom complex. Artifacts and bones came from a black layer about 8 inches thick. Bison of a now extinct type, camel, and elephant were all represented.

Above the Folsom layer at Lindenmeier, there are distinctive projectile points that seem to combine the general shapes of Clovis and Folsom fluted points with the chipping and manufacturing techniques of what is called the Scottsbluff point. This "hybrid" artifact is called the Plainview point, after the type station near Plainview, Texas, which is one of the most interesting of the ancient sites, also discovered by accident. The Plainview site lies in a valley which was filled during a period of accelerated depositional activity. At the base of the fill in the wide valley of Running Water Creek, a layer of bones was discovered during the operation of a quarry. The portion of the bone bed uncovered during the scientific excavation of the site was 62 feet long, varied from 5 to 10 feet in width, and at the center was 18 inches thick. The skeletons of approximately 100 giant wide-horned fossil bison (*Bison antiquus*) had been preserved; evidently the bones are the remains of a mass slaughter or "kill," where a small herd was driven or stampeded over a bluff by the hunters. Eighteen flint points were found in the bone layer, most of them toward the top of the layer. Evidently the hunters had found it necessary to kill the crippled or stunned animals that might have escaped from the top of the heap; presumably the leaders of the herd, on the bottom of the pile, were already dead and motionless, having fallen directly on the bedrock of the original valley, or if they survived the drop, they were probably crushed by the cascade of heavy bodies falling on top of them.

For its clear evidence of the association of animals and artifacts and for the number of flint specimens, the Plainview find takes an important place in the list of early finds attesting to the presence of human beings. It also gives strong testimony of the antiquity of the kill as a favored method of hunting large animals; the kill was still in use in the Plains as late as the 1850s.

Plano Cultures

The next stage of the Paleo-Indian cultures is more obscure than the Folsom just discussed. At many sites, Folsom remains are followed by variants of a widespread, locally variable culture that rests upon the big game economy. The relationship to earlier complexes lies not only in the emphasis upon big game as a subsistence base but also in the general artifact assemblage. There is no general regional name for this group of sites partly because the existence of several well-defined diagnostic point types from several sites has focused student concern upon identification of local complexes, rather than upon synthesis or upon working out chronological equivalence. The term *Plano* (pronounced Plah'no) which has already been used for this time-artifact constellation, has no significance. It serves only as a noncommittal name to identify a cluster of associated traits that so far has no agreed-upon class name. Into the Plano, one could provisionally lump the complexes represented at Eden (Wyoming), Horner (Wyoming), Scottsbluff (Nebraska), Portales Horizon at Blackwater Draw #1 (i.e., the Clovis site in New Mexico), the Long site (South Dakota), Lime Creek (Nebraska), Red Smoke (Nebraska), upper level at MacHaffie (Montana), Meserve (Nebraska), Milnesand (Texas), Brown's Valley (Minnesota), Agate Basin (Wyoming), Hell Gap (Wyoming), and Levi (Texas).

The hallmark of the Plano subcultures is a distinctive point or knife of chipped flint often described as leaf shaped (see Figs. 11, 12, 13). Although "leaf shaped" alone means little, the term has come to mean a long, slender, nearly parallel-sided blade about one-fourth as wide as it is long. The length of the specimens varies from 2 1/2 to more than 5 inches, widths are correspondingly varied. The chipping is usually very well done; the flake scar may be long, slim, and ribbony resulting in a sleek, thin, well-made tool of pleasing symmetry. Often the flake scars run diagonally across the blade and are sometimes large and bold, yet no symmetry is lost. For example, the Eden point, with its bold regular chipping, is an exquisite piece of flint smithing. Most specimens show a definite median ridge—chips were removed from the edge directly toward the center—and this central thickness most probably results from the manufacturing technique. The straight sharp edges and the thick median portion form a sharp diamond/lozenge outline in cross section. The base or butt of the point is usually flat or straight, and a slight, but perfectly shaped, shoulder may appear about an inch up the blade from the butt. Several named artifact types, such as Eden, Scottsbluff, Angostura, Agate Basin, Brown's Valley, and Milnesand points are characteristic of this period.

The several named projectile or knife types grouped here as Plano specimens are much more like each other than they are like either the Folsom or Clovis Fluted types. The game animal with which they are most often found in association is the bison, but these bison remains are not always positively identified as extinct species. So far other artifacts are nondiagnostic, and the major difference between this culture and the preceding Folsom is the presence or absence of the Folsom Fluted point. As far as lifeway is concerned, all the Paleo-Indian cultures (i.e., Llano, Folsom, and Plano) are very like one another and can readily be classed together.

The "fall" or "trap" drive-hunting technique should perhaps be mentioned here. The Plainview, Folsom, Bonfire, and Olsen-Chubbock sites are the scenes of mass slaughters of bison. Plainview is almost certainly a fall; at Folsom a small herd may have been trapped in a box canyon. Scottsbluff, Horner, and Lipscomb (Texas) are other examples of prehistoric mass-kill sites. From 10,000 years ago on down to A.D. 1872 (Ewers, 1949), the drive or some form of mass kill was a common Plains practice; in fact, the drive is a well-developed historic technique lucidly reported by several authors including Lewis and Clark.

Two, prehistoric kills have been carefully described. One is Bonfire Shelter (Dibble and Lorrain, 1968) lying between the Rio Grande and the Pecos River at their confluence in extreme southern Texas. Well south of the usual range of the Folsom points, it was the scene of two bison jump kills. The first kill occurred about 10,200 B.P.; the animals were of the wide-horned species, *Bison antiquus* or *occidentalis*. The artifacts from that lower bone bed included both Folsom Fluted and Plainview points, which supports the contention that the two may be contemporary or that the Plainview type is, in fact, transitional to more distinctive Plano types. The deposits at Bonfire were deep and neatly stratified, the cultural sequence extends from 10,200 B.P. into the Christian era. The location derives its importance from Folsom affiliation and from the clear evidence of a bison jump from the overhanging cliff above the site during Folsom times. So far as our data go today, the bison jump-kill technique must be noted as a Folsom "invention" or innovation.

Another now famous kill site is the Olsen-Chubbock (Colorado) site where, as Wheat (1967, 1972) describes, there must have been an exciting, dangerous event for the hunters. This drive did not culminate in a long drop over a cliff; instead, the herd was stampeded down a steep hill to be trapped in an arroyo. Wheat reconstructed the direction of the drive and the butchery techniques from the data he meticulously unearthed; the butchery technique he inferred from the bones was later corroborated by ethnographic evidence. He found the bison bones piled neatly and conjectured that this had been done after the meat was stripped from the animals in a well-established sequence of dismemberment: First the foreleg was removed and the meat stripped; next the hindleg; then the pelvis, etc. In age, the site, dated about 10,000 B.P., can be equated with Bonfire Shelter. It also yielded Folsom and what appear to me to be Plainview points.

An excellent example of the "trap" kill is the Casper (Wyoming) site, where a modern bison herd was slaughtered between the horns of an active lunate half-moon shaped dune (Frison, 1974).

Regardless of artifact type, culture type, facts of distribution, or dates, the association of extinct herd-animal bones with human debris ends about 8,000 B.P. In two very good studies Jelinek (1957) and Hester (1960), with the aid of the many radiocarbon dates now available, have shown that although the time of extinction varies (and the variations may represent "enclaves" of surviving animals), on present evidence we can safely assign an age of 8,000 B.P. or more to most assemblages of artifacts associated with the remains of the extinct *Bison antiquus* or *Bison occidentalis* (long-horned bison), camel, dire wolf, four-horned antelope, giant beaver, giant armadillo, horse, musk ox, mastodon, mammoth, ground sloth, peccary, and tapir. On the other hand, *Bison bison* (modern bison) occurs as early as 9,000 B.P. at a number of western sites.

Jelinek shows the distribution of six major species, often found together at a single site, and their associated cultures and index artifacts. His work allows us to say, as a general rule, that Clovis Fluted points are found with mammoth, but that Folsom Fluted points are always found with *Bison antiquus;* we cannot say that only these species will be represented. Jelinek lists sequent periods, based on faunal evidence (and includes specific sites or locations for each) that correspond closely to the segregation suggested here for the West. In the eastern Woodlands—from Missouri eastward—mastodon, *not* mammoth, have been found associated with Archaic artifacts. The Pomme de Terre mastodon (Gross, 1951) and the Island 35 find are examples. Quimby (1960) and Mason (1962) believe, but cannot yet prove, that mastodons were taken by both Llano and Archaic hunters in the Great Lakes region.

Artifacts resembling the Clovis and Folsom Fluted points occur nowhere except in North America. They are uniquely American, and their disappearance has not been explained. The Archaic stage tools may be a Eurasiatic complex imported, or transported by immigrants, more or less complete, with the exception that the fluted tools were indigenous. It is equally likely, however, that their development in some places was a response to the varied needs of the exploitative subsistence pattern. This is a point which has not yet been dealt with effectively.

ARCHAIC

Any attempt to relate the historic Indian tribes to the full depth and range of variations/adaptations developed during the next prehistoric stage—the Archaic—is doomed to

failure given our present knowledge, except in the culture areas of the Northeast, Southwest, and Great Basin where the Archaic persisted.

Despite these limits, it is desirable to introduce and briefly discuss the Archaic stage. Characterized by the seasonal selective exploitation of frequently abundant resources, a subsistence pattern adaptive to every ecological zone in the New World, the Archaic culture can be recognized and differentiated over broad areas that are roughly coincident with the cultural area divisions used in organizing this text. Although there is an overall similarity, in each of these prehistoric culture areas the tool complexes, the settlement patterns, the subsistence base, and the seasonal round take on distinctive characteristics; marked differences, for example, distinguish the Eastern and Desert Archaic adaptations. Even local differences can sometimes be perceived in the tools and utensils used to exploit very different ecozones. The Great Basin is an example: Intensive use of lacustrine foods, such as fish, waterfowl, and aquatic plant species from the sinks along the Humboldt River of Nevada, provide the western portion of the Basin with rich resources which are scantily, or not at all, represented in the eastern part.

During Archaic times the "good gray (Archaic) cultures" were to be found over the entire continent. And the details from many areas are surprisingly well known to archeology. Another important fact of this period is that no significant hiatus in the human occupancy of the New World occurs in any area where the archeological record has been studied.

The Archaic cultures of the Mexican Highlands require special mention because there the domestication of indigenous/native and unique American plants occurred, and the process can be charted through archeology. Based on the work of MacNeish (1967), E. Smith (1967), and Callen (1967), positive statements can be made about the *cultivation,* if not yet the *domestication,* by 7000 B.P. of many plants, unique to the Americas, but now enjoying worldwide distribution and of tremendous commercial value in world economy.

Some of the most important species and their apparent dates of cultivation are shown in Figure 18. Of principal interest are maize, the cucurbit (pumpkin-squash) group, the common bean, and probably the amaranth or pigweed (other names are red root and careless weed). The first three are exceedingly versatile in

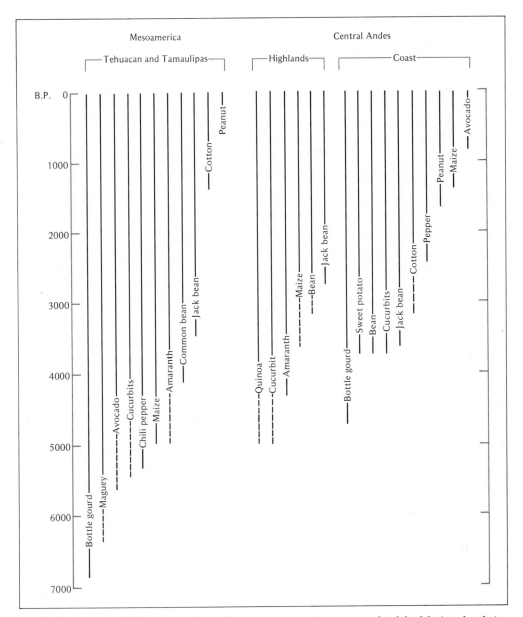

Figure 18 ● Apparent initial dates of use of major cultigens and cultivars in Middle America. (After Meggers, 1972; Jennings, 1974:198)

adapting to temperate zone climates. Additionally, they all require about the same combination of moisture, frost-free growing season, and summer heat to prosper and mature. Between them they provide a well-nigh balanced diet because beans contain essential amino acids not present in the other two; they have long sustained, and still do, millions of American Indians, from deep in prehistoric times to the present (in areas south of the Mexican border).

Although the three primary domesticates listed above eventually came to be cultivated by all the American tribes in the eastern Woodlands, Middle West, Plains, and American Southwest in the prehistoric past, the idea of horticulture or agriculture preceded with the amaranth and marsh elder the first major tended crops. So, at least, the evidence from sites in the eastern Woodlands would indicate.

Without going into great detail (and recognizing the dangers of generalizing culture traits over a continental mass), it is possible to describe the Archaic lifeway for North America.

The key words are *hunters* and *gatherers*. Others have described this subsistence adaptation with the terms "foragers" or even "scroungers." What is meant, of course, is the cluster of subsistence techniques, tools, and utensils focused on food collecting rather than on food production.

Even in the game-filled eastern Woodlands, vegetable foods were the basis of Archaic diet. Game played a varyingly important role in each of the exploitative patterns, but the scheduled collecting of preferred, abundant plant foods (fruits and berries, nuts, tubers, and seeds) in season was the main source of foodstuffs. Tools for collecting (baskets), processing and preparing (mortars, pestles, grinding stones) occur, along with nets and hooks for fishing and stone points and knives for forest game (deer being everywhere the major prey). Tools, such as stone axes and adzes, scrapers and gravers, were made for use in manufacture of other tools of wood or bone. Ornaments of bone, shell, and even turtle shell were made where the raw materials existed.

In summary, the Archaic is to be understood as a richer, technologically more advanced and much more versatile culture than the earlier Paleo-Indian, or Big Game Hunting, stage. Its variety and versatility can best be understood through its subsistence focus because it is characterized by wide, if selective, exploitation of the environment whether this environment was difficult, as in the Great Basin West, or lush and inviting, as in the American Southeast. Hence, in the Archaic stage, there are more varied tools for more varied purposes, and the full artifact complex is astonishingly broad. The cultures tended to be stable—possibly because of a satisfactory balance and adjustment with resources. The ages for the sites range from as early as 10,000 B.P. to as late as A.D. 1850 (until the arrival of the white man in marginal areas). The universality of the Archaic does *not* mean that there is an identity of artifact styles. Nor, considering the climatic variations on the continent, would one expect uniformity. The flora, with its attendant fauna, would control the subsistence bases, and the tools or utensils required for gathering food would be determined by what was gathered. So, the Archaic stage is seen as universal and generalized, whereas the first cultures of the big game hunters were of a special limited sort, constituting an ecological anomaly that could survive only where special

resources were found, for the tools and technology were evidently not adaptable to other circumstances of climate. The Archaic stage, however, brought culture stability and adaptability based on efficiency to all of North America for many millennia. Of course, there were regional specializations, based in part on contact with other cultures, but only where the Archaic base was most efficient (and resources existed) was there later efflorescence.

After recognizing that the ubiquitous Archaic developed and blanketed the continent, the task now is to look for the time and place where the historic American Indian diversity may have arisen. Evidently, all but one of the higher specialized cultures of North America developed out of the local Archaic after the stimulus of a few crucial ideas (the Hohokam of the Southwest is the probable exception). By 3500 B.P. important new traits had been added to the Archaic list: These are the concept of pottery making (evidently borrowed intact as a complex from Asia since there is no experimental stage known to us), and the burial mound (presumably also from Asia, but Chard [1959] thinks it equally likely to have been a local development). Specializations evidently arose, partially by virtue of stimulus or actual contact with Asia and, partially, if Caldwell (1958) is right, by invention in the Archaic cultures where an "enlarged reservoir of innovators" existed in the well-balanced comfort of forest efficiency and intellectual climate conducive to invention and discovery.

WOODLAND

Whatever the source, innovations do appear by 1500 B.C. and mark the end of the Archaic stage. These innovations include a knowledge of pottery making and the erection of earthen tumuli over the important dead. Early Woodland pottery is not elaborate. The shapes are simple—tall, wide-mouthed vessels with conoidal, pointed, or flattened bases. The surfaces are rough as a result of malleation of the surface with a cord-wrapped paddle. The paste is coarse and breaks easily; the temper is grit—crushed rock—or coarse sand. Except for the addition of pottery, there is no change in the Archaic complex. There was as yet no agriculture, the settlements were no larger, and except for the presence of pottery in the debris, there is no way to differentiate the Archaic from the

Early Woodland stage, as the first new manifestation is called. Many students have remarked upon the arbitrariness of the definition of Archaic as "preceramic" because there is in fact no distinction, except for the acceptance of pottery and the occasional mound burial complex, between the Archaic and the Early Woodland. Early Woodland exists then, "by definition"; the lifeway continued to be the forest efficiency pattern described by Caldwell. Most authors, for classificatory and chronological reasons, perceive and establish Early, Middle, and Late Woodland stages, but these distinctions contribute little to the general description offered here. Because the Early Woodland (except for pottery, the use of tobacco (?) in tubular pipes, which probably arose in the South, burial mounds, and perhaps limited horticulture of wild species) is merely an evolving Archaic stage, less attention is given to the Early Woodland stage as such, than to its descendant cultures and to the continuity with the Archaic that it demonstrates. The Early Woodland stage can be considered a transitional one to the Woodland culture climax exemplified by the Adena-Hopewell cultures and the variants of the latter.

The strength and distribution of these transitional cultures were almost equal to the Archaic, for Early Woodland occurs virtually everywhere east of the Rockies except perhaps in the Texas plains. This wide spread took time. The nuclear area of the culture is in the northeastern states from where it spread to the "efficient" Southeast which was immediately receptive to the new ideas. As a general stage the simple Woodland culture never was displaced in most of the eastern woodlands; only in the Mississippi drainage, and this happened in recent times, did the Mississippi culture displace the Woodland. This time span argues for the fundamental excellence of the Woodland cultural (including technological) adaptation to the eastern half of the continent and even to parts of the Plains. It is significant that even when agriculture became part of the subsistence base, there was, over much of the continent, no great relinquishment of the old, old Archaic tradition of total exploitation. The full round of Archaic life—including probably much intangible social behavior—remained appropriate and in use; and agriculture—corn, beans, and squash—and many other complexes were absorbed into the Archaic pattern, without varying the central core of values.

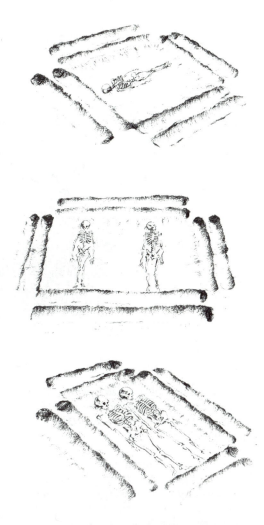

Figure 19 ● Log tomb burials as excavated at the Robbins Mounds. (After W. S. Webb and Elliott, 1942; Jennings 1974:223)

ADENA-HOPEWELL

The highest development in the flowering of the Woodland cultures was in the Ohio-Kentucky area where from 800 B.C. to A.D. 600+ the Adena-Hopewell cultures centered (Webb and Snow, 1945). There is evidence of a large population in a society of considerable complexity, with well-developed religious or ritual practices. Adena sites are characterized by clusters of conical earthen burial mounds of varying size and by vast patterned earthworks, or enclosures composed of long earthen ridges. The mounds may contain only one ritually buried person, enclosed in a tomb of logs (Fig. 19). Or there might be many such interments, each

26' diameter

Figure 20 ● **Postmold plan and cutaway view of restored Adena house showing probable construction (After W. S. Webb, 1941a; Jennings, 1974:224)**

covered by an accretion to the mound. The earthwork enclosures, usually located on high lands, were of many sorts: Square, rectangular, and round were the usual shapes; the enclosures varied from 50 to 500 feet in diameter. There are "gateways" and other evidences that these ramparts of earth were palisaded with posts in the summit, but digging has revealed no enclosed village or evidence of continuous use of the enclosed area. The Adena house, as seen at the Robbins site (Kentucky), was perfectly round, being built of posts that were set into the ground in spaced pairs and slanted outward from the base. Woven mats were hung over the poles to form walls; a roof of rafters and thatch completed the structure. Inside was a packed clay floor and flat fire area (Fig. 20).

More impressive than these houses were the burial mounds. Adena mounds were not simple one-stage construction projects. They were accretional long-term activities, and at the Robbins site, a log-lined tomb was associated with each construction stage or addition. The earth was piled in a mantle over each new bur-

ial. The earth was brought in, a basket load at a time, from different borrow areas. Much human effort was expended on these huge tumuli.

A great deal of care was lavished on the dead, who were presumably important personages. Log tombs were built into shallow rectangular pits, which were lined with logs 8 to 10 inches in diameter. Most were then roofed with logs after the burial and a new earth mantle spread. There were comparable tombs with piled-up earthen walls. The mounds also contained burials not in tombs but merely laid on the mound surface and covered over. The dead were given a variety of treatments. Although cremation—complete or partial—was common and was carried out very elaborately in special pits, inhumation of bodies was even more common. Corpses were laid on their backs, one, two, or three to the grave; objects of value and many nodules of pigment—red ochre, graphite, and galena—were placed with the dead. Grave furniture included objects of polished stone, ornaments of cut sheet mica, tubular pipes of stone, ornate stone tablets intricately carved, cut animal jaws, and other less spectacular specimens (Fig. 21). "Trophy" or single isolated skulls occur at random both in the fill and in tombs.

Probably because their burial mounds have

head

body

wing

leg and foot

tail

Figure 21 ● Engraved Adena tablets. Bird design elements shown at right center. (After W. S. Webb and Baby, 1957; Jennings, 1974:226)

been so extensively excavated while no great villages have been found or worked, the Adena list of material objects tends toward the ornamental or ritual. Of the commonplace tools, chipped flint in the form of large flint blades, rectangular stone hoes, stemmed and diagonally notched blades can be listed. Smoothed or ground stone appears in several throat or chest ornaments called gorgets (the most characteristic of these is the reel shape—a flat plate with four curved and flaring arms), tubular stone pipes, celts with a characteristic circular outline and a socketed poll, and ornately engraved rectangular tablets. In bone, were awls made from scapulae, spines, and split cannon bones of deer, arrow points of antler tip, cut jaws of wolf—used perhaps in masks—handles for tools, and gorgets made from human skulls. Copper, too, was common: bracelets, spiral finger rings, and reel-shaped gorgets of thin plate were the usual forms. Cloth was woven in several techniques. The raptoral bird symbol, often highly conventionalized, is a dominant motif in Adena art. The slate tablets particularly often carry the raptor design, and along with it, the hand-eye motif is sometimes used. These two designs persist in Hopewell and on into the protohistoric period where both are seen in many objects of the so-called "Southern Cult". Pottery, of several named types, was made. If we recognize that there were regional variations and that both utilitarian and special wares were made, the Woodland-style pottery can be generally described. Dominantly plain, although a cord-roughened exterior is frequent, it was made in only a few vessel shapes, the commonest a barrel-shaped body with flattened base. The tempering material is grit, such as sand, crushed granite, or the like, except in Kentucky and farther south where crushed limestone was used. An unusual type is *Fayette* Thick, which bears a regular incised diamond design.

In subsistence the Adena in no way departed from the Archaic pattern. All edible wild foods were collected, as were virtually all animals. Horticulture cannot be proved; although squash, gourd, and sunflower have been found. At one open site or another (some 250± have been explored) the following animal remains have been recovered: deer, elk, rabbit, skunk, muskrat, bear, raccoon, dog, otter, beaver, woodchuck, squirrel, turkey, trumpeter swan, giant horned owl, mussel, snail, box turtle, and several species of fish. Vegetable foods include hickory nuts, walnuts, goosefoot, and raspberry seed. Cultigens (?) are limited to the sunflower, gourd, pumpkin, and squash, the latter three being closely related. From cave sites (not hitherto mentioned, but numerous) other wild vegetable remains, such as chinquapin, acorns, chestnuts, butternuts, paw paw, and honey locust pods, were preserved, as were the seeds of several grasses.

Locally distinguished cultures all over the east are seen as varyingly related to Adena. Examples are the Copena of Alabama, the Tchefuncte of Louisiana, and the Middlesex of New York. Adena must be viewed as a strong Ohio Valley development covering a 1600-year period from 800 B.C. to A.D. 800 exerting varyingly strong influences to east, north, and south. It contributed to, influenced, and coexisted with, the Hopewellian culture of the same area.

Nowhere in North America, during the Woodland stage, until the dominance of Adena had there been such sophistication. Only in the central Ohio Valley province was there "enlightenment." Most of the Woodland groups at this period, from the Plains to Nova Scotia, were hunters, built small (if any) mounds, made conoidal cord-marked or fabric-impressed pottery of poor quality, and left in 10,000 tiny camps scant evidence of their passing. To them, Adena may have stood as Imperial Rome (at about the same time) stood to the barbarian Huns or Saxons. The Early Woodland stage is far from uniform and calls up many and varied images. The Ohio Valley student thinks of Adena and its earthworks; the Plains or Illinois archeologist thinks of a scanty buried camp and a handful of crumbly sherds; the Gulf Coast worker thinks of the transitional shell mounds at Tchefuncte or Stallings Island, and for one who has studied New York, the recall is of the lackluster Middlesex.

Hopewell, coexistent with and much influenced by the Adena, which is the earlier, is again centered in southern Ohio and Illinois. The earliest Hopewell sites seem to lie in the Illinois River valley in central Illinois, but the apogee appears to have been reached in Ohio. A strong, widespread, highly distinctive culture whose diagnostic or index artifacts can be identified wherever found, the Hopewell culture was evidently at its height shortly before the time of Christ. Radiocarbon dates range from 2350 B.P. to as late as A.D. 300.

Although Hopewellian has in it many elements of Adena, it must be recognized as having a distinctive genius of its own and as something more than just a "bigger and better" Adena. In all of North American prehistory, Hopewellian influences were the widest spread of any culture north of Mexico, save the Archaic. The large conical burial mounds and the earthwork patterns continue, but the earthen mounds are sometimes larger and show, in their large single tombs and rich funerary offerings, an even more elaborate cult of the dead than that seen in Adena. Usually the tomb was built into a shallow pit and covered by an enormous mound after the interment of from one to five, six, or more individuals was made. These central tombs were filled with varied artifacts (Fig. 22). The dead are presumed to have been important personages of the society, for the burial of less august members seems to have been in simple pits lacking grave goods.

Such burial practices and the vast tumuli and other public works lead to the belief that there was a strong central control over a large population. Also inferred is a stable and ample food supply. Certainly there was widespread trade (or tribute) over much of what is now the United States. The Hopewellian imports to central Ohio include such things as alligator teeth

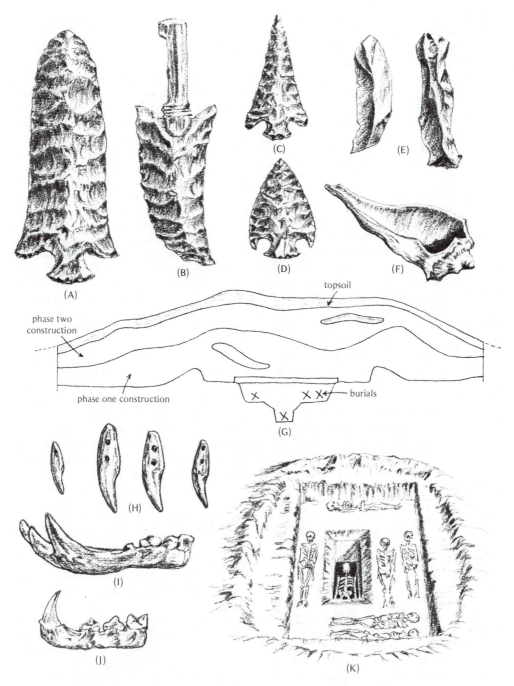

Figure 22 ● Hopewell artifacts and diagram of burial mound. Variable scale. A, obsidian knife or spearhead; B, obsidian knife, wooden handle (restored); C, D, spearheads; E, flake knives; F, conchshell dipper; G, cross section of Wh6 burial mound; H, perforated dog, bear, and wolf canines; I, cut bear jaw; J, cut wolf jaw; K, view of central tomb in Wh6 mound. (A–C after Martin, Quimby, and Collier, 1947; D after Walker, 1952; E after Fowler, 1952; F–K after Neumann and Fowler, 1952; Jennings, 1974:235)

and skulls from Florida, obsidian from Yellowstone Park, mica from North Carolina or Arkansas, copper from the Lake Superior country, and conch shells from the Gulf of Mexico. These were probably imported as raw materials from which the skilled Hopewell artisans wrought objects of surpassing beauty and excellence. Obsidian was used for a variety of ceremonial knives and blades. Copper was used for spool or yo-yo shaped (disclike) ear ornaments, panpipes, ungrooved axes or celts often weighing many pounds, bracelets, rings, and headdresses. Mica sheets were cut into delicate ornaments and headdresses. Conch shells were carved into bowls, gorgets, and beads. Pearls—probably from river mussels—were accumulated by the thousands and used not only as beads but as decorative encrustations on robes or other garments (Fig. 23).

The use of ceramics in both a temporal and cultural interpretation is well exemplified by Hopewell pottery, much of which is standard Woodland, conoidal in form, with wide mouth, the surface roughened with cord-wrapped paddle or stick, and grit tempered. A small but distinctive percentage of the pottery was, however, very ornate, with rocker or toothed zigzag decoration, crosshatched incised rim, and broad-tailed lines. Designs—frequently the raptors already noted in Adena, as well as the roseate spoonbill and the flamingo—were worked out symmetrically over the vessel on which distinct bulges or lobes were fashioned. The designs were based on alternating smooth with roughened or textured zones; the texture was often achieved with the circular or rocker stamp. Vessel forms were still Woodland, but the body was somewhat more globular (or perhaps one should say the neck was more constricted) and the flattened base or bottom was common. Another characteristic was the embossed node below the rim—formed by pushing a reed or round-pointed object into the soft clay from the inside. Although there are a hundred variations in vessel form and perhaps a thousand combinations of design and decorative technique over the Hopewellians' wide sphere of influence, the most distinctive Hopewell complex is ceramic with the rocker stamp, the symmetry of design layout, the alternate use of smooth and textured zones in design, and the crosshatched rim as diagnostic features (Fig. 24, 25). In ceramics, the Hopewell people made also excellent human figurines, from

which many details of dress, posture, hairdress, and even baby care may be learned (Fig. 26).

Some other diagnostic Hopewell artifacts, as listed by Webb and Snow (1945), are shell containers; alligator, shark, and bear teeth; copper breastplates; drills and awls of copper; animal effigies on the monitor (platform) pipe; earspools of stone and copper; cut animal jaws; reel- and bar-shaped gorgets; and cannel coal ornaments. Projectile points and knives were large with deep diagonal notches. There were bone and antler tools of familiar sorts—fishhooks, awls, flaking tools, handles for other tools, and the like (Fig. 27).

One might say that archeological knowledge of the Hopewell is confined almost exclusively to the death cult and its furniture because few details of the day-to-day round have been captured. Few house patterns have been found; they appear to have been round or oval, built of posts set in the ground and joined to form a dome, covered with skins, bark, mats, or clay and thatch.

Although the subsistence pattern was once presumed to have focused on agriculture, almost no documented finds of maize have been made and most of those are not under good control. On the other hand, Struever (1962) reports vast quantities of pigweed, lambs-quarters, and wild grape seeds, as well as hazelnut, walnut, and pecan shells, from the Apple Creek site (Illinois), where maize was almost absent. Struever thinks that the plant species we now consider wild weeds were actually crop plants, and there is good ethnologic evidence for this interpretation. The spread of the culture, its wealth, the ornateness of the burial cult, and the size of the burial/ceremonial tumuli and earthworks all argue for a strong mechanism of social control and a stable, docile work group.

In a triangle covering eastern Iowa, northwest Illinois, and southern Wisconsin, there is an enigmatic Woodland complex called the Effigy Mound culture. Although it resembles the ubiquitous Hopewell in some ways, its age—whether earlier than, contemporary with, or later than Hopewell—is not certainly known. The outstanding attribute of the culture is the scores of mound groups in which some or all of the low earthen forms are well-modeled animals, birds, or reptiles. The animals, modeled in profile or silhouette, are usually found along a ridge crest with the feet, naturally, pointing downhill. Mixed with the effigies are small low

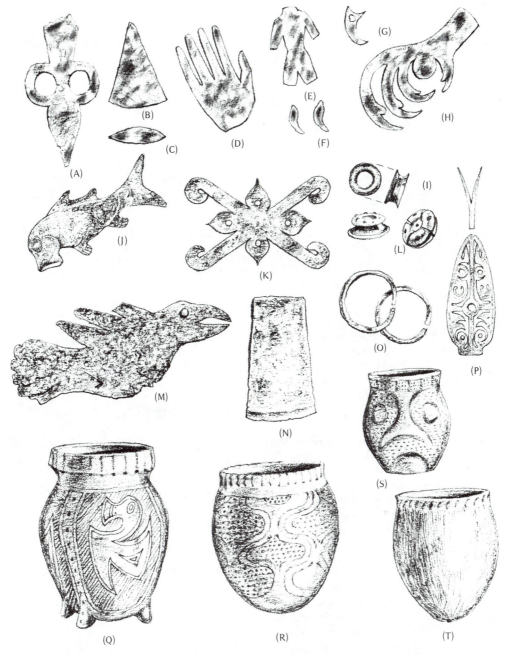

Figure 23 ● Hopewell artifacts. Much reduced scale. Ornaments of sheet mica: A–H (F representing bear claws and G a bird talon); I, stone ear ornament; copper artifacts; J, fish, probably a sucker; K, robe ornament; L, ear ornaments; M, bird with pearl eye; N, ax head; O, bracelets; P, ornament, probably a serpent's head; Q–T, pottery. (A–C after Moorehead, 1910, vol. II; D–P after Martin, Quimby, and Collier, 1947; O after Griffin, 1952a, fig. 32–S; R after Lilly, 1937; S after McGregor, 1952; T after Griffin, 1952b; Jennings, 1974:237)

(A)   (B)   (C)   (D)

(E)   (F)   (G)   (H)

Figure 24 ● **Hopewell pottery types from the Crooks site. A–D, Marksville Plain, 2½ to 3 inches high; E, F, Marksville stamped, both 4 inches high; G, H, Marksville incised, both 4½ inches high. (After Ford and Willey, 1940; Jennings, 1974:240)**

conical mounds and long slender linear mounds or embankments. All these forms are funerary monuments containing one, two, or three individuals. Rarely are there grave goods. No villages of this people can be specifically identified. Chief interest in this culture has lain with the mystery of the effigy cult. In these mounds, the head, shoulders, hips, and rib cages are modeled in correct relief. Forms include panther, raptoral bird, bison, goose, bear, turtle, and lizard. The size of some is surprising; one bird has a 624-foot wingspread. One panther is 575 feet long. Usually, however, the dimensions are smaller, a wingspread or length of 100 feet being more common. According to Hurley (1975), the effigy culture existed from A.D. 300 to 1642; he accords it the status of a distinctive culture developing *in situ*.

Before we close the discussion of the Woodland stage and its substages, the unsatisfactoriness of this classification must be emphasized. In fact, as far as artifact inventory, state of technology, and subsistence pattern is concerned, it is perhaps more accurate to say that the so-called Woodland cultures do not really require a separate taxonomic niche. Actually, the Archaic

Figure 25 ● **Typical Hopewell vessel from the Marksville works. Note roulette decorated area outlining design. Approximately actual size. (After Setzler, 1933; Jennings, 1974:240)**

lifeway never stopped; pottery, the use of pipes, and finally agriculture were simply incorporated into an already satisfactory relationship with nature. Except for Adena-Hopewell (which makes more sense if treated as a unique Mexican superimposition upon a population and adaptation that is a continuum from the Archaic) and the effect this complex seems to have had on certain contemporary and some later cultures, the Woodland does not really exist as a broad uniform stratum such as we have seen in the Archaic.

Figure 26 ● Hopewell ceramic figurines. Approximately three-fourths size. (After McKern, Titterington, and Griffin, 1945; Jennings, 1974:234)

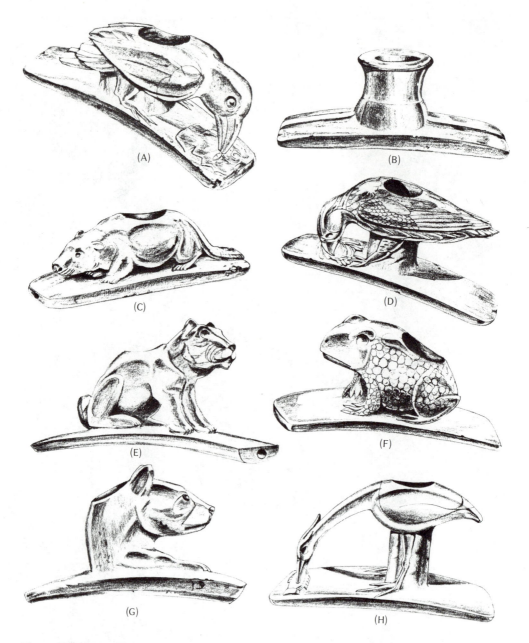

Figure 27 ● Hopewell stone pipe sculptures, slightly reduced. A, hawk or eagle attacking a man; B, highly polished platform pipe; C, beaver; D, hawk or eagle tearing at a small bird; E, cougar or wild cat; F, toad; G, bear; H, tufted heron with a small fish. (A, B drawn from University of Wisconsin color slides of original pipes; C–F, H after Squier and Davis, 1848; G after Neumann and Fowler, 1952; Jennings, 1974:236)

MISSISSIPPIAN

Although the Adena-Hopewellian dominance faded after about A.D. 200 or 400, Hopewell influence moving southward from the Classic phase in Ohio can be seen to have a quasi-ancestral role in the last great culture of the eastern United States, called the Mississippian. As the Woodland cultures passed the central Adena-Hopewell climax, there was actually a regression or slumping in technology, which Griffin (1952)

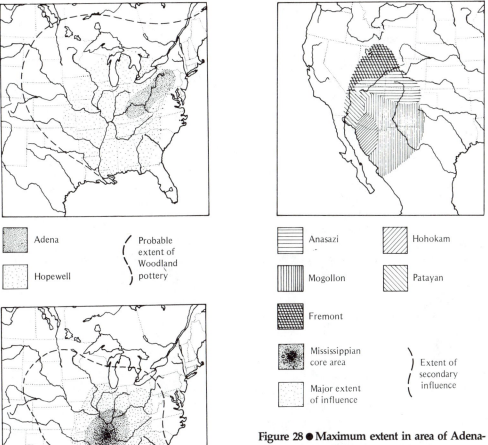

Adena

Hopewell

/ **Probable extent of Woodland pottery** \

Anasazi

Mogollon

Fremont

Mississippian core area

Major extent of influence

Hohokam

Patayan

) **Extent of secondary influence** \

Figure 28 ● Maximum extent in area of Adena-Hopewell, Mississippian, and Southwest cultures at their climaxes. (Jennings, 1974:213)

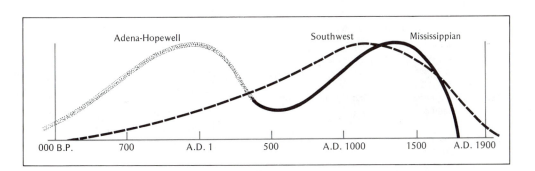

Figure 29 ● Chronology of North American Formative stage climax (Jennings, 1974:212)

persuasively equates with slight but decisive climatic changes including alterations in precipitation and temperature. Whatever the cause, the later Woodland forms, whether in the East, Northeast, Southeast, or Middle West, tend to persist in a sort of tranquility marked by no dramatic change in material culture. This, however, was not true of the Mississippi Valley itself or the valleys of its major tributaries. Here, in ways not at all clear, the most vigorous, most impressive pre-European aboriginal culture came into existence.

The Mississippian culture complex is baffling in a score of ways. Its point of origin is obscure; its antecedents and ancestry are clouded and much debated. Its remains are exceedingly numerous and very large; almost none have been thoroughly excavated because of their size and the expense of proper excavation. Its later stages are obscured by the existence of a flamboyant complex of very special ritual objects— perhaps Death Cult oriented—which, although characteristic of some Mississippian sites, nevertheless are also found in perhaps non-Mississippi sites.

It evolved in the rich lands of the southeastern river valleys climaxing about A.D. 1500, finally to become extinct after A.D. 1700. No further discussion of the Mississippian cultures is given here; the culture is adequately explained and summarized in Chapter 9.

Suggested readings

AIKENS, C. M.
1970   Hogup Cave. *University of Utah Anthropological Papers,* no. 93.

GRIFFIN, J. B.
1964   "The Northeast Woodlands Area." In *Prehistoric Man in the New World,* ed. Jesse D. Jennings and Edward Norbeck, pp. 223–258. Rice University Semicentennial Publications. The University of Chicago Press.
1952   *Archeology of the Eastern United States.* University of Chicago Press.

HALLOWELL, A. I.
1960   "The Beginnings of Anthropology in America." In *Selected Papers from the American Anthropologist, 1888–1920,* ed. Frederica De Laguna, pp. 1–90. New York: Harper & Row.

JENNINGS J. D.
1974   *Prehistory of North America.* 2d ed. New York: McGraw-Hill.
1957   Danger Cave. *University of Utah Anthropological Papers,* no. 27.

JENNINGS, J. D., and NORBECK, E. eds.
1964   *Prehistoric Man in the New World.* University of Chicago Press.

RITCHIE, W. A.
1969   *The Archaeology of New York State.* rev. ed. Garden City, N.Y.: The Natural History Press.

SCHUYLER, R. L.
1971   "The History of American Archaeology: An Examination of Procedure." *American Antiquity,* vol. 36, no. 4, pp. 383–409.

WILLEY, G. R.
1968   "One Hundred Years of Archaeology." In *One Hundred Years of Archaeology,* ed. J. O. Brew, pp. 29–53. Cambridge: Harvard University Press.
1966   *An Introduction to American Archaeology: North and Middle America,* vol. 1. Englewood Cliffs, N.J.: Prentice-Hall.

WILLEY, G. R., and SABLOFF, J. A.
1974   *A History of American Archeology.* San Francisco: Freeman.

II

Language-
American
Babel

Introduction

As one moves from a discussion of the prehistoric past to a consideration of the so-called ethnographic present, one finds that describing native cultures as they were, before the changes brought about by contacts with Europeans, presents many problems of classification. The cultures themselves, their content, such as the inventory one may make of their material and nonmaterial components, permit division into areal groupings, the culture areas delineated in the following sections. But there are also linguistic areas. An initial perspective on the native Americans is given by a review of their language development.

The near and remote past, as gleaned from archeological investigation, obviously allows no suggestion as to what language was spoken by the peoples whose cultures come to light. It can be assumed that cultural continuity also implies continuity of language. This may be so, but some cautions are in order. In the American Southwest, for example, where the pueblo tradition is deeply rooted in time, and where the cultural sequences based on such aspects as agriculture, house types, or pottery are firmly established, it might be expected that the same language has persisted through time. But the difficulty can be seen at once when the Pueblo Indians of the ethnographic present are considered; they speak not one language but have four major speech groupings. This does not count the subdivisions of the major groupings into mutually unintelligible languages, nor the further subdivision into dialects. The pueblos offer a classic example of the point that peoples may share the same general culture patterns even though they speak languages as different from each other as English is from Chinese. Whether the same situation existed during Pueblo III times a thousand years ago, when the monumental building was taking place, is difficult to say. It is known that the strong pueblo culture patterns were able to impress other groups and draw them into the specialized culture and ecological puebloan adaptations. This may account for the linguistic diversity in the face of cultural similarities.

On the other hand, the Eskimo situation is quite different. From Greenland to western Alaska along the Arctic coasts there is essentially the same language, one virtually mutually intelligible over the wide region. This bears out the evidence of the recency of Eskimo movements across the American Arctic. This language distribution tends generally to be congruent with the basic cultural pattern and type. But it is obvious that the language spoken by the Dorset people, or by others representing prehistoric Arctic traditions, cannot be known or even inferred. What can be suggested by an examination of languages and their relationships is an additional perspective on the movements and connections between various groups.

Several misconceptions about the American Indian language picture, or indeed, about language generally, should at once be removed. There were in the nineteenth century, for example, some students of comparative human behavior, philosophers speculating about human society, who assumed that there were tribes of American Indians who spoke such "primitive" languages that it was impossible for the members to communicate with each other in the dark. The languages they spoke, muttered, or grunted were so limited, it was held, that thought and its transference had to be accompanied by gesture in order to make meanings clear. The holders of this view were wrong on two counts. They assumed that Plains Indian sign language, a means of communicating through conventional gestures and symbols made with the hands, which developed in an area of common culture where there was considerable language diversity, was an integral part of the languages themselves. And they also believed that one language can be more primitive, more rudimentary, more reflective of a cruder stage, itself purely hypothetical, of language beginnings. It is not known how language began. It is true that the human being possesses certain biological attributes which suggest how language may have come into being, but the questions of where and when remain unanswered. Moreover, while languages are different in the sounds they possess and in the grammatical structures which each has evolved, so different in fact that each can be said to categorize experience and perception in special ways, no language is "primitive." Certain languages express some ideas with greater facility and economy than others, but any linguistic system developed by human experience is a finished system and has to be seen in these terms.

It must also be noted that a language is an entity which permits analysis even if it is not written. Ancient Mexico did, it is true, develop writing and some of the Plains Indians used written "signs" to record war deeds and time counts on tipi walls, although whether this can be considered true writing is debatable. In the nineteenth century, Sequoia (1760?–1843), a Cherokee, invented a syllabic, alphabetic system applicable to his language, and there followed numerous attempts to develop systems of writing for various formerly unwritten languages. The anthropological linguist, interested in collecting discourses, utterances, and texts from a native language, or the missionary, attempting to translate biblical and other religious materials, have been obliged to reduce a given language to writing. But this is all a postcontact development and the writing systems used, even if ultimately employed by the native peoples themselves, are drawn from a phonetic alphabet based primarily on Latin letters. Except for Mexico, true writing cannot be considered a part of the aboriginal New World culture. Again, however, it must be stressed that because a language is not written, it does not follow that it is somehow debased. Quite the reverse is true. The native American cultures preserved their oral traditions with fidelity, and many valued oratory and drama in speech. The native languages were spoken—as many are spoken even today—with precision and no slovenly quality. The oral traditions of the New World reflect a vast unwritten literature.

Yet another commonly held view must be set aside. Any ethnologist with American Indian experience can attest to having been asked—Do you speak Indian? The mistaken assumption is that all Indians speak a common language. And it is rather discouraging to be asked—Which Indian dialects do you speak? Indian dialects there are, to be sure, just as the English of cockney London, the Deep South, or the American Middle West are dialects of the English mother tongue. Dialects, in the main, are mutually intelligible. When mutual intelligibility ceases, a language boundary has been crossed. There were dialects of the American Indian languages, but there were also numerous separate languages, entities completely remote from each other with no trace of common history.

In 1940 (Voegelin, 1941), a listing was made of native languages in North America north of Mexico which were still being spoken. The list numbers 149 and does not take into account the fact that many of these are broken up into local dialects. Most are still living languages, although in the past decades a few have perished as the last surviving speakers have died. Still others remain in force, possessing several thousands of speakers, as is the case among the populous Navaho of Arizona and New Mexico. Since contact with Europeans, many tribes, and with them their languages, have become extinct, a point especially true of the southeastern United States and California. But at that, in Alaska, Canada, and the United States mainland, about 200 separate languages can be verified for the period just preceding contact. Middle America, Mexico and Central America, had somewhat more, with about 350 languages, the majority of which are still spoken (Driver, 1969:492ff). In South America there is even greater linguistic complexity. McQuown (1955) lists about 1450 languages. In other terms, the 2000 languages listed for both North and South America account for about one-third of the languages of the world.

If one were to speculate on the origins of such diversity, remembering that many of these languages are related to each other, implying that they have branched off from a common parent stock, it might be assumed that man did not enter the New World as a single population with a common language. Now and again, in fact, the suggestion is made that a native American language, such as the Athabascan and Wakashan groupings, or Eskimoan, has affinities in the languages of Eurasia. Some have also seen such relationships in South America. There is no reason to question this claim and with the increasingly refined techniques of linguistic analysis, it may ultimately be established. At this point, however, the evidence is too fragmentary. A long period of time has been involved. What is suggested is that there were multiple movements of peoples over an extended period of time. Since language never remains constant, and like culture, is subject to change, increasing diversity can be expected. Migration of linguistic groups has clearly taken place. With isolation and organic change, it may be seen that the different speech units became increasingly divided rather than the reverse.

CLASSIFICATIONS, RELATIONSHIPS, AND TIME DEPTH

There are two main ways of looking at language. Just as in the case of culture, language can be seen as a finished product, a holistic system, in which the various components— sounds and parts of speech—can be analyzed.

Such an approach asks how the language "works." A second question about how the language came about can be asked. If several languages can be shown to have a common parent, such as the Romance languages of French, Spanish, Italian, and others, which go back to a Vulgar Latin, the ways and processes of their separation can be analyzed largely by a comparison of the elements both of vocabulary or lexicon and the structure which they share. Both approaches are relevant. Applied to North America, both allow some understanding of the scope of the problems of language.

Viewed as a holistic entity, any language has a system of sounds, its phonology, a basic structure, its grammar or morphology, and its syntax, the way in which structured units are put together to give phrases and sentences. Sound, needless to note, is a necessary prerequisite to language, but it is also axiomatic that no two languages have the same exact sets of sounds. This is why, even if the number of sounds in any one language is limited, many of the American Indian languages seemed so unique or peculiar to those who first heard them. The speaker of a European language has difficulty in locating some of the sounds in various of the Indian languages. His phonemes—the basic sound elements composing a given language—are simply different. And of course the reverse is true; an Indian speaker may find troubles in placing his tongue, his lips, or other parts of the speech mechanism in order to pronounce sounds in European languages. One point about sounds: There can be as much difference between the Amerindian languages themselves as between any given Indian language and English, French, or Spanish. There is no problem or special feature associated with the American languages and their pronunciation. Different sounds exist, different, at least, from those of various more familiar languages of Europe, but such sounds all fall into the range of human possibility. Like languages anywhere across the world, those of the American Indian make special selections of sounds, clustering and patterning them in ways peculiarly their own. And, of course, English or any other language does exactly the same thing.

There is a suggestion that sound patterns, like any other element of culture, may spread by diffusion over a wide area. In northern North America, for example, along the Northwest Coast and adjacent regions, where considerable linguistic diversity exists, there is a predilection for fairly heavy glottalizations, which means that some sounds tend to be drawn back into the area of the throat and given a tight, throated quality. The sound pattern appears to have spread across the boundaries of a number of mutually unintelligible languages. Morphological elements can also spread. In the same area, when reference is made to an object, an element of visibility or invisibility must be introduced. Kwakiutl, for example, can refer to a house but the grammatical form used must indicate whether the house is seen or not seen by the speaker or by the person to whom reference is made. This concept spreads beyond the area of Wakashan speech (Boas, 1911:40).

American Indian languages differ from the more familiar languages of Europe in the patterning of sound—even if the sounds of some Indian languages are quite parallel to those of English, German, or other languages—but they become somewhat more distinctive in their morphological and syntactical (i.e., general grammatical) formations. No valuation is implied in such a statement; all that is indicated is that the languages of native America are essentially different in the ways in which they put concepts together. Not only are they different from the general structures of European languages, but they vary considerably in structure among themselves. The languages of native North America, regardless of relationship, have tended toward the development of involved morphological features, as in word building and formation. In forming a word, there is a general inclination toward "agglutination," a combining of various component elements. A problem is created if an attempt is made to enumerate the units of vocabulary. One can sometimes list basic root forms, but when the conjoined elements are taken into account, there is no little difficulty in establishing what precisely a word is. Word counts, in any case, are not a useful index. Suffice it to note that the American Indian languages, as finished systems, can express fully as a wide a range of thought as can the languages of Europe. Because of their structures, they will express the ideas differently. What is clear, when Amerindian linguistic structures are considered, is that the rules of Latin grammar have no application or reality. The native languages have to be appraised in terms of their own grammatical standards.

In English, there is dependence on declarative concepts and certainly, a stress on the ele-

ment of time. No difficulty is encountered with the parts of speech and it is relatively easy to distinguish noun from verb, from pronoun, preposition, or adjective. Distinctions of this kind are not always possible in numerous of the native American languages. It is not that these languages are illogical where English possesses an infallible logic. It is simply that the logical system—one likes to think of it as such—of English is one form, the logic of an American Indian language another. Some languages are not concerned with time and base their verbal differentiations on duration, repetition, or type of action without reference to tense in the European sense. Others are much concerned with the validity of an action, as, for example, whether the action described has taken place within the experience of the speaker or whether he has the information by hearsay. Still others do not differentiate between noun and verb; a root may have the meaning of both and it is the surrounding grammatical elements, the morphemes which, added or inserted, determine the meaning. Definiteness and indefiniteness are fairly common grammatical adjuncts in American languages, not only in verbs, but in such contexts as pronouns, an action being attributed to a definite or indefinite person. Classifications can also be important in some languages, something akin to the English notion of "five head of deer" rather than "five deer." Objects discussed may be classified in this way, resulting in varying definitions and forms relating to round objects, long, thin objects, heavy, bulky objects, and many more. Needless to note, no one language incorporates all of these features but all appear with some frequency over various tongues.

Word building in different languages may take place quite differently. An example or two may demonstrate some of the processes. In Yuman, one of the languages of the lower Colorado River, a series of thematic or causative prefixes exists (Halpern, 1946:271–272). The prefix *k-* means "to cause with the foot, with a large or heavy instrument, or with great force." In combination with *asuly,* "to be ripped" comes *kasuly,* "to rip with great force," or *ka'ak,* "to kick." Or again, *t-* means "to cause by means of an instrument"; from it is derived *taqʷeraqʷer,* "to sharpen to a point," from *qʷeraqʷer* "to be sharp-pointed."

How some of the essentially alien concepts of an American Indian language operate can be illustrated by a short sentence. The language is

Maidu, that of one of the main tribes of central California of the same name:

amá·dikan	món⁹	külém	bǘsstsoia
there and	she	girl	lived (it is said)

On the face of it, the sentence seems eminently simple. What is required is that the speaker and hearer be adapted to the particular linguistic situation which the language puts forth. In the first word, *amá·* is a demonstrative pronoun, with the meaning "that"; *-di* is a locative, that is, it refers to a specific place, while the suffix *-kan* is a conjunction, "and." The compound, *má·dikan*, can best be rendered "and there, in that place." The next element, *món⁹*, has no gender reference at all. It refers conceptually to a kind of midpoint between the article "the" and the demonstrative, "that"; *küĺe* has the meaning "feminine person," thus referring to a woman, girl, or other female. Attached to *küĺe* is the suffix *-m*, which has the function of making the element it modifies a verbal subject. The unit *bis*, from which *bǘss* is derived in compounds, has the root meaning "to continue in one place," hence "to live" (i.e., occupying a residence). Next, *-tsoi* is a verbal morpheme, a suffix which denotes completed action and is quotative or dubitative, that is, the knowledge imparted is dependent on hearsay, not direct experience on the part of the speaker. Finally, the suffixed *-a* relates to the third person, in this instance, the "female" (Dixon, 1911:726). A free translation might be "And in that place there was a girl living." Such a translation fails to catch all the shades of meaning of the Maidu sentence. It is evident from the choice of forms that the speaker never saw the girl—or woman, as the case might be—and that she is no longer living there. That the person in question was a girl can only be gained from the previous sentences of the text, those referring to her parents who were living in the same place. To the Maidu, from the choice of words, it is clear that the girl was not married nor was she very young. In other words, the same subtle understandings which would appear in an English sentence are also characteristic of the Maidu. The implications for culture are considered below.

A slightly different pattern is encountered in Eskimo with its complex synthetic character, that of combining several elements in order to form a single word, one which in English would require translation by a whole sentence.

examples are: *anerquwaatit*, "he begs you to go out." Analyzed into its component parts, the *a* refers to "he," the subject; *aner*, "to go out" (the initial *a* is assimilated by the second); *quwa*, "begs"; *tit*, "you." A similar pattern appears in *aneyaarqerquwaatit*, "he begs you again to go out early." Here, the elements, in addition to those above, are *qer*, "again," and *yaar*, "early." An Eskimo sentence thus consists of numerous bound elements, those put together to connote relationships which do not correspond to the more familiar European usage (cf. Thalbitzer, 1911:1002). To this may be added the elaborated Eskimo nouns, this being a language which differentiates fairly carefully between noun and verb. Examples are: *nuuna*, "land," *nuunak*, "two lands," a dual, referring to two of anything, *nuunat*, "lands," plural; *iglu*, (properly, *i γ ʎu*), "house," *igluk*, "two houses," *iglut*, "houses," plural. Add to this the so-called case endings, such as *iglume*, "from the house," *iglunit*, "from the houses," through several other relational or case concepts, and there is a wide range of forms. But the system goes on. Possessive pronouns, relating to singular, dual, and plural, as well as first, second, and third persons, not to mention several kinds of third personal possessives, "their" as against "their own," are also suffixed to roots with case designations. In such a language, if there are 7 major noun cases, 12 basic possessive pronouns, and 3 numbers—the singular, dual, and plural—there are over 250 possible forms for the noun alone. This of course does not take into account the various combinations of verbs. Eskimo, in short, is heavily inflected and highly synthetic, bringing together various units as it does, all in precisely defined and patterned ways (cf. Swadesh, 1946).

These samples indicate a great range of possible linguistic situations. Turning for the moment away from languages as systems, it is helpful to note the bases on which the various languages of native America are classified. This is a historical problem, one depending for its solution on comparison and a consideration of the relationships between languages.

It is known, and conclusively demonstrated, that English is closely related to German, that both have relationships to Latin, Greek, and to the Sanskrit of ancient India. Throughout these related languages of Europe and southern Asia, certain structural similarities are discernible. Although English has lost sex gender, which characterizes the majority of Indo-European languages to which English belongs, noun-verb distinctions, tense and temporal categories, as well as subordinate or subjunctive categories characterize these languages. There is also the phonological similarity, the fact that Latin *pater* is rather like English *father* and German *Vater*. Meanings and sounds may change over time but an analysis of the kind of change leads to a prediction of change and the establishment of rules of change in language. It can be implied that when a whole cluster of sounds, one running through an extensive vocabulary, reflects patterned and regular changes, a relationship may be admitted. This is to say that languages show relationships to each other, that certain groups of languages may exhibit a common ancestry. Applying this principle to the languages of native America, it can be seen that certain language *Families*, those stemming from an ostensibly common ancestor, emerge quite clearly.

In North America, taking a language family like Algonkin (Algonquian), a precise classification is possible (Bloomfield, 1946:85 ff.). There is a range of Algonkin languages, some more closely and demonstrably related to each other than to others. The major grouping, Algonkin, is divided into the following subdivisions and languages.

I. Central-Eastern: A. Central Type: Cree-Montagnais-Naskapi, Menomini, Fox-Sauk-Kickapoo, Shawnee, Peoria-Miami, Potawatomi, Ojibwa-Ottawa-Algonkin-Saulteaux, Delaware, Powhatan. B. New England Type: Natick-Narragansett, Mohegan-Pequot, Penobscot-Abnaki, Passamaquoddy-Malecite, Micmac
II. Blackfoot
III. Cheyenne
IV. Arapaho-Atsina-Nawathinehena
V. Wiyot, Yurok (Ritwan)

As may be seen, the language names correspond in the main to tribal names, suggesting that tribe and language are often identical. If the distribution is noted, it can be determined that the main clustering of the Algonkin languages occurs on the eastern seaboard and Great Lakes region of the United States and Canada. A second clustering appears in the Plains, with the Blackfoot, Cheyenne, and Arapaho. The comparative method, considering both lexicon and structure, offers wholly supportive evidence for the relationships of these

Algonkin languages; there can be no question of their relationship to each other. The Wiyot and Yurok, so-called Ritwan, division of California is now generally accepted, although the evidence is considerably less clear. Similarly, as has been suggested by Sapir (1929), whether there is justification for including Kutenai in the northern Plateau, and Mosan (Wakashan and Salishan) is again debatable. Mosan, consisting of Salishan, Chimakuan, and Wakashan, three apparently related groupings, suggests Algonkin, but there is no definite proof of relationship (cf. Swadesh, 1953:26-27). Similarily, there are demonstrable relationships to Algonkin in the southeastern United States, such as in the regions bordering the Gulf of Mexico (Haas, 1958a, 1959), a point dependent on lexicostatistical formulation (see below).

Leaving the questionable groups aside, Algonkin emerges as a well defined speech family in the eastern segments of the continent. On comparing a considerable number of words and compounds, Bloomfield (1946) was able to reconstruct a general or proto-Algonkin, a language not spoken, but postulated on the basis of regularized sound shifts between the member languages. Changes are evident, but it is not difficult to see the underlying root and forms:

Reconstructed Proto-Algonkin (Central)	*noohkomehsa	"my grandmother"
Fox	noohkomesa	
Cree	noohkom	
Menomini	noohkomeh	
Ojibwa	nookkomiss	

or:

Proto-Algonkin (Central)	*ehkwa	"louse"
	*netehkoma	"my louse"
Fox	netehkoma	
Cree	nitihkom	
Menomini	neteehkom	
Ojibwa	nintikkom	

*reconstructed or hypothetical

An example such as the above readily points to close linguistic relationship. Languages which are more widely spread geographically, where a question of time depth is raised because of long-term separation, pose rather more intricate questions. Rigorous analysis is then necessary. Greenberg and Swadesh (1953), following a lead of Edward Sapir, a linguistic pioneer and at the same time the most eminent of the investigators of American languages (d. 1939), were able to demonstrate the relationship of Honduran Jicaque and the general Hokan (Hokan-Siouan [Sapir, 1929], Hokan-Coahuiltecan) family. An example or two may illustrate the problem: An interrogative appears in Jicaque as *kanlepa*, "when," and *kat*, "where." In other languages, Chontal shows *kana*, "when," and *kaape*, "where"; Washo (California) *kunya*, "where," *kunyate*, "what"; Tunica (Southeast) *ka-*, general interrogative; Coahuiltec *xat*, (*x=ch*, like German, suggesting a *k* derivation) "how many," *xakat*, "why"; Comecrudo (Coahuiltecan) *xat*, "where," *tokom*, "whatever thing," and Chimariko, *qho*, general interrogative. Close examination reveals that with this example, as well as many others, the words are cognate, that is, they reflect patterned sound changes and retain the same general category of meaning. They exhibit, in short, suggestions of relationship. Clearly, one example is scarcely sufficient; an extensive comparison is necessary to determine the cognates. Implied as well is the establishment of the nature of the modification of sounds from language to language. There is also the suggestion that these languages broke off from a Hokan stem, a hypothetical parent stock, at some point in time, a matter reserved for discussion below.

In any treatment of the relationships of languages, care must be taken to avoid making generalizations on the basis of too little evidence. Remembering that the human speech mechanism can, after all, produce only a limited number of sounds, and that similarities in both vocabulary and structure can occur by chance, it is easily seen why some have contended that some Amerindian or other languages are related to Hebrew, ancient Egyptian, Chinese, or whatever. Carefully controlled comparison would seem to rule out such claims. If there is any such resemblance, as, for example, to the languages of eastern Asia, techniques have been developed which may allow a cautious conclusion. The possibility of the Wakashan relationship to the Altaic languages of central Asia, of Eskimoan to the same, or, as has been claimed, to Indo-European, cannot be wholly discounted but neither can it be adequately demonstrated. The Athabascan languages, as well as some others in native America, are tonal, that is, there is a distinct tone or pitch of the voice associated with the articulation of

vowels. The same is true, of course, of the Chinese languages and of others in East and Southeast Asia. Does this mean that Chinese (or other tonal languages of Asia) and Athabascan share a common ancestry? The answer is possibly, although there are few resemblances of any other kind between them.

The initial attempt to discover language relationships and to define a genetic classification of American languages was made by J. W. Powell and his associates in 1891. His was a remarkably accurate study in spite of fairly fragmentary materials. Powell distributed word lists to Indian agents, missionaries, and others who had contact with a given tribe. The lists, running to little more than one to two hundred words, were compared, the apparent cognates analyzed, and a formulation of language phyla or families for native America north of Mexico given. Since Powell's day some of his 54 families have been shown to be related to others, resulting in a reduction of the original number. It is worth noting that none of his basic stocks has been split further. The same method was later applied to Mexico, Middle, and South America. Powell, of course, was using a method of comparison which had been successfully employed by the nineteenth-century philologists, the historical linguists who were concerned with such relationships as could be demonstrated for Indo-European and other Old World phyla. Powell's was a remarkable achievement; with refinements, his general method continued to be applied for the next half century.

The result of continuing study is that new relationships are seen and languages which were once thought to be far apart may have a common history. As the list of language families is examined, some puzzling features arise. Why, for example, are there so many families, if not for North America, certainly for Middle and South America? New data come to the fore for these areas and relationships are postulated and proved, a synthesis which has been attained more successfully in North America as a result of intensive work over many decades on native languages. If an equation is made with language and the earliest settlers on the American continents, several questions at once arise (Voegelin, 1964). If it can be assumed that human beings came to the New World in waves over a long period of time, it follows that several different languages were introduced, changing from dialect to new language as time progressed. It is only by the most rigorous stretch of the imagination that relationships between New and Old World languages can be found. They either do not exist, or are as yet undemonstrated. A further difficulty, one suggested by Professor Grover Krantz (personal communication), is that hunters tend to stay put. It may be seen as hunting cultures are examined, especially those of the sub-Arctic regions, that migration is unheard of and the group tends to remain in the area which it knows how to exploit. The causes of American Indian movements across the Bering Strait are not fully comprehended despite the many explanations of glaciation, movements of game, population pressures, or others. But what was the nature of the language or languages spoken by such migrants?

Since there seems to be no relation between Asiatic and American languages, it probably may be assumed that the languages and language families of North and South America developed within the continental landmass and were not introduced from the outside (Radin, 1919:492). Or if one or more substratum language had been brought by migrants milennia ago, they cannot be reconstructed. Sounds vary greatly from one American language to another, but by stretching the comparisons, it can be said that there are broad structural similarities between them. Such statements are not very helpful, and any relationship which could conceivably rise out of a linguistic pattern far distant in time remains for pure speculation. Because languages change over time and language families have come into being, the important point is to determine the provable relationships. Temporal depth in language, so far as one can make it meaningful, is important. As linguistic science has developed and devised new methods, some significant statements on language relationships can be made.

Two of these new methods—glottochronology and lexicostatistics—were first proposed by the linguist Morris Swadesh and other linguists to evaluate relationships in time depth (glottochronology) and in terms of enumeration of shared elements (lexicostatistics). The latter is a statistical appraisal of language connections, an evaluation of the number of cognates, related words or roots, shared by languages which belong discernibly to the same stock or family. Temporality is dealt with by glottochronology, primarily a lexicostatistic method of estimating the time span involved in the separation of a language from others to which it is related (cf. Hymes, 1960). When originally developed, it was believed that glottochronological analyses would be as effective a technique for showing time spans in language as those methods employed by archeologists were in establishing temporal sequences, such as carbon 14. There is clear agreement with Sapir's statement that "the greater the degree of linguistic differentiation within a stock, the greater the period of time that must be assumed for the development of such differentiation." (1916:76.) Whether one can find the time span involved and infer a dating on the basis of analyses of cognates is by no means settled. It was originally optimistically believed that glottochronology could assist the archeologist in his need to locate cultural phenomena in time but unfortunately, glottochronology, while not to be wholly discarded, does not work as well as was hoped.

When used with a certain caution and when only a relatively short period of time, a thousand years or less, is considered, dating by glottochronology is worth using. The basis of this dating technique is the assumption that a language will change at a predictable rate. The question can be put hypothetically: If languages A, B, and C are demonstrably related, comparison showing cognates between them, and if A and B are more closely related to each other than to C, it may be assumed that C split off earlier than A or B and that the split between A and B came later; when, therefore, did C diverge and A and B become separate? The answer is based on a comparison of the languages and a statistical count of the number of cognate or related words which each retains. In glottochronological analyses, the choice has been made of basic word lists, consisting of from one to two hundred items. This is a "core vocabulary," one made up of word elements which because of their common occurrence are more readily retained—such items as body parts, lower numerals, pronouns, words referring to common natural objects, as animals and plants, and those denoting universal actions in human experience, as eating, drinking, dying, standing, and the like. Such word elements, not necessarily whole words in themselves, considering that with inflections words as such may be difficult to define, are ostensibly "culture free." This also poses a problem, since special associations with words can be derived from the cultural experience. But admitting this, the core vocabulary can then be compared between two or more related languages to determine the extent to which it is retained. In the example above, A and B possess a greater number of common cognates than either does with C. A time sequence is implied.

A fair number of studies indicates that the loss of cognates is in the range of 19 percent per thousand years. Conversely, a language may be expected to retain 81 percent of its core vocabulary over a thousand year period. When two languages are compared, each is shown to have lost 19 of the basic list of 100, replacing them with borrowed words, or finding other means by which to express the lexical concepts. Since the two languages do not lose the same sets of words, each retains a percentage of what the other loses. Computing this as a fairly constant process, each also retains 81 percent of what the other loses, or, as between the two, there is 66 percent of the basic list in common at the end of one thousand years. If 66 percent cognate retention can thus be demonstrated, it is assumed that one thousand years has elapsed since the divergence of the two languages. When more than two languages are so compared, a gradient is established, a basis of determining the degree of language relationship.

Some examples of glottochronologic dating can be seen in the Eskimo phylum. Eskimoan and Aleut are related languages, a formulation based on cognate comparison, and together form a single language family, Eskaleut in Swadesh's terminology. Eastern (Greenlandic) and Western Eskimo, the latter the Yukon branch, show 66 percent correspondence, suggesting that the split occurred a thousand years ago. This is well borne out by archeological evidence (cf. Swadesh, 1954:364–372; Marsh and Swadesh, 1951:209–216). But where Eskimo diverges from Aleut, the correspondence is considerably less and a 3000 year period of separation is postulated. Corrected for error, the latter figure may include a ±300 year variation. Or again, where comparison of Jicaque and other Hokan languages can be made, Washo (California) and Jicaque may show a divergence of 4500 years, ±450 years.

Do these dates actually hold? In the thousand year dating of the split between Eskimo Yupik and Inupik there may well be some validity. To push dates further back, even if there are some hints of antiquity, seems an attempt to grasp at any technique of dating that comes to hand. There are several serious criticisms of glottochronology, however exciting it may appear

at first. Human language is not a chemical element subject to a predictable series of changes. If there is lexical loss in language, there is also replacement. There is no fundamental reason for languages to change at a consistent rate. The accidents of contact, conquest, diffusion, all of the processes, in short, which are operative in culture building as well as in language structuring, would seem to modify the rate of change. It also seems questionable that a "culture free" list of 200 lexemes (words) is a sufficient sample. Indeed, it may be questioned that words are ever free from associations which lie in cultural systems.

Apart from the use as a technique of dating, lexicostatistics has led to some new formulations and some hints of unsuspected relationships as well. Languages which had not been previously compared can now be shown to share some cognates, with the result that some rethinking of the kind of traditional classifications proposed by Powell is required. The assumption was always that the patterning of language relationships was analogous to the classifications advanced for the plant and animal world by the biologist. Languages were conceived to split off from a parent stock and then to proceed along their independent courses. Although perhaps true in a general way and certainly demonstrable for some languages, the increasing awareness of degree of distance of relationship, as well as of the ways in which languages can influence each other both structurally and in lexicon, begins to suggest that the figure of languages branching off from a parent stock, a tree trunk, so to speak, can no longer be so firmly held. Even if languages have a presumed independent history, the interplay of influences between them and other languages has to be taken into account. Degree of relationship, convergent and divergent influences, when taken into consideration, suggest that the simple family tree has to be discarded in favor of a complex evaluation of many factors. Such meshing of factors—to use Swadesh's concept of a "mesh principle" (1959, 2:7–14)—demonstrates that while the comparative historical method is still applicable, it is possible to perceive it in much greater depth.

A case in point is provided by Yukian. Yuki, a language of native California, was long considered an independent language family, one lacking relatives in any other part of the Americas. Sapir saw Yukian as possibly Hokan, considering one or two elements of its structure and lexicon and the fact of the Hokan speech in the Yuki area. But there was also a tendency, on equally fragmentary evidence, to lump it with Penutian, a point which recent analyses of correspondence have demonstrated (Shipley, 1957). Still later, Swadesh has pointed out that Yukian has cognates with Ritwan, that is with Yurok in northwestern California, which has been generally allied with Algonkin. With Kroeber (1955:104), one may say that a Penutian Yukian influenced by Hokan, or the reverse, is essentially unimportant when compared to language families of greater significance, but when the possibility of an Algonkin influence is suggested, the problem becomes intriguing. It is not that Yuki is now to be assigned to a broader Hokan or Algonkian phylum, it is rather that through Yuki one may work with hitherto unsuspected patterns.

Any group of native Americans can be identified by its language. The tribal name, in fact, is frequently the designation for the tribal language. The Crow speak Crow, the Kwakiutl, Kwakiutl. But if the language relationships are to provide some additional tools of classification and time depth, it is important to note the relationships and to consider their implications. Major phyla there are, such as Athabascan, Algonkin, or Uto-Aztecan. The central focus of these as language families is well defined; there are still margins and thus questionable relationships. Or there are the small and possibly independent enclaves, such as Zuni and Keres, which, like Yukian, may ultimately be shown to have wider affiliations. In any classifications of languages, a particular level of approach can be chosen, one depending on demonstrated relationship or on hypothesis. The latter, buttressed by lexicostatistic comparison, leads to the very broad classification, such as Macro-Penutian, Macro-Otomanguean, or the wider implications of the Hokan phylum. These, in general, are beginning to be more widely accepted. Between Powell (1891), Sapir (1929), Voegelin and Voegelin (1944), Hoijer (1946), and a number of more recent formulations of relationships, an acceptable and usable listing of native American languages emerges. Those which follow are groupings of related languages, not individual languages or their dialects, which can be noted in the pertinent ethnographic sections (see endpaper map; see also Driver, 1961:576).

Classification of native American languages
  I. Eskaleut:
    A. Eskimo
    B. Aleut
  II. Na-Déné:
    A. Athabascan—western sub-Arctic;
       Apachean (Navaho-Apache); Pacific
       Coast Athabascan (Hupa, etc.)
    A-1. Tlingit
    A-2. Eyak (?)
    B. Haida
  III. Algonkin:
    A. Algonkin-Ritwan
    A-1. Algonkin (see above)
    A-2. Ritwan (Yurok, Wiyot)
    B. Kutenai
    C. Beothuk (Newfoundland—extinct)
  IV. Mosan:
    A. Wakashan (Kwakiutl-Nootka, etc.)
    B. Chimakuan (Quileute)
    C. Salishan (Bella Coola, Puget Sound,
       Tillamook)
    Mosan, well defined by Swadesh (1953),
       was assigned by Sapir (1929) to
       Algonkin.
  V. Aztec-Tanoan (Utaztecan-Tanoan):
    A. Uto-Aztecan
    A-1. Shoshonean, or Numic, (Basin
       Shoshonean). Also Hopi, California
       Shoshonean, Piman
    A-2. Aztecan (Nahuatlan)
    B. Tanoan (including Tewa, Tiwa, and
       Towa)
    C. Kiowa
  VI. Penutian:
    A. California Penutian, with divisions of
       Miwok-Costanoan, Yokuts, Maidu,
       and Wintun
    B. Chinook-Tsimshian
    C. Coos-Takelma (including Alsea,
       Siuslaw, Kalapuya, Coos and Takelma)
    D. Klamath-Sahaptin (including
       Lutuamian, or Klamath-Modoc, Sapir's
       Waiilatpuan, or Molala-Cayuse, and
       Sahaptin)
  VII. Hokan-Coahuiltecan
    A. Hokan (Hokan-Siouan)
    A-1. Shasta-Achomawi, Karok,
       Chimariko; Yana; Pomo
    A-2. Washo
    A-3. Esselen
    A-4. Yuman (including, Yuma, Mohave,
       Maricopa, Walapai, Yavapai,

Havasupai, Cocopa, Diegueño, and others)
A-5. Salinan-Seri (possibly Seri-Yuman, including Chumash)
A-6. Tequistlatecan (Chontal)
B. Coahuiltecan
B-1. Coahuilteco-Comecrudo
B-2. Tonkawa
B-3. Karankawa

The Hokan phylum now poses some questions as to its other affiliates. The following are suggestibly assigned to a broader Hokan:

VIII. Siouan-Yuchi (Hokan-Siouan)
IX. Iroquoian (including Cherokee)
X. Caddoan (including Caddo, Wichita, Arikara, and Pawnee)
XI. Gulf (possibly remotely Algonkin)
A. Muskogean
B. Natchez
C. Tunica
D. Atakapa
E. Chitimacha
F. Timucua
XII. Subtiaba-Tlapanec (assignable to Hokan-Coahuiltecan?)

The relations between the Gulf languages and Hokan-Coahuiltecan are fairly well indicated. So also is the suggestion of a Siouan-Caddoan-Iroquoian. Haas has demonstrated the probable affiliation between the Gulf languages and Algonkin (1958), as well as the Tonkawa (Hokan-Coahuiltecan) relationship to Algonkin (1959). It thus begins to appear that the lexicostatistic formulations and the mesh principle noted above have marked application in relation to the ways of viewing the native American languages. This was sensed by Sapir (1929) when he conceived of a Hokan-Siouan phylum. The little problems of Yukian or of Jicaque emerge as keys to a wider comprehension of a broad spectrum of internal linguistic relationships. Certainly, the Algonkian-Ritwan-Kutenai classification posed above must be seen in considerably wider terms.

It is a resolution of this kind which takes place also in respect to Penutian. A Macro-Penutian, while tentative, can permit inclusion of V. (Aztec-Tanoan) above, as well as:
XIII. Totonac-Mayan-Mizoquean-Huave (Mexico) Divisions include Mayan and Huastec; Mizoquean, involving Mixe,

Popoluca, and Zoque, together forming, with Huave, Mizocuavean; Totonacan.

A Macro-Otomanguean takes in:

XIV. Zapotec-Otomian with divisions of:
A. Zapotec
B. Mixtecan (including Mixtec, Trique, etc.)
C. Mazatecan
D. Otomian and Pame
E. Chinantec
F. Chorotegan

Some problematicals remain. XV. Keres (Keresan), spoken in the Rio Grande area by seven Pueblos, was classed by Sapir (1929) as Hokan. In this, as well as XVI. Zuni, and possibly XVII. Tarascan (Michoacan, Mexico) some questions of affiliation and interrelationship remain.

At the present writing, an evident breakthrough is being made in respect to a reclassification and a reformulation of the native American languages, both in North and South America. It is clear that much remains to be done. While it is true that the Crow speak Crow, their Siouan language has broader implications. The time is past when a mere categorization can be made and somehow a history of contact inferred from it. The processes of language, as operative in native America and elsewhere in the world, offer a dynamic tool in the realization of the nature of culture itself.

LANGUAGE AND CULTURE
The point has been made that language is a total system, that is, whether or not the question of historical relationships of a given language can be resolved, the language itself emerges in a finished form. It is an adequate tool for those who speak it. Taking the American languages in historical perspective, it is fairly evident that little correlation exists between type of language and type of culture. In other words, any language may suit any cultural system and there is no necessary relationship between them on this level. The Shoshonean-speakers of the Great Basin, the various Ute and Paiute, had evolved what was probably the simplest of the New World cultures. Yet their language can be shown to be related to Aztec, spoken by a

people with one of the most complex cultural developments. Or again, the northwestern Californian Yurok, Karok, and Hupa are so alike in culture that even a museum specialist cannot differentiate between their baskets and other tools, yet they speak mutually unintelligible languages. The same point can be made for the broader areas that have common culture but great linguistic diversity — the Plains, the Northwest Coast, the Pueblo area. But if language area and culture area fail to coincide, is there any possible relationship between language and culture?

A starting point might lie in vocabulary. A tribe which speaks a given language might be expected to develop a good many words to denote the things in which it is interested or which play a significant role in its culture. It is not wholly true that the Eskimo lack a generic word for "seal," but it is true that their lexicon possesses a great many words for the various species and conditions of seals, such as "a young spotted seal," "a female harbor seal," "a swimming male ribbon seal," and so on. While to the Eskimo, these and other seal species fall into a general class, the giant bearded seal is not a seal at all. Other sets of terms are employed in relation to this animal. In North Alaska, the smaller seals are individually hunted, the bearded seal is always taken cooperatively, factors which may play a part in the way in which seals are conceptualized. Of course, there is a parallel in English. The words "roan," "stallion," "bay," "chestnut," and many others still reflect a major preoccupation with horses.

There is more to language than its vocabulary alone. The Eskimo example above suggests that a people classifies phenomena in certain ways. This is psychological in the sense that it is part of the total personal experience of the individual, but it stems from culture and the classifications which the culture, operating through time, imposes. Any expression of such perception is linguistic. As Sapir has noted, "language is a guide to 'social reality'." The now well-known Sapir-Whorf hypothesis puts forward the proposition that language provides a basis for the classification of experience and reflects the way in which reality is viewed. This hypothesis, although subject to some criticism, is useful in pointing up the important issue that groups, such as the various American Indians, may interpret nature differently than might those of European background. In his various papers, Whorf (1956) emphasizes the ways in which language may mold perception and may classify experience. This view brings language back to its specific structure, stressing its totality and not the mere content of its dictionary.

The point has been made above that the structures of various native American languages, though they may differ markedly among themselves, parallel in no case the familiar structure of English. Simply stated, the Indian language can say the same things as English but says them quite differently, basing the statements on very different kinds of perceptions. English, for example, is much concerned with time and has a tense system built into the language. Unless an action is a purely general one, that is, possessing the force of a law (e.g., "animals eat"), English must say that animals ate, they will eat, they are eating. The result is that the English speaker thinks of such an arrangement as natural and logical and assumes that all other languages must make the same kind of time distinctions. As Whorf has demonstrated, and as anyone who has been concerned with languages as alien as those of the American Indian knows, time can be viewed very differently. Moreover, such a construction as the above "animals eat" really makes no sense. Granted that it satisfies the subject-predicate demand of English syntax, there is still a series of questions which can reasonably be raised: "What animals eat?" "animals eat what?" "frequently?" etc. To put the idea in the past suggests a narrative — "The animals ate quickly," an "and then" being implied. Or again, what are "animals"? English is content with "animals eat"; most other languages are not. They may have to concern themselves with a great variety of elements in connection with the statement. Time is one of them, but there are also concerns of kind of object, type of action, validity of action, nature of the subject, quantity or intensity of action, and so through a range of possibilities. In other terms, what seems to be a wholly valid statement in one language may have no significance at all in another. From Whorf, one can gain an impression of the relative nature of languages.

A case in point is provided by Navaho (cf. Kluckhohn and Leighton, 1946; Hoijer, 1954). To say in English "I drop it" has a meaning which can only be determined by context; the pronoun "it" has an antecedent and thus stands for some object. Navaho cannot express the thought in a way parallel to English. As Kluckhohn shows (1946:204–205), Navaho must specify four particulars: (1) Whether the "it" is definite or an indefinite "something"; (2) the verb stem must define the nature of the object, whether it is round, long, fluid, animate, or falls in yet other categories; (3) whether the act is in progress, about to begin, about to end, habitually carried on, repeatedly carried on, etc.; (4) the extent to which the actor, "I," controls the action, in this instance, the falling or dropping. Navaho seeks to introduce the element of the "hand" into the phrase, suggesting the degree of control. To the Navaho, tense is of less importance than the type of action, whether it is momentaneous, progressing, continuing, customary. The language has aspects, differentiating time completed as against incompleted. Less precise than English in this regard, it is none the less much more exacting in other respects.

A specific example of the Navaho language is seen in (Hoijer, 1954:101) *nìnítį*, "you have lain down," *nìsìnítį*, "you have laid me down;" *n* marks the second person; the form is perfective. In the former example, *nì* means "movement terminating in a position of rest"; *nì* in the latter means: "movement ending at a given point" (movement implied); *tį* means "one animate being moves"; *sì*, in the second case refers to the first person pronomial object, while *i* is a causative infix. By inference, *nì ... tį* can be construed as "one animate being moves to a position of rest." In the second example, *m ... i-tį*, means "to cause movement of one animate being to end at a given point," or "lay an animate being down." The pronouns, both subject and object, serve to identify or delimit classes of animate beings. Hoijer makes the point that the inserted pronomial elements have the effect of referring not to actor-action situations, as in the English pattern, but rather to classes of beings. He thus translates the first unit as "you (belong to, are equal to) a class of animate beings which has moved to rest." The second unit may be rendered "You (as agent) have set a class of animate beings, to which I belong, in motion to a given point."

Hoijer (1954:102) goes on to note that the Navaho thus classifies his universe in terms of entities in action and movement. The world view of the Navaho, that man is subordinate to the universe and must keep order within himself in relation to it, is, in Hoijer's view, borne out in the linguistic structure. The Sapir-Whorf hypothesis does not posit that language is a cause of culture, but rather that there is an interaction between the two. Whorf demonstrates that the universe may be conceptualized differently, that logic may operate differently in different liguistic contexts. From Nootka, "he invites people to a feast," he offers another example of logical differentiation. The Nootka translation is *tl'imshya'isita'itlma*. It can be broken down; *tl'imsh*, "boiling" (i.e., "cooking"); *-ya* "result" (i.e., finished, brought to an end), hence, "cooked"; *is*, "eating," *-ita*, "those who engage in the activity"="those who engage in the activity of eating cooked food"; *-'itl*, "go, in order to get"; *-ma*, "he" (third person singular, undifferentiated). The meaning is thus "someone goes in order to get (invites) eaters of cooked food" (Whorf, 1956:242–243).

Admittedly, the kinds of conceptual ordering of experience as Whorf defines them suggest the great potential range of human endeavor and concept. It is not of course implied that the thoughts of people living in different cultures and speaking different languages are so alien to each other that communication is virtually prohibited, such as in translation and interpretation. A person can become skilled in two languages. What is suggested is important. Languages, just as cultures, tend to be built up over time. As such, they can be examined historically. But if they are not to be analyzed from the point of view of their origins and stages of development, and if, as in the following sections, an attempt is made to see cultures as dynamic, living systems, the kinds of insights suggested by the Sapir-Whorf hypothesis are extremely useful. It is true that the world view of a given people may not always be reflected in their language. Among the Pueblo Indians, for example, where common culture is set off by marked differences of language, what Whorf says about Hopi will not apply to the Zuni or the Keres. The latter two have quite different linguistic structures, both from each other and from Hopi. Like many of the other problems connected with language, this requires further examination.

One likes to think that Sapir and Whorf were right, but while their suggestions are exciting, they do no more than suggest that the total realm of experience is somehow connected with language. On so broad a level the relationship between language and culture is really impossible to prove. In the thirty and more years since the Sapir-Whorf hypothesis was put forward, there have been other developments which may be more revealing, telling less perhaps about language and more about culture, or to put the matter more accurately, relating the two more effectively.

The cultures of the American Indian, differing among themselves and very different from cultures elsewhere in the world, must be seen in their own terms. The foregoing examples of language and its structures in native America reveal that the modes and patterns of thought in each culture have a certain uniqueness. The question then arises whether it is possible to see the universe, the world, the nature of human beings and their interrelations with their total environment through the eyes of the participant in an alien culture. The following chapters are descriptive and detail not only the content of each culture, what is there, but seek to convey the subtleties of perception of each culture. All humans in any cultural setting, by virtue of the language they speak and the cultural system in which they share, possess a cognitive system, that is, a way of classifying the whole range of things that touches their lives.

Classifications vary considerably. One mode of classification can be seen by considering the American Indians whose languages demand that any object talked about be defined in terms of its qualities. In the Klamath language of Oregon, for example, *niwcna* means "hits with a flat object as one moves along," where *n(i-e)* means "to act on a flat object," *cn* "action while moving." *Sliwlga* means "throws down a cloth"; *sl(i)* is a verb "to act upon a clothlike object," while *(e)lg)* refers to "down, to the ground" (Barker, 1964:116–117). These classifications are not arbitrary but are built into the language. Klamath distinguishes between many categories, round or long, flat objects, whether the referent is alive, whether the task is performed with the fingers, and many others all of which reflect, not a choice, but rather a way of using language to define the qualities of experience. If a person speaking Klamath is confronted with a new object, he will perceive it through the categories of his linguistic sphere of experience.

Considerable attention has recently been paid to the perception and categorization of color. Some languages are limited in color vocabulary and it is thus an open question whether color differences have significance in a language whose color designations are limited. This does not mean that the speaker of the language cannot see color differences, but that they are not important or are subsumed under broader categories (Berlin, 1970:8). Different peoples have different ways of dividing up the color spectrum. In Zuni, for example, the word "yellow" covers a much broader spectrum than the English word. It includes shades of orange and even some of the lighter greens. However a language may express its color terms, whether as noun, verb, or adjective, the problem is to see what the culture and the speaker see. The word "blue" in Navaho includes green, purple and other related colors. As these examples of words for colors indicate, a word can have a different meaning to different people, which involves us in semantics. Ethnosemantics is the study of the different meanings attached by peoples to their elements of vocabulary. Conceptual associations follow. An arrow is connected with a bow, but if the bow is used as a drill, it is then related to fire making. An arrow could be connected with something else, for instance, the wood or tree from which it is made. When the lexicon of a given language is seen in the light of the associations of ideas it makes, some sense of the kinds of classifications made by the culture can be obtained.

One can then refine the conceptual tool for the ordering of classificatory principles within a culture. Componential analysis is such a tool aiding in understanding of the classificatory principles of a cultural system. People invariably classify their surroundings but the process is often unconscious. There is cognitive basis for the principles of ordering, a basis for the taxonomies employed. An example can be seen in kinship structure and kinship terminologies, which are important in any analysis of a social system and can be formally examined. A componential analysis reveals not the structural or behavioral factors in kinship, but rather the kinds of classification operative within the system and the kinds of semantic contrasts which appear. In an American Indian case, Lounsbury has compared the kinship patterns of the Crow and the Omaha. These two Plains tribes have social systems very different from each other, the Crow being strongly matrilineal, the Omaha patrilineal. In the Crow case, all the male patrilateral cross-cousins are called by a "father" term, whereas matrilateral cross-cousins are called "son" and "daughter." In the Omaha case, it is the female matrilateral cross-cousin who is designated by a "mother" term. Given two modes of descent, the one is the mirror image of the other (Lounsbury, 1964). Semantic categories reveal, as in these two cases, how kinship classification reflects definitions which the culture has unconsciously established.

A problem in ethnography arises when the observer from the outside imposes his own categories. It is obvious among the Omaha that a mother's brother's son is not a mother's brother, nor is his son's daughter a "mother." The reference is not to the genetic mother but to males and females in the mother's patrilineage. The "mother" term means "female member of my mother's patrilineage," and does not lead to a confusion of role classifications. The problem is to see the mode of classifying from the viewpoint of the Omaha. The terms *emic* and *etic* have come into common use in anthropology to deal with just this problem. Like the linguistic terms *phonetic,* broad comparative systems of speech sounds, and *phonemic,* the idiosyncratic sound system of a given language, they can be used practically to categorize specific kinds of situations. A broad statement on the nature of kinship is an etic approach; the specific case, reflecting uniqueness in a given system, is emic-directed.

As the American Indians are considered here, the aim is to reach a comprehension of the nature of their languages and of their cultures. It must be repeated that these formal institutions must be analyzed in native terms. An Indian language can be learned, but perhaps the learner may be slow—if he is not a native speaker—to think in the language. The learner has to be aware of the classificatory patterns in the system and see the world through the eyes of the native participant; a failure to do so results in only partial communication. What has been said about colors, kinship, and other semantic associations has relevance here. The term "ethnoscience" has come to be used to mean the study of the kinds of classifications of phenomena which various cultures develop internally and express through their language (Sturtevant, 1964:99–131). If a language divides its universe into object categories, such as long, thin, round, bulky, liquid, or the like, this in turn reveals the ordering perception. Each culture may be said to create a paradigm, or series of paradigms, of its experience. In linguistic analysis an attempt is always made to describe with accurate, economical statements that allow

prediction. For instance, "I —, you —, he, she —s", is a pattern which fits virtually any English verb. The final morpheme "s" regularly marks the English third person singular in the present tense. Given this pattern, the observer can predict that almost all English verbs will act in this way. Can the same element of paradigm be introduced to the study of a culture so that the same general kinds of predictive statements can be made of cultural circumstances? Given a patterning of culture, the answer would seem affirmative.

An Eskimo example may illustrate classifications. While religious postulates, family structure, or economy have to be described in any full treatment of the groups, broader institutional portrayal is not the concern here. The point is rather what is said, how the statement relates to a conceptualization, and what the implications of an utterance are for the group. Eskimo kin terms reflect bilateral descent and generational and sex difference. They are generally like those of American English but with some classificatory variations. Side by side with the terms which designate kinsmen, there are words which incorporate nonrelatives into a quasi-kinship status. At least, this is the case among the Eskimo of north Alaska. In the traditional culture, "stranger" and "enemy" were synonymous; unless one could classify persons as belonging to a domain of kinship or quasi-kinship, there could be no peaceful social contact. Thus to live in harmony with others, it was necessary to extend status terms to define not only relationships but respective social positions. It was common for two men to have had sexual relations with the same woman. The two called each other by a term indicating this sexual sharing, *angutawken,* and the term served to unite the two men, who, otherwise strangers to each other, were drawn together by the sexual tie. Conceivably, their children by the woman could be half-siblings to each other, extending the sexual tie to a kinship relationship. The two men in this example acted toward each other in a friendly way, an example being a divorced husband and a current husband. Although the term was polite, proper, accepted, it could be humorously insulting, especially when a bullying man had raped the wife of another. Human roles are classified in every society. In the case of the Eskimo of north Alaska, contrastive role expectations existed (Spencer, 1959:89). These expectations can be seen in the linguistic terminology. The problem of the ethnographer is to discover the contrasts, expectations, and classifications and to place them in a paradigm relevant to the circumstances of the culture examined.

It is not always easy to find the linguistic elements which relate to cultural distinctions. From the same group of Eskimo, there is a song sent by one man to another, his trading partner. There is humor, a slight insult, indicating status conflicts, and a strongly metaphorical language.

kanusik keyaksakimna aylaringnyaymannava
I wonder how person   not bashful
pikuwiyakteruuvlu   puyueamnyunexluat
a lump on neck (has)   crab's big legs
irimawtingaλaatit isiviraaktinearikpik
bending inwards   stretching out again
ikayelura   anootit
I'll help you   little bit

(*Spencer, 1959:175.*)

In free terms, the reference is to a man who is not bashful, is ugly, and like the crab, is menacing, but is not too successful and really needs help. Implied is the classification of status relationships.

Each American Indian language, regardless of the family to which it belongs, has to be seen in its own terms if the goal is to see something of the relations between language and culture. Each language is a complex system, with its sounds (phonology), structure (morphology), and its syntax (ordering of elements or words). In modern times, those languages in native America which are still spoken have had to deal with the problem of change. Even if any human language can express any idea, albeit sometimes awkwardly, native speech has had to adapt to new concepts, for example, to all of the items out of the technology, law, economics, and religion of the imposed Euro-American cultural system. Some languages can borrow very well, simply adapting an English, Spanish, or French word or one from another Indian language, fitting it into the native phonology and structure. Others are so structurally constituted that borrowing is impossible. Navaho, for example, cannot borrow and calls an automobile *chidi* (or *chuggi*), simply imitating the sound. "Gasoline" is then "car's water," *chidi bi to,* and so through other descriptive words drawn from Navaho itself for the parts of an automobile. "Fenders" are "wings," "sparkplug" is "firejumper." On the other hand, a language like

Keres in the Pueblo area, went through a long period of acquiring Spanish loanwords, although there were also loan translations. "Apple" is *mansa·n* (Sp. manzana), horse is *ka ? away,* (Sp. caballo), but "church" combines Spanish *misa,* Keresan *mi's,* "Mass," with *ke ? ,* Keresan "room," as *mi·sake ? .* In other words, the language structure itself will determine the nature of the borrowing. At the present time, too, as the American Indian once again becomes conscious of his heritage and history, language redevelopment takes place and adaptations to the present must be made.

ORAL LITERATURE

There were no aboriginal writing systems north of Mexico. After contact, various ways of writing native American languages were developed, many of them by native speakers themselves, and the emphasis on a writing system continues among many Indian groups today. Pre-Columbian Mexico was the only New World area where true writing was invented. It appeared among the Maya, the Olmec, and the Zapotec, and in somewhat modified form, among the Aztecs. Writing in Mexico used a system not unlike that of China or ancient Egypt, but although the principle was similar, it is eminently clear that writing in Mexico is a completely independent invention.

In the absence of writing, it may be asked how a body of literature can arise among the North American native peoples. That it does is evident. It is an oral literature passed on by tradition, related in turn to the great respect generally accorded to speech, speech making, and narration. As may be inferred from the descriptions of chiefs among many native American tribes, they were individuals with little power as such. Their role depended on the force of personality, the ability to command respect by speaking. Similarly, the individual who could tell a tale, a riddle, or invent word games was in demand in most tribes. A nonliterate culture tends to emphasize language both as a means of communication and as entertainment. There are numerous accounts of the words of a leader. Rhetoric was valued, a play on words prized. Among the Klamath in Oregon, reflecting a pattern common in the Plateau and California, the chief, a speaker, a chief host, a man of virtue, arose daily and addressed the thirty or forty members of the hamlet:

My people. We are here together. Let us have peace within ourselves. Let us not quarrel; let us not have hatred within our minds. Let us work together for serenity (Spencer, 1956).

Obviously, this is a free translation of a fairly concise Klamath convention. There was nothing original in the chief's speech; indeed, people would very likely have been taken aback were he to introduce a new idea into his daily moral harangue. One can note, however, that the repetition of such a speech had an effect of allowing the members of the group to become aware of their own relatedness. Actually, the point of an oral literature, whether of tales, pious exhortations, songs, poetry, or of myth and ritual, is to effect a sense of solidarity within a group.

Much attention has been paid to American Indian folktale and myth. It is here that the forms, styles, and features or an oral literature come to the fore. Most authorities are agreed that it is difficult to differentiate between myth and folktale or folklore. Myth is held to be sacred, related to sets of ritual; folktale is explanatory, possibly historical, or simply for amusement. To draw a line between the two is almost impossible and scarcely necessary (Thompson, 1966:xiv-xxiii).

All the statements made regarding meanings, structure, kinds of classification and definition in language, have relevance in an analysis of oral literature. Further, the element of folklore may contribute some sense of the cultural propositions and premises. Radin, for example, had the Winnebago give an account of their own ethnography by using oral traditions (1950). While it is true that perceptions of time, space, destiny, and many other concepts may lie in language structure, it is in the folktale and myth that one sees the realities of definition, the language structure reified. What, for example, does a culture feel about itself? If oral traditions see the people of the given culture as inferior, fated to suffer, at the whim of forces wholly capricious, then clearly, these moods will appear in folktales. Equally, the reverse may be true and the basic orientations may be wholly optimistic.

There are many other ways of looking at folktales. The great deal of attention paid by the structuralists to myth especially, but also to folktale, has had as its goal an attempt to discover various kinds of universals in the organization of oral literature, or indeed, in all litera-

ture. The organizing principles of structure demonstrate that the folktale seeks to create an order in human affairs. A tale thus is seen as effecting certain reconciliations, such as between heaven and earth, land and water, and the like (Lévi-Strauss, 1967). A structural approach is unquestionably useful but not for purposes of the present account. Here the aim is to note the kinds of tales which occur and the ways in which they are representative of area and culture.

Any extensive collection of tales from either different cultures or from the same people lends itself to multi-dimensional analysis. Over the past few decades, with the development of new research techniques, the range has been drawn from psychological and psychoanalytic interpretations to formal analyses, to computerized methodology in which frequencies and comparisons are elicited. Folklore, including myth and folktale, admits a great many different problems. For present purposes, two aspects are worth examination. The first is historical and deals with the origins and spread of mythological and folkloristic themes among the various American Indians. In synchronic terms, the second is informative of language, culture, and society. It reflects the concerns with time, space, reciprocities, and it serves to introduce certain idealized concepts relevant to a culture. In other words, how does a culture see good and evil? What is proper or improper behavior?

On the historical side, nothing travels so rapidly as a story. Myth and legends offer prime examples of the process of diffusion, the traveling of elements of culture from people to people. The search for linguistic relationships between Asia and America is, as has been seen, generally fruitless. But this is not the case in regard to tales. Motifs have been shown to travel from Eurasia to North America. A motif is a single theme necessary to a plot in a tale. An example is the "magic flight," a motif which appears both in Asia and northern North America. The hero, central figure of the tale, offends an enemy who pursues him. The hero throws down a stone, a comb, and some liquid, all of which turn into mountains, thickets, and a lake or sea and hinder the pursuer. Three elements are involved to defy the pursuer. It is interesting that the Japanese have a version of this tale, written as early as A.D. 712 In the Eskimo, specifically in the western Eskimo variant, the hero, a young boy chased by a man-eating monster, throws down a bead from his headband, thereby making himself invisible. Seen again, he throws down the whole headband and escapes again. Finally, he makes a small stream large and escapes in a kayak.

Obviously, the motif is patterned to the culture in which it appears. Of interest in the comparison above is the flight and pursuit, the presence of three magical objects which aid in the escape. Differences in the details may be expected, but when a continuous distribution of the basic elements is found over a wide geographic area, a historical conclusion may be reached. An impressive list of elements shared among North Americans and Asiatics in myth and folklore can be drawn up (Boas, 1916).

Within native America itself, what kinds of folktales appear to predominate? Some appear to be of considerable temporal depth, as the case of the "lecherous father" motif might indicate. This tale appears among the Californians and reappears in southern South America among the Ona, Yahgan, Alacaluf, and others. The tale is simply that the father lusts after his daughters and devises ways to commit incest. These two occurrences might indicate a relationship between peoples in isolation at the "dead end" which California and Tierra del Fuego seem to be.

Certain favorite themes appear consistently in wide areas of native America. Creation stories are common across the North American continent, but the creation in the west usually is attributed to the figure known as the "Trickster," sometimes called a culture hero. An anthropomorphic or zoomorphic figure, identified in the Basin-Plateau-California with Coyote, by the Northwest Coast and western Eskimo with Raven. But trickster mythology moves to the east as well, although generally, the tales are associated with a human hero who is less capricious than the western Coyote. The Raven among the Eskimo is a culture hero, although he has his puckish side. He creates the world in the sense that he makes it as it is, bringing light and spearing land and raising it from the bottom of the sea. In one Northwest Coast version, Raven sends Turtle down to the bottom of the sea to bring up earth. The counterpart of Raven in the Basin, sections of the Plateau and California, and in some adjacent areas is the generally malicious Coyote. He is much more the "trickster" enjoying success at the expense of others. A common Basin tale introduces another widely spread motif, the "vaginal teeth," the woman who destroyed all her lovers. Coy-

ote sent his friends, deer, muskrat, elk, and others to visit her. They were killed. He then fashioned a sheath of bone (stone) and visited the woman. Penetrating her, the stone sheath destroyed her teeth and she died (went away, swore vengeance with the assistance of her brothers, etc.).

The emphasis on animals and animal spirits by the tribes of hunting North America gives rise to a complex series of tales about animals, their habits, and their role in human affairs. From the Yokuts in California, the following tale again brings in the trickster:

Coyote made it so people die. He made it so because our hands are not closed like his. He wanted our hands to be like his, but a lizard said to him, "No, they must have my hand." He had five fingers and Coyote had only a fist. So now we have an open hand with five fingers. But then Coyote said, "Well, then they will have to die" (Thompson, 1966:38).

Widely scattered in native America is a series of tales relating to the woman who married an animal, or a man with a fox, dog, or bear wife. Animal mythology among hunters generally held that the animals lived in communities like men. On the Northwest Coast, the salmon had villages and wealth, while Eskimo in Alaska spoke of villages of polar bears. The tales relating to marriage with an animal usually take a tragic turn, death for the human or loss of a valuable association. Common too are the tales of the woman who married the moon (stars, sun, etc.). Variations of this motif spread from the Cherokee to the Tlingit, reflecting a complex series of myths relating to "journeys to the other world."

Twin myths, tales of brothers engaged in various heroic or tragic activities spread from California into the Southwest and appear again in South America. Human heroes, such as Manabozho of the Chippewa-Ojibwa and Menomini, take on a trickster character, although the Iroquois Hiawatha, the culture hero, always was measured and dignified. It is of interest that Longfellow's poem "The Song of Hiawatha" puts an Iroquois hero into an Algonkin setting.

It is obvious that the list of motifs common to native America cannot be exhausted here. It is perhaps sufficient to note one or two features regarding them. Deep religious belief and a sense of the historical accuracy of the tale are absent. It is rather that the stories had an entertainment value, but more importantly, they did offer a sense of order in the cosmos, something to which the individual could relate and which served to create a series of definitions common to all in the group.

This of course comes from language. The understandings resident in the folklore motifs, myths, and certainly in whatever the group had developed by way of solemn ritual arose through communication in language. At this point one must return to the question of grammatical categories and the ideas which are ordered and expressed by them. Notions of space, time, validity of action, are variously incorporated, often to the point where even a translation is unintelligible to the Western listener. Whatever one may do with theories of language, the real point remains that language itself is a key to the understandings in a cultural system. To some degree, failing to see the elements resident in the language is to fail to come to grips with the human situation it represents.

Suggested readings

Note: The ways of approaching American Indian languages fall into several categories. The major literature relates to description of specific languages. Earlier works on this level are almost unusable since they lack phonological insight and may often see linguistic structures as analogous to more familiar ones in the west. Not that the writers, such as may be found in F. Boas, ed. 1911. *Handbook of American Indian Languages* (Bureau of American Ethnology, Bulletin 40, pts. 1, 2, and 3), were necessarily wrong; it is simply that methods of description have changed. Boas's "Introduction" (pp. 1–83) to the *Handbook* remains a classic statement on process in culture and language.

More contemporary descriptive methodology has been applied extensively to linguistic description from North, Middle, and South America. These results may be found in a variety of sources. Descriptive, structural, or comparative statements may be found in the journals *Language* (Linguistic Society of America), *International Journal of American Linguistics* (University of Chicago Press), *Anthropological Linguistics* (Archives of the Languages of the World, Anthropology Department, Indiana University), and in various serial publications. Reference may be made to Indiana University Publications in Anthropology and Linguistics, University of California Studies in Linguistics, especially for western American Indian languages, and many more.

Aside from descriptions of specific or local language phenomena, psychological, social, and cultural aspects of various American Indian languages have recently been much taken into account. Nor is historical interest lost, especially as new hypotheses regarding relationships between languages are advanced. It is thus not possible to put together a brief list of pertinent readings. The following, however, may offer a beginning:

HOIJER, H., ed.

1946 *Linguistic Structures of Native America.* Viking Fund Publications in Anthropology, no. 6. New York: Wenner-Gren Foundation for Anthropological Research.

HYMES, D., ed.

1964 *Language in Culture and Society.* New York: Harper & Row.

MANDELBAUM, D., ed.

1949 *Selected Writings of Edward Sapir in Language, Culture, and Personality.* University of California Press.

SAPIR, E. and SWADESH, M.

1946 "American Indian Grammatical Categories." *Word* 2:103–112.

VOEGELIN, C. F.

1941 "North American Indian Languages still Spoken and Their Genetic Relationships." In *Language, Culture, and Personality,* ed. Spier, Hallowell, and Newman, pp. 15–40. Madison, Wis.: Sapir Memorial Fund.

WHORF, B. L.

1956 *Language, Thought, and Reality: Selected Writings of Benjamin Lee Whorf,* ed. J.B. Carroll. New York; Wiley.

III

The Arctic and Sub-Arctic

Introduction

The far north of the American continent is marked by the presence of two basic cultural types. Of these, by far the more dramatic are the specialized Eskimo cultures spread along the coasts from Alaska to Greenland. The second is somewhat less well differentiated and consists of essentially sub-Arctic peoples in the Yukon-Mackenzie country of interior Alaska and northwest Canada. While the Eskimo can be quite readily defined as inhabitants of the treeless tundra, the interior groups are found in the coniferous forests, living along lakes and rivers. Both groups are hunters. To the Eskimo can be assigned both the coastal regions where the hunting of sea mammals is primary and the interior tundra marking the end of the migration route of the vast herds of caribou, the American reindeer. Some groups of Eskimo exploit the caribou exclusively, others mix caribou and sea mammal hunting, while still others are exclusively maritime. In the interior forests, however, the caribou and the moose are the sole dependable bases of subsistence. The result is a marked difference in basic ecological adaptation between the two peoples.

The line of the tundra, the points in northern North America where the barren grounds shade off into incipient forest growth, are highly variable. Even though the territorial expanse covered by the Eskimo is tremendous, there is a remarkable unity to Eskimo culture, permitting a fairly accurate delineation of cultural type. The interior groups, considerably less vigorous in their cultural manifestations, possess a culture area much less easily circumscribed. Just as in the case of the Eskimo, however, language serves in part to delimit the area. The drainage systems of interior Alaska and northwest Canada show the prevailing presence of the Athabascan branch of the great Na-Déné speech family. A rough correlation between Athabascan languages and caribou hunting can be made, it is true, but the interior areas shade off as the cultural influences of immediately adjacent areas make themselves felt. Thus in the south and east, where Athabascan begins to give way to the Algonkin speech family, Plains and Woodland influences are encountered. Along the great cordillera, where there is contact between the Athabascan tribes and those of the Plateau, the other ways of life make their impression, while in a few instances, such as that of the Athabascan-speak-

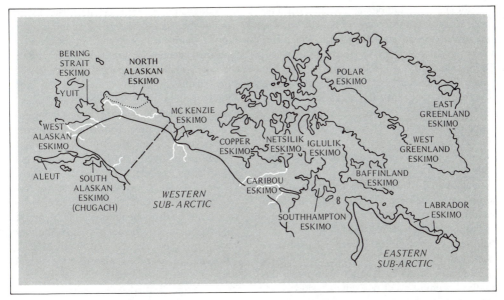

A1 ● Arctic Area

ing Eyak tribe, there is a direct overlay of elements from the vigorous culture of the Northwest Coast. But in general, a range of caribou and a basic dependence on these animals, an adaptation to life in the coniferous forest, permit the designation of a western sub-Arctic culture area (Kroeber, 1939:98-101).

Probably more has been written about the Eskimo than any other nonliterate people, a result of the fascination which these intrepid Arctic dwellers have held for so many. Considerably less is known about the Athabascans of the interior. Their solution to the problems of living is rather less spectacular. Each group has its own specialties, however, and the contrast between them is marked. There is justification for comparing them and noting how each wrests a living from an essentially harsh environment, although far more pressing problems are faced by the Eskimo. Each group has responded in its own way to the challenge of environment, and each has structured a society within the limits imposed by nature. The culture area of the Eskimo is thus set off fairly sharply from that of the interior Athabascans.

THE ESKIMO

It is generally agreed that the Eskimo are one of the few peoples of the world, if not the only one, among whom physical type, language, and culture coincide. Although in the western re-

gions of the American Arctic there tends to be some admixture with Indian types, the classic Eskimo possesses sufficiently distinctive physical traits to designate him a virtual subrace of the Mongoloid stock. In the Eskimo area generally are encountered the short stocky frame, the long head and short face—the cranial disharmony so characteristic of the group—prevailingly lightish skin color, and the distinctive eye fold. The closely related languages of the Eskimo-Aleut family, mutually intelligible from Greenland to Norton Sound in Alaska, accompany the distribution of this physical strain as does the specialized cultural adaptation to tundra and sea.

Estimates of the aboriginal Eskimo population vary. It is clear that the number of Eskimo can never have been very great, a reflection of the need of most groups to cover wide areas in which the food resources could be fully exploited. Actually, none of the native populations of the New World was great, and it is not until one comes to Mexico that an intensive agricultural base gave rise to greater growth and density. Compared with many of the Indian groups to the south, those employing hunting as a subsistence base, the Eskimo total was appreciable. It must be remembered, however, that the Eskimo groups covered a phenomenally large land area, a factor making for minimal population density. The precontact population was certainly considerably under 100,000 even if the non-Eskimo Aleut are included. One estimate runs as low as 54,000 (Birket-Smith, 1958:7), while an earlier figure put the Eskimo number at 73,700, excluding some 16,000 Aleut (Mooney, 1928). The latter is probably too high, and the Eskimo precontact total could conceivably lie somewhere between. Today, the figures must be scaled down. Between the Siberian East Cape through Alaska to Greenland and Labrador there are between 35,000 and 40,000 Eskimo (cf. Laughlin, 1950). Diseases brought by Europeans, such as measles, influenza, and tuberculosis, have considerably reduced the aboriginal numbers (cf. Dobyns, 1966).

Divided into relatively small enclaves, the Eskimo are spread over a tremendously wide area. It is about 3000 miles from the small segment of extreme northeastern Siberia, still inhabited by small groups which have pushed back from the American continent, to the town of Angmassalik in Greenland which marks the northeasternmost point of Eskimo residence. A far greater distance is involved when the coastal indentations of the American Arctic are considered. Eskimo settlements range mainly between 60° and 72° north latitude, but there are also the so-called polar Eskimo on the west coast of Greenland who range as far north as 79° latitude, and the Eskimo of Labrador and Hudson Bay who have pushed fairly far south. As may be seen, the Eskimo have adapted to a variety of topographic and climatic conditions; hunting is always the basic mode of subsistence but several kinds of ecological adjustments occur.

The Indians of native America permit classification in terms of tribal designations, however vague and loosely founded such terms may be. It has not been customary to treat the Eskimo as a series of specific tribes—there are in fact no bases of tribal organization among any of the Eskimo. Attention has instead been paid to the local geographic focus and to the kinds of adjustments which groups have made in respect to a local terrain. On the basis of adaptation to region, one refers to the Greenland Eskimo, those of Labrador, of the central areas, those at the Mackenzie mouth, in northern Alaska, or along the Bering Strait. Other random terms have crept into the literature. The explorer-ethnographer Rasmussen designated the peoples he knew in the central regions of the Arctic by such pointed terms as the Netsilik and Iglulik (1929, 1931). Similarly, the caribou dependence of the peoples of the barren ground has given rise to the term Caribou Eskimo. Again, the hammering of unsmelted copper in the Coronation Gulf region brings about the designation Copper Eskimo. The Eskimo refer to themselves as *inuit,* a noun meaning simply "humans," or "men," a reflection of their own identity as opposed to those groups speaking different languages and possessing other cultures. On the local level, the suffix *-miut* is used to mean "people of ——." This is usually employed to refer to a group living in a small geographic area, such as along a stream, as the Kugmiut, on the Kuk River in north Alaska, on a given stretch of coast, or in a single village, as the Kivalinermiut, "those of Kivalina," a village "to the west," on the Alaskan coast near Point Hope. The word "Eskimo," not used by the groups at all, is derived from Algonkin. In Abnaki and Cree, the word means "raw meat eater" (Birket-Smith, 1958:8).

If there are no tribes, there are the varying kinds of ecological adaptations of the Eskimo of the Arctic coast and adjacent tundra. For convenience of reference, the following listing may be made, one dependent on natural region and resource and reflecting a general consensus in a remarkably extensive literature (Kroeber, 1939; Weyer, 1932).

West: Aleut, Siberian Eskimo (Yuit, including St. Lawrence Island), South Alaskan Eskimo (Chugach), West Alaskan Eskimo (Nunivak Island and adjacent coasts, Norton Sound, Bering Strait, including Diomede Islands, Cape Prince of Wales), North Alaskan Eskimo (Point Hope to Point Barrow and adjacent tundra and foothills).

Center and East: Mackenzie Eskimo, Copper Eskimo, (including Victoria Island), Caribou Eskimo (Barren Ground, Chesterfield Inlet, Back River), Netsilik (including Boothia Peninsula), and Iglulik Eskimo, Polar Eskimo (Smith Sound), Southhampton Eskimo, Baffinland Eskimo, Labrador Eskimo, West Greenland and East Greenland Eskimo. (Northeast Greenland Eskimo are extinct.)

There is some historical justification for dividing the Eskimo culture into two major parts, a central-eastern zone stretching from Mackenzie Bay to Greenland, and a western subregion spread from the mouth of the Mackenzie through coastal Alaska to the tip of Siberia (Kroeber, 1939:20ff.). The specialized Caribou Eskimo of the Canadian Barren Ground can be listed with the former, while the Aleut, as well as the small group in the very tip of Siberia and the Eskimos of southern Alaskan coasts, with the latter. One basis for this division is in a general way a reflection of variation of exploitation of sea mammals. Whale and the Pacific walrus in the west give a basis for a somewhat richer cultural development. Although the seal is universal, appearing in numerous genera and varieties across the Arctic, hunting methods vary somewhat between east and west. What develops in the Eskimo cultures is a series of variations on a major theme; given the common hunting base, the common array of tools and weapons, the local Eskimo culture develops so as to effect maximum efficiency in the pursuit of the game on which livelihood depends. Some groups, for example, have the *kayak* for a single paddler, as opposed to the open or women's boat. Others, because of their particular specialties, lack it. The kayak may be used for individual seal hunting along the shore, or in the caribou drives, where the animals are driven into water and harpooned by hunters in boats. Where there is whaling, as in Alaska, the *umiak,* the open boat covered with skins, is highly developed. Elsewhere, it may be used merely as a freight boat and paddled by women. Where it is necessary to go far out on the winter ice in search of seals, the snow house may become the dwelling. But the snow house is by no means universal, since winter sod houses characterize Alaska, and stone and sod are used for dwellings in Greenland. Despite such differences, there is a consistent thread of culture elements running through the American Arctic and permitting the designation of the Eskimo regions as a precise culture area.

The Land

It is quite erroneous to think of the Eskimo habitat as a barren land of monotonous ice and snow. Remembering that the Eskimo north-and-south range is very great, it may also be expected that there are variations in topography and land form, in climate, vegetation, and in the availability of game and fish. But if in general the land of the Eskimo is equated with the treeless Arctic tundra, some prevailingly similar conditions appear. These lie not so much in land form, although this is important, as in climatic variation and in cold. Land forms tend to change considerably, ranging from the cold fjords of Greenland, backed by the presence of the great Greenland glaciers, to the rocky islands and the flat barren lands of the Canadian Arctic, this same tundra configuration extending across into the Arctic plain of northern Alaska. Southward in Alaska, the coasts remain barren until the forest line is reached and there

is the gradual emergence of sub-Arctic conditions, a feature also true of Labrador. What becomes more significant in Eskimo life is the presence of winter ice, the freezing of the ocean and the inland streams and lakes, and the consequent changes as the ice accumulates and recedes again. Whether the Eskimo makes his home on a rocky or pebble beach or amidst the sea ice in winter, moving to the long unbroken stretches of tundra, he is faced with the problem of meeting the conditions of weather. His hunting and thus his livelihood depend on his response to this challenge.

The Arctic of much of the world is a desert in the truest sense of the word. It is a desert of cold marked by a surprisingly minimal rate of precipitation. The cold so reduces the amount of moisture in the air that many areas have as little as four inches of rainfall in a year. Even if there is slightly more, the Eskimo is usually faced with the difficult problem of obtaining a supply of fresh water. To some degree, the movements of both human and animal life in the Arctic are governed by this problem. Some areas have fresh water streams, frozen in winter, while in the bottomlands of the tundra, the shallow depressions may hold stagnant and often brackish water. Moderately fresh water can also be obtained from the summits of ocean ice packed along the winter shore.

But in this desert of cold there are striking seasonal contrasts. Most dramatic is the change between summer light and winter darkness. Summers, defined as the period when the temperature rises above freezing, are short. Winter can be said to begin with the onset of freezing weather. It must be remembered that the north-south range of the Eskimo between Greenland and Labrador, or between north and south Alaska, is often in excess of a thousand miles. The further north one goes, the longer are the periods of total light in summer and of total darkness in winter. In the general range of the Arctic circle (66° 30' north latitude) daylight begins to decline very sharply after the fall equinox. By late November the sun is lost over the horizon. While it is never totally dark for a dim twilight aura lasts even after the sun has disappeared, the moon and stars are the principal sources of light. The sun begins to appear again by February and the transition from darkness to light is then very rapid. After the spring equinox, the days become longer, and finally by early June, the sun is circling over the horizon a full 24 hours a day, its circle becoming wider and wider as the summer wanes, until at last it again dips over the horizon.

With the onset of summer, streams begin to flow, the tundra pools melt, and the abundant vegetation of the Arctic springs into life. The many species of birds move into the area, the herds of caribou begin their trek northward, smaller animals, ground squirrels, weasels, lemmings, begin to scurry about, and the breaks form in the ocean ice, leaving open water in which the larger sea mammals can be found. Groups of Eskimo begin to move about, some for caribou in the interior, others, such as those in the west, out to sea after whales and walrus, and still others for inland fresh water fishing. Water travel becomes possible, both along the inland streams and in the ocean. Tundra country, in fact, while fairly easily maneuverable by dog sled in winter, makes extremely difficult going in the summer. Undrained except where there are rocky outcroppings or some slope, the land is boggy, stagnant pools appear here and there, and a virtual swamp develops. Walking is arduous on the springy surface, where the foot sinks into mire, and is made more so by the clouds of mosquitoes and flies which attack human and animal viciously and indiscriminately. These swampy conditions are caused by the melting of the surface and the release of surface moisture. Actually, such melting is only a veneer, since below the surface, depending on the penetrating rays of the summer sun, are encountered at varying depths permanently frozen soils. This permafrost, often little more than a foot below the surface, makes modern exploitation of Arctic resources, such as petroleum, natural gas, or minerals, extremely impractical. But for the Eskimo, summer is a time of intensive activity and every effort is made to lay away stores for the bleak period ahead.

With the onset of winter and the shortening of the days, people begin to settle down, returning with the food they have collected to permanent campsites and villages. As the ice forms, travel by dog-drawn sled and sledge becomes the rule, boats being put away. The summer tent is abandoned in favor of the various kinds of winter houses and the period of cold begins. The cold along the Arctic ocean is not so wholly intense as may be popularly believed. There are marked fluctuations, but -30° F. is average for much of the coastline. Days may reach as low as -50° F. but higher temperatures appear as well. Colder weather may actually be encountered in the areas of continental climate in the interior of both Can-

ada and Alaska where ranges to -65° F. and even colder may be experienced. (The North American record is a temperature of -81° F. recorded at Snag, Yukon Territory, while even lower temperatures are known for Siberia, such as at Verkhoyansk to the east of the Lena River.) But the inland situation is not nearly so oppressive as is the maritime Arctic. Clear, windstill days in the interior are matched by the fierce winds of the coasts. In his battle with cold, the Eskimo must often face below zero weather and winds of gale velocity. It is these which are so perilous to life. They sweep the tundra, leaving exposed patches, snow ridges, and drifts, and they pile the ice into fantastic mountain and valley shapes along the shores. Sea ice and black tundra striped here and there with snow is the winter habitat of most Eskimo.

On the flat rolling tundra, once the spring sun returns, the vegetation begins to burst forth. While most Eskimo have not exploited vegetable foods, preferring meat and animal fats, there are untapped vegetal resources in their area. The absence of trees has given rise to a dependence on the driftwood which appears along some coasts in surprising quantities, floating up from the southern rivers. Stands of willow in some of the Arctic gullies are the largest plants, but hardy plants of all kinds burst out in the spring. Many of these are related to plant genera and species in more temperate zones, such as the members of the rose family and many others. In spring and summer, the tundra may be beautifully carpeted with wild flowers. What characterizes the plant cover is its diminutive size; the plants and flowers which enjoy a brief summer life are tiny, becoming larger as the period of summer sun is lengthened in the south. Mosses and lichens abound, covering rock outcroppings and the tundra floor itself. A source of food for the caribou, the moss prompts the movement of these herds.

Since the Eskimo depend entirely on animal life for subsistence, these become the vital element in the Arctic scene. As must be noted, the Eskimo possesses a specialized hunting culture. Groups differ from each other according to the kinds of animals available. In general, the Eskimo distinguish between animals of the land and those of the sea, this distinction becoming for many groups a significant aspect of the world view and tying intimately into the religious patterns. Of the sea mammals, the ubiquitous seals are without doubt the important primary source of food. It can be suggested that the basic Eskimo adaptation to the Arctic revolves around sealing and that such specializations as whaling or caribou dependence are secondary developments, a point borne out by prehistoric investigation. Throughout the Arctic are several different genera of seals with variable habits and distribution. Some are migratory or occur sporadically, others herd, still others remain in an area throughout the year, coming up to breathing holes in the winter ice. If the Eskimo language lacks a specific word for the abstract noun "seal," it is because the many different kinds of seals are viewed in both native culture and language as different animals. The Eskimo lexicon is especially rich in terms which not only distinguish one type of seal from another, but which serve also to point out such features as age, size, activity, coloration, and many other attributes of this important element in the food supply.

The whale and walrus are two very important sources of food among the Eskimo, especially to the west, although right whales appear sporadically in eastern waters along the coasts from the mouth of Hudson Bay. The larger whales of the west are the baleen-bearing bowhead which move in spring northward through the Bering Strait and spend their summers in the neighborhood of the polar ice cap. These huge animals, with their specialized dental development of *baleen*, black, fern-like growths enabling the whale to strain sea water for its food, may run as high as 60 tons in weight and achieve lengths of 50 to 60 feet and more. The whales begin their movement northward as soon as leads form in the ocean ice, in April and May. In the same western regions appear at a somewhat later time, by June and July, the Pacific walrus. This is larger than its Atlantic counterpart, running to 2 or 3 tons in weight. These animals tend to herd and can be found on ice floes in the open sea in the early summer. The walrus, usually a placid animal, though potentially dangerous when attacked, employs its tusks, the source of Eskimo ivory, for uprooting mollusca on the sea bottom. The Atlantic walrus appears in Greenland, Labrador, and as far west as Baffinland. Like the right whale, it is somewhat less important to the Eskimo of this region, being rarer since decimation of the herds by Europeans. Another type of whale, the small white whale, or beluga, appears along the coasts from Alaska eastward. The beluga, 14 to 18 feet in length, runs in

small herds. With the sea mammals must be listed the polar bear, an animal frequently encountered on the winter pack ice where it preys on young seals. While not especially important to the Eskimo economy, polar bear pelts are valued and the meat prized. A last denizen of the western Arctic seas, as well as of the Pacific, is the formidable *orca*, the killer whale. Along with the other animals the killer whale figures prominently in Eskimo folklore, but the ferocious qualities of this 30-foot predator exclude it from the Eskimo economic sphere. No one would attack a killer whale, the "tiger" of the sea.

Many kinds of land animals appear in the American Arctic, all in some measure useful in the Eskimo economy. Of prime importance is the caribou, avidly hunted by all Eskimo groups in contact with caribou herds. This wild American reindeer, a highly gregarious animal, moves through the Arctic regions in amazingly vast herds. Several species and varieties are known, ranging across both Arctic and sub-Arctic, but it is principally the tundra caribou (*Rangifer arcticus*) which is prey to the Eskimo. The caribou herds may number as many as 10,000–20,000 animals, which move seasonally across tundra and mountain range, if such bar their way. The herds winter along the edges of the coniferous forests, migrating in summer to the tundra where they subsist on mosses. Effective caribou hunting ensures vast quantities of meat and hides, the latter a principal source for Eskimo clothing. Both bucks and does carry antlers and range in size from 250 to 400 pounds. Such predators as wolves are often found preying on caribou herds. They, along with foxes and wolverines, are hunted for their pelts. The brown bears, the grizzly bear in some western regions, mountain sheep, weasels, and various rodents, such as squirrels and hares, round out the mammalian inventory (Rausch, 1951).

Nor, as the Arctic fauna are considered, must the various fowl be excluded. Summer in the Arctic sees the return of the many species of ducks and geese, while ptarmigan abound in some sections the year round. Fish are present also, although they are not as vital to the Eskimo economy as may sometimes be thought. Few fish are found in the Arctic Ocean, nor are these widely exploited. Some Eskimo groups move to the inland waterways in summer, netting such freshwater fishes as various salmon, trout, grayling, and others. Except for the polar

Eskimo, North Alaska ● Hunters of the village of Tikeraaq (Point Hope), after lancing a small whale, tow the carcass to the edge of the ocean ice by umiak and begin the task of butchering. The meat is owned by all in the crews who have participated in the kill and is divided between each member of one or several crews. (Courtesy, American Museum of Natural History)

Eskimo, who has developed a special dependence on birds, both fish and fowl are essentially secondary elements in the Eskimo diet (cf. Nelson, 1969).

Aleut. Apart from these Eskimo groups as such, one should mention the Aleut, the aboriginal inhabitants of the long chain of islands extending to the south and west of the Alaskan mainland. Related to the Eskimo in speech, the Aleut, in their fogbound, storm-swept islands, were also adapted to life at sea. Like the Eskimo, their life centered in the local area and community. As nearly as can be judged from the evidence of archeology and from the few Aleuts who managed to survive a long Russian occupation prior to the purchase of Alaska by the United States in 1867 as well as postpurchase disruption, the culture was like that of the southern and western Eskimo of the main-

land, but considerably less rich. As may be anticipated, the adaptation of the Aleuts was toward hunting and the exploitation of their island resources of sea mammals (especially the seal, although some whaling was known) and of fish and birds. Aleut culture, like that of southern Alaska, was not inconsiderably influenced by the virile development of the Northwest Coast. There are suggestions, as a result, of an incipient wealth complex and of some unilineal social structure, although nuclear or conjugal relations were the rule. Nor can the Aleutian chain be ignored as a possible source both for Eskimo culture and as a migration route into the New World.

Thus, as a natural region of the world, a desert of cold, of tundra, rocky island and pebble beach, of ice and silent sea, the Arctic is impressive in the challenge it flings into the face of humankind. For the Eskimo it poses some problems of limits. Why, for instance, have the Eskimo chosen to ignore some of the vegetal resources of their area and to concentrate on the hunting of large game? The orientation toward hunting is the keynote in Eskimo culture; the environment limits but it is secondary to the kinds of choice which men make. Within the limitations of their Arctic environment, the Eskimo and the Aleut choose to concentrate on their hunting skills.

Eskimo Origins

A perplexing question, one which has concerned two generations of archeologists, is where the Eskimo come from. The question can be approached in terms of prehistoric time depth and it can also be viewed ethnologically, through an inductive comparison of the elements of Eskimo culture with those appearing in Eurasia or among American Indians. Do the Eskimo represent one of the last movements of people in the New World, a movement pushed into an inhospitable clime because of the presence of already settled people? In this case, the Eskimo physical type, so markedly Mongoloid at least in its suggestions of Asia rather than America, might be considered, although again the type is specialized and probably highly inbred. Language might also serve as evidence, since there are the suggestions that Eskimo-Aleut may relate to Indo-European or to the Ural-Altaic speech families in Eurasia. But here, too, the evidence is quite fragmentary. An alternative hypothesis, once held rather widely by some Danish Scholars as well as by some Americans, is that the Eskimo were a group of American Indians who, pushing up from the south, either from the regions to the west of Hudson Bay or along the Mackenzie, fanned out across the Arctic and there developed their specialized adaptations (Kroeber, 1939:20–22; Collins, 1951; Birket-Smith, 1929). But the growing mass of information concerning the prehistoric Eskimo would tend to vitiate this point of view.

Arctic Prehistory. Arctic prehistory points to a western source of Eskimo culture. As has been seen, the greatest variety of ancient Eskimo evidence is focused in Alaska. The Aleutian center, with such early cultures as Koniag and Kachemak Bay, is contrasted with the development in the Bering Sea and to the northwest. The sharp line of linguistic demarcation, the fact that from Norton Sound to Greenland there is mutual intelligibility in Eskimo, while to the south, in the Aleutians and in southwestern and southern Alaska, languages, although related, show greater diversity, would suggest that Eskimo culture of the central regions and Greenland spreads from a northwestern center. The discoveries at Cape Denbigh lead to a consideration of the Eskimo cultural sequences. From microliths and burins of a general Mesolithic type arises the suggestion of Asiatic origins (Giddings, 1949). Denbigh flints, found in northwest Alaska as well as in northwest Canada, appear to underlie both the Dorset culture of Canada and points east and the complex prehistoric cultures of Alaska. In the phases of the Old Bering Sea and Ipiutak cultures are seen art forms which bear some resemblance to those of Siberian Neolithic sites (Larsen and Rainey, 1948). Art styles change as the sequences progress, and in the Birnirk culture of north Alaska there are the beginnings of the area hunting specializations characteristic of the Eskimo of the ethnographic present. The artifact array of the Thule period suggests both Birnirk and modern Eskimo. It is in any case substantiated that the Thule people moved eastward, both mixing with the Dorset culture already settled in central and eastern Canada and replacing it. Radiocarbon dates for the earliest Eskimo-type cultures go back little more than 3000 years. The development was gradual, Thule culture reaching Greenland, in fact, by the twelfth century A.D. The conclusion that the Eskimo cultures have Mesolithic affinities stemming from the Old World and that the Eskimo are recent migrants appears well borne out.

Such statements as these are based on broad comparisons. Somewhat more specifically, the prehistory of the Arctic regions can be viewed in terms of temporal span and cultural development. Although the ethnology of the Eskimo has attracted a great deal of attention, knowledge of Arctic prehistory has been so scanty that no credible sequence of cultures, nor any time depth could be defined. The reasons for neglect of pre-Eskimo research are numerous, ranging from lack of opportunity to scholarly myopia. The result has been that most of humankind's possibly 30,000 years in the Arctic has become known only since 1950; the prehistoric Eskimo cultures themselves extend back in time only about 2,000 to 2,500 years. Awareness then of Eskimo roots is recent, and it is only partially understood (Fig. 30).

Standing earliest, and alone, is the Old Crow Flats find, more than 25,000 years old. The record is blank for about 16,000 to 17,000 years, and then there is the splendid record carefully unearthed at the Onion Portage site by Anderson (1968, 1970). Located at a famous camping place and caribou ford on the Kobuk River near the center of the Alaskan Refuge, this site contained a series of thin camp zones or occupation floors, each sealed by subsequent silt layers. The cultural debris and artifacts showed change through time from per-

ARCTIC CULTURE SEQUENCE

	Western (Maritime)	Western (Choris)	Eastern (Dorset)	Southern and Aleutian
Present	Eskimo ↑	Eskimo	Eskimo	
A.D. 1000	Thule ↑	Thule	Thule	Athabaskan
	Punuk ↑			Kachemak III
	Birnirk ↑	Birnirk		
		Ipiutak	Dorset	Kachemak II
A.D. 1	Old Bering Sea			
	Okvik	Norton		
2500 B.P.				
			Sarqaq	Kachemak I (Marpole)
3000 B.P.				
3500 B.P.	British Mt.	Choris		
4000 B.P.	Denbigh Flint Complex			Chaluka
	Arctic Small Tool Tradition		Pre-Dorset (Sarqaq)	
5000 B.P.				
6000 B.P.	Side Notched Points			
	Northern Archaic	Palisades	Plano (?) Tradition	
7000 B.P.	Kobuk			Anangula
10,000 B.P.	Akmak			
12,000 B.P.				
pre-25,000 B.P.	Old Crow Flats			

Figure 30 ● Major pre-Eskimo cultures of the American Arctic (Modified from Dumond, 1973; Jennings, 1974:327)

haps 10,000 B.P. to A.D. 1700. Three major cultural zones were recognized on the basis of artifact typology, typologies that corresponded to collections from scattered single-component (or occupation) Alaskan sites. Thus Onion Portage was not only important in constituting a long record of repetitive use of the site by successive cultures, but it takes on added luster in typing down the chronology of other sites to form a firm chronologic base for the millennia before Christ.

Anderson (1968) identified three early cul-

tures—Akmak (pre-8000 B.P.), northern Archaic (at 6000 B.P.), and the Arctic Small Tool tradition of 4000 B.P. There was even a protohistoric Eskimo dwelling about 300 years old on the surface. The scanty Akmak collection includes cores, large bifacially chipped blades, prismatic flakes, backed microblades (*backed* means that one sharp cutting edge is dulled by chipping). The specimens resemble but not very closely, artifacts from the vicinity of Lake Baikal; a resemblance that is general, at best. The Akmak tools simply do not compare closely to any other Asian or American complex.

The next youngest culture represented at Onion Portage is the Arctic Archaic which has also been called the Palisades complex. The charac-

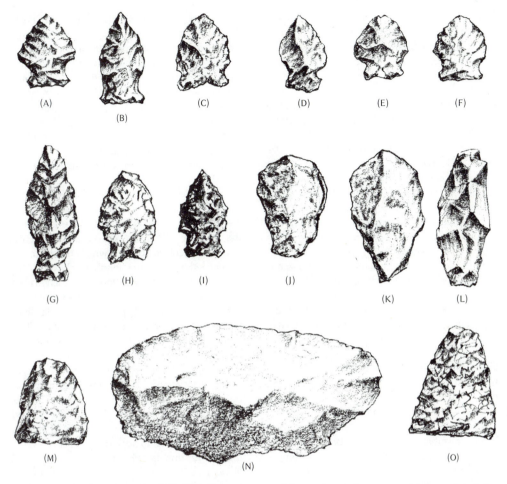

(A)   (B)   (C)   (D)   (E)   (F)

(G)   (H)   (I)   (J)   (K)   (L)

(M)   (N)   (O)

**Figure 31 ● Artifacts from the Palisades site
(After Giddings, 1962; Jennings, 1974:329)**

teristic forms are (Fig. 31) small notched and
stemmed projectile points and some heavy
choppers. The resemblance to the more southerly continental Archaic of Canada and the
United States, though general, is unmistakable.
The complex seems, therefore, to argue for a
deeper penetration into the Arctic of Archaic
peoples, pursuing land mammals, than has
been generally recognized.

By 4500–4000 B.P., the Arctic Small Tool tradition appears in the western Arctic. Represented at Onion Portage, British Mountain, and
across Canada on to Greenland, the type site is
the Denbigh site on Norton Bay. The complex
is important in several ways. First it seems to
represent a clearly Asiatic tool kit and technology of flint working, which may be as old as
8000 B.P. in the Arctic (Laughlin, 1963a, b). It is
ancestral to the Dorset culture, which in turn
contributed to the modern Eskimo tradition,
and it appears to have completely replaced the
Archaic and Paleo-Indian (Plano) cultures in
their spread northward.

The Denbigh collection is the type Arctic
Small Tool tradition, which can be described as
a microblade industry. There are small obsidian
(?) cores from which small prismatic flakes were
removed. The flakes were used just as they
were struck from the core as blades for cutting,
or they were fashioned into burins or beautiful
diagonally flaked lanceolate blades less than 2
inches in length. Larger harpoon points and
scrapers are also part of the complex. Although
the Denbigh site is near the ocean on Norton
Sound, the wide distribution of the Small Tools
across the Arctic and Canada argues a primary
focus on land mammals, which can only mean
that caribou was the game usually sought.

Several prehistoric traditions can be determined. The oldest of these, so far as the legendary emphasis on the sea is concerned, is the
Southern tradition, exemplified best at the
Aleutian site of Anangula dated at about 8000

B.P. Undoubtedly, the Anangula subsistence base and its characteristic artifacts contributed to the historic Eskimo tool assemblage; such things as lamps, stone bowls, a composite harpoon and togglehead harpoon points, eyed needles, drills, *ulus* or crescent-shaped rocker-knife blades and *bolas* (two to three stones at the end of separate cords thrown to entangle game) are examples.

It is the Northern Maritime tradition, the Okvik–Old Bering Sea–Birnirk–Punuk–Thule succession of cultures, which constitutes the most recent 2000 years of direct ancestral lineage to the Eskimo. Until recently, the Maritime tradition was considered as much Asiatic (Siberian) as Alaskan, for it is found on both sides of the Bering Straits. Most scholars, however, now accept the long history of antecedent American cultures that Figure 30 summarizes.

As their artifacts testify, the coastal cultures from Okvik onward were oriented toward the sea, with whale, seals, and walrus the principal game and with villages scattered along the sea shore as they still are today. However, as is later demonstrated, even the Maritime Eskimo heavily exploit interior game—caribou and fish—which they have always done according to Collins (1964) and Spencer (1959).

Since Old Bering Sea times, the houses have been semisubterranean with a long tunnel entrance, a bench across the rear, wooden or whale bone framing covered with sod and usually lined with skins. An incredible array of tools, specialized for Arctic conditions and varied needs, constitute a rich material culture that shows little change (except stylistically) for hundreds of years. Sea hunting was carried on either in the decked-over, one-man kayak or in the open umiak which holds several crew members. Made of skin, these boats were durable yet fragile craft requiring much maintenance. Hunting gear included a clever and complex weapon of many parts—the harpoon—the bow and arrow, the light spear and *atlatl* or throwing board, and an assortment of lines, buoys, drags, and other gear as specialized as plugs to stop up lance or ·harpoon holes so that killed seals would remain afloat. Collins lists other artifacts, such as stone and pottery lamps, sleds, toboggans, adzes, mattocks, the ulu, snow goggles, needles, and needle cases. Even the tamborine drum is ancient (Figs. 32, 33).

From a Birnirk-Punuk (A.D. 500–800) site, Ford (1959) describes the artifacts excavated from a few houses at an old village near Point Barrow. He calls the people "gadget burdened," listing harpoon heads and shaft parts, ice picks, lances, seal mouth and wound plugs, ice scoops, rattles and ice scratchers (to attract seals), bone arrow points, and arrows to name only a few of the hunting tools. Fishing required spears, hooks, and gorges. Tools for men were knives, whetstones, engraving tools, fire sets, whalebone shovels, snow knives, picks, mattocks, and drills. Women's work required an equally long inventory.

The Thule culture, which evolved out of the Punuk by about A.D. 1000, is immediately ancestral to the modern Eskimo. It developed in the western Arctic and spread rapidly all the way to Greenland, during which time it completely submerged the terminal phase of the Arctic Small Tool tradition, by then called the Dorset. Although the Dorset had blanketed the Arctic coast and parts of Canada from about A.D. 1, its contribution to Eskimo culture is nil and no description of Dorset nor its ancestral form Sarqaq is offered here.

It is thus the Thule culture, with its specialized development of sea mammal hunting, that underlies the culture of the modern Eskimo. These earlier cultures, including the Thule, had a surprisingly rich content, so much so, in fact, that some choose to regard the culture of the modern Eskimo as reflecting decline in cultural vigor. This is not necessarily the case, since the Eskimo of ethnography make specialized adaptations of the basic Thule orientations. The central-eastern development of Eskimo cultures sees the underlying strain of Dorset overlaid by Thule. In the west, Thule is a specialized sea mammal culture preceded by Birnirk, Punuk, and the rest. Actually, the Thule movement to Greenland makes this area more like northern Alaska. The central regions show their own unique development and begin to diverge from both Greenland and Alaska (Mathiassen, 1927). A factor relating to this local specializing unquestionably involves some long-range cyclical changes in the distribution of fauna. Except for the beluga and a few smaller cetacean species along the coasts of Baffinland, Greenland, and Labrador, neither whales nor walrus appear in the central areas. It can thus be assumed that the Eskimo groups which depend entirely on caribou, to name one kind of specialty, are those whose development is late in time and whose cultures are impoverished versions of a former maritime adaptation.

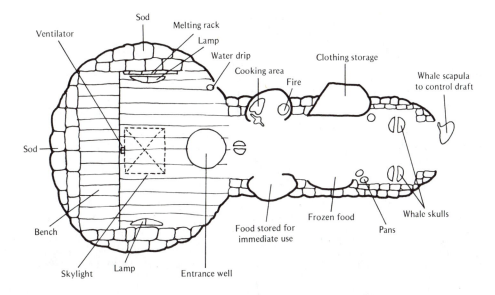

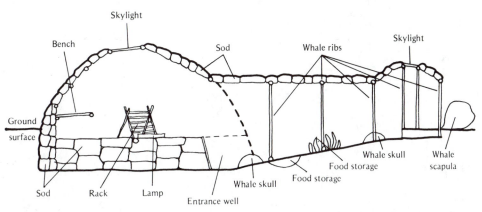

Figure 32 ● Floor plan and cross section of a Point Barrow maritime Eskimo house (After Spencer, 1959; Jennings, 1974:340)

Arctic Ethnology. Leaving the prehistoric record, rich as it is, aside, it is possible to arrive at some indication of the Old World affinities of Eskimo culture by examining inductively single culture traits which appear in both Eurasia and America. In part, these reflect an adaptation to environment and are accordingly shared by a great many peoples of the Arctic and sub-Arctic regions. Such circumpolar features as clothing, weapon assemblage, house types and furnishings, along with many other elements, are parallel in the Old and New Worlds and suggest patterns of historical connection, a diffusion from one area to the other (cf. Bogoraz, 1929). Time depth in the Old World would give priority to Eurasia as against America. A fairly impressive listing of cultural elements which the Eskimo share with the Siberians and similar northern peoples is possible.

As an example, a glance at types of housing suggests at once trans-Bering connections. The semisubterranean house was already in use in the prehistoric Old Bering Sea culture. The house involved an excavation, a roof then being supported by posts and joists. A bench-like arrangement ran around the house at the ground level. Common in this type of dwelling was a roof entrance. Several variations of the structure appear among the Eskimo, but the form is generally much like its Asiatic counterpart. The use by many Eskimo groups of a storm hall may change the shape, and the roof entrance gives way to a skylight, a window covered with translucent gut. The bench retains its prominence. A form of this house appears in the Wei River valley in Neolithic China by 3000 B.C. and modern north Chinese and Ko-

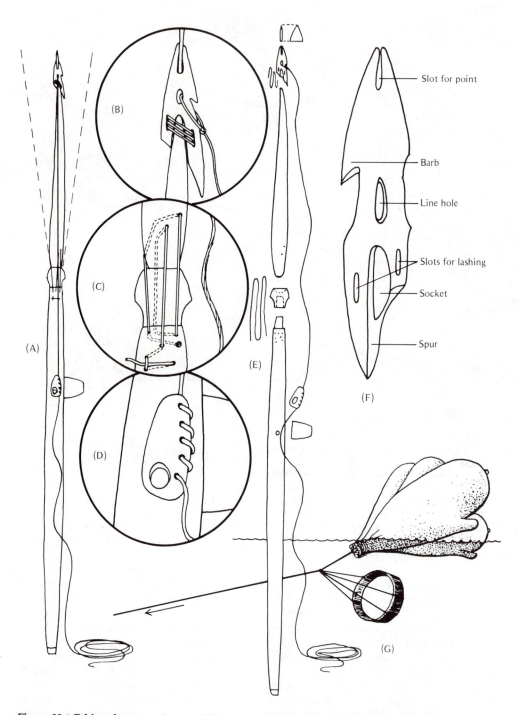

Figure 33 ● Eskimo harpoon. A, assembled harpoon (Dotted lines indicate flexibility of foreshaft); B, harpoon head; C, flexible joint showing shaft, shaft head, and foreshaft lashed together; D, line retainer secured to shaft by knob; E, component parts of harpoon; F, idealized harpoon head; G, sealskin floats and drag attached to end of line. (A–E, G after Boas, 1888; F after Rudenko, 1961; Jennings, 1974:341)

Siberian Eskimo at Plover Bay, 1899 ● The
Eskimo at the extreme northeast corner of Asia
are migrants from America. Shown is a family
residing in a summer tent. The inflated seal
skins serve as floats for sea mammal hunting,
while the harpoons are laid over the top of the
tent. Clothing is placed on lines to dry.
(Smithsonian Institution National
Anthropological Archives)

rean houses retain some vestiges of the style.
Such Asiatic peoples as the Chukchi and Kor-
yak in northeastern Siberia employ this house
type, while in America it diffuses beyond the
Eskimo to the south. The semisubterranean
house is seen in the Plateau and is suggested
in the central fire pit of the plank house of the
Northwest Coast. The peculiar kiva, the ceremonial building of the Pueblo Indians in the
Southwest, has a number of traits, bench, central pit, partial placement underground, which
suggest further affinity. Or, as another manifestation of an Asiatic archetype in housing, the
prominence of the skin tent among hunting
peoples is well known. However, the covering
of such a tent, whatever its form, with snow, is
a trait common both to Siberia and America.
The various Eskimo have several tent types, but

the use of snow as an insulating winter covering suggests wider relationships. It can be
suggested that the unique Eskimo invention,
the domed snow house, reflecting the only authenticated use of the principle of the keystone
arch in America, is derived from the snow-cov-
ered tent.

The weapons of the Eskimo show several
Eurasiatic parallels. Several types of harpoons
are used in different kinds of hunting. Characteristic are those with detachable heads, the
point being buried in the prey, the shaft falling
free, and the head secured with lines. With the
harpoons appears the spear thrower, or atlatl, a
board holding the butt of the harpoon and permitting the thrower to obtain a wider arc and a
more forceful cast. Both of these traits, among
several others like the famous Eskimo lamp,
have been described for the Aurignacian-Mag-
dalenian sequence of the Upper Paleolithic of
western Europe, the glacial hunting age of
25,000 years ago. Whether the Eskimo relate
culturally and perhaps physically to the extinct
humans of the Cro-Magnon type need scarcely
be a question here. The parallels, however, are
indeed striking. The bird arrow, a shaft with a
blunt point to stun and maim birds, is common in both Asia and among the Eskimo. So

Central Eskimo building a snow house ● Characteristic of the central Eskimo regions, the snow house is based on the principal of the arch or dome, the only occurrence of this architectural feature in native America. Cut with snow knives of bone, the blocks were set in place and smoothed. With the Eskimo seal oil lamp, such dwellings were made very warm, an interior problem being the ice melt, which necessitated constant scraping. Although a family might spend a winter in the snow house, a shift was made to a skin tent in summer. (Photograph, 1913–1918, Stefansson Expedition. Smithsonian Institution National Anthropological Archives)

also are the Eskimo woman's knife, the lunate shaped ulu, the forms of the bow, with its trussing and sinew backing, and the corral-impound method for deer hunting.

To this list can be added the lamp, made of stone, especially of steatite or soapstone, and sometimes of pottery. Saucerlike, filled with oil, the lamp is vital to Eskimo life. It heats and cooks with a minimal expenditure of fuel and with notable efficiency. Ancient in the Old World, it has a sporadic distribution there but is well-nigh universal among the Eskimo. The sledge with runners, the kayak, dog traction, all appear widely across the Arctic. Of these

means of transportation, the Eskimo have perfected their own adaptations, such as the double-bladed paddle for the more widely spread kayak. Tailored clothing, generally Arctic in type, again has been accompanied by some distinctive Eskimo adaptations, two relatively light suits of skins affording an insulating area of air warmed by body heat. Eskimo art forms, as in masks and carved figures, suggest Asia rather than the American Indian. Or again, such items as the snow beater, the snow goggles, ice picks, the back scratcher, and the bow drill appear to be of Asiatic origin. On the nonmaterial side, less of course can be said. However, the complex of curing by shamans, as well as the associated behavioral patterns, are considerably more elaborated in northern Asia than among the Eskimo. Associated as well with shamanism in the Arctic, and a prominent feature among the Eskimo, is the tambourine, the one-sided skin drum. This, in fact, is the exclusive Eskimo musical instrument. No full justice is done here to these parallels. Suffice it to say, however, that the Eskimo share traits many of which appear on both sides of the Bering Sea. While they offer their own regional adaptations of them, the Asiatic derivation can reasonably be assumed.

In summary, the Eskimo are a diverse series of groups whose culture is in the main reflective of a boreal adjustment to hunting. It seems indicated that they are recent comers and that they resemble in their overall cultural configuration those northern cultures which have been identified as Mesolithic. An adequate treatment of the totality of Eskimo culture, considering in detail its vigorous and splendid adaptations, is clearly not possible. The post-Thule development, with its sea mammal focus, is perhaps most revealing of the nature of Eskimo culture.

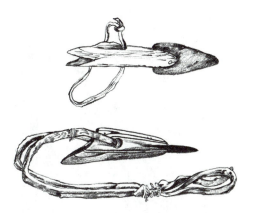

North Alaskan Eskimo ● Detachable harpoon heads for walrus hunting. (After J. Murdoch, 1892)

THE ESKIMO OF NORTHERN ALASKA[2]

The polar, or bowhead whale (*Balaena mysticetus*, Linn.), among the largest of the whales and indeed of living creatures both past and present, spends it summers feeding on the microscopic plankton along the edges of the polar cap. Beginning in April, breaks occur in the ice of the Arctic Sea, forming avenues along which these mammals pass. Swimming up through the Bering Straits, herds pass along the coasts of northern Alaska, rising in the ice leads for air. All along the Alaskan shore, as well as further south in the area of the Northwest Coast around Vancouver Island, settlements have been devoted to the exploitation of this vast food resource. But nowhere perhaps is whaling so fundamental as in the Eskimo subarea stretching in Alaska from Point Hope to Point Barrow. Not, to be sure, that whales form the sole basis of subsistence—other sea mammals as well as caribou occupy important places in the native economy—but in this area so much of social and ceremonial life centers in the whale that this animal can be considered to lend the north Alaskan area its specific focus (cf. Spencer, 1959).

Taking a whale is scarcely an easy task. Even today, following the introduction of European techniques such as the metal lance and the whale bomb, it remains a hazardous occupation. In the past, before European contact, pursuit of whales with such equipment as the fragile skin-covered open boat, the umiak, the stone-tipped harpoon and killing lance, superb

[2] This section on the Eskimo of northern Alaska is drawn from the field work of Robert F. Spencer. This was undertaken principally at Point Barrow during the summer and fall of 1952 and again of 1953. The investigations were sponsored in 1952 by the Office of Naval Research and in 1953 by the Arctic Institute of North America. Grateful acknowledgement is extended both organizations.

inventions though all of these are, was doubly difficult. When the ice leads had formed, crews of men, seven or eight to an umiak, left the ceremonial house, where under the boat captain, the hunt leader whose authority was both economic and religious, they had been preparing for the hunt, and proceeded to the edge of the ice, there to wait until the whales were sighted. The occasion was marked by solemnity, wholly lacking in the banter and jokes so characteristic of the Eskimo. The boat owner, organizer of the crew, had seen to it that each man was wearing new clothes, that new lines had been put on the harpoons and their attached floats, that a new cover had been placed over the frame of the umiak, and that the magical charms were in place. The men sat silently while the boat owner, called the *umealiq*, and the harpooner, a man known for his special throwing and lancing skill, might sing the measured songs designed to compel the whale to come and to effect its capture. When a whale was sighted, the umiak was rushed into the water, each man paddling furiously toward the quarry. In the prow, the harpooner had his gear ready; the umealiq paddled from the stern and steered. Other boats might take off after the same whale or seek to capture another if a herd were present.

Singing the magic songs as they paddled, the crew sought to come as close as possible to the point where it could be estimated that a whale would rise. The harpoon, that intricately fashioned weapon with its complex line, shaft, point, and float arrangement, balanced on a spear thrower, was let fly as soon as possible. The harpooner sang his songs over his weap-

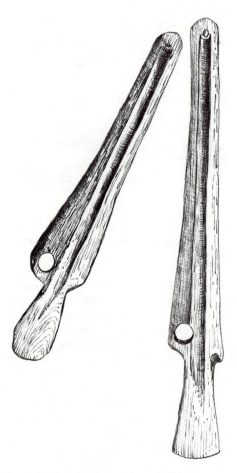

North Alaskan Eskimo ● The atlatl or throwing board. These, made of wood and 15 to 18 inches in length, with carved grip and finger hole, are used to hurl a 5–foot sealing dart or light harpoon. They provide extra length to the thrower's arm and permit a cast of considerable force and distance. At the end away from the grip is a small ivory spur on which the butt of the dart rests. (After J. Murdoch, 1892)

ons as he discharged them. The harpoon head, held by lines of walrus hide, buried itself deep into the whale, the shaft came free. Since the harpoon head was not lethal to so large a mammal, the lines with their attached floats served to tire the quarry. As the whale sounded, the floats, inflated seal skins, or watertight walrus bladders, constituted a drag on his movements. As he rose again, the estimate of where he would do so depending on the experienced judgement of the crew members, another harpoon was fixed. An exhausted whale, fixed by numerous lines, rising gasping to the surface, was now ready to be dispatched. The whaling lance, a stone-headed stabbing tool

with a blade the size of a man's palm, was now brought into play. With it an attempt might be made to cut the sinews of the whale's flukes to prevent the whale from turning and to reduce the danger when an umiak drew alongside. Not that the whale would attack a boat, but his very bulk and a convulsive movement of his flukes, could upset the frail umiak. Here was real danger; no Eskimo can swim, nor in fact can any human being in water so near freezing temperature. Accident took a heavy toll of Eskimo life and, indeed, continues to do so today. Once at the side of the whale, the harpooner went to work with the lance, stabbing at the head, the lungs, the kidneys, the heart. As the whale bled to death, floats were attached at the sides of the carcass to keep it from sinking. Several umiaks working together towed the dead animal to the edge of the ice. Here again was no easy task, the moving of a carcass that might run up to 60 and more tons. Even one whale made for a good season; eight or nine a highly successful one.

As a whale was brought to the edge of the ice, solemnity was forgotten. The members of the community came down to the ice en masse to begin to grab bits of *muktuk*, the highly palatable raw black skin of the whale, to fasten heavy walrus-hide lines on the dead animal, and to play a kind of tug of war with the carcass, inching it onto the ice. First the head, drawn onto the ice edge, was severed with spades. At this point, the wife of the boat owner credited with the capture, herself a kind of priestess and subject to many kinds of restrictions while her husband and his crew were hunting, came forward to offer the head a cup of cold water. "We thank you for coming; you must be thirsty; here is water for you" was her remark. The whale was thus greeted, his spirit released by the severing of the head. The spirit was thanked and urged to return to the land of the whales and tell the living whales how well treated he had been "by those people." Now as the carcass was drawn gradually to the edge of the ice, the butchering process went on. Special fluke parts were put aside as the boat owner's share, piles of meat, blubber, and skin were set aside for the crew members and for the members of the assisting crews. Generosity was the keynote; all in the community could count on piles of meat. Cached in the natural deep freeze of the permafrost, the meat remained as a source of food until the next whaling season.

What has been described here has characterized the settlements along the north Alaskan

● WHALING—NORTH ALASKAN ESKIMO

Drama and danger characterize Eskimo whaling. Among the Eskimo, economic specialization has depended on the kinds of game locally available. As the whales are sighted, the crews are ready. The skin-covered umiak is paddled furiously toward the quarry and the harpooner in the bow seeks to bury as many harpoons as possible into the huge body of the whale.

Here the lines have snapped as the great mammal makes a sudden submerging movement. The harpooner is ready at once with another weapon. The whale will feel the drag of the inflated sealskin and wooden floats and surface again. Yet another harpoon will be thrown. Exhausted from the drag of the floats and lines, the whale will eventually rest at the surface. When its violent swimming ceases, the harpooner will be ready with his stone-pointed lance and will deliver the killing thrusts into the kidneys, heart, or lungs.

But for this crew the victory is not wholly in sight. The snapped lines and the dangerous proximity to the tail flukes call on every man's skill and seamanship. The crew leader, the umealiq, sits in the stern, maneuvering the steering paddle. He has outfitted the boat, provided the lines and weapons, and he has enlisted and maintained his crew through gifts and bribes. He has also acquired the ceremonial furniture of the umiak, the charms hung along the gunwales. About his shoulders he wears the skin of a raven, beak downward, pointing to the whale. And he has also given his crew the rights to sing his personal whaling songs, those which he has obtained by inheritance or purchase and which serve to weaken the whale, to summon the whale, or to prevent the lines from fouling. The men sing as they paddle vigorously.

A successful hunt means a good year for the crew and their families; failure means extra effort at other types of sea mammal hunting over the coming months and a not impossible threat of starvation. But if all goes well, several umiaks will tow the carcass back to the edge of the ice where it is butchered and distributed amidst general rejoicing. The successful whale hunt marks the beginning of a happy year. There is reaffirmation of the relations between the human and the animal world and the economic cycle of Eskimo life runs smoothly on.

THE ARCTIC AND SUB-ARCTIC ■ 73

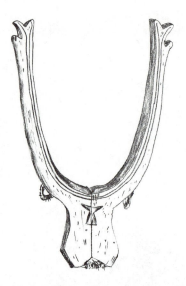

North Alaskan Eskimo ● Ivory crotch to hold whaling harpoons. (After J. Murdoch, 1892)

coast (cf. Rainey, 1947). It is in whaling that a sense of community solidarity developed. A community or village had otherwise no reality and might in fact be torn by feuds and rivalries. There were no chiefs; it was only the leaders of whaling crews who held brief sway over a situation requiring cooperative endeavor for mutual benefit. Sociologically speaking, a village was not a corporate unit and no precise authority could be said to exist in it. Two months of the year might be devoted to whaling, but other activities did not have the same communalistic effect, nor indeed were all of the Eskimo of northern Alaska concerned with whaling. Whaling was an economic specialization limited to the coastal dwellers. Another such specialization lay in caribou hunting as carried on by the interior peoples of the Alaskan north.

Ecological Adaptations and Settlements

North Alaska is tundra country in the truest sense. It is set off from the great river system of the Yukon by the Brooks Mountains, a northern spur of Alaska's great mountain chain. The Brooks Range is a jumble of granite, heavily glaciated, with a fairly precipitous southern flank. The chain, which runs from east to west in Alaska, has a few north-south passes through which the caribou migrate. On its northern side, the Brooks Range slopes gradually to the sea level of the tundra. Here is the moss covered area, boggy and mosquito ridden in summer, black and snow blown in winter.

There are lakes and meandering streams, the latter generally a part of the Colville River and its tributaries. In the interior and along the rivers lived small groups of Eskimo caribou hunters, of which a few small groups still survive. These are to be differentiated from the maritime dwellers, the whalers of the coast. *Nuunamiut*, people of the land, was the name applied to the caribou-hunting nomads, while *Tareumiut* denoted the settled whaling communities on the coasts and the people who lived in them. These were different ecological systems, even if culturally, in terms of formal organization, world view, and basic definitions of man and nature, they were much alike. Because they depended on different means of livelihood, there was, as may be expected, some difference in their material goods. But they spoke the same language and had developed, over the years, a mutual interdependence. Trade between the inland and the coasts kept a stable situation operative. Thus the maritime people wore caribou-skin clothing, while the inland hunters ate seal and whale oil with their meat and used the same material as fuel in their lamps. What the whale was to the *Tareumiut* the caribou was to the *Nuunamiut*. Communal hunting involving great drives of caribou took place in the interior. While these lasted, they had the same effect as did the whaling on the coast of creating a temporary community or group solidarity. North Alaska, isolated by the Brooks Range and stretching on the coast through the areas of concentrated whaling from Point Hope to Point Barrow, thus formed a definable zone of Eskimo culture in which two specialized ecological systems operated (Larsen and Rainey, 1948).

There has been some speculation on which economic system is earlier. More information, it is true, is available from the coastal regions, a result of the depth of archeological remains resulting from long-time settlement. In the interior, people tended to move about more since the caribou herds varied in their migration movements. But the evidence appears to point to a basic maritime adjustment over which is laid a whaling specialization on the one hand, and a movement to the interior with a caribou concentration on the other. The development of both systems may be considered as taking place gradually, with the end result of a system of balance and mutual interdependence.

Today, with the exception of a few small bands of caribou hunters located along the Ko-

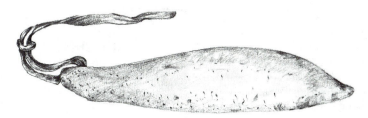

North Alaskan Eskimo ● Carved figures of seals. Figures such as these, in wood and bone, reflect not only the artistic concern with animals and may therefore be regarded as having a ceremonial or magical significance (one designed to attract the seal), but they may have a utilitarian meaning as well. Net floats and sinkers, drag line weights, and many other items may be carved into animal form. (After J. Murdoch, 1892)

buk River and at or near Anaktuvuk Pass in the Brooks Range, population concentration is on the coast in the communities of Point Hope, Point Lay, Wainwright, and Point Barrow. In the precontact present, however, small settlements dotted the coast and there were numerous groups in the interior. The population, 4000 to 5000 a century ago, was greater in the interior. In neither system, however, was provision made for tribal consciousness. Properly speaking, reference can only be made to a concept of *band*, a socio-economic unit with frequently changing membership. When people assembled to form the whaling crews or when a caribou drive took place, an opportunity arose for unrelated people to act together. The social complexities involved remain for discussion below. Suffice it to note here that kinship, real or fictive, was the basis of interpersonal relations. What thus developed was a network of kinship ties across the area. An important theme in Eskimo culture is a concept of freedom—an individual was wholly free to move about as he wished, to engage in whatever economic activity he wished, and to associate himself with any group to which he might have the remotest tie of kinship. In other words, there was a great deal of movement. Coastal villages or interior hunting bands thus found their personnel changing a good deal as individuals and families moved in and out. Such mobility makes any depiction of precise settlement difficult.

There was, it is true, a tendency for those born into a coastal or nomadic interior situation to remain in the ecological situation requiring the special skills associated with it. A man accustomed to sea mammal hunting would be less likely to concentrate exclusively on caribou, although there was nothing to prevent his doing so. But one would encounter at any point along the coast a man from the community of Nuwuk, at Point Barrow, who had chosen to resettle with his family or with part of it, at some more desirable location. The same was true of the people of the interior, all of whom were free to associate themselves with any number of bands along the Colville or the Noatak. The two ecological systems can perhaps best be contrasted in terms of their respective economic activities, their annual cyclical round, and the material elements of culture associated with the specialized kind of life of each possessed.

The Eskimo of the North Alaskan Coast— Tareumiut. On the coast, the year could be said to begin with the increase of daylight and the advent of the whales in the spring. When the drama of whaling was over, usually by early June, when the ceremonies for the whale had been held, the meat and gear put away, the coastal villages were marked by movement. People were free to choose the summer work best suited to their needs or their skills. It was this very freedom which caused households to break up, some members remaining to hunt on the coasts, others moving to the interior for fishing, trapping, and trading. The culture stressed activity; one was free to choose the work he wished but idleness was reprehensible. On the social level, two factors require consideration, the nuclear family and the household. The two might coincide but often did not. In the household might live two or more brothers, a brother and sister, older parents and younger children, all their respective wives and husbands. In the late spring, these nuclear families, coresident in winter, might take out as family units, engage in summer activities, and resume their lives in a single household with the onset of the dark days.

A pattern was established in which the summer activities were carefully planned and timed. Suppose one takes the example of the hunter, Kunuyuq. This man has two wives and five children. In the village of Utkeavik, not far from Point Barrow, he shares a house with his brother Uguruq. The latter is also married, having one wife and two children. Their aged mother as well as a young unmarried brother, a boy of about 14, also live in the village house. Over the past season a recently widowed aunt of Kunuyuq's second wife has moved into the household, although it is not likely that she will stay, since she plans in the late fall to reside with her married daughter in Tikeraaq, the village at Point Hope. When the summer activities are over, Kunuyuq has promised to take her there by dog sled, trading as he goes. In Utkeavik, in a nearby household, lives Kunuyuq's half sister, the child of his deceased father by another wife. She and her husband share a household with other relatives. When Kunuyuq has completed the whaling season, he informs his brother of his intention to go inland for a time, taking his wives and some of the children. The brother, Uguruq, decides he will remain in the community with his family and go later on a trading expedition. The older women and very young children, except the baby not yet weaned, are left home in the village under the protection of Kunuyuq's half sister's husband. The youngest brother accompanies Kunuyuq.

Kunuyuq is now ready. He checks his umiak, loading it with some provisions, extra clothing, fishnets, and smaller harpoons for seals or in the event of encountering a few stray caribou. On the umiak he also loads his sled even though it is now summer and the snow is off the ground. Kunuyuq's twelve dogs are leashed and led along the beach by the younger brother. With his wives and three children, Kunuyuq paddles to the mouth of a nearby stream. The dogs are now leashed to the umiak, and slow progress is made upstream. After several days of camping at sites along the way, a fishing station is reached. Here Kunuyuq pitches a tent and assists his wives in stretching the nets across the stream. Here they will stay until Kunuyuq returns for them, gathering in the catch, gutting it, and storing it in sacks in the permafrost. Mean-

while, they have sewing to do, clothing to make for the winter, boot soles to chew. Other women will join them and together they will spend a happy, gossiping summer. After he returns for them, Kunuyuq will have to carry back to the village six to twelve tons of whitefish.

Kunuyuq, meanwhile, joins some other men at the fish camp. Although not concerned with the caribou drives characteristic of the inland nomads, the men hunt together because a herd has been sighted moving this far north and a supply of fresh meat is welcome. This, with the hides, is returned to the fish camp where the women will do the work of tanning and prepare the meat for freezing. Before Kunuyuq left the village, he had agreed with the boat owner, the umealiq with whom he has been associated in whaling, that he would return to the crew for walrus hunting. These two-and three-ton animals, with their formidable tusks, appear about mid-July, feeding on the molluscs on the ocean floor. Seen on ice floes, they are pursued by umiak and harpooned. An occasional *ugruk*, the giant bearded seal, is encountered at this time as well. Kunuyuq thus returns to the village and the hunt is under way. The walrus is butchered out on the floes of ice which still dot the Arctic Ocean, and the game is divided. Uguruq, Kunuyuq's brother, also joins in this activity. The walrus hides are used for making ropes and whale lines, the meat is frozen and allowed to ferment, being sewed up in sacks. With the walrus there is none of the elaborate ceremonial usage connected with the whale. Still, the walrus's head is split so as to allow its soul to depart, and there are songs for the walrus hunt as well. Meat and gear again stowed, Kunuyuq and members of his crew, including his brother and his sister's husband, prepare for trading.

A long journey now lies ahead of them. Since all the men have partners among the Nuunamiut with whom they have long been accustomed to trade, they prepare to go along the northern coast to the mouth of the Colville where a trading camp exists. Kunuyuq has a fair amount of both whale and seal oil, packed in "pokes," bladders and liquid-tight skins. Because the whaling season was successful, he also has a fair amount of *muktuk*, or whale skin. Some walrus tusks and some driftwood round out his trading items. His brother has some walrus-skin lines for trade as well. Other men have sea birds, ducks and geese, packed in seal oil. These supplies are loaded on the umiaks. With two or three men paddling, the umiaks reach the Colville mouth after two or three stops along the way for brief rests. All speed is taken, since an early arrival promises a trading advantage, and there are others from the home community and from adjacent villages whom Kunuyuq regards as rivals and as essentially hostile. Indeed, it must be remembered that unless Kunuyuq can establish a kinship or partnership relationship with other men, such as has taken place in respect to his boat crew, he tends to regard them as potential enemies.

At the Colville delta, Kunuyuq wastes no time but seeks the inland men, whom he regards as his partners and who have come by umiak down from the interior water courses. Without haggling, Kunuyuq gives generously. His partners—he has several since as a seaman he commands a large supply of oil—are no less so. A poke of oil is traded for six or seven caribou skins. Other items are discussed at length—a piece of driftwood suitable for a piece of umiak frame or a caribou lance, goes for a pair of skins, a poke is given for a wolverine skin, desirable for a ruff on the parka. Kunuyuq is also wearing a pair of ivory *labrets*, the lip plugs which "button" through a perforation in the lower lip. These are very valuable and he trades them to a partner for 25 caribou skins. Into his own lip, he temporarily inserts a pair of slate labrets for he will spend the winter carving a pair of ivory ones again. The trade completed and bales of skins packed into the umiak, the men start back, perhaps pausing along the way to hunt caribou with their partners. Kunuyuq's family will have clothing made of the caribou skins and what is left over he will trade in the home community, getting ugruk skins for boot soles, furs, baleen nets, and similar items.

Kunuyuq has returned slowly along the inland water courses. An occasional portage may delay him and his younger brother for several days, since the other men have now gone their separate ways, and the umiak must be carried and then a return made for its load. The days are growing shorter and there is a sign of freeze. At last Kunuyuq returns to the fish camp where his wives have remained. His children he greets affectionately, inspecting critically the work of his wives. He remains with his family at the fish camp until the freeze starts and there is sufficient snow on the ground. Now the umiak is beached, placed on

North Alaskan Eskimo ● Mukluks, or watertight boots. The sole is seal hide, chewed into shape; the tops are caribou skin. (After J. Murdoch, 1892)

the sled, and the dogs are called into action. The family rides in the umiak on the sled, Kunuyuq steering the dogs, hitched in a fan-wise trace, from behind. He pours water on the runners of the sled. Frozen, this allows rapid motion over the frozen ground and along the icy water courses. Back in the home village, the families making up the household are reunited and the summer discussed. Kunuyuq must make several trips back to the fish camp to pick up the results of his wives' labors of the summer, load his cache of caribou meat, and bring in whatever else has been left. It is now October and the days are very short. By November, the ice has formed on the sea and the house is prepared for the severe winter.

There is just time for Kunuyuq to catch the final southward flight of some of the Arctic birds, those intrepid geese and ducks who summer at the poles. Flying over sandspits, the birds are frightened by posts on which clothing has been placed. Veering in their flight, disturbed by these "scarecrows," the birds pass over a point where the hunters may station themselves. The blunt bird arrow is used, as well as the bola, an ancient American weapon consisting of strings and stone balls. The balls wind the strings about the birds and pull them down. Where he has had time, Kunuyuq also gave attention to duck hunting in the spring. The birds, feathers and all, are preserved in seal oil.

Now that winter has set in, Kunuyuq has somewhat greater freedom to devote himself to taking care of his own special needs. His umiak, his weapons, other bits of paraphernalia require his attention. He makes the necessary repairs, does a bit of carving, sees that the house is properly calked and ventilated. But the economic quest is not over. Traps must be set out for the various predators, the wolf, the fox, and the wolverine. Kunuyuq uses a deadfall and ice block with a figure '4' trigger. The trigger released, the block falls to crush the game. In the late fall, there are ptarmigans, and baleen snares must be set out for them. Land hunting of this kind goes on all winter, and Kunuyuq goes out alone to the areas where he has hunted before and which he knows best. Caught in a storm, he may throw up a shelter of ice blocks, the closest the northern Alaskans come to the "igloo" of the central regions, but he is more likely to carry a tent which he covers with snow. Such tents are small, a pup-tent variety, and like the clothing, made from the ubiquitous caribou skin. He may also put out pieces of sharpened baleen bent over a piece of meat and frozen. These, when snapped down by a wolf, unfreeze and spring out to destroy the animal. But for Kunuyuq, there also remains the sea.

The whale, the walrus, and the ugruk are taken by crew effort, that is communally. The game is shared and everyone's task is allotted. This is not true of the smaller seals which appear under the winter ice and in the open water throughout the year. Kunuyuq has decided that he will go sealing. What he does involves no little preparation, both in terms of gear and clothing. Now the day is gone and Kunuyuq is faced by a dark night over the white world of the sea. Winter clothing is now the rule, a suit of caribou skin, carefully tanned, with the fur turned into the body. Over this another suit, with the fur turned out, allows between the two tanned sides of the skins an area of insulation warmed by the heat of the body. A hood is worn, with a ruff of wolf or wolverine fur drawn closely over the face. Heavy mittens and watertight boots, the sole being of sealhide and the interior lined with soft furs. Down or moss are used as means of keeping the boot

interior dry. A vital part of his equipment is a needle case and sinew for thread. Torn clothing can make the difference between survival and death. For the seals, Kunuyuq carries a few short spears, a light harpoon or two, a scratching tool made of seal claws, ivory clinkers, and most importantly, a baleen net. Eskimo seal-hunting patterns vary somewhat across the Arctic. In north Alaska, netting of seals under the ice is preferred, although stabbing a seal as it rises to a breathing hole in the ice is also common. Holes are drilled in the ice, the net strung near the breathing hole. Seal claw scratchers, imitating the motion and sound of a seal on the ice, serve as a decoy. When the seal strikes the net, usually strangling itself or breaking its neck, the clinkers warn the hunter. Kunuyuq, taking several seals in this way, drags them homeward across the sea ice. He has been careful to make a cut across the neck so as to let the soul of the seal escape and has been careful as well to offer the seal a drink of cold water. Under his parka he has carried a mitten filled with snow, melted by the heat of his body to give a ready supply of water. If successful in spearing a polar bear, a formidable enemy on the ice, he is ready to treat it in the same way.

Kunuyuq, aided by the other men in the household, has amassed no small supply of food. Whale, walrus, seal, caribou, the bags of fish, sea and land birds have all been carefully stored against the needs of the winter and the coming year. Some of the food is placed on racks behind the dwelling house, the rest has been cached in shallow pits in the frozen ground and covered. A storage place in the house keeps food to be cooked readily at hand as well. The women of the household take turns cooking, each one cooking once a day. Apart from this, however, there is no special mealtime, each person eating when hungry, as often as he chooses. Food is cooked by boiling. All food is boiled, in fact, with the exception of fish, which may be eaten raw in a frozen state, and of the oil-soaked sea birds, and a few other foods. Seal meat is boiled with fat, a general tendency, and it is the combination of blubber and meat which appears to give a wholly adequate diet for these inhabitants. Most boiling is done in vessels of a bucketlike shape fashioned of driftwood. Curiously, the Eskimo of north Alaska possess pottery, an unexpected development in this part of the world, the origins of which are not wholly clear. True, it is pottery of

North Alaskan Eskimo ● Harpoon head for walrus hunting with attached walrus-hide line. (After J. Murdoch, 1892)

an inferior grade, made from clay tempered with feathers and blood, but it is adequate for stone boiling, the prevailing North American method, at least among hunting peoples. Heated rocks are introduced into the vessel until the water boils, the stones being heated over the lamp or household fire in this case and handled with wooden tongs. But if Kunuyuq's meat supply seems large, the dozen or so people living in the household will eat at least 100 pounds daily. Twelve dogs will require a like amount.

Kunuyuq engages in sealing and trapping intermittently through the winter. But because his year has been a successful one, he may spend much of December and January, the dark months, in recreational activities. He and his two brothers leave the women at home and spend their waking hours in the *karigi*, the men's house. In the north Alaskan villages, and among the interior peoples as well in their campsites, several such buildings were erected, each one for several crews associated with the various boat owners who maintained the structure. A common phenomenon in Alaska, the men's house begins to fade out to the central regions and Greenland. The karigi (or *kashim*, etc.) was a semiceremonial structure, larger than the usual dwelling, which took a special ceremonial significance during the whaling season.

Prior to the hunt, the men went there as crews, prepared their gear, and sang the magical songs. They avoided sexual relations during this time, such being offensive to the whale. Not barred to women, except at the whaling time, the karigi served as the primary meeting place for men where, during the winter months, it became a recreational center. Feasts were held here, men engaged in banter, games, singing, and other amusements.

Kunuyuq, a respected hunter with two wives, a reputable whaler with trading partners, has a place in the karigi. He jokes with the other men there, enters into games, such as wrestling and feats of strength, joins in the song-making contests, and tells tales and listens to them. As they sit, the men carve, make weapons or netting, repair tools, and engage in other individual tasks. One of Kunuyuq's wives brings his food now and again, as indeed do the wives of the others. Food might be pooled and there is, in any case, the sense of sharing and generosity. Now and again during the dark months a shamanistic seance is held in the karigi, the medicine men engaging in a curing session or simply communing with the helping spirits.

By February, the period of work begins again. Now it is time to think of whaling, and the community, with its various crews acting essentially independently of each other under their hunt leaders, throws itself into the preparations. A special house is built where the umiak is refurbished, the new clothing must be prepared, the weapons made ready. Whaling preoccupies each hunter until June and so the yearly cycle begins again.

The Eskimo of the North Alaskan Interior— Nuunamiut. It is unlikely that the caribou specialization could have developed without the initial commitment to the sea. Caribou is a lean, beeflike meat which could hardly provide adequate subsistence were it not set off by the sea mammal fats and oils. Clearly, caribou driving is easier than whaling, and there are tales of why individuals, fearing the sea and its hazards, chose to live inland. As has been noted, however, the two groups, maritime and caribou hunters, were essentially alike in culture and society; it was subsistence which created any difference.

In the spring, the snow still on the ground, the winds whipping through the passes in the Brooks Range, the first of the caribou began to push northward. If among the maritime Eskimo the whale demanded special treatment, so in the interior the preparations for the caribou required care and ceremonial treatment. Just as on the coast, where whaling became the basis of extra-kin activity, so in the interior, crews were formed under the banner of an umealiq, the men being recruited on the basis of their hunting skills. The various bands used the karigi, the men forming the different crews remaining there in anticipation of the advent of the caribou, and there were the same demands that new clothing be worn, weapons be purged of defilement, and that the proper attitude be preserved.

As among the whalers, the initial caribou hunt of the spring constituted a kind of world renewal ceremony, a reflection of the concept that the world was again being put back into order, that the sequence of events familiar to all would somehow be perpetuated. Among many of the American Indians, both hunters and agriculturalists, this basic religious notion may be considered fundamental.

The caribou came on, the vanguard allowed to pass in favor of the thickly packed herd. The number of animals is truly unbelievable, a single herd running into thousands. The hunting technique was in general one employed throughout the circumpolar zone, the method being that of the impound. The idea was to drive a herd, or at least a section of it, into a stockade which had already been prepared. As the animals milled in the impound, they could be lanced by hunters mounting the fences of the stockade. A variant method was a water drive, where the animals were forced into a lake or stream and lanced by hunters in kayaks.

Even though the term umealiq means boat owner, the reference among the inland people was to the person who owned the stockade and who organized the hunt. The umiak was used by the Nuunamiut principally for travel along the inland streams. The stockade was keyhole shaped, a line of stakes leading to a fenced enclosure. The stakes, spread some distance apart on each side of the keyhole base, were bunches of willow withes dressed in cast-off garments. Increasingly, the gap became narrower until at last the caribou were forced into a wide stockade which was roped around with strands of walrus hide obtained from the maritime groups by trade. Bone- and stone-tipped lances dispatched the milling, frenzied animals and the carcasses piled high. An ideal stockade lay on the far side of a ridge, preferably with a

stream before it. The animals, pushed into the stream, were worried into the stockade as they reached the further shore, Again, men in kayaks kept the herd in line. It is perhaps noteworthy that the kayak appears in northern Alaska only among the inland people; it has scarcely been found practical in the whaling area. Across the path of the caribou movement, once the larger sections of the herd had been taken, were placed V-shaped posts strung with hide ropes. On these many of the survivors entangled their antlers and could be stabbed. Like the whale, the caribou were greeted and required special handling lest their spirits be offended. When the slaughter was over, much time had to be taken to skin, cut the meat into strips for drying, and work over all the by-products of the hunt.

In the spring hunt the bands of inland Eskimo came together. Old enmities were forgotten for the moment and work was the sole preoccupation. When the hunt was over, the various families took out on individual activities, paralleling the people of the coast. Trapping of squirrel, ptarmigan, and rabbit took up the time of some, others went to the fishing camps and did pretty much as their coastal neighbors. The end of the summer found large groups of inland Eskimo at the trading centers on the Colville mouth and in the Noatak valley, meeting their partners and getting the necessary oils and skins from the maritime setting.

Such hunts as have been described here might be repeated several times, as the caribou arrived, as they milled about the tundra, and as they departed for the winter. It is apparent that most inland activity was devoted to the caribou and that the diversity so characteristic of the economic life of the coast was lacking. Winter found the inland bands back at the quasi-permanent campsite, the village of the interior. Here a residence situation quite like that of the coast was operative. The inland villages were located on watercourses both on the tundra and along the rolling higher ground which moved up to the foothills of the Brooks Mountains. Like their maritime counterparts, the Nuunamiut spent the dark days in recreation, with some trapping, both of smaller animals and predators, and with attention to preparations for the coming of light. The men had their ceremonial houses, the personnel made up of crews who worked together in the communal hunts and found their recreation in the social life of the karigi.

North Alaskan Eskimo ● Wooden household bucket. The wood is obtained by trade. It is steamed and bent over a circular bottom; the side is sewed. (After J. Murdoch, 1892)

As one moves away from north Alaska, both to the south and to the east, some variations on the pattern of the economic round, the methods of hunting, and its associated weapon assemblage are encountered. In the area of the Central Eskimo, for example, there is again concentration on seals, although in Baffinland, especially, some whaling and walrus hunting, with the use of the kayak rather than the umiak, has been described (Boas, 1888). The concentration is on winter sealing, however, and nowhere is the development of a mutual interdependence between land and sea adaptations seen except in Alaska. Thus the Central Eskimo devote the winter to sealing and move to the interior after the caribou in the spring and summer. Sealing involves tracking the seals, stealing up on them, and harpooning a laggard as the herd, usually of a small number of animals, breaks for the open water. Waiting at breathing holes, frequently smelled out by dogs, making a peephole covered by an ice window, and the use of the harpoon rather than the net are techniques somewhat different from the Alaskan practises. When the central groups move to the interior, the methods employed for caribou—stockade-impound and kayak spearing—are much the same. The specialized Caribou Eskimo represent one group of the interior which concentrates on land hunting and can be regarded as an impoverished culture, one which lacks the richness which comes to the Alaskan Nuunamiut by trade (cf. Birket-Smith, 1929).

As the economic life of the Eskimo generally is reviewed, it appears that every attempt is made to exploit the available resources in the local habitat. Movement is no problem, what with the umiak where it occurs, or the kayak for water transport, and with the dog team and sled. Specializations lie in the hunting skills associated with a local area. In north Alaska there are whales and caribou, sealing concentration becomes important elsewhere, in yet other regions there is concentration on birds, as at Smith Sound, fish, and even, though rarely, such animals as the musk-ox and mountain sheep. What is striking about the entire range of Eskimo culture is the ability of these groups to live in their environment and to make what in the main is an adequate livelihood within it.

North Alaskan Eskimo Society

Social complexity is not a characteristic of the Eskimo; that is, there is little of elaboration of social structure such as is found among some of the American Indians further to the south. Even if Eskimo society is probably limited by the fact that the food quest requires so much concentration, thus inhibiting the development of elaborated political or corporate organizations, special rules have developed and usages been employed which make for a readily defined set of social activities. No human society is simple; it can only be seen as relatively so and the problem of living with one's fellows has always to be met.

It has been said that the Eskimo lacked political organization. In the sense that authority was not placed in the hands of any one person or group, this was true, although from the foregoing it has been seen that the hunt leaders, in times of communal activity, enjoyed an ephemeral leadership. Leaders there sometimes were, but their task was that of organizing, not commanding. At the same time, and far more important, were the informal social controls in every community, the weapons of gossip, censure, and sometimes of murder. It was true of most Eskimo that political controls rested in the family. A person of status could count on the backing of his kindred; tragedy, to the Eskimo, was the "poor boy," the person who lacked a dependable circle of kindred.

In north Alaska, and true of both ecological groups, village or quasi-permanent settlement in the interior had no reality as such. It was, as has been shown, a place where dwellings were located but from and into which there was a great deal of movement. Society and social relationships began in the household and extended

Alaskan Eskimo with dog-drawn sled ● In addition to the European chimneys on the sod houses, culture change is reflected in the mode of dog traction itself. Tandem hitching was introduced by the Russians late in the contact period. Aboriginal dog traction made use of a fan-wise trace, each dog leashed to a single point on the sled or sledge. (The date of the photograph is unknown. Smithsonian Institution National Anthropological Archives)

beyond the household as far as the ties of kinship could be carried. Thus to the north Alaskan Eskimo, the house itself was focal. Even if, among the maritime groups, the house tended to be more permanent and hence better furnished, much the same structure was employed in the interior.

In approaching a village along the coast, it would be somewhat difficult to determine whether it was really a human settlement. In winter, snow would be piled up along the mounds which were the houses, while in summer the sod of which they were made would blend into the arid landscape. A rack behind the house, umiaks on the beach in summer, overturned by the house in winter, a staked dog team would all be more revealing of the habitation than the dwelling itself. These were sod houses, semisubterranean, dome-shaped, with a passage leading into the main living room. If they were not especially distinctive from the outside, the maritime houses were models of comfort and security within. One entered by the passage, passing through a small door which might be covered with bear skins and outside of which stood a whale scapula to control the ventilation. Once beyond a small storm porch in the passage, one stepped down

to a whale skull, set as a kind of step against the moisture collected in the passageway. By the porch stood a wooden bucket containing the urine of the family. This was used for wounds, for skin tanning, and for bleaching. (Human faeces, mixed with oil, were fed to the dogs.) As one now moved down the hall which sloped gradually to a depth of about five feet, clothing and harpoons would be seen hanging from hooks in the wall. At the left of the passage was an excavation which held frozen food, beyond it a niche to store food ready for preparation. On the right there was first a closet lined with driftwood and supported by whale ribs. Extra clothing, the caribou-skin bales collected in trading, extra utensils, ivory, and many other items necessary to the running of the house were kept here. It was to this room that people also retired for sexual relations. Beyond this on the right was the kitchen, often no more than grease-covered stones on which a pot could be set, a place for driftwood and oil fires where stones for boiling could be heated, and an open space in the sod which could be covered in bad weather and which served as a chimney. In the kitchen hung the cooking aprons of the women of the house. The passage, 10 or 15 feet long (depending on the number of residents), ended at another whale skull, leading to the main chamber itself.

Stepping on the whale skull, one thrust his way up through a round door set in the floor of the main chamber. This could be said to mark the real entrance. The room itself was set a foot or two below ground level, reflecting again that semisubterranean house type so characteristic of the Asiatic and American north. The chamber had been made by a dome of sod, but interior walls of wood supported by whalebone had been erected against the sod

North Alaskan Eskimo ● Two-chambered stone household lamp. One variant of the common Eskimo type, the lamp is filled with seal or other sea mammal oil. Moss wicks are set at the edges and along the partition. Generally smokeless, the lamp provides heat and fairly adequate light. (After J. Murdoch, 1892)

walls, moss being stuffed between for insulation. Both wood and bone were adzed smooth and bleached, making a regular floor and walls with joists at the top to accommodate the dome. At the far end, opposite the entrance well, was a bench which ran along the wall. Near the well stood lamps with racks nearby to dry mittens and boots. At the top of the dome of the house was a skylight, scraped seal- or walrus-gut stretched over a frame. In summer this would be removed and it was sometimes replaced in winter with a sheet of clear ice. Ventilation could be controlled by an aperture with a sliding panel set above the bench, the "nostril" of the house. Of furnishings in the main chamber, beyond the lamps and racks, there was only bedding in the form of various skins.

Such houses were unbelievably warm, as indeed were the domed ice lodges further to the east. The efficient lamp offered more than adequate heat, and it was not unusual for the inside temperatures to reach 90° F. The residents regularly stripped to the waist when at home, and buckets were placed along the walls to catch condensing moisture. When at home, men lolled about the bench at the far end of the house, women and children sat on the floor. Sleeping arrangements followed much the same pattern. It is perhaps of interest to note that there were no special sleeping times, and it was not unusual to find some members of the household asleep while others were busy with

various chores. If the house were crowded, some might sleep in the passageway. In severe weather, the passage could be blocked, and the dogs, usually staked outside, were brought in and quartered there. Puppies were usually kept in the passageway as well.

Several variants of this general house type existed. The most striking was the semipermanent sod house of the interior bands, which was rather like the coastal house but lacked the driftwood and whalebone finishing. Some of the inland bands made use of a T-shaped passage leading off into two chambers. And on the coast a single passage might serve two chambers, or two main rooms were linked together with an interior passage, each having a hallway of its own.

Thus, although the Nuunamiut knew the sod house and used it with passageway and skylight, this was not the usual inland house. A light frame of willow sticks was set up in a dome shape and covered with two layers of caribou skins. This was portable, the willow stakes being notched and easily transportable by sled and umiak. Such tentlike houses were set directly on the ground, no excavation being needed, but a short passage was also made in winter. Even in this tent-type dwelling, the skylight was retained and made from seal gut obtained in trade. Both groups had other tent types, but they were used in hunt expeditions and not for the formal household, which is true of the structures described here.

When a man needed a new house, he called on his relatives or worked alone with his wife, cutting the sod, splitting such wood and bone as were available. Houses were rarely too large, a man with wife and children alone getting by with a room of 6 to 7 feet in diameter. A larger house might run to 15 feet. If a house were abandoned, as might happen when a family moved away, it was discussed for a year or two in the community and then taken over by someone else, not necessarily connected with the builder. Houses were named, possibly after the builder and chief hunter who resided there, after some characteristic such as the direction of the passage, and often after the charm associated with the dwelling.

This was the dwelling as both ecological systems employed it. Detailed attention must be paid to it since it is the house which became the focus of social activity and which served to root the family organization. Reference is made here, however, not so much to the family as to the household itself. The system of relationships, extending beyond the household, was in essence bilateral, that is, with recognition of a system of reciprocal relationships applicable to one's relatives through both father and mother. These familial extensions, relating to grandparents, their siblings, the siblings and descendants of the parents, made for a wide circle of kindred for each individual. A nuclear family, consisting of parents and children, might constitute a household but there was more often a joint arrangement, a man choosing to live with his brother, an uncle, his wife's father, his own parents, all such solutions being possible and depending on the circumstances of the moment. The kinship bond was always present. A skilled hunter might continue to reside with his own parents in the event that there was need on their part for the food he could provide. If his brother could take over this task, he might feel that he wished to move in with others of his kin and work out a cooperative arrangement with them. While it is true that a man felt no special obligation to his wife's parents, they were still the grandparents of his own children. He thus might move into a household with them for the benefits which his children might obtain from the presence of grandparents, the grandparent-grandchild tie being a strong affectional one among the group. Thus although there was little formality connected with the establishment of a household, once it was in operation and the relationships in terms of daily living had been worked out, it tended to hold together.

It did not have to. It was not unusual for two men, even brothers, to enter into a rivalry relationship with each other, especially over sexual dominance in the household. Any man, backed by a dependable group of kindred, might feel free to rape, to capture, or otherwise to dominate women both in his own household and in the households of others. A man of parts in the society, a successful hunter, one capable of asserting himself and bullying his way at the expense of others, found an outlet for domination in interpersonal relations by his success in sexual achievement. A man alone could obviously not so dominate others; only with a backing of kin, of men from his own, but more likely from other households related to his own, he could "steal" wives, could bully his way to the point where he dominated a group. Thus if there were no chiefs, there was certainly a concept of household leader, the chief provider in the

group who succeeded in developing a situation which made others in his joint family, those resident in his own household or in adjacent households related to his own, dependent or subordinate to himself. Among the north Alaskan Eskimo, sexual rights were to a large extent property rights. The successful man in the culture was not only the skilled hunter, but also the man who succeeded in dominating others through women.

Marriage must accordingly be seen in relation to the cultural definitions characteristic of the group. A "legal" definition of marriage concerned itself with no more than cohabitation; there were social sanctions involved with marriage, but religion was obviously not a factor. Marriage extended beyond mere sexual relationships. It was reflective of the gradual building of cooperative relationships, that is, a man, involved with a woman over a period of time, fathering children by her, incurred in time a bond of affection and cooperation with her kindred as well as with his own. Here was the primary extension of kinship to non-kin. The establishment of cooperative relationships with a wife's family, once affirmed, lent position and status in the society.

Who, then, married whom? In groups with unilineal descent, where one belongs to the father's, or especially, to the mother's kin, there are prescribed patterns of mating. Such is true, as among the Haida or Tlingit of the Northwest Coast, for instance, where marriage to the woman classified as the daughter of the mother's brother is mandatory. This was never true of the majority of Eskimo. Only in southern Alaska, where influences from the Northwest Coast made themselves felt and where unilineal descent became more characteristic, were such demands apparent (cf. Lantis, 1946). In north Alaska, the thought was to extend as far as possible the bonds and ties of cooperative activity. An Eskimo question might be phrased something like the following: I do not marry a cousin since I already can count on a cousin for support, assistance, and mutual aid. With what group may I then associate myself in order to achieve ties of mutual assistance? Incestuous unions were thus morally reprehensible only because they failed to create the necessary cooperative climate. If cousins married, or even a brother and a sister, a not wholly unlikely possibility, the union was considered "stupid," failing as it did to establish bonds of mutual relationship between unrelated groups. It was never subject to formal punishment, although the couple would be ridiculed. As in so many nonliterate societies, and indeed, not excluding our own past, marriage was an involvement between groups and not solely between individuals (cf. Burch, 1975:75–119).

Marriage was also involved with capture, rape, and individual ascendancy. There was nothing against a man having several wives (polygyny), provided he could hold them, or a woman having several men (polyandry). Making a marriage was simple to the extreme. Basically, marriage was a sexual relationship involving men and women to whom they were not in any way related. An ideal situation brought a young man and a young woman together. They engaged in sexual relations, and if the two found the situation compatible, they remained together. Not until children were born did the marriage become recognized as stable. Disagreements, strife, and involvement with other men were sufficient to break the marital tie. In such instances, man or woman simply left, returning to his or her own household. A divorce was thus essentially negative; no formality existed, the couple simply stopped living together. As one reads of "divorce" among the American Indians, this pattern is the one to which reference is made. In other words, the legal situation placed a definition of marriage in a concept of continuous cohabitation. It was not unusual to find young people, boys from 16 to 18, once they had amassed the skills necessary to a livelihood in the area, and similarly, girls from 15 to 17, settling down to live with parents on either side in a state of what might be defined as marriage. As time went on, the couple either got along well together or fought. An older man might "steal" a younger man's wife, enticing her to his own house and keeping her captive there. If the younger man failed to get the backing of his kin, he might count the marriage as ended, the girl in question becoming a second or third wife of her abductor. Young men were often "stolen" into marriage by older women. When a woman of 60, past her climacteric, made overtures to a young man, as was not infrequently the case, it was believed that she possessed the ability to work black magic, something denied women who still menstruated and whose cycle was believed to inhibit them from performing magic of any kind. Such old women might become shamans. The fact that

they chose younger husbands insured them a provider. There was of course nothing to prevent such a man from taking another wife. His older wife might in fact assist him in this, welcoming the additional help in the household.

The most striking aspect of Eskimo marriage lay not in any sense of romance, although as men's status related to control of women this was not to be wholly ignored, but rather in the necessity for effecting a sexual balance of labor. Even if young people might "play the field" before settling down with a permanent mate, a stable marriage was essential to a successful life in the hostile environment. The work of men was balanced by that of women. Men were the primary providers, involved as they were in the hunting of sea mammals and caribou. They made weapons and tools, both for themselves and for their household, they built boats and sleds, and cared for dogs. Women, on the other hand, prepared food, engaged in butchering, tanning of skins, making of clothing, manufacture of the all-important boot. In marriage, an economic balance existed in that the work of both sexes was necessary to the successful maintenance of the group. An unmarried person, under these circumstances, was unthinkable. Industry was prized with the result that the man skilled as a hunter or the woman known for her abilities in the home were both in demand as potential mates. If marriages achieved some degree of stability, it was because of such a division of labor. There was also a sense of balance of property rights in marriage which helped make the union permanent. Game taken by a hunter, a seal caught on the ice, for example, was the property of the hunter. Generous to a fault, he would give parts of it away as he dragged it homeward. Once the game was by the house, however, it became the property of his wife. If she chose to give more of it away, the hunter had no argument. In other words, she was free to do with the game as she wished. Such property divisions, it can be seen, would also enhance the stability of a marriage tie. Such a situation developed only over time and continuing cohabitation, there being no property involvements in marriage itself, such as bride price or exchange of goods. As the couple was recognized as married by the group, the man who failed to respect his wife's rights in this way was considered "dishonest." A ritual relationship between husband and wife arose in the case of the whaling leader whose wife remained in the house during the whaling, avoided making cordage or tying knots, thus preventing the whale lines from fouling, and who, with the capture of the whale, came out to make the official greeting.

A wife who was badly treated, or who at least felt herself so to be, a wife who yielded to the persuasive charms of a lover, or yet one who felt herself put upon by undue demands for work, might simply leave. If the husband were aware of her intentions, he might forcibly keep her at home. Whether a woman succeeded in leaving, and so "divorcing" her husband, depended in large measure on the kind of backing she could get from her own relatives. A man's wife who had escaped was pursued if the husband himself could enlist the aid of his own relatives. Taking weapons, five or six men might go over to help recover a woman. But if her case were considered just by her own kin, a similar group would emerge to protect her. Occasionally, this display of strength might erupt into an open feud and blood might be shed. More often, the issue was resolved by argument. The same thing might occur when a woman eloped with a paramour. In this instance it was up to him to enlist his own kin to stand by him and his action. A man who lost his wife in this way was considered "honest" if he made no protest, an interesting facet of the culture when Western or European standards are considered.

But with marriage came children. Here again was women's work, child rearing being wholly in the domain of women. Not until the age of ten or so did a small boy go out with his father to learn the necessary hunting skills. Girls remained at home and learned the necessary skills of housekeeping by imitating their mothers and the other women in the household. Children were much desired. The desire for children, as many as possible, rested in the wish to extend the cooperative kinship circle as broadly as could be. Further, a man with children would be able to count on continuing support through his lifetime. Rasmussen (1928) describes female infanticide among some of the central groups. It is true that such infanticide took place in times of stress, also among the Alaskan Eskimo. While it was not considered shameful to "throw a baby away," that is, abandon it to the elements, it was a sad decision and one which took place only after careful consideration of the demands of the moment. In travelling in storms or under severe

privation this may have been necessary. True also of the aged who might be abandoned if conditions required, it was considered an unhappy recourse, one usually demanded by the old people themselves. Generally in times of stress, periods of starvation, such food as there was was given to the able-bodied on the theory that the whole group needed the labor which these could supply and that the group itself might perish if food went to the less productive very young or old. Children served to bring otherwise unrelated people together; they became the primary factor in promoting the stability of marriage. With children, the essential antagonism which existed between husband and wife was in large measure allayed, and the child became the meeting point of two different kinship groups.

It is thus the kinship group, the household and the extensions of kinship beyond the household, which was focal to a society which lacked so many other formalized institutions. A child was taught to designate relatives by the proper relationship term. Eskimo kinship terms vary slightly across the Arctic, although basically the system reflected in the terms is a bilateral one. Relatives were classified according to generation, but merged. For example, the same terms were used for all ancestors, whether from the father or the mother, for grandparental designations, for the parents' siblings, for cousins and for the children of cousins and for the children of siblings. Such designations as "my older brother," "my younger brother," and "my youngest brother" are characteristically Eskimo, the same applying to sisters. Such terms were extended to involve remoter relationships. A cousin term can be applied to the child of one's father's sister; it could also be directed to the father's father's sister's son and so to an extended collateral range. Out of these designations arose a sense of the extended kinship group. How far this went depended on factors of residence and interest. What was important was that the kinship tie be kept alive. Thus if the descendants of two brothers who had moved to different localities lost touch with each other, the relationship might no longer be observed. In summary, the extent of the circle of kindred was hedged about with practical considerations (cf. Burch, 1975).

The factors maintaining the extended family group were those of mutual aid and support and cooperative activity. Even if there were no residence prescriptions, kindred operated on the level of the household, a wife or husband marrying in and residing there with the spouse's kin being in effect a stranger. This was a factor in creating the basic antagonism between married couples. But members of the extended family of each spouse might reside in adjacent areas, with the result that the force of the kinship tie was for each constantly reaffirmed. When a man travelled he always sought out his kindred. They would offer him food and lodging and aid him in repairing his gear. An additional element in maintaining stability within the extended family was the feud. The law of collective responsibility was ever operative. An injury to an individual was an injury to his circle of kindred as well. If murder took place, as was not infrequent in the rivalry between men over women for status, the kin were all involved and the life of a kinsman of the murderer, not necessarily the murderer himself, was taken, only to perpetuate the feud. The "stranger" was thus suspect; he might be a relative of those with whom a feud was being carried on. Hence if a person were unable to identify himself in a community to which he was a stranger, being unable to locate or relate himself to kindred residing there, he ran the risk of being killed on the spot, his wife made captive, and his children adopted into other families. Adoption was a means of extending kinship relationships. By this reasoning, a "poor" person was one unable to relate himself to a group of kindred.

In summary, the Eskimo of north Alaska established relationships on the level of nuclear family, household, extensions of household within a community, and over a wide area with those kindred who represented the extended family, on both the maternal and paternal sides, and with whom it continued to be practical to preserve the relationships.

Kinship, while thus tremendously important, was scarcely sufficient to effect the maintenance of relationships necessary to satisfactory economic productivity. Unrelated men worked together in a hunting group, traded together, and shared the activities in the men's house together. Ways had to be developed to effect relationships with those to whom one was not related. The ·principle which arose was the extension to non-kin of the privileges and responsibilities of kinship. In other words, if one dealt with a member of a group with which one was not associated by kinship ties, formalized ways had to be found to effect a relationship with him. To fail to do this would be to create the situation of the hostile "stranger." An initial step in this direction was marriage, an institution permitting two unrelated kin groups to interact. But other ways existed, both between men and between women.

The most striking of the means by which one became involved with non-kindred was through the institution of partnership. These were of several different kinds, some purely social, some with economic implications. In north Alaska, some specialized variations on the theme of friendship, hospitality, and social interaction developed. While local to the area, these patterns were in some measure reflective of a general Eskimo solution to the problem of how unrelated people came together. The partnership concept was at base one of friendship, of mutual aid and support. An informal aspect, or rather, one which was somewhat less hedged about with formalized demands, was the joking partnership between men. This usually involved men of different kin groupings who had grown up together in a community, played together as boys, and hunted together. As adults, they continued to "play," using banter and horseplay in their relationship, rolling each other in the snow, playing practical jokes, using such devices as "kidding"· or humorous insults. If both could command a following in a community, they might sing "insult songs," made up on the spur of the moment, at each other, much to the amusement of the assembled groups. In Alaska, such "insult singing" was usually in the form of banter; it did not assume the proportions of the "song duels" which became so characteristic of the Eskimo further to the east and a vital part of their mechanisms of social control. If they had come to live in different communities, they might employ messengers to bring insult songs back and forth and they might also feast each other, a reflection of a friendly rivalry, each attempting to outdo the other in generosity.

More serious partnerships, however, existed within communities, between communities in the same ecological setting, and between the two ecological systems. In a single community, a man who remained behind to engage in some activity could count on a partner to trade for him. Or there was trading of special products obtained by specialized skills. For example, a man might agree to make an umiak for a partner in exchange for so much meat. This was the basis of the trading partnership, a fair exchange of goods and services between individuals who defined their relationship precisely. At the end of the summer, when groups assembled at the trading centers, men sought out their partners, those with whom they had a long-standing relationship. A man without partners was at a distinct disadvantage.

Another variation of partnership lay in the development of the hunting group, the crew assembled for whaling, walrus hunting, or inland, for caribou drives. The men of parts—not chiefs, it will be recalled, but leaders and organizers of the hunt who had achieved sufficient respect to enlist a following—entered into a kind of partnership relationship with members of their crews. They might initially have to bribe them, promising extra shares of meat, or giving gifts of clothing and weapons. As the relationship continued and hunters went out under the same umealiq year after year, the relationship became a fairly fixed one. Similarly, as between members of a crew, quite apart from the umealiq, there developed a camaradarie and a sense of trading and joking partnership. The men in the karigi, those who spent the winter months together in recreational activities, might be regarded as having formed a specialized relationship.

But there was considerably more involved than mere economic interest. The partnership is in effect an extension of kinship, and it is here that some further light is shed on marriage and its meaning in the culture. With the consummation of partnership, a wife exchange took place, temporarily to be sure, but the partners in question engaged in sexual relations with each other's wives. The situation of wife lending has been described for a number of Eskimo groups. In general, in the central regions and in Greenland, this appears to take the form of hospitality. Implicit, however, would be some preexisting relationship between the host who lends his wife and the guest who has relations with her. In north Alaska the arrangement was not one so much of hospitality as a formal agreement, cementing a partnership and implying an onset of mutual and cooperative obligation. Wife exchange, in short, had a significant function in the society.

It is obvious that there was a thin line between adultery and such exchange. Indicated was a situation in which sexual rights became male property rights. Status for men was thus to some extent related to control of such rights, and by the same token, marriage was lent an added stability. A man attempted to hold his wife and regarded it as a violation of his own rights if she took a lover on her own. A man who lent out his wife did so only when he was sure that the partnership relationship so formed would be a promising and honorable one. Nor was there necessarily objection on the part of the woman; she and her family stood to gain by the husband's acquisition of partners. Joking partners did not exchange wives unless the relationship moved to a more formal level. An umealiq might exchange wives with the members of the crew he recruited, thus making the relationship with them more stable and dependable. There was a special term applied to men who had sexual relations with the same woman, as, for instance, between a man and his wife's divorced husband. Although this might lead to partnership and friendly relations between the two men, there was also a sense of rivalry and competition. But in general, when such exchange took place, it was felt that a relationship had been created which worked to mutual benefit. A man could count on his partners to the extent of calling on them for aid, for protection and could in general act toward them as though they were kinsmen. Only if a feud intervened would the partnership relationship be eclipsed by the concerns of family.

Partnership through wife exchange was extended to the children of partners as well. There were in fact special terms which a child applied to his father's partners, a term meaning in effect "man who had sexual intercourse with my mother." Similarly, the term *qatangun* was applied to the children of the father's partners. A child was told: "If you go to such and such a community, seek out so and so; he is your qatangun and will help you." These were thus terms of quasi-kinship, extensions of the principle of the family to non-kindred. There was nothing against marrying a qatangun but it was felt more practical to find a mate outside of the circle even of quasi kin.

Here was thus a society wholly kinship oriented. It has been said that the community was nonexistent as a unit in itself, being made up solely of independent households and extended families. The latter existed not within communities but across community lines. The solution to the problem of meeting the needs of the environment, of cooperatively working together, lay in the extension of kinship to non-kindred. This being so, it can be seen why chieftainship or formality in political organization could not exist. But there was a legal system dependent on the family and enforced by it; the customary procedures followed across the Eskimo area had a force of law.

The Cycle of Life. Children, as has been noted, were much desired. While a concept of biological parenthood existed, it was the sociological relationship of parenthood which was important. It is of course conceivable that wife exchange might result in pregnancy, but the question simply did not arise, for the children of one's wife were regarded as one's own.

The Eskimo did not wholly share the attitudes characteristic of some of the Amerindian cultures to the south that menstrual blood and the postnatal flow were defiling and dangerous. Some suggestions of this attitude existed. For example, it was only the old woman whose menstrual cycle had ceased who might become a shaman, a menstruating woman was not allowed in the main chamber of the house, and the wife of the umealiq could not greet the whale if she were menstruating. But there was no girls' puberty ritual beyond a suggestion or two of what might be an older pattern. A girl was tattooed on the chin following the onset of the menstrual cycle, thus indicating her marriageability. While not wholly formalized, there was also the attitude that a woman giving birth had to be secluded. The rationale for attitudes both toward the parturient woman and the menstruating one was that in this condition they were offensive to the game, driving them away. Hence a snow hut, usually a tent covered with snow, was placed outside the main dwelling as a birth lodge. Actually the inland Eskimo tended to stress this feature rather more than did those on the coast. The woman hung from a beam by her hands while other women pressed downward on her abdomen to expel the fetus. During the birth, the husband was expected to remain quiet and to avoid making cordage and tying knots, a reflection of a modified couvade; that is, the husband was implying his paternal relationship to the child and responsibility for it. After the birth, the mother was under restrictions for four to five days, remaining in the birth hut for this period.

If circumstances were pressing, the child might be "thrown away" although the preference was distinctly against such abandonment. A child so abandoned was not named. Giving the child a name reflected recognition of its existence and was a sign of its acceptance in the community. The native culture had no well

defined notion of a life after death, but a vague concept of reincarnation existed. Names were frequently those of dead relatives. Vaguely it was felt that the deceased had "come home" in the newborn child. But one name was hardly enough. Names could be changed, or rather, names could be added. As many as ten separate names might be given, usually over a several-year period. With each name there was also a food taboo, a concept well developed in Eskimo culture at large. The concept was that such and such a name denied the bearer certain kinds of food, usually quite specific. Thus with a particular name one was forbidden to eat the knuckle bones from the front flippers of the female walrus or with another the taboo extended to the fat from the tenderloin of male caribou. Sickness, it was felt, would result if these taboos were violated. At birth, and as he grew, the child was also given charms, protective amulets worn about the neck or sewed on the clothing. Older relatives gave these as well as new names, and with each one a food taboo was imposed. In later life, ownership of certain songs also carried a food taboo.

The child was carried in the mother's parka resting against her bare skin. He was diapered with moss and fed as he cried. Children were toilet trained quite early but carried in the mother's clothing up until two years of age or even later. After the age of two, children were encouraged to walk and to talk, and their first clothing was made for them. Early childhood was a period of freedom, no particular regimen being established and no special demands being made on the child. Children were free to play, to come and go as they wished, to eat when they were hungry and to sleep when they were tired. In short, very little pressure was put on a child.

Education was also wholly informal. Boys began to hunt with the fathers after about the age of ten, while girls learned household tasks by imitation. The culture is full of children's games, stories, and recreational features. As noted, there was no well-developed puberty rite for girls. Boys, as puberty approached, usually underwent a lip piercing ceremony, the holes just below each corner of the mouth being made for the labrets. A proud moment in the life of the growing boy was where he could appear among his playmates, the childhood gang out of which the adult joking partnerships grew, wearing his labrets. Sexual behavior was not hidden from children nor was there any attempt to discourage sexual experimentation. Chastity, as may be surmised, was not prized, although a girl who was too free with her favors was warned that some man might "capture" her and she would be pushed into a life of drudgery before she was ready for it. If a girl became pregnant as a result of an adolescent affair, no problem arose. Since children were valued, she would have no difficulty in settling down with any man, all of whom were willing to recognize the child as their own. The girl's value was in fact enhanced by proof of fertility. Random affairs were had only in the sense that they took up time and so reduced industry. Since status and sex were linked in the culture, it can be seen that coquetry and exploitation of male rivalry by women were not uncommon.

After marriage, once the marital tie had become more or less permanent, the round of hunting productivity, of household maintenance, of raising a family was the common lot. No special status attached to old age except occasionally to old women, and the ideal was for older people to settle down with their families, frequently becoming the custodians and teachers of grandchildren. A tragic situation was one where old people had lost the extended family ties and were cast adrift without support. Abandonment of the aged, while undesirable, did take place and was a risk which old people faced in times of food shortage.

Of all the world's peoples, probably the one with the least concern for death is the Eskimo. This is not to say that people were indifferent to death or that they did not feel the loss of a family member keenly. Indeed, the closeness of family ties would create a heavy burden of bereavement. But fear of a corpse was not especially marked nor were there any elaborate funerary or memorial observances. When a person died in the house, his corpse was usually taken out through the skylight which was then covered up again. This is a common circumpolar trait, apparently a general reflection of the view that the spirit of the dead will seek to reenter the house through the door out of which the corpse was carried. In some of the Asiatic areas, a special opening is knocked through the wall to take out the corpse and then sealed up again. While this notion is present among these Eskimo only in a rather rudimentary form, the belief is apparently vaguely shared. A man was asked to accompany the corpse away from the community. As he returned, he waved a knife

North Alaskan Eskimo ● Labrets or lip plugs. Valued items in the native culture, these are worn by men, "buttoning" into perforations made just under the corners of the mouth. Boys' lips are pierced at puberty (p. 000). Made of soapstone, bone, and stone, the labret became an item of wealth; more valuable ones are of ivory or with an inset bead. (After J. Murdoch, 1892)

about. So vague was this belief that people were uncertain if the man was cutting the death to prevent its return or frightening the ghost of the dead. The members of the household were expected to remain indoors for four days if the deceased were a woman, five if a man. Among the nomadic groups, hunting was prohibited during this period. When the time had elapsed, the members of the household put on fresh clothes and the time of mourning was at an end. The body of the dead person was brought out to the tundra and left; no concern was felt if it were eaten by wolves and it was, in fact, left out for this purpose. The name of the dead might be added to the names of a child.

The Religion of the North Alaskan Eskimo
Basically, the religion of the Eskimo, and this was generally true for all of hunting North America, was founded on two primary concepts. The first lay in the special relations to the world of the animals, in the view that those animals which were hunted had to be placated, cajoled, or coerced into allowing themselves to be caught. If the animal were offended, his spirit communicated with those of the other animals of his species and they purposely withheld themselves, thus causing humans to starve. The second concept of the Eskimo religious system involved shamans, individuals who possessed special powers to cure, to perform sorcery and magic. Added to these basic features of the religion were a host of miscellaneous beliefs, none too well systematized but

tied in with one or another of the primary concepts (cf. Lantis, 1950).

Religion was not primarily concerned with a world beyond nor particularly interested in explanations of beginnings. True, the creator was the raven, a reflection of an elaborate North American mythology relating to the "trickster," a figure half human, half animal (anthropomorphic, in short), who changed the world to suit his fancy or inclination. In a north Alaskan myth, Raven brings the world into being by harpooning the land from a kayak and thus making it stable. The myths of Raven, like those of Coyote in the Basin or the purely human tricksters of parts of the Plateau, appear to connect widely across northern and western North America and to have relations to Asiatic myth and folktale. The earth, it was said, was flat and mounted on a wooden pillar, or four of them, so that hunters lost at sea were felt to have gone over the edge of the world. Similarly, there were myths about the moon and stars, about the aurora borealis, and other natural phenomena. North Alaska did not have an elaboration of the "moon man" myths found in southern Alaska and the Aleutians. Nor did it share the Sedna myth, the concept of a goddess of the sea, that appears in the central regions. There were beliefs in monsters, such as giant worms and the ten-legged polar bear, in dwarfs and in mermen, and there were those who had seen them. In general, however, religion was an adjunct of socio-economic life, eminently practical, designed to meet the needs of the here and now. Family and household, it has been shown, made up a socio-economic constellation; religion reinforced and supported much of the activity of daily life.

Between humans and animals there existed a specialized relationship founded in the view that animals were superior morally and intellectually, that they allowed themselves to be taken both out of pity for people and through the magic devised by people to coerce them. This idea is one common to virtually all of the hunters of North America and will be encountered again in other areas. At all costs, attempts had to be made to avoid giving offense, the result being that each animal had its special sets of taboos. If any of these were violated, not only might the offended animal withhold itself but the violator himself became ill. This in fact was the theoretical basis of illness in the society, and the curing was done by a religious practitioner, the shaman, who could determine the nature of the offense. The food taboos mentioned in respect to the ownership of names, songs, and charms suggest added aspects of the human-animal relationship.

Characteristic of the Eskimo of north Alaska, and in fact a common element in much of Eskimo life to the east where it reached far greater proportions, was the conceptual division between land and sea animals. This view reached such extremes among some of the Central Eskimo that no game could be taken from the sea when the land hunting season was in progress. Separate weapons had to be used for the two sets of animals. North Alaska did not go this far but there was a strong feeling against using a caribou spear on a seal, or against eating meat from land and sea animals at the same time. Similarly, it was considered necessary to wash the body before caribou hunting, especially if sealing had been a winter activity. Accumulations of seal grease were hateful to the caribou. Both land and sea animals had spirits. Admittedly, the definition of a spirit is always difficult, but to the Eskimo it was a kind of psychic projection of the animal. The soul suffered if it was not released when the animal was killed. Removal of the head of the game, cutting its throat, or opening its brain pan allowed the soul to escape. Failure to do this was dangerous, as was any maltreatment of the game. The guilty hunter might then be subjected to the horrifying experience of having the animal push back the skin of its face, a humanlike face then appearing and speaking to him. Illness and death were a frequent result of such an encounter.

Thus all animals had to be treated with "respect." One could never, in conversation, express contempt for an animal lest the animal spirits hovering about should hear him. But there were also positive injunctions laid on the hunter. Wolves and foxes, as well as the wolverine, were offended if more than five traps were set at a time. When a hunter returned to his traps, finding foxes or wolves, he first slit the animal's throat, then made an offering of a needle case or needles and sinew if the fox or wolf were female, of a stone knife if the animal were male. Failure to observe these rituals often resulted in the hunter falling victim to his own trap when he next set one. After taking a fox or wolf, the hunter was expected to avoid cooked food for four days if the animal were female, five if male. It may be noted that these four and five day periods, applicable to birth, to death, and now, to hunting, reflect the concept of a sacred number—four is characteristically American Indian; five is Eskimo. North Alaska employs both. All sea mammals were offered a drink of cold water. It was believed that because they lived in salt water they were perennially thirsty and could be enticed with a gift of fresh water. Care had also to be taken of the bones and wastes of the animals slaughtered. In the case of the whale, for example, offense was given if dogs were allowed to lick the blood, while the bones could not be given to dogs. Among the western Eskimo, there was some sense of a mourning ritual associated with the disposal of the bones of the game, these being collected at intervals and buried or burned. At the same time, masked impersonations of animals and animal spirits, with dancing, drumming, and singing, formed parts of festivals, and the animal spirits were welcomed with joy and a sense of thanksgiving. This aspect was true of the Bering area and points south and was moving into the region of Point Hope at the southern extension of the north Alaskan area at the time of contact with Europeans (Nelson, 1899; Lantis, 1946).

For the north Alaskan Eskimo, the most noteworthy festivals associated with animals arose in the "cults," that of the whale on the coast, and of the caribou in the interior. These were the high points of the year, constituting, as has been noted, a kind of world renewal rite. A vast number of elements and behavior patterns was involved in these major ceremonies (Lantis, 1938). Already seen have been the restrictions on members of the crew, the absence of levity and of sexual relations, the restrictions on the wife of the umealiq, the offering of water to the decapitated whale. Inland many of the same restrictions applied to the men engaged in the stockade hunt and to their umealiq and his wife. When to this are added the special kinds of clothing, always new, with special headbands and fillets, special gauntlets, the array of songs and charms, the paeans of thanks to the whale or caribou and the general patterns of joyous merrymaking thereafter—for example, throwing the captain, his wife, and the members of the crew up in a blanket—there are seen not only the moment when a community effects some degree of solidarity but also the most elaborate of the north Alaskan group religious activities. Hence the term "cult"; other activities relating to animals tended to be more individualized.

With the pattern of hunting and its religious connections uppermost, it was necessary not only to placate the animals but to achieve some degree of control over them. This was done chiefly by means of songs of which there was a great array. Songs applied to all hunting situations and were considered powerful and efficacious. Not only were there songs for all animals, but songs lent added worth to weapons and gear. Thus the harpooner sang over his darts, over the lines and floats, and the caribou hunters sang special songs over their stockades. Unlike songs for social purposes or the witty insult songs, these songs were measured and slow, frequently containing archaic words, an indication that they must have come down for generations. These songs were property and could be sold and traded. Once formally conferred, the efficacy of a song applied solely to the owner. Owning such songs involved an impersonal power dangerous to possess. The singer was also obliged to observe certain food taboos.

Allied with the song were hunting charms. These were different from the individual charms which every person had in that they were associated with a hunt leader or with an umiak or stockade. They were brought out at the proper time, usually in association with a song. The umealiq was the person obtaining them and they were indeed a prerequisite to achieving the hunt leader status. He generally purchased them, although they might be inherited. With them again went food taboos incumbent on the owner and his wife. Household charms also existed, their ownership vested in the chief hunter of the household, technically the owner of the house, and designed to protect the house.

From animals came power. There were, it is true, the spirits of animals which were specific but there was also a sense of a kind of force, of a *mana*-like emanation which came from the animal world. Such power was invested in songs, names, and charms, but a man of power was one who achieved success, especially in hunting and over women. The concept was vague but meaningfully present as a rationale for successful achievement; it becomes slightly more evolved in the sub-Arctic interior. Specific animal power focused in humans, however, was the peculiar property of those religious practitioners, the shamans in the society.

The term shaman comes out of the Siberian Tungusic and refers to a person who is subject to control by spiritual forces outside of himself. He may become a medium, possessed by a spirit which speaks through his mouth, or he may enter into an ecstatic state, one in which his movements, his speech, and his behavior generally are controlled by spiritual forces without. Eskimo shamanism was of the latter type, as indeed was most shamanism of North America. Not that possessional shamanism was unknown, but the practitioner tended to retain some sense of his own identity. In his shamanistic role, he communed with the spirit world, enlisting the aid of spirit helpers who assisted him in his work. Such spirits were those of the animals, a common belief associating them with land rather than sea. Thus the power of the brown bear was considered especially strong, while wolf power, or fox power as well, were equally valuable. What is apparently encountered here is a common circumpolar concept; bear power, for example, is widely accepted as a source of curing and some sub-Arctic and Arctic peoples, the Ainu of Japan to mention only one, have developed the elaborated bear cult. While there were special omens associated with sea mammals, including the polar bear, and a good many beliefs regarding them, they apparently were not regarded as a source of shamanistic power. An association in temporal depth, perhaps, one relating to the landlocked areas of interior Asia and stemming from a pre-Eskimo, premaritime adjustment may account for the equation of shaman power and animals from the land.

Defining a shaman is by no means an easy task since the line between the shaman and the nonshaman was blurred in the minds of the people themselves. There were shamanistic songs, tokens of power and rapport with the spirit world. But these could be owned by any one, could be bought and sold, and had efficacy in curing certain kinds of ailments, finding lost articles, and discovering causes of death. It was regarded as dangerous to own such songs, "charged" as they were with power, and those who sang them did so with a sense of awe and fear. But when a person owned several, when he was called in by others to effect desired results in curing, and when the attitudes surrounding him in the group were those of anxious respect for his powers, he might be said to be a shaman. The calling was not necessarily a desired one. Too often, in fact, a shaman might be accused of having caused a death by his magic and so be murdered. A shaman became a kind of scapegoat, either in his own or some other group, since he might be regarded as malevolent and have group hatred and hostile expression directed toward him. In other words, he was frequently viewed as a witch or sorceror, again outside of the circle of his own kindred.

Nor was the office, if such it can be called, necessarily consciously sought. Spirits came to a person, marking him as their own and directing him into the shamanistic calling. The point is that unconscious processes were operative, that there were factors of hysteria and of autosuggestion. The shaman was hysterical in his behavior, at least by the standards of Western culture, and his behavior resembled the seizure pattern of the epileptic. The difference, it can be seen, was that the shaman was in some degree in control of himself when he was in a state of ecstasy or trance. Such hysterical reactions happened frequently to some individuals, even if they did not emerge as practicing shamans. Outbursts of madness, at least in patterned form, struck members of the group from time to time. Various authors have discussed the phenomenon of "Arctic Hysteria," a syndrome still imperfectly understood. This involved imitative reactions on the part of the afflicted, the person so touched repeating words spoken to him or making a motion suggested by someone else again and again until falling exhausted. Such behavior has been described for the Aleut, but it does not seem characteristic of the Eskimo. It is important to remember that in cultures such as this one, the line between objective reality and various subjective states was extremely thinly drawn. Eskimo religion, or that of any American Indian, never concerns itself with an issue of faith, of belief or of unbelief, since spirits of animals were fully as real as the animals themselves.

A case such as the following points up the question: Here is a young man, Aarpatuaq, who has interested himself solely in hunting, the thought of becoming a shaman never crossing his mind. However, he meets Kinaliq, an old shaman, who says to him: "I will take away your life and give you the shaman's (*angatquq, angekok,* the latter the usual form as it appears in the literature) life." Kinaliq then tells him that he will go out trapping and that he will capture five wolves. When he has done this, he will become *angekok.* Here then is the suggestion; Aarpatuaq goes out, finds five wolves in his traps, and is immediately overcome by the spiritual forces. He falls down, unconscious. Awakening, he finds his hands tied with the lines he has carried on his sled. Returning, he is greeted by Kinaliq. From there on, he is Kinaliq's disciple, learning the trade, so to speak, the various "tricks" that Kinaliq has been able to perform, and adding some of his own. From his mentor he learns songs, acquiring some of his own, and masters the legerdemain and stage magic that Kinaliq knows. He can, for example, swallow a bladder filled with blood. At the auspicious moment, his stomach muscles break the bladder and he vomits the blood into a pan. His badge is the tambourine, the one-sided skin drum. This, while a general musical instrument among the Eskimo (in fact the only one, although the Eskimo is by no means unmusical, what with their rhythmic counterpoint in drumming), has also become the special instrument of the shaman. In his seances, those held in the dark months in the karigi, he sings, summoning his spirit helpers. Their voices are heard, presumably from his own ventriloquism, in the darkened hallway, a frightening experience for the uninitiated and one demonstrating the power of the shaman in question. Aarpatuaq suggests to his audience that the house is shaking and of course, it is. He tells the groups that another shaman, Masagaroaq, in another community, is throwing power at him. Beating his drum, his eyeballs turning inward, his breath labored, he throws his power back at Masagaroaq. He rides on the wings of the wind to witness his triumph over Masagaroaq, or the latter comes to see his victory. These are frightening and stirring events which take place in the karigi in the winter months, where the shaman makes the most of an audience.

Otherwise, the shaman was as other men. He was married, had children, was a member of a hunting group and a karigi. If he effected a cure, he expected of course to be paid and was quite capable of blackmailing his patients, demanding as much as an umiak or valuable labrets. Similarly, he was able so to intimidate by his power that he demanded either sexual relations with his patient's wife or demanded the wife herself. Again, should this take place, the whole issue of partnership and its involvements arose. What seemingly happened in the case of the shaman was that he was expected to provide for his family but that he had in some measure succumbed to patterns of hysteria which were common to members of

the culture. It may be suggested that the man of parts, the successful hunter, the man able to dominate the situation would rarely be struck by the shamanistic calling. Instead, it was the mediocre individual, the hunter whose success was dubious, the individual with homosexual tendencies, the misanthrope who received the shamanistic call. An umealiq was a man dignified and honorable; a shaman was a potential ne'er-do-well and a misfit. Put another way, the shaman was frequently an individual who failed to measure up to the demands of hunting skill and industriousness.

The shaman was primarily involved with the curing of illness. In cultures which have not invented the microscope, where a scientific theory of illness does not exist, illness must be attributed to malign forces or to an action which the sick person or one of his relatives has performed. Eskimos, living as they did on the knife-edge of their environment, where the illness of the chief provider might mean starvation for the whole group, found sickness particularly anxiety producing. Names, charms, songs, and other supernatural aspects carried with them their taboos. These, as noted, related to food and the violations of food prohibitions. It is of course possible that in a culture where food becomes so important and where anxieties regarding food must exist, food and its relation to illness may become paramount. Such a point, clearly, cannot be proved but it can be affirmed that such anxieties led in turn to illness and that the shaman, if offering in his own way a kind of psychotherapy, was remarkably successful in his cures.

The problem which arises here is one which every culture in some measure faces. If medicine is not seen as art or science, then clearly, its domain is supernatural. Not only the Eskimo, but a wide series of other cultures throughout western North America, down into the Southwest and into Mexico and South America, held to a twofold cause of disease. One cause of illness was soul loss, the idea that the essence of the individual somehow wandered away and had to be enticed back into the body before well-being could result. A second cause was the presence in the body of the patient of an intruded object, one which had been "shot" into the body by an enemy or which entered through the violation of a ritual prohibition. Actually, the latter cause of intrusion was more common among most American Indians, while the Eskimo tended to attribute illness to soul loss. If a food taboo was violated, the individual's soul was offended and wandered away. Or the soul might be "stolen" by a malevolent shaman, captured by him and kept by him in a special prison, such as a mitten. Boys were told never to sleep on their stomachs, since evil shamans wandered about underground and reached up with their power to steal souls, pulling them away and hiding them. If the soul were not returned, the person died. Death was never considered to be the result of natural causes; the belief was that the people would not die were it not for violation of taboo or the machinations of malevolent shamans.

Such a point of view implies that there was a cultural definition of illness. Was a person ill, for example, who broke a bone or suffered from toothache? Clearly not, since the skills of living demanded that anyone have enough practical medicine on hand to set and bandage a broken bone, while an aching tooth was easily knocked out with a hammer and chisel. Only when infection set in, when there were ill-defined pains in the trunk or head, was there a situation requiring the ministrations of the shaman. And such pains, of course, being undifferentiated, arising either from serious organic imbalance or from psychosomatic causes, were still treated in the same way. If the latter, as where a patient felt himself guilty because he offended an animal, the shaman could force a confession, such always taking place in a group. Singing, going into a trance, beating his drum over the entrance well of the house, the shaman evoked so mysterious and eerie an atmosphere that even the guiltless could be persuaded to confess that they had violated a seasonal taboo, failing to observe the eating restrictions or failing to cleanse themselves before whaling or caribou hunting. Confession was thus an aspect of the curing process. Or the patient had offended a shaman. If so, it might be possible to remove from his body an object which had been "shot" there by his enemy. A little harpoon, palmed and mouthed by the shaman, might be spit up on the drum. This was also part of the shaman's array of activity; one cannot of course ask the motivations of the shaman since he was convinced of his own powers and since this was the only way open to a cure.

If the patient died, the shaman was not paid. That shamans were often successful in their cures goes without saying in view of the fact that illness was so often self-induced and fitted into the hysteric behavioral pattern so common to the culture. Hence a shaman made demands for payment in the event of a successful cure. These were met out of fear of the shaman and tended to create some tensions between groups in the community. If the shaman lost a patient, he had a ready excuse that a practitioner more powerful than he was making magic against the patient. He who could cure could also send disease.

Shamanistic seances were also held without regard to illness. Curing, the spiritual battles in which shamans engaged, the shamanistic performance involving legerdemain, ventriloquism, and trickery had an exciting effect. Religion, like any form of recreation, had its value in relieving tedium and in providing an out from boredom.

A religious difference existed between the western Eskimos and those of the central regions as well as of Labrador and Greenland. In the west, as exemplified by the north Alaskan Eskimo, there were clearly no deities; Raven, a trickster-creator, was never a god, nor can one properly identify the animal spirits as gods. As one moves eastward, however, there are encountered Torngarsoak and Sedna, the former the lord of the animal spirits, the latter the goddess of the sea. A parallel is seen in Alaska in the person of the Moonman, although again, among the north Alaskan Eskimo, this figure had no importance (Lantis, 1950:323). The Sedna myth is the one which has preoccupied a number of students of the Eskimo since it appears so strikingly among the eastern and central groups (cf. Boas, 1888). The myth relates to a girl, Sedna, married to the *fulmar*, the seagull, and attempting to escape from him. The girl and her father escape in an umiak, and as they do so, the fulmar follows them, blowing up a storm. To placate him, Sedna's father throws her overboard. She seizes the gunwale and hangs on, but her father, taking a spade, chops away at her fingers. The first joints fall into the sea, becoming whales, the next finger joints become seals, and the last become walrus. She then falls back into the sea, and sinking to the bottom, dwells there with a dog as her companion or guardian (a variant makes her guardian her father). Lacking fingers, she cannot comb her hair which is filled with the vermin of broken taboos. This angers her and she withholds the game over which she presides. Here arises the Eskimo myth offering a

● THE SHAMAN—NORTH ALASKAN ESKIMO

By the flickering light of the seal-oil lamp
(lower left) and the dim winter twilight
filtering through the seal-gut window (above),
the Eskimo shaman begins a cure. The patient,
wrapped in caribou skins, is laid prone before
the kataq, the entrance well leading from the
passage to the inner chamber of the driftwood-
lined house. The shaman, grasping his
tambourine, the one-sided skin drum so
characteristic of the Arctic regions, sings the
curing songs. Their slow measured cadence
will summon up the practitioner's helping
spirits who will seek the patient's errant soul.
The wandering away or the abduction of the
sick man's essence or soul has caused the
illness. Perhaps it has been offended because
the patient violated a food prohibition, or
perhaps it has been stolen by a malevolent
shaman. In either case, it must be captured and
restored before the patient can recover. As he
sings, communing with his spirit helpers, the
shaman will gradually work himself up into a
frenzied ecstasy, sweating and panting, turning
his eyeballs inward, frothing at the mouth. A
skilled ventriloquist, the shaman punctuates

his singing with the voices of his spirit helpers
and the growl of the brown bear or the howl
of the wolf appear to be heard from the
passage way below the entrance well. The
shaman's mittens, tied with strings, will slide
into the passage and in the final climax to the
séance, will be pulled back clutching the sick
man's soul.

The members of the patient's household
watch the shaman's performance with tension
and awe. Stripped to the waist in the muggy
warmth of the slab-lined sod house, the men
occupy their place on the benched platform at
the rear of the house, while women and
children rest on the floor of the main room.
Skin bedding hangs on a rack (right); a
wooden pail hangs on the wall to catch
condensing moisture; boots are drying over the
lamp. The shaman wears a labret, or lip plug.
A costly item in North Alaskan Eskimo
culture, the shaman may demand one as his
curing fee. He might also demand—and get, in
the event of a successful cure—tools, skins, a
kayak or umiak, or the rights to one of the
women in the household.

Illness, so often induced in this culture by

96 ●

the sense of a taboo violation, was frequently successfully cured by the shamanistic performance. The Eskimo theory of soul loss as a cause of illness contrasts with the concept among many other American Indian groups of the intrusion of a foreign object, one causing pain and disease, which the shaman removed by sucking and legerdemain (see p. 94).

rationale of taboo. If game, the sea mammals, cannot be taken, it is the result of offense both to the animals and to Sedna. The shaman, in his spirit form, visits her and discovers the cause of the trouble. He then forces a confession of a broken taboo from members of the group, thereby creating a salutary release and relief for all concerned. Sedna is placated, the game return, and the people themselves are cleansed of "sin."

Various groups of Eskimos had beliefs in anthropomorphic beings but in no case do they emerge as supreme. The issue was power, emanating from such personified sources, or from such superior supernatural beings, or of course from the animals themselves and from their realm. None of these beliefs, however much backed by myth, could be regarded as wholly systematized. There was no development of a theology nor was there more than the simplest philosophical rationale inherent in the system. Put another way, the Eskimo did not speculate. Why this should have been so is readily explainable: the primary focus of the society lay in the solution to the problems of living, to success in the economic quest and in the establishment of interpersonal relations. In this sense, religion was an adjunct feature, not a primary one.

It cannot be said of the Eskimo that they were wholly at the mercy of their environment. The natural surroundings limited, but freedom within these limitations allowed the Eskimo to make choices and to develop variations on the theme of sea mammal hunting. Taken as a whole, the culture area of the Eskimo, spread from Alaska to Greenland, emerges as a resplendent illustration of the human triumph over nature.

Suggested readings

ANDERSON, D. D.
1970   "Akmak: An Early Archeological Assemblage from Onion Portage, Northwest Alaska." *Acta Arctica*, vol. 16. Copenhagen.

1968   "A Stone-Age Campsite at the Gateway to America." *Scientific American,* vol. 218, no. 6, pp. 24–33.

BALIKCI, A.
1970   *The Netsilik Eskimo.* Garden City, N. Y.: Natural History Press.

BANDI, H.
1969   *Eskimo Prehistory.* Translated by A. E. Keep. University of Alaska Press.

BIRKET-SMITH, K.
1959   *The Eskimos.* New York: Humanities Press.

BURCH, E. S., JR.
1975   *Eskimo Kinsmen: Changing Family Relationships in Northwest Alaska.* American Ethnological Society, Monograph 59. St. Paul: West.

COLLINS, H. B., JR.
1964   "The Arctic and Subarctic." In *Prehistoric Man in the New World,* ed. J. D. Jennings and E. Norbeck, pp. 85–114, Rice University Semicentennial Publication. University of Chicago Press.

DAMAS, D.
1968   "The Diversity of Eskimo Societies." In *Man the Hunter,* ed. R. B. Lee and I. DeVore, pp. 111–117. Chicago: Aldine.

1963   *Igluligmiut Kinship and Local Groupings: A Structural Approach.* National Museum of Canada, Bulletin 196.

DUMOND, D. E.
1974   *Archaeology and Prehistory in Alaska.* Andover, Mass.: Warner Modular Publications in Anthropology.

FORD, J. A.
1959   "Eskimo Prehistory in the Vicinity of Point Barrow, Alaska." *American Museum of Natural History, Anthropological Papers,* vol. 47, pt. 1, pp. 1–272.

GUEMPLE, D. L. (ed.)
1972   *Alliance in Eskimo Society.* Supplement to Proceedings, American Ethnological Society, 1971. University of Washington Press.

HUGHES, C. C.
1965   "Under Four Flags: Recent Culture Change among the Eskimos." *Current Anthropology* 6:3–69.

LANTIS, M.
1946   *The Social Culture of the Nunivak Eskimo.* Philadelphia: Transactions of the American Philosophical Society, vol. 35, pt. 3.

LAUGHLIN, W. S.
1963a   "The Earliest Aleuts." *University of Alaska, Anthropological Papers* 10:73–91

1963b   "Eskimos and Aleuts: Their Origins and Evolution." *Science,* vol. 142, no. 3593, pp. 633–645.

NELSON, R. K.
1969   *Hunters of the Northern Ice.* University of Chicago Press.

RASMUSSEN, K.
1929–1932   Reports on Iglulik, Caribou, Netsilik, and

Copper Eskimo. *Reports of the Fifth Thule Expedition,* vols. 7–9. Copenhagen.

SPENCER, R. F.

1959 *The North Alaskan Eskimo: A Study in Ecology and Society.* Bureau of American Ethnology, no. 171.

VAN STONE, J. W.

1962 *Point Hope: An Eskimo Village in Transition.* American Ethnological Society, Monograph. University of Washington Press.

WEYER, E. M., JR.

1932 *The Eskimos, their Environment and Folkways.* New Haven: Yale University Press.

ATHABASCANS OF THE WESTERN SUB-ARCTIC

South of the coastal tundra of the Eskimo, in the watersheds of the Yukon in Alaska and of the Mackenzie in northwest Canada, there is the gradual emergence of the northern coniferous forest. The northern boundary of these vast woods varies as Arctic climates push to the interior and create such barren grounds as those to the west of Hudson Bay where the Caribou Eskimo are encountered. With the onset of the forests, however, a new climatic zone is reached. Continental climates characteristic of the interiors of both North America and Asia have cold winters and warm summers. To be sure, the northern summer period may be short, the winter long and bitter, but the gales and fogs of the coasts are lacking, snowfall is heavier, and there is a marked change from the desertlike land inhabited by the Eskimo. Game of many different kinds abounds in the forests. Barren-ground caribou are encountered on the forest-tundra margin, woodland caribou appear in the forests. There are moose, some deer and elk, bears, wolves, and foxes, various fur-bearing animals and rodents. Fish abound in the interior glacial lakes and in the many streams.

Here, in the northwestern parts of Canada and adjacent interior Alaska, live groups of American Indians all belonging to the Athabascan branch of the Na-Déné speech family. While there is some mutual intelligibility of the languages of the area, there are also shadings off into dialects and separate languages belonging to the Athabascan grouping. It is language or dialect, together with common territory, which sets off these interior tribes from each other. Like the Eskimo, they were lacking in formal tribal organization. Na-Déné, as noted, is divided into four branches—Tlingit and Haida on the Northwest Coast belong to it, as probably does Eyak, an interior group which pushed to the coast along the Copper River in southeastern Alaska. Athabascan is the most widely spread branch. It moves southward, appearing in northwestern California among the Hupa and on the adjacent Oregon coast among the Tolowa-Tututni. The fact that the Navaho and Apache of the American Southwest speak Athabascan languages suggests a recent intrusion of these peoples into the Arizona–New Mexico region, a fact borne out by archeological evidence. Athabascan speakers are thus represented in several different types of culture, evidence of the fact that a linguistic system may persist in spite of adaptations to differing cultural environments. The Yukon-Mackenzie area may well be the homeland of Athabascan speech, although there are suggestions of Asiatic affinities. If so, the Athabascans, essentially recent in the New World, may represent a kind of baseline adaptation to interior sub-Arctic conditions.

Unlike the Eskimo, whose mastery over their environment evokes great admiration, the interior Athabascans lack a precisely definable cultural base. These were—and are—hunting cultures, with exploitation of local natural resources. As hunters, they tended to move about, usually in defined territories, but there are historical evidences of changes in habitat, invasions of each other's territories, and tribal mixtures. Contact with Europeans, largely as a result of the establishment of the fur trade, was early, beginning about 1700, one effect being the use of items of foreign manufacture, another intermixture with outsiders. All such factors make for difficulty in establishing a precise description of the peoples and cultures of the vast region. Even aboriginally, because the cultural base tended to be generalized in the setting of sub-Arctic hunting patterns, it appears to have been highly susceptible to external influences. Where, as on the side of the Pacific drainage, salmon move up the freshwater streams to spawn, the local cultures begin to resemble those of the intermontane Plateau area. Some have also been touched by influences of the elaborate cultures of the Northwest Coast, taking over aspects of societal organization and the patterns of wealth so marked in the coastal cultures. In the far north, Eskimo patterns make their appearance, while still others, pushing to the southern prairies, take on an array of traits from the Plains.

Geographic location thus must be a major

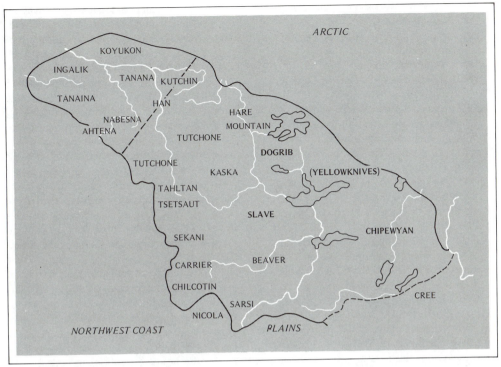

A2 ● Western Sub-Arctic

element in the delineation of the peoples of the area. The Arctic drainage lowlands, generally dominated by the Mackenzie River basin, and including the vast interior freshwater lakes, such as Great Bear Lake, Great Slave Lake, and Lake Athabasca, may be regarded as the focal center of the sub-Arctic. The area is characterized by the boreal forest of spruce, tamarack, willow, and alder. A varying northern timberline marks the entrance into the tundra. Given a baseline of an arctic and sub-arctic hunting culture, one adapted to the variation of forest and tundra topography, such interior peoples as the Chipewyan, Degrib, Slave, or Hare may be regarded as reflecting one major pattern of adaptation. This is the primary caribou-hunting focus. But other peoples of the area, in a somewhat differing terrain, are the mountain dwellers. The cordilleran segments in interior Alaska run southward through the mountain chain to form an eastward parallel to the Plateau area. While caribou are not absent in the cordilleran subarea, there is a greater variety of game there than in the tundra-woodland focus. This mountain mode appears among the Koyukon and runs far southward to the Chilcotin and Carrier. In addition, there are the river basins of Alaska, the Yukon and Kuskokwim, with the

Eskimo-influenced Ingalik and the Tanana. Although some Athabascans pushed early to the sea and such as the Eyak, the Tanaina, at Ceek Inlet, retain something of the adaptation to the interior, they supplement this inland hunting pattern with maritime activities. The western sub-Arctic thus offers a series of differing ecological possibilities with some consequent differences in socio-cultural patterns (cf. VanStone, 1974:7–22).

Tribes

Western Sub-Arctic (note map, cf. Osgood, 1936b; Kroeber, 1939:100; Murdock, 1960:34–47).

Main area (interior Yukon drainage in Alaska; Mackenzie and Arctic drainage, including interior Canadian lakes):

  Kutchin (Loucheux)
  Koyukon (Coyukon)
  Tanana
  Han
  Tutchone
  Mountain
  Kaska (formerly eastern Nahane)
  Sekani
  Beaver
  Slave
  Dogrib
  Chipewyan (easternmost group; some Cree
    [Algonkin] influences as well as Eskimo

contact on the west shore of Hudson Bay;
cf. Birket-Smith, 1930)

Hare (resident on forest edge, exploitation of
interior tundra)

Satudene (interior tundra)

Yellowknives (interior tundra see Chipewyan)

Eskimo and Northwest Coast influences:

Ingalik (name is Eskimo, also known as Tena.
Several groups are located in the lower
Yukon and adjacent Innoko and Kuskokwim
valleys in southwestern Alaska. The Ingalik
are much influenced by the Alaskan Eskimo,
having the *kashim* [*karigi*], the men's house.
Northwest Coast influences are seen in
modified potlatching; cf. Osgood, 1940; 1958;
1959).

Ahtena (strong Northwest Coast influences
especially affecting the Eyak. The latter, on
the Copper River delta, have the phratry
divisions of the Northwest Coast and are
most conveniently listed with that area; cf.
Birket-Smith and De Laguna, 1938).

Nabesna (Upper Tanana, some Northwest
Coast suggestions; cf. McKennan, 1959).

Tanaina (Cook Inlet, Alaska. These groups
show effects stemming from both Eskimo
and Northwest Coast. They are different
from the Tanana; cf. Osgood, 1937).

Tahltan (formerly western Nahane; cf. Emmons,
1911).

Tsetsaut (south of Tahltan and more heavily
influenced by the coastal Tsimshian).

Intermontane (Plateau) influences:

Chilcotin (including Nicola, the latter having
pushed into Salishan territory, cf. Morice,
1895).

Carrier (including Babine).

Plains influences:

Sarsi (Retention of Athabascan speech but
wholly drawn to Plains, specifically, Blackfoot
culture, i.e., bison dependence, tipi, war
patterns).

Other Sub-Arctic Zones:

The Northwest in Canada and Alaska is
paralleled by 1. the central sub-Arctic and
shifts to Algonkin languages, notably with
such groups as the Cree and Saulteaux
(northern Ojibwa), and 2. by the eastern sub-
Arctic, also with Algonkian speech and
represented by such broad linguistic units as
Ojibwa, Montagnais-Naskapi, Beothuk, etc.
These northern Algonkins, in both center
and east, resemble to some degree the
northwestern Athabascans but are generally
outside of the area of caribou distribution
(Helm and Leacock, 1971).

Given the geographic location of the various
Déné peoples, and the fact that the area is subject to external influences from all sides, a type
culture, one representative of the ethnographic
area in its untouched form, is elicited only with
difficulty. There is also considerable debate
what the role of the fur trade was in creating
both a sense of hunting territory and also of
patrilineal systems of society. In the eastern
sub-Arctic such postcontact changes may well
have occurred (Driver, 1969:274–276), but the
western segments of the greater region reflect
such changes only in part. The groups possessing bilateral relationship systems may thus be
those who can be regarded as most representative of an aboriginal situation. This, in addition
to the mainstay of caribou hunting, may permit
the delineation of some typical groups, those
less influenced by other native areas or less affected by postcontact trade.

The basic pattern for the area is varied by
the modes of settlement in woodland, tundra,
lake region, and river basin. The focal area
thus lies in the Yukon Valley of interior Alaska
and in the headwater regions of both the Yukon and Mackenzie, as well as along the Mackenzie River itself. From this basin to the east,
drainage patterns' lead to the Arctic Ocean and
to the Hudson Bay, itself an arm of the Arctic
Sea. Included in the area of interior Athabascan
development are the major lakes—Great Bear
Lake, Great Slave Lake where the Mackenzie
originates, and Lake Athabaska. The representative peoples do not reach the sea but are centered rather in tundra-woodland and wood-
land-tundra. The ecological adaptations were
exclusively hunting, and the economic constellation centered in the caribou. Despite nine
species of caribou, with their two major divisions of woodland and tundra distribution, and
the presence of phenomenally large herds of
these animals, their presence in the area was
uneven, with the result that some of interior
peoples became dependent on other game.
There is, it is true, a series of culture patterns
which might be said to characterize the area,
such as the presence of the socio-economic
band, shamanism, girls' rites, use of caribou
rawhide, and many others. Yet, given the geographic circumstances and some variation in
ecological adaptation, no one group can be said
to be wholly representative of the area. A contrast of several is called for (cf. VanStone, 1974).

Slave, Chipewyan, Dogrib

These three peoples, all speaking generally mutually intelligible Athabascan languages, are chosen as representative of the tundra-woodland mode of life characteristic of the interior western sub-Arctic. The Slave, although they moved rather widely through a vast area, following the Mackenzie from its lake source over to the Liard and south and west as far as Fort Nelson, are always identified with the coniferous boreal forest. One of the larger groups in the area was the Chipewyan. This enclave was spread from Lake Athabaska eastward to Hudson Bay and northward to the northeast of the Great Bear and Great Slave lakes. To the south the Chipewyan intruded on the country of the Cree. Although small in numbers, as are all the interior Athabascan groupings, the Chipewyan had the most extensive territory of any American Indian tribe. A group frequently mentioned in the early literature was the Tatsanotinne, the Yellowknives. If this people ever existed as a separate entity, they were either assimilated early by the Chipewyan and Dogrib or were a northwestern branch of the Chipewyan. Although the Chipewyan hunted the tundra, they, like the Dogrib, had access to the forest. The Dogrib were neither exclusively woodland nor wholly adapted to the tundra (Gillespie, 1970; Helm, 1968; Jenness, 1955; Mason, 1946). As the fragmentary historical data of these people are reviewed, it is clear that considerable contact and movement took place within the area.

Although it is said of the Dogrib that they possessed some tribal sense, they were divided into four main groups, subdivided in turn into territorial socio-economic bands, a pattern generally followed by the peoples of the area. It is thus commonality of territory, as well as language and/or dialect, which permits the designation of the tribe. As noted elsewhere, while convention may refer to the various groups of American Indians as tribes, the term cannot be used to designate the same kind of grouping. If the northern Athabascans were divided into tribelike entities, groups at least called by specific names, it must be understood that one group shades into another, that there are always problems of group definition, and certainly, problems of ascertaining the numbers of people involved.

The populations in the general area were always small, considering the vast landmass in which the people lived. Population potential is significantly reduced by the dependence on hunting and the fact that the game hunted does not reliably appear, year by year, in the same numbers. According to the various population estimates for the extensive area, total numbers seem not to have exceeded 35,000 in precontact times (Kroeber, 1938:141; Mooney, 1928; VanStone, 1974:11). There was a higher concentration of population among such groups as the Carrier on the Upper Fraser in the south, and perhaps among the Canadian-Alaskan Kutchin (cf. Kroeber, 1938). In general, if these interior native peoples are fewer in number than the Eskimo, this probably reflects the absence of a subsistence base as dependable as the Eskimo enjoy. Indeed, lacking the specializations possessed by the Eskimo, the interior peoples appear to have been more susceptible to periods of privation and starvation. A population increase began early in postcontact times with the rise of the Métis, the "mixed" French and Indian population currently so important in the Canadian, although not in the Alaskan, sub-Arctic. VanStone's researches on the various tribes lists 788 Dogrib in 1864, 850 Slave in 1906, possibly 220 Yellowknives in 1859, although these are very likely to be listed as Chipewyan, and 2420 Chipewyan in 1906; and in Alaska, VanStone notes 2000 Ingalik in 1870, 739 Tanaina in 1880, and 1200 Kutchin (VanStone, 1974:11).

Subsistence. These interior hunting cultures exploited all animal resources which the terrain provided. In terms of quantity, it is the caribou which for the peoples of the tundra edge was the chief source of food. But the other sources of subsistence, the moose, musk-ox, arctic hare, and fish, cannot be ignored. The movement of the caribou herds in late summer and early fall brought the Chipewyan and Dogrib out to the tundra to capture them, a situation paralleled in Alaska by the Kutchin, Tanana, and Koyukon. In the past, vast herds of caribou crossed the north arm of the Great Slave Lake in early winter. Even in modern times, between 1943 and 1952, the Dogrib at this location took 53,595 caribou, averaging 36.7 caribou per hunter per year, a figure which seems fairly consistent with the aboriginal situation (Helm, 1972:62). Both the Chipewyan and Dogrib took advantage of the caribou movements in the open tundra. The Slave, however, residents of the forest, never made so extensive a use of the caribou, being limited in any case to the less abundant woodland species and to moose (Mason, 1946; Honigmann, 1946).

The Chipewyan pattern of caribou hunting did not differ essentially from that of the Nuunamiut Eskimo of northern Alaska. Caribou move to the tundra in the spring and return to the edge of the forests in late summer and fall. There was special concentration on the fall, early winter drive. The impound method prevailed, with lines strung along fenceposts leading to the corral or ambush. Water drives were also employed, the swimming animals being lanced, while snares were erected with nooses in which the caribou might catch their antlers. Such snares were also set along the posts leading to the impound.

Snares and lines throughout the area, such lines as might be used in erecting a caribou fence, were made of *babiche*. This is semitanned caribou hide, cut into strands from a single skin. Such lines were used in many of the manufactures of the area, such as for trap lines, impound fences, or for netting. The lines were very long; a single skin could be cut in a circular manner into a 1½–2 inch strip of great length. Moose hides, treated in the same way, were braided. Babiche becomes the virtual material hallmark of the interior Athabascan area.

Unlike the Eskimo, who can count on permafrost storage, the interior groups were obliged to preserve meat, especially with the relatively hot summers of an area of continental climate. Caribou as well as other meat was hung in thin strips and either smoked or dried. But it is pemmican which is most frequently encountered. In the general area pemmican was made by allowing meat to dry and by mixing marrow into it and pounding it. Berries might also be pounded into the mixture, although this was less characteristic of the northern parts of the area. Fish can also be treated in this way. Slabs of pemmican permit long-term storage, although it is remarked that the groups in question rarely had adequate future provision (Mason, 1946:16).

The moose is found in fairly large numbers throughout the forests. A solitary animal, never herding like the caribou, the moose was stalked and shot with arrows, as well as snared with babiche lines. The Slave were especially skilled at moose hunting and this animal became for them the chief staple. (Honigmann, 1946:36). Some social differences arose between the various tribes because of the involvements of cooperative as against individualized hunting. Moose were usually taken by an individual hunter, or at most, by two men working together. Caribou drives, on the other hand, required group effort. The result was the emergence, as among the Eskimo, of temporary

hunt leaders, a feature especially true of the Chipewyan (Birket-Smith, 1930:20–23). The Dogrib, among whom caribou hunting was less well integrated a cultural feature, pursued the herds in sleds or afoot after a stealthy approach, shooting arrows at the game (Mason, 1946:15). The animals which were taken, as well as the methods for taking them, are highly varied. One finds, for example, that bears were speared and snared, that beavers were gaffed, that the Dogrib and Chipewyan made long journeys across the tundra in pursuit of the musk-ox which were again snared and water driven. Rodents, particularly the muskrat and rabbit, were important. The rabbit, tending to increase in population in seven-year cycles, became extremely important to the native economy and could substitute for caribou in the not unlikely event that caribou populations underwent a decline, something which now and again took place. If both rabbits and caribou failed, as sometimes also occurred, some groups suffered great privation and might engage in cannibalism as a result.

The animal inventory of the area is remarkable in terms of the variety of species exploited. What developed as a religious idea among the Eskimo was also characteristic here, the concept that the animal allowed itself to be captured and that proper care had to be taken to avoid giving offense to the game. No Chipewyan woman could walk across the blood and bones of the caribou, for example, and there were also certain parts of the caribou which it would offend that animal to have devoured by dogs however inadvertently. By the same reasoning, certain animals were avoided. It is said of the Dogrib that they would eat no members of the weasel family, even if starving, while the wolf, fox, wolverine, skunk, and dog were taboo as food to most of the groups. Skunk and lynx were eaten by some of the interior Athabascans but avoided by others. A successful hunter could order the game, such as the caribou or musk-ox, to go to a certain place, a river or lake, to be captured. The latter pattern suggests the compulsive song of the Eskimo, although magical singing was by no means so well developed.

Traps, particularly those of the deadfall type, were common in the area. Traplines, both in the forest and at the tundra edge, were put out in the winter months. Birds were eaten, as well as their eggs, but they were considerably less important than fish. Fish were hooked, speared, and netted, the latter again a winter activity, gill nets being strung under the ice. Summer fishing employed fish dams and weirs. Fresh fish was boiled, but fish was also preserved in the same manner as caribou meat dried, smoked, and made into pemmican.

The interior Athabascans, like the Eskimo, boiled most of their fresh meat although spit broiling was not unknown. Copper and iron kettles are much in evidence today but in the past the stone boiling method was usual. The Dogrib and Chipewyan dug a hole in the ground, lining it with a caribou paunch. Hot stones were dropped in to bring the water to a boil.

The interior Athabascans were considerably more dependent on wild vegetable foods than were the Eskimo. Berries of many kinds were collected in the summer months and were often preserved in animal fats. They were also pounded into meat and marrow. The tender shoots of various plants were eaten, such as the various species of willow. Sap, as from the poplar, was eaten and chewed. The women of a band might spend several weeks each summer in gathering wild plant foods.

Among the Eskimo it was possible to define the yearly round with considerable precision. This is not the case among the peoples of the interior whose activities were considerably less well pinpointed. The Chipewyan and Dogrib had their principal caribou drives in the early winter and, like the Slave, spent winter months fishing through the ice. By spring, the bands were on the move in the territories which each knew, beginning caribou, moose, or musk-ox hunting. Men often went far afield for hunting while women and children, as well as older people, remained in a semipermanent summer campsite, fishing, gathering berries, preparing food. Hunting activities were stepped up by fall. Winter found the individual bands at local campsites where semipermanent winter dwellings were erected. As among the Eskimo, there was freedom in choice of activity so that hunters as well as family groups moved in and out of a band through the year.

Because the bands of the peoples in question were required to travel over fairly wide distances, hunting and gathering, they were faced by some problems of transportation. Dog teams were known both to the Dogrib and northern Chipewyan, but the numbers of dogs were considerably less than among the Eskimo. Dogs, moreover, were of a variety different from the Eskimo sled dog and not so tractable,

being allowed to run more freely than among the Eskimo. There is a suggestion that dogs were much mixed with wolves. The Eskimo-derived fan-wise dog trace was used with a toboggan of birchwood. Frozen beaver skins were also used to transport burdens, in themselves becoming a kind of toboggan. Winter travel required the snowshoe, another characteristic feature of the area. Snowshoes throughout the area vary slightly in pattern, but the general type is the familiar tailed snowshoe, an invention which our own culture has taken from the Canadian interior. The frame was made of birch, the mesh of babiche. Tailless snowshoes appear sporadically in the area, although they tend to be more characteristic of the east, such as in Labrador. Burdens were frequently carried by the hunter on foot, supported by snowshoes; a rack, to which the burdens were tied in bags of skin, was borne on his back and supported by a tumpline over the top of his head. Tumpline burden carrying is a general American Indian trait, appearing widely in both North and South America, the line usually running across the forehead. Women carried their children in this manner as well.

Summer travel by water involved the canoe. For the Slave this was of birchbark and probably has cultural affinities to the east and south. Such canoes were as much as 24 feet long, made in sections without a keel. Smaller canoes among the Fort Nelson Slave were made of spruce bark. Canoe types varied, but they were usually light and drew little water. The Dogrib canoes could be carried by a single individual, a necessity considering the need to portage. Canoes, sections of bark sewn together and mounted on frames, were made by men but cared for by women, another reflection of the sexual division of labor. The canoe had to be examined after a day's journey, and any weak seams calked with liquid spruce gum. Unlike the Eskimo umiak, such canoes could carry little, rarely more than two people and a small burden. Difficulties of summer travel arose as a result. Mosquitoes and flies made travel arduous and there were apparently no protective remedies against them. Whether in summer or winter, walking was the main means of transportation. A round moose-skin covered coracle has been described for the Slave and some of the groups further to the south. This was a raft, although log rafts were also known, and suggestive of the bull boat of bison hides known from the Plains tribes of the Upper Missouri.

(cf. p. 324). Canoes were paddled, the paddle made from spruce and described as very short, little more than 18 inches in length. Thus except for the snowshoe and the tumpline burden carrier, the groups in question lacked wholly efficient means of transport.

Tied into the food quest and the problem of mobility within the area, and thus relating to general subsistence, was housing. The basic house type was a conical skin tent, a tipilike structure of skins or bark mounted on poles. Dogrib men, on moving out onto the tundra in pursuit of caribou or musk-ox, are described as bringing tent poles and the necessary covering skins on their toboggans. For the Dogrib, the Chipewyan, and the Slave, the tipi is described as not essentially different from the Plains type, although more squat and covering a greater ground area. A dozen or so poles were used, sometimes transported, sometimes left in place at designated camps. These were covered with skins, the Dogrib using as many as 40 caribou skins, tanned, and sewn together with sinew or babiche. The tipi could be covered with snow in winter. A fire was built in the center and a place of honor accorded to the space opposite to the entrance; no special door covering was used, although the Chipewyan are said to have favored a bearskin flap (Mason, 1946:20–21). It is mentioned that both the Dogrib and the Chipewyan avoided shelter during the bitterest winter weather, preferring to sleep out of doors in skin bags. The point is that rising warm air, passing out through the smokehole, drew in cold air, creating a heavy draught. Among the Slave, where caribou skins were rare, obtainable in the main by trade, a brush or bark covered tipilike structure was more usual.

But where a band settled in a semi-permanent campsite for the winter, dwellings of logs were employed. These were never semi-subterranean, resting simply on the ground itself. The Slave made a kind of wooden tent with a gable rising off the ground, chinks between the logs covered with moss and earth. Such dwellings might be as much as 20 feet long, 10 feet in width. They were inhabited by extended or joint families in the winter encampment.

Tied in with the dwelling, especially the winter campsite, is the *cache,* another distinctive feature of the area. Food was cached on a pole, simply wrapped in hide and hung from a pole from which the bark had been removed; the pole was then lashed with babiche to a tree. Platform caches were also known, pre-

served food being wrapped and laid out on a platform. Caches were considered private property, but a person in need was free to make use of another's cache. The enemies of the cache were the wolf and especially the wolverine, an animal which will wantonly destroy and pollute what it does not eat from a cache.

The severity of the northern winters required no little attention to clothing. Here again, however, the clothing types were interior, not resembling the garments of the Eskimo, although they were of course tailored, a common circumpolar element. The Slave made fairly extensive use of moose hide, using the tanned skins for tailored garments, leggings, mittens, and shirts. Moose-hide blankets were also used. The pattern of clothing did not differ especially among the Dogrib and Chipewyan, although caribou skins tended to be substituted for moose hides. Men wore leggings which were attached to the waist by a belt, over a breechclout. Moccasins were not infrequently sewn onto the leggings themselves. A coat or shirt of buckskin was worn as an upper garment, the skins being carefully tanned with all hair removed. Hats or turbans of rabbitskin, stripped and woven, added to the men's costume. Important to the area, as indeed to western North America, is the use of rabbitskin. The skin was cut into strips and then woven or braided. A winter rabbitskin blanket appeared among the forest groups, the blanket being reinforced by woven elements of fiber. Winter leggings were often lined with rabbitskin as were mittens and moccasins, and a rabbitskin shirt was often worn under the buckskin shirt. Women dressed little differently from the men, employing the leggings and moccasins and winter underclothing of rabbit fur. Women generally wore a longer overshirt, with a knee-length cut. Fringing of garments appeared in the south of the area and there is mention of porcupine quill embroidery, especially on women's garments. Both men and women left their hair long, the men clubbing it under their turbans, women using braids. Some tattooing of women took place, especially on the chin, a reflection of the girls' rite.

It can readily be seen that the material array in the cultures of the interior Athabascans was not great, although it solved adequately the problem of subsistence. At that, the area contained little workable stone, with the result that arrow and dart points were made of antler. Many implements were made of wood, while the ever-present babiche became a virtual necessity in so many aspects of material culture.

Kutchin ● Aboriginal type dwelling. This was a frame dwelling covered with skins. A layer of skins was also placed inside the outer covering to ensure insulation; snow was banked around the house. Seen also is the aboriginal type sled and tailored skin clothing of the interior Alaskan type. (Adapted from A. Murray, *Journal of the Yukon, 1847–1848,* Publication of the Canadian Archives)

Some "native" copper appeared in the area—it was from this actually that the Yellowknives took their name—and this was hammered into knives and projectile points. Bone and ivory knives, frequently of Eskimo manufacture, reached the tribes in the area by trade.

The art of the area was as limited as the material culture. Some painting was done, the designs being mainly geometric. Lines were put on the outside of a tipi, on canoes, moccasins, and paddles. Porcupine quills, those used in embroidery, were dyed, the pigments being made from fungi and berries. Face painting was rare in the past but seems to have become more important following contact with Europeans. The highest artistic development lay in music, although the drum and caribou-hoof rattles were the sole instruments. The tambourine drum, like that of the Eskimo, again suggests the historical circumpolar affinities of these peoples.

Social Patterns

The general diffuseness of interior Athabascan societal organization, the absence of any tribal sense beyond that of common territory and language or dialect, has made delineation of the various groups in the broad area subject to some confusion. But subdivisions of the various groupings there were and it is the subdivision, rather than the linguistically founded major designation, which assumes more meaning (VanStone, 1974:43ff.). No tribe, in fact, had any significant social identity, whether Slave, Dogrib, Chipewyan, or any other. The Dogrib are described as possessing four territorial divisions, frequently called "bands." Yet a review of these local units among the Dogrib shows some fluctuation and movement over time (Helm, 1968:123–124). Similarly, the Slave were divided into territorial and dialect groups, four or five in all, each with a membership of perhaps two hundred individuals (Osgood, 1936b; Honigmann, 1946:64). The suggestion may thus be made that here is a series of population units drawn together by territory, economic purpose, and, as may be seen, by kinship.

A band is a socio-economic unit, a group which moves together in order to exploit the resources of a given terrain. This definition is adequate only to a point and does not take fully into account the realities of aboriginal life in these northern areas. Considerable attention has recently been paid by anthropological theorists to the question of the organization of hunting societies, those marginal socio-economic systems which appear in segments of every landmass in the world. Given a dependence on the fauna of a particular terrain, game with an expanding or contracting population, how do humans organize their social life to meet the demands of the environment? Small populations with utilization of all available manpower, full acquaintance with the land and its resources, along with local social ties are all mandatory.

Within a region (which was generally defined by the drainage patterns, thus permitting movement by canoe in summer and by dog team in winter) local groups came together for some major activity, such as for hunting caribou in the fall, or for intensive summer fishing (VanStone, 1974:45). Such local groups, once the concentrated activity was past, might then return to a more limited area of their own. The problem becomes one of the definition of socio-territorial groups of varying magnitude. The units encountered are fairly easily summarized:

1. Tribe. This, the broadest territorial element, had, as noted above, no primary significance. Tribal names, such as Dogrib or Chipewyan, Koyukon, had meaning only in the sense that commonality of language contributed some notion of identity. The names themselves came to be applied in the postcontact situation when trading posts attracted people from a wide surrounding area. A person might think of himself as associated with the broad tribal group, but other more immediate associations were of greater importance (Helm, 1972:76–77).

2. Regional Band. When it is said of the Dogrib that there were four primary units, each located in a different segment of the broader Dogrib territory, the reference is to a regional unit in which the ecological adaptation is fixed by tradition and time. On this level, the 150 to 200 persons in the region came together periodically for cooperative exploitation of food resources. The size of such a regional band was subject to local variation depending on activity and availability of resources. This was the macrocosmic unit, named, reflecting an identifiable social tie. Such a regional band might consist of some 12 to 50 conjugal pairs, that is, married couples, with their dependents (Helm, 1968:120). The regional band membership assembled only periodically for economic activities and for social and ceremonial reasons, for much of the year its membership was scattered.

3. Local Band. Within the terrain exploited by the regional band was the ultimate microcosm, the functioning local segment. This small unit inclined to concentrate its economic activities within a fairly well defined area, although it could move further afield. A sense of territorial rights was apparently absent in aboriginal times. The local band was made up of from 2 to 12 married couples and their dependents, rarely exceeding 50 persons. These camped together, moved through the local terrain, and periodically joined the regional association with other groups like themselves. Bonds of kinship were operative on this local level, but it is also the case that kinship ties extended to the regional band and frequently beyond. The composition of the local band could change over time with fluctuations in the availability of natural resources as well as changes in membership (Helm, 1968:120; 1972:76–77; VanStone, 1974:66).

On the level of the local band, members could detach themselves in order to engage in a specific or seasonal economic activity. People from one local band might join with members of another to fish, trap, engage in moose hunting, or to go on a trading expedition. A war party, even if war was not highly institutionalized and related mostly to feud and raid, might be considered such a temporary *task force*. The existence of such task groups suggests continuing relations between local bands, associations based on kinship, friendships, and such factors as special skills. The task group could be composed of men only, able-bodied hunters working together with a particular goal in mind, or of locally placed women and children. Married couples could leave the local band, associating with their counterparts from other groups, the women and children to be left at a summer fish camp, while the men sought their own activities. There was no compulsion to stay with the band; it is clear that there was freedom to move in and out as needs and goals dictated.

A band, whether regional or local, had men whose hunting skills and force of personality put them in a position of leadership. As in much of North America, chieftainship was never a formalized institution. The chief lacked enforcing authority as such; his suggestions were followed when he decided the direction of movement or the activity which seemed best suited to the season and moment. Such "chiefs," if such they can be called, lacked even the rudimentary and temporary authority of the Eskimo umealiq, although among the Dogrib there is mention of spiritual power as a source of chieftainship, a reflection of a guardian-spirit experience with some further suggestion of inheritance of the power. But even in the Dogrib case, these chiefs had little authority as such (Mason, 1946:34). Among the Dogrib and Chipewyan, where communal hunting took place, it can be seen that hunt leaders would assume greater importance than among the Slave, where economic activities tended to be more individualized. It is not difficult to picture the place of the hunt leader in any of these societies. Women, children, and older people he might locate for berry picking or at a fishing camp, younger men could be sent far afield for trapping; he could assemble men for any joint enterprise, for caribou drives, for moose hunts, or for intensive fishing and trapping. Even if the chief's role was informal, there was some sense of continuity both to it and within the band itself.

Since warfare, both for offense and defense was not unknown in the area, often resulting from murder and the need to avenge the killing of a relative, war leaders emerged side by side with hunting chiefs. The head of a war party was a "strong man," often a bully, but not especially a respected hunt leader. Regional bands might join together for war, although only temporarily because there was the sense that the war party was an ephemeral task group. Such groups among the Slave are recorded as having fought with the Upper Liard and Mountain Indians. Although the tribe known as the Yellowknives were a western segment of the Chipewyan, they had a history of warfare with other regional groups of this tribe. The Yellowknives also feuded with the adjacent Eskimo and with the Dogrib. The Chipewyan raided into Cree country and were themselves attacked by the Algonkian-speaking Cree. All such hostilities contributed to the movement of peoples within the area. Warfare was mainly by raiding in the early hours of the day, the enemy being unsuspecting. Young women were taken captive, the rest killed. The dead were stripped of their clothing and arms. No

scalps were taken, nor do war honors appear to have been prominent in these societies. A development in the area was the use of armor, more prominent in the west, where it was of the slat type, or of slat pieces with a rod sewn between for pliability, an item appearing both among the peoples of the Northwest Coast and among the Eskimo (Honigmann, 1946:72–76; Mason, 1946:13).

Among the western Athabascans, wealth played a role in leadership and chieftainship. Among the Tanana, for example, Northwest Coast influences reflecting the wealth emphasis came to be important. The result was that those became chiefs who could command a surplus and could enhance a reputation for generosity (VanStone, 1974:49). These same influences are also seen among the Alaskan Eskimo, but are less significant among the peoples of the Canadian Arctic drainage.

Kinship and Marriage. Social relations both within and between bands made for some complexity. There was no sense of genealogy or of extended kinship, largely because the groups in the area tended so to stress the nuclear family. This consisted of a man, his wife—or wives—and their natural or adopted children. Eskimo cooperative patterns, demanding as they did formalized partnerships, were not a feature of this area. Still, attempts to extend the nuclear family by adoption, by capture, in short, by using the ties of kinship to enhance solidarity within the coresident group, were fully as vital. Among the Slave, Dogrib, and Chipewyan, one comes probably as close as possible to the earliest or original form of the Athabascan kinship system. Athabascan kinship terms, wherever they accompany the distribution of the language family, tend to run to a fairly consistent pattern (Kroeber, 1937). The maternal and paternal parents, the grandparents, were merged, but the siblings of the parents were distinguished from each other; that is, there were special nouns for the father's brother as against the mother's brother. An incipient unilineal organization is thus suggested, one which could readily come into fruition as a result of contact with the influence of Northwest Coast or of Eskimo influenced by Northwest Coast. But cousins were called by sibling terms, that is by terms meaning both younger and older brother and sister, a result being that collateral degrees could be extended through sibling terms. Because kinship reckoning went no further than the parents' parents, cousinship did not go very far, rarely beyond the second

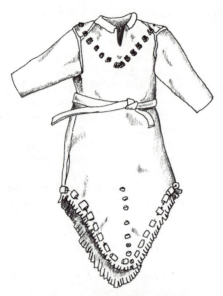

Tanana ● Man's summer shirt, tailed, made of buckskin, decorated with glass beads and red ocher, fringed. Seen here is yet another variation on the pattern of skin clothing, carefully tailored, so characteristic of the native American hunting cultures. (After McKennan, 1959:59. From the Dartmouth College Museum collection)

collateral degree. The kinship system seems thus to bear out the primary emphasis on the nuclear family and to lend added significance to the essentially ephemeral nature of the band.

Like the Eskimo, emphasis could be said to lie in immediate kinship concerns. Unlike the Eskimo, however, there had not developed mechanisms by which extensions to quasi kinship could be made. Mention is made in the literature of wife hospitality, but the implications of such casual sexual relationships are not clear. Both polygyny and polyandry, the latter rare, did take place, and there was a suggestion, characteristic of the whole area, of uxorilocal residence. This implies, in line with the suggestion of incipient unilineal social organization above, that a man came to live in the community or band of his wife after marriage, leaving his own band and of necessity familiarizing himself with a new terrain. Added force was lent to this pattern by the prevailing presence of the levirate, a man inheriting his deceased brother's wife, or at least assuming responsibility for her. If random mating between bands occurred, a man could scarcely occupy a position to effect such provision. The sources are vague on this point. If uxorilocal residence and the

levirate occurred, there must have been preferential mating with bands in a given area. The levirate is lent added force by the kinship system, since a man referred to his brother's children as his own. It is agreed that there was avoidance of cousin marriage, whether to the cross or parallel cousin, although there may have been exceptions. If this is so, the fact of band proximity was unquestionably a factor in marriage. Band endogamy or exogamy was not an issue; the marriage of cousins was. Again, however, like the Eskimo, the problem arose within the group and was censured by gossip and informal controls were operative. What is suggested by the system is that men did not go far afield for their wives, taking them from within the same geographic area and dialect group. No problem arose, since the bonds of formal recognized kinship never went far. Hence, mating with women of nearby bands was the rule (VanStone, 1974:51–54).

In the kinship organization were some joking and some avoidance relationships. In view of the levirate, and its conceptual opposite, the sororate—my husband's brother is my potential husband, or conversely, my wife's sister is my potential wife—a joking relationship existed generally with these relatives, one verging on sex play and sexual innuendo. There was also joking between a man and his father's brother; despite conceptual prohibition of cousin marriage, mating between parallel cousins did apparently occur (Honigmann, 1946:85). Among the Slave, grandparents acted as a socializing force, the result being that there was a close, and often joking, relationship between grandparent and grandchild. Such does not seem to have been the case with the Dogrib or Chipewyan. Some suggestion of avoidance of the wife's mother is contravened by mention of the fact that a man may marry his deceased wife's mother (Petitot, 1891). A man did not avoid his sisters and was indeed expected to provide for them. The pattern of the Eskimo joking partnership apparently did not exist.

Summarizing the formal social organization of the area, it can be seen that the band consisted of related nuclear families brought together under the leadership of a chief hunter. Such families moved in and out and associated with other bands with which they could establish relationships. While kinship did not go far, either in ascending or collateral relationships, there were relationships between the few individuals who made up a band. When marriage occurred, a man first worked for his wife's parents, establishing a right to a wife (bride service) and then remained living independently in the band of his wife. Even here, residence was not wholly fixed, since if a man's parents were destitute, he might bring his wife into his own band. Generally, however, a child belonged to his mother's band, a result of uxorilocal-matrilocal residence and a reflection of the barest beginnings of unilineal kinship. Neither lineage nor clan appear fully fledged in the area.

The last statement does require some qualification. Lineage organization, tending essentially toward the female side, is suggested in the area, although not among the three tribes chosen to exemplify the culture. The Kaska are neighbors to the Slave and possess a dual division (i.e., a moiety system), the two groups being named Crow and Wolf. These were matrilineal and exogamous, they were nonlocalized, and functioned in respect to marriage and to reciprocal feasting (Honigmann, 1949:131–133; Van Stone, 1974:54–57). Actually, this is pretty clearly the potlatch pattern of the Northwest Coast; the moiety names, moreover, are suggestive of that area. Similarly, among the Nabesna (Upper Tanana), while a dual system was in operation in 1930, there is a suggestion of three phratries at a former time (McKennan, 1959:123–124). Here again, the two groups were named Wolf and Raven (Crow) and there was fixed moiety reciprocity, a woman in childbirth, for example, being served by a member of the opposite moiety. To the listing of those tribes which possessed either clan or clans composing phratry or moiety can be added several, the Alaskan Ingalik, other Alaskan groups, and those on the Pacific drainage toward which Northwest Coast influences reached. It is true that the interior Athabascans were receptive to maternal organization by virtue of the special residence and marital patterns they possessed, unilineal organization being implicit in their particularized kinship system. But it took a push from the elaborated societies of the Northwest Coast to send them into a structural formation present in only a highly rudimentary way in the matrilineally slanted band. This is why, in fact, tribes like the Dogrib and Chipewyan reflect greater area typicality than do, say, the Kaska or Ingalik, about which more data are on hand.

Whatever the vagaries of change, even precontact change which was influencing the beginnings of unilineal societal organization, interior Athabascan society offers a practical lesson in terms of the relationships between kinship and territory. Here is the classic case of the hunting culture, one organizing itself around the needs of the environment. The band, whether regional or local, was the primary social entity and the primary territorial unit. It was made up of married pairs, meaning that marriage itself with the implication of the necessary sexual division of labor created the nuclear functioning element in the society. Bilateral descent appears basic (Helm, 1965a).

The Life Cycle. Some consistent patterns appear in the life cycle of the interior Athabascans, customs which have their roots deep in the cultures of western and northern North America. Birth, as among so many of the western American Indians, took place apart from men, even if shamans might work their magic from afar to assist a difficult delivery. They occurred in a special lodge, a brush shelter erected for the purpose. Such lodges might do double duty as places of menstrual seclusion. It is in this area, in fact, that the attitudes toward both the parturient and menstruating woman take on great supernatural importance. It is probably no accident that the Athabascan-speaking Apache of the Southwest make so much of the girls' puberty rite; the distribution of ideas relating to the malefic potential of women giving birth or women menstruating is very wide among the American Indian and may be a very ancient concept. Apart from this attitude, there was little ceremony connected with birth, no special rites surrounding the birth itself, the naming, or the acceptance of the child into the community. Children were kept for about two years in a skin bag lined with moss or rabbit fur. As the child grew, he was instructed informally, boys in the skills of hunting, girls in their role as seamstresses and cooks. The point is important; a sexual division of labor was fully as significant to these cultures as it was to the Eskimo and it followed that the child was prepared for his adult place as man or woman.

Rituals of puberty varied slightly throughout the area, although some patterns are clearly discernible. Properly, there were no puberty rites for boys, no restrictions nor requirement of special behavior. A suggestion exists that boys in some tribes went out at adolescence to seek "power." This was spirit power, to some extent shamanistic power, and may be considered a rather pale reflection of the guardian-spirit concept which becomes so much more emphasized both in the Plains and the Northwest Coast. The Dogrib "chiefs" evidently possessed such power, and it is described for the tribes fringing the Northwest Coast and the Plateau. For girls, the situation was quite different and no little attention was paid to girls' puberty, especially to the onset of the first menses. From childhood the girl was warned by female relatives what could happen and what was expected of her. With the first menstrual period, she left the camp, erecting a special hut, the brush shelter, away from the others. Among the Slave she remained here for a period of about ten days, returning to the hut for a week with each successive period. As she grew older, she might be obliged to remain only for the duration of her uncleanness, for this indeed was the way the period was viewed. The concept was that the woman or girl was dangerous both to herself and to the world at this time. Her diet was limited. Although each tribe had its own sets of taboos, the pattern of food taboo is fairly consistent. Among the Alaskan Nabesna, for example, the girl could eat only liver and kidneys, no other fresh meat, and preferably dried meat and fish. This was brought to her on a bark vessel by other women. Since they were also subject to the menarchy, they could serve her without special danger to themselves. Violation of such food taboos, however a given group saw them, was considered harmful not only to the girl herself, but would be offensive to the animals whose flesh she ate (Driver, 1941).

The complex of menstrual seclusion has a number of associated features which go far beyond the present area. There was a common view that the girl could not look out upon the world during her condition lest she blight it and drive game away. Hence she not only remained in the seclusion hut but often wore a hood or a veil, being careful to keep her eyes cast down. Were the woman to touch a weapon, its potency was wholly lost; were she to lay her body across that of a strong man, his strength and spiritual power would depart. In some of the groups of the Plateau, as a result of this attitude, a cloth or skin dipped in menstrual blood was bound to the cradle board of a child, a powerful antidote against sorcery potentially harmful to the child. The menstruating woman was also restricted in drinking and it was a prevailing custom that she should not bring water—usually the only drink allowed her—to her lips, taking it through a quill or straw. Among the Nabesna, the water could not be drunk cold. The woman was further forbidden to touch her own body with her hands,

being especially warned not to scratch her hair and scalp lest she lose her hair or her body break out in sores. A scratching stick was thus provided. Among the Slave, again reflecting a good many groups, the menstruating woman travelling with a group had to break her own trail and not tread in the footsteps of the band. If water travel were involved, a special canoe might be made for her (Honigmann, 1946:85).

Some groups in the area avoided travelling with menstruating women, not infrequently leaving them behind. Others, while they cannot be said to have made a "festival" or a "coming out" party for girls for their release from the initial seclusion, at least recognized the changed status of a group of girls undergoing the experience during the same season or year. The girls were now nubile and were sought as wives. There were few religious observances among the peoples of the area, excepting again where external influences made themselves felt, but the girls' rite with its associated prohibitions suggests an ancient stratum, a series of practices about which the groups felt most strongly and one deeply rooted in time.

Sexual relations in the area were relatively free. Like the Eskimo, the groups might permit premarital relations as a prelude to settling down to the more or less permanent marital status. Unlike the Eskimo, however, the stress prevailingly on uxorilocal residence, as well as on bride service and in some instances lineage or phratry exogamy, implies a more precise definition of marriage. Adultery was punished by the offended husband who might beat his wife's lover, although again there is the suggestion of the enforcing aid of the kinship group. The Dogrib and northern Chipewyan are, along with some of the others in the northern area, described as permitting wrestling for wives, a strong man taking wives away from a weaker opponent. Polygyny, suggestibly of the sororal type, was not uncommon. As with the Eskimo, the man with plural wives enjoyed prestige as a provider. Wife hospitality did not have the far-reaching implications of partnership exchange as among the Eskimo of northern Alaska. Divorce was not uncommon and was wholly informal, the husband merely leaving the band of his wife. But marriages seem to have been fairly stable, a feature which again arises with a well-defined sexual division of labor.

With the bands of the area moving about in their defined territories, the question of the aged or infirm necessarily arose. Shamanism was the prevailing curing method, but, as among the Eskimo, the sick and old had often to be left behind. Some groups, at least as described by others, were more solicitous of their aged people, or less so, as the case might be. What does seem to have characterized the area was an essentially less dependable supply of food, resulting in periods of famine and starvation. Cannibalism in times of stress, while not unknown among the various Eskimo, seemingly took place more frequently in the interior. In periods of starvation, the survivors might eat the flesh of those who had died, thus preserving their own lives. Still, there was no little stigma attached to such behavior, and it was common in the area that people with reputations as cannibals were pointed at and feared. Among the Algonkins of the Eastern sub-Arctic, such as the various Cree and moving to the Ojibwa, there was the development of a type of insanity, a psychosis affecting those who had eaten human flesh. Such people were said to have become *wittiko* (*wendigo*), and to emulate in their frenzies a mythological flesh-eating giant. Some of this same mythology and the associated attitudes penetrated to the Athabascans.

Death was much feared. Among the Slave, when a person was dying, the whole camp remained awake both to wait for the prophetic power said to be associated with the approach of death and for the sound of the animal spirit associated with the dying person. Never a natural state, death was the result of malevolence and sorcery. The Athabascan attitudes toward death appear intensified among the Navaho and Apache in the Southwest who abandoned the place of death and rushed away in fear. Not quite so extreme, the western sub-Arctic peoples did give up the dwelling in which a death occurred. A pattern of the disposal of the dead runs through northern North America from the Northwest Coast eastward to the Atlantic Algonkins. This was platform burial, either with a structure of poles or in trees. The Slave made log coffins which were suspended above ground or practiced a form of burial, using in the latter case log-lined tombs. Such personal possessions as clothing were placed in the grave. Where Northwest Coast influences appeared, there were funeral feasts, one moiety or phratry feasting another at the time of death. Beliefs in an afterlife were extremely vague. Even where they appear, they may be the result of Christianizing influences (cf. VanStone, 1974:74–86).

Religion. The supernatural was in the main poorly defined. In general, the same attitudes which characterized the Eskimo applied to the western interior, but the same precision, if such it may be called, was lacking. Shared with the Eskimo was the concept of animal spirits as a source of both fear and respect and of power. The latter concept suggests the guardian-spirit belief which appears further to the west and south. Shamanism was also a vital part of religion, as well as having a negative aspect, of witchcraft and sorcery.

Mythology was fairly complex, derived as it was from several adjacent areas. In Alaska and through the north, Raven emerges as the trickster-creator, although in the south, verging on the Plateau, human culture-heroes appear to whom the same feats are ascribed.

Myth lent sanction to the concepts about the animal world. Various animals were especially feared for the power they possessed, and care again had to be taken to avoid giving offense to such economically important animals as the moose and caribou. Among the Slave, wolves and otters were much feared and a wolf was killed only reluctantly. Moose meat could never be given by this group to dogs. The attitudes of respect to all animals carried over to the concept of individualized employment of animal power. Conversely, there were no dramatic group ceremonies such as surrounded the whale or caribou in northern Alaska. The western groups in the area, under coastal influences, or, like the Ingalik, under Eskimo tutelage, tended more to communal feasting in which religious elements played a part. Typical for the area, however, was an absence of feasts and communalism in religion.

With individualism as the essential emphasis in the area, a fact related to the freedom of choice and mobility, lacking even the Eskimo mechanisms of achieving cooperative activity, it can be seen that personal power could become an important element in religion. Such power was sought individually and arose in the animal world. This modified guardian-spirit quest lacked much of the drama associated with that of the Plains. One did not, for example, tell of contacts with one's "medicine" animal, the helping spirit encountered both in visions and in dreams, although one might say which animal it was. Boys were encouraged to seek power, as early in life as possible. A boy would

Tanana ● Drum and drumstick. The
Athabascan peoples of interior Canada and
Alaska shared a number of widely distributed
circumpolar traits with the Eskimo and other
Arctic peoples in Eurasia. The drum type,
although differing in both size and shape from
that of the Eskimo in the Alaskan area, is still
the tambourine, the one-sided skin drum. The
underside was snared for grasping. The
instrument was beaten with a springy stick.
Such drums were used both in social dances
and by shamans. (After McKennan, 1959:43.
From the Dartmouth College Museum
collection)

be told to absent himself from the encampment
and wait until he might perhaps see an animal
which would "tell him something." Power for
hunting, for curing, success in various ventures,
came from the animal world in this way. It is
apparent that all men had power to some degree, stronger or weaker, and for various purposes. Bear power, as an example, led its owner
into curing. There is some suggestion of the
Eskimo pattern of food avoidance with the acquisition of power, usually extending to special
parts of the individual's "medicine" animal.
There is also the appearance of talismans connected with the power animal, charms kept in
boxes or bags. Unlike the Eskimo charms,
which were arbitrarily given, these talismans
came from the vision itself and were intimately
connected with the power animal, thus sug-

gesting the "bundle" pattern of the Plains
(VanStone, 1974:59–71).

Not all the people with curing power became shamans, although they might have the
ability to cure a special disease. A general practitioner, that is, the person occupying the shaman's role, had general powers to cure. As
among the Eskimo, disease and its problems
could not adequately be met by the culture.
There were no herbs, no materia medica. The
shaman diagnosed by asking of offenses to animals, taboo violation, and sought for sorcery.
The concept of intrusion developed among the
Athabascans, so common to much of western
North America, with the result that the shaman
sought to suck out an intruded object, a source
of "pain" which was "shot" into the patient's
body by malevolent beings. This was removed
by legerdemain, the pain object being palmed
or swallowed by the shaman and made to appear or coughed up. The drum was used in
shamanism but was not as well integrated as
among the Eskimo. Sorcery was also practiced
and attributed to those with hatred or evil intent. Since all had power, all were potential curers and sorcerors. Generally, however, evil intent was ascribed to the shamans, especially to
those in other groups. Such patterns imply, of
course, local identification and suspicion of the
outsider, factors unquestionably important to
the cultures. Shamanism was unquestionably
significant, but it lacks the drama of either the
Eskimo shamanism or certainly that of the
Northwest Coast. While there is some suggestion that shamans might sing at various occasions, such as before hunting, and sometimes
in associations with girls' rites, the practices associated with the complex appear essentially
rudimentary and imperfectly developed and integrated.

The problem which the northwestern parts of
Canada and of adjacent Alaska pose is chiefly
that of cultural relationships. Here was an area
of sub-Arctic adaptation, one of inland hunting,
but its principal characteristic is its marginality.
The area is characterized not so much by what
it has as by what it lacks, the cultural groupings within it were essentially impoverished.
Adaptation to the severe winters of the northern continental-type climate, as well as the uniform presence of Athabascan speech, are poor
criteria for the delimitation of culture area, espe-

cially when, in view of the external influences, the various tribes tended to differ among themselves in response to the press of elements from the outside.

Given the marginal character of the western sub-Arctic, the question arises as to whether the classification of the area ought to be seen as a pale rephrasing of the general patterns of Arctic adjustment or whether of the culture complexes of the eastern parts of the continent, those which achieve their greatest development in the maize-raising areas of the so-called Southeast. There is no dramatic transition to the east either in Canada itself or in the area of the Great Lakes. One culture seems to shade imperceptibly into another. On the one hand, as Kroeber (1939:96–101) points out there are elements which suggest again the cultures of the circumpolar zone, such features as the conical skin tent, tailored clothing, or snowshoes and toboggans. Wissler (1938) thinks of the Yukon-Mackenzie as a separate culture area, stressing the dependence on the inland hunting of caribou. Even this, however, does not hold up when the varying kinds of ecological adaptations are considered.

The American Indians are at base a sub-Arctic hunting people, adjusting as they move to new situations and new ecological horizons. This being so, the western sub-Arctic, despite its highly generalized character, may suggest something of the kind of adaptation which for millennia stamped the first comers. The Eskimo were highly specialized with their sea mammal emphasis. Similarly, the Northwest Coast achieved its unique character through its economic mainstay, the salmon. Lack of specialization in the interior posits an archaic strain, and it is this view which justifies a detailed consideration of the region.

Suggested readings

BIRKET-SMITH, K.
1930 Contributions to Chipewyan Ethnology. Report of the Fifth Thule Expedition, 1921–1924, vol. 6, no. 3. Copenhagen.

DARNELL, R., ed.
1970 "Special Issue: Athabascan Studies." Western Canadian Journal of Anthropology, vol. 2, no. 1.

DUMOND, D. E.
1969 "Toward a Prehistory of the Na-Déné, with a General Comment on Population Movements among Nomadic Hunters." American Anthropologist 71:857–863.

HELM, J.
1972 "The Dogrib Indians." In Hunters and Gatherers Today, ed. G. G. Bicchieri, pp. 51–83. New York: Holt, Rinehart and Winston.
1968 "The Nature of Dogrib Socioterritorial Groups." In Man the Hunter, ed. R. B. Lee and I. DeVore, pp. 118–125. Chicago: Aldine.
1965 "Bilaterality in the Socio-Territorial Organization of the Arctic Drainage Déné." Ethnology 4:361–385.
1961 The Lynx Point People: The Dynamics of a Northern Athapaskan Band. National Museum of Canada, Bulletin 176.

HELM, J. and LEACOCK, E. B.
1971 "The Hunting Tribes of Subarctic Canada." In North American Indians in Historical Perspective, ed. E. B. Leacock and N. O. Lurie, pp. 343–374. New York: Random House.

HOIJER, H.
1963 "The Athapaskan Languages." Studies in the Athapaskan Languages, University of California Publications in Linguistics 29:1–29.

HONIGMANN, J. J.
1946 Ethnography and Acculturation of the Fort Nelson Slave. New Haven: Yale University Publications in Anthropology, no. 33.

JENNESS, D.
1958 The Indians of Canada. National Museum of Canada. (First published 1932). Bulletin 65 in Anthropological Series no. 15.

MCKENNAN, R. A.
1969 "Athapaskan Groupings and Social Organization in Central Alaska." National Museum of Canada, Bulletin 228, pp. 92–115.

NELSON, R. K.
1973 Hunters of the Northern Forest. Designs for Survival Among the Alaskan Kutchin. University of Chicago Press.

OSGOOD, C. B.
1936 The Distribution of Northern Athapaskan Indians. New Haven: Yale University Publications in Anthropology, no. 7.

VAN STONE, J. W.
1974 Athapaskan Adaptations. Chicago: Aldine.
1965 The Changing Culture of the Snowdrift Chipewyan. National Museum of Canada, Bulletin 209.

IV

The Northwest Coast

Introduction

Just as the Eskimo suggest a highly specialized adaptation to the circumstances of their environment, so also, although in quite a different way, do the peoples of the North Pacific Coast of North America, a long narrow area stretching from southeastern Alaska to the redwood forests of northwestern California. Unlike most of the culture areas of North America, the Northwest Coast tribes owe little or nothing to the strong cultural influences radiating from Mexico, influences which may still be detected even in so provincial and marginal an area as native California. The particularized configuration of Northwest Coast culture appears to relate, if to anywhere, to eastern Asia, although the cultures themselves became so highly distinctive, so unique, that the area has to be viewed almost as an isolate. More than this, its specialized developments gave this cultural focus a remarkable vigor, one so marked, in fact, that the marginal peoples, such as the western Eskimo, the Alaskan Athabascans, or the tribes of northern California, bore the unmistakable impression of Northwest Coast contact, even if they may be properly assigned to another area. The vitality of the Northwest Coast, its dramatic organization and its inventive spirit, make it one of the most outstanding and at the same time most exciting of the New World culture areas.

The reason for the distinctive developments of the area is not hard to find. The inhabitants were fortunate in locating themselves on the river mouths, the beaches, and the fjords which characterize the coasts of Oregon, Washington, British Columbia, and southeastern Alaska. There were also tribes which settled the many islands off the coast, such as the Queen Charlottes and the large mass of Vancouver Island itself. The sea, abounding in food resources, not only in the prime basis of subsistence, the salmon, but in other fauna as well, became the economic focus of the area. Here were fishing cultures, it is true, but the economic activities were on so vast a scale that it may literally be said that the catches were "harvested." Of agriculture there was none, although some tribes planted an edible clover, and later, tobacco, when it reached the coast from Asia after having made its rapid way around the globe following European settlement of the Southeast. The effects of fishing, dependable as it was, created an atmosphere quite like that appearing among intensive agriculturalists. There were always surpluses of food; mastery of fishing techniques and dominance over nature allowed the native peoples of the area such leisure as to permit in turn continued attention to the non-economic aspects of life. The Eskimo and the interior peoples were constantly preoccupied with the food quest. In the case of the Northwest Coast, since this was never a problem, complexity of social organization in all its forms, of art, and of religion, could and did develop. Further, these institutions took a distinctive direction, one peculiar to the area and reflecting the essential uniqueness of its culture.

The Northwest Coast was not only a well-defined cultural unit, it was a geographic entity as well. The cultural development was exclusively coastal, tied to the sea by the presence of the Coast Range, mountains which rise steeply from the level of the sea with ocean-swept cliffs or the barest foothold along the shore. From southeastern Alaska to Puget Sound the ranges are high, marked by bald granitic peaks rising above the dense coniferous forest. In the north, the high mountains consist of peaks bearing a heavy burden of ice and are "striped" with parallel lines of hanging glaciers. Throughout the area, the glaciers feed the many streams, as indeed does the heavy rainfall. The riverine action, a few fair sized rivers and a myriad of smaller streams, cut the mountain range from east to west. Here and there they have formed canyons which, with an ancient geological subsidence, have produced the cliff-bounded fjord. The land is tremendously rugged with the result that travel through the area, except for some scattered passes, has been unavoidably by boat. From Puget Sound northward the area consists of a spectacular contrast of mountain, forest, and ocean. The great Fraser River empties into the Gulf of Georgia near the modern city of Vancouver, B.C. From here southward through Puget Sound to the mouth of the Columbia and so down the Oregon coast to the borders of what is now California there is a continuation of the coniferous forest, but the mountains become less forbidding and the sandy beaches along the coast suggest the reduction in gradient. Two major types of terrain thus appear (Drucker, 1955:2–3).

Even if there are heavy snows and unmelting glaciers beyond the timber line, the area remains an essentially warm one. Offshore flows the Japanese Current, bringing with it warmer waters and air. The mountain barrier to the interior, the recipient of the benefits of the warmer sea, helps form a pocket to prevent extremes of winter climate. Climatically, the area is temperate. The extremes of heat and cold which characterize the continental-type climates of the North American interior do not appear. Prevailing westerly winds carry the ocean-born vapors which are translated into rain and fog. Rainfall itself is considerable and becomes an important factor in furthering the dense growth of forests. The Northwest Coast is a jungle in a literal sense. Its flora is specialized, with concentration of fir and spruces, red and yellow cedar, yew, and in the extreme southern part of the area, the redwood. The dense forests, along with the rugged terrain, made land travel difficult. The result was that the native peoples lived in relatively small communities accessible to each other mainly by sea.

Just as the flora of the area is somewhat specialized, so also is its animal life. The land animals are many, even if they played an economic role in native life subordinate to those from the sea. Deer and elk abound, and in the higher reaches of the northern and central coast there are mountain sheep. Several species of bear, including the grizzly, and of wolf appear; there are mountain lions and foxes, and a large number of smaller fur-bearing animals, such as otter, beaver, and mink. Where fjord or river leads into the interior, it is possible to hunt animals belonging to the tundra domain, such as caribou and moose. Various birds appear in large numbers, waterfowl becoming especially important economically as they fly along the coasts in their annual migrations. A point of some interest relating to the land fauna has been made. Because of the presence of islands and of isolated segments of the coastal mainland, there are oddly local species and subspecies. The various northern islands, for example, have each their own distinctive subspecies of Alaska brown bear (Drucker, 1955:3).

The native cultures were oriented to the sea even if land animals did play some part in the economy and were important in some phases of religious symbolism. The basic catch was salmon, obtainable in unbelievable quantities. The salmon is an ocean fish but a freshwater breeder. When spawning time comes, the salmon ready to spawn make their way back to the freshwater streams from which they came, leaping falls and overcoming all obstacles in their procreative urge. Salmon species varied slightly up and down the coast, but the native inhabitants could anticipate from five to seven "runs" a year. As the fish made their way upstream, they were ready for the taking. The essential problem faced by the native inhabitants was what to do with the surplus they obtained; this they resolved in a special way. In addition to the salmon, there were runs of herring and smelt, all three possessing commercial importance in the area even today. There was also the run of *oulachon*, the "candle-fish," so called because this little fish is so oily that a string run through it will burn as though it were a wick. For the area, the oulachon was an important source of fish oil. But there were also the great halibut, hooked in the depths of the ocean. Some groups hunted seals and sea otter, while some also practised whaling. Even if the maritime products were not too diverse, they were to be had in such quantity as to create the wholly dependable supply of food which characterized the area.

The point has been made that environment does no more than pose a series of limitations on activities of men. It provides raw materials for living. But the human understandings inherent in the concept of culture as employed by anthropologists may move in a direction quite out of keeping with the natural environment. One can readily note that the human-land relationship on the Northwest Coast was in many ways a factor in the kind of cultural development which took place there. A food resource such as the salmon, for example, required more or less fixed residence. There were at least seasonal periods when everyone in a community was obliged to be present and to devote himself wholeheartedly to capturing, cleaning, and preserving the catch. Permanent houses and settlements were a result even if men could at times go afield for other kinds of hunting on sea or land. But the very kind of hunting which the Northwest Coast peoples developed created a vast surplus. This they chose to equate with a concept of wealth, an institution which becomes a major leitmotif in all the societies of the area. Nature, it is true, provided the basis of the surplus and so permitted a fairly large population growth for the entire area. But the adaptation also allowed periods of freedom from economic activity. The native cultures and societies moved as a result to a high degree of complexity.

TRIBES

One of the difficulties which the Northwest Coast poses—one true of several other areas as well—lies in tribal delineation and naming. While there is general agreement on the designations applied to the major ethnic groupings, it is less easy to define "tribe," especially when it is considered that while villages were focal, there was intervillage visiting, feasting, and occasionally, reciprocal obligations. There were groups which had a sense of identification through community of culture and language, or more precisely, dialect. The area was much split linguistically, and while several major languages are apparent (providing the basis of the commonly used tribal names), for practical purposes, intercourse tended to exist between villages of the same dialect. This was not always true, but sufficiently so as to give a sense of subtribal divisions within a linguistic and so tribally designated group.

A second question on the tribal distribution of the area, remembering that it stretches over a considerable distance on a north-south axis, but remains essentially coastal and so very narrow, relates to tribal regional location and focus. The culture characteristic of the area seems to reach its highest concentration and integration in the north. This suggests in turn that the center and south show slight variations of a northern pattern. They are perhaps not quite so wholly typical. In any case, following Kroeber, it may be useful to define the various subregions of the area and to list the major tribes characteristic of each.

Regional phrasings of Northwest Coast culture (cf. Kroeber, 1939:29–30)
1. Northern Maritime (Tlingit, Haida, Tsimshian).
    1A. Northern Maritime Mainland (northern Tlingit; neighbors to the mainland west are the Eyak [Ahtena] of the Copper River Delta, an interior group with Athabascan affinities which pushed to the sea and became marked by Northwest Coast culture. Beyond the Eyak, one again enters Eskimo country, that of the Chugachmiut).

1B. Northern Maritime Archipelago (insular Tlingit, Haida, and Tsimshian, the latter also appearing on the mainland. These groups and this area represent the focal center of Northwest Coast culture).

1C. Northern Maritime River (Niska, Gitskan, Haisla).

2. Central Maritime (central coasts of British Columbia to Cape Flattery at the northwestern head of the Olympic Peninsula. The landmass of Vancouver Island is included).

2A. North Central Maritime (Kwakiutl, Heiltsuk, Bella Coola, Bella Bella).

2B. South Central Maritime (Nootka, Quinault, Quileute, Makah, possibly Chehalis).

3. Gulf of Georgia (Gulf of Georgia Salish, including Comox, Cowichan; and other coast Salish [cf. Barnett, 1955, 1939]).

4. Puget Sound (Skagit, Lummi, Klallam, Twana, Snuqualmi, Puyallupe [Collins, 1974]).

5. Lower Columbia (Chinook, Tillamook, Alsea, Chehalis).

6. Willamette Valley (Kalapuya).

Each of the above geographic regions might allow individual treatment. In each there are slight variations in land form, in flora and fauna, in rainfall distribution, and as a result some difference in the exploitation of natural resources. The northern and central zones are well defined in terms of ethnic groupings and cultural orientations. The southern reaches, however, pose difficulties both of cultural delineation and of tribal designations. Authorities are not wholly in agreement and it is necessary to exercise some arbitrary judgement. Nor, it must be stressed, is the above listing to be considered complete, especially for the south. Culturally, the south, from Puget Sound through south coastal Washington, the lower Columbia basin including the Willamette Valley, along the mountains and coasts of Oregon until the specialized configurations of northwestern California are reached, suggests a maritime variant of a generalized Plateau pattern. There is a clear suggestion of cultural affiliations with the Northwest Coast further to the north, it is true, especially in the wealth complex, but the southern regions offer little more than a pale reflection of the vitality so characteristic of the northern and central focus of the culture area.

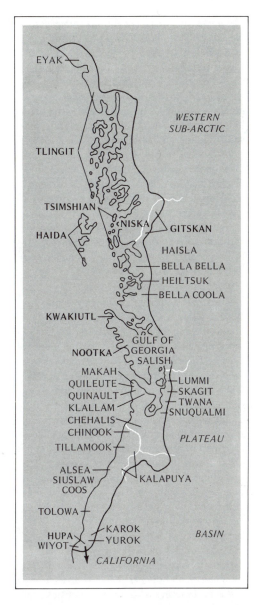

B ● Northwest Coast

A further perspective on the peoples of the area can be had from an examination of the language relationships. These have proved fairly complex, not only because several quite separate linguistic phyla are represented in the area, but also because in some instances it has been problematical to relate them to some of the better defined families of the rest of North America. The Northwest Coast offers an example of peoples speaking quite diverse languages who nonetheless share a common base of culture.

Northwest coast tribes and language groupings
Lanugage family—Na-Déné (Great Athabascan),
   see Chapter 2

The Tlingit, spread from Yakutat Bay in
Alaska over the islands and mainland to Cape
Fox, were divided into fourteen tribal
groupings, all speaking a language related both
to Eyak and to interior Athabascan. The
subfamily can be identified as *Tlingit-Eyak-
Athabascan.* The northernmost Tlingit group is
the Chilkat, a tribe or subtribe noted for
blanket manufacture and lending its name to
the Chilkat blanket, the outstanding example of
weaving art in the area.

The Haida, residents of the Queen Charlottes
and of southern Prince Rupert Island, speaks a
Na-Déné language which forms a subfamily of
its own, the *Haida.*

Language family—Penutian

This language phylum, subject to some
questions as to its overall internal relationships,
is spread along the Pacific Coast, with strong
representation in California. Subfamilies are the
*Chinook-Tsimshian, Coos-Takelman, Klamath-
Sahaptin, and California Penutian* (cf. California).
Tsimshian, neighbors to the Tlingit and Haida
and like these culturally, belongs to the
Chinook-Tsimshian subfamily. Chinook, on the
lower Columbia, forms the other branch. Coos-
Takelman moves down the Oregon coast, while
Klamath-Sahaptin is largely represented in the
area of the Plateau. Returning northward to the
Tsimshian, several tribal entities are represented
in the Tsimshian-speaking area, among them
the Gitskan and the Niska.

Language family—Mosan

Of subfamilies there are two—the
Chemkashan, consisting of Wakashan and
Chimakuan, and the *Salishan.* Mosan as a major
linguistic grouping is somewhat problematical.
There is a possibility of a remote affiliation
with Algonkin but any conclusions regarding
this relationship remain tenuous.

Wakashan appears as the major linguistic
grouping of much of the central regions of the
Northwest Coast. It is represented mainly in
Kwakiutl, including Haisla, Heiltsuk, and
Kwakiutl proper. Bella Bella, Nootka and
Makah also belong to the Wakashan branch.
Chimakuan appeared among the extinct
Chemakum and among the Quileute, cultural
neighbors of the Makah. The third subfamily is
Salishan, a linguistic grouping spread over a
wide area from the Bella Coola on the
mainland north of Vancouver Island, through
the Gulf of Georgia into Puget Sound and so
into much of the Plateau area. Salishan thus
includes the Bella Coola, the Quinault, the
Comox, Lummi, Cowichan, Twana, Puyallup,
Klallam, Snugualmi, Chehalis, Skagit, and
moving down the Oregon coast, Tillamook.

If the Mosan relationship stands, whether or
not it may ultimately be assigned to Algonkin,
the indication is of diverse languages, even
though distantly related, which suggest the
spread of peoples in the area in considerable
time depth. This point is also borne out by the
prehistory of the Northwest Coast. Shell
mounds, up and down the coast, both
extensive and deep, show habitation over a
long period of time.

The above are tribes and peoples about whose
culture fairly extensive descriptions exist. The
many subdivisions, local variations, and the
range of tribal names bar a wholly exhaustive
listing. Unquestionably, one strong reason for
the ethnic complexity lies in the nature of the
terrain. Coastwise travel being of necessity by
boat, local settlements were placed on readily
defended beaches, river mouths, and inlets. The
result was an autonomy of local group, or at
best, of local area. Different ethnic strains appear to have moved into the region at various
times, a fact supported by the linguistic variability. Moreover, as one moves from north to
south along the coast, there are differences in
physical type, those in the north being taller
and more linear than the somewhat stockier
southern groups. There is also evidence of mixture of the various physical types and of one or
two unique physical features, such as more facial hair and, occasionally, lighter hair and eye
color than is true of most American Indians
(Drucker, 1955:16–19). Although language and
physical types varied, these aspects of the area
are completely overshadowed by the dominant
culture patterns themselves; the vigorous sets of
common institutions strikingly overcame the
barriers of language difference and geographic
isolation.

Prehistoric Background. The prehistory of
the rich Northwest Coast tribes is shrouded in
uncertainty and speculation, even controversy.
So little archeologic investigation has been done
that controlled excavated data are lacking. The
many ethnologists who have studied these
spectacular cultures worked before radiocarbon
dating was known and before the time depth
of the Archaic was even suspected. So far as reported work is concerned, there exists no

archeological information about prehistoric cultures antecedent to the historic cultures found from Southern Alaska to the Washington and Oregon coasts with one outstanding exception. This is the incredible Ozette site at Washington (currently being excavated by Richard D. Daugherty). At this location an ancient village, radiocarbon dated at about A.D. 1450, was recently discovered. Like Pompeii, it was covered and preserved in a few hours by a geologic event; in the case of Ozette, however, the event was not a volcano but a massive mud slide which engulfed the village, filling and covering a number of houses along with all their rich contents. Weapons, household implements, personal ornaments, and foodstuffs all were preserved in the moist germ-free environment; the large plank houses were still there, although not always standing. The artifacts range from fine woven textiles to wooden clubs for killing seals. Excavation has been done with hydraulic equipment; the enveloping mud has been washed away rather than dug. The deposits and artifacts testify to a diet largely dependent on the sea—whales, sea otter, seal, fish and shellfish. The historic importance of sea mammals seen in the ethnology is established in Ozette as being ancient.

As for the earlier archeological horizons or traditions, the data are extremely scanty; the few hard facts come from excavations in British Columbia and Washington (Borden, 1962; Campbell, 1962; King, 1950; Sanger, 1967). While interpretations differ, all the evidence points to at least 3000 years of West Coast exploitation of both sea and land mammals to 4000 B.P. or earlier, and the cultures can be equated with (perhaps derived from) the Southern Arctic tradition (see Collins, 1960, 1964; Laughlin, 1963a). For example, Collins lists distinctive artifacts as "oval and round stone lamps, whaling with poisoned lance, the detachable barbed head with hole in tang more important than the toggle harpoon head, composite fishhooks and stone sinkers, specialized forms of slate blades, emphasis on decoration of clothing and the person, high development of woodworking, painting, and especially of weaving."

Borden (1962) reports the Marpole and Lecarno phases, where ground or polished slate blades, points, adzes; and the rocker knife or ulu date back as far as 2900 B.P. Thus, a sea-riverine economy can be shown on the Northwest Coast earlier than the Alaskan Okvik-

Thule sequence of the Maritime tradition. Although his archeological data can be accepted, Borden's complicated interpretation involving interior Canadian contribution to the final rich and elaborate cultures is less persuasive. It is simpler, and markedly more convincing, to derive the cultures from the ancient ones that had a preoccupation with the sea going back to the Aleutian-South Alaskan cultures recorded for Anangula and Umniak islands as of 6000 B.P. or earlier.

This conclusion must suffice because until more systematic archeology at ancient Tlingit and Haida villages is undertaken, it can only be postulated that the Northwest Coast cultures are much older, by thousands of years, than the early writers suspected and that the flamboyant historic cultures are derived from an ancient maritime tradition of comparable richness.

TLINGIT, HAIDA, AND TSIMSHIAN

Northwest Coast culture, considering its depth, vitality, and its totality of integrated patterning, is unquestionably best represented among the peoples to the north, both those on the mainland and on the extensive islands adjacent to the coast. This northern configuration, differing somewhat from the central regions of the area both in social organization and in the ways in which wealth and religious life were structured, is equally represented by the three major groupings of Tlingit, Haida, and Tsimshian. Although there were a few slight differences between the three, their basic patterns of life were essentially uniform. The three tribes can serve as a model for the area, and it may be understood that in the center and south there were rephrasings of the patterns characteristic of the northern tier. The culture, while basically the same throughout the area, remains strong in the center, although many of the institutions are given a reinterpreted cast, and begins to pale out in the south. Thus, in the center, there is a shift away from the maternal institutions of the north in favor of paternal, while the secret society assumes somewhat greater importance. At the same time, however, such material aspects as house and canoe types, and especially art, retain much in common. Tlingit, Haida, and Tsimshian, considered in detail, with attention to some of the main points of difference between them, exemplify the Northwest Coast culture area. It is worth calling attention to the contrasting differences encountered in the center and south of the area.

The Tlingit, it will be recalled, occupied the coast from Yakutat Bay to Cape Fox, settling both the mainland and the islands off the coast as far south as the northern half of Prince of Wales Island. Aboriginally, the northern Tlingit had an estimated population of 2500, while the southern branch, both on the mainland and on the islands numbered 7500. The Haida were exclusively maritime, settling the Queen Charlotte Islands and dispossessing, according to tradition, the Tlingit from south Prince of Wales Island two centuries ago. The Haida numbered 9800. The Tsimshian proper, inhabiting the mainland and the near islands abutting the coast, were about 3500, while their linguistic neighbors, the Gitskan and the Niska on the Nass River, had about the same number. As may be noted, populations for the area were relatively large, the three major groups numbering at the time of contact about 27,000. Insular as against mainland distribution made for some differences in density, the greatest population concentration being that of the Haida (Kroeber, 1939:135).

It may be noted that roughly the same proportion of population applied to the central and southern reaches of the Northwest Coast as well. There is a sharp increase, however, at the lower reaches of the great waterways, the Fraser and the Columbia, the Gulf of Georgia Salish and the Chinook showing some comparative increase. While the population of the general area cannot be regarded as unusual, it may be noted that it was relatively considerably higher than that of the Eskimo or of the interior peoples, a point unquestionably related to the wholly dependable food supply (Oberg, 1973).

Economy and Technology

The abundance of marine life and the presence of the forests were the two primary influences in the life of the peoples of the Northwest Coast. This was no less true of the Tlingit, Haida, and Tsimshian, whose diet was based primarily on the products of the sea and who, like other tribes, were basically wood users. Both features underlie the distinctive character of the native cultures.

It was the use of wood, in fact, so distinctively applied in the area, on which housing, containers, handles and shafts of tools and weapons, canoes, and virtually all aspects of

material elements depended. The Northwest Coast house was a tremendously impressive structure, especially so among these three northern tribes, what with its gabled roof, its massive size, and its distinctive "totem pole." This is the area of the totem pole, a distinctively carved and highly specialized form of native art. Reserving its description for the moment, it may be noted that here again is a wooden item, one relating to the complex artistry of the area.

A Haida, Tlingit, or Tsimshian village was approached from the sea. The village itself consisted of a row of massive communal dwellings on a beach or lagoon above high water mark. The entrances faced the sea. In some of the larger villages, where a short stretch of beach could not accommodate a single line of dwellings, houses were placed in two and sometimes three rows. Visible first were the totem poles, the posts which stood at the gable end of the house, where the entrance was also placed. A not unusual practise was to depict the bottom figure of a 40- to 60-foot pole with its mouth open, this elliptical hole forming the door of the house. In addition, there might be other poles, either memorial or related to graves—that is to the boxes holding corpses or the ashes of the dead—complex in carving and standing at various points in the village.

A great deal has been written about the impressive architecture of the Northwest Coast. Here were permanent houses, built to last, which involved no little effort on the part of artisan and artist. Houses were equated with wealth and with the patterns of reciprocal exchange relationships so vital in the social structure. An average house could measure 40 feet in length by 30 feet in width, although larger houses were known. Much larger festival houses have been described for the Puget Sound area although these lacked the precision and the craft which went into the houses of the Haida and their neighbors. Before erecting the house, the area selected was cleared and measured with strands of cedar-bark rope. Although formalized measurements were lacking, sufficient skill had been acquired to permit exact estimates of the posts, beams, siding, and roof.

And here in fact was where the woodworking skills of the Northwest Coast peoples came to the fore. Logs had to be selected, trees felled, and both split into planks and beams. In the north, the yellow cedar provided the soft, readily workable wood, red cedar was used more extensively in the center and south of the area. Felled logs were preferred and trunks of these huge trees were sought after a storm, but the men skilled in the woodworking craft were quite capable of felling a tree, frequently drilling into it first as a test of its soundness. Logs were sometimes rolled to the water and ferried downstream to the village site. The northern Tlingit, in whose territory cedar was less common, traded with others both for logs and bark. A log was split into planks, such planks also being split off a standing live tree. If necessary to fell a tree, a carefully controlled fire was built into an excavation at the base. This was especially true for trees selected as canoe hulls. Any small log was capable of being cut into several planks.

The preparation of the planks which formed the basis of the elegant houses of the region suggests a complex assemblage of tools. Actually, this was not so much the case. Tools there were, stone adzes (but not axes) and chisels, both hafted into wooden handles, stone mauls, stone carving knives, bone drills, and wooden wedges. There was a minimum of stone for tool making in the area, the result being that many tools were of hardwoods, such as yew, the material from which bows were also made. It was skill and knowledge, rather than an array of tools, which underlay technical excellence. Logs were split with wedges, made of hardwood rather than the sheephorn which marked the central regions. Logs were burned off at the desired lengths and then split from the end with a series of closely placed wedges graduated in size, the largest away from the worker. These were tapped with an unhafted stone maul. The result was a series of boards, remarkable both for their thinness and for their width, the latter reflecting the remarkable size of the cedar trees of the area.

When the area selected for the house had been cleared, holes were dug and four to eight upright planks were eased into them by means of rollers. Planks were morticed into the uprights to form the gable angle and the corner posts were joined by heavy horizontal planks at top and ground level. These were slotted so that the boards making up the siding could be slid into them. A heavy ridgepole, raised by rocking the log chosen over a temporary log scaffolding, was held in place by center posts. These were frequently carved, and the one in front perforated for an entrance. The totem pole

of the house, if such was to be erected, usually involved an additional outlay of wealth, the house itself requiring considerable expenditure, and was often put up some years after the structure was completed. It rested against the central post supporting the ridge pole. When the framework was completed, and this might stand for some time before the necessary wealth was amassed to finish the house, it was ready for the siding of cedar planks forced into the slotted horizontal plates. Such siding boards were often "bent," steamed and forced so as to overlap and form a perfectly weathertight wall. Several roof types were employed, one of double boards, another of bark and boards, or a third of bark layers alone. Lacking windows, the house depended for light on a roof well and smokehole. This could be opened or shut as required by an arrangement of sliding boards. The entire structure depended on notching and morticing; no pegs or "nails" were used.

The northern houses were often built over an excavation. This was rectangular, conforming to the general shape of the house itself. Among the Haida, perhaps the most superb architects of the region, eminent chiefs are said to have had several tiers of benches from the floor at ground level down to the central pit. All floors were carefully finished with planks. Across the ground level floor at the back of the house, away from the entrance, were the sleeping places of the families of the eminent men. Frequently, these were made as apartments, set off from each other by mats or even with small replicas of the greater plank house. It is worth noting that the constellation of a bench opposite the entrance, a roof aperture, a central fire pit associated with an excavation is suggestive of the house types of other areas. Despite different materials, the affinities of this house type to others in western North America and possibly to the general configuration of semisubterranean houses in Northeast Asia as well may be suggested. The question, however, remains open (cf. Olson, 1927:30–31).

The entrance to the houses of the northern tier of tribes, especially that of the Haida, was flanked on each side by carved posts which formed a short passage leading to the interior itself. By these were kept gear for immediate use, such as fishing gear, canoe paddles, and weapons, not excluding suits of mail. The wooden box was a universal item of furniture on the Northwest Coast, and these were seen

Bella Coola, British Columbia, ca. 1901 ● The
gable-roofed house, despite the glass windows,
retains the general style of the area. The mythic
thunderbird is placed at the peak of the house,
while an essentially modern totem pole is set
in front. The thickness of the cedar roof beam
is noteworthy, as are the fishnets drying in the
foreground. (Smithsonian Institution National
Anthropological Archives)

in abundance in every house. The boxes were
made of single planks of cedar, carefully
scraped, scored, and bent up with steam. The
sides of the single piece could then be pegged
together or sewn with cedar fibers. A lid was
made separately. These boxes, some of them
quite large, met a great variety of needs and
were used even as mortuary urns. They were
carved and painted and in the household
served to store foods. Lined up on the ground
level near the entrance, they held fish oil, roe,
seaweed, and berries. Such boxes also appeared
in the sleeping places assigned to the various

nuclear families resident in the house. Some
held family food, others clothing, dishes, and
various personal possessions. A family consisting of husband and wife and small children
had its place, with bedding of furs and skins,
its mats, these both covering the floor and
being used to set off the individual rooms or
apartments, and its ubiquitous boxes. Women
cooked separately for their families, sharing the
central fire.

A large splendid house such as the Tsimshian, Haida, and Tlingit possessed could be
inhabited by several nuclear families, as many
as ten or a dozen. Why they chose to live together in this way relates intimately to the general social organization and is noted below.
Suffice it to say that there was a concept of related families sharing the same or adjacent
houses. A single house, in fact, could be regarded as a village in itself. It sometimes was.
Villages were small and it was rare to find a
community with more than a dozen such communal houses. Economic factors unquestionably

played a part in size of settlement. The natural resources available as well as the manpower necessary to exploit them contributed to community size, although such aspects as defense and social rank and status, so important to the area, had also to be taken into account. Ideally, a village consisted of several separate houses. The village remained a place of permanent residence, complete with its houses, its carved poles, its fish-drying racks, caches, and sweathouses. All economic activities proceeded from the community. If families left from time to time to fish, to gather berries, or to hunt, some members generally remained behind at the house. Men might leave for various seafaring expeditions, including sealing, halibut fishing, and war, while women had their own economic activities. The village thus retained a central focus in the lives of the people. There was a well-defined sexual division of labor and periods of intense economic activity. But the movement which characterized the seasonal ranges of the Eskimo and the interior Athabascans was not so precisely defined.

Travel, since it was so exclusively by water, required the canoe. The occasional travel to the hinterlands for hunting or berries, or along a few well-defined trails between villages, was by foot, and even here the canoe was preferred where possible. The northern tribes were masters of canoe building and distinguished as many as seven different types of canoe. The most impressive was the so-called war canoe. This, while it might be used in warfare, was also involved in the ceremonial visiting which took place between communities. The Haida especially were masters of this type, building the craft from a single log of red cedar as much as 60 or 70 feet in length. The log selected was hollowed out with adzes, then half filled with water which was heated with hot stones. When the wood had been softened in this way, stretching posts of gradually increasing size were forced into the sides so that the canoe was widened. Projecting elements, the bow and stern, were then added, being fitted carefully and "sewn" to the hull with cedar ropes. The perforations drilled to hold the vertically placed prow or bowsprit and the built-up stern were then caulked. The projecting bows served to repel wave action in rough water to prevent swamping. The canoe owner painted his crests on the craft and often added carved figures at the bows. This type of canoe could carry sixty men and as many as three tons of cargo. The

canoe was paddled with leaf-shaped paddles with a crutch-top handle. The steersman in the bows had a longer paddle. A question exists as to whether sails were aboriginal. It is likely that they were not. They were used, and made either of very thin planks reinforced with strips of wood and sewed at top and bottom or of mats. Two canoes could be lashed together and a plank deck laid over them, a pattern reminiscent of Polynesian practise. Unlike the Polynesians, the Haida and their neighbors did not venture far into the open sea. They were not whalers like some of the central and southern peoples and restricted their travels to the coasts.

Other canoe types were generally manufactured according to the same specifications, consisting basically of a dugout; those larger, though not so large as the war canoe, were made with a fore and aft superstructure and sometimes with "sewn" gunwales. As the range of types is considered, there might be noted also a double-ended, the same in bows and stern, for sea hunting, a big bowed craft for short trips at sea, and a small canoe for river travel. Cedar- and spruce-bark canoes have been noted for all three tribes. It may be noted that the large canoes were especially related to the northern sectors of the area; the Nootka, also noted as fine navigators and as whalers, built a different type with a vertical stern and a projecting prow. In general, the dugout principle applies to the area at large.

Canoes were a basic element in the economic life of the area. The entire coast specialized in fishing, developing an extremely complex set of implements for the purpose. It can in fact be said that each fish in the native economy had its special methods of capture and its specialized implements. Salmon were the most important source of food, followed by halibut, herring, smelt, and oulachon. The salmon were taken seasonally, during the salmon runs, when the fish came into the fresh water to spawn. These fish were netted at the beaches at a stream mouth with nets and harpoons, the latter a small arm or projection with a single detachable point of bone or horn containing a single barb. Drag nets were used at stream mouths, while weirs were placed along deeper water in the streams. The weir was a fencelike structure built of wicker and laid across the stream. The fish were taken in baskets set as traps behind the weir. Various traps, consisting of gill nets, baskets, and such devices as dams over which the fish were forced to leap, were used. Platforms, often erected over streams, were used by fisherman for getting close enough to gaff and net the tightly packed fish as they moved upstream. Good salmon fishing spots at the mouths of streams and upstream were owned, a reflection of the attention given in the area to ownership and thus to rank. As the salmon runs began, people frequently left their home communities to camp at the fishing places, men engaging in the fishing, women in cleaning, splitting, and drying the catch.

Sea fishing from canoes was also important. Salmon will strike at a baited hook in deep salt water; angling for these as well as for halibut was an important economic activity from spring to fall. Hooks were of many different kinds. The northern halibut hook was a "bent" piece of yew or cedar, forced into U-shape with a lashed bone or horn barb. Smaller hooks were used for cod, dogfish, and sometimes for herring. The halibut, largest of the ocean fish known to the area, and running often to two hundred-pounds and more, was caught with a hook baited with octopus, using lines of braided or knotted kelp, bark, or fibers. The canoe was anchored with a stone, two or three lines run out, each with a sinker and a float. With a strike, the fish was played, drawn alongside of the canoe, gaffed, and dispatched with a special halibut-killing club. Lures and baited hooks were also used for trolling from canoes.

Dip nets, seines, rakes, and open-mesh baskets were used to capture herring. The rake, a board with horn points, was dragged over a shoal of herring from a canoe, impaling the fish. The oulachon, running at various seasons, were taken in much the same way as salmon with weirs and nets. These oily fish tended to localize, such as at the Nass River in the north. The Tlingit and Haida came here to trade for these fish, the sales made by the Niska who owned the rights to fishing stations along the river. Fishing was thus a full-time activity, one carried on principally from spring to fall, with the winters reserved in the main for noneconomic activities. In addition to the actual fishing, there was gathering of many products from the ocean. These included shellfish of various kinds, clams, crabs, mussels, edible seaweeds, fish roes, octopi, and many others.

Hunting and gathering of various wild foods contributed materially to the diet of the area. Berries were gathered in great quantities by women and stored in boxes, often with rancid oulachon oil, dried, pounded into fish to make

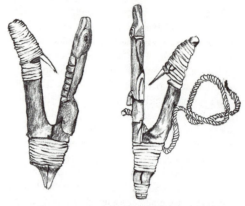

Haida-Tlingit ● Halibut hooks. These were made of spruce branches, steamed into a U-shape, and reinforced; the barb is of bone. The hook was weighted at the end of a line of giant kelp and attached to a short rod. The hook was sufficiently springy to allow the halibut to insert his snout to take the bait. (cf. Drucker, 1955:30. Adapted from photographs, courtesy of The American Museum of Natural History)

a pemmican. Many species of berries were gathered, as well as some roots and tender bark, which, scraped and steamed, were stored and prized. Clover and skunk cabbage were eaten as a kind of salad. There may have been the beginnings of the cultivation of clover, especially by the Kwakiutl. Clover patches, in any case, were privately owned, the same being true of the problematical tobacco.

Hunting, while clearly secondary to the fishing complex, was fairly inclusive. Deer were lured with whistle calls and shot with arrows, bows of cedar and yew being the common types. Large and small bows were for the different types of animals hunted. Bows were unbacked and soaked in oil. Deer were also snared. Deadfalls and nooses were important to the trap assemblage. Bears were taken, either trapped or treed by dogs and shot with arrows. In the treatment of the bear is a suggestion of the bear cult of the circumpolar regions. Special songs had to be sung and efforts made to avoid giving offense to the "Bear People." Sea mammals were hunted for their pelts as well as their meat. Seals, sea lions, and otters were approached and shot with arrows. Sealing in the open sea was also practised, involving a harpoon with detachable head and a float, a pattern not materially different from that of the Eskimo. Quite apart from the bear ritual, there

Makah whale hunters bringing a carcass ashore at Neah Bay, Washington ● The whale is supported with seal-skin floats. While none of the tribes of the southern Northwest Coast were as technologically elaborate as those further to the north, the same general styles, as, for example, in the prow of the canoe, prevailed. (The scene dates from the 1920s. Smithsonian Institution National Anthropological Archives)

was a strong feeling that a hunter should purify himself before taking game. Sweat bathing, fasting, sexual continénce, and avoidance of water were parts of the behavior associated with preparation for hunting—and for war as well.

The food of the area was generally cooked. Salmon and herring roe was often eaten raw as was fresh salmon at the time of the runs. Fish and meats were broiled at an open fire on upright sticks, or boiled. Boiling was done in a watertight basket or a wooden bowl by the familiar method of stone boiling, hot stones being dropped into the water-filled container until the water was brought to a boil. Salmon and halibut heads, roe, and some other foods were allowed to putrefy in boxes and became delicacies. Salmon and other fish, split, dried from racks, or boxed with oil, offered means of developing periods of leisure and a strong institution of hospitality. Food, because of its pro-

fusion, came to underlie the institutions of wealth which so marked these societies. Of privation there was none; the culture was marked by abundance. Caches of food, racked, cached, boxed, and stored were present in quantity in every village. The odor of decaying fish and rancid oil lay heavily over each one.

Food and its preparation and serving involved not only the large storage boxes but other utensils and containers as well. Basketry and wooden vessels were in common use; there was no pottery. Baskets, made generally of spruce and cedar root, as well as cedar bark, were twined. A variety of shapes and types was made, including watertight baskets and openwork baskets which served to store dried salmon. Geometric patterns of dyed elements in the basket were usual, although crests or crest elements were sometimes inserted, also in geometric form, the materials and the nature of manufacture requiring retention of angular designs. The best watertight baskets, those most finely woven, actually come from the far west, the peoples of the Aleutian chain, those related culturally both to the Eskimo and the Northwest Coast, having been noted for the excellence of their basket weaving. Twining was the usual method of basket making among the Tlingit, Haida, and Tsimshian, although coiling, sewing together rings of rods to form a container, was characteristic of the Salishan peo-

Haida ● Carved hardwood club for killing harpooned seal and hooked halibut. (cf. Drucker, 1955:31. Adapted from photographs. Courtesy of The American Museum of Natural History)

ples. The coiled baskets are suggestive of the Plateau and areas to the east and south in North America. Basketry hats were general in the area. Weaving of matting and the making of basketry and textiles lay in the domain of women.

Dishes were made of wood. Troughs, trenchers, and bowls, those for ceremonial use elaborately and beautifully carved, were made of roots, alder wood, and of beryls. There were dishes for daily use while in feasts, guests were given not only the food they were unable to consume, but the dishes as well. Carved bowls of workable slate and steatite, "grease bowls" for holding oil, began to be more common with the advent of metal tools. Spoons and ladles, both of wood and the horn of mountain sheep, were much in evidence. For ceremonial use, the sheephorn ladles, beautifully carved and molded with steam, were much in demand. The horn was traded widely up and down the coast.

True textiles were known to the native groups in the area and different types of weaving practised. The base of textile work lay in spruce roots, wild hemp, and cedar bark. These materials were soaked and spread, the fibers separated and the strands rubbed by the hand against the bare thigh, a common means of cordage making among many of the native American peoples. Braided, such cordage served for ropes and strings. The northern peoples wove from a frame with a suspended warp, although more elaborate techniques, using a simple loom, were known to the Salish. There was considerable variety of woven materials. Blankets and robes of bark, the softer inner barks of red and yellow cedar, of bark and animal fibers, as well as many different kinds of mats offer a marked range of both material and technique. In the northern area, the distinctive woven feature was the so-called Chilkat blanket. Associated with the northern Tlingit, this blanket may possibly be of Tsimshian origin. It was made of the wool of the mountain goat which was spun and twined over a core of cedar bark string. Men hunted the goat for the wool, made the frame, and owned the blanket designs, painting a pattern board from which the women, the weavers, took the design elements. The blankets, in colors of white, black, yellow, and blue, with different design fields to represent the component crests, represent the high point of the weaving art of the north. The Salish, though perhaps more skilled as weavers, did not reach the same artistic heights, but used in their weaving a greater variety of materials, including duck down and the wool of especially bred small dogs which were periodically sheared.

Clothing among the northern tribes generally followed the patterns of the area. It was unique to the area and centered more in ceremonial than practical garb. Only the northern Tlingit made use of tailored garments of buckskin with leggings and moccasins, following in this instance the clothing of the interior Athabascan groups. Elsewhere, remembering that the area is not subject to undue ranges of temperature, preference was for minimal clothing. The Tlingit, Haida, and their neighbors assigned a breechclout to men with a loosely fitting buckskin shirt, made of one or two pieces. Women wore much the same shirt, sometimes lengthening it to a slip, and in colder weather, a buckskin shirt. The center and south preferred shredded bark garments of much the same type. For winter use, robes and blankets, often fitted with thongs, were worn as an outer garment. General in the area was a bark poncho, a single-piece raincoat, usually worn with a tightly woven basketry rain hat. Although fur was used to decorate many of the cloaks and robes, fur garments, again in the form of robes, were used principally by men of status. The head was usually bare, basketry and wooden hats being reserved for festival occasions. Footgear was practically nonexistent and was limited to simple moccasins worn for interior travelling.

Body decoration and personal adornment was fairly well developed. Ear pendants and nose pins were common, the septum being pierced for the latter. The labret, lip plug, was worn in perforations through the lower lip by both men and women. Face painting was common, both daily for cosmetic purposes, and more elaborately for ceremonies. The northern peoples, especially the Haida, painted the heraldic crests on the face. The Haida, however, stressed tattooing, especially for the highborn, making a ceremony of the operation and tattooing crest designs on the arms and legs, the back of the hands, and the chest. Such tattooing was done with charcoal and the color was introduced into the skin with a needle and dyed thread. All tribes in the area knew tattooing, but most appear to have preferred face and body painting, making designs of blue, black, and red. Women braided the hair and wore it down the back in two plaits. Men left their hair free, shearing it at shoulder length and wearing a headband. Men plucked out body and facial hair with shell tweezers. Both sexes decorated the body freely, giving much attention to personal appearance. Bathing was common, not only the ceremonial sweat bathing, but general washing of the hair and body. The hair was smeared with bear grease and often perfumed. Combs were used for hairdressing but not worn. For ceremonial preparation, the hair was washed in stale urine which served as a detergent. The Tsimshian made use of a slate mirror, pouring water over the slate to reflect the image. Jewelry, necklaces and bracelets, as well as the earrings and nose ornaments, were common. Armbands of copper, hammered "cold," of fur, shell, and other materials were widely used. From the Kwakiutl southward, although not practised in the northern sections, there was head deformation. This was done to infants by means of boards pressed against the forehead or designed to taper the head. The practice has also been noted for sections of the Plateau. Shaping the head in this way, common to a number of peoples in the world, seems to have no damaging effects.

Tied up with clothing was the personal array of arms and armor, war being a not unimportant institution in the area. Bows and arrows were of course used in warfare, but there was a variety of weapons used for fighting at close quarters. Clubs, daggers, and thrusting spears or pikes were regularly used. Although the sinew-backed bow was known, it proved less practical in so damp an area. The same bow was used for larger game as for war. The northern peoples made arrow shafts of cedar, tipping the arrow with ground bone or shell. Double-bladed daggers were common, made of whale-bone and there is also some suggestion of pre-European iron, a possible link both in material and form with a Siberian iron-using complex. A picklike club or war hatchet was the so-called slave killer but there were also swordlike warclubs. These, among the Kwakiutl and Nootka, took on the character of heirlooms. They were named and had histories which were recounted as the club was displayed. In war, a sling with a basketry pocket capable of throwing large stones with telling effect was regularly used. Armor was common. In the north, it consisted of several types, the most common being a cuirass of rods sewn with sinew and rawhide. This is the so-called rod-and-slat armor which has a wide distribution in North America as well as in northeast Asia. The northern tribes also employed hide armor, while strips of elk hide were used in the center of the area to wrap the body and limbs. There were also helmets of wood, usually carefully carved, fitted with separate visors.

As the elements of material culture on the Northwest Coast are reviewed—and it may be understood that the foregoing descriptions are by no means exhaustive—several points stand out. The basic dependence was on the sea for subsistence and on wood for the majority of the items in the material array. In terms of the purely tangible aspects of the cultures of the area, these two adjustments lent a peculiar distinction, creating a uniqueness for the Northwest Coast among the cultures of the American Indian. Yet it is again worth stressing that the distinctiveness of the area lay in degree rather than in kind. While such patterns as gift giving, the guardian-spirit experience, unilineal social organization with mystical animal associations, and many other features, including the house type, might suggest that the Northwest Coast cultures offer a marked departure from general—and particularly western—American Indian practise, the basic complexes appear to

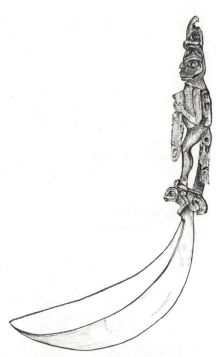

Haida ● "Gravy spoon" of mountain sheep horn. The Haida traded with mainland tribes for sheephorn and carved ornate ladles in line with the traditional artistry of the area. In this striking example, an anthropomorphic supernatural, mounted on a frog and surmounted by a raven head holding salmon, makes up the handle to the spoon. (From the Department of Anthropology collection, University of Minnesota)

be variations of some widely spread features common to many American peoples. The Northwest Coast is fundamentally an American culture area; its special location and its exploitation of abundant natural resources allowed it to achieve cultural specialization in depth. Such specialization was no more than an intensive and localized phrasing of some basic American traits. A few suggestions of Asiatic influences exist, to be sure, but there can be no agreement with the contention that East Asiatic or even trans-Pacific contacts are more important to the area than basic American configurations (cf. Donald and Mertton, 1975).

The Organization of Society

The general area of the Northwest Coast suggests at first glance a remarkable diversity in its societal arrangements. Yet at the same time,

there are some common threads which run through the area. These, although they might be given a slightly different slanting and phrasing by local tribes, are sufficiently precise as to allow some exactness of definition. The economic circumstances of the area, providing such remarkable abundance and ease of life, led in turn to a concept of wealth, to a kind of primitive capitalism in which worth was accorded him who was born to wealth and who then could validate his position by effective employment of wealth. This concept remained uniform through the focal regions of the area even if the ways in which the place of wealth was realized differed slightly from group to group. Some corollaries of the wealth notion arose in the concept of social ranking, in family background and descent, in the cooperative activities of kindred and household groups in amassing and maintaining wealth, and also in the artistic representations of the symbols of status, that is, in the heraldic use of crests which formed so vital a part of the dramatic art of the area. The wealth idea touched all phases of Northwest Coast life; it was this institution which served to create an integration of all social aspects. While the purely formalized features of society can readily be described, they must be seen against the leitmotif of wealth.

The Tlingit, Haida, and Tsimshian possessed a unilineal type of social organization. Characteristic of the northern segment of the area was matrilineal descent, a pattern which differs in the center and south. As one moves through the various cultures of native North America, a considerable range of societal type is encountered. The northern segment of the Northwest Coast thus stands in sharp contrast to the Eskimo and interior Athabascans in this regard. Social organization here was essentially bilateral, although it is worth noting that some of the western Eskimo as well as some of the Alaskan Athabascans had begun to adopt unilineal organization and wealth display and exchange under the strong influences of the Northwest Coast.

Along the entire Northwest Coast there was no sense of nation. There was no idea of tribal territory and although there were chiefs, they were never paramount chiefs or "kings" who might weld together a tribal political unit. Tribes were language groupings. But in addition, even though political unity was lacking, there arose a sense of common purpose and identification through the bonds of relationship. Each unit was organized into precisely defined kinship group-ings. Although these varied in their organization along the coast, they contributed to the stability of the tribal cultures.

The Tsimshian, Haida, and Tlingit, as well as the Haisla, employed the principle of matriline-al descent, meaning that the individual be-longed to a group by virtue of descent through the female line. Correlated with this and similar unilineal descent structures is the principle of exogamy, "marriage out" of the group in which one has one's primary kinship orientation. A man's father was thus in a grouping different from his own. Not that relationships through the father were ignored, but the grouping to which the individual belonged consisted of those related to him through females—the mother, the mother's sisters, decendants through females of the mother's mother, and beyond. The Tlingit and Haida were each orga-nized into two major matrilineal groupings. In other words, the tribes were each split into two major segments or sections. This is commonly referred to as a *moiety* system, one in which the tribe, in its social organization, was "halved." These moieties were highly formalized, named, strictly exogamous, and matrilineal.

Among the Haida, the moieties were called "Raven" and "Eagle" (cf. Swanton, 1905:62ff.; Murdock, 1934). Their primary purpose was the regulation of marriage, a Raven man marrying an Eagle woman or the reverse. There were some services which the members of one group performed for members of the other, al-though this was on a local rather than an in-clusive tribal level. These reciprocal obligations involved house building and conducting funer-als. The moieties were interdependent and there was some sense of rivalry between them. Each moiety had a series of origin myths and a strong sense of descent from a mythological an-cestor. It was this, in fact, which underlay the definition of kinship between members of the same moiety and which enforced the rule of exogamy. Actual kinship between the moiety members was purely fictive and dependent only on mythological definition. Each moiety had the rights to certain crests, names, rituals, and privileges.

While the moiety system cut through the whole Haida tribe and was thus operative among those speaking Haida and allying them-selves with one or another moiety, the more important social units were subdivisions of the moiety. In general, these were local, coresident groups, consisting of groups of actual rather than fictive relationship. Sometimes called "clans," these might more accurately be termed lineages. This group was purely local. Generally it consisted of a village with several house-holds. Occasionally, a single house might repre-sent a lineage. These lineages were named, and each had chiefs. The highest ranking house chief was the chief of the lineage. The group owned rights to areas of economic importance, such as berry and fishing grounds. It was es-sentially politically autonomous, although lin-eages might unite for war and the different lin-eages might feast each other. At the same time, it was not impossible for lineages within the same moiety to engage in feuds with each other, a point indicating that it was the lineage rather than the moiety which assumed impor-tance in the areas of daily life. The lineages must thus be regarded as the primary func-tional unit, although household and nuclear family also played important parts in the social structure.

The subdivisions of the moieties, like the moieties themselves, were matrilineal. But be-cause the communal house, so important to Haida life, was built and managed by males, and because, too, the various rights and privi-leges of status coupled with the use of crests passed into male hands, a socially complex sit-uation arose. Given matrilineal affiliations, it might be expected that uxorilocal residence might logically follow, as indeed it does among many of the world's peoples with similar uni-lineal institutions. This means that a prospec-tive husband would leave his mother's group and, following marriage, reside with the lineage or clan of his wife; his children, by the rule of matrilineal descent, then assuming residence and membership in the group of their mother. But the institution of prestige economy so char-acteristic of the Northwest Coast tended, among the northern tribes, to work against such an arrangement. To gain an impression of the kinds of social relations which existed be-tween lineages among the peoples of the north-ern tier of the Northwest Coast, it is necessary to consider the problems inherent in a matrilin-eal society which stressed the investment in males of certain kinds of rights and privileges. Residence following marriage was intimately linked with the moiety and the lineage subdi-visions of each moiety. The situation is one which has been termed an avunculocal organi-zation. This becomes clear only when the various units are considered and the relations between them appraised.

The house, so important to the life of the area, was communal. In it resided related males, those reckoning their relationship to each other through females. With them lived their wives, and sometimes their daughters even after they were married, and their very young sons. Each nuclear family—a man, his wife, their young children—had its own place in the house, one generally dependent on rank below that of the household chief, the highest ranking person in the house. Some four to ten such nuclear families, all related to each other, representing two and three generations, thus formed the household, an extended family.

The women of the extended household came from the opposite moiety and from other lineages within it. Their children, by the strict rule of matrilineal descent, took the moiety and lineage affiliation of their mothers. At marriage, a man frequently allied himself with the household of his wife's father. This is not so complex as may at first blush appear. Marriages were made with care. Not only did social rank and status have to be considered, there were some preferred forms of mating as well. A man generally married his cross cousin. How this was arranged has in the main to be understood in terms of matrilineal descent, especially as it related to the moiety system.

The marriage-residence arrangements stress the special relationship existing between a man and his mother's brother. Rank, status, and property passed not from father to son—this would involve the transfer of goods and privileges across moiety and lineage lines—but from a man to his sister's son. Moreover, a special relationship existed between the two, maternal uncles becoming social and spiritual sponsors, tutors, in effect, to the sons of their sisters. This is not to say that a father was indifferent to his own sons. On the contrary, the father played an especially benign role toward young sons and at a later time gave feasts for his sons, although in his wife's name. But a boy left his paternal household at about the age of ten and thereafter resided in the household of his mother's brother. This created a close psychic tie between a man and the individual designated as his mother's brother. Any male relative in the lineage and generation of the mother was classed as her brother. A man's father, in turn, had a special relationship to his own sister's sons. This special relationship between a man and his mother's brother is designated an avunculate. The resulting arrangement, among the Haida, and true of the Tlingit as well, created a lineage emphasis on males related to each other through females. The lineage, with its involvements of households, has thus been termed, because of the mother's brother emphasis, an avunclan or avunculineage (Murdock, 1949:72–73).

The preferred form of marriage was thus between a man and a daughter of a mother's brother, the cross cousin. Cross cousins are the children, respectively, of a brother and a sister. When it is remembered that a man took his moiety and his lineage membership from his mother, the brothers of his mother, as well as the sisters of his father, would have been obliged, by the strictly held rule of exogamy, to marry into the opposite moiety. Their children, in turn, would take the membership of their own mother and marriage with daughters so placed was not only legal but preferred. Cross cousins thus stood in opposite moieties. By the same reasoning, parallel cousins, the respective children of brothers or sisters, would fall into the same moiety. Such parallel cousins, in fact, were classified as brothers and sisters, a point to consider in appraising the general mother's brother relationship. Groups of related men, on the level of maternal uncle and sister's son, of brothers, and of parallel cousins resided together and formed the extended household unit as well as the avunculineage at large.

Marriage between a man and his female cross cousin, the daughter of his mother's brother, tended among the Haida and Tlingit to be limited to chiefs. Here was a direct transmission of rank and privilege to an heir. A daughter could hold the titles for a deceased father under such circumstances, passing them to her husband, her cross cousin, at marriage. A man frequently married the daughter of his father's sister, the patrilateral cross cousin. The Haida stressed a special relation to the father's sister, the pattern paralleling the avunculate and often termed an amitate. The sister of the father was called on in many occasions in an individual's life to act in a ceremonial capacity. She assisted at the birth of her nephew's children, at his marriage, and at funerals in his lineage and moiety. For such services she was given gifts. From her nephews she expected courtesy, protection, and generosity. A ceremonial relationship of this kind was another effective way of keeping alive the sense of balanced relations between one's own and one's father's lineage. The daughter of a woman designated as a father's sister was a potential wife. In the Haida language, the kinship term, *sqan,* referred to women of the father's lineage and generation, the paternal aunts. But the term was also extended to include the women of one's own generation, the cross cousins, daughters of these paternal aunts. With them, as a group in the lineage of the father, some premarital sexual freedom was permissible. Since they also married one's brothers, there was a good deal of banter and play with these sisters-in-law, or, as the case might have been, potential sisters-in-law or wives. Before his own marriage, a man could have semisanctioned sexual relations with his brother's wife. A so-called joking relationship between a man and his brothers' wives, his own cross cousins, involving banter and some license, is a common development in social relations of this kind.

Residence after marriage, considering the nature of the moiety system, gave the individual several choices. He could live with the wife's father. If this individual were of the same lineage as the mother—he did not have to be—he was a classificatory mother's brother. He could ally himself with a mother's brother in any case, residing in his house, along with his brothers and male parallel cousins. The wife was thus brought to her husband's matrilineage and resided there. Her children, of course, took her moiety and lineage affiliation. It was this factor which required that a boy of ten leave his parents and live with his mother's brother. The end result was the system of avunculocal residence which characterized both the Haida and the Tlingit.

The general moiety-lineage pattern is reflected in the terms employed by the Haida (and Tlingit) to designate kinship relationships. The system was of the so-called Crow type, or more specially, the avuncu-Crow, referring to a special structuring of kinship terms concordant with matrilineal and avuncular organization. The relatives of the mother were distinguished from those of the father by special sets of terms. Within the lineage, the mother and her sisters were grouped together and referred to as "mothers." A special term existed for the men defined as "mother's brothers," one different from the term used to designate the brothers of the father. It has been noted that the term *sqan* referred to the sisters of the father and also to their daughters, the patrilateral cross cousins in

one's own generation. A separate term existed for the matrilateral cross cousins, sons and daughters of the mother's brother. Brother and sister terms were used to designate parallel cousins in keeping with the moiety-lineage affiliation. The upshot of such a system of nomenclature is to lay stress on the kinds of existing relationships. The term employed for "mother" means in effect "woman of my matrilineage in the parental generation," the mother's brother term "man of my matrilineage in the parental generation." *Sqan* referred to women of the father's matrilineage regardless of generation, although of course behavior toward women so classified differed.

Some precise sets of behavioral rules governed relations between kinsmen. Grandparents were benign figures, for example, both on the maternal and paternal sides. The relations between a man and the mother's brother with whom he resided involved mutual aid and support. One helped one's mother's brother in amassing property and could count on him in assembling one's own wealth. His house was a sanctuary and appeals could be made to him and through him for protection. Brothers were expected to give each other aid, as were parallel cousins. A man and his male cross cousin stood in a kind of partnership relationship, engaging in various activities together. Mention is made above of the joking relationship with the female patrilateral cross cousin. Brothers and sisters, after puberty, were expected to avoid each other; when married, they treated each other with great respect and reserve. The residence arrangements, in any case, precluded their sharing the same house. Avoidance was also extended to the wife's mother, again a paternal aunt. These women were always treated with reserve and respect, despite the permissive play allowed with their daughters. Despite the pattern of such mother-in-law avoidance, the two could live together fairly amicably in a large communal house. Between an uncle and niece there was also reserve. Since a man's daughter-in-law was also his niece in most instances, the pattern of avoidance was also in general practice (Murdock, 1934).

The avunculineage, consisting as it did of males related through females and their wives, was a social unit as well as a political one. Since, among the Haida, at least, it tended to be a localized segment, sometimes retaining associations with lineages in nearby communities, its organization centered in a village.

Each village had its chief or series of chiefs, since there was a chief in every house. The village could be fairly large with several rows of houses, or it could consist of a single dwelling. Numbers are somewhat difficult to estimate, but at the period when Haida culture was at its height, as many as 30 to 50 persons could inhabit a single house. If a village became so large as to be impractical for fishing or hunting, splits could occur in the matrilineages, and sublineages could move away to new sites. In time, the sense of the earlier associations might be lost. In this regard, the Tlingit differed from the Haida. Tlingit lineages tended to retain the sense of linkage. The result was that a sense of nonlocal relationship was kept and a clan, again within the moiety, developed. The clan as a subdivision within the moiety incorporated several lineages which, because of common myth, a sense of common history, and crests, tended to fix the interrelationship between lineages somewhat more precisely.

For Haida and Tlingit, it is possible to offer a general summary of the units to which an individual belonged.

Nuclear family (This consisted of a man, his wife, sometimes wives, since polygyny was permissible though rare, and young children. Boys left early to reside with the maternal uncle; daughters stayed until marriage, although the son-in-law might come as a house resident, he and a daughter forming another nuclear family.)

Extended family (The avunculocal, coresident household. In terms of the daily life of the people, this was important not only because of the close relationship of the men within it, but because the household members worked together, were involved together in fishing, hunting, and other economic activities, and cooperated in the amassing of wealth. The highest ranking male in the house was the household chief. The women, except for the unmarried girls, were from other lineages and the opposite moiety. The household and its associated extended family engendered a strong sense of loyalty; women generally remained loyal to the group of their husband even in the event of strife or a feud between his lineage and their own.)

Sublineage (Such formed only in the event of a group being obliged, by virtue of demands for space to separate from a village and form a new village and sublineage unit. The former association might be kept for a generation or two and then dropped.)

Lineage (This was the local avunculineage usually coterminous with a village. It had its rights to hunting grounds, berry patches, and fishing places. It also possessed ranks and titles along with the important crests. Each house in the lineage had its chief. The chief with highest rank among the household chiefs was the paramount village and lineage chief, a man bearing some special title, such as "village mother," or "village owner.")

Clan (Tlingit only, in association with moieties. The Tsimshian had more inclusive clans which functioned like the Haida and Tlingit moieties. In the Tlingit, this was a major subdivision consisting of several lineages which were associated essentially permanently on a basis of common tradition and symbol.)

Moiety (The twofold division of the tribe which served to regulate marriage and to order the various lineages in one or another section. These were Raven and Eagle among the Haida, Raven and Wolf among the Tlingit. The Tsimshian lacked moieties, see below.)

Tribe (A linguistic grouping in a definable region. Dialect divisions might create subtribes. Like the moiety, the tribe had no political significance but it was important in providing the limits of organizational and culturally defined activity.)

In terms of social organization, the Tlingit were much like the Haida, except that the lineages, as noted above, were grouped into clans. These in turn were aligned with the moiety divisions, Raven and Wolf. Tlingit Wolf and Haida Eagle had many crests in common and there may be some ultimate historical relationship between them. In cases where intertribal relations occurred, especially where intermarriage might take place, an attempt was made to effect an equation of social unit and rank between the two tribes. Despite the presence of formal clans among the Tlingit, linked lineages in effect, it was the lineage which had the basic functions of rights, property, and titles.

Turning to the Tsimshian, while the same general principles of societal organization were in operation, the moiety system gave way to a fourfold division, both among the Coast Tsimshian and the Niska. No longer a moiety, a "halving" of the group, the units regulating marriage were Eagle, Wolf, Raven, and Killerwhale. The last was inclusive of black whale (Blackfish) as well, and was sometimes called Bear, in view of extensive use of bear crests by the lineage subdivisions within it (Garfield,

1951:19). The Gitskan, upriver Tsimshian, had corresponding divisions in Frog-Raven, Wolf, and Fireweed. A fourth Gitskan grouping, although local, was Eagle. These were equated, both in terms of rank and the use of crests, with the coastal divisions. These units, functioning exactly as did the Haida and Tlingit moieties, have variously been termed as phratry or clan. The Tsimshian reflect the Haida lineage pattern rather than the linked lineages or clans which the Tlingit established under each of their moieties. Among the Tsimshian, as among the others, the lineages were local, possessing chiefs, rights, and property, and were ranked within the four main clans. The fourfold division cut across the nine coastal Tsimshian tribes. Lineage, however, remained local with the result that the chief of the lineage of highest rank became a kind of tribal chief in each of the nine components of the Tsimshian. Clan association was matrilineal, resulting again in the feature of avunculocal residence.

Reference has been made to the use of "crests," the heraldic devices, the blazonry, the coats-of-arms—not, indeed, unlike those of medieval Europe—which related to title, to rank and status, and to authority. The art of the area, complex as it was, requires its own special treatment and section (see below). Suffice it to note here that political position, as well as social status, related to the use of such crests, animal figures brought together in various conventional ways. The Haida, Tsimshian, and Tlingit lineages had the rights to certain crests. Their use related both to the lineage as a whole and also to expressions of status by the use of crests by members of the higher social statuses within the lineage. What is suggested is the principle of grading of society.

It has been customary to think of the Northwest Coast as an area marked by rigid, caste-like social strata. In general, the division into chiefs, nobles, commoners, and slaves has suggested a precise hierarchy. There were slaves, it is true, war captives or their descendants, whose status was fixed at the bottom of the system of social ranking. For the rest, however, the line between chief and noble, or that between noble and commoner, was most vague. To some degree, every individual was a noble, at least every person had certain hereditary privileges. These were inherited, it is true, but they required in general some validation through wealth. Birth and wealth together were factors in defining status but the employment of wealth to formalize such status permitted

some slight mobility, upward or downward in the scale, either for one's self or more likely, for one's sister's sons, at least in the northern tier. The end result was the emergence of wealth as vital to the system of ranked statuses characterizing the area.

Within a given lineage, among sublineages, if these were recognized, within a household, there were graded statuses. The highest rank in a lineage was accorded the oldest male in direct line of descent from the lineage founder. Genealogy was important, although stress was laid on the mystic associations in such genealogical reckoning, the relations with the animals whose names and crests were borne by the group. The highest title in the lineage by virtue of descent was thus held by the lineage chief. Below this there were other titles, such as those accruing to sublineage heads, to household chiefs, and so down through the entire lineage. This pattern created a series of gradations within the lineage itself. The lowest person in the group was one who was most distantly related to the lineage founder. Although the native peoples of the area recognized a distinction between noble and commoner, the suggestion being that some people were obviously of higher worth than others, it may be said that in theory, at least, all who were not slaves were nobles. Even those low down in the social scale had the rights to certain names and could participate in ceremonials and exchanges. In practice, however, "poor" people, ne'er-do-wells, or individuals who were unable to define their social position with sufficient exactness, as might occur when a major segment of a lineage died out, were little better than slaves.

On the level of the chiefly status, or for that matter, among nobles, there could be no equality of rank. Descent and wealth as well as traditional ranking combined to make one individual higher than another. Persons could rise or fall slightly in social status, but there was general agreement on what a title was worth and the place in the hierarchy which it gave its holder. The Northwest Coast has been described as an area where individualism was a keynote. This is actually not the case. While it is true that there was a sense of rivalry between chiefs, there was some sense of their working together to maintain the interests of their class (Garfield, 1939:183). But actually, the members of a lineage worked together to support their chief; it was clearly to their advantage to do so, since their prestige rose and fell with his. The several kinds of chiefs, household chiefs, lineage chiefs, in the case of the Tsimshian, chiefs of the subtribes, had considerable power over their following. They directed production and work as well as the products obtained. They also had a marked responsibility to their following. They were expected to be proud and overbearing to outsiders and those counted as their rivals, but on the home scene, they were obliged to be humble, gracious, and generous. They received from other chiefs gifts through the wealth feasting. These they were expected to share with their following. To fail in maintaining loyalty and support might lead to secession of a group to form a new community and sublineage. Purity of birth and the maintenance of wealth again underlay the notion of chieftainship on whatever level.

A chief succeeded to a title through his mother's brother in the northern tribes. Actually, while the title passed on in this way; his heirs presumptive were his own brothers. They in turn passed the office on to the eldest son of a sister. When there was no male successor, a woman could act as regent until the office could be filled. While ideally the eldest eligible person succeeded, a man could be passed over by common consent if he failed to be effective as an organizer, a speaker, or in his qualities of leadership. When a man did succeed, birth created his eligibility, it is true, but the position demanded public validation. Put another way, the individual was born to rank, but this rank had to be validated by a wealth-distributing feast which his parents gave. When the individual then sought to manifest his status, that is, to effect formal justification of his rights to privilege, he also had to provide such a feast. This could be identified as a funeral or commemorative feast for one's mother's brother or one's older brother, the individual from whom one inherited. Failure to do this did not mean that the individual lost his rank, but he suffered loss of status in the eyes of his group. Rights to a title, whether of chiefly or noble rank, had to be validated initially by the parents. Among the Haida, for example, when a boy left his paternal household to reside with his maternal uncle, his father, in the name of his mother, directed a feast for him. The mother's lineage collected wealth and presented it to the father's lineage for the boy. His right to inheritance was thus assured. The wealth-distributing feast, the *potlatch*, indicates the use to which wealth in the area was put.

Moving down from the chiefly status to the nobles and so-called commoners, title and right were assumed in much the same way. In the northern sections of the area, they passed regularly through the female line. Again, no two titles, however superficially corresponding, were quite equal. Within a fairly limited geographic area where people of different lineages and tribal segments came together for feasting, genealogies, relationships, and status were features known to all. So important was the cultural preoccupation with rank and status throughout the area that it can readily be seen that considerations regarding them took paramount attention. Direct lines of descent and proper validation guaranteed high title and chieftainship; lesser ranks were increasingly further removed from such direct lines, as, for example, through descent through younger sisters or by virtue of various collateral kinds of relationship and descent. Since status was thus commonly agreed upon, everyone's rank was more or less fixed. The point is emphasized in respect to seating at a feast or in the conferring of gifts, where protocol was strictly followed and where the most valued gifts were given according to an estimate of the worth of the recipient (Barnett, 1938:354). A newly conferred title, movement of people, or enslavement of those of high title might create some disagreement as to place in an essentially fixed ranking. A man of low title who was valued for skills, such as in carving or in war, might be given a title and the rights to certain crests by a chief. This changed his ranking. A way to avoid according rank to a person of lower status was to confer the title not on the man himself but on his sister's children. In general, the northern tribes stressed the hereditary right with the result that there was little vertical mobility. To the south, as among the Bella Coola, more attention was paid to such mobility (cf. McIlwraith, 1948).

Slaves stood at the bottom of the social scale. They were common up and down the Northwest Coast and known in the Plateau as well, possibly as a result of Northwest Coast contacts. Slaves were obtained by war. Enemy groups, those with whom feuds existed, were raided as were occasionally some of the interior peoples. The slave class was essentially a group apart. Its members were owned outright and lacking in rights. It is of interest to note that the Northwest Coast was perhaps the only area of the world where a nonagricultural society possessed the institution of slavery. As an institution, it was well integrated. Slaves were valued for the work they could contribute and for the prestige they accorded their owner. They lived in the house with their masters, were permitted to marry, and were accorded much the same position as the poorer members of the lineage. However, the children of slaves were slaves. Thus, while not necessarily mistreated, the slave occupied an insecure place. He could be killed at the whim of his owner and often was. Among the Tlingit, for example, the body of a slave was put in the posthole dug to receive the heavy house posts. A sacrificed slave was also often put under a totem pole at its erection. This was not human sacrifice in the religious sense, but rather a reflection of the notion that men of wealth and prestige could afford to dispense with valuable property in so important an undertaking as housebuilding. It is recorded of the central Kwakiutl that slaves were sometimes killed on the beach to make "rollers" for the canoe of an esteemed guest.

Slaves, although some were recruited from tribes outside of the culture area, were generally war captives. Ownership often indicated both success in war and command of wealth. When a member of a neighboring group was enslaved, no effort was spared by his kindred to ransom him. Should his lineage or household fail to do so, they were all stigmatized by the epithet "slave!" Once ransomed, the former captive was obliged to undergo a series of ritual cleansings to remove the taint of slavery. He was then reinstated to his former position but the stigma frequently remained. His former status was never wholly recovered no matter how many face-saving feasts he might give. Men of enemy groups, especially those of high status, were sometimes kidnapped and held for ransom. Slaves did not escape; it was only through the formal payment of ransom that a return to the former status could be achieved.

The emphasis on wealth on the Northwest Coast had its implications for both trade and war. Trade regularly took place among the lineages of the various tribes. A chief would outfit a canoe, inviting men of his lineage to bring the goods they wished to dispose of. Chiefs of two groups would then meet, exchange gifts, and the trade would proceed. It is, however, difficult to distinguish patterns of trading from those of feasting. Trade of some products—slaves, Chilkat blankets, unsmelted copper, and foodstuffs—regularly took place between groups which had established virtual trading partner-

ships. Thus the Haida traded with some of the coastal Tsimshian but waged war on others. Trade was thus formalized and took place as much for preserving good relations and thus enhancing the prestige of men of rank as it did for the commodities involved.

War was both for revenge and for plunder. A lineage, operating on the premise of collective responsibility, felt obliged to defend and avenge its members. On an interlineage or intertribal level, this took the form of continuing feuds. Single lineages might be engaged, but several lineages might unite under the leadership of a high ranking chief, one in fact who might instigate the war party. Canoes were fitted out, armor donned, and ceremonial preparations made. Sexual relations had to be avoided, among the Haida at least, for a month before starting out on war. While the war party was out, the wives of the warriors were obliged to observe restrictions at home. They could not touch their husbands' property, they sang war songs, and were obliged to sleep as though curled up in a canoe. Although pitched battles might occur between enemy groups, as between canoes, the tendency was to surprise in a night or roundabout attack. The enemy was massacred or enslaved, their property taken, and scalps and head trophies brought back. Conflicts between groups which might burst out in wars and feuds could be settled by payment. In such cases, arbitration was made and the full amounts of payment agreed upon. It is worth noting that in paying for lives taken between groups, each paid the full amount; there was no cancellation and payment of difference. The element of property display, again a vital feature of the wealth complex, was important, so much so, in fact, that no occasion was missed where this could take place.

The difference between war and feud was negligible. Large-scale attacks, reflective of a war pattern, received the same attention as less inclusive feuds. The rationale lay in the legal sanctions developed generally in the area. The lineage presented a united front against outsiders and was morally bound to avenge wrongs perpetrated by an outsider against any member. Within the lineage, murder or other wrongdoing, such as sorcery or incest, was a matter of in-group decision. Between lineages, however, action had to be taken. Arbitration, rather than open warfare or feuding, was preferred. Thus if a man of low status from one lineage killed a man of high status from an-

Tlingit potlatch ● Alaska, ca. 1880. This old photograph conveys some impression of the finery worn at so important an occasion. In the left and center may be noted the designs of the Chilkat blanket, woven by women of mountain goat hair according to the crests owned by men. (Smithsonian Institution National Anthropological Archives)

other, the affronted lineage demanded an equivalent in revenge. In such cases, the murderer might go free while one of his higher ranking relatives was killed in his place. Since the two men involved, the man murdered and the man selected to stand in for the murderer, were not of totally equal rank, some further compensatory payment had to be made. After a murder, spokesmen for each lineage met to determine whose life should be forfeit. The man selected stood in his house waiting until his executioner, a man chosen for the purpose, should come for him. The two then fought a mock battle until the man atoning for the murder was slain (Oberg, 1934).

It is evident that some divisive elements were at work in the social structures of the Tlingit, Haida, and Tsimshian. The lineage demanded loyalty. It was considered noble to keep the needs of one's lineage always to the fore, such as being ready to die, if need be, for the benefit of the kindred grouping. On the other hand, there was the emphasis of status,

the fact that the individual had his rank and titles and was expected to follow the role prescribed by the position he held. To some extent the paradox was resolved by lineage interaction in regard to the wealth festivals, the so-called potlatches, which formed so dramatic and significant a part of the culture of the entire area. Through these, there was an interplay between lineage and status. Solidarity within the lineage was in fact enhanced by the presence within it of high titles and the wealth associations which they demanded.

The Potlatch. In Chinook jargon, that curious mixture of structural and lexical elements drawn both from various Amerindian languages and from some European tongues as well, the *lingua franca* of the southern Northwest Coast, an area linguistically diverse, the term "potlatch" has the general meaning of "to give." The institution, in the forms that it took, was distinctive to the Northwest Coast, although the notion of giving in abundance, of open-handed generosity, was characteristic of some other areas as well. For the area, it was a development peculiar to all the tribes from Yakutat Bay to the mouth of the Columbia, each of which gave the institution its own special "twist" but through all of which there generally ran a sense of common purpose. The function was generally everywhere the same even if the behavior patterns and emphases differed slightly from group to group. The potlatch validated status. Status, in turn, was the factor around which the social grouping—lineage, clan, or even tribe—turned. The concept was that of amassing wealth, seen in goods of all kinds, for the purpose of bestowing it on others on special occasions and thereby affirming and validating right and privilege.

Haha hananē! Now, he gave away the four sea otter blankets, ten marten blankets, seven black-bear blankets, thirty-five mink blankets, and fifty deerskin blankets. . . . As soon as he had finished his potlatch, he told the [guests] that he had changed his name. You will call me Lalelit. . . . Thus [he] said to his guests. Therefore I am full of names and privileges. And therefore I have many chiefs as ancestors all over the world; and therefore I feel like laughing at what is said by the lower chiefs, when they claim to belong to the chief, my ancestor. ,Boas, 1921:844..

Although specifically Kwakiutl, statements such as the above are representative of the general pattern. There has sometimes been a tendency to view the potlatch as a form of interaction only between men of high rank. To a degree, this was true, but the general involvement was of a group all the members of which participated. In the north, where the lineage reflected locality and common residence, it was this group which worked together to amass the necessary property and which also acted as a group as hosts to invited guests, usually another such lineage. While men of high rank might assume a place as donor, or chief host, and it was around them that the more property distributions centered, all members were involved and it can be seen that a lesser series of distributions was going on at the same time. In theory any person (except of course a slave or one lacking claim to titles) could institute a potlatch. The issue was never between individuals, however much individuals might profit, or even if validation of the new status of an individual were the ostensible reason for the feast. The local group was alternately host and guest. Chiefs, house chiefs, lineage chiefs or, chiefs of more extended segments were, as might be anticipated, the principal figures at a potlatch. They were, in any case, the custodians of wealth, and they directed labor and wealth accumulation. But every person, down to the lowest rank of commoner, found it to his advantage to share in the proceedings. Because the potlatch was a major group activity, it was an institution which served to maintain the sense of membership and to further the solidarity of the group (Barnett, 1938:349–358).

One did not potlatch members of one's own in-group; the involvement was always between hosts and invited guests. Thus the potlatch was also a way of establishing and maintaining relationships between different local segments of a more extended tribal entity. Property was amassed by the group and prepared for distribution to invited guest. In the area, there was some ambivalence about the place or meaning of the institution of potlatching. On the one hand, there was the concept that it represented an honest requital for services. Among the Tlingit and Haida, for example, there were intermoiety functions in respect to house building, funerals, and other services, even on the local level. A member of the Raven moiety, intent on building a house, called on his wife's kindred, members of the opposite or Eagle moiety, to build it for him. Not only did he have to support the builders, feeding and housing them over a long period of time, but when the house was erected, he established title to it in effect by potlatching the workers. On the other side, there was always some sense of rivalry between chiefs and nobles of different groups, and it is out of this context that the Kwakiutl quotation above comes. While the northern tribes did not go to such extremes in "fighting with property," potlatching for revenge so as to shame a rival, behavior especially true of the Kwakiutl, there was a sense of outdoing another in the magnificence and abundance of gifts. Proud and haughty behavior, boastful remarks of one's descent, about one's titles, privileges, and certainly, about one's use of the valued lineage names and crests were accompanied by a pretended indifference to property. It was not only given away to guests, it was also sometimes destroyed—boxes of oil poured onto the fire, goods dumped into the sea—simply to indicate the vast possessions of the donor (Spradley, 1969).

As a general principle associated with the concept of the gift the world over, it may be said that a gift requires a return. This was theoretically true on the Northwest Coast, especially since the same series of groups tended to potlatch each other. The result was that property changed hands back and forth. Yet it can also be noted that the gifts did not have to be equal; they were essentially commensurate with the occasion for the potlatch. In this sense, the

●TOTEM POLE RAISING POTLATCH—TLINGIT
The second most important potlatch among the
Tlingit of the northern Northwest Coast was
that relating to the erection of the totem pole.
Of first importance was the building of the
house itself, that communal dwelling which
was so intimately involved with the rank and
titles of its inhabitants. But the house, once
built (and as in the case of the Tlingit, the
work done by members of the moiety opposite
that of the owner), was demanding of fearful
expenditure. Wealth was collected for years in
advance by the house owner who depended
on his associates of lesser rank for support and
contributions. Here, indeed, was where the
involvements of kinship and dependency, as
well as marital obligation came to the fore. The
potlatch, any potlatch in fact, was not merely
an event held to signal a precise act; it was a
continuing series of reciprocal exchanges
between and within groups. So it was that
when the totem pole associated with the house,
that splendid blazonry which marked the
statuses and titles of the residents, came to be
erected, a further complex series of exchanges

had to take place. Again it was carved by
members of the opposite moiety, all of whom
had a share in the work to a greater or lesser
degree. During their work, they had to be
supported, and when the work was completed
and the pole about to be raised, they had to be
feasted.

The owner of the house, possessor of the
highest title in the group and hence the chief
of the house, stands in this scene with his
wife. When the discussion of the marriage
arrangements in the moiety-centered societies
of the Tlingit and Haida is recalled, it becomes
apparent that a woman is greeting her own
relatives, members of the group out of which
she married. The chief is dressed in his
gorgeous blanket of mountain sheep hair and
cedar bark, decorated with his crests, and he
wears a formal headdress of ermine tails.
Standing in his door with great dignity, he is
seemingly indifferent to the vast wealth he has
collected, even though his slaves struggle with
a heavy cedar chest full of sea mammal oil or
fish oil. In the house the goods have piled
up—blankets, various utilitarian objects, and

138 ●

phenomenal quantities of food. The guests have been greeted at the beach, already have been given gifts and food, and are now receiving the formal invitation to enter the house. They have come in their canoes, they too dressed in finery and each, according to title and rank, ready to receive the gifts which the members of the host group will bestow on them.

So important an event as the raising of a totem pole is no single day's festival. Many people are involved and the gift giving occupies several days. Marked at the beginning by dignity and great decorum, the tempo of the potlatch will increase, there will be time for dramatic performances, and much religious activity. So important was the potlatch, indeed, that its carrying out took on a quasi-religious character. Added to this was rivalrous display, an air of tension as gifts were given and received, all surrounded by the keen sense of personal status and worth in this society of primitive capitalists.

potlatch involved a payment for services. Among the Tlingit and Haida, where members of one moiety built the house of a man in the opposite moiety, or performed the mortuary services by burying the dead of the opposite group, there was clearly a sense of payment for services rendered, but more was involved. The new house, the associated totem pole, the assumption of the titles of a deceased relative all required validation through potlatching. While it is true that a man who gave a potlatch often sought to offer considerably more than the occasion warranted, he was in effect paying witnesses. But it was his own status that was called into consideration. Guests benefited, it is true, at least from the gifts they received, but the host, affirming his status by his potlatch, was the true gainer. If he was prodigal in his giving, it was to fix the occasion in people's minds. Lavish potlatches were remembered. The concept which was pointedly operative was that an individual could make no claims to status without public validation through giving. Since his kin stood to gain with him, he could count on their cooperation and support.

The property bestowed at a potlatch consisted mainly of nonutilitarian prestige items. Gathering a good many people together of course required food. The guests had to be made welcome and fed. But feasts, involving no more than interdining between different groups, were not always potlatches. It is perhaps worth noting that since the native Northwest Coast lacked alcohol and narcotics—tobacco came in relatively late—eating of vast quantities of food became in some measure a substitute for states which drugs or stimulants might otherwise have produced. Food at potlatches involved the rare, the unusual, always in addition, of course, to regular fare. A slave might be killed and eaten, or a dog, although the latter was part of a Haida potlatch in association with dances held by a secret society. It is difficult to imagine the vast amounts of food which the hosts brought together. It was forced on the guests, often with joking and much horseplay, and the guests too were expected to carry away what they could not consume. Often they brought their own wooden trenchers and horn spoons but these might also be given away as part of the potlatch array. Food, to be sure, was wealth, especially the food collected in quantities far above the subsistence needs, but generally it was merely an expected part of the potlatch ritual.

The Northwest Coast peoples, in their amassing of nonutilitarian objects, involved as they were with the continuous labor of production, were in a sense incipient capitalists. Affirmation of status required an investment. Properly speaking, there was no unit of exchange, no money or currency as such. Yet the area came fairly close to a concept of this kind in employing blankets. When commercial textiles reached the area, it is easy to see how cotton and woolen blankets might meet this need, as indeed, currency does at the present time, but even in the aboriginal setting, blankets of all kinds, excepting the ceremonially worn costume blankets, were employed as elements basic to the potlatch. These, of bark, hair, fibers, might be said to form a unit of capital. So strong is the idea of the potlatch and so deeply is it engrained in the social system that even today blankets and yardgoods are distributed, cash appears, and such items as sewing machines, refrigerators, and similar goods change hands and occur in quantity far out of proportion to their practical use. In the past, blankets and other valued property were distributed, such as boxes of oulachon oil, of oil and berries, seaweeds, dried salmon, but more than food, furs, carved vessels and boxes, weapons, and thus generally, valued surplus goods.

Notable in the potlatch development was the "copper," a piece of raw or unsmelted copper hammered out into the shape of a shield and often decorated with crests and other designs. Among the Kwakiutl, this represented a continuing investment, increasing in value each time it changed hands. In the northern area, however, it tended to take on the quality of an heirloom and was only displayed at a potlatch, although it could be given away. Like food and other articles of value, coppers were sometimes broken and thrown into the sea or the pieces dropped into a fire as signs of the owner's greatness. Such coppers, the metal obtained by trade from the Chilkat country in the north, could be worth several thousands of dollars, to employ a postcontact standard, while in similar terms, a potlatch itself could call for an expenditure of many thousands. When the required labor is considered, the man-hours put in on amassing and manufacturing wealth, the number of people involved, it can be seen that to a wealth-minded group the expenditures were tremendous. A successful potlatch required them absolutely.

Although rank, hierarchy, descent, and kinship might at first glance suggest that the potlatch was a remarkably complex institution, its actual performance can be quite readily related. Those most pointedly involved were of course the chiefs. A chief announced his intention to potlatch to his lineage or to his extended household group and requested their support. He set the time and stated the group to which he intended to extend an invitation. He directed labor, assembled property, and solicited contributions from his kinsmen. Among the northern tribes, the invitation was most frequently extended to the lineage of the wife of the chief, suggesting a continuing involvement between intermarried lineages. The chief's own lineage made their contributions, but he might count on contributions from his male cross cousins, his brothers-in-law, as well. They gave him gifts for the intended potlatch even though they would be among the invited guests. In some instances relating to the potlatch, the concept of borrowing with interest had arisen. This was not the case here; to be sure, as potlatch guests, the brothers-in-law of a host would receive gifts, but their return was in proportion to the kind and importance of the potlatch. Indicated is the element of wealth as a factor promoting societal stability not only within a lineage but between intermarried lineages. A chief's kinsmen were lesser hosts at a potlatch. On a later occasion, when a return invitation would be extended, they became guests. Because of the relations between a chief and his kinsmen in assembling wealth, the potlatch cannot be regarded as an individual enterprise. Once a chief had set the machinery in motion, all members of his group, those with titles to affirm, rights to inherited property to validate, shared the proceedings. The honored names conferred on those assisting the chief host with property raised them in public esteem. It was to the benefit of all members of a household and a lineage to offer their assistance and their substance when the potlatch was announced.

A great potlatch could be several years in the making. Of the potlatches described for the Tsimshian, for example, the chief host began by enlisting his kinsmen. Several years of work might be necessary. The chief, or actually, any person of title who could command a following, sought help from his brothers first, passing messages to them if they were not residents in his house, that he expected each to give so much property—for example, a canoe full of oulachon. His relations to his kinsmen were by no means casual. The preparations required formality and the prospective host stated to his relatives when the potlatch would take place, how much property would be required in all, which other relatives, those, for example, in nearby villages and sublineages, would be asked to assist, and who the intended guests were. His plans found work for everyone. As preparations gathered momentum, vast quantities of berries, boxes of oulachon grease, skins and blankets were assembled. Trade was a factor, since the Tsimshian group could barter with the Haida and other Tsimshian for further needed articles. It can readily be seen that several seasons were necessary for acquisition of the necessary capital (Garfield, 1939:198–199).

In one Tsimshian potlatch, held by a man and his brother, it was agreed that the festivities would be held over a three-year period, a major part of the potlatch being held each year. The main purpose was to permit the house owner to validate his inheritance and the associated titles and to give so momentous a potlatch as to raise the position of the house in everyone's esteem. The two men agreed that the first display would serve to validate the status of three boys, children, each of whom was to be given a supernatural power name. The second feature of the potlatch, held the following year, was ostensibly held to intitiate two girls into secret dance societies. The last festival in the series was held for the purpose of allowing the two brothers to assume ancestral names and so to validate their ownership as well as that of the house. Yet that there was even more involved is indicated by the interest taken by the lineage itself in the proceedings initiated by the brothers. The lineage in council decided on the boys and girls to be honored and initiated (Garfield, 1939:199). Guests from another lineage who came to each event in the series were given gifts. They could estimate initially the extent of the gifts they would ultimately be given. Their chief acted in a sponsoring capacity, calling the names of those who were invested with new names and privileges. In the interim between the series, the brothers called in their father's lineage, made requests for additional property, and feasted their paternal kin. These requests were honored but required repayment. At the final feast in the series, that marked by the assumption of ancestral names and the proper indication of house ownership, the period of mourning for the deceased owner was officially at an end. These titles could now validly be assumed by the living.

The point raised is an important one. A significant element in the potlatches of the northern tribes was that of commemoration and inheritance. The major Tlingit potlatch, for example, was seen as a cycle of ritual activities to mourn the death of a chief. Intermoiety functions among the Tlingit, it may be recalled, required reciprocal burial, the Wolf people being entrusted with the funeral arrangements for deceased Ravens. The potlatch began with the payment to this group for their services. The idea of payment for this service was clearly present, but there were also gifts the value of which went far beyond the requirements of payment. Tied up with the Tlingit mourning ceremonies was the investiture of the new chief. His rights were publicly declared to the guest group. The guests also rebuilt the house of the deceased chief and carved the memorial post. For all this an extensive outlay of property was required.

Mention has already been made of the situation of potlatching among the Haida. Here the concept was to establish a boy as heir presumptive. Before taking up residence with the maternal uncle, the future status of the boy was declared in a potlatch given ostensibly by his father. Actually, the mother's lineage, that to which the boy himself belonged, supplied the property. Later, when the maternal uncle had died and the heir presumptive was to succeed, he validated his position by potlatching again his father's lineage. Like the Tlingit, the Haida also had developed the sense of reciprocity between the lineages in opposite moieties, such reciprocal services calling for funerary observances and for house building.

These major potlatches among the tribes of the northern tier were replete with drama, with elaborations of speech making and protocol. One may imagine the vast amounts of property assembled both in the house and before it. It was uncovered and displayed. Ceremonial dress, elaborate etiquette, great dignity, accompanied by a strong sense of pride and honor all marked the potlatch. And it is also readily seen that to a group which expended so much of its efforts, its hard labor, in assembling items of property, all far in excess of the subsistence needs, events of this kind were tremendously exciting and dramatic, looked forward to and discussed and remembered over years. It may be seen, too, however, that these were not purely secular affairs bound up with the prestige economy. There were some religious aspects, those related to initiation and to the secret societies, religious associations which formed a vital part of the life of the area. Leaving the religious element for discussion below, attention may be shifted to the potlatches which were held among the northern tribes for other than purely commemorative or inheritance purposes.

The competitive potlatch was of a somewhat different order of drama. This striking feature of the complex, so frequently described in the literature on the area, tends to confuse the primary purposes for which the potlatch was held. A potlatch was a unifying, integrating institution, one which brought about cohesion within a lineage and similarly, between lineages. Rivalry there was, and especially on the level of chiefly rank, but such rivalry was not primarily divisive; the system made provision for it. These competitive potlatches have sometimes been associated with a concept of vengeance, the notion that a man of high rank, suffering an insult or believing his honor violated, could shame an opponent by forcing him to match contribution for contribution. Destruction of property could take place in any usual potlatch, although it usually had some relationship to a competitive situation. At a usual potlatch, the host might have oil poured on the fire, ostensibly to "warm" his guests, but in reality enhancing his own prestige by forcing them to move back from the increased heat of the fire. In the vengeance or competitive potlatch, an opponent was challenged to meet and property was destroyed, item by item. Blankets in great quantity were torn up and burned, coppers were broken and destroyed, with the result that thousands of dollars, again in post-contact terms, went up in smoke. The loser of course was the rival who ran out of property first.

The vengeance idea, retaliation for a slight or insult, real or fancied, while not unknown in the northern sections, tended to be more characteristic of the central regions. In the north, the competitive potlatch arose more often because of the attempt to fix rank in the hierarchy. Where potlatches between lineages in different moieties or clans had been taking place over long periods of time, there was never a question of the relative place of each person. Rank was publicly known, publicly defined, protocol was observed with respect to these places in the hierarchy, and because no two positions were equal, there was no necessity to vie with another or to contest his place. As among the Haida, where one could raise one's title for the benefit of one's children or heirs, there might be changes in the hierarchial ordering, but no special problems arose; public opinion in the local area gave confirmation or denial and so kept the ranking of persons and titles fairly well fixed. But where new contacts occurred, or where, after the advent of Europeans, there was greater vertical mobility and an influx of trade goods, resulting in the formation of new federations, it was necessary to define the relative positions of chiefs and nobles between groups not previously in contact. The result was that when two men made claim to the same place in the order, they might be forced into a competitive potlatch. The loser was consigned to a subordinate place. Once vanquished in this way, the individual, and his group with him, had no alternative but to accept what in effect was a decision of public opinion (Drucker, 1955:118).

Another type of potlatch was the so-called face-saving potlatch. An unfortunate slip of the tongue, a public humiliation of some kind necessitated holding a lesser potlatch. If one's child fell into the water and was saved from drowning by a member of the opposite moiety, a small potlatch was held. This was embarrassing, as indeed it was if a chief or noble, descending from a canoe, should fall flat on the beach. One can only imagine an equal occasion for embarrassment if a European monarch or dignitary were to stumble during a solemn event. In such cases the opposite moiety was invited and a distribution was made of blankets. These were usually torn into sections and a piece given to each person of the opposite group who had witnessed the mishap. For anyone thereafter to recall the incident would be a gross insult. A similar pattern of face-saving arose when a person of rank was ransomed after capture or enslavement. Reinstatement required a greater outlay.

It may be seen that the peoples of the Northwest Coast had developed the concept of prestige wealth into an unusually elaborate institution. The patterns of giving and return giving are not unique, especially when Western customs of Christmas giving or interdining are recalled. But here was clearly the major preoccupation of the area, a point made emphatic by the societal solidarity and stability which was created through the potlatch. The native orientation was toward rank and status fixed by the amassing of wealth for the benefits achieved through its distribution.

The Cycle of Life

Among the Haida and Tlingit, girls were preferred. Boys, although invested with property and title, left the parental household; girls remained until marriage and added to the numbers of the lineage. A pregnant woman was not secluded until the actual delivery. This took place in the house. Only the fact that the men absented themselves from the house during birth suggests the widespread American Indian concept of the spiritual uncleanness of the parturient. During pregnancy, a woman was subject to certain restrictions; if she ate foods gathered at low tide, for example, the child would be harmed. The father, too, was expected to remain continent and to avoid certain acts which might harm the unborn child or hinder its delivery. This reflects not only the pattern of a mystic bond between father and child but serves to establish the paternal responsibility for the child in the community. The woman, in a sitting or squatting position and assisted by others, delivered the child.

Reference is made to the interlineage relationship between a man and his paternal aunt. At his own birth, the father's sister cut the umbilical cord, washed and cleaned the child, and cradled it. The name of the newborn child was given by the mother a few days after birth. One of the names of deceased ancestors in the lineage was usually chosen, and there was a vague concept of reincarnation, the thought that the deceased ancestor was reborn in the child through the name. Later, at a house-building potlatch, a funeral observance, or in potlatches held to designate the future status of the child, honorific names associated with the lineage and moiety were given. This practice related especially to those of high rank.

Children were nursed for about two years and confined to a cradle of wood. As small children, they were allowed to run about freely, but restrictions began fairly early. Small boys emulated adult patterns in collecting and distributing pretended property. In short, the major preoccupations of the culture were impressed on the individual at an early age. By the age of ten, when a boy left to reside with his maternal uncle, he was well aware of his role. A potlatch would already have been held for him, especially if he had pretensions to rank. Settled in his uncle's house, he was expected to assist his uncle and show him great respect. After the move away from his parental household, he was also careful to avoid his sisters.

The girls' puberty rite, so strongly entrenched in the cultures of the western and northern American Indian, appears among the Haida and Tlingit in a somewhat less oppressive form. The girl was restricted for several weeks following the onset of her menses. She was limited as to diet and could not touch weapons lest she contaminate them. Her paternal aunts, suggesting again this important relationship, acted as her advisers at this time. When released from the restrictions, she was feted at a dance. While there was no corresponding ritual for boys, the piercing of the septum for a nose ornament was accompanied by a gift distribution, often part of the potlatch cycle given in honor of the boy's assumption of a lineage name. Girls were also included in such a potlatch series when their ears and lips were pierced for ear ornaments and labrets. The piercing itself, symbolic of status, required public validation. In the case of a high-ranking girl, several ear perforations might be made. These could begin when the girl was very small, as part of the potlatch involvement, and might be given again after puberty, or the whole operation might be performed at one time. The paternal aunts either did the piercing or supervised it and were paid for their services. Among the Tsimshian, the number of ear and lip perforations depended on rank; only those with claim to high unsullied status were entitled to multiple perforations. Both sexes wore labrets. Tattooing was also common, especially among the Haida. When a child was tattooed, blackened thread being drawn through the skin, the designs were generally those of the crests and were sometimes done in association with the initiation of a child into one of the religious secret societies.

Sexual freedom before marriage was customary. In love affairs, however, care was taken not to violate the incest prohibitions. Here the lineage itself could take punitive action, even killing the flagrant violators. Because of the marriage regulations, sexual activities between unmarried people generally arose between those who could potentially marry, the young man, for example, seeking out the daughters of his father's sisters. A young man could have sexual relations with the wife of his brother or of his mother's brother. Such affairs, while not openly condoned, were held not improper. While the levirate, marriage between a man and his deceased brother's wife, was not especially strong, it was not unknown; an affair with the brother's wife was by the same reasoning permissible.

Marriages, as might be expected in a society stressing rank, were arranged with an eye to status. Betrothal required gift exchanges and a modified bride service. In the latter case, the intended husband worked for a time before and after marriage for his wife's parents. Because he might reside with them after marriage, he thereby affirmed his special relations to them. At the marriage ceremony itself, gifts were given to the couple and the bride was ceremonially led to the groom by his paternal aunt, also a classificatory mother of the bride. Once married, the individual was conceptually an adult and entered the adult world of status and full participation in the social and religious life of the community. Women continued to hold their own property, apart from that of their husbands, but the couple also worked together as a team, being involved as they were in the moiety-lineage reciprocity system.

Ideally, a person lived a long life, one full of honor and of the memories of potlatches in which he had participated. As he lay dying, his property was assembled about him and his kinsmen of both moieties came to visit him. A male cross cousin was requested to make his grave box and did so in his presence. After death, the body was put seated before the fire, painted and ceremonially dressed. After four days, it was placed in the grave box and carried out of the house, not through the door, again in keeping with a circumpolar culture pattern, but through an aperture in the side of the house. The grave box or coffin was placed in a special hut. In the case of great chiefs and powerful shamans, it was sometimes placed on a scaffold or in a tree. Mourning was complex, requiring as it did the return feasts for the members of the moiety assisting at the funeral, usually the male cross cousins of the deceased. The period of mourning went on for some time and was linked with the elaborate potlatching held to validate the inheritance of rank and privilege. Mourning festivals, as has been noted, were most elaborate in the case of a chief but the general pattern of moiety reciprocity in handling burial and in the memorial potlatches, however minor, were followed for all, men and women alike.

Art

No account of the Northwest Coast can be complete without reference to the lasting achievement of these peoples in the area of decorative art. Among nonliterate peoples the world over, few can rival the artistic splendor which the Northwest Coast of North America developed. Some African and Indonesian groups in the so-called primitive world reached somewhat the same heights, but in the excellence of wood carving, the Northwest Coast is paralleled only perhaps by the Maori of New Zealand. As an art area, the Northwest Coast stands out in native America; not until one comes to Middle America and the artistic brilliance of such peoples as the Maya or Inca is there encountered so dramatic a series of styles.

In the area, and referring again to the northern and central sections where the art forms reached a climax of development, art had some very precise functions. It was decorative art, it is true, and so reflected a strongly evolved aesthetic sense. More than this, it related intimately to the social system. In any consideration of the social structure, the references to rank and status must relate in turn to the consideration of crests. These were the outward symbols of rank and descent. As such, they stand as coats-of-arms, suggesting a remarkable

parallel to the heraldric blazonry of Europe, that also reflected rank and position among the nobility and knighthood in medieval times.

Why the general development should have occurred as it did remains an open question. A foreign stimulus has been suggested and it may not be unlikely that influences reaching the area from northern and central Asia gave the foundation. In some forms of Eskimo art, particularly in Alaska in some of the prehistoric horizons, such as Ipiutak, the Asiatic flavor seems present and some favorable comparisons can be made with the trans-Baikal region of antiquity. Despite speculation and debate, whatever the origin of the distinctive art styles of the Northwest Coast, the native peoples succeeded in fashioning something exclusively their own. When first contacted by explorers and traders in the eighteenth century, the area was introduced to metal tools. These, it is true, along with new types of pigments, gave the artistic development an added impetus. But the basic styles were there already and suggest by their presence a long tradition (Hawthorn, 1967).

The northern and central regions, the focus of the artistic growth, differed slightly from each other in the ways in which they executed their aesthetic conceptions. The Tlingit, Haida, and Tsimshian developed a highly standardized and conventional series of representations, employing these to decorate virtually every object in their material culture. They thus stressed a type of flat and relief work, although they also carved in tri-dimensional patterns with deep relief or in fully rounded proportions, such as in totem poles and house posts. In the center of the area, among such peoples as the Kwakiutl and the Nootka, there was somewhat less standardization and an introduction of a sculptured style, one stressing realism and movement. In historic times, the two forms began to influence each other with the result that the northern tribes began to depict realistic figures on their masks and helmets, while the central groups took on more of the conventionalism of the north. Other local stylistic developments occurred. When one leaves the center of the area and begins to approach the south, however, one finds that the art forms begin to lose their drama. Those of the Salish, for example, begin to be simplified copies of the work of the more northerly peoples. In the lower Columbia some quite different styles appear; archeologically, some highly distinctive manifestations are noted, the traditional Northwest Coast forms changing to a different style of two-dimensional representation. The art center is thus quite precisely located in the center and north.

Apart from regional styles within the subareas, there was also a man's and a woman's art. Men owned the rights to use designs by virtue of inheritance and status. These they could apply to objects, ceremonial and otherwise, belonging to their associated rank and position. Such designs were conceptually the property of clan and lineage and invested in the user. Women, for example, wove. In the north, where the famous Chilkat blanket bore the crests of the owner, the wife of a man wove it for him. He, however, painted a pattern board indicating the placing of his crest elements. Women's work, involving weaving, the making of baskets, and embroidering, did not run to the use of crests. Woven mats or baskets, while they might occasionally have worked into them a crest form, contained fairly simple geometric designs. Woven objects, because of the nature of the techniques and the materials employed, posed some limitations of design. Although not ceremonial, these designs used by women were often called by special names and the rights to their use owned outright. Like virtually everything else in Northwest Coast society, they counted as property.

To the outsider, it is the dramatic art associated with the sculptured flowing portraiture and the conventionalized designs associated with the crest assemblage that are so striking. Art of either type can be regarded as ceremonial. The carved realistic portraitlike masks and helmets were directly associated with secret societies and their functions. They were owned by a lineage which possessed hereditary rights to their carving and use. The art of the crests related to the status rituals and was generally mythologically founded. Both kinds depict supernatural beings, some in human form, some as animals, and still others as mythological monsters.

The traditional crests employed all three forms. In each moiety, phratry, clan, and lineage there ran the sense of relatedness to an ancestor. According to the group tradition, the ancestor in question had been drawn into some special situation where he acquired, through supernatural means, the rights to depict the animal or being as his crest. Myths sometimes related how an animal took human form and so became the founder of the group.

Tlingit ● Helmet mask. The spectacular art of the Northwest Coast area was distinguished not only by the rigid stylizations which create such uniqueness for the area, but by marked attempts at realistic depiction. Carved portraiture reached a surprising level of perfection. Here, the carver shows the paralyzed face of an old man, the one side of the mask being drawn into a grotesque, palsied grimace. Presumably, the carving was done from a living model. (After F. Boas. 1955. Primitive Art. Capitol Publishing Co. Adapted from photographs, courtesy of the American Museum of Natural History)

Such myths provided the rationale for using a particular crest, the forms employed symbolizing the ancestral experience. These crests, most frequently in animal form, were painted and carved on virtually all property of the man entitled to use them. They were put on house posts and siding, on canoes, boxes, horn spoons, carved as dishes, engraved on coppers, and they appeared as elements in memorial and totem poles.

While the idea generally prevailed that an ancestor who founded a line of descent had, according to legend, an encounter or special experience with a supernatural, animal or otherwise, later ancestors, those along direct or collateral lines also had such experiences. The basis of crest usage lay in a concept of family history; crests memorialized these legendary supernatural contacts. Special crests thus became associated with various branches of a group, with lineages and with households. In other words, a clan or lineage could lay claim to several, singly and in combination. The rights to their use, however, were vested in members of the group according to rank. These were among the privileges of rank. If a house made use of a single crest in its posts and furnishings, the rights to the crest were among the prerogatives of the household head. The crest was hence wholly linked with the status concern. Rights to use crests were acquired by descent and also by marriage in some instances. A totem pole is an example of such a compound coat-of-arms, depicting various figures interlocked.

Strictly speaking, the term "totem" is misapplied in relation to the Northwest Coast. The figures, anthropomorphic or zoomorphic, which were represented on the pole were not totems, if by such a term, following the definitions of categories in primitive religions, is meant a specialized and mystic relationship between a group of related humans and a member of the animal world. Usually, where totemism occurs, there is some sense of avoidance of the animal so designated, special treatment, or prohibitions against killing or eating it. This was not the case on the Northwest Coast. A man who used a bear crest, for example, was not required to follow any special observances, other than those which would apply to everyone, when he hunted bear. The idea of special helping spirits from the animal world, a concept applying as much to this area as to so much of general native America, was present and might relate to the special guardian-spirit experience of the clan ancestor. It was this, in fact, which the whole crest complex embodied rather than a totemic idea. Totem poles, as they are popularly called, were of several kinds. The most common were memorial poles set up along the beaches in front of the village. These were erected by a chief's heir on assuming his rank. A variant of this type was the mortuary post, one set up either by the grave of a chief or so made as to support the grave box itself. In some cases, this had a niche in the back to hold the grave box. House posts were often carved with the crest designs, and there was also the central pole lined up with the gable of the house and rising above it. This was slotted to make the door of the house, a crest figure sometimes was carved with an open mouth to serve as the entrance. Among the Haida, there was a special house pole, often erected and validated long after the house itself was built, which combined the crests of the owner and of his wife. It must be emphasized again that the crests carved on all such poles were lineage property. They reflected the conceptual history of the lineage and they were employed by those of the lineage whose rank permitted their use.

On a tri-dimensional object, such as a pole, the figures were made so as to flow into each other. But whether carved in relief or painted, the designs were generally arranged to fit the object which was being decorated. It can readily be seen that a post or pole, the handle of a spoon, a tri-dimensional tureen or trencher could allow for an almost realistic handling by the carver. The artistic concept was to depict the subject in its entirety, showing all of its parts in proper relation to each other—head, eyes, mouth, nose, teeth, limbs, body, tail, all faithfully represented. But where figures move into one another, this is obviously not wholly possible. Or again, if a flat surface, such as house siding, a side of a box, a back rest, was to hold the design, a conceptual difficulty arose. In Western art, there is no objection to a drawing which shows the side of an object, that visible to the viewer. The invisible side is assumed. To the peoples of the Northwest Coast, this kind of approach to art was offensive. Faithful representation required treatment of the whole figure. Thus if an animal has four legs, it is not sufficient to show only two; all four must be faithfully depicted.

It is out of such a concept that the conventionalized forms arise. The problems were resolved in much the same way that a map maker finds different kinds of projections to render a sphere on a flat surface. The animal figure was drawn as though it had been split and laid out flat. There were several ways of doing this. The dimensions of an animal's body could be readily shown on a box with several surfaces, the figure split and the various segments placed on the appropriate sides of the box. Where this was not possible, the figure could be split down the back and each side drawn symmetrically. Two sides of the face could then be shown, the four legs, two parts of the tail, one on each of the symmetrical drawings. An artist could go further since once he had split his figure he felt obliged to show various anatomical features, such as bones and entrails and producing a kind of X-ray effect. This reflected not so much a desire for accuracy as it did a distaste for blank spaces. On many of the flat depictions of animals, the two sides balanced back to back, or the parts variously assembled according to the shape of the object to be decorated, one notes what appear to be extra "eyes." These are generally rectangular

Haida ● Totem poles at old Kasaan village, southeastern Alaska. The poles in the foreground show the crests of Chief Skowl (died 1882) identified as "Raven stealing the sun; Raven putting back his beak after having lost it on the hook of the halibut fisherman; Grizzly bear or the young woman or the cubs." (cf. Marius Barbeau, "Totem Poles," Vol. 1, National Museum of Canada, Bulletin 119, p. 867, 1950. Photograph by Lieut. G. T. Emmons, 1885. Smithsonian Institution National Anthropological Archives)

boxlike shapes containing a lozenge-shaped center. This was a convention employed to represent the joints of the long bones of an animal and thereby to avoid the presence of a blank area.

Although perhaps begun as a naturalistic or realistic art, while such realism was retained in the masks, crest designs became strongly conventionalized. Prominent or characteristic features of the various animals tended to be accentuated so that the observer can tell at a glance what animal was intended. Even if the animal is "dissected," these prominent conventions were retained. The identifying characteristics of each may be noted.

1. *Beaver:* prominent incisor teeth; round large nose; flat tail with crosshatching; forepaws sometimes with a stick or together as though holding a stick.
2. *Bear:* large paws with the characteristic claws; a short snout with large teeth; tongue protruding; short, rounded ears.
3. *Wolf:* long snout with large teeth and pointed canines; erect, pointed ears.
4. *Shark:* a conical snout and depressed mouth; many sharp teeth; curved lines on the cheeks representing gills; shark tail.
5. *Killer whale:* heavy head and large nostrils; blowhole; large mouth and teeth; long dorsal spine or "fin"; forward flukes.
6. *Raven:* long, straight beak; wings, spread or folded, sometimes not shown.
7. *Eagle:* heavy beak with downward curve; wings spread or folded.
8. *Sea monster:* varying mixtures of the features of bear, killer whale, and sometimes, shark.
9. *Frog:* wide toothless mouth; flat nose; no tail.
10. *Mosquito:* long pointed proboscis; segmented body, tapered and elongated wings.

The list is by no means complete. Many other animals, fish, birds, and insects were con-

Haida ● Beaver design on a hat. In keeping with the traditional aims of the art of the Northwest Coast, the animal figures were depicted as though they were split and spread out flat. Any of the animals figuring prominently in the crest assemblage could be handled in this way. On a basketry hat, the beaver face is shown, marked by its short snout and ears and its suggestion of incisors. Proceeding from the snout between the ears is a styled representation of the spine. Moving to the rear of the hat, one sees the distinctive beaver tail and the animal's hind legs. What appear to be "eyes" near the tail are conventionalized representations of the joints of the limbs. In flattening out the animal, convention called for both the external representation and a suggestion of the internal parts of the animal as well. (After F. Boas. 1955. Primitive Art. Capitol Publishing Co. Adapted from photographs, courtesy of The American Museum of Natural History)

ventionally represented. Nor did all of the features mentioned always appear. A tongue between the teeth, for example, was sufficient to represent the bear. These design elements were carved in relief or painted in red and black and they regularly appear in the crest assemblage of the north. As noted, there was somewhat less adherence to convention among the central Kwakiutl and Nootka, and even somewhat more free imagery. This second art style was more tolerant of open spaces in its depictions and more inclined to suppress minor detail.

Of the two major styles appearing in the area, there is no question that both have great artistic power. The culture valued art highly and rewarded the skilled artist. Conventionalized it may have been, but in its variety of forms and structures, in its many applications, the native art allowed room for nuance, latitude for inventiveness within its prescribed range. Along its own lines, it sought fidelity to nature and the natural order as it was conceived by the culture. This was an art which reached high degrees of sophistication, it was flowing and alive, and it is one to which no observer can be indifferent. And because of the ways in which it was employed, Northwest Coast art becomes a prime example of the functional interrelationships between art and society, not to mention, of course, art and religion (cf. Drucker, 1955:161–185; Inverarity, 1950).

Religion

The Tsimshian, Haida, and Tlingit, in their concepts of the supernatural and their approaches to it, did not differ greatly from their neighbors to the south. Their religious life was again reflective of a series of phrasings, variations of a pattern applicable not only to the Northwest Coast itself, but also to a broad segment of western North America and northeastern Asia. Each Northwest Coast tribe, of course, had its own slightly individualized variant, its special interpretation of the common base, and the component elements seem to be deeply rooted in the past, a point inferred by their wide distribution. It is not surprising to note that the basic religious ideas are not wholly different from those of the Eskimo, that they are fairly closely shared in the Plateau and in California, and that there are traces of them in the religious systems of the Southwest and the Plains. As might be expected, the wealth emphasis of the area comes to be intertwined with the religious institutions, but the underlying postulates in the realm of religion are generally those of western and northern North America.

The primary religious ideas on the Northwest Coast permit treatment under the following headings.

1. *Placation of game.* This is the familiar concept that the animals which were hunted allowed themselves to be taken for the benefit of people.
2. *The spirit helper or guardian spirit.* This is the view that humans could put themselves in close rapport with the spirit world and that by so doing, they could achieve certain kinds of success in life. The present world

was considered important; there were a few eschatological concepts (i.e., belief in a life after death), but these were fairly vague and poorly systematized.

3. *Shamanism.* As among the Eskimo, interior Athabascans, and others, the place of the shaman as curer and cleanser was well established.

4. *Secret or dance societies.* These were a specialized development in the area, involving ceremonial, public ritual, and considerable drama. Actually, they represented little more than some basic religious ideas which were carried to a logical conclusion by a people who had the leisure to develop them.

5. *Mythology, relating to cosmology and world view.*

As these religious elements are considered, it is perhaps worth noting that while religion and ceremony were undeniably important, there is little question that the religious institutions played an essentially subordinate role when considered against the system of prestige and status. While crests and names had religious origins, relating as they did to myth and legend and to the special rapport with the world of the supernatural, their use and validation in primarily secular terms was the vital issue. Religious behavior was scarcely an end in itself; it bolstered and fortified the complex social system and cannot be seen out of this context. Evidence for such a view may be adduced from the general lack of systematization in religion. The culture afforded an opportunity to speculate, it is true, and there is a suggestion of the beginnings of a belief in a supreme being, although again, this is by no means limited to the Northwest Coast. The creator-transformer, the trickster mythology of wider distribution, were concepts appearing on the coast and led to an incipient theology, an approach to a belief in gods. But again, such figures were not particularly important; if they existed, they were, in any case, indifferent to the affairs of men.

Although food in the area was available in profusion, so much so that the Northwest Coast has been likened to an agricultural area with its wholly dependable food supply, this was still a development founded in a hunting-gathering economy. As may be thus expected, the world of the animals, one mystically paralleling the human realm, was the immediate source of supernatural power. An animal—or fish—was believed to allow itself to be taken.

Tsimshian ● Owl mask. Masks like this one, strikingly carved in the tradition of the Northwest Coast, were used by the Tsimshian and their northern neighbors in the dramatic enactments of contacts with the spiritual world. (Courtesy of Royal Ontario Museum, Toronto)

Its spirit, released by death, returned again and again provided that the proper care was taken and that no offense to the animal in question was given. The behavior of salmon is clearly a remarkable natural phenomenon, considering that the various species return each year, congregate in great numbers, and move upstream to spawn. Many were taken by the native peoples, but many more ended their life cycle in the freshwater breeding grounds far up the rivers and streams. Their battered and emaciated bodies were then washed downstream. Quite general on the Northwest Coast was the belief that the salmon lived in great houses under the sea. When they lived there, they assumed a human form and carried on feasts and potlatches among themselves. Then, assuming salmon form, they sacrificed themselves. If their bones were returned to the sea, just as the dead salmon were seen returning downstream, they reassumed their human form in their undersea land and would come again. To throw salmon bones carelessly away would prevent the return of the spirit to the sea and give great offense. In such cases, the salmon would withhold themselves and humans would suffer. Out of this reasoning, common to the area, arises the elaborated series of prohibitions associated with the salmon, such as that the bones had to be returned to the sea.

Associated with such beliefs was the elaboration of ritual. All game, but especially the salmon, had to be ritually treated and attempts made to avoid offending it. Such rituals, always observed by an individual hunter, whether on land or sea, became public when group activity was called for. The First Salmon ceremony was an important one for the entire Northwest Coast, although actually it tended to reach more elaborate proportions among the central and southern peoples than it did among the tribes of the northern tier. The ritual was publicly held over the first catch of each species at any place where the salmon run was heavy. It is of interest to note that the social patterns extended to religious observances. There were those who had the lineage rights to conduct the salmon ceremonials, while the first salmon itself was treated as though it were a visiting chief come for a potlatch. The appropriate etiquette, formal speech making, greeting and honoring, were extended to the salmon. It was prepared and cooked in a ceremonial way. Among the various tribes the ceremonial details differed slightly, but the general pattern of greeting the first salmon, either with each run or as a kind of yearly renewal of the world, was fairly constant.

Every ocean species, such as the herring and oulachon which also ran in schools, required similar special treatment, even if not so elaborate as for the salmon. The area did not lay special stress on a land and sea difference; actually, in their religious systematizing, they saw some special and subtle relationships between the various species. Fish other than salmon had their houses under the sea; the various land animals had villages as well. Wolves and bear, especially, had their houses on land and lived in them in human shape. No economic importance can be attached to either wolf or bear, but they required elaborate ceremonial treatment and were thus ritually valuable. To all animals the same concepts carried through: all were immortal, all returned to their natural, and essentially anthropomorphic, state if given proper treatment.

It would be incorrect to speak of the Northwest Coast as developing a special class of priests, ritualists who stand in a special position between the supernaturals and human beings and who carry out the proper observances so as to create a benign relationship to the unseen world. Yet the prohibitions and ceremonials associated with each species of game became so elaborate and required so much knowledge of procedure that specialists had to be called on. These specialists came to own the ritual. Like any other kind of property, it passed through family lines. It may have been repeated for public good and welfare, but it remained one of the prerogatives of a lineage. Those who possessed this knowledge were called on, depending on the circumstances. Thus a man who owned bear ritual was called on to insure success in the hunting of this animal. The area suggests the beginnings of specialized knowledge and concentration.

Turning to the concept of the guardian spirit, a series of beliefs is encountered which has wide following in North America. The notion was that contact with a spiritual being was necessary to success in life. Such contacts were sometimes accidental but more often they were rigorously sought. The spirit gave assurance of ability to achieve some life goal and promise of some control over fate. The promise of wealth might of course be expected, but success in war was also part of the assurance. If the individual acquired curing power, he might become a shaman. Among the northern tribes, there was a strong sense of inheritance of the guardian spirit. The rights to acquire contact with certain supernatural beings were as much a part of the inheritance complex as any other kind of property.

The Tsimshian offer a general example of the guardian-spirit complex as it applied to the three major northern tribes. Spirit power was essential for all persons with any claim to status. Children were rigorously bathed and sometimes made to fast as a first step. A series of ceremonial dances was held in which chiefs "threw" their power into children. The stress on purificatory bathing applied to innumerable situations among the Tsimshian (Garfield, 1951: 38–41). Boys especially, but girls as well, were required to bathe in the ocean in winter and were scourged with switches of spruce boughs and nettles. The process continued after puberty. Before a hunting trip, especially if the game were scarce, as might be the case with mountain sheep, bear, and sea lion, the hunter bathed and recited the proper formulas. Ritual bathing was also called for before assumption of a new name, before initiation into a secret society, in acquiring shaman's powers, and before going on a war party. Related was fasting, urged before any important enterprise. Body purification also involved the use of a purgative. Finally, in all serious activity, there had to be avoidance of sexual relations for a prescribed period. The would-be shaman, for example, isolated himself from his wife and stressed sexual continence. All these features relate to the acquisition of spiritual power. In seeking a contact with a guardian spirit or in reaffirming it, these procedures were regularly followed. An unusual enterprise, in any event, required reestablishment of contact with the guardian spirit. When it is remembered that the spirit realm was a precise reality to the inhabitants of the area, it can readily be seen that the experiences surrounding it could scarcely be questioned. Given the ordeals, the bathing and switching, the fasting, it follows that the individual was prepared from his earliest years to have encounters with the spirit world.

When they came, whether purely by accident or through a conscious quest, the results could be both dramatic and terrifying. A person, intent on his tasks, was suddenly aware of the presence of a spirit. There is little evidence concerning the causes of sudden rapprochement with the spirits. There was the idea of the lonesome vigil, the conscious seeking of a vision. But not infrequently, the spirits came unbidden and it seems not unlikely that the autosuggestion which presumably produced them arose as a group phenomenon. Put another way, a person was suddenly seized by the spirit in front of others. He went into a seizure-like state, frothing at the mouth, or he passed into complete unconsciousness, so much so that others might believe him dead. Whether this was a culturally derived way of meeting the pressures in a social system which did make heavy demands of the individual, creating anxieties about status and wealth, it is difficult to say. Pressures there doubtless were and there was also the sense of being passed over by others of higher position. The reaction described may have been one way of calling attention to one's self. Trance, dream, and vision were all recognized parts of the process. The shamanistic pattern was of the same kind, the spirit power acquired being simply more powerful. The cultures of the area, it is clear, did much to lay a foundation for frenzied states and ecstatic behavior.

When a person had an individual supernatural experience, he was generally given some token of it by his guardian in the form of a mask, songs, or dances. He might test out the spiritual contact, to see whether it was effica-cious for war, wealth acquisition, or general success. Otherwise he did not relate the details to others. At a potlatch, as part of the incidental drama, he might produce the mask or sing his song and thereby make his vision public and establish his rights to it.

The Tlingit, Haida, as well as the Tsimshian, also stressed the inheritance of spirit power. It was validated like other privileges and brought out at an appropriate public gathering. A series of dramatic performances arose, reenactments of the adventures of the clan or lineage ancestors with supernaturals. Masks were used, some of them extremely elaborate, carved so as to permit eyes and mouths to open and close or other parts to move. In the eerie light of the fire, puppets moved on strings and figures strung from cords were propelled across the house. Dramatic performances like these, connected not only with the individual expression of guardian-spirit contact, but often parts of the activities of secret societies, were often enough to induce trancelike states, ecstasies, and compulsive behavior among the witnesses as well as among the performers themselves. Here was a sense of a tie with the past; the ancestors who gave the crests were thought to have obtained them in just such spiritual contacts.

Although spirit power was sought by nearly everyone among the northern tribes of the area, it reached what can be considered its most dramatic and elaborated forms among the class of individuals who followed the shamanistic calling. Curing power, that leading to the office of shaman, was not essentially different from that possessed by any individual, but shamanism was recognized as a calling to cure and as such might be regarded as stronger. The spirits, animal or other, gave the seeker a special kind of healing skill. Although it might be inherited, as was the case with any guardian spirit, the individual, man or woman, might receive this special gift from his guardian. Actually, he did not always want it and resisted it. He might then become ill himself and be forced into the role when another shaman cured him. Generally, as a group, the shamans were set apart because of their skills, not because their power differed in kind from that of other people. The office was also a road to wealth; shamans were paid for their services. It is questionable that a shaman, however skilled, could really amass enough wealth to offer competition to those who enjoyed the fuller backing of household or lineage. He was obliged, like anyone else, to ally himself with his chief and to aid in the wealth procuring. There is not the rivalry between chief and shaman which some other areas exhibited. Even if a shaman ran the risk of being accused of sorcery, the office was still rewarding and some people sought it either consciously or were drawn compulsively to it. To be a shaman was a way to gain some public recognition.

A curing spirit, either inherited or sought, still had to be controlled. There was, in short, a great deal to learn. The aspirant generally allied himself with a tutor, an older relative if the office was inherited, or another shaman. The instruction was paid for, usually by the apprentice's maternal uncle. The theory of the cause of disease in the general area was soul loss, although there was also some attention paid to the intrusion into a person's body of a foreign object which caused "pain." The soul wandered away because of some offense to the spirit world, such as becoming involved with spirits while in an impure state. Sorcery was another cause of illness. A pattern not unlike that of the Eskimo emerged—illness was caused by some infraction of a prohibition. A shaman was hired to diagnose the cause and effect the cure.

Shamanistic cures, as well as performances conducted by shamans to exhibit their powers, were tremendously impressive affairs. Cures were carried out publicly, that is, many assembled in a house where the patient, laid out by the fire, was treated. The shaman sang, went into ecstatic states, summoned his spirits, who conversed with him, and made use of the sleight-of-hand and magical array. Cures and performances were designed to be weird and unusual, thrillingly entertaining for the onlooker. When a shaman engaged in a performance, one designed merely to show off his power, these actions taking place in winter, he swallowed sticks and knives and vomited them up again, sang his power songs, and engaged in contests of strength with other shamans, those in other communities. Shamans, feeling a strong sense of rivalry with their colleagues, attempted to vanquish one another, hurling their powers at each other from a distance. Frequently too, the shaman had to wrestle with his power spirits. In subduing them, as during other aspects of the shamanistic performances, his behavior became frenzied. He frothed at the mouth, went into a trance, appeared dead, and appeared to come alive again. If shamans were initiating an apprentice, as sometimes hap-

pened, although it was rare for a man to announce that he aspired to the role until he was convinced that he had power sufficient to withstand malevolent shamans and their reputed envy, they often went through a staged performance in which the candidate was "killed" then returned to life. The death and resurrection theme was also one which figured in the secret society initiations. Some shamans also practiced fire walking in their trancelike state, again a part of the drama of their role.

Among the Tlingit and Haida, the shaman, once he had assumed office, allowed his hair to grow. Were he to cut or brush it, his power was believed to wane. When acting as a curer, he wore a Chilkat blanket. His paraphernalia included drums—the tambourine, one-sided skin drum of Eskimo and circumpolar derivation, although it moves no further southward than the Tlingit and Haida—rattles, important to the curing rituals, and a special bone tube, used to blow sickness away. In addition to his regalia, although this did differ slightly among the various tribes, the Haida and their neighbors stressed the acquisition of a part of the tutelary source of power. Shamans were buried separately from others, on a low roofed platform. A would-be shaman went to the grave of a dead shaman, took one of his bones, sometimes holding it in his mouth during a nightlong graveside vigil or sucking on the corpse's fingers—all guaranteed to produce spirit contacts. The bone so obtained could then be pointed at an animal who was paralyzed by its power. A small section of its tongue was cut off and kept. The animal was let free. The tongue of the land otter was held to be especially efficacious in thus bringing great power.

Apart from his abilities as a curer, the shaman acted to control weather, although again others who were not shamans had this power. If the salmon run was slow in coming, the shaman might act to snare the souls of the salmon and bring them to the waiting village. In curing, the shaman not only sought the cause of disease and cured by restoring the soul or removing the intruded object and blowing it away, he also had some skill in practical medicine. He gave purgatives, poultices, and even treated teeth with a flint lancet. He could also set bones. No shaman assisted at a childbirth; a delivering woman was unclean, her state abhorrent to the shaman's powers. Like shamans in many other cultures, those of the Northwest Coast were individuals who, avowedly or unconsciously, found in the office a means of attaining status and prestige which might otherwise, because of low birth, have been denied them. In the present area, it was not so much skill as birth which counted. Low birth could never be overcome, but to attract attention, to develop a complex series of magical and soul-stirring acts, to gain wealth by demanding high fees for cures could all in some measure offer compensation.

Another price was paid, however. Shamans were reputedly mean, envious, hard to get along with. Acts of black magic and sorcery, along with incest the greatest crimes in these societies, could be attributed to their malice and evil intentions. A shaman in one's own lineage was treated with respect and deference; he could be depended on if treated with circumspection, but a shaman in another group was a potential enemy. If offended, he could send illness. One might still require his services, especially if he were demonstrably more powerful than the local shamans. All that could be done in such cases was to buy his good will, to bestow lavish gifts on him far in excess of his demanded fee.

Accusations of black magic and witchcraft were fairly common among the peoples of the area. When a person died, sorcery was immediately suspected, and some of the tribes went so far as to perform autopsies in order to determine the magical causes of death. The potlatches, the intervisiting, the moiety exchange of services in the north created a sound base for good relations and peaceful congress between groups. An accusation of sorcery, however, could upset this happy balance. A lasting feud could result. Although shamans were often suspect, any person was a potential witch. He could seek the power or it came to him unbidden, just as guardian-spirit and shaman power. Among the Haida, sorcery was felt to arise when a mouse entered the body of a sleeper and caused him to work black magic against others. The Tlingit were especially horrified by witchcraft and tortured those suspected of it in order to force a confession. The means of making black magic was to secure the exuviae of the one whom one wished to bewitch—the excrement, nail parings, hair, food he had left, an article of clothing—and to take them to a grave box and leave them. The person would then fall ill. A shaman could cure such illness and diagnose the cause. He could also cause a suspected sorceror to confess.

Kwakiutl (?) ● Tambourine, one-sided skin drum, relating to the shamanistic complex, and showing a killer whale design. (Courtesy of The Science Museum, St. Paul, Minnesota)

There were various magical ways of warding off witchcraft.

Beliefs in witchcraft, black magic, and sorcery were by no means uncommon among the American Indian generally. On the Northwest Coast, with its tightly knit social structure, it can be seen, just as in the case of the shaman, that a way was offered by witchcraft for directing one's hatreds against those who arrogantly boasted of their higher status. For most people, participation in the valued institutions of the culture, while possible and certainly gratifying, was sometimes too vicarious and too little rewarding. Sorcery provided an out. So also did the frenzied behavior associated with the guardian-spirit quest.

There can be no question that religion and its patterns were secondary to the major wealth and status preoccupation of the culture. If anything, religion, with its concern with wealth and its justification for the use of crests, provided a rationale for much of the wealth complex. One way in which somewhat wider participation in the life of the culture could be made open to everyone was through the so-called secret societies.

The term secret society is to some extent a misnomer. These were dance groups who performed special series of dances at important public occasions, again part of the potlatch complex. Some dances were owned, along with songs, by people of various ranks. The secret

THE NORTHWEST COAST ■ 153

element arises because there is frequently the association of those with the same guardian spirit. Anyone who was possessed by a spirit was dangerous to those who did not have the same spirit. The result was a sense of initiation into a secret society when someone acquired the appropriate power through a quest. Generally, the development was one of dance groups, associations of people who had particular visions or the rights to them. On various occasions, they brought out their dramatic dance enactments of their spirit power.

At the time of contact, the Tlingit and Haida were just beginning to develop the idea of the religiously inspired dance group. Among the Kwakiutl and Nootka, as well as some of the other central tribes, there was much greater elaboration of the secret society complex. These tribes, in fact, are credited with the original development. From them, it was beginning to spread northward. The Tsimshian, because of contact with the Haisla and Heiltsuk, northern Kwakiutl, had taken over some of the names and organization of the Kwakiutl pattern. Two of the organizations arose as general Tsimshian societies, others were incorporated into the prerogatives of chiefs and so became involved in the system of hereditary privilege. The Tsimshian retained the Heiltsuk names, suggesting the recent diffusion. In some instances, the rights to the dances and the masks associated with them were captured in war. These were then taken over by chiefs as part of their legitimate booty. The differences between the patterns of art in the north and center can be explained by the slight differences in ceremonial interest. The Kwakiutl portraitlike masks, used in the dance society activities, are in contrast to the crest concerns of the Haida and their neighbors.

The two secret societies of central origin which the Tsimshian had integrated into their culture were the Dog Eater and the Dancer. There were other apparently incipient groups among the Tsimshian as well, although the privileges of these, such as the Cannibal and Destroyer dances, were integrated into the system of hereditary right. The two societies are an example of a pattern general in the area. Not only was there the individual quest for the guardian spirit but through the societies, the acquisition of spirit power was made public and took place as part of an initiation ritual. Tsimshian children were subjected at a very early age to a general initiation which was performed under sponsorship of an adult intermediary. From this point, they were encour-

aged to develop the spirit power resident in them. When initiated into either the Dancer or Dog Eater group, an expensive undertaking, since the lineage had to bear the expenses of an initiation, they showed contact with the society spirits and demonstrated their powers publicly. The behavior pattern during such initiatory rituals required the novice to go into a frenzy, to escape, be recaptured, and finally subdued. It was considered that he had been possessed by the spirit of the society and acted under the influences of the spirit. From it he obtained a special song, dance, a name, and some special symbol, such as in the case of one Tsimshian chief, a man who had received a quartz crystal from his spirit (Garfield, 1939:306).

These societies cut across lineages and it was regarded as desirable for the lineage to sponsor memberships in each one for various of its members, male and female alike. It was costly because the sponsors in the dance society, those entrusted with the initiation, had to be compensated. A general initiation feast, again requiring distribution of wealth, had to be given. Those of high status, house chiefs, their heirs, sought to have additional spirit contacts affirmed through the society. This required an outlay of further wealth, but it did increase prestige and it validated hereditary spiritual rights. Only extremely wealthy chiefs could afford several such demonstrations. Out of such a pattern arose a sense of ranking within the dance societies. Such a hierarchial ordering with a number of levels of membership occurred among some of the central tribes.

The two Tsimshian societies performed their demonstrations and their initiations in the winter, although at different times during this season. Everyone in a community was given an opportunity to watch the performances. In the area generally, the winter was the period of most such activity. A vague sense existed of a sacred and profane seasonal division, with winter representing the former. Spirits were held to be closer to humans at this time. In winter, moreover, there was less stress on active economic productivity. The rituals of the secret society were initiated by a chief who held membership. He also terminated the cycle, allowing the "power" to escape through the smokehole in a house.

There is little question that among the northern tribes the emphasis on social rank and crests was infinitely greater than that accorded

Kwakiutl ● Members of a secret society
(Hamatsa) gathered prior to a meeting.
(Photograph C. O. Hastings, 1894, Fort Rupert,
Vancouver Island. Smithsonian Institution
National Anthropological Archives)

religion. In the societies, whether one considers them secret or simply as initiating dance groups, there was a clear association with hereditary privilege. Through his childhood contact with spirit power and through the rigors of his training and upbringing, the person was steered toward the spiritual experience and his ultimate group affiliation. The guardian spirit, acquired individually but with the sense of hereditary right, also pointed toward the secret society membership. The guardian-spirit array then led to public affirmation of acquired power through the societies, group activities which confirmed the hereditary privilege. A complex arose which stabilizes the system of rank in yet another way. And because group membership at this level cut across lineage ties, it afforded another way in which differing lineages could interact. In other words, it made for solidarity within tribes. But as a religious system its basic elements were those of hunting-gathering North America. Its complexity and elaboration lies in its drama, its objects, and its behavior. One may, for example, imagine the thrill of seeing the Dog Eaters, those who were constrained by their familiars, wolf spirits, to kill and eat dogs, or to reenact the experience of

dog eating as it was performed by an ancestor. Or, in another case of spirit-possessed frenzy, Cannibal power represented a society among the southern Kwakiutl, or at least a special class of persons influenced by the Cannibal spirit, but it became a chiefly hereditary privilege among the Tsimshian. In a frenzy, the one possessed bit some of those present when he inherited his title and rank, including the rights to the spirit. This is drama, indeed, but the basic postulates remained essentially simple, making religion secondary to social organization.

Much the same point can be made with regard to the system of myth and of cosmology which evolved in the area. Myths appear in quantity and show not only elaboration but also relations to other sections of North America as well as to Asia, a reflection of the point that mythology diffuses rapidly from one area to another. Despite an extensive mythology and folklore, the area gave it no system. How the world came into being, for example, is treated in the myths, but the tales are never consistent, nor was belief a special issue. The Haida shared the Raven transformer-trickster mythology with a number of the other groups. But Raven played little part in the religious life of the tribe. The Haida also saw the world as covered by a bowllike sky and considered that certain spirits lived on the other side. They also told of an underworld where a spirit being lived on the back of a dog on which rested the islands and the Haida part of the mainland.

Earthquakes were explained as the dog shaking itself. The Haida also had flood myths, and an idea of bringing the earth up from under the water, the "Earth Diver" being, according to the version, Turtle or Raven.

One might, with a number of the earlier investigators in the area, detail the myths at length. But these broader cosmological myths played no prominent role in the life of the northern tribes. What was important was the mythology, truly a sacred one, relating to the origins of the various crests, to the tales of the spiritual experiences of ancestors in the lineage. These were important as history in the native sense. By the same reasoning, the rights to tell certain tales or classes of them were hereditary and passed on through the lineage. From them, some sense of the basic cosmology is obtained. In the important question of the animal realm, that relating to the food quest, myths assigned the salmon and other fishes to a life in the sea and, as noted, attributed a human shape to them. In their natural life, they possessed houses and chiefs. All animals were believed to follow this pattern, as indeed, did the vaguely defined higher spirits, the anthropomorphic beings which suggest the beginnings of a more elaborate system of theology. In other words, the cosmology of the Northwest Coast followed the lead of the native society itself. The spirit world was graded and its inhabitants possessed rights, privileges, and property just as humans did. The status system and all that it involved was carried to such incredible lengths that it seems impossible for the peoples of the area to have conceived of nature in any other way.

THE CENTRAL TRIBES—
KWAKIUTL AND NOOTKA

It is generally held that the northern tier of the Northwest Coast can be regarded as the focus of the area. The integration of moiety-phratry-lineage in the cultures of the Tlingit, Haida, and Tsimshian, coupled with the patterns of wealth, rank, and crest, have suggested that these groups are typical of the culture area in its most vigorous sense. Mention has already been made of the basic difference in the striking art of the area, suggesting that such peoples as the Kwakiutl, Nootka, Bella Bella, and Bella Coola, not to mention the Gulf of Georgia and Puget Sound tribes, had begun to diverge somewhat from the northern model. The Bella Bella, Heiltsuk, and Haisla did, it is true, exert some influences on the Tsimshian. It can be

suggested that the central focus of the area was vigorous in its own way. It had the same kinds of problems to solve, the same general orientations to wealth and rank. But its societal organization differed somewhat, potlatches were somewhat more intense, at least, on certain levels, and there was the development of the religious secret society. Some attention to the central tribes, as well as to those further to the south, may point out how a given culture area may reflect a series of variations on a basic theme.

In all justice to the Kwakiutl, even though their social organization differed from that of the northern tier, they cannot be regarded as a marginal development. If the north is primary, the culture center, Vancouver Island and the adjacent mainland offer a secondary center. In terms of ethnographic reporting, the Kwakiutl especially are among the best known tribes of the area, indeed, the one group most thoroughly worked. Not only did the late Franz Boas, the famous American anthropologist, study the group for more than 50 years, analyzing its customs and behavior, but Ruth Benedict, in her well-known *Patterns of Culture*, made them an example of the so-called Dionysian culture, the individualistic, frenzied, orgiastic character and behavior. Reference is often made to them as a result of Benedict's now-popular book. Actually, Benedict was partially in error in her characterization. It has been seen, among the Haida, for example, that no chief could potlatch alone; he depended on his lineage. All profited from the benefits he assumed and affirmed. This was no less true of the Kwakiutl, the Nootka, or any group which shared in the potlatch institution. The pattern required sharing. How the Kwakiutl, to name one group, arranged this even though the social organization was markedly different from that of the Haida and their neighbors, requires brief attention. Their interrelationships and the patterning of them have led one writer to refer to them as the "amiable Kwakiutl," and so to create a somewhat different picture from Benedict's frenzied, Dionysiac stereotype (Codere, 1956).

The Kwakiutl consisted of about 25 groups who lived on the northern half of Vancouver Island and along the coasts of the adjacent mainland. A group, one might call it a tribe or tribelet, was more or less coincident with a village. There was no total tribal or national consciousness among the people speaking Kwakiutl and there were, in fact, dialect differences among them. As a result, the village was the autonomous unit. These villages followed the pattern already described, a row of plank houses facing the sea. A century and more ago, the Kwakiutl numbered about 3000, although it is suggested that it was once, before the introduction of epidemic diseases of European origin, much larger (Codere, 1950:1). In general, the Kwakiutl, as well as the Nootka, followed the economic organization of the Haida and Tlingit. They were most favorably situated, so much so, in fact, that they amassed an unbelievable amount of food, more of it, if anything, than their neighbors to the north. It was this fact, perhaps, which so blurs any distinction between a subsistence and a prestige economy among them. Food and property were directed to the ends of potlatching on a lavish scale. The Kwakiutl, in fact, seem to have carried the institution to greater lengths. Materially, they were quite well off, living amid a luxury that exceeded, in terms of food and comfort, the lot of any other American Indian—nor does this judgment exclude the farming populations of Middle America and elsewhere.

What made Kwakiutl—and to some extent as well, Nootka—society different from the north was its organization not so much into the unilineal pattern of moiety and clan-lineage as it was into a kind of bilateral extended family with some patrilineal overtones. Matrilineal descent reached as far south as the Heiltsuk but then gave way to the Kwakiutl system. The extended family was the *numaym,* to use Boas's adaptation of the native term (1895). This was a combination of matrilineage and patrilineage, an organization which brought the two elements of descent together in such a way that individual membership in both was possible. The principle which underlay the system was again that of rank. This, in fact, has to be considered the primary factor in the development of the Kwakiutl societal organization, one carried so far that other considerations take on a secondary importance. Rank and privilege were passed on to the eldest son by his father. But all children could and did inherit features of the father's prerogative, although the eldest, by right of primogeniture, usually assumed the greater share. But privilege could also be passed on to the sons of one's daughter. This was done by conferring rights on the daughter and allowing her husband, one's son-in-law, to hold them in trust for his sons. Each male thus drew titular rights from each parent, a special consideration in the case of chiefs. The result of such

an arrangement was not so much an absence as a deemphasis of the stricter rules of exogamy and unilineal descent. Although there was a tendency to avoid marriage with close relatives, first cross and parallel cousins alike, the issue was that of rank and of a careful consideration of the interlocking elements of privilege. The patrilineal bias among the Kwakiutl is seen in the transmission of prime prerogatives to the eldest son and in the fact that a man, following marriage, brought his wife to his father's house.

In practice, the numaym was a group of people related to each other and so forming an interacting extended family. For practical purposes, despite the interwoven series of rights and privileges that passed through the group from the ancestral background, the extended family tended to be local, generally focused in one village. The villages themselves contained from three to seven such units. As in the north, several nuclear families tended to inhabit a single house. Each numaym, whether limited to a single household or at least localized in a community, was invested with defined rights of inherited material and nonmaterial prerogatives. There was the recognition that the group possessed rights to fishing areas, to berry grounds, and to hunting territories. There were also the complex inheritable rights, the array of intangible property, such as crests, rights to dances and rituals, to make certain masks, to acquire special guardian spirits, names, and so through a host of elements of privilege.

Although the principle of rank and wealth was not different from that described for the Haida, the social structure created some variations in application. If anything, the ranking system tended to move to more elaborate extremes, especially in the competitive sense which arose in the culture. Not only were individuals ranked according to the titles and privileges they possessed, but the numaym themselves were ranked against each other and against similar units in other communities. A village itself stood higher or lower in the total social scale because of the titular associations resident in its component numaym. Villages themselves were ranked, again according to the titles to which their component groupings laid claim. The result was that there was a thorough system of ranking throughout the area, one which touched every aspect of life.

Status claims, as in the north, required validation through potlatching. But the Kwakiutl held them more often and attached if anything greater worth to them. Where a Haida chief might potlatch to validate the building of his house, or to ensure the place of his heir, the Kwakiutl potlatches, even if held for the same purposes, were of more frequent occurrence. There was also a greater sense of rivalry between the chiefs potlatching each other, reaching heights of remarkable extravagance. Haida, Tlingit, and Tsimshian potlatches were infinitely more measured; the Kwakiutl seem to have moved to great extremes, certainly, in comparison with their northern neighbors.

The extended family group acted cooperatively to amass the wealth necessary to support the chiefs, those possessing the highest titles in the group. The members were pressured, it is true, but it was again to the advantage of all to rise as a group and as a tribe in total public estimation. The society had its slaves, and there was also the division into chief, noble, and commoner, or so it has been represented in the ethnographic literature. Actually, however, this division must be understood in relation to the principle of primogeniture. Higher titles went to the eldest sons; other sons were relegated to a lesser place. A man who claimed chief's rank could have brothers who inherited relatively little. On this basis there arose some competition between brothers and it could happen that a younger brother might assume titles in his mother's group, were such vacant, a point which indicates the absence of strictly observed patterns of unilineal inheritance. In any case, no man claiming to be a chief held only one title or set of privileges. He had sets of them: in the numaym, in dance societies, in various other rights, all of which could be variously passed on to his descendants, such as to his daughter's sons as well as his own sons. Moreover, through marriage, again requiring careful estimation of associated title, one stood in a position to acquire other rights. Those with fewer rights, younger sons, recalling that they could receive less, were relegated to a lesser place. Conceptually, they might be commoners, but in the native view, this was not the case. They could still achieve high status in a number of ways and could still inherit further. The problem of Kwakiutl society and its organization lay in the fact that there were more persons than titles. Since there was opportunity to acquire greater status by judicious financial dealing, there was greater mobility among the Kwakiutl than among the northern tribes. There was a competition for status, arising from the situation that in the midst of plenty, there was a scarcity of the most valued element, the privileges themselves (Codere, 1950:68). Potential status made everyone a noble in effect. The result has been designated a situation of rank without associated class or caste (Codere, 1957).

It is the feature of competition not only for titles but between titles that has given the Kwakiutl a somewhat distinctive cast when the remainder of the area is considered. The Kwakiutl potlatch also became somewhat differently patterned. Potlatches were given to designate an heir, to reflect a change of name, especially for young men entering manhood, at marriage, involving new titular associations, at the birth of a child, again relating to the inheritance complex, and in the winter initiations into the secret societies. They were also given as feasts where the holder of a position feted those of parallel status. As with the Haida, the Tlingit, or Tsimshian, the potlatch was never an individual matter but rather a series of interlocking distributions in which all those associated with a chief host participated. In such feasts, protocol in relation to rank was very carefully observed. The office of "tally keeper," one who remembered the relative titular positions, was itself a privilege often given to a younger son. The greatest rank holder present was the first to receive a gift and was given the choice and honored seating place.

In the Kwakiutl potlatch, a system of financing arose which, while not unknown to the northern tribes, did not reach such proportions. The point has been made that here was a system of incipient capitalism. The Kwakiutl potlatched so often and with such sense of reciprocal return that it was actually impossible for the labor of the extended group to meet the property demands. The alternative was credit. This was developed and with it a system of interest payments.

Boas (1895:341–342) has presented in detail the career of a Kwakiutl boy stepping into manhood and preparing to engage in the adult status quest. A system developed which permitted him to acquire the necessary capital, one which illustrates the basically fictitious nature of the financial patterns evolved. The boy began by borrowing blankets. These, originally bark and fiber blankets, gave way in historic times to the Hudson Bay trade blanket and were worth, in the period in which Boas writes, about fifty cents. The blanket became a unit of value to the area, one well fixed and serving as a basis of currency among the Kwakiutl, although it never reached this level in the north. Probably the addition of trade goods in postcontact times gave an added wealth impetus; the pattern, however, is clearly aboriginal. In any case, the boy approached men in his own group and those in others to whom he could claim association and borrowed, one may say, 100 blankets. With his blankets he then went to others, men in his own and other numaym, and offered a loan. After a month, the blankets were returned to him at 100 percent interest, meaning that he had now 200 blankets in addition to the 100 he had borrowed. He then repeated the transaction, extending his sphere of business somewhat more widely. At the end of an agreed period, he again recovered his property and received the interest at 100 percent. It is clear that the boy could also count on his father to make him certain gifts of property. He was now in a favorable position to declare himself and to receive his potlatch name and ranking. His initial loan would require a return and an interest payment. Once done, he had acquired sufficient property to carry on by himself, although again, having assumed his place as an adult, he operated within the framework of the social system and cooperated with those of his numaym.

The same general pattern of borrowing and returning with interest ran through the Kwakiutl potlatch system as a whole. In the preparation for any potlatch, the prospective host lent to his own kinsmen and received returns with interest. Actually, this seems no more than a means of creating a basis of cooperation between closely allied individuals. But there was also the sense, when potlatches took place between men of high status, of property distribution and then a return with interest, the interest being equal to double the original investment, or 100 percent. The system, especially as it developed in postcontact times, called for a progressive geometric increase in the amount of property (or money) expended. Actually, there is disagreement on this point among the various anthropologists who have been concerned with the analysis of the potlatch complex. The problem is to understand the bases of high finance among a nonliterate people. The system was one of essentially fictitious capital gains and credits.

It might be thought, for example, that the result of such a procedure would have been to inundate the Kwakiutl with blankets. Contras-tively, in the case of the northern tribes, and among the neighboring Nootka and southern tribes as well, the property distributed at a potlatch was real and tangible. It was collected and covered with skins and other material so that when the guests were assembled and the covers removed, when the chief host and his wife appeared in their finery to begin the occasion, all present could feast their eyes and acclaim the magnificence and the amount of the property assembled. Not of course that the Kwakiutl did not do the same thing. They also went a step beyond. They achieved a system of credit and of marginal capital gains. They were financial experts in the truest Western sense of the word. Various items came to have a monetary value, pretty much as in Western culture. Codere (1950:75), quoting some of Boas's unpublished material, notes that in a village of 150 people, 400 blankets were in circulation but that there was a total indebtedness of 75,000 blankets. Hence, the relations in finance did not have to come out in tangible blankets at all, but in terms of property which had an equivalent value. A canoe, for example, could be expressed as having a worth of 400 blankets. The result was that various tokens could be given, such as a tally stick worth a defined number of blankets, and all individuals were involved in a system with debts owing and debts outstanding. Each man inevitably had his own little financial empire. This remained true even if the more dramatic potlatch involvements were those associated with the chiefs and their transactions. One could call one's debts in, but a financial panic would have been the result. Moreover, since the prestige system and not the wealth itself was the main issue, it was of greater value to keep the system of credits intact.

Codere's analysis of the Kwakiutl potlatch shows the astronomical proportions which the exchange system reached. She argues that the feature which saved the system from destroying itself was the presence of a means by which credit could be erased. The destruction of property introduces the patterned rivalry, the "fighting with property" that so characterized the Kwakiutl. The seeds of it were unquestionably there among the other tribes, but it was the Kwakiutl who carried the concept to its greatest extreme. The destruction was of coppers, the hammered raw copper sheets of unsmelted metal. The system of fictitious values could permit translation into coppers of great worth, those which Boas compares to bank notes of high denomination. Coppers exchanged hands in the course of potlatchings. As each one did so, it was invested with a fictitious value of thousands of blankets. With each exchange the value increased. At last, a chief might feel himself able to destroy a copper, the situation being one in which he sought to discredit a rival. Such instances arose in the competition for place in the hierarchy of rank. The rival, presumably invited as a guest to the potlatch, was bound to equal or outdo the feat by destroying a copper of like or greater value. Here the practical issue of amassing credit was brought to an end. The destruction of the copper, its being broken into pieces or thrown into the sea, ended that particular credit-building sequence. A man's title could then take a higher place, superseding that of a rival. Among the Kwakiutl, title-assuming potlatches and the general pattern of status validation were not concerned with such destruction. This came out only in the system of rivalry and competition and it is this, of course, which has so attracted attention to the group. Moreover, it seems evident that patterned warfare was once the more dominant theme; with European contact, the rivalry potlatch pattern tended to come into its own (Codere, 1950:124). The establishment of the Hudson's Bay Company post at Fort Rupert on Vancouver Island brought several Kwakiutl tribes together in a loose federation. While they knew of each other's relative status, there were still problems of ascendancy of one chief over another. Competitive potlatching went wild (Drucker, 1955:128).

The concept of the secret society was well developed among the Kwakiutl, appearing in its most dramatic forms among the southern groups. In any case, the Kwakiutl are credited with the elaboration of the dance complexes which, because of the initiation feature, have been designated as secret societies. It was this complex which had moved northward to the Tsimshian and which appears also among such southern groups in the area as the Makah and Quinault. The elaboration among both the northern and southern Kwakiutl might suggest that the complex originates among them but the speculations vary. Kwakiutl religion was not essentially different from that described for the north. There were various cosmological ideas, a universe of three realms, peopled by various spirits or divinities (Muller, 1955:15). There were the commonly held views about

animal spirits and a sense of the spiritual guardian. Shamanism and witchcraft were also well developed, but it was in the dance societies that the Kwakiutl again reached an extreme development (Goldman, 1975).

Dances were held in the winter by the members of the various groups. As might be anticipated, the rights to join a secret society or dance house were inherited and the initiation itself required validation through a potlatch. Such initiation, in fact, was one of the rights which a man could confer on the sons of his daughter. If he did so, he might enter into special potlatching arrangements with his son-in-law, again a reflection of the primacy of title over a stress on lineal descent, or in this instance, of the kind of bilateral organization which the Kwakiutl possessed. The grandfather, by passing such a privilege on to his daughter's sons, was partly meeting his own obligations, those incurred through the marriage of his daughter. He was making a return for the bride price and was reaffirming the privileges which arose through the marital union. Any initiation, especially that of the heirs of chiefs, was demanding of an expensive potlatch. A man could step down from his own position in a secret society and confer it on his heirs or a designated heir, who in turn was required to validate his new status. In the Kwakiutl societies there is a suggestion of grading. There were various grades within the dance group itself, each one requiring status validation as the individual achieved it. Only the very wealthy chiefs could aspire to the highest grades. But there were some societies to which only chiefs could be admitted. The societies themselves were thus graded in relation to each other. It can be seen that membership was again an inherited right.

The Kwakiutl of northern Vancouver Island had as the society of first rank the *Hamatsa,* or Cannibal Society. This was followed by Grizzly Bear, *Hamtsamtses,* another Cannibal group, Crazy Man, and Warrior societies. There were grades within them, and the great chiefs of the Hamatsa were the first honored at potlatches (Ford, 1941:23). The pattern which accompanied the winter ceremonials reflects the frenzied character which has been ascribed to the culture of the area. Those to be initiated were captured by the masked members of the group, led to a secret place since they were potentially dangerous to anyone who had not been in contact with the society spirit, and then

Kwakiutl ● Head mask representing a mythical being. The figure is that of the "Cannibal of the Mountain" and was used by the Kwakiutl in the winter dramas staged by the Kwakiutl "secret societies." The figure is carved in the fullblown tradition of the area and painted. The hair is made from shredded cedar bark. (Courtesy of Royal Ontario Museum, Toronto)

brought out at a dance. They threw themselves about in ecstasy, possessed by the spirit, frothed at the mouth, and imitated the character of the spirit which seized them. Part of the initiation in some groups was a ceremonial "killing" of the novice. His lifeless body might be buried in the fire pit. He crept out through a passage and returned, to the presumed wonder of the uninitiated. The death and resurrection theme was a common one. Or in a frenzy, taken by the cannibal spirit, the giant man-eating bird, the dancer cut and ate pieces of skin from selected persons present, people later rewarded with special gifts. Throughout such performances, in keeping with the artistry of the area, a sensational effect was obtained by staging, by use of various props, masks, puppets, and other figures. The secret society aspect of the culture, unlike the secret society developments of some other areas, such as the Southwest, while it did involve some impersonation of the spirits, was mainly for effect. Its religious purpose was clearly subordinated to the social one and it became yet another means by which social worth could be affirmed. Like the potlatch itself, the element of the audience, the concept of display, of enhancing prestige and right were primary (Rohner and Rohner, 1970).

The Nootka, neighbors to the Kwakiutl, are quite like them in the features of material culture and social organization. These groups, numbering about 6000 people, were skilled whalers and shared this ability with some of the peoples along the coasts of Washington, such as the Klallam and Quinault. They went out on the open sea in canoes under the leadership of a chief whaler, one possessing the wealth necessary to the ownership of a canoe. Into the Nootka system of rank and privilege fitted the status of the harpooner, one who possessed the knowledge and also the right to his skills (Drucker, 1951:51ff.). As might be anticipated, the whale figured prominently in the Nootka religious system, requiring magic, hunting preparation, and the commonly encountered spiritual preparation of the participants. Otherwise, however, the Nootka possessed the same food dependence as the remainder of the area; salmon played an important economic role, as did other fish. Nootka society also reflected the interlocking lineage system of the Kwakiutl, with essentially the same bilateral status concerns. The group did not have the same elaboration of the secret societies and was, in fact, more concerned with shamanistic activities; but otherwise, with its chiefs, its ranks, its privileges, its world view, it was a Northwest Coast society. Art also was well developed, but the use of the crest concept begins to shade off slightly. Memorial and mask figures, however, reflect the continuity of the artistic traditions of the area.

What makes the Nootka different from the Kwakiutl, if indeed it is possible to affirm such a difference, lies not so much in the overt features of their culture as in the essentially intangible aspect of their world view and associated personality. The Nootka stressed humor and play, giving a good deal of attention to the role of the comic figure, the clown, a not uncommon development in general native North America. Drucker (1951:456) describes the group as nonviolent, nonaggressive, affectionate, thoroughly open, and amiable. They seem to have lacked the bloody drama of the Kwakiutl, even if, like the Kwakiutl, they could be vicious and sadistic in war and in witchcraft. To return to Benedict's Kwakiutl characterization, there is the impression of the frenzied, orgiastic culture, one overlaid by a sense of brooding, sullen despair. Yet, as has been suggested, the Kwakiutl also had their amiable side, and the dances which they performed also made use of an earthy, ribald humor, just as in the case of the Nootka. Judging from the recent work of Codere, Ford, and others, it may be that the differences are not so great. What the Kwakiutl did was to stress the bloody ceremony, the cannibal spirit and the associated frenzy. Drucker notes that the Nootka are especially drawn to the theatrical performance, a point which can certainly be made for the Kwakiutl. With Ford (1941:27ff.) one is inclined to wonder if the bloody festival and the witchcraft did not become means by which the individual could express himself, give latitude to his feelings and emotions, in the face of a society which suppressed him. Warfare occurred, both among the Kwakiutl and the Nootka, but the same general tendency to avoid open conflict with one's fellows seems characteristic of both. The alternative was the pattern of rivalry, to compete with wealth, and so to shame an opponent. Not everyone could do this; for most there was the purely vicarious experience of watching chiefs affirm their status. Drucker's evaluation of the Nootka person seems borne out by numerous examples. It seems unfortunate that Benedict created a stereotype which surrounds the Kwakiutl with an almost mystic and certainly an exaggeratedly brooding air which makes them considerably less than "amiable." An areal personality there doubtless was, one brought into being by the system of upbringing in the face of the major cultural concerns. But, in general, it is one which seems more like the description put forth by Drucker.

As one leaves the Northwest Coast, moving into the somewhat less vigorous southern reaches of the area, there is a gradual shading off as new ecological zones are encountered. Yet the vital wealth complex is not lost. The forceful cultural stamp appears among the western Eskimo and moves into Oregon, Northwestern California, and the Plateau. Nonliterate, lacking the development of the state as such, yet the Northwest Coast becomes virtually a complex civilization. It unquestionably represents the most elaborate nonagricultural society in the world.

Suggested readings

BARNETT, H. G.
1968   The Nature and Function of the Potlatch. Department of Anthropology, University of Oregon.

BOAS, F.
1966   Kwakiutl Ethnography. Edited by H. Codere. University of Chicago Press.

CODERE, H.
1950   Fighting with Property. American Ethnological Society, Monograph 18. New York: Augustin.

COLLINS, J. M.
1974   Valley of the Spirits: The Upper Skagit Indians of Western Washington. American Ethnological Society, Monograph 56. University of Washington Press.

DRUCKER, P.
1965   Cultures of the North Pacific Coast. New York: Intext.
1955   Indians of the Northwest Coast. New York: American Museum of Natural History.
1951   The Northern and Central Nootkan Tribes. Bureau of American Ethnology, Bulletin 144.

DRUCKER, P. and HEIZER, R. F.
1967   To Make My Name Good: A Reexamination of the Southern Kwakiutl Potlatch. University of California Press.

GARFIELD, V. E.
1939   "Tsimshian Clan and Society," University of Washington Publications in Anthropology 7:167–349.

GARFIELD, V. E. et al.
1951   The Tsimshian: Their Arts and Music. Publications of the American Ethnological Society, no. 18.

GOLDMAN, I.
1975   The Mouth of Heaven: An Introduction to Kwakiutl Religious Thought. New York: Wiley.

HAWTHORN, A.
1967   Art of the Kwakiutl Indians and Other Northwest Coast Tribes. University of Washington Press.

INVERARITY, B. R.
1950   *Art of the Northwest Coast Indians.* University of California Press.

KRAUSE, A.
1955   *The Tlingit Indians.* University of Washington Press. (Translated by E. Gunther. American Ethnological Society, Memoir 26. Original edition: *Die Tlingit Indianer.* Jena, 1885).

LAGUNA, F. DE.
1960   *The Story of a Tlingit Community.* Bureau of American Ethnology, Bulletin 172.

MCILWRAITH, T. F.
1948   *The Bella Coola Indians.* 2 Vols. University of Toronto Press.

OBERG, K.
1973   *The Social Economy of the Tlingit Indians.* American Ethnological Society, Memoir 55. University of Washington Press.

ROHNER, R. P., and ROHNER, E. C.
1970   *The Kwakiutl Indians of British Columbia.* New York: Holt, Rinehart and Winston.

SWANTON, J. R.
1909   *Contributions to the Ethnology of the Haida.* American Museum of Natural History, Memoirs 8:1-300.
1908   "Social Condition, Beliefs and Linguistic Relationship of the Tlingit Indians." *Annual Report of the Bureau of American Ethnology* 26:391–486.

V

Western North America– Plateau, Basin, California

Introduction

Away from the Northwest Coast eastward over the mountains into the Plateau or southward into California and the adjacent Basin, the native cultures are impressive not so much for what they possess but for what they lack. The vigorous cultures of western North America, those which exerted a strong influence and from which there was sometimes extensive borrowing by marginal peoples, can be said to be the specialized adaptations characterized by the Northwest Coast, the Plains, or the agricultural Southwest. Elsewhere there was little by way of distinctiveness, a reflection of the cultural marginality of western North America, a marginality typified by the isolated groups of native California, by the wandering peoples of the Great Basin, and by the essentially impoverished development of the tribes of the Plateau. Like the culture area of the Canadian and Alaskan Athabascans, which, it must be noted, suggests also a Basin-Plateau configuration adapted to sub-Arctic conditions, the area is difficult to define. The wealth complex, modified but none the less present, intrudes into sections of the western Plateau and into northwest California. In both the eastern Plateau and the Basin, following the rise of horse dependence in the Plains, such Plains traits as the tipi, patterned warfare, and the use of the horse give the native cultures a Plainslike stamp. Or again, southern California and Baja California, although nonagricultural, are heavily marked by Southwestern patterns, such as pottery, earth paintings, and spirit impersonation in ceremonials.

The problem is thus to discover a nonmodified series of native cultures, those not subjected to influences from more complex and forceful developments. The three areas are justified; in its own way each is sufficiently distinct to warrant separate consideration. The local configurations are important in demonstrating the variations on the theme of hunting-gathering which characterizes nonagricultural western North America. They are also significant in suggesting the bridging of a gap from the prehistoric past to the ethnological present. In native California, the Great Basin, and the Plateau, while hunting and fishing were not unimportant, these activities tended to be secondary to gathering. On this ecological base there arises justification for consideration of the three sub-

Klamath-Paiute ● The hand game, Klamath versus Paiute. The two men in the center, right, are arranging two sets of "bones" beneath bandanas, while their side sings a power song. One of the opponents must then guess the arrangement. (After Hincks, 1915. Courtesy, Anthropological Archives, University of Oregon)

areas under one heading. If sub-Arctic hunting is to be contrasted with temperate and sub-tropical seed gathering at the earliest levels of New World cultural development, the latter base seems especially exemplified in the Great Basin. The Basketmaker horizons which presage the agricultural growth in the American Southwest imply an adaptation not unlike that of the Great Basin. If division of this vast area into three subregions is possible, although there is disagreement among specialists as to where the lines of division should be drawn, it tends to rest in the specific ecological adjustments within each habitat: wild seeds in the Basin, roots in the Plateau, with considerable added dependence on salmon, and acorns in California. If there is justification for setting the northern Athabascans off from the Plateau, it is essentially because of the difference in food habits; the socio-cultural orientations apart from ecology are not dissimilar.

Local specializations of the seed gathering base appear here and there in the area both because of variations in natural resources and because of influences of adjacent, more vigorous culture centers. In the former case, groups in the Plateau, for example, made extensive use of salmon along with the gathering of wild root crops, factors creating some greater stability of residence and, by extension, a sense of in-group and tribe. These patterns varied to some degree, it is true, but there is enough of commonality to define a Plateau culture area, one somewhat different from either the Great Basin or native California (Ray, 1939:3; Spier, 1930: 224-325). The same point can be made of native California, considering the "uninfluenced" tribes, those drawn neither into the orbit of the Southwest nor of the Northwest Coast. The Californian resource was the acorn; as long as there was a dependable yield of this wild food, the Californian tribes remained in remarkable isolation. But the same precision of definition is not possible for the tribes of the Great Basin. Here band organization and a quasi-nomadism tended to obscure the nature of the tribe and to effect a lack of adequate lines of ethnic demarcation.

Despite the presence of three definable areas in this section of western North America, an underlying series of patterns is discernible. The ecological adaptations vary but there are shared elements of culture. Rephrasings of such complexes as a gathering economy, the girls' puberty rite, basketry and skin work are the merest beginning of a formidable listing of es-

sentially similar cultural elements. There is justification in referring to a great complex which
characterizes the western sections of the continent. Hunting-gathering at base, it differs from
the kinds of developments which arose in areas
touched by agriculture or modifications of the
maize-using theme.

THE PLATEAU

Tribal Groupings

The linguistic affiliations of the peoples of the
Plateau, like those of native California, vary
considerably. Of the language families represented, most extend beyond the boundaries of
the Plateau and are represented in other culture
areas as well.

Language family—Athabascan
> Nicola (an intrusion from the western sub-
> Arctic)

Language family—Penutian
Subfamily—Chinookan
> Wishram

Subfamily—Klamath-Sahaptin (including
> Klamath-Lutuamian, Molala, Cayuse and
> Sahaptin)
> Klamath
> Klikitat
> Molala
> Nez Perce
> Tenino
> Umatilla
> Wallawalla
> Yakima

Language family—Mosan
Subfamily—Salishan
> Coeur d'Alene
> Columbia
> Flathead
> Kalispel
> Lake
> Lillooet
> Okanagon
> Sanpoil-Nespelem
> Shuswap
> Sinkaietk
> Spokan
> Thompson
> Wenatchi

Language family—Algonkin
Subfamily—Kutenai (?)
> Kutenai

The tribes of the Plateau lived in an area of
no little geographic diversity. As a culture area,
the Plateau can be said to lie between the
Rocky Mountains to the east and the Cascades
to the west. Two major river systems drain this
intermontane region, the Fraser and the Columbia. It is the Fraser, in fact, with its great
northern bend, which marks the upper boundary of the Plateau. Mountain systems run north
and south, and there are several ranges appearing in the plateau regions of Oregon, Washington, Idaho, and the adjacent Canadian province
of British Columbia. These are watered and forested, an extension of the western forests. In
the areas of the western drainage, the tributaries of the Fraser and Columbia allow the
passage of salmon, an important native food
source. Along the middle Columbia there is a
gradual southward transition to a sagebrush-ju-
niper vegetal covering, one which gives way
gradually to regions of more intensive dryness
in the Great Basin itself and the Colorado
Plateau. Forested mountain and semidesert are
the major land forms. Some cultural variations
may be anticipated as a result.

For purposes of ethnological description, the
Plateau may be separated from the Basin
largely by the crossing of a language boundary:
Sahaptin leaves off and is replaced in the Great
Basin by the characteristic Shoshonean, a
branch of the major Uto-Aztecan (Aztec-Tanoan) phylum. Similarly, to the far north, the
Athabascan languages of the Yukon-Mackenzie
interior shade off into Salish. While the latter is
also characteristic of the southern reaches of the
Northwest Coast, moving into Puget Sound, it
is strongly represented in the northern Plateau;
the Sahaptin marks the south.

Geographic location and the availability of
natural resources are factors creating some diversity among the hunting-gathering tribes of
the Plateau. But there were also external influences and historic contacts which made for
some variations in the cultures of the area.
Such groups as the Kutenai and Flathead, located to the east of the Rockies, are stamped by
their contacts with the Blackfoot and other
groups from the Plains; much the same imprint
is made on the Nez Perce (Spinden, 1908). In
historic times, the westward trading of horses
caused some changes in the patterns of Plateau
life, especially among those groups living in
terrain suitable for horse maintenance. Slavery,
an institution of the Northwest Coast, was
given some added importance with the advent

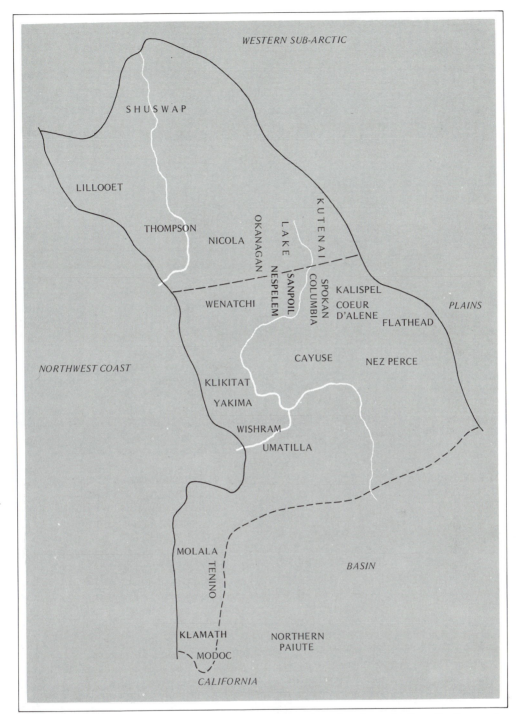

WESTERN SUB-ARCTIC

SHUSWAP

LILLOOET

THOMPSON

NICOLA

OKANAGAN

LAKE

KUTENAI

NESPELEM

SANPOIL

COLUMBIA

SPOKAN

KALISPEL

COEUR D'ALENE

FLATHEAD

PLAINS

WENATCHI

CAYUSE

NEZ PERCE

NORTHWEST COAST

KLIKITAT

YAKIMA

WISHRAM

UMATILLA

MOLALA

TENINO

BASIN

KLAMATH

MODOC

NORTHERN PAIUTE

CALIFORNIA

C1 ● Plateau

of the horse. This was not so much because slaves were incorporated so meaningfully or vitally into Plateau culture as they were in the Pacific tribes, but rather that many Plateau tribes found themselves in the position of mid-

dlemen in a slave-horse trading situation, profiting to the extent of adding horses to their cultural inventory. This in turn increased a stress on raiding, suggesting that in relatively recent times, both Plains and Northwest Coast influences were making themselves more pointedly felt. Such external factors tend to some degree to blur the nature of aboriginal Plateau culture.

The problem is thus to reveal the characteristic uniqueness of Plateau culture and to define the traits which are essentially diagnostic. This is scarcely a task of easy solution, largely because the Plateau, lacking the stirring drama of either the Northwest Coast or the Plains, offers a series of cultural isolates with an absence of cultural intensity. What has been said of such groups as the Slave and peoples like them—Beaver, Carrier, or Chilcotin, as well as other interior Athabascans—can in some measure also be said of the Shuswap and other Plateau Salish. Language, it is true, is different, the caribou are no longer present, and salmon becomes a more dependable food source. Yet the culture patterns are not at base dissimilar. Material culture, appearing in such elements as house types, weapon assemblage, as well as social and political organization, or such religious features as the girls' rite and the sense of guardian-spirit power, all combine to suggest a series of variations within the Plateau on some major configurations generally characteristic of western North America. Shadings of the same general pattern continue into the Basin, although here, while some of the features suggest the Plateau, the orientations are more toward California and the desert Southwest (Kroeber, 1939:55). What is indicated for the Plateau is the absence of any sharply definable lines, boundaries which permit any exact delimitation of a Plateau center.

Lacking cultural focus, the Plateau requires discussion in terms of the relations of the life mode of the native peoples to the natural surroundings. Although virtually all the tribes of the Plateau depended on salmon to a greater or lesser extent, fishing by a variety of methods during the spawning runs from the ocean up the inland streams, differences in terrain, in water distribution and vegetation cover, created some varying patterns in exploitation of the habitat and some cultural differences as well. Despite the presence of such subzones, there is sufficient basic cultural unity in the area to permit one or two diagnostic descriptions (Anastasio, 1972).

The Sanpoil-Nespelem of the Middle Columbia

There is justification for choosing this interior Salish-speaking group, a congeries of peoples around the Big Bend country of what is now

Cayuse, southern Plateau ● Woman smoking buckskin. (Photograph by Major L. Moorehouse, ca. 1900. Smithsonian Institution National Anthropological Archives)

eastern Washington, as exemplary of the aboriginal Plateau. Unlike Plateau dwellers to the east and south, such as the Nez Perce, these tribes were considerably less influenced by the influx of Plains culture traits and so retained something of the flavor of the precontact Plateau pattern into historic times (Ray, 1932:10). The horse, for example, with its associated trappings, was never assimilated into the life of the Sanpoil-Nespelem.

In the Middle Columbia lived—and indeed, continue to live, until recently administered through the Indian Bureau—such "tribes" as the Sanpoil, their neighbors, the Nespelem, the Sinkaietk, or southern Okanagon, the Colville, and segments of other variously named groups. These were much alike in both language and culture, so much so, in fact, that it is well-nigh impossible to draw any sharp lines of demarcation between political units. The pattern, so characteristic of western North America, of local identification and allegiance, in this instance to the autonomous village, prevailed here. Indeed, where there was in the Plateau the development of the tribe in a political sense, it seems evident that this was recent and probably attributable to Plains influences (cf. Ray, 1939:10–24). Common culture and common dialect of Salish made for a sense of identity; this, rather than any formal tribal institution, rested on the emotional designation of "our people." This meant that there could be marriage between villages within the tribe, visiting and trade.

But the local village had its associated territory. With this there were hunting grounds, fishing stations, gathering places. With this territory, too, there was an identification of persons. It is to be stressed that any person might use the lands of another group, but even if trespass was not recognized, the man who did so was regarded as having a guest role. In the Plateau groups which were tribally organized, such as the Kutenai and the Coeur d'Alene, trespass was an offense and strangers barred. In the Middle Columbia, the Sanpoil—and it may be understood that what is true of the Sanpoil is pretty generally true also of the Nespelem, the Sinkaietk, the Colville, and a number of other groups, unless otherwise noted—occupied and considered themselves to own some villages stretched along the Columbia over a distance of about 85 miles (Ray, 1932:13). The four tribes shared about 30 villages between them, all autonomous and independent, but loosely connected by a sense of identity, a fact enhanced by the remarkable pacifism characteristic of these groups. Villages were aligned with territory, with summer encampments and winter settlements.

The Sanpoil-Nespelem population was not so large as that of the groups further to the west along the Columbia, Ray estimating some 1600 for the precontact period (1932:23–24). Villages, spread as they were along the rivers, especially the Columbia, would have held few inhabitants, rarely more than 150 to 200. Estimates are obtained with difficulty, especially in view of the movement of people to summer encampments and back to winter quarters.

The Sanpoil-Nespelem villages in the treeless desert of eastern Washington were located on the benches nearest to the river. Water was plentiful, but the food quest often necessitated movement. Although the Sanpoil hunted in the higher pine-forested mountains, they did not, like the tribes of the Upper Columbia, live in the forests. Theirs was a desert and semidesert adjustment, one affecting their supply of food. The river, however, played an important part in their lives. It was a means of movement and what with trade and fishing, not to mention social visiting, there was often extensive movement in log canoes. These, of two main types, a shallow dugout with a built-out prow and stern, and a deeper sharp-nosed craft, made possible rapid communication between the peoples of the Columbia.

The villages of the Sanpoil, like those of the Plateau generally, were never spectacular. Three to five families, each with its own dwelling, might make up a village which thus contained 30 to 40 people. Some, of course, were slightly larger, as for example, the village of *npui luxu*, the home of the *snpui^u lux^u*, the Salish name from which the corruption Sanpoil arises. Here was a village of importance as a center of salmon fishing; 400 people were estimated to gather there at times, although the permanent winter population seems to have been no more than 75 to 100 (Ray, 1932:18). Around it were several temporary camps, suggesting the essential mobility of the peoples of the Middle Columbia. Offsetting this mobility, however, was the characteristic village identification of the individual as well as the presence of the village chief, a dignitary whose role is described below.

In the village were encountered three, four, five, or occasionally a somewhat greater number of houses. Remembering that the Plateau is elevated and that the winters are severe, no little attention had to be given housing and clothing. In the Plateau generally, housing was complex, consisting of several well-defined types. Probably the oldest, certainly the one with the widest distribution not only in the Plateau, but one having prominence in western North America at large and possessing unquestioned affinities in northern and eastern Asia, was the semisubterranean lodge. The Sanpoil knew this, as well as two different types of mat-covered houses, one for winter, the other for summer. The Sanpoil and Okanagon, in fact, at the center of the Plateau geographically, seem to combine housing elements from several sources.

The earth lodge consisted of a circular pit with a conical or flat roof, the pit itself being 10 to 16 feet in diameter. In the pit was placed a center pole, a large log from which smaller poles radiated to the sides of the excavation. Planks, if such were available, were laid over the radiating poles, or, lacking these, willow mats were used. The roof was then covered with a layer of grass and brush and finally with a thick layer of earth or water-repellent clay. The entrance was located on the roof itself, a well being left to allow both entrance and egress and as a smokehole. One descended into the house by a ladder. It may be noted that roof entrances of this type, associated with the subterranean or semisubterranean house, appear as well in sections of Asia. The *kiva*, the ceremonial house of the Southwestern Pueblos, with its roof entrance, unquestionably relates to the same house complex. The Sanpoil preferred the conical roof which allowed drainage to the flat-roofed type, although the latter was sometimes used. In the house, the fire was placed in the center under the entrance well. This could be closed by a tule mat if no fire was burning or during storms. The interior was covered with a layer of grass which served as a mattress and over which bedding mats or skins were placed. People slept in the earth lodge with their feet toward the fire.

In contrast to the earth lodge was the winter mat lodge, a very different house type with quite different distribution and antecedents. This was a gabled, tentlike structure about 16 feet in width. Its length, however, varied with the number of families resident in it and ranged from 24 to 60-odd feet. This long communal dwelling, 14 feet in height, stood at ground surface. Its entrance, double doors of mats, were placed at the rounded ends of the gable, areas which served for storage. In erecting the mat house, sets of two poles, lashed at the tops, were set into the ground at a slant to form the basis for the tentlike gable. There was no ridge pole, the uprights being held together by transverse rods about 12 feet in length. Matting and grass were laid over the horizontal poles and covered with earth and topped with tule mats. A space was left at the mat course to admit light and as a smokehole. Entering from either round end, a half-tipi-like arrangement, one came through a protected narrow passage, a kind of storm porch, and entered the main dwelling through a second door of matting. A passage, uncovered, ran the entire length of the house. On each side of this four-foot area were mat-covered sections assigned to the resident families. In the middle of the central passage

were fireplaces, each shared by the two families living opposite each other in the house. Each family kept its own place, hanging clothing, weapons, and other gear on the walls, sleeping on soft mats and skins.

The summer lodge was also mat covered but lacked the communal features of the winter dwelling. It was set up by a single family, either in the form of a tipi with three poles and two courses of mats, or merely as a circular windbreak. A further summer variation was a rectangular, flat-roofed structure, most frequently set up at fishing camps. These individual houses were placed end to end and so resembled the communal house of winter. Often little more than windbreaks, these dwellings were closed on one, two, or three sides, sometimes merely with brush. Drying fish might be hung on the lee sides of such structures, protected from the sun by movable mats.

The mat, as may be seen, formed an important element in the Sanpoil material assemblage. Mats were manufactured by women, of both the coarser tule and the softer slough grass. The latter were used for house construction and bedding as well as for a host of other purposes, among them drying berries, holding food, and wrapping corpses. A good deal of skill and time went into mat weaving. For this reason, mats were generally transported. If a family went to a summer camp, it took its mats along, cutting the saplings to support a shelter on the site. Unlike the earth lodge dwellings, the mat houses were always taken down at the close of a season. In the winter lodge, the entire structure was dismantled in spring and the mats taken away. If a death had occurred in the winter, all parts of the house, the uprights and connecting poles, were burned. Unless this was done, it was believed that illness might dog the inhabitants. The supporting poles, sometimes kept and stored until the next winter, were put to some other use than as house posts even if a death had not occurred. Mats, however, were generally kept.

The yearly round of the Sanpoil can be said to begin in the spring, following the period of inactivity which the rather severe winter enforced. Fresh food began to be available and was avidly sought, following a monotonous winter diet of dried foods. Women gathered roots and prickly pears, these eaten when the spines had been burned off, while the men hunted birds and rabbits or gathered freshwater molluscs. Gradually, the winter houses gave way to those of spring and summer, earth lodges were abandoned, and the mat dwellings were dismantled. By late March, groups of four or five families began to trek to the treeless plains south of the Columbia to gather roots. The majority of Sanpoil spent the month of April at these root-gathering grounds, only the aged and infirm remaining in the winter village. Families went off from the village in groups; only rarely did the entire village go en masse. A departing segment notified the chief of its intentions.

While the hunting range of the Sanpoil and other peoples of the Plateau was wide, two items appear consistently in the diet. The intensive fishing of salmon was the work of men, root gathering that of women. Now, in the early spring, women were intensively engaged in gathering a year's supply of roots, those which could be stored and eaten through the next winter, at the gathering grounds. Men's activity did not yet begin, although men accompanied their wives to the plains, there to gossip and gamble while the women went afield for the necessary roots. With the onset of the gathering of any important crop, a simple ceremony was held, a variation on the theme of the first fruits rite. The people came together, the crop was laid out on mats, the chief delivered a short homily, and all took a piece of the crop. The women of four or five families usually went out together under a leader, an older woman of experience who designated the area of each day's activity. The roots were assembled in large quantities at the temporary camp, to be returned at the end of the season for permanent storage in the winter village.

A wide variety of roots was gathered. Most favored was the camas (*Quamasia* sp.) which appeared in several species. The different forms were gathered at different times and prepared for eating in different ways. These starchy roots were roasted, pulverized, made into cakes, eaten raw, stone boiled, among other modes of preparation. In addition, many other wild-growing roots, tubers, and stem plants were gathered. Later in the year women might go afield for berries of many different kinds. Like other groups in many other American Indian areas, the Sanpoil made pemmican, pounding berries with fat and venison. In summary, the Sanpoil and their neighbors made use of a great variety of wild food plants, all of which formed an important part of the native diet.

By the beginning of May the summer fishing began. At this time various small fish as well as sturgeon were taken. Shortly thereafter began the trout and salmon runs. The importance of the salmon to the peoples of the Columbia, or indeed, to the Plateau at large, cannot be underestimated. For the Sanpoil, living as they did on the Columbia itself, salmon unquestionably was the primary staple food. Its importance is further attested by the communal activities and ritual behavior associated with the salmon. While the coastal peoples took salmon in far greater abundance, this does not mean that there was a scarcity of the fish as far inland as the Sanpoil lived. They took four of the five species of salmon common in the Columbia River, the fifth not proceeding so far eastward, and built the basis of their year's food supply on the stored and dried catch. From May until the end of October, the Sanpoil and their neighbors were busy with the fishing activity. There was not exclusive concern with salmon, however; trout, particularly the steelhead, was taken by essentially the same methods.

The methods of catching fish involved spearing and trapping. Although spearing was essentially an individual activity, preparation for it called for no little communal effort. Spear fishing could be done successfully only where the rapids in the river forced the fish into a narrower channel. Camps were built at such sites, and short, artificial channels dug. As the river water rose in early summer, these channels were inundated and permitted a spearer to stand on a platform above them. White rocks placed on the bottom of the four-foot deep channel allowed the passing salmon to be readily seen. In streams smaller than the Columbia, or the Spokane and Okanagon rivers, spearing could be done from the bank or by wading in the water. Channels were dug and platforms built by communal effort. Each man was allowed a turn with his spear, a three-pronged or single-pronged and barbed weapon made of deer bone. When he had taken a fish, he gave his place to the next man.

Spearing was not so productive as trapping. Although nets and seines were known to the Sanpoil and used under certain conditions of weather and river action, weirs were considerably more effective. These were placed at or near the mouths of smaller rivers and streams up which the salmon went to spawn. Fencelike barriers were placed across the stream chosen. The first such allowed the fish through, the second formed a barrier, leaving the fish, with their upstream impetus, with no recourse but to swim into especially prepared traps. Variations of this principle, with willow-withe basket traps, were also widely used, depending on the conditions of the fishing. In small streams, individual families set out their own traps, these being smaller reduced versions of the communally made weirs and traps.

Supervising the activities of salmon fishing was a special dignitary, the Salmon Chief. This was a person to whom absolute power was given in respect to any communal aspect of fishing. The Salmon Chief functioned only during the fishing activity, however, and while his role might relate to the political, in that he kept the village chief informed of his activities, his power was actually dependent on religious sanctions. He either was a shaman or had salmon as one of his guardian spirits. The Salmon Chief set the time for erecting the weir-trap and appointed those who were to assemble it. To him fell the priestly role of supervising the First Salmon Ceremony, unquestionably the most important group religious activity of the Sanpoil. He was thereafter in charge of the actual fishing and the distribution of the catch, designating the men who emptied the trap each morning and evening. Under his eye, too, a fair distribution of the catch was made throughout the village. If the catch was small, the Salmon Chief sat by the trap at night, communed with his spirit, praying that the number of fish might be increased. His place as a priest also called for other duties, such as making sure that no woman approached the trap or crossed the trails leading to it. Nor could a woman take water from a stream where a trap was erected. Women were also expected to remain a few paces away from the place where the salmon was distributed. The idea, of course, related to the possibility of the menstruating woman offending the salmon which then withheld itself. Violation of any of these taboos necessitated the Salmon Chief's communing with the salmon spirit and asking that the insult be overlooked.

If the Salmon Chief happened to be a shaman, other shamans, those in other villages who might possess a malevolent turn of mind, might exert their power to cause a cessation of the salmon runs. In this case, the local Salmon Chief used his power to restore the run if his power were greater, and he might also send illness and death to the offending shaman. Or, if his power were weaker, the salmon run might

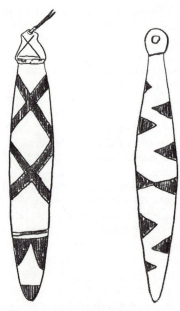

Klamath ● Head scratchers used in girls' puberty rites and by women during menstrual seclusion. During a puberty initiation ordeal, a girl was obliged to remain isolated, to avoid certain foods, and to refrain from touching weapons. She was forbidden to look about and often wore a bark veil. Similarly, she had to drink water from a tube and could not scratch her head with her hands. Head scratchers were especially made for this reason. Failure to comply with any of these restrictions was damaging not only to the community but to the girl herself. (After L. Spier, 1930:70)

cease and he remained powerless to restore it. The point is an interesting one, suggesting as it does the widely spread complex of so-called witchcraft beliefs. The pattern, encountered also on the Northwest Coast, is also clearly defined elsewhere. The notion was simply that the out-group shaman was a potential enemy, one against whom hostile feelings could be directed and a ready explanation for failure.

Women, even if barred from direct participation in fishing, were responsible for the cleaning and drying of the fish. Drying racks were placed by the summer houses at the fish camps, the salmon being hung and spread apart with strips of cedar. In the fall, when the sun was less warm, the salmon were dried in the house, and inadvertently smoked, although this was not the intention. The dried salmon was placed in sewn bags and stored on elevated platforms or in storage houses located on islands in the Columbia. Salmon heads and roe were stored separately in bags. These were dried somewhat longer than the body flesh, the latter process requiring ten days to two weeks. Each family given salmon in the general distribution was expected to dry its own fish.

By the end of October, the intensive fishing of salmon was essentially over. By September, some of the men had gone to higher ground, to the wooded mountains for hunting, while women might take time to go about for berries. Others, still concerned with fishing, visited other communities to see if the catch was any better than on their own ground.

The main hunting involved deer, elk, and antelope. This was done in groups, usually under the leadership of a skilled hunter, one who had one of these animals as his guardian spirit. The men who hunted were supposed to prepare for it by sweating, employing the sweat lodge, a widely spread custom of a hut where steam sweating was brought about by dropping cold water on heated stones. Ten days were supposedly given to sweating prior to hunting. At the same time, the hunter was expected to remain continent, avoiding sexual relations, and not boasting about future success. In sweating, hunting songs to ensure success were sung. Women accompanied the hunting group to cook the food, tend the fires, and act as beaters. The hunt leader appealed to his spirits, the deer were driven by men and women, the latter frequently remaining in camp and coming out only to route the deer if nearby. The deer were driven to a ravine where hunters waited with bows and arrows. On the Columbia, deer were often driven over cliffs. Elk and deer were hunted in essentially the same way, although the antelope, inhabiting the open plains to the south, required a stealthy approach by a single hunter. Bear, black bear and the grizzly, were smoked out of hibernation and hunted also in berry patches with bow and arrow. In keeping with attitudes about the bear, there was some ceremonial, bear songs, in such hunting. At the time of contact, the Sanpoil had begun to hunt the bison, usually in company with the Spokan, but these animals were never economically important. Robes were made from the hide. Smaller animals, the smaller fur bearers as well as wolf and fox, were taken with traps and deadfalls. Rabbits, shot with arrows, were especially important for clothing, such as mittens, caps, and the ubiquitous rabbitskin blanket.

Although furs and skins were important to a people living in an area with cold winters, aboriginal clothing was remarkably scanty. Clothing patterns, in fact, appear to have changed in the century preceding contact, largely as a result of the introduction of buckskin clothing from the Plains. The Plateau in general is not noted as an area in which distinctive types of clothing appear. In summer Sanpoil men wore a breechclout, women an apron, often in front and back. These were woven of bark into which deer hair was sometimes mixed. Over the shoulders was placed a woven poncho. In winter, the same garments were worn, although leggings, of hemp for women, of furs for men, were added. Fur robes and blankets were worn in cold weather. It is said that headgear and footwear were absent in the earlier times. This seems unlikely and it is possible, considering some other Plateau groups, that grass or skins were wrapped about the feet and tied. Moccasins, generally of a western Plains type, were introduced with Plains clothing, as presumably were fur caps. There was some decoration of clothing, along with facial painting both for ceremonial and decorative purposes. Porcupine-quill embroidery was also known. Both men and women braided the hair but there were several coiffure styles for both sexes. Men used bone or wooden tweezers to pull out the scant facial hair, while both sexes plucked the eyebrows to form a straight line. Care of the body was marked, what with sweat bathing, rubbing with oil, and several other practices which suggest that the group had considerable regard for personal appearance.

When the hunting and fishing were over, the Sanpoil settled down into winter quarters in villages and lived off the foods that had been collected. Now, until the spring break-up, was a time of economic inactivity, a social and ceremonial period. The group remained indoors, dances were held, shamans led their performances, there was gambling and recounting of folktales, while any travel was to attend religious festivals in other villages. In the winter, when the families had assembled, the village came into its own and it is thus possible to define some of the social institutions of the group in this context.

Two basic principles dominated the culture of the Sanpoil. These touched and colored the life of the entire group, relating to behavior and to the organization of society. Pacifism was a prime keynote in the culture. Here was a people which sought peace constantly, not only avoiding war and feuds with neighboring peoples and each other, but also refusing to retaliate if attacked. The peaceful life of the community was preserved at all costs. The peaceful ideal carried through into the household without friction. Should tension develop, a person was free to leave. This reflects the second major element in Sanpoil culture—the sense of equality of men and the idea of personal autonomy. There were no social rankings in Sanpoil life. Although the chief was important, especially as one to promote harmony, he was ever one of the group. Unlike neighboring tribes further down the Columbia, the Sanpoil took no slaves and found it unthinkable that one person could be in bondage to another. This premise created a marked communism, all were able to benefit from the work of others, goods were shared, a man need not have participated in fishing but would still be given some of the catch. These two features, equality and the dislike of conflict, minimized the necessity for the development of formal social controls. Torts, offenses against the individual, were kept to a minimum.

Ray (1932:25–27) points out that these features of Sanpoil life, characteristic of the central Plateau, stand in direct contrast to the patterns encountered in both east and west. The stratified society of the Northwest Coast found no place in Sanpoil life, nor did the war orientations of the Plains. This is not to say that war, especially, was absent in the Plateau configuration. Groups such as the Shuswap and the Thompson engaged in raiding, and the pattern was also apparent in the southern Plateau, as among the Klamath. The problem of ranking and war is not readily resolved, especially in view of the influences on the Plateau from the more virile cultures of the coast and the Plains.

Among the Sanpoil, the household, either the earth lodge or the mat-covered house, was inhabited by a group of related people. Exceptions could exist, since the permissive character of the culture enforced no strict rules of residence. The kinship system was basically a bilateral one, although there was a slight tendency toward paternal organization. Even if rules of residence were not rigorously fixed, there was a sense for virilocal residence following marriage. A child frequently continued to live in the area of familiarity but young men often went afield in search of suitable wives, bringing them back to the home community or settling down where the best opportunities for livelihood seemed to exist. A nuclear family might reside with relatives in a settlement and might also travel with these related groups for root gathering and other economic pursuits. The members were free to leave at any time and to associate themselves with relatives in another community or even to settle in a village where there were no kinship ties. Since wives were generally brought from other villages and kinship cut across village lines, affined and collateral kin were widely spread even if wider kinship extensions were lacking. Family and household were important and with the emphasis on harmonious relations, the tendency was for people to get along well together. Marriages became fairly stable, divorce being rare. Both family and household must be seen against the background of the village itself.

Formalism in Sanpoil social organization lay in the political rather than in the kinship realm. The role of the chief in Plateau culture and the various political units which occurred in the area suggest a specialized kind of attention to political structure. Ray's comparative study points up the varying patterns of chieftainship, of structured federations or lack of them, for the area (1938:4–24). The Sanpoil lacked, it is true, any sense of tribe or nation, but accorded to the village something of this character. The village was the prime unit of the group. People were identified as citizens of a particular village. Each village had its chief, its subchief, and its assembly. While it is true that individuals and families could move in and out, claiming full citizenship in any village in which they chose to settle, the village structures remained constant. The result was a fixed political system with mobility of population. Residence constituted citizenship. Citizens were privileged to participate in all community activities, to participate in the assembly and to vote, and to hold office. These rights extended to newcomers as well as to old residents. Marriage, however, was a prerequisite to full citizenship; young men wandered about a good deal and were not given citizenship rights until they settled down as family heads. Women also had a voice in the assembly. Although there was no concept of real property, a village had its berrying and its hunting areas, its rights to these being generally respected. Again the principle of harmony was operative in the culture; kinship and intermarriage between villages created a sense of an extensive in-group even if formal political structures were lacking, tribally or nationally.

Apart from common village territory, solidarity in the community was effected by the presence of the chief. Chieftainship called for persons of responsibility and honesty, of character and integrity. The chief was an adviser, a judge, and a general leader. He directed the movements of the villagers, gave wise counsel, at least in terms of the cultural values, settled disputes, and rendered final verdict in criminal cases. But the chief's powers had weight only as they reflected general consensus; like the chiefs in many other Amerindian tribes, the Sanpoil leader depended on the general respect accorded him and on the force of his personality. At that, Plateau chieftainship tended to be somewhat more precisely structured than was true in a good many areas.

The office was theoretically hereditary, a son following his father, although brother and brother's son might also succeed and there was no definite preference. The assembly, in fact, confirmed the new chief and might select one from a series of eligible candidates. The popular vote was thus also an element in selecting the chief. Nor was the office especially eagerly sought. It entailed responsibilities and only intangible rewards. The chief might have to give of his own store of goods as gifts to litigants or generally to keep peace in his village. The ideal chief was honest, even tempered, and skilled in arbitration. The assembly kept such qualities in mind on selecting a chief. The office was held for life unless a chief resigned or left the community. Women could not be chief although this was not unknown in other Plateau groups.

The chief had an assistant, a subchief, a man either named by him and confirmed by the assembly or selected by the assembly itself. The subchief was assigned certain tasks by the chief and the two were expected to work harmoniously together. Both were served by a spokesman, this again a not uncommon official in the Plateau. At meetings of the assembly, the spokesman delivered oratorically what the chief whispered to him. True of so much of native America, not to mention nonliterate peoples generally, was a high value on oratory; the chief, either through his speaker or by himself, were he able to do so, admonished his people, stressed peace and the desirability of getting along well together.

The assembly consisted of all adults, both men and women. It was not a formal council as such but open to all and allowing equal treatment for all. As noted, membership was usually tied up with a married status; the presence of family responsibilities suggested deeper and more permanent roots. The assembly usually met at the house of the chief. Problems for discussion might involve long sessions. The chief presented the problem and the issue was voted by acclamation. Any person, man or woman, was free to discuss any issue. There was no protocol of seating.

The presence of the chief gave autonomy to a village. Each chief was independent; as mentioned, there was no tribal council, chiefs treating each other with respect but operating independently of each other. The chief stood for peace at all costs. In foreign relations, the chief kept his role as peacemaker constantly to the fore. As could happen, if a village were attacked by such hostile groups as the Lakes, Shuswap, or Coeur d'Alene, with resulting loss of life, the chief urged that no revenge be taken, arguing that lost lives could not be restored by further spilling of blood.

Arguing for peace, the chief continually worked for harmony among his people. In his capacity as judge, he assumed most power in his community. In a society which stressed the worth of the individual yet at the same time demanded conformity to the pattern of harmonious relations, it follows that there would be individuals who stood out for their failure to conform. Witchcraft and sorcery were crimes and it may be seen that here was a patterned approach to the socially unacceptable. Revenge could be taken for this crime or for murder by an injured family, usually with the tacit approval of the chief. Where possible, however, he would seek to arbitrate, levying fines of property and considering the justice of each claim. People accused of misdemeanors were brought before the chief and tried. Witnesses were called and all were free to speak. Stealing, perjury of a witness in a hearing, assault, improper sexual relations such as rape were punished at the decree of the chief. This was done by lashing on the bared back, lashers being appointed by the chief. The number of strokes was in proportion to the offense. In small villages, such as those of the Sanpoil, slanderous gossip and backbiting were frequent and causes of argument and dissension. Again the chief took the role of peacemaker and attempted to smooth over ruffled feelings.

Sanpoil culture, with its particular gathering and fishing economy, its village organization, and its chiefs, allowed a solid measure of security for the individuals within it. From cradle to grave the individual was aware of his obligations and his freedoms. With marriage, one usually arranged by parents although again usually after a young man had made his own choice, one entered into the life of the community, its economic round and its social and political relationships. Further participation, open to all, lay in the religious institutions of Sanpoil life.

The religion of the Sanpoil, like that of the area generally, depended on certain assumptions regarding the supernatural and could be divided, aside from purely speculative beliefs about ghosts, monsters, or omens, into the quest for the guardian spirit, shamanism, and such generally public ceremonies as the First Salmon Rite and the Winter Dance. All three, together with the less formalized range of beliefs, were in some measure interrelated. In religion, the basic theme of individual integrity was again borne out.

In the guardian-spirit quest are seen patterns which cover a wide area, the Plateau being little different basically in this institution from either the Plains or Northwest Coast. But the quest was open to all. It was mandatory for men, but women were not barred from obtaining a spirit helper. Boys were encouraged to go out before puberty, keep a series of one-night vigils, and so make contact with a spirit, which appeared in a vision or dreamlike state on the part of the suppliant. Spirits were, as may be expected, those of animals and covered a phenomenally wide range of insects, fish, land animals—all, in fact, with which the Sanpoil came in contact. The spirit assured the seeker of its aid, as in success in gambling, control of weather, imperviousness to wounds or illness. A song was also frequently given by the supernatural. Any person could have as many guardian spirits as he could encounter, three to six, though rarely more. These became integrally, according to the native concept, a part of the individual personality, so much so, in fact, that individual power remained after death and could be used by another, a relative, who could employ what Ray has termed "spirit-ghost" power (1932:173–174).

An interesting aspect of the guardian-spirit quest was that once the vision had been obtained and the spirit helper present, the whole experience was "forgotten." At least, the idea was that the spirit would return to the individual later in life and then make its presence felt. Ray (1932:186) points out that once the individual had settled down to a responsible life in the community, the spirit could again be called on

and the experience reconstructed to fit the circumstances of the person's life. The return of the spirit caused an illness which was then treated by the shaman. Spirit power had to be used to be successful. Thus a man who had deer power was able to take deer easily and was expected to lest he lose the power.

Shamanism, the second aspect of Sanpoil religion, related to curing. Some guardian spirits gave curing abilities—for instance, the man who had rattlesnake power could cure snakebite—but there was special shaman power which was conferred. Both men and women could be shamans, although the former were more numerous. As is frequently the case in societies admitting shamanism, the Sanpoil being no exception, the shaman was feared. He who could cure illness could also cause it. Although sorcery could be practiced by anyone, accusations of witchcraft were often made against shamans, with care, of course, since it did not do to invite the enmity of a shaman. A chief took care to keep a shaman "on his side," giving him gifts, as did others in the community. Shamans were thus regarded as wealthy, even if wealth among the Sanpoil was not a highly developed concept. It was highly desirable to have a shaman in one's community. During the winter sacred season it was the shaman whose powers protected a village. As may be observed, there were distinct advantages in being a shaman, but at the same time a certain risk. Shamans were reputedly envious, especially those in other villages, and to them were attributed such malicious acts as causing salmon to cease to run. It may be suggested that those with certain personality characteristics, those less competitive, withdrawn, with mystic and also misanthropic orientations, fell into the role.

Shamans cured "unnatural" diseases, those which arose through acts of men or of inhabitants of the spirit world. "Natural" illnesses, injuries, or purely physical afflictions, headaches or colds, did not call for shamanistic treatment. It was rather illness induced by supernatural agencies which were treated. The guardian-spirit return caused illness, as did carelessness in spirit contacts. So also did breaking of prohibitions—menstrual, hunting, burial—which made for the intrusion of foreign matter into the body of the patient. Here again was the common notion of the intruded object as a cause of illness; soul loss was not a Plateau trait. Bewitching by shaman spirits caused a mental illness, delirium, and various psychoses. And there was also witchcraft, the malevolent work of another person. In all cases, the shaman was active. He had to be called, never coming voluntarily. His first task was to diagnose and then to go about his cure. He sang, asperged with water, smoked, and sucked out an intruded object. An assistant, often an apprentice, aided him in his work. Considering the high degree of suggestion operative in illness, it is not surprising to find cures successful. The shaman was paid only for a successful cure.

The public ceremonies were the third element in religion. A First Fruits Rite, as has been noted, was held in respect to the gathering of the first root crops in the spring. With the salmon onset, there was held the more elaborate First Salmon Rite, this under the direction of the Salmon Chief, a priestlike figure who was chosen by the chief, and one who usually had a salmon guardian spirit. The rite involved care not to offend the salmon, to placate it, and to ensure a good catch. In this sense, it was a public activity but one, at least in its ceremonial features, eclipsed by the hard work of fishing. This was not true of the winter dances, public religious activities lasting over the housebound winter period. Guardian spirits were individually received but through the winter dances, public affirmation of the place of the guardian spirit in the culture was made.

People, it is said, became "lonely and despondent" in winter. This mood could only be dispelled by spirit singing and dancing (Ray, 1932:189–200). The dances were guardian-spirit performances held only at the dark of the year. Technically, these were initiation dances, supervised by a shaman, in which the person made ill through contact with his guardian spirit was cured. These dances were organized by a shaman, by the initiate through a shaman, or by anyone at the command of his guardian spirit. Dances lasted three days, so arranged that each village gave one at a different time so as to permit considerable intervisiting. The Sanpoil had not developed the concept or the trappings of the secret guardian-spirit societies which appear further to the east. There were such in incipient form, however, especially since those with bluejay or owl power were expected to police the dances and to protect the dancers. One major idea was that no one might eat during the dance ceremony, a practice enforced by these "sentries." While considerable detail is extant on the nature of the winter spirit dances of the Sanpoil and their neighbors, suffice it to note that the effects were such as to bring people together, to create a solidarity across village lines, and to provide a release from some of the tensions which had built up during the year. The dances brought together and focused the two major cultural configurations of guardian spirit and shamanism.

The Klamath of Southern Oregon

Because the Plateau is lacking in focus and permits description only because of its specialized ecological adjustments, a series of subzones has been suggested. While the Sanpoil reflected life in the desert-plain of the Columbia Basin, there were those Plateau groups who lived in the forests and mountains of the Plateau. One such in the extreme southern part of the area was the Klamath, a tribe with suggestions of Californian traits and one also not entirely removed from the cultures of the Basin. Combining as this group does elements from a number of sources, the Klamath offer a fitting point of transition to the cultural isolates of native California. Here was a tribe which made some specialized adjustments to its habitat, thus differing slightly from the root-gathering, salmon-fishing peoples further to the north. But the Klamath can be regarded as a southern manifestation of Plateau culture and so can be viewed as a primary group in the area.

In a general way, the prehistory of the Klamath may be viewed as illustrative of the Plateau at large. With a few exceptions, of which the Klamath focus is one, the area has been only sketchily worked by archeologists (Jennings, 1974:182–189). Prehistoric investigations point generally to a development over an extremely long period of time of an ecological adaptation of both hunting and gathering. It is evident that the Klamath achieved an efficient and stable mode of life in a rich and rather specialized environment. In their traditions, they combined cultural practices both of the Plateau and the Great Basin.

Thanks to the research of Cressman (1956), the long prehistoric sequence of the Klamath area is understood; archeological work has been carried out in both historic and prehistoric Klamath sites. The very special adaptation of the modern Klamath can be seen as the end product of about 10,000 years of occupancy of the region. Cultural changes through time are well charted; the Klamath tradition is one of some antiquity. The archeological data come from three major archeological locations: Medicine Rock Cave, Kawumkan Springs Midden, and five series of house sites along the Sprague and Williamson rivers in the vicinity of the other two locations.

The oldest of the sites is Medicine Rock Cave, where over three meters depth of deposit lie both above and below a layer of Mount Mazama pumice, dated at 7000 years ago. This site provides the base of cultural succession Cressman suggests for the Klamath; for the most part, however, Kawumkan Springs provides the prehistoric data which chronicle the development of historic Klamath culture. Cressman, on evidence from sites he dug and from other locations in the Northwest, has synthesized a culture sequence that spans a period from about 9000 years ago up to historic contact in the nineteenth century. For the time scale there are only three anchor points—7000 B.P. for Mazama ash, an A.D. 1500 radiocarbon date, and a historic treaty date of 1864. The chronology is therefore based on artifact types and other nonchronometric data (Fig. 34).

Most of the data used came from Kawumkan Midden which was excavated in four arbitrary levels, each 40 cm. thick. Level I is the topmost and youngest, Level IV being the earliest. The midden yielded evidence that until an estimated time of about 2500 B.P., a typically Desert Archaic—Northern Great Basin—assemblage of artifacts and subsistence pattern was dominant, except that river mussels were a continuously popular staple. By the beginning of Level II times, abundant fish bones showed the major food to have been fish, but milling stones for vegetable food, including the mortar and pestle, remain in heavy use. It is estimated that Kawumkan Springs was abandoned as a dwelling site by A.D. 200. Cressman suggests that the special historic subsistence dependence on fish and *Wocas* or water lily seeds may have begun at that time, although to the special two-horned mano or grinding tool, he assigns a late prehistoric development. If he is correct, then a 1500-year depth for the modern Klamath adaptation to the special environment can be claimed.

After A.D. 200, perhaps by A.D. 700, the construction of earth lodges began in the area. The lodges, loosely grouped into villages, were of two sizes. These were rounded or oval shallow saucer-shaped basins with wooden superstructure. The rafters were probably poles arranged around the edge of the pit, slanting toward the center so as to form a conical framework that was covered with mats, bark, or branches over which earth was placed. The large houses were 6 m. or larger in diameter, with either interior basin or mere floor-surface fire areas, and Cressman thinks these were dwellings. The smaller houses, less than 4 m. in diameter, often lack fire areas or other evidence of cookery. Although a number of houses were examined, no post holes or post molds occur in the floor to give evidence of roof supports; historic Klamath houses, however, used post supports, so the prehistoric ones were evidently of an earlier architecture common in the Northwest (Fig. 35).

As suggested earlier, the artifacts from Level II and the later sites were numerous and typical of the Great Basin, with additions believed to presage the Klamath material complex. Inventoried classes of artifacts include a wide variety of chipped-stone projectile points of Great Basin type, including the small triangular-stemmed forms used by the Basin people after A.D. 1, and numerous choppers and scrapers. There were hundreds of whole and broken thick, blocky metates and simple elongated manos. Nearly as common were the conical mortar and pestle, both most often broken. Twenty-nine paint "pallettes," flat slabs with yellow or red pigment on them, were distributed about evenly through the four layers of Kawumkan Midden. In bone and antler there were wedges for splitting wood, harpoons, gorges, awls, flakers, projectile points, and even a needle. Artifact lists from very late prehistoric houses did not include any new items except the two-horned mano and from after contact times, objects of metal.

Cressman is clearly a proponent of long Klamath occupancy of their historic territory. We can agree that the fishing industry—argued by the abundant fish-bone scrap and the gorges and harpoons—is of considerable age and importance. It can also be agreed that Klamath territory has been occupied for thousands of years. Whether the prehistoric continuum is the history of the Klamath cannot be determined, but it seems safe to ascribe perhaps the last 1000 to 1200 years of material to Klamath forebears because it was during this period that permanent housing, the evolution of the two-horned mano, and the present emphasis on fishing developed. We can assume that the Klamath adaptation was a stable, well-established lifeway.

Returning to Klamath ethnography, it can be

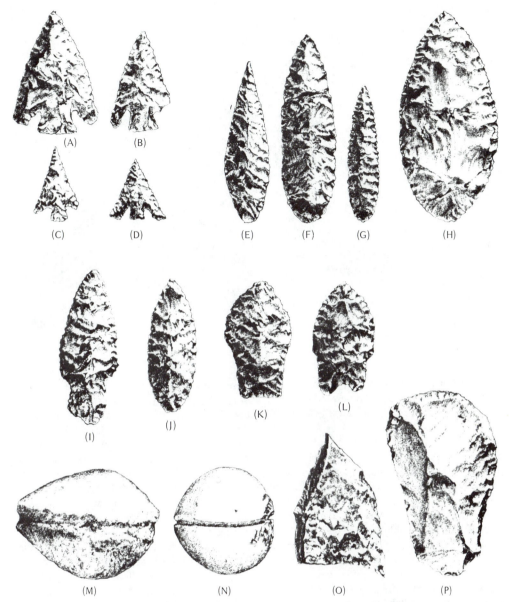

Figure 34 ● A–D, Harder Phase; E–H, Cascade Phase; I–P, Windust Phase. (After Leonhardy and Rice, 1970; Jennings, 1974:184)

seen that hamlet isolation among the Klamath, small hamlets rather than villages having been the rule, both erases any sense of tribal unity and recalls the extreme separatism and isolation which marked native California. Historically, however, and following Spier's analysis of the components and relationships of Klamath culture, the primary orientation to the Plateau can be readily seen (Spier, 1930). Klamath settlements were located away from the salmon area, theirs being an adaptation to highland lake and

marsh. They fished for freshwater whitefish and suckers and gathered *wokas* (*Nymphaea polysepals*), a locally growing wild lily seed. Along with the western American tribes, the Klamath can be assigned to a general ecological configuration of wild food gathering.

The Klamath live today, as in the past, on the 4000-foot-high plateau of central and southern Oregon. Their land verges to higher ground in the west, toward the spectacular geologic formation of Crater Lake. Klamath habitat involved a chain of lakes, headwaters of the Klamath River, located in a shallow depression on the high plateau. In aboriginal times, the Klamath settled on the lake shores (selecting

Figure 35 ● Artist's reconstruction of Harder phase semisubterranean pit houses. (After Leonhardy and Rice, 1970; Jennings, 1974:185)

higher ground for their hamlets) and on the main streams connecting lake and marsh. It is this lake-marsh pattern which lends a certain distinctiveness to the Klamath. The tribe, if such it can be called considering the lack of any centralization, drew its sense of identity from language—although this was shared with the Modoc, a Californian type group—and from common ecology and ideology. It placed its small settlements on lake, river, and marsh. These were largely winter settlements; people moved over the territory in summers, hunting, gathering, and for war, returning to the winter hamlet with the onset of cold weather.

It is evident that the Klamath were split into four or perhaps five subdivisions, depending essentially on proximity. These tribelets, while they might feud with each other, as was sometimes the case, permitted some intermarriage. Small groups of men from different tribelets might occasionally go out as a war party, raiding non-Klamath for booty and slaves. Within each section or tribelet were the permanent winter settlements. Spier (1930:13–21) lists 62 such towns, applying the apt term "hamlet" to them. They were not in any sense centralized

communities. Unlike the Sanpoil, and certainly unlike the Wishram and others to the north of the Plateau, the Klamath made little of chiefs. There were such, rich men, leaders in war, but they were speakers only, offering an example to the group by their success in wealth. The hamlets consisted of semisubterranean earth lodges, with roof entrances, spread out over some distance, although occasionally clustered at random. A single earth lodge could accommodate several related nuclear families. A hamlet could thus consist of just one such or several. Not too large a population is suggested. A century ago, when the culture was still in effective operation, the Klamath probably were somewhat less than 1000, this contrasting with the more numerous and denser populations both to the north and in California (Kroeber, 1939:137).

A quite different tone prevailed in Klamath culture than in the Sanpoil. The latter, with their emphasis on harmony, on the worth of the individual, developed patterns of visiting, hospitality, and generosity. There was a structure to Sanpoil society which made for an essentially predictable and serene world. Although the Klamath were not lacking in the same ideals, they phrased them differently, with the result that certain tensions arose in the society and a quite different set of values emerged. Harmony was stressed, both with the

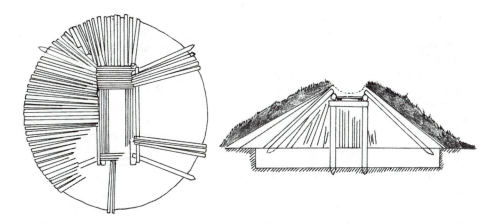

Klamath ● Earth lodge plan. The section and plan here show a common Plateau variant of the widely spread semisubterranean house. Upright posts were linked to girders or studs and logs were placed from these to the edge of the circular pit. Earth was then piled over the roof, the interior lined with yellow pine bark. The entrance in winter led through the roof, while in summer the doorway was dug through a side. The Klamath made special use of a cribbing of logs around the entrance during the winter, a feature serving as protection against rain and snow. Such houses were both large and small, accommodating in the former case as many as a dozen people, in the latter, a single nuclear family. (After L. Spier, 1930:199)

supernatural and with others, but for the latter, especially, there were no enforcing mechanisms. A basic goal was wealth and the prestige derived from it, but unlike the peoples of the northern coasts or even the Yurok and Hupa further down the Klamath River, the Klamath had only the vaguest kind of wealth notion. They collected, amassing a surplus of goods of any kind—skins, food, shells, weapons—in short, any item which could be collected in quantity. It may be suggested that the Klamath offer a marginal phrasing of the strong wealth complex of peoples further to the north. Unlike the Hupa, they had never developed the idea of a unit of wealth. Possessions indeed were valued throughout the whole Plateau; the Sanpoil, as has been seen, had some notions of wealth and possessions, their shamans being reputedly wealthy. But the Klamath stressed the wealth complex rather out of proportion to their material inventory. It was the acquisition of property which colored the life of the individual.

The concept of wealth also led to the place and activity of the individual. Klamath morality called for activity on the part of each member of the group. He was expected to work, to produce, to amass a surplus, this being a moral goal and one reflecting "good" behavior. Something of this moral tone appears as well in native California, an ideal which tended to enforce the separatism so characteristic of this area. People were expected to remain at home, at least in the local community, and to devote themselves to the demands of the local scene. In the Klamath case, the individual was judged on the basis of his application and industry, as a hunter and fisherman, if a man, or as a gatherer, skin-dresser, or cook, if a woman. The word for "chief" in the Klamath language was synonymous with "rich man." There is the distinct impression that the chief used his wealth to dominate social situations. He urged his people to "be good" in formalized harangues and thereby, in a less formal way, succeeded in achieving a position of dominance.

The wealth quest was individual. Persons of "good" reputation worked to produce and to enhance their social status. People were free to do as they wished, finding the economic activity which best suited them. They suffered in reputation only if they were seen as "lazy." Laziness, equated with poverty, created disharmony in the society. The chief gave of his goods to the "poor," albeit grudgingly; nor were the "poor" grateful. Individual achievement was thus a keynote in Klamath society, but there was little room for the somewhat more benign relations which were true of the Sanpoil. There was little hospitality, little sharing of food, and gifts were given reluctantly.

Klamath material culture, like that of the general Plateau and the West exclusive of the

Northwest Coast, was uncomplicated. Basketry was well developed, becoming in fact, the highest artistic achievement. It was made by women and consisted of storage baskets, general containers, cooking baskets, and round basketry hats. Mats were also made, the Klamath employing a mat-covered lodge for summer use. This was a round dwelling, however, suggesting the earth lodge but lacking the excavation and the roof entrance. Clothing was simple, not unlike that of the Sanpoil; moccasins, replacing the footgear of tules, and buckskin appear to have come in with recent trade as Plains traits. Bodily adornment involved tattooing, cuts into which charcoal was rubbed. Head flattening was also practiced; a child's head had the frontal bone depressed while the child was bound in the cradle board, the universal feature of Plateau infancy. Bows were both simple and sinew backed, the latter especially for war, while arrows were both of reed and stone tipped. Armor was both of elkhide and made of slats, the latter suggesting the rod and slat cuirasses of the north. Clubs and a short spear were also in the weapon assemblage. Canoes and snowshoes provided means of transport. The former were simple dugouts, used largely for fish spearing. Work in stone and wood was limited and did not achieve any heights of artistry. Adzes were made of antler rather than stone (cf. Barrett, 1910). Sewing was done with awl and sinew.

Socially, the Klamath had a simple bilateral family, with some suggestion of patrilocal and virilocal residence, although this was not enforced. As among the Sanpoil, polygyny was permitted, although rare, and a bride price legitimized marriages. The marriage price was paid in the form of pelts, skins, fathoms of shell beads, mats, and other property. Bride service was also known, a factor creating temporary uxorilocal residence. Divorce, mere separation, was not uncommon. It was rendered complex, however, by the property involvements at marriage.

The Klamath, with their particular brand of individualism, lacked any elaboration of ceremonial activities. They lacked the First Fruits Rites of some neighboring peoples, even mourning rites being largely individualized. There were social dances, but they were simple and nonceremonial. The institution which brought men from different hamlets and tribal sections together was war. Any man could organize a war party, a group consisting of a few men. A chief was known for his success in war as well as his wealth. Men joined a war party voluntarily, choosing usually to link themselves with a successful strategist. This need not have been a chief, but rather a leader appointed by him. In the event of a large war party, 20 or 30 men, several leaders might be chosen. The basic notion in war was revenge, retaliation for a slain kinsman or an abducted child. Klamath sections could and did feud with each other on this basis. Concerted warfare was directed against neighboring peoples. The Klamath war party, going out ostensibly for revenge, was as much concerned with booty and, especially after new and desired elements such as the horse began to be introduced, with slaves. The war party depended on surprise tactics. They rushed into the enemy settlement, whooping, clubbing, and shooting arrows. Women sometimes went along to add to the din. After the first surprise, the warriors took cover, picking off the enemy with arrows. Booty and slaves were taken and scalps from the enemy warriors. Actually, the dead frequently were dismembered, and following an orgy of killing, the severed parts were brought back as trophies. Scalps, in keeping with western Amerind practice, included the brows and the whole scalp above the ears. The scalp dance, perhaps the only group activity in which the Klamath engaged, was held to rejoice over vengeance taken. The dance lasted over several nights and was marked by frenzied behavior.

Klamath religion was again a variation on the theme of the guardian-spirit quest and on shamanism. The Klamath were fairly heavily drawn to a complex mythology as well, more so than was true of the Sanpoil. Guardian spirits, however, were not so well defined. The concept existed of power, forces which came from animals, it is true, but there was not the same precise relationship to a specific guardian spirit as was true further to the north. Power and songs were linked in the native view; spirits, zoomorphic and anthropomorphic, gave success in various ventures, hunting, gambling, becoming wealthy. They appeared in dreams and visions, conferring songs. Sweating and fasting were part of the spirit-seeking experience, as was a lonely vigil. In keeping with the vague character of the guardian spirit, there was no tendency for those with the same guardian to form associations.

Shamanism had many of the elements which appear in the general area. The shaman was one who had secured more spirit power and was able to use it for curing. Both men and women could be shamans, the vision experience generally being by no means barred to women. Some shamans were reputedly homosexuals, engaging in the wearing of the clothing and the behavior of the opposite sex. Such transvestitism, while by no means unknown among the American Indians generally, was, among the Klamath, allowed only the shaman. Shamans cured and were always summoned by the sick person and his family. The cause of disease was the familiar intruded object, causing illness and sent by an enemy, a malignant shaman, or as a result of breaking a prohibition, such as eating too soon after dreaming. The shaman "doctored," that is, singing his songs, noting the cause of the illness and its location with his "spirit eyes." He then sucked the object out, a dramatic and stirring activity, what with the shaman fighting the "pain," vomiting blood, and struggling with his power. Shamans had apprentices who assisted them, taking the "pain" from the shaman into their own bodies as the curing was done. A shaman was paid for his services. While he may have been wealthy, it was the office itself which called for great respect and fear.

Beside curing, shamans controlled weather, accompanied a war party, made game return, and found lost articles with their power. The most stirring activity of the shaman, however, was the winter seance, held to initiate novice shamans, to demonstrate power, and to prove the strength of one's power. Before an audience of families from his own and adjacent communities, the shaman sang, performed such feats as swallowing fire and arrows, and hurled his power at rival shamans. Winter was not a sacred season since power could be sought at any time, but the shaman employed the time when people were present in the home hamlet to show his might. Chiefs, as has been seen, had little power as such. In Klamath life, it was the shaman who emerged as the feared and respected figure.

Klamath mythology was well developed. It involved not only the various spirits of the animal world, but included anthropomorphic beings as well, such as a quasi-human creator. All the natural features of the Klamath landscape were tied up with tales of how a river, a rock, a cliff, came to be. This is turn was tied up with the sense of power emanating from such natural features. Mountains, lakes, the forest, all were sources of songs of power. The Klamath lived closely in rapport with the natural terrain and found a close mystic bond with it.

Looking back over the Plateau, considering such groups as the Sanpoil-Nespelem and the Klamath, differences in the phrasing of culture traits may be noted. Northwest Coast and Plains influences both made their mark, especially in political and territorial organizations. Chieftainship was a prominent feature, even if among the Klamath it came to have somewhat less meaning. There is the contrast between war and pacifism, between groups which had a strong sense of tribal consciousness as against those which stressed the local autonomy of hamlet or village. In general, however, as the array of cultural elements presented by the Plateau is reviewed, some precisely definable underlying patterns are discernible. Root gathering, fishing, earth lodges and mat lodges, girls' rites, a concept of the guardian spirit in religion, as well as political organization suggest a common cultural base, raw materials worked on by each Plateau group and given in each instance a distinctive slant.

The Plateau—Suggested readings

ANASTASIO, A.
1972 "The Southern Plateau: An Ecological Analysis of Group Relations." *Northwest Anthropological Research Notes* 6:109–229.

RAY, V. F.
1942 "Culture Element Distributions: The Plateau." *Anthropological Records* 8:99–257.

1938 *Cultural Relations in the Plateau of Northwestern America.* Los Angeles: F. W. Hodge Anniversary Fund, Southwest Museum, vol. 3.

1932 *The Sanpoil and Nespelem, Salishan Peoples of Northeastern Washington.* University of Washington Publications in Anthropology, vol. 5.

SPIER, L.
1930 *Klamath Ethnography.* University of California Publications in American Archaeology and Ethnology, vol. 30.

SPIER, L. and SAPIR, E.
1930 "Wishram Ethnography." *University of Washington Publications in Anthropology* 3:151–300.

STERN, T.
1965 *The Klamath Tribe.* American Ethnological Society, Monograph 41. University of Washington Press.

TEIT, J. A.
1930   "The Salishan Tribes of the Western Plateau."
        *Annual Report of the Bureau of American
        Ethnology* 45:295–396.
1928   "The Middle Columbia Salish," *University of
        Washington Publications in Anthropology* 2:83–128.
TURNEY-HIGH, H. H.
1941   *Ethnography of the Kutenai.* American
        Anthropological Association, Memoir 56.
1937   *The Flathead Indians of Montana.* American
        Anthropological Association, Memoir 48.

THE GREAT BASIN

In broad terms, and certainly with respect to subsistence, the western segments of North America, excluding the Northwest Coast and the sub-Arctic north, form a single culture area. The provinces of the area—Plateau, Great Basin, and California—show much in common. Given a concept of culture area, however, it may be expected that the focal and most representative cultures will appear at a center. The cultures which begin to shade off into a boundary area are rarely so reflective of the major or diagnostic pattern. As a culture area in itself, or at least as a segment of a broader domain of western North America, the Great Basin suggests cultural marginality, both in time and space, and is hence defined with difficulty. The three segments are primarily dependent on wild seeds as a subsistence base. The Plateau developed a dependence on gathering, it is true, but was generally able to supplement its food resources with salmon. Similarly, focal California came to specialize on acorns and thus to develop a unique series of patterns. In the Great Basin no such specialization arose, and gathering was directed to all available resources. Similarly, in purely statistical terms, counting the number of elements of culture possessed by the Basin groups, the area is perhaps the simplest of native American cultures.

The point has been made that the earliest levels of native American cultural development were oriented to two primary subsistence forms. There is first the adaptation to hunting, especially in the environment of the sub-Arctic, patterns reflected in the ethnographic present by the various groups of interior Athabascans, or indeed, by the peoples of southern South America. A different ecological mode is found among the seed gatherers of essentially temperate and subtropical regions. In the Great Basin, extensive use was made of the many varieties of wild plants. It is true that the peoples of the Basin hunted virtually every animal in their terrain, not excluding insects, but theirs was always primarily a gathering dependence. The area was never agricultural, despite some evidence of sowing of wild seeds in sections of western Nevada, and it is out of such a gathering economy, elsewhere in the New World, that the ideas which make agriculture possible seemingly come. There is every indication that the temporal depth of the Basin was very great indeed, and that as in the case of the sub-Arctic hunters, here is a remnant of antiquity, a base on which later specializations were built. But the specializations occur elsewhere; the Basin retained its essentially marginal and ancient character.

The generalized gathering pattern and the limitations which it placed on both technological and social development present difficulties in forming an adequate or satisfactory definition of the area. As the literature on the classification of Basin cultures is reviewed, one finds the area linked closely with native California on the one hand or with the Plateau on the other. While it is true that the terrain characteristic of the Basin intrudes into southeastern California, it appears that the native Californian cultures were considerably more specialized. If the general dependence on fish, especially salmon were removed from the cultural inventory of the Plateau, it might be said that this configuration comes closer to that of the Great Basin than does California. All three of these western subareas, to be sure, share many common culture traits, a not unexpected consequence of the primary gathering dependence and a general common history. If the Basin is to be set off as a culture area in its own right, it is probably the geographic focus which lends distinctiveness.

The Great Basin has its main areal concentration in the arid steppe-desert of Nevada, Utah, and sections of what are now the surrounding states. It is a dry southern extension of the intermontane plateau, bordered on the west by the Sierra Nevada of California and the Cascades of Oregon and on the east by the Rocky Mountain chains in central Wyoming and Colorado. The Basin extends northward to verge on the Plateau culture area, including the John Day and Blue mountains of Oregon, the Salmon River and Bitter Root Mountains of Idaho, and takes in the upper waters of the Snake River. To the south, the Basin is

Ute, Uintah Valley, eastern Wasatch range, Utah ● Brush lodge and family scene. (Photograph, John K. Hillers, 1873. Smithsonian Institution National Anthropological Archives)

bounded by the Colorado River which moves westward through the Grand Canyon of Arizona and bends southward to empty into the Gulf of California. Along the reaches of the Colorado are found various peoples with a primary Basin-California type of culture, but who are drawn into modified farming patterns as a result of contacts with the Greater Southwest. Agriculture is significant among the Yuma and Mohave, and there is also modified farming among such erstwhile Basin groups as the Walapai, Yavapai, and Havasupai at the southern and western end of the Grand Canyon. Once away from the river, the arid lands of the Basin proper form the backdrop of the native cultures. The native peoples of the Great Basin inhabited a vast area from the bitter deserts of southeastern California, northward along the dry side of the Sierra Nevada, and across to the Rocky Mountains.

The Great Basin, generally speaking, is exactly that, an area of internal drainage. Although there is some movement of water along the Green, the Colorado, and the Snake rivers, the area is literally turned inward, both geographically and culturally. Basin-range landforms characterize virtually all of the area. There are buttes, short chains of ridges and mountains, all generally oriented on a north-south axis, and there are plains formed by internal drainage. The Sierra Nevada-Cascade complex on the west and the Rockies on the east are mountains higher than those appearing in the Basin proper. It is to be stressed that the area itself is a plateau, and that the many ranges which appear within it may reach elevations of 10,000 feet and more. The presence of the higher mountains at the peripheries of the Basin fairly effectively shut out rainfall, which varies throughout the area but is generally limited. Human settlements may occur in the areas of heavier rains, which are oases within the generally arid environment. Moisture in the Basin generally flows back into the Basin, tending to accumulate in shallow lakes, evaporating slowly and subject to an increase of saline content. Pyramid Lake and Mono Lake have a high salt content, but do not compare with the Great Salt Lake in Utah. The few streams which exist may end in saline marshes or lakes.

Given ranges of varying heights within the area and differences in precipitation, it follows that the distribution of vegetation, so vital to a gathering economy, was also variable. On the Basin floor, in the valleys lying between the ranges, a 5 to 20 inch annual rainfall and a high rate of evaporation, limited vegetal growth to such xerophytic plants as greasewood and sagebrush, neither of significant economic value to the inhabitants. Edible seeds and roots appeared along stream banks and at higher levels in the mountains, but streams were rare and far apart. Where they appeared and in areas along the eastern slopes of the Sierra Nevada and in the Wasatch mountains of Utah, there was some concentration of the limited population. At elevations of 6,000 to 10,000 feet, although generally focused at approximately 8,000 feet, grew the piñon and juniper trees. While juniper was chiefly important for wood, the piñon (*Pinus monophylla* in the north; *P. edulis* in the south) formed the staple food of most of the region. Pine nuts ranged as far north as the Humboldt River in northern Nevada. Other seeds, some from other pine as well as some from other plants, replaced those of the piñon in the northern Basin. Apart from the pine nut staple, however, the tribes of the area used more than seventy-five species of wild food plants (Kroeber, 1939:13–19; Steward, 1938:10–14; Steward, 1955:103–105).

Game in the area was never too plentiful. The central Basin peoples hunted antelope in communal drives when possible, and also engaged in periodic rabbit hunting. In some of the higher mountains where the coniferous forest appears as well as a lusher vegetation, deer were taken. Almost without exception, gathered foods were more important than those hunted. Steward notes that the peoples of the area "probably ate more rats, mice, gophers, locusts, ants, ant eggs, larvae of flies which breed in the salt lakes, snakes and lizards than large game" (Steward, 1955:104). In the rivers which appear at the edges of the Basin, such as the Snake, Truckee, Carson, Walker, John Day, and Humboldt, fish were taken seasonally. The amount of fish cannot compare with that taken in the Plateau, nor were the fish smoked or stored.

In general, the aboriginal Great Basin was an inhospitable area with dry hot summers and bitterly cold winters. It was the home of small groups of humans who drew a precarious living from limited resources.

Peoples of the Great Basin:
Unlike the Plateau or California, the Great Basin is not an area of linguistic diversity; six main languages appear. With the exception of Washo, a Hokan affiliate in the western Basin, and omitting the various languages which intrude on the area from adjacent regions, all groups spoke languages belonging to the Shoshonean branch of the major Uto-Aztecan speech family. Uto-Aztecan poses some problems in the definition of its subgroupings and it is clear that the designation Shoshonean is too general. The term Numic (drawn from the word for "person"; "human being") has been suggested to refer specifically to the Basin Shoshonean languages. Three divisions of Numic—western, central, and southern—each with two principal languages, round out the Basin picture (Miller, 1966:78).

It may be worth noting the place of Numic within the major Uto-Aztecan phylum. As the latter designation implies, the family includes not only the culturally impoverished peoples of the Basin, such as the Ute, but the sophisticated Aztecs as well. It is known that the Aztecs invaded the Valley of Mexico from the

Gosiute, Pleasant Valley, Utah ● Encampment
as drawn by a member of the Simpson
Expedition, 1859. (Courtesy Utah State
Historical Society)

north in late prehistoric times; glottochronologic
reckoning puts the separation between Aztec
and Numic at 4000 to 5000 years (Hale, 1958,
1959). The figure may be somewhat excessive.
In addition to the Aztec relationship, there are
other linguistic ties. The language of the Hopi
towns in Arizona is usually noted as belonging
to Shoshonean; structurally, it is close to Numic. In addition to Numic and Hopi, however,
Uto-Aztecan in the Basin-Southwest-California-
Mexico includes such subdivisions as Tubatulabal, the Takic languages of southern California,
the Pimic, spoken by the Pima-Papago in
southern Arizona, and the languages in northwest Mexico of such groups as the Cahita, Cora
and Huichol, and the Tarahumare of Chihuahua. The problem of Uto-Aztecan is made
somewhat more complex by the presence of the
Tanoan languages, spoken by the eastern Rio
Grande Pueblos. An Aztec-Tanoan phylum is
thus broadened to include the Uto-Aztecan and
the Tanoan and Kiowa languages as well.

Returning to the Numic grouping, it is only
through a linguistic summary that some sense
of the tribal components of the Great Basin can
be reached. Given a gathering economy and
the need to range over a wide area in search of
food, it follows that local groups are necessarily
small and that any sense of tribe as such is
limited to language only. The groups in the Basin are defined by locality and also by language. The six major languages have a curious
distribution. One language in each of the re-

gional phrasings of Numic is wholly localized;
the other fans out widely in the Basin. To sum-
marize:

Western Numic (also designated Mono-Paviotso)
includes the two languages of Mono and
Paviotso. Mono is limited to a small section of
California east of the Sierras, while Paviotso
spreads northward through the entire western
Basin to take in the groups usually called
Northern Paiute.

Central Numic (Shoshone-Comanche) takes in
the small Panamint-speaking area of eastern
California and moves through the Basin to
involve the various Shoshone tribes. Among
them are not only the Shoshone proper but
also groups virtually wholly adapted to the
Plains, such as the Wind River Shoshone, and
the Lemhi at the borders of the Plains-Plateau.
In the southern Plains are the Comanche, quite
clearly speakers of Central Numic.

Southern Numic (Ute-Chemehuevi) takes in the
Ute of Utah and Colorado, the Kawaiisu (and
Chemehuevi) of southeastern California.
Variants are the Gosiute and Southern Paiute.

As a culture area, the Basin is thus clearly
defined by the presence of the Numic languages (Lamb, 1958;1964). The fact that the
Comanche spoke a language mutually intelligible with Shoshone points to a recent
movement of this Plains tribe. The presence in
eastern California of Numic languages and the
fanning out of these languages through the Basin may be suggestive of historical movement.
South of the Grand Canyon and along the
lower reaches of the Colorado another language
family enters the scene. The general Hokan
phylum takes in the Yuman peoples of the
lower Colorado, such as the Mohave, as well as

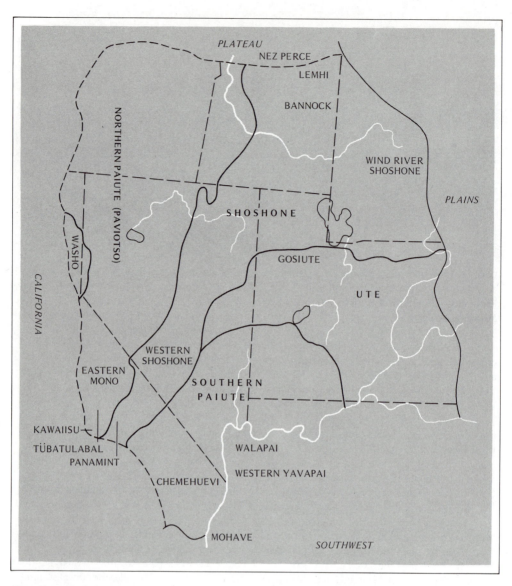

C2 ● Great Basin

the Havasupai, Walapai, and Yavapai. However much, excluding their agriculture, these tribes may resemble Basin culture patterns, they seem essentially different. It may be that Hokan intruded into Uto-Aztecan territory at some prehistoric point. The ethnographic Basin looks like a pre-Pueblo Basketmaker horizon; the Basin and its peoples, never farmers, were linguistically distinct and, given their environment, were culturally definable as well.

Great Basin Prehistory

The cultures of the Great Basin have been recognized as simple and drab. Their artifacts reflect concern with the utilitarian rather than the aesthetic. However, those same cultures are the historic end product of a continuing lifeway some ten millennia in age. The Shoshone can be said to represent the terminal version of the Western Archaic (see Chapter I). The Archaic is antecedent to the historic cultures of the Plateau, Great Basin, most of California and the greater Southwest, and the Central Plateau of Mexico. It can be described as exclusively a hunter-gatherer way of life. Some have labeled the people "Foragers," an apt description but one that does not go far enough. Foraging somehow conjures up a random disorganized pattern of behavior. Such a conception is entirely false. On the contrary, the Archaic lifeway, as reconstructed archeologically and observed historically, was tightly organized, fully attuned to the bounty and parsimony of the arid West. Perhaps it could be cited as a well-nigh perfect and long-successful adaptation to an environment less inviting by far than the Plains or Eastern woodlands, for example.

The Archaic was a subsistence pattern developed around human mobility. The movement of the population in search of varied resources was by no means aimless or blind wandering. Instead, there was a stable, well-known annual round of harvesting, collecting, and storing the varied economic plants, animals, and mineral raw materials. Such a cycle was rooted in an intimate all-pervasive knowledge of a district and its resources.

The desert is not as inhospitable as it appears; a wide variety of plant food is available to those who know the land. Even so, the vagaries of western climate require that the annual subsistence round required knowledge of alternate sources of plant food—the staples of the Archaic larder.

Disregarding the big game hunting, Paleo-Indian, already described, a very brief account of the archeologically known Western Archaic is appropriate here as preface to the Shoshone vignette.

The Archaic seems to be slightly younger than the Llano (Clovis) manifestation but is co-eval with the Folsom finds. The evidence of the lifeway is markedly better. The Archaic is different from the Paleo-Indian on two important counts: (1) it reflects a foraging economy with subsistence focused upon a wide spectrum of species that were seasonally exploited, and (2) the artifact complex contains scores of new tools that indicate new skills. Diagnostic among the new artifacts are the thin slab milling stone and accompanying handstone, the twined flexible basketry or textiles, and before 6000 B.P., sophisticated coiled basketry. A synthesized general description defining the major characteristics of the Archaic Stage follows: A sparse population, very small social groups (extended family), cave and overhanging locations often used for settlement, intensive exploitation of resources, with no reliance on one resource, small seed harvesting with special techniques of preparing and cooking. The Archaic tool inventory includes basketry, netting, fur cloth, woven sandals, the spear thrower, hardwood dart points, stone tools preferably of basalt and quartzite in the early stages (with a shift toward obsidian and other glassy materials later),

flat milling stone, many specialized stone tools, scrapers, choppers, pulping planes of crude appearance, digging stick, curved wooden clubs, fire drill and hearth, tubular pipes, and imported shells from California for ornaments.

One famous Archaic site is Danger Cave, Utah, where a deposit 13 feet deep seems to record the disappearance of the big game tradition followed by thousands of years of Archaic occupancy. The cave yielded literally thousands of stone, bone, leather, and wooden artifacts, which reveal an increasingly complex technology through the centuries but no change in the basic lifeway. The cave was evidently occupied for a few weeks each year while the vast fields of burro weed growing on the salt flats near the Great Salt Desert were harvested. While this harvest was going on, however, many other plant species were collected and hunters concentrated upon the then common mountain sheep. An equally remarkable site is Hogup Cave, also in Utah, where Aikens (1970) discovered and reported a deposit even deeper than Danger. Hogup, richer and more varied in content than Danger, duplicated in every major aspect the finds at Danger, except that the cultural sequence covered a period from about 6000 B.C. almost to modern times. The Danger sequence began earlier, but it is not certain that it extended into the historic period. Even richer, although a little later in time, are Lovelock, Humboldt, Gypsum caves, a cluster of cave locations in Oregon, and several open sites in eastern California, including Karlo.

Farther south in Arizona and Nevada, one of the best documented of the Archaic regional variants is the Cochise sequence. Its earliest manifestation, Sulpher Spring, is associated with extinct fauna, but its later stages, Chiricahua and San Pedro, yield only modern forms. All these cultures are characterized by milling stones and some of the crude chopping tools, in addition to projectile points of typical Archaic form. The Cochise sequence is of particular importance because it has been shown, for example at Tularosa Cave, Cienega Site, and at Wet Leggett, to develop into the earliest of the Pueblo cultures of the Southwest called the Mogollon. In exactly the same way, the northern versions of Desert Archaic form the base from which the northern Pueblo evolved. In California, the full 8000 year sequence reveals the usual Archaic pattern of cyclical seasonal wandering and a wide choice of subsistence resources. California is atypical, however, in that by about A.D. 500 many central California tribes had developed highly specialized and efficient techniques for exploiting the limitless acorn crop, allowing the densest aboriginal population in North America to develop there. At the same time, certain coastal tribes had developed such efficient recovery of sea animals that vegetable resources were almost ignored. Thus we have the interesting phenomenon of an Archaic technology supporting essentially permanent and sedentary villages without the aid of agriculture or reliance upon domesticated animals. In the Basin (excluding, of course, the Southwestern farmers), historic tribes were pursuing the same age-old Archaic pattern of life as recently as 1900.

In Mexico, MacNeish has uncovered a deep sequence of Archaic cultures in Tamaulipas that duplicated the artifacts as well as the general flavor of the Desert Archaic cultures mentioned above. Most scholars see the Archaic of the Mexican plateau as representing the expectable southward diffusion into comparable environment from the more northerly Great Basin. MacNeish surveyed most of Tamaulipas and excavated a series of sites in the Sierras. Beyond documenting the continuous continental distribution of the Western Archaic, which is apparently so efficiently geared to desert resources, the Mexican finds take on particular importance because they contain evidence of agriculture by 5000 B.C. Primitive pod corn appeared by before 1000 B.C., but, interestingly enough, the presence of cultivated species did not reduce dependence upon wild vegetable species until about 500 B.C. For example, during the earliest periods, subsistence was divided about evenly between hunting and gathering. Only a few hundred years before Christ, food gathering still provided about 85 percent of all food, agriculture 10 percent, and hunting the remainder. These Mexican excavations indicate also that the first domesticates were squash and pumpkins, followed soon by several varieties of beans, and finally by corn. The artifacts from this long Archaic column differ only in technological detail from those observed all over the Great Basin and the Southwest. There is heavy reliance on food-grinding tools, much basketry and cordage, and ingenious use of bone for knife handles, scrapers, dart or lance shafts, and other normal uses.

In subsequent work in extreme southern Mexico, at Tehuacan Valley southwest from Mexico City, MacNeish found a comparable Archaic sequence where a similar evolutionary history for corn was documented. Thus, it is apparent that the domestication of food plants and the development of agriculture occurred on the Mexican plateau very early in the Archaic Stage. If we ignore the possibility of Old World influence, we can deduce the development of Mexican high cultures from an Archaic base. The same development in the southwestern United States must be viewed as the result, not of indigenous evolution, but of the stimulus of northward diffusion of both the domesticated species and the concept of agriculture.

The Basin Shoshone

Subsistence, Technology, and Society. Human population in the Great Basin was extremely sparse. In the more favored sections of the area an average might run to 1 person in 5 square miles. In the desert reaches, 1 person to 50 or even 100 square miles is a not impossible ratio (Steward, 1955:103). The area is vast, but population was always necessarily limited. The Basin population has been estimated at 26,700 in 1800 (Kroeber, 1939:143).

One cannot speak of "tribes" in the Great Basin. To a degree there is a parallel with the Eskimo and with the Athabascans of the sub-Arctic, but even band organizations in the pattern of the north were unusual. Family units were primary. Although kinship could unite several nuclear families, those consisting of a man, his wife or wives, dependent children, and perhaps an added relative or two, the nuclear unit was always fundamental. The terrain demanded a special adaptation, one which directed the course of social patterns. It is thus necessary to picture a small group of people essentially alone in a vast region, a group moving through the valleys and up the slopes of the ranges as the food supply dictated. If groups of nuclear families came together as they might for a particular harvest of wild seeds, the units broke off from each other when the task was accomplished. Nuclear groups might also assemble in winter, building shelters together to form villages. By spring, however, the wandering and gathering pattern began again.

In late prehistoric times, the cultures of the Basin were much subject to change, especially in the eastern sections of the area as a result of the introduction of the horse. Two broad subareas may thus be delineated. The peoples of the eastern and northern Basin became equestrian after 1700, assuming Plains patterns of bi-

Nevada Paiute ● Man chipping arrow or dart points. (Photograph by John K. Hillers, ca. 1873. Collection of the Bureau of American Ethnology. Courtesy Utah State Historical Society)

son hunting and war. Plains forms of culture gradually reached the Southern Ute, the Bannock, and the other northern Shoshone, but this change affects the margins of the Basin area. Horses moved westward along the Snake River and into the Columbia, modifying the cultures of such Plateau dwellers as the Nez Perce, Coeur d'Alene, and many others. But the bulk of the Basin remained horseless until at least 1850 (Steward, 1938:234–235).

Because of the assimilation of Plains elements of culture by the eastern Basin peoples, these might be regarded as a general extension of the Plains culture area. They took over the Plains idea of war honors, tipis, the Sun Dance, and all of the technology associated with horses. It is very likely the case that an ecology associated with gathering is probably parallel in both the Basin and the western Plains before the advent of the horse. This is to say that the nonagricultural Plains tribes were not unlike the aboriginal Basin excepting perhaps, even without the horse, a greater dependence on the ubiquitous bison.

A review of the Great Basin cultures as they

were in precontact times has to be found in the center and western sections of the area, principally in Nevada and Utah. The western Shoshone, the northern and southern Paiute are typical of the area. The extreme western tribes, those in eastern California, such as the Chemehuevi, Panamint, Kawaiisu, or Tubatulabal, are more suggestive of the Californian culture area. By the same token, the tribes of the eastern peripheries may be assigned to the Plains.

If the Shoshone are selected as the culture representative of the Great Basin, it must be recalled that they are an extremely widely spread group. There are local differences between the Shoshone segments, not so much in overall culture pattern—the basic cultural orientations and the gathering dependence are consistent from group to group—but rather in specific local adaptations. The terrain offered variable resources; it follows that local groups made capital of whatever regional foods there were. Pine nuts were probably the single most important element in the Basin food supply, but the trees bearing them appear only at high elevations and there were broad areas where no piñon grew. Acorns appear in the far west of the area, near Owens and Death valleys. The mesquite bean was also limited to the Death Valley surroundings. Roots and berries appear more abundantly in the northern fringes of the Great Basin. On a subsistence level, it cannot be said of the Shoshone that they were dependent on a single main food.

To convey an idea of the complexity of Shoshone divisions, recalling that the sole means of defining the Shoshone is by language and that local groups of Shoshone lack tribal or political reality, some of the Nevada divisions may be noted (Steward, 1941:211). By location, groups of Shoshone are found near Death Valley, others at Lida, Beatty, Great Smoky Valley, Smith Creek Valley, Reese River, Ione Valley, Morey, Hamilton, Ely, Spring Valley, Antelope and Snake valleys, Elko, Egan Canyon, Ruby Valley, Battle Mountain, and northward to the Snake River in Idaho. These are, it is true, postcontact locations but they do reflect location in an aboriginal terrain. The same kinds of divisions can be made for the various Paiute, Ute, and others.

Among the Shoshone, gathering was primary; hunting, while clearly important, was given a secondary place. The general gathering complex tended to be quite uniform across the Basin area. Gathering involved every possible plant food; it is estimated that over one hundred wild species of seeds, grasses, roots, and similar plants were collected. At that, it cannot be said with accuracy just how exhaustive the gathering process was. Gathering took place whenever seeds were available, a rich harvest of any wild seeds might call together several families. Both men and women gathered and carried the materials gathered, generally employing a conical burden basket.

Basketry is perhaps the most elaborated Basin technical skill. Baskets of many shapes and sizes were woven, coiled, and twined by women, a reflection of the sexual division of labor so important in an economy of this kind. But the Basin does not reach the same artistic heights in basketry as does central California. The basketry hat, worn by women in the Basin, may be a Californian trait (Steward, 1941:231). The designs on the various baskets represent the height of Basin artistry. Baskets related intimately to the food quest. There were the carrying basket noted above, a basketry seed beater, winnowing baskets, parching trays, and many other forms. Tightly coiled baskets held water, and with a stone rack inside, hot stones were dropped in to bring the water in the basket to a boil, the prevailing American Indian method of stone boiling. There were also basketry jugs or ollas, covered with pitch, which permitted carrying of water.

The seeds collected by the various Shoshone were beaten, winnowed, and variously prepared for eating. Much of the Basin had a simple pottery with limited design (Steward, 1941:294). This, along with the grinding stone, the metate, seems of Southwestern origin. The baskets used in preparing food seem more characteristic and suggest the ancient Basketmaker horizon from which Basin culture seems generally to come. Seeds were variously handled as food. Some could be eaten raw, others required parching. A kind of mush or gruel was made of most seeds, as well as cakes baked from the pulverized seed flour. Roots were obtained with the digging stick and were boiled in pots or baskets and roasted in ashes.

Pine nuts were taken from the cones off the trees. A hooked stick was used to knock down the cones in the fall, when the first frosts at the high altitudes had split the cones. Several families might come together at this time although they would not remain in the mountains for the winter but settle together on lower ground. The extended group might remain together for the winter, having acquired enough pine nuts, a food rich in oil and protein, to see them through the cold season. This situation was about as close as the Basin dwellers came to village life. Houses were built for the winter and the pine nuts and other seeds stored in pits, well guarded against rodents.

Hunting fell generally into the domain of men. Jackrabbits and antelope were the principal sources of meat. Although rabbit populations might rise and decline, antelope drives, because of the limited population of these animals, were less frequent. Individuals hunted both antelope and deer, stalking the game wearing a disguise, but antelope hunts were communal for the most part, resembling both the bison hunting of the Plains and the impound method of the sub-Arctic peoples. The significance of impound hunting of antelope arises because it was in this activity that men from different family groups came together. Further there was a religious aspect to antelope hunting in that shamans performed rituals to attract the souls of the antelope, and by extension, of deer. A shaman, for example, might lie in the impound and perform his magic to draw the game.

It is interesting that ritual should apply to hunting. Despite the fact that gathered foods were more important in the economy, few references can be found to any magic or ritual designed to increase the number of food plants; there are no suggestions of fertility ritual.

Rabbits were hunted not only for their meat but also for their skins. The skin was cut into a long string and woven together with variously selected fibers to make the rabbitskin blanket. While this occurs through the general reaches of western North America, it is important in the Basin, being one of the few elements of clothing to protect against cold. (See Plate, p. 194.)

Virtually all animals were hunted and eaten. An exception appears to have been the coyote. Extremely important in the mythology of the Basin, the coyote was held to have human qualities. Otherwise, mountain sheep, deer, various predators, rodents, birds, and fish where possible were added to the Basin table. To catch rodents, a forked stick was used. Snakes and lizards were also captured in this way. Waterfowl were sometimes hunted on the inland lakes in communal drives. In streams, fish were taken with basketry weirs and nets. Fish, however, were eaten on the spot and there was no adequate means of preserving them. All Basin peoples made extensive use of insect food, eating grasshoppers, locusts, ants, bees, caterpillars, and insect larvae and eggs. The "Mormon crickets," famous in the history of settlement of the Salt Lake area, appeared in vast numbers every seven years and were avidly sought after.

Any game might be hunted individually but communal drives took place when the animal population warranted them. Rabbit hunting, for example, required the use of the long net. This was so important that it might be inherited and the owner became the recognized chief of the hunt. The nets were made from a milk-weed (*Apocynum cannabium L.*), the inner fibers of which were rolled into string by women who rubbed them on their naked thighs. It is said that rabbit nets were sometimes as much as a mile long. Communal rabbit hunting called for equal division of the meat and skins, although the net owners and the hunt organizer might receive a larger portion. Antelope and rabbit drives, as well as the assembly of several families to gather a particular harvest, served to create associations of nuclear families, to bring people together for social and ceremonial as well as economic activities.

Summer shelters in the Great Basin might be no more than windbreaks, temporary shelters of mats. Caves and rock shelters were also used. But considering the sub-zero cold of the area in winter, some more adequate housing had to be developed. A gabled house with a circular ground plan appeared in some Sho-shone groups, but more common was a lodge made with a central pole, a conical house covered with bark, brush, grass, or earth. Some of these houses were semisubterranean (Steward, 1941:233). This house type reflects the circum-polar complex which has so wide a distribution in western North America. A domed willow house was common among the western Sho-shone; willows were bent and tied to form a dome and then covered with whatever material came to hand. Because of the need of the Basin groups to forage widely, houses could never be elaborate or permanent. A house was abandoned when a death occurred in it. The wood which might be used in house construction consisted of dead timbers; there were no tools adequate for the purpose of splitting or chopping wood.

In summer, a winter house might be temporarily inhabited, although it was frequently used at this time for a sweat lodge. The Nevada Shoshone had small willow domed shelters which they used for sweating. Sweat bathing, a complex related to the Plateau and regions further north, was common but not well integrated in the culture. It was considered desirable and might mark a shift from one status to another (e.g., men released from restrictions after a wife gives birth to a child), but notions of ritual purification were vague.

Another structure common to all of the Basin was the menstrual lodge. If houses were placed together to form a "village," they were located at random. The menstrual hut, which did double duty as a place for childbearing, was always placed some distance away from the other dwellings. Classic in the Basin, as in general northern and western North America, is the array of restrictions associated with the menses. A menstruating woman was expected to lag behind the group when it was travelling and to isolate herself in the menstrual hut if the group was temporarily at one place.

Returning again to the concept of a sexual division of labor, houses were generally erected by men. In a gathering economy, both sexes engaged in the seed harvests, although women regularly engaged in general seed gathering, men in hunting. At a piñon site, both sexes worked together, the men knocking down the cones, women picking up the nuts. Both sexes carried water and gathered wood, while insect gathering was women's work. Caches in pits were made by men. Women manufactured baskets and pottery, wove fibers and made clothing. Stone implements, such as the mortar and metate, were made by men. Men also made weapons, chipped stone for knives and arrowpoints, and wove the rabbit nets.

Clothing in the Great Basin was never elaborate. In warmer weather, men wore a breechclout of woven fiber or fur, women wore an apron front and back of the same materials. Some Shoshone are recorded as having gone naked in the summer months. Tailored clothing was known, worn in winter. It was generally of imperfectly dressed skins, often with the animal hair left on. The styles, a long gown of sewed skins with elbow-length sleeves for women, a tailored shirt or poncho for men, may not be indigenous to the Basin but rather introduced from the Plains. Whether clothing was sparse or plentiful, the rabbitskin blanket was the usual winter cloak. While many Shoshone went barefoot all year, moccasins were known and

● COMMUNAL RABBIT HUNTING—
GREAT BASIN

Among the culturally impoverished tribes of
the Great Basin, such as the Shoshone, the
various Paiute, Ute, and others, the basis of
subsistence lay in gathering. While to the east
of the Basin, especially in historic times,
following the introduction of the horse, a
Plains-like configuration developed, the
traditional gathering type of economy
continued to characterize the tribes of Nevada,
Utah, and the adjoining regions. The pine nut
(piñon), although the principal gathered food,
was set against an amazing array of wild seeds
and roots. Hunting was thus not specialized,
although again, virtually every animal which
the environment offered was hunted to a
greater or lesser extent. A focal point of
hunting, however, one which at various times
of the year might draw together several
otherwise independent socio-economic bands,
was the rabbit. Rabbit populations rose and
fell, but when the rangy jackrabbit
abounded in sufficient numbers, a basis for
concerted group activity was present.

Sometimes assembling in the fall, the men
of several bands hunted jackrabbits together,
the women meanwhile gathering up what
piñon nuts remained in the area. The hunt was
frequently called by the older men who
occupied a position of status by virtue of
ownership of nets, these frequently being
family heirlooms, carefully preserved and often
extended to considerable lengths. Some 10 or
12 nets were placed at intervals along the area
chosen for hunting. Here the young men have
raised the rabbits by beating, and have started
the frightened animals down a draw across
which the nets, 1 to 2 feet in height, have been
strung. As the rabbits balk at the net or are
caught in it, they are dispatched with throwing
sticks or killed with arrows. Some hunters
remain concealed near the net to set it upright
should its supporting stakes be upset and to
strike at the quarry as it bounds by. The
purpose of such hunting in the Basin was not
so much for the meat, which was often eaten
on the spot and could not in any case be long
preserved, but rather for the skins. These were
cut into strips and woven with fibers into the

blankets which formed the basis of bedding and winter clothing in so much of western North America.

The rabbit hunt was important, however, as a communal activity in the Great Basin, one which brought several bands together, permitted social activity, allowed arranging of marriages, and so produced a sense of some solidarity among otherwise isolated groups (cf. Steward, 1938:97–98).

varied in manufacture, made either from a single skin with a soft sole or of soft materials sewn to a harder skin sole. Men wore leggings of skins or of woven sage or juniper. Nearly all Basin peoples are reported as having snowshoes of various shapes, predominantly round or oval, with fiber netting. Clothing was sometimes painted or decorated with bead embroidery; tubular beads of bone are prehistoric, glass trade beads appear in postcontact times. In the western Basin, among such tribes as the Northern Paiute, beads came to have a virtual monetary value, an idea undoubtedly drawn from the attenuated wealth complex of northwestern California.

Like clothing, body decorations were not well developed. Both sexes cut their hair to shoulder or neck length. Men and women dressed the hair differently, although both sexes might adorn the head with white or red clay. Faces were painted for social occasions, pigments being mixed with marrow. Women were frequently tattooed on the face, often following puberty. Both sexes might tattoo, however, on the face, arms, and legs. The tattooing was done with a cactus needle, charcoal and burned piñon shells supplying the pigment. All groups bored the ear lobe and had earrings for both sexes. One or two of the western Shoshone bored the septum and encouraged the wearing of a bone nose pin by both sexes.

The northern and eastern Shoshone, heavily influenced by the Plains, took over the buckskin complex, wore feather headdresses and decorated with embroidery of porcupine quills. The central Basin never developed .the skills associated with buckskin tanning. Plains influences also introduced shields, the parfleche, geometric painted designs. Such influences were reflective of the equestrian Basin, a development well after 1800.

The presence of Plains traits suggests raiding and war, but the traditional Basin was anything but war-oriented. The lands which the Numic

speakers inhabited, providing natural resources such as game or foods to be gathered, were not seen as property. Any group, any person was free to exploit the available resources. There was hence no concept of trespass and no resentment if strangers appeared. Not that strangers were likely; even in a wide area, local groups were connected through kinship and marriage or at least by acquaintance. Open violence did sometimes break out between family groups. Disputes might arise over women and there was occasional capture or kidnapping of women. Fear of witchcraft, however, could lead to murder. No one was held to die of natural causes, a malevolent person in another group, usually an unrelated shaman, was always responsible for a death. A suspicion of such a person might result in his death. Unlike the Eskimo situation, however, a concept of collective responsibility was only weakly developed. Feuds seemingly did not last long. It has been indicated that sorcery and witchcraft, the magical causes of death, were effective in social control. Fearing the anger or hatred of an alien shaman, people stayed in line, producing food and avoiding giving offense to anyone. The same attitude apparently acted as a deterrent to war (Whiting, 1950).

According to Steward (1938; 1955), Basin traditional society reflects "a family level of sociocultural integration." The gathering economy, essentially unpredictable, and at the same time demanding a wide foraging area, created a situation in which the local nuclear family was all. A family could camp alone for years at a time. It was obliged to move where food was available. This meant that there was no predictable series of wandering movements. At one time rabbits might abound, bringing several families together for a communal hunt. At another time there might be an exceptional harvest of wild seeds, such as piñon; word would travel and family groups assemble at the place of harvesting. At still another time, limitations of food supply might bring about near starvation. Networks of kinship, however, were operative. Marriages between families gave a sense of relatedness which went considerably beyond the local unit. While there might be relatives scattered through groups other than one's own, it did not follow that there were kinship ties with all adjacent groups. There was thus no broad and all-encompassing web of relationship. The result was that ties between family groups were essentially random, depending on kindred associations. The preference was always to associate most closely with the families bound by such ties.

In a discussion of Basin social life, the terms "unit," "group," "family" have been used. There is probably no more inclusive or adequate term. Band organizations of society, especially patrilineal bands (Steward, 1955:122–142), do occur among some of the southern Californians, but it seems clear that the kinship aspect of the Basin family rules out the more pointed economic implications of band organization. Men, it is true, might come together for a communal activity, such as antelope or rabbit hunts, but when the hunt was over, they returned to the nuclear kinship unit to which they belonged. When families came together, as they might during the winter, the associations were generally with others with whom there were ties of marriage.

Shoshone social organization is best understood through an analysis of marriage patterns. The Basin in general lacked institutions to regulate marriages, such as clans, moieties, or other unilineal forms. Bilateral descent prevailed. The Shoshone forbade marriage between collateral relatives to the second or third degree. This meant that the principals in marriage could not have a common grandparent or great-grandparent. Genealogical reckoning was not an issue; the individual family usually placed its relatives, whether consanguineal or affinal, pragmatically, by simply remembering them. As is the case in many tribal societies, marriage functioned as a contract between groups, serving to effect cooperative and amicable relations between unrelated groups. It introduced ties of kinship, trust, and mutual aid.

Some exceptions existed to the prohibition of cousin marriage. In the north of the Basin, among the northern groups of Shoshone and the northern Paiute, a vague notion of cross cousin marriage existed. This was sometimes a marriage between a man and his father's sister's daughter, or, as sometimes occurred, there was a pseudo-cross cousin marital form, between a man and his father's sister's stepdaughter. The effect of such an arrangement was again to create a tightly knit bond between groups.

The marital tie tended to have some permanence, although a couple might divorce for sterility and also for infidelity. There was no specifically defined residence pattern, although it may have been more usual for women to join the family group of their husbands. A married couple with children could form its own unit, locate itself independently, retaining close ties with the respective families of origin. With a well defined sexual division of labor, it followed that marriage was lent some stability. Marriage was thus an ideal state; widowed persons would either remarry or, if too old, attach themselves to a family group as virtual hangers-on.

The presence of both the sororate and the levirate among the Shoshone conveys some sense of the strength of the marital tie and attests the point that marriage was a contract between groups. A man might not only marry his deceased wife's sister(s), but might often take two sisters at once as his spouses. Similarly, a woman might pass to her husband's brother at her husband's death. Among the Shoshone and the Paiute, both forms were apparently required, clearly a means of effecting continuing group solidarity through the marital bond. Polygyny was generally of the sororal type; conversely, polyandry occurred, and as might be anticipated, was of the fraternal type. There appears to have been no objection to either form of marriage (Steward, 1941:311).

Adultery occurred, a husband was always the offended partner. An unfaithful woman might be killed by her husband but this was seemingly rare, the husband being content with beating or with rubbing the offending spouse with blood. Her paramour, on the other hand, might be severely beaten, his property destroyed or stolen. Men could wrestle over a woman, assembling their kinsmen to back up any claim. A consistently adulterous woman could be abandoned by her husband, thus creating a state of divorce. It seems fairly clear that there was a general puritanical cast to Basin societies, one not wholly different from both California and the Plateau. Men were held to be weakened by overmuch attention to sex. For both men and women, sexual interests were felt to inhibit the ideal of work and production. A "good" person to the Basin dwellers was one who provided for his family, was openhearted and generous to family and such nonrelatives as he might meet, able to suppress his sex drives in favor of diligence and industry. Chastity in women was desirable. In one or two Shoshone groups, a man might offer gifts to his prospective mother-in-law, paying her in effect for sexual rights to the woman destined as his wife. Ideally, however, a man should wait until his betrothed was able to join him as a wife. Marriage arrangements were thus usual, but there was no bride price. Gifts of food, skins, tools, and the like were often exchanged between the groups united in a marriage.

Cycle of Life. The respective roles of husband and wife at a birth illustrate further the stability of marriage. Women about to give birth went to a special lodge, usually a domed willow hut. The child was delivered by the mother either lying flat or kneeling. Relatives often assisted, but any skilled woman might be called in. In cases of difficult delivery, the husband might be called, although he generally remained away. Persons with spirit power might call the baby out. The mother drank warm water and bathed after delivery. A woman was under ritual restrictions after a birth, drinking warm water for as much as three months and variously prohibited from working, eating meat, grease, or salt for as much as thirty days.

The father, meanwhile, was also subject to restrictions. He too bathed, assisted by other men, when the birth occurred and was subject to a series of restrictions. He avoided making cordage and straightening arrows while his wife was in the latter stages of pregnancy, lest by magical transfer the child was strangled by its umbilical cord or was born too soon. After the birth, the father avoided meat and grease for five or for as much as thirty days. He was also forbidden to smoke, to take a sweat bath, or to gamble for varying periods. The restrictions on the father reflect the custom of the couvade, sometimes called the male childbed, where the father is made subject to ritual prohibitions. In the Basin, the function of these taboos served to reflect an acknowledgement on the father's part of responsibility for the child and a spiritual tie to it. In other words, in following the restrictions, the man assumes the status of parent.

A new born child was bathed, then placed in a cradle board. These were of a number of different shapes and sizes, depending on the material resources available. The board, so common in western North America, was made of a frame of basketry and covered with skins. It might be elaborately decorated with beads, feathers, or matched animal skins. In the east, the cradle boards were covered with decorated buckskin. The child was wrapped tightly in the board, but was taken out and cleaned morning and evening. The board usually was made with a subshade. It was regularly carried on the mother's back, taken off and left in a convenient place as she worked.

Children were given names as soon as it was evident that they would survive. Unwanted children were often killed—by sitting on them or thrusting them into a badger hole—while deformed children, and sometimes twins, were similarly destroyed. When a child was named, it was regarded as a member of the group. General in the Basin status terms were used as names. A person was designated by a series of terms indicating his age or growth. A baby was different from a child whose deciduous teeth had erupted, or another who had lost the milk teeth. Names might vary through life, especially as a new status (e.g. marriage) was reached.

Once released from the cradle board, usually simply when he was too large for it, the child learned to walk and talk. He then followed the wandering group, learning by imitation, and learning especially the kinship associations he possessed, not only in his immediate nuclear family, but in units elsewhere. The kinship terms which he used were, usually in the general Basin, of the so-called Hawaiian type. These were generational, reflective of the bilateral societal organization, and potentially encompassing a wide circle of kin. By this system, cousins were merged with brothers and sisters, relatives in the parental generation were called by parent terms, although some exceptions existed on the fringes of the area. The child was drawn into the work ideal, girls following their mothers, boys their fathers, each sex learning the skills appropriate to it.

Puberty rituals for girls follow the general western North American pattern. Girls at their first menstruation did not form a group, but were subject to observances for themselves alone. A girl was confined in the menstrual lodge for as long as thirty days. She might lie in a heated pit or on heated ground and was instructed by her mother or other relative. Her hair was especially combed, she was deloused by her attendant, and she was made subject to such restrictions as avoiding meat, grease, blood, fish, salt, and cold water. She could not talk or laugh; she was obliged to use the scratching stick to touch her body and to avoid hunters, sick people, and in some instances, all males. The time of her confinement following her first menstrual period varied with the local group and ranged from five to thirty days. During her confinement, the girl was obliged to work very hard, carrying wood, and running, always wearing a veil of fibers. Careful observance of these regulations was held to make a girl active, industrious, and suited for marriage.

After the period of initial restriction, women were subject to the same general rules when menstruating. For five days they were required to isolate themselves, to avoid meeting men or watching dances, and to observe certain dietary restrictions. It has been suggested, although precise data are lacking, that the husband of a menstruating woman could not hunt, fish, or gamble while his wife was secluded. If this is the case, it might again indicate the degree of solidarity which existed between married couples.

Boys were not initiated or subjected to any special regimen at puberty. It is said that there were lectures given to the boy at this time, and it may be that special attention was given to the first game taken by an adolescent boy.

When a girl had undergone the trials associated with the onset of the menses, she was eligible for marriage. Boys were felt to be ready when they had demonstrated command of the necessary skills. While there was no ceremony connected with marriage, beyond a gift exchange between the families involved, unions generally took place during the winter months when groups of families came together. At this time marriages could be arranged for the future, suggesting a sense of betrothal. As may be surmised, marriage itself was defined by cohabitation. It is again worth noting that there were no formal rules of residence; the newly married couple could live and move along with the family of the groom, the bride, or establish its own independent unit.

The Shoshone generally feared the dead. The corpse itself was considered impure, and there was a strong view that death was never natural but arose from sorcery. Treatment of the dead varied somewhat through the area. Some groups might abandon a dying person in his shelter. Others made a funeral pyre of the dwelling in which a death had occurred. Some groups buried, others cremated. A relative of the same sex might wash the body and paint it. Persons who did this were ritually impure and thereafter sweat bathed to purify themselves.

General in the Basin was the destruction of the property of the dead, especially of the dwelling of the deceased. This was usually burned even if the corpse had been removed for burial or cremation elsewhere. Relatives might take some of the personal possessions of the deceased. Bereaved relatives engaged in ritual mourning. Both sexes, relatives of the dead, cut their hair, throwing the clippings on the pyre or grave. Women abstained from meat and washing for a time. For men and women, the death of a spouse required a year of waiting before remarriage. Men were under other restrictions; some groups prohibited gambling for a year. There was also a general taboo on the mention of the name of the dead, a trait suggestive of native California and sections of the Plateau. In the western Basin, a Californian type of annual commemoration took place; honors were paid to all who had died during the year.

Social and Religious Life. It is said of the Basin that religious beliefs did little to bring groups of families together (Steward, 1955:113). There was no elaboration of ceremonial. The notion clearly existed that relations to the supernatural were pretty largely a matter of individual choice and experience. The general tenor of Basin life worked against collective social and ceremonial activities; an exception could be said to lie in collective and communal hunting. Dances were often held after such hunts, but one looks in vain for a ceremonial rationale. A circle dance, with a hopping and shuffling step, often held in a brush corral, was the usual Basin form. The purpose was mainly recreational, although there may have been some vague notions connected with it about bringing deer or perhaps increasing the seed crop. Variations on the circle or round dance existed throughout the Basin area. Men and women alternated in choosing partners for the dances and it is clear that this was a social amusement. Musical instruments, a resonator, rattle, and drums, were not highly evolved nor were the dances themselves.

There were variations on the social dances, sometimes with costuming and face and body painting. In the eastern Basin, with the Plains influences, the Sun Dance was known, while new dances entered in historic times, not the least being the forms of the Ghost Dance ritual.

In the religious area, certain basic concepts, common to much of North America, reassert themselves. Considering the subsistence pattern of the societies of the Basin, hunting rituals were not important. Still, the respect accorded to animals suggests an ancient pattern. The Basin was less concerned than elsewhere with placating game but did have the idea that an animal's soul or essence might be coerced, as, for example, in the case of the antelope hunt. Mythology was well developed, although perhaps more as a series of recreational tales than a basis for belief. Among the important figures in myth were the Wolf, a vaguely defined creator, and the Coyote, his younger brother, a trickster or transformer. Aspects of the world, natural phenomena, the nature of living beings are explained as having been brought about by the caprice of Coyote. Animals might also be related to spirit power of various kinds.

Other North American areas, such as the Northwest Coast and the Plains, with some variations in the Plateau, developed the idea of a guardian spirit. The idea was universal in the Basin but poorly defined. Dreams which came in childhood or later life were a source of spiritual power and were usually vaguely tied up with animals but also with heavenly bodies. The dream association gave rise to a vaguely held notion of a helping spirit or guardian, a concept not nearly so well developed as in other areas. The guardian was not discussed, nor were associations formed between persons with the same spirit, points which reflect the individualism of Basin religion.

There were shamans. These were men and women who had received a special curing call, one vaguely identified with an animal such as the bear. Like shamans elsewhere, the Basin practitioner had his array of equipment, his ability to perform sleight-of-hand, and his inclination to enter a trancelike state. His power came from visions, which in turn provided him with talismans, songs, modes of painting, and most of all, his curing talent. Curing was done by sucking, in view of the common North American complex of an intruded object as the cause of disease. From the body of the patient the shaman could suck blood, a worm, a stick, or a snake, all of which had been intruded into a person's body by an enemy in order to make him sick. The shamanistic patterns common to the Northwest Coast, the Plateau, California, and the interior sub-Arctic are also reflected in the Basin. The shaman, like his counterparts in sections of California, might have an assistant, often an apprentice, who aided the doctor in smoking, in blowing away disease, or in getting rid himself of the pain object which he had sucked into his own body. In a quasi trance, the shaman might speak strangely, sometimes in an alien language; the assistant was his interpreter. The shamans of the Basin were skilled at handling fire, standing in the fire, putting live coals in their mouths, picking up fire. Just as the shaman among the Eskimo offered a great deal by way of horrifying and stimulating entertainment, so also in the Basin.

Some shamans were women, even if menstrual blood negated shaman powers. Older women, those past the climacteric, were often shamans. Characteristic of some segments of North America were the transvestites or berdaches, men who dressed as women and assumed a female role. The Basin did allow a degree of homosexuality and the role of the shaman allowed some latitude for such behavior.

The shaman frequently took a position of leadership in certain group activities. He could sing to bring antelope, deer, rabbits, and waterfowl. The rationale appears to be that through his power and his magic, he could command the soul of the animal. In curing, the shamans had various specialties; some could cure rattlesnake bites, others close wounds. Not all could assist in the hunt. It has been noted that shamans of an out-group might be hostile. Witchcraft and sorcery were attributed to malevolent shamans, those offended by another's success or simply, as many Basin-Plateau people said, because they were "mean." Although shamans might assist in hunting, they rarely assumed a position of leadership. Shamans were not greatly respected. Those who received a spiritual call from a spirit offering shaman power might resist it. It is clear that there were psychic mechanisms at work. To become a shaman was a prescribed way of channeling a culturally conditioned neurotic state.

But a shaman, simply through the potential for blackmail which existed, the threat that harmful magic might be used, did play a political role. This was generally operative when family groups came together, such as at a piñon gathering place, for it was at such places that the shaman might encounter nonrelatives who feared him. Similarly, there were men who emerged in such encampments in the role of chiefs. This role might merely be that of a peacemaker, a speaker recognized by the assemblage. Usually, however, such political power was temporary, relating to the men who organized hunts or who simply took on an informal role as recognized leader. Such political leadership, while ill defined institutionally, appears to have carried some weight. A leader could balance the power of others, including that of shamans (cf. Gayton, 1930).

Chiefs became more important in historic times when it was necessary for the Shoshone to deal with outsiders. In the east, with horses and raiding, the rise of war chiefs followed a Plains pattern. In general, however, the Basin lacked a concept of leadership, which is not to say that the population of the area lived in a state of anarchy. As with any human group, informal social controls, public pressures, customary ways of meeting situations were all operative in maintaining the stability of the societies.

Fearful of sorcery, but lacking war and unending feuds, Basin life had its less formalized controls. That there was competition between leaders of family groups is evidenced by the patterns of gambling. Games of chance played an important part in social life among the Shoshone, Paiute, and other Numic peoples. Although a wealth standard was lacking, personal possessions were wagered in the many gambling games of the area. Gambling was a common pastime among many North American Indians but it seems to have reached a particularly high development in the Basin area. Dice were known, split bones marked with numbers; there was a series of guessing games, a stone being placed in one of several moccasins; and there were also various games of skill, the hoop and pole game, among others, where the contestants threw a stick at a rolling hoop. There was strong competition in such games and it was said that men might forfeit their meager possessions if they lost.

Lacking the drama of other areas, able to do little more than meet the demands of their harsh environment, the peoples of the Basin fared poorly at the hands of outsiders. The opprobrious term "Digger" was applied to them because of their gathering economy. Yet, as with many peoples across the world who show a general socio-cultural simplicity, the Shoshone and the Great Basin offer an interesting example of the one possible avenue of human activity. The family level of integration suggested by Steward seems to be the solution which the Shoshone found to their problem of adaptation to their environment. These were not, as some have suggested, anomalous or patrilineal bands (Service, 1971:52), but one solution adequate for life in an arid land. It is true that the Shoshone and their neighbors are perhaps the simplest of the native Americans. They compare with other desert hunters-gatherers elsewhere in the world, such as the South African Bushman, or the tribes of Australia, lacking of course the social complexity of the latter. For the Americas, the area is important since it is from a pattern

like this, a kin-oriented, bandless social system, that New World economy and society take their direction.

In history, the Shoshone have contributed some important figures. There was Sacajawea, the woman who guided Lewis and Clarke, and the chief Washakie (1804–1900), who was instrumental in establishing the Wyoming reservation for his people. It was two Paiutes, Wodziwob, in 1869, and Wowoka, in 1889, who founded the messianic movements which have come to be known as the Ghost Dance. Basin cultures changed rapidly, even early in the period of contact, largely as a result of the pressures exerted by surrounding tribes, especially those of the Plains. Changed they may be, but even today, the American Indian of the Great Basin stress their identity as Indians.

The Great Basin—Suggested readings

DOWNS, J. F.
1966   *The Two Worlds of the Washo: An Indian Tribe of California and Nevada.* New York: Holt, Rinehart and Winston. (Case Studies in Cultural Anthropology.)

HARRIS, J. S.
1940   "The White Knife Shoshoni of Nevada." In *Acculturation in Seven American Indian Tribes,* ed. R. Linton, pp. 39–118. Englewood Cliffs, N.J.: Prentice-Hall.

KELLY, I. T.
1932   "Ethnography of the Surprise Valley Paiute." *University of California Publications in American Archaeology and Ethnology* 31:67–210.

LOWIE, R. H.
1924   "Notes on Shoshonean Ethnography." *American Museum of Natural History Anthropological Papers* 20:185–314.

OPLER, M. K.
1971   "The Ute and Paiute Indians of the Great Basin Southern Rim," In *North American Indians in Historical Perspective,* ed. E. B. Leacock and N. O. Lurie, pp. 257–288. New York: Random House.

STEWARD, J. H.
1938   *Basin-Plateau Aboriginal Socio-Political Groups.* Bureau of American Ethnology, Bulletin 120.
1933   "Ethnography of the Owens Valley Paiute." *University of California Publications in American Archaeology and Ethnology* 33:233–350.

WHITING, B. B.
1950   *Paiute Sorcery.* Viking Fund Publications in Anthropology, 15.

CALIFORNIA

Tribal Groupings
Language family — Athabascan
  Hupa, Tolowa, Wailaki
Language family — Algonkin (Algonkan-Ritwan)
  Wiyot, Yurok (?)
Language family — Hokan (Hokan-Coahuiltecan)
  Achomawi (including Atsugewi)
  Shasta
  Karok
  Chimariko
  Yana
  Pomo
  Salinan (including Esselen)
  Chumash
  Yuma
  Mohave
  Cochimi
  Diegueño
  Kamia
Language family — Aztec-Tanoan (Uto-Aztecan)
Subfamily — Numic (Basin)
  Tübatulabal
  Luiseñan
  Cahuilla
  Gabrielino Subfamily Takic
  Kawaiisu
  Serrano
Numic, Tübatulabal and Takic form a unit
frequently called Shoshonean.
Language family — Penutian
Subfamily — California Penutian
  Yokuts
  Miwok (including Olamentke)
  Costanoan
  Maidu
  Wintun
Language family — Yukian (?)
  Wappo
  Yuki

Backgrounds of Native California
Within the present state of California formerly lived an exceptionally large number of Indians who varied among themselves somewhat in appearance, differed considerably in language, but shared a number of fundamental cultural activities. Favorable conditions of the geographical environment permitted the considerable number of inhabitants, for California was in many respects a land particularly well suited for peoples living under primitive conditions. The climate was mild and temperate, native food resources occurred in unusual variety and abundance, and there existed ample and diversified raw materials from which to fashion material equipment. The great number of native people, estimated as around 133,000 at the beginning of European contact, contrasts with the comparative scantiness of population found in most other sections of aboriginal North America, north of the Rio Grande. With about 5 percent of the total land area, California held 13 percent of the native inhabitants, having a density 3 to 4 times that of the remainder of what is now Anglo-America. The population was by no means evenly distributed over the entire region. Most thickly settled were the coastal belt and the lower courses of large rivers and streams. Inland the density diminished, tapering off markedly in mountain and arid districts.

In a number of physical traits the Californians were homogeneous. All exhibited the common American Indian characteristics of coarse, black, and uniformly straight hair, dark-brown eyes, brownish complexion and broad, heavy faces. In other features such as stature, head and nose form they showed extreme variability. Among the native inhabitants were examples of the tallest (Mohave) and shortest (Yuki) people of the whole American continent. Practically all the variations in head form found among North American Indians were present. Some groups had long heads whereas others were typically broad-headed. Pronounced contrast in nose form also occurred.

More exceptional than physical variation of the Californians was their astonishing diversity in speech. Between the Oregon and Mexican boundaries lived peoples who spoke more than one hundred separate dialects and languages belonging to no fewer than six linguistic families. Some of the stocks included a fair number of distinct languages; others seem to have been limited to a few or, in one instance, to a single idiom. The separate languages making up a family often diverged considerably from one another in vocabulary, phonetics and grammatical structure. Four of the native linguistic groupings — Athabascan, Algonkin, Hokan and Numic — have representation elsewhere among North American Indians. The two others — Penutian and Yukian — may be purely Californian though certain wider affiliations have been suggested. Lutuamian, a subbranch of Penutian, included speakers in southern Oregon. The multiplicity of idioms implies that various peoples by no means uniform in speech infiltrated California from time to time. Geographi-

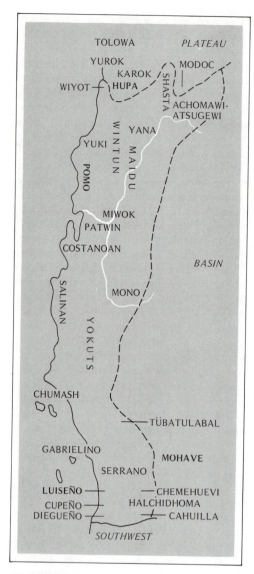

C3 ● California

by any other language family there. More restricted in distribution and far fewer in number were the remaining stocks, all confined to north-central and northern California. Inserted among Penutian, Hokan, and Athabascan speakers in the north-central region dwelt 4000 Yukians. Northern California contained 7000 Athabascans and 3500 Algonkins. Lutuamians in California, represented solely by the Modoc at the Oregon border, consisted of only 500 individuals.

No corresponding complexity in custom existed, however, for the Californians, excluding only the Colorado River valley tribes, exhibited a basic uniformity in economy, material equipment, social organization, and religion. Most of their food came from the gathering of wild plant products, particularly acorns, combined in varying degrees, with hunting and fishing. Their material culture was not elaborate. Only in basket weaving did they display exceptional aptitude. Art found expression primarily in geometric designs applied to articles of daily or religious usage.

Aside from the ever-present family, the basis of California Indian society was the independent village, often made up of families related through the male line, or the "tribelet," composed of one main settlement and a couple of minor outlying ones. Definite tribal organization such as functioned in other parts of native North America were wanting. Each local group, averaging one hundred or so persons, stayed self-contained in its own territory to which its members held rights in common. Generally a headman whose position was hereditary provided leadership and handled civil affairs. The Californians number among the least warlike of the North American Indians and mostly lived in peace with each other. Only occasionally did feuds or petty wars, most frequently motivated by revenge, break out. The overwhelming majority of the state's aboriginal inhabitants remained unreceptive to notions of social stratification.

Among religious practices shared by all or nearly all California Indians were an observance for adolescent girls and a ceremonial dance for war or victory. Ritual otherwise included collective ceremonies, often enactments of mythological events. In common with the majority of North American Indians, the California peoples gave prominence to shamanism. Shamanistic practices were fairly consistent with an absence of fasting or other vision-producing acts.

Although the California Indians showed a

cal isolation between groups with the same tongue resulted in profound dialect differences.

In extent of territory and number of speakers, the linguistic stocks varied tremendously. Of them, Penutian, occupying a continuous tract in central California, had the most representatives, an estimated 57,000. To the second major group, Hokan, belonged 37,500 speakers. Hokan territory included a series of disconnected areas, extending from northern California to the extreme southern border. Some 23,500 Indians living in the narrow desert strip along the state's eastern boundary and in coastal southern California spoke Numic languages. The land held by Shoshoneans exceeded in size that held pronounced uniformity in their manner of living, this does not mean that it was the same everywhere. Numerous and often important local variations in custom existed and on the basis of these the state can be split up into four regional subdivisions. In the northwestern section and extending over into southwestern Oregon prevailed a somewhat specialized mode of life, profoundly affected by elements diffused from the North Pacific Coast. By far the most widespread and typical was the native culture which covered the central portion of the state. Southward, and marked off from the central area particularly by differences in religious beliefs and practices, lay the southern province. To the southeast, the Colorado River valley constituted a fourth subdivision. Here flourished a unique way of life, in many ways non-Californian. The river peoples enlarged their food supply by farming, made few and extremely crude baskets, possessed a semblance of tribal organization, fought frequently and well, and lacked group dances. Both of the latter two areas had been subjected to influences emanating from the Southwest.

To some degree these provincial subdivisions reflected adjustments to differing geographical conditions since each corresponded in a measure to a distinct natural habitat. But local innovation and influences from adjacent areas had played the major part in their shaping. None of the four ever appears to have been more widespread than it was at the time of first European contact, so it can be assumed that each originated mainly on the spot and endured. In addition to the four regional specializations, two other forms of culture, both intrusions from the outside, can be recognized. The eastern desert fringe of the state, inhabited almost exclusively by Numic-speakers, belonged to the Great Basin area. The Modoc in northeastern California formed a small enclave of Plateau culture, somewhat like that of the Klamath, with adaptation to an unusual lake-marsh environment.

Archeology records that California has been a region of gradual and unspectacular cultural change, the course of development being along lines of increasing regional differentiation. So far as acceptable evidence goes, human history begins in California with the appearance around 10,000–11,000 years ago of small bands of wandering people whose life revolved around the pursuit of game animals. Their campsites are marked by heavy projectile points and other stone items consistent with a hunting economy. The nature of their quarry remains conjectural, however, for animal bones are lacking or very scarce. Most likely, they stalked and killed big beasts of species still alive. Lesser game must also have received attention. A noticeable absence of seed-grinding implements suggests that the early hunters did not avail themselves of the abundant and diversified edible plants.

Infiltration by two separate hunting populations, each identified by its own characteristic projectile points, is indicated by the archeological discoveries. One group employed fluted points that resemble those of the Clovis-Folsom hunters of the Great Plains. Their spear or dart heads have been found at two major sites—Borax Lake in the coastal ranges of north-central California and around Tulare Lake in the southern San Joaquin Valley. Stray specimens with channels on one or both faces have turned up at a number of other places. Leaf-shaped and shouldered points were used by the second group of hunters. Two localities, Lake Mohave in the center of the Mohave Desert and the San Dieguito River in the southwestern coastal district, represent important encampments. Scattered finds demonstrate that these people roamed over a wide area of southern California. Their antecedents are uncertain. Apparently the two hunting populations overlapped at least in part in time and space.

A shift to an emphasis upon foraging for wild plant foods is reflected in the archeological record for the period between 6000 and 3000 B.C. The importance of vegetal products in the native diet can be seen in the wealth of stone implements suited for their processing. Mills and mullers, the bottom and top stones used to grind seeds, make up a high proportion of the finds from habitation sites falling within this time span. The remainder of the artifact inventory is meager and commonly includes pebble choppers, flake scrapers and rather poorly chipped projectile points. The size of the seed collectors' dwelling places and the depth of occupational debris shows that they enjoyed a more settled life than their predecessors.

Food-collecting cultures are best represented on the south coast where they have been subsumed under a Milling Stone horizon. Outside southern California, they occur in the southern San Joaquin Valley, the northern Coast Ranges, and on the western foothills of the northern Sierra Nevada. Their presence can also be dimly perceived in the lower Sacramento Valley. Once established, the food-gathering way of life endured, uninterrupted and relatively unchanged, for several millennia.

After about 3000 B.C. a trend toward more diversified economics and distinct regional variants of culture developed as the various populations began to adjust better to their local environments and more thoroughly exploit the rich and varied food resources. The introduction of the mortar and pestle implies that the vast acorn crop was being tapped. Cultures of greater complexity emerge. The best known is the Early Horizon (Windmiller) of the lower Sacramento Valley. Early Horizon economy probably rested primarily upon hunting, but fish and plant foods appear to have been regular items in the daily diet. The artifacts exhibit great variety and fine workmanship.

By the end of the third millennium, B.C., the new ways and techniques had become firmly established and form the basis for succeeding cultures. An expansion in population is evident. For the first time the well-favored shores of San Francisco Bay became heavily settled, and the great shell mounds which once lined the bay's shores experienced their greatest growth. In the nearby Sacramento Valley archeological sites attributable to this stage, designated the Middle Horizon, are much larger and more widespread. Though the mode of life shows continuity with the preceding Early Horizon, it also displays a continuing elaboration. Bone tools, for example, are more widely used.

Later prehistoric cultures, taking form in the early centuries of the Christian Era, can be firmly linked with the historic tribes. Most archeological artifacts show a close similarity to, or identity with, ethnographic forms. Innovations include the replacement of the dart- or spear-thrower by the bow and arrow as the principal weapon and, in the south, knowledge of pottery making. Noteworthy is the elaborate, sea-oriented culture that flourished in the Santa Barbara Coast–Channel Island region. There is little doubt that its members were the immediate ancestors of the Chumash, or as the Spanish explorers preferred to call them, Canaliño.

Such is the broad outline of California's aboriginal history as revealed by archeology. Its course has been one of slow progression and development as the native peoples gradually learned to take advantage of the region's rich food supplies. Their successful exploitation of

these resources brought an unusually heavy population, a semi- or completely sedentary existence and a more complex lifeway than that of the tribes inhabiting the adjacent and more impoverished Basin-Plateau. Although the native Californian cultures grew largely from within as local groups developed new skills and ideas of their own, they were not without outside stimulus. Influences radiating from the Southwest seem to have reached both the south and central sections. And the highly developed North Pacific Coast manner of living played a dominant role in shaping the culture of the Indians inhabiting the northwest corner of the area.

The Hupa Indians of Northwestern California

In the extreme northwestern portion of California lived a number of Indian groups whose mode of life, though less elaborate, showed many relationships to the remarkable and distinctive culture of the North Pacific Coast. Shared traits included a great dependence on salmon, the building of substantial wooden houses, an emphasis on woodworking, wealth as a criterion of social position, and spectacular group ceremonials. But the culture of these peoples was not merely a pale reflection of the richer life of the more northerly tribes, for it contained many characteristic Californian features, notably acorn leaching and an advanced basket-weaving industry, as well as a number of unique local developments.

This northwestern Californian way of life found typical expression among the Hupa Indians of the lower Trinity River in Humboldt County and their Klamath River neighbors, the Yurok and Karok. Although speaking entirely unrelated languages, members of each group visited back and forth, attended and even participated in one another's religious ceremonies, and intermarried. As a consequence their customs varied remarkably little.

The center of the Hupa homeland was the 6-mile-long valley which still bears their name. Through it winds the Trinity River, a swift-flowing stream of considerable volume and the main tributary of the Klamath. Aside from the level valley floor, the country is mountainous and difficult of access. A temperate climate without prolonged spells of cold or heat prevails. Rain, in excess of 40 inches annually, falls mainly between November and March. The remainder of the year is normally quite dry.

Most of the region has a dense cover of

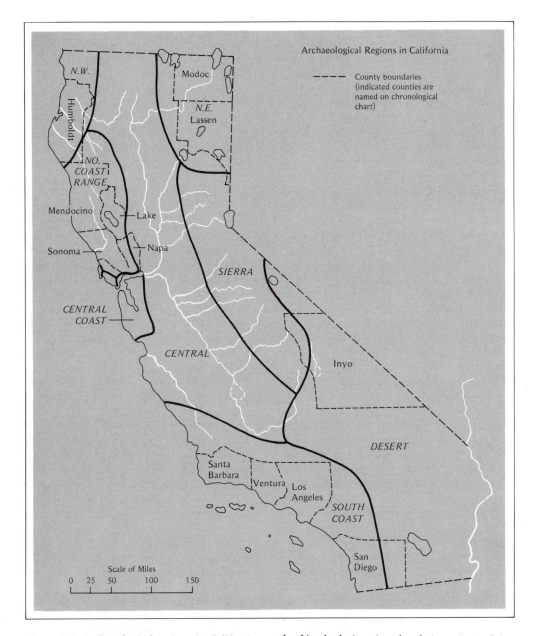

Figure 36 ● Archaeological regions in California

vegetation. Evergreen forests made up of pines, cedars, and Douglas firs clothe the surrounding mountains. Oak trees of several species grow on the valley floor. Less fertile sections of the valley and the lower mountain slopes are covered with dense chaparral. A varied and plentiful animal and bird life inhabits the country and many fish are present in the river.

The term "Hupa" refers to the 1000–1500 Indians who spoke the Hupa language. The name is not a native word but a rendering of the Yurok designation for their territory. Like so many other primitive peoples, the Hupa had no term for themselves as a group. In physical appearance these Indians closely resembled their neighbors. They were moderately broad-headed, with heavy faces and dark skins. As a group they were of medium to tall stature, muscular, and stocky. Hupa speech was one of a number of Athabascan languages spoken along the Pacific Coast from Washington to northern California.

Their Athabascan speech indicates that the ancestral Hupa originally came from the far north. How and when they reached Hoopa Valley and what type of culture they carried with them remain matters of speculation. Archeology has nothing to tell for no systematic investigations have been carried out in Hupa territory. It can be surmised, however, that the migrants were nomadic hunters and gatherers who rather quickly adopted the implements and techniques of an already existing lifeway. A current problem for archeologists is to determine the antiquity of the distinctive culture of the northwest Californians. Prehistoric manifestations of it have been recognized in four excavated sites in coastal territory occupied at the beginning of the historic period by Wiyot, Yurok, and Tolowa. That it already flourished in distinguishable form at least a thousand years ago is demonstrated by a radiocarbon date of A.D. 900 for the basal layer of a large prehistoric settlement on an island in Humboldt Bay. Perceptible changes can be detected in the native culture during the next 1000 years, but these are of a rather trifling nature, reflected in variations in harpoon points and the like. No convincing evidences of earlier occupations have yet been unearthed in the northwest.

The Hupa earned their living mainly by fishing and collecting edible wild plants. Of the varied food resources, two—salmon and acorns—far exceeded all others in importance. Each spring and fall vast numbers of salmon entered the Trinity from the Klamath and swam upstream to spawn in its upper reaches. At these times, intense activity occurred and the year's supply was secured. Salmon were taken by a variety of devices. During the spring run, platforms were erected over suitable pools and eddies and fish were dipped out with long-handled nets. In the shallow water of the fall a stout weir of poles and withes was built across the river. It was constructed communally and placed in alternate years near one of the two principal Hupa settlements. Fishermen standing on small platforms along its top scooped up salmon as they swarmed against the obstruction. Other methods of capturing salmon included gill nets set in still pools and drag nets hauled by a group of men. Where water conditions permitted, a harpoon provided with a detachable bone point was employed.

A variety of other fish were available seasonally. Steelhead, sea-running trout which returned to the river to spawn, were second only to salmon in the quantity caught and eaten.

Sturgeon were valued not only for their flesh but also for the glue obtained from their heads. Lamprey eels, migrating upstream in the spring, were highly esteemed as food.

The emphasis was upon mass taking of fish, so little effort was expended on angling with hook and line. Trout and other small fish present in the river throughout the year were sometimes caught by means of a V-shaped hook, made by binding a sharp-pointed piece of bone at an acute angle between two split sticks. The swift current of the Trinity precluded drugging fish with narcotic plants, a method frequently resorted to by other Californian Indians.

While the catching of fish, by whatever means, was the work of men, their handling from this point on was almost exclusively by women who attended to their transporting, butchering, and drying. The commonest cooking process was broiling on pointed sticks propped up before the fire. Vast quantities of salmon were preserved for winter use by drying and smoking on racks. In this state their flesh was most often consumed without cooking. Lamprey eels, sturgeon and steelhead were also preserved for future eating.

A rich harvest of acorns was gathered by the Hupa women when the nuts started to drop from the trees during the fall of the year. Those of the tan oak were most esteemed. Acorns were gathered in conical baskets, each large enough to hold a bushel or two. They were prepared for storage and eating in the regular Californian Indian manner. The nuts were shelled, split, dried, and kept in huge baskets. When needed for meals, they were placed on a hard, smooth stone provided with a basketry hopper and pounded into a fine flour with a stone pestle. Next the meal was leached in a shallow excavation in the sand to remove the bitter tannin. Acorn meal usually was served as a thin mush, cooked by dropping heated stones into it. It was stirred about with a carved wooden paddle, two to four feet in length. Less commonly, dampened flour was baked on a hot stone. In this form it was carried as rations by travellers and hunters.

A wide range of other plant foods—nuts, seeds, berries, fruits, roots, and greens—were also consumed. Pine nuts, chinquapins, and hazel nuts were harvested and eaten raw. Seeds of certain grasses and herbs were beaten into a basket with a basketry seed beater, crushed in a mortar, parched with live coals, and then eaten.

Various berries and fruits were picked and consumed without cooking or other preparation. Manzanita berries, however, were parched and the flour eaten dry. Bulbs, mostly of the lily family, were dug up with a pointed hardwood stick and steamed in a rock-lined pit for several days before eating. Largest and most plentiful were those of the soap-root. Tender young leaves and stalks of many kinds of plants were eaten raw.

Game, though a valuable adjunct to the food supply during the winter and early spring, was of lesser importance in the Hupa diet. Deer and elk, the principal large game animals, were stalked in the forests or driven by trained dogs toward waiting huntsmen. At times, a hunter disguised with a deer head and skin, simulated movements of the animals in order to get within bowshot of a grazing herd. Deer and elk were sometimes driven into the river by shouting men and barking dogs and then pursued in canoes. A short, wide sinew-backed bow with stone-tipped arrow was the standard weapon of the chase. Noose-snares of strong iris-fiber rope were commonly set along trails followed by deer or elk. Smaller game such as rabbits, squirrels, and quail were shot with a simple bow and arrows lacking stone heads, or were captured in snares or traps. Meat was roasted on the coals, broiled on skewers, or stone boiled. Deer and elk flesh were preserved by drying and smoking.

A number of potential food resources were not exploited. Several species of birds and mammals were not killed for food because of religious taboos. All reptiles, except the tortoise or turtle, were shunned. Grasshoppers, caterpillars, other insects and larvae, relished by Indians elsewhere in California, were also avoided.

Though the Hupa occasionally went hungry, particularly during the winter and early spring, they almost never knew famine. In a normal year there was plenty to eat and a sizable reserve of dried salmon, acorns and other foodstuffs provided insurance against want. The comparative ease with which it was possible to secure an adequate food supply during a few months of the year, combined with efficient techniques for its preservation and storage, allowed for leisure time which could be devoted to activities other than making a living.

Hupa dwellings were square or rectangular wooden structures reminiscent of those of the North Pacific Coast. Their walls, of upright cedar planks attached to a sturdy framework of poles and beams, enclosed an area measuring 18 by 20 feet. Overlapping boards covered a three-pitched roof. Inside, the central section, a 10 by 12 foot space, was excavated to a depth of 4 or 5 feet, leaving an elevated earthen shelf between it and the walls. Entrance was through a circular doorway, placed at one end of the house and just large enough to squeeze through. A notched plank served as a stairway down into the pit. Often the ground in front of the dwelling was neatly paved with cobbles.

Customarily a dwelling housed a single family. In the dirt-floored, cellarlike room, its members gathered for meals and here the women and children slept. A centrally placed fire kept the living area warm. Space on the earthen shelf above, next to the walls, was utilized for storing stocks of food, fuel, and family possessions. Only temporarily during the summer and fall harvesting season did the family residence stand deserted.

The sweathouse represented the only other type of structure in a Hupa village. Smaller than the dwelling, it consisted of a rectangular pit, about 4 feet deep and lined with planks to prevent a cave-in. Only its pitched board roof and surrounding stone pavement showed above ground level. Each sudatory was provided with a rock-ringed hearth and wooden floor. It was entered through an opening in one side of the roof and descended into by means of a plank with cut footholds.

Among the Hupa, the sudatory served not only for daily sweatbathing but also as workshop, clubhouse, and sleeping quarters for men and older boys. As in central California, direct heat from a fire rather than steam was used for sweating. Because a plunge in cold water followed a sweat, the structure stood close to the river bank. A single sweathouse usually sufficed for males of several adjoining dwellings. Generally it was built and used by a group of kinsmen related to one another through the male line.

As the climate was seldom severe, the Hupa regularly wore little clothing. A deerskin wrapped about the hips was the only article of dress constantly worn by men. Elderly males, lounging about the sweathouse or walking through the village, commonly dispensed with even this. On special occasions men donned a more elaborate garment made of two pieces of deerskin, joined along one side and meeting over the left shoulder. Summer and winter, they went about barefoot without apparent discomfort, putting on buckskin moccasins only when leaving on a long journey. Hunters and travellers, passing through brushy country, covered their thighs with knee-length leggings of the same material. For warmth, men and women alike relied upon robes of deer or other animal skins thrown over the shoulders like a cape or wrapped around the body.

The daily clothing of the women was more elaborate. It consisted of a two-piece buckskin garment, extending from the waist to below the knees. The larger section, its border fringed, covered the back and sides of the body whereas an apronlike piece, a foot wide, concealed the front. The latter was a length of buckskin, cut into narrow strips, each wrapped with bear-grass or strung with pine nuts. A bowl-shaped basketry cap, designed to protect the forehead from the carrying strap whereby burdens were borne, was worn almost constantly. Like the men, women donned footwear only while on the trail.

Styles of dressing the hair were much the same for men and women. Both sexes wore the hair long. Males tied theirs in two bunches, which hung in front of the shoulders, or in a single one which fell behind. Females arranged their hair in two rolls, each held together with a thong. A few men had scanty beards but the majority plucked out facial hairs as soon as they appeared. To enhance their beauty, women had three broad vertical bands tattooed on their chins. The ear lobes of all individuals were perforated for the insertion of shell ornaments. Face painting formed part of a man's make-up only on special occasions. For festivities there were also necklaces of shell beads, feather headdresses, and other ornaments.

The most important Hupa industries were woodworking and basket making. Cedar furnished a soft, easily worked material for the manufacture of house planks, chests for the storage of ceremonial regalia, household utensils, low stools, sweathouse headrests, and many other articles. Where tougher wood was needed, as in making bows and tobacco pipes, there was yew, manzanita or other hardwoods. Hupa craftsmen achieved excellent results with a limited stock of tools. Since they had no axes with which to chop down trees, they had to depend upon fallen logs or fell trees with the aid of fire. Large slabs were split off from logs by antler wedges driven in with unhafted stone mauls. Objects were shaped and reduced to de-

Yurok ● Woman wearing a basketry hat. Broadbrimmed hats of basket weave characterized a number of tribes of the Northwest Coast. In northwestern California, as well as in adjacent portions of the southwestern Plateau, brimless basketry caps, tightly woven, and good rain gear were worn by both sexes. (After Kroeber, 1925:741. Courtesy of Bureau of American Ethnology, Smithsonian Institution)

sired smoothness with knives, adzes, scrapers and abrasives. Most wooden articles went undecorated, noteworthy exceptions being mush stirrers with geometric designs cut into their handles. The Hupa woodcarver's art differs strikingly from that of the North Pacific Coast which was dominated by conventionalized animal and human motives.

Basket weaving, carried on exclusively by females, provided the Hupa with most of their household utensils as well as with storage containers, cradles, caps, and special dance ornaments. All baskets were fashioned by one technique—twining. The absence of coiled weaves of any kind distinguishes northwestern California from the central portion of the state where twining and coiling occurred together. Slim hazel shoots, carefully peeled, provided the weaver with stiff, straight warps: flexible strips of pine or other tree roots served as wefts. Ornamentation was achieved by overlaying wefts with white bear grass and introducing patterns in black and red. The glossy outer covering of maidenhair fern stems supplied black strands: fibers taken from stems of giant ferns and dyed in alder-bark juice furnished the red color. Design elements were geometric, consisting of parallelograms, triangles, bands, and related forms. Although named from supposed likenesses to living or nonliving things, the patterns had no symbolic meaning.

Work in horn, particularly elk, was another craft in which men had achieved tolerable skill. Large horn spoons, cut and steamed into shape, had zigzag or notched handles. These spoons were used by males only, ordinary mussel shells sufficed for females. Neat money boxes ornamented with incised geometric designs were also fashioned from antler. Other horn articles included net-mesh measures, wedges, and stone-flaking tools. Harpoons, awls, and scratching sticks were made of bone. The men were fairly proficient in manufacturing arrowpoints and other weapons and tools of stone. Outstanding and highly valued were huge blades of obsidian, a material for which there was no local source. Males also braided rope and twine and wove nets. The handling of animal skins from flaying the carcass to the final tanning of the hide was likewise their job.

Travel was mostly in dugout canoes obtained in trade from the Yurok. Constructed from half of a redwood log, these vessels were round bottomed with blunt ends. Despite their somewhat clumsy appearance, they were exceptionally maneuverable and capable of carrying a number of persons or a cargo of several thousand pounds. The canoe was propelled with a narrow-bladed, flat-ended paddle.

Pathways joined the various Hupa villages and there was considerable foot traffic over them. Crossing the mountain ridges in any direction entailed severe physical exertion but such journeys were undertaken from time to time. Along each well-travelled trail were traditional stopping places where passers-by removed their packs and rested, special trees into which arrows were shot for luck, and spots where each traveller dropped a stick or a stone and prayed for safety on his journey.

Commerce was chiefly with the Yurok living along the coast near the mouth of the Klamath. In return for dried seaweed, which furnished the salt supply, surf fish, and other marine products, the Hupa supplied the coast people with acorns and other inland foods. The Hupa carried on considerably less trade with the Karok because the products of the two groups were too alike to allow for much barter. Sporadic commerce was also conducted with other Indian peoples.

Dentalium-shell money was sometimes used to purchase products instead of bartering for them. The source of supply of these thin, tube-like shells lay in the waters off the west coast of Vancouver Island, many miles to the north, so that they had passed through many hands by the time they reached the Hupa. Each dentalium had a fixed value according to its length. There were standardized ways of measurement for an individual shell, five of the same length strung together, and longer strings. The principal method of evaluation was matching five strung shells with one of a number of marks tattooed on the inside of the left forearm of a man. Dentalia were frequently ornamented with scratched designs, spiral wrappings of fish- or snake-skin, or scarlet woodpecker feathers, but these decorations did not increase their monetary worth.

Hupa society was characterized by a minimum of formal organization. The fundamental basis of social life was the family. A typical unit of this sort, numbering six to seven persons, consisted of spouses, their children and an unattached relative or two. Claims of kinship extended beyond the family, however, and linked together several households into a larger, informal division. Close kinsmen through the male line resided near one another, worked together, built and occupied the same sweathouse.

Generally several such kin groups made up a village, though the inhabitants of a small settlement were sometimes all paternal kin or nearly so. Despite common residence no real community sense existed and a village was likely to operate as a unit only if its inhabitants were all related. Formal political structure was conspicuous by its absence. There were neither headmen nor village councils.

The permanent Hupa settlements, numbering 11 or 12, were strung out along the banks of the Trinity, less than a mile apart. Almost without exception, they were located near a spring or tributary stream from which drinking water could be obtained. Each also had ready access to a sandy stretch for beaching canoes. Communities varied considerably in population, ranging from 50 to 200 persons.

Other than a loose grouping of settlements into up-river and down-river divisions for purposes of holding important religious ceremonies and for constructing the communal fish-weir, there was no unit above the village. Any sort of tribal feeling or organization was lacking. Hupa, like peoples everywhere, recognized that certain neighbors shared the same language and customs but felt no unity of common interest on that account.

Despite this lack of political machinery, a highly intricate and precise code of laws regulated conduct. Its underlying principle was that every wrong, intentional or not, had to be compensated for, preferably in money. In theory at least there was no infringement which could not be smoothed over by a payment, though the threat of force and blood revenge was always present. A great range of offenses was recognized—murder, mayhem, rape, adultery, theft, cursing, and other insults—and for each there was a more or less clearly indicated fine. The social status of the injured person was always considered in calculating the indemnity.

Wrongs were against individuals and redress had to be sought by the offended party or his family. A go-between employed to arrange a settlement conferred with both sides in a dispute until satisfactory recompense was decided upon. Prolonged haggling was basic to the judicial process because an aggrieved person had to either insist upon his rights or lose face. The power of the kin groups involved, their numbers, wealth and prestige, as well as resolution, gave advantage in the settlement of legal cases so that justice was not always done.

Though there were many person-to-person quarrels, the Hupa disliked fighting and bloodshed. Hostilities did, however, flare up from time to time. Reprisal for an unatoned slaying or the belief that an illness or death had resulted from witchcraft were the most frequent causes of armed clashes. Fighting normally involved only a few individuals and usually took the form of feuds between Hupa kin groups or with corresponding divisions among a neighboring people. Occasionally entire communities became involved but never the Hupa as a whole. Conflicts were generally short-lived and casualties few.

Military equipment comprised bows and arrows, short stabbing spears, stone knives, and rocks. Corselets of vertical wooden rods or stiff elkhide shirts protected a few warriors. Both forms of armor successfully turned arrows but were awkward to wear. Shields were unknown. Ambushes and sudden raids were the preferred tactics. The scalps of fallen enemies were not taken. Hostilities ended with a formal peacemaking, arranged by an intermediary, during which each death and injury to either

side was paid for separately and indemnity was made for all property taken or destroyed.

The Hupa and their immediate neighbors were unique among the Californian Indians in grading individuals into a series of higher or lower statuses on the basis of their wealth or lack of it. Though it was theoretically possible for an individual to better his station in life or that of his children, upward mobility was only rarely achieved. Because wealth was inherited, a person's status approximated that of his parents.

In addition to shell currency, wealth meant albino or other unusually colored deerskins, great blades of black or red obsidian, scarlet feathered woodpecker scalps glued to wide bands of buckskin and a number of lesser items. These rare and precious objects, proudly displayed at large ceremonies, exchanged hands only in important transactions such as in payment of a bride price, shaman's fee or indemnity for a killing. Certain other forms of private property—house sites, the choicest and most productive fishing, hunting, and gathering spots—were also highly prized. In contrast, ordinary utilitarian articles had a very low value.

Rank distinctions were evident in the deference paid to a wealthy man, in the valuation placed upon a person involved in a legal suit, in the niceties of behavior of the rich and wellborn, and in dozens of other ways. A man of wealth usually had clustered about him a group of kinsmen, close and remote, and other hangers-on, who were willing to follow his advice and do his bidding. Sometimes he also had a slave, a man reduced to temporary servitude through nonpayment of a debt.

The Hupa's overwhelming interest in wealth and social position allies them with the North Pacific Coast tribes. But the latter's distribution or destruction of property during a potlatch was to the Hupa a preposterous idea and quite beyond their comprehension. Wealth in the Hupa mind was something to be accumulated, nurtured, displayed, and passed on to one's children but not given away or destroyed.

The pursuit of wealth was carried on at the expense of sexual gratification because continence was considered essential for its acquisition. This belief combined with the practice of maintaining separate sleeping quarters for males and females limited sexual relations between spouses and kept families small. Cohabitation was confined largely to the summer and autumn when the entire family camped out together. Understandably it was during this period that practically all conceptions occurred.

A pregnant woman was subjected to many regulations. She had to be careful of her diet, avoiding meat and fish and eating sparingly of other foods. To insure an easy birth and to protect the well-being of her unborn child, magical formulas were recited over the expectant mother by a formulist. Aside from being obliged to refrain from sexual intercourse, her husband had no special restrictions placed on his behavior.

When her time approached, the mother-to-be retired to the dwelling, attended only by an older woman, generally a relative. During parturition she assumed a sitting position and held fast to a leather strap suspended from a roof beam. If the delivery proved difficult, a formulist was called in. Immediately following the birth, the midwife cut and tied the naval cord, bathed the infant, and then placed it on an openwork basketry tray and held it over a cooking basket containing boiling water and herbs. This steaming process was repeated at intervals for ten days.

After childbirth the mother remained indoors for ten days lying in a pit lined with heated stones covered with damp wormwood or sand. The resultant steaming was designed to hasten her recovery. Meat, fresh fish, and cold water were excluded from her diet. The father ate no meat for ten days and refrained from hunting or gambling. When the remaining stub of the infant's umbilical cord dropped off, he deposited it in a gash cut into a young pine tree. It was believed that as the tree grew, so grew the child.

For the first few days of its life, the newborn was not nursed. Instead it was fed a thin gruel of mashed pine or hazel nut meats in water. Thereafter it was given the breast whenever it showed signs of hunger. Nursing continued for two to three years. On the tenth day following its birth, the baby, wrapped in a soft deerskin, was strapped into a basketry cradle of the sitting variety. Feet and legs dangled free, but its body, hands, and arms were confined. Here it remained, except for bathing and exercise periods, until it learned to walk. A child was not given a personal name but was addressed as "baby," "little girl," or by an affectionate term until it reached the age of five to ten years.

Children were left pretty much to their own devices. Most of their time was passed in play. Boys and girls romped in the sand along creeks, swam, imitated adult activities, and engaged in other simple diversions. They were carefully instructed in etiquette and morality with particular attention given to correct eating habits. Their formal education, aside from this, was sporadic and incidental. Necessary skills were acquired gradually, largely by seeing and doing. Disciplinary methods were mild, the usual punishment being a reprimand. When approximately eight years of age a boy joined his father and other kinsmen in the sweathouse.

At the onset of puberty, a girl was considered unclean and her glance contaminating, so she had to be isolated in the dwelling for ten days. When it was necessary for her to go outdoors, a deerskin covered her head. During her isolation, the menstruant was prohibited from eating meat or fresh fish and was allowed to drink only warm water. Scratching with fingernails was forbidden and a carved piece of bone, ornamented with incised geometric designs, was provided for this purpose. As the pubescent's actions at this time were thought to influence her future behavior, she was urged by her mother and other female relatives, who visited her daily, to be clean, good-tempered, and industrious. In families of high station the coming of age of a girl provided an occasion for a public ceremony. No rite marked a boy's arrival at adulthood.

Marriage customarily took place at fifteen or sixteen for a girl, a year or two later for a boy. The choice of a mate was limited by blood relationship and social position. Near kin, whether on the father's or mother's side, were not allowed to marry, and it was regarded as desirable that a person take a spouse of corresponding social rank. Marriage was conceived of more as a formal contract between kin groups than as an arrangement between individuals. Negotiations were initiated by the boy's relatives through an intermediary, and a bride price, partly in shell currency and partly in other valuables, agreed upon. Though closely bargained, the sum was generous because the status of the couple and their children depended upon it. A bride brought a dowry of essential household goods to the marriage. No wedding ceremony was held, though a feast and mutual exchange of gifts between the two families took place. As a rule, the young married couple resided in the husband's home or village.

If a youth's kin were too poor to afford the

entire bride price, or if for some reason they refused to raise it, he entered into "half-marriage." Under this arrangement, about one half of the purchase money was paid and the groom went to live in his father-in-law's house. Various other situations, such as a parent being unwilling to have his daughter leave home, also led to this marital form. Children resulting from a "half marriage" were regarded as belonging to the wife's family.

Polygyny was permitted but only very rich men could afford more than one spouse. There were few formal regulations governing relationships between relatives by marriage. A man could talk freely to his wife's mother and his bride to his relatives. Upon the death of her husband, a widow was expected to marry one of his brothers, though this was not strictly enforced. Similarly, if a woman died without bearing children, her family provided a sister or other kinswoman as a substitute.

Marriages regarded as failures were dissolved. If, for legitimate reasons, a man sent his wife back to her people, and there were no children, the entire bride price was refunded. If she had just cause, a woman left her husband. Again, if the union had been childless, the full purchase money was returned by her relatives.

Hard, steady labor, considered as a virtue, characterized adult life. But industrious as they were, the Hupa found time for visiting, games, storytelling and other diversions. Great pleasure was derived from visiting relatives and friends in neighboring villages and from trading trips to the coast. Whenever a group of any size congregated, there was gambling. The favorite of the men was the hand game, played with a bundle of sticks, one of which was marked with a black band. Women wagered on the toss of four mussel-shell discs. Athletic contests included wrestling and shinny. Storytelling helped pass many a long winter night with tales of the adventures of the mischievous Trickster, Coyote, preferred. Anecdotes of past events, often including supernatural incidents, were also enjoyed. Pipe smoking provided bedtime relaxation for males. The Hupa pipe, fashioned from hardwood and with a soapstone inset, was short and tubular in form. Tobacco smoked in it was a cultivated variety.

As in most primitive societies, only a small proportion of the population survived to old age. Persons of advanced years were well treated but did not receive exaggerated respect merely because of their longevity. Their wants were taken care of by relatives. If, however, an individual had outlived all of his kinsmen, others saw to it that his needs were provided for. Old people idled away their time sitting in the sun or near the fire. They often tended the children while their parents were busy elsewhere.

When a person died, the body was disposed of as soon as burial arrangements could be completed. The corpse, wrapped in deerskin and tied to a board, was passed out of the house through an opening made in one wall. Still lashed to the plank, it was lowered into a shallow, plank-lined grave. A board placed over the top made a complete box which was then covered with earth. No large amount of property was placed in the grave, but utensils, implements, and clothes, broken or torn so as to render them useless, were deposited on top of it. Those in attendance at the burial expressed grief by loud wailing.

The funeral over, grave diggers, corpse handlers and members of the bereaved family underwent purification which included recitation of a special formula to remove contaminating effects of the dead. Close relatives, men and women alike, cropped their hair as a sign of mourning. In addition, members of the household wore necklaces of twisted grass to protect them from dreaming of the deceased. The name of the departed person was never again mentioned in the presence of his kinsmen.

Before journeying to the land of the dead, an individual's soul was said to linger about the village for four days, attempting to reenter its former residence. On the fifth day it descended to a damp, dark underworld. Only the spirits of shamans and singers in the major ceremonies followed a trail to a more pleasant abode in the sky. Disembodied souls were thought to reappear at times to plague the living, particularly their relatives.

Religious beliefs and practices deeply influenced everyday living. An almost endless series of taboos had to be scrupulously observed. Also there were daily supplications for health and wealth and various preventive acts to avoid ill luck. And finally each person was supposed to maintain a devout frame of mind throughout the day. This was especially necessary during an important group ritual when reverent thoughts by participants and onlookers alike were considered essential for its successful performance.

Annually, in the late fall or summer, the Hupa celebrated elaborate group rituals de-

Hupa, northwestern California ● Men performing the Readheaded Woodpecker Dance at the Yurok town of Pekwan, California. (Photograph by A. W. Ericson, ca. 1890–1900. Smithsonian Institution National Anthropological Archives)

signed to revitalize the world for another year and to ward off famine, disease, or other disaster. Providing regalia was the privilege of certain influential family or kin groups and afforded them an opportunity for publicly exhibiting their treasures, as much of the paraphernalia consisted of objects of high value. The conventional procedure of these public spectacles, carried out by males, was precisely prescribed and inseparably linked to particular sacred spots or localities. Ritual cleanliness, achieved by fasting, abstinence from water, and continence was required of participants.

There were two of these world-renewal and wealth-display ceremonies—the White Deerskin and Jumping Dances, both lasting ten days. Though they shared many features, each had its own dance steps, songs, finery, and equipment. During the White Deerskin Dance per-

formers carried albino or other oddly colored deerskins mounted on long poles along with obsidian blades wrapped around with a piece of buckskin. In the Jumping Dance, the principal regalia consisted of woodpecker scalp headbands and tubular-shaped dance baskets. The really sacred part of the observances was the recital by a ritualist of a long formula. This was not a prayer to a deity but a narrative explaining how the ceremony had been established by a race of supernatural beings who formerly inhabited the earth. Recounting their actions and the ensuing results was believed to produce similar effects.

First-food observances were held each year for salmon and acorns, the two foods upon which the people depended. The Acorn Feast was celebrated in the autumn as soon as nuts began to fall from tan oak trees and the First Salmon Ceremony was performed when the spring run of fish began. In each case the product was obtained and prepared by a qualified functionary who recited a formula and carried out ritual acts. Until this was done, no one ate the food. These solemnities were conducted in the public interest, their purpose being to

●THE WHITE DEERSKIN DANCE—HUPA

The Hupa, along with the Karok and Yurok, those peculiarly money-oriented tribes of northwestern California, offer essentially the same array of ceremonies. Basically, the concept associated with dance rituals is one of world renewal, of restoring food, averting disaster, and so of recreating order in the universe. Present, too, is an element of a first fruits offering, signalizing the beginning of a year and thus again relating to the concept of maintaining and initiating a regularized cycle of life. Emerging from these ceremonial dances are two major preoccupations of northwestern Californian life. There is first the sense of extreme localization, seen in the recitations which initiate the dances, long formulas in which precise and highly local place names figure prominently. The dances indeed may be held only at precisely defined places. The second feature is the concern with wealth, so dominant a theme in these cultures. As the dance develops over a several-day period, it grows in intensity and in the amount of wealth items assembled for display purposes.

Obsidian blades, woodpecker scalps, dentalium shells, and the white deerskins themselves are part of the splendid and lavish display.

Kroeber's description (1925:55–56) of the dance depicted here is to the point:

The Deerskin dancers wear aprons of civet cat or a deerhide blanket about the waist, masses of dentalium necklaces, and forehead bands of wolf fur that shade the eyes. From the head rises a stick on which are fastened two or four black and white eagle or condor feathers, so put together as to look like a single feather of enormous length, its quill covered with woodpecker scalp; or, three slender rods of sinew, scarlet with attached bits of scalp rise from the stick. The dancers also hold poles on which are white, light grey, black, or mottled deerskins, the heads stuffed, the ears, mouths, throats, and false tongues decorated with woodpecker scalps, the hide of the body and legs hanging loose. A slightly swaying row of these skins looks really splendid. The singer in the center of the line, and his two assistants, add to the costume of the others a light net, reaching from the forehead to the middle of the shoulders and terminating in a fringe of feathers. Their apron is always of civet cat skins. The step of the entire row is merely a short stamp with one foot. At the end of the line and in front of it is a dancer who carries an obsidian blade instead of a deerskin. Over his wolf-fur forehead band is a strap from which project like hooks half a dozen or more curve-cut canine teeth of sea lions. From the head hangs down a long close-woven or crocheted net, painted in diamonds or triangles, and feather fringed. A double deerskin blanket passes over one shoulder and covers part of the body, or is replaced by an apron of civet or raccoon skins ... These two dancers advance and pass each other in front of the row of deerskins several times during each song, crouching, blowing a whistle, and holding their obsidians conspicuously. In the final drama of the ceremony, they may number four instead of two ...

honor the foodstuff or its controller and thus to insure a continuing supply. The first eel taken each spring received similar treatment.

Besides the regular group ceremonies there were others enacted for the benefit of an individual—a sick child, a pubescent girl, or a novice shaman. When pestilence threatened, a special dance was executed to keep it away. Simple ritual acts were performed by men embarking on fishing or hunting expeditions. These preparatory observances had as their aim the securing of good luck.

The Hupa believed in the existence of a host of supernatural beings. Prominent in their thoughts and mythology was the culture hero, establisher of present conditions and human institutions. Another deity, born of the union of sun and earth, was invoked by young men seeking wealth. A third, bearded but of dwarf stature, controlled the vegetable world. On the whole these divinities, thought to dwell beyond limits of the known world, received little ritual attention. Living on earth were numerous local spirits, each with his own abode in a mountain, rock, riffle, or other feature of the landscape. Prayers were said to these supernaturals to ensure safe passage or success in the endeavor of the passer-by.

Hupa myths contained no account of creation, for according to Hupa belief, the world has always existed in much the same form. It was once inhabited by a race of beings, human

in form but supernatural in character. They lived for a time on earth and then left to dwell forever in a land across the ocean. In this prehuman period Hupa customs, industries, and arts were founded, many by the culture hero.

Humans were not created any more than was the universe. They merely sprang into existence, their coming signalled by smoke on the mountain sides. It was at this time that the prehuman race, their work finished, fled downriver in canoes and disappeared across the sea. Since their ancestors were believed to have come into being within their own territory, the Hupa had no legend of migration from another land.

Illnesses were attributed mostly to supernatural causes, and for diagnosing and curing them there were the usual shamans. Shamanism in northwestern California took on a unique aspect in that the profession was predominantly a female one. Although men as well as women could become healers, few males actually did. Another peculiar feature lay in the absence of the almost universal American Indian idea of a close and continued association between shaman and spirit helper. A Hupa healer acquired her curative powers through swallowing a small, semianimate object or "pain," an inch or two long, placed in her mouth by the ghost of a dead mother or other relative once engaged in the profession. Customarily this occurred during a dream but a few women deliberately sought power through nightly dancing in solitude on a mountain top. After acquiring a "pain," the novice learned to control it under the direction of an older medicine woman. A public dance terminated her training and publicly announced her readiness for practice.

A "pain" entering the body of an ordinary individual, either caught out of the air or shot in by an evil person, produced illness and had to be removed by a shaman. Called to a patient, the healer smoked a special pipe and finally applied her lips to the affected part and sucked with great force until the harmful, disease-causing object was removed.

Another sort of shaman possessed no "pain" but diagnosed the cause of illness by clairvoyance. These functionaries sang, danced, smoked tobacco, and shook a deer-hoof rattle until the cause of the disease was finally seen. They then suggested necessary steps for the patient's recovery and advised on what healer to hire. Such individuals could also locate lost persons

Hupa, northwestern California ● Beginning of the White Deerskin Dance (see p. 214). The men of status are carrying the sacred obsidian blades reflecting heirlooms and wealth. (Photograph by A. W. Ericson, near the Yurok town of Weitchpec, Humboldt County, California, ca. 1890. Smithsonian Institution National Anthropological Archives)

or property. A curing shaman was often a diagnostician as well.

Doctoring was a lucrative profession, for shamans charged high fees, payable in advance, for their services. If a patient failed to show improvement or died within a year, the payment was refunded. An unsuccessful practitioner was not killed if her patient died, but she might be if she refused recompense. Shamans were people of consequence and powerful ones were known far and wide. They formed the sole professional group in Hupa society and were the only persons who could hope to accumulate wealth by means other than inheritance.

Lesser disorders like an upset stomach or headache were treated by spoken formulas, secret possessions of certain individuals. Almost always an herbal medicine accompanied their delivery but these medications were administered in such minute quantity or in such a way as to have little or no effect. Relief was supposed to stem from the set form of words muttered rather than from any plant substance. Formulas, handed down in family lines were valuable property, as a stiff charge was made for their recital. Cuts, bruises, and the like needed no magical words but were cared for by home remedies known to everyone.

Certain formulas, sometimes repeated over

and over again, could be used to destroy an enemy or cause him to fall ill. Evil could also be worked by burying a nail paring, a lock of hair, or a bit of the intended victim's clothing near a grave or in a damp spot or by introducing "poisons" into his food or tobacco. Most dreaded were individuals who, under the cover of darkness, struck down their fellows with invisible missiles loosed from a miniature bow shaped from a section of human rib and strung with sinew taken from the wrist of a recently interred corpse. Sorcery was a practice open to anyone who knew the correct procedure but was believed to be worked most often by males.

In their contacts with Europeans the Hupa have fared better than other California Indians. They remained secluded in their nearly inaccessible valley until a little over a century ago. The first Caucasians to enter their country were fur trappers, passing through en route to other destinations. Their earliest sustained contact with outsiders came in 1850, following discovery of gold on the upper Trinity. Miners, white and Chinese, suddenly appeared in the valley. Several bars of pay-gravel were discovered but these were soon worked out.

A few miners took up farms and settlers began to drift in. Troubled conditions in the surrounding country led to the stationing of federal troops in Hoopa Valley in 1855 for the protection of whites and Indians alike. It was not until 1892, long after need for it had passed, that the little military post was abandoned. The idle soldiers were a continuing menace to the well-being of the Indians, and their presence resulted in a large infusion of Caucasian blood into the native population. In 1864 Congress authorized the setting aside of nearly the entire Hupa habitat for a reservation. White settlers were reimbursed for their improvements and moved out. An Indian boarding school and government-run hospital were subsequently established.

Uninterrupted occupancy of their homeland has benefited the Hupa. It has resulted in the proportion of survivors being one of the highest among Californian Indian groups. In combination with the remoteness of the country, it prevented a sudden disruption of native life. Though the old customs have by now largely disappeared, they have dropped out slowly so that the people have been able to adjust to changing conditions. Pressure from American civilization did not lead to messianic religious movements as it did elsewhere in California. Though cognizant of the Ghost Dance of 1870, accepted by the Yurok and Karok, the Hupa did not take it over, presumably because their traditional religion still had a strong hold on them.

Gradually the Hupa settled into a rural American life. They began to farm small plots of land and to keep livestock, though no great success was achieved in either endeavor. Men found employment on the reservation, in seasonal work on nearby ranches, in logging and road building. Missionaries, active on the reservation for many years, inspired most of the Indians to become at least nominal Christians. The Indian Shaker Church was introduced in the 1930s but never took firm root.

The Hoopa Valley Reservation, the largest in California (87,000 acres) is extremely rich in timber, and when trees are felled by private lumbermen, the tribe is compensated. A portion of the revenue, which today exceeds $1 million, is distributed semiannually to the more than 1100 persons currently on the tribal rolls and a $1 million reserve is maintained.

Prosperity and modernization followed World War II. The postwar lumber boom created an abundance of well-paid jobs in the woods and four mills. New businesses, mostly owned and operated by whites, added to the number of goods and services available to the community. The shift to a wage economy and the funds from timber brought an end to virtually all farming and stock raising. The present standard of living, though not high, is far superior to that of most California Indians.

Despite the changes which have taken place in their manner of living, the Hupa retain a strong sense of ethnic identity. The native language is still widely spoken, though many younger Indians feel more at home in English. Efforts are being made to perpetuate or to revive certain aspects of aboriginal life. This growing concern for the fate of their native legacy has little reference to the current generalized pan-Indian movement. The Hupa insist that their traditions be kept just as they were given to their ancestors by the mythical prehuman race and the culture hero, and not mixed with imports from other tribes or pseudo-Indian practices.

The Pomo Indians of Central California

Most characteristic of California was the aboriginal culture which covered the central two-thirds of the present state. Exceptionally well provided with foodstuffs and useful raw materials, this region, consisting of the Great Central Valley, drained by the Sacramento and San Joaquin rivers, and the adjoining Coast Ranges, Pacific shoreline, and western Sierra Nevada foothills, supported a dense native population. In this advantageous environment, largely cut off from outside influences, lived settled groups of food gatherers, estimated to have numbered at least 75,000 to 80,000 persons. Notwithstanding a bewildering diversity of language and dialect, a certain likeness ran through the manner of living of all these peoples.

Acorn eating was the most characteristic feature of Central Californian Indian life. The discovery of an efficient method for leaching objectionable tannic acid from the nuts of oaks, which grew nearly everywhere, made available a vast food supply of highly nutritive value. Another noteworthy development was basket weaving. All of the Indians in this section were skilled makers of both twined and coiled baskets in a variety of forms.

Representative of the Central Californian manner of living, though they had woven into its fabric specializations of their own, were the Pomo. These Indians occupied a considerable portion of north-central California, north of San Francisco Bay. Except for a small detached group inhabiting the fringe of the Sacramento Valley, the Pomo lived entirely within the temperate, wooded and well-watered Coast Range country of modern Sonoma, Lake, and Mendocino counties.

The Pomo homeland divided naturally into three geographical provinces. Least favorable was the precipitous, surf-beaten coastline, backed by an unbroken redwood forest. Though possessing marine resources not found elsewhere, acorn-bearing oaks and other edible plants as well as land mammals, aside from deer, were restricted in quantity. Near the center of Pomo territory lay the Russian River country, a succession of grassy, oak-dotted valleys separated from one another by rolling hills. This region furnished a larger and more dependable supply of plant foods and game than did the coast. Providing the most advantageous living conditions was the land surrounding Clear Lake. The former, a 25-mile-long freshwater lake up to 7½ miles wide, teemed with fish and, seasonally, with water fowl. Vegetal foods, game animals, and useful minerals were plentiful in the neighborhood. The influence of

the three geographical environments, though considerably mollified by intergroup travel and trade, were clearly seen in some aspects of Pomo economic and material culture.

Within this area lived an estimated 8000 Pomo. As might have been expected, the Clear Lake region had the heaviest concentration of population and the coast the lowest density. Physically the Pomo resembled most other Central Californian Indians. They were dark-skinned, moderately broad-headed, of short to medium stature, and sturdily built. Both males and females possessed large, heavy faces and, particularly the latter, tended to become corpulent with age.

Originally Pomo speech was considered a distinctive linguistic stock (Kulanapan) with no affinity to other North American Indian languages. Now it is regarded as an isolated member of the widely scattered Hokan family. Historical linguistic inferences agree in placing Hokan idioms among the most ancient in California, with a time-depth of 5000 or more years. The entrance of Penutian speakers into the central region apparently broke apart a solid block of Hokans, thereby isolating the Pomo from speakers of related languages. Pomo was spoken in seven dialects which exhibited considerable difference one from another, almost to the point of being separate languages. Divergences existed in each of the subdivisions but these were minor.

Pomo archeology has received much less attention than ethnology. But enough information has been gathered to demonstrate a lengthy human occupation of the tribal territory. Hunters who camped at Borax Lake, located just east of Clear Lake, appear to have been the region's first inhabitants. Their characteristic fluted points and other artifacts have been found at a few additional localities in the northern coast ranges. Archeologists remain divided in their opinions as to the antiquity of the Borax Lake materials, though the evidence is not incompatible with a dating of at least 10,000 years. Later in time and more widely distributed are the milling and handstones and other implements left behind by a foraging people. Their food-collecting lifeway persisted for a long time. A change in subsistence is reflected in the prehistoric remains assigned to the 3000–1000 B.C. interval. Mortars and pestles suggest acorn processing whereas a relative abundance of stone weapon tips implies that considerable attention was given to hunting. Cultural materials from the final prehistoric period, which began around A.D. 500, can with some certainty be tied to the ancestral Pomo. That some of the earlier cultures were carried by more remote forebears of this tribe is a reasonable inference. Their Hokan speech argues that the Pomo had established themselves in north-central California, if not in their historic homeland, at a very early date.

Like other Central Californian Indians, the Pomo depended heavily upon wild plants for their livelihood. Of first importance were acorns. In the fall the ripened nuts were harvested by the women, often aided by boys and men who climbed the trees and shook down the acorns or dislodged them with long poles. White Oaks (*Quercus lobata*), the most common species, yielded the main supply. Enormous quantities were collected and stored in granaries holding up to a dozen bushels.

Preparing acorns for eating required much labor. First the nuts had to be dried and hulled. Next they were pounded into flour with a stone pestle. Finally the meal was spread out in a shallow, sandy basin and hot water poured through it to remove the bitter tannin. The latter process left a sticky mass, which, combined with water, was placed in a tightly woven basket and cooked by dropping in hot stones. The resultant product consisted of a tasteless gruel or mush. Occasionally acorn meal was molded into unleavened cakes and baked in hot ashes. Only rarely was this food seasoned with salt.

In addition to acorns, a wide variety of other plants were gathered and eaten. Seeds of grasses and small, flowering herbs, harvested with the aid of a long-handled basketry seed beater, were parched, ground into flour, and consumed as dry meal or formed into cakes. Roots, bulbs, and tubers, dug from the ground with a hardwood digging stick, were eaten uncooked or roasted in hot ashes. Berries of several kinds were picked and devoured raw. The Pomo were extremely fond of tender leaves and stems of plants. In the spring, clover ranked high as a subsidiary food, nibbled off as it grew in the fields instead of being pulled up.

Game was varied and plentiful and provided a good share of Pomo diet. Meat came mostly from deer, rabbit, quail, and, in the lake region, from water fowl. Lone hunters, lying in wait along a game trail or at a salt lick, frequently slew deer with bow and arrow. But cooperative hunting was far more important. Often a small party of men drove deer toward a good marksman, disguised with deerhead mask, who shot them down with relative ease. A more ambitious group project involved construction of a pole and brush corral into which frightened animals were driven and slaughtered at will. The sinew-backed bow provided with a string of sinew or nettle fiber and obsidian-headed arrows used in hunting large animals were the same as those employed in warfare.

Smaller game animals and birds were mostly taken in snares and traps, though they were sometimes shot with simple, unbacked bows and wooden-tipped arrows. Mass drives forced rabbits into a brush fence or net. A number of special devices—blinds, nets, and slings for throwing clay balls—had been developed for capturing water birds. Game was usually broiled on live coals. Venison, the only meat stored for winter use, was cut into thin strips and sun dried.

Most Pomo groups consumed large amounts of fish. Certain species, like salmon, inhabited the streams only briefly during their spawning season; others could be obtained at almost any time of the year. The principal kinds available were salmon, trout, perch, suckers, and a variety locally called blackfish. Fish were caught in many different ways but netting was by far the commonest method. Seines, often of great length, gill and dip nets all were employed. For taking salmon, a pole and brush weir was constructed across a stream, leaving a foot-wide opening near one bank. Fish ascending the stream had to pass through the narrow aperture and were easily stabbed with a bone-tipped spear. Sometimes a long cylindrical basketry trap was set at the upstream side of the opening. Crushed pulp of the soap-root bulb or leaves of the turkey mullen, dropped into quiet pools formed behind brush dams, stupefied the fish and caused them to float to the surface belly up from whence they were readily gathered. Angling with hook and line was done only occasionally. The hook consisted of a piece of bone sharpened at either end. A line was attached at its center so that when swallowed it turned sidewise in the fish's mouth. Fresh-caught fish were usually broiled on hot coals. When a considerable catch had been made a portion of it was sun dried for future consumption.

A wealth of clams, mussels, abalones, and other shellfish as well as ocean fish and sea mammals were available to coast dwellers and interior peoples alike. The latter made periodic journeys to the shore to collect these marine products. To vary the diet, there were various insects. Army worms, small and nearly hairless caterpillars, captured by the hundreds in shallow trenches dug around trees on which they were feeding, were roasted in hot ashes or boiled, with the surplus spread out in the sun and dried for winter use. Grasshoppers, killed by firing the grass, hornet and yellow jacket grubs, angleworms, and various other insects were also relished. Shunned, however, was the flesh of all reptiles save the turtle.

While there was normally a sufficiency of food, hunger and famine were not unknown. A widespread failure of the acorn crop, which occurred rarely, was most dreaded. If this happened the Pomo enlarged their dietary range by eating such things as buckeye nuts, made edible by leaching. Large stores of foodstuffs, especially dried acorns, provided a safeguard against want.

Their rich economy permitted the Pomo a permanency of residence denied most food gatherers. For a good part of the year they occupied fairly substantial dwellings in fixed villages. Their houses varied in details of construction and in materials in the three geographical provinces. Smallest and least elaborate were the single-family, conical residences of the coastal people formed by setting slabs of redwood bark or wood in a circle, 10 to 15 feet across, and leaning them together against a center post. More pretentious and sheltering several families were the dome-shaped Russian River houses. Slender, flexible poles stuck in the ground in a circular or oval arrangement and bent over and tied at the top made up the basic framework to which strengthening poles, running horizontally, were added. Bunches of long coarse grass in a series of overlapping layers covered the framework. The long axis of such a structure measured up to 25 or 30 feet. The Clear Lake Pomo built similar dwellings but thatched them with bundles of tules instead of grass. Within a community the houses clustered together without plan. For summer or fall use while temporarily away from their homes in search of vegetable foods or game animals, the Pomo inhabited simple, hastily constructed brush shelters.

In every settlement there stood at least one structure in which the men took daily sweat baths. The sudatory, built around a 4-foot-deep circular pit, 15 to 20 feet in diameter, had a thick covering of brush and earth to conserve the heat. Warmth for sweating came directly

Pomo ● Fish trap. Traps such as these represent yet another application of the basketry technology of the California Indians. (After Kroeber, 1925:173. Courtesy of Bureau of American Ethnology. Smithsonian Institution)

from a fire, the smoke of which found its way out through a hole in the roof. Men and boys spent much time lounging about the sweathouse, particularly on winter days.

Centrally located in each larger Pomo community was a dance house. Circular in form, it measured 40 to 60 feet across. Like the sudatory it was semisubterranean and earth covered. Entrance was by means of a descending side tunnel. Construction of a dance house, attended with much ceremony, involved all of the males.

In keeping with the generally mild climate, the Pomo needed and wore little clothing. Men regularly went about stark naked. Women, on the other hand, never appeared in public unclothed. The essential female garment consisted of a two-piece skirt, extending from the waist to below the knees, donned for modesty and

Pomo, central California ● Woman pounding acorns with stone pestle and basket mortar. Shapes of the remarkably diverse types of Californian utility baskets may be noted. (Photo by H. W. Henshaw, date not recorded. Smithsonian Institution National Anthropological Archives)

style rather than for protection. This standard Californian Indian female costume comprised a narrow apron in front and a much larger back piece joined at the hips. It was fashioned from plant fibers—redwood bark on the coast, willow bark in the Russian River area, and tule around Clear Lake—shredded into strips and gathered on a waist cord. Buckskin skirts with the lower half slit into fringes were occasionally worn.

When necessary, both sexes wrapped themselves in thick, warm blankets made from strips of rabbit skin twined together. Mostly the Pomo went barefoot, though men protected their feet with simple skin moccasins while travelling in rough country. No covering was worn on the head except at dances. Males and females allowed their hair to grow to full length and, normally, to hang loosely. To keep the hair out of the way while performing certain tasks, men confined it in string hairnets. Tattooing was rather sparingly done and had only aesthetic significance. Women had a few lines radiating from the corner of the mouth across the cheeks and perhaps forehead and chin markings as well. Only a few males possessed tattooing. Early in life both sexes had the ear lobes punctured for insertion on festive occasions of sticks decorated at either end with shell beads and feathers. Boys underwent piercing of the nasal septum for the introduction of a wooden rod or bone tube.

In contrast to the scantiness and simplicity of daily attire, gala dress was elaborate. Of the various items reserved for special occasions, none was more striking than the orange and black headbands of flicker feathers. Skirts of turkey vulture feathers, necklaces of shell, bone, and stone beads, all formed part of Pomo ceremonial dress. Decorating the face, in fact all exposed parts of the body, with black, red, and white paints also constituted an important feature of ritual costume.

In a region noted for its uniform excellence of basket making, the Pomo were unrivaled. It is evident that this craft had undergone a special development among them and their finely woven baskets rank with the finest examples of aboriginal handiwork found anywhere in the world. Basket making was essentially woman's work though men wove a few coarse, openmesh articles.

Employing an unusual variety of techniques, the Pomo were by far the most versatile of the

California Indian basket weavers. They coiled and twined to about an equal extent, utilizing several variants of each process. Wickerwork, comparatively rare in native North America, was also known but was confined to fabricating seed beaters. Of the 30 or more plant materials used, they preferred slender, peeled willow shoots for warps and foundation rods. Common flexible fibers which provided wefts for twining or wrapping material for coiling comprised strips of sedge and bulrush root or redbud bark.

Baskets served many purposes. In addition to tightly woven, bowl-shaped containers of various sizes for cooking, Pomo women wove burden and storage baskets, mortar or grinding hoppers, winnowing trays, sifters and many more utilitarian forms. Unusual were elliptical or boat-shaped receptacles, often quite large, used as gifts, in ceremonies, or for storing valuables. Basketry articles prepared by men consisted of openwork carrying baskets, fish traps, and cradles.

In ornamenting baskets the Pomo reached their highest and almost only expression of art. Their geometric designs in black and red displayed a greater variety of arrangement than was regularly found on baskets of other native Californians. Whole patterns and individual design elements received names, from some real or fancied likeness to an animal, bird, or object, but had no symbolic meaning. Clam-shell disc beads were often attached to the surfaces of containers for additional ornamentation. Highly distinctive coiled baskets covered with brilliant feathers arranged in patterns of two or three colors, and sometimes with abalone-shell pendants attached, served as gifts and treasures and, above all, as sacrifices at funerals.

The Pomo were also conspicuous for their manufacturing of shell beads and magnesite cylinders. Men fashioned quantities of discoidal beads from heavy clam shells and traded them widely. The beads, strung according to size, functioned as money as well as for ornaments. When needed for paying off a debt or giving a present they were counted off and moved along the string. Clam-shell beads were enumerated in units up to 10,000 and 40,000 and through these computations the Pomo had developed a special mathematical facility.

Lumps of magnesite, a fine-grained, creamy-white mineral, roasted in the ashes until they took on a reddish or yellowish hue, were ground into cylinders and drilled. One or more

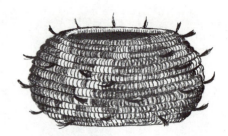

Pomo ● Small basket (diameter, 7 inches). Basketry craftsmanship of the California Indians was unsurpassed in native America. In this small, tightly coiled basket, quails' crests have been inserted to lend an added element of decoration. The use of quail, woodpecker, and hummingbird features in basketry decoration was especially characteristic of the Pomo. (Courtesy of The Science Museum, St. Paul, Minnesota)

of these valuable objects was often inserted into a necklace or placed with the body of a deceased person as a death offering.

In other handicrafts the Pomo exhibited only ordinary skill. Though fortunate in having in their country unlimited quantities of an excellent grade of obsidian, their arrowheads, spear points, and knife blades fashioned from this material were not outstanding products. Wood was employed in manufacturing a variety of articles including the familiar fire drill and a tubular tobacco pipe, 12 to 18 inches long, with an enlarged bowl. But the Pomo did not qualify as expert woodworkers. The primary bone tool consisted of the awl, indispensable in fabricating coiled baskets, formed from a shaped and sharpened deer bone. Tanning animal skins constituted a minor activity and the Pomo practiced no loom weaving or pottery making.

Having no beasts of burden, the Pomo travelled on foot and transported loads on their own backs. Women were almost invariably the carriers, bearing burdens in large conical baskets nested in nets supported by a tumpline passing over the forehead. A broad band woven into the net with a pad of grass, moss, or tule beneath it eased the strain on the forehead. Polished shell beads, placed so as to roll over when the load swayed, prevented sidewise chafing. This special headband took the place of the protecting basketry cap worn by Indian women in northern and southern California.

Water transportation was confined to two types of craft, neither seaworthy. Tule balsas, canoe-shaped rafts of buoyant dry reeds lashed together, could be navigated safely only on the quiet waters of lakes and sloughs. They were frequently poled but in deep water had to be paddled. Log rafts, temporary affairs made up of a few drift logs tied together, were used by coast dwellers in crossing river mouths and in making short voyages to offshore mussel and seal rocks. While sometimes propelled with a paddle, log rafts were customarily pushed by swimmers.

No overall sense of political unity existed among the Pomo, as they were split into more than 50 self-governing local groups. Characteristically each unit consisted of a main village and one or two lesser settlements. The primary community, aside from seasonal dispersal to gather and hunt, was continuously occupied over many generations; the smaller ones were less permanently fixed. Ordinarily a local group had no special name except for that of its locality or its major village. The usual designation included a place name with -pomo or -poma added, thus *Sedam-pomo, Shanil-pomo* and so on. It is this feature, the meaning of which is not wholly clear, that gave rise to the current name for the language group. Nearly every political unit spoke a slightly different subdialect.

Local groups numbered from 75 to 300 persons, averaging 150 to 200. Each owned a particular territory, ordinarily comprising 100 to 150 miles, to which its members had strong sentimental ties. Usually such a tract included a stream valley or part of one and some adjacent hilly country. Though boundaries were not regularly marked, they were known and respected by adjoining peoples. The land was owned collectively and every group member had the right to use its resources. In some localities, however, certain oak trees or open places which yielded plentiful supplies of seeds or other products were considered as private property.

Little formal government existed. Matters of common concern were discussed at gatherings attended by all male members of the local group. Each unit had an acknowledged headman, residing in the main settlement, who was accorded a good deal of respect but possessed only slight authority. Traditionally a son followed his father in this office but inheritance was subject to his having the necessary personality qualities—friendliness, fairness, evenness of temper, good speaking ability—as well as receiving community approval. A headman's suc-

cessor sometimes came from the female line, a nephew replacing his maternal uncle.

Although his right to command or to act was limited, the duties of a headman were many. Of paramount importance was his obligation to see that the proper religious ceremonies were held. Welcoming and entertaining visitors with a lavish hospitality constituted a second important duty. Another of his functions involved delivering frequent speeches on current events to his people and moral lectures to the children. He also tried to keep things going smoothly by mediating disputes, his primary aim here being to restore good relations, not to punish offenders. A herald or messenger acted as his assistant. Normally a headman possessed greater wealth than others and his family enjoyed considerable social prestige. Aside from this, no sharply crystallized distinctions in rank prevailed.

Prevailingly friendly relations existed between local groups and warfare was infrequent. The commonest cause for armed conflict lay in seeking revenge for a death ascribed to enemy witchcraft. Hostilities were also precipitated by unauthorized trespass. An individual who had previously displayed skill and courage in combat, rather than the headman, usually led a war party.

Fighting was carried on principally with bow and arrow. Other armaments included a short, obsidian-tipped thrusting spear and a sling. The latter had the same form as that used in stunning water birds but its ammunition consisted of small stones rather than clay balls. Handy cobblestones were frequently picked up and hurled at foes. A few Pomo fighters donned wooden-rod armor which covered the trunk, front and back. While affording protection against arrows, the clumsy and rigid armor reduced a warrior's mobility. Shields were unknown.

Battles regularly consisted of brief skirmishes, often sudden surprise attacks, with little loss of life. Each side was so anxious to see the fighting end that the first blood drawn frequently terminated a conflict. When possible the scalp of a slain enemy, a good-sized affair composed of the skin of the head down to and including the ears, was removed. Dried and carefully kept, scalps were brought out and danced over following a victory. Women and children seized in battle were often adopted by their captors; male prisoners were never taken. If hostilities persisted, it became the duty of the headmen of the groups involved to attempt a reconciliation.

Within the local group closely related families formed a lineage under the leadership of one man. Generally these units were paternally constituted, though some Pomo groups placed emphasis upon the maternal side of the family. Two or more lineages were usually represented in the community and their leaders made up a sort of informal council which cooperated with the headman.

Lineage members had mutual loyalty and gave aid when called upon. The kin group also provided the main basis for settling disputes. Offenses committed against nonmembers had to be compensated for in money, but as no fixed rates existed, negotiation always occurred. To forestall blood revenge following murder of an outsider, a sum of money was collected and paid to the victim's relatives. In parts of central California lineages were grouped into exogamous moieties but the Pomo had no such organizations.

It was, however, the single family rather than the lineage which formed the basic social and economic unit. Often this group had to be expanded to include an unattached kinsman or two. In the Russian River and Clear Lake districts several closely related families shared a common habitation and comprised a tightly knit household.

Every Pomo family desired children and as soon as it was known that one had been conceived, both parents took precautions to insure its safe delivery. The expectant mother, though continuing her regular household duties, was particularly circumspect in her behavior. Throughout her pregnancy she ate sparingly, avoided meat, and observed other dietary restrictions. Looking at the sun and weaving baskets became forbidden acts.

Childbirth took place in the family dwelling or in a small temporary hut. During delivery, the mother-to-be, attended by one or more kinswomen, sat on a bundle of tules or other soft material. If labor proved difficult, a shaman was called in for consultation. Immediately after birth the infant's umbilical cord was cut by one of the female attendants who also bathed the newborn. The severed cord was subsequently placed in a hollow tree or buried in a secluded spot. To rid her of the effects of childbirth, the mother submitted to steaming in a pit twice daily for a month or more.

Following birth of an infant, its parents still had to be extremely careful lest their actions be detrimental to its well-being. As in many Californian Indian groups the father observed a mild couvade, remaining quietly indoors for four days and refraining from hunting, travelling, and gambling for about a month. For her part, the mother limited her diet largely to vegetable foods and avoided scratching her body, face, and hair with her fingernails, employing instead a special stick.

A newly born baby was not suckled for several days but received instead a thin acorn gruel. Later it was given the breast whenever it exhibited signs of hunger. The nursing period frequently lasted from two to three years with other foods gradually introduced until complete weaning occurred. A few days after birth an infant was placed in a sitting cradle which resembled half of a basket. A hood shaded the baby's face. With its arms and body securely strapped but with its feet and legs dangling free, the infant remained confined in its cradle day and night with only brief periods of freedom until it reached the age of walking. An ancestral name, often that of a deceased grandparent, was bestowed upon a young child. No special ritual accompanied the name giving.

While growing up, children led a free and easy existence. Their parents displayed great indulgence towards them but discipline was not entirely lacking. Though rarely struck or whipped, youngsters were frequently admonished and exhorted by their elders. The headman also provided moral advice. Between five and ten years of age boys and girls underwent a health-giving rite as part of an important religious ceremony. They lay on the ground in a row and an old man scratched each in turn on the back with a piece of shell, breaking the skin slightly so that blood flowed.

The education of children proceeded with a minimum of formal instruction. Largely through conscious and unconscious imitation of their elders, they acquired the skills necessary in adult life. Much time was devoted to amusements. Toys, however, were few and simple, consisting of acorn tops and buzzers and dolls fashioned from clay or woven tules. Natural objects like seashells often served as playthings. A game indulged in primarily by boys involved seeing who could hurl a slender stick or arrow the greatest distance.

When a Pomo girl experienced her first menses, she was considered to be a source of contamination and was kept isolated in a corner of the family residence or in a special hut for four to eight days. Most of the time she lay in a heated pit and many of the same restrictions applied to a new mother prevailed. For her own well-being, the menstruant refrained from eating meat and scratching herself with her fingernails. She went outdoors only after sundown or early in the morning and then with her head veiled or covered. No public ceremony was held in her honor. The coming of age of a boy received no attention, although around puberty there occurred their initiation into religious cults.

When a youth reached marriageable age, his family entered into negotiations with the kindred of a suitable girl. The only important restriction on choice of a mate rested upon blood relationship. Unions between fellow villagers were permitted if no known blood ties existed. Before marital arrangements were settled upon, the wishes and feelings of the couple were considered so as not to force a young person into a distasteful match. The marriage pact concluded with an exchange of money and goods between the two families involved with the groom's relatives giving more than they received. This simple interchange of gifts involved more of a pledge of goodwill between two kin groups rather than actual bride purchase.

Final postnuptial residence was regularly with the groom's people but a fair number of young married couples settled in the girl's community. A man felt restraint in the presence of his wife's folk. In particular he avoided seeing or talking to his mother-in-law. A certain reserve also prevailed between a woman and her husband's parents. Polygyny, though allowed, occurred infrequently. Divorce, simple to achieve, was not lightly resorted to.

Once married and settled down, a young couple began a busy though uneventful life. The division of labor between spouses followed the usual primitive pattern. The male hunted, fished, made his own weapons and tools, and did the house building; his wife supplied the vegetable fare, cooked meals, cared for the children, and wove baskets. The Pomo woman, far from being a drudge, enjoyed a higher status than females did in many other Californian Indian groups.

When not occupied with more serious concerns, adults amused themselves by calling upon friends, gambling, or participating in athletic contests. Considerable visiting back and forth occurred between inhabitants of adjacent villages and between coast and interior peoples. Both sexes exhibited a fondness for gambling games and devoted considerable time to them. Men preferred the hand game, concealing two short sticks, one plain and the other marked, in small bunches of grass; women indulged in dice throwing, utilizing six willow sticks, unmarked on one side and bearing burned-in designs on the other. Males and females alike wagered on the toss of a single bone die, a deer or elk astragalus. Whenever a large group assembled, footraces were run. Teams of either males or females competed in shinny contests, played with hooked stick and wooden ball.

Pipe smoking provided another diversion, particularly for older men. The size and form of the Pomo pipe made it necessary to hold it almost vertically so that it was mostly used while reclining. In common with other Californian Indians, Pomo men smoked only moderately. Storytelling also afforded entertainment, for adults as well as children enjoyed listening to talented narrators. In addition to their sacred myths, the Pomo had a rich stock of tales recounted for amusement only. Animal characters possessing human attributes were common characters in these stories and a telling of the exploits of Coyote, the braggart Trickster, produced much merriment. Myths and tales were customarily related only at night.

Persons of advanced age were respected and humanely treated. They received food and care from their kinsmen, often becoming part of the household of a son or daughter. On rare occasions a decrepit oldster who had become a burden or hopelessly ill was strangled with a stick pressed down at either end across the throat. This practice was resorted to out of pity rather than from necessity.

As soon as relatives and friends of an elderly or seriously ill individual became convinced that he was dying, they gathered about him and began wailing. While lamenting, women often scratched their cheeks with fingernails until blood streamed over the face. Almost immediately after life had departed, the corpse was dressed and readied for cremation on a pyre built over a shallow pit. Personal effects of the deceased, together with practically all of those of his immediate kin, were burned with the body. More distant relatives and friends also contributed valuables, including feather baskets and shell beads. Following the funeral, remaining charred bones were gathered together and buried in a cemetery near the village.

Pomo mourning practices, essentially personal and nonceremonial, were neither as ostentatious nor as prolonged as those of some neighboring groups. Near relatives of the deceased, particularly females, cut and singed their hair but no severe restrictions were placed upon their behavior. Formal mourning lasted about a year and was not followed by a mortuary anniversary comparable to the elaborate rituals of south-central and southern California. The name of a dead person was never mentioned in the presence of his kinfolk. Under the levirate custom, a widow sometimes became the wife of her dead husband's brother but she did not have to accept this arrangement. Marriage of a widower to his deceased wife's sister also occurred.

It was believed that a person's soul, released at death, lingered about the village for four days before journeying to the land of the dead located at the southern extremity of the world or, according to another version, in the sky. Conceptions of the hereafter and how departed souls fared there were vague. Ghosts occasionally returned from the afterworld and, because the sight of one could cause illness, were regarded with apprehension. Dreaming of the nonliving endangered a person and had to be counteracted by chewing angelica, an herb of the carrot family, or rubbing it over the body.

A well-developed ceremonialism characterized Pomo religion but the reason for holding many of the rituals was not precisely expressed. Presumably their performance produced generalized benefits. Religion found its greatest visible expression in the solemnities associated with two spirit-impersonating rituals—the Ghost and Kuksu ceremonies. The masquerading and dancing associated with these took place in the earth-covered dance house from which all females and uninitiated boys were barred.

Outstanding was the four-day Ghost Ceremony. Male participants, disguised by paint and with faces distorted from twigs thrust into nostrils and cheeks, assumed the character of dead persons. Before entering the dance house, the masqueraders dashed wildly about the village, terrorizing women and children who remained out of sight as much as possible. Dancing, fire eating, handling hot coals, and manipulating live rattlesnakes formed part of the ritual. Regularly used was the footdrum composed of half of a hollow log, six to ten feet long. Placed over a shallow pit, which acted as a resonance chamber, this instrument, when stamped upon with bare feet, produced a deep, booming sound. There was also whirling of the bull-roarer, believed by outsiders to be the voice of the dead, and the shaking of cocoon rattles. Initiation of boys during which the novices were tossed back and forth through a large fire constituted an important part of the performance. The Ghost Ceremony concluded with an all-night dance.

The second cult centered around impersonation of Kuksu, a deity living at the southern end of the world, and several other supernatural beings. Kuksu, represented by one or more men wearing elaborate headdresses and false noses, was regarded as a healer of the sick and by some as presiding over the realm of the dead. The Kuksu ritual, an affair lasting six days, included a series of dances and dramatizations. Dancers carried bone whistles upon which they blew from time to time. Youths were initiated through being symbolically "killed" by mock stabbing and being brought back to life. The health-giving rite for children formed part of the Kuksu ceremony.

God-impersonating cults were not limited to the Pomo. In the central California province the Patwin, Maidu, Miwok, Yuki, and several more tribes participated in them. A fair number of the practices connected with the rituals recur in the ceremonies of the Pueblo Indians of Arizona and New Mexico. These parallels suggest that religious influences emanating from the Southwest may have reached north-central California and were worked into the god-impersonating observances of the Pomo and their neighbors. Other ritual performances were less spectacular. Though men enacted most of these, there were some in which women participated and two that they conducted alone. Minor ritual acts included praying to the new moon for health and making a great noise when an eclipse of the sun occurred, the latter designed to drive off a bear supposed to be devouring it.

The Pomo believed in the existence of a host of supernatural beings. Prominent in myth, along with Kuksu, were Madumda, regarded by some as creator of the world and occasionally identified with Coyote, Sun-man, and Thunder-man. These three deities, conceived in the image of man, were remote and ideas concerning them were hazy. The Pomo held no communion with them and they played no prominent role in religious beliefs and practices. Also there was Gilak, a fearsome, birdlike creature, reputed to soar over the earth in search of victims to devour.

Local spirits, potentially malevolent, produced greater concern. The Pomo imagined their homeland to be overrun with beings who inhabited springs, rocks, crevices, caves, mountains, in fact any spot of unusual configuration. Such places, fraught with danger, had to be avoided.

General forces of evil could, in Pomo thought, be warded off by charms. Strangely formed pebbles and artificially shaped stones served as amulets as did certain roots and herbs, such as angelica. Charms possessed the power not only to counteract malevolent agencies but to insure success in hunting, fishing, gambling, and other endeavors as well. Various omens foretold good or bad luck. Hearing an owl's call near one's residence, for example, signaled impending disaster or death, whereas seeing a bull snake portended good fortune.

For their religion, the Pomo had no organized priesthood. The only religious specialists were the shamans who cured the sick. Pomo practitioners, mostly men, were of two types. The first group obtained their healing power in the usual fashion, directly from a spirit. It came to them unsought, often during an illness. In their cures, these medicine men followed the widespread primitive practice of feigning to suck a disease object out of the patient's body. Treatment by a healer of this kind was considered particularly efficacious in sudden seizures believed due to witchcraft.

Another class of medicine men acquired curative powers by virtue of special training under older practitioners, regularly a father or maternal uncle. Their healing was effected by singing, dancing, and simple ritual acts such as pressing heated objects rubbed with special herbs against the seat of the pain. Essential paraphernalia consisted of a medicine bundle, containing such miscellaneous objects as oddly shaped rocks, bones, roots, a cocoon rattle, and an obsidian blade. A shaman of this sort was called upon for any type of serious disorder.

Medicine men enjoyed high respect. They received good pay for their service though no man made his living by this means alone. A deeply rooted belief held that a shaman, when he so desired, could turn his power to evil purposes and injure or kill a person and much illness was attributed to such hostile magic.

Not all illnesses required the services of a professional medicine man. Kuksu dancers were sometimes called in to minister to the sick, and home remedies—potions, poultices, and fumigants concocted from herbs, barks, roots, and the like—sufficed for ordinary ailments not ascribed to supernatural agencies. Another medical technique, considered effective for most disorders, was the sweat bath.

Much dreaded by the Pomo were "bearmen" who roamed about plundering and murdering. Whereas elsewhere in central and southern California certain individuals were credited with having the power to turn themselves into grizzly bears at will, the Pomo thought that such persons merely wore bearskin disguises. These special suits, however, endowed their wearers with great speed and endurance. For slaying his victims a Pomo bear-man carried a special elkhorn or bone dagger. Bands of clam-shell beads wrapped around his body served as protective armor. Though a bear-man inspired extraordinary fear, he was frequently looked upon as a benefactor by members of his own local group in the belief that he exercised his destructive powers only against foes. Referred to as "bear-doctors" by modern Indians, these individuals did not have shamanistic powers. Evidently they received instruction in this evil pursuit from older persons, either practicing or former bearmen.

The Pomo possessed a mass of myths and legends which accounted for or explained many of their ideas regarding the supernatural. But these had not been arranged in any sort of orderly system and they contained the glaring inconsistencies and contradictory beliefs generally found in the mythology of primitive peoples. It was the custom to recount a sacred tale in the form of a long, composite narrative, the episodes of which followed one another without logical sequence. In Pomo myths the universe was conceived of as being made up of three worlds or levels. The earth proper upon which human beings now dwell had been inhabited in a former era by the supernatural "Bird People," later transformed into actual birds, reptiles, and mammals. Directly above lay the first Upper World, the abode of Madumda. Over this was a nebulous, second Upper World where lived Madumda's brother and about which people possessed little knowledge. There also existed four outer worlds situated in the cardinal directions.

Comparatively little information dealing with the creation of this universe was found in the myths, and ideas concerning its origin differed greatly. Some Pomo assumed that it had always existed much as it is now; others maintained that there had been a definite creation. Coyote, who enacted the dual role of culture hero and mischievous Trickster, brought humans into being out of feathers or sticks. Many mythological incidents explained how present usages and conditions came about. There were also accounts of the destruction of the world by fire and flood in prehuman times and its subsequent rehabilitation. In common with Indian peoples of northwestern and central California, the Pomo lacked a tradition of migration.

Pomo culture continued to flourish until around the middle of the nineteenth century. During much of the Spanish period in California (1769–1822), the region north of San Francisco Bay remained uninhabited by whites. But with the founding of a Russian colony on the Mendocino coast in 1812, the Spaniards and later the Mexicans gradually extended their frontier northward to counteract the intrusion. In 1823, shortly after Mexico had won its freedom from Spain, a Franciscan mission was established at Sonoma and cattle ranching began in the fertile valleys of the southern Pomo country. However, on the whole, this Hispanic expansion northward had no great effect on Pomo life.

With the annexation of California by the United States in 1846, there began a period of rapid disintegration of native culture. The Pomo region, lacking gold, did not experience an invasion by the first wave of immigrants, the gold seekers. But as soon as the gold excitement died down, settlers moved in and began ranching. The Pomo were ruthlessly dispossessed and, as the white population increased, they declined in numbers. Disease, starvation, and indiscriminate killing combined to take a heavy toll. To alleviate the Indians' plight, the federal government set up a reservation on the Mendocino coast in 1856 to which Indians were brought from the Russian River and Clear Lake districts. Never a success, the reservation failed to check the decline in native population. When the Mendocino establishment was abolished, 12 years after its founding, most Pomo returned to their home localities only to find that their lands had been taken over by white ranchers. The Indians were often permitted to settle on the larger ranches by owners, eager to have a pool of cheap labor close at hand.

More and more the Pomo became dependent upon Caucasians for their livelihood. They became harvesters in the grain and hop fields, wood choppers, and unskilled farm and domestic workers. These early years of hand-to-mouth existence proved difficult and demoralizing and, like many other aboriginal peoples, the Pomo reacted to their unhappy state by turning to a revivalistic religion. The Ghost Dance of 1870, which swept northern and central California, reached the Pomo early in 1872 in the form of two special cults, outgrowths of the original movement. The new doctrines, stressing the end of the world and concepts of afterlife and the Supreme Being, took firm root and led to a resurgence and making over of the old Kuksu ceremonies. Local prophets arose and the cults, which have maintained themselves in some degree to the present, became elaborated through the addition of new songs, paraphernalia, and ritual acts.

Today the Pomo live in tiny groups on small government-bought or privately purchased parcels of land scattered throughout their old territory. Although numbering only a fraction of their original total, they constitute one of the most populous Indian peoples within the boundaries of California. There are well over 1000 survivors, pure and mixed. Though their standard of living has improved, they are still on the economic level of poor, rural whites. Only bits of the old Indian life persist and each year, as the elderly pass on, even these vestiges disappear. The long aboriginal occupancy has left slight if any impress on the modern culture of central California. Apparently the Pomo had little else to offer to settlers other than their labor and a few geographical place names.

The Luiseño Indians of Southern California

The southern California coastal region, from north of Point Conception to the Mexican border, contained a series of native peoples whose mode of life exhibited a basic uniformity. Essential qualities of this culture included a predominantly gathering type of economy, a relatively meager technology, a simple set of social and political institutions, an intense interest in adolescence and death, considerable religious symbolism, and a complicated cosmogony. Only the Chumash (or Canaliño) of the Santa Barbara region, with their greater maritime adaptation and superior craftsmanship diverged markedly from this general pattern.

With the exception of the Chumash and the Diegueño, the Indians of southern California spoke languages belonging to the Shoshonean branch of the major Uto-Aztecan phylum, closely related to the Numic of the Great Basin. The Shoshoneans appear to have been late-comers, migrants from the interior deserts who pushed to the coast and adapted themselves quickly and successfully to a new geographical and cultural environment. It is thought that they displaced Hokan-speaking peoples, leaving the Chumash on the north and the Diegueño at the south as the only remaining representatives of this linguistic stock. The exact time of the Shoshonean thrust westward cannot be fixed definitely but presumably it occurred before A.D. 1000.

Most southerly of the coastal Shoshoneans were the Luiseño. Originally called "San Luiseño,"they derived their name from San Luis Rey de Francia, the mission established in their country in 1798. This designation was later shortened to its present form. Like most aboriginal groups, the Luiseño lacked a name for themselves other than one meaning "people." All of their neighbors, save for the Diegueño to the south, consisted of fellow Shoshoneans with whom the Luiseño had close affiliations, linguistically and culturally. To the east lived the Mountain Cahuilla and Cupeño; at the north they were bordered by the Juaneño, Gabrielino and Serrano.

Roughly defined, Luiseño territory included what is now the northwestern corner of San Diego County and the contiguous portion of Riverside County. Along the coast their land extended for about 20 miles; inland it ran back 30 to nearly 50 miles. Adjacent to the shoreline it comprises a pleasant region of alluvial valleys, diversified by low hills and infrequent watercourses. Eastward stretches a hinterland of rugged mountains fringing the interior desert. The climate is mild with long, dry summers and brief, never severe winters. Nearly all precipitation falls in one period, December to March inclusive. The seasonal amount averages around 15 inches but varies considerably from year to year. A deficiency of perennial streams characterizes the region because most watercourses, including the main San Luis Rey river system, become dry or practically so during the rainless summer and fall.

Most of the land has a cover of woody shrubs, often of considerable density, with here and there tracts of grassland. On the whole, the area is scantly forested. Oaks, of primary importance to the Luiseño as a source of food, are restricted to valleys and gentler hillslopes. Willows and sycamores line stream bottoms and pines and other conifers clothe the mountainsides. The natural environment supports a diversified, though only moderately abundant wildlife. Fish and sea mammals formerly abounded in the coastal waters. Shellfish of many kinds are obtainable along the shoreline.

Roughly 4000 Luiseño inhabited this section in precontact times. The greatest concentration of people lay in the coastal district with the interior uplands the least populated. Typical Californian Indian in physical appearance, the Luiseño attained only a medium stature, had good physiques and moderately round heads. Their complexion had a deep brown tone and they exhibited the common aboriginal American characteristics of coarse, black hair, dark-brown eyes and rather heavy faces. Only small regional variations existed in their language with dialectic differences most noticeable between the extreme nothern and southern groups. Luiseño speech showed many likenesses to that of their northern neighbors, the Juaneño, and the two languages must have been largely intelligible.

Recent archeological work has produced information regarding the immediate ancestry of Luiseño culture. It can now be traced through two closely related prehistoric phases, designated San Luis Rey I and II. The artifact assemblages and the mixed hunting-gathering economy mirrored in the finds shows that the prehistoric peoples lived in much the same fashion as the Indians encountered by Spanish explorers in the latter half of the eighteenth century. The second of the two phases witnessed the inception of pottery making. At present it is difficult to give precise dates for the San Luis Rey occupations but there is little doubt that the first goes back to A.D. 1000 or beyond. Material remains belonging to several preceding societies afford proof that the San Luis Rey peoples were not the country's first settlers. Surface finds of projectile points and associated objects corresponding to those recovered farther south along the San Dieguito River suggest that ancient hunters once roamed the land. Much more in evidence are the grinding stones and other implements of a later population who depended largely upon plant foods for their livelihood. Conditions of increasing aridity inland may have led to the coastward movement of foraging groups. The simple food-collecting mode of existence, which began

Diegueño, southern California ● Man and woman sorting beans or seeds outside brush house. (Photograph by H. W. Henshaw, date not recorded. Smithsonian Institution National Anthropological Archives)

before 5000 B.C., persisted for several thousands of years. A degree of obscurity surrounds the nature of the cultural development that took place between the occupation of the milling-stone users and that of the San Luis Rey people.

The local environment provided a wealth of natural products in the form of wild plants, animals, and seafoods from which the Luiseño procured a good livelihood. Here, as generally in aboriginal California, there was a marked concentration upon the gathering and eating of acorns. At least six species of acorn-bearing oaks grew in the area with those of the black oak most eagerly sought. Each fall, when the nuts became ready for harvesting, an effort was made to secure and store away enough of them to tide the family, if need be, over a year of scarcity. The accumulated acorns were placed in granaries resembling huge birds' nests. Made by rough coiling from willow or other plant material, these receptacles held from eight to twelve bushels. They were provided with lids

and mounted on low platforms to protect their contents from the ravages of rodents.

When needed for the family meal, the acorns were hulled and then pulverized. Crushing with a stone pestle took place in a hole worn into a rock outcrop or in a basket-hopper mortar. The pestle consisted of a conveniently shaped stream cobble. The tannic bitterness of the nuts was leached out in a loosely woven basket which allowed the hot water to filter through or, as among the central and northwestern Californians, in a basin scooped out of the sand. Acorn meal generally was cooked in an earthenware vessel as a thin gruel or soup.

Acorns, though providing the chief sustenance, constituted but one of the 60 or so wild plant foods collected. Next in importance were seeds obtained from various shrubs and grasses. Tiny gray seeds of Chia, one of the smallest of the sage family, provided much good food. Others came from black, white, and thistle sage, pepper grass, several species of the sunflower family, and from native grasses which have since disappeared. Seeds were knocked into a shallow basket with a small, fanlike beater of open-twined work. When a sufficient quantity had been harvested, they were emptied into a large bowl-shaped burden basket, held on the back in a special carrying

Cahuilla, southeastern California ● Examples of
Desert Cahuilla storage baskets. (Photograph
H. W. Henshaw, ca. 1890.)

net. Before grinding, seeds were winnowed
and parched by shaking them together with
live coals upon a basketry tray. They were
spread on a rectangular stone slab and ground
into flour with an oval cobble handstone. The
meal, mixed with water, ordinarily was consumed cold. Surplus seeds were kept in pottery
jars, often three feet in height.

Other items of diet included fruits and berries. Succulent fruits of the prickly pear cactus,
pulled off with simple tongs and their thorns
removed by burning or scraping, were much
enjoyed. Pulp of the wild plum as well as its
kernel served as food. The latter, ground into
meal, underwent leaching and cooking in exactly the same manner as acorn flour. Toyon or
Christmas berries, after toasting, were eaten
without further preparation. Choke-cherries,
wild grapes, and berries of several varieties also
provided the Luiseño with food.

Green stalks of the Whipple Yucca, roasted in
a preheated, stone-lined pit, furnished a valuable though fibrous supplement to the spring

diet. Large, creamy-white flowers of this plant
as well as those of the less common Mohave
Yucca (Spanish Dagger) were boiled in water
before eating. Green pods of the latter were
consumed after roasting on hot embers. Tender
foliage and shoots of many plants, including
clover, lamb's quarters (white pigweed), Indian
lettuce, watercress, eaten fresh or boiled, added
greens to spring meals. Roots and bulbs provided comparatively little food because the generally dry soil supported few edible varieties.
Included among those consumed were bulbs of
the lily family and yucca roots, both pried up
with hardwood digging sticks.

The seasonal yield of wild plants produced a
varied diet, marked with momentary abun-
dances. Ordinarily, a plentitude of vegetable
foods existed so that failure of even a highly
important one could be compensated for by
more intensive gathering of others or by drawing upon previously accumulated stores.
Women and girls did most of the foraging, but
men and boys occasionally helped, particularly
with the acorn harvest when tree climbing had
to be done.

The Luiseño did not, of course, subsist upon
plant foods alone. Game, fish, shellfish, and in-

sects rounded out their prevailing vegetable fare. Living in a country where big game was not especially plentiful, they relied upon rabbits for their primary source of meat. Hunters secured these creatures in several different ways. They hurled flat, curved sticks at running animals to kill or cripple them, shot them with bow and arrow, and caught them in snares placed along their runs. Occasionally an enormous net woven of tough plant fibers was strung across a suitable spot and entire families spread themselves out and beat the brush so as to force the frightened rabbits into it. Once entrapped the animals were speedily dispatched with clubs. Woodrats, mice, and ground squirrels were poked out of their burrows with sticks; quail and other birds were taken in snares. The flesh of these smaller creatures was broiled on hot coals.

Deer constituted the most desirable game. Armed with bows and arrows, men went out singly to stalk them or to lie in ambush. Sometimes a hunter put on a stuffed deerhead disguise and mimicked the actions of a grazing animal in order to get within arrow range. Nooses placed along deer trails entangled the feet or antlers of running animals. Customarily venison was broiled on coals or roasted in an earth oven; less often it was boiled. Huntsmen occasionally killed bears for their skins and claws but the flesh of these animals was never eaten.

The hunting bow, about five feet long and quite narrow, most commonly was made of willow, but alder and ash also served. The Luiseño bow lacked the sinew backing characteristic of most northwestern and central Californian weapons. Its string consisted of twisted fibers of Indian hemp, milkweed, or nettle. Arrows usually had cane shafts fitted with foreshafts of sharpened hardwood with only those intended for big game hunting or warfare stone tipped. A quiver fashioned from the pelt of a fox, bobcat, or other animal and worn slung over the shoulder, protected a man's bow and arrows. For skinning and butchering, a hunter employed a stone-bladed knife.

Sea otters, seals, and sea lions provided meat for the seacoast dwellers. These animals were harpooned or otherwise killed by hunters who ventured a short distance out from shore on tule balsas or in small dugout canoes. So far as is known, the Luiseño did not make use of the type of plank canoe employed on sea mammal hunting, fishing, and trading expeditions by the Chumash and Gabrielino.

Fish formed an important staple of the coastal groups. Many varieties were netted, speared, or caught with curved hooks made from abalone shell and attached to lines of twisted plant fiber. Shellfish also furnished the shoreline peoples with much food. For most inland Luiseño, fishing had minor importance because the intermittent watercourses contained no fish. Trout were present on the upper San Luis Rey River and in some of the mountain streams emptying into it. A narcotic, prepared from crushed roots, was dropped into pools causing the drugged trout to rise to the surface where they were easily captured by hand or scooped up in baskets.

Although they shunned frogs, lizards, snakes, and turtles, the Luiseño eagerly sought certain insects for food. When swarms of young grasshoppers appeared, a good-sized pit was dug and surrounded at a distance by a circle of men, women, and children. With boughs in hand with which to beat the grass, they slowly drove the grasshoppers into the excavation. A quick fire of dried grass and brush killed and toasted the entrapped insects. In this condition grasshoppers not eaten on the spot could be stored for months. Large green caterpillars, flavored with salt and boiled, were relished.

An unusual food consisted of exudations of sucking insects such as aphids, generally deposited upon rushes. Gathering the product involved considerable labor—cutting the stalks, spreading them out in the sun to dry and beating them so as to dislodge the "honey dew" onto an animal hide or woven mat. Collected and pressed into balls, the tiny particles formed a sweet, pasty substance, a much favored delicacy. The use of "honey dew" centered among the Shoshoneans of southern California and the Great Basin. A few central Californian groups also utilized it.

The Luiseño kept no domesticated animals other than a few dogs. These creatures did little more than roam around the village, scavenging for food and barking at strangers. Apparently they received no formal training and never were put to work as aids to hunters.

Clothing was minimal. Males most often went about nude; feminine attire followed the usual native California style of a small front apron and a larger back piece. The former consisted of cords of Indian hemp or milkweed; the rear garment was made of strips obtained from the inner bark of willow trees. In winter adults wrapped themselves in robes formed of twisted strips of rabbitskin or highly prized sea otter pelts. Men wore no head covering but women put on coiled basketry caps when they had burdens to carry. This headgear, a truncated cone, eased the strain of the carrying net cord and prevented its chafing the forehead. As a rule, both sexes went barefoot but sandals protected their feet while travelling in rough country or over hot soil. The sandals, fashioned from yucca fibers, formed pads nearly an inch thick, fastened to the feet with loops of cordage.

Customarily the hair of either sex flowed long and loose, men's being somewhat shorter than women's. Males had their foreheads marked with tattoo designs and horizontal or radiating lines on the cheeks. Females were more profusely tattooed. Lines radiated from the lower lip to the chin in the usual California Indian fashion. In addition each woman had a vertical line drawn down the center of her forehead and a small circle inscribed on each cheek. Bands of tattooing encircled a female's wrists, and a curved bar from which lines descended downward decorated her chest. For special occasions both sexes painted their faces and bodies with black, red, and white designs and adorned their persons with necklaces of shell, steatite, or bone beads. The ear lobes of males were pierced for the insertion of bone pins; their nasal septums had perforations for suspension of shell pendants.

A cone-shaped, thatched house afforded shelter for each Luiseño family. Construction began with excavation of a circular pit, perhaps 2 feet deep and 8 feet across. A half dozen or so heavy wooden supports, set solidly in the ground around the circle and with their crotched ends hooked together, formed the basic framework. Lighter poles were leaned against these and others were lashed on horizontally. A thick thatching of rushes, arrowweed, bark, or locally available material then was added. Some dwellings also had a partial or entire earth covering. A low opening left at one side, covered during unusually cold weather with a suspended mat, served as the doorway. A vent in the roof allowed for escape of smoke.

Little in the way of furnishings existed inside the house. Beds of the occupants—rabbitskin blankets, mats or even bundles of dried grass—lay on the earthen floor around a central hearth. The rabbitskin robes also served, when needed, as blankets. Various family belongings were thrust into the thatching or stood against the wall.

Cooking and other common domestic activi-

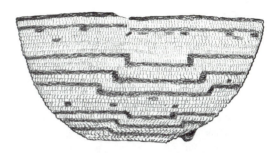

Yuki ● Simple utility basket (top diameter 15 inches). Reflecting the ubiquitous concern with baskets in native California, a Yuki household basket such as this might be used for cooking by filling with water and dropping heated stones inside. A rack prevented burning. (After Kroeber, 1925:822. Courtesy of Bureau of American Ethnology, Smithsonian Institution)

ties generally took place beneath an unwalled shade which stood adjacent to the dwelling. The structure's flat roof found support on four heavy, forked uprights set firmly in the earth at each of the four corners of a rectangle. Rafters and poles were laid across them and a layer of brush spread on. The shade offered relief on even the hottest days, for its open sides permitted free circulation of air and its roof formed a shield against the sun's rays. On warm nights the entire family slept under it.

A third type of building, similar in form and construction to the dwelling but smaller and earth covered, functioned as a sweathouse for the men. Here adult males carried on their daily sweating and, on occasion, engaged in competitive heat trials. A centrally placed fire furnished the heat necessary for inducing perspiration. Men did not sleep in the sweathouse nor did it serve them as a workshop. Now and then minor curing took place in it.

As elsewhere in native California, basket weaving, wholly in the hands of women, dominated the industrial arts. But considering its importance, the craft showed a remarkable limitation in weaves, materials, and forms. Coiling preponderated. Twined baskets were made but they consisted of roughly fashioned open work affairs which served only for the most ordinary domestic purposes. The Luiseño did not employ simple in-and-out weaves such as checker, twilling, and wickerwork.

Only three materials found regular use in the manufacture of coiled baskets. A bundle of long and coarse stems of Epicampes grass composed the foundation; strips of either Juncus rush or sumac provided the sewing elements. Though well made, Luiseño coiled containers did not have as fine a texture as those fashioned by central California Indians because the grass bundle foundation produced a certain thickness and thus precluded delicate work.

Most coiled baskets were bowl shaped. Even the burden basket, typically conical and deep elsewhere in California, consisted of a comparatively shallow bowl with either a rounded or flat bottom. All coiled containers bore decorations in contrasting colors. The Juncus rush which comes in a variety of natural hues—cream, yellow, red, brown, and olive—provided most of the ornamental strands. Black, the only artificial color, was produced by boiling sumac strips in water containing marsh mud. Patterns comprised simple geometric motifs, predominantly combinations of bars, triangles, and quadrilaterals. The design lacked symbolic meaning.

Luiseño women also made earthenware vessels of fairly good quality. Built up by adding coils of clay, vessel walls were thinned by patting them between a smooth, rounded pebble held inside and a wooden paddle. The forms made included globular, wide-mouthed cooking pots, smaller-mouthed jars of large size for the storage of seeds, and shallow, bowl-shaped serving dishes. Vertical or slanting lines, pressed into the soft clay, decorated a few vessels. Firing took place in a pit partially filled with dry oak bark and the finished products emerged with a lusterless, brown surface.

Luiseño pottery represents a local variety of a plainware (designated Tizon Brown by archeologists) with wide distribution in southern California and western Arizona. There is general agreement that its manufacture began quite late among the Luiseño. However, no satisfactory means by which to date its first appearance is yet available; it may have been around A.D. 1200–1300. Everything points to the knowledge of pottery making having reached the Luiseño from their southern neighbors, the Diegueño.

The remainder of the Luiseño's equipment was composed of simply made but serviceable articles. Included were the usual wooden fire drill, a small brush of soap-root fibers for sweeping acorn meal from the mortar, and a sharp-pointed bone awl, indispensable in fabricating coiled baskets. Pipes, in which wild tobacco was smoked, consisted of short tubes of fired clay, tapering rather abruptly toward the mouth end. Bits of clam shell, worked into small perforated disks and strung, served as money. A string's value was determined by measuring it around the circumference of the hand.

Because it suffered an early breakdown, Luiseño social structure is difficult to reconstruct. Little doubt exists, however, that it rested upon the paternal lineage. The core of such a group consisted of a number of men related to one another through the male line; their wives came from other kin units. Component families regularly inhabited the same village and cooperated with one another. Certain plots of land, containing oak trees or other useful resources, were traditionally used by and generally recognized as belonging to particular lineages.

It is not altogether clear whether lineages formed part of larger kinship units. Throughout much of south-central and southern California, such groups had been arranged into moieties which traced descent through the father. Of the southern peoples, the Cahuilla, Serrano, Cupeño, and perhaps others had this form of dual organization. The moieties, regularly called Wildcat and Coyote, stressed exogamy and performed various services, generally of a ritual nature, for one another. Certain plants, animals, and natural phenomena were linked to each grouping.

Families belonging to several lineages habitually resided together in local groups composed of 200 or so persons. This was the primary landholding unit, for its members claimed a stretch of territory which they alone had the right to exploit. Each group's tract of land, which included about 30 square miles of varied terrain, contained sufficiently large and varied food resources to support the local population during a normal year. Its boundaries, clearly defined by natural landmarks, were jealously guarded against encroachment by outsiders.

At least one major village was situated in the group territory, usually in a valley near the center of the landholding. Here stood the cluster of houses in which the people resided for a considerable part of the year. The community broke up seasonally when its members dispersed to smaller settlements while harvesting acorns or other wild crops.

Each local group acknowledged the leadership of a headman; although accorded high respect, this functionary wielded only a small degree of authority. He presided over the village council, acted as an advisor to his people, and exerted what pressure he could to settle minor disputes but he had no power to command or to punish. The headman occupied the largest house in the settlement and frequently possessed several wives. When a leader died, his son ordinarily succeeded to the office. But if the normal heir lacked essential qualifications such as generosity, intelligence, and knowledge, a more capable man, often a brother of the deceased, took over.

In addition to the headman, there was a religious leader whose house served as a center for ritual activity. Entrusted to his care was the sacred bundle of the lineage. This contained an assortment of religious paraphernalia—eagle feathers, dance costumes, magic wands, and other items—kept wrapped in matting and brought out for use in ceremonies. It was his obligation to know all of the essential rituals, to decide when they should be held and to assume a leading role in them. An assistant kept order during the ceremonies and did the announcing. There were other religious officials as well. Each of these functionaries was the head of a lineage and transmitted his powers, office, and functions to his selected male heir.

Adjoining local groups sometimes came together for joint ceremonies. Intermarriage and ties of friendship also linked them. But no formal and permanent political unions developed and each remained totally independent. The only known amalgamations occurred in modern times when units, greatly reduced in numbers, combined to form religious "parties" for the purpose of conducting rituals.

Conflicts between local groups developed from time to time as a result of trespass or from other wrongs, real or imagined, such as murder or suspected witchcraft. But serious trouble seldom occurred and the clashes which did take place tended to be short-lived and not attended with much bloodshed. Ambushing a lone enemy or attacking a settlement by surprise were preferred tactics. Weapons included the bow and, for in-fighting, a stone knife, the same one employed in hunting. Warriors carried no shields and wore no protective armor. The scalping of fallen enemies does not seem to have been practiced.

As in all primitive societies, the course of an individual's life was surrounded at critical times with prohibitions and rituals. Particular attention centered upon adolescence and death. Numerous and elaborate group activities accompanied these events. In contrast, observances attending pregnancy and birth were few, simple, and private. As soon as a woman became aware of her pregnancy, she excluded meat, fat, and salt from her diet and avoided sexual intercourse. At parturition, she delivered her child in a sitting position in the family's dwelling. A midwife assisted supporting the mother from the rear during her labor. Following delivery, the woman rested quietly in a heated pit for several days. When necessary she scratched herself with a special stick rather than with her fingernails. For a month or more, she abstained from drinking cold water, eating meat, fat, or salt, and from working. Because the Luiseño believed that the father's actions could affect the newly born, he did no hunting, gambling, or travelling for a brief period. The same foods denied his wife were forbidden to him. Sex restrictions between spouses persisted until the child could walk.

Shortly after birth, the infant was tied to a ladderlike cradle fashioned of sticks. Some time later it received its name in a brief ceremony. If a male, its ear lobes were pierced during the first year of life. Twin children, regarded as having special powers, received gifts from persons seeking good luck. The treatment and training of children followed much the same course as among other Californian Indian peoples.

Luiseño boys received initiation into manhood during a lengthy and complicated ceremony, held whenever there was a sufficient number of candidates. The initial and central ritual involved drinking a potent decoction prepared from roots of the Jimsonweed or Toloache plant. The roots, which had earlier been gathered and dried, were crushed in a special stone mortar and then steeped in water. Administered to the initiates, gathered together at night in a special enclosure, the drink quickly produced unconsciousness. Great care had to be exerted not to give too much because taken in excess the infusion caused death. The period of stupor lasted two to three days or, with a heavy dose, four. While under influence of the drug, neophytes experienced visions during which they acquired personal guardian spirits. Their revelations usually took the character of visitations by animal spirits from whom the boys obtained supernatural power and at times learned special songs.

The drinking of Jimsonweed formed part of the boys' initiation rite among all coastal groups of southern California. A similar custom also prevailed among the Yokuts of the southern San Joaquin valley.

Sandpainting played a prominent part in the boys' initiation. Made by pouring dry colors on a circle of carefully smoothed earth, the figures measured from 4 up to 15 or 18 feet across. Three colors—white, red, and black—predominated. Ashes or crushed steatite provided the white pigment; red was obtained from pulverized hematite; powdered charcoal served for the black color. The finished work, representing the earth or universe, consisted of concentric circles and other simple geometric forms. It depicted such things as the Milky Way, sky or night, and agents or "watchers" of the god Chungichnish. The comparatively simple designs indicated the existence of these objects rather than attempting to portray their form or supposed appearance. In the center lay a hole, symbolic of death and the burial of human ashes. While the boys, properly painted, stood in a circle around the picture, an old man explained the meaning of its various characters. At the conclusion of the ceremony, he obliterated the painting by pushing it from the edges toward the center.

The sandpaintings, also made by the Gabrielino, Juaneño, Fernandeño, Cupeño and Diegueño, strongly suggest a historical relationship to those made in the Southwest by Pueblo and Navaho Indians. But the style, subject matter, symbolism, and function of the representations differed considerably between the two regions. No equivalent practice existed among the geographically intervening tribes living in the Colorado River valley.

Another act in the prolonged initiation symbolized descent into the grave and out again, or death and resurrection. A pit, about 4 feet long, 15 inches wide and 2 feet deep, was prepared. In the bottom lay a crude string outline of a human, fastened with stakes, and three flat stones. In turn, each boy descended into the pit and sprang from stone to stone and out again. If a youth stumbled while passing through, this presaged a short life.

A final severe test—an ordeal by ants—had to be undergone. One by one, the boys laid down in a pit and biting ants were sprinkled over them. While older men sang special songs, the youths remained motionless, permitting the ants to run over their bodies and to bite them. When the sufferers arose, men whipped away the insects with nettles. The making of a second sandpainting and a foot race concluded the ant ordeal.

Education and moral training formed an important part of the initiation. Throughout the protracted ceremony, boys received lectures on proper rules for life and frequent exhortations to become good men. The initiates also obtained considerable knowledge of religious and mythological matters. Food taboos, singing, and dancing entered into all of the ritual activities.

The corresponding ceremony for young females was less elaborate. Normally several girls went through the initiation together. Only one needed to be pubescent; the others might be younger. For several days and nights the girls stayed side by side in a warmed pit. At night men danced around the pit and sang; in the daytime women performed to the accompaniment of a different set of songs. Female relatives admonished the girls against being lazy, stingy, or deceitful and provided other advice. When the initiates left the pit for any reason, their heads were covered with large, openwork baskets or with special brush visors.

Each girl swallowed a ball of tobacco, followed by a drink of warm water. If she vomited, it was taken as a sign that she had not been virtuous. While lying in the pit and for several months thereafter, the initiates ate no meat, fish, or foods seasoned with salt, and drank only warm water. Because they could not use their nails, they scratched themselves with a piece of wood.

The ritual closed with a sandpainting and a race. The sandpainting was smaller and slightly different in style from those employed in the boys' initiation. After its symbols had been explained, the girls raced to a rock formation or huge boulder near the village upon the surface of which they painted designs. These paintings consisted of lines, zigzags and other simple figures in red, usually arranged in vertical patterns several feet high. Some time later the young females received their tattoo marks.

Marriage received comparatively little attention. When a youth had reached the proper age, his family contracted for a bride. Since marriage within the lineage was forbidden, they sought a suitable girl in another kin group. Incest rules also prohibited unions between near-kin in the mother's line. Gifts of shell money, ornaments, and other goods were presented to the bride's family and a feast marked the wedding. Monogamy prevailed but cases of polygyny were not unknown. Generally only a headman had more than one wife but other males occasionally took a second or even third spouse. The usual form of polygyny consisted of a man marrying two or more sisters, one after another.

A married couple resided with the husband's

group. Parent-in-law taboos appear to have been unknown. If her husband died, a widow ordinarily became the wife of his younger brother, or, if the wife died, a younger sister took her place. Neither of these customs was obligatory, however. Little difficulty surrounded divorce. The parties separated because of laziness, incompatibility, or infidelity on the part of either spouse. Presumed or actual barrenness of a wife also terminated marriage.

Death assumed extreme importance among the Luiseño and provided a focal point for rites and observances. Just after a person passed away or while he hovered at the point of death, fellow lineage members prepared his funeral pyre. First they dug a trench six or seven feet long and two feet deep into which they piled brush and logs. The corpse was placed on the pile, face up and with the head to the north, and the pyre ignited. While flames consumed the body, close relatives sat nearby weeping and lamenting. As soon as the coals had cooled, the calcined bones and ashes of the deceased were gathered up and placed in a basket, later to be buried. Remaining ashes and charcoal were pushed in and the trench was filled and leveled so as to obliterate all traces of the burning. As signs of mourning, a widow wore her hair closely cropped and kept her face blackened. Other close kin also cut their hair. The name of the dead person became indefinitely or permanently tabooed.

After being liberated from the body, the soul of the deceased lingered about the village for a time before journeying over the Milky Way to the sky where it became a star. To assist the soul in reaching its destination, everyone at a funeral motioned upward.

Several separate mourning ceremonies followed cremation. The first and simplest, the washing of the dead person's clothing, took place a few days to a week after the funeral. Subsequently the garments were burned. These two rites symbolized the individual's severance from his life on earth and prevented his soul from staying about. Supposedly the deceased's spirit would not depart for the hereafter unless the clothes had been properly washed and burned. A special observance may also have accompanied the destruction by fire of his house.

A more complicated commemorative rite, the burning of the images, supposedly occurred a year after the death of one or more lineage members. Actually it took place only when the group had a number of dead to mourn. A considerable amount of advance preparation was necessary. Property had to be assembled, for it was customary to give presents to members of the outside lineage who carried on the ceremony and whose headman presided over it. In addition, valuable articles destined to be burned with the images had to be collected. An image, believed actually to resemble the individual, was prepared for each deceased person. These life-sized figures consisted of bundles of rushes or arrowweed woven together with sticks inserted at the shoulders and hips. The face had a covering of buckskin upon which the image makers indicated the various features. For eyes they sewed on circles of abalone shell. Human hair was fastened to the head and the figure dressed as in life. Before dawn on the last night of the week-long ceremony, the piled-up images and offerings were burned to the accompaniment of sad lamentations. Just prior to this act, the religious paraphernalia of dead males had received ritual burial in the center hole of a sandpainting.

Another mourning ceremony, the Eagle Dance, was performed in remembrance of a departed headman. Well in advance of the ritual, a young eagle or, rarely, a condor had been taken from its nest and confined in a special cage under care of the lineage leader. When mature and in full plumage, the captive was taken from its cage and reverently slain during the course of a night-long performance. Men took turns dancing around the fire with the bird, slowly and surreptitiously pressing it to death. Spectactors, however, believed that it had been slain by magical power. After its skin had been carefully removed, the eagle's body was cremated with proper rites and offerings. The feathers became dance regalia.

The various Luiseño performances connected with death, as well as those associated with boys' initiation, though diverse as to detail, presented many points of similarity. They all took place in a roughly circular enclosure, open to the sky. Constructed of willow boughs and brush, its walls stood about the height of a man or even less, so that it could be looked into from the outside. The eastern end remained open; a fire burned in the middle. Ritual costuming was never elaborate. A simple skirt of netting, from which dangled eagle or condor feathers, and a topknot of owl or hawk plumage constituted the standard ritual garb. Participants painted their faces and bodies but wore no masks or disguises. Objects which figured prominently in religious acts included magical wooden bands tipped with quartz crystals and turtle-shell rattles. Whirring of the bull-roarer summoned people to ceremonies.

Dancing figured in all collective rituals, with two dances regularly performed. The first, the Whirling Dance, involved a single male participant whose repeated rapid turnings caused his feathered skirt to stand out horizontally. During the Fire Dance, a spectacular climax to most rituals, male performers stamped out hot embers with their bare feet. Other standardized procedures included singing special songs, nearly all of mythological import, the use of double names in referring to animals (e.g., "bear–mountain lion"), objects, places, and other phenomena, and frequent allusions to or symbolical representations of death.

Aside from ceremonies which served to initiate boys and girls into adulthood or to commemorate the dead, the Luiseño had few collective rituals and none of these was elaborate. When the new moon shone in the sky, boys raced toward it, for its rising symbolized resurrection of the culture hero, Wiyot. At the eclipse of the sun or moon, everyone shouted, clapped hands, and made other loud noises to frighten off the celestial animal or monster believed to be devouring the orb. To bring rain, to ensure an abundance of wild crops such as acorns and Chia, and to cause rabbits to multiply, songs were sung and special acts performed.

The Luiseño recognized two higher supernatural beings—Wiyot, the culture hero, and Chungichnish, a wise and powerful deity. Wiyot, met with in the origin myth, taught the first people many arts and crafts and established other customs. Though an outstanding character in folklore, he figured but slightly in religious activities. Chungichnish, also acknowledged by the Gabrielino and Juaneño, played a more important role. Credited with having instituted the Jimsonweed initiation and certain other ritual practices, he also laid down stringent rules of conduct and punished those who committed religious infractions or misdeeds. His many "watchers"—certain animal and plant species or even celestial bodies—saw to it that people did right. These agents of Chungichnish appeared symbolically in the sandpaintings.

The concept of a moralistic deity is unexpected in religions such as those of the Luiseño and their neighbors, and it seems quite probable that Chungichnish represents the Spanish padres' God, given a native name and tailored to fit into existing belief, introduced by Indian converts to Christianity. The Luiseño ascribed Chungichnish to another tribe, presumably the Juaneño, who were missionized earlier than themselves. They, as well as the Gabrielino and Juaneño, recognized the Gabrielino island of Santa Catalina as the original source of Chungichnish and associated ideas. The spread of the concept of this god into Luiseño territory went on at least in part, and may have taken place entirely, within the mission period. The recency of his introduction is demonstrated by the fact that Chungichnish enters hardly at all into the Luiseño story of origins.

Of the other spiritual beings, only the guardian spirits acquired while under the influence of Jimsonweed loomed large in Luiseño religion. Of subordinate importance were localized spirits, inhabitants of certain springs and pools. These beings, thought to resent having humans around their abodes, dragged individuals who bathed nearby under water in order to drown them. Another variety of ill-favored water spirits stole souls. The Luiseño thought it best to avoid the places where these beings resided or to approach them with great circumspection. Much feared was Takwish, a cannibal spirit who made his home on San Jacinto, the great mountain peak where Luiseño country adjoined that of the Cahuilla and Serrano. This monster, usually appearing as a ball of lightning or low-flying meteor, carried off and devoured human victims. Mere sight of him portended disaster and death.

A large body of beliefs and practices centered around a mysterious supernatural power which existed everywhere and took a number of forms and modes of expression. Certain individuals possessed it at birth; other acquired it later. Power could also vanish. The supernatural force engendered a strongly respectful attitude and definite rules applied to its employment. It had always to be used on appropriate occasions and according to set procedures. In Luiseño thinking, this mystic essence had become associated with knowledge, much, if not all, of which was believed to have supernatural qualities.

The treatment of disease was almost exclusively the function of shamans. Any adult could become a medicine man but normally only males entered the profession. Power to cure and to perform other miraculous deeds emanated from a quartz crystal or other supernatural object present in the person's body at birth. In addition a medicine man dreamed of a guardian spirit and received special songs and curing methods during a revelation. But the concept of a special spiritual helper was only weakly developed. Before taking on his first patient, a novice danced and sang to publicly announce his readiness to practice.

A shaman diagnosed the cause or location of an illness by singing special songs, dancing, and smoking a sacred pipe. The common primitive theory of disease, ascribing an ailment to a foreign object lodged in the patient's body prevailed, so that treatment consisted principally of sucking the afflicted part to extract the disease-causing agent. The supposed offending object—splinter of wood, stone, beetle, or whatnot—was exhibited to the sufferer. Other medical techniques included blowing on or rubbing the painful part. Sometimes the latter was effected with a pebble of peculiar form. Herbal medicines were administered for a few maladies. For his services, a practitioner received gifts commensurate with his client's gratitude.

Particular shamans became known for their specialties. Some claimed the ability to bring rain or to otherwise control the weather; others handled rattlesnakes and cured snake bites, a few aided in the hunt. Certain individuals were credited with having the power to transform themselves into bears in order to devour enemies. Medicine men also prepared love potions. Mere possession of the substance was thought to attract members of the opposite sex, a little rubbed on the desired person's body had an even greater effect.

Supposedly all medicine men had some acquaintance with black magic and could exercise their supernatural power to kill as well as to heal. Sorcery followed the common practices of contagion and imitation. To bewitch a person, an evilly disposed shaman secured something personal, a little hair, a few nail parings, or the like, and recited incantations over it. Harm was also inflicted through making an image of the individual. A doctor with a sinister reputation sometimes came to an untimely end. Apparently non-shamans also occasionally practiced the evil art.

The Luiseño myth of their origins revealed a surprising loftiness of concept, centering around the notion of an original void or nothingness. In this appeared the creative principles—Sky Male and Earth Female. From their union came all things—plants, animals, humans, or their spirit, and so on. A conspicuous episode embodied in the cosmogony and a feature absent in myths of Indians of northwestern and central California concerned migration of the "first people" from the north. After wandering a great distance, they arrived at Temecula in Riverside County, regarded by the Luiseño as their most sacred place and center of the world, where Wiyot died by sorcery at the hands of Frog, his daughter. As a result of his demise, which constituted the first death, people lost their immortality. The burning of the culture hero's body instituted cremation and the mourning ceremonies. Wiyot later returned as the new moon. Found in Luiseño folklore were many stories about stars, regarded as souls of the dead. Coyote, the deceitful Trickster, played a prominent role in several mythological episodes and provided the main character for numerous nonsacred stories.

Aesthetic aspects of Luiseño life were not developed. Native art reached its highest achievement in the decorative patterns woven into coiled baskets. Painting found representation in the dots, lines, circles, and other motifs employed in facial and bodily adornment, in the designs of the sandpaintings, and in pictographs prepared by girls during their adolescence ceremony. The Luiseño knew no true sculpture or carving in wood or stone. Music found primary expression in the songs which accompanied initiation, mourning, and other rituals. Musical instruments comprised the turtle-shell rattle, an accessory of most ceremonies, a whistle of cane or bone blown during the boys' rite, and a flute of cane or wood played for amusement. Nothing corresponding to a true drum existed.

Recreational activities included competitive sports and gambling games. Shinny, played with a curved stick and wooden ball, provided a popular sport for women as well as men. Additional masculine sports included a ball race, in which a wooden ball was propelled by the feet, and hoop-and-pole contests. Above all other amusements, men, inveterate gamblers all, preferred the hand game and indulged in it on every possible occasion. Looped cords attached to the small bones used in the game encircled the contestants' fingers so that the gaming pieces could not be juggled after a guess had been made. Females, young and old, enjoyed playing ring-and-pin with acorn cups strung together.

As a result of nearly two centuries of exposure to Western civilization, the Luiseño's manner of living has undergone considerable change. Contacts with the outside world were few and slight until the Spanish founded permanent settlements in California in the last part of the eighteenth century. Like other southern California Indians, the Luiseño soon became missionized. In 1798, San Luis Rey de Francia, the eighteenth Franciscan mission in the state, was established in their territory. Situated in the fertile San Luis Rey River Valley with other arable lands within easy distance, San Luis Rey became the largest and one of the most prosperous of the Franciscan establishments, with 2000 to 3000 Indians living on its various farms and cattle ranches. Profound changes in nearly all aspects of native life resulted, for the padres sought not only to convert the peoples but to prepare them for useful lives in a Spanish colony. The Luiseño became acquainted with agriculture, animal husbandry, and many European arts and crafts as well as with Christianity. Mission life proved disastrous for the Indians, however. Crowded together, they suffered from epidemics of newly introduced diseases and died by the hundreds. Unfamiliar foods and ways of living also seem to have contributed to their decline.

When Mexico became independent of Spain and took California with her, the mission system was broken up with passage of the Secularization Act of 1833–1834. As a consequence, the Luiseño and other Mission Indians found themselves freed of Franciscan domination. But the long period of dependency upon the padres had poorly prepared them for taking care of themselves and they suffered greatly. Cheated, in most instances, of the share of mission properties which was supposed to become theirs, some Luiseño were permitted to take up residence on land included in huge Mexican grants; others became ranch workers, receiving little or no pay for their services; still others drifted about in helpless vagrancy, scrabbling for a living as best they could.

Their situation gradually worsened following annexation of California by the United States in 1846. Though the flood of migration that poured into the state during the Gold Rush bypassed southern California, a steady increase in population began. As land became more and more scarce the former Mission Indians were thrust aside. The condition of the Luiseno and other Mission Indians finally became so deplorable that, beginning in 1870, small parcels of land, usually of poor quality, were set aside for them by the federal government. Most of them settled eventually on tiny reservations.

These events have combined to substantially eliminate the Luiseño as an ethnic and cultural group. The several hundreds who survive today have been acculturated to a greater or lesser degree. Not all of the old native life is gone but it is fading fast. Noteworthy is the persistence of a few of the old mortuary rituals, though much modified. The Indian's economic situation has ameliorated somewhat but the majority of them live in shacks and remain very poor by majority standards.

The Mohave Indians of the Lower Colorado River

In the lower Colorado River valley, extending from south of the gorge to its mouth in the Gulf of California, lived a group of Yuman-speaking peoples fundamentally alike in appearance, speech, and culture. Most northerly were the Mohave and then, in order downstream, the major tribes were the Halchidhoma, Yuma, and Cocopa. The middle Gila drainage was occupied by a similar people, the Maricopa, who are believed to have left the Colorado not many generations ago. In their riverbottom country, these Yumans had developed a distinctive and self-contained manner of living, different from that found in the adjacent Southwestern and Californian regions, though sharing features of both.

River Yuman culture found its most vigorous expression among the Mohave. Their territory centered around Mohave Valley, lying within the present-day states of Arizona, California, and Nevada. They inhabited the floodplain on both sides of the Colorado, but as most of the bottom lands lay on the east bank, it was here that the majority dwelt. On either side of Mohave Valley rise rocky, flat-topped mesas and barren mountains beyond which stretches a far-reaching desert.

The fertile and well-watered Mohave Valley forms a green oasis in a hot desert region. The summer season is long with maximum daily temperatures reaching as high as 125° F. Winters are pleasantly warm with only occasional cool or cold days. Rainfall is scanty, around four and one-half inches annually. The effects of the negligible precipitation are offset, however, by the presence of the river.

Every summer the Colorado, swollen by melting snow and rain in its Rocky Mountain headwaters, rose and inundated a great part of Mohave Valley with silt-laden waters. The yearly period of high water began in May and reached its peak near the end of June. Sloughs and ponds formed from the overflow lasted for months or, in some instances, throughout the entire year. The receding river left a coating of rich alluvium over the land and its evaporating floodwaters moistened the air.

A tangled growth of brush and trees covered much of the flooded land and its borders. Groves of cottonwoods and willows and nearly impenetrable thickets of arrowweed, cane, and rushes lined the river margins. Farther back on occasionally flooded land grew mesquite and screwbean trees. Wildlife was rather limited. Most numerous were rabbits and rodents and the coyotes, foxes, and other predators which preyed upon them. Beaver, raccoon, and musk-rat lived along the river banks. But larger game animals were few, being limited to deer which sporadically ventured into the mesquite groves. Quail and doves were abundant in some local-ities and water birds appeared seasonally in great numbers.

In this narrow strip of bottom land lived 3000 Mohave. Their outstanding physical character-istic was their tall stature, many males standing six feet tall. Mohave men were long-limbed, spare and muscular. Women had an inclination toward corpulence. Though burned dark brown by exposure to desert sun and wind, their skin had a distinctly yellowish tinge. Mohave speech showed a great degree of uniformity without perceptible dialectic differences. Closely related but unintelligible were the languages of the neighboring Colorado River Halchidhoma and Yuma and the middle Gila Maricopa.

Little is known of Mohave life as it was be-fore the first Spanish explorers entered their country. In large part this ignorance stems from the sparseness of the archeological record. Silt deposited when muddy floodwaters stretched over the land has buried the material remains of the people who inhabited the floodplain. What information exists has come primarily from higher ground bordering the plain. Dur-ing the periodic inundations many valley dwellers retired to terraces, sand dunes, and spurs to await the recession of the water and here are found their broken and discarded tools and implements.

The later prehistoric materials have been as-signed to a vaguely defined culture, variously known as Yuman, Laquish, Lowland Patayan or Hakatayan. As artifacts other than potsherds are rare, no clear idea of its nature, other than seeming poverty, has been obtained. Actually this poverty may be more fancied than real, since many objects must have been fashioned from perishable substances as were the prod-ucts of the Mohave and fellow Colorado River tribes. The pottery, a paddle-anvil buff ware, was almost certainly made by the forebears of the Mohave. Present evidence indicates that the pottery-making culture had its origins around A.D. 800.

From higher ground too have come assem-blages of stone tools unassociated with ceramic materials. These are judged to belong to an ear-lier phase of river valley culture. Excavations at Willow Beach, an important campsite and trad-ing center located 15 miles below Hoover Dam, produced remains of several preceramic cul-tures, stratigraphically below a layer containing potsherds left behind by Mohave visitors in the period between A.D. 900 and 1150. Quite prob-ably some of the stone tools were made by an-cestors of the Mohave or some other Yuman-speaking tribe, for linguistic evidence points to representatives of this stock residing in the Col-orado River valley and adjacent regions for the past 1500 to 2000 years. Presumably they moved in from the west.

The Mohave were basically a farming people. They raised the three usual crops of agricultural tribes of native North America—maize, beans, and pumpkins—the first overshadowing the others in importance. Mohave maize was mostly of the white variety, though like peoples of the Southwest, they also cultivated ears with colored kernels. Two kinds of tepary beans and two forms of squashes were grown. Kidney beans, native to the Southwest, were not culti-vated.

Besides these familiar American Indian prod-ucts, several other crops were raised. The Mo-have were unique among the River Yumans in growing sunflowers. Nonedible plants consisted of tobacco and gourds. Most interesting were several indigenous grasses and herbs. As these species were wholly unknown to other New World farmers, the Mohave or one of their Yu-man neighbors must have domesticated them.

The Mohave method of raising crops was a simple process of clearing fields and planting. They practiced no irrigation but depended en-tirely upon the annual flooding of their land and the moisture surviving from it. Men and women cooperated in farming with the former doing the major part of the work. Planting be-gan almost immediately after the recession of high water.

Farm land was privately owned and regularly inherited through the male line. An individ-ual's holding normally comprised a continuous strip, up to several acres in extent, the plot varying in shape according to the configuration of the land. There always existed plenty of vacant acreage so that when a man wanted to plant a new piece of ground, he merely sought out a suitable spot and cleared it of growth.

Most of any Mohave field was planted to maize. A half dozen corn kernals were sown in a hole, six or so inches deep, punched into the moist soil with a wedge-ended planting stick. As the holes, a pace apart, were irregularly spaced, the plants came up in scattered clumps rather than in even rows. Both beans and pumpkins were frequently sown in the same field. Seeds of the native grasses and herbs were scattered broadcast on wet ground.

Under the heat of the burning summer sun the plants, with their roots deep in the moisture-laden soil, grew rapidly. They needed and received little attention aside from weeding. This was done with a knife-like paddle of mesquite wood. Harvesting took place whenever the products matured or sometimes before they ripened. Magic and ritualism centering around the growing and harvesting of crops was almost totally absent.

A large percentage of the maize crop was roasted and eaten while the ears were still green. The remainder, after being thoroughly dried by spreading it in the sun, was stored in huge, nestlike baskets, often five to six feet across. Provided with conical covers, these granaries rested upon low platforms or on the roofs of shades. Dried corn was always ground on an oblong milling stone with a cylindrical stone muller before being used. Beans were prepared by boiling or were parched and ground. Their pods were sometimes cooked before being fully ripened. Pumpkins were cooked whole or in pieces. Those for storage were either cut spirally into long strips and sun dried or were placed whole in pits lined with arrowweed. Pumpkin seeds were parched and eaten.

Domestic crops were supplemented by wild plants gathered by women. The native flora, largely independent of seasonal local rainfall, regularly produced an abundant and dependable harvest of foodstuffs. Of paramount importance were the sweet and nutritious bean-like pods of mesquite trees. Plentiful in July, they were collected from the ground, plucked from branches with the aid of a wooden crook, and pilfered from rodents' nests. Claim was laid to the yield of certain trees by hanging bunches of arrowweed in their branches. Dried

mesquite pods were crushed by means of a long stone or wooden pestle in a mortar hollowed out of a cottonwood or mesquite log. Heavier fibers and seeds were removed, only the pulp being saved. Sometimes this substance was eaten raw; more often it was mixed with water to make a sweet drink. The fresh dough was also molded into cakes, baked hard in the ashes. Quantities of dried mesquite pods were put aside in granaries for winter eating.

Coiled pods of the screwbean tree, which ripened in August, supplied only slightly less food. Unlike mesquite, screwbean pods are bitter at maturity and had to be stored in pits lined with arrowweed for a month and sprinkled with water before they became palatable. Seeds and other edible parts of plants which sprang up following recession of the annual overflow were collected but none of these served to give more than variety to meals.

Fishing, carried on by men, contributed the main flesh food. Although never teeming with fish, the Colorado provided an adequate supply of this resource. Its yearly flooding and falling away left landlocked bodies of water well stocked with fish. Only four species—squaw fish, hump-backed suckers, mullet, and bony tail—were regularly taken. Though scaly, bony, and tasteless, they were relished by the Mohave.

Most fish were caught in nets or by similar devices. When the river was high, small baglike nets were dipped into the muddy waters whereas large seines were hauled through shallow ponds or set in the river when it was low and quiet. An enormous fence of interlaced branches, pushed forward by 20 to 30 men, drove fish into one end of a pond where they were easily picked up. Fish were enticed by bait into semicircular stick pounds constructed in the shallow water of the shelving river bank.

Lifting fish out of the water with handled basketry scoops, measuring five to six feet across, was a frequent practice. Dormant fish were caught by hand by swimmers groping in holes and under snags along the river bank. This method provided great sport for men and boys. Angling with hook and line and shooting fish with bow and arrow were engaged in only sporadically. Neither fish spear nor harpoon was employed, probably because the water was normally too turbid for their successful use. Drugging fish by dropping narcotic plants into the water was also unknown, though it would have been effective in the landlocked bodies of water.

The Mohave generally prepared fish in the

form of a stew, bones, guts, and scales all being included. Corn meal or other ingredients were sometimes added. Whole fish were also roasted in the ashes and coals. That part of a day's catch not immediately needed was sun dried and stored away. The desiccated flesh could be kept for only a week or so before it spoiled in the warm and often damp atmosphere.

Hunting played little part in Mohave economy. The men, at best, were indifferent hunters and most of them devoted little time to the chase. They were primarily hunters of small game. Rabbits were pursued by a lone individual or sometimes by a group of men who combined their efforts in a collective drive. The rabbits were dispatched with bow and arrow; they were also caught in snares and nets. Other small creatures taken and eaten included woodrats, and a smaller number of squirrels, raccoons, muskrats, beavers, and badgers. Birds were relatively unimportant as a food source. Those most frequently taken were quail, ducks, mudhens, and doves.

Methods of taking the few deer that strayed into the country were simple. A hunter, after sighting his quarry, waited in ambush or stalked his prey until he could shoot it with bow and arrow. Occasionally small parties of men ventured into nearby mountains in search of deer or mountain sheep. Most meat was cooked by covering it with hot ashes and coals; sometimes it was boiled.

No scarcity of food occurred except under unusual circumstances. Normally, Mohave fields yielded a bountiful harvest and there was plenty for everyone. But there were years when the Colorado waters did not rise sufficiently to overflow the land or when a partial or complete crop failure resulted from a second, unexpected flood. At such times critical food shortages and even famines occurred. Stocks stored against times of want were small and soon depleted and other resources—wild plants, fish, and game—were hardly sufficient to support the entire population.

For much of the year the Mohave lived in open-sided, flat-topped shades. Posts set in a rectangle supported a roof of poles and arrow-weed. These structures furnished protection from summer sun and, on their tops, convenient storage places for foodstuffs. For winter residences the Mohave built earth-covered rectangular structures with sloping sides and ends. Customarily a low rise of ground near a pond or river bank was selected as a desirable site. Housebuilding was man's work; women did

not regularly assist. Two or four main posts connected by heavy beams with smaller poles leaned against them formed the framework of a dwelling. Over this a thatch of arrowweed was applied and earth piled over it to a depth of several inches. The earth covering made these houses quite warm and comparatively waterproof. A low doorway, facing south and closed with a bark mat at night, served as entrance. It also provided the only means of escape for smoke issuing from the household fire. Dwellings of this kind stood for years, requiring little maintenance. They were meagerly furnished.

Each family had its own winter house but often its members slept elsewhere. Prominent men, aided by relatives and friends, put up exceptionally large structures in which a considerable number of adults and children slept each winter night. Such a house was the owner's dwelling, not a communal building, but others used it because they considered their own residences too cold for comfortable sleeping. The Mohave were without sweathouses.

As the daily temperature in Mohave country was seldom sufficiently cool to require that clothing be worn for warmth, it was put on almost exclusively for modesty. Everyday dress for both sexes was quite scanty. The only men's garment consisted of a breechclout, less than a foot wide, woven of strands of the inner bark of willow trees. Drawn up between the legs, it passed under a belt of the same material, so as to leave a short overhanging flap in the front and a longer one in the back. The basic female garment, reaching from waist to knees, comprised separate front and back aprons made of strips of willow inner-bark and hung from a cord belt. The thick, bunched rear apron produced a bustlelike effect. Rabbitskin blankets, mostly obtained from Paiute or Walapai Indians, covered the upper body in inclement weather. Sandals were put on only when travelling; at home the Mohave went barefoot. For the head there was no covering.

Intense pride was taken in personal appearance, with particular care lavished upon the hair. Both sexes wore the hair hanging to the waist in back and banged over the forehead. But while that of females hung loosely, men twisted their hair into twenty or so long, pencillike strands. The hair was frequently washed in a decoction of mesquite-bark gum and water to make it black and glossy. To kill vermin, mud was plastered on the head and allowed to remain there for two or three days. Paint was used freely on the face. Much of it was for ornamentation and applied whenever the inclination arose. Young people painted their faces daily, if possible. Red and black pigments were used; white paint was sometimes smeared on the hair or body. Tattooing was universal. Men and women had vertical lines inscribed on their chins and a few marks on the forehead as well. Personal ornaments were not too numerous. A few shell beads served as jewelry and most old women wore at the throat a highly valued shell pendant cut into frog shape. The ear lobes of both sexes were pierced and adorned with beads on festive occasions. The nasal septum of young males was slit for the insertion of a shell pendant.

Good workmanship was not prized by the Mohave and most of their tools, weapons, and other articles of daily use were made just well enough to do what was necessary. There was also considerable indifference in their handling and maintenance. Characteristically an object was used without repair until it became completely unserviceable, then it was thrown away and another made.

Quantities of reddish-buff pottery vessels, the chief household utensils, were manufactured by Mohave women. These were formed by coiling, adding one roll of damp clay after another until the desired size and shape was reached. Walls of the receptacles were thinned by beating them with a wooden paddle; a smooth cobble held inside received the force of the blows. A variety of forms was produced—bowls, cooking pots, large water jars, parching trays, and ladles. Carelessly executed red designs, mostly repeated angular elements such as zigzags, hexagons, oblongs, squares, and triangles, adorned many vessels. Though descriptively named, the patterns had no symbolic meaning.

Mohave basketry was poor in quality and limited in variety. Besides granaries and fish scoops, virtually the only baskets made were twined winnowing trays and coarse burden baskets, the latter manufactured by men for transporting fish. Finely made baskets were obtained in trade from other tribes. Woven bags for carrying smaller objects were fashioned from tough fibers of bean or other plants. Gourds, a few of which were grown, served as containers, dippers, and rattles.

Though much basic Mohave equipment like planting sticks, weeding implements, mortars, pestles, fire drills, bows and other articles were fashioned from wood, this craft was little developed and there was no decorative carving.

Work in stone was likewise rudimentary. Knife blades, pestles, milling stones and mullers comprised the major articles fashioned from this material. The Mohave had no stone axes; split cobbles lashed to handles served as rude substitutes. These were suitable only for hacking off smaller limbs and not for felling trees. Very few articles were made of bone or animal hide.

Though a river people, the Mohave had no canoes. When they needed to cross the river or other body of water they usually swam it. A log held under one arm often acted as a swimming aid or was straddled for going downstream. Rude rafts fabricated of bundles of tules held together with wooden skewers or, rarely, of logs lashed together were employed if goods and supplies needed to be transported across water. These were pushed along with poles or allowed to drift with the current. Large pots, up to a yard in diameter, served for ferrying young children, a swimmer pushing the vessel before him. On land, burdens were transported on the back in rough, netted carrying frames or in burden baskets. For balancing pots or loads on the head, women employed willow-bark rings.

Mohave men made frequent trips to northern Arizona to trade with upland Yuman peoples and into the desert to exchange products with Numic-speaking groups. For baskets, rabbitskin blankets, buckskin, and red paint, they gave maize and other farm produce. The men also enjoyed travelling from place to place merely to see new lands and other tribes. Carrying bags of parched corn and pumpkin seeds and small gourd or pottery canteens, individuals or small parties journeyed to the Pacific Coast, to the Gulf of California, into the Pueblo country, and to other distant lands. They habitually moved at a distance-consuming dogtrot. Along well-traveled trails were shrines at which passersby placed offerings of stones, arrows, or other articles.

The Mohave shared a peculiar clan system with other River Yumans. Membership in one of their twenty or so kinship divisions was through the father's line but, strangely, only the females bore the clan name. The designations for these social units were understood to have been derived from animals, plants, natural phenomena, or objects but were not current Mohave words for these things. Thus all women of a particular clan were called "hipa," said to mean coyote although in everyday speech the term for this animal was *hukthar*. There were no taboos surrounding the plant, animal, or other object from which a grouping derived its name, nor was it held in veneration. Although males did not share the clan designation, they were well aware of their affiliation. Within these social divisions, marriage was prohibited, but aside from this, they had little or no function. Not all members of a clan inhabited the same locality.

The essential kinship unit was not the clan but the individual family which formed the basis of day-to-day economic and social life. This domestic unit of husband, wife, and children was often joined by an unattached relative or two. There was also an almost continuous stream of daily visitors, relatives or otherwise, who came to gossip, and to share the ever-ready meal. Status differences between families hardly existed.

Mohave families did not congregate in villages; instead they lived in straggling rural neighborhoods. Wherever suitable bottomlands existed there stood a dozen or more homesteads, each a hundred yards or more from its neighbor. These settlements, if they can be called such, were situated as much as a mile from one another. Customarily each cluster consisted of families related through the male line. Considerable shifting of residence took place because quite often, for one reason or another, a family transferred to another locality.

Despite their lack of well-defined communities, the Mohave exhibited a strong sense of tribal solidarity. They conceived of their country as a whole and regarded themselves as distinct from all other human groups. Within the tribe people interacted freely with one another. Their conscious feeling of tribal cohesion enabled them to present a united front against all enemies, whether in attack or defense.

Little formal government existed, however. The Mohave had no tribal council or other governing body. They did have a tribal chief but he had few duties and little personal authority. In the main, he functioned in an advisory capacity. The office descended in one family, passing from father to son. Prominent men were recognized as leaders in the various settlements but they possessed no formal status.

Ordinarily considerable harmony prevailed in interpersonal relationships. Minor quarrels were usually settled amicably by the individuals involved or by their families. But from time to time more serious disputes arose over ownership of agricultural fields, the boundaries of which had been obliterated by flooding. Such quarrels were settled by more violent procedures. First a pushing match was arranged in which each claimant was surrounded by supporters who endeavored to push him across the contested piece of land. If the losers were dissatisfied, they appeared the next day carrying willow poles with which to beat their opponents over the head and with shorter sticks for parrying blows. Their antagonists came similarly armed. The aim of each party was to drive the other back across the disputed tract.

Warfare occupied a large place in Mohave thought and life. Prestige was the reward of a man who fought well and bravely. Most fighting was with other river tribes; nearby desert and mountain peoples were not regarded as fit opponents. The Halchidhoma, Maricopa, and Cocopa were chronic enemies; the Yuma dependable allies. All able-bodied men participated in military campaigns. They were led by a single war chief with warriors divided into archers, clubbers, and stick-men.

Bows and arrows were employed for long-range fighting. The Mohave war bow, five feet or so long, was of the unbacked variety. Staves were of willow, or, for better bows, of mesquite or screwbean wood. They were strung with deer sinew. Arrows commonly had arrowweed shafts, sharpened at one end, but were without foreshaft or stone tip. Each bore three feather vanes. Combating forces always sought to come to close quarters so that mallet-headed clubs and sturdy sticks could be used in hand-to-hand fighting. The former consisted of short, bulky instruments with their heavy heads and handles carved from a single piece of mesquite or ironwood. With an upward swing these weapons smashed into the faces of antagonists. The straight sticks, each about two feet long and fashioned from screwbean wood, were designed for breaking heads. Some warriors protected themselves from enemy arrows with circular hide shields but none wore armor.

Fighting frequently took on a stylized character with the two forces drawn up in opposing ranks. Surprise raids involving smaller bodies of men were also undertaken. Fallen antagonists were scalped, the skin of the whole head being removed. During raids on enemy settlements, captives were taken. The lot of military prisoners, almost exclusively girls and young women, was generally an easy one; they were not mistreated and performed only the usual daily tasks. Enemy slayers abstained from salt and meat and purified themselves of the effects of defiling enemy contacts by repeated bathing. A scalp dance followed the return of a fighting force within a day or two.

At the core of Mohave religion, in fact dominating their entire life, was individual dreaming. These Indians were firmly convinced that dreams were the source of all special abilities and success in any important endeavor, whether it be fighting, doctoring, gambling, or lovemaking. While it was recognized that a person acquired certain skills and knowledge through learning and practice, it was felt that any activity would not be wholly successful unless validated or reinforced by the requisite revelation.

Often it was thought that a "great dream," which brought a special gift or bestowed some ability or promised success in an important activity, had occurred first while an unborn child was still in its mother's womb. The prenatal fantasy, forgotten during infancy and childhood, came back to a youth as he heard others telling of similar experiences or was repeated later in life so as to refresh the memory. A power-bestowing dream was not deliberately sought by fasting, self-torture, or taking narcotics; it passed through the mind involuntarily during sleep. Many of these experiences were unusual in that the sleeper's soul was believed to have journeyed to the scene of creation and to have been impelled backward in time so as to have viewed the beginning of things. "Great dreams" were often recited to audiences and not uncommonly evoked criticisms and corrections from older men if the ritualized telling went contrary to the traditional form. Endowments secured through these experiences could not be transferred to other persons. Though not expressly excluded from having "great dreams," few females obtained them.

Although clearly distinguished from the power-bestowing dreams, regular nightly sleep experiences were not ignored. Ordinary dreams were believed to shed light on forthcoming events so their contents were interpreted directly or searched for symbolic meanings. Apart from dreams, there were omens which almost without exception presaged failure or disaster.

Because of their preoccupation with individual dreaming, the Mohave devoted little time or interest to other aspects of supernaturalism. They had surprisingly little group ceremonial, the ritualized telling of dream experiences and myths or singing taking its place. Their songs were arranged in long cycles of 50 to 200, forming the framework of a myth. There were 30 cycles, designated by such names as Goose, Turtle, Raven, and Pleiades. A singer was supposed to have dreamed his cycle but sometimes admitted he had learned it from a relative but had later experienced it during sleep. Occasions for singing were many and often a night was spent by a singer entertaining a house full of people. Shaking a gourd rattle or drumming on an overturned basket provided accompaniment. The use of regalia and ritual dancing were reduced nearly to the vanishing point.

Of superior beings, the Mohave had none who played an active role in religious practices. Their gods were remote figures whose legendary activities explained the origin of things and human institutions. The leading divinity, Matavilya, first-born of a union of Sky and Earth, offended his daughter Frog Woman. By means of black magic she caused his death. Mastamho, his younger brother or son, superseded Matavilya. To him was ascribed the widening of the river valley, the bringing of food products, the creation of the characteristic elements of Mohave culture, and the killing of Sky Rattlesnake, a sea monster. Having completed his work, Mastamho turned himself into a fish eagle and flew off. As their deities no longer existed, they were not venerated or directly invoked in prayer. Nor were gifts or sacrifices offered to them. The gods did, however, remain as enduring sources of supernatural power, seen or even contacted by a person's soul projected back in time during a "great dream."

Other supernatural beings were few and unimportant. Curiously for a farming people, they had no conception of agricultural deities. Nor did they have a god of their life-giver, the river. A few local spirits were thought to inhabit Mohave country. One of these was believed to dwell in a large rock in the river below Mohave valley.

Mohave shamans acquired their power just as other men did, through a "great dream." Most received their gift directly from Mastamho who taught them ritual practices and special songs. A medicine man's competency to cure was limited to certain illnesses, depending upon the scope of his dream and the nature of instruction conferred by Mastamho.

Sickness was understood as being caused mainly by the individual's soul being taken away or otherwise affected by injury, fright, shock, or by sorcerers or ghosts. The common American Indian idea of a disease object projected into the patient's body was only weakly developed. In doctoring the chief means employed consisted of singing, laying on of hands, and blowing a spray of saliva. The songs described acquisition of the supernatural power which was being used. Payments for successful cures were given as gifts; there were no stipulated fees. Mohave shamans were assumed to be able to cause illness as well as to heal. A practitioner who had failed frequently was accused of bewitching his patients and was killed by their relatives.

The earlier crises of life—birth and puberty—were treated casually by the Mohave. True, an expectant mother took a few precautions for the benefit of her unborn child, such as avoiding looking at unpleasant things and having sexual intercourse with her husband. She also ate sparingly. But activity was considered desirable, so she continued her daily tasks. The fetus was believed to have a conscious existence of its own and could express itself. If it became displeased or unhappy, it caused trouble for the mother. This was also the period during which a developing male might have his "great dream."

When the time came for her child to be born, a woman remained in her own house. Assisted by two midwives, preferably relatives, she delivered the baby in a seated position. One of the attendants cut the umbilical cord, later to be buried by the father. The newborn was then dipped in warm water, dried, and a chalky powder applied to its body. Following the birth both parents observed a few simple restrictions on their diet and behavior for the benefit of their offspring.

During the first four days, the only nourishment an infant received consisted of the sweet liquid derived from mesquite-pod pulp. After this it was given the breast. Mothers suckled their babies for as long as two years with adult foods gradually introduced. On the fourth day, a newborn child was bound in its cradle, an arch of willow or mesquite wood with long parallel sides to which transverse rods were tied. A broad basketry hood provided shade and protection. The baby remained confined to this cradle most of its waking and sleeping hours until it was able to walk. There was no naming ceremony. At birth a girl received her clan name and another which bore some relationship to it (e.g., "Spotted Coyote"). A male child, however, was called merely "boy" or "male child" or by an affectionate term until he

learned to walk. Then he was given a name descriptive of a physical or personality trait (e.g., "Tall and Light," or "Mean Boy"). During his lifetime, a male's name might change a number of times but a female's remained the same.

Childhood was a carefree and happy time, for Mohave parents were very indulgent. The children played a great deal and their pastimes, often in imitation of adult life, were numerous and varied. Many of the boys' diversions were in reality mock battles or contests developing physical hardiness and thus preparing them for a warrior's life. Swimming and water games provided favorite sports for both sexes. Socialization was informal, the child becoming a Mohave by easy stages. That little effort was made to educate children reflected the belief that knowledge came through dreaming rather than learning. Disciplinary methods, only rarely invoked, were mild.

The observance of a girl's puberty was a private, unobtrusive family matter which did not include dancing, singing, or any public performance. At the onset of her first menses, a girl remained quiescent for four days in one corner of the family dwelling. During this period of seclusion she ate little, eschewing salt, meat, and cold water, and avoided scratching herself with her fingernails. Each night she lay down in a pit scooped out of the sand and previously warmed by a fire. Although the pubescent was shunned by men, particularly warriors and hunters, the concept of a pubescent's ritual uncleanliness, strongly developed in many North American Indian tribes, was weak among the Mohave. At this time a girl's dreams were regarded as of particular importance as foretellers of her future. The sole observance for boys approaching adolescence involved piercing of the nasal septum. It can hardly be called a puberty rite since seven or eight years was considered the best age for the operation.

The years between puberty and marriage constituted a time of experimental love affairs. Marriage itself was casual. It meant no more than a couple living together without bride price, gift exchange, or wedding ceremony. Girls tended to marry younger than males, usually two or three years after puberty. The only limitations on whom one might marry lay in incest rules. A man could not take as a spouse a woman to whom direct blood relationship could be traced either through his mother or father or who was a member of his own clan.

A married couple took up residence with the husband's parents. No formal regulations, such as in-law avoidances, governed the behavior of affinal relatives. Marriages were normally monogamous, though plural unions occasionally occurred. Divorce involved only separation when either spouse felt so inclined. Marital break-ups took place frequently among young adults who remarried easily.

Adult life proceeded at a leisurely and relaxed pace. There was no systematic daily routine; the Mohave worked in their gardens or performed other tasks whenever the spirit moved them. They did not enjoy the slow, steady labor towards which Californian and Puebloan peoples inclined. Rather they, men especially, preferred to lounge about in complete idleness and then plunge into sudden and vigorous activity until a job was completed. Women had a greater freedom of action than was customary among American Indians. They regularly sat, ate, and conversed with the men. It was only in religion that females labored under disabilities. Because they rarely experienced the requisite "great dream," they could not join in the men's singing or mythtelling or become shamans.

Mohave adults filled their leisure time with visiting, storytelling, and games. Older males also relaxed by smoking either wild or cultivated tobacco in short clay pipes. Great emphasis was placed upon hospitality, generosity, and good humor and people were prone to gather together for talking and eating. Listening to expert narrators of both sacred and nonsacred stories was thoroughly enjoyed. A long complicated narrative recounted how, in the beginning, Earth and Sky, male and female, came together and from this union were born the gods, all men, and beings. Equally lengthy were the "Great Tales," assumed to be legends of clan migrations, which took an entire night or sometimes three or four to recount. The narrators were men, supposed to have dreamed the stories they told. Coyote tales, often quite brief, were also told. Men indulged in two strenuous field sports—shinny and kickball—and in archery contests. But their most popular pastime was casting a long pole at a rolling hoop. Another favorite was the hand game played by opposing teams. Contestants and onlookers wagered on the outcome of this and most other games. Women gambled with four decorated willow sticks. Ring-and-pin, consisting of a

stick to which was tied a string threaded with pumpkin rind rings of different sizes, provided amusement for all, as did water sports.

As a person aged and became helpless, the duty of caring for him fell upon a son. If this was not feasible, a daughter or other kin took charge. The older people idled away their remaining years, doing little other than occasionally caring for youngsters while the parents were busy elsewhere. The Mohave were extremely kind to aged relatives. The hopelessly ill or infirm were not killed.

Death provided the occasion for the Mohaves' most elaborate ritual observances. When a person lay dying, his relatives and friends gathered about and prolonged wailing began. Songs dreamed by the dying man were sung and ceremonial speeches extolling him were made. As quickly as possible after death, the corpse was laid on a waiting funeral pyre and cremated. The pyre had been prepared by scooping a shallow trench out of the sand and stacking logs above it. Belongings of the deceased and combustible goods provided by others were piled on the logs and body.

Once the pyre was lighted, considerable emotion was expressed. In a hysterical state, mourners divested themselves of their own personal belongings, even clothing, and cast them on the fire. Whipped into a frenzy of grief, a bereaved woman sometimes attempted to throw herself upon the pyre of a spouse or close relative. When the fire had burned out and its charcoal and ashes had sunk into the pit, sand was pushed over it so that every evidence was obliterated, for the Mohave could tolerate no reminder of the dead. A wholesale destruction of the deceased's property took place. The dead man's dwelling and everything within it was burned. Granaries were also set afire and standing crops were destroyed or given away. The bereaved family then moved, at least temporarily, to another locality. The removal from sight and thought of anything which might remind the living of the dead extended to all references to the deceased. There was a strong repugnance to mentioning the name of the departed and a death was alluded to by an elaborate circumlocution to avoid giving offense to kinsmen.

For four days following a funeral, mourning relatives ate no salt, meat, or fish, and drank no cold water. Purification by bathing with a decoction made of arrowweed roots steeped in water and fumigation from the pungent smoke from the burning of the same plant was necessary for them, the speechmakers, and everyone who had touched or tended the corpse. Female mourners cropped their hair to ear level, males cut theirs to shoulder length. A special public memorial service, a one-day affair, was held for distinguished warriors and chiefs. Dramatization of a battle formed part of the ceremony.

For four days and nights following death, a soul lingered in the neighborhood in which it had lived and sought to revisit its former home. It then moved on to a land of the dead downstream. The soul of a person who had died untattooed was not permitted to enter the dwelling but had to go down a rodent's hole instead.

Western civilization touched the Mohave only lightly until well into the nineteenth century. The earliest Spanish explorers to reach the Colorado did not penetrate into their territory. Contacts with later Spanish expeditions were brief. No missions were established within their country. The coming of the Spaniards had no appreciable effect on Mohave life, other than introducing wheat as an important crop. Even this seems to have reached them through the agency of other tribes. Through trade with the California coastal tribes, missionized by the Spaniards, such items as glass beads were introduced. During the Mexican regime the Mohave were left pretty much alone, though the lure of horses and cattle led them to raid outlying ranches in southern California.

Euro-American influences began to be felt before the middle of the nineteenth century. First came the fur trappers in search of beaver skins and other valuable animal pelts. Later arrived the immigrant parties moving to California. The main overland tide of travel, however, passed to the south, through the land of the Yuma. Despite their warlike disposition, the Mohave made no notable resistance to these Americans. Aside from a few sporadic clashes with trappers and an attack on a wagon train, there were no hostilities.

No treaty was ever made with the Mohave regarding their tribal lands, the United States government merely assuming title to them. By an act of Congress in 1865 the present Colorado River Agency, located largely on the east bank of the river around Parker, Arizona, was established for them and for neighboring peoples such as the Chemehuevi. It was subsequently enlarged so as to encompass nearly a quarter million acres. Many Mohave persistently refused to go to the reservation, preferring to live in the area of Needles, California.

Today there are perhaps 1500 Mohave. Agriculture, as it has for centuries, forms the basis of subsistence for the reservation Indians. But today men work for wages. Formerly a considerable number found employment on the railroad; more recently, they have had government work on roads and dams. On the whole, the Mohave have adjusted well to changed conditions.

Little of the aboriginal culture survives. The old varieties of domesticated plants, dress, houses, and implements have disappeared. Nonmaterial elements have persisted to a degree. Clan names and affiliations are remembered; the office of chief still exists, though there are several claimants. No one today experiences a "great dream," but considerable attention is still paid to nightly sleep experiences as portents of things to come. Although little of the native religion remains alive, surprisingly few persons have turned to Christianity. Cremation in the old manner is still practiced by conservative Mohaves. Nowadays the old culture finds its greatest expression in intangibles such as attitudes, mannerisms, and interpersonal reactions. The Mohave language is still very much alive, notwithstanding the fact that virtually all of the younger and middle-aged people speak English as well. Much of the valley which they once claimed lies today beneath the waters of reservoirs created by the building of dams across the Colorado.

Suggested readings

CURTIS, E. S.
1924–1926   *The North American Indian.* Volumes 13, 14, 15. Norwood, Mass.: The Plimpton Press.
HEIZER, R. F. and WHIPPLE, M. A.
1971   *The California Indians. A Source Book.* 2d ed. University of California Press.
KROEBER, A. L.
1973   *Handbook of the Indians of California.* 3rd printing. Berkeley: California Book Company.

VI

The Southwest

The greater southwest

The most spectacular archeological sites and the best-preserved aboriginal cultures in the United States are to be found in that arid but magnificently scenic region known to anthropologists as the Southwest. The areal characterization of the cultural Southwest was at first limited essentially to the prehistoric and historic Indian cultures of Arizona and New Mexico, with only minor extensions into adjacent states. Pliny E. Goddard in his book *Indians of the Southwest,* first published in 1913, concentrated upon the archeology and ethnology of Arizona and New Mexico, with little mention of contiguous areas.

Soon, however, anthropologists began to enlarge their conception of the Southwest to include the tribes of a much wider area. Archeologists were discovering prehistoric sites related to those of Arizona and New Mexico not only in southern Utah and southwestern Colorado, but also in northern Mexico. It was becoming apparent also that the cultures of the simpler Southwestern tribes had much in common with those of other Indian groupings distributed over vast expanses of arid North America, and that aboriginal farmers with cultures similar to those of the agricultural Southwesterners extended deep into old Mexico. A. L. Kroeber, discussing the expanding conception of the native American Southwest in 1928, extended the southern boundaries of the Southwest culture area almost to the Tropic of Cancer, thus including half of Mexico (Kroeber, 1928).

The concept of a "Greater Southwest" culture area was gradually emerging, although the term was not yet in use. At the Third Round Table Conference on Problems of Mexico and Central America in 1943, Ralph L. Beals proposed the abandonment of the terms "Southwest" and "Northern Mexico" in favor of the larger region, the "Greater Southwest," which would include not only Arizona and New Mexico, but also all of northern Mexico and the peoples of the Sierra Madre Mountains in Mexico down to and including the Cora and Huichol tribes. Beals' Greater Southwest further includes most of southern and eastern California, and takes in Utah, Nevada, west Texas, and parts of adjacent states, (Beals, 1943a:193–194). Paul Kirchhoff in 1954 argued that the Greater Southwest should include, in addition to Arizona and New Mexico, the areas of southern coastal Texas, the Great Basin, Central California, Southern California, Baja

California, and northern Mexico as far south as the Sinaloa and Panuco rivers. Kirchhoff further suggested that the Southwest contains not one basic culture, but two, and that it should be divided into two culture areas rather than one: an "Arid American Culture Area" inhabited mainly by hunting and gathering peoples, and an "American Oasis Culture Area," encompassing the settled agriculturalists (Kirchhoff, 1954:533 ff.).

Anthropologists continued to discuss the Greater Southwest and its boundaries, and there is general agreement that it includes much more than Arizona and New Mexico. The present writer considers the Greater Southwest a valid culture area, but will nevertheless focus his discussion upon the Indians of Arizona and New Mexico, inasmuch as in this book the Indians of Mexico, California, and the Great Basin are treated in other chapters.

Kirchhoff's delineation of an Arid American culture area had been anticipated by other writers, who suggested that a preagricultural, Basin-like hunting and gathering cultural substratum had once been widespread over the region that we now call the Greater Southwest (Lowie, 1923; Drucker, 1941; Beals, 1943a). It has become increasingly evident that in prehistoric times the Indians of vast areas of arid North America participated in a basically similar cultural substratum, with local variations resulting from adaptations to differing ecological conditions. These Indians eked out a living primarily by collecting wild food plants and by hunting small game, following a seminomadic plan of life to best take advantage of the natural resources during the seasons when they became available. Limited by the exigencies of the food quest, the material culture, social structure, and ceremonialism of these peoples remained at uncomplicated levels. With the introduction of agriculture from Mexico as early as 4000 B.C., further local differentiations gradually developed: some peoples became horticulturalists; others continued to hunt small game while continuing to rely mainly upon gathered foods for their subsistence; and still others became, to use Kirchhoff's term, "part-farmers," supplementing their often meager crops with foods supplied by the natural environment.

ARCHEOLOGY

For the southwestern United States our information about archeology is fullest, our chronology is the most nearly absolute, the scholarly concern is longest, and the general story is known to millions of Americans who have visited the several national parks and monuments of the Southwest where extensive prehistoric evidence is preserved.

There are two ways to think of the Southwest cultures, both accurate on different levels of generality. One is to view the entire area as a series of regional variants of the same basic culture tradition. Martin and Plog (1973) take this approach. This view is, of course, defensible. All the cultures—Anasazi, Mogollon, Hohokam, and Patayan—stemmed from one or another regional variant of the western Archaic. All were gardeners. All also continued to rely heavily on a variety of seasonally available wild plant foods so that the concept of total dependence on the Mexican triad—corn, beans, and squash—has been overemphasized. It must be understood that the Archaic exploitation of many wild plants did *not* diminish greatly. All the cultures made excellent pottery and were adept (at one time or another) at masonry construction.

It is of particular interest that Southwestern cultures developed in a region not at all adaptable to farming. For example, the Anasazi in Colorado were concentrated in highlands, or plateaus, where vast tablelands alternate with deep gorges, where steep mountains nurture swift little streams in narrow valleys, where cold winters contrast with blistering hot, dry summers. The plateaus and mountains are forested with various conifers; the valleys and plains are covered with shrubs and grass. It is, to be sure, an area rich in desert game and plants, but it is not lush. In most years rainfall is inadequate for dry farming as practiced by modern farmers. Permanent water for human use has been a crucial problem in the Southwest at all times, even as now; for crops, it has always been scarce. Indian gardening techniques were specially developed to utilize the limited moisture. Aside from moisture problems, the higher plateaus have short growing seasons, with late and early frosts a constant hazard.

Farther south, in Mogollon territory in New Mexico and Arizona, the problems were not different—they were merely intensified. The winters perhaps are less cold, but the country is as rough as any in the Southwest. Here, on the New Mexico–Arizona border are a half dozen ranges—steep mountains and narrow valleys—with little arable land. Although better watered than most of the Southwest and, therefore, better timbered and with more game species and

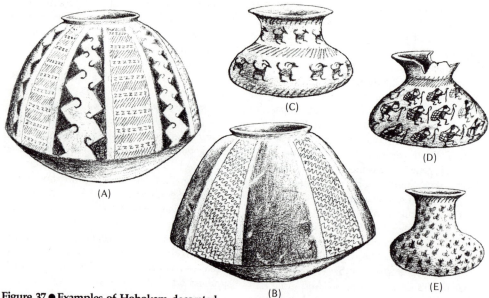

Figure 37 ● Examples of Hohokam decorated pottery. A, B, Sacaton Red-on-buff, both approximately 18½ inches high and 25½ inches in diameter; C–E, Santa Cruz Red-on-buff, all about 5½ inches high. (A, B after Haury, 1937c; C–E after Wasley and Johnson, 1965; Jennings, 1974:288)

edible plants, the rough dissected terrain restricts gardening to small areas.

In south central Arizona where the Hohokam flourished, the land was unquestionably desert. Low, hot, and rarely rained upon, this country was entirely dependent upon the streams arising in the mountains to the east (where the Mogollon peoples were located). These major Hohokam streams were the Salt and Gila rivers, along which Hohokam agriculture was carried on with a complex, well-developed system of irrigation dams and ditches.

In sum the Southwest gardeners, with three still cultivated species and numerous plants now regarded as weeds, established technologically advanced cultures in the least likely place on the continent. The problem to be faced was not soil fertility; no land is richer. The problem has been, and remains, one of water. Great ingenuity, patience, and industry must be credited to all the aboriginal groups that survived in the deserts and mountains.

Whether the stimulus of new ideas from Mexico first reached the Mogollon area or that of the Hohokam is debated. At the famous Snaketown site, where the Hohokam series of phases was first found and described, Haury (1967 and personal communication) excavated several additional acres of the huge village. As a result of this second study, the evidence now

favors the Hohokam as the locus of Mexican inspiration/impact on local Arizona Archaic cultures. Many scholars resist this conclusion because it reverses earlier thinking which favored the Mogollon area as the impact point; or they even deny that there was "impact," preferring the idea that there was a slower process of diffusion of such key elements as pottery, horticulture, and permanent dwellings to the San Pedro, the last phase of the Cochise Archaic.

The Hohokam

If, as assumed here, the strong Mexican flavor of all three Southwestern cultures originates with the Hohokam in the Gila and Salt river valleys, the question arises "How did the Mexican elements arrive?" Haury thinks that an actual migration of a band of Mexican colonists about 2300 years ago is supported by the evidence. They arrived with a full cultural kit that included a knowledge of irrigation and water management, a full complement of cultivated plants, an incipient cult or religion that called for special architectural forms, such as low earthen platforms or higher truncated pyramidal mounds, a well-understood ceramic technology, and a domestic dwelling architectural pattern calling for semisubterranean houses built in pits or mud and post surface houses called *jacales.* Dozens of exotic artifacts, and the

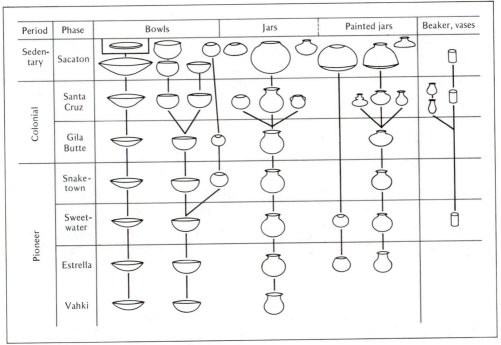

Period	Phase	Bowls	Jars	Painted jars	Beaker, vases
Seden-tary	Sacaton				
Colonial	Santa Cruz				
Colonial	Gila Butte				
Pioneer	Snake-town				
Pioneer	Sweet-water				
Pioneer	Estrella				
Pioneer	Vahki				

Figure 38 ● Evolution of dominant Hohokam vessel forms (After Haury, 1937c; Jennings, 1974:289)

brilliantly feathered macaws kept as pets or religious objects, are all new in the Southwest, but had been long established in Mexico. Because the artifacts appear suddenly and there are no antecedent forms, we may be sure the Hohokam were not Archaic peoples who instantly adopted the niceties of a complex culture; instead, since they possessed a full blown complex of alien origin, we can only agree that the first Hohokam were no doubt a group of transplanted Mexican Indians establishing a northern outpost with a technology appropriate for subduing the desert wastes of the Gila and Salt valleys where Phoenix, Arizona, now stands.

The most impressive accomplishment of the Hohokam is the vast network of irrigation canals, evidently begun in the Colonial period. The main Snaketown canal proper seems to have been in use from A.D. 800 to 1300, but there were many earlier canals. From diversion dams on the Salt and Gila, the major canals led 30 and more miles away, with distributary canals and laterals branching off at intervals. Dug by hand, these large canals (one at Pueblo Grande, near Phoenix, is 6 feet deep by 30 feet wide; another is 10 feet deep by 15 feet wide)

represent tremendous effort, to say nothing of the later labor of constant tending, repair, and maintenance (Woodbury, 1960).

In pottery, the dominant Hohokam pattern was a quite distinctive ceramic complex. Buff colored, it is somewhat lighter in weight than is usual, made by paddling (as opposed to coiling and paddling), and has decorative style not noted elsewhere in the Southwest. One favored decor was the endless repetition, in red paint on buff ground, of small, usually stylized, zoomorphic forms. Special vessel shapes were developed (Figs. 37, 38).

In such architectural forms as ball courts and stepped pyramids, the Mexican stimulus for Hohokam is obvious. Equally Mexican were the slate mirrors encrusted with pyrites, elaborate bracelets, rings, and ornaments of shell. Houses were simple huts of mud and sticks, scattered around inside compounds enclosed by low mud walls. By A.D. 1100 the influences of Mogollon and Pueblo began to be felt and the distinctive features of Hohokam began to blur (Fig. 39).

The Mogollon

Some two hundred miles east of the small area of Hohokam dominance, where the headwaters of the rivers—the Salt and Gila—rise, is the heart of the Mogollon tradition. Early Mogollon can be identified as an Archaic complex to

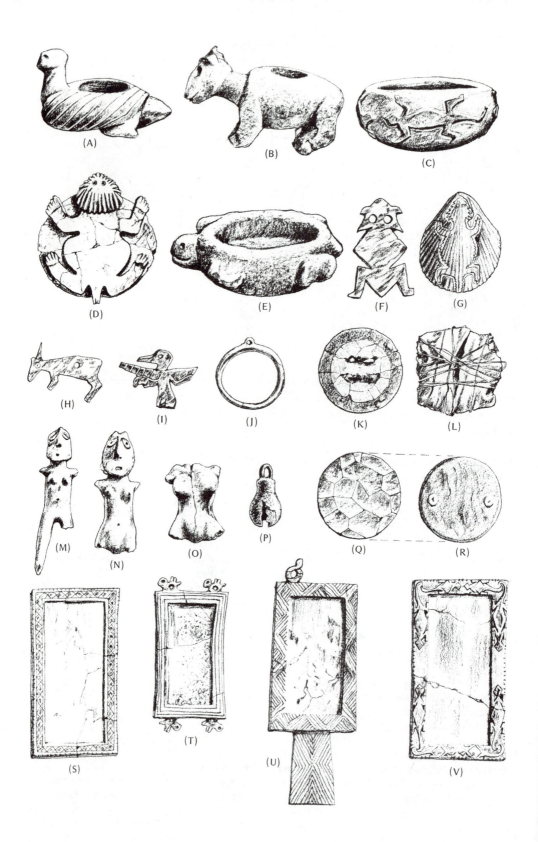

(A)　　(B)　　(C)

(D)　　(E)　　(F)　　(G)

(H)　　(I)　　(J)　　(K)　　(L)

(M)　　(N)　　(O)　　(P)　　(Q)　　(R)

(S)　　(T)　　(U)　　(V)

which horticulture and pottery had been added; the idea of pottery had arrived, possibly from the nearby Hohokam to the west, by 2000 years ago. In the Mogollon, we find horticulture, milling stones—slab and basin type—chipped-stone implements of specialized function, shallow oval pit houses, a knowledge of weaving and basketry, and well-established techniques for exploiting all available plants and animals.

The Mogollon sequence has been exhaustively studied. On the basis of artifacts and architecture, several phases have been distinguished, which cover a period of about 1700 years from 2300 B.P. to about A.D. 1400. The sequence begins arbitrarily at 2300 B.P. as the approximate time pottery was added to the trait inventory.

Wheat (1955) uses numbers—Mogollon 1 through 5—to separate the Mogollon into five major time periods, as follows:

Period 1. 300 B.C.–A.D. 400
Period 2. A.D. 400–600
Period 3. A.D. 600–900
Period 4. A.D. 900–1000
Period 5. A.D. 1000–1350

The Mogollon culture, which has been seen as a parent, or as an agent of transmission of ideas, to the more northerly Anasazi, has its greatest importance to us as its content or culture inventory was constituted during the Mogollon 1 (or Pine Lawn) phase because it was during that period that the northward spread occurred.

There were permanent houses during Mogollon 1 times but no architectural uniformity; Wheat identifies eighteen different patterns of dwelling houses. Usually they were set in shal-

Figure 39 ● Hohokam artifacts from Snaketown. Variable scale. Stone effigies: A, duck; B, mountain sheep (?), 2½ inches high; C, lizard, 3 inches in diameter; D, horned toad, 9 inches long; E, turtle, 4½ inches long; F–I, cut and etched; G, shell ornaments; J, shell bracelet; K, stone-backed plaque or mirror, 4½ inches in diameter, encrusted with iron pyrites; L, Q, R, (from Tempe, Arizona), three views of plaque, 4½ inches in diameter, similar to K; L, plaque in original wrapping; Q, front of plaque showing pyrite polygons; R, back of plaque; M–O, clay figurines (M is 4½ inches high); P, copper bell, ⅜ inches high; S–V, stone palettes, 7 to 12½ inches long. (A–E after Sayles, 1937b; F–V after Haury, 1937a, b, d, e.; Jennings, 1974:290–91)

low pits; about half had a narrow, roofed entryway coming in on the side. The floor was not often level or smooth but irregular, having storage (?) pits sunk into it. The fireplace was usually only a simple unlined depression in the floor. The major roofing elements were supported by central or peripheral posts or both; the rafters, in turn, supported sticks, branches, or reeds. House shape shows regional patterns but cannot be generalized for the whole Mogollon province except to say that about half of the Mogollon 1 houses were roundish; others were D-shaped, kidney shaped, or rectangular. Later the house types stabilized: houses were larger in floor area, set deeper into the ground, and of quadrangular plan with lateral entryways. From earliest times onward, large ceremonial buildings were a feature of most villages; in shape, these show about the same changes through time as do dwellings, but they were always larger and sunk even deeper into the ground. These ceremonial structures were often truly subterranean. No stone masonry is noted during this period. Outside the houses, straight-sided and belled storage or cache pits occur, as well as large fire areas or hearths.

No systematic or recurring village plan or pattern can be detected. Houses were scattered along the summits of ridges, conforming to no perceptible scheme. Only a few houses occur together. The preferred location was an elevated and isolated spot near a strip of cultivable land. Villages were continuously occupied; Wheat says that some were occupied for 1000 years. This fact can, of course, be deduced from the cultural debris and the stratified house remains and other evidence. Towns grew larger, and in some cases after about A.D. 1050 or 1100 are located on level land, when aboveground masonry began to be used for dwellings. Masonry as an architectural technique was evidently a return borrowing from the Anasazi to the north.

Mogollon pottery is of good quality and shows mastery of all the basic techniques involved in all aboriginal American pottery except decorative ones. The earliest pottery is plain, brown or red, usually polished; these two plain wares never disappeared from the Mogollon complex. This ubiquitous ware, called Alma Plain, is recognized all over the province, with variants of paste differences noted and described from place to place. Vessel shapes were actually as varied—from the dominant shallow and hemispherical bowls to slender, small-necked bottles—in the early period as at any later time. None of the shapes was complex or bizarre, however. Wheat has remarked that the Mogollon ceramic tradition is distinctive and moves smoothly through time to a uniform, widely distributed complex with relatively little borrowing or internal innovation. Also in clay, the Mogollones made human and animal figurines, miniature vessels and ladles, and other minor items.

A wide assortment of ground or pecked stone was included in Mogollon technology. Such things as milling stones, of course, were common, as were mortars and pestles. Stone tubular pipes were common at an early date, but gave over later to cane cigarettes. Stone bowls, whetstones and abrading stones, axes, stone balls, discs, pot covers, hoes, and tubes were also made. Special flat stone utensils called palettes, upon which pigments were evidently mixed, are present but not common in Mogollon collections. Chipped stone includes the expectable variety of projectile points, knives, drills, and scrapers. They are usually not large and they are usually somewhat rough in execution, lacking the delicacy of retouch or finish associated with some Anasazi specimens. A special form is a saw made by chipping smooth, even notches in the side of a long flake.

Because of the deep, rich deposits of Tularosa Cave (Martin et al., 1952), a long list of Mogollon perishable artifacts and attendant technologies is available to us. Many of these types are distinctive in technical detail. The collections include sandals, feather ornaments, aprons and girdles of string, fur- and feather-woven robes, snares, flexible cradles, net bags, tumplines, atlatls and darts, bows and arrows, weaving tools and loom parts, reed flutes and wooden dice, miniature bows and arrows, as well as evidence of 23 (?) separate plant species gathered for food or as raw material for manufactures. Ornaments and tools of shell (including Olivella) and bone were also common at all periods.

Possibly because farmlands were scarce or because the well-watered uplands supported more game or perhaps by choice, the Mogollones never depended exclusively upon horticulture for subsistence. Haury (1936) points out that a major dependence on hunting is inferable from two or three villages; Martin et al. (1952) show, from Tularosa Cave, a heavy reliance on gathered wild foods and game animals, a reliance that varies from period to period.

However, all authors are evidently agreed that Mogollon subsistence was more evenly divided between hunting, gathering, and agricultural pursuits than were other Southwestern cultures. And in this, resemblance to the Desert Archaic is noted.

It is generally agreed that the modern Zuni tribe fully described later in this chapter, is descended from the prehistoric Mogollones (Reed, 1955).

The Anasazi

The most recent of the Southwestern local cultures is the Anasazi. It too arose from the Desert base. The Anasazi took on its distinctive form by A.D. 500 or 600 in the southwestern United States, developing to a cultural apogee by A.D. 1200. It soon covered the largest area of all the Southwestern cultures and achieved a great richness. Best known in the Four Corners area, where fabled Mesa Verde lies, the Anasazi passed through several developmental stages. The Anasazi culture is another of the archeologically defined cultures that can today be identified with living American tribes, in this case, specifically with the Rio Grande and Hopi Pueblo (Fig. 40).

The Anasazi culture may well have developed from the local Desert base in response to altogether different influences from those acting on the Hohokam or Mogollon. For example, the first house types resemble nothing else in America, being beehive domes of cribbed logs laid up horizontally with mud mortar, and accompanied by elaborate storage cysts of several types which appear as a separate architectural concept also new to the Southwest. The first corn identified with the Basketmakers of the area is not the Mexican pyramidal seen in the Mogollon but a broad dent type commonest in the southeastern United States. Also, in pottery, there was an early flamboyance of such odd shapes as the trilobed pot, boot-shaped vessels, animal effigies, water bottles with long slender necks and gourd-shaped bodies—all without counterpart elsewhere in the Southwest. The shapes were common, however, in the Southeast during Mississippian times. Although few other scholars would agree, one can see in the architectural differences (e.g., wattle and daub cists) and the early ceramic tradition sources for the first Anasazi stimuli entirely different from, and in addition to, those affected by the Mogollones.

The familiar Pueblo culture can best be de-

(A)

(B)

Figure 40 ● Mesa Verde, Classic Pueblo III A, Doublehouse B, Cliff Palace (After D. Watson, 1950)

scribed in terms of the stages archeologists have come to use. These stages tend to emphasize the explosive growth and richness which the Pueblo culture generated from the simple Desert base. These periods are Basketmaker II, A.D. 1–500; Basketmaker III, A.D. 450–750; Pueblo I and II, A.D. 750–1100; and Pueblo III, A.D. 1100–1300.

The first and all-important new trait to be re-

ceived by the Desert people in Basketmaker times was agriculture—corn and squash and knowledge of how to raise them—which marks the beginning of a new era. Houses, with central fireplaces, were made of horizontal logs laid in mud mortar. Basketry techniques and forms became more elaborate with complicated designs in color worked into the baskets. Beautiful flexible bags for storage, for carrying supplies, and even for burial shrouds were woven of vegetable fibers. Sandals, also woven, were triumphs of color, design, and craftsmanship; the colors remain bright even today. The major weapon was still the dart and spear thrower; clothing included the same materials—woven rabbit-fur robes, string aprons, and belts. At least two varieties of dogs were bred, apparently as companions and possibly for hunting. There is no evidence they were used for food.

Surplus food and personal objects were stored in stone slab-lined storage pits or aboveground chambers called cists. In abandoned cists dead were sometimes placed, in tightly flexed positions, knees to chest. Many possessions were interred; such items as beads, sandals, digging sticks, blankets, and conical smoking pipes are common with burials. Although burials were sometimes made in empty cists, the grave usually was only a hole in the dirt. In most cases baskets and mats were laid over the body before the hole was filled. Here then, in Basketmaker times, are the germs of a new life—agriculture, permanent houses, careful burial, and long-term living in one spot.

By A.D. 500–700 the changes were more marked. There were larger clusters of circular houses, now built as pit houses, and food storage structures of mud and stone. These were in larger organized communities, often built in the huge caves or overhangs so common in the Four Corners area. The design of these pit houses is quite different from the earlier type. They were lined with stone slabs and had wooden roofs; they could be entered either from the roof or by way of an antechamber and passageway. With corn already present and beans, a prime source of protein, now having been introduced, the people were perhaps less dependent upon meat from the hunt. The bow and arrow, a weapon vastly superior to the atlatl, appeared at the end of the period, but did not displace the atlatl and associated dart entirely. Clay pottery (fired not in kilns but under conical piles of bark), turquoise jewelry, and crude clay figurines also are found for the first time in this period. The skills in basketry and textiles continued to flourish, with sandals at their most elaborate at this time.

Thus, by the end of Basketmaker times the inventory of new resources is complete: corn, beans, and squash provided a balanced and fairly certain food supply; permanent housing and small villages existed; pottery making was understood; and the development of the religious system (inferred from the figurines) continued. Two new tools, the grooved axe and a grooved maul, appear for the first time. Upon

these innovations and their refinement, the flowering of the culture came.

In the Pueblo I and II stages which started by A.D. 750 and lasted until A.D. 1050 or 1100, there were changes, but none so revolutionary as had come earlier. For example, the dart and atlatl were abandoned, being replaced entirely by the bow and arrow. Sandals, though still made, were coarser and less carefully made; other weaving, however, was even more elaborate. The potter's art was greatly developed. A wide range of vessel forms and a variety of decorative styles evolved. Black paint over a white base was the color combination more commonly used. Cooking pottery became specialized; the coils from construction were left visible so the surface was corrugated. Cotton was introduced from the south as a new crop, and cotton blankets replaced the earlier fur robes. Weaving was done on a loom, leading apparently to a decline of twining as a textile art. Turkeys were kept as domestic fowl. The pit house began to be less popular because the idea of building aboveground houses, out of stone mortared with mud and arranged in rows, was adopted; the pit house, however, evolved into the very special round subterranean *kiva*, or sacred men's room, where a variety of religious ceremonies were held, which began to take up a great deal of time. *Jacal* construction for walls of dwellings became popular, however (Fig. 41).

Ceremonies to insure crop fertility, to bring rain, to ward off storms and crop damage were developed. The entire religious system probably focused on the world of nature and on agriculture. Dance courts or plazas in the towns resulted from the need for space for the public parts of various religious ceremonies. By the end of the period, there were fairly large towns or pueblos (a Spanish word meaning town) composed of many houses built as one continuous square, L-shaped, or semicircular unit enclosing a plaza or court. Because burials are very rare from this period, it is not known just how disposal of the dead was handled.

But with the Pueblo III period between A.D. 1100 and 1300 came the culture climax. At this time the cliff dwellings and terraced apartment houses were built of mud, stone, and wood; here scores of families lived together. The skill with which these houses were built is just another expression of the high levels attained in all handicraft. The famous Mesa Verde black-

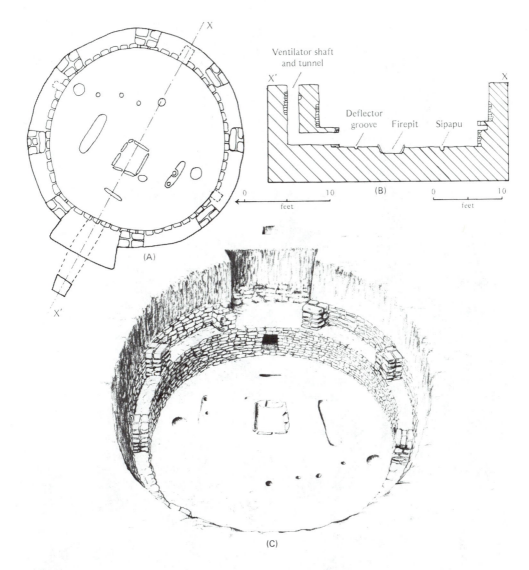

Ventilator shaft
and tunnel

Deflector groove Firepit Sipapu

(A)

(B)

(C)

Figure 41 ● Pueblo II. Kiva at Mesa Verde National Park. A, Place view B, Cross section C, Excavated Kiva. (After Lancaster and Pinkley, 1954)

on-white pottery—pots, mugs, and ladles—was made at this time.

We can appreciate the Anasazi on many counts. They developed a rich culture in difficult surroundings by learning to exploit the land. As farmers on the mesas and in the desert they were superbly ingenious, especially in their techniques for saving water. Their farms were small patches (more like the gardens of today) wherever there was water. Sand dunes, lying at the foot of long, slop-

ing hillsides, collected and conserved water to form favorite garden spots. Here the water running off the bare rock oozed slowly down through the dunes and watered the crops at the edges of the dune. Thus a natural subsurface irrigation was utilized. In other places, along the small streams, there were dikes and little dams that diverted or fanned flood waters out over a wider area where the gardens were located. This was called flood irrigation. Sometimes the sloping hillsides were leveled into a series of terraces that conserved flood and runoff water by slowing its run and allowing it to soak into the thirsty gardens planted on the terraces. This is another form of flood irrigation. Farming was done by both men and women.

Zuni ● Dance of the Uwanami (Rain makers). (After Stevenson, 1904. Smithsonian Institution National Anthropological Archives)

Success with crops was a year-round concern and the focus of many religious ceremonies.

In all other arts, the Pueblo skills excite admiration. Normal household tools, utensils, and furnishings were many and varied. In a Pueblo III house one would find a score of corrugated cooking and storage pots, decorated ladles, mugs, and bowls, cotton blankets (woven by the men), turquoise, coral, and Pacific shell wristlets, necklaces and pendants, flint knives on wooden handles, stout little bows and many specialized arrows, feather robes, gaudy sandals, belts, or girdles, a hundred different tools of bone, string, and cord.

Then in 1276 there was a very dry year followed by another and another. The drought, which lasted until 1299, may be a major reason for the abandonment of settlements and migration to the south, or south and east, and no doubt thousands of Pueblo people died of hunger as both wild and domestic foods became scarce or disappeared entirely. Additionally, there was perhaps fighting between towns, and occasional pueblos seem to have been burned after their inhabitants were killed. Some students have thought also that the Navaho and other Apache reached Utah from the north during this century and, through their raids, helped drive the nonwarlike Pueblo people southward. Whatever the cause, it is known that northern pueblos and towns were abandoned by 1300. (Schoenwetter, 1962, offers an entirely new explanation of Pueblo expansion and abandonment, involving a change in rainfall pattern over two centuries, which throws doubt on the classic explanation given above.)

Little mention has been made of the course of Southwestern culture after about A.D. 1300, although it seems clear that the contraction of the Anasazi domain in the late 1200s reflected an enormous loss of population. There was a removal of the remnant population to the Rio Grande Valley and the mesas of central Arizona. The descendants of the Anasazi still reside in these areas at Hopi, Zia, Taos, and other modern villages. Similarly there is evidence that the Mogollones moved to east-central Arizona where their descendants—the Zuni—now dwell. The historic tribes of southern Arizona, the Pima and Papago, are the lineal descendants of the Hohokam and exploit the same original area in about the same way.

LINGUISTIC AFFILIATIONS

The languages of the historic tribes of the Southwest have been classified as affiliated with six linguistic families: Uto-Aztecan, Tanoan, Keresan, Zunian, Athabascan, and Yuman. Various attempts have been made by linguists to merge certain of these stocks into larger families, with differing degrees of certitude.

The affiliations of the Hopi and the Pimans with the widespread Uto-Aztecan stock are well established. J. W. Powell long ago linked the Hopi language with the Shoshoneans of southern California and the Numic of the Great Basin as it later came to be called (Powell, 1891:110). Sapir in 1913 established the Uto-Aztecan stock, consisting of the Shoshonean, Piman-Sonoran, and Náhuatl (in Mexico) branches (Sapir, 1913). The language of the Tepehuane in Mexico has been shown to be closely related to those of the Pimans (Mason, 1950), and the Taracahitan branch of Uto-Azte-

can includes the languages of the Cahita, Opata, and Tarahumara of northern Mexico (Whorf and Trager, 1937).

The Tanoan languages spoken at some of the Rio Grande pueblos are internally diverse, and have been divided into three mutually unintelligible subfamilies: Tewa, Towa, and Tiwa. The Tewa subfamily includes the present villages of Tesuque, Pojoaque, Nambe, San Ildefonso, Santa Clara, and San Juan, plus the village of Hano among the Hopi on the First Mesa. Towa is represented today by the single village of Jemez, although the now extinct pueblo of Pecos is believed to have belonged to this subfamily (Swanton, 1952:336). Tiwa comprises the villages of Taos, Picuris, Sandia, and Isleta and was formerly spoken in the Galisteo Basin area south of Santa Fe and among the extinct Piro in the vicinity of the present city of Las Cruces, New Mexico.

Whorf and Trager (1937:609–624), following Sapir (1929), have presented strong but not entirely conclusive evidence that Uto-Aztecan and Tanoan should be amalgamated into an Aztec-Tanoan family, which is now accepted by many linguists. Suggested linkages of Aztec-Tanoan with other stocks are as yet not supported by adequate evidence.

Similarly, Sapir's suggestion that Keresan should be grouped in a Hokan-Siouan (Hokan, etc.) superstock (Sapir, 1929) remains to be demonstrated, although the Voegelins have concurred in it (Voegelin and Voegelin, 1944). The Keresan family is usually divided into a western group, consisting of the pueblos of Acoma and Laguna, and an eastern division, comprising the villages of Santo Domingo, Santa Ana, Zia, San Felipe, and Cochití (Newman, 1954:631).

The language of the Zuni is customarily classed in a distinct and separate family, the Zunian, which has never been proved to be related to any other known stock. Sapir's suggestion that Zuni should be included in Aztec-Tanoan remains without adequate supportive evidence (Sapir, 1929).

The Athabascan languages of the Southwest are divided by Hoijer into Eastern Apachean, consisting of Jicarilla, Kiowa-Apache, and Lipan, and Western Apachean, comprising Chiricahua, Mescalero, San Carlos, and Navaho (Hoijer, 1938). Powell in 1891 linked the Apachean languages with those of the Northern Athabascan and Pacific Coast Athabascan groups. Sapir (1915) postulated a Na-Dené stock, including Athabascan and Haida and Tlingit on the Northwest Coast, a classification with which many but not all linguists concur.

Finally, the Yuman family includes the Upland Yumans of Arizona (Walapai, Yavapai, Havasupai) and the River Yumans (Mohave, Yuma, Cocopa, and Maricopa), as well as the Diegueño of southern California and various Baja California groups (Kroeber, 1943). Less certainly, the Yuman languages have been grouped with a number of other stocks from widely separated areas into a Hokan-Coahuiltecan family, (Kroeber, 1915; Dixon and Kroeber, 1913, 1919; Sapir, 1917) and even more tenuously by Sapir into a Hokan-Siouan (Hokan, etc.) superstock (Sapir, 1929).

THE NATURAL ENVIRONMENT

Although important environmental contrasts exist in the Southwest, the whole area is uniformly a relatively arid one. Altitude, rather than latitude, is perhaps the most important determining factor in variations of climate and vegetation. Rainfall in general is light, averaging less than 20 inches a year in most sections, and reaching a minimum of under 4 inches in the desert near Yuma, Arizona. The atmosphere in most parts of the Southwest is usually clear and dry, permitting visibility over great distances. Day after day, in this land of maximum possible sunshine, the sun traverses an almost cloudless sky. Temperatures often vary greatly within a span of twenty-four hours; during the desert summer, frying hot days may be succeeded by refreshing cool nights.

The heaviest concentrations of aboriginal population in the Southwest were in the valleys of such rivers as the Colorado, Gila, Salt, and Rio Grande. In certain other areas, such as the Hopi country of northern Arizona, a limited amount of dry farming was possible with a careful conservation and utilization of the scanty precipitation. Seminomadic peoples like the Apache, Navaho, Walapai, and Yavapai were "part-farmers," planting where they could in the vicinity of smaller streams and oasislike springs, but relying heavily upon nonagricultural food sources for their subsistence.

Physiographically, Arizona and New Mexico may be divided into three main regions, with the plains of eastern New Mexico, a westward extension of the High Plains, as a fourth. The principal divisions are the high, cool, plateau area of the north, the hot, low-lying desert of the south, and the mountainous central region lying between the plateau and the desert. Vegetation and climate in these three zones differ in accordance with altitude and precipitation.

The northern section, physiographically a southward extension of the great Colorado Plateau Province, is drained by the Colorado River and its tributaries, the Little Colorado and the San Juan. The average elevation of this high plateau country surpasses 5,000 feet, and a few peaks rise to heights of nearly 13,000 feet. A colorful land of high, flat-topped mesas, and fantastically shaped buttes, the plateau is gashed with many sheer-walled canyons, including the famed Grand Canyon of the Colorado River. Here and there over the plateau are evidences of past volcanic activity: cinder and lava cones, extinct craters, and extensive lava flows. The higher elevations are clothed with forests of yellow pine, and at the middle altitudes are smaller trees such as piñon and juniper. The lower elevations are quite dry; the sparse vegetation includes sagebrush and other typical desert plants. Rain over the plateau comes mostly in the form of thunderstorm activity in late summer, sometimes in violent downpours which quickly transform the dry arroyos into torrents. Snowfall, like rainfall, is erratic, but occasionally heavy snows drift down to shroud the mesas and desert plains in a blanket of white. The growing season on this high plateau is so brief that Indian farmers are always apprehensive that unseasonal frosts may blight their crops.

Scattered over the plateau area are many ruins abandoned by the prehistoric Anasazi peoples, whose modern descendants, the Hopi and Zuni, still farm near their villages. The Navaho, relative newcomers to the Southwest, practice both agriculture and pastoralism on the plateau, moving with their flocks of sheep between summer and winter grazing lands. The Yuman-speaking Havasupai are farmers, in an idyllic natural setting in a branch of the Grand Canyon, using the waters of a creek for irrigation. The Walapai, another Yuman people in northwest Arizona, farmed where they could, but a dearth of water in their environment necessitated primary reliance upon hunting and gathering, prior to the adoption of stock raising in modern times.

The central mountain region, which was the homeland of the prehistoric Mogollon culture,

Old Oraibi ● A Hopi village. (Voth Collection, Arizona Historical Foundation)

is physiographically a part of the Mexican Highlands division of the Basin and Range Province. It is another land of scenic grandeur, one of rugged topography, with many deep canyons and spectacularly eroded slopes. Cool in summer, with lofty pines and sparkling streams, the mountain area has become a vacationland for fugitives from the sizzling summers of the southern desert. The beautiful mountain valleys are for the most part rather narrow, but some of them were farmed by the prehistoric Mogollones. In more recent years the mountain region was occupied by roving Yavapai and Apache bands, who practiced little agriculture and whose descendants are now primarily cattlemen.

The lowland desert of southern Arizona lies within the Sonoran Desert portion of the Basin and Range Province. It is a land of hot summers and mild winters and of a low annual precipitation, which falls erratically and unpredictably as rain in winter and in late summer. The rolling desert plain, marked by wide alluvial valleys broken by networks of arroyos, averages between 1000 and 2000 feet in elevation. Numerous low ranges of serrated mountains rise to elevations of 1000 to 3000 feet above the desert floor. The xerophytic vegetation includes yuccas, agave, creosote bush, and various species of cacti, notably the giant saguaro. When watered, the soil is extremely fertile and was farmed intensively by the prehistoric Hohokam irrigators in the valleys of the Gila and Salt rivers. Today the Pima farmers and their congeners, the Papago, live in scattered villages in the desert. Near the Pima are the agricultural Maricopa, the remnant of several Yuman tribes who fled across the desert from the lower Colorado River in hope of escaping their enemies, the Yuma and Mohave.

Cultural Divisions

The Southwest has been subdivided into culture provinces by various writers, each of whom presents a somewhat different classification (Kroeber, 1939:34–45; Beals, 1932: 134–146; Kirchhoff, 1954:542–550; Underhill, 1954:656.) In the present chapter, primarily for the sake of convenience, the tribes will be grouped under the following categories: 1. Upland Yumans 2. Athabascans 3. Pueblos 4. Pimans 5. Northern Mexico.

The Upland Yumans. The Upland Yuman (or Plateau Ranchería) tribes of Arizona, the Walapai, Havasupai, and Yavapai, have prob-

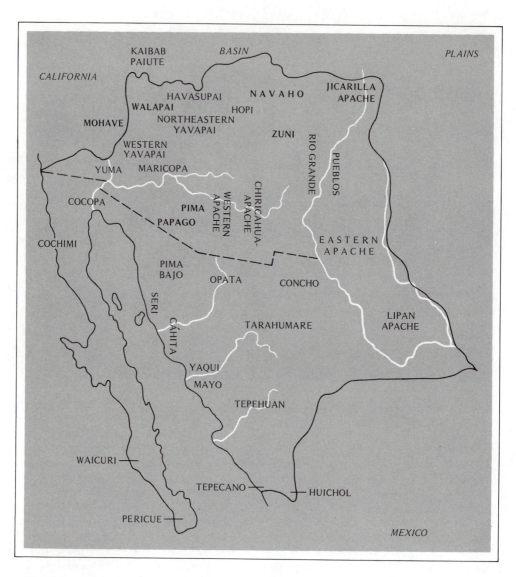

Map labels:
KAIBAB PAIUTE · BASIN · PLAINS · CALIFORNIA · HAVASUPAI · NAVAHO · JICARILLA APACHE · WALAPAI · HOPI · MOHAVE · NORTHEASTERN YAVAPAI · ZUNI · WESTERN YAVAPAI · RIO GRANDE · PUEBLOS · YUMA · MARICOPA · WESTERN APACHE · CHIRICAHUA-APACHE · COCOPA · PIMA · PAPAGO · EASTERN APACHE · COCHIMI · PIMA BAJO · OPATA · CONCHO · SERI · CÁHITA · TARAHUMARE · LIPAN APACHE · YAQUI · MAYO · TEPEHUAN · WAICURI · TEPECANO · HUICHOL · PERICUE · MEXICO

D ● Greater Southwest

ably remained closer to the old Desert culture substratum than any other tribes in Arizona and New Mexico, with the possible exception of the Kaibab band of Paiutes, who are actually a Great Basin people, and live in the "Arizona Strip" country between the north rim of the Grand Canyon and the Utah border. In particular, the culture of the Walapai suggests the ancient substratum, although the Walapai have been culturally influenced to a minor degree by their neighbors to the west on the lower Colorado River, the Mohave. The Havasupai appear to be an offshoot of the Walapai who have acquired a degree of cultural distinctiveness in consequence of contacts with the Hopi and as a

result of their occupation of a somewhat different ecological zone, which includes Cataract Canyon, a side branch of the Grand Canyon. Western Apache influence is apparent among the Southeastern Yavapai, and the Western Yavapai were to some extent affected culturally by the Yuma and Mohave.

In general, the Upland Yuman tribes are characterized by simplicity in material culture, social structure, and ritual. For their subsistence, they relied mainly upon hunting and gathering, except for the Havasupai, who imitated certain Hopi agricultural techniques and were able to farm by using the waters of a creek for irrigation.

The Walapai ("Pine Tree People"), who live on a reservation south of the Grand Canyon, farmed where they could, but their habitat was arid and the soil poor, and only a few spots near springs and streams were suitable for cultivation. They remained essentially a nonagricultural people, leaving their villages in the spring and summer in quest of wild foods. The women gathered fruits, seeds, berries, and roots. Hunting was the main occupation of the men, who stalked a variety of animals, including deer, antelope, mountain sheep, and rabbit. With the father functioning as instructor, the education of a boy was chiefly in the relatively rich variety of hunting techniques.

Walapai material culture, in its lack of complexity, again suggests the Great Basin. Houses were of a type common in the Basin; dome-shaped huts constructed of branches and poles on a four-pole foundation, covered over with juniper bark or thatch. Clothing was of buckskin or bark fiber: women wore bark skirts or front and back aprons of buckskin; men wore short-sleeved buckskin shirts and breechclouts of either buckskin or bark. Rabbitskin blankets, similar to those made by the ancient Basketmakers, were used in cold weather both as robes and for bedding.

The art of pottery making was never highly developed, and the only surviving craft is basketry, which is made in both the coiling and twining techniques and is very similar to the basketry of the Western Apaches.

As in other phases of Walapai life, the political pattern and the distribution of population were conditioned by the natural environment. The tribe was loosely organized, with a division into subtribes and patrilineal bands. Headmen of the bands had little authority, but attained their positions by virtue of prowess in warfare, oratorical ability, and qualities of personality, although there was a tendency for the position to be roughly hereditary in the male line. The location of the several villages in each division was inevitably determined primarily by the availability of water. Today, the tribe is governed by a Tribal Council, consisting of one hereditary chief and eight elected representatives.

The religious leader was the shaman, who received a "call" in a dream. The shaman was also the medical practitioner and functioned mainly in curing rites, during which he became possessed by a spirit which entered his body and spoke through his mouth. Disease was attributed to the intrusion of malignant objects. The shaman sang to the accompaniment of a gourd rattle, blew on the patient's body, and sucked out the disease object. Shamans were feared and were often suspected of causing disease. In former times, shamans were sometimes killed by the friends and relatives of deceased patients.

The Walapai seem to have admired the Mohave, from whom they adopted a few cultural features, including the Mohave mourning anniversary and certain song cycles. The Walapai used the Mohave type "potato masher" war club, particularly against their most insistent enemies the Yavapai, who raided them almost yearly. The Walapai cremated the dead in a manner similar to Mohave practices and adopted the Mohave commemorative mourning anniversary, a conventionalized pantomime of warfare, held in honor of the recent dead.

At present the Walapai number approximately 1000, and depend for their income primarily on cattle raising and on the sale of timber from the reservation, supplemented by wage work in neighboring towns.

Although it has been customary to distinguish a Havasupai ("People of the Blue Green Water") tribe, it would be more accurate to group them with the Walapai and call them simply the Pai, as has been done by recent authors. The differences between the Walapai and Havasupai seem to be the result of differential culture contacts and adaptations to varying ecological conditions. In spite of having adopted certain ceremonial features and agricultural methods from the Hopi, the Havasupai remain essentially similar to the Walapai in their basic culture. The Havasupai language is nearly identical to that of their Walapai neighbors, with whom intermarriages are frequent. Again, social structure, technology, artifacts, and subsistence habits (except for agriculture) are similar to those of the Great Basin peoples to the north of the Grand Canyon. But from the Hopi the Havasupai adopted such agricultural items as the planting of cotton and tobacco, together with ceremonial features, including prayers at the time of planting corn, a rain dance, masked dancing, and prayer sticks.

Always a small tribe, the Havasupai number at present no more than 350. Far from the turbulence of modern life, they live in a setting of breathtaking natural beauty, secluded deep in a green valley surrounded by precipitous canyon walls of limestone and red sandstone.

The Yavapai ("People of the Sun" or "Crooked Mouth People") in native times were divided into three tribes or subtribes, the Southeastern, Northeastern, and Western Yavapai, each of which was again subdivided into localized bands. Basically, the cultures of the Yavapai resembled those of the Walapai and Havasupai, to whom linguistic resemblances were also close. The Southeastern Yavapai, who ranged primarily over the Mazatzal, Pinal, and Superstition mountains, to the east and northeast of the present city of Phoenix, were on cordial terms with the San Carlos and Tonto Apaches, with whom there was some intermarriage. Yavapai and Apaches sometimes joined forces in raids on the Walapai and Havasupai and on such desert tribes as the Maricopa and Pima. As a result of their associations with the Athabascan-speaking Apache, the Yuman-speaking Yavapai have sometimes been called by the rather confusing names of "Mohave-Apache" or "Yuma-Apache." The simple culture of the Southeastern Yavapai was also affected by Apache contacts, with the adoption by the Yavapai of matrilineal clans, the mother-in-law taboo, masked performances, and the use of tule pollen in ceremonies. The Western Yavapai (or Tolkepaya), in consequence of contacts with the Yuma and Mohave, adopted the Yuma style of house and engaged in a limited amount of farming along the lower Colorado River, in imitation of River Yuman methods. Few of the Yavapai farmed, however, and they relied for their subsistence mainly upon hunting and gathering, with each band roaming over a delimited area, moving seasonally from place to place as the different wild plants ripened. As with the other Upland Yumans, Yavapai social structure, material culture, and ceremonialism were unspecialized. Basketry was the chief craft, made by techniques and in styles similar to those of the Western Apache.

The Yavapai, in all probability, never numbered more then 1,500, although they ranged over a territory of some 20,000 square miles, and no more than 800 Yavapai can be counted at present. They do a little subsistence farming, raise livestock, and work for wages off the reservations.

The Athabascans. The Athabascan-speaking peoples of the Southwest consist of the Apache, last of the hostile tribes to submit to the Whites, and their close linguistic relatives, the Navaho, to be discussed in detail later in this chapter. Of northern provenience, the Navaho

and Apache are believed to have drifted into the Southwest at least four or five centuries ago.

At present the Apache number approximately 15,000 individuals, usually classed in six distinct tribes or divisions, all speaking closely related Athabascan languages and manifesting a genetic relationship in social structure and ceremonial organization, but with cultural variations as a result of differing cultural contacts and adaptations to different environmental conditions. The Jicarilla Apache of northernmost New Mexico show many influences from the Plains, particularly in material culture, and they engaged in some buffalo hunting. They also farmed relatively extensively, as a result of pueblo contacts, with some pueblo influence also apparent in their ceremonies. The Lipan Apache, now almost extinct, were apparently an offshoot of the Jicarilla. They were less agricultural and more mobile than the Jicarilla, ranging over eastern New Mexico and west Texas, hunting and gathering, until they were pushed down toward the Gulf of Mexico and into old Mexico by the Comanche. The Mescalero of south-central New Mexico also show Plains elements in their culture, although to a much lesser degree than the Jicarilla, and they remained a hunting and gathering people. Culturally much like the Mescaleros were the Chiricahua, who centered around the Chiricahua Mountains of southeastern Arizona and also ranged over adjacent southwestern New Mexico and parts of Chihuahua. Another nonagricultural people, the Chiricahua became the most famous of the Apache, in consequence of their raids in the nineteenth century under their leaders Cochise and Geronimo. The Western Apache of east-central Arizona farmed on a larger scale, and of all the Apache they are linguistically and culturally closest to the Navaho, from whom they probably separated at no distant date. The Western Apache are divided into several groups, such as the White Mountain, Cibecue, San Carlos, Southern Tonto, and Northern Tonto, each of which is in turn subdivided into several bands.

It is even more difficult to trace the origins of the Apache than it is that of the Navaho. The Apache apparently drifted into the Southwest during the prehistoric period, perhaps following a route along the eastern slopes of the Rocky Mountains, and there are suggestions that at least the more easterly Apache divisions

Apache ● Women building a wickiup. (Arizona Historical Foundation, Hayden Library, Arizona State University, Tempe, Arizona)

entered the Southwest from the southern Plains. There is no evidence of Apache in Arizona before the middle of the sixteenth century, but Spanish accounts indicate that by the late sixteenth century they were numerous in southern Colorado and northern New Mexico. With the acquisition of horses they made forays from their mountain strongholds, raiding such sedentary Indians as the Pimans and Puebloans and pillaging deep into the interior of the Mexican states of Sonora and Chihuahua. After the war with Mexico the United States inherited the headache of the Apache and their fierce resistance to encroachment upon their native lands. The Apache wars are associated particularly with the period between 1870 and 1886, when small bands of restless, dissatisfied warriors recurrently broke out of their inadequate reservations and resumed their harassment of the frontier settlements, defying the efforts of numerically superior army forces to pacify them.

In early days the Apache roved the mountains, totally dependent for their subsistence

● GIRLS' PUBERTY RITE—APACHE

Among the Apache generally, despite the varied groupings into which these Athabascan peoples are now divided, the girls' puberty rite assumes primary importance in the ceremonial calendar. The point is of interest when it is remembered that among the Athabascan-speaking tribes of northwest Canada and Alaska the girls' rite is the principal element of religious activity. The Apache, despite their affinities to the culture area of the Southwest, still retain, along with their language, this vestige of their northern origin.

Part of a four-day ceremony is depicted here, one which takes place in the summer. The girls remain secluded, the pattern usually involving several girls of the same age. Under the tutelage of older women, they will appear at the end of the four-day cycle, dancing before the dawn. Like so many of the ceremonies of the American Southwest, not only the girls are involved but the entire community as well. And again, the element of god impersonation, one so strongly developed in the Southwest, impinges on the Apache. The Gans, the masked figures representing the Mountain Spirits, with their kilts and wooden slat headdresses, dramatize the proximity of the spiritual world. Their badge is the black mask and the wooden sword. Behind them sing a chorus of older women and the impersonators dance about a bright fire. Spectators in the background thrill to the dancing, the singing, the drum beat, and to the mystic sound of the bull-roarer, the resonating device which appears off and on in the ceremony.

The same spirit impersonations may occur at another time of the year, when again directed to the promotion of communal well-being. Just as the Navaho concern themselves in their religious practice with curing, the same element is not lost to the Apache. Gans dancers appear in curing ceremonials, although these are secondary in the Apache religious system to the girls' rite. Pueblo designs are suggested in the headdresses, and present also is the buffoon. Although not depicted here, the clown forms a vital part of Southwestern ceremonial and is by no means absent in much of North America.

268 ●

In summary, the Apache offer a variation on the theme of the widespread girls' rite, one with its roots deep in the native American past. Added to this are the elements from the strongly entrenched and vital cultures of the American Southwest. The result is to give the Apache an ancient and northern flavor, but one in which the neighboring cultures have played a significant contributing role. The keynote of communal well-being promoted through ritual is as fully characteristic of the Apache as it is of the Pueblos and the Navaho.

upon wild plant and animal foods. Some later practiced a limited amount of farming, particularly the Jicarilla and Western Apache, but most had little interest in agriculture, leaving their small farm plots untended while they roamed about. After the acquisition of the horse, the Apache entered a period of a "raiding economy," depending to a great extent upon booty captured from other Indians and from Mexicans. Since the establishment of the reservations the Apache have become excellent cattlemen, raising fine herds of Hereford cattle. Wage work is also important at present in the Apache economy.

In consequence of the mobility of their roving life, the Apache had few possessions, and arts and crafts were limited mainly to basketry and the dressing of buckskin. They did not weave and produced only a little pottery, a simple utility ware. They excelled in basketry, which was artistically woven of split willow in both the coiling and twining techniques. The attractive Apache baskets are sometimes fringed with buckskin and decorated with black geometric figures and life forms on a light-colored background. A watertight twined water bottle, called a *tus,* was thickly coated on both the exterior and the interior with piñon pitch.

The dwellings of most of the Jicarilla and Mescaleros were tipis of the Plains type. Some of the Western Apache still live in their native-style house, called a wickiup, which consists of a framework of saplings thrust in the ground and covered with grass and brush, or today with canvas.

In native times the Apache dressed in buckskin. Today, the men wear cowboy garb, and the women are clothed in a style of women's dress worn toward the end of the last century by Caucasian women (the so-called squaw dress), which consists of a full skirt of bright calico and a loose blouse hanging to the hips.

Western Apache women wear their hair shoulder length, with bangs above the eyebrows, while the women of the Jicarilla part their hair in the middle and wear it in two braids, Plains-fashion.

Like the Navaho, the Apache had no centralized tribal organization. Political control was of an informal, fluid nature. But the component bands of each tribe possessed a certain feeling of unity as opposed to all outsiders. The loosely organized bands, each of which was strictly autonomous, were the real war-making units. The bands were in turn divided into local groups, and the strongest of the local headmen acted informally as "chief" of the band. Leadership was not hereditary, but depended upon military prowess, demonstrated ability, and force of personality. Each local group was composed of several matrilocal extended families, which were the basic units of the social organization. The local groups of a band sometimes joined forces for raiding, but the extended family functioned as a relatively independent economic unit.

Details of the loose social and political organization varied from one Apache tribe to another. Kinship systems are bilateral, except for the Western Apache, who have developed a matrilineal clan system similar to that of the Navaho. Western Apache local groups center around farm lands controlled by the clans, which are linked in three large phratries. The Apache in general have mother-in-law avoidance, the levirate and sororate, and permissible sororal polygyny.

In warfare the Apache stressed individual initiative and aggressiveness in combat. The ideal of manhood held up to the Apache boy was to become a brave warrior. In the training of the boy the development of physical endurance was stressed, a regime which produced notably hardy and skillful warriors. Apache tactics were those of surprise and ambush, rather than of open combat, and the horse gave them great mobility. A quick attack was followed by a speedy escape, the warriors scattering in all directions, thus making successful pursuit all but impossible. The warriors would then reassemble at a prearranged place to divide the loot.

The Apache share the Navaho horror of the dead. The corpse is buried as expeditiously as possible by the nearest male relatives. The wickiup and possessions of the deceased are burned, the mourners purify themselves with

Apache (White Mountain) ● Shallow coiled basket. Basketry of this type is common to the Greater Southwest, appearing among the Pueblos, as well as the Navaho and Pima-Papago. Such tightly coiled baskets are often used to hold corn pollen used on ceremonial occasions. (Courtesy of The Science Museum, St. Paul, Minnesota)

sagebrush smoke, and the family moves to a new locality. Again in resemblance to Navaho belief, fear of the dead rests upon a dread of ghosts, which may harm the living, bringing on "ghost sickness," a condition of fright and extreme nervousness.

Many Apache myths and ceremonies are similar to those of the Navaho, although in general less complex in form. Some Apache ceremonies are curing rites, intended to ward off evil, to "set things right." These require the services of a medicine man and in some of them a simplified drypainting, or "medicine disk," is made. Other rituals are connected with hunting, warfare, rainmaking, and the growth of crops. The most spectacular of the Apache ceremonies is the girl's puberty rite (sometimes erroneously called the "Devil Dance" by whites), a four-day ceremony in which the Mountain Spirits, or Gans, are impersonated. The rite dramatizes a triumph of good over evil. The girl sways in a fatiguing dance to the

accompaniment of a chorus of chanters. The impersonators of the Mountain Spirits are black-masked men wearing kilts and towering painted wooden headdresses. In the blaze of a huge fire they wave wooden swords and utter eerie cries, performing elaborate contortions and gyrations, twisting and turning to the beat of the drums.

The Gans are comparable to the Navaho Holy People and are believed to live at present in certain mountains and beneath the horizon. White Painted Woman is the Apache version of the Navaho Changing Woman, and Killer of Enemies and Child of the Water correspond to the Navaho Hero Twins. Also prominent in Apache region are natural forces such as the sun, moon, and winds. The Apache believe, too, in an impersonal force called Yusn, a being without sex or place, which influences the affairs of men and is the source of all power. Among the Chiricahua, Yusn, or Life-Giver, is a "nebulous and remote Supreme Being," and is credited with the creation of the universe (Opler, 1941:280).

After they were confined on the reservations, the Apache underwent a depressing period of poverty, disease, and bitterness, but at present they are a thriving, peaceful people, with less severe economic problems than the Navaho. Some of the older ceremonies and beliefs persist, together with parts of the material culture, but the Apache have been strongly exposed to acculturation. The old political systems have been replaced by active Tribal Councils. Associations of cattlemen are strong, and facilities for schooling on the Apache reservations are good. The descendants of the raiders are now, on the whole, good-natured but reserved cowboys and wage workers.

The Pueblos. Descendants of the prehistoric Anasazi peoples still live in towns along the upper Rio Grande in New Mexico, in the Hopi villages of northeastern Arizona, and at Zuni, in western New Mexico. The pueblo peoples are noteworthy for their cultural conservatism. They adhere tenaciously to their traditional way of life, which in many respects persists with remarkably little alteration from that reported by the Spaniards four centuries ago. Ceremonial systems are still vigorously functioning, the social structure continues relatively intact, and even much of the material culture persists, although the pueblos have adopted foreign artifacts and technologies of obvious utility. Despite the increasing encroachments of the alien world around them, the Pueblos continue to

● PUEBLO INDIAN AGRICULTURE

The agricultural complex of the Pueblo
Indians, from Hopi and Zuni in the west to
Taos in the northeast and so southward along
the Rio Grande drainage, is deserving of the
highest admiration. It has involved the creation
of an intensive agriculture, a primary
dependence on the maize complex in the face
of an arid desert, an environment offering a
minimum of water and rainfall. It is small
wonder that the Pueblo peoples have come to
focus much of their religious and social activity
on the group efforts to promote fertility and to
bring rain.

Today, as in the past, an individual has
rights to the land he cultivates. Should he
cease to develop it, it reverts to the tightly knit
community and can be assigned to another.
Corn is planted in the vicinity of the Pueblo,
the town which to its inhabitants forms the
veritable center of the world. The arid
conditions demand strategic locating of the
fields, near a flat-topped mesa, perhaps, where
every available bit of moisture may be caught,
or again, where irrigation waters can be
effectively controlled. A special planting
technique is also required, with corn "hills"

spaced at least 6 feet apart, the better for each
plant to thrive. Squashes and beans, the other
major elements in the American maize
complex, may be planted with each cornstalk.

Here, at one of the Rio Grande Pueblos, the
farmer discusses his allotment of water with
the ditch boss, the elected official whose task is
to supervise individual water shares. This
office was introduced to the Pueblos by the
Spanish, along with that of some other secular
officials, a reflection of the integration of some
European elements over the several centuries of
Spanish contact. Hopi and Zuni in the west
never developed these offices and continue to
relegate these functions to members of the
ceremonial hierarchy.

But regardless of internal social and political
organization, the Pueblos are uniform in their
agricultural practices and in the view which
they take of the universal powers which
promote fertility, rain, and human welfare. A
man is not only a farmer; he is a priest and
ritualist, a member of numerous of the
associations which the Pueblo peoples have
developed to further their communal
domination of nature. In the background is
the town itself, a citadel of societal solidarity.

THE SOUTHWEST ■ 271

Acoma (Keresan Pueblo) ● Polychrome water jar (height, 15 inches). Although modern, this piece reflects the general pattern of pottery making so characteristic of the Pueblos. Made by women, the pot is created from coiled clay, then smoothed by a "paddle and anvil" process, painted, and fired. (Courtesy of The Science Museum, St. Paul, Minnesota)

find satisfaction in their rich and complex ceremonial systems, around which the cultures are integrated as functional wholes.

Two main cultural divisions are apparent among the pueblo peoples: Western and Eastern. The Western Pueblo include Zuni (to be described below), the twelve Hopi villages, and the Keresan-speaking towns of Acoma and Laguna in western New Mexico, which in many ways are transitional between the Hopi and Zuni and the Eastern Pueblo Indians. The Eastern, or Rio Grande Pueblo peoples of New Mexico include five Keresan villages (Zia, Santo Domingo, Santa Ana, San Felipe, and Cochití), and a number of pueblos speaking languages of the Tanoan family (Jemez, Taos, Picurís, Sandia, Isleta, San Juan, Santa Clara, San Ildefonso, Tesuque, and Nambé).

These are all that remain of the 80 pueblos inhabited at the time of the Coronado expedition of 1540, 66 of which were in the Rio Grande area. Before the arrival of the Spanish there had been an even greater shrinkage of the number of towns, with the earlier depopulation of literally hundreds of pueblos. Prolonged drought conditions account for this in part; when water supplies fail, people must migrate. Other villages were probably abandoned in consequence of the depredations of such raiders as the Navaho, Apache, Ute, and Comanche. In postcontact times still more towns were deserted after the general pueblo rebellion of 1680 and the subsequent return of the Spaniards.

Despite significant cultural differences between the Eastern and Western peoples, subsistence in both groups formerly depended upon intensive agriculture. Corn is everywhere the main crop in this arid environment, where the rainfall seldom exceeds ten inches a year and where seasonal rains have made the difference between times of plenty and of starvation. The Hopi and Zuni are dry farmers, situating their fields at the mouths of washes to take advantage of the runoff from rains and relying upon subsurface seepage for germination. Along the Rio Grande, irrigated fields are situated in the river bottoms near the villages. In addition to corn, such crops as squash, beans, gourds, cotton, and tobacco are raised, cultivated with simple wooden digging sticks, hoes, and weed cutters. Men do most of the agricultural work, although women may assist at times of planting and harvest. Providently, a portion of each year's crop was stored against the possibility of famine.

Although primarily dependent upon agriculture, the pueblo peoples also formerly did considerable hunting and gathering. Members of special hunting societies in the Rio Grande villages stalked deer and antelope in the mountains, and men of the northern towns of Taos and Picurís sometimes even made trips into the Plains for buffalo. People of all the villages engaged in communal rabbit hunts. The women gathered a variety of wild foods: berries, piñon nuts, and fruits of yucca and cacti, which became of crucial importance in times of famine. The dog and the turkey were the only domesticated animals in pre-Spanish times.

The people lived in compact communities, many of which were built on the tops of steep-sided mesas for defensive purposes. At present few of the multistoried "apartment house" structures survive, but formerly in some villages stone and adobe dwellings, grouped around plazas, rose to heights of several stories in terraced tiers. Ladders provided access to apartments on the upper levels. Most of the pueblos have kivas, or secret ceremonial chambers, often partially underground, where the esoteric rites of the religious fraternities are conducted, and from which the uninitiated are excluded. Kivas are also used as clubs and workshops by the men.

Each pueblo is politically autonomous, a closely knit entity in which the individual is

Eagle Dance ● **At the pueblo of Tesuque, New Mexico. (Arizona Historical Foundation)**

distinctly subordinated to the group, for the sake of community solidarity. Governments are typically "priestly," with the heads of religious societies constituting a council which governs the town. Among the Hopi, one member of the council acts as the village chief, dealing with relations to the outside. Generally, too, there used to be a war chief even though pueblo warfare was primarily defensive in nature.

Among the Western Pueblos, residence is matrilocal, and the matrilineal clan is an important social unit. The women own the crops, houses, and all the furnishings. Clans are either weak or lacking among the Tanoans and are usually replaced by bilocal extended family units. Most of the Rio Grande villages are divided into ceremonial moieties, known as the Squash People and the Turquoise People, or as the Summer People and the Winter People, with all the people of the village belonging to one moiety or the other. The moieties are patrilineal, and the ceremonial activity of the pueblo is divided between them. The Squash moiety is in charge of the summer ceremonials, while those in winter are conducted by the Turquoise moiety. Each moiety has certain kiva societies associated with it. A functionary known as the *cacique*, a term of West Indian origin introduced by the Spanish, is the religious head

of a moiety or a village and is assisted by several society chiefs and other officials. In addition, each of the Rio Grande Pueblos has, under Spanish influence, a governor, who is appointed to serve for one year only, and who also has several assistants.

Pueblo culture is strikingly integrated by the native religion, which permeates all aspects of life. An endless pageant of ceremonials continues throughout the year, especially among the Western peoples, intended to bring the rain and keep the crops growing. Pueblo thought and activity is centered around the religious system, dramatized in the elaborate ceremonials, which blend song, dance, poetry, and mythology. Costumes and paraphernalia are strikingly beautiful. Much imitative magic is practiced in the rites, and sun and rain symbolism are prominent.

Since many of the ceremonies in the annual cycle last for nine days, one is hardly ended before another begins. Preliminary rites are conducted in the kivas, where, under the direction of the priests, members of the religious societies fast, purify themselves, prepare altars, and make offerings of feathered prayer sticks. Some of the ceremonies feature public performances in which masked dancers impersonate the katcina rainmakers, the ancestral spirits. The deep satisfaction which the Pueblo Indians derive from their religion is reflected in their extreme cultural conservatism. They see little

THE SOUTHWEST ■ 273

profit in adopting the distasteful ways of the white man, aside from certain practical technological features.

The Pimans. The Piman branch of the Uto-Aztecan linguistic stock is represented in the Southwest today by the Pima and Papago, peaceful farming tribes of the southern Arizona desert. The Pima and Papago are essentially one people, with only slight cultural distinctions between them as a result of differing environments. They speak the same language with only minor variations between the two tribes. The Pima, known as the River People, number over 8,000 today, and practice agriculture with irrigation along the Gila and Salt rivers. The 12,000 Papagos, or Desert People, live in a more forbidding desert habitat along the Mexican border, to the south of the Pima. The Papago were unable to farm as intensively as the Pima, since their extreme desert country is totally devoid of rivers or permanent streams; hence they were forced to rely more upon hunting and gathering, shifting their residences at different seasons of the year in search of water. Across the international boundary live Mexican Papagos, and the remnants of the Pima Bajo, both now considerably Mexicanized. Several other Piman-speaking groups in Arizona have lost their tribal identity, among them the Sobaipuri, who formerly lived in the valleys of the San Pedro and Santa Cruz Rivers, but fled to the west under Apache attacks, to be absorbed by the Pima and Papago.

It is probable that the Pima and Papago are descendants of the prehistoric Hohokam people, who occupied much the same territory as the present Piman tribes. The Pima culture shows many similarities to that of the Hohokam: the Pima farmed by irrigation, lived in one-room houses, and made pottery similar to Hohokam wares. The Jesuit missionary Father Kino, in the closing years of the seventeenth century, found the Pimans living in much the same localities that they inhabit today. Contacts between the Spaniards and the Pimans were sporadic during the next century and a half, and the Papago in particular remained relatively unknown and almost unvisited. During this period the calm of the easy-going Pimans was frequently shattered when bands of marauding Apache would stream out of the mountains to the east and attack the villages of the peaceful farmers.

During the gold rush to California in 1849, and in later years, white American pioneers toiled through Arizona, following the waters of the Gila through Pima territory. The affable Pimas sold food to the whites and convoyed them through Apache territory, and later served as scouts with the United States Army in the wars against the Apache. By the 1880s Pima culture was disintegrating rapidly as the whites settled the river valleys in increasing numbers. The Pima are at present a thoroughly acculturated tribe, but the more remote Papago have had less contact with the whites, and have retained more of their native culture.

Cultural differences between the Pima and Papago are largely the result of environmental differences, farming being more difficult and uncertain for the Papago in their barren habitat. In consequence, the Papago were more dependent than the Pima upon foods obtained through hunting and gathering. For the Pima, hunting and gathering were merely supplementary to agriculture and became of crucial importance only in times of drought. In extremely dry years, occurring on an average of about every fifth year, Pima crops would fail, and the Pima would be reduced to eating jackrabbits and mesquite beans (Russell, 1908:66). Castetter and Bell have estimated that wild foods constituted more than 75 percent of the total food supply for the Papago. In contrast, wild foods made up no more than 40 percent of the usual diet of the Pima (Castetter and Bell, 1942:57). The Papago relied upon hunting and gathering to a much greater degree, and some villages were totally dependent upon them. Nevertheless, mesquite beans were at all times an important item in the Pima diet, supplemented by screw beans, cholla buds, and the fruit of the saguaro cactus. The Pima also caught fish in the rivers, but fish formed no part of the Papago diet, since there were no permanent watercourses in the Papago country. Inasmuch as the Pima usually obtained an early farm crop in June, their quest for wild foods was less crucial than that of the Papago.

The early Pima dug irrigation ditches with primitive wooden tools, diverting the waters of the rivers to their fields, where they cultivated crops of corn, beans, and squash. Today they also raise wheat and alfalfa, which were acquired from the Spaniards. Irrigation made it possible for the Pima to be sedentary, living in larger villages than the Papago, inhabited probably by several hundred individuals (Hackenberg, 1962:190). The political structure of the Pima villages was also more complex than that

Pima Indians ● Their traditional houses, ki. (Goldwater Collection, Arizona Collection, Hayden Library, Arizona State University, Tempe, Arizona)

of the Papago. The Pima headman had more authority than his Papago counterpart in directing the communal enterprises in irrigation and in protection against alien tribes (Hill, 1936). Pima planting and harvesting were organized on a cooperative basis.

The desert lands of the Papago are in one of the hottest and driest regions in the United States, where subsistence is ever precarious, a land where the water supply is scanty and uncertain, averaging only five inches a year in some districts. The Papago were well adapted to the harsh environmental conditions, yet to stay alive they were obliged to be semi-nomadic, to "follow the water" at different seasons of the year, utilizing to the utmost the rainfall and runoff. Thus they were forced to maintain several residences. In summer they lived in their "field villages," adjacent to the fields used for floodwater farming, but in the winter they were obliged to go to their "well villages," located near springs in the mountains. Water was scarce even in the mountains, and the women often had to make a daily trip of several miles to the spring or waterhole (*tinaja*) to fetch water in pottery *ollas.*

The Papago families usually did not move down to the field villages until after the summer rains had already begun, in order to be sure that drinking water would be available in the depressions which had been dug near the farming villages. The rains are concentrated in July and August, at which time summer cloudbursts may temporarily flood the plains. The Papago store up the runoff in primitive reservoirs called *charcos,* which are natural waterholes along channels where the floodwaters spread. Dikes and ditches are constructed to help impound the floodwaters.

The Papago practice flash-flood farming in the valleys where the washes fan out, where the floodwaters can spread over the ground. In some places ditches are dug to conduct the waters to the fields. Seeds are planted in the moist ground after the first rains. The planter punches holes about four to six inches deep in the damp earth with a simple wooden digging stick, then inserts the corn seeds in the holes. The principal crops in native times were an ancient yellow flour corn, pumpkins, and a kind of bean native to northern Mexico, the tepary bean. Because of the Papago dependence upon tepary beans in lean years, and possibly also upon the wild mesquite beans, other Indians sometimes called them the "Bean People."

The men did most of the agricultural labor, while the women spent their days trudging over the desert collecting a rich variety of wild plant foods. The Papago learned to utilize to the utmost every sort of wild food which the desert provided, including grass seeds, mesquite beans, and cactus fruits.

After the harvest had been dehydrated under the desert sun, and stored to furnish food during the dry months to come, and when the charcos which had supplied drinking water were dry (in late September or October), the Papagos moved to the "well villages" in the mountains to spend the winter. There the men hunted deer, rabbits, bighorn sheep, and peccaries.

In recent years the United States government has improved the water resources of the Papago Reservation by building dams and drilling deep wells near many of the villages, thus making it unnecessary for the Papagos to migrate seasonally to the "well villages." Stock raising, first learned from the Spaniards, and wage work have become important in the Papago economy.

The Pima and Papago formerly lived in round, flat-topped houses thatched with grass and covered with earth, which in shape resembled inverted washbasins. The old dwellings have been superseded by rectangular Mexican-style houses of adobe or wattle and daub. Near the houses are *ramadas* or shades, which are essentially roofs on four posts, without walls, through which the breezes can circulate, and under which the family spends much of its time during the torrid summer months.

Little clothing was needed in the warm southern Arizona desert, and in former days Pima and Papago men wore only a breechclout of cotton or buckskin, and the women wore wraparound skirts of the same materials. Hide sandals were worn on journeys, for protection against the sharp rocks of the desert. At present most of the people wear "store clothes." The men dress in cowboy garb, and the older women wear long cotton dresses and loose blouses, with *rebozos* (shawls) wrapped tightly around their heads.

Basketry and pottery are the principal surviving crafts. Both Pima and Papago formerly made many artifacts of wood and did some weaving in cotton down to the late nineteenth century. Basketry is almost extinct among the Pima, but the Papago women still make many finely woven baskets in the coiling technique as well as some plaited baskets. The Pima formerly made decorated pottery, with some designs in imitation of those on Hohokam potsherds. The Papago still make a decorated ware with black designs on a red background. Large red ollas are used as water containers, which are hung under ramadas, and in consequence of their porosity keep the water cool by evaporation.

The Pima had a fairly strong tribal organization, at least in Spanish times, with a chief for the whole tribe elected by the chiefs of the various villages. The political organization of the Papago, who had no central government, was quite loose and informal. The Papago village units, each consisting of several related villages, were autonomous. These were important in both the economic and the ceremonial life of the Papago. There was a tendency for villages to be composed of related patrilineal extended families, and residence after marriage was patrilocal. The dialect groups, of which there are six, were also important social entities to the Papago, but they had no ceremonial or governmental significance.

The villages were governed by headmen or village chiefs, assisted by councils consisting of all adult males. Leadership depended mainly upon personal qualities rather than upon vested authority. Unanimous agreement was necessary to decide anything in the council, which was dominated by the elders, in whose presence young men were expected to remain silent. The nonindividualistic Papago disapprove of aggressive striving for personal prestige or wealth.

Both tribes were divided into two moieties, called by the Papago the Coyote People and the Buzzard People, but sometimes referred to by the Pima as the Red Ant People and the White Ant People. Both Pima and Papago have patrilineal clans, which are nonexogamous and which seem to have few connections with political or ceremonial functioning.

The native religion of the Pima is little known, since the Pima have long been Christianized, and as long ago as 1900 only fragments of ceremonies were to be found among them. Most of the Papagos, too, are now either Presbyterians or Catholics, but more of the old ceremonies and beliefs persist among them. Papago ceremonial life was primarily concerned with bringing rain and health, featuring curing rites and ceremonies connected with the economic cycle. One of the most important ceremonials of the Papago was the summer rain ceremony, centering around the drinking of a wine made from the fermented juice of the saguaro cactus. The Papago believed that the ritual drunkenness induced a purification of the mind and heart, which would impel the rains to come. The Papago also made ritual pilgrimages to the salt flats along the shores of the Gulf of California, beseeching the rain spirits to follow them home. Both the Pima and Papago held an important harvest festival, the *Viikita*, every four years, at which sacred clowns and masked dancers performed. The principal deities in both tribes were Earthmaker, creator of the world, and I'itoi (Elder Brother), a culture hero. The main ceremonial official in each village is called "Keeper of the Smoke." He lives in a large ceremonial house and cares for the village fetishes.

The Pima suffered considerably for many years from a water shortage when the white men dammed the waters of the Gila River, and many of them were forced to eke out a living cutting mesquite wood. Some of the Pima are now making the necessary adjustments to large-scale, mechanized farming. The economic problems of the Papago are no less severe than those of the Navaho. The reservation land of the Papago is not adequate to support an increasing population, and many of them must leave their homes to work for wages. Thus, the Papago are confronted with problems very similar to those of the Navaho—the enigma of how to adjust to the pressures of increasingly strong acculturative forces, and how to make a living on unproductive, overpopulated lands.

Northern Mexico. Although the southern boundary of the Southwest culture area has never been definitely agreed upon by anthropologists, it has long been recognized that tribes of essentially Southwestern culture extend deep into Mexico. Uto-Aztecan–speaking tribes showing close cultural resemblances to the Pimans of southern Arizona stretch in an almost unbroken series south to about 26° north latitude. Most of these tribes farmed, wherever environmental conditions were suitable, and many of them irrigated. Most of them lived in houses of wattle and daub, raised cotton, and made cotton garments. Physiographically, as well as culturally, northern Mexico is a southern continuation of the Southwest. The region is of particular interest to anthropologists as a probable funnel for the past diffusion of Mesoamerican cultural influences into the southwestern United States.

Except for the Yaqui and Seri, the tribes of the Mexican state of Sonora have now for the most part lost their cultural and ethnic identity. The Mexican Papago, closely related to the Papago of Arizona, are now largely intermixed with village Mexicans. The Opata of the central valleys of Sonora, who were culturally very similar to the Pimans, have now been almost completely assimilated and lost in the general Mexican population. The Pima Bajo, or Nevome, too, are now assimilated. Since the aboriginal cultures are gone, ethnographic infor-

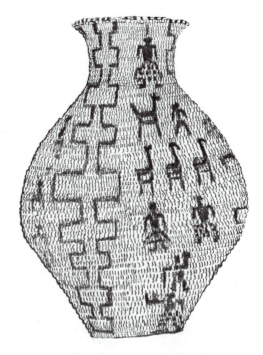

Pima-Papago ● Water basket (height, 26 inches). Modern period. Of the Southwestern peoples, the Pima and their neighbors, the Papago, have developed a basketry specialization. Tightly coiled, such baskets serve quite adequately as containers for water. (Courtesy of The Science Museum, St. Paul Minnesota)

mation on these peoples must of necessity come from Spanish documentary sources.

Along the beaches of the Gulf of California and on the island of Tiburon, to the west of the former Opata territory, are the people known as the Seri (actually the remnants of several bands, whose language may be distantly related to Yuman). The Seri are nonagricultural, depending for their subsistence upon marine products supplemented by hunting and gathering. Kroeber raised the possibility that the Seri may have come across the Gulf of California, noting cultural resemblances of the Seri to the Yumans of Baja California. He pointed out that the environment of the Seri is very similar to that of Baja California, being almost rainless and devoid of perennial streams. Kroeber suggested that the Seri are "a nonfarming element that came in to occupy the coastal desert which was worthless to the surrounding agricultural tribes." (Kroeber, 1939:41).

The Cáhita-speaking tribes, including the Yaqui and Mayo, lived in the lower river valleys and deltas of the Yaqui, Mayo, Fuerte, and Sinaloa rivers, in southern Sonora and northern Sinaloa. The Cáhita are Uto-Aztecans, whose languages and cultures differed only in minor details, although they were divided into a number of politically independent tribes. Beals estimated that the Cáhita numbered between 90,000 and 120,000 although most of the tribes have now either become extinct or been absorbed into the general Mexican population or into the Mayo, of whom many still survive in the valleys of the Mayo and Fuerte rivers. The Cáhita practiced floodwater agriculture in the rich bottomlands along the rivers. Today the Yaqui alone among the tribes of Sonora show the vigorous maintenance of a distinctive cultural life, in the face of the persistent encroachments of Mexican civilization (Spicer, 1954:10).

The Yaqui homeland was along the lower course of the Yaqui River, in southern Sonora, but many Yaqui have been dispersed over Sonora and other Mexican states, and 3000 or 4000 now live in Arizona. The Yaqui have a warlike reputation, earned in a series of uprisings and rebellions against the Spanish and Mexicans, notably under the leadership of a strong personality named Cajeme in the 1880s. Even after they were decisively defeated by Mexican troops in 1886, the Yaqui were not easily pacified, and small bands escaped to strongholds in the Bacatete Mountains, whence they continued to harass the Mexican villages and garrisons. The last serious Yaqui uprising was as recently as 1920.

During the turbulent years many Yaqui fled as refugees to Arizona, where they now live in six villages, including Pascua, near Tucson, and Guadalupe, near Phoenix. Present-day Yaqui culture, in both Sonora and Arizona, represents a fusion of sixteenth-century Spanish culture with the indigenous Yaqui ways. As Spicer says, "Their present culture is as strongly rooted in the militant Christian culture of sixteenth century Spain as in aboriginal traditions. It is this Indian-modifed village culture of an earlier Europe to which the Yaquis cling ..." (Spicer, 1954:10). Yaqui ceremonials are a blend of Spanish Catholicism with native Yaqui rites. They reach a climax during the 40 days of Lent, at which time Yaqui ceremonial societies enact a colorful Easter Passion Play. Of interest is their tradition that Jesus was born and lived in the Yaqui country.

The mountainous, pine-clad country of the Sierra Madre, a southern extension of the Rocky Mountains, lies to the east of the Cáhita,

Pima Bajo, and Opata territories, in the state of Chihuahua. There live some 50,000 Tarahumare Indians, who speak a Uto-Aztecan language closely allied to the Cáhita languages. Culturally, too, they show many similarities to the Cáhita, Opata, and Pima Bajo, but ceremonially their relations seem to be mainly with the south. The Tarahumara live in a region of rugged terrain, inhospitable to farming, but they have made a fine ecological adjustment in adapting the general agricultural methods of Mexican tribes to local conditions.

The southern Sierra Madres were the habitat of a number of Uto-Aztecan tribes, of which the Huichol, Cora, and Tepecano have the best preserved aboriginal cultures. Kroeber would class these tribes as Mexican rather than Southwestern (Kroeber, 1939:127), but Beals includes them in the Greater Southwest (Beals, 1943a). The agriculture of these peoples remained simple because of their stern mountain environment, but the Cora and Huichol developed elaborate ceremonies and handicrafts. The languages of the Tepecano and of the Tepehuane, farther north in the Sierra Madre, are closely related to those of the Pimans. In fact, Whorf classifies Tepecano, Tepehuane, and Piman as one language, with separate dialects (Whorf, 1935:608).

THE ZUNI

Background

Zuni, a sun-drenched village in western New Mexico, is the largest and one of the most representative of the surviving pueblos of the Southwest. Some 5500 conservative Indians still live there, clinging tenaciously to the ancient rituals of their elaborate ceremonial cycle, living much as they did when the Spaniards first entered the Southwest more than four centuries ago. An agricultural people in an arid land, the Zuni rely upon their rituals to bring the blessing of the indispensable rain, as well as the beneficences of health, long life, and fecundity, which in Zuni ideology is dependent upon the maintenance of an orderliness in the universe. Although the Zuni have been exposed to stronger acculturative influences than have their friends the Hopi, and while changes in the sphere of material culture are more apparent at Zuni, the Zuni have nevertheless preserved the core of their culture in a relatively intact configuration, despite all the encroachments of modern civilization. Indeed, a nativistic trend has become more pronounced in recent years.

Zuni is situated 40 miles to the southwest of Gallup, New Mexico, near the Arizona border. The village lies in a fertile valley, rimmed by flat-topped mesas, its brown houses of stone and adobe sprawling along a low hill beside the tiny Zuni River, which wends its sluggish way toward a confluence with the Little Colorado. Three miles to the southeast of the pueblo, towering 1000 feet above the plain and dominating the landscape, is the sacred Corn Mountain (or Thunder Mountain), on which are important Zuni shrines and which has several times in the troubled past provided a refuge for all the people of Zuni. At the time of the Spanish entradas into the Southwest during the sixteenth century there were six Zuni villages, but today the people are concentrated in one large pueblo, with the outlying farming settlements of Nutria, Pescado, Tekapo, and Ojo Caliente inhabited for the most part only in summer. These farming villages have no civil or religious organization of their own, nor are rituals performed in any of them. Most of the people return to Zuni after the harvest for the great ceremonies in December and January, although in recent years a few people have shown a tendency to remain in these outposts all year.

The little Zuni reservation lies in the Datil section of the arid Colorado Plateau Province (Fenneman, 1931:318). The average elevation is 6500 feet above sea level, and the pine-clad Zuni Mountains to the northeast attain an altitude of 9200 feet. Topographically, the land consists of brightly colored sandstone mesas and high, broad valleys, with rugged, forested mountains and precipitous-walled canyons to the northeast. West of the pueblo of Zuni, the land slopes rather abruptly to relatively open rolling country. Although water is not abundant, the Zuni in comparison with the Hopi have a relatively dependable supply. Several creeks flow out of the Zuni Mountains, combining to form the perennial Zuni River, which in dry seasons may become a mere trickle. Summer cloudbursts intermittently turn the river into a briefly raging torrent, and many of the arroyos debouching into the valley also course with water at such times.

Climatically, the keynotes are aridity and marked fluctuations of temperature between seasons, and even daily at certain times of the year. Precipitation, which averages 12.43 inches a year, comes during two seasons: the period of late summer thunder showers from early July to the middle of September, and the time of the light snowfalls between December and March. As a consequence of the high elevation, winters are cold, but not severe, and snow is often on the ground in December and January. Summers are marked by many hot days, with pleasantly cool nights. The sky is normally of a crystalline blue, and there are few days during the year when the sun does not shine. In the spring gusty winds from the west often blow clouds of dust and sand across the Zuni country. The growing season is short, averaging only 156 days, because of frosts which may come as late as the middle of May or as early as the middle of September, but by centuries of careful selection and experimentation the Zuni have produced hardy crops which are well adapted to this limitation.

The Zuni country lies within the Upper Sonoran Life Zone. Pine trees grow in the higher mountains, and cedars, piñons, and junipers appear at the lesser elevations. The flora in the valleys consists of grasses, small cacti, sagebrush, yucca, greasewood, and other plants well adapted to semidesert conditions, with some poplar and cottonwood trees along the watercourses. The native fauna, while varied, is not abundant, save for the ubiquitous rabbits. Formerly, deer and bear were fairly plentiful. A few muskrats, minks, and weasels have been reported for the reservation, and prairie dogs, pack rats, skunks, and coyotes are common.

As compared with other sections of the Southwest, the Zuni area provides a relatively favorable environment for an aboriginal people. The water supply is comparatively adequate and dependable, and the soil in the valleys is fertile and deep. In common with other pueblo peoples, the Zuni have manifested considerable ingenuity in their agricultural methods, enabling them to survive as dry farmers despite the aridity of their habitat, supplementing their diet by hunting and gathering.

Zuni was the first of the Southwestern pueblos to be sighted by Europeans. By 1539 the number of Zuni villages had been reduced to six, including the old pueblo of Hálona, on the site of the present village of Zuni. Gold-hungry Spaniards were tempted by rumors filtering into Mexico of the reputedly large and fabulously wealthy "Seven Cities of Cíbola," somewhere in the vast, unexplored land to the

**The pueblo of Zuni ● Mid-twentieth century.
(Arizona Historical Foundation)**

north. In 1539 the small party of the Franciscan friar Marcos de Niza, an Italian in the service of Spain, headed north in quest of Cíbola, guided by a Barbary Negro, one Esteban (or Estevanico). Esteban, with some Indian companions, preceded the party into what is now New Mexico, reached "Cíbola," where he was killed by the Zuni. Fray Marcos, approaching within sight of Zuni, learned of Esteban's fate. Not daring to continue, he hastily retreated to Mexico. De Niza had seen the golden glow of the setting sun on the roofs of Zuni and returned with a tale of buildings made of gold, which spurred the Spaniards on to further endeavors.

The following year, 1540, the Spanish nobleman Francisco Vasquez de Coronado organized a stronger expedition consisting of several hundred mailed and armored Spanish horsemen, accompanied by Mexican Indian servants. The objective was the conquest of Cíbola. The Spaniards first encountered the Zuni near the mouth of the Zuni River and subsequently entered the Zuni pueblo of Hawikuh, where there was some fighting with the Zuni, who ineffectually shot arrows and threw rocks at the Spaniards from the roofs of their houses. In anticipation of the Spanish attack, the Zuni had already moved their women and children and most of their possessions to the summit of Corn Mountain, to which the men now also retreated. The Spaniards were bitterly disappointed to find no gold in Zuni and continued their quest for riches into the Rio Grande area and ultimately into the Plains, where they likewise met with frustration. In 1542, after two years of fruitless treasure seeking, the Spaniards withdrew to Mexico, leaving the pueblos in peace for an additional four decades.

The Zuni were visited by Chamuscado in 1580, by Espejo in 1583, and by Don Juan de Oñate, the colonizer of New Mexico, in 1598. In 1629 the Franciscans established the first mission among the Zuni, at Hawikuh, but in 1632 the Zuni killed the missionary and fled once again to Corn Mountain, where they remained for three years. In 1643 the Spaniards reestablished missions among the Zuni, with the central mission at Halona. By 1680 the Zuni occupied only three villages. Resentment against the Spaniards was by this time acute among all the pueblos. The Spaniards had harshly exploited the Indians, requisitioned their corn and pastured horses in the corn fields, and had made strenuous efforts to destroy the beloved native religion, thus threatening to upset the entire harmony of the pueblo scheme of things. Resistance on the part of the natives to Spanish demands for labor and female companionship was ruthlessly punished by flogging and hanging, and many Indians were sold into slavery. Tension mounted, and in 1680 the Zuni joined in the general Pueblo Rebellion, engineered by one Popé, a Tewa Indian of the pueblo of San Juan. This was the only time in history that the autonomous pueblo villages, including those of the Hopi and the Rio Grande peoples, acted in unison. The missions were burned, many Spaniards were killed, and the rest were temporarily expelled from the land of the pueblos. The Zuni again withdrew to their stronghold on Corn Mountain, where they lived for twelve years until the Spaniards under de Vargas returned in 1693 to subjugate the pueblo peoples and reestablish control.

The Zuni people at the time of the reconquest were concentrated in a single large village, the present Zuni, where the Spanish built a new mission in 1699. The Indians continued to resist conversion, and after another uprising in 1703, a Spanish garrison was stationed at Zuni for some years.

An understanding of these historical events helps to explain the persistent resistence of the Zuni to Christianization, and their still strong suspicion and distrust of the Mexicans, descendants of the hated Spaniards. The Zuni to this day bar Mexicans from their ceremonies. The American period began in 1846, after the Mexican War. At first the Anglo-Americans were more cordially received by the Zuni, but secretiveness and reaction have increased among the Indians through the years. Missionary influence was never as strong at Zuni as among the Rio Grande Pueblos. Despite strong acculturative pressures during the Spanish-Mexican period (1539–1846) and during the later American period, much of the ancient Zuni culture persists, although with certain important modifications.

Physically, the Zuni are much like the Hopi and a majority of other Pueblo Indians. They have been classed as of the "Southwest Plateau physical type." (Seltzer, 1944:23–27). The Zuni are typically brachycephalic and of a short, stocky build, the men averaging 5 feet 4 inches in stature. In other physical traits they show such generally typical Indian characteristics as wide faces, straight black hair, and reddish-brown skins.

Economy and Technology

The aboriginal Zuni subsistence depended basically upon dry farming, although the diet was supplemented from the available flora and fauna. The principal native crops include six colors of hardy, deep-rooted corn, well suited to arid conditions, plus beans and squash. The Zuni did not raise cotton, but obtained it from the Hopi. Wheat, introduced by the Spaniards, has become important in recent years.

In 1909 the United States government built a dam diverting the waters of one fork of the Zuni River to permit the irrigation of certain fields. This was not the native method, however, and to survive as dry farmers the Zuni were formerly forced to locate their fields at the mouths of sandy washes emerging from the hills, where the crops might benefit from the overflow during the infrequent rains and where they could depend upon seepage for germination. In wresting a living from an inhospitably arid environment, the Zuni developed numerous ingenious agricultural techniques, meticulously utilizing all available sources of water.

Men till the fields and do most of the work in connection with the growing and harvesting of the crops. The work is done cooperatively by all the men of a household, together with their relatives, who cultivate one field together, then move on to another. The fields belong either to matrilineal households or to individual males. A man may farm any strip of land on the reservation, providing it is not already in use. With the help of kinsmen, the Zuni burns over the brush and clears his plot, builds an earthen diversion dam across the arroyo to retain the water and mud brought down by the rains, and then borders or dykes his field in accordance with the natural contours, to conserve the runoff.

The Zuni plant in May, using a digging stick to punch holes in the parched earth, about 6 feet or more apart. In each mound 15 or 20 kernals of corn are placed, 8 to 12 inches deep. The holes are then covered with earth. During the growing season the fields are guarded against birds, and are carefully weeded and tended with a knifelike wooden hoe. A sagebrush windbreak is constructed to protect the crops against strong winds. After the first frost, in late September or October, the crop is harvested. Although the men have done most of the agricultural labor, the crop is considered the collective property of all the women of the Zuni household. The corn is dried in the sun on the roofs of buildings, then stored away in the inner rooms of houses, where a year's supply of corn is kept in reserve against the periodic crop failures. The fields are inherited by the daughters, since it is felt that a man can always clear more land for himself, and it is considered best to keep the land in the matrilineal household. The Zuni maintain, in contrast to the Hopi, that the land was never owned by the clans.

Women own and tend the small, picturesque "waffle gardens," planting onions, tomatoes, and chili peppers in shallow, rectangular depressions separated by raised partitions of soil, which when viewed from above look like waffle squares. An adobe wall is built around the entire garden plot to shelter the crops from destructive winds, and to keep out foraging animals. These garden patches are watered by hand, the women carrying water from the river in pottery ollas. Women also own fruit trees, especially the peach, which was acquired from the Spaniards. Peach trees are owned apart from the land on which they stand, which may belong to someone else.

Hunting and gathering are of slight importance today, although they were of more significance in the past, especially in years of crop failure. The women gather wild fruits, seeds, and roots, and go to the mountains for piñon nuts. Rabbits are hunted in occasional communal drives, mainly for the fun of it. Men and boys beat the brush for rabbits, driving them into the low, open spaces, and then dispatching the animals with bows and arrows or with flat, curved throwing sticks shaped like boomerangs (which are, however, nonreturning). Like many Southwestern Indians, the Zuni have a dread of anything living in the water, and taboo the eating of fish.

The only native domestic animals are the dog, which is not eaten, and the turkey, raised not for meat but for its feathers. Sheepherding is today a major source of income, with cash coming from the sale of wool and lambs. The introduction of sheep by the Spaniards at an early date has resulted in economic concepts alien to the Zuni, introducing a profit motive, one foreign to the aboriginal Zuni economic system. Sheep are individually owned by the men, in contrast to the prevailing pattern of land ownership by the matrilineal household. The sheep are identified by earmarks, and are inherited in the male line. Groups of male kinsmen cooperate in herding their sheep in the more remote parts of the reservation, taking turns in watching them, with each man going out for a month. Older kinsmen will present a young man with sheep, until soon he has a flock of his own. The chief meat of the Zuni to-day is mutton, of which great quantities are consumed at ceremonies.

Zuni foods are varied, including savory meat stews and several varieties of excellent corn bread, in which the women take great pride. Corn, which is considered sacred, is ground into meal on metates and forms the principal ingredient of many dishes. The paper-thin cornmeal bread (*héwe*), resembling the many-colored *piki* bread of the Hopi, is a staple and is baked on gray sandstone slabs. Human urine is an element in its preparation. Parched corn is another favorite food. Meat stews are highly flavored with chili peppers. At meals all the members of the family sit on rolled-up blankets on the stone-paved floor around a big bowl, and dip in with their fingers.

Salt, which has important ceremonial uses, was obtained on annual journeys to a sacred lake, 42 miles to the southeast of Zuni, from which the Zuni also supplied their Hopi congeners.

Zuni was formerly a compact village of multistoried apartment houses of the traditional Pueblo type. The village was intersected by a number of streets or passageways, and some of the buildings rose in tiers or terraces to a height of five stories and were irregularly grouped around plazas. The roof of one story formed the floor of the one next above. Few of the houses, however, had more than two stories. Upper stories were reached by ladders, and some of the rooms were entered by means of ladders descending through hatchways in the roof. Rooms on the upper stories had external doors opening onto the terraces. Doors were so low and small that in many cases it was difficult to squeeze through them. Small windows were, during the Spanish period, covered with semitranslucent slabs of selenite. The houses were constructed of stone masonry, cemented and plastered with adobe mud. Interior doors connected many of the dwelling units, so that it was possible to pass from one to another without ever going outside the communal building.

The men do the heavy construction work, laying the stone foundations, putting up the stone and adobe walls, and placing the huge crossbeams which support the roof, which consists of successive layers of willow boughs, brush, and trampled earth. Women smooth the mud floor, cover both the exterior and interior with brown adobe plaster, and whitewash the inside with burned gypsum. In keeping with the matrilineal and matrilocal system, the houses are owned by the women.

The average Zuni house of today is of one story and is constructed of cut stone and adobe. The Zuni house is larger than those in many of the other pueblos, consisting of 4 or 5 rooms, some of which measure as much as 40 feet in length. Many of the houses now have glass windowpanes, and are equipped with such manufactured items as steel ranges, sewing machines, cooking utensils, and other furniture. Today the roofs of many Zuni houses sport television antennae, and late model automobiles are parked in front of some of the houses.

The ancestral Zuni home contained little furniture, save for a low built-in bench along the wall, and a few small stool-blocks or three-legged stools carved from the trunks of piñon trees. The people slept on blankets and skins spread on the floor, which in some houses was flagged with large, flat stones. A pole suspended from the rafters served as a rack for wearing apparel, robes, and extra blankets, while the more precious religious costumes and ceremonial paraphernalia were carefully wrapped and stored in a dark inner room. Small niches in the walls, formed by filling in a window with a thin wall, served as cupboards. The houses, which are cool in summer, are readily heated in winter by corner fireplaces, large enough to hold three-foot logs. In every house, usually in the living room, there is a three-compartment "milling box" for grinding corn, usually consisting of three slanting stone slabs set side by side, tilted at an angle of 45 degrees, separated and enclosed by other upright slabs of stone. Thus three women can engage in the task of corn grinding simultaneously, using manos or handstones. Outside the houses are picturesque dome-shaped ovens, of Mexican derivation and common to the Pueblo of the Rio Grande. These ovens are made of clay and stone, smoothly plastered over, and as many as twenty loaves of bread at a time can be baked in one of them.

At Zuni there are six kivas, the secret ceremonial chambers in which are held the esoteric rites of the *Katcina* society; the priests go there for "retreats" while seeking purification from profane contamination and to rehearse for the ceremonial performances. Zuni kivas are square, oriented east and west, and unlike the circular kivas of the Rio Grande Pueblo peoples, they are not underground, but are built into the house blocks.

With the exceptions of silverwork and beadwork, Zuni arts and crafts today are either extinct or moribund. Formerly, the Zuni men were expert weavers in both wool and cotton, making women's dresses, kilts, sashes, belts, and a variety of ceremonial garments, but the Zuni now trade with the Hopi for their ceremonial garb. Basketry is also a lost art, but in past times the Zuni made a variety of coarse utility baskets of willow and dogwood, including wicker carrying baskets and winnowing baskets. Plaited baskets were woven from yucca leaves attached to a heavy wooden rim. The Zuni of today purchase baskets from the Hopi and Apache, and at present, only the Hopi among the Pueblo Indians make decorative baskets.

Even Zuni pottery has now almost passed into oblivion. While it may not be considered as having the same high artistic quality as that of the Hopi, it is nevertheless attractive. Shaped in the coiling technique, Zuni pottery is fired by covering it with sheep manure and burning for several hours. It is typically a polychrome ware, with contrasting designs of red and black on a chalky-white slip (*kaolin*). The designs are often bold and startling, with the frequent depiction of mountains, clouds, birds, squash blossoms, and such animals as the deer, antelope, and frog. Characteristically, the lifeline (or "breathline") of the animal is painted in, running from the nose to a quite visible heart. Beadwork, a recent development, since the Zuni had no glass beads before the coming of Europeans, has displaced pottery economically within the last 25 years and has become an important craft for the women. Women and girls sew colored beads on padded rabbits' feet which take the shape of miniature animal heads and tiny dolls. These are sold to traders and have proved popular with the tourists.

Silverwork is today the chief craft among the Zuni, who make more silver jewelry than all the other Pueblo combined. It is not an ancient art with them, but was learned in the 1870s from the Navaho, who in turn had learned it from Mexican silversmiths. Early Zuni silver jewelry was in imitation of simple and massive Navaho models, but in later years it acquired a distinctiveness of its own. Zuni jewelry is often of an intricate and rococo quality and can be identified by rows and clusters of exquisitely tiny turquoise sets in the silver. It is more delicate than the jewelry of the Navaho and includes a great variety of pieces, such as brace-

San Ildefonso Pueblo ● Modern black pottery. Such black ware, as opposed to the traditional polychrome Pueblo pottery, was developed in the twentieth century by the famous artist, Maria, at the Tanoan Pueblo of San Ildefonso. The black sheen is created by special techniques of firing. The pottery is now widely imitated in the Pueblo area. (From the Department of Anthropology collections, University of Minnesota)

lets, squash-blossom necklaces, rings, earrings, bow guards, brooches, and concho belts. Inlay work of turquoise, onyx, and shell is outstanding, two of the favorite designs being Knife-Wing, and the sacred Dragonfly. While silverwork itself is a recent development, the Zuni in prehistoric times made mosaics in turquoise on objects of shell, bone, or wood.

Since the 1920s the commercialization of Zuni silverworking has resulted in a type of economic revolution in the pueblo. Modern tools, introduced by the traders, have facilitated the craft, until today there are numerous silversmiths at Zuni. Few of them devote full time to the craft, but the income from jewelry provides an important monetary supplement to the sale of wheat, sheep, and wool. Silversmithing is a household affair, and there is a smith in practically every family. In recent years a few Zuni women have become silversmiths, and others help their husbands, particularly with the delicate inlay work.

The early costume of the Zuni men was a short cotton kilt. Later, under Spanish influence, they began to wear loose, white cotton trousers, with slits up the side, and white cotton shirts girded with a cotton belt or with a concho belt, a broad leather belt studded with silver disks. The shirts are worn with the tails out. On their feet the men wear well-tanned reddish-brown deerskin moccasins with hard rawhide soles. The hair is cut square in bangs over the eyes and at the sides on the level of the mouth and is tied up with yarn in a single club in back. A

bright silk or cotton band is worn around the head to keep the hair out of the eyes. The Zuni man often wears a silver bow guard on his left wrist, plus necklaces and other miscellaneous items of jewelry.

The *manta*, traditional dress of the Zuni woman, is a knee-length one-piece gown of black, diagonal cloth, embroidered in dark blue at the top and bottom. It is fastened over the right shoulder, leaving the left shoulder bare. A long woven belt or sash is wrapped several times around the waist. This hand-loomed dress is at present worn mainly on ceremonial occasions, when the woman may also wear over her shoulders a white Hopi robe.

More frequently, Zuni women wear full cotton skirts and cotton blouses, with a white apron tied around the waist and an imported flowered shawl covering the head and falling to the hips. On the feet are white, hard-soled buckskin moccasins, above which are wrapped stiff leggings of white doeskin reaching to the knees. Underneath the moccasins are knitted, footless stockings of blue or black woolen yarn. Zuni maidens, like the Hopi girls, formerly wore their hair in immense whorls over each ear, symbolizing the squash blossom, while the older women let their long hair hang in two braids, one over each shoulder. The hairdress of the Zuni women today is very similar to that of the men. Zuni women are also adorned with silver jewelry and often wear Navaho blankets. A woman never goes outdoors without wearing her *piʻtoni*, a square of silk or cloth which is tied in front and hangs across the back and shoulders, lest a man might speak to her disrespectfully; without it she feels naked.

Society

Tribal organization at Zuni is stronger and more cohesive than is that of the Hopi, who manifest a divisive tendency. Hopi villages have tended to split up and form new villages, with each new village politically independent. On the contrary, at Zuni there has been a consolidation and unification into one large pueblo of the people of villages which were formerly separate entities. Zuni may be termed a theocracy, inasmuch as what governmental authority exists is centralized in a council composed of three members of the principal priesthood and the heads of three other priesthoods. The priests pass judgement in cases of witchcraft, make ritual appointments, and initiate the major events in the Zuni ceremonial calendar. The

Bow priesthood acts as an executive arm for the priestly council in matters of crime and warfare. But since the priests are holy men who must never feel anger while fulfilling their duties and who are solely occupied with matters of religion, they are considered too sacred to contaminate themselves by settling mundane disputes. Hence, there is also a secular government, the officers of which are appointed by the priestly council. The secular officers constitute a tribal council composed of a governor, a lieutenant governor, and eight assistants called *tenientes*, whose duties consist in conducting relations with the United States government and other outsiders, settling disputes within the pueblo, and dealing with matters of civil law. Control is still ultimately in the hands of the council of priests, since they may depose the secular officials at any time. The secular offices carry little prestige, and are by no means sought after by the individual Zuni, who tries to evade them as an onerous responsibility rather than a privilege, in accord with the noncompetitive Zuni ethos.

The basic economic and social unit at Zuni, which is the most important in the business of daily living, is the household, an extended family of which the core is the matrilineage, based upon matrilocal residence. The household occupies a single house, in which there are several connecting rooms. When a woman's daughters marry and their husbands come to live with them, additional rooms may be added onto the house if necessary. A woman normally resides for life in the household of her birth. As many as 25 persons may live in a household, which may include a grandmother, her daughters and granddaughters, their husbands and children, together with unmarried brothers and sons. Since descent is matrilineal, and the women comprising a matrilineage own the houses, the husbands are regarded more or less as outsiders in the household, and they continue to regard their real home as in the households of their mothers and sisters, where they also retain ceremonial affiliations.

The men of the household together cultivate the fields belonging to the women of the household, and the crops pass into a collective storehouse, where they are considered the common property of all the women in the household. A man may not even enter the storeroom. Within the household there are no officials and no formal organization which exercises authority. A household owns and cares for certain fet-

ishes, and particular rites are linked with specific households. In ritual matters of the household, again, the husbands are outsiders and return to their natal homes for ritual activities.

The Zuni clan is not quite so strong an institution as that of the Hopi and is actually of less importance in the Zuni social structure than is the household. Today at Zuni there are 13 matrilineal, exogamous, totemically named clans, and other clans have become extinct in the past. Zuni clans have no political functions, lacking both a clan head and a clan council. Despite the totemic names of the clans, there are no food taboos on eating the totem and no belief in descent from the totem. Zuni clans do play a part in marriage regulations and in the allocation of ceremonial offices, and there is a feeling of closeness to one's fellow clan members, whose aid is sought in cooperative enterprises such as housebuilding and harvesting. A link with the ceremonial system is apparent in that each clan has a fetish, which is kept in one of the clan households, and certain ritual activities are performed in connection with the fetish. Some of the larger clans are divided into named subclans, which are not functionally important. A clan is normally composed of several unnamed lineages. Formerly, the clans may have been grouped on a ceremonial basis into phratries associated with the six directions. Whether or not the Zuni ever had moieties is a matter on which the evidence is inconclusive, although there are hints in the mythology of a past dual division.

Life Cycle. Observances in connection with the crisis rites of the life cycle are rather weakly developed at Zuni in comparison with the elaborate rituals associated with the ceremonial calendar. The life crises of birth, puberty, marriage, and death are considered matters of concern to the individual rather than to the community as a whole, and little note is taken of them, in striking contrast to the strongly socialized practices of the communal religion.

At the birth of a child the maternal grandmother assists, after which the paternal grandmother bathes the child in warm yucca-root suds. She then rubs wood ashes moistened with water on the body of the child for purification purposes and prepares a bed of warm sand on which the baby lies beside its mother. A perfect ear of corn is placed beside the infant as a symbol of life and a divided ear beside the mother as a symbol of fertility. The child's ears are pierced, and a small bit of turquoise is placed in each. During an eight-day confinement period there are restrictions on the behavior of both mother and father. On the eighth day after birth the infant is taken out at dawn by the paternal grandfather and presented to the rising sun, the great Sun Father, to the accompaniment of short prayers and the scattering of sacred cornmeal. After the rite, the child is bathed and fastened to a cradle.

The child is not named until later, until after is has shown promise of surviving. The name is bestowed by the father's mother. The Zuni are loath to use their personal names, however, and in address teknonymous and kinship terms are common.

Zuni children are treated with kindness and grow up under little physical restraint. The parents humor them, and rarely resort to physical punishment, but shaming is strongly used as a sanction against nonconformity. The child learns early that he must adjust to the cooperative framework of Zuni society, that he must be polite, gentle, unaggressive, and sober, lest he be called "childish." Unruly children may also be frightened into conformity by threats, rather than by punishment. A fear of owls is instilled in the child. A mother will tell a naughty child that she will call the "bogey" Katcinas to come and eat him or cut off his head or carry him away in a basket. A Zuni mother will say to an unruly child, "I am going to send Su'ukyi to eat you up." (Parsons, 1939:50.) Or she may threaten that a Navaho or a witch will come and get the child.

The grandparents on both sides of the family take an active part in the education of the children, telling stories which inculcate the lore and the values of the tribe.

While the child is yet a toddler, his parents take him to the colorful Katcina dances, where he begins to become absorbed in the ceremonial life of his elders. At the age of nine the boy begins to enter into the economic life of the village by assisting in the herding of his father's sheep, a task in which he delights. Little girls follow the mother about the home, and soon begin to learn the household skills.

True puberty rites are lacking at Zuni, but are in certain respects paralleled by the initiation of the boys into the tribal Katcina cult. The first initiation is held when the boys are between the ages of five and nine, at which time they are whipped by the "scare Katcinas," the punitive masked gods. These carry yucca blades for puri-

ficatory purposes, and perform a rite of exorcism. After that the boys receive names from their ceremonial fathers. The ceremonial father is usually a man of the boy's father's clan and the household of the father's sisters or the husband of a woman who was present at the birth of the boy. The second initiation comes when the boys are between the ages of eleven and fourteen, at which time they are whipped again and learn the previously carefully guarded secret that the masked Katcinas are really men whom they know. The boy at this time becomes a member of the kiva society of his ceremonial father.

No note is taken of the attainment of puberty of a Zuni girl, other than that at the time of her first menstruation she is taken to the house of her paternal aunt, where she spends the day grinding corn while kneeling on heated sand, meanwhile observing certain restrictions. The father's sister then bathes the girl in yucca suds. In contrast to Hopi practice, Zuni girls are not ordinarily initiated into the Katcina society.

Marriage is considered a matter primarily of concern to the bridal couple, and attracts little public attention. There is a minimum of courtship, and the marriage is casually arranged.

Marriage being matrilocal, the groom moves into the bride's household. Marriage within one's own clan is prohibited, and is disapproved within the father's clan. The institutions of the levirate and the sororate are absent among the Zuni.

The Zuni, like the Hopi, are strictly monogamous, but their monogamy has been characterized as "brittle." Divorce may be very simply effected at the will of either party, but since the Zuni deplore quarreling and bickering, most marriages are ostensibly harmonious, and many endure for a lifetime. But if the couple are unhappy together, divorce may be effected simply by a return of the husband to his mother's house. In most cases, however, it is the wife who takes the initiative in divorce. She indicates her wishes by placing her husband's belongings outside the door, and he, strongly conditioned by the culture as to what is proper, accepts dismissal without remonstrance; although he may weep a little, he returns to his mother's household. Often the woman has already selected a new husband, who then moves into her household. The children remain with the mother and are looked after by the new husband.

Death and illness are attributed to witchcraft. The Zuni share the common Southwestern

Hopi ● Katcina effigy. Such katcina representations, or dolls, are still commonly obtainable from the various Pueblos in Arizona and New Mexico. They are models of the masks used by the dancers impersonating the celestials who relate to rain and fertility. This, the so-called Malo katcina, has a black face with red, green, and white overlay. In the actual dance, the mask covers the dancer's head, his body is painted red, and he wears a white kilt with black and red geometric designs on it, the latter symbolizing rain and lightning. In practice, the actual masks are kept in the ceremonial houses, the kivas, and are treated ceremonially, are fed, and given tobacco. (Courtesy of The Science Museum, St. Paul, Minnesota)

dread of the ghosts of the dead, who may try to take the survivors with them. The corpse is buried in the churchyard with its head to the east, by paternal kinsmen, as expeditiously as possible. Funeral rites are simple and as little as possible is made of the death. The surviving husband or wife fasts for four days, during which time the ghost is believed to be hovering about. The mourner takes emetics and scatters black cornmeal for purificatory purposes. On the fourth day after death, if the deceased has been a member of the Katcina society, his soul is believed to depart for the Katcina village under the waters of the Sacred Lake, 65 miles to the southwest of Zuni near St. Johns, Arizona, where it is believed to become one of the "rainmakers." After this four-day interval, further purification of the survivors takes place, and the belongings of the deceased are burned or buried on the river bank.

Religion

The whole of Zuni culture is functionally integrated by the native religion, and there is accordingly a diversified and complex series of ritual organizations interlocking with the governmental, kinship, and household institutions. Basic to Zuni ceremonialism in general is the cult of the ancestors, in which every Zuni participates. On the foundation of this tribal cult, six specialized, esoteric cults have developed, including the cult of the Sun, the cult of the Uwanami ("rainmakers"), the cult of the Katcinas, the cult of the Priests of the Katcinas, the cult of the War Gods, and the cult of the Beast Gods with its twelve medicine societies or curing fraternities. Each of the cults has its priesthood, its fetishes, its places of worship, its own secret rituals, and it observes a calendric cycle of ceremonies in worship of particular supernaturals. As Bunzel has expressed it, "The functions, activities, and personnel of these groups overlap and interweave in a bewildering intricacy that baffles analysis." (Bunzel, 1932a.)

The fundamental cult, that of the ancestors (alacinawe), plays a part in every ceremony and in the worship of all the other cults. The cult of the ancestors is not esoteric; it has no priests, and any individual may approach the ancestors directly. Every Zuni, regardless of other ceremonial affiliations and without regard to age or sex, participates in the cult of the ancestors and prays to the ancestors in general, not merely to his own particular ancestors. In Zuni belief the ancestors, "those who have attained the blessed place of the waters," are beneficent beings who protect, nourish, and guide the living. They are identified with the clouds and rain, and in response to Zuni prayers, they come clothed in rain, bestowing not only the indispensable rain upon this agricultural people, but also such other blessings as health, fecundity, and general well-being. The Zuni accompanies his prayers to the ancestors with offerings of plumed prayer sticks and sacred cornmeal. At each meal a bit of food is cast into the fire for the ancestors, so that the "gone-aways" will know that they are remembered. At nightfall each ceremonial official throws offerings of food into the Zuni River, which carries it to the supernaturals in the Katcina village at the bottom of the Sacred Lake. At the great autumn harvest ceremony dedicated to the ancestors, Grandmothers' Day, large quantities of food are cast into the fire and into the river in honor of the ancients.

The six specialized, esoteric cults have more restricted memberships than does the cult of the ancestors. Each is devoted to the worship of a particular group of supernaturals, and each has a special priesthood. The cult of the Sun is an important and sacred one, since the Sun Father, to whom many people make offerings of sacred cornmeal each morning at sunrise, is considered the source of all life. A priest known as the Pekwin, who is believed to derive his power directly from the Sun Father, presides over the cult of the Sun. He is, according to Bunzel, "the most revered and the most holy man in Zuni" and is "ultimately held responsible for the welfare of the community." (Bunzel, 1932b:512.) The Pekwin, who is always a member of the Dogwood clan, the largest clan at Zuni, is in charge of the ceremonial calendar, and he calculates the dates for the solstice ceremonies on the basis of his observations of the sunrise and sunset. The Pekwin installs new priests, all of whom participate in the ceremonies of the cult of the Sun, and he officiates at all rituals in which the priests of the several cults function jointly.

The cult of the Uwanami, or "rainmakers," water spirits who are believed to inhabit all the waters of the earth, is an extremely complex cult in the charge of twelve priesthoods. The most important priest of the Uwanami cult is the Rain Priest of the North, the Kiakwemosi, who like the Pekwin of the Sun cult is a member of the Dogwood clan. Membership in the Uwanami priesthoods is hereditary in particular matrilineages (Eggan, 1950:205). The rain priests are very holy men who must not engage in quarrels and who hold themselves aloof from worldly affairs, absorbing themselves in the matter of utmost concern to the Zuni, the bringing of rain. These priests conduct no pub-

Hopi ● "Prayer stick." Such short sticks, decorated with eagle feathers and down, sometimes painted, are placed at shrines, springs, and at altars, reflecting a point of contact with the forces of the supernatural. (From the Department of Anthropology collections, University of Minnesota)

lic ceremonies, but undergo a series of "retreats" in certain households in which the sacred fetishes are kept, particularly during the crucial period between July and September, when they perform secret rain-bringing rites. The power of the priests resides in their sacred medicine bundles, which are kept in inner rooms of the priests' houses. During their retreats the priests must sit motionless, fixing their thoughts upon ceremonial things. Associated with the worship of the Uwanami is the plumed water serpent, Kolowisi, who is believed to guard certain springs.

A third and very important cult is that of the Katcinas, the most vital, pervasive, and popular cult at Zuni. This is also a tribal cult, in that all males are initiated into the Katcina society and are required to participate in its ceremonies, and it also has a very few female members, who may be initiated to "save their lives." The

Katcina society has as its officers a Katcina chief, his assistant, and two Bow Priests. The society is organized into six divisions, associated with the six directions (including up and down), each with its own officers and with its own kiva (ceremonial chamber). The priests of the Katcina cult are in charge of all matters concerning the masked dances. Each kiva group dances at least three times during the year. Membership in a kiva group has no connection with clan affiliation, but is determined rather by the sponsorship of a boy at his initiation by his ceremonial father, whose kiva group the boy joins.

In Zuni belief the first Katcinas were children who were lost long ago while fording a stream and were transformed into beautiful and happy beings, now living beneath the surface of the Whispering Waters, the Sacred Lake. The Katcinas are thought, in part, to be the spirits of the dead, since certain of the deceased, members of the Katcina cult, go to join them there, although others of the dead have different destinations. Members of the cult of the Beast Gods, for instance, go to join the latter in their home at the east. The Katcinas are also associated with clouds and with rain, and when they come to dance at Zuni, they bring rain.

The Katcinas, of whom there are more than a hundred, spend their time singing and dancing in their village. They are believed to return to Zuni each year for a series of dances between the summer solstice and November, during which they are impersonated by masked dancers, members of the Katcina society. The elaborate Katcina masks are treated with the utmost reverence and are individually owned. They are made of leather, painted and adorned with feathers, in shape resembling helmets of inverted buckets, covering the entire head and resting on the shoulders. The masks are believed to contain a divine substance and are burned at the death of the owners. When the dancer puts on the mask, he is believed actually to become transformed into the Katcina for the time being. Should a dancer be incontinent during a Katcina dance, it is believed that the mask will stick to his face or choke him. "The mask is the corporeal substance of the god, and in donning it, the wearer, through a miracle akin to the Mass in Roman Catholic ritual, becomes the god." (Bunzel, 1932a:517.) Each Katcina has a distinctive costume, consisting of a cotton kilt and embroidered mantle decorated with spruce boughs and parrot or eagle feathers, and each Katcina has his own peculiar cry.

The cult of the Katcina Priests is closely connected with that of the Katcina society, but is nevertheless distinguishable. The Katcina Priests are concerned primarily with fecundity rather than with the bringing of rain. They are the priests of the supernatural world, the priestly hierarchy that rules the Katcina in their village under the Sacred Lake, and they are also represented by masked impersonators in certain Zuni rites.

For each of the Katcina Priests, there is a sacrosanct mask, which is passed down from generation to generation in certain family lines. Each Katcina Priest is represented as having a distinct personality: the chief among them, Pautiwa, is regarded as epitomizing the qualities most admired by the Zuni (dignity, beauty, kindliness), while his assistant, Kauklo, is officious and bustling. One group of Katcina Priests, the Koyemshi or Mudheads, consists of sacred clowns, corresponding to the Koshare clowns of the Rio Grande villages. The Koyemshi are explained in Zuni mythology as the offspring of an incestuous union between brother and sister. Grotesque in appearance, the Koyemshi indulge in indecorous obscenities and are privileged to mock or satirize anyone or anything. At every ceremony in which they perform they are the center of attention; they are the comedians of the performance. They wear mud-daubed, knobby masks, and their actions are those of muddle-headed people. Nevertheless, their position in the ranks of the gods is high, and they are greatly respected as well as feared. In contrast to the Koyemshi are the dignified Shalako, giant duck-billed couriers of the "rainmakers," the Uwanami.

A fifth cult is that of the War Gods, the Ahayuta, twin children of the Sun, who in mythical times led the Zuni to victory and taught them the rites of war. Like the Hopi, the Zuni are peaceably inclined, but in past years it was necessary for them to defend themselves periodically and to retaliate against marauding enemies, particularly the Navaho. Hence, the cult of the War Gods, presided over by the Bow Priests, once performed important ceremonies. As officers the Bow Priests had a society chief and a battle chief. Membership in the cult was restricted to those who had slain and scalped an enemy, for whom affiliation with the cult became imperative. To escape vengeance from the malevolent magic of the enemy ghost, the slayer must be initiated into the cult at the Scalp Dance. The slayer underwent a retreat in a kiva, sitting silently, abstaining from food, and taking emetics. As a result of the elaborate rites of the Scalp Dance, the enemy scalp was believed to be converted into one of the Zuni rainmaking supernaturals.

The Bow Priests, who have been described as "the defenders and executive arm of the religious hierarchy" (Bunzel, 1932a:526), led in war and protected the village. They also took measures against suspected witches, lest these malevolent persons cause sickness and death among the people.

The cult of the Beast Gods, composed of 12 Medicine Societies or curing fraternities, is open to both men and women. The predatory and rapacious Beast Gods, the most fearsome and violent of Zuni gods, are the patrons of the Medicine Societies. Of them, Bear, who is impersonated in certain ceremonies, is the most powerful. Instead of masks, these dancers pull over their arms the skin of bear paws, with the claws still in place, and they growl ferociously like bears. Each Medicine Society has male officers, and each is in fact an esoteric medical guild, with jealously guarded secrets and rites from which nonmembers are excluded. Each society practices general medicine, but also has a specialty: one cures bullet wounds, another epilepsy, another sore throat, and so on. Membership is obligatory for anyone who has been healed by a Medicine Society, but initiation demands an outlay of goods and may not be completed for many years. Gradually, the members learn the esoteric techniques, like swallowing wooden swords or walking over red hot coals. Each Medicine Society has a highly developed ritual of its own, with elaborate altars, fetishes, and other paraphernalia kept in the house in which the meetings are held. The Medicine Societies conduct public ceremonies in the fall and winter, but not in summer. A point of interest is that the behavior characteristic of the individualized shamans in other areas is translated by the pueblos to group activity.

The Zuni world is pervaded by a sense of human oneness with the universe. Although the Zuni have little interest in cosmology or metaphysical concepts, they conceive of the whole world as animate, as having a spiritual essence. All animals and natural forces, the wind, clouds, trees, night and day, even artifacts such as pots, clothing, and houses are

Hopi ● Gourd rattle (length, 8 inches), with eagle feather decoration, used in ceremonial dances. (From the Department of Anthropology collections, University of Minnesota)

conceived as living and sentient, neither friendly nor hostile to people, since the nondualistic Zuni religion does not conceive of an antithesis between good and evil (Bunzel, 1932b:483). If humans, who are conceived as an integral part of the animate universe, are to receive the blessings of the supernaturals, the parts of the universe must be maintained as a harmonious whole, by prayers, offerings, magical practices, and above all by ceremonies. As Bunzel said, "... the great divinity, the sun, and all the lesser divinities, the katcinas, the rain-makers, the beast gods, the war gods, and the ancients must be reminded that man is dependent upon their generosity; and that they, in turn, derive sustenance and joy from man's companionship." (Bunzel, 1932:488.) Ritual techniques, then, are in essence a request by human beings for supernatural favor. The more personal approaches to the divinities include prayers, purification, mild forms of abstinence, and the offering of plumed prayer sticks and sacred cornmeal. In the collective rituals appear the more mechanistic techniques of dancing in groups with rhythmic movements, singing, incantations and formulae, and imitative magic. In the "retreats" of the priests designed to bring rain, imitative magic is important, water

Hopi ● The Altar of the Antelope Society at Mishongnovi. This altar has been completed by the Antelope Priests in their kiva in this Hopi town. It consists of a sandpainting (drypainting) with figures representing the cardinal points and rain. Prayer sticks in small pottery pedestals surround the figure and a vessel with a corn tassel is put behind it. Water jars, an asperging brush, and a plaque holding corn pollen stand before the altar. In keeping with the patterns of Pueblo Indian religion, the predominant emphases on rain and fertility are sharply defined in this ceremonial assemblage. Only the initiated, members of the Antelope Society, could participate in the making and ceremonials of the kiva. Other societies showed different altar forms, as indeed, do other Pueblos, among whom the religious complex is by no means extinct. (After J. W. Fewkes. 1900. "Tusayan Flute and Snake Ceremonies," Annual Report of the Bureau of American Ethnology, 19:2:966–967. Courtesy of Bureau of American Ethnology, Smithsonian Institution)

is sprinkled in imitation of falling rain, stones are rolled across the floor to simulate thunder, and tobacco smoke is blown, "that the gods may not withhold their misty breath." (Benedict, 1934:55.)

The Zuni, who have been called one of the most thoroughly religious peoples in the world, center much of their thought and endeavor around an elaborate series of rites designed to win divine blessings. Ceremonialism, which pervades and integrates all phases of Zuni life, is more highly developed among the Zuni and other pueblo peoples than among any other Indians north of Mexico. The observances of the cults are coordinated and intermeshed in an extremely complex way, precisely fitted into a complicated ceremonial calendar. Few weeks in the years are devoid of ceremonies. The year is divided into two cycles of six months each, separated by the winter and summer solstices. The summer ceremonies concentrate on the bringing of rain and rich harvests, while the rites of the winter cycle are concerned with fertility, medicine, and war.

Zuni life, then, is oriented around religious observances, which find their prime expression in rituals, of which the most important and spectacular are the masked performances. The prime objective of these is to bring rain and ensure bountiful harvests. Since rain is of supreme importance to this agricultural people, it follows that rain occupies a prominent place in the ceremonials, which must be performed in traditional, specified ways, with all details observed most meticulously, or else the gods will not respond to the Zuni prayers. Each detail is believed to be magically efficacious. Hardly a week passes during the year without some ceremonial observance, some symbolic portrayal of a prayer. The ritual calendar neatly binds all the cults into a synchronized pattern in which there are no conflicting dates even for a man with several cult affiliations. Each cult has rites throughout the annual cycle, from the summer solstice through the winter solstice and back to the summer solstice. The Zuni word for the period of the solstice is *itiwana,* meaning "middle," a name which they also give to their village, which they believe to be the center of the world, just as the solstice is regarded as the center of time.

The most impressive of the Zuni ceremonies is the Shalako, a rite of the Katcina Priests held in early December as a winter solstice festival. This inaugurates the New Year for the Zuni. The season of the Shalako is opened when the Rain Priest of the North gives a string tied in 49 knots to the leader of the Koyemshi or Mudheads, the sacred clowns. Each day a knot is untied, and on the 49th day the string is straight, and the Shalako are due to arrive. The Shalako, wearing fantastic twelve-foot-high wooden masks, appear. They represent the great courier gods of the rainmakers. The Shalako bless the whole village, light new fire, and inspect all the houses which have been constructed during the past year.

The ceremonious Zuni place a high value on inoffensiveness and sobriety. They deplore an authoritative manner and strongly disapprove of aggressiveness and qualities of leadership. A man who manifests such traits is suspect as a witch and would formerly have been hung up from the ceiling by his wrists or thumbs until he confessed. The fear of being accused of witchcraft is a strong sanction enforcing conformity, as is the fear of being talked about or ridiculed. "The worst thing you can call anyone is a witch." (Parsons, 1939:280.)

Individualistic qualities are held in low esteem in the collectivized culture of Zuni, where the maintenance of oneness with the universe is believed to depend upon the subordination of individual ambition for the benefit of the group, lest the supernatural powers look with disfavor upon Zuni and withhold their blessings. Hence, all the complex ritual is designed to bring rain, health, and fertility to the pueblo as a whole; this basic goal is reflected throughout the entirety of the markedly noncompetitive Zuni culture. Such a deeply entrenched, highly integrated ethos as that of Zuni is not likely to succumb quickly to acculturative pressures, which are nevertheless becoming ever stronger. The Zuni, in turn, are obviously strengthening their resistance to the distasteful and disruptive foreign influences.

THE NAVAHO

Background

The Navaho, a proud and independent-spirited people with a composite culture which is still vigorously functioning, number at present more than 140,000 individuals, constituting the largest Indian tribe in the United States. Speaking an Athabascan language of remarkable linguistic purity, closely related to the languages of the Athabascans of the interior of northwestern Canada and Alaska, the Navaho are relative newcomers to the Southwest, having arrived from the north a few centuries ago at an as yet unascertained date. In contrast to the linguistic conservatism, Navaho culture is markedly syncretistic, and the tribe is composed of heterogeneous ethnic elements. Arriving in the Southwest with a simple culture and an economy based upon hunting and gathering, the Navahos were strongly influenced by the sophisticated, sedentary pueblo peoples, from whom they learned to farm and to weave. The pueblos also had a significant influence upon the developing Navaho religious and ceremonial system. In later years, the Navaho acquired livestock from the Spaniards by raiding and trading, and in the nineteenth century they learned silverworking from Mexican smiths.

Despite historical vicissitudes the Navaho have manifested great vitality, having increased to the present 140,000 from a total of no more than 15,000 in 1868. The high rate of increase, more than twice that for the United States as a whole, is estimated at 2.25 percent per annum and is the result of a tremendous birth rate, which offsets an abnormally high death rate, especially among infants and children. The Navaho population explosion continues unabated, resulting in acute economic problems accompanying a ruinous erosion of the land, and precipitating a crisis which the United States government has been making strenuous efforts to alleviate. Despite the economic dilemma, Navaho culture is still viable, retaining its distinctive flavor and maintaining its structural integrity by a complex system of ceremonials or "chants," while at the same time incorporating alien material elements and economic devices. In the world view of the Navaho, the chants are mechanistic techniques for preserving a harmonious wholeness in the cosmos and for restoring health to the individual.

The average Navaho is proud but poverty-stricken, eking out a meager subsistence on the arid, polychromatic plateau of northeastern Arizona and northwestern New Mexico, a magnificently scenic but barren country, a region of sagebrush wastelands and inaccessible buttes and canyons. The Navaho country, much of which is desiccated and badly eroded, comprises an area of nearly 25,000 square miles, mainly in Arizona and New Mexico, but spilling over into southeastern Utah and encompassing nearly 16 million acres. The main reservation is about the size of the state of West Virginia, but not all the Navahos live on it, since many reside on railroad lands, on areas of public domain, and on individual Indian allotments. Three small nonreservation colonies, all in New Mexico, are the following: at Ramah, south of Gallup, near El Morro National Monument and not far from the pueblo of Zuni; at Puertocito, 80 miles southwest of Albuquerque; and at Canyoncito, 40 miles southwest of Albuquerque.

The population density on the Navaho reservation is only 5 persons per square mile, which sounds low, but in view of the unproductive nature of the land, the reservation is actually crowded. More than a million acres are too barren and too inaccessible to be suitable even for grazing. It has been estimated that the reservation can support no more than 35,000 at a minimum subsistence level without the development of new ways of making a living, thus necessitating the resettlement of thousands of Navaho off the reservation. The intense devotion of the Navaho to their scenic homeland, however, makes them extremely reluctant to leave the reservation permanently.

The pastoral Navaho in past decades permitted their increasingly large flocks of sheep to nibble away persistently at the grass cover, thus exposing the topsoil to the gusty winds which sweep across the country. Much of the best topsoil on the reservation was blown away into the Colorado River, where it was carried as silt into Lake Mead, behind Hoover Dam. The forces of erosion scarred the denuded hills and valleys with deep gullies, damaging thousands of acres and threatening the range-land economy of the reservation. The runoff after heavy rains, unchecked by vegetation, rushes down the unprotected slopes in torrents, cutting deep gullies.

Despite its low productivity, the Navaho reservation contains some of the most spectacular scenery found in the United States: rugged mountain ranges, towering flat-topped mesas,

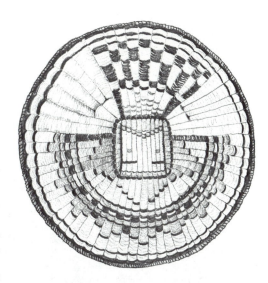

Hopi ● Polychrome basketry plaque. Preoccupation with the realm of the supernatural again appears in so simple a motif as that connected with a basketry geometric design. Such plaques have been used at the Hopi towns to hold the sacred corn pollen. (From the Department of Anthropology collections, University of Minnesota)

high plateaus and deep gorges, wind-carved buttes of many colors, and great expanses of desert sand and gravel plains. Elevations range from 3,500 to 4,500 feet in the river valleys and desert country up to between 8,000 and 10,000 feet in the mountains. Approximately half of the reservation, which is part of the Colorado Plateau, is more than 6,000 feet above sea level. The highest point on the reservation is the sacred Navaho Mountain, looming majestically above the landscape of northwestern Navaholand at a height of 10,416 feet. A range of mountains, the Lukachukai-Tunitcha-Chuska chain, runs in a northwest to southeast direction near the Arizona–New Mexico boundary, separating the eastern and western sections of the reservation. In the north, 14,000 square miles of the reservation drain into the Little Colorado, Puerco, and Colorado rivers.

The climate may best be characterized as arid or semiarid, although precipitation varies from 5 inches annually at the lower elevations to more than 20 inches in the mountains. The threat of drought is an omnipresent reality. Precipitation and temperatures vary greatly with the altitude. Much of the rainfall comes in torrential thunderstorms in late summer, and snow sometimes falls on the higher elevations

● SHALAKO — ZUNI

In the chill December moonlight blanketed spectators stand in rapt attention watching the approach of the towering Shalako, gigantic couriers of the Rain Gods. Behind them rises one of the great communal buildings of Zuni, the "Middle Ant Hill of the World," its dwellings piled up on terraces. Around the tall effigies of the giant birds caper the sacred clowns, the Mudheads or Koyemshi.

The tremendous masks of the Shalako, 10 to 12 feet in height, contrast with the seemingly tiny brown-moccasined feet of the impersonators. Each mask is supported by a slender pole attached to the waist of the dancer. The mask is constructed like a crinoline, with a hoop sewn inside a long cylinder which narrows toward the top. The dancer is able to look out through a hole in the midriff. The heavy white textile material, elaborately embroidered at the bottom, bulges over the hoop. The turquoise-colored cylindrical head of the mask has protruding eyes which roll up and down, long black hair, upward curving horns, and a long tubular beak with which a loud clacking noise is

made. Around the neck is a ruff of raven feathers, while a tall crest of black and white eagle feathers surmounts the head. The dancers are not at all ungainly, moving with bird-like grace despite the bulk of the mask and repeating a single bird call as they swoop and whirl.

The bodies of the little Mudheads are nude save for a kilt of cotton cloth of black. They wear brown moccasins and carry fawn skin bags over their shoulders. Their bodies are daubed with the same pinkish clay with which their knobby masks, also of cotton cloth, are stained. The mask of each of the ten Mudheads is slightly different, but all have gaping mouths, large warts, and bulging doughnut-like eyes. On the tops of their heads are either fleshy nodes or antennae resembling those of a catfish. The uncouth Mudheads cavort about, speaking in a high falsetto or a gruff bass, heckling the spectators. Skipping about, they may play a bean bag game — a kind of tag — and at times they may burlesque the dances.

The Shalako, a winter ceremonial, is a rite also known as the "Coming of the Gods." It is the most impressive of all the Zuni ceremonials. The six Shalako supernaturals come to bless new homes and to promote fecundity. Other members of the Zuni pantheon are also impersonated during the season of the winter solstice. But at Shalako time all the spirits of all the Zuni who ever lived are believed to be present in the pueblo. This festival represents a culmination of a cycle of ritual activities carried on through the cult of the Katcina Priests.

from December through March. However, the sun shines brilliantly in an azure sky approximately 80 percent of the time. The brief growing season is not infrequently blighted by unseasonal frosts. Subzero temperatures are not unusual in winter, and the lower elevations are quite hot in summer. In the spring of the year violent winds often blow up dust storms.

Vegetation differs with the elevation. At the lower altitudes are found such typical desert plants as grasses, cacti, yucca, and sagebrush. At elevations of between 5500 and 6500 feet the sagebrush combines with piñon and juniper trees. In the mountains are splendid forests of yellow pine, as well as oak, aspen, and fir.

Wildlife is varied, but no longer abundant. Forty-seven species of birds have been reported, including hawks, eagles, magpies, bluebirds, and mourning doves. The most numerous mammals are rabbits, prairie dogs, and squirrels. Coyotes, mountain lions, bobcats, foxes, badgers, and skunks are still found on the reservation, but the bear, mule deer, mountain sheep, beaver, and wild turkey are gone, victims not only of the hunters, but of the overgrazing and the erosion cycle, which have affected the subsistence of the wild animals, as well as of the sheep and the Indians.

In summary, the Navaho entered the Southwest with a hunting and gathering economy, learned agricultural methods from the pueblo peoples, and changed to a basically farming subsistence, cultivating fields where they could despite the scanty nature of the water resources. The addition of livestock, particularly sheep, resulted in a further alteration in the nature of the economy, as well as in seasonal shifts of population in search of pasturage. Hunting and gathering declined considerably in importance, as the game was depleted and many of the wild plants were consumed by the livestock. A natural erosion cycle beginning in the 1880s was accelerated by overgrazing, until

artificial conservation measures became imperative. The deterioration of the land and the depletion of the natural resources have necessitated an increasing dependence upon wage work by the Navaho, many of whom now periodically and reluctantly leave the reservation to work at least temporarily in the outside world.

Linguistic analyses have demonstrated a close relationship between the Navaho and Apache languages and those of the Athabascans of the north, indicating that the separation of these peoples is fairly recent. Navahos can actually understand some of the words used by such Athabascans of western Canada as the Sekani, Beaver, and Carrier. Other hints of a northern origin are found in the material culture, social organization, religion, and mythology. The old "forked-stick" hogan or traditional house of the Navaho is much like a former dwelling of the Sekani. The Navaho also possessed sinewbacked bows similar to those of the northern Athabascans, much superior to the simpler bows of the pueblos. Doubtless at the time of their arrival in the Southwest, the Navaho were simple nomads, like the northern Athabascans, with no knowledge of agriculture, and with no domestic animal but the dog.

The precise time of arrival of the Navaho and their linguistic relatives, the Apache, in the Southwest is still shrouded in mysteries which the archeologists have been unable to penetrate, although it is generally conceded that Athabascans have been in the region for at least 400 or 500 years. Some authorities are of the opinion that the Navaho began to drift into the Southwest by about A.D. 1000, or perhaps even earlier, but there is no convincing supportive evidence at present. Athabascans may well have been in the Southwest by about A.D. 1300, at which time the pueblos were abandoning many of their villages, perhaps in part because of pressure from marauding nomads, who may or may not have been Navaho. The earliest Navaho hogan sites thus far dated by the dendrochronological method are in Governador Canyon in north-central New Mexico, yielding dates circa A.D. 1491 to 1541, although it is probable that Navahos were in the Southwest prior to that time. The marginal Anasazi Largo-Gallina Phase in New Mexico, dated between A.D. 1100 and 1250, shows crude settlements with pointed-bottom pottery of a type later made by the Navaho, in association with definitely puebloan wares, raising the interesting

Navaho ● Horseman herding his sheep.
(Arizona Historical Foundation)

speculation that Navaho may have been living among these people. However, this is by no means specific evidence of Navaho occupation, since essentially the same type of pottery was also made by the Ute, Paiute, and Western Apache.

Whether the Navaho and Apache all entered the Southwest at the same period, and whether they all came by the same route, are questions to which we still have no answers. As Evon Z. Vogt expresses it, "As matters now stand, there is not a shred of solid archaeological evidence indicating which of a number of routes the Athabascans may have followed in their migration from Canada to the Southwest nor the time (or times) that the movement occurred." (In Spicer, 1961:285.) A favorable route of migration from Canada would have been along the eastern foothills of the Rocky Mountains. In western and central Colorado ruins resembling hogans have been discovered, some of which are dated as having been built prior to A.D. 1000 (Huscher and Huscher, 1942, 1943), but again it is totally uncertain whether these are Athabascan remains. Another possible but un-

proved route for the southward migrations of the Navaho is through the intermontane region of Utah. The Promontory cultural assemblage discovered in caves in the Salt Lake valley is probably an Athabascan manifestation, but it was probably quite late, dating between A.D. 1600 and 1700.

Navaho history remains obscure until the late 1600s, at which time the heart of the Navaho country was in north-central New Mexico, in a region known to the Navaho as Dinetkah ("Home of the People"). Navaho were already mixing both racially and culturally with other groups of Indians, and their culture was undergoing radical transformations. By 1630 the "Apaches de Navajo," as described in Benavides' report, were practicing agriculture with techniques learned from the pueblos, and were no longer a completely migratory people. The adoption of agriculture was making them at least partially sedentary. They gradually began to imitate the rituals of the pueblos, adopting at as yet unascertained times such pueblo ceremonial features as ceremonial wands, feathered prayer sticks, masked dances, and the use of cornmeal and pollen in their rites. They had probably not yet begun to expand to the more westerly regions which they now occupy, which seem at this period to have been a vast, empty territory.

Benavides' account does not mention livestock or weaving, but both of these are described in the Rabal documents, which were reports to the Spanish Viceroy of Mexico during the period from 1706 to 1743 and which give us our first detailed accounts of the Navaho. At that time the Navaho were living in small, compact communities on the tops of mesas near their fields. It is uncertain from the Spanish accounts whether the Navaho had at this time adopted matrilineal institutions.

The coming of the Spanish conquistadores to the Southwest in the sixteenth century set the stage for further important alterations in Navaho culture. Oñate and his Spanish colonists brought sheep, goats, and cattle to New Mexico in 1598, and soon the Navaho were obtaining these animals, mainly by raiding. The horse increased the scope of their raids, and before long they were harassing Spanish settlements and pueblo villages more intensively. After the general Pueblo rebellion against the Spaniards in 1680 many pueblo Indians from the Rio Grande towns fled to escape Spanish reprisals, and some of them, particularly from the pueblo of Jemez, sought refuge among the Navaho for a number of years, building the "pueblitos" that are found in association with Navaho hogans, especially in the Governador area. Some pueblo Indians intermarried with the Navaho, introducing more of their own arts and crafts, such as the making of painted pottery, and other pueblo traits were incorporated into the Navaho culture pattern, including social and religious concepts such as altars, sandpaintings, the origin myth, and perhaps even certain features of the matrilineal clan system. Some of the present-day Navaho clans originated in groups of pueblo refugees, such as the Sia and Jemez clans.

The Navaho, who were at this period divided into bands under the leadership of local headmen, began to spread out over northwestern New Mexico. By 1750 they had spread as far to the west as Canyon de Chelly, and local cultural differences between the bands were becoming more marked. In the 1700s a number of Hopi, seeking refuge from drought and famine, settled with the Navaho in Canyon de Chelly.

When the United States took possession of the southwestern territories in 1846 after the war with Mexico, the inhabitants were promised protection from marauding Navaho and Apache, who had become a serious threat to the tranquility of the Rio Grande Valley. Military posts were established in Navaho territory, but attempts to halt the raiding through negotiations during the next fifteen years were failures, since the Navaho had no centralized authority, and no autonomous Navaho band felt obligated to observe an agreement made by another band. The white men never understood the autonomous nature of the Navaho bands, and came to regard the Navaho as hopelessly treacherous. The raids increased in intensity while the Army was preoccupied with the Civil War, until in 1863 Colonel Kit Carson, the famous frontiersman, was ordered to subdue the Navaho and the Mescalero Apache and to resettle them at Bosque Redondo along the Pecos River, 180 miles southeast of Santa Fe, where Fort Sumner was established as a headquarters for the garrison. Carson had succeeded in rounding up most of the Mescaleros by midsummer of 1863 and then began to pursue a "scorched earth" policy against the Navaho by systematically destroying their crops and taking their sheep. By early 1864 groups of starving Navaho began to straggle in to Fort Defiance to surrender. Some bands never capitulated, but hid out in the Grand Canyon and other inaccessible places.

Eventually, 8000 Navaho made the "Long Walk" of 300 miles from Fort Defiance to Fort Sumner. There the Indians were to be taught a new way of life, to make them into "civilized" citizens. On this 40-mile-square reservation, a flat, treeless plain in an alien region, the proud, homesick Navaho were held in captivity for 4 years, along with 400 Mescaleros. They underwent many hardships during their detention at Fort Sumner, which had a literally traumatic effect on them and resulted in much bitterness and distrust of the white Americans, a residue of which persists to the present. The only major change in Navaho culture which resulted from their captivity was the elimination of their raiding complex.

In 1868 a treaty was signed with the Navaho which established a reservation for them in northwestern New Mexico and northeastern Arizona, setting aside a total of 3 million acres, which was actually much less than they had occupied prior to their detention. The return to their desolated homeland began and further privations awaited them there. For years they existed on rations before the government managed to circumvent bureaucratic red tape and issue enough tools, seed, and livestock to make them once again self-supporting. Several successive years of drought increased their suffering. Even after the economy began to recover, the Navaho were subjected to additional pressures which increased their bitterness and disillusionment. Many of the early Indian agents were bungling and corrupt politicians. Broken promises and changes of administrative policy in Washington confused the Navaho beyond measure. They were forced to surrender much of their best winter grazing land and finest watering places when the Santa Fe Railroad was built through their territory in the 1880s. White men established towns on the margins of the reservation, bringing disease, discrimination, and drunkenness. At this period the Indians resisted sending their children to school, since they emerged fitted to live neither as white men nor as Indians.

Despite their travails, the Navaho increased notably in numbers, and the reservation was enlarged from time to time, although the additions never kept pace with the population growth. Pastoralism recovered and flourished, until the land began to erode and deteriorate from overgrazing. An absolutely essential livestock reduction program in the 1930s, which required the Navaho to cut down their herds and flocks of horses, sheep, and goats in the interest of long-range conservation, was misunderstood by the Indians, who bitterly resisted what they believed was the government's attempt to arbitrarily confiscate their sheep and destroy their livelihood without giving them any means of making a living in return.

During World War II more than 15,000 Navaho were recruited by railroads and war industries, and 3,500 more served in the Armed Forces. Navaho Marines in the South Pacific developed a code in their own language which the Japanese were never able to crack. After the war, the Navaho were ready for important cultural changes and began to demand better school facilities for their children, most of whom had never spent a day in the classroom.

By 1947 the economic plight of the Navaho had become acute, and the news that they were starving swept the country. Shocked into a belated realization of the severity of the problem, the American public took up collections of food and clothing in cities all over the United States. Congress appropriated money for Navaho relief, and the Red Cross and American Friends Service Committee sent additional aid.

Charity, however, was embarrassing to the proud Navaho, who wanted not relief, but an opportunity to earn a living, to become self-supporting.

Congress, apprised of the plight of the Navaho, voted $88 million in 1950 for Navaho-Hopi rehabilitation. This long-range program provided for roads, wells, irrigation projects, the development of coal and timber resources, and has attempted to develop new sources of livelihood for the Navaho. Schools and health services have been improved; by 1955, for the first time in history, nearly every Navaho child was in school. There had been a great increase in off-reservation employment. Uranium has been discovered in Navaho territory, and oil leases have poured millions of dollars into the tribal coffers. Still, the average income remains at a very low level.

As a result of interbreeding with Mexicans and with other Indians, particularly with pueblo peoples, the Navaho show considerable variability in physical type. Some with short, stocky physiques, are indistinguishable physically from Pueblos. Others are taller, leaner, and bigger boned. In general, Navahos are taller than the pueblos, but shorter than the Pimans and Mohave. Navaho men average 5 feet 6 inches in height, and the women 5 feet 1 inch. Navahos are less inclined to obesity than many Southwest Indians, and the body build may best be described as "medium." Most Navaho are brachycephalic, and many of the skulls show evidence of cradle-board flattening. The Mongoloid eye fold is seen fairly commonly.

Economy and Technology

The basis of the subsistence economy among the Navaho has been agriculture for hundreds of years, since farming techniques were acquired from the Pueblo Indians. Almost every family raises at least some of its food. The principal crops are maize, beans, and squash, and melons are also raised. Fruit trees are popular, particularly the peaches of Canyon de Chelly. These fruits were acquired from the Spaniards, as were the oats and wheat which are important in some areas. Navaho agriculture methods are basically like those of the pueblos, commonly of the dry farming type. Irrigation is practiced to a limited extent in certain areas, but in many places the Navaho farmer relies upon the summer rains for the growth of the crops. Some families even leave the fields untended after the planting, moving elsewhere to pasture the sheep and returning only to harvest the crops. In parts of the reservation, more advanced methods and tools have increased the productivity of the fields.

Livestock have been important in the Navaho economy since Spanish times, but as a result of the stock reduction program of the 1930s, have supplied a decreasing proportion of Navaho income in recent decades. A few prosperous families own a relatively large proportion of the sheep. Many of the sheep are of poor quality and yield relatively little wool, although the government has long been trying to improve the stock. The country, although overgrazed, is very well suited to a pastoral economy and to sheep raising in particular.

Animal husbandry techniques were learned first from the Spanish, later from government stockmen. Sheep are often herded by the children, when they are not in school. The sheep are kept on the move from early morning until sunset, after which they are returned to the corral for the night. Many adults herd sheep on horseback. Goats and a few cattle are also herded, and horses have a prestige value for the Navaho, who have kept too many of them on the range, a practice which has contributed to the overgrazing of the land. Many of the sheep are owned by the women, which gives them a source of prestige and additional income.

Although they are not true nomads, the Navaho still shift their residences at different times of the year, moving their flocks to higher elevations in search of pasturage in summer, then back to the lower altitudes with the onset of colder weather in autumn. Availability of wood and water also play an important part in impelling this seasonal transhumance.

The Navaho place little reliance upon hunting and gathering today, inasmuch as both the wild plants and the game resources of the reservation have been considerably depleted. Their hunting methods resembled those of the Great Basin and included the use of pitfalls, encircling by fire, stalking with disguises, driving game toward hunters in ambush, and the tracking and running down of game. Hunting rituals also were personal shamanistic performances, resembling those of the Great Basin.

At certain seasons of the year cactus fruits and wild greens are eaten and rabbits and prairie dogs are sometimes hunted. Every few years a large harvest of piñon nuts is gathered in some areas and is sold to the traders for commercial outlets.

In recent years income from wages has become increasingly important, supplemented by the sale of silver jewelry and the famed Navaho rugs. Navaho are being drawn more and more into the money and market economy.

Daily life is leisurely, without pressure or haste. Men tend the fields, herd the horses, and haul wood and water, often singing as they go about their work, to keep peace with the supernatural powers, the Holy People. Children tend the grazing flocks of sheep and goats. Women weave the rugs, clean the hogan, and cook the meals of mutton, bread, and coffee, sometimes opening cans of peaches or tomatoes from the trading post.

It is an isolated life, but one with humor and fun, since the Navaho is sociable and is fond of jests and practical jokes. Native games are played, horse races are popular, and the elders relate folktales and myths on the long winter evenings. Families frequently meet their friends at the medicine "sings" and at the trading posts. A trip to the trading post becomes a social occasion, an opportunity to chat with friends, to receive and discuss mail, to trade wool and rugs for the white man's canned goods. The trading post is also, in a sense, a bank, since the Navaho usually invests his surplus cash in silver jewelry, which may be pawned at the trading post in times of economic need.

Navaho dwellings, called "hogans," are low, unpretentious structures of logs and mud which blend into the landscape. The typical hogan of today is a windowless, polysided structure with a blanket-covered door facing east, as prescribed in the mythology. The floor plan is circular, symbolizing the sun. The hogan resembles a low log cabin, the logs of which are gradually built in toward the center to form a dome-shaped crib-work roof. The roof is covered with tamped earth, with an opening about three or four feet square left in the center for a smoke hole. A more ancient type of dwelling, still seen in some parts of the reservation, is the conical "forked-stick" or "pile-stick" hogan, which has a foundation of three upright forked cedar poles locked together at the apex. Additional logs are leaned together over this foundation, and the whole is plastered over with mud and earth. Most families have several hogans, situated in various localities and occupied at different seasons of the year. Some of the more well-to-do Navahos now have stone hogans with glass windows, and others live in frame or stone houses like those of the whites. But in Navaho belief, a ceremonial cannot be conducted in a dwelling other than a hogan.

Within the traditional hogan there is little or no furniture, and the family sleeps on the dirt floor on sheep pelts arranged around the centrally located fire like the spokes of a wheel. Belongings are stored in boxes from the trading post or are hung from poles or cached in crevices between the logs of the hogan. At some distance from the hogan is located the sweat lodge, a smaller replica of the "forked-stick" hogan but without the smokehole. Near the hogan are such auxiliary structures as the brush corral, one or more dugouts for storage, and a brush-covered, flat-topped *ramada* or shade, a roof without walls, beneath which a woman may sometimes be seen weaving at an upright loom. Ramadas are also constructed at the temporary summer camps. Cool and shady, they are well adapted to the hot summer weather.

Navaho informants say that in the early days the people wore scanty clothing made of yucca- and grass-fibers twisted together, much like the attire of the Indians of the Great Basin. The men wore breechclouts, and the women were clad in skirts and sandals. In cold weather both sexes wore rabbitskin blankets. By 1750 the men were dressed in buckskin shirts and breeches, and on occasion they wore cotton pants slit on the outside of the legs. The women at this period wore black woven dresses made by sewing two woolen blankets together, leaving holes for the head and arms. At present Navaho men usually wear blue denim pants, brightly colored shirts, wide-brimmed felt hats, and either work shoes or cowboy boots. Many men wear a colored scarf tied across the forehead. Most Navaho men still wear breechclouts under their trousers. The garb of the women is more colorful, consisting of long, full-flounced skirts of calico or sateen, and bright blouses of plush or velveteen decorated with silver buttons. The hairdress of the long-haired conservative men and of the women is in imitation of that of the pueblos; the hair is drawn up in back in a compact club and tied with yarn. A woman never goes out in public without wearing or carrying her Pendleton blanket, manufactured in Oregon. The Navaho blankets are now only woven for commercial purposes or are used as saddle blankets. On festive occasions both men and women wear as much silver jewelry as they possess or can borrow.

The Navaho first learned to work silver sometime between the years 1853 and 1858, probably from Mexican smiths and using the silver coins of Mexico, although the Navaho made little silver jewelry until after the captivity at Bosque Redondo. Most of the smiths are men, but many of them receive help from their wives. Navaho silverwork went into a temporary decline in artistic excellence as a result of commercial demands for quantity, but attempts to improve the quality in recent years have resulted in a renaissance of the craft. The beautiful silver and turquoise jewelry includes rings, pendants, and bracelets of silver inlaid with turquoise, broad leather concho belts studded with large silver disks, and silver necklaces, often with squash-blossom symbols. As mentioned, the Navaho invests his surplus capital in silver jewelry, hence every trading post has its rack of pawn jewelry, each piece tagged with the owner's name.

The only other Navaho craft of importance at present is weaving, which was learned from the pueblos by A.D. 1700, probably in the Governador area of New Mexico. All the basic technical processes in Navaho weaving are those of the Pueblo, who use the simple upright loom, which can be easily dismantled as the semi-nomadic Navaho practice their seasonal transhumance. Women do the weaving, in contrast to the Pueblo Indians, whose men are the weavers.

According to Navaho mythology, it was the supernatural Spider Woman who taught the Navahos weaving, so formerly, in the center of every blanket, the weaver left a "spider hole" in gratitude. This practice was abandoned when traders refused to buy the "spider hole" blankets.

Weaving became increasingly important among the Navahos between 1700 and 1850, and they began to outstrip their Pueblo mentors as the principal producers of native woven textiles in the Southwest. Early Navaho blankets were simple in design, with patterns of narrow stripes woven in native dyes or natural wool colors. These blankets were traded to other tribes and to Mexicans for use as wearing apparel.

It was from the Mexicans that the weavers learned to use indigo blue and a brilliant red made from the cochineal insects which are found on cactus leaves. The Navahos also procured a colored cloth material called "bayeta" (baize) which they wove into their blankets. Between 1850 and 1875 Navaho blankets reached a peak of excellence, as the women created imaginative and attractive designs in soft, natural colors.

Traders introduced cheap aniline dyes in the 1880s, and for a time the blankets deteriorated badly, as the weavers hastily wove great numbers of sloppily made blankets in gaudy color combinations for the commercial markets. By the end of the nineteenth century the Navaho were weaving only rugs, using brilliant Germantown yarns from Pennsylvania. Today, standards are again higher, and efforts are made to use better wool, improved dyes and patterns, and better spinning and weaving techniques. Many of the patterns are associated with rain and the clouds, with jagged symbols of lightning and square mountains used for borders. Some are ceremonial blankets, depicting ritual dancers. Considering the amount of time and effort necessary to weave a rug, the Navaho woman still receives relatively little monetary return for these high-quality rugs.

The other Navaho arts and crafts are today either extinct or nearly so. True native pottery was a rough cooking ware, typically a tall gray pot with a pointed bottom. Decorated pottery was produced in rather inept imitation of pueblo models for a brief period around 1680 and was made by a few women in some areas until recently. Basketry was never widely practiced as a craft, but the Navaho made a basketry water bottle in the coiling technique, smeared with pitch to make it watertight, similar to those made by the Great Basin Indians. The Navaho now use baskets and pots only for ceremonial purposes and prefer to obtain both their basketry and pottery through trade with other tribes. Many articles of buckskin were also formerly made, but in more recent years the Navaho bartered with the Utes for such objects of leather and hide as they required. They now use the white man's manufactured articles for their everyday needs, showing a lack of emotional resistance to abandoning the laborious native crafts in favor of the serviceable artifacts of the white man.

Although the Navaho have been quite willing to accept changes in their material culture and economic life, they have proved to be much more conservative in their social organization and religious patterns, and in general the traditional Navaho values still prevail.

Society

Society is based upon the bonds of kinship, the importance of which cannot be overstressed. The nuclear family, consisting of husband, wife, and unmarried children, is the basic social unit. Navaho society is both matrilineal and matrilocal; the line of descent is through the mother, and the married couple usually (but not invariably) builds a hogan near the dwelling of the wife's mother. Consequently, the children ordinarily grow up in close association with their matrilineal relatives, and the mother is considered the center of the family. The position of women in Navaho society is unquestionably a very strong and influential one, and they play an important part not only in social and economic life, but also in political and religious affairs. Women control a large share of the property, which is usually inherited by the female descendants, thus keeping it in the matrilineal family line. They have little conception of joint property between husband and wife. A woman may actually have more cash than her husband, since she markets the wool from her sheep and has a ready source of income in weaving. The husband continues to retain ceremonial, economic, and other ties with his mother's family, and he visits frequently at his mother's hogan, where he returns in case of divorce. He is expected to attend ceremonials at his old home and to share in the expense of them.

Members of a larger group of relatives, the extended family, consisting of an older woman and her husband and unmarried children, together with her married daughters and their husbands and unmarried children, usually live in the same general locality, and constitute a functioning group of relatives which cooperates in such tasks as agriculture, house building, and animal husbandry. The "outfit" comprises a wider circle of relatives than the extended family and consists of two or more extended families living in a specific area which regularly cooperate or pool their resources in economic activities and in giving ceremonies. The male head of a prominent family is usually informally considered as the leader of an "outfit," the membership of which varies from 50 to more than 200 persons.

Navaho kinship terminology reflects the matrilineal organization of society and distinguishes specific categories of relatives. The mother's sisters are called "mother," and their children are called by the same terms as are actual biological brothers and sisters. Relatives on the mother's side of the family are in general

●WEAVING—NAVAHO

The hallmark of the modern Navaho, the most
populous of native American tribes today, is
both the manufacture of silver jewelry and of
rugs or blankets. Neither can be regarded as
aboriginal, although the techniques of weaving
are attributed to influences from the Pueblo
Indians, especially the Hopi, whose material,
social, and even ceremonial life left
innumerable imprints on Navaho culture.
Despite such borrowings, however, the Navaho
made of Hopi patterns things which became
distinctively their own. Weaving is an example
of such specialized integration by the Navaho.
While the pueblos continue to weave on the
same types of loom, theirs are simpler designs.
The Navaho have forged imaginatively ahead
to create new and elaborate patterns and have
raised their weaving to the level of a high art.
Women are the weavers, unlike the Hopi with
whom weaving falls to the lot of men. To the
contemporary Navaho, silver jewelry and rugs
provide the main sources of cash, both being
made for trade and sale.

It has been the sheep, a domesticated animal

introduced from the European setting, that has
made Navaho life possible in an essentially
hostile desert environment. But despite the
changes in way of life which a dependence on
livestock implies, the society and ceremonial
system of the Navaho people remains precisely
their own. It proves highly resistant to outside
pressures. The strongly maternal society places
women in a key role in the economy of family
and household. Through her weaving, the
woman makes an important contribution to the
family which surrounds her. Its members in
turn assist the women who weave by
providing the materials and tools, by making
the loom and its associated artifacts, in sheep
shearing, and in the assembling of dyestuffs,
whether from the desert itself or, as today,
from commercial sources. Although weaving
among the Navaho probably developed in the
remote past, it is only in the late nineteenth
century, with intensive herding of sheep, that
rug making came into its own. The techniques
have remained constant, although the styles of
design and color have tended to change. The
earlier, or antique rugs, those made with

threads dyed from local vegetable and mineral materials, are valued collectors' items at present.

Characteristic of Navaho life is a measured rhythm, one stressing the avoidance of excess and calling for a self-effacing and modest character. Virtually all women weave although no woman specializes exclusively on weaving. To do so would be to invite the spiritual disaster which inevitably follows excess activity. Similarly, no design, whether on rug, blanket, or basket, is ever wholly completed. A minor and often scarcely detectable element is left unconnected or undone. The same thought applies to the song and ritual cycles so important in the life of the group, and sometimes to the ceremonial sandpaintings as well. To achieve completeness might work to some degree to the detriment of the artisan or ritualist (cf. Kluckhohn and Leighton, 1946a:225–226).

called by different terms than are corresponding types of relatives on the father's side of the family. In the kinship terminology there are also distinctions between older and younger brothers and sisters. There are prescribed ways of behaving toward different classes of relatives.

Cross cousins, the children of siblings of the opposite sex, are addressed by different kinship terms than are parallel cousins, the children of siblings of the same sex. There is a joking relationship between cross cousins, often of a teasing and sometimes obscene nature. A type of avoidance exists between brothers and sisters, which is characterized by affection and respect, but with speech restrictions and avoidance of physical contact. It is strictly taboo for a Navaho man and his mother-in-law to converse, to meet face-to-face, or to be in the same room together, lest supernatural powers strike them blind. If a man is seen suddenly rushing out of a trading post, the probability is that his mother-in-law has just entered!

The institution of the avunculate is strongly developed, and the maternal uncle accordingly has many obligations and responsibilities to his nephews and nieces. The uncle disciplines and instructs his sister's sons, and may arrange or veto the marriage of his sister's daughters, exercising many functions which are the province of the father in the general American society.

Navaho families are also grouped into 60 or more large matrilineal clans, which bear for the most part the names of localities, suggesting that the clans may at one time have been local

groups. Some clans are named for the alien tribes or peoples from which their ancestors came to the Navaho, such as the Ute, Zuni, Mexican, Jemez, Hopi, and Apache clans. The most important function of the clans today is in regulating marriage, since a Navaho may not marry either into his own clan (i.e., his mother's clan) or into his father's clan. Violation of these exogamic prohibitions is regarded as incest, one of the most repulsive of crimes. This feeling is so strong that clan brothers and sisters may not even dance together. Members of the same clan feel a strong sentimental bond with one another, although they may meet only occasionally, or never if their homes are in widely separated parts of the reservation. Many kinship obligations are connected with the clan system, but there are only traces of political and religious functions among the clans. The clan was traditionally a strong agency of social control, since the Navaho had the concept of collective responsibility, and the clan as a whole was responsible for the deeds or misdeeds of its members.

Formerly, "linked clans" were important. Each clan considered itself especially close to several other clans and observed obligations and marriage restrictions with reference to other clans in the linkage. The linked clans are no longer significant and many of the younger Navaho are not even aware of them.

Navaho political organization has always been characterized by its extreme informality. There was never an indigenous centralized tribal organization, and a tribal or national consciousness is something which is only in the process of developing. The Navaho Tribal Council, consisting of 74 elected members, is now a major decision-making body, controlling important tribal assets, but it has been in existence only since 1923, when it was instituted primarily because of the necessity of dealing with the government of the white men and with economic matters foreign to the traditional Navaho culture. Despite the traditional decentralization of social control, the Navaho call themselves Dinneh, "The People," implying a sense of distinctiveness and an awareness of a certain cultural, linguistic, and territorial unity among themselves as opposed to all outsiders.

Formerly, the Navaho were divided into autonomous bands, each with a definite territory. According to Vogt, by 1846 "political organization had developed to the point that there was apparently both a local band headman or peace *natani*, chosen for life and inducted into office by a ceremony, and one or more war leaders whose choice was entirely dependent upon ritual attainment. To some extent during limited periods of time headmen from several bands may have been controlled by a pre-eminent natani. ..." (In Spicer, 1961:306.) Today there are local groups or "communities," composed of groups of "outfits" occupying specific localities, which have been described as "the largest effective units of social and political cooperation" (McCombe, Vogt, and Kluckhohn, 1951:138), and which in certain respects resemble the bands of the past. Membership in local groups is determined upon the principle of locality rather than that of kinship. Many local groups have elective headmen, individuals who have no coercive powers, but who do have responsibilities, and whose influence depends largely upon personal qualities. Decisions relating to local policy are reached by consensus at public meetings attended by both men and women. The local groups should in no sense be thought of as "towns" or "villages," since the Navaho do not live in compact communities, but rather in sprawling settlements of hogans scattered over a considerable area.

Life Cycle.   Children are greatly desired and are welcomed. No important ceremonial observances attend the birth, at which the mother is usually assisted by a female relative as the midwife. Corn pollen is sprinkled over the head of the infant immediately after it is delivered, and the child is then bathed and swathed in cotton cloth or a woolen blanket. Its ears are pierced for earrings within the first 24 hours. The midwife "shapes" the baby by kneading and molding the various parts of the body, so that they may grow strong and straight. The afterbirth is carefully buried to hide it from witches, who might use it to work contagious magic against the child. Everything which has been stained with blood is burned or buried, or wrapped in a bundle and hidden in the upper branches of a tree. If the baby is puny, it may be rubbed with sage while a medicine man sings over it as a preventive measure.

The infant is almost constantly in close physical contact with the mother, who responds readily to every sign of hunger or discomfort on the part of the child. At about four weeks of age the child is placed on a cradle board, where for a period of months it will spend much of its time tightly swathed in cloth wrappings.

These effectively restrict its movements, except at the time of the daily bath. The mother takes the infant with her wherever she goes, hanging the cradle board on a wall or suspending it from a tree while she goes about her duties. Nursing is never hurried, and the mother gives the child the breast whenever it cries. All Navaho make a great fuss over babies, and indulgent relatives are constantly patting and fondling the child. If another child is born to the mother, weaning may be abrupt, but otherwise it is gradual and protracted.

Toilet training likewise is usually not sudden, and the child experiences few "don'ts" in connection with its biological impulses. Little pressure is put on the child to learn bowel and bladder control before he can talk. Great gentleness and permissiveness is shown the child, who is in general encouraged rather than coerced into "growing up." Adults are very tolerant of temper tantrums and other displays of aggression. The child is permitted to sleep when and where he pleases and to eat what he chooses. The Navaho say, "The baby knows what is best for him." Consequently, the child understands that he is loved and valued, and develops a feeling of self-confidence.

Gradually, the child becomes more responsible, as he begins to learn the expectations and values of the adults. At an early age (six or seven) he begins to perform such tasks as fetching firewood, watering the animals, and helping with the herding of the sheep.

At the time of her first menstruation the Navaho girl undergoes an impressive puberty rite, the *Kinalda,* a four-night ceremonial with an all-night "sing" on the fourth night. During the Kinalda the girl must not eat certain foods and is under other restrictions. Each day she undergoes the "molding ceremony," in which an older woman kneads the girl's body to make her beautiful and shapely like Changing Woman, the favorite figure among the Holy People. The girl grinds a quantity of corn, races to the east each day at dawn, and has her hair ceremonially washed. After the Kinalda is over, the girl is considered eligible for marriage. Puberty observances for boys are simpler and begin at about the time the boy's voice begins to change.

Both boys and girls at some time between the ages of 7 and 13 are initiated into participation in the ceremonial life of the adults on the last night of a Night Way chant. Two masked figures appear, representing Grandfather of the

Monsters and Female Divinity. Each of the boys, naked to the waist, is in turn led out into the firelight, where one of the masked figures places sacred cornmeal on his shoulders, while uttering falsetto cries, and the other impersonator strikes the boy with a bundle of reeds. Finally, these awesome beings remove their masks, and the black mask representing Grandfather of the Monsters is placed over the face of each child in turn. Thus, the children learn that the masked figures are merely impersonators, a secret which they are admonished not to reveal to the uninitiated.

Marriage is regarded as the normal state of affairs by the Navaho, and there are few bachelors or spinsters among them. In fact, a person is not considered a responsible adult until he has married and had children. Formerly, girls married within a year or two after their first menstruation and boys at the age of 17 or 18, but at present most people are a few years older at the time of marriage, due to school and other factors. The initiative in arranging the marriage is usually taken by the boy's father, who discusses the matter with the girl's relatives, particularly her maternal uncle. If the marriage negotiations are successful, a gift, generally of livestock, is made to the girl's family by the family of the groom. The concept of romantic love plays little part in the choice of a bride; the Navaho idea is that one woman is about as good as another, if her health is good and providing she is industrious and competent. Economic considerations are important, as well as the factor of establishing or strengthening the bonds between the two families. The wedding ceremony is held at the hogan of the bride's parents and is attended by the relatives of both young people. The bridal couple eats ceremonially from a new wedding basket of corn mush, after which the wedding guests begin to feast on a repast of mutton and coffee.

Divorce is not difficult and may be accomplished at the will of either party, but often the families of the couple exert pressure to prevent a divorce, since it is regarded as indicative of failure on the part of the individuals and may be injurious to good relations between the two families. Family instability appears to have been quite common in the past. A woman could inform her husband that his presence was no longer desired simply by putting his saddle outside the hogan, whereupon he would return to the home of his mother. If the couple were incompatible, the man also had the right to leave his wife, particularly if she were lazy or disobedient. The Navaho say, "She does not *always* have to obey her husband, but she ought sometimes to get along." (Reichard, 1928:58.) In the case of divorce the wife retains her property and her children.

Some Navaho men still practice polygyny, despite all efforts of the missionaries and the government to eradicate the practice. The joint wives are usually sisters, each of whom occupies a separate hogan with her children.

Death and everything connected with it is frightening and horrible to the Navaho, who have a strong fear of the *chindi* (ghosts), who may return to harm the living, no matter how close or affectionate they were while alive. Every human being is believed to have an evil portion which becomes a dangerous ghost after death. Hence, the Navaho are reluctant to speak of death or the dead. A dying person is removed from a hogan, or if a death should take place in the dwelling, the corpse is removed through a hole broken in the wall to the north, the direction of evil. The hogan is then abandoned and is either burned or henceforth avoided with horror by the living as a "chindi hogan." The corpse is buried as quickly as possible, and all mourners must observe elaborate precautions and undergo purification by bathing and burning incense to avoid contamination. Four days of mourning are observed after the burial. If at all possible, the Navaho try to prevail upon white men to undertake the abhorrent responsibility of burying the dead. In former times captive slaves were forced to bury the corpse, and were then killed at the grave. Burial is usually in a secluded and distant place, such as a rock niche, the opening of which is sealed with rock to prevent the intrusion of wild animals. Many valuable possessions of the deceased, including jewelry, are buried with the corpse, and other belongings are destroyed. The fear of the dead, as Reichard says, amounts to a tribal phobia. The Navaho believe that the worst possible thing that can happen to a person is to come into contact with a corpse, and much of the ceremonialism is intended to exorcise the evil effects of unintentional encounters with the dead (Reichard, 1949:67).

Religion

In Navaho belief there is no concept of a glorious immortality. "As soon as he dies ... he loses his individuality—that which is good in him becomes amalgamated with the great concept of universal harmony; that which was bad, earthly, fleshly is his 'dead part' his 'ghost.' Nothing anyone can do in this life can change this maleficent part of man." (Reichard, 1949:69.) Thus, life on this earth is not considered a preparation for life in the hereafter; this life is what counts. The afterworld is conceived as a shadowy place to the north, somewhat like this earth, but underground, an uninviting realm so that life after death is not considered a desirable thing. Deceased relatives guide the dying to the afterworld on a journey that requires four days. Because of these concepts, the Ghost Dance religion of 1890 was unacceptable to the Navaho. As Hill has expressed it, "The Navaho were frightened out of their wits for fear that the tenets of the movement were true." (Hill, 1944:523.) The last thing the Navaho wanted was for the ghosts of their dead ancestors to return!

All ghosts are thought to be malevolent and are always potential threats, since they may return to seek revenge for any offense or neglect, such as not burying enough property with the corpse. They are believed to appear only after dark, in human form or in the shape of coyotes, owls, whirlwinds, or as formless dark objects. They may chase people or throw dirt on them, or jump on them. Hence, Navaho are afraid to go about alone after dark. The sound of whistling in the dark is attributed to ghosts. Seeing a ghost is an omen of impending disaster. If a Navaho dreams of a ghost or thinks he has seen one, he must have a ceremonial performed for him, lest he or a close relative die.

The Navaho conceive of the universe as a dangerous place, since it is an all-inclusive entity, containing both good and evil. Any disturbance of the universal harmony, causing an imbalance in the cosmos, results in danger and evil and must be ritualistically corrected. Above all, upsets in the universal scheme cause illness or other misfortune.

All sickness and disease, physical or mental, is believed to be due to supernatural causes: an attack by a ghost or a witch, or by one of the Holy People, or in consequence of the breach of some taboo. Hence the cure, to set things right and restore the proper balance, depends upon having a ceremony or chant held for a patient. To determine the cause of the ailment, upon which the choice of the proper chant depends, a rite of divination must first be held.

The diviner, or diagnostician, probably represents a survival from an earlier shamanistic tradition in Navaho culture since he receives his power suddenly, as a "gift," or may even be born with it. Two of the older modes of divination—"star-gazing" and "listening"—are no longer common. The usual method of divination employed today is "hand-trembling." The "hand-trembler," a hired specialist in divination, places corn pollen on the patient's body, then traces a trail with pollen along his own arm, meanwhile reciting a prayer. He goes through this procedure four times (four is a ritual number among the Navaho), then begins to sing a sacred song, gradually passing into a trancelike state. His hand begins to tremble and shake involuntarily, and its movements are then interpreted as indicating the proper chant to be held for the patient, to restore health to the sufferer and equilibrium to the universe.

Diseases are categorized according to the assumed cause, and the chants likewise fall into a number of groupings based upon mythological associations and etiological factors. For instance, Holy Way Chants are indicated for illnesses attributed to natural forces or animals, Life Way Chants are the choice in case of bodily injuries, and Mountain Top Way is the treatment for troubles attributed to contact with bears. Evil Way chants are used in curing "ghost sickness." Other chants are held for illnesses caused by breach of taboos, by lightning, by snakes, or by witchcraft. All of the chants have potentialities for harming rather than helping, if mistakes are made by the participants. The whole system is believed to work mechanically according to fixed rules.

Not only the ghosts of the dead are ever-threatening; witches are also menacing. Witches are malevolent men and women who, operating chiefly at night, may steal property or may use ritual means to cause illness and death. They are believed to rob graves and to practice incest, and some of them, called "Navaho wolves" or "human wolves," are thought to wear the hides of wolves as disguises. A witch may surreptitiously feed his victim "corpse poison," made from powdered human flesh, or he may utter spells over fingernail clippings, a lock of hair, or an article of clothing. He may magically shoot into the victim a small bit of bone. Many individuals are suspected as witches by the Navaho, and occasionally "witch killings" are carried out. Various substances, such as certain plants, are used as protection against witches. If a person is convinced that he is ill because of having been bewitched, he will have the ceremony known as Enemy Way performed for him. If the rite is successful, it is believed to cause the death of the witch before long.

Although the Navaho have adopted many ritual elements from the pueblos, they have altered and rephrased them to fit with their own cultural emphases, with their own basic religion. In contrast to the communal rites of the pueblos, Navaho religion places great stress upon the welfare of the individual. Navaho religion is a type of central control over the supernatural powers, manifested in a great number of religious, magical, and practical observances. The rituals are long and detailed, comprising many acts which must be carried out in a prescribed traditional sequence. Lengthy songs or prayers, sometimes several hundred to a chant, must be sung or recited word-perfectly. An apprentice Singer must master a formidable number of ritualistic procedures.

Fundamental to Navaho religion are the curing chants of which there are more than 50 principal varieties, each with numerous possible variations. The prime emphasis in religion is on curing sickness, and chants are believed to rectify imbalances in the universe and restore health to the individual. The Navaho conceive of the individual as a functioning entity in whom mind and body must be put in harmonious accord with the universe by means of the chants. Thus, as in modern psychosomatic medicine, the mind and body are conceived as intimately connected parts of a whole, and to restore or maintain health the whole person must be treated.

In Navaho belief the universe contains two categories of beings: the Holy People and the Earth Surface People. The Holy People are mysterious, supernatural beings, who have great powers to aid or to harm the ordinary mortals, the Earth Surface People. While the Holy People are always a potential danger they are not all-powerful and are certainly not wholly moral, being capable of either good or evil. They may be manipulated and coerced, as well as supplicated, by the Earth Surface People, by means of performing the proper ceremonial actions. If the ritual observances are successful in consequence of being correctly carried out, they exert a compulsive effect on the Holy People,

thus maintaining or restoring harmony in the universe, between the Earth Surface People and the Holy People, and within the individual human beings.

To the Navaho, the world is a dangerous place, since they are continually threatened not only by ghosts and by witches among the Earth Surface People, but also by the Holy People. The only one of the Holy People who is trustworthy, who is consistently benevolent and well-wishing to the Earth Surface People, is Changing Woman (also known as Turquoise Woman), who seems to be a personification of nature and of the seasons. Changing Woman is the principal figure among the Holy People, and she played a prominent role in the creation of the Earth Surface People, to whom she gave the important gift of maize. She is conceived as eternally young and radiant in beauty, and she now lives in a marvelous dwelling on western waters. Her husband, the Sun, is also prominent among Holy People, and in Navaho religion there is much sun symbolism. The children of Changing Woman and the Sun are the Hero Twins, Monster Slayer and Child of the Waters, who are invoked in almost every Navaho ceremony and who might almost be called the Navaho war gods, since their exploits in slaying monsters in mythological times serve as models for the conduct of Navaho young men. Navaho religion includes also many other groups or categories of Holy People, including the Thunder People, the Wind People, and other personalized natural forces. Animals like Coyote, the Crooked Snake People, and Big Snake Man are another type of Holy People. The Failed-to-Speak People are impersonated by masked dancers at the chants. First Man and First Woman are also Holy People, who are believed to have been transformed from two ears of white and yellow corn. In some myths First Man is portrayed as the creator of the universe; in other versions the creator is a shadowy being called Begochidi.

According to the origin myth, the Holy People at first lived beneath the surface of the earth, gradually making their way through 12 superimposed subterranean worlds. At last, because of a great flood underground, they ascended to the present world through a reed. At this time Changing Woman was born, and natural objects were created. After reaching puberty, Changing Woman was impregnated by the rays of the Sun and by water from a water-

●DRYPAINTING AND CURING—NAVAHO
Although many of the outward forms of
Navaho ceremonial life are direct importations
from the pueblos, they assume a specialized
character when adopted by the Navaho. No
exception is the curing ritual. Although such
features as the painting itself, one made on
clean sand or on buckskin with powdered
mineral or vegetable material, is known to the
pueblos, along with emetics, pollen sprinkling,
ritual blowing of breath, the Navaho curing
complex, the combination of these elements, is
peculiarly their own. The curing procedure is
generally part of a cycle, a series of rites and
ceremonies which may extend over a
considerable period of time. Many so-called
chants exist, all with associated procedures,
drypaintings, paraphernalia, and sometimes,
public dance activity. Details of ritual may vary
with each cycle, the one chosen being pertinent
to the illness and the ability of a family to pay.
The idea in all such curing chants remains
constant, however, that the patient through the
chant is restored to a normal state.

Here the Singers, those with the knowledge

of the curing rituals, are completing a small
drypainting for the benefit of an ailing child.
Although in this instance, the painting is made
in a sheltered place out of doors, a more
elaborate ritual and a more complex painting
might be made in a hogan. As one Singer
completes the drypainting, drawing his colored
materials from small bark vessels nearby,
another holds a gourd rattle, a common
element in a curing ceremony. The Singer at
the left holds tubes through which sacred
breath is blown. When the painting is
completed, the patient will be placed in a
seated position on it. The infusion of
ceremonially prepared herbs will be given him
to drink and the principal Singer will touch
the painting and then the afflicted parts of the
patient's body (see p. 309). The sacred painting
is then to be destroyed, the materials taken
away in the order in which the painting was
made. The process may be repeated; the sacred
number four calls for a fourfold repetition of
the ritual. At the end of the cycle, the patient's
family may walk over the place where the
painting was made, treading where the feet of

the Holy People, the spiritual figures represented in the painting, have themselves trod.

While the religion of the pueblos relates to the concept of fertility, that of the Navaho is directed primarily toward curing, the establishment of a balance between man and the spiritual forces of the universe, one exemplified through health and well-being. The curing act depends not on the activities of the individual practitioner, as, for example, the shaman (see p. 307), but is a communal phenomenon. Not only do the Singers represent a group, but they involve not merely the patient but his family as well and so by indirection the society itself. Curing benefits the patient, it is true, but it also reaches out to promote the well-being of all.

fall, and she gave birth to the Hero Twins, who subsequently journeyed to the house of their father, the Sun, undergoing many adventures and slaying monsters en route. Most of the monsters were killed, but Old Age, Dirt, Poverty, and Hunger survived as eternal enemies of the Earth Surface People. The lava fields in part of the Navaho country are believed to be the dried blood of the monsters.

Finally, the Holy People met at a great conclave, at which they created the Earth Surface People and instructed them in the techniques necessary for living on this earth. In one of their key ceremonials, Blessing Way, the Navahos reenact this meeting of the Holy People.

The great chants of the Navaho are ritual dramas, each of which has its rationale in an accompanying myth, which recounts the origin of the rite and prescribes how it should be conducted. The chants are solemn and complicated religious liturgies, involving the singing of sacred songs and the recitation of artistic religious poems, sometimes several hundred verses in length, which for full effectiveness must be recited word-perfectly by the Singer (hatali). Masked impersonators of the Holy People enact impressive sacred dramas in the light of the fire.

The Singers use elaborate ceremonial paraphernalia, and for most chants there are accompanying drypaintings (sometimes erroneously called sandpaintings), which are sacred pictures of events in the lives of the Holy People. More than 500 different drypaintings are known; each one is traditional for a particular ceremonial. In a ceremonial hogan the Singer and his assis-

tants sift varicolored pulverized vegetable and mineral materials in fine streams through their fingers onto a background of buckskin or clean sand, skillfully portraying mountains, lightning, clouds, rainbows, the elongated figures of the Holy People, and the four sacred plants, corn, squash, beans, and tobacco. Some paintings are very small, only a foot or two in diameter, whereas others are very large, measuring as much as fifteen feet across. Fifteen men, working during most of the day, are needed to make the largest paintings. The beautiful drypaintings must be obliterated before sundown on each day of the ceremony. The materials are swept into a cloth or deerskin and carried away from the hogan and deposited at the foot of trees at the four cardinal points.

When a drypainting is completed, the patient is seated on it in a prescribed fashion, to bring him into direct communion with the Holy People. The Singer has the patient drink an infusion of herbs. After this, the Singer touches the feet of a figure in the drypainting, then touches the feet of the patient, saying, "May his feet be well. His feet restore unto him." (Kluckhohn and Leighton, 1946:154.) The same procedure is repeated for various other parts of the patient's body.

All chants are for purificatory purposes, and all participants must observe sexual and other taboos, also taking emetics, purgatives, and sweat baths. During the rite they must think only good and beautiful thoughts.

Among the great chants of the Navaho are Night Way and Mountain Top Way, of which there are both five- and nine-day forms, and which may be given only in late autumn or early winter, when the snakes are hibernating, and "when the thunder sleeps." In the nine-day forms, the first four days are given over to the purification of the patient by emetics and sweat baths, to the planting of prayer sticks as sacrifices, and to the preparation of ritual equipment. Drypaintings are made on each of the ensuing four days, and the patient is visited and treated by impersonators of the Holy People. The ninth night culminates in a spectacular public performance. That in Night Way is called the Yeibichai, in which masked impersonators sing a hypnotic chant in a weird falsetto and shuffle to the rhythm of rattles all night long. The eerie Fire Dance is held on the final night of Mountain Top Way. A dozen lithe Navaho men, their bodies naked above the waist and painted with white clay, bound into the circle of firelight. They light torches of bundles of shredded cedar bark from the huge bonfire, and then leap around in the darkness, shrieking and beating each other on the backs with their flaming torches.

The chants are important social occasions, which bring great crowds of Navaho together, and which heighten their feeling of social and cultural unity. Chants are often quite expensive, since the Singer and his assistants must be paid, ceremonial equipment must be purchased, and all those present must be fed. Although all members of a family are expected to share in the expense, it may prove quite burdensome in the event of a succession of persistent ailments among family members.

Blessing Way, which reenacts the great meeting of the Holy People in mythological times at which mankind was created, is today the only important Navaho ceremony which is held primarily for preventive and precautionary rather than curing purposes. Blessing Way is intended to ensure health and well-being, to place the Navaho "in tune with the Holy People," "for good hope," as they say. Thus, Blessing Way may be held for an expectant mother, for a young man leaving to enter the Army, or for Navaho going off the reservation to work for wages. Songs from Blessing Way are also sung at marriage ceremonies and at the girl's puberty rite.

Enemy Way formerly had as its purpose the protection of warriors from "ghost sickness," which was believed to result from contamination due to contact with the enemy or with foreigners in general. In recent years it has been held for returning service men, and for others who have been closely associated with white people. The Squaw Dance, originally a part of the Enemy Way chant, has now become an important social entertainment on the reservation, and it serves as a type of "coming-out party," to present eligible maidens to the Navaho bachelors. Girls take the initiative in selecting their partners, tugging at the clothing of the chosen men. If a man wishes to decline or to cease dancing, he must pay the girl a coin, which she adds to her dowry.

Religion to the Navaho is not distinct and separate from mundane life, nor are religious observances reserved for ceremonial occasions. The supernatural powers are conceived as ever present and ever threatening; hence, ritual is integrated and interwoven with all phases of daily life, and the observance of taboos and the performance of positive actions is believed essential to the maintenance of harmony in the universe. Thus, nearly every act of daily life contains ritual elements; for instance, singing is important in keeping one's peace with the Holy People, so the Navaho sings as he lets the sheep out of the corral, he sings as he rides, and the Navaho woman sings as she weaves. Songs from Blessing Way are sung upon rising in the morning and when retiring at night. Minor rituals are performed to assure safe journeys, and in connection with agriculture, hunting, and house building.

In recent years pressures from the outside world have become stronger, resulting in increasing anxiety and personal disorganization in individual Navahos, who find themselves in a confusing and disturbing position "between two worlds." The old techniques for manipulating the Holy People and maintaining the equilibrium of the universe seem ineffective in coping with current economic pressures and with the encroaching world of the Whites. The Navaho clings to his native religion and view of life, but has been forced to make concessions to the disrupting forces. A shift from a pastoral to a wage economy is in progress, and many Navahos must leave the reservation to seek employment. The Navaho's emotional roots in his scenic homeland are deep, however, and he always wants to return to the land of the Navaho. Thus, while their culture persists in its ideological essentials, the Navaho are today a people in transition, and it may be anticipated that the native culture will slowly but inexorably undergo further changes.

Suggested readings

ABERLE, D. F.
1966 *The Peyote Religion Among the Navaho.* Chicago: Aldine.

ADAIR, J.
1944 *The Navajo and Pueblo Silversmiths.* University of Oklahoma Press.

BASSO, K. H., and OPLER, M. E.
1971 *Apachean Culture History and Ethnology.* Anthropological Papers of the University of Arizona, 21.

BEALS, R. L.
1945 *The Contemporary Culture of the Cahita Indians.* Bureau of American Ethnology, Bulletin 142.

BENNETT, W. C., and ZINGG, R. M.

1935   *The Tarahumara: An Inland Tribe of Northern Mexico*. University of Chicago Press.

BUNZEL, R. L.

1932   "An Introduction to Zuni Ceremonialism." *Annual Report of the Bureau of American Ethnology* 47:467–544.

DOZIER, E. P.

1970   *The Pueblo Indians of North America*. New York: Holt, Rinehart and Winston.

EGGAN, F.

1950   *Social Organization of the Western Pueblos*. University of Chicago Press.

GOODWIN, G.

1942   *The Social Organization of the Western Apache*. University of Chicago Press.

KLUCKHOHN, C.

1944   *Navaho Witchcraft*. Papers of the Peabody Museum, no. 22.

KLUCKHOHN, C., and LEIGHTON, D. C.

1946   *The Navaho*. Cambridge: Harvard University Press.

LANGE, C. H.

1959   *Cochiti*. University of Texas Press.

LEIGHTON, D. C., and ADAIR, J.

1966   *People of the Middle Place: A Study of the Zuni Indians*. New Haven: Human Relations Area Files.

OPLER, M. E.

1941   *An Apache Life-Way*. University of Chicago Press.

ORTIZ, A.

1969   *The Tewa World*. University of Chicago Press.

1972   ed. *New Perspectives on the Pueblos*. University of New Mexico Press.

PARSONS, E. C.

1939   *Pueblo Indian Religion*. 2 vols. University of Chicago Press.

REICHARD, G. A.

1950   *Navaho Indian Religion: A Study of Symbolism*. 2 vols. New York: Pantheon Books.

SPICER, E. H.

1954   *Potam: A Yaqui Village in Sonora*. American Anthropological Association, Memoir 77.

1962   *Cycles of Conquest*. University of Arizona Press.

SPIER, L.

1933   *Yuman Tribes of the Gila River*. University of Chicago Press.

1928   "Havasupai Ethnography." *American Museum of Natural History, Anthropological Papers* 29:81–392.

THOMPSON, L., and JOSEPH, A.

1945   *The Hopi Way*. University of Chicago Press.

TITIEV, M.

1944   "Old Oraibi." *Peabody Museum Papers* 22:1–277.

UNDERHILL, R. M.

1946   *Papago Indian Religion*. New York: Columbia University Press.

WHITE, L. A.

1962   *The Pueblo of Sia, New Mexico*. Bureau of American Ethnology, Bulletin 184.

1935   *The Pueblo of Santo Domingo*. American Anthropological Association, Memoir 43.

VII

The Great Plains

Introduction

Sioux, Cheyenne, Comanche, Kiowa are names well known to the first European traders and trappers on the great plains of North America and equally well known today. These and other Indian tribes of the Plains produced a culture that changed dramatically after the arrival of the horse on the grasslands and culminated in the nineteenth century nomadic bison-hunting societies described here. Just as much at home on the Plains were a second group of peoples, perhaps less well known today but equally important in the functioning Plains culture of the eighteenth and nineteenth centuries. These were the sedentary farming peoples like the Mandan, Hidatsa, Omaha, Kansa, Missouri, and others who occupied the timbered Missouri River valley and some of its major tributaries on the eastern Plains. Both the nomadic bison hunters and the sedentary village farmers shared a vast number of culture traits, and both groups are Plains Indians. The variation in their subsistence systems is reflected in significant differences in settlement pattern and social structure, but the dynamics of change of each group toward a cultural adaptation to grassland and horse is one of the remarkable episodes in human culture history.

The Land

The geographic area encompassed by the North American Plains includes the heartland of North America. This vast area stretches as an unbroken grassland from northern Alberta and Saskatchewan in Canada to the Rio Grande border of Texas. Its distinct western margin lies along the foothills of the Rocky Mountain chain while the less distinct eastern boundary follows longitude 97° west. Physiographically, the Plains area is a uniformly elevated steppe, though there are local variations seen in the Black Hills of South Dakota, the flat lake bed of the Red River Valley of the North, or the Wichita Mountains of Oklahoma. There is a general rise in elevation from east to west, and the more elevated western half of the Plains shows much more desiccation and erosion than the gently rolling eastern portion. The area is dominated by the Missouri-Mississippi river drainage system, flowing from west to east across the northern Plains and thence southward along the eastern Plains margin to the Gulf of Mexico. Tributary streams feed this major drainage system by crossing the Plains from west to east bringing waters from the eastern slopes of the Rockies.

The Plains area is dominated by a continental climate having a wide seasonal range in temperature. The winter months of December through mid-March may exhibit temperatures considerably below zero Fahrenheit, though the temperature severity increases from south to north. The summer months from June through August may exhibit equally severe high temperatures. It is not unknown for temperatures to reach as high as 110° F. The spring months of mid-March through May and the fall months of September through November are transitional climatically. Moisture patterns on the Plains are dominated by warm Gulf air masses moving up from the south and southwest meeting dry Arctic continental air masses from the north. Moisture is fairly equally distributed throughout the year, but there are peaks in late fall and spring months. From an average of 15 inches of moisture per year in the western Plains, the annual moisture increment increases toward the eastern margins of the Plains to approximately 25 or 30 inches. Cold winter temperatures allow accumulations of snow which, when combined with frequent rapid melting in the early spring, sometimes cause major flooding. Cyclonic storms in the summer months are also quite common, though they decrease in frequency, but not intensity, from south to north.

The moisture pattern strongly influences the vegetation areas of the Plains, particularly in the southeastern Plains where the so-called tall-grass prairies merge into a deciduous forest on the margins of the southern Plains. In the central Plains, the tall-grass savannah extends eastward as a tongue across northern Missouri, Iowa, and southern Minnesota, into Illinois and Indiana. The western Plains are generally termed a "short-grass" vegetation area in contrast to the eastern Plains. As the aridity increases from east to west, the presence of many forms of cactus, yucca, and sagebrush can be noted. The flanks of eroded buttes and mesas of the western Plains are often forested with scrub cedar and juniper trees, and the Rocky Mountain foothills have both deciduous and coniferous timber.

The grassland of the Plains, where it is crossed by major west-to-east flowing streams, is penetrated by fingers of the eastern deciduous forests which follow these watercourses. The alluvial valleys of these streams are timbered with oak and elm in the east; oak, box elder, and cottonwood further west. Smaller shrubs are also found in the bottom lands and in interior ravines and coulees. Willow is a frequent floodplain plant. Vegetable foods occurring naturally include wild plum, chokecherry, buffalo berry, and several tuberous wild plants. The northeastern Plains bordering the glacial-lake area of Minnesota also has limited amounts of wild rice in the slower moving streams and lakes.

Animal life on the Plains was dominated by the bison, a nomadic, grazing, herd animal which aboriginally occurred in tremendous numbers. This animal, as will be seen, was a primary source of food and was equally important as a source of raw materials for clothing, shelter, and tools. Another grazing animal, the antelope, was important in the northwestern Plains, and browsing animals such as deer and elk which lived in the timbered river bottom lands, also contributed to the aboriginal economy. Badgers, coyote, brush wolf, grizzly bear, and other carnivores were found, and numerous rodents, such as rabbits, squirrels, prairie dogs, and others abound and were sometimes utilized for food.

Bird life on the prairies is specialized and includes some species which were used for food. Varieties of native grouse, particularly the prairie chicken and sharp-tailed grouse, were abundant in some areas. Migratory waterfowl in the northern and central Plains were present in large numbers seasonally. Varieties of hawks and eagles are also found, and though they were not used as sources of food, they were important as sources of feathers for decorative and ceremonial use. The rivers provided a source of fish, though most of the rivers are slow moving and silt laden, and most of the fish would be classified today as "rough fish."

It is within this distinctive and specialized ecologic area that the Mandan, the Teton Dakota, and the Kiowa, together with the other Plains Indian tribes, developed two distinctive ways of life, both adjusted to the environment. Traditionally, the Teton Dakota and the Kiowa are classed with the "typical" Plains tribes which had been described by Clark Wissler (1917, 1938). A more satisfactory phrase might be "nomadic Plains" tribes, for this is exactly what the Teton and the culturally similar tribes of the high Plains were. The Teton and Kiowa had, by 1850, developed a highly specialized way of life centered on two animals: the domesticated horse, introduced into the Plains in the seventeenth century, and the bison, native to the Plains. The horse, as it became available in large numbers, provided the mobility necessary to sustain large numbers of people whose existence depended on procuring quantities of bison from the large nomadic herds. Around this horse-bison complex, the nomadic tribes of the Plains geared their whole society and culture so that their patterns of warfare, the organization of their society, their religion, and their understanding of the world about them reflected their daily concern with these two animals. The nomadic way of life, in its climactic form on the Plains in the nineteenth century, was then a development dependent upon European contact and the arrival of the horse. This does not mean that nomadism of the Plains is entirely post-European, for bison formed one of the staple foods for the very early post-Pleistocene hunters of the high Plains, and it is known that similar small bands of wandering hunters continued these hunting practices on the western and southern Plains throughout the prehistoric period. Archeological and historic evidence also indicates that bison hunting, utilizing many of the techniques followed later by the nomadic Plains tribes, was practiced in the Eastern Prairie area. The developed Plains nomadism of the historic period is unique, however, despite the fact that it draws upon prehistoric cultural antecedents, for it reaches its climax only after European contacts and the introduction of the horse.

Languages and Tribes

The nomadic and sedentary tribes of the Plains speak languages representative of several linguistic families. None of these language families exhibits a distribution limited to the Plains area but they are distributed to the east, west, and north, a fact which indicates the eclectic origins of Plains culture. Both the Mandan and the Teton Dakota speak Siouan languages, but the languages are not mutually intelligible. Only among recently separated tribes such as the Crow-Hidatsa and the Atsina-Arapaho, or among such very closely related tribes as the Yanktonai and Teton Dakota can members of different tribes converse with one another, albeit with some difficulty. For all others, membership in a common language family indicates a genetic relationship linguistically but does not imply a mutual intelligibility of the languages.

In this fluid and mobile area where intra-

tribal contacts were numerous, and where communication between groups was vital at times, the welter of distinct languages was a formidable handicap. A hand "sign" language which developed in the area partially overcame this serious obstacle. Utilizing fixed hand and finger positions as symbols of ideas, known and accepted by the majority of Plains Indians, this sign language was in no sense a method of spelling out a particular language. As Wissler remarked, it is a purely arbitrary system (Wissler, 1927:142). The origins of this sign language are obscure, but limited though it was, it was a system of communication contributing to the exchange of ideas and information among these peoples.

The table of languages below groups tribes according to their dominant mode of subsistence, listing them roughly by their geographic distribution from north to south. (See also Chapter II.)

Language family	Nomadic tribes	Sedentary tribes
Algonkin	Plains Cree	
	Blackfoot	
	(Blackfoot,	
	Blood,	
	Piegan)	
	Plains Ojibwa	
	Atsina (Gros	
	Ventre)	
	Cheyenne	
	(Northern,	
	Southern,	
	Sutai)	
	Arapaho	
Athabascan	Sarsi	
	Kiowa-Apache	
		Arikara,
Caddoan	Pawnee	Pawnee,
		Wichita
Kiowan	Kiowa	
	Northern	
Shoshonean	Shoshone	
(Numic)	Wind River	
	Shoshone	
	Comanche	
		Mandan,
	Assiniboine	Hidatsa,
	Crow	Ponca,
	Dakota	Omaha,
Siouan	(Teton,	Iowa,
	Yanktonai,	Oto,
	Yankton,	Missouri,
	Sisseton)	Kansa,
		Osage,

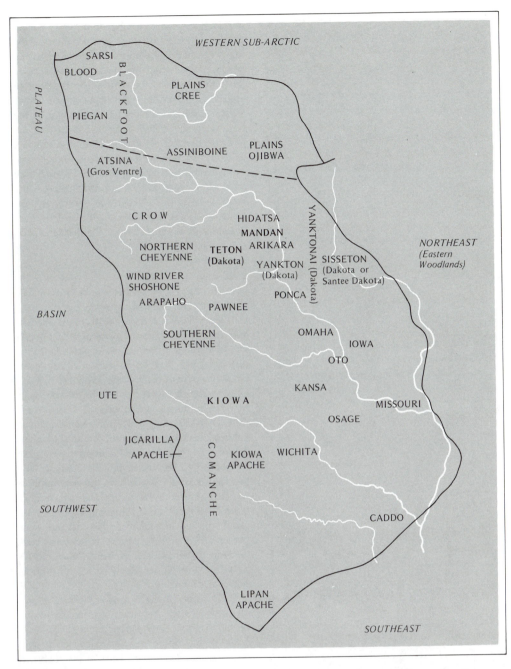

WESTERN SUB-ARCTIC

SARSI
BLOOD
PLATEAU
PIEGAN
B L A C K F O O T
PLAINS CREE
ASSINIBOINE
PLAINS OJIBWA
ATSINA (Gros Ventre)
C R O W
HIDATSA
MANDAN
ARIKARA
NORTHERN CHEYENNE
TETON (Dakota)
YANKTONAI (Dakota)
YANKTON (Dakota)
SISSETON (Dakota or Santee Dakota)
NORTHEAST (Eastern Woodlands)
WIND RIVER SHOSHONE
ARAPAHO
PAWNEE
PONCA
BASIN
SOUTHERN CHEYENNE
OMAHA
IOWA
OTO
UTE
KANSA
K I O W A
MISSOURI
OSAGE
JICARILLA APACHE
C O M A N C H E
KIOWA APACHE
WICHITA
SOUTHWEST
CADDO
LIPAN APACHE
SOUTHEAST

E ● Plains Area

Many Shoshone (Numic) speakers on the western margins of the Plains, extending to the Plateau and into the Great Basin, show strong cultural influences from the Plains area in the nineteenth century. Some of these tribes, particularly the Nez Percé, the Bannock, and the Ute have been classed by some writers as Plains tribes, but they are marginal to the nomadic Plains culture climax. Southwestern tribes are sometimes included as marginal Plains nomads, particularly the Jicarilla and Mescalero Apache whose languages are Athabascan.

THE MANDAN

The Mandan may have the longest documented archeological tradition of any American Indian tribe, except for the general documentation for

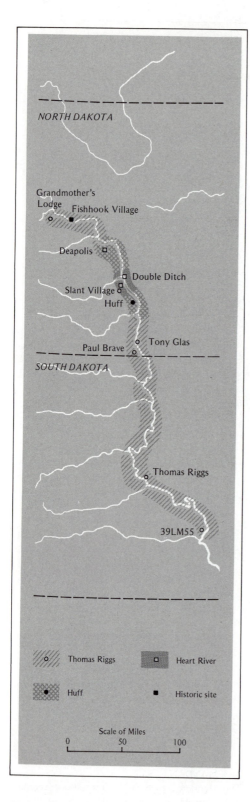

Figure 42 ● Prehistoric sites in the Middle Missouri

the Pueblo groups of the Southwest. Siouan speakers, the Mandan were the vanguard of the many Sioux tribes who eventually came to the Missouri Valley and the Plains out of the eastern and southern Woodlands. The evidence of linguistics is that they pulled away from other Siouan speakers perhaps 1000 years ago; by the time of white contact their dialect was not intelligible to other Sioux. They were a numerous tribe and friendly to the European and American explorers and traders, perhaps because they themselves were traders and middlemen. They were also a well-established entirely typical Eastern Plains village tribe, relying on both gardening and hunting for a rich/abundant subsistence base.

Prehistory

Mandan archeology has been studied by a succession of competent students since about 1900. By 1944, Will and Hecker (1944), the most diligent of Mandan scholars, were able to publish and document three stages of Mandan prehistory which have not been seriously challenged in subsequent years. Wood (1967) has released the definitive volume on the evolving Mandan tradition, which can be traced from A.D. 1100–1200 to the late nineteenth century. Lehmer (various) has contributed to Mandan studies by defining and refining the Middle Missouri tradition concept. The roots of the Mandan tradition go back to the beginning of the Plains horticultural tradition, an amalgam of both Woodland and Mississippian elements, called the Chamberlain Aspect, dating back perhaps to A.D. 700. It bears an ancestral relationship to all the later Plains farming groups including the Upper Republican and Middle Missouri cultures.

The Middle Missouri area is defined as the Missouri River Valley from the mouth of the White River in southeastern South Dakota almost to the mouth of the Yellowstone River near the Montana–North Dakota line (Lehmer, 1971). The three earliest Middle Missouri cultures of typical Plains village farmers are the Monroe focus, A.D. 700+; the Over, A.D. 850–1100; and the Anderson, after A.D. 1100. The basic cultural inventory (aside from diagnostic details) of these foci is listed by Wood as:
Pottery: Grit tempered, mass modeled, shaped by paddle and anvil, globular, with rounded or angular shoulders, flared and recurved (S-shaped or collared) rim forms, incised and cord-impressed rim designs.

Chipped stone: Triangular side-notched or unnotched arrowpoints, triangular and leaf-shaped broad knives, elongated, narrow two-edged knives, drills, planoconvex end scrapers. Ground stone: Grooved mauls, hammerstones, grooved pumice or sandstone abraders, elbow pipes, diorite celts.
Bone: Scapula hoes, bison horn core-frontal bone scoops, arrowshaft wrenches, scapula knives, serrated metapodial fleshers, pottery modeling tools (or quill flatteners), split metapodial awls.
Shell and antler: Shell disk beads and disks, broad antler bracelets.

From the early Middle Missouri cultures there developed the Thomas Riggs focus, found over most of the area. Thomas Riggs is attributed to the early Mandan and dated A.D. 1100 to 1400. Out of the Riggs focus comes the Huff focus A.D. 1400 to 1600 and then the Heart River A.D. 1600 to 1800 which becomes the historic tribe described later in the chapter. As Figure 42 shows, the territory held by the Mandan shrank through the years from the 500 mile long distribution shown for the Thomas Riggs focus to the tight cluster of villages near the Heart River of record in 1797. With the Mandan sequence known with considerable assurance in the 700 to 800 year sequence above, we turn now to the brief descriptions of the several phases. In order to show continuity, as well as change through time, the descriptions will tend to be comparisons from one phase to the next.

The villages of the Thomas Riggs focus number an estimated 100 or so, and their extended distribution marks the first upriver location on the Missouri River by the farmer-villagers. The villages consisted of scattered houses, often clustered around a central open space or plaza. Very infrequently a fortification or palisade surrounded the village, or at least the portions where no natural obstacles (cliff or stream) occurred. The small number of houses in each village (14 to 15), the scattered village locations, and the 500-mile-long distribution leads Wood (1967) to think that the period was relatively peaceful, despite the infrequent palisades, and that the upriver expansion to the very extreme northern limits of corn agriculture was largely unopposed by other tribes.

The houses themselves were rectangular, of ridgepole construction, with wall posts only on the long sides. The ends must have been closed with curtains of hide or matting. The houses tended to be aligned NE-SW, with a narrow entrance hallway or passage made of posts opening to the southwest. The pottery is clearly derived from the Chamberlain Aspect cultures, being paddle shaped with a grooved paddle from a lump of clay and being subsequently partially smoothed. The standard vessel form was globular, with flared or collared rims. Other artifacts of bone, stone, antler, and clay are of the kinds listed earlier, but with few changes in fabrication detail.

In Huff times there is marked change in settlement pattern. The population is now concentrated in large villages, with the rectangular houses built close together along what appear to be streets. If the Riggs villages can be characterized as "loose," Huff and later period arrangement can well be labeled "tight." The rectangular houses in shallow pits varied slightly from the Riggs pattern in having the ends closed with leaning poles as in Figure 43. A new house type, probably introduced from the central plains region, which is a square but round-cornered structure supported on four heavy central posts, comes into use. Quite different in concept, it is a domed, earth-covered lodge not at all resembling the longer ridgepole structures. It presages the round lodges with center posts that remained in use until the building of earth lodges was abandoned late in the nineteenth century. Noteworthy were the bastioned fortifications entirely surrounding some villages. These were made of close-spaced posts with an encircling moat in front of the palisade. It is argued that the reduced territorial distribution of the Huff sites, the larger villages, and the fortifications themselves testify to intensifying pressure by other tribes upon the Mandan. This suspicion is strengthened by legend, but even more by the knowledge that European pressures for territory on the east coast had set in motion a chain reaction affecting in some degree all the tribes east of the Rockies— a pressure which became greater and greater with time.

One of the most impressive of the Middle Missouri sites of any period is the Huff site itself, now preserved as a State Archeological site in the North Dakota Historical Park system. Figure 44 shows many details of this interesting location.

Spanning the years between archeology's data and the historic accounts of the Mandan, the Heart River focus, or protohistoric Mandan, occupies only a few dozen miles of territory. Its

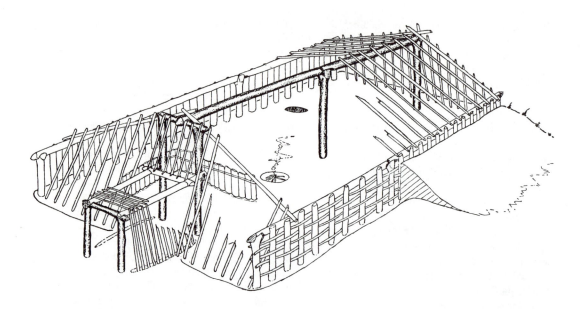

Figure 43 ● Mandan prehistory, speculative reconstruction of the Huff long rectangular houses. (After Wood, 1967:103)

fortified villages are compact clusters of round lodges, usually located on the west bank of the Missouri River from the Heart to Knife rivers.

For the entire 700 years of Mandan prehistory touched upon above, and even before that time, the subsistence base was a combined hunting-gathering-farming one. The resources were numerous, and living was in a sense easy. At least 95 percent of the meat food was supplied by the bison, which were taken and consumed in large numbers. Crops were grown in the loose rich soils of the alluvial plain along the river, soils annually renewed by flooding.

Early in the historic period, the Mandan became associated with the fur trade and their villages became centers of trade goods distribution. As early as 1738 the Mandan were visited by Verendrye who crossed the border lakes country from Lake Superior. Stories were told of red-haired Mandan, and in the early nineteenth century, stories were circulated of their Welsh origin. The fact that they used a hide coracle boat akin to that used in Wales added credence to these stories.

The earliest useful ethnographic information on the Mandan and the Hidatsa, who lived adjacent to them, comes from the early nineteenth century when they were visited by Alexander Henry and David Thompson, Lewis and Clark, George Catlin, Prince Maximilian, and others.

The records of these men furnish most of the data on the Mandan.

Economy and Technology

In the early nineteenth century, the Mandan were living in nine separate villages in the vicinity of the Heart River in central North Dakota. The Hidatsa lived near them as allies, and to the south, along the Grand River, lived the Arikara. Early in the century, smallpox had begun to take its toll of the Mandan, but they were still at the peak of their power, fighting both the Dakota tribes and the Arikara and trading with other northern Plains groups. In 1837, however, smallpox epidemics struck again with devastating results. After the attack only 125 Mandan survived. These few merged later with the Hidatsa and the Arikara, but their former strength and position on the northern Plains was gone. Completely encircled by hostile Dakota, the Mandan dared not even venture out for their summer bison hunt.

Before this depopulation, however, their settlements consisted of several villages located on benches or terraces along the Missouri River, usually at points where tributary streams entered. These locations gave them steep river banks as protection on two sides of their villages, and to protect the open sides, they constructed palisades of upright posts surrounded by a 10- to 15-foot-wide ditch. Early descriptions of their villages indicate a formal town plan with streets and a central plaza, but this plan was not seen in the nineteenth-century

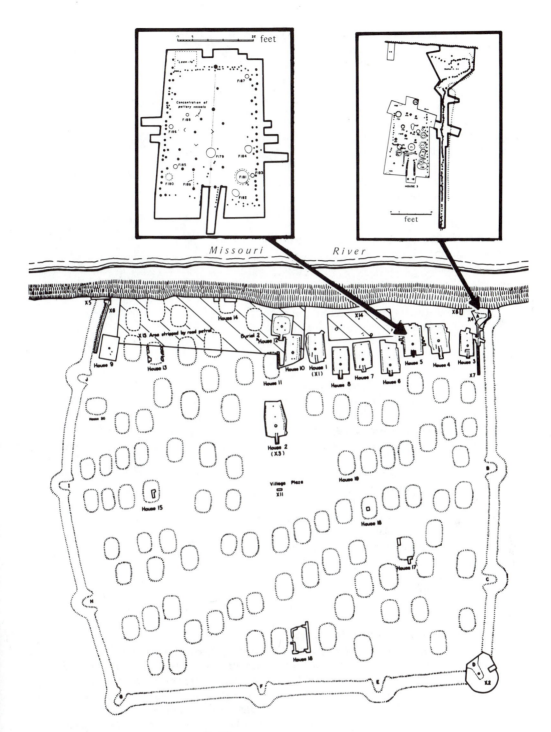

Figure 44 ● Mandan prehistory, Huff village
site (After Wood, 1967)

villages when the houses were clustered close together, and the intervening area was covered with drying racks. Their houses were large and comfortable earth lodges, clustered about a large open space in the center of the village where the Sacred Ark was located. The central plaza was the focal point of the community for it was here that the ceremonies were held and the competitive games were played.

The Mandan earth lodge was a circular semi-subterranean house which varied in size from 40 to 80 feet on the outside wall in circumference. The floor of the earth lodge consisted of packed earth on a level about 2 feet below the ground surface. The earth excavated to form this floor was thrown up around the perimeter of the floor. Four huge cottonwood center posts were set in the center of this circle and a ring of heavy posts about 5 feet high were set about the edge of the circle. The four center posts were topped by horizontal cross beams, and a continuous series of cross beams was set on the tops of the outer ring of posts. Pole rafters radiated from the tops of the center posts to the outer post ring and short slanting poles were set in the ground outside the ring. The long rafter poles did not meet at the center of the lodge, but left an opening which was used as a smokehole. Thick mattings of willow branches were then placed over the rafters and the exterior surface covered with layers of firmly packed earth. The doorway opened into an upward slanted passageway which was roofed and which could be closed with a rawhide door. A series of upright planks was set immediately inside the door to serve as a baffle to keep out the cold winds. The fire pit was in the center of the lodge, directly beneath the smokehole. The tops of the earth lodges were frequently flattened to provide a platform which could be used for drying maize and which doubled as a cool porch on hot summer evenings. The lodge itself was very spacious, warm and draft free in the winter and cool in the summer, for the thick earth walls insulated the interior of the lodge from temperature extremes.

An excellent account of the construction of a lodge was written by Gilbert Wilson (1934) who studied Hidatsa ethnology. Wilson's account, plus the descriptions of early travelers and artists, gives us an excellent idea of the interior furnishings of the lodge. Boxlike rawhide beds built on a raised platform lined the walls

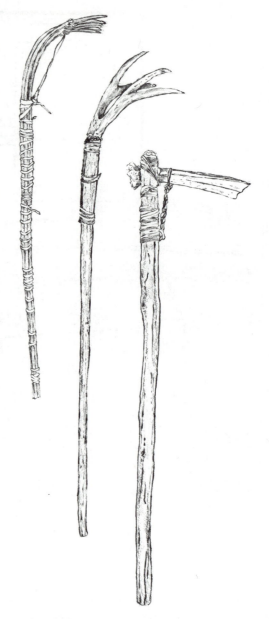

Mandan ● Left: Wooden pronged cultivator. The prongs of this rakelike tool, bent, are held in place with rawhide. Center: Scapula hoe. The essentially sedentary Mandan, along with other agricultural groups in the Plains, developed a series of simple farming tools. Here, a bison scapula is attached with rawhide to a staff, creating a crude but serviceable hoe. Right: Antler cultivator. A farming tool of the semisedentary Plains. (From the Department of Anthropology collections, University of Minnesota)

of the lodge. Areas for storage lay behind the beds and against the walls, and the floors of the lodges were honeycombed with deep storage pits excavated into the earth. These pits were sometimes eight feet deep and tapered from a wide base to a narrow upper opening. When lined with dried grass, they gave good dry storage for shelled corn and other harvested crops. Those that became damp and soured after use served as refuse collectors until they were filled.

The altar and the storage area for weapons and ceremonial bundles was on the right side of the lodge. Cooking took place in the central area during the winter, though as among the nomadic tribes, summer cooking normally took place outdoors. Willow backrests and bison-robe couches lay between the fire and the doorway, and it was here that the older males of the house sat and visitors were received. Some Mandan houses also had a partitioned area at one side of the doorway where favorite horses could be kept during the coldest weather.

Most of Mandan and Hidatsa material culture did not differ markedly from that of the Teton and other tribes of the central and northern Plains. Where it differed significantly, it reflected the sedentary mode of existence. For example, the Mandan, Hidatsa, and Arikara, together with the more southerly village tribes, manufactured pottery, a trait dropped by those nomadic tribes which had once utilized it. Such things as heavy wooden mortars and pestles were also found in each earth lodge. Bison shoulder blade hoes, antler rakes, and wooden digging sticks were used to cultivate their crops.

Another Mandan manufacture which is interesting is the bull boat or coracle. This circular, basin-shaped boat was made of a bent willow frame and covered with a green bison hide which was sewn to the upper edge of the frame. The rawhide dried and formed a drum-tight covering. The bison tail was left attached, and when the boat was in use, a driftwood drag was attached to the tail. The single paddler knelt in the front of the boat and reached forward with his paddle. The drag acted to prevent the boat from revolving and to keep it on course.

Mandan clothing, too, resembled that of the Teton, though in some respects their ceremonial clothing was even more elaborate. Consid-

Mandan ● Burden basket. (From the Department of Anthropology collections. University of Minnesota)

erable use was made of the white weasel or ermine, and Mandan painted bison robes were famous in the Plains. Hair style differed in that the men allowed their hair to grow very long and then fashioned it into several plaits plastered with clay and wound with beaver skin. The lock of hair hanging over the nose did not differ from the Teton and Yanktonai custom.

The strongest contrast between the Mandan and the Teton lies in subsistence patterns. The Mandan were hoe horticulturalists and hunters living on the extreme northern margin of effective agriculture. The primary crops raised were maize, beans, squash, pumpkin, sunflower, and tobacco. Although little precise ethnographic information exists on Mandan cultivation practices, there is an excellent study of the Hidatsa, who, according to tradition, were taught horticultural techniques by the Mandan (Wilson, 1917).

The small garden plots cultivated by the women lay in the river bottoms below the villages. The soil was soft and easily worked, as it was not covered with the tough prairie sod of the uplands. The brush and timber was cut "in such a way that the trees all fell in one direction. Some of the timber that was fit might be taken home for firewood; the rest was left to dry until spring when it was fired. The object of felling the trees in one direction was to make them cover the ground as much as possible, since firing them softened the soil and left it loose and mellow for planting" (Wilson, 1917:13). The burning probably destroyed weed seeds as well, and the ash deposited on the surface undoubtedly had some effectiveness as

Blackfoot ● Man's pipe. This is a simple elbow pipe of the general Plains area. It is not to be confused with the ceremonial pipes which so frequently appear in association with sacred bundles and ceremonies. The same elbow pipe design appears in the Northeast where it is identified with the pipestem itself, the so-called calumet. Ceremonial pipes throughout the Plains and Northeast were elaborately carved and decorated with feathers, beads, and fur. A simple pipe, modestly decorated, was for daily use. (After Lowie, 1954:27. Adapted from photographs. Courtesy of The American Museum of Natural History)

a fertilizer. There was no great competition for land, as the Missouri River bottom lands are wide enough to easily encompass the number of fields needed by any one village. Plots were cultivated for two or three years and then allowed to lie fallow for a period of years. River bottom lands thus provided soft, alluvial soils which could be worked with the technological equipment the Mandan possessed. These agricultural implements were not suitable for use on the tough prairie sod of the uplands, however; thus the villages of the sedentary tribes were restricted to major riverine areas.

In the Mandan area, the river bottom lands also afforded a more certain supply of moisture necessary for the production of crops in an area of marginal rainfall. Where crops might fail on the uplands, the high water table of the river bottoms aided in keeping the soil moist. The bottom lands also offered the growing crops protection from the hot, dry summer winds and from the late spring and early fall killing frosts. The Mandan had developed varieties of maize adapted to the short growing season; some of these special varieties have been hybridized and are still grown by modern farmers in the northern Plains.

Sunflowers were grown around the edges of the maize plots. Early in the spring, three or four seeds were planted in hills spaced approximately ten feet apart. Several varieties of sunflower were grown and all were treated alike

after harvesting. The seeds were parched and then ground into a meal which was used to thicken boiled vegetable and meat dishes. Balls of sunflower meal were also carried by men on hunting or warfare expedition just as pemmican was used by others.

Maize provided the staple vegetable food in the Hidatsa and Mandan diet, and most of the garden plots were used for maize cultivation. The digging stick and hoe were used to loosen the soil and to form small hills spaced in rows about four feet apart. Six to eight seeds were planted shallowly in each hill simply by pressing the seeds into the ground with the thumb. The fields were rectangular in outline and early accounts indicate that each field was five or six acres in size. Adjacent fields were separated by an uncultivated area about four feet wide. Beans were commonly planted in hills between the rows of maize, though occasionally they were planted separately. Squash grew separately since the plants were quite large and did not thrive when shaded by the taller maize plants.

When the maize plants were three inches high the plots were hoed to cut down the young weeds. Hills that showed no sprouting plants were replanted with seeds that had been soaked briefly in tepid water. During the growing season platforms with a sunshade were constructed in the fields, and women and children alternated in guarding the growing plots to prevent damage from birds, stray horses, and deer. Small boys were fond of green corn and were apparently quite adept at "stalking" a garden unobserved.

Fresh green corn was harvested, boiled, and eaten. Successive planting insured the availability of green corn till late in the season. Some green ears were picked and allowed to lie overnight in the field. They were carried to the village the next morning and husked by hand. The ears were then boiled briefly and placed on drying racks overnight. The cobs were shelled by running a pointed stick between the rows of kernels and then forcing the loosened kernels off with the thumb. The shelled corn was placed on skins and laid on the drying stage where it dried in a few days and was then winnowed to remove chaff. Corn was stored in skin bags in the underground cache pits.

Most of the corn, however, was allowed to ripen completely before it was picked. The whole family took part in the harvesting of the major crop, and the harvesters were given a feast in the field at the conclusion of their work. The largest and finest ears were partially husked, braided into long strings, and carried on ponies back to the village where the strings were hung on the drying stages. Most of the ears, carried back in baskets after they had been husked, were placed on the drying racks for about a week. The choice, braided ears were kept for seed for the following year, and some were used to trade. The rest of the dried corn was threshed on a platform with hardwood flails. The clean cobs were placed in a pile and burned and the grains of corn were sacked and stored in the pits. When this corn was used, it was pounded in a wooden mortar set into the floor of the earth lodge, and the resulting corn meal was cooked with other vegetables and meat.

Several color phases of squash were grown, but all were small and round and were handled in the same way. The squash were sliced and strung on a long pole to dry in the sun. This dried squash could be stored for long periods and was used with corn meal and meat in cooking.

Tobacco cultivation was a special task of the older men among the Hidatsa and the Mandan. Tobacco was a sacred crop among Plains Indians and considerable ritual surrounded its cultivation. Even some of the nomadic tribes, particularly the Crow, continued tobacco cultivation long after they had abandoned other farming practices.

The Mandan surrounded their horticultural activities with ceremonials intended to bring supernatural assistance to the growing of the crops. Certain ceremonials were annual events, but others could be given at any time the need arose. The elaboration of rituals surrounding cultivation attests to the importance of domesticated crops to these people. The degree of ceremonial association with farming seems usually to offer an index of the intensity of agriculture among North American Indians, and in this respect, the Mandan rank very high.

Here the rights to offer ceremonies were owned by individuals who had inherited or had purchased the sacred ceremonial bundles. The owner of the Robe bundle, for example, officiated as a priest at all horticultural ceremonies involving that ceremonial bundle. Long mythological traditions were associated with the efficacy of the bundle and could not be doubted. Bowers relates, for example, that the

corn bundle owner was expected to ask the help of the spirits who sent good crops. In the spring before seeding time, he held the ceremony of cleansing the seeds so that they would germinate. Early on the appointed day he went to the top of his earth lodge where he faced to the south singing the Corn bundle songs to call the spirits of the corn back from the south. He held a vessel containing shelled corn. Each woman making a garden came to him and received two seeds of each kind of corn, beans, sunflowers, and squash, paying for them and the prayers he addressed to the gods. Payment was made in elk robes, blankets, and other clothing (Bowers, 1950:192).

Work in the fields was done by the women, each working in the fields cultivated and held by her household. Younger children participated, and when the seasonal activities required many workers, even the young men aided the women. The produce of the fields was owned by the women, and it was they who distributed it to the family units in the household. Mandan men were hunters and warriors, for bison, elk, deer and smaller mammals were important in the diet. An annual bison hunt was held during the summer, and the meat was treated for preservation in the same ways as among the nomadic tribes. The Mandan also supplemented their diet by taking fish in the Missouri River with small elongate basket traps placed at the apex of V-shaped willow-stake weirs set into the river.

Organization of Society
In Mandan society, descent was traced unilineally, and residence after marriage was with the family of the wife's mother. The household group which occupied the earth lodge consisted of several nuclear families related through the females, and early writers indicate that each lodge held from 20 to 40 persons. This matrilineal extended family was the functioning economic unit, as the women of the household cooperated in working the cultivated fields and the men hunted together. The household as a unit controlled the garden plots, but it did not own them in the sense of being able to buy

Mandan ● Bull-boat or coracle. The 6 foot
bullboat spread up the headwaters of the
Missouri River as far as the Blackfoot and into
the Plateau. It was a single bison skin spread
tightly over a circular frame and served as an
adequate ferrying craft. (From the Department
of Anthropology, University of Minnesota)

and sell the land. The land was held by groups
of related matrilineal extended families grouped
into larger kin units known as lineages. The
right to land within the lineage was based on
the principle of the usufruct, which simply
means that the family controlled and worked
the gardens as long as they had enough
women to cultivate the land. If family fortunes
fell and the family diminished in size, the lineage assigned some of the garden space to
other families.

Each lineage and the extended families
which composed it were self-sufficient economic groups. They were grouped into larger
kin units, however, which had different functions. These larger groups were organized on
the same principle as the lineages, in that they
were composed of several lineages related
through maternal lines. This matri-sib, or female clan, as it is frequently called, was a corporate group with an organization and formalized leadership. Older men were the dominant
figures with the matri-sibs, but these men were
not associated with the households within the
sib. Marriage was exogamous for sib members,
which meant that each member of a particular
sib had to marry someone from another sib.
Membership in a lineage and matri-sib was
determined at the time of birth, for one auto-
matically belonged to the lineage and sib of his
or her mother. This affiliation never changed
during one's lifetime. At marriage, then, the
man married a woman from another lineage
and sib and moved to the household of his
wife. His children belonged not to his lineage
and sib, but to that of their mother. The man
did not function as a leader in the lineage in
which he resided after marriage, but in the lin-

eage and sib in which he grew up, thus they
functioned as fathers to their children in one
household, but might serve as leaders in the
matrilineal sib of their mother and sisters.

The matri-sib was then a large kin group
composed of individuals related only through
their mothers. The sib was not localized in one
village, as the lineage probably was, but the 13
matri-sibs of the early nineteenth century were
found scattered throughout the several Mandan
villages. Some matri-sibs were even shared
with the Hidatsa, who were organized in a
similar fashion. The Mandan matri-sib served
to regulate marriage according to exogamy and
extensions of the incest taboo. The matri-sib
was also a mutual-aid society in that sib members were bound to assist each other with matters of economic cooperation, vengeance, and
other obligations.

Certain of the matri-sibs were ranked above
others, though the ranking was informal and
based largely on the size and ritual importance
of the group. Certain sibs had owned the more
important sacred bundles for many generations,
which gave them greater prestige. Other sibs
had traditional roles in the tribal Okipa ceremony and were allotted space for their lodges
near the central village plaza and again accorded more prestige and honor among their
fellows. There was considerable rivalry between
sibs, particularly in warfare which the Mandan
had developed to much the same degree as
had the nomadic tribes.

One further grouping complicated the picture
of Mandan society. Matri-sibs in each village
were divided into two units of approximately
equal size which are technically termed
moieties. This dual division of Mandan society
was important, for the two leaders of each village, somewhat akin in their functions to a war
leader and a peace chief, came from opposite
moieties as well as from specific lineages
within each. Moieties also competed against
each other in games and contests, and the joking relationship applied between members of
opposite moieties. It is believed that in the
nineteenth century, eagle trapping grounds
were owned by the moieties and that the pits
dug into the high bluffs to capture these sacred
birds could be used only by men belonging to
the moiety. It is also probable that the moieties
were exogamous at one time, which meant that
a mate must not only be selected from another
matri-sib, but from matri-sibs in the moiety
opposite one's own.

This societal organization was found among the Mandan and the Hidatsa and among the nomadic Crow as well. The Crow had split recently from the Hidatsa, and their matrilineal organization was retained although it did conflict with their new way of life and was in the process of change. The Mandan social system offered a cohesive kin group and a regularized system of descent and inheritance. The latter is particularly important in a horticultural society where stability and continuity in the system of land use and property distribution is necessary. This unilineal system of organization with the associated corporate kin groups is found among all of the sedentary tribes of the Plains and varies only in the emphasis on matrilineal or patrilineal descent.

The Mandan kinship system is classed as a "Crow" type which emphasizes the maternal relatives. Kinsmen of the maternal side of the family are distinguished from those of the paternal side which has only two basic kin terms. These terms for father's kinsmen have no equivalent in English but mean, "male of my father's matrilineage" or "female of my father's matrilineage," and apply to males or females without regard to age or generation differences. Kinsmen on the maternal side of the family are distinguished more specifically; there are separate terms for mother, mother's brother, maternal cross cousins, children, and grandchildren. The patrilineal reverse of this Crow system, called the Omaha kinship type, is found among the patrilineal sedentary Siouan peoples of the central Plains and is also found further to the east among such groups as the Winnebago.

Preferential marriage for a Mandan male was with mother's brother's daughter, in the classificatory sense, and for a female with father's sister's son. Residence was matrilocal, but village exogamy was not practiced so one could remain in the same village after marriage.

The Mandan had men's and women's associations, which were more elaborate and more highly structured than comparable Teton societies. One would expect to find the status of women and their roles more important among the Mandan, and this importance is reflected in the associations as well as in the kinship system and ceremonial organization. Both men's and women's societies were graded; they were ranked in successive order based on the ages of society members. At the head of the men's war societies were the Buffalo Bulls composed of the older males of the society, irrespective of kin

group membership. To reach the Buffalo Bull society a man needed to prove his abilities through roughly the same deeds and personality characteristics as marked the Teton system. This was necessary before an invitation was extended to him. In addition, he had to have been a member of each age-graded society leading to the Buffalo Bull society at the top. Membership in each of these societies had to be purchased from a present member, who then purchased his way into the next higher society. Each step up this ladder of prestige was more expensive than the previous, and only a select few reached the highest society. Kinsmen were obligated to assist in filling the economic needs of prospective members. They helped to furnish the goods necessary for membership both because of the obligation of kinship and because a kinsman who was a member of one of the higher societies added to the prestige of his kin group as a whole. Here, as among the Teton and generally on the Plains, we see the competitiveness which characterizes all of these societies.

Age grading of the associations probably originated among the Mandan as did many other culture traits which characterize the tribes of the northern Plains. Similar systems were found among the nomadic Blackfoot and Arapaho, for example, as was the concept of private ownership of sacred bundles.

The Mandan shared the idea of camp and tribal hunt police with the Teton and other Plains tribes. The Black Mouth society, composed of young active men, traditionally held this role among the Mandan and they functioned in much the same manner as did the Teton *akicita*. The Mandan were governed by a council of older males, and the tribal leaders were persuaders rather than autocrats. The Mandan sedentary villages were similar to the bands of the nomadic groups, each operating as a unit, but each a part of the tribal whole.

Religion

Mandan religion centered about the personal-vision quest, but the elaboration of tribal ritual and ceremonial was geared to sacred bundles; some were tribal fetishes similar to the Arapaho flat pipe, but all were privately owned and could be transferred or sold. Each bundle was also associated with a detailed mythology and each functioned for the tribal good in some way. Alfred W. Bowers, in a detailed study of Mandan ceremonialism, described the characteristics of Mandan sacred bundles as follows:

Each contained objects representing the characters and incidents of the myth; the rites were dramatizations of the sacred myth; there were prescribed rules of behavior when in the presence of the bundle or while it was open; an incense was always burned while the bundle rites were being performed or when the rites were terminated; there were songs and a sacred myth which belonged to the bundle; each bundle included a buffalo skull; the ritualistic lore was secret, and payment must be made to the bundle-owner for a knowledge of the rites; there were fixed rules of inheritance for the sale and transfer of a bundle; tribal sanction of a bundle transfer was at a public feast to which those owning related bundles were invited; feasts were made to the bundle by non-owners as a social obligation; and bundle-owners on occasion would give Bundle Renewal feasts to their own bundles to which were invited those owning important tribal bundles (Bowers, 1950;107).

Some of the bundles and the associated rites were quite specialized in that they pertained to specific activities, such as fishing and eagle trapping. Others were general curing bundles and the owners served as curers. Many were associated with fertility, crops, and the control of weather essential to successful cultivation. The most important of the bundle ceremonies was the *Okipa* which was held annually in midsummer. According to Bowers:

The Okipa ceremony was an elaborate and complicated affair. It was a dramatization of the creation of the earth, its people, plants, and animals, together with the struggles the Mandan endured to attain their present position. The history of the tribe was a part of the secret lore held by the officers of the ceremony. The uninformed could pay to have the creation myths told but could not repeat them. The songs, chants, and rituals were conducted by men who by virtue of inheritance and purchase had acquired that right, but the words were unintelligible to the population at large, being, according to tradition, in an ancient Nuptadi dialect. Only the legitimate officers understood their meaning, and that information was never divulged to another except when purchase was being made into the ceremony (Bowers, 1950:111).

The Okipa ceremony was a four-day series of progressive rituals reenacting the Mandan creation myth and offered to insure the welfare of the people. As in the Sun Dance, an individual pledged to offer the ceremony as the result of a vision. More than one individual might pledge

the ceremony in a year, and if that happened, the ceremony would be given more than once. It was offered either before or after the midsummer tribal bison hunt.

The elements of self-torture were very strong in the Okipa, and the officers of the Okipa society had to be assured that the young man pledging the ceremony could fulfill the obligations this imposed. Those whose ability to do so was questioned were told to participate in warfare to test the legitimacy of their vision, and those who were successful were accepted as Okipa Makers. While there was only one pledger for each ceremony, other youths participated in the fasting and self-torture portions of the ceremony. The latter were not required to have had visions to participate, but like the successful Sun Dance candidates, they would expect to receive a vision after successfully completing the ritual.

The Okipa ceremony was held in the village ceremonial lodge at the edge of the open plaza. This lodge was built by members of both moieties, each of whom worked on the half of the lodge which was owned by their moiety. Traditionally, a man in a specific matri-sib was selected to live in the ceremonial lodge with his family and act as caretaker. He was a member of the WaxikEna matri-sib, "to which Lone Man, traditional founder of the ceremony, belonged . . ." (Bowers, 1950:115), and which owned the sacred Okipa bundle. The sacred Okipa bundle could be inherited by women, but they could not participate in the ceremony, for the entire ceremonial lodge was taboo to all women during the four days of ritual. The owner of the bundle, a member of the WaxikEna matri-sib, functioned as the Lone Man during the ceremonies. The other ceremonial leader functioned as Hoita who was responsible for most of the organization of the ritual. The Lone Man was the Mandan culture hero, who according to their mythology,

established the custom of leaving an open area within each village for dancing. Later, when he was leaving the tribe, he erected a Red-painted cedar, as a symbol of his body and of all the Mandans who had lived before. The cedar was surrounded by a wall of cottonwood planks as a symbol of the wall he erected to protect the people from the flood. A water willow surrounding the planks marked the highest advance of the flood waters. He also established the custom of maintaining a special ceremonial lodge in each village and taught the ceremonies associated with its con-

struction. The lodge was the symbol of Dog Den Butte where Hoita (the speckled eagle) imprisoned all living things. Six central posts were used making it oblong in form, with a flat side facing the open circle (Bowers, 1950:113).

After the pledger had been accepted by the members of the Okipa society, the village criers announced the fact. Frequently the decision was made nearly a year in advance of the ceremony, for considerable amounts of goods had to be acquired by the Okipa Maker. In addition to giving feasts for the Okipa officers, the pledger had to have "at least one hundred articles consisting of robes, elkskin dresses, dress goods, shirts with porcupine work, knives, and men's leggings" (Bowers, 1950:123). The accumulation of this amount of property demanded help from kinsmen, for no individual could possibly provide this. Members of the lineage and sib aided the young man, for the honor of the kin group was at stake. Men who had pledged and successfully completed the Okipa ceremony in the past achieved great prestige and were important leaders in the village. They could participate in any future Okipa rites and in so doing they elevated the prestige of their kin group.

The rituals, directed by the Hoita and the Lone Man, began on the day preceding the four-day ceremony. The many officers, singers, and impersonators who would take part in the rites had been selected and the ceremonial lodge had been made ready for the activities. The pledger and the other young men who had volunteered to fast and participate in the torture dances had been instructed in the sacred lore and moved into the ceremonial lodge where they fasted and rested quietly on beds of sage placed around the outer walls.

To begin the rites, the Lone Man approached the village to enact his arrival from the supernatural world. He was conducted to the ceremonial lodge where he recited the myths pertaining to his previous existence with them and then made a round through the village relating similar myths. That evening, a ceremony, in the sacred lodge, invested the pledger with the right to perform the ceremony through transfer of Lone Man's pipe to him. The other fasters were also dedicated so that the rituals could proceed the following morning.

The rituals which followed for four successive days reenacted the Okipa mythology with impersonators taking the roles of the supernatural deities. Singing and dancing were important parts of the rituals, and in these dances, members of the Buffalo Bull society took prominent roles. All of these men had participated in the Okipa rites as young men, for this was one of the prerequisites to membership in the Bull society. An interesting aspect of the ceremony took place on the third day when the Foolish One who "symbolized those who did not respect the sacred things" (Bowers, 1950:144) appeared from outside the village. The impersonator of the Foolish One acted like a clown and symbolized also the malevolent forces present in the world. "He was challenged by the Okipa Maker who approached him with the Lone One's pipe, challenging that one's right to come among the people to frighten them and bring misfortune or death at the hands of enemies by breaking up the dances for the buffaloes" (Bowers, 1950:145). The Foolish One, before being vanquished and driven from the village, provided a great deal of merriment to the onlookers as he imitated breeding bison bulls and approached men who were dressed in female clothing. When he was finally vanquished, his cap and necklace were tied to a pole in front of the Okipa lodge as an offering to "the Foolish One who lived in the Sun."

The torture of the Okipa Maker and the other volunteers took place during three days and was considerably more elaborate than the Teton torture during the Sun Dance. Torture began on the second day when the young man selected a man of his father's sib to cut holes through the skin of his back, breast, and legs. Wooden skewers were inserted in these, and thongs attached to those in the breast and back were used to hoist the candidates above the ground within the lodge. Bison skulls were attached to the thongs and skewers in the legs. The candidates were raised by the thongs and held suspended as the Buffalo Bulls danced. They were lowered when they became unconscious but were allowed to regain consciousness without assistance.

The candidates were taken from the Okipa lodge on the afternoon of the third day as the Buffalo Bulls danced about the sacred ark. A pole was raised near the ark, and the candidates were suspended from this pole as the dance progressed. The tortures of the final day were similar to those of the previous days.

The Okipa ceremony reached its climax on the fourth day when a symbolic chant took place. Bowers describes it as follows:

After the calling of the buffaloes from the four direc-

tions, the remaining portion of the ceremony progressed rapidly. The drummers began beating rapidly, and the hunters formed a circle about the sacred cedar, holding to the willow hoops. The four Bulls threw off their masks and danced around the circle as rapidly as possible. Each of the remaining fasters was led out of the Okipa lodge by two of his father's clansmen who had the right half of their bodies painted blue and the left side red. They held straps wrapped around the faster's arms. Each faster had one or more buffalo skulls dragging from skewers fastened through the skin; those who had struck an enemy were permitted to wear a skull as a necklace. The father's clansmen led or dragged the young men around the sacred cedar in clockwise direction as fast as they could travel until the victim fell unconscious. When the last faster fell to the ground, the drumming ceased, and the hunters threw their hoops into the air. All the fasters returned to the Okipa lodge where those on the west side moiety rubbed their wounds with buffalo marrow while those of the opposite moiety rubbed theirs with ground yellow corn (Bowers, 1950:149–150).

The ceremony ended quickly and with its closing, the Mandan had revitalized their world and renewed the strength of their society.

THE TETON DAKOTA

Background

While the sedentary village farming tribes had been residents on the eastern margins of the Plains for many years and had incorporated many of the culture patterns involving the horse, the dominant societies of the Plains were the nomadic hunters. These horse nomads subsisted primarily on bison, lived in portable skin tipis, had a technology which produced light and durable articles of skin, emphasized war and military societies, were usually bilateral in social organization and in kinship, and emphasized the Sun Dance as the major tribal ceremony. The horse nomads were competitive and aggressive people among whom social status was earned and individual social mobility was rapid. Mobility was also very important for the bands or residential groups which formed the tribe, for these people ranged over vast areas and survival depended upon quickness and speed of movement. The Teton Dakota were typical of the nomads living on the northern Plains, and like many of the tribes of this region, were drawn onto the high Plains in the

historic period. Some of the nomadic Plains tribes, like the Cheyenne and the Crow, had been village farming peoples who had shifted to hunting with the arrival of the horse. Other tribes, like the Comanche and the Northern Shoshone, had been hunters and gatherers in the Great Basin before moving onto the western Plains where they adapted their cultures to the bison and the horse.

The Teton Dakota are recent migrants onto the northern Plains. Early historical records indicate that they crossed the Missouri River to the western high Plains about 1750, the date at which the horse first appeared in the northern Plains. In the hundred years before 1750, and probably for some time before that, the Teton Dakota apparently hunted the eastern banks of the Missouri River, the James River basin in present-day South Dakota, and the upper Minnesota River Valley in Minnesota. The first maps of that area by French traders and explorers invariably name the present Big Stone–Traverse lakes at the head of the Minnesota River "Lake of the Tetons." The Teton name for themselves is "Lakota," indicative of their close linguistic-cultural relationship to the Yankton, Yanktonai, and Assiniboine, who call themselves "Nakota," and the Santee or eastern Dakota comprised of Sisseton, Wahpeton, Wakpekute, and Mdewakanton, all of whom designate themselves as "Dakota." These Dakota tribes have often been spoken of as forming a "loose confederacy," but there is no basis in fact for this. At no time did these eight tribes act together as a political unit, though seven of them did not make war upon each other. The eighth group, the Assiniboin, were outside this informal nonaggression pact. They were frequently at war with other Dakota groups, particularly as allies of the Cree against the Yanktonai. It is from this latter group that the Assiniboine traditionally separated in the late prehistoric period somewhere in northwestern Minnesota. From here the Assiniboine moved west and north to the Plains proper.

The Dakota as a group, therefore, are representative of the movement of peoples onto the central and northern Plains in late prehistoric and early historic times. The Cheyenne, for example, have traditions of having lived in the upper Minnesota River Valley, then moving to the Sheyenne River area of eastern North Dakota, where their late prehistoric village has been documented archeologically. From there they moved to the Missouri River and appar-

Cheyenne, Lame Deer, Montana ● The wife of
Black Horse shows a dog travois made by her
husband in the traditional manner. The basket
is of willows tied with leather thongs. The
floor of the basket is cowhide; bison hide
would have been used in the remoter past.
(Photograph by Thomas M. Galey, ca. 1922.
Smithsonian Institution National
Anthropological Archives)

ently settled as horticulturalists alongside the
Mandan until sometime in the early eighteenth
century when they abandoned their sedentary
existence and moved to the Black Hills region
as nomadic hunters. It is possible that the other
Algonkin-speakers following the classic nomadic hunting existence on the Plains in historic times preceded the Cheyenne onto the
northern Plains, following much the same route
of movement. Whether they moved onto the
Plains as horticulturalists like the Cheyenne, or
as Woodland hunters like the later Plains Cree
and Plains Ojibwa is not known. The movement of the Shoshonean-speaking Comanche

onto the Plains from the Great Basin area in
relatively late times indicates that attractions
operated to draw Basin-Plateau hunters and
gatherers into the Plains culture as they did to
the east.

The Teton moved onto the Plains as an Eastern Prairie tribe, not as a Woodland hunting
people as is often thought. The area in which
they lived when first mentioned by French
sources is a prairie zone adjacent to the mixed
grassland–deciduous forest area of central Minnesota. Here they probably practiced a mixed
horticultural-hunting economy as did the other
Dakota tribes. Certainly the bison was important to their subsistence as it was to all of the
Dakota, and perhaps wild rice was gathered
annually in the early fall and used as it was
among other Dakota groups.

The Teton had left this eastern prairie fringe
before the period of French contact in the upper Mississippi Valley and the western Great
Lakes and so were not drawn directly into the
northern fur trade and the conflicts with the
westward-pushing Algonkins as were their

● HORSE AND BISON IN THE PLAINS

The cultures of the western Plains reached
their zenith as, beginning in the eighteenth
century, they began to center their economic
and social life more and more in the horse.
Before the horse reached them, they had
employed several methods of bison hunting,
none so effective as the mounted forays against
the bison herds. Both antelope and bison had
been taken in surrounds or impounds and
slaughtered, or they were forced to stampede
over cliffs and bluffs by the use of grass fires
or beaters. But the horse, coming to the Plains
from the south after European expansion,
allowed fuller exploitation of the incredibly vast
herds of bison. While even the semisedentary
agricultural tribes, such as the Omaha or
Mandan, left their villages for the summer
hunt and came to depend on horses, it was in
the west, among the Blackfoot, Crow,
Cheyenne, and others of the nomadic Plains,
that horse and bison together assumed primary
economic importance.

While the bison might be hunted during the
entire year, the great communal hunts of
spring and summer, those which brought
together large segments of a tribe, required
careful preparation and supervision. Every care
was taken to ensure the amassing of as much
meat as possible. The war orientations of the
Plains cultures made the hunt a virtual military
procedure. Warriors, members of special
groups or clubs, were delegated to police the
hunt so as to ensure uniform communal action.
Punishment, usually destruction of property,
awaited the man who, perhaps carried away by
excitement, might step out of line and so
endanger the communal enterprise.

The hunters here have driven their mounts
directly into the bison herd. Each has selected
an animal he wishes to kill. Dispatching one
with arrow or lance, the hunter moves on to
the next, leaving the carcasses to be butchered
later. The slaughter will continue until horses
and men are exhausted or until night calls for
a halt. A variation of this hunting procedure,
applicable to a somewhat smaller herd of
bison, might involve its surrounding by riders
who again work with lance and arrow.

Much information exists on the role of the

horse in the cultures of the Plains. A good mount, one trained both for war and the hunt, was a priceless possession. It could be ridden without a bridle, although most were not, and was able to respond to the rider's commands which were given either by a pressure of the knee or a shifting of weight. The horse accorded not only wealth and status but its relation to the food quest became vital. It is small wonder that raiding for horses became so significant a part of the Plains war pattern.

After the kill, with virtually everyone in an encampment assisting, the butchering went on. The bison meat was stripped, jerked, pounded into pemmican. The hides were made into robes and generally tanned for a host of uses. Sinews were pulled for thread and there was use for the horn, hooves, and intestines (cf. Ewers et al., 1955).

Dakota ● The method of "stone boiling," in this instance meat being boiled in the stomach of a cow, was a technique prevalent in virtually all of native America. Stones heated in the fire were dropped into any liquid in order to bring it fairly quickly to a brisk boil. Any container might be used. In this instance, a cow paunch was filled with water and a soup of boiled meat made, care being taken to avoid touching the sides of the container with the hot stones. Cool stones were so arranged as to make a rack in this container or in a basket. Pottery vessels were also used to boil in this way. (Smithsonian Institution National Anthropological Archives)

eastern relatives. The Yanktonai, Yankton, Sisseton, and Wahpeton were drawn into direct participation in the fur trade during the late seventeenth and early eighteenth centuries. The attractions of the horse and bison nomadism in the eighteenth and early nineteenth centuries ended this direct adaptation to fur trading for them and turned these groups toward the Plains. But they continued to function as middlemen in trade, distributing guns, ammunition, and other trade goods to the peoples of the Northern Plains in exchange for horses, bison robes, dried meat, and other products. The Teton benefited from this arrangement for they annually returned to the upper Minnesota to trade with their eastern relatives (Jablow, 1951).

As the Missouri River trade developed in the nineteenth century, and American traders and trappers moved upriver from St. Louis to the village tribes on the upper Missouri, the Teton acted as a militant wedge separating the traders from the northern groups. The St. Louis source of trade upset the traditional pattern established earlier by the Dakota tribes and much of the early nineteenth-century Teton conflict with Europeans centered on attempts to disrupt the Missouri River trade. The Teton benefited from trade, but it was the more easterly Dakota who participated most actively. The Yankton, for example, who controlled the famous catlinite, or "red pipestone," quarry in southwestern Minnesota, were particularly oriented toward trade and supplied most of the northern Plains groups with catlinite, either directly, or indirectly through the Teton.

Teton history in the nineteenth century is well documented and is a history of conflict for Indian and European alike. The Teton were the most numerous group on the northern Plains, a people with a reputation for irascibility, impetuosity, and in some cases, sheer delight in causing trouble. They dominated the village horticulturalists, placing the Arikara in a position approaching complete subjugation, forcing them to trade agricultural products at rates of exchange set by the Teton. They raided the Mandan and Hidatsa and were continual enemies of the surrounding nomadic tribes. The Teton constantly harassed the keelboats bringing trade goods up the Missouri, and later they were a threat to wagon trains crossing the Plains to the west. Only in the late nineteenth century when gold was discovered in the Black

Hills and when white settlers finally began competing for land, did the Teton and the surrounding tribes submerge their differences and attempt to ally against a common enemy.

The Battle of the Little Big Horn in 1876 was fought against the troops of General Custer by some of the Teton with Cheyenne allies. These struggles against overwhelming odds were successful for a time, but the Teton were finally subjugated and assigned to reservations. The last military action against them took place in 1891 in the infamous "battle" of Wounded Knee when the Teton, agitated by the messianic Ghost Dance brought to them from the Basin-Plateau, attempted a religio-magical revival of their former way of life.

Throughout the nineteenth century, names of Tetons, like the Oglala war leaders Crazy Horse and Red Cloud and the Hunkpapa shaman Sitting Bull, were widely known. The tribal eclipse ended the freedom of the Teton and all of the tribes of the Plains. In a brief span of a little over a century, horse nomadism on the northern Plains developed, flourished, and was finally destroyed.

The Teton today live on reservations, most of which are in South Dakota. The Pine Ridge, Rosebud, Lower Brule, Crow Creek, and the Cheyenne reservations are here. Standing Rock lies split between North and South Dakota and is populated by Teton and some Yanktonai. A few Teton are located at Fort Peck, in Santee, Nebraska, and Fort Totten, North Dakota. The Teton, after a population decrease during the earlier periods of reservation life, are again gaining in numbers, so that they are the second most populous Indian tribe in the United States today.

Material Culture

The Teton, as recent migrants onto the western Plains, quickly adapted to the classic nomadism of the area as it developed in the eighteenth and nineteenth centuries. This adaptation is nowhere seen more clearly than in their material culture and their patterns of subsistence. Lightness of weight, durability, and ease of transport are the keystones for their patterns of nomadism, to be effective, required all of these characteristics. The Teton developed a material culture using animal hides as the primary raw material.

The tipi itself exemplified the main attributes of the total material culture. This structure, generally used by a single nuclear family for shelter throughout the year, was a conical skin tent, round at the base, and tilted slightly forward. Most single-dwelling tipis were 12 to 16 feet in diameter at the base and tapered evenly to the open smokehole at the top. They were constructed of 8 to 12 bison skins, all carefully tanned and trimmed to fit exactly. The skins were sewn together with sinew by using a bone awl to punch through the skin. Together they formed a rough semicircle when laid flat on the ground. The tipi was erected over a conical pole framework built up over a tripod base. Two skin flaps at the smokehole were attached at their peaks to long poles which could be moved to open or close the flaps, depending on wind and weather. The lower edge of the tipi cover was usually held in place by placing stones around the margin, but in the hot summer periods the edge was frequently rolled up for a few feet to provide ventilation. When the tipi cover was in place, the seam was fastened with wooden or bone pins, and the small, elevated doorway was covered with a rawhide door. The interior of the structure was made more comfortable against cold winter winds by a skin tipi liner attached to the poles four or five feet above the floor and dropping vertically to the ground. The fire hearth was in the center of the tipi directly under the smokehole. Tanned bison robes were used as both bed and bed covering, and the tipi in winter has been described as warm and comfortable, although a bit smoky at times.

The suitability of this structure for year-round living in a harsh environment was perhaps not ideal, but its adaptability to a nomadic existence was excellent. The whole structure could be dismantled and packed in a matter of minutes. It was light and compact and could be easily transported, especially when the tipi poles were lashed at one end and placed over a horse's back in an inverted V-shape to drag behind the horse as a travois. The poles extending behind the horse were fitted with a willow framework platform on which the tipi cover was lashed and carried to the next camping place.

The tipi is an example of still another aspect of Plains Indian culture—the adaptation of a more general and widely distributed culture practice to the specialized nomadic existence of the western Plains. The tipi as a dwelling is not unique to the Plains and in fact is not unique to the North American Indian. It is a circumpolar trait, found in the northern boreal areas of both North America and Asia. Among many

Blackfoot ● Stone Club. This double headed stone club was sewed into a rawhide loop, the hide then folded down a 3-foot handle and seamed. The wrist loop suggests the use of the club by a mounted hunter or warrior. (Courtesy of The Science Museum, St. Paul, Minnesota)

boreal forest groups, the tipi is the common dwelling, but unlike the Plains tipi, it is normally covered with sheets of bark, heavy moose hides, and sometimes, branches. In some northern groups where the tipi is not the common dwelling form, it is frequently used as a temporary hunting shelter that can be built quickly with immediately available materials. The Plains Indian tipi is a modification of this basic circumpolar tipi type. In an area where timber is rare and straight lodge poles hard to replace, the problem of a pole framework was solved by carrying the poles along on the move. Rather than acting as an extra burden, however, the poles were made to serve a useful function on the move and were fashioned into a travois on which not only the tipi cover but

other camp gear was transported. The beautifully fashioned skin cover was durable and could be used again and again. When it was damaged, it could be repaired quickly and easily. The streamlined nature of the tipi and its adaptability to both the rigors of the environment and the necessities of mobility is characteristic of all Plains Indian material culture.

The use of skin, particularly bison skin, was universal among both the sedentary and the nomadic Plains tribes. Methods of tanning skins were well developed and involved a minimum of paraphernalia. A fresh bison skin was staked out on the ground with the hair side down. Women used a short elk-antler scraper with a stone or iron blade attached to carefully scrape all of the tissue and fat from the exposed inner surface of the skin. If the skin was to be used as a robe for either clothing or bedding, the hair was left on; if it was to be used as a section of a tipi cover, the skin was soaked and the hair scraped away from the exterior surface. The skin was then submerged in water or buried in damp earth to keep it pliable until the tanning process took place. Tanning involved working natural animal fats and oils into the skin. Generally, the Teton used animal brains for this purpose, but other internal organs could also be used. The hide was twisted many times and also pulled back and forth over a fallen limb or tight thong to break down the internal fibers and to work the oily tanning material into the skin. Teton hides were sometimes placed over a small tripod framework of green poles erected over a green-wood smudge fire. This smoked the hide, and while the tanning effect of the smoke is debatable, the smoke did impart an even yellow-brown color to the hide. Other Plains tribes such as the Crow were famous for their "smoke tanned" hides, and one group, the Kutenai, who lived west of the Blackfoot, produced beautiful white-tanned deerhides much in demand for use in ceremonial clothing.

Other animal skins were tanned in much the same fashion. Deer and elk hides were in demand for they were used in place of the heavier bison hide for most articles of clothing. Some hide was not tanned, but used in a natural state as rawhide. Here again, the Plains Indians have adapted a more widespread practice to their immediate needs. Rawhide is a peculiar material in that when fresh or "green" it is very plastic. It can be applied to the surface of nearly any solid form by sewing it in place. When

Crow ● An example of tree burial. Although burial was not unknown in the Plains, some tribes put corpses in trees or, lacking these, on a four-pole scaffold. The body was allowed to decay and the bones then put in rocky areas (Lowie, 1935:66–68). This pattern may be a marginal reflection of the more elaborate death rituals which appear east of the Mississippi. (Smithsonian Insititution National Anthropological Archives)

rawhide dries, however, it is extremely hard, it shrinks considerably, and it keeps its form. The Teton and other Plains groups utilized these properties in fashioning several tools used daily. The stone hammer or pemmican maul, used by the women to pound dry meat, was constructed by placing a split-willow handle around the center of an oval or round grooved hammer stone. The short wooden handle and the stone hammer head, except for its pounding face, were then completely covered with a single piece of green rawhide, sewn in place. When the rawhide dried, it had shrunk and was very hard. It held the hafted hammer head and willow handle together as a rigid tool.

Similar uses for rawhide are seen in the manufacture of the stone-headed "war club," made in much the same fashion as the pemmican maul, and in the wooden pack saddle. This

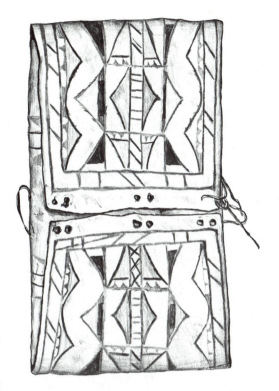

Blackfoot ● Parfleche. The rawhide, envelope-like container was regularly decorated with painted geometric designs, a highly distinctive development in the Plains. (Courtesy of The Science Museum, St. Paul, Minnesota)

Blackfoot ● Men's ceremonial buckskin shirt. Shirts such as this, made of carefully tanned deerskin, came to characterize the northern Plains especially in the historic period. The soft buckskin was fringed and decorated with ermine and beadwork. The garment is ceremonial in the sense that it was worn on special occasions by men of standing (cf. Lowie, 1954:49. Courtesy of The Science Museum, St. Paul, Minnesota)

simple wooden saddle, made in imitation of the Spanish colonial prototype, has high wooden cantles at front and back, a simple wooden or antler frame lashed together with rawhide strips, and a complete covering of rawhide which serves to bind the saddle into a single, rigid unit.

Smaller utensils and containers were sometimes made of rawhide, sometimes of tanned skin. The *parfleche* is a single piece of rawhide which folds much like an envelope to form a container in which dried meat and other food were stored. Saddlebags, tubular headdress containers, small pouches for personal belongings, amulets, and medicines, were all made of light and durable tanned skin or rawhide.

In early historic times, most tools were made of chipped stone. Contact with traders quickly altered this practice, for metal knives and iron arrowpoints, frequently made from metal barrel hoops, proved much more satisfactory. The Teton arrow tipped with a long, thin iron point proved quite effective as a hunting weapon.

The bow was a simple wooden self bow, made of ash or other local hardwood. The bow was frequently given greater strength and power by gluing a thin strip of green sinew over the entire back of the bow. This allowed a shorter bow, important to a hunter who was mounted and would be handicapped by a very long wooden bow. The lance was another weapon used by the Teton, though it perhaps had greater use as a ceremonial object carried by leaders of the several military societies.

Cooking utensils were as light and durable as the other aspects of Teton material culture. Though the Teton probably made pottery at one time, as did other Nomadic Plains tribes such as the Cheyenne and Crow, they abandoned this art as they adapted their way of life to pure nomadism. Pottery is much too fragile for a people like the Teton. Instead they used skin containers and frequently cooked in skin-lined pits where water could be boiled by plac-

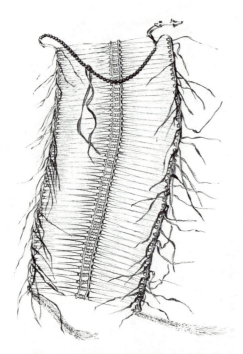

Teton Dakota ● "Hair pipe" necklace or breastplate. Worn as a gorget, or breastplate, this decorative piece reflects the great attention given by the Indians of the Plains to personal adornment and finery. It is made of carefully carved tubular bone beads, each about 4 1/2 inches long, and joined to blue trade beads and buckskin cord. A buckskin fringe and animal tails are set at the outer edges of the necklace. Like so many other features of Plains Indian dress, this was used at festive occasions of many kinds. (Courtesy of The Science Museum, St. Paul, Minnesota)

ing red-hot stones into the container. In this domestic side of life, they also benefited from trade contacts, for the brass trade kettle was admirably suited to their life of frequent movement. Spoons were normally made of bison horn, which, when boiled, became soft and pliable, and thus easily fashioned into a long-handled spoon. The spoon served only as a serving utensil, for food was generally eaten with the fingers. Plates were sometimes made by carving out a knot or burl from an elm or box elder tree.

Teton clothing was quite simple. The basic male winter apparel consisted of a skin turban, a simple sleeveless shirt, breechclout of skin, high leggings, moccasins, and a bison robe. The women wore a tubelike skin dress, short knee-length leggings, moccasins, and a bison-

skin robe. Both sexes used deer or elk hide for their clothing rather than the much heavier bison hide, and in the summer body painting and personal ornament took the place of much of the clothing. Tattooing was frequently practiced by the females who often had lip and facial tattoo marks. The ears of young boys and girls were commonly pierced when the children were five or six years old. An older male made the perforation, using a bone needle, at the request of the parents and was given gifts in exchange for his services. The perforation was kept open with a small piece of sinew until the healing was completed. Short strings of colored beads obtained from traders were hung from these ear perforations.

Both men and women wore the hair in two braids, sometimes artificially lengthened by braiding in extra strands of human or horse hair. The braids were often decorated by intertwining colored woolen cloth or wrapping them with mink or otter skin. Some younger men trained a forelock of hair to hang down in the middle of the forehead; this they frequently lengthened by attaching a small string of beads. Other Plains groups to the south sometimes wore the hair loose, and older women among the Teton also did this. Some Teton males wore their hair in a roach by shaving the sides of the head, leaving a central ridge of hair standing. This hair style was common in the eastern Prairie area and was also found among some of the western Great Lakes peoples.

The decorative art of the Teton was quite elaborate and was frequently applied to articles of apparel. Two major forms of decorative art were used. The first consisted of painting, the second of sewn quill or beads. Two major art styles were also seen—a realistic or naturalistic style, and an angular geometric style. The tendency was to associate the naturalistic style with the painted art form, and the angular geometric style with the quill and beaded art form. Women produced the latter type of art, and males generally, though not exclusively, the former. Early nineteenth-century accounts of the Teton by scholars and artists indicate a prevalence of decorated clothing, particularly the specialized clothing worn on ceremonial occasions. Prince Maximilian of Wied, a German naturalist who travelled up the Missouri River from St. Louis in 1832–1833, describes such clothing for the Teton and for the sedentary tribes further north. Accompanying Maximilian was a young Swiss artist named Carl Bodmer, who made many watercolor sketches of Teton men and women, most of these showing a considerable use of highly decorated clothing. The American artist George Catlin also visited the upper Missouri during this same period, and his records agree with those of Maximilian and Bodmer. Earlier, Lewis and Clark in their journals give some indication of these same practices.

Teton painting was applied to the surface of bison-skin robes, often to the exterior of tipis, to the skin tipi liner, and, of course, to the human body. One of the most interesting examples of Teton painting is seen in the "winter count" where a significant event marking one year was symbolized in some way and that symbol painted onto a hide. The symbols themselves are pictographs, some of them conventionalized, used as mnemonic aids in recalling events of past years. A man kept a personal record of events important to him in this way; one year he might have recalled capturing three Crow horses, another year may have been memorable because of an extreme drought, another perhaps the year that he pledged the Sun Dance.

Quill and beadwork were applied directly to clothing or attached to strips of skin or woolen trade cloth and these applied to the clothing. Teton women gained considerable skill in the application of this decoration, and certain women, more skillful than others, gained prestige in this manner. The art style associated with this form of art is geometric, utilizing small triangles, rectangles, short straight lines, and other simple geometric motifs. The Teton had a preference for blue and red dyed quill or colored beads to form the design, and a preference for blue or white colored quill or beadwork to form the background color. Black was never used, but yellow and green appeared in limited amounts. The colors selected are bright and the resultant decorative art is stunning. The geometric motifs of this art form were not symbolic, and the decorative pattern was not intended to have any particular meaning. Names were apparently given some of the more common motifs but this does not indicate a symbolic significance. Clothing decorated in this manner was frequently augmented by the addition of strips of horsehair hanging in rows or, more commonly among the Blackfoot and other northern groups, the use of strips of white weasel skin hanging in the same fashion. Women's dresses were commonly decorated with quill and beadwork on the yoke, though

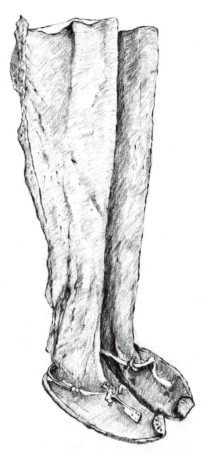

Comanche ● Combination leggings and hard soled moccasins. The hard sole characterizes the southern Plains and differs from the soft sole moccasin of the north. With the attached leggings, also a southern trait, the complex may reflect Southwestern influences (cf. Wissler, 1927:44–46. Courtesy of The Science Museum, St. Paul, Minnesota)

Pacific northwest dentalium shell or large elk incisors were often perforated and hung on the dresses. Many of the dance costumes were decorated with objects which produced noise when moved. Small metal cone-shaped "tinklers" were made from the tin covers of tobacco cans and added to the fringes of leggings or to moccasins. The two-piece Teton moccasin, an upper of tanned skin and a sole of rawhide, frequently was decorated on the toe, and as among the Mandan, often had animal tails extending behind the heel.

The featherwork of the Teton and other Plains tribes was a distinctive part of their material culture. Single feathers were worn in the hair by young Teton men to indicate achieve-

Blackfoot ● Beaded buckskin pouch or carrying bag. The equestrian life of the Plains made leather bags a necessity. Bags such as this, along with rawhide bags and parfleches. (see p. 335), were of many types and were variously decorated. The beadwork is, of course recent, replacing the older decoration by means of porcupine quills. (Courtesy of The Science Museum, St. Paul, Minnesota)

ment in warfare. The large feather bonnet, often associated with the Plains in particular, and in the reservation period practically an American Indian universal, was not the common type of headgear. The Teton bonnet, probably adopted from the Cheyenne, was restricted to certain war leaders and served as a mark of status. Many of the military societies also had distinctive headgear, sometimes made of feathers, and frequently utilizing other animal parts such as bison horn. Feathers used on society headdresses were often owl and grouse feathers, split down the central rib so that they curled. Feathers used for the large bonnet and those worn in the hair were eagle feathers and because of the sacred nature of the eagle as a bird, the headgear constructed of their feathers took on some of these sacred attributes. The capture of an eagle was a serious and significant event.

As mentioned previously, some of the Teton men wore their hair in a roach form. Artificial roaches were sometimes constructed of procupine quill and deer tails and were worn at dances and for ceremonial occasions. This artificial roach does not differ significantly from that worn by the prairie people further to the

east. The winter turban of animal skin is more characteristic of the Mandan and other sedentary tribes, but again, the Teton also used this type of headgear.

Nowhere is the Teton dependence upon the bison seen more clearly than in their patterns of subsistence and economics. Hunting was the major male occupation, and the Teton were adept at all of the methods of bison hunting common to the Plains. Individuals, or small parties of men, hunted on horseback using the bow and the lance to kill bison. Frequently they rode down individual animals, and shot from their horses, but they also practiced stalking. The stalking technique was also used to hunt deer and elk in the timbered bottom lands, particularly when the large Teton bands broke up into smaller units that lived during the winter in the sheltered cottonwood groves of the valleys.

The main bison hunt took place during the summer when the entire band was together. This hunt was a communal affair in which all of the able males participated, and with luck, enough bison were killed to provide food for the band to last many months. The communal hunt utilized different hunting techniques, depending upon the terrain and the size of the bison herd. One method used with success was the "surround by fire." In this technique, the bison herd was quietly surrounded and a circle of fire kindled around the entire herd. As the fire burned in toward the herd, the panic-stricken bison were slaughtered by the men. A similar technique utilized a bluff edge or sometimes a corral into which the bison were lured. Here the Teton constructed a V-shaped arrangement of stone piles and brush with the apex of the "V" at the cliff edge or a ravine. The stone piles fanned out onto the open prairie, and when a herd was sighted, a shaman covered with the skin of a bison calf, placed himself between the herd and the open end of the "V." By imitating a lost calf in action and sound, he enticed the herd slowly into the mouth of the "V." When the herd was in this position, horsemen stampeded the herd from behind to move them in the direction of the cliff edge. Women, young men, and boys stationed behind the rock piles and brush stood as the herd approached, waved blankets, and shouted to keep the herd from veering to the side. If the drive was successful, many animals plunged over the edge of the cliff where they were killed with clubs by the men waiting below.

The communal hunt gave a huge meat supply, if successful, and the success of the hunt was critical in the life of the Teton. Success or failure could mean the difference between a year of plenty and a year of hardship and perhaps starvation. For this reason, the cooperation of every member of the society was demanded during this period. A military society was given absolute powers of policing at this time. Anyone who through carelessness or intent engaged in any activity which threatened the success of the communal hunt was severely punished by the military society. His entire belongings, and those of his family were destroyed, his horses driven off, and at times he was driven from the land.

The communal bison hunt is again a practice which was not unique to the Plains. Early French records describe similar hunts by the eastern prairie horticulturalists during the summer months. They also record the presence of absolute authority over the band at this time. However, once the Teton and the other Plains nomads obtained the horse, they were able to develop this subsistence technique to its ultimate. The horse gave mobility and the chance to obtain bison in greater quantities than when hunting was on foot. The mobility also provided a means of locating the wandering herds at much greater distances than before. The Teton economy was a surplus food economy in a successful year and much of the rapid population growth among the Teton can be attributed to this fact.

The communal hunt was not solely a male affair. It is seen that the women participated to some extent in the actual hunt. They also provided most of the effort at the successful conclusion of the hunt, for they were given the responsibility of skinning the fallen bison, preparing the meat for packing back to the camp, and taking the hides. This period was one of intense activity for the women. The meat had to serve as food for many months to come and they needed to preserve it. To do this they cut it into thin strips and hung it on pole racks to dry. The skins, too, had to be worked rapidly before they began to decay, and this involved an enormous amount of effort. Some of the dried meat was pounded with dried berries and tallow to form the concentrated pemmican used by hunting and war parties. The major portion was packed in parfleches and used later as food by boiling it in water, with dried berries and tubers. Women also collected these wild vegetable plants and

dried them, and occasionally a Teton woman would plant a little maize. Other domesticated vegetable products were raided or bartered from the sedentary village tribes to the north.

In all of this activity, there was an obvious and rather strict division of labor, which generally followed sex lines, with the men the hunters and the women the collectors and preparers of food and clothing. There was also a division of labor by age differential inasmuch as the elderly men and women could not participate in the most active pursuits, and the younger children did not have strength and skill. The younger boys and girls did take an active part in some of these activities, however limited their contributions were. They helped their parents and were taught the techniques in the process, and their games commonly were models of adult activities. The aged were at a disadvantage in this society, despite the fact that in their lifetime they may have accumulated considerable prestige. No longer able to participate actively, those older members of the Teton had to lean on younger members of their families for support. This was gladly given, for age and wisdom were respected, but at times the burden became too great, and the aged were left behind in a shelter with a limited supply of food and water. This was not an action forced upon them, but in many cases voluntary on the part of the older individual, and apparently it was always accepted as inevitable.

Specialization of labor other than by lines of sex and age is not found in Teton society. Some males were expert craftsmen in bow construction and their services were valued. Women, too, frequently enjoyed prestige because of particular skills. None of these people was a full-time specialist, however. All participated in the normal round of activities. The only real exceptions to this generalization are the shamans or curers, who occasionally, because of great powers and abilities, became nearly full-time religious specialists, and the berdache, or transvestite males, who adopted the woman's role for life. Neither of these individuals is common, however, and in each case they are exceptions to the general rule.

Society

The Teton comprised seven bands known as the Brule or Burnt Thighs, Hunkpapa, Miniconjou, Oglala, Oohenonpa or Two Kettle, Sans Arc, and Sihapsa or Blackfoot. Of these groups, the Oglala were the most populous and occupied the greatest extent of territory. In form and organization the Oglala approach a tribe composed of subunits or bands. During the nineteenth century, however, these bands did not function as a single tribe in the sense of having any sort of political unity. The Oglala were quite independent, for example, and in the area of southwestern South Dakota, western Nebraska, and southeastern Wyoming which they occupied, they actually functioned as a tribe in the political sense used here. The character of the environment and the type of hunting existence followed by the Oglala combined to form a fluid society which came together as a unit only during the summer months of the communal bison hunt and the Sun Dance. During this period, fresh meat in quantity was available so that a large group could function as a unit. The demands of the communal hunt also required the band as a whole for effective bison surrounds. During the remainder of the year, the Oglala broke up into smaller units, largely composed of patrilineally related families, which followed the food resources as they became available. During the cold winter months even smaller groups separated to camp in sheltered spots, generally remaining in one area for most of the winter. John Ewers, in his monograph on the horse in Blackfoot culture (1955), gives a lucid description of the winter camps and seasonal round of the Blackfoot, much of which applies equally well to all the Teton bands.

The summer Sun Dance camp which brought all of the Oglala small bands together formed a huge circle in which each incoming band occupied a definite position. The circle opened to the east and its center was dominated by the Sun Dance circle. This was a time of excitement for the Oglala and the other Teton bands who followed similar practices. The reunion was within a religious framework, for it was the Sun Dance which ostensibly brought them together. More than that, however, it was a time when food supplies would be replenished through the summer hunt, a time for renewing acquaintances with friends and relatives not seen since the previous summer, a period of gossip and matchmaking, gambling and gaming, oratory and debate. Young men vied in contests like horse racing and archery, older men recounted experiences of the past year and the years before, and discussed problems of a serious nature affecting the band as a whole, and younger ambitious men organized war parties for the period after the summer

hunt. This was surely the high point of the Oglala year as it was for the other Teton bands and most of the other nomadic Plains tribes.

The nuclear or biological family was the basic structural unit in Teton society. A band was composed of a series of these nuclear families living together as an organized society. The band tended to be composed of families related through the male heads of families. At marriage, a boy would likely bring his wife to live in the band in which he had grown up. This patrilineal residence pattern was not strictly enforced, however, and the newly married couple could decide to live in the band of the wife's parents, if that was different, or they could live in another band entirely. Band membership was also fluid during one's lifetime. As the band was not a corporate kin group and band affiliation was not strictly kin determined, a couple could shift their band affiliation during their lifetime. New bands were formed, as among the Oglala, when band size grew above the optimum size and a series of families broke away to form their own band. New bands were also created when conflicts and factions formed within a band. When these reached such a proportion that fragmentation of the original band was the only solution to the mounting tensions, one or more new bands formed.

Unlike the sedentary tribes, which were organized on a unilineal kinship basis and in which the lineage and sib groups were kin organizations dominating the structure of the society, the Teton, like all other nomadic Plains groups except the Crow, organized around the family and band. Bands tended to have fairly well defined hunting areas and in a sense they were also territorial groups, just as the tribe as a whole had a defined territory. As may be seen, some of the early conflict on the Plains centered about hunting rights and territorial disputes between neighboring tribes.

The Teton family, as the basic unit of this society, was composed of mother and father, younger unmarried children, frequently an adopted child, and perhaps a male or female of the oldest generation. The usual marriage system was monogamous and most Teton males had but one wife. Polygyny, or plural wives, was the ideal type of marriage, although the incidence of polygyny was low. The preferred form of polygynous marriage was marriage to sisters, or sororal polygyny. The polygynous households lived adjacent to each other, or if children were not numerous, which was usually the case, sisters married to the same man might share the same lodge. Marriage partners were sought from one's own band or an adjacent band, and the only restriction was that they should not be closely related. Cross cousin marriage was not practiced among the Teton.

Marriage itself was not highly formalized nor was it usually marked by ceremonies. Most marriages were arranged by the parents of the bride and groom as there was little socially sanctioned opportunity for young unmarried men and women to meet alone. The marriage was marked by gift exchange between the families, though again, this was not formalized into a bride price. Marriages were often lifetime associations, but divorce was relatively easy and apparently quite common. A man could divorce a wife for adultery, laziness, slothfulness, or even excessive nagging. A woman did not have as many causes for divorce, though if the marriage were impossible to her, some means of divorce could always be found. Divorce was sometimes merely separation by mutual agreement, though a man could humiliate a wife by casting her off publicly at a dance or other band ceremony. Suicide by hanging was not uncommon for women cast out by men in this fashion. Adultery, as was indicated, might lead to divorce, though it need not. A man with evidence of adultery on the part of his wife might punish her by cutting off her nose, and he could demand a payment from the wife's paramour. A truly great and generous man, however, might divorce his wife and force the adulterous couple to leave the band. This was looked upon as a magnanimous gesture by a man who was not to be upset by such trivial events. His gift of a horse and other property to the erring couple further reinforced his generous nature in the eyes of his fellow band members.

Both the levirate and the sororate were present in Teton society. Both functioned as mechanisms of social stability in that they were means of preserving family unity upon the death of one parent. Under the levirate, a man was obligated to marry the wife of his deceased brother and under the sororate, a younger sister of a recently deceased woman was obligated to marry her brother-in-law, or the husband of her deceased sister. These marriage practices did more than establish rights to sexual intercourse. They were means by which the brother or sister assumed the obligations of caring for and rearing the children and also assumed the obligation of economic participation in family duties. Both practices also indicate the necessity of marriage as a joint economic arrangement whereby the specialized knowledge and skills of a man and woman were combined. Single adults of either sex were not found in Teton society, for life in this harsh area demanded the joint participation of a man and a woman in the yearly economic round.

Marriage was not always arranged nor was it always without ceremony. A couple, wealthy by Teton standards, might keep a girl severely restricted during her period of growth, giving feasts in her honor, and at the time of her marriage, shower the groom with gifts. Such a girl, publicly labelled a virgin at a ceremony after her puberty, brought great prestige to her family and to the groom. Elopement gave an alternative to the rather rigid arranged marriage. Love matches were not unknown, and the Teton did have a concept of romantic love. A young man attracted to a particular girl might serenade her on warm summer evenings by playing love songs on his long wooden flute. He might also see her alone frequently by hiding in the brush along the path she would take to the stream to get water. A young couple behaving in this manner might, if their parents did not approve of the match, elope and live alone for some months, until they returned to the band and were usually then accepted.

Children were highly desired among the Teton and male children were particularly welcome. A child born into a family was born into a large kin group and his relationships with many members of his band were determined at the time of his birth. Kinship organization and the patterns of prescribed reciprocal behavior associated with particular classes of kin were well developed. As in our own society, however, the Teton reckoned kinship equally between the mother's and the father's side of the family. Theirs was a bilateral kinship system, rather than a unilateral system like that found among the Mandan and the other sedentary peoples.

The Teton kinship system and its terminology is highly classificatory. That is, the Teton grouped various genetic and affinal kin into categories of relatives. These terms were used in address more commonly than were individual names. These latter were given a short time after birth but were frequently changed during a lifetime as a result of deeds and exploits or

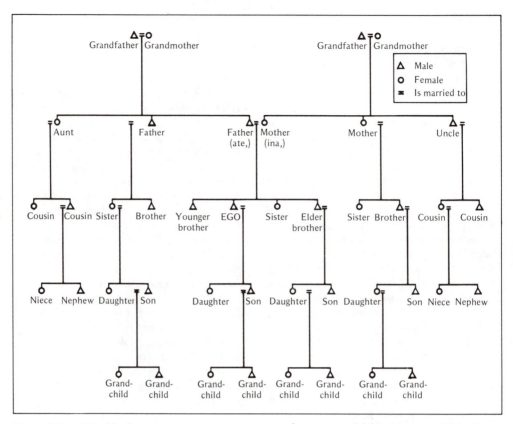

Teton Dakota Kinship System

due to some physical or mental peculiarity. Teton kinship does more than give a set of kin terms, however, for between each set of designated kin, special behavioral patterns were fixed in Teton culture. Between *ate* and son, for example, a relationship was established which is best termed a "respect" relationship. Behavior between these categories of kinsmen were marked by seriousness and respect, joking was not allowed, and the popular erotic tales current in the culture could not be told to these close kin. The system then established a series of behavior patterns operative whenever persons wearing these labels interacted. The system did more, however, for it also established a series of duties and responsibilities between these designated kinsmen. *Ate* was responsible for training his son or anyone he called son in the arts of hunting and warfare; he was obligated to provide economic support; and it is he who was normally obligated to provide goods for distribution to the members of the military society his son joined. A similar respect relationship was enjoyed under the mother-daughter relationship, and to some degree between

grandparent-grandchild kinsmen. This latter relationship was freer, however, and Teton grandparents were notorious for the indulgence of their grandchildren. To some degree the respect relationship in an attenuated form applied between older and younger siblings. An older brother felt the same degree of responsibility toward a younger brother as did the father.

Relationships between members of the opposite sex were also clearly prescribed. Brother and sister relationships were marked by an extreme respect relationship which, between the ages of infancy and marriage, was marked by what approaches complete avoidance. Young boys and girls did not play together after infancy, and brothers and sisters never joked in each other's presence. The elaborate avoidance relationship applied between a mother-in-law and her son-in-law. This relationship was so strict that in theory, and probably in practice, these two individuals never spoke directly to one another. When the mother-in-law entered the lodge, the young husband left or he turned his back so that he did not face her. If they met on a path near the encampment, the mother-in-law would likely leave the path and hide in the brush until the young man had passed. When forced to converse with one another, they did so through a third party who transmitted the conversation. Some writers have indicated that a father-in-law avoided a daughter-in-law in much this same way. This may be true, but if so, it was not as highly institutionalized and was probably more like the well-defined respect relationship described earlier.

All inter-kin behavior among the Teton was not as somber as may seem from the above description. Even between those under the respect relationship, the interpersonal relationship was marked by warmth and friendliness. Among other kin there were fewer restrictions of this sort. A joking relationship applied between males who stood in the brother-in-law relationship, and under this, great freedom of action was allowed. Males and those women who were potential spouses under the marriage rules of the levirate and sororate, could indulge in considerable freedom of behavior, and mild sex play between these individuals was sanctioned.

Teton society was of such a size and nature that nearly any stranger could be accommodated within the framework of kinship. All that would be needed would be one ancestor in common and the correct kin designates could be found. The kinship system was capable, then, of nearly infinite extension laterally and could include nearly any band member if need arose. Those kinsmen distantly removed laterally from the individual speaker were treated with less formality and intensity than similar kinsmen more closely related. The duties and obligations of kinship could be applied when needed beyond the immediate family, and it was this quality of Teton society which made it a strongly knit group.

Kinship thus formed the framework around which the majority of interpersonal relations functioned. In Teton society, as in all societies, there were individuals who did not or could not adapt themselves to the situation. The individual who consistently did not follow these behavioral norms could be ejected from the band. Those individuals whose behavioral lapses were infrequent were not treated as severely. In most cases gossip and ridicule sufficed as a means of controlling deviant individuals, and in a small society, this method of social control can be extremely effective. A young man who consistently disregarded normative behavioral codes in his dealings with a female parallel cousin would probably be subjected to ridicule by his peers as

well as chastisement by his elders. The personal shame felt as a result of this ridicule was frequently enough to stop the deviant behavior.

For more serious offenses, such as murder of a kinsman, the close kin were obligated to avenge his death and internal conflict of significant proportions could arise through this means. When such conflicts did appear, the council of older males sought to intervene and settle the dispute to the satisfaction of both parties by a property settlement. The council had no real authority, however, nor did they have any force to back their decisions. They depended upon their great prestige and upon the willingness of the disputing parties to settle a grievance which might lead to dissolution of the band.

The only period during which a true force had control of the Teton band and during which council decisions were absolute was the period of the communal hunt when one of the military societies would be appointed as akacita or camp police. At this time all assembled bands functioned under a single authority. This application of authority to a period of crisis also appeared in Teton warfare. Here a war party was under the authority of the war leader or organizer. His authority extended only to those individual members of the party, however, and was absolute only during the period in which the party was absent from the camp.

Social control rested in kinship and in the face-to-face contacts of members of the band. Sanctions of ridicule and shame, applied by those within the living unit, were most common and effective. Serious matters of band and even tribal interest were difficult to resolve for the structure of Teton society provided no institutionalized mechanism to function in these circumstances. In these cases, reliance had to be placed on the powers of persuasion of prestigeful men, backed by supernatural symbols of their office and status. This tale of the origin of the White Buffalo Calf Pipe related by Black Elk (Neihardt, 1972) illustrates one of these symbolic objects which served to buttress the arguments of the chiefs as they offered a means of settlement to disputants.

A very long time ago, they say, two scouts were out looking for bison; and when they came to the top of a high hill and looked north, they saw something coming a long way off, and when it came closer they cried out, "It is a woman!," and it was. Then one of the scouts, being foolish, had bad thoughts and spoke them; but the other said: "That is a sacred woman; throw all bad thoughts away." When she came still closer, they saw that she wore a fine white buckskin dress, that her hair was very long and that she was young and very beautiful. And she knew their thoughts and said in a voice that was like singing: "You do not know me, but if you want to do as you think, you may come." And the foolish one went; but just as he stood before her, there was a white cloud that came and covered them. And the beautiful young woman came out of the cloud, and when it blew away the foolish man was a skeleton covered with worms.

Then the woman spoke to the one who was not foolish: "You shall go home and tell your people that I am coming and that a big tepee shall be built for me in the center of the nation." And the man, who was very much afraid, went quickly and told the people, who did at once as they were told; and there around the big tepee they waited for the sacred woman. And after a while she came, very beautiful and singing, and as she went into the tepee this is what she sang:

"With visible breath I am walking.
A voice I am sending as I walk.
In a sacred manner I am walking
With visible tracks I am walking.
In a sacred manner I walk."

And as she sang, there came from her mouth a white cloud that was good to smell. Then she gave something to the chief, and it was a pipe with a bison calf carved on one side to mean the earth that bears and feeds us, and with twelve eagle feathers hanging from the stem to mean the sky and the twelve moons, and these were tied with a grass that never breaks. "Behold!" she said. "With this you shall multiply and be a good nation. Nothing but good shall come from it. Only the hands of the good shall take care of it and the bad shall not even see it." Then she sang again and went out of the tepee; and as the people watched her going, suddenly it was a white bison galloping away and snorting and soon it was gone (Neihardt, 1975:3–4).

In this society where individual male action was valued, where younger men prided themselves on their aggressiveness and where competition for status was strong, informal methods of social control were not always successful. Serious personal antagonisms were not unknown and disruptions of band solidarity were relatively frequent. It was only when band and tribe were pressed by a common enemy that many of these internal differences were sub-merged. Late in the nineteenth century, when the Teton were sorely pressed by encroaching miners, settlers, railway building crews with their professional bison hunters, and the United States Cavalry brought in to protect all of these groups, did the tribal and even intertribal differences become forgotten in the face of a common enemy.

Leadership and authority were diffuse in Teton society. The general North American Indian pattern of "democratic" leadership prevailed here as elsewhere. Chiefs were men past the age of active participation in warfare; men who had achieved prominence as war leaders in their youth; those who had mature, respected judgment and great ability as orators; and those whose past actions were above reproach, who were noted for their generosity, who fulfilled Teton ideals of male behavior. Bands were governed by a loose council of these chiefs, always older men, many of whom fulfilled all of the criteria listed above. A man need not have been a noted warrior, however, as chiefly status could be achieved with the combination of the other attributes alone. The council acted as a unit, their deliberations were calm, and their unanimous decisions were made within the framework of the consensus of the band as a whole. Their actions were not arbitrary nor authoritarian and they lacked the force necessary to back their decisions.

Wissler describes a more complex organization among the Red Cloud band of the Oglala on the Pine Ridge Reservation in the latter part of the nineteenth century. According to Wissler, the Chiefs society organized here elected seven of its own members.

Independent of its organization, it elected seven chiefs to govern the people. These chiefs were elected for life. Since it was customary for vacancies to be filled by the election of a worthy son or relative these offices were partially hereditary. These seven chiefs did not actually participate in the daily government but delegated powers to younger and more virile men, by the appointment of four councilors to serve for life, though they could resign at any time. These may or may not be members of the chiefs society but the seven chiefs are not eligible to the office. They are spoken of as the "owners of the tribe," but more particularly as the "shirt wearers" since upon investment in office they are given a special form of hair-fringed shirt. These shirts are spoken of as "owned by the tribe." Their owners are the supreme councilors and exec-

utives. They are charged with the general welfare; to see that good hunting is provided, healthful campsites selected, etc. Thus, though theoretically deputies, these four men are the real power in the government.

The seven chiefs, often assisted by the four shirt wearers and the whole chiefs society, elect four officers (wakic'un) to organize and control the camp. All except the four shirt wearers are eligible to this office. These men serve for about one year. It seems to have been the custom to reelect two or three of them so as to have experienced men in office. . . .

The wakic'un are after all the true executives, the shirt men standing as councilors. A tipi was set up in the center of the camp circle as the office of the wakicun in which they occupied "the seats of honor." The shirt men as well as the seven chiefs had seats there as councilors, but did not sit continuously like the wakicun. As soon as invested in office, the wakic'un appointed two young men to act as orderlies, see that food were provided, etc. They appointed a herald to promulgate their orders. They also selected two head akicita. . . . (Wissler, 1912:8.)

This specialized development in Red Cloud's band was mirrored in another Oglala band called the Kiaksai, but is not reported for other Oglala bands or for other Teton bands. It seems to be a very late formalization of governmental structure lacking in earlier periods.

It is difficult to say if the Teton at one time had hereditary chiefs as their eastern relatives the Mdewakanton did in historic times. Keating, writing in his journal as he accompanied Major Stephen Long up the Minnesota River in 1823, describes hereditary chiefs for each of the Mdewakanton villages. His description of the village of Kaposia, for example, tells of their chief, Little Crow, who "is a very distinguished man, and [who] belongs to one of the oldest families of chiefs among the Dacotas, he being the fourth of his family in direct line." Keating further indicates a possible hierarchy of chiefs when he states:

At a meeting of many Indian nations which took place at Lake Traverse about four or five years ago, there were present, besides some men from all the tribes of Dacotas, many for the Assiniboins, Mandans, Minnetarees (Hidatsa), Iawas, and other nations, who all addressed him (Little Crow) by the name "father," acknowledging thereby, not only his superiority over all the other Dacota chiefs, but even that of the Dacota nation over theirs. . . . (Keating, 1825:94.)

The above quote indicates the probable primacy of the Mdewakanton and certainly documents hereditary chieftainship within a family or lineage among them. Many authors feel, however, that the hereditary chieftainship in historic times is a pattern arising after trade contacts with Europeans and due directly to that contact. Accustomed to authority and seeking to establish trade relationships with the Indian band or tribe, the European trader preferred to deal with one man, conferring on him gifts which brought him prestige, and insisting on dealing with him in future relationships, thereby validating his position. It would be quite simple to transform this pattern into a hereditary system, especially among a group such as the Mdewakanton who seem to have had a stronger tendency toward unilineal descent in the male line than did the Teton. One author writing of the Eastern Dakota states specifically that "the chieftainship is of modern date; that is, since the Indians first became acquainted with the whites. Tradition says they knew of no chiefs until the white people began to make distinctions. The first Sioux that was ever made a chief among the Dacotas was Wahba-shaw, and this was done by the British. Since that time, chieftainship has been hereditary." (Wissler, 1912:11–12.) This statement should not be taken at face value, but does indicate the probability that hereditary chieftainship is of recent origin for all of the Dakota.

Men reached the status of chief among the Teton when public opinion supported their claims. This same public opinion might depose a chief, for continued correct actions were required. The man who did not live up to the obligations of the rank was quickly relieved of his position and was powerless to avoid this. Strong pressures were applied to an individual chief and he had to continually validate his status by showing his generosity to the poor, by demonstrating his judgment, even temper, and concern for the welfare of the band. In the words of a Hunkpapa informant, "chiefs were always poor men" because property distribution through gift-giving was the prevalent way of validating status.

Symbols of office were well developed among the Teton. Chiefs, the leaders of the military societies, camp criers or heralds, and even Oglala women in their organizations wore specially ornamented clothing, carried symbolic lances, staffs, coup sticks, and other paraphernalia when acting in their official capacities. Keating describes Major Long's meeting with Wanotan, a Yanktonai chief associated with the British in the War of 1812. The first day's meeting took place in a huge pavilion formed by the erection of several skin lodges. Wanotan at this time wore a mixture of European regalia and feasted Long with quantities of food including the "much esteemed" dog meat. The following day, the festivities were repeated, and Keating describes Wanotan as he appeared

in the full habit of an Indian chief. We have never seen a more dignified looking person, or a more becoming dress. The most prominent part of his apparel was a splendid cloak or mantle of buffalo skins, dressed so as to be of fine white colour; it was decorated with small tufts of owl's feathers, and others of various hues. . . . A splendid necklace, formed of about sixty claws of the grizzly bear, imparted a manly character to his whole appearance. His leggings, jacket, and moccasins were in real Dacota fashion, being made of white skins, profusely decorated with human hair; his moccasins were variegated with the plumage of several birds. In his hair he wore nine sticks neatly cut and smoothed, and painted with vermillion; these designated the number of gunshot wounds which he had recieved [probably coups counter — Editor]; they were secured with a strip of red cloth; two plaited tresses of his hair were allowed to hang forward; his face was tastefully painted with vermillion; in his hand he wore a large fan of the feathers of the turkey, which he frequently used.

Having requested that the warriors favour us with a dance Wanotan had one performed for us in the afternoon. . . . The dresses which they wore were more carefully arranged than usual, and indicated that some pains had been taken for the occasion . . . one of the warriors was conspicuous. In his hand he held a wand about ten feet long and about six inches wide; one of the edges of this band was fastened to the staff, the other was furnished with black and white feathers, closely secured to it by their quills, and forming a sort of a fringe. This was one of the two insignis of the Assn. of the Nanpashene. . . . (Keating, 1825: 455–457).

This description indicates the elaboration of dress and costume among the Dakota in historic times. It also indicates the use of a feather fan as a symbol of chiefly office among the Yanktonai as it was among the Teton. The military society staff carried by the dance leader is also symbolic, as will be seen when these societies are described. It should be noted here, however, that apparently among only the Oglala, chiefs themselves formed a distinctly organized society known as the Chiefs Society, thought by Lowie to be borrowed by them from the Mandan Buffalo Bull society.

Leadership in Teton society was not restricted to chiefs or war leaders. Some leaders, generally called shamans in the anthropological literature, were individuals who had achieved reputations as skilled manipulators of the supernatural. Their powers were gained individually through direct contacts with the Teton supernatural world, and many of these men wielded considerable power. Their functions were largely outside the political sphere, however, though some men, such as the Hunkpapa shaman Sitting Bull, used their prestige gained in other areas of behavior to advantage in more mundane matters.

Much of the prestige accumulated by individuals came to those active in warfare. Plains Indian warfare has been described and analyzed by many authors, and the interpretations have varied from describing warfare as a sport or game to emphasizing the purely economic motivations. Neither of these extreme interpretations is correct, of course, for Plains warfare combines these attributes and others.

Foremost in Teton warfare in the early nineteenth century was a system of war honors usually called counting "coup." Honor and prestige went to those who exhibited bravery and daring in the face of the enemy. The deeds of these men included touching a fallen enemy, wresting a rifle or bow from the hand of an enemy, striking an enemy in the thick of combat, stealing a horse picketed within an enemy village, making a vow to stand steadfast in one place during a battle, and other heroic efforts of this nature. Killing and scalping were accorded honor, but they fell far below the previously named activities in the hierarchy of prestige. The goal of most men was to accumulate war honors to gain the prestige afforded the successful warrior by the society. From the time they were able to play together, boys fashioned their games after the war activities of the adults. Mock battles, simulated horse-stealing raids, archery practice, and counting and recounting of coup on small animals occupied the day of most boys. The first animal killed by a boy was a signal for a feast given by his father in honor of this deed. Horsemanship was learned early and practiced constantly. Boys of twelve and even younger begged to be allowed to accompany their father or another relative on a war party. Training to endure hardship was a regular part of the life of these boys. A Hunkpapa informant told of his grandfather telling of being awakened at dawn by his father and rushed outside to plunge into an ice-clogged stream. This same Hunkpapa man as a youth accompanied an older relative on a war party for the first time. A few days away from their camp, they stopped near a thicket to rest. The following day they moved north along a river, keeping to the timber to avoid being seen. When they camped that night, the boy was told by one of the men, "Here now, I left some arrows at the place we camped last night. You go and get them." The boy had to travel back at night to the previous camp and then return with the arrows. As the informant said, "This was the way that they would test his courage."

Each war party was headed by a single leader. These men were normally not chiefs and council members, but were younger men anxious to make a place for themselves in the Teton world. Any man might organize a war party. He needed only to hang his decorated rawhide shield before his lodge to publicly announce his intentions. If he were a man who had been successful in the past, or a man who had dreamed of a successful war venture, he would undoubtedly attract young men to his standard. Those who accompanied him did so voluntarily. There was no external compulsion to go, no overt force applied. The drive for status, the need to avenge a death within the family, the possibility of gaining horses or a second wife, the chance for loot and booty might all be factors in motivating the men who accompanied the war leader. Their only obligation, once they left the camp, was to follow the leader of the party. A man might leave the party, and men often did so if a dream or another omen indicated an unsuccessful venture to them. When they left the party, however, they returned to their camp. Before leaving, all members of the party needed to be ritually pure. Sexual abstinence for four days was necessary and most commonly the men took purifying baths in the sweat lodge.

Many war parties in the nineteenth century were horse-stealing raids with no other object. Counting of coup was purely secondary, and the really successful party of this sort was one which returned with horses taken from the vicinity of an enemy camp, but taken unobserved. These parties frequently left their camp on foot, depending on enemy horses to bring them home. Horses were wealth to the Teton as they were to the other nomadic Plains tribes. Vast herds, such as the Comanche accumulated on their raids into northern Mexico, were not found on the northern Plains and the Teton cannot be counted rich in horses. The severity of the winter limited the number of animals that could be kept, for grazing land was frozen and often covered with snow. Favorite horses were kept in the timber near the winter camp, and Teton stories relate that often these horses were fed small branches and tree bark to keep them alive over the winter. The Cheyenne functioned as middlemen in the trade of horses from the southern Plains to the village tribes and nomads of the north-central Plains. Tribes of the northern intermountain plateau also served as suppliers of horses to the northern Plains. This area, centered on the Snake River in present-day Idaho, was an optimum area for horse herding, and tribes such as the Nez Perce and Flathead raised numbers of horses which were funneled onto the northern Plains through the Crow and the Blackfoot.

Teton warfare also had its economic motivations. The Arikara, a sedentary Caddoan-speaking people living along the Missouri River below the Mandan and Hidatsa, were virtual serfs of the Teton in the nineteenth century. Completely dominated, they were forced to furnish maize and other vegetable foods to the Teton bands. The Mandan and Hidatsa also suffered from Teton and Yanktonai depredations. After the smallpox epidemic of 1837, the Mandan were so reduced in size that they could no longer leave their village for the summer bison hunt. The Teton were too numerous and the Mandan could not afford the chance of being caught away from their protected village. Crow and northern Cheyenne bands offered some protection to both Mandan and Hidatsa. The Crow were recently separated from the Hidatsa and annually returned to the Hidatsa villages for summer trading. Teton war parties were conspicuously absent from the area when the Crow were visiting. This pattern does indicate the role of economic forces in shaping Teton warfare. They needed vegetable foods, dried and preserved for winter use; they grew maize

●RETURNING TO THE CAMP—NOMADIC
PLAINS

Among the tribes of the Great Plains, those
concerned primarily with the intensive hunting
of the bison, tribal assemblages took place
when, toward the early summer, the bison
herds themselves began to gather. As they
grew fat in the summer pasturage in the vast
windy plains, they became the focus of human
activity. Among the Plains Indians, small
bands and groups of kindred spent their
winters in essential isolation from each other.
Then the summer hunt called them from their
local residence areas. Hunting was their prime
activity, and a tremendous amount of labor
went into the chase, into the gathering of meat,
fat, and hides. But there were other activities as
well. War, so vital to the culture of the Plains,
was an almost equally important occupation;
much time was also found for ceremonial and
ritual. In the camps, the kindred groupings
pitched their tipis together at special places.
Men rejoined their warrior groupings and

ceremonial associations. In the now greater
community every effort was directed toward
the achievement of success both in the
carefully organized and policed hunt and in
forays against tribal enemies.

Here, in the Great Plains of a century ago
(the rifle suggesting the period), a man and his
wives return to the greater camp circle. Their
belongings, including the hides for the lodge,
are packed on a travois, the poles of which
will serve as partial support for the tipi. The
decorations at the back of the travois suggest
the Blackfoot, but the pattern was much the
same for all the tribes of the High Plains. In
earlier times, it was the ubiquitous dogs which
drew the travois, but with the advent of the
horse, it was a device which lent itself readily
to transfer. Weary from a long trek and from
the short rations of winter, the hunter and his
family reach the point where they can
reaffirm their ties with others in the tribe. The
yearly cycle begins again.

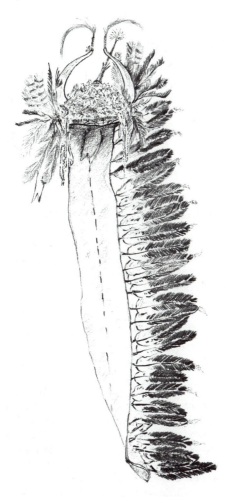

Blackfoot ● Bison horn headdress with eagle feather streamer. Headgear in the Plains was reserved for festive occasions and the use of a horned cap such as this was generally permitted only to especially distinguished men. Of the Plains tribes, the Dakota had the greatest elaboration of headgear, relating it both to military exploits and to personal charms. The latter aspect characterized the Blackfoot, among whom even the single eagle feather in the hair had significance as a charm. The streamers on this horned headdress are 68 inches long. (Courtesy of The Science Museum, St. Paul, Minnesota)

only sporadically and depended on the village tribes for their supply. Raids on the villages gave them these needed foods, and in these raids their warriors gained the honors needed in the mobile Teton status system.

Large pitched battles were not common, though traditions describing the early period on the northern Plains indicate that the practice was known and large battles did take place between tribes contesting for hunting territories. It was only in the final phases of Plains culture, during the middle and latter portions of the nineteenth century, that this pattern of warfare again assumed importance. These later battles against the common foe sometimes involved as many as 3000 active warriors from several bands and often from neighboring tribes. The Teton were not completely effective in these battles, as their patterns of warfare which emphasized individual heroics and hand-to-hand combat did not always suffice against the more disciplined foe. Lacking this discipline, the Teton often failed to follow up the advantage gained in their initial surges. Long sieges were not attempted; they were content to hit a foe hard, withdraw, hit again, and then disappear. The quality of these Plains warriors in battle is well attested in the historic literature, and the Teton achieved a reputation in the northern Plains comparable to that of the Comanche in the south. No Plains tribe in conflict with the white man, however, can recall a struggle of the proportions of that waged by the northern Cheyenne under Dull Knife as they eluded the cavalry for months in their epic march north from Oklahoma territory to their homeland. All of the Plains Indian skills of maneuver and tactics are displayed in this story; but it is a story of desperation where individual glory and war honors were forgotten.

As indicated previously, leadership for Teton war parties came from the younger men. These individuals were sometimes denied chieftainship, for they sometimes lacked the other personality attributes necessary for this high status. Again, however, in the final phases of warfare against the white man, some of the war leaders gained a position of authority in their bands impossible in earlier periods. The nearly continual state of war elevated these men so that their authority became practically continuous.

A type of organization which was highly elaborated on the Plains was that known to anthropologists as the voluntary association. The akicita or camp police, composed of members of a military society, formed an organization of this sort. There are no complete studies of these societies for all of the Teton bands, but Wissler (1912) describes those present among the Oglala in the late nineteenth century. He groups Oglala societies into (1) societies for men, (2) feast and dance societies, and (3) dream cults. The first named are men's military societies whose function in warfare was important. The feast

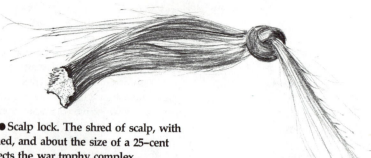

Blackfoot ● Scalp lock. The shred of scalp, with hair attached, and about the size of a 25–cent piece, reflects the war trophy complex characteristic of so much of native America. In the Plains, these small scalp locks were taken. Although to some extent related to the war honors associated with "counting coup", the Plains generally stressed scalping far less than other exploits of war, such as touching the enemy or running off his horses. Only the Teton set a high value on scalping. (cf. Lowie, 1954:106–108. Courtesy of The Science Museum, St. Paul, Minnesota)

and dance societies are generally social but include specialized women's groups. Dream cult societies are shamanistic or religiously oriented societies which will be discussed later.

Oglala societies seem to have been rather fluid in that their membership and their importance fluctuated, some even disappearing entirely or temporarily until reactivated later. All of these societies were voluntary associations in that membership was not compulsory. In most cases membership was by invitation and usually the initiate distributed gifts to the officers and members of the society. Most Oglala youths desired membership, and the nonmember, unless he were a shaman or a berdache, was severely handicapped in the quest for status. Rarely could such a person achieve any real distinction.

The Oglala had many societies. Wissler groups the Men's societies into Akicita societies, Head Men's societies, and war societies. The subdivision is somewhat arbitrary in that the akicita and war societies are both military societies composed of younger men, the distinction being that only certain of the military societies were selected as camp police. It seems probable that these were the older societies and that those military societies which did not serve as akicita were more recently borrowed from neighboring groups.

The Head Men's societies were composed of older men, past the age of active warfare, who had distinguished themselves in the past.

Wissler lists the four found among the Oglala as (1) the Chiefs, (2) Ska Yuha, (3) Miwatani, and (4) Omaha societies. The Miwatani seemed to be a recent adoption from the Mandan as it closely parallels their Buffalo Bull society. The Omaha society was borrowed from that tribe in the nineteenth century. While Teton societies were not age-graded as were the societies of the Mandan, the societies were loosely ranked in a prestige hierarchy and they competed against each other for status. All Oglala were unanimous in their statements regarding the Chiefs society, for Wissler states that "all were of one mind as to the rank of the chiefs, it being the 'oldest as well as the one of highest rank.' Boys were not taken into it and a man seldom won sufficient recognition to be chosen before reaching the age of thirty or forty. None of our informants seemed to know the exact number of members at any definite time, but estimated them at forty to fifty." (Wissler, 1912:38.)

The strongest of the military societies and that which was most often selected for camp police was that called the Braves (ca^nte ti^nza or the dauntless) among the Oglala. The organization of this society included two leaders, two warbonnet wearers, four lance bearers, two whip bearers, one herald, one food passer, four drummers, eight singers (four of each sex), and thirty to forty additional members. Like all military societies, membership was not restricted to those in one band and, as in all societies, those who failed to conform to the ideals of the society could be expelled. The Oglala Braves were a society in which the leaders vowed never to turn in battle. The bonnet wearers, for example, wore headdresses with bison horns attached. In battle, they fastened themselves in one position with a small stake and, once in this position, were required to remain until the enemy was driven away or until they had been released by another member of the society. Variant forms of this society are found among Yankton, Yanktonai, Sisseton, and other Dakota groups. The Yanktonai No Flight society has a similar organization and similar requirements.

Membership in the Braves came through invitation and a candidate was informed of his selection by the herald. Members carried rattles and a bone whistle, and when participating in the society ceremonies and dances, they painted their faces red. Leaders had further signs of rank which they carried or wore, and the society lances were distinctive. A primary function of this society and all others was that of feasting and fostering comradeship within the bands. Society processions around the camp preceded feasts and dances, and some society members, like those in the Brave society, were permitted to take food from anyone. The Braves had songs and dances the knowledge of which was restricted to the membership. They also competed with members of other societies in contests within the camp and in warfare. Societies rarely fought as units in warfare, but any society officer on a war party was expected to carry the insignia of his organization. Intense competition for coup between members of different societies was common. The Oglala, like the societies of the Crow tribe, also participated in "wife-stealing." This practice involved the forcible abduction of a wife or wives of members of competitive societies. In the camp competition, usually in the form of horse races or hand games, society members wagered horses and other property. Competition in recitation of coup and war exploits was formalized and was tied in with distribution of property. In this, two societies might face each other: A member of one society recited a deed, then a member of the other; and as time progressed, horses and other property were given away, sometimes culminating in giving away wives.

The other Teton societies had some of the qualities of the military societies, but the membership was determined by supernatural visions. The *Heyoka* were one of the most important of these and Heyoka societies are found as well among other more easterly Dakota groups. Heyoka, or clowns, were a religious cult organization composed of individuals who had a vision requiring them to become Heyoka. Their behavior patterns were the reverse of normal. They might wear winter dress on the hottest summer day; they had the ability to put their

Crow ● Shield cover. The traditional shield of the hunting Plains was a toughened and steamed piece of bison hide about 18 inches in diameter. While its utility as a protective device was apparently adequate—it is said that a properly cured shield could stop a rifle ball—the shield was far more significant as a war fetish. Among the Cheyenne and Blackfoot, the shield was painted in accord with the directions of the supernatural guardian obtained in visions. The Dakota and Crow tended to put these same types of designs on the buckskin cover of the shield. Decorated covers were also used by the Cheyenne. To be effective as a powerful spiritual protector, the shield has to be made in special ways; songs were sung and rituals followed in its manufacture and in the making of the covers. (From R. H. Lowie, 1954:75. Adapted from photographs. Courtesy of The American Museum of Natural History)

hand in boiling water without being burned; during the Sun Dance, they participated as a group engaging in their own dances. Membership in Heyoka and the other religious cult groups depended on similarity in vision experience among the members; some had curing abilities and in this way resembled more the highly elaborated curing societies found among the Plains Siouan tribes such as the Omaha.

Women and children also had societies. Some women were associates of military societies, but purely female organizations also existed as the guildlike association of renowned quill and beadworkers among the Oglala. Young boys formed informal societies patterned after those of the adults and simulated the activities of their elders.

Status and rank were thus highly fluid among the Teton. Wealth, as such, was not an attribute which could bring prestige. Bravery, oratorical ability, supernatural powers, generosity, and many other factors were much more important. Teton society emphasized individual achievement above all else and ascribed status was extremely rare. Kinsmen and wealth were no hindrance to gaining status, however, for both were needed to gain admittance to important societies. Teton tales often tell of the poor orphan boy, without relatives and without horses, who lived on the fringe of the society and could never hope to achieve any status in the normal channels. There were apparently many such people in a Teton camp, and chiefs are often described as generously giving food to such people.

The Teton are also a society which presents few alternatives of behavior to the individual. To succeed, a man must achieve his success; if he has the help of kinsmen or help from the supernatural, that is to his advantage. But he can succeed only in a restricted number of ways. Those unable to compete in this system were relegated to a marginal position in the society, except for the very few males who assumed the role of shaman or of berdache. These latter were men, some of them homosexuals, who adopted women's clothing and women's role for life. They were often secondary wives of famous men, and many achieved considerable success as craftsmen in skin tanning, clothing preparation, beadwork, and other normally female tasks. The berdache was not an object of ridicule or scorn for he was *wakan*, or sacred, and his role was looked upon as inevitable—perhaps unfortunate, but certainly not of his own doing.

Life Cycle. The life cycle of the Tetons was marked by a series of rites of passage which served to indicate changes in status. Those associated with childbirth were not highly elaborated, and the period of pregnancy was not surrounded by highly restrictive taboos. During pregnancy women did avoid certain foods so as not to influence the growing fetus. At the time of delivery, an area was cleared in the lodge and then covered with soft tanned skins. The parturient woman knelt over these skins and grasped a pole for support. Men and boys absented themselves from the lodge, as did the younger girls. Older women assisted at

the birth, and if a difficult birth ensued, an older woman placed her arms around the abdomen of the parturient woman and exerted pressure. After the delivery, this same procedure was followed to help expel the placenta. The older woman who had assisted with the delivery then cut the umbilical cord, saving a section approximately six inches in length to dry. This section of the cord was later placed in a small decorated pouch which was hung from the child's cradle board as an amulet.

The newly born infant was carefully wiped and wrapped in soft skin robes. The mother rested and did not begin to nurse the child for at least one day, though the Teton preferred to wait four days. The first milk was viewed as unhealthy and was extracted manually. The child first nursed at the breast of another woman, preferably a relative. The placenta, which was looked upon as dangerous, was wrapped carefully and taken away from the camp to a place where it could be set high in the crotch of a tree and thus protected from animals.

During the first few months of life the infant spent most of its time wrapped tightly in a decorated sash which was placed firmly on a wooden cradle board. Only the infant's head and arms were not restricted in the cradle board. The infant slept at night with the mother and was allowed to nurse any time it indicated hunger.

The naming of the child took place within the first few weeks after its birth, though no specific period was necessary. An older man or woman, again usually a relative, named the child and frequently selected a name held by an ancestor two or three generations back. Naming a child was an honor and invested the name giver with a responsibility for the child's welfare. The father of the child, if he were able, gave gifts to the person naming the child and, if possible, gave a feast with additional gifts for others.

The infant, particularly if he were a boy never suffered for lack of attention. He followed his mother on her round of duties, as the cradle board could be strapped to her back. If she were working outside the lodge, the cradle board was frequently hung from a drying rack or a tree so that the infant could watch the activity. Older sisters helped care for the child, as did the grandmothers. Teton children learned very early that they should be unobtrusive when guests were present in the lodge, and although they were rarely struck or given any sort of corporal punishment, they were occasionally threatened with stories of *Iktome* or with stories of ghosts. As they grew older, they were allowed to play anywhere within the camp and in the long winter evenings were quieted with tales told by grandparents.

Infancy ended in the fifth or sixth year, at the time of the ear-piercing ceremony. This came shortly after weaning of the child, for the Teton mother nursed her child about four years. During this period the child was the center of attention for he rarely had the competition of a younger sibling. Ideally sexual intercourse between husband and wife was forbidden until after weaning, and genealogical records indicate that this prohibition was apparently observed rather rigidly among many families. The child was toilet trained by this time, though in this area the behavior of adults toward the child was quite permissive. An infant was simply placed outside the lodge where he could relieve himself. If a toilet accident took place within the lodge, there were no serious recriminations, though the older infant would be reminded of his carelessness.

Boys and girls until the age of puberty played together, though brothers and sisters were expected to play apart. As indicated previously, the activities of children were frequently modeled after adult patterns of behavior, and children also received a considerable amount of informal advice and instruction from their elders. Puberty marked the most important change in status for a Teton as this biological change signaled an even more important sociological change from child to adult.

Girls at their first menstruation were secluded in a menstrual hut built behind the camp. Their activities were restricted because at this time the girls exuded danger to man and animal alike. The restriction lasted only a few days, but during that time they were not allowed to leave the hut except at night in the company of their mother or another older woman. Food was brought to them by the women, and the girl was expected to devote all of her time to practicing the handicraft arts. She was harangued by older women who visited her to give advice on craft work and, more important, lengthy lectures on the behavioral ideals associated with adult women.

A father, if he were able, gave a public ceremony for his daughter two or three weeks after her first menstruation. The ceremony, directed by a shaman, was intended to serve to bring supernatural aid to the young woman, to publicly announce her status as an adult woman, and to bring prestige to both herself and her family. The greater the prestige of the shaman and the more lavish the gifts distributed by her father, the higher the status accorded the family. The ceremony, described by Walker as the Buffalo Ceremony, involved construction within a lodge of an altar on which a bison skull was placed and around which the shaman used sage and sweet grass incense, smoked to the six directions, and sang to call upon the Buffalo Woman to aid the young woman in her future life so that she might exhibit "chastity, fecundity, industry, and hospitality, the virtues most to be desired of a woman." (Walker, 1917:141.) At the conclusion of the ceremony, the young woman sat facing the shaman with her legs crossed (the seated position of men and children) and was instructed to sit as women do with their legs together and at one side. The shaman

painted red the right side of the young woman's forehead and a red stripe at the parting of her hair, and while doing so he said, "You see your oldest sister on the altar. Her forehead is painted red. This is to show that she is sacred. Red is a sacred color. Your first menstrual flow was red. Then you were sacred. You have taken of the red water this day [red chokecherry juice]. This is to show that you are akin to the Buffalo God and are his woman. . . . You are entitled to paint your face in this manner." He then tied the eagle plume at the crown of her head and said, "The spirit of the eagle and the duck are with you. They will give you the influence of the Sun and the South Wind. They will give you many children." (Walker, 1917:149–150.)

The girl's clothing had been removed during the ceremony, and at its conclusion she was dressed in new garments. Gifts from the father to the shaman and the others present concluded the ceremony itself. The feast which followed featured dog meat and lasted several hours.

The girl was now a woman, ready for marriage, and thoroughly inculcated with the ideals of Teton society. From this time forward she observed the decorum of an adult woman, she avoided any contact with men or their weapons during her subsequent menstrual periods, and she ideally avoided sexual relations with anyone but her husband after marriage. Virginity before marriage, continence, and lack of promiscuity after marriage were all Teton cultural ideals. An older woman who could publicly testify to a life in which these ideals were followed achieved considerable prestige.

Young boys did not undergo a specific puberty ceremony akin to that for girls. A boy's puberty was marked by a series of events over some length of time. His first successful bison hunt, his first war party, his first capture of enemy horses, and other deeds of this sort proved his status as an adult and might be marked by feasts and gifts to others on the part of his father. None of these practices was highly formalized, however, and some Teton males passed through this period without recognition. The most important aspect of this period of a young man's life was his personal-vision quest. This was a supernatural experience, actively sought, which gave him a "familiar spirit" for life, and sometimes indicated the course his adult life would take.

A boy was usually prepared for the vision quest by a shaman who instructed him in the necessary ritual preparation and in the way he should conduct himself while seeking the vision. Preparation through a shaman was not required, for an older man could offer this same instruction, but with less chance of success, for the boy in his quest. The vision quest itself involved fasting, isolation, and self-torture. The young boy fasted for four days before leaving the camp and took ritually purifying sweat baths in the small dome-shaped sweat lodge. On leaving the camp, the boy found an isolated place where he waited for four days and nights or until he received a supernatural vision. This place was frequently a butte top or other elevated spot. The boy fasted and frequently gashed his arms and legs. The vision came to the boy when a supernatural being took pity on the boy and instructed him. The content of the vision was variable, but not completely so, for many individuals received visions from the same supernatural beings or forces. Those whose vision came from the thunders in the west were forced to become Heyoka, for example.

The vision quest, if successful, gave the boy a guardian spirit on whom he could call in times of need throughout his life. Men frequently fasted and sought renewals of their visions during their lives. The boy would also be told in the vision what items he should collect to carry in a small pouch on his person for protective purposes. Most also received songs which were theirs and which, when sung, gave

supernatural aid. The vision was a highly personal experience and an experience vital to success in Teton society. The shaman received his calling through a vision and the warrior received supernatural aid for life. All visions were not of equal potency, however, and the Teton looked upon variable success in warfare among several men, or the differing powers of shamans as indicative of the power of their separate supernatural guardians. All boys did not receive visions either, and he who was not successful suffered in consequence. The unsuccessful candidate tried again for a vision experience, and some men received their first vision rather late in life. It was not necessary to actively seek the vision experience, although this was the usual practice. Black Elk, an Oglala shaman whose biography has been recorded, received his vision as a result of illness when he was nine years old. Women also received visions, although they did not usually actively seek this experience. Teton women could be shamans, however, and vision experience was necessary for this.

Marriage took place at a relatively early age, though earlier for girls than for young men. The man must first have proved himself an adult in hunting and warfare, and if the marriage were with the daughter of a prominent man, he must also have accumulated sufficient goods for distribution. It is clear that marriage did not involve complex ceremonies nor did it have any religious overtones. It did set up a new series of obligations for the young couple, however, and it marked their recognition as full adults. Children were strongly desired by the Teton and boys in particular were highly desired in a family. A form of ritual adoption was institutionalized and in this manner a childless man could formally adopt a young boy. This ritual adoption, called *Hunka*, could also be used to bind two men of approximately the same age together in a ritual-brotherhood association which lasted for life. The bonds established by this ceremony were ideally stronger even than the bonds of kinship. The ceremony itself resembled strongly the girl's puberty rite, and when completed the man became *Hunka Ate* or "father Hunka" and the boy *Hunka*.

The period of adult married life was the time of greatest competition for status on the part of both the man and the woman. This was the period of life which the Teton viewed as most significant and most rewarding. All events of importance in the life of an individual really took place during this time, and the period of old age, which began after the children were grown and married and active competition ceased, was the time for reflection and reminiscence. A person whose active adult life had been full and who had numbers of exploits and deeds to recount received the positions of status due him. He was still required to validate this status through distribution of property, however, and depended on the younger active males in his family to provide him with the goods to do this.

Death in old age was not feared, and although the ghost of a recently deceased person might continue to remain for a time, the ghost or spirit was usually not malevolent and therefore not disturbing. The Teton did not place great emphasis on genealogy, many not being able to recount their progenitors back beyond two or three generations. At the time of death, the corpse was sometimes placed in a mourning lodge at which time female relatives participated in a ritualized mourning. If the deceased were young, and particularly if a child, the mourning often involved gashing of the arms and legs as well as the ritual crying. Women in mourning wore their hair loose, and a widow was not expected to remarry until some months had passed. Burial took place in the open. The corpse was wrapped tightly in a robe with his or her personal pipe, medicines, and weapons or tools. It was then placed on a scaffold or platform erected outside the village, or it was laid in a tree. In the late nineteenth century, there are evidences that a favorite horse was sometimes killed and placed beneath the scaffold. Food and other small offerings were placed beneath the scaffold burial. In former times, the Teton, along with the other Dakota tribes, undoubtedly practised inhumation in an earth mound, although such inhumation took place after the original exposed burial. The secondary mound burial involved collection of the bones which were then grouped into a small bundle and buried without any accompanying grave goods. On the Plains, the Teton abandoned the secondary burial and used only the scaffold type. There are evidences, however, that the burial was sometimes revisited after a lapse of time, for older widows sometimes wore the jaw bone of their deceased husbands.

Religion

The supernatural world of the Teton consisted of everything that was *wakan* or sacred. As Walker states:

Teton or Oglala (Sioux) ● Ceremonial bag of otter skin. Part of the complex of the "medicine bundle," this bag might hold sacred tobacco as well as fetish objects assembled through guardian-spirit direction. The bag might then be wrapped in buckskin and taken out at auspicious times for communal and individual good and well-being. This talisman was individually owned, as were the songs sung when it was displayed. Individual medicine bundles, mementos of spiritual contacts, contrast with the great tribal bundles, such as the sacred pipe bundle of the Blackfoot or the Eveningstar bundle of the Pawnee (cf. Wissler, 1927:113–119. Courtesy of The Science Museum, St. Paul, Minnesota)

The supernatural is Wakan Tanka, *or the Great Mystery that no one of mankind can comprehend. It may be pleased or displeased by the conduct of any one of mankind. It may be propitiated or placated by a proper ceremony correctly performed. Its aid may be secured by appropriate sacrifice. . . .*

Therefore, it is the Great God. This Great God communicates with mankind through various media and in various manners. The chosen medium is a *Wicasa Wakan*, or Shaman. Other media are called *Akicita Wakan*, or *Sacred Messengers*. A sacred Messenger may be anything animate or inanimate, other than mankind, which makes itself known as such. (Walker, 1917:79.)

The world of the *wakan* is populated by deities and spirits of a variety of forms and a variety of degrees of supernatural powers. The Teton did not organize this world into a highly regularized pantheon, though they did recognize classes of benevolent and malevolent supernatural beings. Foremost among the deities were *Wi*, the Sun, and *Skan*, the Sky, both looked upon as having male attributes. *Maka* who was the Earth was a female deity whose name means the "all-mother." Beneath these highest deities were a host of lesser forms which included the Winds or four directions, the Moon, Buffalo, Bear, Whirlwind, Thunders, and many others. Lesser spirits could take any form and could be either animate or inanimate. Ghosts and bodily spirits were also *wakan*.

The attributes of the deities were variable, and in some cases the deities could assume differing roles. *Wakinyan* or Thunder is described by Walker, for example, as

visible only when he so wills. His properties are wakan and anti-natural. He abides in his lodge on the top of the mountain at the edge of the world where the Sun goes down to the regions under the world. He is many, but they are as only one; he is shapeless, but has wings with four joints each; he has no feet, yet he has huge talons; he has no head, yet has a huge beak with rows of teeth in it, like the teeth of a wolf; his voice is the thunder clap and rolling thunder is caused by the beating of his wings on the clouds; he has an eye, and its glance is lightning. In a great cedar tree beside his lodge he has his nest made of dry bones, and in it is an enormous egg from which his young continuously issue. He devours his young and they each become one of his many selves. He had issue by the Rock and it was Iktome, the oldest son of the Rock. He flies through all the domain of the Sky, hidden in a robe of clouds, and if one of mankind sees his substance he is thereby made a heyoka, and must ever afterwards speak and act clownishly and in an anti-natural manner. Yet, if he so wills, he may appear to mankind in the form of a giant man, and if so, he is then the God, Heyoka. One who looks upon the God, Heyoka, is not thereby

made a heyoka. The potency of the Winged God cannot be imparted to anything. His functions are to cleanse the world of filth and to fight the Monsters who defile the waters and to cause all increase by growth from the ground.

The acceptable manner of addressing him is by taunt and vilification, the opposite of the intent of the address. He may be visualized as a bird whose wings have four joints. His symbol is a zig zag red line forked at each end. His akicita are the dog, swallow, snowbird, night hawk, lizard, frog, and dragon fly, and if either of these is seen in a vision, the one to whom it appears is thereby made a heyoka. (Walker, 1917:83–84.)

It is impossible to say to what degree detailed knowledge of the supernatural world was held by the population as a whole. Most accounts, like that quoted above from Walker, are taken from shamans who were more sophisticated and perhaps more philosophically inclined. There was also a body of esoteric knowledge which was the property of the shamans alone, for only they could interpret the sometimes strange language of the deities and many of the strange natural events which were looked upon as due directly to supernatural causes.

The shaman, as the only religious functionary, had an important role in Teton society and in the other tribes of the Plains. As a direct intermediary between humans and the supernatural world, the shaman filled an important position in the society. One of his prime responsibilities involved the curing of illness, which the Teton viewed as due to supernatural causes. Malevolent spirits could cause illness, and did so, but illness could also be due to failure of the individual to respond correctly to the biddings of the supernatural. As the shaman could manipulate the supernatural, it was possible for him to cause illness through sorcery. Sorcery was of slight importance to the Teton, however, and though it did occur, it was not common and a shaman suspected of sorcery was often expelled from the band. The Teton recognized this phenomenon as more highly elaborated among the Sisseton than among themselves. Teton women did take considerable care to see that their menstrual blood, for example, was carefully disposed of as possession of this by a shaman could be used against them.

Herbal remedies for common ailments such as dysentery, headache, and other such complaints were known. Women were herbalists, and shamanistic knowledge or experience was not necessary for this type of curing. Most adult women knew which plants were efficacious and collected specimens which were dried and kept in the lodge.

Serious illness, however, was difficult to deal with and required the services of a shaman. As noted previously, certain shamans had greater prestige than others, due either to their past success or to the type of vision they had experienced. The shamanistic curing performance centered about a ceremony in which the shaman called upon his familiar spirit for aid in determining the cause of the disease. The ceremony might be lengthy and usually took place within the lodge of the patient. Sage and sweet grass were used, as the aroma of these plants was pleasing to the supernatural beings. Normally, tobacco was smoked, and as the curing ceremony progressed the shaman sang and danced, using a rawhide rattle for accompaniment. The songs were the personal property of the shaman and had been given to him by his familiar spirit. In the successful curing ceremony, the shaman received knowledge of the specific cause of the illness and also its location in the body. He could then ask supernatural aid in curing, but also frequently administered herbals and gave advice on activities the patient should follow. The actual cure involved expulsion of a foreign object from the patient through the normal means of elimination.

The shaman received a gift at the conclusion of the ceremony, and if the cure were successful might receive additional gifts. He would also benefit in reputation following a successful cure. All shamanistic curing ceremonies were not successful, however, and a shaman might learn during the cure that the illness demanded the services of another shaman with a different familiar spirit. Shamans were not required to accept every "case" and could, after examining the patient, refuse a request.

Shamans were also important in matters of everyday life in that some of them had powers which enabled them to foretell events. They were called upon to predict the location of bison herds, to indicate the probable success of a war party, to locate lost property, and, most important, to direct the annual band and tribal Sun Dance.

As the leader of the Sun Dance, the Teton shaman filled another role, and one which differed considerably from his others. In this role he functioned as a priest learned in the complex ritual and ceremonial aspects of the Teton's most important tribal ceremony. The shaman was responsible for instructing Sun Dance candidates both in the required behavior, and in correct step-by-step ritual which culminated in the dance itself. Actually, several shamans were involved in the Sun Dance preparation and instruction but one was chosen to act as the superior shaman and the total responsibility rested on him. Other Plains tribes, both sedentary and nomadic, also held the annual Sun Dance, though it was not performed by the Comanche nor by the Mandan. In the Plains as a whole, this ceremony is remarkable for its homogeneity among the tribes, despite tribal variations. As a complex, it reached its highest degree of elaboration among the Arapaho, the Cheyenne, and the Oglala bands of the Teton.

Information on the Teton Sun Dance rests primarily on the data presented by J. R. Walker (1917) in his monograph on the Oglala. Detailed ethnographic studies of the Sun Dance among the other Teton bands is lacking, though there is considerable information in Frances Densmore's *Teton Sioux Music* (1918).

The Oglala Sun Dance was an annual ceremony given at midsummer when all of the bands congregated at a predetermined location. According to Oglala lore this was the time when the bison were fat, when the new sprouts of sage were one span long, when the chokecherries were ripening, and when the moon rose as the sun set. Each year's ceremony was held on the initiative of an individual who had vowed to participate in the dance. His vow was made during the previous year when he had pledged to hold the dance in return for supernatural assistance. This vow might be made as a request for supernatural aid in curing oneself or a kinsman, or it might be made by a young man in response to a shamanistic vision. Once a man had made this pledge, he announced the fact and approached an older shaman to act as his instructor. A shaman thus approached need not accept this request, but if convinced of the pledger's ability to perform the dance and the sincerity of the vow, he normally would accept. The mentor then appointed two assistants whose duty it was to function as akicita or messengers. The messengers dressed in their finest regalia and travelled with a message stick, made from the branch of a plum tree, to the other bands. As they approached the camp of each band in daylight, singing joyful songs, they were escorted to the council lodge. There the invitation to assemble was delivered.

It usually happened that more than one person vowed to offer the Sun Dance each year so that there were several candidates, each with their instructor. The instructor of the man first announcing his intention was given the superior role among the instructors unless he were not a shaman. If this were the case, the shaman-instructors selected one of their own to act in this capacity.

The first important ritual act took place before the bands assembled. Each candidate participated in a ceremony directed by his instructor in which the candidate was consecrated or dedicated to the Buffalo deity. In this solemn ceremony the candidate and the Buffalo deity actually assumed the *hunka* relationship toward one another. At the consecration, each candidate indicated his desire to dance one of the three most significant dances. These were called Gaze-at-Sun-Buffalo; Gaze-at-Sun-Staked; and Gaze-at-Sun-Suspended. All involved self-torture and all were considered more efficacious than the Gaze-at-Sun dance which others could do. Once the candidate was consecrated, he was expected to follow these "invariable rules."

1. He must subordinate himself to his Mentor.
2. He must meditate continually on his undertaking.
3. He must speak little with others than his Mentor.
4. He must use only consecrated implements and utensils.

In addition to following these restrictions on his behavior, each candidate was expected to refrain from becoming angry, to avoid any contact with ribald speech, he must not go into water, and he must abstain from sexual intercourse.

The candidate, who was usually a young man, was expected to exhibit the four great virtues of the Oglala which they termed bravery, generosity, fortitude, and integrity. He also needed the support of relatives and friends, perhaps fellow members of his soldier society, for much of the food and gifts distributed to the shamans and to the populace had to be provided by the candidates. Each young man after his consecration was provided with a red painted skirt of tanned skin, an otterskin cape, two bison-hair armlets, two rabbitskin anklets, a whistle made from an eagle wing bone, and a hoop made from a willow branch. In contrast

to the merriment which pervaded the camp, the candidate kept to himself to prepare for the dance.

As the time for the ceremony approached the various bands, brought together again for the late spring and early summer hunts, began to move toward the selected place. Each band moved slowly during the day and timed their travel so that they would finally approach the Sun Dance camp in the last of four days of equal movement. The members of the bands were carefree during these days and considerably more freedom of action was allowed than usual. On the last day of their march, all dressed in their finest and covered the last few miles singing as they approached the camp. They were greeted by those already present, and found their position in the camp circle.

The four days after all bands were assembled were filled with preliminary preparations. These were all highly ritualized and took place in a definite sequence. All rituals were under the supervision of the leading shaman and the other instructors or mentors. Heralds and marshals were selected the first day, and on the second, children who were to have their ears pierced during the ceremony were named, as were the children who would participate in the Sacred Tree procession. Female attendants for each candidate were picked, and as they were necessarily virginal, their claims were made known and the right to challenge was allowed. At the conclusion of the second day, a feast for the participating shamans was given which featured the favorite dish—succulent young dog meat.

On the third day the activities in the preliminary camp centered on selection of the hunter or scout who would locate the Sacred Tree, the digger who would prepare the hole in which the Sacred Tree would be set, the escort who would lead the mock war party to the Sacred Tree and bring it to the Sun Dance circle after it had been symbolically captured and felled. Each of these men was selected by the superior shaman and each was painted in a distinctive fashion. Any man selected for one of these sacred positions could paint himself in the same fashion at any future time. The shamans also selected the four drummers, the four men who would use the rattles, and the chorus of male and female singers. The third day again ended with a feast for the shamans and selected participants which this time featured bison tongue, another Oglala delicacy. These were furnished

Ponca ● Participants in the Sun Dance.
(Photograph by G. A. Dorsey, 1905)

by the families of the candidates who had procured them earlier in the summer.

The fourth and final day of the preliminary
rituals involved selection of the woman to chop
the Sacred Tree and the woman who would finally fell it. These were older women,
frequently mothers of the candidates, but again
they must have unclouded reputations and
they too could be challenged.

This concluded the four preliminary days of
ritual. These were days of happiness and excitement about the large camp. Sexual license
was allowed and the descriptions of the Oglala
indicate considerable lively banter and sexual
byplay. The candidates did not participate in
these activities. Each day they viewed the rising sun with their shaman-instructors; during
the day they took ritually purifying sweat baths
and received detailed instructions on the ceremonies lying ahead; and at night they occupied
beds of sacred sage.

The rituals of the actual Sun Dance occupied
four days, and began on the day following the

last of the preliminary days. The sequence of
rituals within the four days followed a prescribed order which began with a procession
on the first of the four sacred days of midsummer. The procession wound around and
through the camp and then to the area selected
for the dance lodge. Mock battles against the
malevolent deities marked the procession
which culminated in the location of the sacred
spot where the center Sun Dance pole would
be erected. A new sacred lodge was erected by
the women. This lodge was occupied by the
candidates and their instructors during the ceremonies and needed to be constructed of new
lodge poles and a newly fashioned cover. The
altar within was dedicated to the Bison deity.
During this same day, the hunter-scout located
the sacred tree and marked it with red paint.
Later the bands moved to the ceremonial camp
which surrounded the sacred lodge and the
dance circle. The day ended again with a bison
feast.

The second day was filled with symbolic ritual as had been the previous days. The sacred
tree was "captured," felled by the women, carried to camp in a procession marked by relays

of runners, painted red on its west side, blue on its north, green on its east, and yellow on its south side. Finally a rawhide bison effigy figure was attached to the top of the pole. The day concluded with the members of the military societies feasting.

The procession to raise the pole and to construct the round, brush-walled dance lodge took place on the third day. Each of these three days, plus the four preliminary days, had been filled with jesting, good humor, sexual play, and some licensed sexual promiscuity. As the third of the sacred days came to a close, the obscene deities were banished and the attitude of the camp shifted to contemplation of the sacred rites to take place on the following day. At dusk, all entered their lodges and the camp was quiet until the following morning.

On the morning of the fourth day, the candidates viewed the rising sun and then in a procession moved slowly to the dance lodge. Here they were formally installed as dancers and each candidate was instructed as to his actions, depending on which form of the dance he was to follow.

The dancing began with a Buffalo Dance, danced only by those who were to dance the three self-torture types of Sun Dance and by men who had danced the Sun Dance on previous years. The Buffalo Dance completed the dedication to the Bison deity and each man who danced successfully received a wand fashioned from a buffalo tail. Children whose parents had dedicated them, then had their ears pierced and the Sun-Gaze Dance itself could begin.

The Sun-Gaze Dance symbolized capture, torture, captivity, and escape. Those candidates dedicated to the self-torture Sun-Gaze Dance had the wounds made in the flesh of their breast or back through which wooden skewers could be passed. Four variations on the type of self-torture were used. Skewers placed through the skin of the back were attached with thongs to bison skulls which the dancer dragged behind him as he danced. Another form bound the dancer with four thongs to four posts with the dancer in the center. The third form used wooden skewers through the skin of the breast and the dancer was attached with thongs to the Sacred Pole. The final form was similar to the third, except that the dancer was attached to the crotch of the Sacred Pole with loose thongs so that he could actually be raised from the ground.

The dance itself consisted of 24 songs, any of which other than the first and last could be repeated any number of times. Brief intermissions took place during which the dancers rested. During the dancing, each dancer gazed steadfastly at the Sacred Pole, and each blew continual short notes on an eagle-bone whistle. The dance frequently took many hours and often continued into the night. At its climax, the dancers jerked and pulled against the thongs in an attempt to break free. Those who did so by tearing the thongs from their flesh had danced the Sun-Gaze Dance in the most praiseworthy manner. Some did not complete the dance in the proper way as many fainted and had to have the thongs and skewers removed. Others might have the thongs torn from them by their female relatives after they had fainted.

The dance ended when each of the candidates had "escaped" the capture and torture and had been led back to his lodge by his band members. Successful candidates enjoyed great prestige from that time on. Their scars marked them as having participated in the dance, and each could expect to receive a vision from the Sun during the following year. They could also participate in any aspect of any future Sun Dance simply by drawing blood and entering the dance circle.

The ceremonial camp broke up quickly and each band left the circle to move to its late summer hunting grounds. The Dance lodge was left intact and the Sacred Pole left standing.

No single event served to bind the Oglala and the other Teton bands together as a unit as did the Sun Dance. Here they came together at one time during the year for a deeply emotional religious experience in which supernatural aid was called upon to assure the tribe of a plentiful supply of bison for the coming year. Renewal of kin ties, the arranging of marriages, exchange of property, recitation of the past year's deeds and exploits, political maneuvering, and all of the other associated activities were secondary to the central group ritual.

THE KIOWA

The tribes of the southern Plains were dominated by the Comanche, the largest and most powerful group in that area. For many years after the arrival of the Spanish and the introduction of the horse into the southern Plains, groups like the Comanche and Kiowa incorporated the horse and gun complex into their cultures and moved from the northern and central Plains toward the south. The southern Plains were inviting to these tribes, for nearby were the Spanish settlements of the Rio Grande and Mexico. The southern Plains tribes, like the tribes to the north, dependent upon the bison, soon developed aggressive patterns of raiding Spanish settlements for horses, guns, and food. As the tribes grew in size, their raids became more effective, and the range of their raiding parties became extended to points far into northern Mexico. The resultant economic gain made the nineteenth-century southern Plains tribes rich in horses and even more powerful than they had been previously. Many of the tribes of the central and northern Plains obtained their horses from the tribes to the south and from a second area of concentration of horses in the northern Plateau, but none of the northern Plains tribes had herds of the size held by the southern tribes.

The Kiowa were a small tribe which numbered approximately 2000 persons in the early nineteenth century. "You know, everything had to begin, and this is how it was: the Kiowas came one by one into the world through a hollow log. They were many more than now, but not all of them got out. There was a woman whose body was swollen up with child, and she got stuck in the log. After that, no one could get through, and that is why the Kiowas are a small tribe in number. They looked all around and saw the world. It made them glad to see so many things. They called themselves *Kwuda*, 'coming out.' " They had moved into the southern Plains from the north in the eighteenth century and were in conflict with the Comanche during this period. By the early nineteenth century the Kiowa had resolved their difficulties with the Comanche and had begun an existence in which both tribes cooperated in raids to the south. The Kiowa territory in the early nineteenth century was in western Oklahoma, north of the Comanche yet near the Spanish settlements. A moving account of the Kiowa move to the southern Plains is N. Scott Momaday's, *The Way to Rainy Mountain* (1969).

Like the Teton, the Kiowa were subdivided into small residential bands, but unlike the Teton, they did not have to cope with the severe winters known in the north. The southern Plains were more hospitable, for winters were milder, bison plentiful, and water and timber present in localized areas. Kiowa culture contained most of the major characteristics described for the Teton, but they elaborated their patterns of behavior surrounding wealth and male rank to a degree unknown to the Teton. Kiowa emphasis on warfare, particularly the raiding party, resulted in the acquisition of large quantities of horses and Spanish goods, and the associated Kiowa emphasis on wealth and status was dependent upon their activities in warfare.

The accumulation of wealth was important to all Plains tribes and was directly tied to the system of status achievement. The base for status achievement, however, rested in success in warfare, for through this means, new wealth in the form of horses and goods was obtained. For most Plains tribes, wealth was not important in itself, but assumed significance in that the wealthy man was necessarily a successful warrior. Among the Teton, for example, accumulated wealth was distributed through gifts and thus served mainly as a vehicle for validating status. The successful Teton man demonstrated his prowess to others in his band through his generosity. The Kiowa, however, far richer in horses than the Teton and in an area where accumulation of horses through raiding gave greater promise of new wealth, had developed what were essentially a series of economic classes. Kiowa values also emphasized generosity and a rich Kiowa man was called upon to aid his less fortunate relatives, but a successful Kiowa man accumulated wealth and this wealth was retained by family groups through inheritance. Wealthy families were able to perpetuate their position in Kiowa society for as Mishkin points out:

The wealthy class could afford to set their offspring on the path to military careers while the poor, for the most part, were compelled to specialize in the prosaic activities, hunting, camp duties, etc. The propertied group could advance the interests of their descendants because they controlled the channels of publicity. Finally, the achievement of great war renown and the winning of leadership in war opened the way to further wealth accumulation. Thus the mechanism for rank perpetuation acted to create an aristocratic caste. (Mishkin, 1940:62–63.)

The formal Kiowa system of rank included four named categories. The first or *ngop* included those whom Mishkin has classed as an aristocratic caste, men with skills in horsemanship, wealth, a generous nature, and distinguished in warfare. Men lacking in war honors, even though they had wealth and a generous nature, could not qualify for this highest rank. The *dapom* were Kiowa who were the hangers-on, men with no property, no skills, and, according to Mishkin, "virtual outcasts," Between these two categories of rank were the *ondeigupa,* or second best, and the *K ə n,* or propertyless people. Captives taken in warfare were also incorporated into Kiowa society, though they did not qualify for positions in the four-scale system of rank. Female captives were frequently taken as wives, and male captives sometimes served as assistants to their captors.

While wealth and property assumed large proportions in Kiowa society, and wealth was used to validate status, the highest status for males was achieved through success in warfare. Kiowa deeds or coup in warfare were like those of other Plains groups, and as was general on the Plains, killing an enemy did not rank as the highest of honors. Most of the deeds which served to elevate the status of a warrior were those which came through individual feats of bravery. Warfare was a group activity, but in combat the individual warrior acted to accumulate honors and to demonstrate his prowess.

Successful leadership in warfare was also a means to an increase in status. Raiding parties were generally small and were organized by an individual who recruited a small group of men, usually from his kin group, and led them to an enemy camp or settlement for horses or plunder. The larger revenge war party was organized formally after the Sun Dance when a man of demonstrated skill in warfare sent a pipe to the leaders of each military society. If the leader smoked the pipe, it signified his acceptance of the invitation. Revenge parties were often large, numbering up to 200 men, and they acted out of an obligation to avenge the death of Kiowa warriors during the previous year. The participants also had a religious rationalization for revenge warfare.

The man who successfully led a raiding party gained prestige and in the future would have little difficulty in attracting warriors. He who did not succeed not only failed to gain prestige but suffered a loss of status. The successful war leader and the individual warrior who had counted coup were each honored when the war party returned. These men recited their deeds in public at this time, and at any future

Crow ● **Painted power shield. In this instance, the Crow has painted his power signs on the bison-hide shield itself. To be effective as a power shield, the cover would also be necessary. (After Lowie, 1954:74. Adapted from photographs. Courtesy of The American Museum of Natural History)**

event where they wished to speak formally or be recognized, deeds were also recited.

Kiowa warfare, like that of the majority of Plains tribes, thus had both an economic motive, seen in the raiding party, and a motivation toward improving one's position in the society. Both motives were important and both contributed to the emphasis placed on warfare by the peoples of the Plains.

With the building of railroads across the Plains, the movement of immigrant wagon trains, and the beginnings of European settlement of the Plains, warfare by the native tribes against the intruder became a strong unifying factor. Tribes which had formerly wrangled among themselves, and even adjacent tribes who had long considered each other hereditary enemies, united against the common outside foe. Plains warfare in the latter half of the nineteenth century thus became warfare for survival. Very large organized groups of warriors engaged the enemy in pitched battles, a form of conflict not unknown previously on the Plains, but one certainly not emphasized. In many of these large engagements, the Plains Indian was successful—skill in horsemanship, intimate knowledge of the terrain, the ability to maneuver for long periods without logistic support were all in his favor. Ultimately sheer numbers of the enemy combined with superior fire power ended the resistance of the Plains Indian; reservation areas were set up and the former nomadic groups were restricted. With the reservation system and the collapse of the economic base of Plains Indian society, the system of status and rank was completely undermined and the culture of the inhabitants of the reservations changed radically.

Suggested readings

BOWERS, A. W.
1950   *Mandan Social and Ceremonial Organization.* University of Chicago Press.

HASSRICK, R. B.
1964   *The Sioux: Life and Customs of a Warrior Society.* University of Oklahoma Press.

LOWIE, R. H.
1963   *Indians of the Plains.* American Museum of Natural History, Science Books.
1956   *The Crow Indians.* New York: Holt, Rinehart and Winston.

MARRIOTT, A.
1945   *The Ten Grandmothers.* University of Oklahoma Press.

MOMADAY, N. S.
1969   *The Way to Rainy Mountain.* University of New Mexico Press.

NEIHARDT, J. G.
1972   *Black Elk Speaks: Being the Life of a Holy Man of the Oglala Sioux.* New York: Pocket Books.

VIII

Eastern Woodlands

Introduction

Any line differentiating the three eastern culture areas of the United States and Canada is not easily drawn because of the spread of agriculture and native dependence on the maize complex. The eastern Plains Indians were farmers as well as bison hunters; in the northeast, the area here designated as the Eastern Woodlands, there was also some concern with farming. It was the Southeast, however, the area of the contemporary Gulf States, which may be regarded as an area of fairly intensive agriculture. True, the Southeast was not so vitally drawn to maize cultivation as were the Southwestern Pueblos or the precursors of the Pima and Papago of Arizona. But the Southeast developed a strong dependence on farming largely because of its proximity to Mexico. The diffusion of agriculture can be traced from eastern Mexico into the prehistoric Southeast. From the Southeast, cultivation spreads northward up the Mississippi, up the Missouri to affect the sedentary Plains tribes, and up the Ohio to New England and the St. Lawrence Valley.

The northeast and the settled, farming Plains tribes are marginal areas. They were farmers in part, although never to the same degree as the groups to the south. Their agriculture was generally spotty, except perhaps for the Iroquois, and stood side by side with hunting and trapping. A line can be drawn at the northern zone where agriculture stops. The Eastern Woodlands thus has farmers as well as hunters. North of the woodlands, away from the boreal forest and in a tundralike configuration, tribes with a sub-Arctic adjustment are encountered, hunters whose societies resemble those of the Athabascan northwest. Thus in the Eastern Woodlands, as in the Plains, there is a variation of economic mode from farming to hunting. The result is some cultural variation, which makes it necessary to consider several peoples representative of the area.

The Eastern Woodlands surrounds the five Great Lakes, follows the boreal forest north of the lakes from Manitoba, Minnesota, and Wisconsin to the St. Lawrence Valley and follows the Atlantic Coast from Newfoundland southward to Virginia. To the north is the taiga, the spruce-birch-pine forest which gives the Woodlands its name. This is the area of the pre-Cambrian Shield, the Laurentian highland which stretches from Minnesota where the western plains-prairie ends across the northern tier, to the St. Lawrence. These forest areas are highly glaciated, with few streams and many lakes. South of the Great Lakes, from Iowa to the Appalachians, the boreal forest fades away into a prairie-parkland (Kroeber, 1938:88,182–183). To the east, in the Appalachian areas of New York and Pennsylvania, there are deciduous and coniferous trees, especially at the higher elevations of these geologically old mountains.

Variation in landform, vegetation, drainage, climate, as well as in the availability of natural resources, created some differences in the aboriginal culture patterns. Although such variations in ecological adaptation may be determined by a review of the complex prehistory of the area, further changes occurred as a result of European colonization and of the movement of peoples within the area. At the time immediately before contact, several population centers existed, each reflecting a somewhat specialized ecological adaptation. The Wisconsin-Minnesota region had a twofold economic dependence: a northern sector which made use of the wild rice (*Zazania* sp.), essentially a gathered product but sowed broadcast in the northern lakes and marshes; a second sector, which was agricultural, stretched to the border of central Lake Michigan (Kroeber, 1939:88–89). This subarea may have had a population of 45,000 in 1750. The northern reaches of the Ohio Valley, in prehistoric times something of a major center probably related to the Southeast, were relatively sparsely populated. The historic tribes there cultivated maize, it is true, but exhibited little of the pre-Columbian system of complex villages, earthworks, and mounds, which indicates a break in tradition raising some still unanswered questions about this area. This subarea extends from Illinois eastward to West Virginia, and parts of Ohio, Kentucky, and West Virginia were uninhabited in the eighteenth century despite a rich series of prehistoric sites.

The eastern Great Lakes take in an area of some aboriginal importance. Included are lakes Ontario and Erie, upstate New York, and the central St. Lawrence Valley. The woodlands of hemlock and pine differ somewhat from the northern forests and maize cultivation was possible. This subarea was the home of the famous Iroquois, a group somewhat different in culture from many of their neighbors. The Atlantic coastal regions involve a northern and central slope. (Here were the tribes first encountered by settlers from England and the Netherlands, tribes with simple agriculture.) The north Atlantic slope, taking in Maine, New Brunswick, and Nova Scotia, represents the northernmost limit of maize cultivation. The middle coast takes in the region from Maine to New Jersey, an area of maize farmers, but the agricultural complex along the coast was less well integrated than, for example, in the eastern Great Lakes region.

The problem of describing the native cultures of the Eastern Woodlands as they were is further complicated by the fact that the seventeenth century witnessed the wholesale migrations of Europeans. The French in Canada, the British in New England, the Dutch in New York saw the native peoples as an annoyance, souls to be saved, perhaps, but second-class citizens at best. Whether it is true that Peter Minuit purchased Manhattan Island from the Delaware for $24.00, the story has a ring of authenticity. In any case, the French and Dutch were interested in furs, however much the English were seeking freedom from religious persecution. From French Canada, the fur trade of the seventeenth century brought trappers and traders as far west as the Mississippi and Lake Winnipeg, and in the next century further north and west. With the fur traders came the missionaries, especially the French Jesuits whose writings, the many volumes of the *Jesuit Relations*, offer a mine of information on the events, ethnography, and geography of the Woodlands area.

Seventeenth-century Europeanization was essentially destructive of the native cultures. The Huron, for example, abandoned their villages in 1649, an act of despair following epidemics of the introduced diseases measles and smallpox and pressures from the French and the hostile Iroquois (Trigger, 1969:2). Although the Huron scattered, as did many Woodlands tribes in succeeding years, other groups pushed westward. A virtual chain reaction took place, with the result that wholesale migrations occurred. The Chippewa (Ojibwa), now in Wisconsin, Minnesota, and Ontario, left the region around Sault Ste. Marie in the central Great Lakes and pushed into their present habitat. Their place was in turn taken by others. The factor of such movements creates difficulties in describing the native cultures as they were. Considering the changes which had taken place in prehistoric times, however, it seems clear that the Woodlands area was never stable.

The effects of European settlement, aside from the enforced movement of many tribes and not infrequently their break-up, go back three centuries and are apparent in many ways. Metal was introduced; not only cooking kettles traps, and beads, but in addition, liquor and guns. Trapping and the demand for furs led many tribesmen further afield, away from the traditional habitat, while the gun lent added weight to an already existing war pattern. The part played by the Woodlands tribes in the colonial history of both the United States and Canada cannot be underestimated. The seventeenth and eighteenth centuries saw the Indian used as a political pawn in the wars between European powers. The frontier pushed ever westward.

Some ideas out of the European cultural sphere reached many native cultures indirectly. The Woodlands, especially among the western Algonkins, had the concept of the "Great Spirit," and some developed a notion of a "Happy Hunting Ground." Neither concept, that of a supreme being or that of life after death, seems compatible with cultures possessing ceremonial associations, curing, or hunting and fertility rituals. Christian ideas had evidently spread from tribe to tribe in advance of the missionaries and were incorporated somewhat vaguely into a native world view.

LANGUAGES AND TRIBES

With one or two exceptions, the languages of the Woodland area belong to the great Algonkin speech phylum. Algonkin, although widely represented in other native American areas, characterizes the area. Exceptions appear in the lower Great Lakes and east where Iroquoian languages have intruded. Iroquoian is generally assigned to a broader Hokan speech family and appears to represent an invasion of the Woodlands, clearly in prehistoric times, from the south. There are Siouan speakers to the west of the area, not only the Wisconsin Winnebago, but the various Dakota who inhabited the forest-prairie edge in Minnesota.

The Algonkin-speakers were spread widely over the area. A large number of tribes inhabited the western sections in the seventeenth century. Some of these had adapted to wild rice harvesting, others had moved into the area and were adapting to it. The Chippewa (Ojibwa) were becoming settled in the north of the area, and there were also the Menomini, Sauk and Fox, the Kickapoo, and Potawatomi. The latter were located to the east, in the Michigan pen-

insula, while the Sauk, Fox, and Kickapoo were driven out. The Sauk and Fox, after a turbulent career, settled in the eastern Plains. The Chippewa continued to enter the area and to adjust to wild rice use, while the Winnebago and Menomini remained and carried on their cultural traditions with some success.

In the Ohio Valley were encountered the Illinois, Miami, and several groups of Shawnee. The Kickapoo and Potawatomi moved into the area as a result of the stresses occurring in the western Great Lakes. Little is known of these upper Ohio drainage groups. They were maize farmers, it is true, but there appears to have been some depopulation after the decline of the prehistoric, so-called Mound Builder cultures. There is a tradition that groups of Siouan-speakers were in the area or passed through it in a series of movements to the west. The Illinois and segments of the Miami lived in an oak parkland. As a result, their native cultures appear more closely linked to a Plains-Prairie pattern (Kroeber, 1939:90).

North of the Great Lakes, once the Chippewa had moved westward from the central segment, were found the Ottawa, Huron, and Algonquin tribes, the last being the group from which the language family takes its name. The speech of the area belonged to Algonkin excepting the Huron, who spoke an Iroquoian language. Algonkin speech then moved northward into the eastern sub-Arctic to include the Montagnais and Naskapi, spreading westward from this area to include the northern Chippewa (Saulteaux) and the Cree whose territory borders on the western sub-Arctic. The Huron, Ottawa, and Algonquin had a modified farming, although it seems to have been secondary to a hunting economy.

Along the Atlantic Coast, classic Woodland culture is encountered. To the north, maize cultivation gradually phased out. The Micmac and Malecite of New Brunswick were not farmers, although the neighboring Abnaki (Wabnaki) of Maine did raise corn. Algonkin speech appears among these tribes as it does in the middle Atlantic slope. The Penobscot, Pennacook, Mahican, and Massachusett were modified maize farmers in New England along with a number of other tribes whose names survive in history, such as the Wappinger, Conoy, and Nanticoke, but whose cultural position can only be inferred. From the south shore of Connecticut to the New Jersey coast were found the Delaware, not a single tribe, but a confederation of Algonkin-speakers modeled on that of the league of the Iroquois.

Algonkin speech moves south along the east coast. The Jamestown colony in Virginia met the Powhatan league, again a confederation of the kind so common in the eastern and southeastern United States. In his dealings with the Powhatan, Captain John Smith encountered the Susquehanna and Conestoga in Maryland in 1608. These tribes, particularly the former, were much respected by the English settlers in Maryland. Wars and colonial pressures drove these Iroquoian-speakers further to the north.

Iroquoian intrudes into the Algonkin domain. The language family, apparently a general Hokan offshoot, appears in the southeast among the Cherokee. It is known that the famous political federation of the Iroquois was already in existence at the time of contact, tradition placing its formation in the fifteenth century. The five main tribes making up the Iroquois confederacy, the Seneca, Cayuga, Onondaga, Oneida, and Mohawk, were settled in upstate New York and had spread to the St. Lawrence Valley. In this region they waged war on many of their Algonkin neighbors. As a result they may be considered the dominant group in the area. The relations between the Iroquois and the southeast are open to some question. Their southern background, however remote in time it may be, is attested by their farming dependence, one considerably more intensive than that of the adjacent Algonkins. The Tuscarora were an Iroquoian-speaking tribe in the Carolinas. After continuous war with European settlers there, they moved northward to join the Iroquois federation between 1712 and 1715. The association with the south may thus be present both culturally and linguistically. At the same time, however, the mode of Iroquois farming seems to have roots in considerable antiquity (see pp. 374–378).

Eastern woodlands — tribal summary:
Algonkin
West: Chippewa (Ojibwa), Menomini, Sauk, Fox, Kickapoo, Potawatomi
Ohio Valley: Illinois, Miami, Shawnee
Northern Great Lakes: Chippewa, Ottawa, Algonquin
Atlantic Slope: Micmac, Malecite, Abnaki, Passamaquoddy, Penobscot, Pennacook, Mahican, Massachusett, Metoac, Wappinger, Conoy, Nanticoke, Delaware
Siouan (Hokan Siouan)

West: Dakota (Santee, Sisseton) in Plains: Winnebago
Iroquoian (Hokan)
Lower Great Lakes: Iroquois federation (Seneca, Cayuga, Onondaga, Oneida, Mohawk, and after 1715, Tuscarora) Erie, Susquehanna, Conestoga
Northern Great Lakes: Huron, Neutrals

THE MICMAC

The Micmac speak an eastern Algonkin language. They are located today, as in the past, east and northeast of the Penobscot and Passamaquoddy along the southern and eastern shores of the Gaspé Peninsula into New Brunswick and sections of Nova Scotia. Micmac population was an estimated 2000 in 1612, with some increase through the historic period. There were perhaps 3000 Micmac in 1760, 4000 in 1911 (Wallis, 1955:16–17). At the present time, the tribe has increased in numbers, has a strong sense of identity, and is seeking to keep its language alive.

The Micmac are chosen for discussion because they represent a Woodland group not involved in maize farming. In this sense, they are at one end of a spectrum which runs from the essentially intensive agriculture of the Iroquois, through the modified farmers of the upper Great Lakes and New England, to a baseline group which lacked the dependence on cultivation. The Micmac with their primary hunting dependence suggest the general eastern sub-Arctic. The tribes of the general area, Micmac, Malecite, Penobscot, Passamaquoddy, and Abnaki, appear to have been at the point of developing agriculture at the time of contact. The Malecite, for example, were adapting to maize in 1600, and the Micmac were apparently aware of cultivation but their short cool summers precluded its development. One legend states that the Micmac knew agriculture but had "forgotten" it (Wallis, 1955:19–20). Maize, along with beans, squash, and tobacco, was planted by the New England tribes. Massachusetts Bay Colony in the seventeenth century not only adopted Indian corn, but also the method used by such tribes as the Massachusett for fertilizing and storage. The use of fish heads and entrails for fertilizer was seemingly indigenous to New England; similarly, the corn crib, a container set slightly off the ground, was also taken over by Europeans.

Like the Algonkin tribes further to the north,

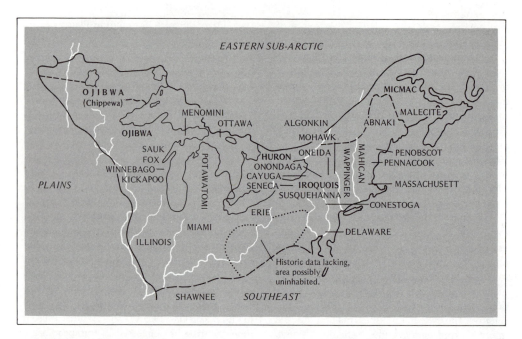

Map labels: EASTERN SUB-ARCTIC; OJIBWA (Chippewa); MENOMINI; OTTAWA; ALGONKIN; MICMAC; MALECITE; ABNAKI; OJIBWA; MOHAWK; SAUK; FOX; HURON; ONEIDA; WAPPINGER; MAHICAN; PENOBSCOT; PENNACOOK; WINNEBAGO—KICKAPOO; POTAWATOMI; ONONDAGA; CAYUGA; SENECA — IROQUOIS; MASSACHUSETT; PLAINS; SUSQUEHANNA; ERIE; CONESTOGA; MIAMI; DELAWARE; ILLINOIS; Historic data lacking, area possibly uninhabited; SHAWNEE; SOUTHEAST

F1 ● Ultra-Mississippi Northeast (Eastern Woodlands)

the Micmac were primarily hunters. Gathering was limited essentially to the berries which abound in forested land. Although there was a wide variety of animals to be hunted for meat and skins, the Eastern Woodlands as well as the eastern Sub-Arctic lacked any single animal around which it could build its economy. There were no caribou or jackrabbits, which characterized other native areas, and while fish were taken with spears, weirs of sticks, and long birchbark nets, there was no single dependable species. Because the Micmac lived near the sea, they could make considerable use of shellfish and crustaceans, taken in the tide flats. Formerly, there was some dependence on sea mammals, particularly seals. But the Micmac were not primarily a maritime people; like other Algonkins, their orientation was to inland hunting.

This meant a fair complexity of skills, knowledge, and technology. Beaver were an important element in the food supply and valued also for their furs, especially after the fur trade began. A beaver dam was cut and the animals clubbed as they sought to escape. Deadfalls were put over beaver paths and split-log traps were placed in the water near a beaver dam. Bears were enticed with a baited snare made of a bough or bush, which was meant to strangle the bear, although this trap may be postcontact. Bears were speared while hibernating. The

moose is perhaps the most important animal for food. Since moose do not herd, they had always to be taken singly. Both deer and moose were trapped with overhead snares made of twisted birch branches. Moose were stalked by hunters wearing decoy costumes with antlers. Men, wearing the tailed snowshoe, often ran a moose down in the winter snow. At all times of the year, although chiefly in the autumn during the rutting season of the moose, the hunter used a moose call of birchbark (Speck and Dexter, 1951).

Meat was preserved by smoking. A special structure made of branches and covered with birchbark was used to smoke food; this was a long lodge, open at the ends, constructed by several men together. Fish were smoked on racks, moose and deer meat cut into slabs and dried by the smoking process, and birds—partridge, ducks, geese, and owls—might be smoked. Food was roasted fresh when available. Porcupine, beaver, and dog were also eaten, although some dogs were kept for hunting and tracking.

Mention has already been made of the ever-present birchbark, an important element in the cultures of nearly all of the Woodlands people. Although some of the Algonkins made pottery, this stood side by side with vessels of bark. The Micmac had no pottery and made their containers, cups, canoes, and houses with birchbark. The American birch (*Betula lutea*) or yellow birch grows through the entire Woodlands from the Atlantic coast to the junction of the Woodlands and Plains in Minnesota. The original growth, which was used by the native peoples (much changed today by deforestation), was of trees two to three feet in diameter from which large segments of bark could be taken. The bark was scored, bent, and sewed to make boxes, trays, buckets, and many other items. Meat was often boiled in a birchbark container, using a stone boiling method, with a rack at the bottom to prevent burning.

The Micmac shared the birchbark canoe with other Algonkins far to the west. The canoe had a frame of cedar splints, carefully curved by soaking and curing and carefully fitted. Over the frame were laid pieces of birchbark, sewed together, and calked with spruce gum (Wallis, 1955:43–45). The birchbark canoe became famous through the area and was used regularly by Europeans as well as Indians for lake and river travel. This is the canoe of the *voyageur*, the French fur trader of the seventeenth and eighteenth centuries.

Winter travel was by snowshoe, of the tailed type adopted from the Algonkins by Europeans, and by toboggans. The latter is an Algonkin word. These were six to eight feet in length, bent wood slabs with a curved end, sewed or tied together with strips of rawhide.

The universal birchbark was also used in housing. A tipilike skin tent was sometimes built but the preference was for the *wigwam*, an Algonkin term which has been much misused. The Micmac built a tipilike structure, a conical wigwam, by clearing the ground, erecting four poles bent together, and covering the frame with sewed bark. Additional supports were added as needed. An inside lining made of mats of swamp grass both gave insulation and prevented leaking of rain. The entrance was covered with a skin flap. Houses of this type varied in size depending on number of residents. The inside was lined with fir branches overlaid by moose hides. Other Algonkins built their lodges in the same way, but the ground plan and the size varied locally and regionally. Such wigwams were transportable. In the main, however, they were a winter dwelling, several located together to form a village. At some distance from the family house was the menstrual lodge.

Micmac clothing was fairly specialized, given that the long winters required skin clothing. It was tailored but reflected the natural resources available, generally being made from the belly of a moose, including the fore part of the animal, with shoulders and forelegs. This provided material for sleeves, which made it a serviceable jacket. The jacket was tied at the waist by a belt, which also held up the moose-skin trousers. Both sexes wore the same type of garments, but a longer shirt was worn by women. A cloak of moose hide with sleeves was added in the colder days of winter. Summer dress for both sexes was a skin loin cloth or girdle. A light jacket of deer hide was used as protection against the sun.

Winter footgear was leggings and moccasins, made of a folded piece of deerskin sewed at both ends. Sealskin footgear was apparently used at one time. Headgear was not usual, but there were caps of moose hide, pointed and tied to the winter cloak. Birchbark caps were also known. Both sexes wore their hair long, parted in the middle; the two sections were then doubled back on themselves and tied with a thong. Hair was carefully combed, oiled, and indicated the concern felt by the Micmac for personal adornment.

All clothing was carefully decorated. The main aboriginal decoration, a complex which moves far to the west, was embroidery of porcupine quills. The hollow quills were fitted into each other from point to butt and appliqued over the dress. Eagle feathers were used on social occasions and much jewelry was made of shell. With quill embroidery, beadwork, moosehair weaving, many dyes, the Micmac achieved considerable variety and skill in decoration. Floral, animal, and geometric designs painted on or applied to clothing, utensils, and wigwam walls made up an active artistry.

The economic life of the Micmac, based as it was on hunting, indicates that the tribe would necessarily be divided into segments. A few related families inhabited a region where the food resources could be exploited, which meant that there was no sense of an extended tribe and that the factor of relationship was primary. An extended family, in this instance a series of bilateral relatives, might take in several smaller social units. As is so often the case among hunting peoples, the smallest unit was the nuclear family. There were small settlements, each with a chief, consisting of groups of related families. But a nuclear family might move out in the winter, wandering through the woods in search of game, and returning to the more permanent encampment in spring. Social structure was simple compared to some of the other Algonkins and seems to represent a basic level of Algonkin organization.

The nuclear family, consisting of the chief hunter, his wife, or wives, children, and at times a dependent relative, inhabited a wigwam. Social usages were quite precise. Each person in the dwelling was assigned his place according to age, sex, and role in the family. Conventionally, there were two entrances to the dwelling, a hunters' door, through which the men entered, and a girls' entrance. Only males could use the hunters' entrance, but widows were free to use either, and the household head and other older men could enter through either door. Within the wigwam there were especially assigned places. The chief hunter and his wife slept at the center of the south wall. Near them were placed the unmarried girls of the family and at their left the older people, parents of either the head of the house or of his wife. At the far wall, opposite the sleeping place of their parents, with a central fire between, were placed the boys of the household. The Micmac had strong views on sexual purity. Brother-sister avoidance, even in the same dwelling, was the rule. A girl, in fact, was carefully supervised. Should she mistakenly enter the house through the hunters' door, she was seen as "spoiled," no longer a girl, and it was felt that she must marry at once (Wallis, 1955:227).

The wife and mother in the household was expected to assign the proper place to each resident. The head of the house tended the fire. Etiquette was taught by both parents. The teaching was strict and involved physical punishment, such as striking a boy's leg with a stick if he stretched it out to the fire. Boys were expected to sleep curled up lest they lose their swiftness. Women were forbidden to step over the legs of a man, which probably relates to the menstrual restrictions.

As nearly as can be judged from the scanty data, the kinship system of the Micmac is of the so-called Eskimo type, general bilateral descent, differentiating cousins from siblings. Additional attention is paid in the kinship system, however, to the marital status of the kindred; conceivably, this points up the importance of marriage in Micmac society.

Like some of the western native Americans, the Micmac and other Algonkins were careful to distinguish the status of any member of the society. There were special terms relating to status, applied to kindred as well as to nonrelatives. Sex was a factor, but in addition there were terms for the infant, young child, young adult, middle-aged people, and the aged. It is of interest in this connection that people were expected to behave according to the status assigned to them and in line with the term used.

Marriage and residence after marriage was a matter of choice. When a couple married, it might set up a wigwam of its own, usually with a single entrance. Not until there were children was the second entrance built. Marriages were not formally arranged, although parents might express a feeling about a possible mate for a child. Marriage within the extended bilateral kinship grouping was generally felt to be improper. Contact between different settlements brought young people together. At an annual meeting of many family groups during the summer, an occasion when feasting, dancing, and general sociability took place, young people had an opportunity to meet. Along with the chief and assistant chief who might direct such events locally, there was an official "Watcher of the Young People" who informed the chief and by extension the community of the names of marriageable young people.

Young men and women did not speak to each other. Virginity was prized, and an ideal situation was one in which young men and women kept themselves apart. Even when a boy spoke to a girl, it was considered a sexual overture and might result in a forced marriage. During the summer festivities, the Watcher of the Young People might try to effect matches, between the boys and girls who came in separate canoes (Wallis, 1955:238). The marriage was simply a festival between the families. Some bride service is suggested. A boy wishing to marry a girl might enter into a relationship with her father to work for him for a period. Several forms of betrothal were thus possible but premarital sexual relations were never permitted. The idea of bride service may operate in respect to postmarital residence. While there was clearly freedom of choice, there was also a sense that the couple, after marriage, should live with the bride's family for a year or more, thereafter being free to settle where they chose. There are many Micmac traditions on marriage, some statements describing exchanges between the principals, use of smoke, and shamanistic practices (Wallis, 1955:242–243). A problem, however, in obtaining such data is that older Micmac culture is now a matter of legend. One point seems eminently clear—the Micmac

Micmac ● Camp with birchbark tipi at
Dartmouth, Nova Scotia, in 1860. (Photographer
unknown. Smithsonian Institution National
Anthropological Archives)

stressed the sanctity of marriage, had used
marriage as a primary way of cementing relations between kinship groupings, and founded
much of their social system on the marital tie.

With the birth of a child, marriage was held
to be successful. A pregnant women was under
restrictions lest her behavior damage the unborn child. Food restrictions, however, were not
included. It was important that quarrels be
avoided. At birth, a woman went to her own
wigwam. Her husband was expected to remain
outside, although there were no other restrictions on him. The parturient knelt, was assisted
by two older women, and after delivery, was
regarded as unclean for forty days. The child
was washed, wrapped, and placed in a cradle
board. This was carried on the mother's back
and held by a strap over her forehead. As a
mother, a women had status. Two days after
birth children were named and recognized as
members of the group. As a child grew, he was
continually made aware of his sexual status: as
a male, he was obliged to avoid girls and playing with their toys. Boys were more desired
than girls. A father might hold a feast for a
boy's first hunt, or even his first step (Wallis,
1955:225).

Boys at age 12 or 13 (i.e., once the voice
changed) were recognized as young men and
expected to behave accordingly. They formed
close friendships with others of the same age
group, hunting and fishing together and engaging in joking behavior. Girls were subject to
the menstrual restrictions and to the status
change which followed on the first menstruation. There was a lodge away from the
main wigwam, which the pubescent girl shared
with other menstruating women and with
women who had given birth, for although the
birth occurred in the family house, the mother
was expected to remain in some seclusion.
Menstruating women were expected to eat
from their own dishes. There was the view, so
common in native America, especially in the
hunting cultures, that game would be offended
if they came into contact, however it happened,
with menstrual blood.

According to the accounts left by French ad-
ministrators, explorers, and missionaries, death
to the Micmac was surrounded with complex
ceremonials. A dying person told by a shaman
he could not be cured dressed in his finest
clothes, otter or beaver skins, sang his death
song, and recited his achievements. He might,
if supplies were on hand, feast all who came to
visit him. If he failed to die, pails of water were
poured over him or he was buried alive. Formal mourning commenced at his death. A
corpse was carried out of the wigwam through

a special aperture—the place where the dying person had last looked. The idea of not using the door is a trait encountered in other northern regions and seems to be a trans-Bering trait. Traditionally, the body was tightly wrapped into a fetal position and buried, seated in a deep grave. Mourners blackened their faces and, gathering at the house of deceased, gave a funeral feast. Orations were given in praise of the dead, for women as well as men. Although relatives mourned for a year, they did not visit the cemetery, fearing the ghosts of the dead. Algonkin burial practises vary considerably over the area. Unlike some of the central tribes, the Micmac do not move to new grounds and thus do not practice the removal of the bones of the dead.

A Micmac settlement made up of several unrelated groups usually had a chief. It is not known how the chief was chosen, although there is some indication that the office passed from father to son (Wallis, 1955:171). If so, this might indicate some paternal bias among the Micmac, a point which other aspects of their social organization, such as modified bride service, might suggest. The chief was a speaker and chief host. He met strangers and either welcomed them or turned them away. Apparently, a chief acted as a diplomat, representing his group in meetings with other chiefs of like status, or he acted as the leader of a war party. The Micmac were primarily loyal to their local group, but they did not wage war on other Micmac settlements. Unlike other tribes in the Woodlands, especially where the Iroquois influence makes itself felt, there was no federation of Micmac. That chiefs of settlements might meet to discuss tribal business suggests the kind of situation out of which might grow the idea of a confederacy.

Chiefs might adjudicate disputes, but the force of public opinion and gossip had equal weight in so small a community. The principal crime was murder, and the factor of intent was taken into account; thus if a man accidentally killed another, he was not punished. The men of the group passed on the fate of a murderer. A blood feud seems not to have arisen; the community at large acted to take a murderer's life by pulling at cords attached to his limbs. This point is interesting, for a blood feud might have been expected; yet the notion of murder as a crime rather than as a tort (i.e., an offense against an individual or family) is characteristic of both the Woodlands and the Southeast.

Adultery was also a crime and an offense against the society at large, in some areas. The stability of marriage among the Micmac may have hindered adulterous relationships; at least, the group have claimed that such never occurred.

Micmac religion died out early, largely as a result of Christian pressures. Some reconstruction is possible when the practices of adjacent peoples, such as the Penobscot (Speck, 1940), are considered and when one reads between the lines of the early missionary accounts, prejudiced though they were. Attention has been called to religious phenomena common along North American hunting cultures, such as those of the Eskimo, the interior Athabascans, or the Northwest Coast. The concepts that illness was caused by the wandering of the personal essence or soul, or by the intrusion into the body of the sick of some "pain" object was common. So also were the ideas about the animal realm, that animals allowed themselves to be taken or could be magically entrapped. Similarly, shamanism was a major element, not only for curing, but also for control of natural and other phenomena.

Shamanism and shamanistic cures were a part of Micmac life. Disease was caused by sorcery; a shaman diagnosed by divining, seeking to discover the nature of the cause of illness, predicting the life expectancy of the patient. Early descriptions mention the shaman's bag of magical items and stress his frenzied behavior. A shaman entered combat with the spiritual cause of illness, a dramatic and wild exhibition involving a virtual trance on the part of the shaman. He was paid for his services.

If shamanism was fairly well developed, hunting ritual was minimal. Animals were offended if contaminated with menstrual blood, but the idea that offense to the animal was a cause of illness seems not to have appeared. More attention was given to natural phenomena, the sun, especially. Connected with the veneration of the sun was the idea that power, or *Manitou*, an Algonkin word meaning a being with power, could be directed for personal advantage. Personal power of various kinds was sought, including shaman power, but among the Micmac, at least, the idea of a special guardian spirit seems not to have developed. The manitou notion is also present among other Algonkins. Tied up with it, across the Algonkin Woodland area, is a concept of "mana," the term employed to refer to an impersonal, supernatural force. The Micmac used the word *keskamzit,* a power which one possesses, secretly, improving one's life and working to general personal advantage. A peculiarly shaped stone, a fungus, any unusual object may accord the finder this kind of power of well-being.

Signs, omens, everyday magic, a host of treatments for illness involving roots, herbs, brews, and many other ingredients achieved a degree of complexity among the Micmac. As with most Amerindian tribes, these remedies and beliefs stood side by side with more formal aspects of shamanism.

Religious concepts also involved ghosts, the essence of the dead, which were much feared. There was also a culture hero, a mythic figure associated with all the eastern Algonkins. This was Gluskap, the transformer. He was a human figure, by no means a divinity, but like Coyote in the west, changed elements in the world largely for his own amusement. He was capable of bringing rain or changing the wind, and native folklore is full of his exploits. He turned people into frogs, gave the beaver its tail, and on the more modern side, helped the Micmac fight the Europeans. Other religious ideas involved signs and portents. There was also the concept of witchcraft, a power related to shamanism. To dream of a *buoin* is to invite his power and is a source of illness. The Micmac seem to have been confronted with a not unusual problem. Was the shaman in one's own family good? Obviously, as a relative, he must be. The shaman of another group, however, with which hostilities might exist, was to be feared as a sorcerer.

The foregoing reflects the Micmac as they were prior to contact. In historic times, beginning in the seventeenth century, the Micmac joined other tribes for mutual defense and for war against Europeans, particularly the English, but also against the Iroquois Mohawk. The idea of a federation took hold rather early, and the Abnaki, Malecite, and Micmac were one of the earlier historical unions. The pattern followed was the exchange of plans, news, and embassies. The associations of tribes varied from century to century. At one time, prior to the American Revolution, the Ottawa acted as arbiters between the Abnaki federation and the Mohawk. When ambassadors went to another tribe, they carried with them their badge of accreditation, *wampum,* which was not money, as is frequently and popularly believed. Strings of tubular beads, made aboriginally from the purple sections of hard clamshells, were originally intended merely as a form of identification, but strings of wampum were used by the Iroquois as compensation for various issues. In general, however, the wampum strings were symbolic of treaty, a trait which characterizes the Woodlands area (cf. Wallis, 1955:222–225).

THE IROQUOIAN TRIBES

Iroquoian speech, including a series of languages belonging to the family (or subfamily) of the same name, possibly to a broader Hokan phylum, evidently came to the Eastern Woodlands at some remote point in time. Considering the distribution of Iroquoian and the fact that these languages intrude on areas of Algonkin speech, the Southeast is indicated as the probable area of origin. The language family has affinities with Siouan. It is known that Siouan groups moved from the Southeast into the Plains, while its remote relative, Iroquoian, pushed northward. Included in Iroquoian are not only the five tribes making up the political confederation, but several others as well, especially the Huron and the Neutrals north of the eastern Great Lakes. To the south, but still in the Woodlands, were the Erie, Conestoga, and Susquehanna, while in the Southeast two important tribes were the Cherokee and Tuscarora.

The fact that the Huron were typically Woodland in culture, generally assignable to an eastern maize configuration, raises the question of why they were not more like the tribes of the federation. The Conestoga and Susquehanna were also Woodland in cultural type. The former allied with their Algonkin neighbors in the seventeenth century against the Iroquois league. Even if the Iroquoian languages point to the Southeast, it seems that the break away from that area occurred long before contact. A conservative glottochronological estimate puts the departure at A.D. 800, while archeology brings the separation back earlier. If the latter is the case, the Iroquoian-speakers of the Eastern Woodlands are not recent migrants but created their variant of Woodland culture in such a development as the League or, like the Huron, had developed essentially within the framework of the area.

It has perhaps been noticed that the knowledge of some tribes seems to begin with European contact, while for others there is an identified, well-described prehistoric foundation, so that change through time and evidence of acculturation to European standards can be documented varyingly deeply into the past. The data can never be stretched so far as to allow a statement that a given tribe, speaking an identified language, lived in the same region for millennia or even centuries because linguistic data are not recovered archeologically. What can be said, however, is that a given tribe did possess a material culture, a subsistence base, a settlement pattern, and an overall adaptation to an environment that is traceable deep into prehistoric times and showing a clear-cut "genetic" or developmental relationship to well-known early cultures.

Among those tribes whose seventeenth-century culture has a long and well-understood pedigree, the Iroquois are a prime example. Despite legends (supported to a degree by linguistic evidence) that the tribes pushed into New England from the area north of the Great Lakes, there is ample archeological reason to suppose a long period of occupancy in New York State in a cultural continuum from 1000 to 2000 years old. The following account is drawn largely from the contributions of Griffin (1964), MacNeish (1952), and Ritchie (1969). The historically noted mixed subsistence model—horticulture along with hunting, fishing, and gathering—developed from the hunting-fishing-collecting base, characteristic of all the eastern Woodland tribes at about A.D. 1000–1100. The culture, called Owasco, lends its name to many related local variants in New York, Pennsylvania, and adjacent states which are grouped under the name Owascoid because of the close similarity. The late Woodland Owascoid culture is linked through ceramic, subsistence, and other traits with earlier Middle Woodland cultures including the Point Peninsula and Hopewellian. (The colorful Hopewell cultures, or more properly the Hopewell cult, blanketed the United States east of the Mississippi and contributed importantly to all later manifestations. Dated at 2300 to 1500 B.P., it cannot be identified with any historic tribe and is not described in this volume except for the paragraphs on pp. 25ff; 404 ff.)

The Owasco settlement location preference seems to have been for river or lake side situations, with the villages built in a somewhat elevated spot upon the second terrace, above the alluvial plain where corn, beans, and squash were grown. Gardening of the three staples mentioned above, tobacco, and several

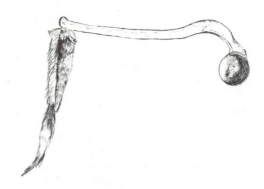

Iroquois ● "Tomahawk" or ball-headed club. Such clubs, about 2 feet in length, often with a 6-inch ball head, were common weapons among the Great Lakes tribes in the eighteenth century. As metal came more and more into use, a knife point was sometimes inserted into the ball. Later still, this gave way to a metal axe, the "tomahawk" of fame. The ball was often made from a beryl and the entire item was occasionally carved from a single piece of wood.

plants now considered weeds was first practiced in this region by the Owasco. It was evidently done in a swidden pattern, a technique requiring the abandonment of fields and a shift of village location every few years as soil fertility declined and wood for fuel and construction became scarce.

Based on the information produced by the excavation of several sites (Maxon-Derby, Levanna, Bates, Sacket sites in New York and the Miller site in Ontario), it is possible to describe the Owasco villages and some other aspects of the culture. The houses were long, evidently multi-family affairs as much as 25 feet by 60 feet in size. The houses were built of flexible saplings "screwed" into the ground to form the parallel sides and rounded ends. They were bent over to form a loaf-shaped framework that was covered with sheets of birchbark. Shallow firebasins were found aligned between the walls and the centerline. Thus, by A.D. 1100, the Maxon site shows a cluster of prototypical Iroquois long houses. Ten house patterns, scattered over a two acre area on a low ridge, comprised the village. Several of the houses had been repaired or rebuilt. Occupancy had been once interrupted (perhaps to let the forest and fields regenerate) and new houses were built directly upon the old house sites but along different axes. Thick trash or midden deposits attest to a reasonably long total period of occu-

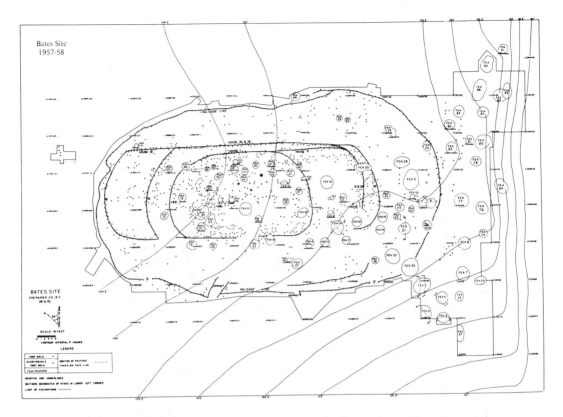

Bates Site
1957-58

BATES SITE
CHENANGO CO., N.Y.
(W.A.R.)

SCALE IN FEET

CONTOUR INTERVAL 8 INCHES

LEGEND

HEARTHS ARE UNDERLINED

Figure 45 ● Iroquois prehistory, map of the subsoil features of the Bates site, showing stockade line, postmold outline of probable oval house, enlarged four times, storage pits, hearths (underlined), and burial. Canandaigua phase, Owasco culture. (After Ritchie, 1969)

pancy. No surrounding palisade existed, although this feature characterized later Owasco and the descendant prehistoric Iroquois villages (Figs. 45, 46).

The tools for a farming-gathering technology were recovered during excavation. These include double-ended bone gorges and fishhooks, bone hide-dressing tools, bone awls for basketry and leather work, a curved bone and a needle for mat weaving and, of course, many chipped-flint tools for cutting, scraping, and piercing. Ornaments were bird-bone beads, "tinklers" carved from toe bones of deer, canine teeth from bears, wolves, or dogs grooved or pierced for suspension, and breast plates or pendants of freshwater clam shells. Antler combs, presaging the Iroquois style are also part of the Owasco ornament trait list. Woodworking tools of stone are numerous and varied, including axes, adzes, and chisels. Wedges of antler, carving tools made from beaver in-

cisors, and other tools anticipate Iroquois versions of the same tools.

Perhaps best known is the simple but sturdy diagnostic amphora-shaped pottery, made by the paddle and anvil technique and decorated around the neck with cord-wrapped stick impressions. Clay pipes of pottery and stone, with the elongated bowl at an obtuse angle to the stem, were made in highly distinctive styles. Some of the pipes are sculptured to represent animals and even the human face. Again the Iroquois design is seen in ancestral form.

There is no evidence of trade or warfare. Ritchie believes the people were self-sufficient within the resources of their lands. He also says that lack of palisades or of large numbers of weapons bespeaks a people at peace, with no demographic pressures upon them in the early phases of the culture. Before A.D. 1300, however, palisades occur.

By A.D. 1400, what can be called proto-Iroquois villages can be recognized and by A.D. 1600, of course, historic locations can be identified. The long-house village, the double-rowed palisades, the long list of tools, weapons, utensils, and ornaments, and the subsistence pattern all indicate the several hundred years of evolution of Iroquois culture from Owasco be-

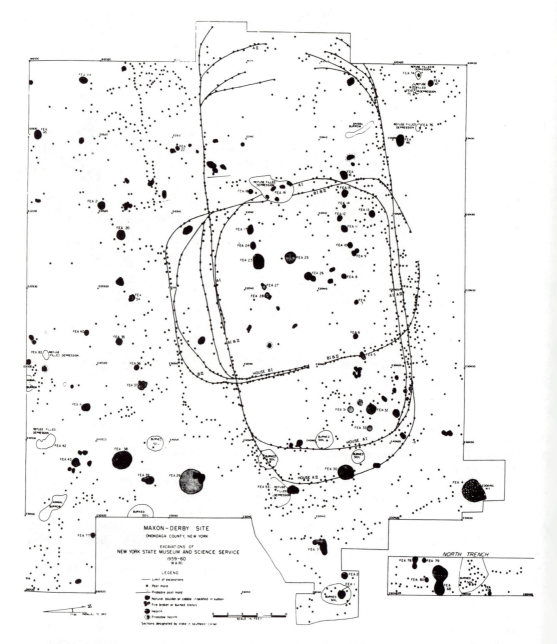

Figure 46 ● Iroquois prehistory, portion of excavated area at the Maxon-Derby site, showing overlapping house floors A and B, hearths, and other features. Note evidence of several stages of construction in both houses. Carpenter Brook phase, Owasco culture. (After Ritchie, 1969)

ginnings in the New York area. Archeologists would perhaps disregard the legendary stories of a recent arrival of the Iroquois in New England; at least their entire life cycle and style are clearly rooted in earlier local cultures. The sophistication of their social organization and government, including the famous Confederacy, is not hinted at in their technology.

There are, of course, differences between the Iroquois and Owasco material culture. One example is in the Iroquois pottery, which is characterized by elaborate modification of the rims. While the basic vessel form remained amphoralike, the simple Owasco rim was replaced by a taller rim with four "peaks" making the orifice somewhat square. In general, cord mark-

Figure 47 ● Iroquois prehistory, restorations of pottery vessels. A, restored jar of Castle Creek Beaded type, check-stamped malleated body, height 21 inches; B, vessel (intact) of Castle Creek Punctate type, height 3¼ inches; C, restored pot of Owasco Corded Collar type; D, restored pottery vessel from Lakeside Park site, Auburn, Cayuga Co., N.Y., Canandaigua phase, Owasco culture, Wickham Corded Punctate type; E, restored Iroquois pottery vessel from the Oakfield Fort site, Genesee Co., N.Y., Oakfield phase; F, restored Iroquois pottery vessel of Oak Hill Corded type from the Clarke site, Willow Point, Broome Co., N.Y., Oak Hill phase. (After Ritchie, 1969)

ing gave over to incised decoration and the vessel bodies were more smoothly finished. But it was in the manufacture of pipes that Iroquois artistry showed itself. A new form, the "trumpet" bowl was developed; also, the Owasco carry-over sculptured forms became more numerous, with the carving more skillfully executed (Figs. 47, 48, 49).

In architecture some changes occured. Fortification palisades were double- or triple-walled enclosures. Simple surface fireplaces tended to be along the central axis of the long house, which continued. At one of the sites, Kalso, the long houses were over 125 feet long by 22 feet wide (Fig. 50).

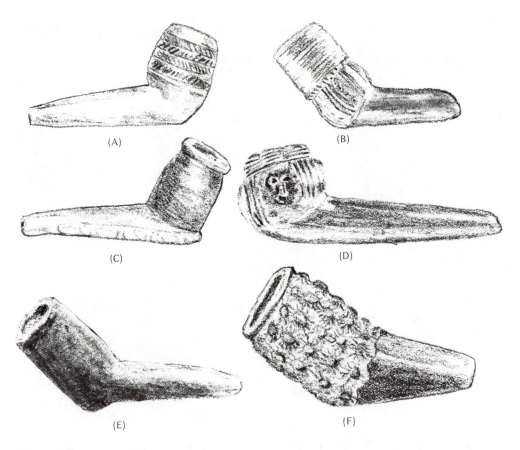

(A)

(B)

(C)

(D)

(E)

(F)

Figure 48 ● Iroquois prehistory, tobacco pipes. Pottery, A, B, D, E, F, and stone, C, elbow pipes of the Owasco culture. Natural size. (After Ritchie, 1969:294)

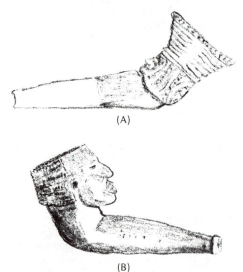

(A)

(B)

Figure 49 ● Early Iroquois pipe styles. A, Chance phase; B, Oak Hill phase. (After Ritchie, 1969:311)

The archeological record of Iroquois prehistory sketched above attests to the development of the Iroquois over several hundred years and suggests an antiquity in the area of fifteen hundred years or more.

The Huron

Attention was paid to the Micmac tribe of New Brunswick because a general base of Woodlands culture was encountered there. The other tribes of the Woodlands share an essentially similar mode of life but add two major elements. An agricultural mode of subsistence stands side by side with a hunting dependence, while, in addition, an emphasis on war has far-reaching implications. The settled economy associated with farming meant that a somewhat more elaborated material culture might develop, but in general it has its roots in the same orientation and adaptation which marked the Micmac.

One of the characteristic features of native American life in the eastern sections of the continent was the federation of various tribes both for offense and defense. The classic example is, of course, the famous League of the Iroquois,

Figure 50 ● Chippewa. Pole framework of arbor-roofed longhouse, medicine lodge of the Seine River band of Chippewa of the Rainy River district of Ontario. (Drawn after Ritchie, 1969:283)

but even the basically simple Micmac culture moved into this pattern, and in the Southeast, the pattern of formal political alliances between tribes also appeared. Not all of the Woodlands peoples were drawn into the making of inter-tribal federations, but the Huron, the Neutrals, and many of the Algonkins developed leagues of longer or shorter duration. At times, a con-federacy might develop both for protection against, or at the urging of, various European powers, but the political patterns were clearly pre-Columbian. The influence of the Iroquois was evident; confederations were formed as protection against Iroquois imperialism. The re-lation to the emphasis on war is obvious.

The Huron followed these Woodland pat-terns. From a base not unlike that of the Mic-mac, the Huron developed a sedentary mode of life with permanent villages and farmlands. Four tribes, the Attignawantan, Attigneenogna-hac, Arendahronon, and Tahontaenrat, shared a common language although each had a sense of its own traditions. (Tooker, 1964:9). The tribes were bound together in a confederation which according to missionary accounts had

been in existence for more than two centuries (Trigger, 1969:14). The Attignawantan, the larg-est tribe, was traditionally involved in the founding of the league, had the largest number of seats in the council, and incorporated per-haps half the total Huron population. Each tribe had chiefs, representatives to the league council, and there were also chiefs of villages. The em-phasis on political organization so characteristic of eastern North America is well exemplified by the Huron.

The population of the total federation of the Huron has been estimated as between 30,000 and 40,000 in the early seventeenth century. This is in keeping with the large populations of the total area (Kroeber, 1939:143). The problem of obtaining any accuracy in respect to Huron population can be seen when it is considered that perhaps half of the Huron had died off from European diseases by 1640–1650. A figure of 18,000 Huron by 1750 may be generally cor-rect (Kroeber, 1939:140).

Each of the four component tribes was di-vided into villages, excepting the Tahontaenrat, a late comer to the federation (1610) and limited to one large village. Huron country was not ex-tensive, the four tribes living in an essentially limited region between Lake Simcoe and Geor-gian Bay, an arm of Lake Huron. Villages were spaced fairly close together, a reflection of the dense population and undoubtedly of the fact that farming could be successfully carried on in Huron country. The French explorer, Champlain, lists eighteen Huron villages. Larger villages, it is said that there were six in all, were located on lower ground and palisaded with wooden stakes. The palisades were sharpened at the top, forced into the ground, and bound together. Three rows made up a defensible wall. Galleries were run at the top of the sixteen-foot wall and there were also watchtowers. Such a village might also have a ditch surrounding it. Unfortified villages were placed on high ground. In the event of an enemy attack, the residents took refuge in a fortified town. Archeology reveals the pattern of locating a village on high ground near a suitable stream. Fortifications may be historic. Villages were named and related to the respective tribes: the Attignawantan are recorded as living in fourteen villages in 1636.

Within the village, fortified or not, were houses, which were smaller and less elaborate variations of the "long house" of the League of the Iroquois. A house was set on a ground plan of 20 by 30 feet; the poles making up the frame were apparently lashed together to give support for the outer covering, which was of bark, preferably cedar, although any bark at hand could be used. Given the dense population in the relatively few villages, houses were placed only a few feet apart, thus creating a problem of fire, especially since fires were built in the houses themselves. It is said that the Huron put valuables in containers and buried them.

Inside the house, with an entrance at each end, a row of fires ran down the center. Nuclear families had sleeping places on one side of the house and shared a fire with the family in the section across the central aisle. In each house fires were spaced 2 to 3 paces apart. In a house 30 feet in length there might be 5 fires, each serving 2 families. If a nuclear family consisted of a man, his wife, 2 to 3 children, and perhaps a few dependent relatives, 60 to 80 people could inhabit a single house. There were smokeholes in the roof, but even so, according to French accounts, the house was smoky, the people naked, and dogs were everywhere (Tooker, 1964:40). Along the sides of the house were platforms where goods could be kept and where people slept. Villages might also have a larger structure which served as a meeting place and perhaps as the residence of a chief. In some villages there were two such larger houses, one for a civil chief and his rela-

tives, another for a war chief. A division of war and peace chiefs suggests the Southeast and may ultimately be traced to Mexico.

Huron economy was based on agriculture. Farming accounted for perhaps three-quarters of the food eaten (Trigger, 1969:27). Wild plants of many kinds were gathered, and in addition, hunting and fishing were important. Huron society was essentially classless with the result that the primary division was between the sexes. A certain uneasiness appears to have existed between the sexes creating some sense of avoidance and formality. The worlds of men and women were well defined. Men cleared the fields, often by burning off the brush, hunted, went to war, and cultivated tobacco. Women, apart from the usual household tasks of cooking and child rearing, did the maize cultivation, gathering and grinding of foods, sewing of clothing, as well as many other kinds of work.

Maize planting was done in spring. Kernels of corn were selected, soaked for a few days, nine or ten kernels then placed in a single hole. When the corn began to sprout, a hill of earth was erected around the sturdiest stalks, forming the traditional corn "hill" of the Woodlands area. Placed several feet apart, they dotted the landscape throughout the Huron territory (Trigger, 1969:28). The same hills were used every year. The Huron tended to clear off as much forest as possible and to leave open land between villages. This pattern differed from that of the Iroquois who kept forest tracts available for hunting between villages. At that, there were forested areas in Huron territory. The brush was cleared when new fields were needed. There is some question how much land would have been needed to support the large population of the Huron. But maize is a nourishing crop; perhaps no more than 7,000 acres could support 20,000 people (Trigger: 1969:28).

The usual plants of the maize complex appeared among the Huron, but it is not known whether the corn hills accommodated beans and squashes as well as corn itself. It is clear that these were planted by women in the fields. Men planted tobacco around the dwelling. Women, especially if a plot were free from raids, might spend days on end in the fields, living in small shacks. Harvested corn was hung in the houses on poles under the roof. Dried, the corn was shelled by women who stored it in large casks made for the purpose (Tooker, 1964:61).

Although not so economically important as

agriculture, the products of hunting and fishing played a role in Huron society. The birchbark canoe of the Woodlands was used by the Huron, although this was more directed to travel. Fishing stations on lakes were established with several bark lodges for the fishermen. The fish (largely whitefish) was netted and hooked; winter fishing was done by netting through holes in the ice. Fish taken were dried and smoked, larger fish boiled for oil. The men engaged in serious rituals for fishing. Each fishing house tried to have a fish preacher, a man skilled in the ritual, who "preached" to the fish, telling them that the Huron did not burn fish bones. This was felt to encourage the fish to come to the net. Tobacco was offered to the water and in one ceremony, aimed at successful fishing, two virgin girls were "married" to the fish nets (Tooker, 1964:64).

Hunting was more important, not for meat so much as for clothing, which was generally made from deerskin and beaver pelts. The Huron were somewhat less skilled in skin tanning, preparation, and sewing than some of the neighboring Algonkins, with whom the Huron traded for skins and clothing. Although the moose appeared in Huron territory, it was not plentiful. Deer were shot with arrows and snared. There were many ways of getting beaver, an animal desired both for food and skins.

Despite the presence of agriculture, the material culture of the Huron was not elaborate. Each person and family made what was needed. Pottery was known, made of clay, with several shapes, although a globular pot was the most common. It was generally of poor grade, unable to hold water without becoming soft after a time. Men chipped stones for dart points and made knives and choppers. They also rolled fibers on the thigh to make twine for lines and netting. Although men carved pipes of soft stone, pottery pipes were also known. Bone tools such as harpoon points were common. Men manufactured tubular beads of bone, shell, and red steatite. Body decoration was usual, as were bracelets and arm- and head-bands. The body was painted, frequently covered with grease into which different colors had been introduced. The hair was carefully cared for, combed, oiled, and plaited in various ways. Women wore the hair in a single braid down the back; men arranged their hair in many different ways, more frequently with large rolls over the ears.

The Huron traded widely, in fact controlling the aboriginal trade from the St. Lawrence Valley into Ontario. When European contact began, trade became much more important. The Huron traded ground corn northward to the Algonkins for skins. They got a better grade of tobacco from the Neutrals and other tribes to the south, offering in turn black squirrel skins which were much prized as cloaks. Pottery was traded northward in aboriginal times and is found in Algonkin sites. Located as they were, the Huron were in a position to exert a degree of control over trade routes. There were specific routes owned by individuals. Trading on them required the owner's permission. It is of interest that the *lingua franca* of the region was Huron, meaning that Algonkin tribes and such westerly Siouan groups as the Winnebago had to use Huron. Although there were tentative exchanges with the Iroquois, the situation was generally one of war. Trade was important to the extent of creating good relations with other groups. There was gift exchange; trading partners might hold one another's children, virtually as hostages. Although trading could help to ensure peace, tensions could arise and create open hostility, feud, and warfare.

The Iroquoian-speakers of the Eastern Woodlands were always involved in a state of war. Although the League of the Iroquois itself was partly concerned with conquest in order both to expand its hunting grounds and to dominate neighboring tribes, this was less true of the Huron. War was a ritual, a means of advancing individual prestige as well as that of the group at large. Wars were also fought for revenge, parties being organized by relatives of a slain warrior, in which case, the struggle, a virtual feud, could be averted by gift giving. Failure to give atoning gifts was regarded as an act of hostility.

It has been said that wars in the Eastern Woodlands arose as a result of an Iroquois invasion, assuming that the Iroquois upset a normal balance by moving in from the Southeast. Since it is clear that the Iroquois had been long in the area and that the Algonkins themselves were frequently at war, the condition of rivalry, hostility, and aggression between tribes must be regarded as an ancient pattern. War patterns of the Plains area are in some measure different, what with the emphasis on counting coup and horse stealing, but in the Woodlands and in the Southeast variations on a theme are encountered. There can be no question that the eastern sections of North America were war-oriented; however, the complex had its specific integration in each area.

The Huron were closest to the Seneca and were in a state of permanent war with them. Mutual raids took place, and the Huron, not unlike modern nations, were much concerned lest the enemy discover the raiding plans. A war leader was always circumspect and tried to learn of the war plans of enemy tribes by giving gifts to neutral chiefs or even placing spies. Wars were fought through the summer months because most tribes were too occupied in winter to fight, and travel, in any case, was difficult. If a group of Huron attacked a Seneca village, several hundred men came together, made their way by canoe to the enemy country, hunting and fishing along the way, and then by stealth entered Iroquois territory. Enemy met by chance were killed or captured, and the Huron warriors then advanced to the Seneca palisades to try to set fire to them. A pitched battle could be fought, several men killed, and the invaders would withdraw before reinforcements could come. The wounded, tightly bound in a flexed position, were carried home in baskets on the backs of the unscathed. On the retreat, older warriors were placed in the center, while the younger and lustier men made up the sides.

Some five or six hundred Huron warriors might gather for a raid. They traveled in groups of five or six, hiding in the forest or fields and trying to capture or kill an enemy. Brave men might steal into an enemy village and try to set fire to houses. Any prisoners taken were brought back to the Huron region if possible or else killed on the spot, clubbed or shot to death. Heads or scalps were taken as trophies, later to be put up on the palisades to frighten off attackers. Prisoners taken back to the home community were subjected to a variety of tortures lasting until the victim died. The flesh of the prisoner was cut away, and hot stones, later irons, were thrust into the wounds. Prisoners resisted crying out, thus showing contempt for their torturers, whose efforts were at once increased. The flesh of the war captives was sometimes eaten at a victory celebration (Tooker, 1964:29), which seems to reflect a ritual cannibalism, a trait rather rare among the American Indian. The taking of heads was also unusual in general North America, although it is probable that the concept of scalping can be traced back to an ancient complex of beheading and the use of the skull as a trophy.

Information on the social organization of the Huron depends on the few remarks made by visiting Frenchmen in the seventeenth century.

Both in social and in political organization, there is a resemblance to the general Iroquoian five tribes. The descent system among the Huron was matrilineal. An individual belonged to one of four tribes and to one of eight clans, membership in which cut across tribal lines. A man belonged to the group of his mother, married outside his maternal clan, and presumably went to live in the community of his wife (Trigger, 1969:54–59). Within the clans were certain offices which passed through the female line, that is, from a man to his sister's son. The clan was represented locally in villages and, if extensive, might have several chieftainships within it. These officials both dealt with the internal affairs of the clan on the village level, and represented it on councils, whether in the village itself, where several clans might appear, on the tribal level, or within the federation. The system looks at first glance like that of the Iroquois. One has the impression, however, that the League of the Iroquois had both its chieftainships and its clan associations far better structured.

The eight clans of the Huron are only questionably known by name. The neighboring Wyandot, however, had eight clans with animal names—Turtle, Wolf, Bear, Beaver, Deer, Hawk, Porcupine, and Snake. Since the Seneca, Cayuga, and Onondaga also had eight clans with the same names, it is assumed that the Huron fell into the same pattern (Connelley, 1890). The names, as well as the clan system itself, may have arisen from what were originally autonomous hunting groups (Trigger, 1969:57), and the animal names are not unexpected in aboriginal North America. No special attitude seems to have been directed by the members of a clan to the animal whose name it bore. Other tribes in the area linked clans in various ways. Interclan marriage was of course, an element, but the Wyandot had three groupings of clans. These, the phratries, may have functioned among the Huron in a ceremonial way. Phratry organization, in any case, is a feature associated with many unilineal systems in the Eastern Woodlands.

It has been said of the Huron that it was a classless society. Although chieftainships were inherited in the maternal clan line, a chief, to secure his office, had to demonstrate his force of personality, his ability to lead, his general equanimity. While he might inherit his office from his maternal uncle, public opinion had to endorse his status. These civil chiefs, a war leader was somewhat differently viewed, worked toward peace and harmony within the tribe, at confederacy convocations, or in the village. A chief exhorted, rendered his opinion, and was oriented to caution. A man who called a war party, for example, might meet with the objections of the civil chiefs who argued that possible retaliation would place all in danger.

Although chiefs had no judicial powers, a well-defined system of law employed public opinion as an enforcing agent. Treason and sorcery were crimes against the society at large. Traitors were those who told secrets to the enemy, while witches were feared both because they caused illness and drained people's possessions away by forcing them to pay a curer. As has been demonstrated among some other native American tribes, accusations of sorcery were a way of effecting social control, forcing an individual toward proper behavior in order to avoid being called a witch. There was also a channel and a rationale for hostile and aggressive reactions, since one person could accuse someone he disliked in the group (Kluckhohn, 1944). Traitors and sorcerors were killed. Murder was a matter to be resolved between families; a murderer was obliged to pay an indemnity to the relatives of his victim, either in the form of wampum beads or by labor. A thief, if caught, ran the risk of having his victim take all his possessions.

Whether adultery was seen as a social offense or as a matter to be resolved by any affronted individual is not wholly clear. The Huron were notoriously modest and it is clear that there were tensions between the sexes. A man's orientations lay with his own maternal clan, never with that of his wife. Sexual relations were avoided for a long period after the birth of a child. But the presence of a child appeared to cement the marital union. Prior to parenthood, infidelity was common and divorces frequent.

Huron religion involved three major aspects—general festivals, curing, and the attitudes toward the dead. Some fundamental beliefs underlay these features, such as an elaborate mythology and a series of common attitudes toward the supernatural. Ritual was minimal and there were no priestly classes. Given the political structure of the Huron where chiefs met in conclave once a year, it follows that these assemblies should have a ritual quality. To some extent these festivals, however political in tone, had the effect of restoring order in the world. Each village also had a winter festival for restoring health. While curing was often done by an individual practitioner, one

who had the special shamanic powers, there were also curing societies. These were associations of persons who underwent an initiation and learned the modes of curing. The initiation of one such society called for pretended killing of the initiate. The societies had special rituals, paraphernalia, and dances. Several such fraternities existed, admitting both men and women.

The individual shaman is said to have sought power by isolation and fasting. His primary power was curing, but there were other shamans who could control the weather, find lost objects, or predict future events. Even if women could join a curing society, individual practitioners were always men; some women could predict by divination.

The tone of Huron religion, however, introduces special attitudes and thought patterns, which have been described as the "desires of the soul." The Huron—and the Iroquois—had developed an oddly conceived theory of the human fate and condition, oddly, in that it resembles aspects of psychological theory. The soul, an unconscious element, makes its desires known through dreams. When, for example, a shaman found a patient about to die, he suggested that the soul desired unattainable things. The wishes of the soul had a well-defined social function, bringing about a kind of commonality and cooperation. One person, or more, attempted to define the soul desires of another and to assist him in satisfying them. For example, a warrior dreamed that he would be captured and burned at the stake. In order to prevent this, he was taken by his fellow villagers, tortured as he might be were he captured, but a dog was killed in his place (Trigger, 1969:116–117). The community was thus able to interact to hinder the destructive desires of the person's soul. Curing ceremonies generally were conceptualized to meet the desires of the soul which arose through dreams (Wallace, 1969:59–75). This aspect of Huron—and Iroquois—life is extremely important in understanding societal behavior. The culture stressed the freedom of the individual. At the same time, the individual needed the society and found a rationale in this philosophical formulation for the interaction of persons in groups.

Death in Huron society was a source of anxiety. It was related to a fear of separation and was tied in turn with a ritual of separation. Formalized mourning, feasting, and gift exchange marked the ceremony. The body was placed in a bark coffin on stilts, eight to ten feet off the ground. People who had died a violent death were not treated in this way but buried at once in the ground. Every ten to twelve years the bones of the dead were collected and placed in a pit. Why this was done is subject to variable interpretation. Villages might move, especially if new fields had to be cleared. On moving, the village took its dead along. It must be recalled, however, that secondary burial is common in the eastern United States among the native tribes. It seems a southeastern complex, one taken over by some of the Algonkins. A ten-day feast accompanied the removal. The bones were cleaned, sometimes wrapped in beaver skins and placed carefully in a pit, the bones mixed together. A social aspect of such secondary burial might be noted. People from several villages might be buried together in such an ossuary. The living then argued that since the dead were at peace, so also should the living be. A pattern of ritual friendship existed among the Huron. A man might request that he be buried with his friend.

The Huron in effect are gone. Their language disappeared and the tribe was scattered. Yet the detail of their culture comes through clearly from the seventeenth-century visitors who described them.

The League of the Iroquois

The activities of the Iroquois proper, or the five tribes who made up the federation, extended from the Atlantic Coast and the St. Lawrence Valley as far west as the Mississippi. This extension was the result of military conquests, reflecting wars fought simply for the sake of the victory and sometimes for political advantage and territorial aggrandizement. Protectorates were established over some Algonkin tribes; with others, the Iroquois were constantly in a state of war. This is surprising in view of the low estimates of Iroquois population. Mooney and Kroeber agree on a figure of 5500 for the five tribes in 1600 (Kroeber, 1939:133,140). An estimate which may be correct if the Iroquois tribes at the time of contact represent a decline of the quasi states which existed in prehistoric times. Apparently the success of the Iroquois lay not in numbers but in a tremendously effective war machine.

There is little doubt that the origins of the confederacy, the League of the Iroquois, consisting of the Seneca, Cayuga, Onondaga, Oneida, and Mohawk, were aboriginal. Myths relating to the founding of the league tell of the spirit, Dekanawidah, who imparted the idea of

peace between what were five warring tribes to the hero, Hiawatha. Given an aboriginal background, however, it seems clear that the League could adapt itself very well to the changing situation brought about by Europeans. The tribes were a power in the area before the American Revolutionary War.

Because of the distinctive politico-kinship nature of the organization of the League, anthropological interest in the Iroquois has been marked. The famous Lewis Henry Morgan[1] began this latter concern with the publication of his *League of the Ho-De-No Sau-Nee* in 1851. The particular anthropological concern for the Iroquois has centered on the structure and operation of the confederacy, on their socio-political organization, which perhaps comes closest to the classic "matriarchate," and, more recently, on the tenacity and persistence of Iroquois culture in the twentieth century.

The confederation of the five Iroquois tribes operated under a council composed of fifty *sachems*. The sachems represented each of the five constituent tribes, and the positions on the League council were hereditary within each tribe. The distributions of sachem positions was unequal, however, for the Onondaga, the smallest tribe in numbers, held 14 sachem positions, the Mohawk 9, the Oneida 9, the Cayuga 10, and the Seneca 8. Each sachem position was named and each was associated with a particular duty or series of duties. To a degree, the sachem positions were ranked. The Onondaga, for example, held three sachem positions which were of greatest importance. The man holding one of these positions or titles acted as the head of the Council of Fifty, while two of his Onondaga sachems acted as councillors. One Seneca sachem was keeper of the long house; an Onondaga sachem, keeper of the Council wampum, the tubular shell beads which had a sense of exchange value and also a badge of ambassadorial accreditation. The wampum was also used in ceremonial recitations, as a kind of "prayer bead."

Sachems were always male, though a woman could act as a regent for a boy too young to serve as an active sachem. The men of the Council of Fifty controlled the external affairs of

---

[1] L. H. Morgan (1818–1881), a lawyer in Rochester, N.Y., was led by his Iroquois studies into social theory. He became a pioneer social philosopher, one of the first on the American scene.

the League and in their meetings deliberated matters of war and peace and problems which were common to all of the constituent tribes. The Council had no voice in the internal affairs of the separate tribes, however. Each tribe had its own council, composed of the sachems they had as representatives on the confederacy council. The tribal council dealt with internal problems and could act on matters which concerned only their tribe's relations with outside groups. Both confederacy and tribal councils operated in a similar fashion. Problems which were raised were discussed deliberately and each member was given an opportunity to speak. The gift orator was honored and ample opportunity to develop an oratorical skill was present. Council decisions reflected a consensus, for the decisions arrived at were unanimous.

Iroquois involvement with the French and the fur trade strengthened the League, for the Iroquois fought the French for control of the lower Great Lakes and upper St. Lawrence valley, a territory which, had the Iroquois held it, would have given them control over the western trade. The resultant warfare increased the feeling of solidarity among the members of the League and also increased the number of external problems which the Council of Fifty had to face. Iroquois power and strength as a confederacy grew until the American Revolution, when the tribes were divided in their allegiances. Coupled with the westward expansion of American settlers, the effects of the American Revolution ended the military power of the League.

Warfare was a pre-European pattern among the Iroquois, for they expanded their territories at the expense of Algonkin tribes and sent raiding parties long distance. When Hennepin first saw the Illinois in the seventeenth century, they told him of Iroquois raids on their villages. The Iroquois-speaking Huron who lived in eastern Ontario were traditional enemies of the tribes of the League, and even the Algonkin of the Gaspé Peninsula knew and feared Iroquois war parties. The historic period brought an intensification of these patterns of warfare and out of this situation the Iroquois developed a new series of honorific titles to recognize those who had been courageous and successful in warfare but who were not sachems. These "Pine Tree Chiefs" were given the title by the Council as public recognition of their contributions in warfare. The titles were originally not hereditary, though they tended to become so during the reservation period of the nineteenth century (Wallace, 1970).

Active young men of warrior age who received this recognition became the war leaders during the intense conflicts with Europeans, and the Council of Sachems, traditionally a council of peace chiefs, was faced with increasing problems in controlling the warfare activities of the younger men. Success in warfare brought increased prestige to the warrior, many of whom, having no possibility of becoming sachems, could not receive the prestige accorded a sachem, and thus they continually demanded the right to organize a war party. During the period of intense and continual conflict with Europeans, the Pine Tree Chiefs were extremely powerful and the Council of Fifty was pressed by demands for action in warfare.

The fifty sachem titles were thus restricted, not available to all worthy candidates but only to males who were members of the tribes and kin groups who held the titles. Iroquois kin groups were matrilineal and certain matri-sibs and matrilineages within these sibs were the traditional holders of the named sachem titles. Only from the kin group holding a sachem title could a successor be chosen. The sachem titles were therefore hereditary within specific kin groups, and as these groups were matrilineal and the matri-sib exogamous, a son could never succeed his father, for the son belonged to a different matri-sib, that of his mother. The successor of a deceased sachem was nominated by the women of the lineage and matri-sib from among the male members of the kin group. Frequently a younger brother of the former sachem was selected, or a sister's son might be so designated. There was no specific rule of succession within the kin group, so that in theory the male chosen might be anyone. The regent rule of an older female member of the kin group occurred when the new sachem was too young to participate as a sib, tribal, and confederacy leader. The role of the females in selecting the nominee and in acting as regent on occasion gave them particular power and importance in these societies, a fact which has led to the designation of the Iroquois as resembling a matriarchate.

The nomination of a successor meant that the sib agreed on the person to become sachem. The western Iroquois tribes were also organized on a moiety basis where the constituent sibs of the tribe were grouped into two units, both exogamous like the sib. In these tribes the nomination was confirmed by the moiety to which the nominating sib belonged, and then the opposite moiety and the tribe approved the nominee. When this had been accomplished, the other tribes of the League were informed and the Council met to perform the condolence ceremony where the deceased sachem was officially mourned and his successor accepted into the Council. This moving ceremony, practiced also by opposite moiety members at the death of any Iroquois male, acted to confirm the traditional right of a sib to hold a sachem title and publically informed the people that the position had been filled.

Even on the level of the common person in Iroquois society, the condolence rituals at death were solemn mourning rites. F. G. Speck recorded a portion of such a ceremony given at the Cayuga reserve at Sour Springs in this century. The members of the opposite moiety responsible for the ritual offered their condolences to the mourners by reciting a series of messages associated with wampum strings.

Now when a person is in deep grief the tears blind away his eyes and he cannot see. By these words we wipe the tears away from your eyes that you may again see. . . . When a person is mourning the loss of a loved one his ears are stopped and he cannot hear. By these words we remove that obstruction so that you may again hear. . . . When a person is mourning his throat becomes stopped so that he cannot breathe well nor can he consume food which the Creator has given him to eat. By these words we remove that obstruction so that you may breathe and enjoy your food. . . . In your grief your entire body has become very uncomfortable. We now remove all discomfort. . . . Your bed is uncomfortable and you cannot rest well at night. We now remove all discomfort from your resting place. . . . During your grief you have been in darkness. We now restore the light. . . . You have lost the sight of the sky. We remove the cloud so that you may regain sight of the sky. . . . You have lost the sun. By these words we cause you to see the sun. . . . The mourners are thinking of the two kinds of weather from which they must protect the grave of their loved one, the hot rays of the sun and the cold rain. So you throw grass on the grave to protect it from the hot rays of the sun and place a flat board on it to protect it from the cold rain. . . . During your sorrow you have allowed your mind to dwell on the great loss which you have sustained. You must not let your minds dwell on

this loss lest you suffer from a serious illness. . . . Since our brother has died the light has dropped from the sky. We now lift up the light and replace it in the sky. (Speck, 1949:160–162.)

Iroquois tribal and confederacy political structure rested upon the social structure through which political leaders were selected. Kin relationships were therefore of considerable importance and the lineages and sibs which formed the corporate kin groups had significance beyond that of their primary economic and social functions (lineage) and their mutual aid functions (sib). The Iroquois had a dual obligation to kin group and to tribe and confederacy. The seeds of conflict present in a society organized on both a kinship and larger territorial basis were resolved in Iroquois society by giving the kin group a major role in providing leadership and political authority for the territorial-political group. Iroquois political structure was a form of "kinship state" and in certain aspects of social and political structure resembles, and is probably related to, the cultures of the Southeast. It is in this area of their culture that the Iroquois appear to be a culturally intrusive element in the basic Woodland cultures of the Algonkin Northeast.

Iroquois culture was not simply a Southeastern culture in a northern Woodland setting, for many elements of their material culture and technology were Woodland. Wooden mortars and pestles were used and many of the containers were of bark and splint basketry. Their clothing of tanned deer hide was similar to that of the other tribes of the Woodland northeast and ornamentation of clothing using dyed porcupine quill applied by sewing in curvilinear motifs was a widespread northeastern tradition.

Iroquois villages in the historic period were built along streams or lakes on elevated flat terraces which offered the protection of one or more steep banks at the village edges. The use of palisade walls of logs was common as a protective device. The villages were permanent and in use during the entire year. In the timbered lowlands surrounding the villages, garden plots were cleared for maize horticulture in much the same way as among the Prairie and the Plains sedentary tribes.

Within each village matrilineal extended family groups formed a household occupying a long house. The long house was rectangular in floor plan, roofed by a gable framework of poles, and covered with horizontal strips of elm bark. Further north and west, the Algonkin tribes built a similar, though smaller, domed structure using the more suitable birchbark as the covering of the lodge. Within the long house, individual nuclear families occupied designated sections along each side of the structure and pairs of these family groups shared one of the central aisle fireplaces. Sleeping platforms were arranged along each wall with areas for storage below the platforms and on shelves fastened beneath the eaves.

The matrilineal family group living in the long house constituted the basic cooperative economic unit in Iroquois society. The women of this family group held gardening tools and plots in common and worked together in the cultivation of crops. The men hunted and fished together and the subsistence produce of both sexes was used by the entire family group. The long house was controlled by the elder females, for the husbands were outsiders who came into the family unit at marriage. Sons born to women of the long house left the household when they married a woman from another moiety and sib. Family continuity was channeled through the women and through this mechanism of matrilineal descent and kin affiliation, property and goods were inherited through the female line and kept within the family group.

Household groups forming a matrilineage were localized within a single village, but the matri-sib was not localized. Tribes with several villages would have some members of most of the sibs (normally there were eight sibs in the tribe) resident in the village. Ties of kinship to fellow members of an individual's matri-sib were strong and sib members were obligated to assist each other. The revenge motive for warfare or for injury by a member of another sib called for mutual assistance. Sib members shared the honor of a distinguished sachem from their group and the prestige of the Pine Tree Chief reflected on his fellow sib members.

The group of sibs forming one of the tribal moieties was responsible for conducting the burial rites and condolence ceremony for a deceased member of the opposite moiety. In addition, moiety members competed in games against members of the opposite moiety. Many of the Iroquois tribal ceremonials also involved paired and reciprocal functions of moieties.

These ceremonials were tribal rather than confederacy-wide. The Council of Sachems was not a body with religious functions except as the Condolence Ceremony for a sachem involved religious concepts. The major tribal ceremonies centered on horticulture, curing of illness, and thanksgiving and were ordered in a sequence tied to the calendrical year. The degree of dependence upon horticulture among a North American Indian society can be measured by the number and complexity of ceremonials associated with crops and the attendant natural phenomena. By this scale, Iroquois horticulture was intensive, for they, like the tribes of the prairies and the Southeast, practiced a series of ceremonials during the cycle of maize cultivation. One widespread ceremony in the eastern United States was the Green Corn ceremony given annually when the first of the crop of green corn was ready to harvest. Morgan describes parts of such a ceremony he recorded for the Seneca.

When the green corn became fit for use, the season of plenty with the Indian had emphatically arrived. They made it another occasion of general thanksgiving to the Great Spirit, and of feasting and rejoicing among themselves. Corn has ever been the staple article of consumption among the Iroquois. They cultivated this plant, and also the bean and the squash, before the formation of the League. From the most remote period to which tradition reaches, the knowledge of cultivation and use of these plants has been handed down among them. They raised sufficient quantities of each to supply their utmost wants, preparing them for food in a great variety of ways, and making them at least the basis of their sustenance. In their own mode of expressing the idea, these plants are mentioned together, under the figurative name of "Our Life," or "Our Supporters."...

On the first day of this festival after the introductory speeches had been made, the Feather Dance, the thanksgiving address, with the burning of tobacco, and three or four other dances, made up the principal religious exercises. This address was introduced in the midst of one of the dances which succeeded the first. One more specimen of these brief prayers of the Iroquois, as made by the Senecas, will be furnished. Having placed the leaves of tobacco on the fire, as usual, the keeper of the faith thus addressed Ha-wen-ne-yu: "Great Spirit in heaven, listen to our words. We have assembled to perform a sacred duty, as thou hast commanded. This institution has descended to us from our fathers. We salute thee with our thanks, that thou hast preserved so many of us another year, to participate in the ceremonies of this occasion.

"Great Spirit, continue to listen: We thank thee for thy great goodness in causing our mother, the earth, again to bring forth her fruits. We thank thee that thou has caused Our Supporters to yield abundantly.

"Great Spirit, our words still continue to flow towards thee. . . . Preserve us from all danger. Preserve our aged men. Preserve our mothers. Preserve our warriors. Preserve our children. We burn this tobacco; may its smoke arise to thee. May our thanks, ascending with it, be pleasing to thee. Give wisdom to the keepers of the faith, they they may direct these ceremonies with propriety. Strengthen our warriors that they may celebrate with pleasure the sacred dances of thy appointment.

"Great Spirit, the council here assembled, the aged men and women, the strong warriors, the women and children, unite their voice of thanksgiving to thee."

Before partaking of the feast, the people went out to witness some of those games which were often introduced, as an amusement, to accompany the other exercises of these festive days.

The second day commenced with the usual address, after which they had the Thanksgiving dance, Ga-na-o-uh, which was the principal religious exercise of the day. This dance was not necessarily a costume performance, although it was usually given by a select band in full dress. In figure, step, and music, it was precisely like the Feather dance, the chief difference between them being the introduction of short thanksgiving speeches between the songs of the dance . . . the music consisted of a series of thanksgiving songs, performed by select singers, who accompanied themselves with turtle-shell rattles, to mark time. Each song lasted about two minutes, during which the band danced around the room, in column, which great animation. When the song ceased, the dancers walked around the councilhouse, about the same length of time, to the beat of rattles. The thanksgiving speeches were made between the songs. A person arose, and perhaps thanked the Maple as follows: "We return thanks to the Maple, which yields its sweet waters for the good of man." Again the dance was resumed, and another song danced out, after which another speech was made by some other person, perhaps as follows: "We return thanks to the bushes and trees, which provide us with fruit." The dance was then resumed as before. In this manner the thanksgiving speeches, the songs and the dance were continued, until all prominent objects in nature had been made the subjects of special notice. . . .

The third morning was set apart for a thanks-giving concert, called the Ah-do-weh, which constituted the chief ceremony of the day. The council was opened by an introductory speech by one of the keepers of the faith, upon its nature, objects, and institution. This novelty in their worship was a succession of short speeches made by different persons, one after another, returning thanks to a great variety of objects, each one following his speech with an appropriate song, the words of which were of his own composing, and often times the music also. In a chorus to each song all the people joined, thus sending forth a united anthem of praise. They passed through the whole range of natural objects, thanking each one directly, as in the Thanksgiving dance; but they were not . . . confined either to the natural or spiritual world. Acts of kindness, personal achievements, political events, in a word, all the affairs of public and private life were open on this occasion to the indulgence of grateful affections. . . .

On the fourth day, the festival was concluded with the peach-stone game . . . a game of chance, on which they bet profusely, and to which they were extravagantly attached. It was not in the nature of a religious exercise, but a favorite entertainment, with which to terminate the Green Corn ceremonial. . . .

At the close of each day, the people regaled themselves upon a sumptuous feast of succotash. This was always the entertainment at the green corn season. It was made of corn, beans, and squashes, and was always a favorite article of food with the red man. It may also be well to state in this connection, that among the Iroquois at the present day, they do not sit down together to a common repast, except at religious councils of unusual interest. The feast, after being prepared at the place of the council, is distributed at its close, and carried by the women, in vessels brought for the purpose, to their respective homes, where it is enjoyed by each family at their own fireside. But when the people feasted together after the ancient fashion . . . they selected the hour of twilight. The huge kettles of soup, or hominy, or succotash, as the case might be, were brought into their midst, smoking from the fire. Before partaking of this evening banquet, they never omitted to say grace, which, with them, was a simple ceremonial, but in perfect harmony with their mode of worship. It was a prolonged exclamation, upon a high key, by the solitary voice of one of the keepers of the faith, followed by the swelling chorus from the multitude, upon a lower note. It was designed as an acknowledgement to each other of their gratitude to the great Giver of the feast. (Morgan, 1954:190–197.)

Within Morgan's brief description of a traditional Iroquois ceremonial, we can see several practices and themes which characterize all such Iroquois ceremonials and some of which were general eastern North American cultural patterns. The cycle of four-day ceremonials, with many repetitive elements, was a general pattern. Song cycles accompanied by male dancing was also general, as were the associated competitive games and gambling. Feasting and food distribution formed a part of all Iroquois ceremonies, and prayers of thanksgiving were repeated. The use of a master of ceremonies or individual responsible for the correct sequence of the ceremony is like that of the Sun Dance, the Mandan *Okipa,* and ceremonies of the southeastern tribes.

An integral part of the Iroquois ceremonial cycle were the Midwinter Rites, a sequence of thanksgiving, propitiatory, and curing ceremonies held annually. Curing ceremonies were conducted by members of societies or associations of individuals who had been cured by members of a society. Illness was understood to be of supernatural cause and the curing of illness demanded rituals which dealt with the supernatural. There were several curing societies among the Iroquois, both those which were restricted to members and those which gave ceremonies in which the nonmembers could participate. Perhaps the best known of Iroquois curing societies is the False Face society whose origins were mythological and whose curing rituals were accomplished through carved wooden masks worn by the society members. Speck describes contemporary Cayuga wooden masks as "representations of the spirits . . . made of the wood of the forest: maple, white pine, basswood, and poplar. In making a False Face the features are first carved upon a living tree, then cut free. During the process, prayer is addressed to the spirit force it represents, and tobacco is burned before it. The particular kind of spirit reveals itself to the maker when he has burned tobacco and prayed and started to carve its features. It is then painted and the long horse-hair arranged on it. Tradition says that before horses were known to the Iroquois, plaited corn-husks were used for hair, as some specimens still show. . . ." The appellation "False Face" refers to the distorted facial features which the carved masks present (Speck, 1949).

Curing ceremonies were actually private affairs held in the long house of the patient.

When curing societies participated in the public midwinter ceremonies, they were performed for a person who had previously been cured by the society, an act necessary to prevent the recurrence of the illness. Curing ceremonies involved group shamanistic practices used in conjunction with medicinal herbs and were directed toward propitiating the supernatural agent responsible for the illness. Much of the ritual in curing ceremonies consisted of specialized songs and dances, the use of which was restricted to members of the society.

Supernatural associations of curing societies can also be seen in the way in which many members of the society were originally recruited. Iroquois youths and adults, like most northern North American Indians, sought supernatural visions or experiences where they directly perceived and communicated with a supernatural spirit. In so doing, they were frequently directed into membership in curing societies, a practice also common to the prairie horticulturalists further west.

The supernatural world was important to the Iroquois, and though they had no ordered and regularized pantheon of deities and spirits, this group of supernatural beings encompassed such variant personalized forces as mother earth, sun, bear, eagle, winds, unusual places and objects, and other natural phenomena. Reference is often made, as in the Green Corn ceremony (pp. 387–88), to the "Great Spirit." This concept is usually attributed to the Northeast, both to Iroquois and Algonkins. The idea is a vague one, reflecting no monotheism and may possibly stem from the earliest Christian contacts. The relations with the supernatural world were both individual, through vision experiences, and group, through tribal ceremony. Though there were not full-time religious specialists among the Iroquois, certain men appointed as keepers of the faith or others who were recognized for curing ability had frequent religious duties and were accorded considerable prestige.

The origins of curing societies were captured in myths and stories, as were the origins of the confederacy itself. The mythological culture heroes of the Iroquois, Deganawidah and Hiawatha, originated the confederacy in the mythological infancy of the Iroquois. In their creation of the sachem titles, each was given a name and each was given specific duties, both of which were retained by the Iroquois. Each man, upon being elevated to a position of a sa-

●FALSE FACE CURING—IROQUOIS

Noted especially for their strongly defined and
impressive political organization, not to
mention the ways in which politics dovetailed
with complex matrilineal institutions, the five,
then six, tribes which formed the historic
league of the Iroquois were no less elaborate in
their religious practices. A well-defined
cosmology, an elaborated mythology,
anthropomorphic deities, complex ceremonies
for fertility and communal good, as well as a
highly sophisticated theological concept of
impersonalized spiritual power, were all part of
the religious array of the Iroquois tribes. Nor,
even today, despite the long time
encroachment of Euro-American influences
(those dating back to the eighteenth century)
have these religious ideas entirely disappeared.

As is so frequently encountered in native
America, religious concepts applied to the
restoration of well-being for the community
and health for the individual. Curing, for the
Iroquois, was as vital a part of the religious
system as it was among the Eskimo or Navaho.
And, like the pueblos or Navaho, although

quite different in basic premise and external
form, the Iroquois devoted considerable
thought to the cause of disease and its cure.
Medicine societies developed, groups of
associated individuals whose task was to
diagnose, to placate, and to effect cures by
manipulation of supernatural forces. Many
such societies are recorded for the various
Iroquois tribes, as many as 19 for the Cayuga,
11 for the Seneca, varying numbers for the
remaining tribes. All had special techniques
and rituals. Of these curing associations,
however, the best known is unquestionably
that of the False Faces. The members wore
masks, representing the faces of spiritual
beings, control of which could be turned to
curing benefit. Always acting as a group, the
members were summoned by a sick person or
his family. Creeping grotesquely to the
patient's house, muttering, grunting, and
uttering a characteristic weird cry, the False
Faces made several starts into the patient's
house, scraping their rattles, made of a turtle
carapace, against the door. Once in, they
sprinkled the sick person with ashes, rattled

over him, and so drove away the cause of illness. Tobacco also figured in the curing ritual. The group of curers was given gifts for its services, often in the form of specially prepared foods.

The masks themselves are made of wood and carved according to a well-defined procedure. The mask was first carved on the trunk of a tree especially selected, and then removed from the living trunk. If the carver began work in the morning, the mask was painted red, if in the afternoon, black. Hair was originally made of an inner bark, but has been replaced with horsehair.

Just as in the case of a number of other American tribes, the effect of group activity in a matter such as curing was to effect a sense of social cohesion. Through such activities individuals were brought to a fuller awareness of participation in society and universe. Recognizing this, the Iroquois themselves sought to involve as many persons as possible in the curing societies, noting that the more involved the more spiritually efficacious their activities.

chem, dropped his personal name and became known by the title to which he had succeeded. The mythological base of League organization and curing society origins forms a stable and traditional charter, important in the continuity of Iroquois culture.

Complete stability and cultural continuity were not possible for the Iroquois in the historic period, however. Conflicts with European and Indian, the introduction of trade goods of European manufacture, the rise in power and importance of the Pine Tree Chiefs, and finally, the loss of land with the intrusion of the American colonist, markedly modified Iroquois culture. Many of the modifications were absorbed and integrated into the culture without highly disruptive effects, but some, including alcoholic drinks, were disorganizing. The Iroquois, like many societies under these severe pressures from an outside dominant group, reacted by attempting to revitalize their society and culture through supernatural directive. About 1800, a Seneca sachem named Handsome Lake, a rather ordinary man, fell ill and during his illness received a series of supernatural visions through which he was instructed in the ways through which the Iroquois could regain their former cultural integrity. Handsome Lake, a half brother of Cornplanter, brought his message to the Iroquois and attempted to cause

the Iroquois to accept the regulations of behavior and conduct which his vision had ordered. Handsome Lake later travelled from village to village bringing his message to each tribe, and after his death the message was perpetuated with the appointment of a successor (Wallace, 1970).

The message which Handsome Lake received was one which prescribed correct conduct according to traditional Iroquois practices. In addition, however, the Iroquois were told that they must reject the use of liquor and must hold the lands which were still theirs. Supernatural aid was promised those who followed the message. This message was received in the traditional Iroquois manner through direct communication with the supernatural world and contained much that was Iroquois in origin. It also contained many elements of Christian belief, and in the generations which followed, those who practiced the Handsome Lake religion wove many elements of Christian belief into the myth traditions. Handsome Lake himself was a messianic leader and his rules of conduct resemble, in some ways, the Christian commandments. This intermingling of native and Christian beliefs and practices was not restricted to the Iroquois, for most of the messianic movements, like the Ghost Dance of the west, and the quite recent Peyote cult, were based on similar syncretic movements.

It is interesting to note that the Iroquois, despite the long period of contact and conflict with Europeans and Americans in a region which was settled by these outsiders at a very early time, have retained their social being and many of their cultural practices to this day. On reserves in New York and Ontario, the Iroquois still exist as a people. Even many of those who have left the reserves for employment and residence outside Iroquois society return each year for the midwinter ceremonies and retain their kinship and cultural ties. Iroquois cohesion and social solidarity rested upon a firm structural base, much of which has persisted to the present day (Fenton and Gulick, 1961).

WESTERN ALGONKINS: THE OJIBWA

In the western regions of the Eastern Woodlands, Algonkin-speakers are again encountered. The most notable, tribal segments variously carrying on their patterns of culture in the northwest, even today, are unquestionably the Ojibwa. The names Ojibwa and Chippewa are two transliterations of the same Algonkin word; native preference is toward the Ojibwa (Ojibwe) spelling. To the north, at the southern limits of Hudson Bay, or more specifically, of James Bay, the forest-dwelling Ojibwa are often called the Saulteaux.

The Ojibwa offer an interesting example of the direct effects of the European fur trade upon the northern Algonkin groups. At the beginning of the historic period, the Ojibwa were located both north and south of what is today Sault Ste. Marie, in the central Great Lakes region. Closely related culturally to the Ottawa and culturally more similar to the Micmac than to the Central Algonkins, the Ojibwa moved their territory west into the Lake Superior basin as the French expanded their trade routes in that direction. In the late sixteenth century, the Ojibwa were in the region of Chequamagon Bay of Lake Superior and were also moving west along the lake's north shore. They reached the St. Louis River, which empties into the Bay of Duluth, and began a series of continual meetings with the eastern Dakota who occupied villages west and south of Lake Superior. These first contacts with the Dakota were friendly, for the Ojibwa and their French allies had trade goods to offer and the Dakota had much to gain (Hickerson, 1970).

In a short time, however, the Dakota and Ojibwa began a series of conflicts, most of them in the nature of skirmishes and small raids, that did not end until the ejection of the Dakota from Minnesota in the middle of the nineteenth century. The conflicts had developed as the Ojibwa moved into Dakota territory in the upper Mississippi River basin to trap and take furs.

Ojibwa reliance on the fur trade for a large part of their subsistence and for the specialized trade goods which they desired changed many aspects of their culture. The movement into the western wild rice area, and for some segments of the Ojibwa, into the northern Plains contributed further impetus to change.

The early French and British patterns of fur trade were built upon a system of utilizing the native populations as the labor force for obtaining pelts. Fur trading posts were constructed throughout the wooded areas, posts staffed by French or British employees of the licensed trader. These men exchanged European goods for the pelts the local Indians took from animals they had trapped. It was vital that the European trader maintain a friendly position with

the local Indian group, since his economic success was largely dependent on them. One aspect of culture change which seems to have resulted from the close association of the Ojibwa with the trader was the strengthening of the role of the band headman from that of a relatively weak leader to a strong hereditary position. Northern and eastern Algonkin concepts of the role of the headman in the early historic period ascribed little power to the position. The European trader, dealing with a band, sought out an individual with whom he could bargain. Such an individual gained prestige with the local group, and with the reinforcement of gifts of European goods which he distributed, his position became more secure. Continued European contacts through the same individual intermediary acted as a further reinforcement. Thus the Ojibwa headman became a person of considerable power and authority. This, combined with the patrilineal tendency throughout the culture, probably gave rise to the inheritance of headmanship positions through the paternal line of descent (Hickerson, 1970).

Fur trade involvement also changed the economic and subsistence patterns of the Ojibwa, but equally important for the southwestern Ojibwa was their movement into the heart of the wild rice area. In this former Dakota territory, the Ojibwa, like the Menomini of northwestern Wisconsin, became intensive users of wild rice. The practices of wild rice utilization were quite complex and involved subdivision of rice beds into units which individual families were allowed to harvest.

Wild rice ripens in late summer, but before the harvest, the Ojibwa band headman divided the rice bed into family units. Family members went into their area of the rice bed and tied several stems of the ripening rice plants together, then bent the seed-bearing heads over. This practice hastened the ripening process and also improved the quality of the rice, as it shed the rain from grain heads. At the time of harvest, men and women, usually one man and one woman to each canoe, paddled slowly through the rice. The woman sat in the rear of the canoe holding two short wooden sticks. With one stick she reached out and bent a tied clump of rice over the canoe and then struck the rice clump several times with the second stick. The ripened grains fell to the bottom of the canoe.

When a load of rice had been collected, the pair returned to the shore where the rice was

Chippewa ● Birchbark "wigwams" on the Red River. (Photograph by M. L. Hime, 1858. Smithsonian Institution National Anthropological Archives)

winnowed on a birchbark tray and then parched in a metal drum or kettle. Rice was originally husked in a pit, dug into the earth, and lined with a skin. A man or woman in moccasins then trod on the rice in the pit. The husked rice was stored in birchbark containers and was used as the main vegetable food during the winter months.

The quantity of rice harvested varied seasonally, since climatic conditions could affect the growth of the crop. Yet it remained a dependable food supply and was present in such an amount that it enabled the Ojibwa to survive in an area of otherwise limited resources after the fur trade had ended and the means to European goods had disappeared.

Although Ojibwa social organization varied from the south to the regions north of Lake Superior, it was similar to that of the Micmac, but tended to be somewhat more definably structured. The Ojibwa generally had paternal clans or gentes, which bore animal names; the some fifteen listed moved beyond any local unit. The clan functioned to regulate marriage exogamously, and the aboriginal choice of mate was with the persons designated as cross cousins (i.e., father's sister's child), although the mother's brother's child was not ruled out. While the strong maternal clans of the Iroquoians fit neatly into these social systems, clanship among the Ojibwa seems less well defined. A patrilineal system is suggested by the marriage arrangements, it is true, but there are many features in the social organization which look like the bilateral patterning of a group like the Micmac. While it may be that influences from the unilineal systems of the area made their impression on Ojibwa organization, there is also the factor of the relations between family and hunting territory (Landes, 1937:30–52).

Algonkin hunting areas are common through these tribes. Nowhere, however, does the idea of ownership, or at least, of rights to a section of land appear as strongly as among the Ojibwa. Rights to such hunting domain were inherited, bilaterally, rather than unilaterally, since one could lay claim to a territory through one's mother as well as inherit rights from the father (Landes, 1937:89). The land could be lent but seems otherwise to have remained in a single person's hands. The owner had the right to kill trespassers. He could exploit the hunting and trapping resources alone, if he chose, but he usually hunted the area with members of his bilateral kindred (Landes, 1937:90). There has been some theoretical speculation on the relations between social structure and hunting territory among the northern Algonkins (Speck, 1915; Speck and Eiseley, 1939). The stress on the concept of rights to land and on their inheritance may underlie a transition to a unilineal and, in this instance, a changing descent system.

In the vast forests of Ontario, Minnesota, and Wisconsin, along the banks of the many lakes left by the glaciers of the Pleistocene, the Ojibwa lived in essentially isolated units of

Ojibwa ● Birchbark canoe (length, 11 feet, 6 inches). (From the Department of Anthropology collections, University of Minnesota)

from 3 to 15 small families. They exploited their respective hunting lands through much of the year and came together in fall and winter to live as an informal village, building wigwams of layers of birchbark. The villages had no special function except as a place where people could come together. Chiefs were present in these villages but here again, lack of formalism was characteristic. A chief led an enterprise momentarily; when the task was completed, he stepped down (Landes, 1937:2). Elders were important in any decisions affecting a group. Shamans emerged as persons with some political power. In general, Algonkin life might be described as a strongly focused democratic mode of life. Yet recent studies of the Ojibwa have tended to stress the atomistic nature of their social systems.

There is a cultural orientation which stresses individuality at the expense of cooperation. In part, this reflects the subsistence-economic patterns where the separation of groups was necessary for long periods of time and where the practices of subsistence activities in hunting and trapping were confined to an individual or a very small group.

This emphasis of Ojibwa culture is reflected in the personality of the Ojibwa adult who was self-reliant, but whose emotions were repressed to a remarkable degree. Anger, hate, and even overt expression of love were held internalized within the individual. Fighting and conflict were rare, and even in warfare the Ojibwa were not enthusiasts. Associated with these emotionally repressive aspects of Ojibwa personality were the ever-present fear of hunger and starvation coupled with a fear of malevolent sorcery. The Ojibwa personality manifested itself in patience and self-control added to the generous sense of humor found among these people.

Hostility expressed itself in the form of sorcery whereby an individual could cause illness in another. Such sorcery was secret and thus particularly feared. The illness could be caused

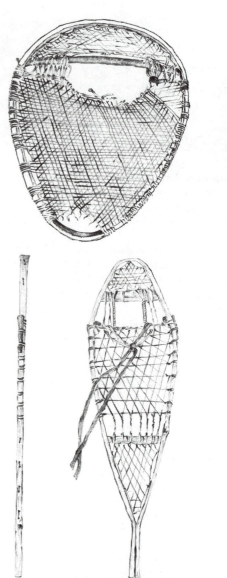

Ojibwa ● Snowshoes. Above: shows the oval or bearpaw snowshoe. Below: the tailed snowshoe. Both were made with a wooden frame strung with greased rawhide. The tailed snowshoe was taken over by western culture directly from the northern Algonkin peoples and persists today. (Courtesy of The Science Museum, St. Paul, Minnesota)

Ojibwa ● Makik, birchbark vessel. The birch, so common to the forests of the Great Lakes region, lent itself to a greater variety of uses in the native cultures. The bark was employed for making containers, such as this one, for covering the wigwam and the canoe frame, as well as for wrapping of different kinds. A vessel such as this one could hold water and could lend itself to cooking through the method of stone boiling, a rack being placed in the bottom to prevent the heated stones from burning through the bark. (Courtesy of The Science Museum, St. Paul, Minnesota)

by the intrusion of a foreign object into the victim or by stealing of his soul through supernatural means.

Illness could also be caused by conduct contrary to the established cultural norms and ideals. Violation of these precepts resulted in punishment which took the form of illness. Release from the effects of illness demanded the shaman, or in some cases, public confession of deviant behavior. The most severe reaction of the Ojibwa to the fears of sorcery, illness, and starvation took the form of a psychosis where the individual was captured by *Windigo,* one of the monsters of the supernatural world.

While most of the cultural traits mentioned for the Ojibwa are those found in the more northern Algonkin groups, influences from the central Algonkin cultures were also present. One such cultural form, common to the Ojibwa and the central Algonkin, was the Grand Medicine Society, or *Midewewin.* The Midewewin is similar in organization and in function to the curing societies found in some of the eastern Prairie Siouan groups as well. Walter Hoffman's 1891 report on *The Midewewin or Grand Medicine Society of the Ojibwa* is the best report available on such medicine societies. In it he describes in detail the practices of the society which revolved around the vision quest and direct contact with the supernatural world. An initiate, who should have had a supernatural vision, was inducted into the society at an an-

nual ceremony during which he was instructed in the practices of the medicine lodge by an older member of the society and was "shot" with a white shell by another member during the initiation ritual. Each member of the society owned a medicine bag, usually an otter skin, and the initiate was shot with a shell from this bag. The shell carried supernatural power into the initiate. The Midewewin ceremonies and associated dances involved the use of trance, for as members "shot" each other with the shells during the ritual, they fell unconscious. As they regained consciousness, the shell with which they had been "shot" was spit from the mouth.

Though the society was a curing society, the initiated members were not shamans and did not have the individual power to cure. Initiation of an ill person into the society could cure his illness and many entered for that reason. Most obtained membership because such membership gave them the supernatural assistance necessary to a long life. A strong secondary motive for joining the society was added prestige which membership brought. The society was divided into four grades through which a member might pass, each grade marked for the individual by changes in facial painting and by the type of medicine bag which he could use. As membership and increase in rank also demanded payment to the officers in charge of the ceremony, a man's economic status was indicated by the rank he achieved.

The birchbark scrolls used as mnemonic devices in the Midewewin contained an outline of the Midewewin lodge constructed for the ceremony and through a series of symbols, a set of instructions for the initiate (Landes, 1968:82–83).

EASTERN SIOUANS: THE WINNEBAGO

The home of Winnebago was the area around Green Bay, Wisconsin, westward to the Wisconsin River and southward to the Fox River. Never a large tribe, estimates run between 3800 and 5000 in 1800 (Kroeber, 1939:140), the Winnebago are important for the way in which they bring together elements from the Plains and from the Eastern Woodlands. The tribe spoke a Siouan language, one related fairly closely to Omaha and Osage (Radin, 1932:54). On the material level, the Winnebago were clearly Woodland, sharing many traits with the neighboring Algonkins. Society and religion were complex, with social patterns in some respects like those of the southern Algonkins, but equally suggestive of Plains Siouan organization. The religious system, one involving a complex cosmology and demanding a vision quest not unlike that of the Plains, bridges a gap between the Plains and Woodlands. The notion of religious power is given a special phrasing, one slightly different from the Chippewa-Ojibwa and also from the Dakota and Omaha.

The Winnebago were farmers, raising the usual crops associated with the maize complex, but like the Algonkins of the area, the Winnebago were not intensive agriculturalists, stressing hunting and trapping, and sharing with·the Ojibwa and Menomini the gathering of wild rice. Birchbark canoes, containers, and the birchbark lodge reflect the Winnebago adaptation to the Woodlands. Some pottery was made, but wooden vessels were fully as common. It has been suggested that the Winnebago were gradually being drawn into the Woodland focus. Pottery, once more important, gave way to wood as a result of Menomini influence (Radin, 1916:119). Netted bags, tailored skin clothing, moccasins, snowshoes, reflect the Woodlands. Face and body painting, clothing styles, design, and decoration were more like those of the Plains.

The Woodland-Plains patterns appear in Winnebago society. Dual organization (i.e., moieties) moves across the Mississippi into some tribes of the southern Woodlands, and the Winnebago were divided into two units, in turn divided into paternal clans. As a result there were two phratries, or linked clans, and it was these which regulated marriage and its consequent social ties. The twofold division was defined as *Wangeregi*, "Those-above," and *Manegi*, "Those on earth." The former contained four clans, all of which bore names conceptually connected with things above the earth, such as Thunderbird, Hawk (or Warrior), Eagle, and Pigeon. The *Manegi* division had eight clans, Bear, Wolf, Water-spirit, Deer, Elk, Bison, Fish, Snake. Winnebago clans had special relations to each other within the moiety; and beyond, relating to the opposite moiety, the rules of marriage operated. There were thus social and ritual functions in the general organization. What emerges from this ordering of the society is a sense of universal order, the fact that the earth is symbolically divided into an above and a below.

In addition to regulating marriage, the moieties played a determining role in village organization, in arranging clan positions in war, in the giving of feasts, and in the ceremonial games. In any village, since the Winnebago tended toward some permanence in this regard, a line separated the residential sections from each other. At the ceremonial game, the so-called lacrosse or field hockey, one phratry opposed the other, a trait shared by the Sauk, Fox, and Omaha and suggestive of southeastern influences.

Descent in both clan and moiety was patrilineal. The clan association was strictly kept, which means that clan members always located themselves in specific places in any assemblage. Thunderbird usually took the center of the half circle, and was referred to as Chief. Water-spirit was reckoned as Leader among the other moiety. Each clan, however, had specific functions, both political and religious, and it was this feature which lent stability to Winnebago society. The Hawk clan, for example, had functions of planning and organization for war. The Bear clan members policed the camp and enforced conformity both on the hunt and at war. The Bison clan contributed the public crier who gave the announcements of the Thunderbird chief. All clans appear to have specific duties.

The chief was a spokesman and an arbiter of peace, who could not lead a war party. His lodge was a sanctuary; all wrongdoers could find refuge there and escape punishment. In his peaceful role, the chief could use his authority to prevent a war party from leaving a village, especially if he felt their foray was doomed to defeat. The Bear clan, in the opposite moiety, was perhaps the most important unit among the *Manegi*. The members kept the sacred war bundle and in their behavior, suggest the enforcing police of the Plains. The Bear people were guards of the village, watched over the gathering of wild rice, and punished the seducer of a woman. In general, the precise definition of moiety relationships and the exact position of clans in Winnebago society created an infinitely more regulated system than was true of the neighboring Algonkins.

The same precision applied to Winnebago religion. It may be anticipated that the content of the belief system was not especially different from that of Plains or other Woodland cultures. Yet the way the system was integrated, how it brought together elements in its own distinctive way, illustrates integrated specialization. The Winnebago structuring of both society and religion gives this tribe an idiosyncratic character. With the Omaha, the Ojibwa, and even the Iroquois, the Winnebago shared the concept of a diffuse, impersonal, supernatural power. *Wakonda, manitou, orenda* are the names for this power, a force which exists without any spiritual or divine direction, significant for a person psychologically prepared to receive it. To some degree, the notion of such power may be equated with a strong religious emotion, one not uncharacteristic of many American tribes. The term *wak'an* applied to sanctity and to power. In the Winnebago case, the strong sense of impersonal supernatural power was ever present. Religious attitudes were always operative in this society (Radin, 1916:277–283). The Winnebago appear to have achieved a verbalized relation between spiritual and life values, something not nearly so well articulated among most peoples.

As part of their cosmology, the Winnebago peopled the universe with an indefinite number of spirits. These were both anthropomorphic and zoomorphic, the latter especially being conceptually related to the clan units. In addition to some attention paid to celestial bodies, such as the Sun, Moon, and Morning Star, the Winnebago ascribed a sanctity to Earth. These were all concepts which have parallels in the Plains. There were also godlike figures: such as Life-Giver, or Earth-Maker; Disease-Giver, who gave war and curing power; the Water Spirit, or water monster, who controlled the earth; and the Thunderbirds, which possibly relate to the eagle and were depicted as bald although clan names separate the two. Although the Winnebago linked these spirits with a host of other less definable entities, and so fashioned an elaborate spirit world, the general view was that this realm was essentially indifferent to man. Approached in the right way, the spirits could become sources of power for individuals. In other words, the Winnebago laid stress on the rituals which brought power from these beings (Radin, 1932:274).

The quest for power, however impersonally conceived, was related to the concept of the guardian spirit. Contacts with the spirit world brought socioeconomic benefits to human beings. The point is an interesting one, considering the religious theories of hunters in other areas. The Eskimo notion, to name one, that animals can be cajoled by ritual and magic or will allow themselves to be taken if the appropriate ritual procedures are followed, is given a

somewhat different phrasing both in the Plains and among the Winnebago. Of course the concept of social and economic good associated with religious phenomena is widespread in native America. The guardian-spirit idea, again seen in the Plains, carries out this basic theory. Success in economic activities, in war, in status was linked by the Winnebago to the spiritual mentor. The guardian made its presence felt in various crucial activities; success in hunting or fishing was attributed to the spirit, and there was also a sense of inheritance of the spirit. As in the Plains, there was both the idea of a quest in the search for the guardian and a test of the experience by the elders to determine its authenticity. The Winnebago stressed fasting in the spirit encounter and made a pubertal initiation rite of it as well. Women as well as men could obtain spirit help. Radin gives an account of the guardian-spirit experience:

One of the Bear people felt grieved and went out into the wilderness to fast. His desire was to be blessed by those spirits who are in control of war, and in his longing to be blessed by them he cried bitterly. Soon he heard someone saying, "Do not cry any more, we have come after you from above. The spirits have blessed you. You are going to be taken to the lodge of your friends." When the young man got there he saw four men. They were called cannibals and they were brothers. "Our friends have blessed you and we also bless you," said the four spirits. These four spirits were catfish. Then some white crane spirits said, "Our friends have blessed you. With spears they have blessed you. Indeed, for good reason was your heart sad. With victory on the warpath do we bless you. Here is your bundle. Here also are your spears and your bow and arrows. This bundle you must use when you go on the warpath. Here also are some songs to use when you start out and when you return. With these songs I bless you. Here they are:

   Hósto kᵐine djaᵃedja rahíje
   Where they gathered, there did you go?
   K'aró hitcak'âró hágixewìre
   Friend, shout it out for him.

When the enemy is close upon you and aims at you, if you sing these songs they will not be able to hit you. If you sing these songs then, those who gave you a name will honor you. Thus we bless you. With life also we bless you." (Radin, 1916:296.)

The vision described is not essentially different from those recorded for Plains tribes, but the spirit figures are Woodland and thus give a somewhat different tone to the Winnebago experience. The presence of the bundle is not exclusively Plains. Sacred objects obtained in a vision, such as a pipe stem (calumet), or any wrapped fetish object, appear consistently in the Woodlands and are also characteristic of the Southeast.

In addition to the individual vision, the Winnebago had a well-defined ceremonial organization. There were four main kinds of ceremonies aside from purely social events such as feasts. There were clan ceremonies, carried on by each of the twelve clans and limited to members. Such rituals involved the display of the war bundle of the clan. Religious societies were made up of people who had the same general vision and a common guardian spirit. Men who had contact with the bison spirit, for example, met periodically to dance, sing their sacred songs, and to feast. A special lodge was built and the bundles of the society were displayed. Bison heads, decorated and painted, were set out ceremonially. To obtain bison, the Winnebago had to trek west and were often involved in war with the western tribes as a result. Visions and the emphasis on war are suggestive of the Siouan background of the Winnebago. Yet war was carried on without the horse, a suggestion that in the Plains case, there had been an underlying structure like that of the Winnebago.

The most complex ritual of the tribe was the Medicine Dance, which called for a chief host and a series of invitations. Secondary hosts and their assistants were concerned with the organization of the dance as well. The ceremonial offering of food, formal speech making, and the rituals taking place during the four-day series suggest much the same pattern as marked the Midewewin of the Ojibwa. Common to both was a process of initiation. Other rituals concerned the men who had brought scalps from a successful war party, bringing scalps and the Woodland variation of coup counting (Radin, 1916:317).

Of more recent interest in Winnebago religion is the Peyote cult. The association with the drug, the pre-Columbian Mexican cactus, of Christian symbolism arose among many western tribes. The Wisconsin Winnebago, apparently drawn into the cult through contact with Oklahoma members of the tribe, who had been forced into migration by outside pressures, succeeded in bringing it together with aboriginal ritual. The drug produces visions, with the re-

sult that its effects supplanted to some extent the vision quest. The dramatic account of Crashing Thunder, the Winnebago who failed to obtain a vision but found it in the peyote, is an example not only of a changing culture but a reflection of the way many native Americans have succeeded in bringing together the old and the new. The Winnebago developed a complex peyote ritual in which many of the traditional elements of their past religion appear (Radin, 1916:388–426; 1926).

With the exception of the Iroquois, the tribes of the Eastern Woodlands may be defined as marginal, meaning that they were in an isolated geographic position and that elements of their culture frequently came to them by being borrowed. The Winnebago were no exception. Their Siouan speech relates them to the Plains, but their social system, and certainly their material culture, is Woodland. Considering the social organization, the Winnebago, like the Ojibwa and the Ottawa, had paternal clans. This complex spreads southward and eastward from the Winnebago as well. A relation to the Omaha is suggested not only because of language but also because of the war pattern and a concept of a dual tribal division with specific functions. Dual divisions appear among some adjacent Algonkins also, however, and the question may be raised of the point of origin of the clan-moiety complex. The Ojibwa lacked a dual division, but the pattern existed among the Menomini, with a Bear-Thunderbird division, and among the Sauk and Fox of southern Wisconsin. All these tribes appear to have had clans linked with the moieties, each clan having special duties, names, badges, and restrictions. Nor did the moiety always relate to marriage and exogamy; among some tribes, the moiety was purely ceremonial. The Kickapoo and Potawatomi had dual divisions with clans, although the relation between clan and moiety is not fully understood. Further, given the strength of these institutions, it would not be unexpected to discover the organization of the Illinois and Miami to be an extension of the same western Woodlands pattern. The point is important if the cultural location of both Winnebago and Algonkin tribes is to be determined.

Considering the problem of relationship, it seems difficult to define the Woodlands. The Iroquois clearly was the most stable group. The New England and northern Algonkins possessed an essentially sub-Arctic cultural mode.

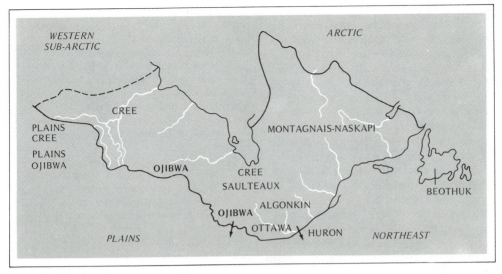

F2 ● Eastern Sub-Arctic

The sporadic superimposition of horticulture changes the basic Woodland pattern. Because the northeastern Algonkins were the first groups of North Americans north of Mexico to enter into protracted contact with Europeans, their cultures were among the first to be disrupted. Nor did the presence of the vigorous and bellicose Iroquois, the fur trade, introduced epidemics, and the colonial wars of the seventeenth and eighteenth centuries assist them in maintaining their cultural integrity. Some elements remain, it is true, especially among the western Ojibwa in Wisconsin, Minnesota, and adjacent Ontario. But it is also clear that many tribes were dispossessed, forced to leave their home grounds and settle in Oklahoma or other designated areas; the Winnebago, Sauk, Fox, Kickapoo offer cases in point. Movement and change have broken down the native structures and many traditions are gone.

THE EASTERN SUB-ARCTIC

The western sub-Arctic (see Chapter III) was an area in which forest and tundra came together. Extensive trapping and fishing were basic to the western area, but there was the addition of vast herds of caribou which gave a generally predictable basis of subsistence. Caribou, particularly of the woodland type, moved as far south as the forested regions of northern Minnesota and were hunted at times by the northern Ojibwa, but the caribou stop at that point. Thus while the trap-

ping and fishing bases of the human food supply might still persist in the east, there was no such dependable animal. The moose was hunted extensively in the northern forests. The Micmac of New Brunswick, however much they fall into the New England Algonkin sphere, had a cultural system like that of the eastern sub-Arctic. If anything, the cultures to the north, to the interior of Quebec and to the Canadian coasts, were like the Micmac but even more impoverished.

In general, the eastern sub-Arctic suggests a basic Woodland horizon. The Micmac, Malecite, and Penobscot could at times exploit maritime resources. This was not true of the Montagnais-Naskapi, the principal tribes of an enormous geographical region. They might move up as far as Labrador but were effectively kept from the sea by the Eskimo. The area was characterized again by Algonkin speech, the main tribes emerging as speakers of what was evidently a northeastern linguistic substratum. The forest to tundra or barren ground movement suggests the west, but the linguistic uniformity makes any line of demarcation from the Woodlands to the sub-Arctic difficult to draw. Encountered is a series of shadings, varying with environment, such as lake, forest, tundra, or high and low ground.

The Montagnais and Naskapi were tribes only in a linguistic sense. There were perhaps some 5500 inhabitants in the total area of the Montagnais-Naskapi, with some additional population of Tête de Boule Cree and the extinct Beothuk. The main language groups were broken up into socioeconomic bands, groups with hunting territories. This feature, ownership of hunting lands, is apparently deeply rooted in time among the Algonkins of the north; the Ojibwa, to name one, stressed this complex. One can map the location of subtribes of each main unit, somewhat broader sections encompassing several bands (Driver et al., 1953). Within each tribelet lay the sense of hunting territorial ownership (Leacock, 1954).

The Montagnais-Naskapi bands were exogamous, the rule being marriage within the local subtribe. They did not, however, develop any strong unilineal system nor were the practices concerning residence fixed. Men, for example, might reside in the band of the wife, which apparently occurred with some frequency with the result that the two tribes may have been in process of shifting toward matrilocality, one adjunct of a maternal system (Leacock, 1955).

The Beothuk of Newfoundland became extinct early in the historic period, victims of European diseases. Early descriptions of their culture suggest some Eskimo-like patterns, not unexpected in an economy built around the sea in a northern climate. The Cabots, in their discovery of the area, remark on the "redness" of the Beothuk. These are the original "Red Indians," of British usage, who daubed their bodies with grease and red ocher, both as a decoration and as protection against mosquitoes. The Beothuk were puzzling to ethnology for a time, since it was unclear where they belonged linguistically and culturally. As a result of comparisons of materials in early records their language has now been demonstrated as Algonkin (Hewson, 1968).

The boundary between the Woodlands and the sub-Arctic involves groups with varying ecological adaptations. The Ojibwa, to name one, has a northerly branch, while the Cree spread far west, entering tundra, woodland, and the plains-prairie as well. But given the Algonkin base for the area, the gradual shift from woodland to the north suggests no more than that the Eastern sub-Arctic peoples connect more with the Algonkin Eastern Woodlands than they do with the Athabascans of the Western sub-Arctic.

Suggested readings

CALLENDER, C.
1962   *Social Organization of the Central Algonkin Indians.* Milwaukee Public Museum Publications in Anthropology, no. 7.

FENTON, W. N.
1953   *The Iroquois Eagle Dance.* Bureau of American Ethnology, Bulletin 156.
1940   "Problems Arising from the Historic Northeastern Position of the Iroquois." *Smithsonian Miscellaneous Collections* 100:159–252. Washington.

FENTON, W. N. and GULICK, J., eds.
1961   *Symposium on Cherokee and Iroquois Culture.* Bureau of American Ethnology, Bulletin 180.

HALLOWELL, A. I.
1955   *Culture and Experience.* University of Pennsylvania Press. (Part II. World View, Personality Structure and the Self: The Ojibwa Indians; Part III. The Cultural Patterning of Personal Experience and Behavior: The Ojibwa Indians.)

HICKERSON, H.
1970   *The Chippewa and their Neighbors: A Study in Ethnohistory.* New York: Holt, Rinehart and Winston.

LANDES, R.
1968   *Ojibwa Religion and the Midewiwin.* University of Wisconsin Press.
1937   *Ojibwa Sociology.* New York: Columbia University Contributions to Anthropology, vol. 29.

MORGAN, L. H.
1851   (1901, 1954) *League of the Ho-De-No-Sau-Nee or Iroquois.* New Haven: Yale University Press, 1954.

RADIN, P.
1916   *The Winnebago Tribe.* Annual Report of the Bureau of American Ethnology, 37.

SPECK, F. G.
1940   *Penobscot Man.* University of Pennsylvania Press.

THWAITES, R. G.
1896–1901   *The Jesuit Relations and Allied Documents (Travels and Explorations of the Jesuit Missionaries in New France).* 73 Vols. Cleveland: Burrows Brothers Co.

TOOKER, E.
1964   *An Ethnography of the Huron Indians.* Bureau of American Ethnology, Bulletin 190.

TRIGGER, B. G.
1969   *The Huron: Farmers of the North.* New York: Holt, Rinehart and Winston

WALLACE, A. F. C.
1970   *The Death and Rebirth of the Seneca.* New York: Knopf.

WALLIS, W. D., and WALLIS, R. S.
1955   *The Micmac Indians of Eastern Canada.* University of Minnesota Press.

WRIGHT, J. V.
1966   *The Ontario Iroquois Tradition.* National Museum of Canada, Bulletin 210.

IX

The Southeast

The land

The cultural province of the Southeast in its most characteristic phases represents an accommodation to a broad coastal plain, extending inland for 100 to 300 miles. Along the shore, behind barrier reefs, tidal lagoons, and saltwater marshes lies the coastal belt known as the Flatwoods, some 20 to 40 miles wide, its monotony broken only by sandy hillocks and swamps. Some conifers and scrub oak stud the Flatwoods in the north, but toward the south they give way to salt palmetto and coarse savannah grasses, to cypress, tupelo, and cane.

The inner belt of the Coastal Plain lies at a higher elevation, less than 200 to 300 feet in the north rising to 500 to 600 feet in Alabama, Tennessee, Arkansas, and Texas. The rivers, sluggish and aggrading, meander through the outer margin of the coastal plains and in their estuaries build alluvial floodplains. Indeed, the broad valley of the Mississippi forms a plain cut in places through loess deposits, with a braided valley and a rich alluvium, 20 to 75 miles broad and approximately 600 in length. In the river valleys, stands of cypress, tupelo, and red gum are found; the remaining coastal plain has a cover of longleaf and loblolly pine and scrub oak, save where hammocks of hardwoods in the north border lakes in the high pinelands.

Upriver, the transition to Piedmont is abrupt and along the river courses marked by rapids which have given the margin the name "fall line." The Piedmont is a plateau fringing the highest lands to the west, some 200 miles long, and some 150 miles wide at its widest point in North Carolina. Its outer margin ranges in elevation from sea level to about 800 feet; its inner border from 700 to 1500 feet. Here the conifers give way to a mixed oak-pine forest and sassafras, gum, and sycamore.

Successively, then, the land mounts abruptly with passage into the Blue Ridge Province, rising some 2000 feet in three or four miles to form the Eastern Escarpment of the Southern Appalachian Mountains, which trends from northeast to southwest, with its highest peak in North Carolina rising 6684 feet. The Appalachians form a barrier to east-west travel, save where rivers traverse them or wind gaps occur. Though game was formerly abundant, agriculture is only possible in the valley bottoms or on the lower slopes of the mountains. Here are found the southern hardwood forests of chestnut, chestnut-oak, yellow poplar, and hickory, in the upper elevations meeting the southward marching birch, beech, sugar maple, and hemlock.

To the west, between the Appalachians and the Cumberland Plateau, lies the Great Valley, an elevated series of depressions which widens to 60 miles in Tennessee and provides an avenue of communication from Maryland south into middle Alabama. Below its southern margin, in a great crescent, lies the fertile Black Belt. Many rivers rise in the valley, which in southwestern Virginia stands at an elevation of 2700 feet. From here the Shenandoah, the James, and the Roanoke course to the Atlantic, the Coosa into the Alabama and thence to the Gulf, and the Tennessee flows westward across the Cumberland Plateau to empty into the Mississippi.

North of the Appalachian Plateau, of which the Cumberland forms a part, northern Tennessee falls away in the Blue Grass Basins, to make part of the Great Interior Plain that stretches to the north and west. Beyond the Mississippi, the Coastal Plains become prairie and only the Ozark and Ouachita plateaus provide a resumption of the elevated plateaus west of the Mississippi.

The Southeast thus lies open to the north and west, just as it is accessible by water from the south. Indeed, the Everglades in the low-lying tip of Florida lie within the tropical region. Most of the Southeast is characterized by mild winters with 210 to 240 frost-free days each year and by an abundant rainfall exceeding 40 inches in the Gulf zone. It is an area with abundant game and edible nuts, fruits, and roots.

Archeology and Cultural Relationships

The region known ethnologically as the province of the Southeast is the result of complex cultural development within a diverse and changing environment. Although some scholars take the position that "the Southeast was at no time a single culture area any more than it was a single ecological area" (Lewis and Kneberg, 1959:161), diffusion and migration have repeatedly brought about a cultural levelling. The earliest population came in post-Pleistocene times, about 9000 B.C., when Paleo-Indian big game hunters moved in, perhaps from the north, but more probably from the grasslands and prairies which stretch to the Rockies. Some may later have returned to the Plains, if there is warranty for the view that the Fluted Point

complex, so characteristic of the later Big Game tradition, developed within the Southeast (Griffin, 1967:176). For those who settled in the East, the coniferous forests of the north, the deciduous forests of the interior, and the coastal plain provided a rich ecological diversity, within which there gradually emerged a number of cultures, termed Archaic, subsisting by a combination of hunting, fishing, and gathering. Within the deciduous forests, in particular, river valleys gave access to fish, freshwater molluscs, edible plants, and migratory birds; the uplands to nuts, berries, and game. In favored localities, as upon the fall line along the Savannah River and along the Green and Tennessee rivers of the interior, shell middens attest to a semisedentary existence. Archaic cultures, which are attested from about 8000 B.C., may at first have overlapped remaining Paleo-Indian cultures. By some three millennia later, they had received the domesticated dog, which was given burial along with humans at Indian Knoll in Kentucky, and their cultural inventory had come to include a number of polished stone artifacts. Characteristically, cultures of the Southeastern Archaic possessed woodworking tools, such as the grooved stone axe, and the atlatl spear, bone gorges, fishhooks, harpoons, awls for basketry (Jennings, 1974:129), skin clothing, and needles, together with stone vessels and stone mullers and pestles. To these they subsequently added the tubular pipe and a rich array of objects, some of them made from exotic materials, such as copper from the Great Lakes and marine shells from the Gulf, which evince an interregional trade. Such objects, buried with the dead, reflect status distinctions (Winters, 1968:219).

Taken as a whole, the Archaic development in the East was convergent over time, so that later cultures came to parallel one another in content, while retaining stylistic distinctiveness (Caldwell, 1958:17). Those of the Southeast tended to influence those of the Northeast (Jennings, 1974:150), but there were regional lags, and in Kentucky and Tennessee, and perhaps elsewhere, some Archaic cultures may have lasted into the first millennium A.D. (Lewis and Kneberg, 1959:180ff.).

Late in the Archaic, a modeled, fiber-tempered pottery was added to the cultural inventory of the Southeastern Coast, appearing in dissimilar wares in the Stalling's Island culture of Georgia about 2500 B.C. and in the Orange period of peninsular Florida some five hundred years later. These wares resemble in some degree indigenous stone vessels, and Bullen holds them to be possibly a local development (Bullen, 1961, 1972). Ford (1966, 1969) has seen them as ultimately stemming, via colonies in Mesoamerica, from the Colonial Formative of South America, and even compares the sequent phases of the Florida wares with developments in distant Ecuador, suggestive of repeated contacts. As Stoltman (1972; and see Ford, 1966:794) points out, the Stalling's Island culture in its other aspects is unchanged by the advent of pottery. It seems likely, as he suggests, that this combination may reflect a stimulus-diffusion from the south, rather than a wholesale cultural importation.

The Woodland tradition that succeeded the Archaic was marked by the development of horticulture, by the construction of mounds and earthworks, and by the development of a distinctive range of ceramic wares, often cord marked or decorated with paddle stamping (Willey, 1966:267). Ford (1966, 1969) and Webb (1968) detect a major impetus for these developments in the Poverty Point culture, which appeared in the lower valley of the Mississippi about 1500 B.C. and three centuries later had moved upriver, to a site which combines local Archaic features with a mound complex and extensive earthworks, together with traits such as mano and metate, greenstone celts, and a lamellar flake industry reminiscent of the Olmec culture of Veracruz.

The horticultural base of the Woodland cultures has been debated. Caldwell has taken the position that the combination of food-getting techniques of the Archaic was capable as well of supporting the more elaborate Woodland manifestations. Thus he cites the Kellog site in northern Georgia, which shows in its cache pits a heavy reliance upon acorns; and he adduces evidence that the bow and arrow was added in Early Woodland times, thus increasing hunting efficiency (1958:25ff.). It may be noted that the historic Calusa, at the southern tip of Florida, maintained a complex, stratified society, with mounds and a rich ceremonial art—the wood carvings of Key Marco are to be ascribed to them—by means of a mixed economy heavily dependent upon fishing, but without horticulture (Goggin and Sturtevant, 1964).

The usual assumption, however, has been that in its major developments the Woodland tradition included farming. Streuver and Vickery (1973) are of the view that cultivation had

its inception in the bottom lands of the middle Mississippi, where Indians may first have gathered, then domesticated, such native plants as the sunflower and marsh elder, probably—and later—goosefoot, and possibly others, such as amaranth (Sauer, 1950:496–498). To these local crops tropical cultigens were added, first squash and the bottle gourd, later maize, then beans. Ford (1969:191) holds that the metate at Poverty Point is evidence for the cultivation of maize in Early Woodland times; but at present the earliest surviving specimen of maize comes from the Middle Woodland and is dated at about 500 B.C. As Streuver (1968) has shown from the Illinois valley, Woodland farmers continued to rely heavily on hunting, fishing, and gathering to supplement their crops.

Woodland pottery is quite distinct from the fiber-tempered wares of the Archaic. The earliest specimen in this tradition, dating from about 1000 B.C., comes from New York. Its resemblance to that of the Eurasian Boreal is so strong that despite large gaps in distribution between the Northeast and comparable—and later—wares in Alaska and despite a paucity of evidence supporting a trans-Atlantic diffusion (Kehoe, 1962), Ford (1969:91) concedes a northern origin for this paddle-stamped ware. Within the Southeast, the subsequent development and diffusion of Woodland ceramic forms delineate two major regional divisions, which in turn parallel divisions which Lewis and Kneberg (1959) had found in the Archaic. Within the interior there emerged the Middle Eastern regional tradition; while somewhat later a Southern Appalachian tradition arose in Georgia and northern Florida, its complicated stamped wares being borne into the highlands and Piedmont, to supplant fabric-impressed wares of the Middle Eastern tradition, and being carried downriver onto the Coastal Plain from Florida to the Carolinas.

Poverty Point, like its Archaic predecessors, drew upon a trade in exotic wares (Ford and Webb, 1956), along with which trade cultural innovations were transferred. Among the early beneficiaries was the Adena culture of the Ohio valley, the emergence of which, about 1000 B.C., marks so dramatic an advance that Willey (1958:268;1966:272f.) sees it as the product of a migration from Mesoamerica. He is supported, not only by some of the cultural inventory, but by the circumstance that the Adena people were broadheads—though admittedly there had also been brachycephals among the Archaic

Figure 51 ● Cahokia "Monks Mound" (East St. Louis, Ill.) with human figure on first level for scale. (After Grimm, 1950; Jennings, 1974:252)

populations east of the Appalachians—supplanting a local long-headed population.

The climactic centers of Woodland times lay in the valleys of the Ohio and Illinois, just beyond the Southeast as here defined. The Adena culture, distinctive of Early Woodland developments, combined dispersed hamlets suggestive of informal living arrangements, with burial mounds, sometimes of considerable size, often associated with extensive earthworks, and with diverse burials accompanied by elaborate grave goods, suggestive of well-defined status distinctions. The combination of dispersed settlements and ceremonial centers finds a parallel in Mesoamerica among such peoples as the lowland Maya.

In turn, about 300 B.C., the Hopewell culture arose in the Illinois Valley. Unlike the Adena, its population were physically the continuation of their Archaic predecessors, and their culture shares features both with Archaic and Northern traditions and with the Adena (Spaulding, 1955:22f.). Soon, Hopewell peoples moved into the Ohio Valley, where their culture reached its peak in the centuries just before our era, continuing until about A.D. 850. Far from being extinguished by this manifestation of the

Middle Woodland, Adena culture continued in Kentucky and elsewhere well into the first millennium of our era (Webb and Baby, 1957, Griffin, 1952:368ff.). The ascendancy of Hopewell was marked by a rapid increase in population (Streuver, 1968:288), dwelling in organized villages, and supported by a crop inventory in which maize had become a major cultigen (Prufer, 1964:98).

As in Adena, the impressive ceremonial centers and the lavish display of wealth in burials attest to the organization and hierarchical ordering of society in what, following Gearing (1962), we may term its "ceremonial pose." Again, an extensive trading network supplied materials for the grave goods: obsidian came from the Yellowstone region, grizzly bear canines from the Rockies, copper from the Great Lakes, mica from the Appalachians, and conch and other marine shells from the Gulf (Prufer, 1964:93). These materials were not simply relayed in intertribal barter but seem to have been sought at their sources by trading parties (Griffin, 1967:184). In this manner, Hopewell influences radiated throughout the East. While in some instances it may have been borne by actual migration of populations, in a number of sites there seems to have been a diffusion of the ceremonial complex alone. Caldwell (1958: Fig. 5) is of the view that the major spread of Hopewellian influences within the Southeast

Figure 52 ● Artifacts from the Spiro and Etowah mounds. Variable scale. A, embossed sheet copper eagle, 11½ inches high; B, embossed sheet copper head; C, copper covered earspools; D, embossed sheet copper feather; E, embossed sheet copper snake; F, shell gorget of hand symbol, 3¼ inches high; G, embossed sheet copper design; H, shell gorget of world symbol with woodpeckers; I, shell design of animal snakes representing world symbol, 8 inches in diameter; J, shell design of two snake dancers, 12⅜ inches long; K, embossed sheet copper design of dancer wearing eagle paraphernalia, 20 incles long; L, sheet copper symbol. (A–G, I, J after Hamilton, 1952; H, K, L after Willoughby, 1932; Jennings, 1974:260)

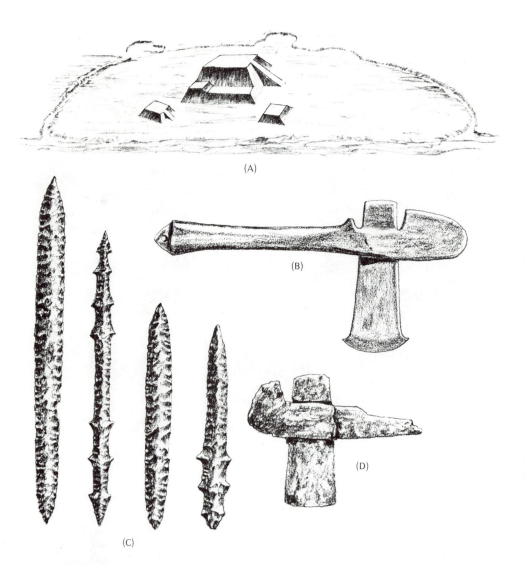

(A)

(B)

(C)

(D)

Figure 53 ● Etowah (Georgia) and associated artifacts. A, reconstruction of site with human figure at foot of ramp for scale; B, monolithic stone ax; C, problematical flint forms; D, copper axhead with handle fragment; artifacts are variable scale. (A after Willoughby, 1932; B–D after Moorehead, 1932; Jennings, 1974:262)

was confined to the interior region of deciduous forests; but Hopewellian features strongly mark cultures in the Coastal Plain of Georgia (Deptford) and of Gulf Florida (Santa Rosa–Swift Creek), as well as the lower Mississippi (Marksville-Troyville). Within the Southeast, the domestic aspects of Hopewellian cultures retain a local character and a continuity with the past.

Decline in the Hopewellian throughout much of the Midwest and North set in from about A.D. 300 to 900 (Griffin, 1967:186). In the Ohio

Valley, about A.D. 750, the Hopewell people abandoned their valley sites and began to erect their earthworks on hill-top locations in what Prufer (1964) sees as refuge places. Streuver and Vickery (1973:1215) follow Griffin (1960) in suggesting that a climatic shift to wetter weather had so shortened the growing season that the cultivation of maize had to be discontinued. It may also have made valley sites untenable. The networks by which Hopewellian ceremonial community was maintained seem to have failed, and resurgent local cultures once more became prominent.

Meanwhile, on the lower Mississippi and along the Gulf Coast, cultures had exhibited a continuity over time which Caldwell (1958:52ff.) denominates the Gulf tradition and which Griffin (1967:187,189) prefers to regard as expression of a Hopewellian persistence. From time to

Figure 54 ● Artifacts from Spiro mound. Variable scale. A, shell inlaid mask of red cedar, 11⅜ inches high; B, monolithic stone ax, 5½ inches long; C, hafted copper ax, 13 inches long (pileated woodpecker effigy, shell-inlaid eye); D, turtle effigy rattle of red cedar, 6⅞ inches long; E, front and side views of human sacrifice clay effigy pipe, 9¾ inches long; polished stone mace, 13¾ inches long; H, polished stone spuds, longest is 23 inches; I, human effigy of red cedar, 11¼ inches high; J, composite animal-bird stone effigy pipe, two inches long at base; K, stone effigy pipe, 9⅞ inches high (woman with mortar and ear of corn). (After Hamilton, 1952; Jennings, 1974:259)

time, the Gulf cultures were enriched by a succession of Mesoamerican contacts. One example may be cited from the west coast of peninsular Florida, where the Crystal River site, dating from the fifth century A.D., contains a group of mounds together with crudely carved stelae which Bullen (1965) declares would not be out of place in the Mexican Huasteca.

It was in the years A.D. 700–1700 that renewed influences from Mesoamerica spurred

Figure 55 ● Moundville and associated artifacts. A, reconstruction of site, square pyramid at upper left is almost 60 feet high; B, stone pendant; C, ceremonial disc; D, pottery beaker; E, frog effigy pot; F, G, incised pottery. Artifacts are variable scale. (After Alabama Museum of Natural History, 1942; Jennings, 1974:261)

(A)

(B)

(C)

(D)

(E)

(F)

(G)

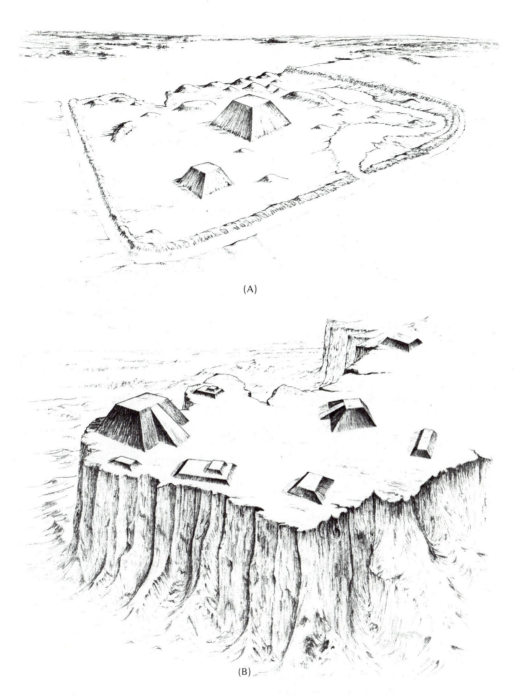

(A)

(B)

Figure 56 ● Reconstructed Mississippian mound groups. A, Lake George in the flat "Delta" near Holly Bluff, Miss.; B, Anna on the bluffs north of Natchez, Miss. At both sites, dominant pyramid is about 60 feet high. (After Griffin, 1952a, fig. 142B, C; Jennings, 1974:250–251)

THE SOUTHEAST ■ 409

the development of the Mississippian tradition, which found its center in the rich alluvial valley of the middle course of the Mississippi from the mouth of the Missouri down to Vicksburg. The best present view would derive those influences from the Huasteca region of coastal Tamaulipas (Ekholm, 1944; MacNeish, 1947) and bring them overland through Texas, where the Alto focus of East Texas presents Mississippian features in a Gulf tradition site with a radiocarbon date of approximately A.D. 400 (Newell and Krieger, 1949; Krieger, 1951). Sears (1954:345) sees the major influences upon the Gulf tradition as Circum-Caribbean in character, and as coming, perhaps by water, from the coastal area south of the Yucatan peninsula. It seems plausible that seminal features passed up the Mississippi River by way of the Gulf tradition (Ford and Willey, 1941; Krieger, 1951; 1953:257; Caldwell, 1958:61ff.), and that at a later date influences from the mature Mississippian culture moved again downriver to produce an impress upon Gulf culture (Willey and Phillips, 1958:164).

The possibility of an Antillean route for exotic influences into the Southeast has steadily lost ground (Sturtevant, 1960). The archeological culture most proximate to the West Indies, the Glades tradition of southern Florida, presents the most obvious resemblances, particularly in the late site of Key Marco, with its famous wood carvings, preserved by the muck. Yet this site is evidently too late, for it bears the evidence of mature Mississippian contacts. Indeed, Rouse (1949) reverses the direction of influence, asserting that the Glades tradition, which has its roots in the Southeastern Archaic, passed southward, to give rise to the variant Ciboney culture of western Cuba and southwestern Hispaniola. At a later period—perhaps in the time of Key Marco—renewed contact brought burial mounds and certain shell tools to the Ciboney. Of counter-influence by the Arawakan-speaking sub-Taino or Taino upon either Gulf or Mississippian traditions the evidence is insubstantial.

The Mississippian development gave rise to a new climax culture in the East. Its participants were many. Willey (1958) proposes the Siouan and Caddoan peoples, but undoubtedly the Muskogeans were involved as well; and with expansion to the north the Algonkin-speaking Illinois and Shawnee were also drawn in (Griffin, 1952:362–364). Mississippian culture rested upon an efficient maize horticulture, with associated crops, involving bottom-land farming, and was characterized by compact towns, often

fortified, and with a ceremonial nucleus typically comprising a plaza fronted on one or more sides by flat-topped mounds bearing a temple or chief's house (Sears, 1968; Brown, 1971). Although these features vary from site to site and are not always associated, they are accompanied by a number of domestic artifacts which lend a familiar stamp to Mississippian culture wherever encountered. Expansion carried radiations wide afield. In the North it is seen in Aztalan, Wisconsin; in the Northeast it penetrated the upper Ohio River and its influences were felt by the Iroquois. In the Southeast, migration carried it by river valley over the uplands, until it reached the coast in Georgia, Florida, and the lower Mississippi Valley. In the years A.D. 1100–1400, there spread through the Southeast a movement known as the Southern Cult which in its motifs shows generic relationships with Mesoamerica (Waring and Holder, 1945; Griffin, 1967:190), the while including features already present in Adena and Hopewell (Krieger, 1945:503–507; Webb and Baby, 1957:102–108). Although centrally associated with the Mississippian culture, the cult moved far beyond its limits, where many of the most impressive manifestations are to be found (Caldwell, 1958:68–70; Willey and Phillips, 1958:166).

The radiation of Mississippian cultures into the Southeast brought Creek, Choctaw, and Chickasaw, together with other peoples, into their historic locations, probably not many centuries before De Soto encountered them in 1540. The movements were made at the expense of local cultures, including Gulf cultures within the Coastal Plain. Surveying the ethnological data, Swanton (1928a:718; 1946:823) calls attention to special resemblances between the entrant Siouans and southeastern Algonkins of the Atlantic Coast and the Choctaw, Chitimacha, Tunica, and Natchez of the lower Mississippi Valley and vicinity, as well as between some of the latter and the Timucua of northern Florida. These resemblances in the Coastal Plain were not shared in general with the peoples of the interior (excepting the Choctaw), largely dominated by Mississippian invaders. Some features, such as the "bone house" ossuary complex were still moving northward along the Atlantic in historic times, for one band of Delaware had taken it over, presumably from the Nanticoke (Speck, 1924:191, fn. 1).

The Mississippian movement had brought its Southeastern settlers into areas somewhat less favored for maize agriculture. Among some of them, the compact, isolated large town gave way to small-town or village clusters, often strung out along the bank of river or creek, and hunting and gathering came to assume a larger role in their subsistence economy. Meanwhile their warlike preoccupation—it is here that Spaulding (1955:25) would place the introduction of the bow and arrow—had brought about a decline in other phases of their culture both in the Southeast and in the heartland of Mississippian culture, so that by the time of De Soto it was everywhere in decline. It may well be that a contributing factor was the temporary cessation of Mesoamerican influences; and it is worth noting that the Gulf tradition had passed its prime somewhat earlier, perhaps in the twelfth or thirteenth century A.D., with the failure of external stimulus (Sears, 1954).

Thus the picture of early historic times is one of a series of local cultural amalgams in the hinterlands of the interior and upon the Coastal Plain, preserving some features of earlier cultures, and of two major entities, the Gulf tradition of the Coastal Plain, expanding on the northern periphery, though on the wane in its centers, and an aggressive, expansive Mississippian tradition, dominating the river systems of the interior. Though the latter was in decline in its heartland, it was even then in the process of absorbing its predecessors and effecting a new consolidation of Southeastern cultures.

Historic Tribes

The major lines of the scene encountered by early European observers, and from which our ethnological data proceed, are simply drawn; but a more extended examination reveals evidence of the complex prehistory we have just reviewed. The Southeast is far from a bounded entity, and its earlier treatment as a distinct unit (Mason, 1907:428; Wissler, 1917:222–224) has given way to the view which merges it into a larger East, extending to the Great Lakes and the St. Lawrence (Kroeber, 1939:60–61, Map 6; Driver and Massey, 1957:173, Map 2). Within this larger area, the Southeast, in the words of Kroeber (1939:61ff.) "must be accorded such cultural primacy as there was east of the Rocky Mountains."

Among the peoples of the greater East, the most significant resemblances to the Southeastern cultures are shown by the Iroquois, who lie along the northern limits of the area, with their horticultural maize economy, nucleated villages, matrilineal clan organization, moieties, and annual series of first-fruit ceremonies marking the agricultural cycle (Fenton, 1940:164ff.). A number of these shared features seem on archeological grounds to be old within the Iroquois homeland (Griffin, 1944), while Eggan (1952:43) has suggested that the basic features of Iroquois social and political organization, which have their counterparts in the Southeast, may have arisen out of a local setting. Whatever the native component of the Iroquoian confederacies and those of the Southeast, in their most elaborate form they were a product of the contact situation with European cultures (Kroeber, 1939:62ff.; 92), and their resemblance may to that degree have been convergent.

Finally, such other specific resemblances as the blowgun and the Eagle Dance may have diffused to the Iroquois during historic times (Fenton, 1940:165). Consequently earlier theories which cited these resemblances as evidence that the Iroquois had migrated directly out of the Southeast have had to be rejected in favor of more complex explanations of relationship.

Within the greater East, are there special features which set off the Southeast? To a considerable extent, they consist less of gross presences or absences than of what Kroeber (1957) has impressionistically referred to as regional styles of living. Nonetheless, a comparison of those cultural traits examined by Driver and Massey (1957) reveals a few that distinguish the Southeast from immediately neighboring areas. They include the use of fish poisons; distinctive, though diverse, methods of processing acorns; the "black drink"; a rectangular, gabled house, thatched and with walls of mud wattle or other earth covering; the practice of going barefoot most of the time; and societies with five matricentered traits. There are other features which are largely confined to the Southeast though not everywhere present. Included among them are houselike storage structures; gourd ladles; chewing, eating, drinking, or licking of tobacco; the litter for nobility; carved wooden stools with legs; the blowgun with unpoisoned dart; and Crow kinship terminology for sister and female cousins. Others could be added, such as the manufacture of nested twilled baskets, but even this list gives some intimation of a Southeastern distinctiveness.

While trait lists help to demarcate the Southeast, they do not establish firm limits, and in a part of the continent which is not set off by natural features assessments of those boundaries have varied. Wissler (1917:223) found the typical culture of the Southeast among the

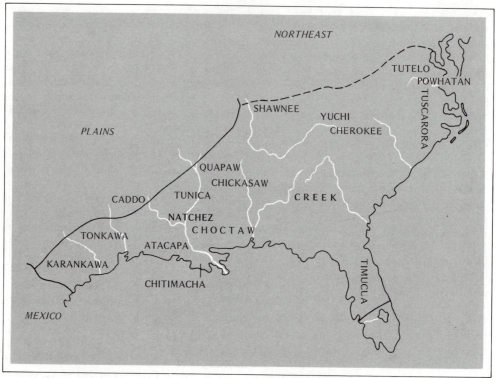

G. Ultra-Mississippi: Southeast

Muskogean speakers, Yuchi, and Cherokee; Swanton's (1928a) initial formulation is criticized by Kroeber (1939:64) as giving undue weight to the inland tribes, and particularly the Creek; while Eggan (1952:44ff. Fig. 11) in turn, although otherwise following Kroeber, finds unwarranted his elevation of the Natchez as a distinct, climax culture for the Southeast. The agreements and points of issue may be made clearer by the following list which compares the views of Swanton (1928e:713; 1946:812–816) and Kroeber (1939).

Swanton (1928c, 1946)   Kroeber (1939)
(divisions renumbered)

Core area
(1946:822, Map 1)

1. Creek area, with Georgia coast, Yuchi, Cherokee and Chickasaw marginal. (In 1946, Yuchi are inferentially included with Creeks, Chickasaw have independent status, but are in-   1A Southeast (Includes as well the Eastern Shawnee, whom Swanton considers marginal.)

cluded, while Cherokee are omitted from the core area. Two Siouan tribes, the Ofo and Biloxi, are admitted.)

2. Choctaw
3. Tunican group proper
4. Chitimacha
5. Natchez and allies   1B Southeastern Climax
6. Florida, especially the Timucua. Reference to distinctions between North and South Florida   1C North Florida (Timucua)
                        2 South Florida
7. Caddo   4A (Part of Red River, Caddo)

Greater Southeast:

8. Eastern Siouans (1946:813) calls attention to linguistic distinction between Virginia Piedmont (e.g., Tutelo) and Caro-   North Atlantic Slope:
12A Piedmont
12B Lowland
(The latter including also the Iroquoian Tuscarora, Nottoway,

lina groups.
9. Southeastern Algonkins (e.g., Powhatan).

10. Cherokee (See 1 above.)

and Meherrin.)
South Atlantic Slope:
12C Carolina Sound
12D Virginia Tidewater
13 Appalachian Summit (Cherokee)

There is a solid consensus between the two schemes. Of Swanton's revised core group, Kroeber excludes Southern Florida, with its impoverished culture based upon a reliance on seafood and the uncultivated Zamia root, together with the Caddo, transitional as they are between the Southeast and the Plains. Reflection upon the data, together with Kroeber's comments, has led Swanton to transfer the Cherokee from the inner area Creek group (1928) to his outer area (1946). Swanton still rules out the Shawnee, the eastern branch of whom Kroeber admits.

Linguistic affiliation can sometimes offer an important commentary upon assessments of cultural relationship. If we examine the Southeast as a whole, the principal linguistic blocks, arrayed almost concentrically about the south coast, are the Gulf languages, Caddoan, Yuchian, Iroquoian, Siouan, and Algonkin. Of these, the Gulf languages form an inner core. Muskogean, the best-known member of this stock, includes a western division, comprising Choctaw-Chickasaw, and an eastern division, comprising Alabama-Koasati, Hitchiti-Mikasuki, and Creek-Seminole (Haas, 1941:54f.). Members of these divisions dominate the interior uplands of Swanton's inner area, while closely related members extend fan-wise upon the Coastal Plain, from the lower Mississippi into South Carolina. Linguistic ties link coastal and inland members: for example, the special affinities of Choctaw-Chickasaw lie within coastal Mobile, Houma, and Pensacola, while those of Hitchiti-Mikasuki similarly link them with the Sawokli (Swanton, 1922:11; Kroeber, 1939:65–67). In southern Florida, the now-extinct Calusa and their neighbors are judged by Swanton to have spoken languages closely related to Muskogean (Swanton, 1946:238–240). Muskogean languages, then, with minor exceptions lie east of the Mississippi and below the Ohio. Timucua, in northern Florida, presents a problem. Swanton (1929b; 1946:239) finds it linked, though more remotely, with Muskogean, while Haas (1951:77) is uncertain as to its inclusion among the Gulf languages. Lamb (1959:44) tentatively includes it as a stock within that larger phylum.

The remaining members of Gulf extend from the lower Mississippi westward into Texas and are confined to the littoral: thus, Tunica, Natchez, Chitimacha, and Atakapa (Haas, 1951; 1952; 1958). Swanton (1924) had seen a special relationship between Natchez and Muskogean, and (1919) among the other three, and other special relationships have also been proposed, but Haas (1941:56, fn. 24; 1956:61) reserves judgment, and Swanton himself (1946:240) attests to the linguistic diversity of this region, not attributable to natural barriers. The distribution of component stocks places the center of gravity for proto-Gulf somewhere upon the Coastal Plain, perhaps in the vicinity of the lower Mississippi (cf. Eggan, 1952:43). At the time of contact, all members of the phylum were to be found entirely within the core area of the Southeast, with the exception of Atakapa, immediately to the west, which both Swanton and Kroeber exclude entirely from this area. Haas (1958a:258) estimates that proto-Gulf lies back in time some two or three millennia. The lexico-statistical time depth secured by Swadesh (1954:362) for the separation of Chitimacha and Atakapa is somewhat greater (4700 years).

Although it is always possible that these stocks were already distinct when they entered the area, standard interpretation of these data would appear to confirm the long-term association of Gulf speakers with Southeastern prehistory, extending back perhaps into Archaic times. Indeed, on the basis of Haas' further demonstration of Gulf-Algonkin linguistic relationship, of an estimated order of five or six millennia in depth, Willey (1958:266ff.) sees them jointly responsible for the Archaic of the entire Eastern area.

Bordering the Mississippi on the west are the Caddoan speakers, of whom the Caddo proper have already been mentioned. To the north, in the valley, but also in strength in the Piedmont and tidewater of the south Atlantic slope, and with one tribe, the Biloxi, on the Gulf coast, are the Siouans, later to spill out upon the western prairies. Their center of dispersal may have lain along the lower Ohio (Swanton, 1946:241; Eggan, 1952:45). In the Appalachian fastnesses are the Cherokee mountaineers, with their congeners, Tuscarora and related tribes, on the South Atlantic littoral. Together they constitute the southern Iroquoians. West of the Cherokee, but subsequently to be encountered widely in the Southeast, are the Yuchi. Iroquois-Caddoan and Siouan-Yuchi, along with the languages already considered under the Gulf phylum, had been included by Sapir (1929) in a proposed Hokan-Siouan phylum; Lamb (1959:44ff.) more conservatively classifies them as three distinct phyla. Willey (1958:268–269) sees the Iroquoians as vectors of Mesoamerica influences into Adena and the Caddoans and Siouans as the propagators of similar influences in Mississippian times.

The last group to be mentioned, the members of the far-flung Algonkin stock, have already figured in this discussion. Their distribution at the time of contact, earlier relations with proto-Gulf aside, suggests late reentrance from the North. Along the seaboard, they extend southward in a wedge with its point on the Carolina sound, flanked by Siouans and Iroquoians. In the interior, the principal member is the Shawnee.

Finally, it might be mentioned that still more remote relationships have been posited by Haas (1954:61; 1959) which would confirm relationships of Gulf, on the one hand with proto–Hokan-Coahuiltecan, and on the other with Tonkawa (neighboring Atakapa on the West) and Algonkin (see p. 47).

Whatever the fate of the identifications of linguistic groups and archeological cultures and of the more remote affiliations, the linguistic research offers valuable confirmatory evidence of the long-term identification of Gulf speakers with the development of the Southeastern cultural province. Of these peoples, we have made a time-honored choice in selecting for description the Natchez, who embody a Gulf tradition which survived best in the lower valley, although affected by Mississippian influences, and the Creek of the interior plateaus, a people whose culture may be regarded as an amalgam of Mississippian and Southern Appalachian constituents (Caldwell, 1958:52).

THE NATCHEZ

Historic Background

In the rich bottom lands of the lower Mississippi valley lay a number of small enclaves, such tribes as the Muskogean-speaking Houma, Bayougoula, and Mugulasha, the Tunican-speaking Koroa, Yazoo, and Tunica proper, and the Natchezan-speaking Natchez, Taensa

and Avoyel. Near the mouth of the river, in a lacustrine setting, dwelt the Chitimacha. None of these peoples was numerically strong. For the entire population of the lower valley in 1698, Swanton (1911:43) estimates less than 21,000 and Kroeber's figures (1939:138ff.) are but little higher. Certain cultural features in greater or lesser degree characterized them all, and aligned them in turn with the Caddo to the west and the Choctaw to the northeast (Quimby, 1942). From a political standpoint, such peoples as the Natchez, with their nobility and associated temple cult, may be taken to constitute politically organized chiefdoms, of a sort originally defined for the circum-Caribbean region (Oberg, 1955:484ff.). The stability of Natchez culture over time is suggested by radiocarbon dates from the mounds of the ceremonial square of the Great Village. These show that with repeated rebuildings they had been continuously in use from the thirteenth century to their abandonment in colonial times some five centuries later (Neitzel, 1965:86–99).

The Natchez star may have been in the ascendant in 1542, when they joined in harrying De Soto's survivors down the Mississippi, and their "Province of Quigualtam" was said to be the most powerful in the Lower Valley (U.S. De Soto Expedition Commission, 1939:271ff.). But from the time they emerge clearly in history with the visit of La Salle 140 years later, they were fated for quick decline. Scarcely half a century was to pass before they had been crushed in a series of wars, some 400 had been sold into slavery in the West Indies, and the remainder had taken refuge among the Chickasaw. The major accounts of Natchez culture stem from that brief period when, buffeted by change, it gave way before colonial rivalries; and they should be read in the light of those conditions.

The population figures for the Natchez are eloquent testimony of that decline. Early French authors concur in crediting them with greater numbers in aboriginal times, the best modern estimates ranging between 4000 (Swanton, 1946:161) and 4500 (Mooney, 1928:8). In 1698, they may have totalled some 3500 persons, as against 875 Taensa and 280 Avoyel (Swanton, 1911:43). De la Vente (in Swanton, 1911:39) avers that by six years after that date the Natchez had already lost one-third of their population. By the end of the half-century, the surviving Natchez amounted to fewer than a quarter of their aboriginal number (Swanton, 1911:44).

When the French first encountered them, the Natchez dwelt in some nine villages along St. Catherine's Creek, which empties into the Mississippi from the east. The Great Village, the seat of the principal chief known as the Great Sun, lay several leagues upstream from the confluence, with three villages below it, about half a league apart (cf. Albrecht, 1944). In later times the names of the other communities have been given, among which may be noted the Flour, White Apple, and Hickory villages. One or more settlements were inhabited by the Tiou and Grigra, Tunican-speaking dependents. If Iberville's estimate (in Margry, 1881, IV:177) in 1699 of a total of 300 to 400 cabins is held to apply both to Natchez and to subject villages, the average community may have contained about 30 to 40 cabins and a population of some 400. At a somewhat later time, the White Apple village counted more than 80 cabins (Du Pratz, 1758, III:235, fn. 1).

As Iberville (Margry, 1881, IV:411) discovered, the Natchez village was widely dispersed. After climbing the bluffs from the landing on the Mississippi, he reported, "... one finds a country of plains, prairies, filled with hillocks, in some places groves of trees, some oaks, and a great many paths which intersect, going from one hamlet to another or to cabins." The main path led to the ceremonial nucleus of the Great Village, lying in a bend of the creek, and containing cabins variously estimated at four (Gravier, in Thwaites, 1900, 68:139) and nine (Iberville, loc. cit.).

The cabins, . . . (said Charlevoix [1744, VI:172]) . . . are in the shape of a square pavilion, quite low and without windows, the roof is rounded almost like an oven. The majority are covered with leaves and stalks of Maize; some of them are built of a kind of mud . . . covered outside and within by very thin Mats. That of the great Chief is quite neatly plastered on the inside; it is also larger and higher than the others, placed on a somewhat elevated site, and is isolated on all sides. It gives upon a large Plaza . . .

Both the cabin of the Great Sun and the temple stood upon low mounds, facing each other across the plaza. The placement of these structures which has been variously stated (Iberville, loc. cit.; Charlevoix, loc. cit.; Le Petit, in Thwaites, 1900, 68:127; Du Pratz, 1758, III:16)

has now been resolved by an excavation of the site, which shows that the mounds lay on the northern and southern sides of the plaza, with the temple on the latter (Ford, 1936:59ff.; Neitzel, 1965; cf. Swanton, 1911:163). Another cabin upon the plaza was that of the Head War Chief, younger brother of the Great Sun (Du Pratz, 1758, III:52). A low burial mound lay some distance to the southeast of the temple. The dwellings of the village at large lay across the creek from the ceremonial center, sprawling over some five acres of higher land (Ford, 1936:59ff., 64ff.). Each community had a temple (Le Petit, in Thwaites, 1900, 68:135) and may have duplicated other features of the ceremonial center as well.

Subsistence

Such villages spelled a sedentary existence, and agriculture provided the base. The thirteen month names of the year, beginning in March, reflect concern with wild and domestic foods: Deer, Strawberries, Little Corn, Watermelons, Peaches, Mulberries, Great Corn, Turkeys, Bison, Bears, Cold Meal, Chestnuts, and Nuts. After the Great Corn festival in September and the hunting of turkeys near the settlements in the following month, the able-bodied left their towns for the communal bison hunts, and as Du Pratz (1758, II:38) says, "In these hunting seasons the feasts are not larger, because the warriors, being all away from home, take away many of the people with them." During the latter part of the winter months, nuts supplemented the diet, but the month of the Little Corn was, in the words of Du Pratz (1758, II:361ff.), "often awaited with impatience, their crop of the great corn never sufficing to nourish them from one harvest to another."

The staple crop of the Natchez was maize, of which at least two varieties seem to have been known. What may have been a wild rice was sown on sand banks along the Mississippi (Swanton, 1911:76; 1946:291). Other seeds were gathered from a wild cane and what may have been cockspur grass. Subsidiary crops were beans and pumpkins. By the time of French colonization, watermelons (possibly from the Spanish settlements) and peaches (from the Atlantic coast, according to Du Pratz) were already under cultivation; and it is interesting that two months bore the name of these exotic fruits. In addition many wild fruits, including persimmon and the scuppernong grape, berries, edible fungi, and nuts were gathered. When their grains failed, the Natchez had recourse to roots and chestnuts, but these were considered famine foods (Du Pratz, 1758 III:9 ff.). Tobacco was a cultivated crop. Salt was obtained by trade from the Caddoans to the northwest.

Agriculture was a community concern. The men girdled the trees and cut down the canes upon the field and when they were dry burned them. For planting, the entire village gathered, danced and feasted together, and then worked and sowed each field in rotation, starting with that of the Great Sun. The land was worked with a mattock made from a hickory fork, the maize kernels being set into holes made with the hand. Women, seemingly, had the major responsibility in the weeding of the crops, but the people as a whole harvested together (Dumont, in Swanton, 1911:75).

Fishing seems to have occupied a minor place in the domestic economy. In spring a run of "sardines" made its way up the Mississippi and were caught in bass-fiber nets. Iberville (Margry, 1881, IV:410) found several men fishing for carp in that river from a scaffold projecting over the water. Large fish like carp, sucker, and catfish, were shot with bone-tipped harpoon arrows provided with a line and wooden float (Du Pratz 1758, II:168). A concentration of Natchez fishing activities upon the Mississippi may account for the absence among them of such widespread Southeastern devices as the weir, the fyke, and fish poisons.

Hunting was a major occupation of the men. The Natchez hunter used a bow of black locust with cord of twisted bark or sinew and feathered arrows with fire-hardened tips. For big game, the arrow bore a bone head, bound with feather midriffs soaked in fish glue; for war a gar-fish scale served as point. Arrows were feathered (Du Pratz, 1758, II:168). Cane spears with flint points are mentioned by modern Natchez as formerly employed against large animals (Swanton, 1946:583).

On occasion, the hunter worked alone or with another man. Dogs were used chiefly to tree turkeys, when they could be shot from the roost. Hibernating bears were driven from hollow trees by fire and dispatched. Deer were stalked by a hunter disguised in a deer head and cleverly imitating the gestures of the beast.

The major hunts were group affairs. Bands of hunters sought ducks and other migratory fowl. Deer were driven within a circle of hunters, of-ten at the behest of the Great Sun, who then distributed the flesh. For the bison—that beast formerly ranged at some distance from the Natchez country—all able-bodied villagers took part (Dumont in Swanton, 1911:67–71; Du Pratz, 1758, II:67–73, 381f.).

When the hunt was close to home, the hunter merely brought in the head or tongue, and his wife or her servants set out to bring it back. It then seems to have become the property of the wife, since in later times she was free to sell the surplus to the French. Some might be preserved by smoke drying (Dumont, in Swanton, 1911:71ff.).

While men might prepare the flesh of game killed some distance from the settlements, cooking was generally woman's work. Maize was parched, then pounded in wooden mortars and made into a meal which would keep for six months. It was eaten as a gruel or, mixed with beans or nuts, as a bread. Other grains were similarly prepared, and persimmon was made into a bread. Boiling in earthware pots and roasting were the chief methods of cooking, and salt, obtained in trade from the Caddoans, was used for seasoning. There were no special times for eating, but men and boys ate before their womenfolk, and only at feasts did people make a point of eating together. Tobacco was smoked mixed with sumac leaves (Du Pratz 1758, III:8ff., 11, 18–20, 345ff., 360ff., II:45; and Dumont in Swanton, 1911:74–78, 89ff.).

The sole domesticated animal was a wolflike dog, used in hunting turkeys and commonly eaten. Soon after contact, however, Natchez women took up chicken raising, though only for the flesh (Du Pratz, 1758, II:74; and Dumont in Swanton, 1911:72ff.).

Material Culture

Many of the major crafts were in the hands of women and did not necessitate cooperation or labor exchange. It was the men who worked together in building cabins, cultivating the sacred fields, in hunting and warring, and in games. Men also cut firewood, which the women carried in, dressed skins, which women made into clothing, and made their dugouts and lesser implements. Pottery making, basket and net weaving, feather- and bead-work were women's tasks, along with weeding the fields and general housework.

Stone was little employed in Natchez technology—knives were of split cane—but ground stone axes were local and stone pipes may have been traded in. (See also Swanton, 1946:543.) Fire was produced by the hand drill. The women were skilled potters, their pebble-polished, red-slipped, incised ware, in a variety of forms, sometimes attained a capacity of 40 pints (Du Pratz 1758, II:178ff.; Quimby, 1942:262–269). Skins were soaked and stretched, scraped, and treated with cooked brains, afterwards being smoked to render them impervious to shrinkage (Dumont, in Swanton, 1911:64ff.). The wide array of nets, sifters, covered trinket cases, and other baskets were made from cane splints, often dyed with vegetable dyes to produce designs in the finished article (Du Pratz 1758, II:179, 183ff.). The textile arts were rudimentary: mantles of twisted mulberry bast were finger woven on a suspended warp, and garters, belts, and ribbons were perhaps braided of bison wool or oppossum fur (Du Pratz, 1758, II:192ff.; Dumont, in Swanton, 1911:63ff.). Women also made turkey- or swan-feather mantles on a fish net or woven bast base and rectilinear decoration in dyed porcupine-quill work. (The quills seem to have been traded from the north.) Dressed skins might be dyed black or painted in various designs (Du Pratz 1758, II:19ff.; Dumont, in Swanton, 1911:63ff.).

Much of the Natchez travel was by river, in pirogues such as those in which they had joined in the pursuit of the retreating De Soto. These canoes, sometimes 40 feet long, were shaped and hollowed by charring and scraping cypress or poplar logs, burning being checked by the application of clay. Such canoes were propelled by paddles. When overland travellers had to cross water, cane rafts might be improvised. In bearing burdens, women employed bear-skin shoulder straps and the tumpline, or a bass-bark carrying collar. The litter was reserved for the Great Sun and his ranking kindred (Du Pratz, 1758, II:180, 184, 188ff.).

Within the village, dwellings reflected rank differences in their location, size, and richness of furnishing; yet even the house of the Great Sun struck the French as comparatively bare within. Like most houses, it had platform beds ranged along the wall, each provided with mats, a wooden pillow, and a bison-skin coverlet. The bed of the Great Sun himself stood alone on the left side, set off by a post or stone in the floor which all must circle before approaching (Le Petit, in Thwaites, 1900, 68:126). A fire ordinarily burned in the middle of the floor. Small seats with legs, carved of a single piece of wood, were used infrequently, perhaps on special occasions, and one served as a throne for the Great Sun, reminiscent of the *duhos* of the West Indies and their counterparts in Central and South America (Du Pratz, 1758, II:181–183; Le Petit, in Thwaites, 1900, 68:127).

The Natchez lavished much attention upon their persons. In infancy, the head was deformed, probably fronto-occipitally, upon the cradle board. Most of the women blackened their teeth daily with a mixture of the ashes of wood and tobacco. From youth, boys and girls bore a tattoo across the nose, and added to it according to later rank or valor. The designs, made with a needle and tattooing frame in the form of suns, serpents, war clubs and other patterns, might cover the entire body of warriors and wives of the nobility. Face and even head might also be painted. Through the pierced and distended lobes of the ears women inserted spiked shell ear plugs; men wore wire earrings in later times. Shell gorgets and bead necklaces may have been general, but pearls, deposited in the temple, were worn only by noble children below the age of ten (Swanton, 1911:54–56). Axillary hair and beard were plucked out; that of the head was prepared in different ways, sometimes long on one side, shaved on the other, or symmetrically shorn. These differences in the men may have been significant for rank or age. Women wore their hair in several braids or a queue with beads or porcupine quills interlaced.

Boys and girls ran naked until, at about the age of eight to ten, the girl donned a two-piece apron of mulberry tassels with net foundation. When she had once entered into sexual relationships, she replaced it by the knee-length skirt. When about twelve or thirteen, the boy donned a buckskin breechclout, the garment of the man. In warm weather a deerskin, dyed white or black, and painted, might be worn by both sexes. When it grew colder, men added a deerskin shirt and even a buffalo robe, and donned leggings tucked into the high, laced puckered moccasins worn by both sexes. Women sometimes wore feather or woven mulberry-bast mantles.

Like bodily adornment, clothing might indicate differences of rank. Du Pratz (1758, II:190) asserts of the breechclout that "few save Chiefs wear breech-clouts of black skin"; the remainder wore white. A similar distinction may then have held for the deerskin mantles. Swan or Indian duck feathers were reserved for the mantles of women of the Honored grade, and swan-feather diadems were worn by the rulers (Du Pratz, 1758, II:113, 192).

Social Organization

From the time he was first bound to his cane cradle, padded with Spanish moss, the child was shaped to Natchez ways, his head strapped down to flatten it, bison-wool garters wrapped about the legs, his body rubbed with bear oil. Yet with restraint went assistance. When the child began to walk after a year, a young girl held it under the armpits. Until the mother became pregnant again, the child was free to suckle. From about the age of three, children were taken to the water and taught to swim. Discipline of the boys soon passed to an old man, who presided over their swimming and their foot racing, and when they were old enough to don the breechclout, instructed them in archery. It is said he never beat them, but he was feared and respected, and the threat of ostracism is said to have been sufficient to discourage fighting. Le Petit, however, states that if a youth passing the temple failed to pay reverence, his father or mother "would punish him immediately with several blows of a stick." (In Thwaites, 1900, 68:140.) Girls seem to have remained under the tutelage of the mother and were encouraged to industry and submissiveness to men. Controlled competition is seen in the ball game of the boys or the chunkey game of the young men, the latter often accompanied by lively betting; while the women were restricted to a quiet dice game without wagers (Du Pratz, 1758, II:309–321).

Premarital license among the Natchez contrasted with postmarital chastity. The girl might indeed amass a dowry through her person, and Penicaut states that only girls who had been free with their favors could pass after death over the bridge to the afterworld. A child born before marriage might be strangled if the mother was unwilling to nourish it.

Marriage took place only at the age of 25. The boy made his request to the senior male of the girl's family, often her father, presented his future in-laws with gifts, and, after a ceremony and feast at her home in which the two families participated, returned with his bride to his home, where they might continue to reside. If there was no room, a cabin might be built nearby for the newlyweds. The elaborateness seems to have varied with the rank of the couple, for chiefs, who married commoners, did so with less ceremony. They alone might have several wives, one or two in their cabin, the remainder living each with her parents upon call. Commoners had no more than one or two.

The husband of equal or superior rank to his wife had control over her sexual favors and might lend her at will. She, on the other hand, was enjoined to strict fidelity. Du Pratz claims to have witnessed but one divorce in eight years of residence near the Natchez, and Dumont agrees. The Luxembourg Memoir speaks of some women "who desire neither lovers nor husbands," and presumably remained single. According to Dumont, there were male transvestites, termed "the chief of the women" who assumed a woman's role and, if no woman was available, performed feminine duties on the hunt or warpath (Swanton, 1911:94–100).

Within the family, the man was preeminent. Du Pratz asserts that within a cabin might be found the househead, his sons, and their families down indeed to his grandchildren, and that his authority might extend as far as his great-great-grandchildren. His household, indeed, might contain nephews and grandnephews: no matter, they called him "father" and deferred to his counsels. "It is only death," observes Du Pratz, "that puts an end to his empire." (1758, II:386.)

Natchez family relationship, as in much of the Southeast, was matrilineal. Kinship terminology as it is now known has been greatly influenced by Creek practice (Swanton, 1928a:91–97; Haas, 1939:605–609). Murdock (1949:247) classifies it as patri-Crow, thus distinguishing it in the Southeast from the matrilineal Cherokee, Choctaw, and Creek, whose system was normal-Crow, and the Yuchi, who have double descent and thus are duo-Crow. Natchez terminology differs from that of the other tribes chiefly in keeping distinct the terms for father's brother and father, and those for mother's sisters and mother, a divergency which it shares with the system of the Chitimacha, below them on the Mississippi (Haas, 1939:609ff.). The shared features may be historically related to the prominence of hereditary classes among the Natchez and endogamous castes among the Chitimacha (Swanton, 1911:348ff.). Indeed, it was only after they had settled at the Creek town of Abihka that the Natchez took on the clan system of their hosts (Haas, 1939:597–603).

Undoubtedly, the unique Natchez class system has provoked the greatest discussion. Basically, there were two classes, a graded nobility claiming remote origin from the Sun and the commoners. The latter were termed by the nobility Stinkards, but only, apparently, in reference, since they took great offense at the name. The grades of nobility were, in descending order, Suns, Nobles, and Honored. The ruler himself, the Great Sun, stemmed from the highest grade.

An elaborate deference regulated behavior between classes, most exaggerated in respect to the Great Sun himself. There were distinctive forms of speech. The utterance of the Great Sun was greeted with three "hous," that of a simple Sun with a single "hou." They in turn greeted the Great Sun daily with a single "hou." When meeting them, the commoner stood aside, and always faced them while approaching and withdrawing. Only elders, leading men and his wives might enter the cabin of the Great Sun, and his bed and eating utensils were not to be profaned by others (Du Pratz 1758, III:54; De Montigny in Swanton, 1911:93; cf. Dumont, *ibid.*, 104).

Coupled with this behavior were sumptuary practices of dress and housing already mentioned and ceremonial practices, such as the use of a litter, which centered especially about the person of the Great Sun and the White Woman.

Chief, then, among the nobility was the family of the Great Sun, themselves termed Suns. Descent was matrilineal, and for all members of the nobility it was obligatory to marry a Stinkard. It was accordingly through the female Suns that Sunly status was maintained. The Great Sun held his office as the eldest son of his mother, whose title was "White Woman." His second brother, says Dumont (Swanton, 1911:104), was designated "Little Sun," and held the office of Great War Chief, while the remaining brothers merely bore the rank of Sun. For their descendants in the male line there was a stepwise generational regression. Thus, counting only through males, the son of the Great Sun was Noble, his grandson, Honored, and his great-grandson, Stinkard.

In the female line, the picture presents some ambiguities. Dumont states that all daughters of the White Woman assume that title, which he equates with female Sun; but others restrict the title to a single individual. Succession to the title, says Du Pratz (1758, II:396), falls to the female Sun most closely related to the incumbent White Woman, the first princess of the blood,

says Le Petit (Thwaites, 1900, 68:133ff.): in most instances she must have been the eldest sister of the Great Sun. Some observers give the impression that all female Suns perpetuated Sunly matrilineages. Penicaut, not without some ambiguity, asserts that the children of a Noble woman were themselves Noble, a rule which Swanton (1911:107) has extended to the Honored woman and her children. In this he has been followed by most scholars (Josselin de Jong, 1928; Davis, 1940). However, White et al. (1971) have shown that the French sources make no reference to an Honored woman born to that status. MacLeod (1924:205ff.), drawing upon remarks by Penicaut, proposes that only the direct line yielding the Great Sun maintained indefinitely Sunly status, all collateral maternal lineages reverting after three generations to Noble rank. Thus Sunship would have ranged only in the immediate family of the Great Sun, the White Woman, and her descendants.

Much comment has dwelt upon the asymmetrical marital system of the Natchez. The nobility must always have been proportionately few. La Harpe in 1700 credited them with 17 Suns, and Le Petit, 30 years later, with "6 little villages and 11 Suns." (Swanton, 1911:44, 107.) The numbers of the lower grades of nobility are nowhere stated. It has always been assumed that the preponderance of the tribe were commoners and that the great majority of marriages were within that class. Some writers (White et al., 1971; cf. Tooker 1963, Mason, 1964) see Honored as a rank within the commoner class. The plebeian body was further enlarged by the incorporation of Tunican-speaking groups as Stinkard (Swanton, 1911:334, 336; Quimby, 1946). Nonetheless, as Hart has shown, within a few generations the system as set forth would have drained the commoner class in providing mates for the nobility, unless the matrilineal rule for females is enlarged to prescribe that the daughter of a Stinkard woman inherit her mother's rank (Hart, 1943; see also Fischer, 1964: White et al., 1971).

Thus far described, the class system was hereditary, but there were likewise opportunities for advancement. Through warlike exploits, an Honored man might rise to Noble rank (Du Pratz, 1758, II:395). Similarly, a Stinkard might rise to Honored position by taking a scalp or performing an equivalent deed of prowess. In the latter instance, his wife rose with him (Dumont, in Swanton, 1911:104). A Stinkard couple who immolated their child at the bier of a Great Sun might gain Honored rank, a special instance of achieving status through the sacrifice of a relation. Du Pratz (1758, III:46–49) tells of a commoner who declined to die with his wife, a Sun, or with another Sun. Two old women, his relatives, took his place; he helped strangle them and thereupon entered Honored station.

The lot of a Stinkard husband of a Sun was not an enviable one. He did not eat with her, stood in her presence like her servants, must observe strict fidelity while his royal spouse might consort freely—at least one had a child by a Frenchman (Du Pratz, 1758, III:247)—and at her death was killed to accompany her. He did not work, however, and had authority over his wife's servants (Charlevoix, 1744, VI:182).

When a child destined to be the Great Sun was born, each family brought forward its infants, from among whom his lifelong retainers were chosen. When they came of age, some became hunters or fishermen for the heir's house, others farmers, while still others became his guards (Le Petit, in Thwaites, 1900, 68:131). The White Woman was similarly served. Among the retainers of the Head War Chief at his death, Du Pratz (1758, III:36, 44) enumerates a speaker, doctor, head servant, and pipe bearer; Dumont (Swanton, 1911:151) says the head servant was of Honored rank and seems to equate him with the speaker; he mentions in addition a first warrior.

The power of the Great Sun and White Woman was very great. "As soon," notes Charlevoix (1744, VI:177), "as some one has the misfortune to displease one or the other, they command their Guards ... to slay him. 'Go rid me of this Dog,' say they, and they are obeyed upon the spot." During a war with the French, the Head War Chief intervened on behalf of a Frenchman whom he admired and put to death his captors (Du Pratz, 1758, II:353). Suns, on the other hand, might not be slain. At least after the advent of the French, the Great Village lost inhabitants, who moved away in order to evade levies and formed new hamlets at a safer distance (Charlevoix, 1744, VI:172).

Sunly estate, it must be emphasized, was a limited affair, within a single matrilineage. It was buttressed by the myth of descent from a divine pair, emissaries of the sun, and genealogies seem to have been maintained in which the names of some 45 to 50 chiefs were recorded (Du Pratz, 1758, II:331–336; De la Vente,

in Swanton, 1911:185). The Luxembourg Memoir states of the kindred of the Great Sun that they were "more or less respected according to their degree of proximity to the chief, and, in turn, regard the other savages as dirt." (Swanton, 1911:100, 106.) The Great Sun at least had to be without physical blemish. It was from this line, and perhaps from maternal uncles of the Great Sun, that major posts were filled. Thus The Bearded, maternal uncle of the Great Sun, was Great War Chief until the French executed him in 1716, after which the Great Sun's brother succeeded him. "The Festivals which I have seen celebrated in the great village of the Natchez, where the Great Sun resides," says Du Pratz (1758, II:383), "are celebrated in like manner in all the Villages of the Nation, which are each governed by a Sun, to whom the people show the same respects and make the same presents. These Suns are all subordinate to the Great Sun, whose authority absolutely no one shares." The chief of the Flour village, who held the additional office of Master of Temple Ceremonies, is known to have been a brother of the Great Sun, while the war chief of another village was either a nephew or brother. War chieftainships and secondary offices seem to have been open to Nobles (Swanton, 1911:107).

In this theocracy, duality was an important principle. Du Pratz quotes the head guardian of the Great Village temple to the effect that in the past there were two temples, each with eight wise men to guard its fire (1758, II:335ff.). "The Natchez," Charlevoix (1744, VI:182ff.) tells us, "have two war chiefs, two Masters of Ceremony for the Temple, two Officers to regulate what must be done in the Treaties of peace or of war; one who has the inspection of works, and four others who are charged with arranging everything in the public feasts. It is the Great Chief who grants these offices and those upon whom they are bestowed are respected and obeyed as would he himself." Indeed, officialdom may well have been still more complex, for Dumont speaks of the "second war chief of the Flour village," and again of the "chief of the grain," who supervised sowing and harvest (Swanton, 1911:150). As MacLeod points out (1924:202, note 4), there was at least incipient centralization akin to that of the Taensa, for the war chief just referred to lived not in his own village but in the Great Village near the temple.

War offices were to a marked degree intertwined with those of the civil organization. The Great Sun himself might lead in war, but was then shielded from harm by his followers (Charlevoix, 1744, VI:187). In the council of war, both the Great Sun and his brother, the Great War Chief, were "only a witness, for the opinion of the old warriors always prevails over those of the two chiefs, who subscribe willingly to it on account of the respect and the great consideration which they have for the experience and wisdom of these venerable persons." (Du Pratz, 1758, II:414.) Yet Tattooed Serpent, then the Great War Chief, was in his own right a man who had slain 46 enemies (Du Pratz, 1758, III:35). War was an avenue for advancement. A Stinkard was an "apprentice warrior" until he had taken a scalp or performed an equivalent deed, after which he advanced to Honored rank and was known as a "warrior." (The condition for a novice of noble class may have been the same.) Both tattoo marks and a war name testified to his new status. It is uncertain whether such an individual could again move upward. At least those born Honored could move on to Noble status, perhaps by performing the deed of a "true warrior," or "great man slayer," that is by taking 10 captives or 20 scalps. It is from these men of Noble rank, together with Suns, that the functional war chiefs were in all probability chosen. As MacLeod (1924:210) has pointed out, even though the Great Sun was present, it was the oldest of the venerable warriors who bore the title of Ancient War Chief, who passed about the war calumet and bestowed names and ranks upon warriors. Moreover, while it was the Great War Chief who addressed the council and held a war feast and dance in his cabin, war parties might also be independently recruited by other war chiefs, who would lead them against enemy tribes (MacLeod, 1924:211).

A Natchez war party gathered at the cabin of the leader, where they partook of the "war medicine," an emetic drink, feasted on dog meat, and struck the war post. After making preparations they set out, often 20 or 30, but sometimes 300 strong, with scouts out. The leader carried his war medicine and at night suspended it on a pole leaning toward the enemy. Inauspicious dreams along the way might lead them to turn back. They sought surprise; if their enemies had learned of their coming they withdrew, leaving behind a few men to lie in wait for hunters. In the attack bows and arrows, axes, or sword-clubs were used, and bison-hide bucklers for defense, and the attack fell if possible at dawn. Circular palisades were erected to defend villages, and the Natchez soon learned from the French and from Negro slaves how to improve them. When a raid had been carried out, markers bearing the symbol of a sun were left at the scene to identify the attackers. Men were scalped or captured, and women and children brought back as slaves. Captured warriors were made to sing and dance several days before the temple, then were bound to frames, where they were tortured to death by fire. However, a young widow whose husband had fallen in war might demand a captive to replace him. A warrior who had taken his first scalp or prisoner underwent a six months' abstinence from meat and from intercourse with his wife, in order to protect himself from the spirit of his victim (Swanton, 1911:123–134). The Great War Chief paid compensation to the families of those warriors he failed to bring back (Du Pratz, 1758, II:437).

War might be concluded by securing the mediation of a neutral tribe, sending slaves and presents to secure the good will of the erstwhile foe. Peace embassies to the Natchez came with the calumet and gifts and were received in state by the Great Sun himself. When war was concluded between the Natchez and Taensa, offerings were made at the Taensa temple by the Natchez deputies.

Ceremonial and Religious Life

In their efforts to control supernatural events, the Natchez had recourse to shamans. The acquisition of spiritual power follows lines familiar in the Americas, and indeed, in many other parts of the world. The novice fasted in his cabin for nine days, invoking a supernatural to the accompaniment of his gourd rattle, and with contortions that may have been a sign of possession (Luxembourg Memoir, in Swanton, 1911:178ff.). A distinction seems to have been made, according to the power granted, between curers, rain shamans, and good-weather shamans (Charlevoix, 1744, VI:187ff.). Curers fasted and smoked, dancing with a basket of "what they call their spirits, that is to say, small roots of different kinds, heads of owls, small parcels of the hair of a fallow deer, some teeth of animals, some small stones or pebbles, and other similar trifles." With invocation, they scarified the patient upon the afflicted part and sucked out the foreign object. Recovery of the patient spelled a large fee; his death brought the death of the shaman at the hands of relatives (Le Petit in Thwaites, 1900, 68:151ff.). Like other shamans, the curers were principally old men; but herbalists might include women, and sometimes those of rank (Swanton, 1911:80–86, 145). Curers employed a sweating frame, upon which the patient lay covered with Spanish moss, while charcoal burned on the ground beneath him. Rain shamans were given payments in the spring from public contributions to bring rain for the newly planted crops. They sprayed water through a perforated reed, shaking their rattles and holding their power objects. For good weather, the shamans mounted the roof and sought to drive away the clouds. Like the curer, the weather shamans braved death for failure (Charlevoix, 1744, VI:187ff.; Le Petit in Thwaites, 1900, 68:153). On occasion, even the Great Sun himself fasted for nine days and bathed himself to bring rain (Du Pratz and Dumont, in Swanton, 1911:155, 169).

Shamans otherwise played but little part in public performances. After the death of the Head War Chief, Dumont's source observed a shaman and the official known as "chief of the grain" praying to the celestial sun, and a shaman later blessed the tobacco pills to be swallowed by the retainers to be strangled at the feast (Swanton, 1911:150, 156). Aside from this, ceremonies tended to be in the hands of the Great Sun and his officials and centered about the temple.

The Natchez temple was a quadrangular structure atop a mound on the south side of the plaza, upon which it fronted. The mats with which its wattle-and-daub walls were covered were ceremonially renewed each year. Upon its roof were three painted birds carved of wood. Within, a partition divided a larger antechamber from the sanctum. In the antechamber burned a perpetual fire of three hickory logs, and behind it stood a table upon which the bones of ancestral Suns rested, to whom offerings of food and drink were periodically made. Other palladia, such as carved images and the pearl necklace worn by the White Woman, were kept there. In the sanctum there were carved boards and a buried stone, perhaps an image, said to be the divine progenitor of the Sunly line who, as St. Cosme was told, "became so terrible that he had men die merely by his look; so that in order to prevent it he had a cabin made for himself into which he entered and had changed into a stone statue

for fear that his flesh would be corrupted in the earth." (Swanton, 1911:158–173.)

Great respect was shown the temple, before which the people prostrated themselves as they did before the Great Sun. Only that chief, the White Woman, and some Honored men might enter there. Daily the Great Sun greeted the celestial Sun before the door of the temple. Morning and evening he and the White Woman went there to worship and commune and to recount to the people from the door what had been foretold to them. At those times a fire was lit before the door. At each new moon offerings of food were made, perhaps to the ancestors whose bones were enshrined there; perhaps also to the stone image buried in its wooden case (Penicaut, in Swanton, 1911:159f.). Seed was presented at the temple before sowing and the first fruits of harvest were offered there (Charlevoix, 1744, VI:183).

The perpetual fire was intimately connected with the welfare of the tribe, and its extinction required that fire be taken forcefully from another temple, that of the Mobile, said Charlevoix erroneously, that of the Tunica, said Father Poisson (Swanton, 1911:165–172). The fire in the cabin of the Great War Chief, at least after his death, was kindled from the temple (Dumont, in Swanton, 1911:152). The sacred fire might not be profaned by use for ordinary purposes, for it burned in honor of the sun (Charlevoix, 1744, VI:173). Eight guardians, presided over by a chief guardian, tended the fire in four shifts, each pair being responsible for a quarter of a month (Du Pratz, 1758, III:19).

It is perhaps because of his sacerdotal role that the Great Sun had to be without blemish (Du Pratz, 1758, II:399). That he was not the only official with access to the temple divinity is evident. During the funeral of the Great War Chief, "the principal guardian of the temple came out and told them what he had learned from the Spirit," and the old chief of the Flour village, a brother of the Great Sun (MacLeod, 1924:202, note 4), assisted the latter as master of ceremonies (Dumont, in Swanton, 1911:152, 156).

In the cyclical festivals of the Natchez the sacred role of the Great Sun was also evident. Each new moon of the thirteen-month year was celebrated with a feast marked by thanksgiving to the Supreme Being and by tribute made to the Great Sun who set the time for the feasts (Penicaut, in Swanton, 1911:121). Two have merited special description, the Deer feast, initiating the Natchez year in March, and the feast of Maize, the Green Corn festival of the Southeast.

The Deer festival had three ceremonial segments. In the first the Great Sun was rescued by the White warriors from an attack of Red "enemies," led by the Great War Chief. Next followed an act of worship of the four directions and the temple by the Great Sun, assisted by the Great Master of Ceremonies and the Great War Chief. Finally, the Great Sun came out in ceremonial diadem and pearl necklace to sit in state on his throne before his people and receive their gifts. Dancing then followed.

The harvest ceremony fell in either the month of Little Corn (July) or that of the Great Corn (September-November); or two ceremonies were held. Du Pratz describes a sacred field cleared from virgin forest, tilled and harvested by warriors alone, but other foods seem to have been brought in to supplement the maize it yielded. The corn was stored in a granary erected in a clearing habitually used for the harvest ceremony. Around the clearing cabins were built, that of the Great War Chief beside the granary facing that of the Great Sun, on its low mound. In ceremonial attire, the Great Sun and White Woman were borne to the scene on a litter by swift relays of warriors, eight to a relay. There the Great Sun made the circuit of the grounds, saluting the maize in its granary as one would a lord. A new fire was now kindled; and the grain ceremonially distributed by the Great War Chief was prepared by the women and eaten by men, then by boys, and finally by women and children. Thereafter, led by the Great War Chief, warriors struck the war post and recounted their deeds. At night, there was dancing, with sexual freedom for the young folk, but seemingly no license for the married. In the morning there followed a ball game between the White and Red warriors, the cabins of the Great Sun and Great War Chiefs serving as goals. The feasting lasted three or more days, until the provisions were exhausted. Before they returned to the village, the Great Sun addressed them, exhorting them to their duties to the temple and the instruction of their children, and praising those who had set such an example (Du Pratz, 1758, II:363–381).

Of the occasional ceremonies, none was more spectacular than the funeral of a person of Sun rank. Commoners, on the other hand, were interred with their possessions, and mourners cut their hair, abstained from public gatherings,

and visited the grave daily for a period up to three months. The lower nobility may have followed similar practices.

At the death of a Sun, however, his wives, guards, and retainers prepared for death. The commoner husband of a White Woman was at once strangled by his firstborn son. In addition, those who had earlier pledged their lives and any others who desired to do so prepared to accompany their master into the afterworld. Parents might strangle an infant to form part of that procession. They and eight of the relatives of those to be strangled gained Honored status. Among those who offered themselves to accompany a ruler were Nobles; indeed when the Great War Chief, Tattooed Serpent, died, the French had difficulty dissuading his brother, the Great Sun, from slaying himself. When the Great Sun died, all fires were extinguished.

During the period of preparation, much was made of the persons marked for death. Those who had volunteered stood upon scaffolds erected in the plaza, and, attended by their nearest kin, climbed down at intervals to dance together. Some four days later, at sunset, the bier bearing the deceased and his spouse was borne in pomp toward the temple by six men, under whose feet the strangled infants were cast. While the principal dead and his wives were buried in the temple, those to accompany him sat upon the ground, took tobacco pills to lose consciousness, and were strangled by their kindred. Nobles were buried on either side of the door of the temples. Those from other villages were returned to be interred in the temples there. The cabin of the deceased was burned. If he was a Great Sun, his successor's cabin was built upon a new mound, probably an innovation of the old one. After two to ten months the bones of the Great Sun were exhumed and placed in a cane basket within the temple, and the long bones of his principal servants were added. At the time of secondary burial, temple guardians might also be strangled (Swanton, 1911:138–157).

The realm to which good spirits now made their way was an attractive one to the Natchez. True, those who had violated ethical precept were destined to an afterworld covered with water, swarming with mosquitoes, and poor in food. For persons who had conducted themselves well, however, there was the world described by the favorite wife of the Tattooed Serpent, as she looked forward to her imminent death. "Do not grieve yourselves," she told the

French (Du Pratz, 1758, III:37ff.), "We shall be friends far longer in the realm of the Spirits than in this one, for there one dies no more. The weather is always fine; one is never hungry, for nothing is lacking there to live better than in this country. Men make no war there, because they are no more than all one Nation."

Both ethical conduct and their system of government had been ordained to the ancestors of the Natchez by a divine pair, ancestral to the lineage of chiefs, who by their radiance betrayed their descent from the sun. The visible orb was merely termed "Supreme Fire," but within its radiance dwelt the "Supreme Spirit," who, like the Great Sun on earth, was ministered to by "servant spirits." In the time of the creation, these deputies had given shape to all on earth, save man, whom the Supreme Spirit himself had modelled from clay. Beside them, there were other spirits of the air of varying malevolence and, if we consider the talismans of power carried by shamans, spirits in natural form as well.

Natchez culture, in Swanton's (1911:185ff., 146, 239) view, was a product of fusion between a Muskogean people and Tunican predecessors (see also Brain, 1971). A broader base, however, is suggested by the presence of hierarchically structured social systems in the Chitimacha castes (Swanton, 1911:348ff.) and the analogous Timucuan organization (Swanton, 1922:370–372). Neither of these can be demonstrated to be of composite origin. The many features shared by the tribes of the lower Mississippi with the Natchez (Swanton, 1911; Quimby, 1942) also render it less likely that the latter were the unique product of a cultural fusion.

In its somewhat rigid form, that culture survived half a century of intense contact (Albrecht, 1946). There was an initial enrichment from the French trade, but a decline from introduced disease. Colonial maneuverings by French and English soon split the little nation. The French directed their diplomacy to the Great Sun, though executing hostile members of the ruling class, and only the Great and Flour villages remained loyal. Even before the death of Tattooed Serpent (1725) and the Great Sun, (1728), chiefly power had dwindled, and the White Woman even made overtures to Du Pratz to marry her daughter and successor, alleging the desire to break away from the old social order (Du Pratz, 1728, II:397–403). The end was hastened by the malfeasance of a colonial administrator, who paid with his life in the subsequent uprising. With Choctaw levies, the French crushed the rebellion. By 1731 the new ruler had been taken and with many of his followers was sold into slavery. The remaining members of the tribe took refuge among the Chickasaw and eventually joined the Creek and Cherokee.

THE CREEK

History

The people known to the early settlers as Creeks, from the old name of one of their rivers (Swanton, 1946:217), were of composite origin. Migration legends bring the principal people, the Muskogee, from the northwest, the Alabama from northwest and southwest, the Koasati and Tuskegee from the north, and the Hitchiti from the Gulf region (Swanton, 1922; 1946, Map 10). Both archeologically (Fairbanks, 1952) and historically they were principally a people of the interior plateau, situated at the margin of Piedmont and Coastal Plain, and the Great Valley seems to have provided them an avenue of movement. In his *entrada* in 1540–1542, De Soto encountered Creek towns as far north as the present Augusta, Georgia, and Creek are said to have comprised an element of the Guale, on the Georgia Coast. In time, the Creek withdrew toward their central settlements when they constituted two groups and some fifty towns, the more numerous Upper Creek on the Coosa-Tallapoosa-Alabama drainage, with a Koasati segment on the Tennessee, and the Lower Creek on the Chattahoochee-Flint system, extending upon the Coastal Plain. In the early nineteenth century the Confederacy numbered 21,733, of whom almost 18,000 were Muskogee.

The recorded history of the Creek opens with the expeditions of De Soto and of the explorers who followed him. Eventually, Spain established colonies along the southern Atlantic and Gulf coasts, made up of mission settlements containing pacified Indians under monastic tutelage, guarded by a handful of soldiers. The Spanish were soon to be challenged by the English settlement of Carolina and subsequently by that of the French on the lower Mississippi and on the Gulf Coast. The secular colonies of the English and French depended heavily on trade, both for support of their colonies and as an instrument of Indian policy. The Creek, initially drawn into the English sphere, soon became dependent on the deerskin trade for the firearms and ammunition which had become necessities. Indeed, about 1690, a number of the Lower Creek towns moved eastward to the Ocmulgee River to be closer to the source of trade. As allies, they assisted the Carolinians in slave raids, in 1704 devastating the Spanish mission settlements of the Apalachee. Soon thereafter, however, widespread discontent at the high-handed behavior of the English traders erupted in the Yamassee War (1715). Behind it lay the hand of the Creek, who were related to the Yamassee, and at the end of the hostilities the Lower Creek withdrew their towns from the Ocmulgee to the Chattahoochee. They then established a policy of nonalignment with the various contending European nations. The most influential voice in this policy was that of the chief of the leading Lower Creek town, Coweta, a man to whom the British and French alike referred as the "Emperor" Brims. Although it is probable, as both Swanton (1908:257) and Corkran (1967:42) assert, that some elements of the Creek Confederacy already existed in De Soto's time, it was only in the aftermath of the Yamassee War that it emerged as a conspicuous presence in the Southeast.

In the colonial struggle, with its intensification of intertribal warfare, the Creek found themselves at one time or another pitted against the Cherokee and even the Iroquois in the north, with the Chickasaw to the west, and with the Choctaw to the south. When colonial pressures reduced the power of some of these enemies, the Creek were willing to receive elements from among them within the confederation. Meanwhile, the nearly complete elimination of the French after Queen Anne's War and the decline of the Spanish left the English colonies with a virtual monopoly of the Indian trade. During the American Revolution, it was the superior British ability to supply that trade which led the Creek Confederacy to side with them. Afterwards, and for a decade, the Creek leader, Alexander McGillivray, son of a Scotch Tory trader and a Creek mother, skillfully maneuvered to maintain a precarious position by playing the Spanish in Florida against the Americans.

By this time, intermarriage with whites had diversified the Creek. Agent Benjamin Hawkins set afoot a program of acculturation through which many Creeks, particularly in the Lower towns, became substantial farmers, with livestock and black slaves. In the growing split between such "progressives" and those who sought to maintain an Indian way of life, the latter were receptive in 1811 to a visit by Tecumseh, the Shawnee leader, who had been born among them. With British backing, he sought an alliance of the western tribes to stem the American advance. From his visit arose a Creek prophetic movement, which in 1813 inspired Creek conservatives to attempt to impose a militant nativism upon their fellows. This Red Stick faction soon embroiled Americans in their civil war. Finally victorious, the Americans then forced land cessions from all Creeks alike (Nuñez, 1958).

Meanwhile, local white agents were pressing the Creek leaders to sell their remaining land, although they lacked the authority to do so. In 1825, one leader, William MacIntosh, signed such a treaty, but the Creek put him to death and denounced the treaty. Nonetheless, the United States Government insisted upon the legality of this document and in 1835–1840 undertook to move the Creek to Indian Territory beyond the Mississippi. In Florida, a Creek offshoot, the Seminole, resisted a similar move, in warfare which lasted from 1835 to 1842. Finally, the removal was effected, and the Seminole joined the Creek, Choctaw, Chickasaw, and Cherokee, constituting the "Five Civilized Tribes" of Indian Territory, the area which became the State of Oklahoma. Behind them, they left small groups too devoted to their homeland to consent to leave it. The loss in property, life, and human suffering that attended the removal along what has been referred to as the "Trail of Tears" was appalling and might have been expected permanently to embitter them against the United States. Nonetheless, the Creek Nation, under its own government, took up life in the new homeland with courage and energy, and, though divided during the Civil War, at its end they made such progress that the "Wild Tribes" of the Southern Plains turned to them for advice. In time, the pressures of whites for Oklahoma statehood made the Indian Nations anachronistic, and in 1906 they were effectively dissolved (Caughey, 1938; Debo, 1941; Foreman, 1934; Swanton, 1922; 1946).

Subsistence

The twelve-month Creek year began in the month corresponding to August with the busk, or Green Corn ceremony, and was divided into two seasons. The "Winter" months, from August through January, were Much Heat, Little Chestnut, Big Chestnut, Frost, Big Winter, and Little Winter. From Big Chestnut through this

Southern Algonkin tribes. Virginia ● "Their Manner of Fishynge in Virginia." DeBry, engraving 13; after White. Courtesy, Rare Book Division, The New York Public Library, Astor, Lennox and Tilden Foundations.

period and into Little Spring of the subsequent season, the Creek went off on the hunt, leaving the aged and the infirm behind to watch the village. The "Summer" months, commencing with February, were Wind, Little Spring, Big Spring, Mulberry, Blackberry, and Little Heat. At approximately Little Spring (March), though sometimes much beyond, the Creek returned to work their fields and sow their crops. Soon afterwards war parties sallied forth against hostile towns, while those remaining behind settled into town routine. There they remained as long as two months after the busk, getting in and storing their harvest. It was especially while the crops were ripening that fishing parties worked the low streams and pools with fish poison, for

"... until ripening of the new corn," observed Swan (in Schoolcraft, 1856, V:274), "they are all straitened. . . ." It was during the months in town that religious and social life reached ceremonial heights.

By contrast with the Natchez, who forsook their villages for the hunt only in part and, at the most, only for one or two months, the Creek were absent over some six or seven months of the year. The Natchez also exceeded the Creek in population density, with 19.1 persons per 100 km², as against 12.2, a figure only exceeded among the interior tribes by the Choctaw, with 21.9 (Kroeber, 1939:145). The difference for Natchez and Creek may lie, however, less in the effectiveness of farming than in the availability of wild game close to the settlements. The deerskin trade in colonial times did much to foster hunting. In one year (1748), South Carolina and Georgia shipped out 160,000 skins (Crane, 1928:112). Whatever its cause, the seasonal dissolution of the Creek town had consequences for the organization of social life.

The Creek town (*talwa*) ranged in population from 100 or so to approximately 1000, and physically comprised some 30 to 100 houses, sometimes strung out in hamlets along the river, loosely clustered about a ceremonial nucleus, and with fields and forest intervening.

Each house had a small garden plot nearby, worked by the women of the family. Near the settlement was the town plantation, a common field in which boundaries marked off household allotments. An overseer, appointed annually, called together the men and women of the town to work the field, and shirkers were fined. The household tracts were worked and planted in rotation, to the accompaniment of songs; afternoons were given over to ball games and evenings to dancing. Yet there seems to have been some individual work, for Adair (1930:147) says that the relatives of a newly married Creek hoed out the cornfields of each of his wives. Hoes and digging sticks were the chief implements of cultivation; and since no use was made of fertilizers, the fields were soon exhausted and had to be abandoned. Corn in three varieties seems to have been raised, as well as beans, squashes, pumpkins and melons, and sunflowers, the seeds of which were eaten. When the crop began to ripen, the old women mounted scaffolds as watchers to drive off wild birds and animals. Each household harvested its own crop from the general plantation and stored it in its granary, but a portion went to the "chief's crib," as a reserve for public purposes. The plot of the *hilis-haya* (medicine-maker) of the town was planted and worked by old women in return for his services.

In addition to these crops, many wild plants were gathered and utilized, including wild rice, cane seed, persimmon, made into a cake, wild sweet potato, and other fruits, berries, and nuts. From a "saltish kind of grass" they extracted a saline condiment (Adair, 1930:122).

Each town owned hunting lands adjacent to it, though Bossu (Swanton, 1928a:405) reported of the Alabama that hunting parties went 60 to 100 leagues from town to hunt. Such parties left the old people behind, travelling by pirogue, camping by groups of related families, and returned with skins and smoked meat.

The chief animals hunted were the deer and bear. Individuals stalked deer with deer-head decoy. The Alabama hunter sweated before hunting and used an emetic to purify himself. When a party of hunters joined in a drive, a shaman accompanied them and, if they were successful, was paid a skin by each hunter. Each party decided on the division of game; and, after his return, each hunter divided the flesh among all the houses in the yard, sending some also to his own parents (Swanton, 1928a:405, 444–446). A piece of the deer, especially the first kill of the season, was sacrificed (Adair, 1930:124), and special treatment was accorded bear bones (Swanton, 1928a:445). Smaller animals such as the rabbit seem to have been hunted by men or boys armed with rabbit clubs. From time to time the forest underbrush was put to the torch to destroy the cover that impeded the hunt. Traps and snares were employed to take both animals and birds. Turtles and their eggs were simply gathered. Some of the animals taken were used only secondarily for food—thus bear grease was much sought to dress the hair and turkey feathers were attached to a textile foundation to make a feather cloak. Individual weapons used in the hunt included the bow and arrow, the latter with a feathered cane or wood shaft and a head of fish bone or stone. The blowgun, employed against small animals and birds, was made from a cane and shot an unpoisoned dart with thistle wadding.

Fish were taken with hook and line, with spear, or were shot with arrow. At night they might be speared by jacklight from a canoe.

North Carolina Algonkins ● The Town of Pomeiooc, a palisaded village, 1585. According to Hariot (after Swanton, 1946:630), "The townes of this contrie are in a manner like vnto those which are in Florida, yet they are not soe strong nor yet preserued with soe great care. They are compassed abowt with poles starcke fast in the grownde, but they are not verye stronge. The entrance os verye narrowe as may be seene by this picture, which is made accordinge to the forme of the towne of Pomeiooc. Ther are but few howses therin, saue those which belonge to the kinge and his nobles. On the one side is their tempel separated from the other howses, and marked with the letter A. Yt is builded rownde, and covered with skynne mats, and as it wear compassed abowt with cortynes without windowes, and hath noe lighte but by the doore. On the other side is the kings lodginge marked with the letter B. Their dwellinges are builded with certaine poles fastened together, and couered with matts which they turne op as high as they thinke good, and soe receive in the lighte and other. Some are also couered with boughes of trees, as euery man lusteth or liketh best. They keepe their feasts and make good cheer together in the midds of the towne as yt is described in the ... Figure. When the towne standeth fare from the water they digg a great ponde ... wherhence they fetche as muche water as they neede." (Courtesy, Rare Book Division, The New York Public Library, Astor, Lennox and Tilden Foundations.)

Weirs set across streams forced fish into traps set at their openings. Adair (1930:432ff.) describes fishermen driving their prey before them into their traps, as well as the use of hand nets and baskets. In summer, when the water was low, narcotic roots were mashed and thrown in, stupefying the fish, which rose to the surface and could be gathered by men, women, and children. It might be observed parenthetically that the Natchez, who exhibit so many evidences of affinity to the south, lacked both blowgun and fish poison, which were widespread in the Southeast.

Of domesticated animals, the Creek had only the dog, used somewhat by hunters, and sometimes eaten. Occasionally birds were kept as pets.

Creek cuisine employed an extensive variety of implements, from the wooden mortar and pestle through a wide variety of vessels of gourd, basketry, wood, and pottery, wooden or gourd stirring paddles and ladles, and shell or buffalo-horn spoons. Maize, of course, figured widely in their dishes, and grits, *sofki* (hominy), and succotash are still favorites. Many vegetable foods could be preserved; the flesh of fish and animals was frequently dried in the sun or on racks set over a fire. Even grapes were fire dried and stored (Bartram, 1958:254). "It is surprising," observes Adair (1930:439) "to see the great variety of dishes they make out of wild flesh, corn, beans, peas, potatoes, pompions, dried fruits, herbs and roots."

Material Culture

The Creek family occupied from one to four dwellings according to their wealth. When there were four, they were arranged around a yard; one served as kitchen and winter lodge, the second as summer and guest house, the third as granary and storehouse, as well as for a shade in hot weather, while the fourth was a warehouse for skins, furs, and other raw materials. All these structures were rectangular in ground plan and comprised a wooden frame upon which wattle-and-daub walls were built, the whole being roofed with cypress bark or shingles held down by poles laid across them. Some granaries were two stories in height, the lower floor being reserved for storage. Swan (in Schoolcraft, 1856, V:692ff.) attributed the frequent movement of towns to the flimsiness of house construction, but it is more probably to be attributed to soil exhaustion and the rapid growth of weeds. In early times the house had a fireplace in the middle without corresponding smokehole, but chimneys came to be popular soon after white contact. The fire was made with the wooden drill, and in moving was carried in a torch of burning oak bark. The bed was a low bench, extending around the wall and covered with animal skins. Adair (1930:452), speaking generally, mentions stools cut out of single blocks of poplar and chests made of boards sewn upon crossbars. Each household cooked separately; when eating they made frequent use of a large wooden spoon which was passed around to each in turn.

Each town had a ceremonial center, containing three special features. At one end was the rotunda, or "hot house." Sometimes situated on an elevation, it was circular in plan, with eight central posts and two concentric circles of posts supporting a roof daubed with clay and covered with pine bark. The walls likewise were plastered, and the only entrance lay variously to the east or south (Swanton, 1927; 1928a:174–190). The rotunda was used particularly for large meetings, and participants sat by rank and affiliation on seats covered with reeds or mats in the space between the two circles of posts. Its fairweather counterpart was the square ground, which lay beyond the entrance, and comprised a central plaza with four cabins or "beds," fronting upon it, often oriented to the cardinal directions. It was Swanton's view (1928a:191) that the cabins on the square ground were a subtropical development which largely duplicated the functions of the rotunda; in subsequent Creek history the latter disappeared.

Opposite the rotunda was the chunk yard, so called because the game of chunkey, a local variant of the hoop-and-pole game, was played here. Posts stood here at which captives were burnt, in addition to a tall pole, sometimes bearing an emblem of the town (Swanton, 1928a:190).

North Carolina Algonkins ● The Town of Secota(n), a village without palisades, 1585. According to Hariot (after Swanton, 1946:631), "Their townes that are not enclosed with poles are commonlye fayrer then such as are inclosed, as appereth in this figure which liuelye expresseth the towne of Secotam. For the howses are Scattered heer and ther, and they haue a gardein expressed by the letter E, wherin groweth Tobacco which the inhabitants call Vppowoc. They hauve also groaues wherin thei take deer, and fields wherin they sowe their corne. In their corne fields they builde as yt weare a scaffolde wher on they sett a cottage like to a rownde chaire, signiffied by F, wherin they place one to watche, for there are soch a nomber of fowles, and beasts, that vnless they keep the better watche, they would soone deuoure all their corne. For which cause the watcheman maketh continual cryes and noyse.

They sowe their corne with a certaine distance noted by H, other wise one stalke would choke the growthe of another and the corne would nnot come vnto his rypenes G. For the leaves thereof are large, like vnto the leaues of great reedes. They haue also a seuerall broade plotte C where after they haue ended their feaste they make merrie togither. Ouer against this place they haue a rownd plotte B, where they assemble themselues to make their solemne prayers. Not far from which place ther is a lardge buildinge A wherin are the tombes of their kings and princes ... Likewise, they haue garden notted bey the letter I wherin they use to sowe pomplons. Also a place marked with K wherin they make a fayre att their solemne feasts, and hard without the towne a riuer L, from whence they fetche their water. (Courtesy, Rare Book Division, The New York Public Library, Astor, Lenox and Tilden Foundations)

Early Creek towns, at least those upon the frontiers, were defended by stockades. The Upper Creek Red town of Ullibahali in De Soto's time was enclosed with a fence "of large timber sunk deep and firmly into the earth, having many long poles the size of the arm, placed crosswise to nearly the height of a lance, with embrasures, and coated with mud inside and out, having loop-holes for archery." (Lewis, 1907:185; Swanton, 1946:433.) With the growing success of Creek arms, town fortifications became less necessary. The sprawling towns of later history may only have been possible in the heyday of the Confederacy.

There was little specialization among the Creeks, save that dictated by the division of labor between the sexes. With the exception of a few civil and ceremonial town officials, there seem to have been no full-time specialists. Shamans were probably part-time practitioners. The distribution of raw materials led to some trade between the Coastal Plain and the interior, and it may be significant that in the time of De Soto the town of Cofitachequi, which seems to have been a market, lay on the fall line between them (Swanton, 1928a:452f.; 1946:736–742, Map 13). Private knowledge and skill apparently lay behind one person, a man from the Natchez town, who near the end of the eighteenth century is reported to have manufactured all the pipes used by the Creeks, since he alone knew where the pipestone was to be found (Swan, in Schoolcraft, 1855, V:692).

With the development of the fur trade, some men readily took up trading, and Romans (quoted in Swanton, 1928a:453), writing in the late eighteenth century, found "'few towns ... where there is not some savage residing, who either trades of his own flock, or is employed as a factor.'"

For the rest, most domestic utensils and weapons were made by members of the household that would use them, nor does there seem to have been an appreciable exchange of skills between households. In general, women made the baskets and mats, did the weaving and pottery making, prepared skins and made clothing, while the men did the wood and stone working and made the tools and utensils for their own use.

In basketry, the most frequent material was cane splints, often dyed in black or red before being woven into the desired vessel. Twilling was the favored technique, by which a large variety of baskets and sieves were made, as well as the mats so widely used in the house (Swanton, 1946:604–606). Coarse cordage was made from twisted mulberry or bass bark, finer stuff from silk-grass fiber. According to Adair (1930:453ff.), spinning was in the hands of old women; weaving took place on a weaving frame equipped with two heddles. The finished piece was painted on both sides in symbolic designs. Carpets, garters, sashes, shot pouches, and belts as well as women's clothing seem to have been so made. Occasionally, feathers of the turkey or flamingo were woven into the cloth to form feather cloaks.

Pottery was made from clay gathered from a community clay pit (Bartram, 1958:288), to which sand or crushed stone was added, the vessel being built up by coiling a fillet spirally upon a disc base. It was then shaped with a mussel shell, decorated by incising or by rubbing with a corn cob, and burnished with a stone. After drying, it was fired in a self kiln. Such vessels, usually with a rounded base, were of capacities that ranged from one pint to as much as ten gallons (Swanton, 1946:551–553).

The processing of skins, formerly the task of both sexes, came later to be the province of the women alone. The rawhide was first dried on a frame, then soaked in water for two days, after which it was scraped to remove fat and hair. After being dried again it was immersed in a solution of animal brains, then stretched, smoked, and finally dipped, for coloring, into an oak-bark solution. Presumably Creek women were unaware that the oak-bark dip produced true tanning of the hide.

The men on their part hollowed out the poplar pirogues which were the most common means of transportation, the largest holding 20 to 30 men. They also made the mortars, flaked flint blades and points, and pecked and polished into shape the stone disks used in the chunkey game. After the coming of the Europeans, some of them took up silversmithing, working Mexican coins into a variety of ornaments (Swanton, 1946:495, 559ff., 594).

Clothing, produced by the women, made large use of buckskin, though buffalo hide was also used for moccasins. With the exception of the latter, clothing was untailored; it was stitched together by means of a bone awl and thread of twisted sinew. The richness of clothing in De Soto's time is hinted at by that seen in the town of Cofitachequi, on the Savannah River. "In the barbacoas were large quantities of clothing, shawls of thread, made from the bark of trees, and others of feathers, white, gray, vermilion, and yellow, rich and proper for winter. There were also many well-dressed deer-skins, of colors drawn over with designs, of which had been made shoes, stockings, and hose." (Lewis, 1907:174.)

Men wore a breechclout thrust through a belt with flaps hanging down before and behind, together with leggings and moccasins, the latter apparently made from a single piece of soft buckskin. The basic costume of the women, in either textile or skin, was a knee-length skirt, held about the waist with a belt, to which they added moccasins which extended up to the calf of the leg (Bartram, 1958:319). Aboriginally women went bare from the waist up, but soon learned to add a short cloth jacket. In the winter both sexes often added a mantle. Boys went naked until they reached the age of puberty, while girls were invested with skirt and moccasins from the time they began to walk.

A large variety of ornaments were in use, including a silver ring set through the septum of the nose, wire wound about the margin of the dandy's ear (women wore small earrings), and necklaces, collars, gorgets, bracelets, and rings made in later times of silver. The head was not deformed. Men shaved off their hair, leaving only a roach running down the center and a fringe at the brow. Women in Bartram's day wore their hair in a "wreathed top-knot," decorated with many ribbons (1958:319). Both sexes frequently treated their hair with bear grease

and a red rouge. At an early age symbols were tattooed with needle and dye upon the arms, trunk, and thighs. The most elaborate designs were to be found on the bodies of the leading men. During the operation, the youth was expected to bear tattooing stoically as a sign of fortitude. As a boy of four exclaimed when the operation was at an end, "'Now, I'm a man, and a warrior too.'" (Pope, quoted in Swanton, 1946:533.) In addition, men might paint head, neck, and breast with vermilion and on occasion lay on other designs. Among the women, only prostitutes painted themselves.

Differences of rank were exhibited in clothing as well as adornment. Individuals of higher rank are said to have worn mantles of muskrat fur and feather mosaic. Leading warriors or chiefs are often depicted wearing a fillet decorated with porcupine-quill work or wampum and set in the front with crane or heron feathers. Shamans frequently wore clothing of white buckskin, and neophytes are said to have held a stuffed owl, worn on the head or carried in the hand (Bartram, 1958:320).

Social Organization

The basic household unit was the family, comprising a woman, who owned the house, her husband, and their children. This was home for the owner's classificatory "uncles," "brothers," and "sons," who ordinarily dwelt with their wives. In addition, aged dependents and orphans or war captives might form part of the household. Until old age the husband was expected to live with his wife, but he might often be found in those predominantly masculine retreats, the square ground or the rotunda. Particularly if he was wealthy, he might take two or more wives, preferably sisters, who might then share the same house and husband amicably. If they were unrelated, he might wisely establish them in separate domiciles. To take a second wife required the permission of the clan of his first wife, and the latter retained primacy within the family.

Proposals of marriage were opened by negotiation, sometimes by proxy, the brothers and uncles of the women being consulted. It was essential that she not belong to the clan of her swain's mother, and disfavor was shown to a marriage within his father's clan. Of a man marrying his father's clansmen it was said, scornfully, "He has fallen into his own [sofki] pot." (Swanton, 1928a:166.) Although the desires of the couple might initiate the matter, the

**North Carolina Algonkin ● Body painting and
dress of a noble. (After John White, illustrator
of Thomas Hariot's** *Narrative of the First
English Plantation of Virginia.* **London, 1588
and 1590. Hariot and White were members of
Raleigh's expedition. (Courtesy of Bureau of
American Ethnology, Smithsonian Institution)**

entire clan of the woman was sometimes
drawn into the discussion. If the man had
proven himself a good provider and was otherwise acceptable to her relatives, he paid a bride
price to them, and the pair went through a ceremony which sealed the union. Thereafter in
some towns it was forbidden for the man to
speak to his mother-in-law or the wife to her
father-in-law. Adair (1930:147) states of the
Creek men that, "if newly married [they] are
obliged by ancient custom, to get their own
relatives to hoe out the cornfields of each of
their wives, that their marriages may be continued: and the more jealous repeat the custom
every year, to make their wives subject to the
laws against adultery." Standards of sexual conduct made a clear distinction between premarital permissiveness, restricted only by the
rules of clan exogamy, and the exclusiveness of
the marital bond. Adultery was strongly con-
demned and harshly punished. In a marriage
dissolved on grounds of adultery or through
simple separation of the couple, the children
and house went with the mother. On the death

of a spouse, the survivor underwent a period of
mourning, four years for a widow, four months
for a widower. At the end of a year, Adair says
generally, the brother of the deceased might release the mourning woman by having intercourse with her, a release, Adair adds (1930:198)
eagerly sought by "the warm-constitutioned
young widows." At the end of the period of
mourning, the clan of the deceased selected
from its midst a new mate for the survivor. If
he declined their choice, he was free to marry
into some other clan. Widows and divorced
women sometimes became prostitutes.

Children born to a couple became the responsibility of the mother's clan, although her
husband was obliged to support them. Illegiti-
mate children or those born into needy families
might be killed in the first month of life by the
mother; after that it was adjudged murder
(Swan in Schoolcraft, 1856, V:272; Milfort
1959:155). Twins were considered blessed, and
it was thought that the younger would become
a great prophet. Shortly after birth the child
was named, and the girl's name was retained
for life. The boy was named for his totem or
from a physical peculiarity, the girl by kinship
term or some event connected with her birth.
Some names of men and women given by
Swanton (1928a:99ff.) suggest that both bore
names recalling the war exploit of a relative. In
illness the name might be changed. Elderly
parents sometimes took a teknonymous name.

"The invariable custom," says Swan (in
Schoolcraft, 1856, V:273ff.), "is, for the women
to keep and rear all the children, having the
entire control over them until they are able to
provide for themselves. They appear to have a
sufficient natural affection for them; they never
strike or whip a child for its faults. Their mode
of correction is singular: if a child requires punishment, the mother scratches its leg and thigh
with the point of a pin or needle until it
bleeds; some keep a jaw-bone of a garfish, having two teeth, entirely for the purpose." Ordinarily, the skin was wet before scratching; the
"dry-scratch" employed as punishment might,
in the case of adults, run down the middle of
the back from neck to heel. Children learned
early to follow the practice of their elders and
bathe in a stream before eating. Each clan in a
town had an elderly man of influence designated as "uncle," and the boys of the clan as
they grew older came under his tutelage, to be
instructed, admonished, and on occasion
whipped. If Adair's Chickasaw instance

(1930:163ff.) has a Creek counterpart, boys were whipped as a preventive as well as for punishment. Gradually, they became skilled in men's activities but took inferior places and performed menial roles for the men. It was not until he had won distinction in war or had secured eagle feathers that the boy received a busk title that gave him manly estate. Such titles, which might be taken in succession, consisted of the name of a totem animal, his or his father's, or of his town or a foreign tribe followed by some such epithet as "crazy," "heartless," or "warrior." Occasionally titles were bestowed upon women, and in later times upon a successful hunter. It would seem as well that they came to be bestowed upon boys (Swanton, 1928c:102).

Other avenues of choice were few for the Creek youth. Swanton, who speaks of transvestites as forming "an important factor in the social institution" in most parts of the Southeast outside of the northeastern segment (1928c:700) is silent as to their presence among the Creeks. Those individuals who were inclined to a shamanistic career might elect to take instruction in one of the schools conducted by practitioners.

For the girl, education continued under her mother and other clan women, her training including both practical and moral instruction. At her first menstruation, as in all recurrences and in confinement, she withdrew to a small hut at some distance from the dwellings to avoid polluting others. "The nonobservance of this separation, a breach of the marriage-law, and murder," says Adair (1930:130), "they esteem the most capital crimes." While the boy's attainment of adult status was public and formal and marked by the acquisition of a title, the girl's was signaled only by this biological event.

Beyond marriage and parenthood, the major life crisis recognized was death and its attendant rites. Upon the request of an ailing elder, his end might be hastened by his relatives. Afterwards, a hole was dug in the floor beneath the bed of the deceased, says Bartram (1958:328), lined with cypress bark, and here "they place the corps (sic) in a sitting posture, as if it were alive; depositing with him his gun, tomahawk, pipe and such other matters as he had the greatest value for in his life time." In later times, in Oklahoma, extended burial replaced the earlier sitting form, and the personal property buried with the deceased was reduced in favor of inheritance. In a subfloor burial, the family might prefer to build a new house, but

they might instead purify the old one, kindle a new fire in the hearth, and exorcise the ghost (Swanton, 1928a:395–397). Only among some of the northeastern Creek towns in De Soto's day are there indications of secondary burial and the ossuary. (Lewis, 1907:174; Swanton, 1946:45ff.)

Throughout his life, the individual was strongly conditioned in his relationships by the ties of kinship. Creek kinship terminology was of the normal Crow type (Murdock, 1949:247), merging parents' parallel siblings and their spouses with each other and classifying their offspring with one's own siblings. Parents' cross siblings were distinguished from each other, father's sister and her female descendants being equated with grandmother while mother's brother, the "uncle" of clan terminology, was given a distinct term and his children identified with one's own. Among his siblings the individual distinguished by age those of his own sex and merged their offspring with his own. Cross siblings were not thus distinguished and their children were given distinct terms. As Eggan (1937, 1966) and Spoehr (1947) have shown, this original terminology, which is consonant with a matrilineal kinship system, underwent changes under acculturative agencies toward a patrilineal emphasis, while stress upon lineage became instead generational, and range was increasingly restricted to the bilateral family.

Although by birth a person was a lifelong member of his mother's clan, that of his father likewise had importance for him. He did not ordinarily marry into it, for father's brother's children were equated with one's own siblings, and those terms were extended to all children of men in father's clan. A joking relationship obtained between persons whose parents—paternal as well as maternal—were clansmen. One was expected to show deference toward father's clan, praising it while belittling one's own clan, and to see to the proper respect of the eponym of both father's and one's own clan.

Perhaps the clearest expression of the paternal relationship was the conferring of the busk title. Owned by the clan, the busk title became available only at the death of the incumbent. If none was available in his own clan, a person might be assigned one for his lifetime from the clan of his father. Quite possibly this tendency gained strength in the growing patrilineal influence of later times.

Even in the eighteenth century, however,

there were already in evidence strong bonds between father and son, not only among the Creek, but also among the Choctaw, Chickasaw, and Cherokee. A wealthy man occasionally distributed his livestock among his children. When son or father was slain, the other avenged him. A man's son and his nephew sometimes vied for his favor. Indeed, a chief was not infrequently succeeded in office by his son. The most notable is the "Emperor" Brims of Coweta. During his lifetime he proposed two of his sons as his successors. When these died before him, two twin sons were named instead. Since they were minors, guardians were appointed for each, one guardian being a brother of the deceased chief. Finally, in the third generation, a minor grandson, again under guardianship, followed in office. It may be added that Brims did not neglect clan ties in his diplomacy, sealing a bond with the British by giving his sister's daughter in marriage to the son of an officer (Corkran, 1967). The ties between father and son in the eighteenth century were recorded primarily for leading men and may in fact have been largely limited to them, becoming general only at a later date. Willis (1963) who has brought these data together, suggests that the colonial presence, with its stress on Indian hunting, trading, warfare, and politics—and, it might be added, the example of the patrilineal traders—elevated the relative status of Creek men and fostered paternal ties.

In historic Creek society, however, the maternal clan was preeminent in personal loyalties. It was a source of strength that men like Alexander MacGillivray had secure status among the Creek as a member of his mother's clan and indeed was heir to a minor chieftainship in it (Caughey, 1938:8). Creek clans, like those of most other tribes of the Southeast, bore names drawn predominantly from local biota, through the range as indicated by the following, drawn from Swanton's list (1928a:115–117) of some 46 Creek clans: Alligator, Arrow, Bear, Beaver, Bison, Cane, Corn, Deer, Fish, Lye Drip, Panther, Salt, Spanish, Wind, and Wolf. In the traditional past, clans are said to have lived separately, but historic Creek towns contained from 4 to 28 clans. Within the town, clan dwellings were not clustered within a special clan quarter, but were interspersed. Members of a clan were considered related to each other through some distant ancestor, and to have a special relationship to the clan eponym. The social flow of borrowing and hospitality lay chiefly within the clan. A visitor to another town sought out the house of a clansman, where he would remain for the duration of his stay. Stiggins (in Nunez, 1958:132), through his Natchez mother a member of the Confederacy, saw in Creek clanship, crosscutting as it did town loyalties, "the strongest link in their political and social standing as a nation...."

Clansmen were jealous of the proper treatment of the clan totem, and a person of another clan treating the eponym with disrespect might be fined by the offended clan. Speck (1907:115) insists of the Tuskegee Creek that a clansman might neither kill nor eat his eponym, but Swanton (1928a:168) takes a more moderate view, pointing to the general use of deer and bear meat, despite the circumstance that clans of those names were prominent among the Creek.

Clansmen sat together in public ceremonies, and each clan usually had an annual council, held during the busk, at which each clan or group of clans was addressed by the senior "uncle," who reviewed the year, bestowing praise and blame where they were due.

Although in general clans were on an equal footing, a few enjoyed a certain prominence. The Wind clan, for example, frequently furnished either the town chief or his *heniha*, its women were addressed deferentially as "grandmother," and in the punishment of adulterers it alone might take up again clubs once laid aside. On the other hand, there were some clans, often the smaller, which were deemed inferior.

There were two larger groupings of clans, the phratry and the moiety. The phratry was usually nameless and might include from two to nine clans, considered in some way related. Sometimes a small clan was regarded as an offshoot of a larger member clan, but often they were held to be coordinate. A myth or legend often accounted for the linkage. Thus Panther and Deer were associated through the mythic friendship of their eponyms, an amity disrupted at noon when the former slew Deer. Their association was accordingly said to last through noon. On the other hand, Alligator and Turkey clans were said to be linked because both came from eggs. A clan, linked in one phratry in one town might have quite different associations in another. Within the phratry, one clan might be given precedence, being termed the "uncle" clan, and it was not always the largest or the most influential. Thus, the Wind clan, in both instances more numerous, was "nephew" within phratries respectively to Skunk and Fish clans. Phratries often met together, during the busk to review the year, rather than as separate clans. Analysis of square-ground seating shows that phratry-linked clans tended to occupy the same "bed." Because of the putative linkage between them, members of the same phratry were considered to be related, and in consequence were forbidden to marry. A point of conflict sometimes arose when a man sought the hand of a girl in another town whose clan, though locally not in phratry with his, was so linked in her town.

An analysis of phratry size, in number of component clan, as listed by Swanton (1928a:123–127), shows that the more populous Upper Creek had far smaller phratries than the Lower Creek, with the Seminole, containing a large Creek element, intermediate. It seems possible that there was an upper limit for phratry associations and that the larger the size of the clans the fewer were the number to be found associated in phratries.

Within each town there was a second grouping of clans into two moieties, termed "White" and "Chiloki" ("of a different speech"). The origin of the moiety division was mythically linked with the ball game, and its chief function, at least in historic times, was to determine the sides for intratown practice games, although the distinctions were also recognized in the feathers worn at the Feather Dance. The moiety did not regulate marriage, at least in recent times. (It will be recalled that ceremonial moieties, White and Red, seem to play a part in the ball game, as well as other ritual occasions, among the Natchez.)

It is theoretically possible to establish a moiety division that does not transgress phratry lines, and this situation was to be found at some towns, such as the Upper Creek town of Talledaga. On the other hand, it was also frequent to find towns, such as Abihka-in-the-West, in which phratry-linked clans were in opposite moieties. The latter, in the view of Swanton (1928a:163–165) is unusual. While some clans were in one moiety in one town and the opposite in another, certain clans were almost everywhere identified with one moiety. Thus the Wind and Bear clans were almost always White, the Raccoon, Water Moccasin, and Potato, Chiloki.

There was a further functional relationship.

White clans were associated with peace and Chiloki with war. The distinction, related in a measure to the division between "White" and "Red" towns, referred to functions or offices transmitted within clan lines, rather than to individuals, for White clans provided warriors as well as did the Chiloki.

Thus there is evident an interaction between a principle of paired, opposed duality, with some functional specialization of clans and an order of phratry association based upon putative kinship. The organization of the town itself further exemplifies that conflict.

The Creek town formed a strong governmental unit. Each town had a ceremonial center, possessed such property as the discoidal chunkey stones (Adair, 1930:431), and owned land in habitual use. Some seem to have had as well a distinctive symbol. Each week, and daily in the leading town of Tukabahchee, the men of the town met together in the square to take the emetic black drink and to discuss public affairs. "No doubt," opined Stiggins (in Nunez, 1958:36), "but their custom of drinking the black drink originated through political motives, viz., for the purpose of assembling the townspeople frequently at their town house or square in order to keep them united, for the harmony subsisting among the people of a town is noted ... as the usages and customs of every town is (sic) similar and the men all know the unity and simpathy (sic) of a town people, the men of one town will approach another town with seeming diffidence. . . ." The solidarity of town loyalties has continued to be a force in modern times (Opler, in Spicer, 1952).

A dual division into civil and war officials was to be found. At the head of the civil administration was the chief, or *miko*, drawn in Red towns usually from the Chiloki, in White towns from White clans. Save in unusual circumstances, he was chosen from the same clan as his predecessor, the choice being exercised during a session in the square ground. In that selection, White clans had special voice and it was they that inducted him. The candidate was humble before the honor and might later resign, but while in office he was given precedent, occupied the seat of honor in the rotunda and town square, and in ceremony was borne in a litter. At least in later times the chief was masculine, but the De Soto expedition has left a memorable picture of the Lady of Cofitachequi, niece of the woman chief of that town (Lewis, 1907:172–177).

Associated with the miko in his civil administration was a "twin chief"—note the duality—sometimes drawn from a different clan. His council comprised three classes of officials. The precinct officers (also called miko) were usually of the same clan as the town chief. The *heniha* were usually from a White clan and were originally drawn from the Wind clan itself. Finally, the "beloved men" were those retired from a distinguished career as war leaders, precinct-officers, and those who had otherwise made their mark in public service. In council, the miko was served by a speaker and by a war speaker, usually drawn from his clan.

Together with his counselors, the miko ruled the town, presiding in sessions in the rotunda and town square, and was responsible for the food stored in the public granary and for the feasts for which it was expended. It was he who set the busk time and his "beloved men" and heniha who made the arrangements for it. The heniha were responsible for the direction of public works, for the construction of houses for new settlers, for communal work in the fields, and served as well in the busk, having charge of the black drink. The miko and his council, at least in later times, served as a court of arbitration and decision in legal matters, and they took the lead in deciding for peace or war.

Centralization of legal control in early Creek history was at best incipient. The miko and his council acted more as an expression of public opinion than as an intervening authority, and execution was at the hands of the clansmen of the victim. Murder, within which were construed the consequences of sorcery, of carelessness in menstrual withdrawal, or of sheer accident, could only be avenged by a corresponding loss to the clan of the murderer. If the victim was inferior in status to his murderer, the latter's younger brother might be slain in his stead, or the offended clan might choose to adopt the murderer in the place of the man he had slain (Hewitt, 1939:147–149). Public interest might be subordinated to clan vengeance. In 1808, the Singer, a ranking chief of the Creek Nation, was deliberately slain in retribution for the act of his brother, who had killed another Creek mistaken for an enemy and who was even then on his way to explain the accident (Stiggins, in Nunez 1958:134ff.).

While other crimes found amnesty at the annual busk, unavenged murder was always kept green. The murderer might gain sanctuary by fleeing to a White town, although should he be driven out again he might be slain. Bartram (1958:246ff.) recalls that old Apalachicola, a Lower Creek White town, was abandoned after a series of misfortunes attributed to a breach of sanctuary in the massacre of European traders who had taken refuge there. With the centralization of legal authority under the promptings of American officials, public trial by the miko and his council was substituted for clan vengeance and the White towns lost their character as sanctuaries.

Discipline in premarital sexual affairs was in the hands of the clan council and sarcastic censure, dry-scratching, or flogging might be administered. Incest between phratry members brought the long scratch, while between clan members it might bring death. The stringency with which adultery was punished has been marked since De Soto's time. Under changes instituted by Abihka, the punishment at the hands of the husband and his kin was graduated: a beating and cropped hair and ears for the wife, a beating and cropped ears for her lover. Subsequent offenses brought a cropped nose and upper lip, and finally, death. When in more recent times theft became a problem, a similar gradation was maintained for frequent offenses: whipping, then ear-crop, and for the incorrigible, death.

A person failing to attend the busk or spring planting, or remiss in other duties, was liable to fine or confiscation of property by the town council. In disputes over the payment of debts, the council mediated differences.

Some persons sought by flight to avoid retribution for murder, adultery, or another offense; several towns were founded by such fugitives.

Police action in time of peace and leadership in war were in the hands of the principal *tastanagi*, the main war chief, and associated tastanagi. These officials also participated in important council discussions. The war chief was chosen by the miko and his beloved men; the tastanagi as a whole might come from either White or Red clans, with some preference for the latter. Swanton (1928a:304ff.) sees a clan principle emergent in their selection. Two lower grades of warriors included the assistants of the tastanagi and the warriors with busk title.

War was decided in council and announced by the head war chief. When endemic hostility existed against any other people, any war leader might gather two or three followers, but it was the head war chief of the town who or-

● THE GAME OF LACROSSE—CHOCTAW
A great variety of games was played across native America. These ranged, apart from the many gambling games, from such team sports as the unstructured kick-ball of the Eskimo to the highly formalized ball-court games of the Maya. Among the Indians of the Southeast, the court or playing field can be traced to influences stemming from Middle America. The games themselves, however, consisted of chunkey, a variant of the widely spread hoop-and-pole game, and of the game suggestive of field hockey, generally called lacrosse. The game of lacrosse has been credited to the various Algonkin tribes of the Great Lakes region (Swanton, 1946:674). These tribes played the game with a single racquet or stick, while the Southeastern peoples added a second. This was made on a frame and strung with twisted squirrel skin or hemp. The ball was made of tightly packed deerskin and covered with deer hide.

This Choctaw game, played by men of status, warriors, and nobles resplendent in the finery of egret feather costumes, wearing the insignia of town, clan, and moiety, is best described by Catlin's eyewitness account.

"Then the game was commenced, by the judges throwing up the ball at the firing of a gun. At that instant the struggle ensued between the players, who were six or seven hundred in numbers, and were mutually endeavoring to catch the ball in their sticks and throw it home between their respective goals. Whenever this was successfully accomplished it counted one point for the game. In these desperate struggles for the ball, hundreds of strong young Indian athletes were running together and leaping, actually over each other's heads and darting between their adversary's legs, tripping and throwing, and foiling each other in every possible manner, and every voice raised to its highest key in shrill yelps and barks! Every mode is used that can be devised to oppose the progress of the foremost who is likely to get possession of the ball; and these obstructions often meet desperate resistance, which terminate in violent scuffles and sometimes in fisticuffs; when their sticks are dropped and the parties are unmolested whilst settling matters between themselves ... There are times when the ball gets to the ground, and such a confused mass rushing together around it ... when the condensed mass of ball-sticks, and shins, and bloody noses is carried around different parts of the playing field ... Each time the ball is passed between the goal posts of either party, one was counted toward their game and there was a halt of about a minute. Then the game was again started by the judges, and another similar struggle ensued."

Surprising to the European is the number of players involved. In the accounts of some of the other Southeastern tribes, such as the Creek or Cherokee, it is said that not so many players took part and there is some suggestion of equal numbers playing on opposing teams.

But it must not be thought that here was a mere social pastime. True, heavy wagers could be laid on the outcome of a day-long game and there was also present the sense of sport and play. As among many of the North American tribes, games came to relate to the ceremonial calendar. In the Southeast as elsewhere, they came to be a part of the religious complex of world renewal, a part of the rituals designed to restore order in the universe and to bring about the continued welfare of man through another cycle of a year. All of the peoples of the area approached the ball game, as indeed the other aspects of the great yearly festivals, with a sense of religious feeling. The players in the game were expected to remain continent, avoiding sexual relations for a prescribed period beforehand, they fasted, and they took emetics. The game, as part of an elaborate body of ceremonial, thus drew the groups together and reinforced the sense of solidarity in clan and tribe.

dinarily led a party that numbered forty warriors. The Confederacy made possible larger forces and a body of nearly 1000 warriors is on record (Swanton, 1928a:409, note 1).

The conduct of war was hedged about with ritual. When the war leader beat the drum and the warriors assembled, they fasted for three days together and partook of an emetic before starting out to war. Each warrior provided his own weapons, carrying bow and arrows, knife, tomahawk, war club, and spear, as well as parched corn for provisions. Early Spanish sources mention also rawhide armor, helmets, and shields. On the warpath, the leader acted

as a war priest, assisted by the "beloved waiter," taking turns in carrying the sacred ark, with its ritual vessels and sacred objects. The waiter fed each warrior in order to preserve his purity (Adair, 1930:168ff.) A warrior who had an inauspicious dream might without ridicule return home. The party as organized stressed duality: leaders included the war chief and his assistant, warrior and assistant, scout and assistant, as well as supply officers.

A special power may have been felt to reside in the head war chief. Milfort, who claims to have led the combined forces of the Confederacy, states that should the head war chief be in danger of being taken by the enemy, the warrior closest to him slew and scalped him himself; then all withdrew on signal to select his successor. On returning from a campaign, the minor band leaders stripped the head war chief of his clothing, which they tore into small pieces to be made part of their individual medicine bundles (Milfort, 1959:156, 197).

In the conduct of their war, the raiders sought to penetrate the enemy's heartland, and the scalps of women and children were highly valued as evidence that they had succeeded. Since towns were often defended by moats and palisades, surprise and a dawn attack were favored, fire arrows being used to burn out the foe. After the first onslaught, the dead were scalped and the captives led back. Seasoned warriors among the prisoners in early days could only look forward to being burned at the stake by the women of the victorious towns. They could escape their fate only by making good their flight to sanctuary in the house of the head priest or in a White town (Swanton, 1946:695).

When the party returned in triumph from the war, bearing trophies and escorting prisoners, they were ceremoniously received. Each person who had taken a scalp either deposited it in the town square or divided it among his friends. In the public acclaim, says Milfort (1959:154–155), scalps were graded by the leaders according to the dangers run in taking them—an outlook, it may be added, suggestive of that of the Plains Indians in counting coup upon the enemy. "It is in proportion to the number and merit of these scalps," he asserts, "that advancement takes place, both in civil and military life."

Peace was restored with solemn ceremonies, in which the *cassina* emetic, the calumet, and the color white were prominent, and the miko and his council were the principal representatives of the town.

Captives were enslaved, unless prior to going out on the warpath the Creeks had "devoted to death" all of that town or region. There was to be sure a certain onus to their position, and an adult slave might sometimes be killed in revenge for an earlier death at the hands of his tribesman, but it was principally in lack of freedom and of political voice that they suffered. Their children bore no stigma and were free. In colonial times, slaves became a valuable commodity in trade, and thus added an incentive for intertribal warfare (Crane, 1928).

In peace and war, such concerted action as existed was dominated by the Confederacy. Two geographical divisions were known, the more numerous Upper Creek and the Lower Creek. In each, towns were characterized in two "fires," as either White or Red, the designation following in the main the moiety of the miko's clan (Swanton, 1928a:196ff.). White towns, in their character as sanctuaries, often took in foreign towns, as the Natchez were received by Abihka, and the Yuchi by Kasihta. The Yuchi towns were united under their own head chief within the Confederacy (Woodward, 1939:40) and for a long time retained their own customs and laws (Hawkins, quoted in Swanton, 1922:310). Offshoot towns retained affiliation in the "fire" of the mother town. Intertown matches in the two-stick ball game known as "the younger brother to war" were conducted only between "fires," and were preceded by a contract between towns. At least in more recent times the head war chief took a principal part in these negotiations, and a town losing a stipulated number of games went over to the "fire" of the victor (Haas, 1940; Spoehr, 1941).

Within each geographical division, there was a leading town for each "fire," although the fortunes of individual towns led to occasional replacement. Among the Upper Creek, Coosa, on the river of the same name, had anciently been the leading White town. By about 1700 it had so declined that its place was taken by Abihka, often linked in migration legends with the principal Lower towns and important as the "door-shutter" against the Cherokee and Chickasaw. The principal Red town of the Upper Creek, Tukabahchee, lay upon the Tallapoosa. It had special ties with the Shawnee, and it has in fact been suggested that it was Shawnee in origin (Swanton, 1922:277ff.; Witthoft and Hunter, 1955). The principal Lower towns in the eighteenth century were Coweta (Red) and Apalachicola (White). Subsequently, Kasihta, closely linked in legend with Coweta (Swanton, 1922:216), and like it a Red town (Corkran, 1967:5, note 1), replaced Apalachicola as the leading White town. The leaders were thereafter known as "the four foundation towns" of the Confederacy. A rivalry existed between the leaders of each "fire." A council of the Confederacy was held annually in spring or fall at one of the leading towns, chosen, says Bartram (1958:246) according to the topic for discussion. War was debated in a Red Town, while proposals for peace were put forward in a White one. At this time mikos met, sitting by order of personal status, in ceremonious consultation. In their deliberations, oratory was highly valued. Decisions appear to have been made by a consensus of a few leaders and were imparted to the people by a speaker.

Milfort (1959:33–35, 142, 184) mentions bead belts which served as mnemonic devices and records of past events, including the legendary migrations. These he saw in the custody of the "old chiefs," the beloved men. They seem to have figured in negotiations with the Choctaw and Cherokee, as well as with other tribes, and to have functioned like the "wampum" belts of the tribes of the Northeast.

As late as the eighteenth century, the Confederacy was still loosely knit. Councils were held irregularly and separately by Upper and Lower divisions, and council decisions were not considered by dissident towns to be binding. When the chiefs, sitting in council, had determined that a Creek, having broken the terms of a treaty, must be put to death, the accord of his clan had first to be secured to avoid a vendetta. In a war against the Chickasaw, at the end of the century, Abihka, which linked itself with that people, refused to participate and later mediated the restoration of peace (Hawkins, in Swanton, 1928a:49–51). The Abihka action had many a counterpart in dealings with Whites, in which in general the more acculturated Lower Creek towns took the initiative.

In the late decades of the century, the Confederacy became increasingly close knit, reaching a brief pinnacle under the leadership of Alexander McGillivray. In 1783 he was simultaneously invested by the council of chiefs with the offices of head chief and head war chief of the Confederacy (Cotterill, 1954:56). The better to place the nation on a war footing—for the main body of the Creek had sided with the

British—he instituted internal reforms, giving the war chiefs control in their towns, supplanting the mikos. It was a measure resisted by the mikos, but in the end McGillivray prevailed. When he died after a decade of leadership, no successor again attained a like concentration of powers (Swanton, 1928a:324–327; Caughey, 1938; Cotterill, 1954:57–99). The subsequent changes within the Nation are well described by Swanton (1928a), Foreman (1934), and above all by Debo (1941).

The success of the Confederacy may be attributed to its strategic position athwart routes of communication (Myer, 1928), to its success in minimizing internal, and concerting external, warfare, and to the incorporation of foreign peoples, like the Alabama, Shawnee, and Yuchi, by which the Creek losses were made up.

Ceremonial and Religious Life

Town life was focused upon the ceremonial center, in the rotunda or square of which the miko and his council were to be seen in daily session, drinking the cassina emetic, called by Europeans the "black drink," smoking, and deliberating upon civic affairs. The seating arrangement differed from town to town. Bartram, (1958:285) thus describes Atasi, Red town of the Upper Creeks "... the aged chiefs and warriors [are], seated on their cabbins or sophas, on the side of the house opposite the door [of the rotunda], in three classes or ranks, rising a little, one above or behind the other; and the white people and red people of confederate towns in the like order on the left hand; a transverse range of pillars, supporting a thin clay wall about breast high, separates them: the king's cabbin or seat is in front, the next back of it the head warriors, and the third or last accommodates the young warriors, &c., the great war chief's seat or place is on the same cabbin with, and immediately to the left hand of the king and next to the white people, and to the right hand of the mico or king the most venerable head men and warriors are seated." As noted above, the square-ground seatings of later days (Swanton, 1928a:205–296) show a tendency for phratry-linked clans to occupy the same "bed." Of the four "beds," oriented to the cardinal directions, that of the warriors often faced either that of the miko, or of the henihas, the boys and visitors occupying the remaining "bed." The arrangement, however, varied widely between towns. The "beds" seem at times to have borne painted and sculptured depictions of clan totems, and the pillars of the council house that of the town tutelary animal (Bartram, 1958:288; cf. Swanton, 1928a:235).

The rotunda, with its spiral cane fire, possessed certain elements of the sacred. Thus Swanton (1928a:626) points out that certain illnesses might be cured by an offering to it. However, the principal repository lay in the miko's "bed." "It is partitioned off by a mud-wall about breast-high, behind the white seat, which always stands to the left hand of the red-painted war-seat," says Adair (1930:84), "there they deposit their consecrated vessels, and supposed holy utensils, none of the laity daring to approach that sacred place, for fear of particular damage to themselves, and general hurt to the people, from the supposed divinity of the place." Here, in the town of Tukabahchee, were kept the sacred brass plates which were brought out during the busk.

Chief among the priests was the *hilis haya,* or "medicine-maker," who had charge of the sacred objects which were used in the preparation of the cassina and other emetics for the busk, and who besides had responsibility for community health. In match games between towns, the hilis haya prepared the emetic to be taken by the players (Swanton, 1928a:462, 464ff.), a practice similar to that of hunters (*ibid,* p. 445), and was responsible as well for the war medicines (Hewitt, 1939:156). He alone of the religious practitioners had his fields tilled for him. Sometimes heads of the miko's clan (indeed, Bartram says that on occasion the miko himself) were "medicine-makers" (Swanton, 1928b:620ff.).

The cult of the hilis haya thus was more immediately connected with concepts of ritual purity than with special divinities. Yet there was a connection between the Supreme Being of the Creek, the heavenly Breath Holder, and the sacred fire kindled at the busk, and he seems, like the Natchez deity, to have been in some way linked with the sun. It was he who ordained Creek clans (Speck, 1907:146–148), and to him offerings were made of the first buck killed in the spring, and thereafter a morsel of flesh at each meal. Likewise connected with the sacred emetic were two other celestials, Yahola and Hayuya, whose names were recited by the libation bearers as they offered up the conch shell of emetic (Bartram, 1958:286). Other such beings, however, Thunder and Wind, had no direct relationship with the busk.

In Creek conception, the Breath Holder presided over the realm of the blessed dead. Below his realm lay the mundane world, square in shape and floating upon the waters, and beneath it there was the domain from which mankind had ascended in its emergence. After death, the spirit followed along the Milky Way, passing perils along the path. Only those who had led an upright life found their way at last to the land of the blessed.

The Creek world was peopled by supernatural creatures, of which the snakes had a peculiar fascination, for there were many, the horned snake, the celestial snake, tie snake, and sharp-breasted snake, among others. Some snakes were linked with the waters, while on land such preternatural beings as the "little people" and giants were at home. Birds and animals likewise were endowed with supernatural powers and dwelt apart from men in their own towns.

Powers were everywhere. He who found the *sabia*, a lustrous colored crystal believed to be the product of a plant, gained with it the sacred song formula and could then lure deer and women to him. The world was replete with supernatural forces which could help or harm mankind. The warrior who ate the heart of a slain enemy, the Creek who eschewed possum and mole, were aware of those powers, and dreams and visions were a token of a mystic communication.

Of the practitioners in the supernatural, the "knowers" or prophets were often the younger of twins, so that their sacred power may have been by that measure inherent. The prophets, always men, were few in number, and principally devoted to clairvoyance and the diagnosis of disease. Their performance included sleight of hand, and, at least among the Alabama, involved also a variant of the shaking tent rite (Bossu, in Swanton, 1928b:616). While the latter performance is often thought of as principally northern (Hallowell, 1942; Ray, 1941), possible cognates are to be found in the tropical forests of South America (Lowie, 1948:49ff.). "Knowers" might at times act as weather shamans, but the rainmakers at least seem to have been distinct.

The second class of sacred persons were known as "fasting men," or doctors, of whom the medicine makers were the most prominent. They received instruction in a series of graduated medicine schools, in which, isolated in the forest under the ministration of a teacher, a small group of novices fasted, partook of magi-

cal emetic, and received instructions. After four days the novice took a sweat bath and returned home. For the next twelve months, he had to observe dietary and other restrictions, use the scratching stick, and end by sweating again. After five or six such sessions, there was an eight-day session. Instruction was directed to the graduated curing of wounds, and a vision during the fast was an omen for the future. "Fasters" from the fifth degree on wore special insignia. They frequently scratched their limbs to preserve their health and observed dietary taboos.

Curing required initial diagnosis, often by a "knower," for the cure must be matched with the ailment. There were many ailments linked with animals, birds, fish, and other beings, including the spirits of the dead, and for each there was an appropriate medicine or medicines and formulas (Speck, 1907:121–133, 148ff.). Witches were a second source of illness, for they flew, disguised as owls, to poison their victim, to steal heart or spirit, or to shoot a foreign object or "pain" into his body. There were protective practices, such as scarifying the limbs to cleanse the body of "bad" blood, and the use of "old man's tobacco" to avert the spirits of the dead; and medicines were hung over the door to ward off malevolent forces.

When the source of disease was known, the "faster" who had the appropriate powers set about the cure. He might prescribe a sweat bath, using water which had been enchanted. Often the patient would be laid heading east, and treated with medicines ritually gathered and prepared in an infusion, into which the shaman blew through a reed, while reciting the sacred formulas. In such ritual, the colors, green, red, black, and white, the cardinal directions, and the number, four, were ceremonial constants. The patient drank some of the infusion and some was rubbed on his body. Scarification and sucking were employed to extract a foreign body. Such cures might be performed by a woman (Swan, in Schoolcraft, 1856, V:271), but more usually the "fasters" were men. Women may have been more numerous among those who healed with herbal simples.

While there was much concern with the rituals of curing, shamans granted the proper power served as weather shamans and to bring success in hunting. Failure in weather control was likely to be attributed by the shaman to the immorality of his clients (Adair, 1930:93ff.)

while they in turn were likely to blame a destructive flood upon him, for which a shaman was indeed shot (Adair, 1930:91). Like the curer, the successful weather shaman was well rewarded.

Shamans sometimes held public contests of their prowess. As persons of great power they were envied and feared, but along with old people they were often suspected of malevolence. Both witch and shaman might have the same teacher, but the indwelling powers of the witch were lizards that compelled him periodically to slay others, beginning with a member of his own family. If he were reluctant, his powers might be exorcised. When a patient died, the shaman treating him attempted to divert suspicion upon another, but often suffered a beating or death at the hands of the outraged bereaved. If his powers became too strong for the witch or shaman, they might destroy him and resume their animal form.

The rich socio-ceremonial life of the Creek town was punctuated by dances, often held near the full moon, and accompanied by such instruments as the pottery water drum, gourd rattle, and turtle-shell leglets. Many dances bore animal names, though by no means all, and there is no indication of a special connection between such dances and the correspondingly named clans. Indeed, Bartram (1958:321) states that some of their favorite dances and songs came from their foe, the Choctaw, who had a reputation for talent in composing new songs. Some dances were seasonal, like the popular Horned Owl dance, held in September, or the Buffalo dance, held during the busk, and these, as well as such others as the Snake and Skunk dances, had a decidedly ceremonial cast. Some, for example those of Fox and Skunk, were danced only by women, and "dog whippers" served to regulate the former. The Old Man's dance, a clownish dance, was performed by youths wearing gourd masks.

Such dances, which may have tended to outlive sacred associations, may at one time have been part of a yearly cycle, initiated by the busk. This "fast," as the Creek term, *poskita*, has it, fell in August, at the harvest of the main maize crop, and constituted a ceremonial purification of the town, marked by the extinction of the old fire and the kindling of the new, the purging of all by the drinking of the sacred emetic and by fasting, and the ritual washing away of sins. It marked the amnesty for all crimes save those construed as murder, the public award of war titles, and exceptionally a period of sexual license connected with fecundity (Speck, 1907:139, 144). New marriages were not considered binding until they had passed the first busk. Clan or phratry councils met apart to hear "uncles" admonish them, and dances and a ball game formed ceremonial segments. In the four- or eight-day ceremony, the town sat in the square in their proper "beds," and after a day of feasting watched the medicine maker (sometimes the miko himself) kindle the new fire with a drill, from which in turn the fires of the rotunda and individual hearths, swept clean, were relit. Upon sunset of the eighth day, the men washed themselves ritually pure in the river, and the proceedings were brought to a close by an address of counsel by the miko. In this ceremony the Creek town redefined its social order, phrased anew its position in the cosmos, and, cleansed and rededicated, entered upon the new year.

Suggested readings

General

COTTERILL, R. S.
1954   *The Southern Indians: The Story of the Civilized Tribes before Removal.* University of Oklahoma Press.

FOREMAN, G.
1934   *The Five Civilized Tribes.* University of Oklahoma Press.

SWANTON, J. R.
1946   *The Indians of the Southeastern United States.* Bureau of American Ethnology, Bulletin 137.

Catawba

HUDSON, C. M.
1970   *The Catawba Nation.* University of Georgia Press.

Cherokee

DEBO, A.
1940   *And Still the Waters Run.* Princeton University Press.

GEARING, F.
1962   *Priests and Warriors: Social Structures for Cherokee Politics in the 18th Century.* American Anthropological Association, Memoir 93.

GILBERT, W. H.
1943   *The Eastern Cherokees.* Bureau of American Ethnology, Bulletin 133.

Chickasaw

GIBSON, A. M.
1971   *The Chickasaws.* University of Oklahoma Press.

Choctaw

DEBO, A.

1961   *The Rise and Fall of the Choctaw Republic.*
University of Oklahoma Press.

SWANTON, J. R.

1931   *Source Material for the Social and Ceremonial Life
of the Choctaw Indians.* Bureau of American
Ethnology, Bulletin 103.

Creek

CORKRAN, D. H.

1967   *The Creek Frontier, 1540–1783.* University of
Oklahoma Press.

DEBO, A.

1941   *The Road to Disappearance.* University of
Oklahoma Press.

SWANTON, J. R.

1928   *Social Organization and Social Usages of the
Indians of the Creek Confederacy.* Bureau of
American Ethnology, Report 42.

1928   *Religious Beliefs and Medical Practices of the
Creek Indians.* Bureau of American Ethnology,
Report 42.

1922   *Early History of the Creek Indians and Their
Neighbors.* Bureau of American Ethnology,
Bulletin 73.

Natchez and Neighbors

SWANTON, J. R.

1911   *Indian Tribes of the Lower Mississippi Valley and
Adjacent Coast of the Gulf of Mexico.* Bureau of
American Ethnology, Bulletin 43.

Powhatan

STERN, T.

1952   "Chickahominy: The Changing Culture of a
Virginia Indian Community." *Proceedings of the
American Philosophical Society* 96: 157–225.

Yuchi

SPECK, F. G.

1909   *Ethnology of the Yuchi Indians.* University of
Pennsylvania Museum, Anthropological
Publications, no. 1.

X

Meso-america

Introduction

The consideration of Mesoamerica must not only include a description of the ethnographic present, in this instance the Spanish Conquest in the early sixteenth century, but must also take as one of its most important components the culture history as a whole. The chief reason for this departure from the general approach of this volume is that here we are dealing with human groups possessing a complex civilization. This implies the possession of writing, cities, complex division of labor, the presence of social status differentiation to the point of classes, and the presence of political states, to mention some of the more important attributes of civilization. Consequently, the approach will be threefold: (1) a generalized description of the area at the time of Spanish Conquest, giving a picture of the culture for the ethnographic present; (2) a summary treatment of the culture history of Mesoamerica indicating the major points of cultural change, and; (3) the ethnographic treatment of two ethnic groups as representative of the culture history of the area—the Classic Maya and the Aztec.

Mesoamerica is the term proposed by Paul Kirchhoff (Kirchhoff, 1952:17–30) to distinguish a region bounded on the north by a line running from the mouth of the Rio Panuco in northern Vera Cruz southwestward to the Rio Lerma in central Mexico and thence northwestward to the state of Sinaloa; bounded on the south by a line from the mouth of the Rio Motagua in northern Guatemala southeastward through Lake Nicaragua to the Gulf of Nicoya on the Pacific shore of Costa Rica. This area, Mesoamerica, is defined on the basis of distinctive culture traits and patterns shared at the time of the Spanish Conquest; the boundaries of Mesoamerica undoubtedly shifted at various times in its history, nor has the appended map adhered rigorously to Kirchhoff's definition. For a generalized picture of the culture pattern at the time of the Spanish Conquest one can do no better than quote Kirchhoff's listing of culture traits. Such a sharing of culture is indicative of a common history, enabling the consideration of the area as a unit.

A certain type of digging stick (*coa*); the construction of gardens by reclaiming land from lakes (*chinampas*); the cultivation of lime-leaved sage (*chia*) and its use for a beverage and for oil to give luster to paints; the cultivation of the century plant (*maguey*) for its juice (*aguamiel*), fiber for clothing and paper, and maguey beer (*pulque*); the cultivation of cacao; the grinding of corn softened with ashes or lime.

Clay bullets for blowguns; lip plugs and other trinkets of clay; the polishing of obsidian; pyrites mirrors; copper tubes to drill stones; the use of rabbit hair to adorn textiles; wooden swords with flint or obsidian chips along their edges (*macuahuitl*); corselets padded with cotton (*ichcahuipulli*); shields with two hand grips.

Turbans; sandals with heels; one-piece suits for warriors.

Step pyramids; stucco floors, ball courts with rings.

Hieroglyphic writings; signs for numerals and relative value of these according to position; books folded screen style; historical annals and maps.

Year of 18 months of 20 days, plus 5 additional days; combination of 20 signs and 13 numerals to form a period of 260 days; combination of the two previous periods to form a cycle of 52 years; festivals at the end of certain periods; good- and bad-omen days; persons named according to the day of their birth.

Ritual use of paper and rubber; sacrifice of quail; certain forms of human sacrifice (burning people alive, dancing dressed in the skin of the victim); certain forms of self-sacrifice (extraction of one's blood from the tongue, ears, legs, or sexual organs); the flying game or ritual (*juego de volador*); 13 as a ritual number; a series of divinities, Tlaloc, for example; concept of several other worlds and of a difficult journey to them; drinking the water in which the deceased relative has been bathed.

Specialized markets or markets subdivided according to specialties; merchants who are at the same time spies; military orders (eagle knights and jaguar knights); wars for the purpose of securing sacrificial victims (Kirchhoff, 1952:24–25).

This listing of traits represents the end point of Mesoamerican culture history, and the archeological record shows many differences of emphasis in culture from that indicated, which complex represents only one, the last, of the several phases of Mesoamerican culture history which dominated the region.

Physiography and Climate

The physiographic organization and boundaries of Mexico and Central America do not coincide with the cultural boundaries of Mesoamerica given above. A casual glance at a relief map of this area would lead one to believe that the Rocky Mountain system runs the length of the continent. In reality, the Rocky Mountain system ends in southern Mexico at the Great Scarp of Oaxaca, after having run the length of Mexico north of this area in the form of a plateau, the Mesa Central. From the coastal regions it appears that the Mesa Central is bounded on the east and the west by the Sierra Madre Oriental and the Sierra Madre Occidental, respectively. However, from the plateau, the two mountain ranges are far less impressive and are seen to be part of a single structure. South of the Great Scarp one encounters two geological structures completely dissociated from the Rocky Mountain system. One runs the length of Lower California, gradually turning eastwards through Oaxaca through the Sierra Madre del Sur of Mexico, the Isthmus of Tehuantepec, the highlands of Chiapas and Guatemala, and finally ending in Cuba. The second structure originates in Oaxaca running northwest to southeast to Honduras where it turns sharply northeastward and terminates in Puerto Rico after passing through Hispaniola. The regions affected by these structures show a series of ridges and valleys running parallel with the structures. Much of this underlying system has been covered by recent volcanic activity. Areas of instability along the Great Scarp of Mexico and the along Pacific slope from Tehuantepec to Costa Rica result in heavy volcanic activity. Two major features, the Balsas and Tehuantepec portals, formerly connected Atlantic and Pacific. The former, which runs between the Great Scarp and the Sierra Madre del Sur, was open in late Cretaceous times and although somewhat obscured by recent volcanic activity, it is still a major geologic feature of southern Mexico. The latter is today the Isthmus of Tehuantepec and was open in late Pliocene times. This, too, has been greatly obscured by volcanic activity. The lowlands of the Atlantic, such as the Peten in northern Guatemala, Yucatan, and the coastal plain of the Gulf of Mexico in Tabasco, Vera Cruz, Tamaulipas, and the Gulf Coast states of southeastern United States, all are part of a limestone structure extending far beyond the shoreline into the Gulf of Mexico. The shoreline here is typified by numerous indentations resulting in many bays and inlets. The Pacific coastal plain, which in contrast, shows little complexity with very few gulfs and harbors, is extremely narrow.

This region shows such a diversity of altitudes within a relatively small distance that to speak in general of the temperature and rainfall is extremely difficult. The temperature shows a direct relationship to the altitude and decreases inland. In the coastal regions the temperatures are high and the rainfall is usually greater and less subject to seasonal variation than in the highlands.

Language and Ethnic History

The linguistic composition of Mesoamerica and the relationships between the languages are still far from clearly determined. Here there is as complex a linguistic condition as in any similar area in the world. "In one small portion of the area, in Mexico just north of the Isthmus of Tehuantepec, one finds a diversity of linguistic type hard to match on an entire continent in the Old World." (McQuown, 1955:501.) Because of this, the intention here is to present Mesoamerica linguistically in as simplified a fashion as possible. This involves the use of several proposed superfamilies of languages which have not yet been fully demonstrated, let alone accepted, by linguists. This lack of agreement is due mainly to certain problems of comparative linguistics: Chiefly, many of the relationships claimed are based on inadequate linguistic methodology; uncertainty of the validity of this scheme is caused by the lack of sufficient linguistic data. Despite these difficulties the following listing will provide a general idea of linguistic relationships not only in Mesoamerica itself, but also of these languages with those in the remainder of North America (see Chapter II).

For Mesoamerica we are concerned with three or four linguistic superfamilies and one independent language: Macro-Penutian or Aztec-Tanoan (Macro-Mayan, including Mizoquean and Huave, is held by some authorities to be clearly separate from the other languages of this group), Hokan-Siouan, Macro-Otomaguean, and Tarascan. The listing of the major subdivisions of these groupings and some relationships beyond Mesoamerica are as follows:

Macro-Penutian
Mesoamerican subdivisions
Mizocuavean (mostly southern Mexico)
Aztec-Tanoan
Mayan
Totonac (northern Vera Cruz)

Of this group we are chiefly interested in two: Aztec-Tanoan in which Nahua, the language of the Aztecs, is classified, Mayan with

its many subdivisions—Huastec (Vera Cruz), Chol-Tzeltal (southern Mexico and northern Guatemala), Chuh-Kanhobalan (southern Mexico and western Guatemala), Moto-Mamean (western Guatemala), Quiche-Kekchi (central Guatemala), Maya (the Peten and Yucatan).

Extra-Mesoamerican relationships: In North America such groups as Ute, Comanche, Tanoan pueblos, Pima-Papago, Zuni, and Kiowa are considered by some linguists to be of the same superfamily. In the regions to the south such migrant groups as the Nicarao of Nicaragua and the Sigua of northern Panama are related languages.

Hokan-Siouan (Hokan-Coahuiltecan)
Mesoamerican subdivisions: Hokaltecan— Tequistlatec and Chontal with Tlapanec in southern Mexico, and Subtiaba in northern Nicaragua, the latter two forming a possibly separate phylum.

Extra-Mesoamerican relationships: Most of the languages of this superfamily are widely scattered in North America. Pomo and Chumash of California, Yuman of the lower Colorado drainage, the Siouan languages of the central and northern Plains, Caddo of the southern Plains, Iroquoian of northeastern North America, and Muskogean of southeastern United States are some of the better known groups.

Macro-Otomangue
Mesoamerican subdivisions: Otomanguean:
Mazatecan]
Otomian]
Popolocan] southern
Triquean] Mexico
Chorotegan]

Mixtecan] mainly southern Mexico; some
Chinantecan] partial extensions into Nicaragua
Zapotecan] and Costa Rica.

Extra-Mesoamerican relationships: This is the only one of the three major linguistic groupings confined wholly to Mesoamerica.

Tarascan
Mesoamerican subdivisions: Tarascan, the most important of the few isolated languages in the region is centered in the Mexican state of Michoacan. Affiliations with other American Indian languages have not yet been established.

The distribution of these linguistic groups, their cultural relationships, as well as linguistic affiliations, within and without the area, would appear to indicate that the Mizocuavean,

Map labels (clockwise/top-to-bottom): PLAINS, SOUTHEAST, SOUTHWEST, LAGUNERO, COAHUILTEC, TAMAULIPEC, ZACATEC, HUASTEC, TOTONAC, OTOMI, TARASCAN, AZTEC (Nahua), MIXTEC, ZAPOTEC, MIXE CHONTAL ZOQUE, Yucatan Maya, MAYA, Lacandon Maya, CHORTI, LENCA, JICAQUE, MOSQUITO, CHOROTEGA SUBTIABA, NICARAO, CHIBCHAN AREA (South America)

H1 ● Mesoamerica

Mayan, Totonacan, and Tarascan were basic to Mesoamerica linguistically and probably cultur- ally—perhaps even were the languages of the originators of the Mesoamerican culture pattern as revealed in archeology and ethnography. Nahua seems to have appeared late in spite of its full commitment to Mesoamerican culture; its close linguistic relationships northward from Mesoamerica and distinctive migration tales correlate with each other closely. In addition, it is the opinion of certain cultural analysts that the Nahua speakers contributed relatively little to the Mesoamerican culture pattern, but merely adopted it upon arrival in the area. Macro-Otomangue also does not appear to be deeply rooted linguistically or culturally because of its widespread distribution and its curious association with Nahua in both the far south- ern and northern reaches of the area. The lan- guages purported to be Hokan-Siouan have a sparse distribution, and on this basis appear to

indicate late arrival and unimportance in Mesoamerican culture history.

The linguistic boundaries of Mesoamerica re- veal an unstable situation in the north where there appears to have been a shifting line through time, more or less correlating with the contacts of the Mesoamericans with the "bar- barian" tribes to the north. An alternation of spread of high cultivators (in Kirchhoff's sense) north and a push southward of low level cul- tivators, or hunters and gatherers, is seen in both linguistic and ethnohistorical data. Move- ments of Nahua-speaking groups or tribes is often utilized as a demonstration of this. In contrast, the southern boundary of Meso- america was stable linguistically. Kirchhoff (1952:17–30) attributes this to the fact that there were stable high cultivators to the south sepa- rated by a relatively small area of simple cul- tivators. According to this proposition there would have been less incentive for these groups to move into the southern parts of Mesoamerica than for those northern groups to

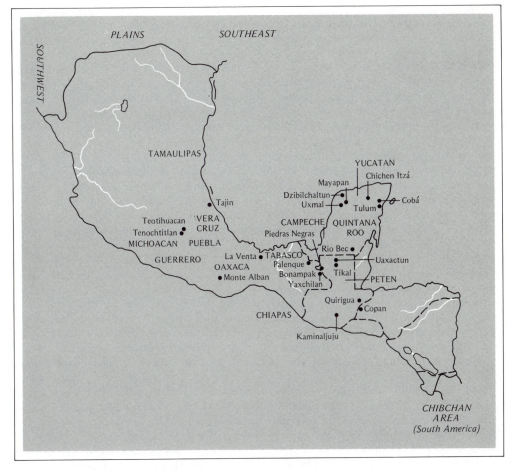

H2 ● Mesoamerica Archeological Areas Sites

move into the area. There is suggestibly corroborative proof for this in the methods of lexicostatistical dating developed by Swadesh and others (Swadesh, 1967:79–116). As an example, a brief glance at some of the dating for Mesoamerica does reveal closer relations of Nahua with the North American Papago and Paiute than with any of the Mesoamerican members of the proposed Macro-Penutian superfamily of languages.

Culture History

Until recent years the study of the culture history of Mesoamerica has been confined to cultures with an agricultural base. In fact, one of the most serious problems has been the origin of plant domestication and the associated archeological cultures. What once seemed a sudden appearance of sedentary cultures with plant domestication left us with a gap between the hunters and gatherers of Paleo-Indian identification and the pre-Classic culture of nuclear America, both in Mesoamerica and the Central Andean region. In the last 25 years, however, archeological excavations in both areas have begun to reveal the preagricultural base from which the pre-Classic cultures were derived. Nevertheless, it should be cautioned that only part of the hiatus between the early hunters and gatherers and the first pre-Classic cultures has been closed. One further introductory comment is in order here. Unlike those in the remainder of the New World, archeologists and culture historians of Mesoamerica have had the advantage of dealing with a culture history which for a significant part of its span presents calendrical dating and, for its final two or three centuries, written records in the form of native histories and annals. However, as will be seen, this condition has not been an unmitigated blessing.

The earliest evidences of human occupation in Mesoamerica come from Mexico. In 1947 at

Tepexpan, valley of Mexico (de Terra, 1949), in the lower levels of the Bercerra formation, a human skeleton was discovered in association with the remains of a mammoth. Radiocarbon dating of materials from this level has been given at 10,000 B.C. Certain projectile points and scrapers from Valsequillo and Tlacopan may date to 20,000 B.C.; however, there is still dispute over the nature of the tools found and their chronological position. Other early finds come from Santa Isabel Iztapan (Aveleyra, 1953:332–340) where mammoth remains and a Plano Scottsbluff projectile point were found in association in the upper Bercerra (Armenta) formation. Radiocarbon dating on this find gives 9,000 B.C. The work of MacNeish (1950:79–96; 1954:323–327; 1971:307–315) in Tamaulipas, Chiapas, and the Tehuacan Valley in Puebla more clearly suggests the culture sequence preceding the pre-Classic. Tamaulipas cave deposits yielded the following from early to latest: Diablo (choppers and scrapers) and Lerma (Plano projectile points) — in sequence, showing hunting emphasis; Nogales — mortars, metates, and hunting tools indicating these were semi-gatherers and hunters; La Perra — mixed hunting-gathering and plant cultivation with the former predominant, gourds and primitive maize, baskets, metates, matting and nets, radiocarbon date 2,492 B.C. ±280. Later phases possessing pottery, hybrid maize, cotton cloth and terra cotta figurines appear to directly succeed the La Perra phase. This sequence of events was more clearly demonstrated by MacNeish's intensive Tehuacan valley survey of the 9 distinct cultural phases apparent; the first 5 are pertinent to the problem of the origin of the pre-Classic: Ajuereado (10,000–6,600 B.C.) with Lerma and Absolo projectile points, a wide range of choppers, blades and scrapers, and a nomadic microband organization; El Riego (6,700–5,000 B.C.) showing an increase in gathering subsistence to 40 percent and possible cultivated plant food 10 percent, evidence for seasonal macro-microbands and scheduled subsistence system; Coxcatlan (5,000–3,400 B.C.) wild plant gathering increases to 54 percent and the horticulture of maize, beans, zapote, gourds, and other plants rises to 14 percent, evidence of an increasing demand for scheduling food production; Abejas (3,400–2,300 B.C.) shows a shift from a wide variety of horticultural plants to an emphasis on a few good producers especially vigorous hybrids, these plants now constitute 25 percent of the diet, which reflects the increased interaction of the central based bands

society; Purron (2,300–1,500 B.C.) is notable, although not as fully known as the preceding, because of the first ceramics in Mesoamerica and the probable presence of food surpluses. Although more is likely to be discovered about the origin of the pre-Classic, this list serves to point up the fact that the pre-Classic emerged from a long series of experiments on, and the consequent accumulation of knowledge of, edible plants in a broad area of the New World.

The sequential culture history of Mesoamerica as a distinctive culture pattern begins with the full dependence on domesticated plants which, as in many other parts of the world, permitted the formation of larger population groups settled in permanent locations. Usually this culture history is conceived in three chronological divisions: Pre-Classic, 2000 B.C.–A.D. 300; Classic, A.D. 300–900; Post-Classic, A.D. 900–1500. The long-standing controversy concerning the correlation of the European calendar with those of Mesoamerica, despite greatly increased archeological knowledge and the discovery of radiocarbon dating, still has not been settled in favor of either the Spinden (200 years earlier than those given above) or the Goodman-Martinez-Thompson correlations. In addition, these chronological divisions have other designations: Pre-Classic — Formative, Developmental; Classic — Florescent; Post-Classic — Militaristic, Expansionistic, Historic. Further, some authorities see a Proto-Classic separating the Pre-Classic and Classic.

Terminology for the temporal and cultural historical divisions of Mesoamerica are still fraught with confusion and contradiction as the foregoing suggests. There have been many calls for a standardization of terminology (Wauchope, 1950, 1964; Sabloff, 1973) but the deposit of past terms in print seems impervious to conceptual excavation and ordering by Mesoamerican archeologists. Some workers such as Tolstoy (1974) have called for the recognition of Mesoamerican culture complexes analogous to those in the pre-Columbian Central Andean area termed horizons. These complexes circumscribe large areas of cultural organization that affect the entire region under consideration — Mesoamerica or the Central Andes. The culture horizons do not obliterate local or regional cultural traditions but serve to unite them areally. Hence, in Mesoamerica one can argue for an Olmec horizon, a Teotihuacan horizon, and an Aztec horizon.

The Pre-Classic refers to that phase of

Mesoamerican culture history in which the bases of civilizations of the Classic phase were laid. During this time the development of an agricultural economy accompanied technological development in ceramics and construction. Also, closely associated with the agricultural complex was an accumulation of knowledge concerning the movement of celestial bodies and the change of seasons, so that by the end of the period there were sufficient astronomical observations and records to gear a ceremonial cycle to a calendar count. There was, then, an early correlation of the calendar and its related attributes with the agricultural, ceremonial, and religious needs of the population as a whole. The mastery of agricultural production, the close interrelationship of economy and religion, and the derivative technological and observational attributes of this concern, such as the calendrical and astronomical knowledge, form the basis of the Classic phase.

The earliest expressions of the Pre-Classic appear to be those of the Purron phase from Tehuacan, and the Pox phase from Puerto Marquez and Zanja in Guerrero, dating between 2300 and 1500 B.C. Typical of early Pre-Classic sites are large village settlements, manos, metates, incised and simple ceramics, well-made hand-modeled figurines. During the middle Pre-Classic flat-topped and platform mounds appear, marking the presence of ceremonial sites. It is at this time that we encounter the rise of a distinctive unifying culture pattern for Mesoamerica as a whole, the Olmec of southern Vera Cruz and Tabasco. Most of the attributes necessary to a civilization it is generally agreed are found in this pattern: calendrics, monumental construction, full-time sculptors and engineers, great importance of trade, strong evidence for social classes and priesthood, and the development of an agricultural-religious complex. Perhaps the most distinctive aspect of what has been termed the Olmec horizon by some (cf. Tolstoy, 1974) is the art style, especially its iconographic aspect. Here the representation of felines, humanoids with feline characteristics, and other motifs constitutes the visual expression of an ideology that spread far beyond the apparent place of origin. These Olmec traits were disseminated through the Izapan style, so named after a ceremonial center in Mexico near the Guatemalan border on the Pacific slope. This spread was not only a geographical one but also continued through time. The middle Pre-Classic period saw the consolidation of a distinctive Mesoamerican culture pattern. This

was true not only for the regions mentioned but also for highland Guatemala, the Peten, Michoacan, and the Huasteca of Vera Cruz.

Most Mesoamerican culture historians and archeologists would recognize a phase of cultural development between the Pre-Classic and the appearance of a full-blown Classic (e.g., Wauchope, 1950, 1964). In some instances this would equate, in part, with what has been called late Pre-Classic. In essence, what is designated in this interim, or introductory, phase is the foreshadowing of the cultural features which so clearly distinguish the Classic, and which, at the same time, show clear regional differences and display their common origins. Many authors see the rise of an urban Pre-Classic, as indicated by wealth differences and richer grave offerings, made possible by the fully developed Pre-Classic economic base. Archeological evidence shows an increase in the size of settlements as well as overall complexity of culture. This was nowhere more apparent than at Teotihuacan. The culture pattern that developed there foreshadowed the coming dominance this city was to exercise over most of Mesoamerica during the major portion of the Classic. For an increasing number of authorities this reflects a basic preeminence of the highlands in the cultural development of Mesoamerica. Teotihuacan was already a planned city by 300 B.C., and it becomes increasingly likely with new archeological evidence, that it dominated Mesoamerica during the Classic between A.D. 300 and 600. Further, a continuity of strong use of feline representations (albeit reflecting culture change through time) and some human sacrifice adumbrates the development of religious ideas later on. Likewise, the earliest inscriptions which occur at Monte Alban I in Oaxaca and Izapan in Chiapas have dates and mature hieroglyphic writing which clearly demonstrate the complex base from which the Classic arose.

Essentially, the Classic in Mesoamerica means the appearance of civilization, some of the criteria for which are visible here. The rise of cities, complex division of labor, writing, the maturation of a specialized priesthood, secular planning and management are only a few important features. Of these, there is a question only whether all of Mesoamerica during Classic times had true cities; in the sense that these are permanently occupied complexes of constructions and buildings, such seem to be absent in the lowland areas. The pattern of a ceremonial center alone being occupied permanently by a priestly hierarchy and the necessary assistants and maintenance staff was typical of the larger settlements of the Peten and the Usumacinta, and, in fact, most of the lowland region of Mesoamerica during the Classic times.

The beginnings of the Classic are generally associated with the appearance of the first Initial Series (Long Count calendrical inscriptions) in the Peten, Teotihuacan III, Monte Alban III, Aurora-Esperanza phase at Kaminaljuyu. There is some disagreement that these early Classic expressions are contemporaneous. Again the argument revolves around the system of calendrical equation utilized. However, the trends in cultural development are essentially the same although regional differences obtain.

There are many continuities from Pre-Classic times such as figurine forms in Mexico, Zapotec continuation of hieroglyphic forms, and the continuation of Mayan ceramic forms. However, the ceremonial architecture became more complex and elaborate with the complicated use of stone in construction. The ceremonial centers themselves, the flat-topped mounds, the plazas, the temples, and the so-called palaces, were more numerous and more carefully planned in Classic as compared with late Pre-Classic time. There was a general tendency toward the production of more finely decorated pottery through the use of polychrome painting and ornate modeling, and a corresponding esthetic refinement in other craft products—although it should be noted that a marked contrast between the objects associated with religious ritual and the simplicity of utilitarian objects existed. But it was with the appearance of stelae—large stone monoliths carved in low relief sculpture and inscribed with hieroglyphs and dates—well-developed sculpture in stone and wood, the corbelled vault or arch, writing, and a well-developed and accurate calendar that the Classic assumed its identity. Although we see continuities from the Formative for many aspects of culture, the sudden, almost precipitate, area-wide appearance of these characteristics fully developed is still not fully understood. However, the influence of Teotihuacan in mòst areas allows agreement with Willey's earlier conclusion that "the trait diffusions of the Classic, particularly the Early Classic, must have resulted from a rapid process of the dissemination of ideas and products (trade), whereas the Formative diffusions seem to have been much more general" (Willey, 1955:571–593).

The end of the Classic period comes with surprising swiftness and contemporaneity. This is especially true for the lowland Maya area. Many explanations have been put forth for this event. Certainly the abandonment of the cities of the Peten, and the Usumacinta and Motagua drainages shortly after the beginning of the tenth cycle of the long count marks some area-wide event. It has been suggested that the priestly hierarchy became so widely estranged from the mass of the population that the latter no longer supported the ceremonial centers (Thompson, 1954). Nevertheless, as Willey indicates for British Honduras, there is evidence that the peasant and the priest disappeared together (Willey, 1956a:777–782). These, and other factors, will be discussed more fully in reference to the Classic Maya. Other regions of Mesoamerica offer less mystery concerning the downfall of the Classic. Around A.D. 700 Classic Teotihuacan ended with a catastrophic destruction of the site and the appearance of new styles and, perhaps, new populations. As more and more information becomes available it is clear this event was an extremely complicated one. Suffice it to say that the Toltecs of Tula as well as others were intimately involved in a religio-political rivalry with strong economic overtones and that out of this, in combination with "barbarian" elements from the north, three distinctive central Mexican Post-Classic centers emerged: Tula, Cholula, Xochicalco.

The Post-Classic period of Mesoamerican culture history essentially amounts to reorientation in Mesoamerican cultural foci. Although many of the characteristics which are typical of the Post-Classic were present in the Classic period, they did not assume the proportions of the guiding values. In general, the Post-Classic has been characterized in terms which are antithetical to those which typify the Classic. Thus, such words as militaristic, expansionistic, secularized, and urbanized do describe the result of cultural reorientation in Mesoamerica as a whole, but this does not hold for every region. Certainly the basic social dichotomy of Classic Mesoamerica loses its sharpness with the increased secularization-militarization of the priesthood, and thus the means of social control change in nature. There is every indication of an increase in warfare, fortifications, and fortified sites in many regions. For this reason the term militaristic is generally applicable. Likewise, both archeological evidence and direct historical sources record that political domains increased in size. Certainly this is evident in the spread of Mexican groups to Yucatan in what appear to be Toltec conquests and/or domination of the area. Further, the development and expansion of the various Nahua city states with their tribute regions are well documented. Of these, the Aztecan Tenochca are best known. Whether these cultural changes and military conquests were as secular as some authors contend is still open to question. Brainerd (1954) has suggested, at least in the case of Yucatan and probably in other regions, that the conquest may have been as much one of religious conversion as military conquest. (See Benson, 1970, for recent interpretations.) There is sufficiently strong evidence that the decline of the Classic preceded strong Mexican influence in this area, and that decline meant the abandonment of the ceremonial centers for the most part, and, presumably, the loss of faith in the priesthood. New religious ideas came in with the military conquerors, possibly in two phases—emphasis on human sacrifice, and, later, a figurine cult which some authorities see as a resurgence of earlier Pre-Classic religious ideas. The impression of secularism is enhanced by the dominance of the secular over the sacred, but this did not mean that the religious aspect of culture was submerged by the secular.

Mesoamerica has been characterized as possessing a civilization; however, the presence of true cities during the Mesoamerican Classic was not uniform. Teotihuacan and other highland centers were settlements of this nature while the urban character of the lowland centers has been open to serious doubt. Some new interpretations of the settlement patterns of such centers as Tikal make the highland-lowland contrast suspect. Certainly all the other attributes of a civilization developed in the various regions of the Mesoamerican area. It must be stated, however, that most of the intellectual achievements were made in the lowland region, and, as Brainerd points out, this is remarkable because this is one of the few areas in the world (Southeast Asia being another) where a high culture or something closely approximating a civilization arose in tropical rain forest. The highland regions of Mesoamerica seem to have developed a true urban life before the lowland areas, and there was a diffusion of the culture patterns associated with true city life to the lowlands. Classic Teotihuacan in Mexico appears to be the earliest urban center with a permanent population, a well-developed market center, and all the other attributes mentioned above. Certainly true urbanism was easier to achieve by Post-Classic times, not only in terms of increase in population size and density, but, as well, in the increase in the complexity of culture and its subsequent reflection in a more diversified divison of labor. It is important to note that the urbanism of which we are speaking seems to be Mexican-stimulated. It is in the general Mexican area that several city states grew during the Post-Classic. Further, it is in the Mexican-influenced regions of the remainder of Mesoamerica that true cities developed— especially the cities of the League of Mayapan (more so for the namesake) and Dzibilchaltun in Yucatan.

Certain distinctive cultural elements were area-wide during Post-Classic time. In pottery, plumbate ware and fine orange ware are widely traded over the area in the early part of the period. Later, Mixteca-Puebla polychrome ware and certain related forms became widely traded. This would seem to indicate, along with other forms of evidence, a more secular emphasis in culture through the renewal of wide trade contacts and trade routes—although the utilization of traders as spies was an important function of this activity. It is notable that in the craft products, as well as in the sculpture and masonry, there is an esthetic decline for the Post-Classic. One speculates whether there is sufficient evidence for indications of an accompanying decline in other intellectual activities. A cursory scanning of Mesoamerican specialists leaves one with the impression that if one is wedded through experience and knowledge to the Classic Maya, decline is certainly emphasized, but that if one is oriented as a specialist to other regions, decline is questioned.

This summary survey of Mesoamerican culture history of course ends with the Spanish conquest of the region under the leadership of Cortez. As in the case of the conquest of the Incas of Peru, there is the conquest of a large population organized for warfare by a small band of dedicated, even fanatical, Spaniards. While in both Mexico and Peru there is something of the incredible, closer examination of the cultural situation at the time of Spanish contact removes much of the mystery from the event of the conquest. The importance of Mexican influence during Post-Classic times has been indicated above. What has not been made emphatic, however, was the fact that Mesoamerica consisted of a number of relatively small warring states. This was true for Mexico,

Yucatan, and highland Guatemala especially. The closely intertwined elements of Mexican religion and the warring political state are more fully explained below, but suffice it to say that the Mesoamerican state was not one of complete conquest, colonization, and rule. Conquest was motivated by desire for tribute, not only in the form of material products, but also for supplies of candidates for human sacrifice. It is still uncertain if a true conquest state developed in Mesoamerica. Likewise, attempts at confederation were either abortive as in Mexico or had run their course as in the case of Yucatan. Every Mesoamerican state had a waiting line of enemies and potential conquerors, and this was especially true of the Aztecs of Tenochtitlan. So it is not to be wondered that Cortez easily swelled the sparse ranks of his conquistadores with the warriors of other Mexican states. Further, there is the little matter of native Mesoamerican warfare: its purpose, strategy, armament, and the like. Mesoamericans entered battle with little overall strategy when compared with Europeans of that time. Every battle was likely to develop into a series of individual contests. Further, although the Aztecs were sometimes exceptions, long-range planning and tactical movement of troops was not agreeable to the Mesoamerican warriors or military leaders; ambush, surprise attack, and unorganized mass assault were more to their liking and inclination by culture conditioning and content. Also, the logistics of large-scale campaigns in distant regions were confronted with the difficulties of lack of transport and the inability to depend upon neighboring groups for supplies. The Mesoamerican did not have the cultural background and knowledge in military matters to cope with the Spaniards. Lastly, one should not overlook the motivations and situation of the Spaniards in Cortez's company. They were in Mexico against orders and knew that unless conquest of what seemed to them a great and rich empire was achieved, return to Spain or the West Indian colonies would be impossible without severe penalties. They chose to alter their situation by the conquest of Mexico. This they initiated by the destruction and sack of Tenochtitlan in 1519–1522. With this, Mesoamerica as an independent cultural unit was lost. The conquest of the remainder of the area soon followed. Although some of the Yucatecan Maya, the Itza, remained independent at Tayasal in the Peten until 1697, the sixteenth century

marks the end of the native Mesoamerican culture history.

THE CLASSIC MAYA

Introduction

It has long been contended that the culture history of Mesoamerica was marked by major shifts in the orientation of the culture patterning. Usually this shift is seen in the differences between the Classic and the Post-Classic, which is distinguished by a change from a peaceful, calm way of life with an emphasis on intellectual achievement to a militaristic, blood-thirsty, and unstable patterning typifying the Post-Classic. Although the change may not have been as dramatic as is maintained by some authorities, it is certain that major culture changes marked the end of the Classic and the full development of the Post-Classic. The Classic of Mesoamerica is known from several regions in the area: the Classic Maya of the Peten, and the Chiapas and Tabasco lowlands, the Zapotec of Oaxaca (especially Monte Alban), Teotihuacan in the Valley of Mexico, La Venta in lowland Vera Cruz, and El Tajin (Totonac) of the northern Vera Cruz coastal lowlands were all centers during the Classic period. There is still much argument concerning the earliest of the true Classic cultures. The first inscriptions appear in Monte Alban I, and there are other dates associated with La Venta which may have priority over those in the lowland Maya area. Whatever may be the final outcome, the present concern is with the Classic of the lowland Maya for the simple reason that it is best known from this region.

Confining discussion to the Classic Maya forces one to work almost completely with the archeological record. While it is true that the Classic Maya possessed hieroglyphic writing and a complex system of calendrical dating, few of the written records that remain in stone and wood have been completely deciphered. What written records have been preserved from the Post-Classic are still imperfectly understood and suffer from the additional disadvantage of not depicting the Classic Maya, but the Maya of Yucatan after the decline of the Classic Maya and the effects of heavy Mexican cultural influence. Consequently, proto- and post-Conquest records of the Yucatecan Maya must be used cautiously and with a heavy reliance on archeological data. The reconstruction of Classic Maya culture must then be a judicious combination of what may be inferred from archeological data and post-Conquest documentation. Fortunately, it appears that the life of the commoners, or peasants, of this region changed relatively little compared to that of the priestly group, so that this aspect of the culture has more validity when post-Conquest data are utilized in the reconstruction.

Physiography and Climate

The area of the Classic Maya was a region which coincides generally with the Maya-speaking area today, comprising most of the Guatemalan highlands, the Chiapas uplands, the Peten district of Guatemala, and the peninsula of Yucatan. Thompson (1954) divides this area into southern, central, and northern regions. The southern region, consisting mainly of the Guatemalan highlands, is mountainous with a temperate climate and in Classic times undoubtedly served as a supplier of raw materials to the Maya of the lowlands. Cacao beans and quetzal feathers were two important items. Although this region possessed relatively great natural wealth and was on the main trade routes, it did not achieve the full Maya scheme of culture. The central region consisted of the Peten of Guatemala and the adjacent regions of Mexico and British Honduras where the full development of the Classic Maya took place. The northern region included Yucatan, most of Campeche, and all of Quintana Roo. This region displays greater dryness and lacks raw materials present in the south. It is the view of most Mayanists that the northern region was marginal to the main area of Maya cultural achievement—the central region centered in the Peten. However, recent work at Dzibilchaltun in northern Yucatan indicates a parallel development took place in that region (Andrews, 1960:254–265).

The central region, which displayed the highest development of Classic Maya, was confined mostly to the Peten, an area characterized by interior drainage basins, low-lying hills, tropical forest, and savannahs. The central drainage basin runs approximately 60 miles east and west, and is not more than 20 miles north and south. On the north and south of this basin lie ranges of low hills varying in altitude from 100 to 600 feet and averaging about 500 feet. Along the northern boundary of the

Maya, Classic ● **Pottery whistle in the form of an attendant or dignitary. (Courtesy of The Minneapolis Institute of Arts)**

basin lies a series of lakes of which the largest is Lake Peten Itzá, home of the last Maya to defy the Spaniards. Beyond the range of hills to the south lies the central savannah of the Peten which appears never to have been occupied in pre-Columbian times. However, in the hills to the north of the central drainage basin the Classic Maya built their cities. It was in the valleys and on the northern slopes of the ridges separating the central basin from the north that the Classic Maya built their ceremonial centers. It is worthy of note that the Maya centers were located wherever there was tropical forest growth.

On the basis of the distribution of the larger ceremonial centers with hieroglyphic inscriptions and dates, Thompson (1954) points out that only Copan across the Motagua River to the south and some of the sites in the Chiapas uplands represent a successful establishment of the Classic Maya outside the tropical lowlands. The Peten-centered area is far warmer than the southern highlands and more humid than Yucatan. The rainy season usually runs from May until January with high annual rainfall—70 inches in the north to 150 inches in the south. In addition, temperatures are high, running to 100° F. in April and May when the dry season reaches its height. On occasion the temperatures will lower to the fifties when cold fronts come in from the north but on the whole, the climate is one which shows a high average temperature with an accompanying high humidity.

This is a region of tropical forest with some trees reaching to 120 feet. In general, the undergrowth is not heavy, but where there are open spaces caused by the fall of the larger trees a new growth presents impassable barriers. The region is rich in animal and insect life, with corresponding destruction of the garden and field crops and discomfort to people which is compounded by the high rainfall and humidity. Further, the central Maya area is highly deficient in raw materials. Nowhere in the area are there igneous rocks except for a small deposit of granite in British Honduras from which material for metates was traded. However, there was an abundance of limestone which was easily worked with the stone tools possessed by the Classic Maya. Further, when burned, this yielded lime. Likewise, there was a ubiquitous supply of a friable, granular limestone which the Maya utilized for mortar.

The region is drained by the Rio Pasión flowing into the Usumacinta and thence to the Gulf of Mexico. Rio San Pedro Matir also drains the northern hills. And a series of smaller rivers drains eastward into the Caribbean Sea. In addition to the lakes of the central Peten, there are many other small lakes and ponds scattered throughout the area. Many which were formerly active have now turned into swampy areas. Despite these water resources, there was and is a continuing problem of water supply due to the paucity of surface streams.

On the whole, it should be emphasized that the achievement of the Classic Maya in a tropical forest region was one of considerable magnitude. As stated previously, the Maya of the southern highlands did not reach the apogee of the central Maya, being more influenced in their later development from Mexico. The Yucatan Maya were marginal and later in their development, although it should be indicated that the last efflorescence of the Classic Maya may have taken place in the *serranía* region of central Yucatan as seen in the Puuc, Rio Bec, and Chenes cultural expressions.

Culture History, Abridged

The date of the emergence of the Classic Maya from the Formative period is open to question, for there is equivocal evidence for the Goodman-Martinez-Thompson correlation or for the Spinden correlation with the European calendars. A second difficulty has to do with the first appearance of the cultural traits which typify the Classic since it is undecided whether the La Venta culture and its art expression, the Olmec, was created by Maya speakers. However, here one may follow the more commonly accepted dates, and utilize the Goodman-Martinez-Thompson correlation and the Peten as the locus of the first Classic Maya.

A number of cultural features marked the distinctiveness of the Classic Maya. First, there was a marked homogeneity of writing, calendrics, corbelled arch, and art forms over a widespread area. Second, a strong contrast between the objects associated with religious ritual and the simplicity of utilitarian objects existed. Third, there was never a large population in the central Maya area during Classic times; it has been estimated that there were never more than 30 individuals per square mile—there was no true urbanization. Fourth, although there is comparatively little evidence of mass conscription of labor, there was a great amount of energy spent in skilled work compared with the other parts of the world which were on this level of cultural complexity. It would appear that the construction of the Classic Maya centers involved skill rather than size, quality rather than quantity. There was a cultural conservatism in the priestly monopolies of writing, calendrics, religious art, and architecture, while the lay arts and crafts revealed what might be termed a more usual rate of change over the 570 years of the Classic Maya. This conservatism yielded a uniformity not only through time but over a broad area as well. Compared with the Post-Classic, there is the near absence of evidence for warfare; evidence of widespread trade reflects the conditions under which this cultural conservatism perpetuated itself.

The dates which one assigns to the Classic will depend upon the minor differences in judgments concerning the minutiae of Classic cultural development. Likewise, the number of subdivisions one makes for this period is dependent on one's purpose. We recognize here an Early Classic (A.D. 292–593) and a Late Classic (A.D. 593–889). The Early Classic sees the spread of Maya-style stelae and corbelled vault architecture. This architecture shows a consistent refinement and improvement during this time. Sculpture is naturalistic and vigorous, and similar refinement in other arts and crafts accompanies these items. The Late Classic ends with the last of the Initial Series inscriptions. In the beginning of the period, there had been an acceleration of cultural activity evinced in the increased refinement in architecture and art associated with extensive religious activity in the west and east of the area in such centers as Piedras Negras, Yaxchilan, Palenque, and Copan. During this time some 90 cities erected stelae or buildings with inscribed hieroglyphic writing and dates. The finest pottery, the best lapidary work, the highest development of architecture, all occur during these times. Great progress in astronomy and advanced arithmetic was achieved. A great expansion in the number of ceremonial centers resulted also in an increase in markets and trade. A.D. 790 was the last time a large number of centers erected stelae marking the end of a ceremonial cycle; 19 centers did so. After this date there was a progressive decline in the cultural vigor of the Classic Maya.

Factors involved in the decline and collapse of the Classic Maya culture have been alluded to; it is certain that this was not an event peculiar to the Classic Maya. However, there is doubt that the same factors apply here as in the central Mexican region, the Guatemalan Highlands, and in Yucatan where there is strong evidence that military conquest and religious proselytization was involved. Among the Classic Maya there was something more in the nature of the disjuncture of culture. Thompson (1954) and others have suggested that too wide a discrepancy developed between the esoteric development of the priestly knowledge and religion on the one hand and that of the peasants on the other. However, this apparently did not mean the abandonment of the ceremonial centers by the peasants since we know they were used after the decline. Likewise, Willey (1956:777–782) has used archeological evidence to demonstrate the coincidental disappearance of the priestly class and the peasants in Classic localities of British Honduras.

A recent conference on the collapse of the Classic Maya civilization came to the conclusion that the Classic Maya in effect filled the gap left by the fall of Teotihuacan in A.D. 600, but that the level of organization and cultural integration was inadequate to maintain the role (Willey and Shimkin, 1971). This despite the fact that the period between A.D. 711 and 790 saw the

Late Classic period of Colima-Nayarit region of Western Mexico. ● Ceramic figurine in the form of a warrior dressed in what is apparently basketry armor and a helmet. (Courtesy of The Minneapolis Institute of Arts)

climax of lowland Maya civilization. The conferees inferred several stress factors among the lowland Maya, some of which are: the limits of ecological-demographic in terms of cultural capabilities (any short term disaster would have become a long term one), internal competition between ceremonial centers, the collapse of peasant support, and the expansion of exploitation into marginal lands. It was pointed out that the Classic Maya retained a form of organization that originated in Olmec times, which made them particularly vulnerable to developments taking place in other parts of Mesoamerica in the eighth and ninth centuries. The spread of the collapse was from west to east over a forty-year period which began twenty years after the peak of Maya expansion. There is some archeological evidence of strong contact with highland cultures, but the exact course of events is still unclear. Whatever the case, the lowland Maya displayed an inability to recover from this decline. "In effect, these lowlands, and especially their southern regions, had been bypassed during the progress of

Mesoamerican civilization, for they lacked the resources necessary to the formation of a state of the new type." (Willey and Shimkin, 1971:14.)

Whatever the factors may have been, it is evident that the Maya Classic reached its climax in A.D. 790, and a progressive and accelerating decline began thereafter. The central area returned to a Pre-Classic level of complexity and the Guatemalan Highlands and Yucatan came under strong Mexican influence.

Population and Settlement Patterns

The estimate of pre-Columbian population is notoriously speculative due to the lack of satisfactory historical records. However, on the basis of archeological data and inference from modern census materials, it is possible to arrive at some idea of the number of people in the central area during Classic times. Even here there is considerable disparity between estimates. The estimates for the entire Maya region during Classic times range from 13 million given by Morley (1956) to 1.25 million listed by Kroeber (1939). Archeological evidence seems to indicate that the Guatemalan Highland population was greater than that in the lowlands, especially during Early Classic times. On the basis of modern estimates of Yucatan for example, an area similar to the central region since the central region is mostly uninhabited today, the usual density amounts to approximately 30 persons per square mile. On the basis of archeological evidence it seems that population was not sufficiently concentrated in the ceremonial centers to make them true cities. The permanent population of the ceremonial centers was small, and the majority of the people were scattered over the neighboring countryside, in small rural settlements or in dispersed country neighborhoods. Although dispersed, the populations of the lowlands had much greater focus than formerly assumed. The results of the long archeological campaign at Tikal suggest that the actual center contained around 39,000 persons. If an additional 100 square kilometers is added, to reach 163 square kilometers, there is the likelihood that nearly 45,000 people centered on Tikal for religious and political purposes.

Typical of the Classic period was a ceremonial center with a dispersed farmer population surrounding it. The construction of the ceremonial centers was primarily for religious pur-

poses. However, archeological work by Willey (1956:777–782) in the eastern fringes of the central region in Belize Valley, British Honduras, seems to point to a different possibility. It is argued that the separation between the theocratic hierarchy and the majority of the Maya farmers was not as great as has been concluded. Here archeological exploration reveals a semi-sophisticated peasantry rather than a rustic and primitive folk, and the rural village and the ceremonial center possessed close ties and relationships. Willey describes the occurrence of minor ceremonial mounds in the village housemound clusters, and this seems to strengthen the idea of a widespread ceremonial and religious life which was associated with structures similar to those in the large ceremonial centers. The impression is one of a well-integrated network of theocratic stations and substations, all supported by a peasantry sharing the ideology of the urban centers. The ideology was not markedly different in the smaller settlements from that in the larger ones. The chief differences lay in the possession of great architecture, monumental art, and writing in the major centers. An inference to be drawn from this is that the major centers recruited artisans, retainers, and even some levels of priesthood from the peasant groups and that close contact was maintained through a chain of priestly command from the larger to smaller centers of population. If Willey's proposals are verified through excavations in other areas, we will have to conclude that there was a greater cultural homogeneity and interinfluence between the ceremonial centers and the peasantry than has been thought.

The Classic period saw a great expansion in the number of ceremonial centers in the central area. Not only were these expanded for the primary purpose of religious activities, but also there was evidently an increase in the designation and size of market areas within the centers themselves, although the latter is still a matter of hot debate among experts. Physically, the centers consisted of two main forms of structures: the large monumental structures utilized for religious purposes which were of stone and incorporated the advances in Mayan art, and the living quarters of the peasant worshipers, and possibly those of the permanent population of the ceremonial centers as well, fringing the religious complex. The so-called Classic Maya cities appear to have been occupied by a

● LINTEL 12, YAXCHILAN, MEXICO – CLASSIC MAYA

The sculptured figures on the stelae and other stone monuments from the Maya lowlands have recently been demonstrated by T. Proskouriakoff to represent actual historical individuals and not simply gods or god impersonators. The principal figures of these sculptures most often are magnificently attired personages whom Proskouriakoff has identified as rulers from evidence in the associated hieroglyphic texts. Yaxchilan Lintel 12 seems to depict one of these rulers at a significant moment in his career. Attended by another person who seems to be a warrior, the ruler is apparently making a disposition of the four persons kneeling about him. Judging by the symbolism on the ruler's costume, the prisoners' futures are not too bright. The priest-king wears a long tunic with decorations of crossed bones on it and a human trophy head suspended from his neck. An elaborate headdress and ornaments, presumably of jade, complete the costume. The ruler grasps a spear

as does his retainer, emphasizing the warlike nature of the scene. The kneeling figures are roped together and each of the prisoners is identified by a set of glyphs on his person.

Lintel 12 was found bridging a doorway in Structure 20 at the great site of Yaxchilan located on the Usumacinta River. This is in the southwest region of the Maya lowlands and on the frontier of the Maya area during the Classic period. Lintel 12 is only one of many sculptures from Yaxchilan and other sites of the region showing scenes of warfare and indicating that toward the end of the Classic period relations among the Maya political units were frequently not peaceful. Lintel 12 is of special interest since it is one of the latest sculptures from Yaxchilan, dating from about 900 A.D., and just before the start of the events bringing about the sudden collapse of Maya civilization. The sculpture measures 6 feet 10 inches by 3 feet 4 inches. (After Herbert Spinden, 1913. *A Study of Maya Art.* Memoirs of the Peabody Museum, Harvard University, Vol. VI, Fig. 10.)

relatively small population between the times of religious ceremonies and markets. However, on specified occasions visiting groups of Maya peasantry occupied the town for religious worship, ceremonial dances, ceremonial ball games, and market purposes. The general ground plan centered on a ceremonial court flanked by masonry terraces, pyramids topped by temples, ceremonial platforms, and stelae. In addition, there were possibly bachelor and virgin houses, sweat baths, and complex drainage systems which completed the architectural complex. Inside the city, and connecting some cities, were roads with raised and well-finished roadbeds. The monumental structures were ill-suited for living quarters as they contained mostly daises for the religious leaders and rooms apparently used only for ceremonies and the storage of ceremonial paraphernalia. For the greater part of the Classic period there are few evidences of structures or fortifications for defense, and the picture is one emphasizing peaceful diffusion throughout the area of the cultural patternings which gave such a widespread homogeneity during these times.

Some idea of the number and geographical extent of the Classic Maya cities has already been mentioned. It is certain that some of these centers were more important than others if only by reason of size. However, other criteria can be employed for the assessment of importance. The number and extent of architectural remains, of course, are important since they indicate the intensity of ceremonial life, and the number and excellence of sculptured monuments are equally good guides. However, considering the cultural emphasis of the Classic Maya on the relationship of time, ceremonies, and gods, the erection of hieroglyphic monuments marking major ceremonial events would seem to be the most important criterion for judging the importance of the center. Using these criteria as a means of designating important centers, it is possible to arrive at some ranking of their relative importance. However, a full accounting is beyond the scope of this section and the mention of only a few of the more important centers will have to suffice. Thus: the neighboring centers of Tikal and Uaxactun in the heart of the central area; Palenque, Yaxchilan, and Piedras Negras in the west; and Copan in the southern part of the central area are prime examples of the Classic Maya ceremonial complexes and concentrations.

Tikal, the largest, and probably the oldest, of the Maya centers is located in north-central Peten. The main concentration of structures at Tikal covers about one square mile, but there are several minor groups stretching away from the central area for distances up to three miles. The central group consists of nine complexes, some of which are connected by causeways spanning the ravines which intersect the site. Here are found the highest structures of the Maya area, 6 great temples measuring 143 feet, 155 feet, 178 feet, 188 feet, and 229 feet from the base of the pyramid platform to the top of the temple roof combs. A fuller description of Maya architecture is found below.

Recently, Joy Marcus (1973) building on the ideas of Willey and others proposed that between 600 and 900 A.D. there was an overall organization of the Maya lowlands based upon the Maya quadripartite view of the universe. There were always four capitals each located in one quadrant of the lowlands (not necessarily always the same cities), and each was a center for a series of secondary capitals and smaller settlements. Marcus maintains hieroglyphic inscriptions verify this. Thus, at 730 A.D. a Copan glyph mentions by association that Copan, Calakmul, Tikal, and Palenque were capitals. This hypothesis offers an interesting test of the association between the value aspects of culture and its social geography, for, as we shall see below, the Maya organization of the universe was in terms of the four cardinal directions.

Economy

The economic base of the Classic Maya originated during the Pre-Classic period and was held in common with the whole of Mesoamerica. The underpinnings lay in the domestication of plants, in which the Indians of Mesoamerica probably have had no equals. The almost inordinate emphasis on the domestication of food plants provided the peoples of pre-Columbian Mesoamerica with the necessary food surplus upon which to build the civilizations which flowered in the Classic Period. With regard to the Classic Maya, however, it now seems that those of the central area contributed relatively few domesticated plants to the food inventory. Unlike formerly held conclusions, it now appears that the most important food plant, maize, was domesticated elsewhere. As another example, the elaborate domestication of beans centered in the uplands of the southern Maya area and the southern Mexican region. Nevertheless, the long span of the Pre-Classic allowed the gradual diffusion of such food plants so that the central region Maya possessed nearly the same food inventory as other Mesoamericans at the beginning of the Classic. It is notable that of all the early centers of civilization in the world, the Classic Maya achieved this status without the mastery of large water resources through irrigation and other means of control.

The cultivation of relatively small plots of land under what is generally termed the *milpa* system typified the food production of the Classic Maya. Technologically, this form of plant cultivation is known as slash-and-burn and/or swidden, and due to lack of fertilization techniques leads to rapid exhaustion of the soil in a given plot. Usually two to three years, or four years at most, will see the farmer seek out virgin land for new plots. From what is known of the population distribution during Classic times, it is apparent that the system of cultivation has changed relatively little since then. Therefore, one can analogize with some accuracy from the present to the past. The sequence of events usually runs as follows: The first step is locating a proper plot. This is followed by the men felling the forest and brush (in Classic times with a stone axe). After the felled plant life has dried sufficiently, it is burned and the ashes then serve as fertilizer. Fencing of the plot against potential depredation of animals such as deer and wild swine precedes planting. Planting involves the use of a digging stick with a fire-hardened point to open holes, into which are dropped a number of kernels of maize; often, beans are planted between the maize. For the next several months, depending upon the length of the growing season, which varies according to altitude, time will be spent in weeding and protecting the gardens from birds and animals. Upon the proper maturation of the maize ears, harvesting the entire plot ensues, although some green ears are taken as delicacies before this time. The maize is then stored, usually on the ear, in the house or in small storehouses nearby.

It should be emphasized that all this work was done with a digging stick and a stone axe. The milpa was exclusively men's work. If they followed the present schedule, work began in the fields between four and five in the morning. The chief connection of women with food

Post Classic ● Chacmul stone sculpture from the vicinity of Teotihuacan, Mexico. (Courtesy of The Minneapolis Institute of Arts)

Classic period of Colima-Nayarit region of Western Mexico ● (Height, 10 inches, maximum width, 8 1/4 inches). Ceramic figure holds a conch shell on its knee. (Courtesy of The Minneapolis Institute of Arts)

plants lay in its preparation, especially maize. Maize was, and is, first soaked in warm water and allowed to stand. The following morning the hulls are washed loose from the kernels, which are then ground into a meal. From this, certain forms of food are made, such as various forms of *posole*, a ubiquitous, general purpose dish which varies in viscosity from that of a beverage to that of a pudding, and *tortillas,* a thin pancake cooked in a flat pottery griddle, although there is some uncertainty regarding the pre-Columbian presence of the latter.

Maize was the most important crop of the Maya, and the chief economic activity of the bulk of the Classic period population was the production of milpa which included not only maize but other products. One of the most important problems associated with the Classic Maya lies in the determination of the methods used in the recruitment and the use of labor in the construction of the ceremonial centers. Obviously, this is closely related to the time spent in milpa production. On the basis of extended studies of production and diet in present-day Yucatan (Morley, 1956), it has been discovered that 72 acres are needed to support a family of five—this of course includes land lying fallow. However, in experimenting with weeding techniques it was discovered that hand weeding prolonged the productive life of a plot to as much as 7 to 8 years, compared with the usual 2 years for plots weeded with machetes. Thus, a larger population may have been supported in the same area of land in Classic times. At present, the Yucatecan spends 190 days working the milpa, but much of this product is for livestock and surplus for trading in imported products. It is estimated that the Classic Maya could have produced all that was needed for a family of five by 48 days of work. Consequently, the Classic Maya farmer could have had 9 to 10 months in which to devote his time to the construction of ceremonial centers and the practice of his religion. Whether or not these estimates are precise, they answer most of the question regarding the source of the labor supply needed by the theocratic leaders in the ceremonial centers.

The food plant inventory of the Classic Mesoamerican was extensive. Although maize overshadowed all others, additional food plants occupied an important position in the diet. Black and red beans, two varieties of squash, chayote, tomatoes, sweet potatoes, yams, and manioc were some of the more important. Such condiments as chili peppers, vanilla, and all-spice were raised. Cacao, the source of chocolate, was used not only as a beverage, but also in religious contexts and as an important item of trade and exchange. In addition to the food plants, cotton—the chief source of fiber for weaving—tobacco, gourds, and other fiber plants such as agave were produced. There is

some doubt of the abilities of the central area Maya in plant domestication, and Thompson (1954) considers that only cacao, papaya, and aguacate (avocado, alligator pear) are definitely indentifiable with the Maya.

The domesticated animals of the Classic Maya were few. The ubiquitous dog was used for hunting and as a pet. Turkeys and muscovy ducks were important fowl in every household, kept not only for food but for their feathers as well. Beekeeping apparently was an ancient form of animal husbandry among the Maya, a form of economic activity enhanced by the presence of stingless honey bees in this area. Bees were kept in hives made of hollowed logs and demanded the care of an experienced person. Among the Maya of today, turkeys and bees still occupy an important place.

Milpa means more than a type of cultivation or the production of certain plant foods. The milpa as it is known today, and as can be inferred for the Classic Maya because of their preoccupation with a religion oriented to plants, climate, season and the like, involves a way of life rather than a means of production of food. The Maya farmer today views the universe and all within it, including himself and the supernaturals, as part of the total unity of existence. The Maya farmer attempts to adjust himself to the totality of things, to become part of it, and this is most strongly striven for through the cultivation of the milpa plot and the practice of religious ceremonies associated with it. As will be seen below, the complexity of Maya religion appears to have grown from this base, from the preoccupation not only with the growing of plants and with the supernaturals associated with them, but also with the all-embracing qualities of growth, greenness, and the necessary knowledge of the regular passage of time as seen in the growing and harvesting seasons.

Economically, the majority of the ancient Maya were confined to milpa production. In another, though more extended, sense the Maya peasant contributed to the economy of the area through his efforts in the construction of the monumental architecture, the quarrying of the limestone used in construction, and in the preparation of the blocks and the mortar used. There was evidently sufficient time during each year to devote to these activities. In addition to such workers, there were part-time and resident craftsmen in the ceremonial centers who contributed their time and skills to the theocratic leaders. The role of the peasant women appears to have been confined to three main activities, weaving, some pottery making, and the preparation of food.

Little is known of trade during the Classic period in the central area, although Sabloff (1973) sees the Classic Maya filling the gap between the fall of Teotihuacan and the rise of Tula by controlling trade in the manner learned from Teotihuacan. However, the material resources of this area were few, and such things as quetzal feathers, jade, and obsidian were traded from the highlands. Likewise, it appears that a certain amount of cacao beans were imported from the same area. We have already mentioned the trading for granite for metates from the highlands of British Honduras. In addition to trade carried on from without the area, the general cultural homogeneity would seem to indicate widespread trading within the area itself.

Architecture and Construction

For present purposes one can consider Maya structures under two main categories: the steeply pitched, thatched-roof houses of the farmer, and the monumental architecture of the ceremonial centers. The differences between these provide one of the most striking contrasts in Classic and Post-Classic times; nevertheless, there appears to be an intimate genetic relationship between the two forms.

While the excavations of house mounds in the Maya area provide little information concerning the exact nature of the peasant's house in Classic times, the ground plans and the existence of sculptured examples of houses from the Classic point to a strong continuity to the present. It is with some confidence that one can say that the commoner in Classic times lived in a house with a rectangular ground plan, in some instances with rounded ends. The walls, if analogy to the present is made, could have been constructed of poles, wattle-and-daub, or, in rare instances, of stone. The roof was two-sloped, steeply pitched, and thatched. Inside were pounded earth floors and, usually, four main posts supporting the roof structure. In many areas, the houses were built on individual mounds of earth, and these were used again and again so that several houses occupied the same spot.

If further analogy to the present day may be made, the house furnishing would likely consist of the following items: A fireplace made of three large stones which supported cooking pots. The smoke from the fire found its way out through the thatching. Most of the pottery in the house would have been plain since it appears that most of the highly elaborate pottery of the Classic Maya was associated with religious activity or for the use of the theocracy. More common forms were bowls, jars, and pottery griddles, usually termed *comales*, for the cooking of tortillas. In addition to these containers, half gourds for drinking cups, large gourds for keeping tortillas warm, and figure-eight gourds for water were used. A ubiquitous item would be the metate and mano used for grinding maize. Woven bags would contain such things as maize and beans. Rectangular slat beds or matting on the floor were used for sleeping. In addition to all these items there would be the gardening tools, a throwing stick for hunting, and some obsidian or flint knives. Also, a rolled-up belt loom with some partially finished cloth would be found in all houses.

The monumental structures are the eye-catchers of Classic Maya sites. Here are the evidences of the great strength of Maya religion. The basic organization of a Maya ceremonial center usually involved the arrangement of a series of structures on low or high pyramidal substructures around a plaza or court. Before some of these were to be found the sculptured and inscribed stone monoliths known as stelae, marking a significant ceremonial date in Maya history. The substructures, or pyramids as some of the higher ones are termed, range from 2 to 3 feet in height to the great ones of Tikal ranging to 229 feet. These are usually stone-faced rubble structures arranged in a series of terraces with broad, steep stairways on one or more sides. The apex of these substructures is truncated, and the temple or other structure found on it is set back from the front toward the back and side edges, giving an open area before the building. It appears that these substructures find their origin in the house mounds of Formative times since the superstructures of late Pre-Classic times were placed on low platforms.

The superstructures of Classic times have been given many names, but they usually settle down to temple or palace. The best evidence would seem to indicate that most, if not all, were temples or associated with governing activities of the theocratic group. The structures were decorated by facades which were divided by a medial molding running around the building. Flat roofs with the centers slightly higher for drainage, and roof combs, sometimes as high as the building itself but serving a purely decorative purpose, completed the structure. It is notable that these superstructures contained no windows and appear to have been covered with lime plaster and painted. Whether one of these superstructures was a temple or a palace is difficult to determine. Morley (1956) maintained the ground plan would reveal the purpose, stating that a temple ground plan consisted of two chambers, one behind the other, but entered only through the front, while the palace type consisted of two long ranges of rooms, sometimes entered only from the front and at other times with entrances front and back. In the latter there was no connection through the center wall. In all these structures the area taken up by the walls is usually greater than the floor space, and the rooms were dark and damp. Some of the rooms have large platforms or daises which occupy most of the floor space. Even if these were not directly used for religious ceremonies, there was no room left for living quarters. In other words, there is very little evidence that any of the monumental construction of the Classic Maya was occupied by the ruling theocracy, and it has been reasonably maintained that this social group probably lived in much the same type of house as the commoners. Despite this, it is difficult to explain the proliferation of multi-roomed palacelike structures as part of a massive increase in sheer architectural volume ranging from 10 to 1 and 100 to 1 between the eighth and ninth centuries (Willey and Shimkin, 1971:5).

The raw materials used for the stone buildings were limestone blocks, limestone reduced by burning to a lime cement, and lime gravel used in mortar. The construction of the pyramidal substructures usually did not involve the construction of a totally new one, but was accomplished by placing a rubble covering of stone and mortar over an older one and then facing the rubble with fitted stone. Evidently this type of construction was associated with the end of the ceremonial long count and the erection of new stelae marking the date. It would be fruitless in the space available to try to discuss all the details of Maya architecture and construction techniques. However, the Maya, as all groups having the desire for large construction, was faced with the problem of the spanning of space. This the Maya, like other New World groups, did not solve satisfactorily, for they confined their architectural inventiveness to the principle of the corbelled arch. The corbelled arch, in spanning a given space, must employ the principle of balance so that as stonework extends over a space a counterweight must be used to balance it. This obviously had great disadvantages when compared to the true arch and resulted in the rooms of the structures being small and narrow or long and passagelike. Although the Maya later substituted concrete for balanced stones, the corbelled arch principle still demanded careful planning of stress in the problem of stability. In Post-Classic times in Yucatan a more spacious effect was achieved by placing the arches on columns. But it is doubtful that the Maya priesthood would have desired lighter more spacious rooms, for it was here the mysteries of Maya religion dwelled.

The decoration of the superstructures, and sometimes the substructures, of Classic Maya building was an integral part of the architecture. In the early part of the Classic there was relatively little decoration. However, with the full development of the Classic both the lower and upper zones of the facade were elaborately decorated with modeled hard-lime stucco. There was some stone sculptural decoration, but this was not highly developed in the central area. With the exceptions of Quirigua and Copan, full development of decoration in stone sculpture was reached only in the northern area, and this was confined mostly to the upper zone of the facade. Morley (1956) maintained that at this point sculpture became a part of architecture with a consequent decline in sculpture as an art in itself; the flamboyance of the sculptural mosaics for buildings in the late Classic Puuc is a good example.

Of course the temples and "palaces" do not exhaust the varieties of structures found in a Classic ceremonial center. There were ball courts where a wild and dangerous game was played with a solid rubber ball, there were structures erected for the purposes of making astronomical observations (but usually not of the observatory form familiar to our culture), and also many platforms and similar constructions about the use of which there is uncertainty.

There remains one spectacular aspect of Classic Maya engineering and construction abilities—the roads. Evidently these were constructed to connect ceremonial centers for religious purposes. Although there are such roads connecting Uaxactun and other Peten centers of Classic times, the most spectacular runs from Cobá, Quintana Roo, to Yaxuna a few miles south of Chichen Itzá in Yucatan. Its length is 62.5 miles and it averages 32 feet in width. "For the greater part of its length it is a little over two feet high, but in crossing swampy depressions, its height increases, in one case to slightly more than eight feet. Walls of rough dressed stone form the sides; large boulders topped with smaller stones laid in cement compose the bed, and the surface, not badly disintegrated, was of cement and stucco. A sort of a platform 40 feet long and 16½ feet high covers the road just before the road reached the outer suburbs of Cobá, and it seems probable that processions halted there to make sacrifices before entering the city." (Thompson, 1954:161–162.)

Dress and Ornament

The basic dress of the commoners and the theocracy was the same in Classic Maya times, and it appears that the basic forms of dress have continued down to the present day. The major differences in clothing lay in the greater elaborateness of theocratic dress.

The basic dress for men consisted of a loincloth, sandals, and a square shoulder cloth. The loincloth was made of woven textile, the sandals of deer hide with ties made of sisal fiber, while the shoulder cloth was woven material which served not only as protection against the elements but also as a bed covering at night. The sandals especially showed great elaboration in theocratic dress in Classic times. The dress of women consisted of a skirt, a blouse of varying length, and sandals. Although dress was basically the same for all, the ruling group did possess an additional item. This was the elaborate headdress used both in ceremonial context and daily life. In fact, much of the difference between the commoners and the hierarchy and among the theocracy itself, lay in the variety of headdress. This item was essentially a base of wickerwork or of wood which was formed to represent jaguars, serpents, birds, or one of the gods. The base was then covered with skin, feather mosaic, carved jades, and a high panache of feathers.

The other elaborate quality of the theocratic dress, then, was in the materials used. Thus, the commoners used sisal fibers, aloes fibers, painted barkcloth (made from the inner bark of certain trees, especially the wild fig, fused together in the manner of paper), and, possibly, rough cotton muslin cloth. Feathers and most of the cotton textiles were reserved for the priestly class.

The materials for clothing were prepared mostly by women, since weaving was their prerogative. According to the Maya mythology, the moon goddess was considered the originator of this craft. In murals and ceramic painting, for the actual remains of Classic Maya textiles are very rare, a complex use of cotton cloth is indicated: Such weaves as muslin with brocade and some embroidery, as well as tie-dyeing, are discernible; there are certain representations of what appear to be tapestry; quilting was another technique, and featherwork was done on a net base.

Hair dressing and other decoration allowed for sex differentiation. Men wore their hair long, with a spot burned bare on top of the head; lengths of hair were braided and wrapped around the head, with the exception of a queue which hung behind. Women also wore their hair long and well dressed, and there are indications that differences in style indicated married status. Body paint was widely used by men with the following associations of colors: warriors—blue and red; prisoners—black and white stripes; priests—blue, a color associated with sacrificial rites. In addition, men were tattooed over most of the body while women were tattooed from the waist up with the exception of the breasts.

In addition to the alteration of the body through tatooing, the Maya practiced cranial deformation of the fronto-occipital type. This was accomplished by placing boards on the front and the back of the heads of infants and securing them with ties. The resulting head shape in the adult provided the individual with a physical trait which made him socially acceptable. The use of jade was not confined to ornament and jewelry, for many of the high-ranking Maya advertised their high status by jade insets in the faces of the incisor teeth.

The additional ornamentation worn by the priestly class was highly elaborate and, in conjunction with the feather headdresses mentioned above, permitted one to distinguish social gradations and statuses. "Costume accessories consisted of collars, necklaces, wristlets, anklets, and knee bands. They were made of feathers, jade beads, shells, jaguar teeth and claws, crocodile teeth, and, in later times, of gold and copper. Other kinds of jewelry were nose ornaments, earrings, and lip plugs of jade, stone, obsidian, and less valuable materials. Ornaments of the lower class were confined largely to simple nose plugs, lip plugs, and earrings of bone, wood, shell, and stone." (Morley, 1956:175.)

Art

A most significant feature of Classic Maya culture was the complex development of the art forms. It was not that the forms and the motifs of Classic Maya art were so varied or that they were so greatly elaborated, but that the art was the chief way in which the Classic Maya communicated the complex patterning that was the closely interrelated and interdependent religion, social structure, and world view. Classic Maya culture cannot be understood unless one has some glimmering of the nature and the uses of Maya art. Here it is necessary to be brief, although some aspects of art will become clearer in the discussion of religion. Entire volumes have been written analyzing Maya art forms and their change through time. This section can only hope to adumbrate its significance.

As in any culture whose manufactured products depend upon handicraft technology, the art of the Classic Maya was intimately connected with the hand technology of the times. Maya art forms are extensions of the motor habits and form conceptions used in the manufacture of tools and utensils of daily life. That it achieved the status of a separate art is somewhat open to question since one must be able to determine whether or not there were full-time resident artists in the ceremonial centers. Some authorities have argued that the high quality and complexity of Maya art required full-time artists, while others have stated that the planning of the art was done by the priestly class, but that the execution was performed by part-time peasant artists under their direction. Whatever the case, Maya art stands as one of the major esthetic achievements of man.

The subject matter of Maya art was the glorification of the priestly class and the representation of religious ideas. Never are the commoners, the peasant bulk of the population, represented. When the human subject is at hand it always is an important chief or priest, or one of these representing some aspect of a god. Great attention is paid to detail, which makes it possible to derive a great wealth of knowledge from the art forms about the external trappings of social differentiation as well as the detailed attributes of gods. According to Covarrubias (1957) the mask of Chac, the rain god, is ever present in Maya art, and Covarrubias maintains this derives from the jaguar masks of Olmec art, and indeed it may have been transferred from the Olmec via Izapan. Many other animals are represented in Classic Maya art, for the gods of the Maya pantheon all had their animal counterparts.

During the Classic period there were four different art styles represented in sculpture: Teotihuacan, Monte Alban, Tajin, Classic Maya. For the most part, there was little interinfluence between these styles with the exception of motifs attributable to Teotihuacan and Monte Alban and Kaminaljuyu in the Guatemalan Highlands. Classic Maya sculpture was differentiated from these other styles by the almost complete absence of sculpture in the round; bas-relief sculpture was emphasized and, despite the presence of the stelae monoliths and a few giant altars such as that at Piedras Negras, as a result, became intimately integrated with architecture. In sculpture, as in the other aspects of Classic Maya art, the primary goal was the reproduction of godly attributes conforming to the traditional style of presentation. The necessity of introducing much religious symbolism grew to become an overelaboration of certain parts of the subject matter and the failure of the design to stand out from the background. Despite this, the depiction of the human figure more nearly approached a true naturalism than did the other art styles of Classic Mesoamerica. Whether the sculpture was found on stelae, altars, or as bas-relief on some part of a building, certain principles and characteristics stand out. Primarily, the head and the headdress may occupy one third of the height of the figure. This seems to be the result of the desire to fully represent the identity of the deity and its aspect. The stelae figures display three main styles: (1) full face with feet turned out to a straight line running from heel to heel; (2) the head in profile with the body full face; (3) a full figure profile. In one sense, there is a stiffness and lack of foreshortening in such representation. However, this was due to religious and symbolic demands of the figure since subsidiary figures in the same panel or composition show complete naturalism with mastery of foreshortening. Usually the figures did not fill the full composition and the Maya, in order to achieve balance, would fill the area with glyphs. In such compositions differences in the size of the figures meant difference in social rank, not the lack of perspective in art. Depth was sometimes achieved by combining low and high relief, or allowing the quetzal feathers of the headdress to overflow the frame. Compared with the sculpture of other Mesoamerican styles at this time, Classic Maya sculpture is static, calm, and self-assured. It is the art of a secure pantheon of gods and priestly hierarchy.

As stated previously, the facades of Early Classic structures were not elaborately decorated. Bas-relief sculpture in stone did not appear until the Late Classic Puuc style of southwestern Yucatan. However, this lack may be due to the decline in stucco modeling which was widely used in the exterior decoration of buildings. Closely related to this more free form was clay modeling which represented a continuation of hand-modeled figurines of the Formative. Classic mold-made figurines of superb execution reach their height in the eighth and ninth centuries in Campeche and Tabasco.

Mural painting on the interior walls constitutes another and perhaps more interesting form of Maya art. Here the Maya artist demonstrates complete mastery of naturalistic art. Murals have great animation compared with the sculpture. Foreshortening is mastered although scale is not important. Perspective is achieved through the upward continuation of the scene to indicate distance as in certain periods of Chinese painting. The mural scenes also emphasize high-ranking personages and symbolic aspects of religion. Compared with sculpture, murals are not common in the central Maya area, and the spectacular discovery of Bonampak in southeastern Chiapas provides us with the most complete example of this art form. Here is a structure of several rooms with the interior walls completely covered with scenes depicting social and religious life, such as the treatment of war captives, the meeting of chiefs, the representation of what are obviously wives of prominent individuals, significant because female figures are rare in Maya art, and an endless detail of ceremonial costumes. Bonampak demonstrates a mastery of line and spectacular use of color. Other murals are known from Uaxactun, Santa Rita, British Honduras, Tulum on the eastern shore of Yucatan, and at Palenque. The colors so far identified are: red and pink—red iron oxide; yellow—hy-

drous iron oxide; black—carbon; blue—beidelite; green—a mixture of yellow and blue.

For the archeologist, ceramic remains are the most certain way of determining cultural change and cultural diffusion. These artifacts not only better withstand deterioration, but as a more plastic form, they reflect minute cultural changes. Pre-Classic pottery was an excellently made monochrome, with some bichrome and polychrome painted wares found in the Late phase in the Guatemalan Highlands. On this base, ceramics developed as a Classic art form. In the Early Classic, polychrome painted wares appear in the Peten, and following this, painted pottery in the mural tradition, showing life scenes as well as geometric designs, reaches a high degree of artistic achievement. Further, modeled pottery in human and animal forms was a well-developed tradition during Classic times. In Late Classic times carved pottery, bringing bas-relief technique to the ceramic medium, was made in two mold pieces. In addition to a plethora of ceremonial pottery forms, such as bowls, jars, and the like, pottery was utilized for many other things. Idols, incense burners, braziers, drain pipes, drums, flutes, whistles, ear plugs, beads, sinkers, stamps, molds, griddles, and many utilitarian vessel forms are but a few examples.

Maya art was found in many other media. Especially noteworthy is the fine low relief work done in jade. Although this is on a minute scale compared with the other sculptures, infinite detail is achieved. Pressure-flaked blades and eccentric shapes of flint and obsidian are works of art, not only in the superb mastery of technique, but in the eccentric depiction of gods and animals. Bone and shell art work is little known from the Classic Maya, but what is known follows the same art canons developed for the other forms. Low relief sculpture in wood is of high quality with every detail of Maya style evoked to its greatest expression. On door lintels and ceiling beams of sapodilla wood from Tikal and Tzibanche, human figures and hieroglyphic writing are found which parallel low relief sculpture in stone.

Metals do not play a part in Maya art or technology until the end of the Classic period. At that time, copper and some gold and bronze make their way into the central area and Yucatan. The copper and bronze appear to come from Mexico while the gold is in sheet forms of repousse design originating in Panama, although the designs are Maya. Copper and bronze bells of small size were the most common objects, but many small items such as cups, rings, sandals, and ear plugs are found as well. All the work in metal is either the result of imported craftsmen or the importation of the finished metal. The significant fact to note here is that the achievements of the Classic Maya in architecture and other aspects of construction, and in art, let alone the intellectual achievements in writing and calendrics, were all accomplished without the aid of metal tools.

Social and Political Organization

Aside from the theocratic-peasant dichotomy, there is little concrete evidence of the nature of the social and political structure of the Classic Maya. Most reconstructions of Classic Maya society have leaned heavily on the records from the time of the Spanish Conquest. Due to the conservatism of Maya culture there is some basis for analogizing from that date to Classic times. To a certain extent, post-Conquest knowledge is verified by the archeological record as seen in murals and by the traditional histories of the Maya, such as the Books of Chilam Balam. Nevertheless, such reconstructions must be used with extreme caution because Conquest records are concerned with Yucatecan Maya, and this after the long centuries of Mexican influence. So we then begin with the certain knowledge of a theocratic-peasant dichotomy with possibly, as Willey suggests, a religio-political chain of command from the large ceremonial centers to smaller and smaller settlements with social status a correlate of geography. One question remains entirely unclear: Was there a clear-cut division between religious and political officials? In Post-Classic times this was true, but this was the result of Mexican influence and the Mexican orientation was far more secular.

Classic Maya society was stratified on the basis of a combination of political, religious, and social factors. There were apparently four social groupings: rulers (royalty and nobility), priests, peasant-commoners, and slaves. It is probable that in Classic times the rulers and priests were a combined group with individuals having dual functions.

The political hierarchy was headed by the halach uinic, the "true man," and his position was hereditary, based on patrilineal descent and primogeniture. This personage possessed broad powers and determined foreign and domestic policies with the aid of a council of the chiefs, priests, and special counselors; he appointed town and village chiefs; in addition, he was the highest ecclesiastical authority. His various roles were reflected in his costumes. For civil affairs he held a mannikin scepter in the right hand and a round shield in the left. For religious roles he had a double-headed ceremonial bar, possibly a god's-head mask, across the breast or diagonally with one end on the shoulder. For military occasions a weapon was held, usually a spear, occasionally a throwing stick. This picture, however, is one heavily influenced by Mexican culture. In the murals of Bonampak there appear to be a number of individuals of equally high rank. Lesser chiefs who acted as local magistrates and executives were appointed by the halach uinic. These were members of hereditary families and headed local councils and collected taxes. Two types of war captains, the hereditary and the elected, the nacom, give a strong flavor of Mexican influence; the former led the battle, and the latter formulated plans and had to remain ceremonially pure for the three years of his elected term. Usually, there were two or three town councilors who were powerful in local affairs. Beneath these in importance were deputy assistants to the hereditary war chief and advisors on foreign policy who also acted as the masters of the men's house. Finally, there were a number of town constables charged with law enforcement.

The priesthood showed a similar hierarchical arrangement. The head of the hierarchy was known as Ah Kin Mai, or Ahau Kan Mai, and had many duties. Administratively he examined and assigned priests. He was charged with the supervision of instruction in writing, genealogies, curing ceremonies, calendrical computations, astronomy, divination, and the ritualistic round. He was an important advisor to civil officials and laymen through his knowledge of astrology and helped elect the successor to the chief. However, despite this myriad of duties his was mainly a supervisory position and he officiated only at the most important ceremonies. At the time of the Spanish Conquest in Yucatan the position was passed from father to son, who must be of noble family, with close ties to the chief civil authorities. Beneath the Ah Kin Mai were the ordinary priests, the Ah Kin—"he of the sun," who conducted the communal sacrifices and divination rituals. The chilans were soothsayers, prophets who employed the sacred books in their work. Probably these were priests with a special spiritual vision. Another specialized priestly group was the *nacon* who tore out the hearts of the sacrificial victims. Finally, there were the *chacs,* four elderly laymen who held sacrificial victims and kindled the new fire on the proper ceremonial occasions. Thus, the duties of the priesthood were many and varied, but the most important were the various forms of divination through the use of the 260-day ceremonial calendar, the *tzolkin,* and the relationships of time periods with the gods. There were simpler forms of divination in which corn kernels, other seeds, and pebbles were used. Also, the priests were charged with the treatment of sickness which consisted of diagnosis and the prescription of cure through magic and the native pharmacopoeia.

We need say little more about the peasant-commoners. These were, of course, basically farmers who contributed their labor to the construction of ceremonial centers, paid tribute to the halach uinic and the lesser officials, and gave offerings to the gods through the priests.

Slavery seems to have been practiced in Classic and Post-Classic times. However, we have little information on its status in Classic times.

There is little information concerning the nature of political units among the Classic Maya. Since there are few indications of organized warfare, the general assumption is that the Classic Maya were committed to peaceful living and that the ceremonial centers and their tribute areas were self-contained political units, but this is extremely difficult to verify. The best tentative conclusion would be that formal political organization was little developed except on the local basis until the appearance of Mexican influence during Post-Classic times. The description given above would apply more to Post-Classic times, and we would be justified in concluding that social control operated on the local level through councils of the village elders who utilized compromise and consensus in disputes and decisions, and through the supernatural as interpreted by the priesthood.

When questions of kinship, kinship terminology, marriage and the like are considered, there are the problems of reconstruction. Utilizing the same arguments as previously, modern analogy plus the conservatism of the Mayan peasant will again permit some leeway of description of conditions in Classic Maya times (Eggan, 1934:188–202).

The basic kinship unit of the Maya was a patrilineal, named, exogamous group of kin. It is not clear whether these were lineages or clans although some believe there were clans and even larger inclusive kin units among the Maya. The kinship terminology was classificatory and based on sibling terms. Likewise, the system placed emphasis on generation stratification, but recognized special affiliation through the linkage of alternate generations with the same or similar terminology. Strongly stressed was the recognition of a bilateral cross cousin terminology which designated eligible and preferred mates.

Marriage among the Maya was monogamous. Usually the bilateral cross cousins in related households were considered the desired mates, the children of the mother's brother and father's sister. It was desirable for households to exchange daughters in this fashion, and the eldest child in the family would marry the eldest cross cousin, the others following in order. Recent epigraphic work on the stelae of these times suggest there were royal dynasties in the Classic cities and that there may have been close political, if not kin, relationships between them (Proskouriakoff, 1960:454–475; Marcus, 1973). In addition to kinship preference there was also preference that the spouse be of the same social class and the same locality. Tabooed marriages were with a person of the same surname, a stepmother, and a maternal aunt. The levirate and the sororate were likewise prohibited. There is little evidence regarding age at marriage. Bishop Landa reports 12 to 14 years as the usual age in the sixteenth century.

The chain of events which culminated in marriage was usually set in motion through specified patterns of courtship in which the eligible couple would meet in public places and once preference was established meet with greater frequency. A man must have demonstrated his hunting ability before negotiations could be initiated. Once the decision had been made, the boy would consult with his father, and a professional matchmaker or marriage broker would be hired. The matchmaker, in the company of the boy's parents, would then repair to the house of the girl's parents where long, drawn-out bargaining would take place. This resulted in an agreed bride price consisting of bride service during which time the boy would work in the fields, hunt, gather firewood, and work with the bees, and payments of cacao, beads of spondylus shell, copal incense, and cotton. When agreement was reached, the boy's father notified his son who had been waiting in the men's house. The local priest was then called in and a horoscope for marriage suitability and wedding date would be cast. The wedding was timed so that the slack season of work in the fields was at hand, for during the time preceding the wedding a house would be raised near the bride's home by kinsmen and friends. When the new house was completed, the priest consecrated the structure. The wedding took place at the house of the bride's father before invited relatives and guests. On the wedding day the bridegroom's mother presented the bride with a skirt and blouse and the bridegroom with a loin cloth. The bridegroom's father presented his son with a pair of sandals. The ceremony took place in the evening preceded by, and accompanied by, feasting and ceremonial drinking. When the priest arrived the fathers presented the bride and groom to the assembled group by means of long speeches. The priest then stated the marriage agreement after which the priest and the bridal couple retired to the newly erected house, accompanied by members of the wedding party, where the couple were seated on a mat and blessed. Ceremonial incensing of the house preceded a blessing of the couple by the priest. Not until this process had been completed did the couple speak to one another.

There was temporary matrilocal residence, its duration dependent upon the length of bride service agreed upon—four to seven years was usual. Following this, patrilocal residence was the rule.

Widows and widowers found remarriage easy. All that was needed was acceptance of each other, although a person had to wait a year after the death of his spouse. Divorce seems to have been similarly easy, simple repudiation being the only step necessary.

In Classic Maya culture the course of one's life depended on the day of the *tzolkin,* the sacred 260-day ceremonial year, upon which he was born. The names he received, his role in ceremonies, when he married, and so on were determined by this day. Morley (1956) believes that the ceremony of the *hetzmek* represents a possible survival from pre-Columbian times. Among the modern Yucatecan Maya, when a child is first carried astride the hip, usually at three months for a girl and four months for a boy, a ceremony symbolically introducing the child to adult life is performed. Two god-

Maya, Classic period ● Polychrome goblet, ca. eighth century A.D. (Courtesy of the Minneapolis Institute of Arts)

parents, man and wife, carry the child nine times around a table on which nine sacred objects are located. Each of these objects, representing tools and implements of adult life, are placed in the hand of the infant. With proper feasting and drinking the ceremony is then concluded. Among the Maya of the past a child received four names: a personal name; his father's family name; a combination of his father's and mother's family names; and a nickname. In their early years all children were raised by the mother. When a boy was three or four years of age he began to accompany his father in his daily activities. During childhood fronto-occipital cranial deformation of the head was accomplished since this was a sign of great beauty among the ancient Maya. Likewise, there is good evidence that a cross-eyed condition was achieved by dangling an object between the infant's eyes. This was considered highly desirable since it was a condition of some of the important gods. This practice persists to this day among many of the Maya-speaking groups.

When children reached puberty an important ceremony was performed which admitted them to certain privileges of adult life. After this, girls were considered eligible for marriage and they had to adopt a highly circumspect behavior. Boys would assume membership in the men's house after a few years. The puberty ceremony, like all others, was preceded by the casting of a horoscope for good omens. An important man in the community sponsored the ceremony and four *chacs* would assist the priest during the ceremony. Old people would act as godparents to the children. The children would assemble in the courtyard of a chosen house, and after the priest had expelled evil from the house, he turned and asked the children if they had done any evil. A benediction followed, after which the sponsor tapped each child on the forehead nine times with a bone and placed water on their foreheads and between their toes and fingers. The children then gave gifts to the priest and the four chacs. After ceremonially smoking and drinking, the children were symbolically relieved of child status by the removal of a red bead symbolizing virginity tied around the waist of the girls and the removal of white beads symbolizing child status tied to the hair of the boys. The girls and boys were then dismissed and feasting and drinking concluded the ceremony.

The age at which boys entered the men's houses seems to have been around 16, and they remained there until married, usually 19 to 20 years of age. This house was set apart from all others and served as a rendezvous and work house for males of this age group as well as a guest house for male travellers and traders.

In addition to the aspects of status mentioned previously, three other forms are seen in the fact that the son-in-law deferred to his father-in-law, a woman always deferred to her husband, and age was an important factor in all social situations. The last was especially true with regard to the village elders who were presumed to possess great wisdom and thus were permitted the power of judgment in situations of dispute and policy.

According to the earliest records the Maya greatly feared death. Sickness and disease were always considered the result of wrongdoing, and healing and curing was magical in outlook. However, a large pharmacopoeia was used in combination with magical treatment. When death occurred a long period of mourning ensued. However, during the day no vocalizing was permitted. A commoner was buried in the floor of the house or behind it, and then the house was usually abandoned. The burial of high-ranked individuals was in the courtyards of the ceremonial centers, sometimes in the pyramids themselves, or in specially constructed tombs. Burial furniture was placed in all graves, and here again the class differences were maintained.

The Problem and Obsession of Time

For the Classic Maya the concept of time and the problems it posed amounted to what might almost be termed an obsession. In the treatment of time and the related endeavors of arithmetic and astronomy, the Maya reveal their greatest intellectual achievements. It should be stated at the outset, however, that their concern was not primarily an abstract intellectual one. The Maya were primarily concerned with the magical interpretation, manipulation, and prediction of natural phenomena which directly affected the well-being of Maya society, which was oriented towards natural phenomena and their relationship to the milpa—the means by which man identified himself with the universe. The Classic Maya viewed the world in a highly animistic fashion and this extended beyond the limits of natural phenomena.

The implications of the milpa as a combined economic and world-view mechanism have already been discussed. The association of man, plants, seasons and seasonal change, water, and all of their associated supernatural qualities formed the base of conception of the universe for the peasant farmer. The primary goal in the life of the Mayan peasant, and, by extension, the priestly hierarchy, was adjustment to the universe. The Classic Maya, as do the present Maya peasants, demanded an orderliness in the universe in order to achieve their goal. The means were at hand for this, the use of magic, whereby the various aspects of the universe could be influenced if not controlled for the benefit of man.

These central concerns of the Maya must have led to increasing observation of natural phenomena during the pre-Classic period. Since the Classic is marked by a complex set of calendrical observations and associated ceremonies and priesthood, a long period of observation during the Formative must have led to the recognition of repetition in seasons, positions of the sun, moon, and other heavenly bodies at given points in time, which gradually moved the Maya to a conception of cycles of time of varying durations. By the beginning of the Classic the Maya, through the development of a highly specialized priesthood, conceived of time divisions as burdens carried through eternity by relays of divine bearers. The different time periods were distinguished by these bearers. But the Maya were not concerned with vague recognition of temporal generalities and their supernatural associations. "Each day is not merely influenced by some god; it is a god, or, rather a pair of gods, for each day is a combination of number and name, i.e., 1 Ik, 5 Imix, 13 Ahau, and so on—and both parts are gods." (Thompson, 1954:138.) Further, day and night gods exchanged the burden of the sky. In addition to these factors there were benevolent and malevolent aspects of the gods for each day, as well as for the gods associated with the other time divisions. As an example, the year bearers were viewed in this fashion: Kan was good and associated with a fine maize crop; Muluc, an aspect of the rain god, assured a good crop, but the other two year bearers, Ix and Cauuc, were malevolent. Since the Mayas recognized several cycles of time operating simultaneously, it was apparent that the beginnings and endings of two or more time periods would with regularity occur on the same day. Consequently, gods with different aspects and qualities would occupy the same time space. In order to determine what that particular day meant for people and what ceremonies should be performed, the Maya somehow had to make a judgment of the relative strength of the gods and their attributes. This led to two things, recording of what had happened in the past, and an exploration of the past for other conjunctions of these gods in order to predict the future and thus permit prediction of behavior demanded on days of particular conjunctions. In this way the Maya priesthood attempted to ameliorate malevolencies and sought the beginnings of time. In their search they extended time into the distant past, accurately determining temporal events as far as 90 and 400 million years before. Thompson (1954) believes that the Classic Maya concluded that time had no beginning. There developed an overriding concern that history would repeat itself. That is, that the end of given time periods represented the culmination of evil influences. This appears to have led to two consequences: confounding the future with the past, and introducing a conception of cycles of time which partly conflicted with the concept of the eternity of time—the unending march of the bearers. The future was less important than the past. The Maya projected time forward only four millennia.

As the Classic period began and developed, the Maya found themselves observing a number of time cycles, and they developed a great concern over the correct designation of the conjunction of these cycles. Since the cycles were based upon ceremonial day counts which did not coincide with the true solar year, serious errors began to occur in their calculations regarding these conjunctions. This led to more exact observations through the development of suitable mathematical notation and arithmetical systems.

Basic to the observations of time cycles was the *tzolkin* sacred year, or the sacred divinatory almanac of 260 days, consisting of 13 day numbers and 20 day names. All time cycles reentered the time count in terms of a specific day name and number of the *tzolkin*. In addition to this base were the following: a vague year of 18 months of 20 days plus 1 month of 5 unlucky days; the *tun*, a ceremonial year of 360 days approximating the true year; the *katun* consisting of 20 tuns; a Venus cycle of 584 days; a lunar cycle in which lunar half years were recognized for greater accuracy; cycles of sky gods, and 9 nights and 7 days each associated with given gods; and a cycle of solar eclipses.

The main problem of the Maya priest-astronomer was to discover when two or more of these cycles coincided and to weigh the benevolent-malevolent qualities of the gods associated with the day coincidences. Among the more important of these conjunctions were the following. The conjunction of the 365-day year with the 260-day tzolkin comes only every 52 years. This was known as the calendar round. The Maya New Year was written O Pop and only 52 of the 260 days of the tzolkin could occupy the O Pop position. Hence the tzolkin revolves 73 times and the vague year calendar 52 times before the original position is achieved. In all, there were 18,980 different positions of day name, day number, and month position in the calendar round. The conjunction of the tzolkin and the katun could recur only every 260 tuns or approximately every 256 years. A katun could only end on the day Ahau, but a katun of a given name could recur only in the specified time stated above. The katun cycle was of great importance to the Maya since only 3 of the 13 katuns possessed good omens. A third important conjunction was that of the tzolkin, the vague year, and Venus. With these attempts at correlation the Maya were forced to devise correction formulas which amount to some of the major intellectual achievements in the history of man.

By the time of the Classic it was apparent to the priest-astronomers that to maintain some sort of order among the cycles a systematization of time designation was needed. This resulted in a mathematical notation system based on vigesimal units—sequential groupings of twenties. From this they developed a system of positional notation which permitted the achievement of mathematical computations which in turn allowed the correction of observational errors in the prediction of cyclical conjunction. However, apparently due to the fact that the calendrical units preceded the systematization of numbers, the calendrical progression does not follow the vigesimal progression. Thus the regularization of time notation which could be applied to total time and all cycles ran in this way:

20 kins	1 uinal (20 days)
18 uinals	1 tun (360 days—approximation of solar year)
20 tuns	1 katun (7200 days)
20 katuns	1 baktun (144,000 days)
20 baktuns	1 pictun (2,880,000 days)
20 pictuns	1 calabtun (57,600,000 days)
20 calabtuns	1 kinchiltun (1,152,000,000 days)
20 kinchiltuns	1 alautun (23,040,000,000 days)

Having once achieved the tools to cope with the complexities of the growing astronomical knowledge, the Maya then set about making corrections in their observations which would allow the proper conjunctions of the various cycles. This was necessary since each of the cycles possessed a given tzolkin day for reentering the cycle of time with which it was associated. Because the cycles of time with which the Maya were concerned did not divide themselves evenly into units of 24-hour days it is obvious that there would be accumulative errors as time passed. In order to obviate the increasing disconjunction of these cycles, correction formulas were needed. This was achieved in a number of ways. One of the great intellectual feats of the Maya was the exact measurement of the tropical year. By this they were able to correct the solar calendar with great accuracy. Using 3113 B.C. as their base the Classic Maya were able to correct, for time elapsed from that date, the accumulated error to one or two days less than what the solar year demands, while our Gregorian calendar with its leap years corrects to a day too much for the same period. Also correction of the error in the tzolkin, vague year, Venus conjunction was of the order of an error of one day in slightly over 6000 years.

Coincident with the development of the calendrical and mathematical systems came the inscriptions needed to note the correct date of the conjunctions and the associated gods. These are found in the numerical and hieroglyphic inscriptions made on the monolithic stone stelae. As noted previously, these stelae were placed before temples in the ceremonial centers and were important parts of the religion of Classic times. The glyph forms used to indicate the dates were of two types: (a) a zero, a dot for 1, and a bar for 5; (b) god's head variant numerals, comparable to the Arabic system, in which there are head forms for 1 to 13. The head variant for 10 is death and a fleshless lower jaw is added to the head variants for 4 to 9 to gain numerals 14 to 19.

The Maya numbers were placed in vertical position, and the concept of the zero did not exactly correspond to ours, but was in essence a space filler indicating completion of a specific category in the vigesimal system. The vigesimal system progresses in this manner: 1, 20, 400, 8000, 160,000, 3,200,000, 64,000,000, and the use of the bar, dot, and completion sign (zero) would indicate how many of each order was meant. As mentioned, the numerical notation of the calendar did not follow the vigesimal system. Examples of the two Maya forms of positional notation follow:

Vigesimal

8000's			•	•
400's		••	•̄	••
20's	•		—	••
1's		—	—	≡
	20	806	10,145	10,951

Chronological (calendar count)

7200's		•	(katun)
360's	—	•••	(tun)
20's	•••	••	(uinal)
1's	≡	•	(kin or day)
	1977	9866	

As is seen, the bars equal 5 and the dots 1. The position from top to bottom allows the rapid designation of date or number in the same way that our 1977 means 1 thousands, 9 hundreds, 7 tens, and 7 ones.

The Classic Maya thus were able to inscribe hieroglyphs dedicating stelae on particular conjunction days. These were all counted from a hypothetical beginning point that was 7 baktuns earlier than the inaugural date inscribed. It is believed that the inaugural date was at the end of baktun 7. The two correlations give 7.0.0.0.0 (353 B.C.) and 7.6.0.0.0 (235 B.C.). During the Early and Middle Classic the inscriptions consisted of three parts: the Initial series or long count; the Supplementary series or moon count; and the Secondary series or calendar correction formulas of that date. These inscriptions were made up as follows: a large initial glyph at the top with the central element varied according to the month deity on which the date fell; this was followed by two rows of glyphs read from left to right and from top to bottom. The first five glyphs are the number of baktuns, katuns, tuns, uinals, and kins which have elapsed since the starting point of Maya chronology. So when the Classic Maya wrote the Initial series 9.17.0.0.0 13 Ahau 18 Cumhu they meant that 9 periods of 144,000 days (9 baktuns), 17 periods of 7200 days (17 katuns), 0 periods of 360 days (0 tuns), 0 periods of 20 days (0 uinals), and 0 periods of 1 day (0 kins) had elapsed since the beginning of their chronology. The sixth position on the inscription, 13 Ahau 18 Cumhu, was the terminal date, and the seventh position was the glyph of one of the gods of the lower world. The Supplementary series or moon count noted the age of the moon, the length of the month, and the number of the lunar position in the lunar half-year period. When the Secondary series, or calendar correction formula, was added, the Maya could work out a cyclical conjunction date involving so many different time cycles that a particular day could not recur before a cycle of 374,440 years had passed. By the middle of the Late Classic the Initial series began to pass out of use and only three of the original ten glyphs were in use, giving rise to what has been termed the Short Count. This permitted accurate dating for a 19,000-year period with less than a one-day error. By late Post-Classic times there was a further abbreviation, so that accuracy only within a 256-year period was attained. This required only one glyph to express—the katun ending days.

Writing

As we have seen, the growth of writing accompanied the development of calendrical and arithmetical notation. The Maya, Zapotec, and La Venta (Olmec) were the only people in the New World to develop an embryonic form of true writing, and it is the general opinion that the Maya extended the basic ideas of the Early Classic farther than any of the three. The Aztec did not have true hieroglyphic writing but a pictographic form. The stelae cult had writing as one of its integral parts. For this reason, it is proposed by some authorities that the first inscriptions appeared outside the central Maya area. Special reference is made to the La Venta culture. However, the earliest of the certainly dated inscribed objects come from the central Maya area: Stela 29 from Tikal 8.12.14.8.15 (A.D. 292) (Shook, 1960:28–35), the Leyden Plate, apparently from Tikal—8.12.14.8.15 (A.D. 292), Uaxactun 8.14.10.13.15 (A.D. 328). It will be remembered that the inaugural date of the Maya calendar was proposed as the end of baktun 7; either 7.0.0.0.0 (353 B.C.) or 7.6.0.0.0 (235 B.C.), depending on the correlation system used. This all points to a long-term development.

Almost all the Maya glyphs have two distinct forms: one is a head form, the other is a symbolic or ideographic form, usually some attribute or element, often highly conventionalized. Most of the glyphs are compounds consisting of a main element with various affixes—prefix to left or above, and suffix to right or below. There was a considerable use of simple phonetic writing which might be described as an advanced form of rebus writing in which the original object is no longer recognizable. Ideographic glyphs were used rather extensively, but only simple sentences were written. (See Y. V. Knorozov, 1958:284–291, for different ideas on the phonetic nature of the writing.) The texts of the Classic period all seem to have dealt overwhelmingly with time, astronomy, god associations, and ceremonies. As mentioned above, a minor but important part of the texts had to do with town names, royal dynastic identity, and political relationships between them.

In addition to the inscriptions on stone and wood, the Maya wrote their religious texts on paper books known as codices. These were single sheets of paper made from the inner bark of the *copo* tree. They were folded like a screen so that there were several pages, to be read on the front in serial fashion and then read on the back. The surface was covered with a fine coating of white lime which served as the writing base. Usually these were organized into a series of chapters of several pages. Only three unquestioned codices have survived, mainly due to the sixteenth-century religious zeal of the Spaniards in wiping out Mayan religion. The Madrid Codex, which is 23½ feet long and consists of 56 leaves or sections 9¼ inches high and 5 inches wide, is a textbook of horoscopes for divination by priests. The Dresden Codex, which is 11¾ feet long and consists of 39 leaves 8 inches high and 3½ inches wide, is a treatise on astronomy. The Paris Codex is a fragment 4¾ feet long of 11 leaves and contains ritualistic formulas.

However, it is known that the Maya had more than divinatory and astronomical codices. It is reported that the Maya had a series of historical codices relating the history of the various Maya groups. There are three such forms of literature surviving: the Books of Chilam Balam, the Popol Vuh, and the Annals of the Cakchiquels. The Books of the Chilam Balam were written soon after the Conquest, in Mayan with a Spanish devised script, and contained, in part, the remains of the historical codices of the Maya. The Popol Vuh and the Annals of the Cakchiquels are the work of the Highland Maya in Guatemala and serve a like purpose for this area. They preserve many of the aspects of the total life and history of the Highland Maya, with the Annals of the Cakchiquel emphasizing the historical more than the Popol Vuh.

Religion

Mention has been made of the milpa basis of Maya religion. The dominant feature among the Maya of the past and the Maya speakers of today is the desire to achieve an accommodation to the universe, for the individual to become part of the functioning whole of the universe. From this concern, grew the need for greater predictability of natural phenomena, and a need for specialists, so the priest-scholar-astronomer group emerged. In the milpa system relatively greater emphasis was placed on maize than on any other aspect. This emphasis evidently preceded the full development of Maya religion, for this was, and still is, the primary concern of the Maya peasant. As the specialized priesthood emerged and developed, it became more concerned with other gods and the philosophical implications of the increase in astronomical and mathematical knowledge.

As can be seen from the discussion of calendrical systems, Maya religion became so involved in the functional interrelationships of infinite detail that a full treatment of Maya religion would embrace volumes. Here only the major outlines are discussed. Thompson (1954) lists six characteristics of Classic Maya religion which will serve us well here: (1) Reptilian origin of the deities of the rain and of the earth; features of snakes and crocodiles, merged and fantastically elaborated, alone or blended with human characteristics, distinguished those gods. Deities with purely human form are not common in Maya art. (2) Quadruplicity of various gods together with association with world direction and colors, yet a mystic merging of the four in one, a process somewhat comparable to the Christian mystery of the Trinity. (3) Duality of aspect, for deities could be both benevolent and malevolent and, in some cases, seemingly could change sex. This duality also extended to age, for in the case of several deities, functions are shared between a youthful and an aged god. (4) Indiscriminate marshalling of gods in large categories so that a god might belong to two diametrically opposed bodies, becoming, for instance, a member of a sky group as well as an underworld group. (5) Great importance of the groups of gods connected with time periods. (6) Inconsistencies and duplication of functions arising from the imposition of concepts originating among the hierarchy on the simpler structure of the gods of nature worshiped by the early Maya.

There were apparently a number of gods associated with the creation of the earth in Maya mythology. Among these Hunab is sometimes designated as the chief one. According to the legend, after the creation of the earth and the filling of it with plant and animal life, the gods found nothing with intelligence, and they therefore created men of mud. But these could not speak and were destroyed. The gods then created beings of wood, but these were not grateful, had limited intelligence, and acted so badly towards all things that waters were sent to destroy all life on earth. Some of these escaped and became monkeys. The final creation was that of four men from a gruel of white and yellow maize, but these humans were too gifted and the gods had to place a light mist before their eyes or the secrets of the universe would be revealed to them. The foregoing version is from the Popol Vuh of the Maya-speaking Quiche. The Maya also believed that there had been five creations of the world and four destructions. Part of the Mayan concern about calendrical conjunction derived from an attempt to anticipate the fifth destruction.

The Maya world was arranged in a complex fashion. The sky was conceived to be thirteen compartments inhabited by specified gods, six ascending on the east and six descending on the west with one and thirteen on an equal plane. The sky was supported by four gods at the sides of the world—the *Bacabs*. These four were associated with world directions and colors: red and east, white and north, black and west, yellow and south, and possibly center with green. The association of world directions and colors with the gods was of supreme importance for the Maya. At the four sides of the world stood sacred ceiba trees (wild cotton trees) which in turn were associated with the colors. And the world rested on the back of a huge alligator or crocodile floating in a vast pond. Thompson (1954) thinks there may have been four of these reptiles. Finally, there were nine underworlds with steps down to five and then up again. Each of these was associated with gods known as the lords of the night.

The Maya believed in the immortality of the soul and in an afterlife, but we are not certain what the nature of the afterworld paradise or hell was conceived to be in Classic Maya times. In Post-Classic times, after Mexican influence was strong, paradise was conceived to be a place of delights, no pains or suffering, with an abundance of food and drink, rest and happiness. However, only those dead by hanging, in battle, in sacrifice, and in childbirth, and all priests went directly to paradise. There was a hell, *xibal*, where the souls were tormented by evil gods with hunger, cold, weariness, and grief. Since the soul was immortal all pleasure and torture went on forever.

Most Maya gods were found in groups of four; thus each was associated with a color and direction. As mentioned, each had good and bad aspects, and each showed a blending of features of animals and plants with a human aspect. Of the sky gods, the sun and the moon were the most important. These were the first inhabitants of the world and the sun became patron of music and hunting while the moon was associated with weaving and childbirth. These were the first to cohabit, but the moon was unfaithful and thus became associated with sexual looseness. Itzamna was outstanding in the hierarchic pantheon, but apparently had little devotion among the rank and file of the Maya. There were probably four Itzamna associated with the colors and directions, but they seem also to be confused with the Chacs in the form of celestial monsters with rain attributes. The Post-Classic Maya of Yucatan viewed Itzamna as benevolent and always a friend of man. The Chacs, rain gods possibly associated with Itzamna, but they may be part of an older religious set than Itzamna, were four gods with the associated directions and colors. They caused rain by sprinkling from gourds and hurled stone axes as thunderbolts. They were thought to be gigantic beings with little frog attendants. With the basis of Maya religion in mind, it can be seen that these gods occupied a very important place in the religious life of the Maya, priestly and peasant. There were many other gods associated with the sky of which the planet Venus was among the more important, with hieroglyphic and calendrical associations.

The earth gods likewise were many and varied; the most important was the youthful maize god, the god of all vegetation. All other growing things had in-dwelling gods. A jaguar god of the interior and surface of the earth was singularly important, while Mam, an old god who carried the year symbol on his back, was believed to cause earthquakes while moving about in his underground abode. All of the earth gods had common symbols: water, lily, shells, aquatic symbols, the Imix sign, and death attributes.

The nine gods of the underworld are widespread throughout Mesoamerica. They have been identified in the Classic Maya inscriptions, but their names are not known. They were apparently associated with the paradise and the hells of the Maya, and if we can analogize from the Aztec or Mexican-influenced Yucatecan Maya, *Ah Puch*, the god of death, was associated with the fifth, the lowest, of the underworlds.

The almost endless time and number gods offer a good example of the shifting quality of the Mayan gods. Some were more important than others, but their importance varied according to the conjunction of days.

In one sense Maya religion was one continuous round of ceremonies. These demanded ritual cleanliness, ritualistic drinking, and ritual purification afterwards. This cleanliness applied equally to all the participants and the objects used in the ceremony. There were ceremonies for war, for any new construction from a peasant's hut to a temple, for puberty rites, for communal and individual hunting, for all aspects of plant cultivation such as clearing, sowing, planting, and harvesting. In fact, all ceremonies public and private demanded continence, fasting, offerings, and sacrifice. Among the more important ceremonies were those associated with the katun endings, the New Year, and the 52-year cycle. The complex divinatory forecasting demanded that all the restrictions mentioned be highly intensified.

Intimately associated with the religious ceremonies were the dance and various forms of sacrifice. Dancing was important during ceremonies of sacrifice and during those for hunting and good crops. Impersonation of the gods was the chief duty and the dancers were subject to special restrictions. Dance was essentially a religious ritual, and very little of it was social in our sense of the term. The Maya believed that sacrifice was demanded by the gods in order that the world may move and work. Unlike the Post-Classic times, there was no abasement on the part of the Classic Maya. Human sacrifice was practiced by all Maya, but its great elaboration did not occur until after the Mexican influence. Apparently children were much in demand because of ceremonial cleanliness, but the bloody forms of human sacrifice seemingly were mostly Post-Classic in date. In addition to humans, animals, agricultural products, cooked meat in sauces, copal (an incense of great ceremonial value), rubber, flowers, jade, shell beads, and prized feathers were sacrificed. Also very common was the sacrifice of blood from the tongue, ears, the genitals, and various other parts of the body. The priests engaged in this most often.

The world view, or basic values, of the Classic Maya has been mentioned in several contexts. Adjustment to the universe and moderation in all things apparently were what the Maya valued most. This would seemingly have been the result of high value placed on compromise and cooperation coupled with a deeply religious character. There was in addition devoutness, discipline, and respect for authority which conduced to the development of the priesthood. Also, the doctrine of orderly predestination either predisposed to the development of the calendrical systems, or derived from it. One gets the impression of great endurance in the Maya, not on the level of the priestly hierarchy, but on the peasant level where the same basic religious features persist to this day. To be sure, this approach to the pan-human problems of the universe demands the suppression of the individual.

Classic Maya civilization, contrasted with total Classic Maya culture, achieved great intellectual attainments. The great central value was the passage of time: "... the flow of days from the eternity of the future into the eternity of the past." (Thompson, 1954:13.)

THE AZTECS

Introduction

The Aztecs (more properly the Tenochca, or Mexica, since the Nahua-speaking tribes of the Valley of Mexico are more correctly referred to as Aztecs collectively) were late comers to Mesoamerica. From the beginning of the Classic period onward, the instability of the northern cultural frontier of Mesoamerica was a reflection of the constant recruitment of "barbarian" tribes to the Mesoamerican way of life. As Kirchhoff (1952:17–30) has noted, the boundaries of Mesoamerica shifted in accord with the movements of these barbarians southward and the Mesoamericans northward. The Aztecs were one of the later barbarian groups, along with other Nahua-speaking tribes, who acquired Mesoamerican culture. Temporally, the Aztecs fall entirely into the Post-Classic period. As a distinctive group they apparently never came in contact with the Classic cultures of Mesoamerica. The destruction of Classic Teotihuacan long preceded their advent. Other Nahua- and non–Nahua-speaking groups were fully engaged in the development of the Post-Classic culture pattern when they appeared on the scene. However, the Aztecs adopted wholeheartedly the Mixteca-Puebla tradition derived from Teotihuacan. The Post-Classic marks the widespread presence of true cities in Mesoamerica although, as we have seen, Teotihuacan in the late pre-Classic along with others in the Classic could lay valid claim to that form of settlement. We have mentioned the various descriptive terms applied to the cultural reorientation of the Post-Classic, noting especially militarism, secularism, and expanded urbanism.

For the Post-Classic in the Valley of Mexico there are a number of historical records written soon after the Conquest. From these there arises an idea of the nature of the political organization and military history of the region. The term Chichimec, which plays an important role in the Post-Classic history of this region, is nearly always used when referring to the wild tribes to the north or to the late comers and adherents to Mesoamerican culture. Generally, the term Toltec referred to the bearers of Mesoamerican culture. In this sense then the Toltecs long preceded the Aztecs, but one must remember that this apparently was a generic term, so that at the Conquest both the Toltecs of Tula and the Aztecs were called Toltec. This is important to note because it has long been maintained that the Toltecs were a completely separate group who reorganized Mesoamerican culture following the disintegration of the Classic. Toltec is a term best utilized for the Mexican Post-Classic Mesoamericans whatever their linguistic affiliations or origins were (Kirchhoff, 1948).

Physiography and Climate

The environment of the Aztecs stands in high contrast to that of the Classic Maya. The Valley of Mexico marks the southern limit of the *Mesa Central* of Mexico. It is a basin which was filled with lakes and marshy land and surrounded by high mountains at the time of the Aztecs. In the valley floor the altitude runs between 7000 and 8000 feet while high mountains rim most of the circumference of the valley. Standing with their crests high above the snow line are the volcanic peaks of Popocateptl and Ixtaccihuatl, Smoking Mountain and White Woman, respectively, in Nahua. The former rises to a height of 17,893 feet and the latter to 17,343 feet. It is believed that during early Classic times the area was well forested with pine; however, as the population increased these trees were so decimated for firewood that most of the mountain slopes were denuded by the end of the Classic. Added to this, the rainfall is relatively low in this region, and the natural cover of the Valley of Mexico at the advent of the Aztec was extremely sparse. In fact, the control of water resources became one of the major tasks of the tribes of the area.

Living in a region which presented the dual problems of a semiarid climate and a basin which collected the available water in lakes and marshes, measures were needed which would both preserve the water for use and control the accumulation in the lakes. During Classic times most of the settlement was confined to the slopes of the adjacent mountains and the level land away from the marshy regions. Thus, the Classic occupation of Teotihuacan resorted to irrigation in order to utilize the water for the production of food. It was not until Post-Classic times that the water resources of the lakes were fully exploited, although before this the natural edible lacustrine life was used. By the fourteenth century, population pressures in the region generated a group of warring towns in the valley. In fact, the Tenochca found little space in which to settle and much of their history prior to the founding of Tenochtitlan was motivated by a search for cultivable land. The founding of Tenochtitlan on an island in Lake Texcoco brought into full use the *chinampa* system of cultivation. Essentially this is a means of constructing fields which amount to floating islands, and it was the answer to the land shortage of Post-Classic times. The floating fields, or gardens, consisted of a woven mat base covered with soil. As the plants grew on this raft plot, the roots sought out, and anchored the plot to, the bottom of the shallow lake, and soon new static land had been created. The economic and population expansion of the Tenochca was made possible by the full exploitation of the chinampa method of cultivation. It is not implied that the Tenochca were the only group who practiced this method, for it was widely used in southern Mexico at the time of the Spanish Conquest. Today the remnants of these chinampas can be seen in the still-cultivated floating gardens of Xochimilco.

Unlike the Classic Maya, the Post-Classic peoples of the Valley of Mexico, through the direction and organization of large populations, paralleled other areas of the world in which the appearance of civilization has required the control of water resources through major public works. Not only were the water resources of the valley controlled through the irrigation systems of Classic times and the chinampas of Post-Classic, but major efforts were exerted in changing the character of the lakes themselves by means of dikes.

The Valley of Mexico presents what we would term temperate climate throughout the year. A rainy and a dry season indicate the more southerly latitude of the area. Moreover, while the nights are cool and sometimes cold, only rarely does snow fall, but hail is not uncommon. In Mesoamerica, the environmental contrast between the Aztec and the Classic Maya could not be greater.

History

The traditional history of the Aztecs begins in A.D. 1168. Their origin was supposedly an island in the middle of a lake to the north or northwest of the Valley of Mexico. Here they began their wandering by building boats to take them ashore. On the shore they discovered a cave or seven caves, in which a stone image of Huitzilopochtli, the hummingbird god, spoke to them and advised them on their journey to the Valley of Mexico. At each stop his advice was heard and those who did not wish to follow it always met with dire results. The Tenochca tribe of the Aztecs claim to have come into the Valley of Mexico from the northwest, via Tula and Zumpango, and settled first in the area known today as Chapultepec. Little attention was paid them upon their arrival and they made their way to Chapultepec without any great interference on the part of other groups already occupying the region. However, they appeared at a time when the population was beginning to show signs of increase and settlements were expanding. The traditional date was A.D. 1248. According to the traditional histories, the previously quiet and peaceful Tenochcas began to generate enmity among their neighbors because of their wife-stealing habits and their generally disgusting—to their neighbors at least—religious practices which emphasized human sacrifice. As a result, the towns of Tepanec, Xochimilco, and Culhua banded together and crushed the Tenochcas. The chief, Huitzilihuitl I, and most of the tribe became serfs of the town of Culhuacan. The date traditionally is ca. 1300. However, some escaped to a low-lying island in the lake and there founded Tenochtitlan. The date of the actual founding of Tenochtitlan is in some doubt, but those most often cited center in the fourteenth century. Between the founding of Tenochtitlan and ca. 1375, when the Aztecs became a distinct, organized tribe again, they went through a period of learning Mesoamerican culture better and distinguishing themselves in battle.

Coxcox, the King of Culhuacan, found himself at war with Xochimilco and asked his captives for aid. During this war the Tenochcas distinguished themselves and asked for a daughter of Coxcox to found a dynasty with their own chief. However, the Tenochcas sacrificed the girl, flayed her, and performed a ceremonial dance wearing her skin as a costume. Coxcox in his anger drove them all into the lake where some of the more acculturated are said to have introduced stone architecture to Tenochtitlan. Before 1375, the Tenochcas gradually became more powerful. So much so, that at that date, they asked Culhuacan for a chief who then became Acamapichtle under whose rule the Tenochcas were tributaries and allies of the Tepanec of Azcapotzalco against Tenayuca and Culhuacan. His successor, Huitzilhuitl II, mar-

Aztec ● Polychrome tripod vessel. The design elements, especially the stepped design, are suggestive of pottery designs in the Pueblo area of the Greater Southwest. Tripod forms, however, are distinctively Mesoamerican. (Courtesy of The Minneapolis Institute of Arts)

ried the daughter of Tezocomoc of Texcoco, and thus insured the position of the Tenochca during the major struggle for power between Texcoco and Tepanecs. In the end, Texcoco was defeated. However, Maxtla, one of the sons of Tezozomoc, gained the leadership of Texcoco through murder and intrigue, exiling Nezahualcoyotl the rightful heir. Maxtla attempted to gain control of the entire valley, and when he murdered Chimalpopoca, the Tenochca chief, the Tenochca, those Texcocans under Nezahualcoyotl, and the town of Tlacopan joined in alliance against him. Under Itzacoatl, the new Tenochca chief, and Nezahualcoyotl, Maxtla was overthrown. With this victory the Tenochcas won their freedom supported by a military class which came to the fore mainly through land division of the mainland. Itzcoatl (1428–1440) reorganized the Tenochcas. Temples were constructed, the city was planned, constructed, and connected with the mainland by causeways, and a religious hierarchy and civil government were founded. Also, Itzcoatl began a systematic conquest of tribes not subject to Tenochtitlan and Texcoco. In this way, Xochimilco and Chalco had acknowledged supremacy of the allies by the death of Itzcoatl. Moctezuma I, who succeeded Itzcoatl in 1440 and was in power until 1469, had been the general during the conquest of Chalco in the preceding regime. He continued the alliance with Texcoco, and also extended the conquests to Puebla, Vera Cruz, Morelos, and Guerrero. The reign of Moctezuma I was marked by a number of important events. The conquest of Puebla introduced many new religious ideas and gods to the Tenochcas. Tenochtitlan grew mightily, creating a necessity for the construction of an aqueduct from Chapultepec to bring fresh water to the city. Also, the lake was diked for better control of the water resources. More important was the overall incorporation of the Aztec into Mesoamerican culture, albeit they added their own interpretation. Axayacatl succeeded his father, Moctezuma I, in 1469 and continued conquests to the west of Matlatzinca, and southwards to Oaxaca, Tehauantepec, and possibly to the Guatemalan border. However, he was severly beaten by the Tarascans of Michoacan, and this remained the only defeat until that by the Spaniards. Tizoc succeeded his brother in 1479 and, although not noted for his military successes, constructed the great temple to Huitzilopochtli the War God, and Tlaloc the rain god. It is said that the military advisors poisoned Tizoc for his lack of military success. Ahuitzotl succeeded his brother in 1486 and immediately, through a continuance of the alliance with Texcoco, reconquered Oaxaca and returned with 20,000 sacrificial victims. He also conducted a campaign against the Huasteca in northern Vera Cruz, but it appears that most of his time was spent in maintaining control over tribute peoples who apparently were in continuous revolt. Tenochtitlan continued to grow, so much so that a second aqueduct had to be constructed to bring water from the mainland. Ahuitzotl was a lover of war, women, and, generally, of lusty living. During supervision of public works against serious flooding of the city, he received a serious head injury and died. A nephew, Moctezuma II, succeeded to power in 1502 and his reign was filled with increasing disaster, not only from the continued revolts among the conquered tribes and towns, but also through the breaking of the long alliance with Texcoco. More ominous than all these, the omens for the 1507 New Fire (52-year cycle) ceremony were the worst possible, and news of Spanish probing on the east coasts created an air of impending doom. Moctezuma II died in 1519, whether by disease or at the hands of the Spaniards is not known. His successor, Cuitlahuac, died of smallpox within a month, and Cuauhtemoc, who led the fight against the Spaniards, was the last free ruler of the Aztecs. He met his death at the hands of the Spaniards in 1524 during Cortez's march to Honduras.

The history of the Tenochcas, who became the foremost Aztec group, is one of increasing use of the Post-Classic culture. They contributed little in the way of originality to Mesoamerican culture, but what they adopted they utilized and developed in an intensive manner. It was they who brought the trends of secularism and militarism to the greatest heights. It was the Tenochcas who brought the development of true urban centers to full completion. The contrast with the Classic Maya is one which at first glance would seem to indicate an insuperable gap between the two. However, it must be remembered that most of the cultural elements and even cultural patternings which the Tenochcas so fully expanded were present among the Classic Maya. The differences between the two appear to be far greater than they really were. The Classic Maya and the other cultures of Classic times laid the base of Mesoamerican culture and developed much of its potential, and while the Aztec immigrants displayed different emphases in the use of Mesoamerican culture, it should not be forgotten that Mesoamerica was an area unified by culture history.

Population and Settlement Patterns

At the end of the fifteenth century the Valley of Mexico was typified by settlements of a size and complexity which could be termed urban. These were not the ceremonial centers of the Classic Maya, but were fully occupied, fully functioning cities in the sense in which we think of the term. The Tenochcas were the dominant Aztec group, and their city, Tenochtitlan, was the largest and most powerful center in all of southern Mexico. However, the analogy to a modern city must not be carried too far, since much of the urban organization was still based on extended kinship groupings and, consequently, a fully developed class system had not emerged although there was a complex system of social stratification.

It will be remembered that Tenochtitlan was built on a low-lying island in Lake Texcoco and had expanded its land area by constructing chinampa plots. The general plan of the city was rectangular and this form appears to have been maintained throughout its expansion. The entire city, termed the *altepetl* Tenochtitlan, was divided into four major sections, the *campans,* or the *barrios grandes* of early Spanish terminology. The altepetl and the campan appear to have been territorial divisions; however, each campan consisted of several *calpulli barrios* which were also kinship units. The exact number of calpulli is somewhat in doubt although the most commonly accepted number is 20, and the number in each campan apparently varied. Each calpulli in turn consisted of several smaller subdivisions with a kinship base known as *tlaxilacalli* (*calles* or *barrios chicos*). The number of tlaxilacalli in each calpulli is also open to question, but it appears there were two and sometimes three. Each tlaxilacalli was made up of family plots known as chinampa. The division and use of the land was more complex than the territorial arrangement of the city and will be discussed below.

One approached Tenochtitlan from the mainland over wide causeways running from the north, west, and south to the city. The edges of the city were a mass of greenery, the cultivated chinampa, and behind them could be seen the white masonry buildings with the pyramidal temples standing above all other structures. When the edge of the city was reached the broad causeways ended, and the main thoroughfares became canals with foot paths running alongside crossed by bridges at intervals. The main canals led to a central plaza which was used for communal gatherings. Here also were the main temples (the *teocalli*), a huge wooden rack for the skulls of sacrificial victims, the living quarters for the royalty, and the market. As well, each of the calpulli sections had its own ceremonial center. The city was served by two large aqueducts bringing fresh water from the mainland. The one entering from the west came from Chapultepec and consisted of two channels which allowed for alternate cleaning of the conduits. The one entering from the south from Coyoacan was constructed later by Ahuizotl. The problem of sanitation was solved by stationing canoes at specified locations, which were taken when filled to the chinampa as fertilizer. Urine was collected in pottery vessels to be used as a mordant in dyeing cloth. The continued existence of Tenochtitlan required a well-organized system because the city was estimated to have had a population of between 100,000 and 300,000 at the time of Cortez, depending upon the size of the area included in the estimate. From the description given by the Spaniards it would appear that public sanitation and water distribution were better than any with which the Spaniards were familiar.

Housing varied according to social status. The commoners occupied rectangular, one- or two-roomed houses with earthen floors, wattle-and-daub walls, and thatched roofs. Wealthier individuals lived in houses constructed on a raised platform which was usually faced with stone. The walls possessed stone bases and the body of the wall was completed either in stone or adobe brick. Large cross beams, covered by small poles, and then a lime plaster, formed the roof. Even for the wealthy the house was not spacious, but usually shallow with a depth of two rooms with the back room open only to the front and containing the hearth. The other rooms were open, fronted by a colonnade which formed a rectangular courtyard in the rear, but no room possessed a window. However, social, sleeping, cooking, storage, and slave quarters were distinct from one another.

The living quarters of the ruling family were in essence more extensive forms of the houses of the wealthy. There were many patios arranged at different levels, and the rooms were more spacious and open to the air. As would be expected in a household which required 3000 attendants, guards, and specialized workers to function, the size and purpose of the rooms and patios varied greatly. The descriptions left by the Spanish conquistadors, however exaggerated they might have been, leave one with an impression of sumptuousness and barbaric splendor which could only have made these men more determined to win Aztec territory for their own.

Tenochtitlan was a true city. Busy with trade, mass movement of people on the causeways, and the center of a complex network of fiefs paying tribute which demanded an intricate combination of secular and religious administrative machinery; it marked the peak of Post-Classic cultural complexity. However, all was not well with the Aztecs in 1519, and a major element in the Spanish Conquest was the inability of Aztec cultural complexity to maintain itself as an integrated and cohesive unit.

Economy

As in the remainder of Mesoamerica, the economic base of the Aztec lay in the milpa production of food plants. The plant inventory, and the tools and techniques used, were very much the same as those of the Classic Maya and of Mesoamerica today. However, among the Aztec there seems to have been little of the goals and philosophy associated with the Mayan peasant and his desire to adjust to the universe, for the Aztec dealt with the universe in other ways.

The full development of the potentialities of the chinampa distinguished the Aztecs from other parts of Mesoamerica, but the food plants would be familiar to every inhabitant of the region. Maize, as always, dominated, but beans, squash, gourds, sweet potatoes, green and red peppers, avocados, and tomatoes were all produced to diversify the diet. The maguey, or so-called century plant, was important in the manufacture of the fermented beverage pulque. Pulque was important in the diet of the Aztec since it made up for the lack of greens. Maguey was also important in religious ceremonies; from it was produced a fiber used in making twine, rope, and woven containers, and it supplied thorn needles as well as leaves for roofing and walls. Cotton and tobacco were raised. Other vegetable products were imported from Vera Cruz: chocolate, vanilla, pineapple, copal, and rubber. The number and variety of domesticated animals were few among the Aztec. Dogs, turkeys, ducks, geese, and quail were domesticated, but only the first two were important. One of the several types of dogs was fattened for food. The cochineal bug was kept for the manufacture of crimson dye, and the maguey slug may have been domesticated for food.

The Aztecs made full use of their lacustrine environment. The great abundance of water fowl during seasonal migrations made them important as a food. They were taken with nets and the throwing stick. Large quantities of small fish were taken each day and traded in the markets. In addition to these products, several edible invertebrates were taken from the lakes (Deevey, 1957:213–328). The *axayácatl*, a corixid water bug, laid eggs in bundles of tule placed in the water by fishermen. The pupal and larval stages of the salt fly, *cuclin* and *izcauitli* respectively, were harvested. These were combined in various ways to make *ahuautli* cake sold in the markets. An algae, the purple Oscillatoria or Nostoc, was collected and made into *tecuitlatl*—another cake form. Crustaceans were represented by crayfish.

It will be remembered that the total cultural situation among the Aztecs was one differentiated from the Classic Maya by the presence of true urban centers. In terms of cultural generalization, there is thus a condition of food surplus which in turn implies the possibility of a more complex division of labor. This is seen in Tenochtitlan by the specialization of economic activities. Although much of the craft production was in the homes, there was craft specialization by some levels of kin group organization. Individual families were no longer completely independent in economic activity, as is seen by the expansion of markets and the existence of such distinct groups as traders and merchants.

Craft production was specialized socially in terms of calpulli and tlaxilacalli although not to the degree that there was a complete exclusion of some craft work in all households, such as weaving by women. There was the beginning of a division of labor which has led many authorities to claim the existence of guilds among the Aztec and to assign social status and rank to these. However, it may be seen that social status and rank were based on the principle of those who governed and those who were governed in each kin and sectional division of Tenochtitlan. There were specialized craftsmen who worked with stone. Some specialized in the flaking of flint and obsidian, making flaked-flint sacrificial knives and the long slender blades of obsidian used as knives. Others pecked, ground, and polished stone into the form of manos and metates, stone boxes for burning and storing the hearts of sacrificial victims, and incense burners. Some specialized only in working obsidian, grinding and polishing mirrors and vessels from this extremely hard and difficult volcanic glass. Others specialized in stonework associated with the public buildings, dressing masses of stone for construction and sculpture. Closely associated with the last activities were the masons who worked in stone fitting and in the uses of mortar. Although weaving was done by most women, there were those who specialized in textiles for the ruling classes and for trade. Most of the weaving was done with the belt loom so common throughout Mesoamerica and the techniques were highly varied. The most common characteristic was the almost exclusive use of cotton fibers; there was also the development of rectangular patterning, along with fine embroidery with curvilinear as well as naturalistic design, batik and tie-dyeing, and velvet and brocade weaving in addition to the usual muslin weaves. Closely related to the weaving of textiles was feather mosaic work made into shields and cloaks which were used as ceremonial insignia.

Other mosaic work was done with shell and turquoise, the latter being the one most prized material of the Aztecs. Sacrificial knives, masks, and shields were covered with intricately fitted pieces of shell and stone depicting gods and ceremonial scenes.

Woodworking was also done by specialists and consisted of two sorts, ceremonial and utilitarian. Masks, idols, drums, and ceremonial throwing sticks were all elaborately and tastefully carved with ceremonial designs and very often combined shell and turquoise mosaic with the woodcarver's art. The drums were of two sorts, a vertical cylindrical form with a skin head and the horizontal slit gong so typical of the Maya. Utilitarian aspects of woodworking were very important to the Aztecs. Wooden beams instead of planks were cut from pine, and since the Aztec did not employ the corbelled vault with any great frequency, these were important in all construction. The lake environment made canoes extremely important, and some woodworkers devoted all their time to the making of dugout canoes, although plank canoes were known as well. Given the canals of Tenochtitlan, some means of traveling from one section of town to another was necessary. This was accomplished by portable bridges which were placed at specified crossings when needed.

One important craft distinguished the Aztecs from the Classic Maya. This was metallurgy. It will be remembered that the Classic Maya knew little of metals, and what was known either came in by trade or the importation of craftsmen. The Aztecs, as was the case with most of Post-Classic Mesoamerica, knew metallurgical techniques and made use of metal tools and implements. However, these had not superseded stone tools and implements by the time of the Spanish Conquest. This craft was very late in Mesoamerica and was never as well developed as it was in the circum-Caribbean and the Central Andes to the south from whence it had presumably diffused. Mining techniques among the Aztecs were simple, and the smelting of ores was accomplished by a forced draft using blow tubes. Copper was worked in its native state as well as being gilded. They also alloyed copper and gold which was cast by the *cire perdue* or lost wax method into bells and ornaments.

Ceramics were highly developed among the Aztecs and showed a much wider use than among the Maya. The techniques, however, were not as numerous as among the Classic Maya since the Aztecs used neither molds nor the primitive potter's wheel, the *kabal* (a rotating base moved by the foot without the benefit of the weighted wheel). All pottery was handmade, and the vessels were decorated with polychrome designs emphasizing naturalism. There seem to have been vessel forms for every conceivable use. The most common were goblets for pulque, graters for chili, an oval eating platter with a separate compartment for sauces, and *comales* for cooking tortillas. Decorated spindle weights, or whorls, were ceramic for the most part. Ceramics were used in construction to make large roof ornaments for temples, fired bricks for the back of fireplaces and sometimes for building corners in the place of stone.

Merchants and traders did not work in the fields and were organized into groups similar to the calpulli. This condition developed from the increased specialization in the handicrafts and the demand for raw materials from outside the Valley of Mexico. Further, the traders performed a dual function by acting as spies. Trade was carried on over large distances with shells from the Caribbean, pottery from Salvador, and gold ornaments from Panama. The market system was well developed with each town of any size holding one at specified intervals. Some of these were very large and were conducted daily, such as the one at Tlatelolco, a town adjacent to Tenochtitlan. The wealth and variety of this market astounded the Spaniards, some of whom estimated that 60,000 people occupied the marketplace on given days. Barter was the chief means of exchange, although cacao beans, gold-filled quills, and crescent knives of copper served as a medium of exchange as did the more highly valued jade and turquoise on occasion.

The implications of the size and complexity of the market system among the Aztec are many. Foremost is that by the latter part of the fifteenth century large segments of the population were not seriously engaged in food production but instead in manufactures, administration, and other activities characteristic of true cities. This implies an increasingly complex but fragile cultural organization whose interdependence of specialized parts reflects the strengths and weaknesses of the Aztec empire. (See Kurtz, 1974, for an extended discussion of this subject.)

Theoretically, the tribe of the Tenochca owned all of the land held; however, the immediate controlling unit was the calpulli. Monzon (1949) maintains that the calpulli occupied the land they were originally assigned at the settlement of Tenochtitlan. According to the rules of land ownership, a calpulli could not take the land of another when their population expanded, although a family could gain the use of calpulli land other than its own. The chinampa system allowed for the growth both of arable land and of the city. However, land use and ownership was closely tied to the social system which consisted of two main groupings: the *macehuales*, or common people and manual laborers, and the *pilli*, those who directed or coordinated work. These two social divisions cut across the tribe, the calpulli, and the tlaxilacalli and were intimately associated with the division of what was produced on the land. In one sense, the calpulli was, then, a closed group of landowners. However, the land of the calpulli was divided into two classes, that cultivated for tribute and that cultivated for sustenance. The latter was divided into private land and the common land of the calpulli. The tribute land was worked by the macehuales under the direction of the pillis, and the products were paid as tribute to the chiefs and the temples. This applied to both the tribal and calpulli categories. Private land was owned only in the sense that a given family had the right to work it. On the death of a man his sons inherited this right, but if there were no heirs or if it was not worked within a two-year period, the land reverted to the calpulli and could be reassigned.

Despite the expansion of the chinampas, the Aztecs were suffering from a land shortage by the early sixteenth century and conquest was being used as a technique for alleviating it. Those warriors who showed themselves valiant in battle were given grants in the conquered territory, and small Tenochca colonies were settled there to oversee the conquered peoples who worked the land. However, conquest served for more than alleviating land shortage. Tribute became an important part of the economy of the Aztec, although it seems certain that tribute in the form of sacrificial victims was more important than other kinds.

Dress and Ornament

The Aztec strove to accentuate social status and rank through dress and ornament. In general, four main groups could be distinguished in any social gathering; within these groupings were differences in status and rank. The commoner men wore their hair long and uncovered as a sign of their status. The dress was simple, consisting of a loin cloth, a mantle knotted over one shoulder, and sandals of woven maguey fiber or leather worn only in cold weather. The commoner women wore a two-piece outfit of a finely woven wraparound skirt held in place by a belt, and a woven blouse or *huipil*. Their hair was worn long and dressed in braids with interwoven ribbons of cotton or coarsely woven maguey. On occasion, the braids were twisted around the head.

The higher-ranked pillis wore the same basic clothing, of similar materials but better made, usually decorated with elaborate embroidery. The chiefs and the wealthy wore feather cloaks, and the chiefs of all ranks wore a leather fillet from which hung two tassels. The highest-ranking chiefs wore a diadem of gold or jade and turquoise as a badge of their office.

Men in their role as warriors were distinguished by costumes modeled on the ocelot or the eagle, thus indicating their affiliation with one of the two important military orders. Rich mantles and ornate feather headdresses, the latter, consisting of a wicker harness held on the shoulders and covered with huge feather mosaics, further indicated the high social position of the military groups.

The priests and priestesses were as elaborately dressed as the warriors with their costumes representing specific gods and goddesses. In addition, ornate ritualistic marks set this group apart.

Jewelry corresponded in complexity and richness to the social position of the wearer. Copper, gold, silver, jade, turquoise, emeralds, opals, moonstones, mosaics, and shells were all used, alone and in combination. Both men and women wore ear plugs, but men were usually more elaborately ornamented than women. A well-dressed male displayed nose and lip plugs, other ornaments in these features, necklaces, pendants, armlets, and leglets.

As well, the Aztec utilized elaborate body painting as a means of designating social status and role. Red, blue, yellow, grey, and black were colors which indicated specific social and religious significance.

Art

As with Classic Maya the major motivating force in Aztec art was religion. In all aspects of artistic expression the quality of monumental-ism is its most prominent feature. Sculpture was the most highly developed form and its religious motivation made it an integral part of architecture or imparted architectural qualities to it. Painting and drawing were most weakly developed although even there monumentality and strict attention to detail are the clear characteristics. The Aztecs were stark realists in their approach to life and in their religious art. It has a severe realism and austerity which applies to both humans and animals. But this was not the whole of the art, for, while being realistic, the Aztec could express deeply religious esoteric ideas. This art has a ferocious quality, and the subject of death is so preponderant, that religious awe and respect for the Aztec military power must have been inspired in most who viewed it.

Stone sculpture was essentially cubist in style. Huge blocks of stone were worked into figures of gods with only small openings in the stone to indicate arms and legs as separate from the great mass of the cube. Sculpture in the round emphasized form as volume, while low relief sculpture possessed a lightness and attention to detail. Coatlicue, the "Lady of the Serpent Skirt," mother of Huitzilopochtli, was a powerful and awesome goddess who embodied the ever-present fear for the universe with which the Aztec were so preoccupied. The Aztec sculptor attempted to translate these qualities into stone. The head of Coatlicue is twin serpents, the hands and feet are armed with terrifying claws, the necklace is made of human hands and hearts, and the skirt is a writhing mass of serpents—all of this in monumental passivity combined with the dynamism of the horrors of a threatening universe. Low relief sculpture depicted young gods and goddesses of crops with a passive, calm demeanor, and usually showed some of the animal qualities of these gods. The Aztecs also modeled life-size figures and intricate, huge braziers in clay. The same qualities mentioned above were found in wood, bone, mosaic, semiprecious stone, and gold.

There was also a secular art among the Aztec, and all the techniques and materials of the religious art were utilized in depicting everyday objects and activities.

In painting and drawing found on pottery and in the codices, lavish use was made of color. To the modern eye it was a crabbed style and highly conventionalized limitations were placed on the artist. His chief concern was the correct delineation of ceremonial elements. However, the pictographic annals made after the conquest lose much of the stuffy correctness and display humor in the depiction of the activities and events of daily life.

Although we know the Aztecs developed the other arts to a high degree, all of music and dance, and most of the oral literature have been lost.

Social and Political Organization

The territorial division of Tenochtitlan with its four campans, twenty calpullis, and the smaller units of the tlaxilacallis and the individual family plots have already been described. Residence in any one of these territorial divisions, however, was not a matter of free choice, but was dependent upon kinship affiliations of which the calpulli was the most important.

The nature of the calpulli has long been a matter of contention along Mexicanists. It has been maintained that they were only territorial divisions, that they were clans, that they were guilds, and so on. It is not the present purpose to discuss the evidence for these differing claims. However, it appears that Monzon (1949) has more clearly delineated the nature and form of the calpulli, and his analysis is followed here. The calpulli were ambilateral, endogamous clans based upon common descent from the ancestral settlers of Tenochtitlan. These kinship units were also territorial units, and a person gained his economic rights and privileges through this social group. These calpulli were not the relatively simple clans found among some of the North American Indian tribes, for they were aristocratically organized and highly stratified socially. Closeness of relationship to the ancestors resulted in a strong internal social differentiation which amounted to a true pyramid of social ranks and economic positions. According to Monzon's analysis the principal social relations of all Tenochtitlan were determined by the calpulli. Social stratification was not independent of the clans although many investigators have thought there were social classes or beginnings of social classes. The social division of labor was based on calpulli membership and not guilds as has been maintained. Also, land ownership and usage was not based on class, but on calpulli membership, although there were some macehuales and pilli not subject to these restrictions. Marriage rules were endogamous, although ruling families sometimes married outside as did a few of the calpullis. One was born into his kin group, the calpulli, and with it he inherited a number of ascribed social and economic positions. In this, the stratified society of Tenochtitlan most clearly expresses itself.

It has been the complex association of social stratification and kinship which has led to so much confusion concerning the nature of Aztec society. Basic to social status was the division between those who paid tribute and those who received it. This form of taxation allowed for social stratifications both within and without the calpulli. However, this was not a simple social division, for there were those who paid taxes to all who ranked above them, those who paid only the high-ranking individuals of the calpulli, those who neither paid nor received tribute. From this economic and kinship base developed the social dichotomy of the mace-huales—the commoners—and the pilli—the nobility. However, this was not a rigid social division, for marriage did occur between macehuale and pilli, and the offspring from this union occupied a social position between the two. In fact, there was a wide range of social positions from the highest and purest noble to the lowest commoner.

A social division of labor accompanied membership in a calpulli. And it is here that many authorities have identified the existence of guilds among the Aztec. Not all macehuales were farmers, and not all the calpulli were predominantly concerned with the production of food. Day laborers, artisans, such as carpenters, masons, feather workers, silver workers, and merchants were all grouped in calpullis with their macehuale and pilli divisions. A person gained his economic role through inheritance in the same way he became the member of a kin group. In this way each calpulli had its own occupation, gods, and fiestas. Whatever the economic nature of the calpulli, they were not democratic and egalitarian but highly aristocratic. The calpulli always had a chief who came from that calpulli. Further, they were elected for life and new ones always came from the same families. Purportedly these were the ancient families which led the Tenochca to Mexico.

Not all the calpulli were of equal rank in Tenochtitlan, nor were the other territorial and social divisions. Only six of the calpulli had schools of the nobles—the calmecac. One of these six was ranked higher than the other five.

As a result, the calpulli could be ranked as follows: the one cited highest, the other five with noble schools, and all other calpulli. Each of the four campans had a calpulli with a calmecac, but one of these was ranked above the other four. Thus, an Aztec leader such as Moctezuma gained his position because of his membership in the highest-ranked family, tlaxilacalli, calpulli, and campan. It should be emphasized that the basic allegiance of any Aztec was to his calpulli and not to the social status he occupied.

Although social stratification was, for the most part, the result of inherited social and economic position, there were ways whereby an individual could achieve higher social status and rank. Success as a warrior was the most common means. One gained prestige for the number of captives he made, which in turn gave him the right to wear increasingly elaborate costumes. If his prowess maintained itself, he became a member of the knights of the Eagle or the knights of the Ocelot (or Jaguar), military orders of high social rank privileged to perform special dances and rituals. As a man climbed this social ladder he would have the obligation of tribute to the pilli removed and he would be given land rights in addition to those he inherited. If a warrior displayed outstanding prowess he was given additional grants of land which became private property, and he gained importance in the councils of the Aztecs, possibly even attaining the high position of a place on the tribal council.

However, prowess in war alone was not sufficient to gain a man these high positions. One also had to distinguish himself in religious observance, by his probity, and by faithful performance of civic duties. If a man brought notice to himself through his bravery in war he was given many petty civic offices which he had to fulfill while performing his regular economic duties. Such things as keeping order in the markets, acting in the tribunals during calpulli disputes, as a teacher in the youth's house, or as a record keeper of the tribute, all contributed to his eligibility. When these positions were satisfactorily filled a man could become a chief, a tecuhtli. However, unless a man belonged to the correct family and tlaxilacalli, his position never ranked with the highest leaders of the calpulli or tribe.

If a person belonged to the calpulli of the merchants or the artisans there was the possibility of gaining higher social rank by planning the journeys and supplying the traders who travelled abroad from Tenochtitlan. These men acted the part of wholesalers and sales managers, and if their wisdom was gained through success in planning, high rank was achieved. However, it is uncertain whether these men were the chiefs of the merchant and artisan calpulli. There were certain other social groups which stood apart from the regular membership of the calpulli. The head of a school, singers and instrumentalists, and painters occupied anomalous positions although they belonged to a calpulli. Usually they received tribute, which suggests a pilli rank.

The position of the priesthood is so intertwined with political position that it is difficult to say whether or not they were a special social group despite their calpulli membership.

All nonhereditary social positions were not socially mobile upwards, for slaves constituted a well-established group among the Aztec. One became a slave in a number of ways: as a prisoner of war, because of criminal acts, voluntarily, or by being sold by one's parents. Military captives were usually sacrificed, but if a person was a craftsman, he would be used by the community as a whole. It is maintained that most of the craftsmen of Tenochtitlan originated in this fashion. One became a criminal slave for failure to denounce treachery, by being a traitor or a member of a traitor's family, by kidnapping a free man, or by stealing. Criminal slaves were usually held by those against whom the crime was committed. A person placed himself in voluntary servitude if he was poor and landless, indolent, a gambler, or a prostitute, although social pressure was strong in the case of the last two categories. Children were sold by destitute parents, but restrictions were placed on the owner since he was held responsible for the well-being of the child if the debt was discharged. One did not inherit the position of a slave, but was born free. However, although the child of a slave could own property and own slaves, he lost eligibility for tribal office and thus the opportunity of raising his own social status.

Although the role of the sexes was complicated by the varying degrees of social status, the Aztecs held that the man was dominant in all affairs. A woman was supposed to be chaste and above reproach in all her actions. Consequently, her legal position was low, but the personal influence of high-ranked women was great, especially when they acted as regents for sons and when they played a central role in the cementing of alliances with other tribes through marriage. In addition, some women reached high rank as priestesses although this was likewise exceptional.

The social organization of the Aztecs was based upon the calpulli with its ambilateral, endogamous character. Within the calpulli social stratification was complex and aristocratically organized, but it was not independent of this kin organization. At the time of the Spanish Conquest class structure was oriented within the calpulli, but there was a developing social mobility made possible by the increase in trade and private ownership of land. While social mobility was possible, the higher ranks of Aztec society were inaccessible to one not born in the ranking families. However, the fact that such uniformity of class structure did extend throughout Aztec society may have foreshadowed the development of a true society-wide class system. The different rankings of the calpulli, the campans, and the increase in the number of private property owners, as well as the development of specialized economic groups, all pointed in the direction of a city-wide social stratification. Monzon (1949) maintains that the economic potential for the Aztecs to have developed a more complex class system was not available. Whatever may have been the outcome without European interference, the Spanish found a wonderfully rich and complex society when they entered the Valley of Mexico.

An Aztec entered the world with the aid of a midwife who washed and swaddled the newborn infant. As soon as possible, a priest was called in to cast the horoscope of the child by consulting the *tonalamatl,* the book of the sacred almanac, to determine if the birth date was lucky or unlucky. If the day was unlucky there were several ways of changing the true birth date to a lucky one. Four days after birth a feast was celebrated to name the child. At this time pulque was thrown over the fire as a sacrifice to the rain god, and the child was shown or given toy copies of the tools and implements associated with his role in adult life. A boy was given the name of the birth date, or of an animal, or of an ancestor, or some event which took place during his birth. A girl frequently received a name which was compounded with the word for flower. A child was weaned at the age of four, and from that time on his education into adult life was pushed as rapidly as possible. The techniques and obligations of adult life were passed on to sons by their fathers and to daughters by their mothers. Until the age of six this education consisted of advice, homilies, and minor duties around the house, but after this time entrance into adult life was approached with vigor and strictness. According to early Spanish chronicles, the life of the Aztec child was highly regimented, even to the point of age proscriptions in diet. Until the child was three he received a half a tortilla, from four to five years of age he received one tortilla each meal, between six and twelve one and a half tortillas, and from thirteen to twenty, tortillas were supplemented with beans and game. At the age of eight the child was placed under strict discipline and was subjected to strong admonition and corporal punishment, such as exposure to a mountain night, or being bound and forced to lie in a cold puddle of water. When a boy reached the age of 15 or 16 he was placed in the school of the calpulli, the *telpuchcalli* or the house of youth. Here he learned the duties of citizenship, the art of war, and crafts, as well as the history, traditions, and ordinary religious observances of the Aztec. Mention has been made of the fact that there was another type of school, the calmecac, which was attended by the sons of high-ranking families. This was always in addition to the telpuchcalli, and it emphasized religious and priestly knowledge and duties. However, high political roles and priestly roles were closely related to Aztec culture, and the sons of the chiefs were trained for these contingencies. Girls were rarely educated beyond what was learned in the home. There were special schools for priestesses who learned religious duties and wove special cloth and made featherwork for the priests.

The Spaniards reported that a male Aztec usually married around the age of twenty and that the bride was four years younger. The marriage was arranged by parents, although the consent of the couple was necessary. In order to be eligible mates, the couple had to be of the same calpulli, although there was some indication that tlaxilacalli exogamy was demanded. Before any final arrangements could be made, a priest had to cast the horoscope of the young couple to determine if the omens were favorable for such a marriage. Once this had been determined two elderly clanswomen of the boy acted as go-betweens in negotiations with the girl's family. These negotiations were an attempt to balance the dowry of the girl and the bride price of the suitor. First offers always

received a rejection, but after this, detailed negotiations resulted in a satisfactory settlement. Marriage among the Aztec was usually monogamous. However, if a man was wealthy or of high social rank, polygyny and concubinage were permissible. Divorce was possible under certain circumstances, but it had to be by rulings of the calpulli court. A man could seek divorce if his wife was sterile, or if she was a shrew, or if she persistently neglected her household duties. A wife could seek divorce if she were deserted, or if the husband failed to support her or educate her children. A divorcee could remarry as she pleased, but a widow was forced to practice the levirate. On the day of the wedding the bride was carried over the threshold of the groom's house by one of the matchmakers. This was followed by speeches of advice and warning from married persons after which the mantles of the young couple were tied together. Then followed more advice by elderly individuals, and the ceremony was completed with feasting. However, the marriage was not consummated until after four days of fasting and penance on the part of the newly wedded couple. The gods and the forces of the universe were also members of the wedding.

Kinship, social stratification, and political position were intricately intertwined. There were two classes of political officials, those who gained their offices through achievement, and those who occupied the higher social positions because of their membership in high-ranking families. A person had to be elected to all the political offices, but nomination was highly restricted. Each calpulli elected a number of officers. The lower positions were filled by the tecuhtli, those men who had shown their worth through meritorious service to the calpulli. The high-ranked officials were usually three. The *calpullec* was a form of secretary-treasurer of the calpulli whose duty it was to see that economic order was maintained in the calpulli in such matters as distribution of tribute and land. He could draw on the tecuhtli to aid him. The *teochcautin* preserved order and enforced the law, and he also commanded the forces of the calpulli in time of war. The highest-ranked political official was the chief, a member of the *tlatoani,* or the speakers, who linked the calpulli to the tribe, making up a supreme council with juridical and directive functions. Each chief had a council made up of the most honored men in the calpulli to advise him. The council of the tlatoani selected four officials, apparently one from each campan, whose duty it was to maintain order among the calpulli and solve disputes whose resolution could not be found within the calpulli. Two of these officials dealt with judicial matters, one was the chief executioner, and one acted as intermediary in civil and military affairs. These positions were the proving ground for the highest office of the Aztec, that of the *tlacatecuhtli,* the "chief of men." The holder of this office was chosen from the four campan chiefs, and very often he had occupied the position of Snake Woman, the supervisor of the temples, the form of rituals, and the internal affairs of the priesthood. In this way, the high offices of the priesthood and government were part of a system which emphasized social rank in all things. The tlacatecuhtli represented the tribe in foreign affairs, especially in war and alliances. The "chief of men" could be deposed by the council at any time, but his successor came from a limited number of family lines.

The increasing complexity of Aztec culture brought about the need for more formal organization of social control although the ostracism from his kin group was basic to the punishment of an antisocial individual. Nevertheless, in order to cope with the increased complexity of Aztec life, calpulli and tribal tribunals were organized. These were concerned only with civil suits since it was felt that crime against religion brought its own punishment from the gods. The Aztec tribunals acted under the theory that antisocial acts evoked the need for restitution, and cases were tried publicly in conjunction with the markets. A short list of crimes and punishments illustrates this principle. Theft—slavery until restitution, or double the amount of the theft as a fine to the individual and calpulli; highway robbery—death; market theft—stoning to death immediately; corn theft—death if growing in the field, but one could take an ear or two if near the road; theft of precious materials for religious purposes—a mortal crime; murder—death even if it was a slave; rebels and traitors—death; kidnapping—slavery; drunkenness and intemperate behavior was a serious crime; witchcraft or the impersonation of a high official—death; slander—the loss of lips and sometimes the ears; adultery—severe corporal punishment or death; incest—hanging. The brief inventory reveals that Aztec law was efficacious if brutal. However, a strong sense of community solidarity supported the system.

In many ways, it is incorrect to speak of the Aztec empire, for the demand for city cultural autonomy among the Aztec tribes played down the development of a true political empire. The Aztecs made conquests, but these were mainly for the purpose of the tribute to be gained rather than new lands to be colonized and directly governed. Tribute was the chief political method of the Aztec, and the expansion of trading was not so much to gain economic control over other groups as knowledge of new lands, or old ones needing reconquering. There was also the goal of exacting tribute in the form of human sacrificial victims and attendant wealth.

Whether the Aztecs developed a true empire state is still being debated on these grounds. The conquered peoples were divided into 38 provinces each with a governor, tax collectors, capital cities, and garrisons. As Sanders and Marino (1970) point out, these demonstrate departmentalization and a chain of command, both critical features of true states.

War

It will be remembered that the Post-Classic period was typified by war and warlike activities which, at least in degree, placed it in contrast with the Classic. In large part, this was a concomitant of a new religious orientation which demanded human sacrifice as the central feature of its ceremonies and dogma. As the city states developed, the organization and the motives behind warfare became more complex and demanded more efficient organization.

Warfare was important in Aztec economy and religion, but the major motivation was obscured by a number of secondary factors. In the main, the two important motives were economic tribute and sacrificial victims, and the latter seemed to overshadow the former. However, many campaigns were fought for ostensible reasons of defense, revenge, and purely economic motives. But throughout all Aztec warfare the central goal was to take captives for human sacrifice. The human sacrificial victim and war captive was held in such high esteem that a special heaven existed for them alone.

The Aztec army organization reflected the calpulli of Tenochtitlan. Thus, groups of 20 men were combined into larger units of 200 to 400 men. Each one of these larger units possessed a special flying squad of 4 to 6 men who acted as scouts and raiders. The units of 200 to 400 were grouped together to form the calpulli unit under the command of the calpulli chief. These, in turn, were combined into 4 divisions under the

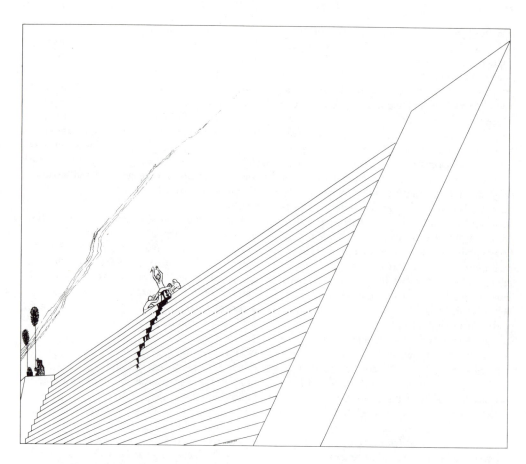

●AZTEC HUMAN SACRIFICE

The exact details of the sacrificial complex of the Aztecs are not easily obtainable; the sources differ among themselves as to the procedures. But some of the codices which describe the spectacular culture of the Aztecs provide insight into the sacrificial behavior. Further, Aztec religion is sufficiently well understood as to leave no question why the rituals of sacrifice were performed.

The speculative theology of the priesthoods in the various Mesoamerican cultures, of which the Aztec were only one (although the group which stressed the element of human sacrifice), evolved the concept that the gods, in order to work for the benefit of man, must themselves be nourished by man. And indeed, the pantheon of the Aztecs, with its many anthropomorphic beings, offered a high degree of theological complexity. Behavior toward the gods required prayer, offerings of food and incense, dramatic performances, but above all—and by far the most dramatic—the sacrifice of captives. The theory arose among the Aztecs that the gods thrived best when nourished by

the hearts of the sacrificial victims. Actually, it was this quest for victims which was in part responsible for the conquests of other peoples by the Aztecs. Bravery in war was prized here as it was among some of the peoples further to the north; the sacrifice of a brave warrior was of special value in providing sustenance to the gods.

Atop the many ceremonial structures which abounded in the capital of Tenochtitlan were altars on which human sacrifices might take place. Whether the rite was a simple one, such as the dispatching of a slave for a minor deity or festival, or whether the involvement was one of hundreds of war captives, the procedures were much the same. The sacrificial victim was held fast to an altar, a so-called eagle bowl, a stone with a blood rill and a receptacle was used to hold the heart. Four priests held the victim's extremities while the sacrificial officiant, holding a flint knife, made a cut under the rib cage and ripped out the heart. This was burned for the benefit of the gods. The victim's corpse was flung down the steps of the pyramid. Among other practices, there was present at the temple of

Tezcatlipoca (one of the great gods), a skull rack on which the heads of victims were also kept. Tied up with this god was the pattern of impersonation, a perfect young man being selected to behave as the god for a year, at the end of which he too was sacrificed.

Here, on one of the great pyramids, that of Tezcatlipoca (cf. Marquina, 1960), the sacrificing priest holds aloft the heart of his victim. The smoke of incense wafts by the feather standards. The blood of the many victims leaves a dark stain on the stuccoed steps of the pyramid.

Grisly though such a practice may seem, it is to be stressed that through such religious ceremonies peoples such as the Aztecs found a religious rationale and created through it a solidarity of religion and society. By contemporary standards, theirs was a conquest state and, as such, scarcely admirable. Yet it would be erroneous to ascribe to the Aztecs a quality of bloodthirsty sadism. This element was present, it is true, as indeed it has been in many societies across the world which have developed sacrificial patterns. Aztec religion was not solely based on such rites. As Vaillant (1941: chapter X) points out, their system was based on a complex series of reckonings of time and space. These served to create a sense of world renewal regularly repeated with each major ritual.

The Aztecs evolved what few other American peoples did. By virtue of their heritage in strategically located Mesoamerica, they brought together the contributions of many peoples. Despite their conquering character, many aspects of their culture—their significant human contributions—persist today in Mexico.

4 campan chiefs, although sometimes a campan's troops were divided into brigades made up of 2 or 3 calpulli. The high command of the army consisted of the tribal war chiefs.

The officers of the Aztec army were the executives of peacetime. Those who commanded the larger units of the army were the high tribal chiefs, the war chief, the campan chiefs, and the calpulli chiefs. The smaller units were directed by the ordinary chiefs—the tecuhtli, and the members of the warrior orders of the Knights of the Eagle and the Jaguar. The soldiers were all the able-bodied men of the tribe who had received their training in the telpuchcalli and in battle as squires to the knights.

The armament of the Aztec army was specialized into offensive and defensive forms. The most common offensive weapons were the wooden, obsidian-edged sword-club, the throwing stick and dart, and the thrusting spear. Also used, but less preferred, were slings and the throwing javelin. The Aztec warrior protected himself with a shield of wickerwork covered with hide, body armor of quilted cotton, and wooden helmets, although the last were more decorative than protective. As the Spaniards soon discovered, the quilted armor offered more protection against Aztec weapons than did the European metal form, and during the latter part of the Conquest a conquistador was more often seen wearing Aztec armor than his own. Although all warriors used the same weapons, each one could elaborate his costume according to his social position. Thus, the amenities of social stratification were preserved even in war. Each campan possessed its arsenal (*tlacochcalco*) which was situated near the chief temple of the quarter, and its readiness was one of the chief duties of a campan chief or one of his deputies.

An offensive campaign was difficult to mount due to the nature of the territorial organization of political units which emphasized the city-state autonomy. Further, the lack of large domesticated animals made it difficult to provision a large army for an extended campaign, and the multitude of potential enemies made it extremely difficult to live off the country since a commander did not wish to engage more than one army at a time. For all these reasons, siege operations were similarly difficult. Defense works became relatively unimportant, although every town and city took advantage of natural barriers and obstacles, and although defensive purposes were taken into account in town planning, purely defensive construction such as fortifications were rarely built. Strategical concepts were little developed among the Aztecs. There was little planned movement of troops, and the main forms of battle tactics consisted of feigned retreat, ambush, and surprise. More common, as war strategy, were political manipulations through political alliance and the spy systems of the merchants and traders.

The religious nature of Aztec warfare is seen in their conception of this activity as an earthly reenactment of the titanic battle of the opposing forces of nature, especially the Sacred War of the Sun against evil forces each day. This was so important to the Aztecs that in times of rela-

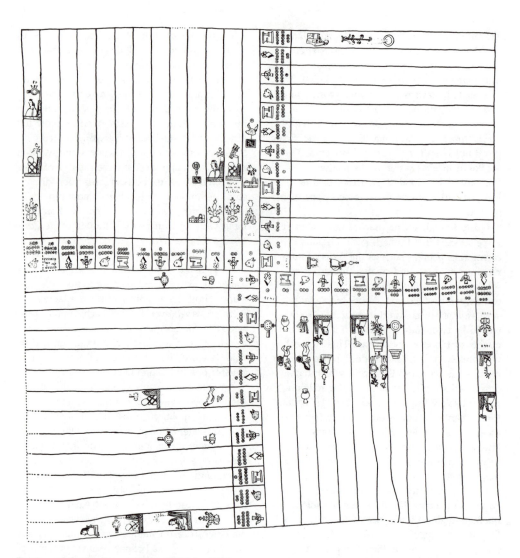

Portion of the Codice en Cruz (Dibble, 1942) ●
**Reading from One Rabbit (the rabbit figure in
the center with the single dot over it), and
counterclockwise, the historic record emerges
year by year.**

tive peace the "War of the Flowers," a ceremonial contest between the warriors of two tribes
or groups of tribes, was conducted, in order
that prisoners might be taken for sacrifice without the costs of a formal war.

Writing

Much more is known about Aztec writing than
Maya hieroglyphics, because the Aztec were a
flourishing culture at the time of the Spanish
Conquest and because far more was preserved
by the Spaniards than in Yucatan, partly
through the interest of the Spanish themselves

and partly because the Aztecs displayed greater
resistance to European culture. In the main, Aztec writing can be termed a pictographic form
of rebus writing. There was little which could
be called phonetic compared with Maya hieroglyphics. In fact, much of the writing seems to
have been an elaborate mnemonic device, for
according to Spanish records the writings were
supplemented by complex oral traditions. But if
the Aztec writing system lacked in versatility, it
seems to have been put to far more varied uses
than that of the Classic Maya. Of course, it is
recognized that there is little knowledge of the
uses to which Classic Maya writing was applied, but the extreme emphasis on sacred matters appears to have culturally limited its utilization. The Aztec, on the other hand, left
behind annals of ancient times, records of contemporary events, year counts, yearly tribute

accounts, specific records of each year, books concerning the events of each day, and even diaries. The Aztec tribes also attempted history. Events, the peoples or tribes involved, and places with name pictographs as well as year names were all carefully recorded. These histories were written in terms of a succession of years showing the whole time covered by the history and the important events recorded in their proper chronological position. Tribal records were also kept showing names of towns and tribute paid, the lines of descent of the important families, the land occupied, land ownership and so on.

Even though Aztec writing was a far less efficient device than that of the Maya, it may again be noted that the Aztecs had an urban culture with all its attendant complexity. The need for records, economic and otherwise, was much greater. Add to this the development of a true state with its need for records of places, population, tribute, etc., and the reason for the expanded use of writing by the Aztecs is not hard to understand.

Time Measurement and Calendar

Like the Maya, the Aztecs measured time as a function of religion. However, the Aztec measurement of time, although they shared the same basic calendrical systems with other Mesoamericans, was not so accurate as that of the Classic Maya. Nor did they observe the number and length of time cycles which the Classic Maya so elaborately spun out. The Aztecs had two time counts, the *tonalpohualli*—the ritual year—and the solar year. These two were combined to give a 52-year cycle. However, the Aztec did not give numerical value to the 52-year cycles so that Aztec history is still highly confused, for although the years in a given 52-year cycle are in sequence, the order of the cycles is mostly unknown. It is as if there were only the last two digits of our time count to mark an event, let us say 76 to mark the American Revolution, but nothing to indicate whether it was 1776 or 1876.

The tonalpohualli was a sacred almanac of days written in a sacred book, the *tonalamatl*, which was a complex association of day names, day numbers, and gods similar to the tzolkin of the Classic Maya. The tonalpohualli consisted of 260 days divided into: (a) thirteen 20-day months consisting of the 20 day names of the Aztec solar month, and thirteen day numbers;

Fasting enclosure, after the Codex Borgia ● The association is with the day of rain and its patron deity, the Sun God, Tonatiuh.

the designation of these days was by name, then number; (b) twenty 13-day weeks, the number of the day preceded the day name here so that every week began with number 1, and, thus, every week day could be distinguished from every other day. With these two systems every day could be distinguished in two ways. There were gods associated with each of the 20 days and each of the 20 weeks. At times, 9 gods and goddesses were sequentially associated with the rights of the tonalpohualli. The same 9 gods were associated with the 13 stations of the day and the 9 stations of the night. It was by determining the juxtaposition of day names, numbers, and associated gods that an Aztec priest was able to cast a horoscope for any event. Like the Maya, the Aztecs found it necessary to propitiate the supernaturals appropriately before any event of importance, and the only way this could be done was through the consultation of the priest and his reading of the tonalpohualli.

However, it was for the solar calendar that the Aztecs reserved their great ceremonies. Each solar year was named for the day of the tonalpohualli on which it began. The 365 days were divided into eighteen 20-day months and an unlucky 5-day period at the end of each year. Each of these months was named for agricultural pursuits of products, indicating the origin of this calendar. Each of the 20 days of the month was numbered, this in addition to the tonalpohualli numbers and names. Because of the limited combinations of day names and numbers, only 4 of the 20 day names could begin a year: House, Rabbit, Reed, and Flint Knife. Also, the relationship of the 13 day numbers to the 365-day year brought about a condition whereby the number of the day beginning the year increased by one each year: 1 Rabbit, 2 Reed, 3 House, 4 Flint Knife, 5 Rabbit, etc. In this way, every year of the 52-year cycle was distinguishable, since the 13 day numbers and the 4 day names could repeat themselves only every 52 years.

Mention has been made of some of the shortcomings of the Aztec calendar when compared with the Maya. Added to the paucity of cyclical observance is the fact that there is no certain evidence that the Aztec reached a solution to time lag by the recognition of the leap year, nor did they make any of the complex calendric corrections achieved by the Classic Maya.

The Aztec numerical system was vigesimal although they had no way of marking place notation. Dots or circles were used up to 20. A flag indicated a value of 20 and was used in repetition up to 400. A fir tree-like sign indicating many hairs indicated 400 (20 × 20), and a bag signifying innumerable cacao beans equaled 8000 (20 × 20 × 20).

Religion

The Aztec approach to the universe and the supernatural reflected their urban life and the greater control of the universe which they possessed compared with the Classic Maya. Some authorities have contended that Aztec culture could only be understood if one assumed that basically all things revolved around religious affairs and concepts; but the Aztec was not as closely meshed with the total universe as the Maya. The greater control over human affairs, and the elaborate and organized attempts to control nature, give one the impression that the Aztec stood apart from nature; and if he did not view himself as an individual so much as he viewed himself a member of a human group apart from the universe and nature, this does not detract from the idea that he was interested in religious matters with a secular end in view. Here we are not attempting to ascribe modern western European secularism to the Aztec, but we are trying to place the Aztec and his religion in contrast to the Classic Maya. The Aztec was much concerned with nature, and thus with a series of observable cycles and rhythms of growth and the movements of heavenly bodies. The Aztec viewed the supernatural very much as if it were in great degree a counterpart of the human world, and because of this, supernatural beings were capable of

Aztec ● Detail of the Codice en Cruz (Dibble, 1942). Reference here is to the events of year Twelve Rabbit (1478), giving details of a military expedition.

494 ●

Aztec ● Above: Stone of Tizoc. This is believed to have been erected in Tenochtitlan at the order of the war chief Tizoc, ruler from A.D. 1481 to 1486. The Sun Disk (Tonatiuh), a variant of the carving seen on the famous calendar stone, appears at the top. Around the side appear the images of Tizoc shown conquering various peoples. In each case Tizoc is wearing the insignia of the warrior god, Tezcatlipoca. The glyphs representing the names of the conquered towns and areas appear above the figures at the side of the stone. All have been deciphered and are prime examples of the Mesoamerican writing system. (From Instituto Nacional de Antropología e Historia, Mexico, D.F.)

Right: Detail of the Stone of Tizoc (Piedra de Tizoc).

good and evil in the way of human beings. The major importance of the religion was that it was concerned with the determination of the cycles and rhythms of the universe in order to protect people. These rhythms and cyclical forms were the major source of ritual and daily life.

In the Aztec's view, the world had undergone five creations and four destructions. Since these were all associated with cycles of nature and the affairs of gods, there was much concern over the portents for the fifth destruction. These five ages of the world were termed Suns.

The first age of the world was 4 Ocelot, during which time Tezcatlipoca, the Smoking Mirror, presided and became the sun at the end when jaguars devoured the men and giants occupying the earth. The second era, 4 Wind, presided over by Quetzalcoatl, the Feathered Serpent, was destroyed by hurricanes and all men became monkeys. The third age of the world, 4 Rain, presided over by Tlaloc, the Rain God, came to its end through the fall of a fiery rain. During the fourth era, 4 Water, Chalchihuitlicue (Our Lady of the Turquoise Skirt), the water goddess, presided, and destruction came in the form of a flood and all men were changed to fish. The fifth, and contemporary, age of the world was 4 Earthquake, presided over by Tonatiuh, the Sun God, and was slated to be destroyed by earthquakes. Vaillant (1941) views this sequence as a recapitulation of the disasters which beset the Mexican communities. Much of the Aztec religious life was an attempt to avert the fifth destruction of the world.

To the Aztecs the universe was a religious concept rather than a geographical one. This, at least, is the view of many Mexicanists. However, the Aztecs were excellent map makers, and grasped the extent of Mesoamerica through their conquests and travels of their merchants and traders. Records were kept of this secular knowledge of the universe, and again there is the problem of deciding to what extent the Aztec were secular or sacred in their orientation. The religious universe was viewed in horizontal and vertical dimensions. Horizontally the universe consisted of the four cardinal directions and a center. The horizontal dimensions of the universe were associated with gods and their qualities which determined the portents for human affairs and destiny. The center direction was controlled by Xiuhtecuhtli, the Fire God, who apparently was one of the ancient gods of the Aztec. East was under the control of Tlaloc, the Rain God, and Mixcoatl, the Cloud God, and signified abundance. It has been suggested that this referred to Vera Cruz where the lower altitudes and abundant rainfall resulted in a lush growth. South was dominated by Xipe, the Flayed One, and Macuilxochitl, Five Flower, both of whom were associated with spring, flowers, and growth, but at the same time this direction was considered evil. West was identified with Venus, and the god of knowledge and learning, Quetzalcoatl, presided over this favorable direction. Mictlantecuhtli, the Lord of Death, dominated the gloomy and awful northern direction. Although the preceding is a simplified version of the horizontal universe, one might view this dimension as the association of the divine with geography and climate.

The vertical dimensions of the universe consisted of 13 overworlds and 9 underworlds, heavens and hells. These had no moral significance. The 13 heavens were occupied by gods in order of their rank in the pantheon, with the top heaven dominated by the original creator, Tloque Nahauque. One of these heavens was the home of Tlaloc, the Rain God, who received those dead by drowning, lightning, and other forms of water demise. Another heaven was divided into east and west sections, the east became the home of dead warriors and the west the home of women who died in childbirth. The remainder of the dead passed to the underworld, *Mictlan,* but this was no easy journey. These souls had to overcome many hazards on a four-day journey which took them between two mountains which threatened to crush them, past a giant snake and a monstrous alligator, across eight deserts and over eight hills, through a freezing wind filled with stone and obsidian blades, and finally across a broad river on the back of a small red dog. When the traveler reached the end of his journey, he made offerings to the lord of the dead and was then assigned to one or more of the nine hells for a probationary period of four years before admission to Mictlan was given. Vaillant (1941) associates the vertical dimensions of the universe with social stratification and rank among the gods and men, and the exaltation of the warriors and those who produced warriors for Tenochtitlan would seem to bear this out.

The pantheon of Aztec gods is heavily populated, and in many ways is contradictory, duplicative, and highly complicated. As an example, Vaillant (1941) lists 63 gods. (However, compare this with Nicholson's (1971) more recent summary.) These he categorizes as great gods (3), creative gods (4), fertility gods (15), rain and moisture gods (6), fire gods (3), pulque gods (4), planetary and stellar gods (12), death and earth gods (6), god variants (6), and a miscellaneous group (4). But the complicated association of aspects, directions, colors, and the like, precludes any full treatment here. The following represents a small but distinctive sample of this godly world.

Three powerful and complex gods dominated the supernatural world of the Aztecs: Huitzilopochtli, Tezcatlipoca, and Quetzalcoatl. Huitzilopochtli, the Hummingbird Wizard, was the war and sun god, and the chief god of Tenochtitlan. Tezcatlipoca, Smoking Mirror, was the chief god of the Aztec pantheon and the main god of Texcoco, the main adversary of Tenochtitlan among the Aztec city states. Tezcatlipoca, sometimes the adversary of Quetzalcoatl, was widely worshiped throughout the Aztec world, and a complicated and powerful cult was associated with this worship. Tezcatlipoca shared powers with many gods, but the cult dogma depicts him presiding over the four directions identified in his four aspects by sacred colors. The Red Tezcatlipoca was identified with Xipe, or with Camaxtli the god of Tlaxcala, and dominated the west. The Blue Tezcatlipoca dominated the south identified with Huitzilopochtli's warlike and sun god aspects. The Black Tezcatlipoca was known by this name, and dominated the night and the north, acting as the most implacable adversary and opposite to the Blue Tezcatlipoca. The White Tezcatlipoca was identified with Quetzalcoatl, and while he dominated the east signifying morning, he often dominated the west signifying evening. From this shortened version, it is apparent that the cult of Tezcatlipoca was moving in the direction of a synthesis of Aztec religion, but it had not assumed the proportions of domination by the time of the Spaniards.

Quetzalcoatl, the Feathered Serpent, was the god of learning, civilization, the priesthood, and the planet Venus. He was widely worshiped, and in several forms his qualities were shared with other divinities. In Tenochtitlan a feathered serpent cult called him Xiuhcoatl who assumed two guises, that of the fire snake and the standard feathered serpent. He was also identified as Ehecoatl, the Wind God, and was shown as a bearded personage whose face was covered by a projecting mask. Quetzalcoatl was also viewed as a historical personage, a great king of the Toltecs who purportedly went to the east to Yucatan and after founding Post-Classic cities returned to Mexico. The Catholic priests tried to identify him with the blond St. Thomas, but in Mexico he was always associated with the color black.

There were four creator deities, less closely associated with the affairs of men than most of the pantheon. Tloque Nahuaque was supreme and ineffable, in one sense the creative spirit in the universe, and distant to people and their affairs. Only in Texcoco was there an organized cult for his worship. Tonacatecuhtli and Tonacacihuatl, Lord and Lady of Our Subsistence, were the creators and the parents or originators of other deities, supposedly heading the pantheon. Ometecuhtli was equal to the two preceding deities and was the Lord of duality, a concept with which the Aztec were much concerned.

The gods associated with the earth, rain, and growth were very important to the Aztec, for they intervened in everyday affairs of the people. Tlaloc, the Rain God, was an ancient god usually represented by eye rings, fangs, and a volute over the lips. In Tenochtitlan he shared a temple with Huitzilopochtli. Tlaloc, in addition to his identification with rain, was joined with Chalchihuitlicue and associated with growth and fertility, growth and vegetation, lakes and rivers—a constant coupling of dualities. A highly important god in this category was Xipe, the Flayed One. His special association was with spring, and he was always represented wearing a distinctive costume of flayed human skin which symbolized the casting off of skin of the old year and the spring life renewal. Many other gods were associated with growth, youth, and games in this category, but among the most important were a special group associated with pulque. *Mayauel,* goddess of the maguey plant, possessed a special cult and has 400 sons associated with pulque in one way or another.

The gods of the earth and death were very important to the Aztec, since all things could be associated with the earth—even death. Tlaltecuhtli, the Lord of the Earth, was a male monster who consumed the sun each day. However, two goddesses were more widely worshiped in this category. Coatlicue, Our Lady of the Serpent Skirt, was the mother of the stellar gods, the mother of Huitzilopochtli, and in one sense was conceived of as the mother principle in the universe. Tlazolteotl was the goddess of dirt, the eater of filth, a mother of many gods, and the Earth Mother. She was worshiped under many synonyms, but her importance lay in the fact that great moral significance was attached to her, for the filth she ate was all the sins of man, and a rite of confession was part of her worship.

Tonatiuh, the Sun God, was the heavenly overlord and was very closely associated with all Aztec life and religious practice since he daily engaged in mortal struggle with Tlaltechutli, an event the Aztec were much exercised about since they wished to prevent the fifth destruction of the world. There were several other gods who intervened in human affairs and were, in one sense, venerated above all others. These were mostly sky gods.

We have previously noted the duplication of political and priestly roles in Aztec society. This was especially true in the higher ranks of the priesthood. In the special cults and temples and to a certain extent among the lower ranks, there seems to have been a clearer delineation between priestly and secular statuses and roles. At the head of the Aztec tribe and Aztec priesthood was the tlacatecuhtli, the "chief of men," who was the active leader in all important religious ceremonies. On the same level of importance, or perhaps slightly below, was the Snake Woman who supervised the temples of Tenochtitlan, the form of rituals, and the internal affairs of the priesthood. Very often the "chief of men" had occupied the role of Snake Woman before his election. Two high priests of equal rank directed the cult activities of Huitzilopochtli and Tlaloc, Quetzalcoatl-Toltec-Tlamacazqui and Quetzalcoatl-Tlaloc-Tlamacazqui. Quetzalcoatl was an honorific term because he was the god of learning and priestly lore. Mexicatl-Teohuatzin was the priest who supervised general religious business in Tenochtitlan and the conquered towns, while his two assistants directed the instruction in the lay and priestly schools. There were other assistants for the pulque ceremonies. Each temple erected for a specific god or goddess had its special priest whose main role was to impersonate the god in rituals. These foregoing priests were aided by a series of assistants who in turn were supplemented by priestly aspirants occupying the bottom of the hierarchy. A number of temples were directed by priestesses and some had schools attached. However, the rank of the priestesses is not clear. There were religious practitioners outside the priesthood. These were the male and female practitioners of magic, in many ways analogous to the shamans among the North American tribes.

The role of the priesthood was to direct intellectual life, to keep the calendars in harmony, and to supervise the religious dramas that were the major ceremonial acts of the Aztecs. Because of the great importance of the religion in Aztec life, some Mexicanists have gone so far as to term the Aztec state a theocracy. However, the close interrelationship of priestly and political roles does not appear to justify this concept, and when one considers the complicated social stratification and its calpulli and kin group identification, a theocracy seems hardly the term to characterize Tenochtitlan or any other Aztec town.

Central to all ceremonies was the practice of sacrifice. Although the Aztecs carried this farthest of all Mesoamerican groups, the idea was not restricted to this area. Blood sacrifice, especially through blood letting from the tongue, ears, and genitals, was widely practiced by the Classic Maya. Likewise, the development of human sacrifice by tearing out the beating heart was not unknown to the Maya. The full development of this form of sacrifice appears to have taken place in and around the Valley of Mexico, and the Mexican invaders of the Maya area took this complex with them. Just how many new concepts the Aztecs as a whole, or the Tenochca specifically, originated, is difficult to say. Certainly many authorities believe the Aztecs contributed little new to the Mesoamerican culture pattern. It is known that the Aztec received much of their godly pantheon and religious concept from the Puebla-Mexteca area. Whatever may have been the case, the Aztecs elaborated and intensified the practice of human sacrifice to a very high degree.

War captives were considered the best candidates for sacrifice, but slaves could be used in minor ceremonies with impunity. Women and children were sacrificed in fertility ceremonies, and there was, on occasion, ceremonial cannibalism. Self-sacrifice through blood letting was very common and accompanied almost every ceremony, no matter its relative importance. The higher the social position, the greater amount of blood. The number of sacrificial victims in a ceremony varied according to its importance, but the high point was reached when 20,000 captives were disposed of by Ahuitzotl after a two-year campaign in northern Oaxaca. Human sacrifice was the means whereby the Aztecs attempted to balance the good and evil forces in the universe or even to tip the scales in favor of man. Consequently, human sacrifice was necessary for the well-being of the tribe. But this became a vicious circle, for only through war could victims be gained and only through sacrificial victims could war be waged successfully.

The New Fire Ceremony, marking the end of the 52-year cycle, was the most important of all religious events. At this time, the beginnings of the tonalpohualli and the solar calendar coincided, with all of the attendant gods and qualities. The Aztecs believed that great danger lurked, for at this point in time the gods and nature could most easily withhold existence for human beings. The older altar fires were extinguished and signs propitious for the kindling of new ones were anxiously watched for. The five unlucky, or useless days of the last year of the cycle saw all fires out, all furniture destroyed, much lamentation, fasting, and a general fear of catastrophe. At sunset of the last day the priests went to a volcanic crater in the floor of the Valley, the Hill of the Star, to await the passing at meridian of the Pleiades, a sign that the world would continue. When this occurred a new fire was kindled in the open breast of a freshly slain victim, and from this all the fires in the area were rekindled, first in the temples and then in the homes. The next day saw a hurricane of activity. Temples were renovated, houses were refurbished and refurnished, there was feasting on special food, and much blood letting and human sacrifice. The world was safe for 52 years more.

The ceremony of the day 4 Earthquake symbolized the passing of the sun through the sky. At dawn a victim, personifying Tonatiuh, the Sun God, was sacrificed. This was followed by ceremonial feasting and general blood letting by gashing until noon. In the afternoon an Eagle Knight and a Jaguar Knight killed a prominent captive in gladiatorial sacrifice symbolizing the death of the sun who is reborn the following day.

The fire sacrifice to the god Huehueteotl was one of the most brutal and terrifying of all Aztec ceremonies. The first day, prisoners of war and their captors danced together in honor of the god. The second day the captives were taken to the top of a ceremonial platform where they were stupefied with the drug *yauhtli* (variously identified as Indian hemp powder, *Apocynum* sp., or the sweet scented marigold, *Tagetes lucida*). They were then bound hand and foot, hoisted on the backs of priests who danced around a huge fire. One by one the captives were dumped in the fire and allowed to roast, but before death they were hooked out and sacrificed while the heart still beat.

The cult of Tezcatlipoca is possibly the beginning of an attempt in religious synthesis. Certainly, the ceremony in honor of the Smoking Mirror was one of the most poignant of all Aztec religious rites. The handsomest and bravest prisoner of war became Tezcatlipoca, and was under the instruction of priests for a year. During the last month four handmaidens dressed as goddesses cared for his every want, and throughout Tenochtitlan he was the most honored of men. On the day of death he led a procession in his honor as the personified Tezcatlipoca through the city, showered by flowers, and amid much weeping. Upon his return to his living quarters he left for a small temple which he ascended, breaking a flute for each step, symbolizing the end of his happy incarnation. The victim was sacrificed in the usual manner by the wrenching out of the still-beating heart, but because of his great honor his body was carried down the steps by the priests rather than being cast down as was usual.

In Aztec religion the priesthood strove to keep man attuned to the rhythms of the universe and the gods, not by becoming a whole-hearted part of it, but in order to avert the cyclical destruction of the world. There was a duality in Aztec religion in which good and evil forces, such as north and south, were constantly opposed. Certainly, there was an apprehension of impending doom and much uncertainty in Aztec religion. It was the task of the priesthood to alleviate this. But the Aztec ethos was not wholly centered on religion, for moral and ethical proscriptions were entirely within the social framework, and what the highly fluid social status system might have developed is open to conjecture. The impression one receives is that the Aztec more easily separated the religious from the secular than did the Maya, that although religion through priestly geomancy entered all aspects of life, the Aztec in the Post-Classic world of a vastly expanded universe of knowledge and experience was either on the verge of becoming increasingly urban or returning to the Formative way of life much as the Classic Maya had done before him.

Suggested readings

BENSON, E. P. ed.

1972 *The Cult of the Feline: A Conference on Pre-Columbian Iconography*. Washington: Dumbarton Oaks.

COE, M. D.

1966 *The Maya*. Ancient Peoples and Places series. New York: Praeger (paperback P-224).

1962 *Mexico*. Ancient Peoples and Places series. New York: Praeger (paperback P-212).

NICHOLSON, H. B.

1971 "Religion in Pre-Hispanic Central Mexico." In *Archaeology of Northern Mesoamerica, Part 1, Handbook of Middle American Indians*, ed. R. Wauchope, vol. 10, pp. 395–446. University of Texas Press.

PETERSON, F.

1962 *Ancient Mexico: An Introduction to the Pre-Hispanic Cultures*. New York: Capricorn Books (CAP Giant 221).

PORTER-WEAVER, M.

1972 *The Aztecs, Maya, and Their Predecessors: Archaeology of Mesoamerica*. New York: Academic Press.

PROSKOURIAKOFF, T.

1946 *An Album of Maya Architecture*. Washington.

SANDERS, W. T., and PRICE, B. J.

1968   *Mesoamerica: The Evolution of a Civilization.*
       New York: Random House (AS 9).

THOMPSON, J. E. S.

1973   *The Rise and Fall of Maya Civilization.*
       University of Oklahoma Press.

TOZZER, A. M.

1941   *Landa's Relación de las Cosas de Yucatán.*
       Cambridge, Mass.

VAILLANT, G. C.

1962   *Aztecs of Mexico: Origin, Rise, and Fall of the
       Aztec Nation.* Revised and annotated by S. B.
       Vaillant. Garden City, N.Y: Doubleday.

WAUCHOPE, R.

1970   *The Indian Background of Latin American History:
       The Maya, Aztec, Inca, and Their Predecessors.*
       New York: Knopf (Borzoi Books on Latin
       America).

1964   ed. *Handbook of Middle American Indians.* 13
       volumes. University of Texas Press.

WILLEY, G. R., and SHIMKIN, D. B.

1971   "The Collapse of Classic Maya Civilization in
       the Southern Lowlands: A Symposium
       Summary Statement." *Southwestern Journal of
       Anthropology* 27:1, 1–18.

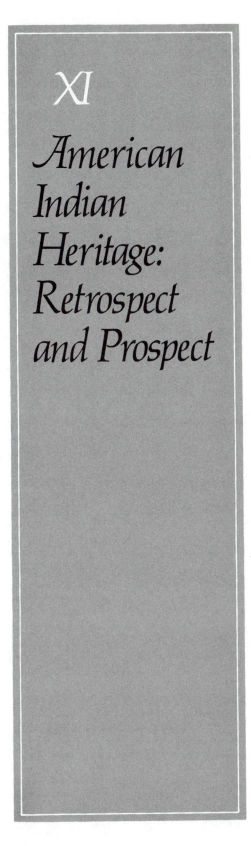

XI

American Indian Heritage: Retrospect and Prospect

We are the Ancient People;
Our father is the Sun;
Our mother, the Earth, where the mountains tower
And the rivers seaward run;
The stars are the children of the sky,
The red men, of the plain;
And ages over us both had rolled
Before you crossed the main;
For we are the Ancient People,
Born with the wind and rain.

EDNA DEAN PROCTOR

The Ancient People still live. The Navaho herds his sheep in the vast silence of the panchromatic plateau of the Southwest. High on his mesas the Hopi enacts his traditional pleas for rain. The Seminole poles his pirogue through the waters of the strange green land of the Everglades. Eskimo sea hunters skillfully paddle their kayaks through the ice-infested waters along the shores of the Arctic. Indian women in Mexico patiently grind corn on ancient metates. In contrast, sure-footed Mohawk structural steel workers now make their way along the girders of new skyscrapers, high above the roar of New York City's traffic. Zuni and Apache are flown to fight forest fires in western states. Indians of many tribes work on the assembly lines in the aircraft industries of southern California and Seattle.

Once the Ancient People seemed to be the "vanishing Americans." Their ranks thinned by the white man's bullets, bottles, and diseases, they appeared to be nearing the "end of the trail," slipping rapidly down the path to racial oblivion. But the trend toward extinction was halted and reversed in the early 1920s, and now the red man, in proportion to his numbers, is increasing faster proportionately than any other ethnic group in the United States. Many of the ancient cultural traditions in the United States are still viable, and more than 150 Indian languages are still spoken.

The Indian has accepted much of the white man's civilization. Even at the conservative pueblo of Zuni, where the Shalako reappear each winter, television aerials now rise above the little brown houses, beside which compact cars and pick-up trucks are parked. Electricity is at last coming to the Hopi villages, where ancestral Hopis were living at Old Oraibi three and a half centuries before Columbus first landed in the New World. While the Native Americans have been receptive to the white man's material culture, many tribes cling to their venerable customs and rituals. But acculturation is a two-way process; the white man is also profoundly indebted to the Indian.

Almost every time we sit down to a meal, we see before us foods of American Indian derivation. After the discovery of America more than 50 food plants diffused even to remote parts of the Old World, enriching the diets of every continent. These American Indian foods influenced the striking increase in the world's population after 1650.

With our meat courses, we usually have "Irish" potatoes, which were originally domesticated by the Indians of the Andean highlands in South America. The potato now exceeds in total tonnage all of the other crops of the world, except for rice. Maize, a sacred plant to many Indians, ranks third in total tonnage, having surpassed wheat in volume. Indian methods of cultivating corn, too, were imitated by white pioneers. Our diet has also been augmented by such other American Indian crops as manioc (the source of tapioca), squashes and pumpkins, sweet potatoes, avocados, the "Jerusalem" artichoke, chili peppers, chocolate (from the cacao bean), pineapples, guava, peanuts, cashew nuts, several varieties of beans (including Lima and kidney beans), and many lesser known plants. Such foods as succotash (made of corn and Lima beans), cornbread, hominy, persimmon bread, tamales, tortillas, and even toasted cornflakes originated with the Indians! So did maple sugar. Not only was the "Irish" potato originally Indian, but so were "Hungarian" paprika and "Spanish" sauce.

When we don a cotton garment, it is usually made of cotton of American Indian derivation, although cotton was also domesticated in the Old World. Sisal (agave fiber), formerly much used by Mesoamerican Indians as a clothing material, is still fabricated into cordage.

Many of us enjoy smoking, despite the controversy over its alleged harmful effects. American Indians, too, liked to smoke, and originated the various ways of using tobacco, in pipes, cigars, cigarettes, and as snuff. Tobacco, another sacred Indian plant, was first domesticated in tropical America, whence it spread to the Indians of most of North and South America, without, however, ever reaching the Eskimo. The Spaniards in the West Indies and the Portuguese in South America found the Indians puffing away on cigars, some of which were two feet long and were held in two-pronged holders. The Indians of the eastern United States smoked tobacco in pipes, while the red men of Mexico smoked cigarettes made of tobacco rolled in cornhusks.

After the discovery of the New World, tobacco diffused over the eastern hemisphere with startling rapidity. The plant was introduced into Europe at two points. In 1558 it was taken to Spain in the guise of a medicine, and was for a time regarded as a cure-all. In 1586 Sir Walter Raleigh introduced the custom of smoking to court circles in England, and it spread quickly among the commoners.[1] From Spain and England tobacco spread swiftly over the Old World, despite all opposition of priests and rulers and regardless of the infliction of such harsh punishments for smoking as flogging, excommunication, and even execution. Tobacco users were tortured in Russia, fined and imprisoned in Switzerland, and executed in Turkey. Nevertheless, people in all parts of Europe were soon smoking, as were Siberian natives, Japanese, Malays, and even aboriginal tribesmen in the interiors of Africa and New Guinea who had never seen a white man! By the year 1700 tobacco had encircled the globe, and was reintroduced into America from Siberia at Alaska, where the Eskimo at last became familiar with the properties of nicotine.

The Native Americans never had as many domesticated animals as the peoples of the Old World, for there were no real American equivalents of horses, cattle, or asses during the time when the Indians were the sole inhabitants of the Western Hemisphere. The native American horse had become extinct, and was never domesticated; hence the Indians had no horses prior to their introduction from the Old World by the Spaniards. Save for the untamed bison and caribou, the New World had no large animals which might have served as draft animals in pre-Columbian times. The sole beast of burden known to the Indians was the llama of the Andean Highlands—a small, humpless relative of the camel. Llamas thrive only at high elevations and are not strong enough to carry riders or very heavy loads; neither could they have pulled wheeled vehicles even if such had been invented by the Indians. The llama and its relatives, the alpaca and the wilder vicuña, are still used for their meat and wool by Andean In-

[1] Raleigh, incidentally, according to one version, is also credited with the introduction of the potato to Ireland. The last thing Raleigh did before he was beheaded in 1619 (although not for initiating the habit of smoking among the English!) was to smoke a pipeful of tobacco.

dians, but they are not milked. Dairying was a practice unknown to American Indians.

When we carve into a Thanksgiving turkey, we are once again beholden to American Indians. Native to North America, turkeys were taken to Europe by Hernando Cortez after his sixteenth-century expedition of discovery and conquest in Mexico. The turkey was probably domesticated first in Mexico, where it was an article of diet, and it spread to the Indians of the Southwest, who kept it principally for its feathers. Mesoamerican Indians also kept stingless bees for their honey.

The musk duck, a fowl which is almost as large as a goose, was first domesticated by Andean Indians. This bird is sometimes misleadingly called the muscovy duck, because it was taken to Russia and subsequently reintroduced into the New World. Also domesticated in the Andean Highlands of South America was the guinea pig, so important in present-day laboratory experiments. Guinea pigs are still prized for their meat by Indians of the Andes, some of whom also use them as "bedding," covering themselves with living guinea pigs for warmth on the cold mountain nights.

Although few Indians north of Mexico possessed any alcoholic beverages in pre-Columbian times, the Indians of Mexico made pulque (or agave wine) from the fermented sap of the maguey plant. An inexpensive beverage, pulque is still popular with modern Mexicans, despite its unpleasant odor and sour taste to those unaccustomed to it. Distilled liquors were unknown in America in native times, but after the Spanish Conquest the Indians of Mexico learned to distill their native drinks into such hard liquors as tequila and mescal. Chicha, a fermented drink which can be made from several fruits and vegetables, as well as maize, is still imbibed in great quantities by South American Indians, especially at fiesta time.

Modern pharmacies stock numerous commercial derivatives of American Indian remedies. Quinine, or "Peruvian bark," from the bark of the cinchona tree, is a specific for malaria. The Spaniards introduced quinine to Europe, and it was soon brought back to the English colonies in America, where it reduced appreciably the number of deaths from malaria. Ephedra, in ephedrine, is useful in clearing nasal passages and sinuses and was used by the Aztecs in treating the common cold. The leaves of the coca shrub, first used by Peruvian In-

dians, are the source of cocaine and novocaine. Several balsams, such as sweetgum, Tolu balsam, balsam of Peru, and copaiva balsam, were obtained from the Indians. Other drugs of Indian derivation include curare (used in anesthetics), datura (in pain-relievers), witch hazel (for muscular aches and pains), jalap (a cathartic from Mexico), cascara (in laxatives), and ipecac, used as stomachic tonic and as an expectorant.

In colonial times and later, various other American Indian remedies were highly valued by whites, although many of these folk medicines have since lapsed into disuse as pharmacology has progressed. For instance, the Virginia House of Burgesses in 1738 rewarded Dr. John Tennent with one hundred pounds for using Seneca rattlesnake root in treating pleurisy. The image of the Indian as a healer has been a persistent one, perpetuated until recent decades particularly in the midlands of America by traveling medicine shows which featured Kickapoo Indians.

Frontiersmen found such items of Indian clothing as moccasins, leggings, and buckskin shirts well suited to life in the wilds. The house slipper of today is patterned after the Indian moccasin, as are moccasin-toed shoes. The so-called squaw dress, popular today among white women, particularly in the Southwest, is actually not of Indian origin, since Indian women patterned it after styles worn by the wives of American Army officers in the last century. In Mexico today many women wear the Indian-style *huipil,* a sleeveless blouse, and the *quesquemetl,* a poncholike upper garment. The poncho, a blanket with a hole in the middle for the head, is still worn by most Andean Indians, and its style has been imitated in commercial raincoats. The hooded parka of the Eskimo has been copied in winter sports costumes and for use by ski troops. In fact, many Eskimo techniques of survival under the rigorous Arctic conditions were taught to members of the armed forces during World War II.

The Indians were the first to become familiar with the properties of rubber, making from it enema syringes and tubes, hollow rubber balls, and waterproof fabrics. Columbus took samples of rubber to Europe, but it was almost 250 years before its commercial potentialities were appreciated. The English were the first to use the word "rubber," applying the product to the rubbing out or erasing of pencil marks.

Pioneers used the forest trails of the Indians, some of which were later developed into roads and highways. Communication by water was of great importance to the early settlers, who adopted certain Indian modes of water transport. Colonial traders in the eastern United States used the dugout canoe of the Indians, and white men in the north adopted the fragile birchbark canoe of the Algonkins, which is now imitated in craft of more durable canvas. White men in the Arctic area have used the hide boats of the Eskimo, and modern rubber or canvas-covered copies of the Eskimo kayak, propelled with double-bladed paddles, are used today by sportsmen in running the rapids of streams. The Eskimo use of dogsleds has also been imitated in the north, although tandem, rather than fan-wise hitching comes from Eurasia, and both toboggans and snowshoes were copied after those of the northern Athabascan Indians. In Mexico some Indian porters still use the tumpline or forehead strap, which is also occasionally used by backpackers in the wilderness areas of the United States and Canada.

Certain dyestuffs, such as cochineal, Brazil wood (used in red ink), and logwood, are of Indian derivation. The hammock, so important as a sleeping place to the navies of the world and to backyard loafers, was invented by the Indians of the tropical forests in South America.

In architecture the influence of the Indian has been minor, although in the Southwest a few houses and public buildings emulate the Pueblo style. The Sibley tents of the Army are modifications of the Plains Indian tipis. In Mexico in recent years there has been a certain revival of Indian styles in dwellings, and some of the public buildings show features of Indian architecture. The national art style of Mexico is, in fact, a blend of Indian and Spanish influences. The work of such artists as Miguel Covarrubias, Diego Rivera, and Juan O'Gorman may be seen in public places in Mexico today, where there are huge indoor murals in the composite style, and the buildings of the national university are ornamented with such motifs from Indian art as sun symbols, eagles, serpents, and jaguars.

Artists in the United States have been less influenced by Indian art styles than have those in Mexico, although Indians have long been popular subjects in our sculpture and painting. Native Indian arts and crafts are increasingly appreciated by whites. Navaho rugs are treasured in many homes, particularly in the Southwest, where numerous Indian stores and trading posts also display for sale Indian baskets, Pueblo pottery, and Navaho and Pueblo silver jewelry, as well as the paintings of contemporary Indian artists. In Latin America various Indian arts and crafts have also been commercialized, including the weaving of mats, baskets, and bags, and the making of metal jewelry and hand-made pottery.

American Indian music has never been as widely appreciated as that of the Black, although certain composers have utilized Indian themes. The first American opera, "Tammany" (1794), used Cherokee motifs. Most noteworthy was Edward McDowell's "Indian Suite," which introduced Indian themes to American concert music and was first performed in 1896. Also deserving of mention are Skilton's "Indian Dances" (1915) and such popular songs as Cadman's "Land of the Sky Blue Water" (1909) and Lieurance's "By the Waters of the Minnetonka" (1921). In Latin America such composers as Carlos Chavez in Mexico and Heitor Villa-Lobos in Brazil have borrowed from Indian musical motifs.

The Indian has also been a subject of many American folksongs. Some of these romanticize the Indian, while others tell of episodes in the relations of Indians and whites. Certain Indian songs and other features of Indian lore, including camping and woodcraft techniques, have been borrowed by such organizations as the Boy Scouts, Girl Scouts, and Campfire Girls, as an examination of their handbooks will readily show. Thousands of American boys have qualified for the merit badge in Indian lore, which requires that, among other things, they be able to "sing three Indian songs, including the Omaha tribal prayer and tell something of their meaning."

The Indian has long been a favorite topic in our drama, poetry, and fiction. Plays about Indians had a great vogue in the nineteenth century, after J. N. Barker's *The Indian Princess*, concerning the life of Pocahontas, was first staged in 1808. The peak in popularity of Indian dramas falls between 1830 and 1870. The most important of these was a drama entitled *Metamora, or the last of the Wampanoags*, which became one of the most popular of all American plays, and was seen by probably more Americans than later attended such long-running Broadway productions as *Abie's Irish Rose* or *Tobacco Road*. (Hallowell, 1957a:246.)

A pioneer in the use of Indian material for poetic purposes was Philip Freneau (1752–1832), sometimes called the "father of American poetry." The most outstanding poem about the American Indian is Longfellow's "Hiawatha" (1855), which was based upon Ojibwa legends in the "Algic Researches" (1839) collected by Henry R. Schoolcraft. Literary classics also are James Fenimore Cooper's *Leather-Stocking Tales.* Indians play a prominent part in eleven of Cooper's books, written between 1823 and 1851, and Cooper perhaps more than any other writer impressed the American as well as the European reading public with his conception of the Indian. Cooper's *The Last of the Mohicans* may be the best-known American novel in the world (Hallowell, 1957b:231). Although Henry David Thoreau published little dealing specifically with the red man, he was intensely interested in Indians, and left at his death eleven unpublished notebooks of some 2,800 pages and approximately 540,000 words, replete with "Extracts Relating to the Indians." Joaquin Miller, in his *Life among the Modocs* (1873) and other works, stirringly defends the red men of California. Helen Hunt Jackson's *Ramona* (1884), recognized as among the better American novels, sympathetically portrays the plight of the Mission Indians in California. Almost every novel of the American pioneer period of necessity deals with Indians. Some of this writing is exceptional, but much of it is mediocre or worse, and suffers from uncritical acceptance of the current stereotypes of the Indian. At a later date a notable exception to such inaccurate portrayals of Indians was Oliver LaFarge's *Laughing Boy* (1929), a novel of the Navaho which won a Pulitzer Prize. Charles L. McNichols' *Crazy Weather* (1944), a novel which depicts Mohave culture at about the turn of the present century, is also well written and ethnographically accurate. In 1969 a superb novel *House Made of Dawn,* written by N. Scott Momaday, a young Kiowa author, won the Pulitzer prize. The book describes the inner and outer conflicts of a young American, returned from a foreign war, and being torn apart by two worlds.

The Indian now appears even in comic books, as well as in television and motion picture dramas. Too often still, in such portrayals, the Indian is stereotyped as a sadistic enemy.

Indian loan words, or translations of Indian words, have been incorporated into all the languages of European origin spoken in America today. Nearly half of our states have Indian names: Alabama, Alaska, Arizona, Arkansas, Connecticut, Dakota, Idaho, Illinois, Iowa, Kansas, Kentucky, Massachusetts, Michigan, Minnesota, Mississippi, Missouri, Nebraska, Ohio, Oklahoma, Tennessee, Texas, Utah, Wisconsin, and Wyoming. Literally thousands of cities, towns, lakes, rivers, and mountains bear Indian names, often in a corrupted form. Witness, at random: Chicago, Minneapolis, Appomattox, Erie, Seattle, Tucson, Omaha, Mackinac, Miami, Mobile, Tacoma, Wichita, Tallahassee, Penobscot, Peoria, Potomac, Spokane, Susquehanna, Topeka, Oshkosh, and Schenectady. Incidentally, one version of the name Manhattan, from the language of the Lenape Indians, is that it means "the place where we all became drunk," in consequence of the hospitality of Henry Hudson in 1608. More probably, Manhattan should be translated "island of hills." Many words or expressions in American English are either of Indian origin or Indian influence: papoose, Tammany, caucus, wampum, wigwam, powwow, and sachem; "going on the warpath," "burying the hatchet," "running the gauntlet," "smoking the peacepipe," and "happy hunting ground." In Latin America, also, thousands of Indian words have been incorporated into Spanish.

The Indian also influenced certain religious developments among white Americans, specifically those of the Church of Latter-Day Saints (Mormons), the Spiritualists, and the United Society of Believers (Shakers). There are songs about Indians in Mormon hymnals, and in the *Book of Mormon* the red men are represented as the descendants of a group of Israelites, the Lamanites, who are believed by the Mormons to have migrated to the New World before the beginning of the Christian era. Mediums of the Spiritualists often "speak in Indian tongues," or are believed to have Indian "controls" or "guides." Shakers on occasion think themselves to be possessed by Indian spirits, and it is also one of their beliefs that some of them have received songs from Indian spirits while in trances (Hallowell, 1957b:242).

The democratic traditions of the Indians may have contributed to the statement in our Declaration of Independence that "all men are created equal, that they are endowed by their Creator with certain inalienable rights." It is even possible that information about the League of the Iroquois, acquired by Benjamin Franklin and others of our founding fathers at councils with the Indians, may have affected the development of a pattern for the government of the infant United States of America. The League of the Five Nations balanced the sovereignty of each of the component tribes against sovereignty delegated to the superordinate League, and the Iroquois constitution provided for such things as initiative, referendum, and recall, as well as suffrage for both men and women.

And what of the psychological effects of the Indian upon the American national character structure? We know little about these intangible factors, but it is probable that Indian influences have been important. The noted psychoanalyst, Dr. Carl Jung, believed that in the character of his American patients he could detect an Indian component. It has also been suggested that "The frontier, of which the Indian was so intimately a part, is usually credited with the development of the traditional American characteristics of courage, resourcefulness, energy, and tolerance. Though the frontier is gone, these qualities still characterize, in the eyes of Americans, the ideal-stereotype of their national group" (Heizer, 1952:29, after McLeod, 1928).

The persisting influence of the Indian is even more apparent in Latin America than in the United States. Indian race, language, and culture survive to a high degree in most parts of Latin America. The face of Mexico, for example, is still an Indian face; probably 80 percent of the ancestry of the people of Mexico today is Indian. Such South American countries as Bolivia and Paraguay are predominantly Indian. The cultures of Latin America today are a blend of the Indian and the European. As George Foster expresses it: "Even in the non-Indian areas of Mexico, for all the influence of Spain and the modern world, one is impressed with how thoroughly native American culture has left its imprint ... Hispanic American culture cannot be described as Indian any more than it can be described as Spanish. It is a new, distinctive culture, with roots deep in two separate historical traditions, but with a unique and valid ethos of its own." (Foster, 1951:316f.)

Indian cultures in Mexico vary along a scale of acculturation, some being more Europeanized than others. At one end of the continuum are approximately one million people who speak only Indian languages, who are racially Indian and show little or no intermixture with Europeans and who retain culture patterns which are in part analogous to those of their ancestors. Another million Indians of Mexico remain racially and culturally Indian, but speak Spanish in addition to their native languages.

Several million others are still racially Indian, and retain many aboriginal customs, but have forgotten their Indian tongues and speak only Spanish (Gamio, 1945:406f.).

Two contrasting "images" of the Indian have affected the historical relations of the red man and the white man: the Indian as a "Noble Savage" (or "Child of Nature"), and the Indian as a "Bloodthirsty Savage" who delighted in scalping and torturing white people. The image of the Noble Savage has often been associated with the writings of the French philosopher, Jean Jacques Rousseau, but Rousseau did not originate the concept. Its roots are much more ancient. The belief in a golden age of natural man had long been prominent in European literature and can be traced back to such writers of antiquity as Ovid and Tacitus. Europeans had yearned for the simplicity and innocence of a primeval era, antedating the corruptions of civilization. The French essayist and moral philosopher, Michel de Montaigne, in the sixteenth century found descriptions of the fabled virtues of the Noble Savage in the accounts of explorers of the New World. Christopher Columbus, for instance, had written of the Indians, "They are loving people, without covetousness, and fit for anything. . . . They love their neighbors as themselves, and their speech is the sweetest and gentlest in the world." Here, said Montaigne of the Indians, is a nation which "hath no kind of traffic, no knowledge of letters, no intelligence of numbers, no name of magistrate, nor of politics, no use of service, of riches, or of poverty; no contracts, no successions, no partitions, no occupation but idle, no apparel but natural, no manuring of lands, no use of wine ... the very words that import a lie, falsehood, treason, covetousness, envy, detraction, were not heard among them. . . . Furthermore, they live in a country of so exceedingly pleasant and temperate situation that as my testimonies have told me, it is very rare to see a sick body amongst them. . . . They spend the whole day in dancing. The young men go ahunting after wild beasts with bows and arrows. Their women busy themselves there whilst. . . ." Other European writers, too, were enamored with the image of the Indian as a romantic embodiment of what all men should be, minus the tarnishing influence of civilization.

Probably the most influential of the eighteenth-century writers who speculated about the Noble Savage and the blissful innocence of his natural state was Jean Jacques Rousseau.

However, Rousseau's portrait of natural man is less idyllic than that of Montaigne. Rousseau discourses on another factor, man's faculty for self-improvement: "In the operations of the brute, nature is the sole agent, whereas man has some share in his own operations in his character as a free agent."

Not all contemporary European writers were in sympathy with Rousseau's conception of a Noble Savage. Wrote Johnson, "Pity is not natural to man. Children are always cruel. Savages are always cruel. Pity is acquired and improved by the cultivation of reason." Johnson was also skeptical about the felicity of pristine living, writing, "The savages have no bodily advantages beyond those of civilized man. They have not better health; and as to care or mental uneasiness, they are not above it, but below it, like bears." (Quoted in Fairchild, 1928:331f.)

To most of the European colonists, the Indian way of life was inferior to their own. The colonists appear to have shared with Rousseau the idea that the Noble Savage could be improved upon. The Europeans were, however, unwilling to trust the Indian, as a free agent, to improve himself voluntarily. The Europeans brought with them an idea of *order,* which must be *imposed* upon the red man, in order that he might attain his highest potentialities (Pearce, 1953:3). The aim of the colonists at first was to live peacefully with the Indians, to confer upon them the benefits of civilization, that they might live like Europeans. Thus, as early as 1619, as many as 50 missionaries had already been sent to Virginia to educate Indian children in the blessings of Christianity and of civilization.

Soon it became apparent, however, that Indians were unwilling to acquiesce so complacently to being civilized." Ere long the Indians began to resist encroachment upon their lands; in 1622 the Indians of Virginia suddenly rose up and killed at least 347 Englishmen within a hundred-mile area. Angered by the refusal of the Indians to accept the values and customs of the civilization which was being so magnanimously proffered to them, Europeans came to regard the red men as obstacles squarely in the path of the advance of civilization, as impediments which must be removed or destroyed. With their smug convictions of their own cultural superiority and with their unrealistic ideas about "natural men," Europeans had little incentive to try to understand the Indians. Disregarding the diver-

sity of Indian cultures, the colonists insisted on regarding all Indians as alike. There was no place in the colonies for uncivilized Indians. Pearce writes of this: "Americans who were setting out to make a new society could find a place in it for the Indian only if he would become what they were—settled, steady, civilized. Yet somehow he would not be anything but what he was—roaming, unreliable, savage. So they concluded that they were destined to try to civilize him and, in trying, to destroy him, because he could not, and would not be civilized." (Pearce, 1953:53.)

And, as the Indians resisted, the image of the Indian as a Bloodthirsty Savage became predominant in the minds of the colonists. By 1703 the government of Massachusetts was paying twelve pounds for every Indian scalp. Widely read at that time was Mary Rowlandson's narrative of her captivity by the Indians during King Philip's War, in which she described the Indians as "atheistical, proud, wild, cruel, barbarous, brutish." She wrote of her horrendous memory, "That was the dolefulest night that ever my eyes saw. Oh, the roaring, and singing, and dancing and yelling of those black creatures in the night, which made the place a lively resemblance of hell." Cotton Mather similarly horrified his Puritan congregations with tales of Indian bloodlust and cruelty, of red men knocking the heads of captive white children against trees, or gouging out their eyes if they cried too much. Mather believed that the Indians were in America because "probably the Devil decoyed (them) ... hither, in hopes that the gospel of the Lord Jesus Christ would never come here to destroy or disturb his absolute empire over them." John Adams wrote in 1790, "I am not of Rousseau's Opinion. His Notions of the purity of Morals in savage nations and the earliest Ages of civilized Nations are mere Chimeras."

At the time of the initial European colonization, there were probably one million Indians in North America north of Mexico; in Mexico, several million more. Thinly scattered, linguistically and physically heterogeneous, there were hundreds of tribes, with numerous distinctive cultures, some of which were as different from each other as were the cultures of England and China at that period. Misunderstanding Indian concepts of land use and tenure, the Europeans generally assumed that in their primitive condition the Indians had failed to develop a property system, that the land was therefore free for the taking. And so began the greatest "land grab" in history. Despite resistance by the Indians, the colonies were established relatively easily, with the use of force and intimidation by the Europeans.

In Mexico the Spaniards seldom entered into negotiations with the tribes as sovereign states, and confiscated the Indian lands rather than purchase them or make treaties with the Indians. The Spanish exploited the Indians, pressing them into service as laborers on huge estates or *encomiendas*. Nevertheless, the Indians were regarded as subjects of the crown and the church, and the Spaniards attempted to assimilate the red men by establishing missions and undertaking the Christianization of the natives. The Spanish class structure was transplanted to Mexico, but Spanish colonists were never numerous. And even on the upper-class levels there was considerable intermarriage with the Indians. Many Indians underwent a rapid acculturation during the early post-Conquest years, hoping thereby to progress under the new social system.

North of Mexico, the French came mainly as traders rather than as colonists and often married Indian women. The Dutch set a precedent of paying the Indians for their land, buying Manhattan Island for a mere $24, and the English began to emulate this policy of purchasing Indian lands. Usually, the Indians had no idea of what they were relinquishing, and thought that they were merely selling the use of the land, rather than giving over permanent possession to the whites. The maximum density of Indian population was not on the East Coast, but in such western regions as California and the Rio Grande Valley, so the colonists experienced little difficulty in getting a foothold on the Atlantic seaboard. Soon the eastern tribes had been defeated and decimated, and the frontier moved ever westward.

During the early years of settlement each English colony had been permitted to deal directly with the Indians within its borders as it saw fit. Consequently, the Indian policies of the several colonies varied greatly. But in 1763 the British Crown announced a new policy which removed jurisdiction over the Indians from the individual colonies. Under terms of the new policy, the tribes were henceforth to be considered as independent nations, and it became illegal for any individual or group to seize or buy land from the Indians. Indian lands were now considered inalienable unless they were voluntarily surrendered to the Crown. The opposition of the incensed colonists to this British governmental policy was one of the issues eventuating in the Revolutionary War.

The new American government in essence took over the British Crown policy of regarding the Indian tribes as independent sovereign nations. During the period between 1778 and 1871 the federal government entered into many treaties with Indian tribes. But when the tribes failed to yield to pressures to cede their land, military force was often applied. Significantly, the Indian Office was first established in 1824 under the War Department, since the Indian problem at that period was considered to be chiefly a military one. Often the whites ignored treaties which had already been made with the Indians, in their eagerness to possess the remaining Indian lands. Thousands of Indians perished in wars and massacres initiated by the white men, and some of the eastern tribes were completely exterminated. Among the more famous Indian wars fought east of the Mississippi were the Black Hawk War in Illinois and the Seminole Wars in Florida. Intertribal conflicts among the Indians increased, too, as the whites pushed Indians from the east onto the territories of tribes farther to the west.

In 1830 President Andrew Jackson signed the Indian Removal Act, which gave the President authority to order the removal of all the remaining eastern Indians to territory west of the Mississippi River. During the next ten years more than 70,000 tribesmen were resettled across the great river. Soon most of the tribes of the east had been moved to the Indian territory in what is now Oklahoma, except for remnant groups in New York, Florida, Maine, and Virginia, and with the exception also of a large group of Cherokee who had resisted so strongly that they were allowed to stay in the Great Smoky Mountain region of North Carolina. During the period of removal few attempts were made to alter the Indian cultures; the only concern of the white man at this time was to get the Indian out of the way, to open up the country to white land-seekers.

The tragedy of defeat and expropriation was not long delayed for the tribes of the west. Soon the old stories of warfare, treaties, and land cessions were reenacted west of the Mississippi. Gold was discovered in California, and wagon trains of gold-seekers and emigrants began to rumble across the Plains. Western tribes were settled on reservations and were issued rations in compensation for their loss of hunting opportunities, but frequently bands of dissatisfied warriors would rebel and break out of bounds. Among the uprisings were those in the Southern Plains in 1874 (the Red River War), of the Sioux in 1876, the Cheyenne in 1878, the Nez Perce in 1877, the Bannock in 1878, the Utes in 1879, and farther west in northeast California the Modocs in 1872–1873. The Apache in the Southwest went on the warpath many times in the 1870s and 1880s.

Once again, the aim of the frontiersmen was to get rid of the Indian, to get him out of the way, in order that the young nation might fulfill its "Manifest Destiny" to expand from coast to coast. The image of the Indian as a Bloodthirsty Savage moved west along with the frontier. As the struggle increased in fury, Indian rights were ignored, and countless atrocities were committed by both sides. The Indian came to be considered as less than human, as a game animal to be hunted down and destroyed. The prevalent frontier sentiment was manifested in the oft-repeated opinion that "the only good Indian is a dead Indian." One of the first debates in the Colorado legislature was over a bill authorizing bounties for dead skunks and dead Indians (McWilliams, 1943:68). In 1867 the Topeka *Weekly Leader* called the Indians "a set of miserable, dirty, lousy, blanketed, thieving, lying, sneaking, murdering, graceless, faithless, gut-eating skunks as the Lord ever permitted to infect the earth, and whose immediate and final extermination all men, except Indian agents and traders, should pray for." (Taft, 1953:66.) At Sand Creek in Colorado in 1864 militiamen descended upon an encampment of Cheyenne who had been guaranteed safe conduct and viciously slaughtered them. In the words of a congressional committee which investigated the massacre: "It scarcely had its parallel in records of Indian barbarity. Fleeing women, holding up their hands and praying for mercy, were shot down; infants were killed and scalped in derision; men were tortured and mutilated. . . . A war ensued which cost the government $30,000,000 and carried conflagration and death into the border settlements." (Fey and McNickle, 1970:33f.) After Sand Creek a collection of a hundred Cheyenne scalps was exhibited between the acts in a Denver theater.

As the whites poured into the western lands in swelling numbers, killing off the game animals even as they slew the Indians, many of the tribesmen lapsed into despondency. Like other frustrated, dispirited peoples in various parts of the world, whose survival and way of life was being threatened, the Indians began to yearn for supernatural deliverance from their tribulations. The situation was conducive to the rise of prophets or messiahs who would promise a withdrawal of the intruders and a revival of the old ways. Such messiahs did indeed appear among North American Indians, attracting numerous red men to their revivalistic cults.

An earlier nativistic movement had been that among the Pueblo Indians in the late seventeenth century, led by Popé, a Tewa medicine man and prophet in New Mexico. In the ensuing Pueblo Rebellion of 1680 the Spanish oppressors were temporarily expelled from the Southwest. The Delaware Prophet in the eighteenth century preached a return to the old customs and attempted to exclude Christianity and revive a modified form of the old-time religion. The Shawnee Prophet, Tenskwatawa, brother of Chief Tecumseh, in the early nineteenth century preached a doctrine which may have been a revival of that of the Delaware Prophet. In 1801 in southern California a nativistic movement started among the Chumash Indians and spread to the tribes of the interior valley and the Sierra Nevada. In 1884 Smohalla, a Sahaptin Indian of the Columbia River area, originated a revivalistic cult which combined ancient shamanistic elements with certain ceremonial features of the Catholic Church. The Seneca prophet, Handsome Lake, who had been influenced by Quaker missionaries, between 1799 and 1815 preached Gaiwiio, the "Great Message" of abandoning the white man's ways and reverting to the Indian mode of life, a doctrine which still survives in altered form among the Iroquois. In the Puget Sound area the Indian Shaker religion was founded by John Slocum in 1881. This cult, which combines Indian style visions with Christian elements, still flourishes among the Indians of that area.

Among the more interesting of the messianic movements were the two waves of the Ghost Dance religion. In 1869 a Northern Paiute (or Paviotso) in Nevada named Wodziwob began to prophesy certain events which he claimed had been supernaturally revealed to him: that the old, worn-out world would end, thus getting rid of all the white men, and the dead Indians would all return to help rebuild the world. The prophet Wodziwob was subject to trances, during which he professed to be in communication with the dead. He instructed his followers to dance the traditional circle dance of the Great Basin, and to sing certain songs which he announced had been divinely revealed to him. The movement picked up momentum as it spread to the tribes of southern Oregon and northern California, and developed into three variant submovements in California. As the cult diffused, a number of local prophets and dreamers arose in different tribes. Since the supposedly imminent events promised by the prophets did not occur, the people lost faith in their leaders, and the movement subsided.

A resurgence of the Ghost Dance began in 1889, led by another Paiute messiah whose doctrine was essentially the same as that of the original Ghost Dance. The new Paiute prophet, who may have been the son of Wodziwob, was a marginal man who lived between two worlds, the Indian and the white. His Indian name was Wovoka ("Cutter"), but he was also known as Jack Wilson. After the death of his Paiute father, Wovoka had gone to work as a ranch hand for a white family named Wilson, whose surname he adopted. He acquired a close friend of about his own age in the person of the son of the Wilson family, Bill by name, as well as a degree of knowledge of the English language and some familiarity with the Bible and the teachings of Jesus. Wovoka seems also to have been influenced to some extent by Mormonism, and as a youth he traveled to Oregon and Washington, where he learned of the Shaker Cult, from which he derived some of his ideas. After returning to his own people, he acquired a certain reputation as a medicine man, prior to the time in 1888 when he fell ill with a severe fever. During his illness an eclipse of the sun spread excitement among the Indians.

When he revived, Wovoka claimed that he had died and had been taken to the spirit world, where he saw God and received a direct revelation. Wovoka then began to preach the spiritual regeneration of the Indians, with the promise that it would eventuate in the restoration of their world. He professed that God had directed him to instruct the living Indians that they should be good and love one another, that they must live peacefully and return to the old ways, and that they were to sing certain songs and hasten the millennium by dancing. If they did these things, the white men would disappear and the living and dead Indians would

be reunited in a renovated world, where all would live in happiness, in deliverance from misery, death, and disease.

In the dance prescribed by Wovoka, the dancers formed a circle, holding hands, men and women alternately, facing toward the center, moving slowly in a counterclockwise direction, keeping time to the songs that were sung. There was no instrumental accompaniment. The songs, with simple words, included such as the following:

The rocks are ringing,
The rocks are ringing,
The rocks are ringing,
They are ringing in the mountains,
They are ringing in the mountains,
They are ringing in the mountains (Mooney,
1896:1055).

Hypnotic trances were a common feature of the dance. Wovoka believed that magical powers had been conferred upon him and that he was able to control the elements. He could perform certain feats of sleight of hand which helped to convince those who observed him that his message was genuine.

Wovoka himself apparently never made any attempt to spread his doctrine to other tribes, but other Paiutes did, and soon emissaries began to come from the faraway Plains tribes to learn of his teachings. Wovoka himself, apparently, remained at home at Walker Lake, Nevada, for the remainder of his life. The noted Smithsonian Institution anthropologist James Mooney made a thorough and classic study of the Ghost Dance at the time of its occurrence, travelling 32,000 miles by horse and buggy among the tribes that had taken up the cult, and even interviewing Wovoka in 1892. He was convinced of Wovoka's sincerity.

Mooney reproduced a letter which sets forth the doctrine of Wovoka as it was delivered to Cheyenne and Arapaho delegates, who came to him seeking to learn of the cult. A free rendering of the Messiah Letter:

When you get home you must make a dance to continue five days. Dance four successive nights, and the last night keep up the dance until the morning of the fifth day, when all must bathe in the river and disperse to their homes. You must all do in the same way.

I, Jack Wilson, love you all, and my heart is full of gladness for the gifts you have brought me. When you get home I shall give you a good cloud [rain?] *which will make you feel good. I give you a good spirit and give you all good paint. I want you to come again in three months, some from each tribe here [the Indian Territory].*

There will be a good deal of snow this year and some rain. In the fall there will be such a rain as I have never given you before.

Grandfather [a universal title of reverence among Indians and here meaning the messiah] says, when your friends die you must not cry. You must not hurt anybody or do harm to anyone. You must not fight. Do right always. It will give you satisfaction in life. This young man has a good father and mother [Possibly this refers to Casper Edson, the young Arapaho who wrote down this message of Wovoka for the delegation.]

Do not tell the white people about this, Jesus is now upon the earth. He appears like a cloud. The dead are all alive again. I do not know when they will be here; maybe this fall or in the spring. When the time comes there will be no more sickness and everyone will be young.

Do not refuse to work for the whites and do not make any trouble with them until you leave them. When the earth shakes [at the coming of the new world] do not be afraid. It will not hurt you.

I want you to dance every six weeks. Make a feast at the dance and have food that everybody may eat. Then bathe in the water. That is all. You will receive good words again from me sometime. Do not tell lies. (Mooney, 1896:781.)

The California Indians in their disillusionment were unreceptive to the revitalized Ghost Dance, and this time the cult had its principal acceptance among tribes farther east. Beyond the Rockies it was received with enthusiasm by such tribes as the Sioux, Arapaho, Cheyenne, and Comanche. Among the frustrated Plains Indians the movement underwent modifications and became a more hysterical, militant cult than it had been with its originators. The buffalo on whom the hunters of the Plains had so largely relied had been nearly exterminated by this time, and the old prestige hierarchy which had depended upon exploits in warfare had been shattered. The demoralized Plains tribes had been confined on reservations, where they were dependent for their subsistence mainly upon rations issued by the government. They were unwilling to adapt to the life of farmers; to the erstwhile warriors, farming was women's work. In the Plains tribes some shamans began to preach an active resistance to the encroachment of the whites. The

Sioux began to wear "ghost shirts," which bore magic symbols and were thought to be impervious to bullets, and they held all-night gatherings at which the participants would dance until they collapsed into a trancelike state. Apprehensive white authorities alerted the military and tried to stop the assemblies of the Ghost Dance adherents. Finally, nearly three hundred Sioux, including women and children, were massacred at Wounded Knee, South Dakota, where they had gathered to perform Ghost Dance rituals. Soon the followers of the prophets lost faith and the movement faded away, although a few of the old people still sing the songs of the Ghost Dance.

By 1880 most of the tribes had been defeated and were disarmed and concentrated on reservations. The treaty-making period had ended in 1871, when Congress decreed that henceforth "no Indian tribe shall be acknowledged or recognized an independent nation, tribe, or power, with whom the United States may contract by treaty." This marked the beginning of a new phase in the relations between the whites and Indians, during which the Indians were considered to be "wards" of the government. The wardship status, however, was intended to apply to the tribes rather than to individual Indians. It was meant to have application only to certain types of property, in particular to the reservation land, which was to be held in trust for the tribes. Although the wardship status was in the years to come often misinterpreted and misapplied, it was not originally intended as a warrant for paternalistic domination of the Indians, nor was it for the purpose of controlling their comings and goings.

It had proved impossible to exterminate the red man; in fact, in 1870 it was estimated that it had cost the United States government about $1 million for every dead Indian (Loram and McIlwaith, 1943:142). Since it seemed cheaper to feed the Indians than to kill them, the tribesmen had been concentrated on reservations where, impoverished, diseased, and greatly reduced in numbers, they now existed in a slough of despondency and were often not far from actual starvation.

By 1880 certain segments of the American public began to feel ashamed of the part they had played in the betrayal of the Indians, and a few people began to work for some measure of reform in Indian affairs. The reformers were well meaning, but most of their proposals at that time were unenlightened. While they did not see the Indian as the Bloodthirsty Savage, they still believed that *order* must be imposed upon the Indians, that the only solution to the Indian problem was to civilize the Indian, to make him over into a white man.

The policies in Indian affairs which emerged from the thinking of the reform element in the late nineteenth century were those of "forced assimilation." No longer was the aim to exterminate the Indians, who appeared to be a vanishing race anyway. Now, instead of destroying the Indian, the objective was to extinguish the Indian cultures, which when viewed through the ethnocentric lens of the white observers still seemed inferior. This, it was decided arbitrarily (and with no consideration of the wishes of the Indians themselves), was all that was necessary to "Americanize" the Native Americans. Accordingly, strenuous efforts were to be made to eradicate the Indian cultures: Indian tribal governments, native religions, systems of land-ownership—all were to be destroyed. In order to facilitate this extirpation of the Indian heritage, children were snatched from their parents and taken to boarding schools, which were in many cases far from their reservation homes. The children were to be kept in the schools for from four to eight years, and usually were not permitted to visit their parents even during vacations. In school the hair of the children was cut short, and they were subjected to rigorous discipline of military nature. Indian languages, styles of dress, and religious practices were all strictly forbidden.

The experience of Sun Chief, a Hopi, was not unusual. Educated in a boarding school, he decided while convalescing from a severe illness to return to the ways of his ancestors:

As I lay on my blanket I thought about my school days and all that I had learned. I could talk like a gentleman, read, write, and cipher. I could name all the states of the Union, with their capitals, repeat the names of all the books of the Bible, quote a hundred verses of scripture, sing more than two dozen Christian hymns and patriotic songs, debate, shout football yells, swing my partners in square dances, bake bread, sew well enough to make a pair of trousers, and tell "dirty stories" by the hour. It was important that I had learned how to get along with white men and earn money by helping them. But my death experience had taught me that I had a Hopi Spirit Guide whom I must follow if I wished to live. I wanted to become a real Hopi again, to sing the good old Katcina songs, and to feel free to make love without the fear of sin or a rawhide (Simmons, 1942:134).

In civilizing the red man, it was also deemed expedient to break up the tribal lands and divide them among individual Indians, with the aim of making them small freehold farmers. Such was the intent of the Dawes Act of 1887 (General Allotment Act). But many of the Indians were without experience in farming and had no taste for it. Nomadic hunters did not take readily to a circumscribed life of tilling the soil. Indians in general lacked the necessary capital for developing the land, much of which was unsuitable for agriculture and might have been more profitably used for grazing livestock. For instance, the Blackfoot in Montana valiantly planted crops year after year, but the growing season was so short that the crops were often frozen before they could be harvested. Inexperienced in financial matters, many Indians quickly sold or leased their allotments to white men; often, indeed, they were swindled out of the land. Within 60 years, 86 million acres of the best Indian lands had been lost, and some 90,000 Indians were landless. The Indians of Alaska and the Southwest were more fortunate, since most of their reservation land was never allotted.

The policy of forced assimilation was a failure and succeeded only in further impoverishing and demoralizing the Indians. By 1920 the health conditions on the reservations were deplorable, and the poverty-stricken, depressed survivors of the once proud tribes had dwindled to little more than a quarter of a million. The "vanishing American" seemed to be sliding rapidly down the road to extinction. Ostensibly educated Indian youths emerged from the boarding schools as marginal personalities, fitted neither to make their way in the world of the whites nor to successfully readjust to reservation life. Even the more acculturated Indians soon learned that the color consciousness and racist prejudices of the dominant-status white Americans hampered the adjustment of the educated Indian to white society. Under the circumstances many Indians found their only escape from their wretched situation in the bottled solace of the bootleggers.

Only since the 1930s have the Indians gotten a "new deal" in the form of governmental policies more in line with their needs, with a greater recognition of their right to personal dignity as Indians. In the 1920s, at the request of Secretary of the Interior Hubert Work, the Brookings Institute, a private agency for government research, undertook an intensive study of the problems of Indian administration. Usually called the Meriam Survey, the monumental report (1928) of this two-year study laid the foundation for momentous changes in Indian affairs. Most significantly, this study stressed the fact that the assimilation of the Indians could not successfully be forced.

Beginning in 1929, under Commissioner Charles J. Rhoads, a new governmental policy in Indian affairs was inaugurated, one which gradually nullified the previous policy of disrupting tribal cultures and allotting Indian lands. The new philosophy in Indian affairs was strengthened in 1933 during the first term of President Franklin D. Roosevelt, when John Collier was appointed Indian Commissioner, an office which he was to hold until 1946. Collier had the advantage of having done extensive research and field work among Indians, and had served as the Executive Secretary of the Indian Defense Association. To Collier the real problem lay in America's blindness to the wisdom and beauty of the Indian cultures, and at his suggestion, the tribes themselves were consulted prior to the drawing up of a new governmental program for them. Many of the recommendations of the Meriam Survey, plus suggestions from the tribes and from Commissioner Collier, were incorporated into the Indian Reorganization Act of 1934 (Wheeler-Howard Act). In brief, the philosophy of the act was the opposite of forced assimilation, since it encouraged the Indians to retain their tribal identifications and cultures, offered them assistance in becoming self-sustaining, and held out the promise of their integration into the national life as Indians. The new policy stopped all allotment of Indian lands, gave the tribes the opportunity to organize for increased self-government with elected tribal councils, and made it possible for organized tribes to borrow money from the government for such enterprises as cooperative cattle raising. Health and school services were improved, and the Indians were given back their constitutional right of religious freedom. Native arts and crafts were encouraged, and it became possible for the first time to teach Indian languages in the schools. No tribe was compelled to accept the provisions of the Indian Reorganization Act; rather, each was permitted to vote upon its acceptance or rejection by secret ballot.

Although much progress was made under Collier, he was often handicapped by inadequate financial and moral support and by the ingrained (and justifiable) suspicion of governmental proposals on the part of many Indians. So many promises had been broken in the past, so many times had the Indians been confused by reversals in policy as one administration succeeded another, that the Indian suspicion that "the white man speaks with a forked tongue" carried over to hinder full implementation of the provisions of the Indian Reorganization Act.

Indians of today disagree about Collier's accomplishments, but many of them in retrospect take a favorable view of Collier's efforts adjudging his administration to have been an enlightened one on the whole, conceding that, at least in comparison with earlier commissioners, Collier knew what Indians wanted and needed. His administration was, however, hampered by limitations on funds during the depression years and subsequently by the onset of the Second World War. As the defense expenditures mounted, the federal budget for Indian affairs was ruthlessly slashed. After the war, the climate of opinion in government had changed, and strong pressures were felt in Congress to divest the government of as many obligations to the Indians as possible and as rapidly as feasible.

Accordingly, during the 1950s there was an unfortunate reversal in governmental proposals and policies for the Indians. Partly as a consequence of pressures for the reduction of the number of federal employees and for economy in government in general, it now became the official aim to accelerate the liquidation of the government's responsibility to the Indians as speedily as possible. By 1950, as Nancy Lurie has expressed it, "... the time-honored philosophy of the Indian as the Problem again was dominant in official thinking. In the last decade policy regressed to the nineteenth century with startling speed and with a vengeance. The earlier philosophy assumed that if the Indians' specific problems were taken care of, they would stop being Indians, and the Indian Problem would be solved. Now, however, the idea was to get rid of the Indians by dispersing them and relieving the government of all responsibility for their specific problems." (Lurie, 1961a:480.)

The new aim was to "get the government out of the Indian business" as rapidly as possible, by a policy of termination of governmental services to the Indians, by transferring federal jurisdiction of law and order on Indian lands to the states, and by the relocation of as many Indians as possible off the reservations, in order to hasten, once again, their assimilation, and to alleviate the pressure of increasing population upon the inadequate resources of the reservations.

Legally, Congress has the authority to determine when the federal government shall terminate its special relationships with the Indian tribes. In line with the demand for the liquidation of the Bureau of Indian Affairs and for expediting the termination process, the House of Representatives in 1953 passed Concurrent Resolution 108, which stated that federal supervision of the Indians of five designated states and for seven specified tribes located elsewhere should be swiftly brought to a conclusion. In part, the resolution stated that: "It is the policy of the Congress, as rapidly as possible, to make the Indians within the territorial limits of the United States subject to the same laws and entitled to the same privileges and responsibilities as are applicable to other citizens of the United States, to end their status as wards of the United States, and to grant them all the rights and prerogatives pertaining to American citizenship."

In consequence, termination laws were enacted for the Menomini of Wisconsin, the Klamath of Oregon, the "mixed-blood" members of the Utes, and a few other small groups. As originally promulgated, termination would have meant the dissolution of tribal organizations in many cases, and the division of tribal assets among individual Indians. But the termination proposals stirred up a storm of protest by alarmed Indians and their friends all over the United States, evidencing with emphasis the intensity of Indian opposition to such a program. Several of the termination bills never got beyond the hearing stage, since the groups concerned were obviously quite unprepared for termination: for example, the Turtle Mountain Chippewa of North Dakota were among the most destitute Indians in the nation and many of the Seminoles in Florida spoke no English and had received little schooling. At their own

request, the Alabama and Coushatta tribes of Texas (about 400 Indians in all) were partially terminated and the state of Texas took over the reservation in trust and assumed certain responsibilities for the Indians, but almost immediately there was agitation among whites to "get Texas out of the Indian business." The Menomini and Klamath both happened to have on their reservations valuable tracts of timber and had expressed consent to the principle of termination, but the Indians were not permitted to vote on the specific bills affecting them. They were, in effect, pressured into termination, being told that if they refused to accept it, the moneys which belonged to the tribes would not be distributed among them. Both tribes were unhappy about the hasty, impatient way in which they were being terminated. Two of the strongest arguments against speedy termination are, first, that many Indians are still quite unprepared to enter the world of the whites on a competitive basis, and secondly, that the burden of assuming the payment of taxes on the reservation lands would bankrupt the Indians in short order. The Indians maintain that under the provisions of the treaties whereby they ceded other lands to the government their remaining lands should not be taxed.

The prospect of the transfer of jurisdiction over Indian lands to the states frightens the Indians. In many cases the financial resources of state and local governments are inadequate to carry the added burden of services to the Indians. Organized pressure groups in the states are eager to obtain the remaining Indian lands. Prejudice and discrimination against the Indians are often strongest in the areas surrounding the reservations, where the old frontier conception of the Indians as shiftless and drunken inferiors tends to persist. Indians often have been Jim-Crowed in towns near the reservations and have not infrequently been abused by the local police.

The effects of termination upon the Menomini and Klamath tribes were disastrous. Before they were terminated in 1961 the Menomini had been a relatively self-sufficient people, operating a tribally owned sawmill and with good schools and community services. After termination the state of Wisconsin created a county out of the former Menomini Reservation, and the Menomini were immediately billed for taxes on their lands that they were unable to pay. At the same time the Menomini had to assume the responsibility for paying for such county services as sanitation, police and fire protection, and highway maintenance, the cost of which the revenue base of the tribe was quite inadequate to meet. The tax base was too small to support adequate schools and health services, and the Menomini hospital had to close. The sawmill and the forest holdings of the tribe were endangered, as were the Indian land-holdings. Many Menominis lost their homes and life savings, and as a result the state of Wisconsin was faced with a massive welfare problem. Thus termination had tragic consequences for a formerly comparatively prosperous tribe. Within ten years after the termination, Menominee County, Wisconsin, was ranked as one of the ten most depressed counties in the nation. Finally, the federal government recognized that the termination of the Menomini had been a mistake, and on December 22, 1973, President Nixon signed the Menomini Restoration Act, which nullified the termination of the Menomini and restored the tribe to federal trust status.

The Klamath tribe of Oregon, also terminated in 1961, fared no better than the Menomini. The Klamath were unable to cope with altered conditions after their termination, and lost $32 million in timber sales almost immediately. Payments to individual members of the tribe were soon exhausted, and before long many Klamath, demoralized and angry, were totally dependent upon welfare for their support.

In an effort to alleviate the pressures of excessive populations upon the resources of the reservations, the Indian Bureau has been encouraging the relocation of Indians in cities off the reservations. For many Indians this seems to be the only solution, and thousands of Indians had set a precedent for it in previous decades, by voluntarily leaving their homes in search of off-reservation employment, mostly in urban areas. Under the new relocation program the Bureau assisted those Indians who wished to move to such cities as Los Angeles, Chicago, Denver, and Oakland, furnishing them money for transportation and moving costs, helping them to find jobs and housing, and providing them with a year's Blue Cross medical protection and a month's subsistence allowance.

Under the resettlement program of the Bureau of Indian Affairs, more than 100,000 Indians have been relocated in cities from the West Coast to the Middle West since 1952, and more than twice that number have moved from reservations to urban areas on their own initiative and without government support. The migration from the reservation to the cities is currently probably the most important trend in Indian affairs. More than half of the Native Americans may now be city residents.

Many Indians are, however, reluctant to emigrate from the reservations to the cities. Accustomed to rural life, with little job experience, speaking English only with difficulty, they view with trepidation the transition to the tension and congestion of city life. The reservations are home to the Indians, few of whom wish to leave the security of family and tribe for the unfamiliar life of the cities, where most of them can obtain only unskilled and poorly paying jobs and where they are often subjected to discrimination and permitted to live only in dilapidated districts. Some of the relocatees have successfully made the adjustment to city life, others have become unhappy, dispirited, and homesick.

According to recent estimates by the Bureau of Indian Affairs, 35 percent of the Indians who have been resettled in the cities have given up and gone back to the reservations.

Along with the growing pressures for termination of the Indians, Congress in 1946 established a special Indian Claims Commission, to hear and settle once and for all the claims of Indian tribes for lands taken from them. During a period of five years, Indian tribes filed 852 claims for reimbursement against the United States government. Many of the claims involved grievances of a social and cultural nature not covered by the usual interpretations of American law, such as the socioeconomic effects on the disintegration of cultures of such governmental policies as the abolition of polygyny and the kidnapping of Indian children and sending them to boarding schools far from the reservation. Difficult problems arose in determining tribal boundaries, over questions of use and occupancy of the lands, and of the actual value of the land. As expert witnesses, at least 50 anthropologists played important roles in the claims litigation, some for the Indians, some for the government. Evidence presented was based not only upon ethnographic field work, but also upon critical analyses of the ethnohistorical literature. Archeological data also provided valuable information in instances where prehistoric sites could be linked up with historic groups. The process of adjudicating the claims has of necessity been slow, and it has been necessary for Congress to extend the tenure of the Indian Claims Commission several times. By 1973 some 300 claims had been heard, and over $300 million had been awarded to claimant tribes, but the awards represent less than 4 percent of the amount claimed. Some of the decisions were quite favorable to the tribes, as when the Ute Mountain Utes shared with other Ute bands in an award of $31.2 million. Adding to their windfall were royalties from oil and natural gas discoveries on their barren reservation. In contrast, over 100 claims have been dismissed by the commission without any award whatsoever, and in other cases the award has been far less than that asked by the tribes; in certain instances as little as a few hundred dollars was awarded.

During the later years of the Eisenhower administration, pressures for the hasty and mandatory termination of the Indians abated, and governmental policies once again veered back to the principles embodied in the Indian Reorganization Act, with emphasis upon improved educational facilities for Indians, particularly in vocational training, plus the development and encouragement of new industries on or near the reservations for Indian employment, with increased financial assistance to aid the Indians in becoming self-supporting. This trend was continued and strengthened under President Kennedy, with the appointment of Philleo Nash, an anthropologist, as Commissioner of Indian Affairs in 1961. Kennedy, also in 1961, halted further termination of tribes, at least temporarily. The administrations of Presidents Lyndon B. Johnson and Richard M. Nixon likewise expressed the opinions that the termination policy had been in error, admitting that the terminated tribes were worse off than before, and proposing that termination should be replaced with a policy of fostering Indian self-determination, with continuing governmental assistance and services. Nevertheless, the tribes live in fear that a future national government might revert to the termination policy.

Now, in the 1970s, we appear to have entered a new era in Indian affairs. The Indians are currently increasing at a much faster rate than the general population. The 1970 census listed 827,091 Indians and Alaska natives, as compared with a total of 523,591 in 1960. The resources of the reservations are inadequate to support the Indian population explosion; for those Indians who do not wish to resettle off the reservations, new modes of livelihood must be developed.

In the attempts to force the assimilation of the Indians, an important fact was not understood: that peoples cannot be swiftly remodeled to adapt to cultural patterns which are not in harmony with their ideals and aspirations. Despite all the pressures, the rate of acculturation of the Indians to the ways of life of the white Americans has been slow. Indians have not been swallowed up in the great melting pot of America, and numerous basically Indian cultures persist as cultural islands. Surprisingly large segments of Indian cultures do survive, at least in modified forms, and many Indians still retain their tribal identifications, and remain culturally and socially "Indian." No Indian cultures have been completely unaltered by contact with the whites; Indian religions and social structures in general have undergone significant modifications. The biggest changes have been in material culture, in which the emotional resistance to change is less intense, and most of the Indian artifacts have been replaced by those of modern industrial society. Indians have of necessity become increasingly involved in our economic system. Even those cultures which have changed the least have nevertheless undergone important functional changes and modifications in form, in consequence of which the emerging cultural patterns differ in many ways from the aboriginal. Indian basic personality structures are persistent, and as John Collier suggests, the Indians have never lost their power for living, their "passion and reverence for the human personality and for the web of life and of the earth." (Collier, 1947:8.)

At present Indians live on approximately 200 reservations in 26 of the United States, mainly in isolated localities. In the East the most prominent remaining groups are the Iroquois of upper New York State, the Seminoles in the Everglades of Florida, the Eastern Cherokee in the Great Smoky Mountains of North Carolina, and several Algonkin tribes in the woods of Minnesota, Michigan, and Wisconsin. Here and there are small remnant groups such as the Penobscot and Passamaquoddy of Maine, the Shinnecock on Long Island, and survivors of the Powhatan Confederacy in Virginia. About 3200 Choctaw live on small reservations in Mississippi.

Many of the Prairie and Plains tribes were

resettled in Oklahoma, along with the "Five Civilized Tribes" and others removed from the Southeast. Outside of Arizona and New Mexico, Oklahoma still has the greatest concentration of Indians in the United States, totaling about 75,000 in 1970. Large numbers of Sioux remain on reservations in the Dakotas, and other Plains tribes such as the Crow, Cheyenne, Assiniboin, and Blackfoot, are in Montana. Small tribes include the Ponca and Omaha in Nebraska, and the Fox (or Mesquakie) in Iowa.

In the Southwest are the largest and most conservative Indian populations in the United States, including the numerous Navaho, Apache, Pueblo, and Papago. In 1970 there were more than 200,000 Indians in the Southwest, or nearly a quarter of all the Indians in the United States. Remnants of the Pacific Coast tribes are intermittently scattered on small reservations in the states which were their aboriginal homes.

In Canada in 1968 the Indian population was estimated at 250,000, a majority of whom were living on reservations. Mexico is today predominantly a *mestizo* nation, but there are still many large groups of relatively unacculturated and unassimilated Indians. The social system of Mexico is such that various Indian groups are able to move relatively easily along the continuum of acculturation to a fuller integration in the national life, and it is possible for talented and ambitious Indians to rise in the social scale. For instance, Benito Juarez, a Zapotec Indian from Oaxaca, became one of Mexico's greatest presidents.

Economic deprivation continues to be one of the most serious problems for the Indians of the United States in the 1970s; Indians in general are poor, many of them extremely poor. Oil-rich Indians, such as the Osages of Oklahoma, are very much the exception. A few other individual Indians and tribes have good incomes from timber, oil, and gas, but a majority are still deeply mired in the bog of poverty and must be classed on the lowest economic levels in the United States. In 1970 the unemployment rate among Indians was still ten times the national average, running as high as 80 percent on some reservations. The annual income for 80 percent of the reservation families was still below the poverty line, with an average annual income of only $1500 per family.

Indians on reservations frequently supplement their income from livestock and agricul-ture with the wages of seasonal and periodic work in the alien world beyond the reservation boundaries. Usually they work as agricultural laborers or in unskilled occupations and often are paid less than whites employed in the same kind of work. As previously mentioned, the federal government has attempted to alleviate the economic plight of the Indians by encouraging them to resettle in urban areas, by developing some of the resources on reservations, and recently by bringing new industries to certain reservations.

In 1969 it was estimated that 70 percent of Indian housing was still substandard (Cahn, 1969:19). Senator Edward M. Kennedy, chairman of the United States Senate subcommittee on Indian education, pointed out in the same year that 50,000 Indian families were living in unsanitary dilapidated dwellings, many of them in shanties, huts, or even abandoned automobiles.

Health problems continue to be acute on reservations; the health of Indians in general lags 20–25 years behind that of the general population. The life span of the Indian is abbreviated; in 1970 the average age at death for Indians was only 44, or about a third less than the national average. Great numbers of Indian babies do not survive the first year of life; the infant mortality rate for Indians is nearly 50 percent higher than that in the general population. Indians are still stricken with infectious diseases such as trachoma and dysentery that have become rare in most other segments of the American population. In 1974 statistics gathered by the Senate permanent investigations committee showed that Indians suffered from ten times more tuberculosis than other Americans, as well as from thirty times more strep throat, eleven times more hepatitis, and sixty times more dysentery. Although in the past ten years there has been some improvement in death rates among the Native Americans, they are still forty times greater, in all age groups, than the death rate for all Americans. Enteritis, influenza, and pneumonia take a high toll of Indian lives. For many Indians living in crowded, unsanitary conditions, health standards are far below those of the general population in the United States. The high rates of death and disease are in spite of the fact that many improvements have been made in medical care for Indians since 1955, when all medical services on the reservations were transferred to the United States Public Health Service. Still, many of the hospitals of the Indian Health Service branch remain understaffed and under-funded. Budgets have been consistently cut, and in the past ten years the Indian Health Service has received only about half of the funds it regarded as necessary to upgrade its facilities.

Although advances in the education of Indians have been made in recent years, the sad fact is that the educational level of the Indians remains below that of the general population, at less than six years of schooling for all Indians under federal supervision. The dropout rates of Indian children are twice the national average; between 48 percent and 60 percent of Indian high school students drop out of school before graduation (Sorkin, 1969:30).

Until recently, many Indians resisted education and did not wish their children to be tutored in the white man's tradition. This has changed; all the tribes are now seeking better educational facilities, and for the first time in history, instruction is now available for nearly all Indian children. A few tribes such as the Navaho and the Jicarilla Apache now provide scholarships for the higher education of their young people. Other youthful Indians are being trained to take their place as technicians in the mechanized world of today.

With greater education, the political participation of Indians is increasing, and able, informed Indians are rising to leadership in their own tribes. All Indians of the United States have been citizens since 1924, but several states still denied them the vote. In consequence of court rulings in Arizona and New Mexico in 1948, Indians in all states have now been enfranchised. Tribal councils and the National Council of American Indians have encouraged the political participation of the Indian people, and have assisted them with information about candidates and with explanations of the mechanics of voting.

Tens of thousands of Indians are now members of various Christian denominations. But many native religions still survive, especially in the Southwest, and even Christianized Indians often retain some of the ancient beliefs. Certain "amalgamation" religions have compounded Indian and Christian elements. Among these are the aforementioned cult of Handsome Lake among the Iroquois and the Indian Shaker religion of Puget Sound. The most widespread of these syncretistic religions is the Peyote Cult, whose adherents have been brought together in the Native American Church, which is now

the principal religion of a majority of Indians between the Mississippi River and the Rocky Mountains, and is also represented in parts of the Great Basin, southern Canada, and east-central California. The Peyote Cult combines social ethics with old Indian practices and beliefs. Members consume the nonnarcotic dried buttons of the peyote cactus, which induce visions and hallucinations of varied colors. Although the native components seem to be dominant in the Peyote Cult, it includes also various elements of Christian derivation, such as baptism, the Trinity, the Cross, and other Christian symbolism. At meetings of the cult there is singing, prayers, and testimonials.

The Peyote Cult appears to be a manifestation of the emergence of what has been called "Pan-Indianism," which has been developing in consequence of the growing recognition among Indians that they have common interests and problems, regardless of tribal affiliations. The culture elements in the Pan-Indian movement are a synthesis from diverse Indian cultures, but many of them are drawn from the Plains area, such as the Plains-type war dance, the warbonnet, Plains modes of dancing, and others which appear to have become symbols of Indianism to Indians of a variety of tribes in other culture areas. Intertribal visiting and intermarriage is on the increase, and in the future the Pan-Indian movement may acquire a greater political significance than it has at present.

The Pan-Indian movement reflects a new and growing Indian nationalism, a vital social movement in which Indians of many tribes are coming together in increasing numbers to affirm and intensify their Indian identity, regardless of the multiplicity of their tribal origins. Tribes have been overcoming ancient antagonisms to one another, in recognition of their shared "Indianness."

A number of new Indian organizations, intertribal and Pan-Indian in nature, have appeared in recent years, coincident with the neo-Indian nationalistic trend and the recognition of the need for unity among the Native Americans. The oldest of these major intertribal associations, organized by and for the Indian people, is the National Congress of American Indians (NCAI), founded in 1944, which until 1961 was the only such organization among Indian Americans. The membership includes both tribes and individuals, and while non-Indians are accepted into membership, they are required to pay double membership fees and are without voting rights in the organization. The political philosophy of the NCAI is relatively moderate, but its purpose is political action, and it has used the political technique of lobbying for the advancement of Indian interests. It has strongly opposed legislation that proposes the transfer of federal functions concerning Indians to the states. When the tribes in 1954 were faced with the threat of termination, the NCAI developed a program which was intended to foster self-determination among Indian communities. The slogan was, "Self-determination rather than termination!" The NCAI has also tried to use political pressure to force changes in the Bureau of Indian Affairs. It has insisted that the Indian land base under old treaties should be protected, and that individuals should have the choice of assimilation or nonassimilation. Proper educational facilities should be provided for all Indians, and individuals should have the opportunity to enter the larger society at a favorable socioeconomic level if they choose, or they should be able to remain in Indian communities with a decent standard of living.

The founders of the NCAI were mainly relatively acculturated and well-educated Indians, including business and professional men, Indian employees of the Bureau of Indian Affairs, and anthropologists of Indian ancestry. It has been charged by members of certain newer organizations that the NCAI does not represent the "real Indians," that is, the impoverished, more traditionally oriented people.

In 1961 a new all-Indian organization, the National Indian Youth Council, was started by Indian college students and recent college graduates. More radical and more militant than the NCAI, the National Indian Youth Council (NIYC) clearly shows the influence of the civil rights movements of the period. It has been extremely critical of the NCAI as well as the established tribal governments, charging them with being too conservative. It has used tactics of picketing, confrontation, and demonstration. The NIYC sponsored the "fish-ins" in 1964 among Indians along the Puyallup, Nisqually, and other rivers in the state of Washington, in opposition to the efforts of the state to cancel Indian fishing rights guaranteed by federal treaties and to impose the customary fish and game laws upon the Indians. In the "fish-ins" many Indians deliberately violated the state fishing regulations, and went to jail as a result.

In 1963 members of the NIYC joined in the poverty march on Washington, D.C., and began to use the term "Red Power." The NIYC advocates the abolition of the Bureau of Indian Affairs, which it accuses of paternalism and exploitation, and its replacement by agencies which could advise and counsel Indians, but not attempt to control them.

By the late 1960s, in strong contrast with the habitual passivity of the Native Americans over most of the past century, a wave of Indian activism forced itself upon the attention of the general public. On November 19, 1969 a group of young Indians occupied an abandoned federal prison, which had been declared excess property, on Alcatraz Island in San Francisco Bay. Calling themselves Indians of All Tribes, they were mostly students from various colleges and universities in the Bay area. They proposed to establish an Indian cultural center on Alcatraz and offered to buy the island from the federal government for "$24 in glass beads and red cloth."

A majority of the Indians in the nation were now under the age of 20, and throughout the year of 1970 angry young Indians, mainly in the West Coast area, also calling themselves Indians of All Tribes, occupied other isolated islands and abandoned army posts, demanding the return of lands that had been taken from their ancestors.

Along beaches in the state of Washington other incensed Indians set up road blocks and closed fifty miles of reservation seashore to non-Indians, who had been wantonly littering the beaches with beer cans and broken bottles.

Among other Indian groups, similar to the NIYC and organized during the 1960s, were the Young American Indian Council, the United Native Americans, the Organization of Native American Citizens, and the Native Alliance for Red Power in Canada. A highly militant organization, the American Indian Movement (AIM), was started by a group of young Chippewas in Minneapolis in 1966 to protest alleged police brutality and has gone on to become the most substantial (and most controversial) activist group among Indians in the United States. Minneapolis has one of the few Indian ghettoes to be found in any city in the nation, in a rundown district around Franklin Avenue, often called "the reservation" by both Indians and the police. The members of AIM organized an Indian Patrol for surveillance of police activities. AIM soon expanded into other cities in the

Midwest, particularly Cleveland, and to other parts of the nation. In 1972 AIM spearheaded the forcible occupation of the main offices of the Bureau of Indian Affairs in Washington, D.C., in a movement of Indians to the nation's capital called the "Trail of Broken Treaties." Three months later AIM occupied by force of arms the hamlet of Wounded Knee, South Dakota, on the Pine Ridge Reservation, scene of a massacre of nearly 300 Sioux by United States cavalry in 1890. AIM responded to a complaint by certain members of the tribe of what they termed corruption in the tribal government and of bungling by the Bureau of Indian Affairs. Some 200 Indians armed with shotguns and rifles took over Wounded Knee on February 27, 1973, and occupied it for 71 days. AIM set up roadblocks, and the village was surrounded by Federal Bureau of Investigation agents and United States Marshals. More than 130 Indians were later indicted, and their leaders were accused of conspiracy and of assaulting federal officers. AIM has also played a prominent part in a number of other Indian protest incidents, using tactics of direct confrontation, including picketing and disruption. It is ever alert to expose instances of discrimination and racism and seeks full rights and redress for Indians, including the return of federal lands. It opposes what it considers the exploitation of Indians in performing tribal dances at the annual Inter-Tribal Ceremonial in Gallup, New Mexico.

In 1964 the American Indian Historical Society was founded by Indians in San Francisco, stating its goals to be: "To promote the culture, education, and general welfare of the American Indian; To inform and educate the general public concerning America's Native, original people; To preserve the philosophy, culture, and languages of the land's First People." The Society has published books of high quality about Indians, as well as a quarterly journal, *The Indian Historian* and a monthly newspaper, *Wassaja,* subtitled "A National Newspaper of Indian America." A major aim has been to improve the Indian image in textbooks and other publications, to correct distortions and expose exploitation and falsehoods concerning the Native Americans.

In June of 1961, with Dr. Sol Tax as coordinator, the American Indian Chicago Conference (subtitled "The Voice of the American Indian") was held on the campus of the University of Chicago, with the objective of affording Indians an opportunity to express their conceptions of their rights and needs and their ideas of proper governmental policies in Indian affairs. The conference was attended by more than 500 Indians, representing 90 tribes and bands. The outcome was a document entitled "The Declaration of Indian Purpose," in which the delegates expressed a strong unity in insisting upon their desire to maintain their identity as Indians and their right to what may be termed selective acculturation, to pick and choose appropriate aspects of the culture of the white men, while rejecting others. They expressed their opposition to mandatory termination, and made known their wish for help and assistance in developing their own resources and programs. In the document the Indians say: "What we ask of America is not charity, not paternalism, even when benevolent. We ask only that the nature of our situation be recognized and made the basis of policy and action. In short, the Indians ask for assistance, technical and financial, for the time needed, however long that may be, to regain in the America of the space age some measure of the adjustment they enjoyed as the original possessors of their native land." (Declaration of Indian Purpose, 1961:20.)

The Native Americans have made it increasingly clear in recent years that most of them do not want to relinquish their identity as Indians, that assimilation into the larger society is not their goal. Among young Indians in particular there is apparent an insistence upon the retention of ethnic distinctiveness and the preservation of Indian cultural patterns. The former possessors of the continent demand a right to determine their own destinies, rather than having decisions made for them by paternalistic governmental agencies. They insist upon more voice in controlling their own affairs and especially in handling their own money. They maintain also that it is their rightful prerogative to go on living as Indians, but with economic assistance from the usurpers of their native lands in order to raise the general level of Native American life. They want equality in economic and political opportunities, as well as in health and educational services. They want Indian school boards to control the reservation schools. They will no longer countenance governmental treatment of reservations as domestic "colonies."

The Indian of today is neither the Noble Savage nor the Bloodthirsty Savage. A real human being rather than an image of fantasy, the

Indian now lives in a world of automation, of expanding urbanization, and of persistent international tensions. The Indian is being inexorably drawn into the maelstrom of this complex outside world with its multitudinous problems which baffle not only the red man but the white man as well. Both races are entangled in this intricate situation. The white man must still assist the Indians, the original possessors of the continent from which they have been displaced. Perhaps the Indian can also help the white man. We are already culturally indebted to the Indians in so many ways; perhaps we could learn still more from them. We might profit by reexamining the world views of the Indians, to see what they still have that we seem to have lost, what it is that has enabled them to survive and preserve so much of their native traditions, despite the profound pressures to remake them. As Mrs. Martha Grass, a Ponca, addressing a meeting of non-Indian human rights workers in Tulsa, Oklahoma, said: "We got along fine before you people came to this continent. You could learn a beautiful culture from the Indians. We still have a lot to teach you."

Indians believe that they can function with competence in modern society *as Indians*. Like most Americans, they believe in freedom and in the right of self-determination, with which attempts at coercive assimilation are incompatible. Voluntary assimilation is another matter: over a period of decades, countless Indians have been assimilated as individuals, leaving the reservations of their own accord to seek a livelihood in the wider society. There is no evidence that a hasty termination of federal services to the Indians or a breaking-up of the reservations would accelerate this process. And why should the prospect that Indian cultures may survive for a few more generations be so alarming? In America we already have many other cultural islands, such as certain groups of orthodox Jews, Amish farming communities, and Spanish-American villages in New Mexico; their existence has not been detrimental to the general American life, so rich in its diversity. We can anticipate continual modifications in Indian customs and value systems; eventually, Indian cultures may fade away. Meanwhile, we have moral obligations to assist the dispossessed red men in their problems of health, education, and economics. This is what the Native Americans want.

Our deep canals are furrows faint
  On the wide and desert plain:
Of the grandeur of our temple-walls
  But mounds of earth remain.
And over our altars and our graves
  Your towns rise proud and high!
The bison is gone, and the antelope
  And the mountain sheep will follow.
And all our lands your restless bands
  Will search from height to hollow:
And the world we knew and the life we lived
  Will pass as the shadows fly
When the morning wind blows fresh and
    free
  And daylight floods the sky.
Alas for us who once were lords
  Of stream and peak and plain!
By ages done, by Star and Sun,
  We will not brook disdain!
No! though your strength were
    thousand-fold
  From farthest main to main;
For we are the Ancient People,
  Born with the wind and rain!
                        EDNA DEAN PROCTOR

Suggested readings

BROPHY, W. A., and ABERLE, S. D.
1966   *The Indian: America's Unfinished Business.* University of Oklahoma Press.
CAHN, E. S., ed.
1969   *Our Brother's Keeper: The Indian in White America.* New York: New Community Press.
DELORIA, V., JR.
1969   Custer Died for Your Sins: An Indian Manifesto. London: McMillan.
FEY, H. E., and MCNICKLE, D.
1970   *Indians and Other Americans: Two Ways of Life Meet.* New York: Harper & Row.
HALLOWELL, A. I.
1957   "The Backwash of the Frontier: The Impact of the Indian on American Culture." In *The Frontier in Perspective*, ed. W. D. Wyman and C. B. Kroeber. The University of Wisconsin Press.
1957   "The Impact of the Indian on American Culture." *American Anthropologist* 59:201–217.
JOSEPHY, A.
1971   *Red Power: The American Indian's Fight for Freedom.* New York: American Heritage.

LEACOCK, E. B., and LURIE, N. O.
1971   *American Indians in Historical Perspective.* New
        York: Random House.
LEVINE, S., and LURIE, N. O.
1971   *The American Indian Today.* University of
        Toronto Press.
MCNICKLE, D.
1973   *Native American Tribalism: Indian Survivals and
        Renewals.* London, Oxford, and New York:
        Oxford University Press.
STEINER, S.
1968   *The New Indians.* New York: Dell.
WAX, M. L.
1971   *Indian Americans: Unity and Diversity.*
        Englewood Cliffs, N.J.: Prentice-Hall.

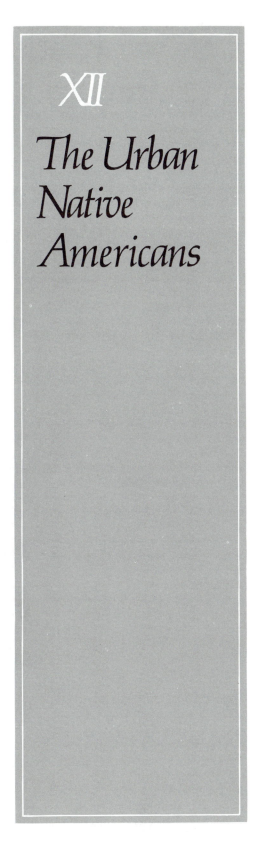

XII

The Urban Native Americans

One of the most noteworthy developments in Indian affairs in recent decades has been the sizable migration of Native Americans into the cities. This movement is not an entirely new phenomenon, but it has been accelerated in the decades just past. Some Indian individuals and families have been moving into urban areas ever since pioneer times and especially since the reservation system was established in the 1870s. The volume of migration was merely a trickle, however, prior to the Second World War and the inception of the Voluntary Relocation Program of the Bureau of Indian Affairs in the 1950s. Since that time the intensified rate at which Indians have been emigrating from the reservations has become so important a trend that it is estimated that more than half of the Native Americans now live in urban areas (Bahr, Chadwick, and Day, 1972:ix).

The problems that Indian migrants encounter in the cities are grave. In leaving the intimacy of their primary groups and other secure relationships on the reservations, the Native Americans enter a complex industrial situation in quest of the employment that has been scarce or lacking on their native soil. The migrants are still tribal people, and they bring with them tribal customs and values, many of which are directly counter to the premises of urban life.

When the federal government fostered the resettlement of Indians in the cities, away from the low employment areas on the reservation, the intent was to hasten the assimilation of Indians into the so-called mainstream of American life. While it is true that urbanization has been influential in expediting the acculturation of many Indian persons, it has at the same time brought new problems and aggravated old dilemmas. There has been, moreover, a consequence that was never intended by the federal government: the migrations have encouraged among Native Americans an unanticipated trend toward Pan-Indianism. As American Indians of many tribes came together in the cities, they began to comprehend more fully the fact that they share common interests and problems which override tribal considerations. Now, indeed, it appears that a new Indian nationalism is in the process of emerging.

On the whole, the Native American migrants have preferred to maintain their identity as Indians, rather than being swallowed up in the great American "melting pot." Better educated and more sophisticated on the whole than the Indians who have remained on the reservations, the urban Indians have provided most of the leaders in recent Indian activist and nationalistic movements.

The urbanization of Native Americans has been in progress for many years. For more than half a century the Bureau of Indian Affairs has made some effort to find jobs for Indians off the reservations. By the late 1920s Indians were sufficiently numerous in the cities that in the Meriam survey, a comprehensive summary of a large-scale study of Indian affairs and problems undertaken by the Brookings Institute for Government Research, a section was devoted to the "migrated Indians" (Meriam, 1928:667–742). The migrated Indians had come to the cities on their own initiative, as individuals or as families, many of them seeking the wherewithal to survive. Some came after selling or leasing lands that had earlier been allotted to them under the provisions of the Dawes Act of 1887. Others had decided not to return to the reservations after having attended off-reservation boarding schools, particularly in such cities as Phoenix and Albuquerque, or after having participated in the so-called outing program, in which young Indians were placed temporarily away from the reservation with white families for employment, mainly in agriculture or housekeeping.

After a period of residence in the cities, some of these Indians shifted their identifications from their tribes of origin to the general urban population and ceased to keep up any contacts with the reservations. Since these Indians were relatively few in number, their visibility in the cities was comparatively low, and some began to "pass" for white, no longer identifying themselves as Indian if that seemed economically or socially beneficial.

The numbers of the urban Indian migrants remained relatively small until the time of the Second World War. During the 1930s a few desultory attempts had been made to encourage Indians to seek employment in cities, but these efforts were hindered by the prevailing conditions of economic depression. Jobs were at a premium for white workers already living in the cities, let alone for darker-complexioned migrants from the plains and cactus country.

With the revival of employment opportunities during World War II, there was an exodus of an estimated 40,000 Indians from the reservations, attracted by war-related work in heavy industries. Following the war, many of these were laid off, and many returned to the reservations. Some Indians, having learned skills that were in demand by employers, having developed a craving for material possessions, and having made a satisfactory adjustment to urban life, managed to find new employment and remained in the cities permanently.

More than 25,000 Native Americans served in the armed forces during the war, and quite a few of them were stationed in or near cities. More acculturated as a result of their wartime experiences, and having acquired a taste for urban life, some of these veterans settled in the cities after discharge from the services. Other Indian veterans returned to the reservations only temporarily after demobilization. After a sample of reservation conditions, restless and bored, and finding no employment on or near the reservations, a number of these veterans, too, headed for the cities.

The great majority of Native Americans on the reservations were still living in abject poverty during the post-war years, as the reservation economies remained relatively stagnant. The general pattern on reservations throughout the country was one of economic underdevelopment, with the rural Indians remaining among the most deprived groups in America. Conditions were so depressed on some reservations that they have been described as "open-air slums." As D'Arcy McNickle has summarized the situation, "Infant mortality rates were excessive and life expectancy short, housing was deplorable, unemployment rates ran nine and ten times higher than the national rate" (McNickle, 1973:vii).

To escape from the mire of poverty, Indians of many tribes had begun to leave the comparative emotional security of the tranquil reservation life to make their way to the cities in search of employment. Most of them would probably have preferred to remain on the reservation if they could have had equivalent economic opportunities there.

Although the motivations behind the Indian migrations to the cities have been complex and varied, a major impetus to the emigration to urban areas has been the indisputable fact of economic deprivation on the reservations, at a time when the Indian population was on the increase. The birthrate of Indian babies continued to soar, while Indian death rates, although still high in comparison with those of the general populations, were declining because of advances in modern medicine and improvements in the medical facilities available to Indians.

The land base and the available resources became increasingly inadequate to support the burgeoning reservation populations. Much of the reservation land was not productive enough for the maintenance of the tribesmen by farming, stock raising, and timber production alone. Some reservations were deficient in natural resources; on other reservations potentially valuable resources remained in an undeveloped condition. Most Indians lacked the capital to start new enterprises on their own and were unable to obtain adequate financing for that purpose.

Rates of unemployment on the reservations were persistently high. There was a lessening need for agricultural manpower on the reservations, and for all too many Indians, agriculture had been the only source of intermittent employment. Simultaneously, there was a persistent dearth of other job opportunities of any kind for Indians on or near the reservations.

The description of the situation among the Hopi would have fitted the condition of underdevelopment and impoverishment on most reservations all over the nation: ". . . a growing population but a young one, a decreasing and already inadequate land base, . . . high unemployment, low incomes" (Waddell and Watson, 1971:147). For many of the Hopi, as for Navahos living nearby under similar conditions, emigration to urban areas became a matter of necessity rather than choice.

Such conditions still prevail to a large extent on reservations all over the United States, as indicated by recent statistics on Indian income and unemployment on the reservations. In 1960 the unemployment rate for Indian males was 51.3 percent compared with only 5.4 percent for all males in the United States. By 1970 Indian unemployment was still ten times the national average, running as high as 80 percent on some reservations. Raymond Nakai, then chairman of the Navaho Tribal Council, reported in 1970 that there were 35,000 unemployed among a total of 140,000 Navaho.

On most reservations the economic circumstances remained considerably below those of nearby communities where the population was predominantly white. In 1964 the median income for reservation males was a mere $1,800 per annum, as contrasted with a median income for all United States males of $6,283. Furthermore, 80 percent of reservation Indian families had annual incomes below the poverty line, defined as $3,500 for a family of four, with an average annual income of $1,500 for such Indian families. Ninety percent of the reservation housing was substandard. Typical of the housing situation on many reservations was that described for the Sioux of the Pine Ridge Reservation:

A great majority of the homes on the Pine Ridge Reservation are one- or two-room cabins, poorly furnished and commonly constructed of rough plank, with the roof made weather resistant by a covering of tarpaper or sod. A stove, centrally placed, supplies heat. Auxiliary buildings usually include an outhouse, a shed, and one or more tents. The tents not infrequently provide the only sleeping area for some members of the family or for relatives even in the most severe weather (Brophy and Aberle, 1966:168).

In view of the deplorable economic conditions on many reservations at the end of the Second World War, the United States government adopted a major policy of encouraging and assisting the migration of Indians to cities. At the same time pressures were intensifying in Congress to, once and for all, "get the government out of the Indian business," to terminate the reservation system altogether. Accordingly, government aid to Indian migration began on a small scale in 1948, at first with a Labor Recruitment Program designed specifically for Navaho and Hopi, on whose reservations the problems of pressure of population on resources had become particularly acute, for the population had increased rapidly on reservation land that was badly depleted and eroded. The winter of 1947 was an excessively severe one in the Navaho-Hopi country, and the sad plight of those Indians, starving in their scenic but barren homeland, was widely publicized by newspapers, magazines, and radio. The Labor Recruitment Program was designed to ameliorate the situation in part, and it provided for assistance to Navahos and Hopis in obtaining employment in a few selected cities which included Phoenix, Salt Lake City, Denver, and Los Angeles.

The year 1952 marked the beginning of a much more ambitious project, the Voluntary Relocation Program, with the opening of a placement center for Indians in Chicago. The program was expanded in 1957, appropriations were increased, and by 1960 a dozen relocation centers had been opened in various cities to assist in the placement of Indians from reservations all over the nation. The name of the program was considered, however, to have undesirable connotations, reminiscent of the War Relocation Authority, under the auspices of which Japanese-Americans had been detained in relocation centers in the desert and mountain states, after their enforced removal from the Pacific Coast states in the hysterical atmosphere that followed the bombing of Pearl Harbor in 1941 by the military forces of the Japanese nation. Accordingly, the name of the relocation program for Indians was in 1962 changed to the Employment Assistance Program, which was the responsibility of a branch of the Bureau of Indian Affairs. Under the Employment Assistance Program services to Native Americans were expanded to include job placement on or near the reservations, as well as in urban centers.

Despite the predominance of economic factors, the motivations impelling the migrations from the reservations have actually been multiple. Many young Indians, desirous of escaping reservation boredom, have been lured to the cities by the prospect of adventure and excitement amid the bright lights, as well as by hopes of economic betterment. It should be noted that by this time, no Indians, even those who had never before visited a city, were completely uninformed about the cities, no matter how isolated their reservations might have been. They had developed preconceptions about city life, having learned something about it in schools, as well as through the media of mass communication, and from hearing other Indians who had been to the cities and subsequently returned to the reservation tell of their experiences. Some Indians were drawn to the cities because of a wish to evade the responsibilities of what they had come to feel as the constricting burdens of tribal and kinship ties, or to escape from what they felt was the stifling pressure to conform to traditional behavior and values, which was exerted by the older generations of reservation Indians. Other miscellaneous family and personal problems were involved in individual decisions to abandon the reservations. Some young Indian migrants had no intention of becoming permanent city residents, but merely expected to have a good time in the city at government expense and then return to the reservation.

The goals of the resettlement program were summarized in a Bureau of Indian Affairs area office report as follows:

(1) Develop employment opportunities for Indian people with some degree of skill who are employable but unable to find jobs. (2) Make institutional training available for all Indian boarding school and public school graduates who do not plan to or cannot go on to higher education. (3) Provide on-the-job training for the unskilled to meet the labor demands of the increased industrial development occurring on or near Indian reservations. (4) Provide vocational counseling and guidance to the unemployed or underemployed reservation Indians. (5) Participate in community development programs on the reservation and provide work orientation and motivation.

The potential emigrants were first screened on the reservations, and only those who were considered to be best fitted for successful adjustment to urban life were selected for aid in resettlement. In theory, the only Indians accepted for relocation were those who could meet certain standards of health, education, and acculturation. To make it more difficult for the resettled Indians to leave the cities and return to the reservations without having made a realistic attempt at adjustment to urban life, the Bureau of Indian Affairs adopted the official policy of not relocating Indians in communities near their own reservations, but placing them, rather, in distant cities. The assumption was that the relocated Indians would become part of the general society, and would cease to be part of the "Indian problem." Accordingly, the Bureau of Indian Affairs opened Employment Assistance Centers in thirteen cities, the first in Chicago, Los Angeles, and Denver, and others were added later. The resettlement program continues in 1976, and ten of the centers are still functioning, with offices in Los Angeles, Chicago, Oakland, Seattle, Cleveland, Denver, San Jose, Dallas, Tulsa, and Oklahoma City.

Since the beginning of the Voluntary Relocation Program in 1952 more than 100,000 Native Americans have been resettled in thirteen cities. At least twice as many Indians have moved off the reservations during that period on their own initiative and without government assistance, many of them to smaller cities near their own reservations. The shorter move tends to lessen the culture shock of the transition to urban life, and it makes it easier for migrants to return to the reservations to attend ceremonials and to visit with friends and relatives.

Some of the relocated Indians, as well as others who went to the cities without benefit of government assistance, never intended to become permanent urban residents, but migrated only in search of temporary employment, with the objective of, for instance, earning enough money to buy an automobile, intending then to return to the reservation.

In the early days of the Voluntary Relocation Program, the Bureau of Indian Affairs provided the migrants only with one-way travel expense, assistance in finding a job, and money for subsistence until the first pay check was received. After that, the migrant was on his own. Later, as appropriations for the resettlement program were increased, other services were added, including assistance in finding housing, transportation for all members of the family from the reservation to the city, payment for the shipment of household goods, a clothing allowance if necessary, various orientation and counselling services, and other benefits. After the migrant is placed in a job, he is entitled to receive follow-up counselling services for one year.

In 1956 the program was expanded to include adult vocational training for prospective migrants, with the aim of increasing their employability. Training was made available to Indians between the ages of 18 and 35 in basic language skills and a variety of vocational skills, including welding, upholstery, and secretarial work, at the Intermountain Indian School at Brigham City, Utah. Also approved to offer training to Indians under this program were 350 other institutions, mainly business colleges and technical schools, located both in urban centers and near reservations. These schools have turned out Indian graduates with a variety of skills and specializations in demand by employers, including draftsmen, electricians, technical illustrators, barbers, nurses, beauty operators, and other types of craftsmen and specialists.

In the 1960s the off-reservation training and placement program was greatly enlarged in terms of appropriations. Residential training centers were established where families could live while their breadwinners were undergoing vocational training. In 1967 the Bureau of Indian Affairs began to make available grants for down payments on the purchase of homes in urban areas by the resettled Indians.

In 1968 the Bureau of Indian Affairs estimated that within the preceding decade some 200,000 Indians had moved from the reservations to urban areas, more than half of them on their own initiative and without government aid (Bureau of Indian Affairs, 1968:23). The largest concentrations of urban Indians were now in such metropolitan centers as Los Angeles, Chicago, the San Francisco Bay area, and Minneapolis–St. Paul. California in particular had become a goal for Indian migrants. The population of Native Americans in that state had nearly quadrupled during the decade preceding 1960, with the migrants coming mainly from reservations outside the state of California. Los Angeles now had the largest Indian Population of any city in the United States, with nearly 50,000 Indians estimated to be living in the metropolitan area. Other migrants had been going in augmented numbers to cities near their reservations or rural homes, such as Phoenix and Tucson in Arizona, Albuquerque in New Mexico, Portland in Oregon, Rapid City in South Dakota, and Oklahoma City. Incidentally, there are no legal reservations in Oklahoma; Indians live, rather, among the general population in both rural and urban areas.

The United States census of 1970 enumerated 827,091 Indians and Alaska Natives in the United States, and indicated that there were approximately 310,000 Indians in large metropolitan areas, with another 50,000 Native Americans in smaller urbanized areas with populations of 2,500 and up. The magnitude of the increase in the numbers of urban Indians becomes apparent when the 1970 figures are compared with the relevant figures from earlier censuses. According to the 1960 census there were 165,922 urban Indians, while the 1950 census counted only 56,000 Indians in cities.

In Canada, too, Native Americans have been moving into cities for much the same reasons as have the Indian migrants in the United States. Reasons given for leaving the reservations to move to Canadian cities include inadequate resources and lack of employment opportunities on the reservations, the desire to take advantage of urban educational opportunities, and the quest for excitement in city life. Canadian census data indicate that between 1951 and 1961 the Indian population of Toronto increased ten-fold, that of Winnipeg five-fold, and that of Montreal two-fold. In 1957 the Individual Placements Program was inaugurated by the Canadian government, with the objective of using the facilities of the National Employment Service to place reservation Indians in urban employment. Since resources and employment opportunities continue to be limited on Canadian reservations, the trend of migration to the cities by Canadian Indians may be expected to accelerate.

The census figures probably understate the total numbers of Indians in the United States as a whole, as well as the number of Indians in the cities. Some estimates place the total number of Indians in the United States in 1970 closer to a million, and suggest that there may be as many as 10 million persons in the United States with some degree of Indian ancestry (Taylor, 1972:2). It is further considered likely that more than half of the Indian Americans (or an estimated half a million) are now urban residents.

In 1970 the metropolitan areas with the greatest number of Indian residents, according to census statistics, were the following:

1. Los Angeles–Long Beach 24,509
2. Tulsa 15,519
3. Oklahoma City 13,033
4. New York City 12,160
5. San Francisco–Oakland 12,011
6. Phoenix 11,159
7. Minneapolis–St. Paul 9,852
8. Seattle 9,496
9. Chicago 8,996
10. Tucson 8,837
11. San Bernardino–Riverside 6,378
12. San Diego 5,880
13. Albuquerque 5,839
14. Detroit 5,683
15. Dallas 5,022
16. Denver 4,348
17. Milwaukee 4,075
18. San Jose 4,048
19. Portland, Oregon 4,011
20. Philadelphia 3,631
21. Tacoma 3,343
22. Washington, D.C. 3,300
23. Houston 3,215

Statistics on Indians are notoriously unreliable, in part because of the difficulty in locating and identifying people of Indian descent in the cities and partly because many people are not easily recognizable as Indian unless they choose to be explicit about their Indian ancestry to census enumerators. As a result, they are often listed in other categories in census reports. Furthermore, some Indians reside in the cities only briefly, or they shift from one neighborhood to another, obscured by the anonymity of the urban milieu, and appreciable numbers of

them are doubtless missed by the census takers. According to the Bureau of Indian Affairs, in the year 1969, the year just preceding the last census count, the number of Indians in Los Angeles county alone was as high as 50,000, although the number reported by the census the following year was much less. Similarly, one study put the number of Indians in Seattle in 1970 at 12,000 while another estimate placed the number of Indians in Chicago also at 12,000, and again the census figures in both instances were lower.

The Bureau of Indian Affairs in 1969 also reported sizable concentrations of Indians in such cities as Buffalo (New York), Great Falls (Montana), Duluth (Minnesota), Gallup (New Mexico), Sioux City (Iowa), Tacoma and Spokane in Washington, and Fresno, Sacramento, and Eureka-Crescent City in California. Considerable numbers of Indians have also moved to smaller urban centers near their own reservations. Such cities include Winslow, Arizona, where there is a Hopi colony of 400 persons, and Holbrook and Flagstaff, also in Arizona, where the Indian residents are mainly Hopi and Navaho. Indians are numerous in Ponca City, Oklahoma, as well as in Scottsbluff, Nebraska, and Yankton, South Dakota. Most of the Indians living in the latter two communities are Sioux.

Another recent development has been the emergence of small urban centers directly on the reservations, including Tuba City, Fort Defiance, Shiprock, Chinle, and Crownpoint on the Navaho Reservation. Certain Bureau of Indian Affairs agency towns on the reservations, too, are taking on some urban characteristics. Examples of this incipient urbanism at agency towns are Window Rock (Navaho), Sells (Papago), Sacaton (Pima), San Carlos (San Carlos Apache), all in Arizona, and Dulce, New Mexico (Jicarilla Apache).

A few reservations have become integral parts of urban areas, as the cities have expanded to encompass the reservations wholly or in part. Examples are the Oneida Reservation, now surrounded by Green Bay, Wisconsin, and the Salt River Reservation (Pima-Maricopa) in Arizona, adjacent to the three cities of Mesa, Scottsdale, and Tempe. The Yaqui Indians in Arizona, who came as refugees from Sonora in Mexico in the late nineteenth and early twentieth centuries, are now for the most part urban, as cities have expanded around the Yaqui communities. The Yaqui settlements include Guadalupe, now in the shadow of a free-way near Phoenix and Tempe, and Pascua and Barrio Libre, on the outskirts of Tucson. As the city of El Paso, Texas, has spread out, it has encircled the southernmost community of Pueblo Indians, that of the Tigua of Ysleta del Sur.

Numerous Indian migrants have made the transition to city life successfully and have become permanent urban residents. But by no means all of the resettled Indians have remained in the cities permanently. Some, in fact, have stayed in the cities only briefly before returning to the reservation. Others have relocated two or three different times, if they have been able to convince the Bureau of Indian Affairs that their reasons for having left the city and returned to the reservation were legitimate. Philleo Nash, former United States Commissioner of Indian Affairs, expressed an opinion that the return to the reservations has been about as frequent as the permanent resettlement. Joan Ablon estimated that in the San Francisco Bay area during the early years of the Relocation Program, about three-quarters of the Indians who had resettled in the cities of that area had moved back to the reservations (Ablon, 1965:365). The rate of return to the reservations later slowed down, but Ablon was of the opinion that 50 percent of the relocated Indians eventually moved back to the reservations. Recent Bureau of Indian Affairs figures have placed the number of returnees to the reservations at 35 percent. One study reported that three out of ten relocatees return home in the same year in which they have been resettled and suggested that the number who eventually return to the reservations is much higher, although no figures are available to corroborate this opinion.

In contrast, quite a few Indian migrants to the cities have made successful accommodations to urban life and have prospered. Even among these, many hope eventually to retire to the reservations, after what seems to them a term of exile in the cities.

One problem in ascertaining the numbers of Native American urban residents is the fact that some Indians literally alternate their places of residence between the tribal communities and urban areas, shuttling back and forth between the reservations and the cities. There is also a floating migrant population of Indians, in which there are several fluctuations, as Indians move off the reservations for brief periods for the specific purpose of earning money, after which they return home to the reservations, or move on elsewhere for other work.

A study made under the auspices of the Navaho Agency illuminates some of the reasons why relocated Indians have returned to the reservations from the impersonal city milieu. The causes most frequently given by the returnees were alcoholism (19 percent), illness (23 percent), and military service (8 percent). About 25 percent returned for social and emotional reasons, 3 percent because of language difficulties, and 19 percent for economic reasons. The Navahos who remained in the cities tended to have greater fluency in the English language, to be between 20 and 40 years old, and to have attended public schools rather than government or mission schools (Navajo Yearbook, 1958:367–369). But Weppner found that of the Navahos who had been resettled in Denver, over half returned to the reservation within three months (Waddell and Watson, 1971:254).

La Nada Means, a young Shoshone-Bannock woman from the Fort Hall Reservation in Idaho, explained the fact that 80 percent of those relocated from her tribe had returned to the reservation by saying, " ... things in the slums where you wind up are even worse than on the reservation, and you don't have your people to support you" (quoted in Collier, 1970). Without a doubt, resettled Indians from many tribes return to the reservations because of homesickness and a longing for the support and security of the primary group ties on the reservations.

Dr. Joan Ablon has commented on the attitudes toward living in the city upon the part of urban Indian residents:

Most Indians do not like the city, although they appreciate the many conveniences of urban life. They do not like the crowds, the many buildings pushed together, the constant restraints, the bills, the lack of privacy. Yet most enjoy the varied amusements a metropolitan area can offer them, as well as the educational experiences of seeing new things. Indians come to the city seeking work, not to become white men nor to stop being Indian. Most of them sorely miss their families and reservation life. Their feelings about returning are ambivalent, and negative and positive attitudes occur in their every utterance. If comparable job opportunities at home were available, it is probable that more than 75 percent of the Indians who have relocated would choose to return to their reservations as soon as possible. (Ablon, 1965:365.)

The resettled Native Americans have been

confronted with serious problems in making adjustments to urban life, difficulties which have been more acute for some persons than for others. It is not easy to make the transition from the relatively tranquil life of the reservation to the fast-paced, highly competitive life of the metropolis.

Among the most severe handicaps has been inadequate vocational preparation, which has made it impossible for many Indians to get employment in other than unskilled and low-paying work, in jobs of uncertain duration. The problem is aggravated by the fact that many Indians have not had an adequate education and are insufficiently skilled in reading and writing the English language. In 1970 the average educational level of Indians under federal supervision was only that of the sixth grade. The rate of Indian dropouts from school was twice the national average.

Finding suitable housing in the cities has been another serious problem, and the Indian migrant has often been able to afford to live only in decaying areas of the city, too frequently under truly deplorable conditions. He has sometimes been the target of discrimination by other city residents, and in some cases there has been conflict with other ethnic groups, as for example between Indians and Puerto Ricans on the north side of Chicago.

Transportation has been a problem for many Indians, who have not been able to afford to buy automobiles and who have had consequent difficulties in getting to their places of employment. Obtaining adequate medical care, too, has been difficult for urban Indians, since the migrants lose the medical services provided on reservations. The Indian Health Service branch of the United States Public Health Service assists resettled Indians when they first come to the cities, but only for as long as they remain ineligible for local health services because of residence requirements, and the Indian will later be eligible for assistance from the local health services only if he is indigent.

It is similarly difficult for Indians to obtain access to social services in the cities, since the local welfare agencies have persisted in regarding urban Indians as the responsibility of the federal government, while the federal government has taken the contrary point of view. The fact that the Bureau of Indian Affairs does not provide the city dwellers with the same range of services that it does to reservation Indians has persistently been a source of bitterness among the urban Indians.

To all of these and other problems must be added those of psychological stress and culture shock in making an adjustment to urban life, so different from that of the reservation. The individualistic social milieu in the cities contrasts sharply with the closely knit, supportive environment on the reservations. For some Indian migrants, uprooted from their traditional backgrounds and bewildered by the swirl of urban life among anonymous strangers, the consequence has been personal disorganization.

In an article entitled "The Indian in Suburbia," *The American Indian,* a publication of the San Francisco Indian Center, offered the following precautionary information to resettled tribesmen:

> *When an Indian family first comes to Oakland, or San Francisco, they will find thousands of cement streets running in every direction.*
>
> *On these streets will be tens of thousands of automobiles. These automobiles are filled with people who are trying to kill each other off with these monsters as fast as the white man killed off the buffalo.*
>
> *To find his way around this cement prairie, the white man uses a map, and so must the Indian.*
>
> *All of these houses have numbers, and some of the streets are called by numbers. Some streets have other names, and in many cases streets are not called streets but avenues, places, boulevards, and freeways. Freeways are the most dangerous, and no one walks on them, and sometimes it is even hard to drive on them.*

A high rate of alcoholism has been noted among urban Indians, and this has resulted in an excessive number of arrests for drunkenness and related offenses. Indian children, many with the linguistic handicap of knowing little English, often face difficulties in the urban schools, and this is reflected in a disproportionate dropout rate. The ultimate escape of suicide is all too frequent among urban Indians. The suicide rate for all Indians (including both urban and rural residents) is more than three times the national average (Josephy, 1971:208).

Some of these problems of urban Indians merit further discussion. To begin with the matter of employment, the urban migrant usually has difficulty in finding a job if he is not assisted by the Bureau of Indian Affairs, often because his educational background and vocational training have been inadequate and because he is insufficiently skilled in handling the English language. Employers may discriminate against Indians in hiring, regarding them as unreliable and incompetent workers. The traditional values of the migrant's native culture often are in contrast with the western work ethic prevalent in the cities, and this factor contributes to the pattern of job instability among the migrants. The white employer's emphasis on promptness and reliability, and the requirement that the worker maintain a certain level of production are unlikely to have been part of the migrant's prior work experience. An employer is not apt to be sympathetic to the Indian's desire to stay away from work, perhaps for days at a time, to go to the reservation to attend a ceremonial or to help out relatives. The Indian may not be motivated to work at a job eight hours a day, five days a week, and he may compromise by seeking employment as a day laborer, working only irregularly and being paid by the day.

With an imperfect knowledge of the English language, the migrant may have trouble understanding the job requirements. He may furthermore be at a disadvantage because, in contrast to the white man's ways, Indian cultures do not usually stress aggressiveness or emphasize the importance of competition. On the contrary, the values of generosity, cooperation, and sharing with others are stressed in Indian cultures. Rather than expressing himself constructively in a conflict situation, the Indian usually tends to withdraw.

The jobs available to the unskilled Indian worker frequently are seasonal in nature. Layoffs of Indian workers are common, in a job market which demands increasingly skilled workers rather than the reverse. In times of economic recession Indian workers suffer disproportionately from being thrown out of work, but nevertheless the rent still has to be paid and food has to be purchased. A related problem is the fact that the migrants may have difficulty in learning to live with the higher prices of essential commodities in the cities. Their experience on the reservation has given them little practice in budgeting and the management of money so necessary in the urban milieu.

A consequence of all this has been that, although there are exceptions, too many Indians in the cities have remained poor. Having attempted to escape the poverty of the reservations by migrating to the cities, they have, ironically enough, too often succeeded only in exchanging rural poverty for the poverty of the urban slums. In 1970 it was estimated that three-quarters of all urban Indians were still living in poverty, with incomes below the currently specified poverty line of $3,500 per year for a family of four.

If, in his job experience in the city, the Native American experiences early economic disappointments and frustrations, these may be psychologically shattering, and the odds against his making a successful adjustment to city life are increased. Too many migrants, after losing jobs or being evicted from housing, have become stranded in an alien environment, some of them gravitating to the skid row districts.

In the words of Mary Lou Payne, a Cherokee woman who herself had the experience of moving to the city:

It was shameful to force rural Indians into urban ghettos. It's no answer to poverty to dump these people into the cities. They are so unprepared for city life, paying bills each month, going to work every day, that they filter out to the very bottom of society.

This shipping out of unprepared people is just shameful. It doesn't work out. They just go back to doing what they did before, which is picking up odd jobs. But doing it in the cities. (quoted in Steiner, 1968:180–181.)

The fact that Indians often have large families increases their difficulty in obtaining suitable housing in the cities. Landlords may refuse to rent to large families, or they may evade renting to Indians at all. Charging high rentals to Indians is also common. In order to pay the rent, it may be necessary for members of an extended family, or even a number of unrelated people, to live together. A survey in Minneapolis discovered that up to fifteen Indian people might be crowded together in a two-room apartment, while other Indians were found sleeping in hallways or bathtubs. Many of the accommodations available to Indians in the cities are substandard. Too frequently, they are run-down, infested with cockroaches, and located in slum neighborhoods.

Drunkenness and drinking behavior have loomed large among the problems of urban Indians, but these are directly related to the marginal social and economic positions that so many of the urban Indians occupy, and they are by no means restricted to Indians only. Theodore D. Graves, who made a study of the drinking patterns of resettled Navahos in Denver, concluded that "... the vast majority of Navajo drunkenness, at least in Denver, can be accounted for *without resource to the fact that the subjects are Indians*," and he maintained that the role of economic marginality is of fundamental importance in the migrant's adjustment problems in the city, (Graves, 1970:51).

It cannot be denied that too many Indians have sought solace and alleviation of emotional conflicts in alcohol. In the central districts of some cities are "Indian bars," so-called because the patrons are mainly Indians. These taverns have become centers of sociability for the urban Indians, where Indians go to meet drinking companions, and the camaraderie thus engendered encourages and reinforces the drinking patterns.

Indians are frequently arrested for drunkenness, since they are conspicuous because of their physical distinctiveness and because of their patterns of drinking in public. Graves reported that in Denver 93 percent of the arrests of Navaho relocatees were for drinking-related offenses, and this pattern is similarly characteristic of other cities to which the migrant Indians have gone (Ibid., 282). A study by Daniel Swett of 610 Indian arrests in San Francisco concluded that in every case the consumption of alcohol was a contributing factor either to the offense or to the arrest (Swett, 1963:2).

The late Dr. Edward Dozier, himself a Native American from Santa Clara Pueblo, considered the pattern of excessive drinking among American Indians to be a response to cultural, social, and historical factors that produced a sense of frustration and inadequacy among the Indians (Dozier, 1966).

Indian families have often been reluctant to enroll their children in city schools, and too frequently have not insisted upon the child's regular attendance once enrolled. Shy Indian children, suspicious and fearful of strangers and with a sketchy knowledge of the English language, may thwart the attempts of teachers to communicate with them. Their teachers frequently are deficient in cross-cultural sensitivity or knowledge of Indian life-styles. Little has been done by educators to correct these deficiencies, but in Minneapolis, where 8000 Chippewas live, a program of bi-cultural educa-

tion has been started, which emphasizes the involvement of Indian parents in the school situation, in the hope of overcoming the high dropout rate of Indian children.

Throughout their lives, many Indians remain handicapped by the fact that they have never learned to read and write well enough to function adequately in the competitive world outside the reservation. Fuchs and Havighurst have commented on the unfortunately high rate of school dropouts among Indian adolescents:

At present the Indian adolescents appear to have special difficulty in adapting to urban conditions. They drop out of school in large numbers after reaching the eighth grade. Many of them become chronically truant at ages 14 and 15, and then are dropped from the school rolls when they reach 16. . . . The urban schools that Indian children attend differ from most other schools serving Indian children in that the numbers of Indian children attending are relatively small, indeed sometimes not even noticed by school authorities. The Indian children tend to be merged into the ranks of the "disadvantaged," attend predominantly lower class schools in the inner city, and little attention is paid to their unique characteristics as Indians (Fuchs and Havighurst, 1972:290).

Studies of the residential patterns of Indians in the cities have shown that, in general, Indians do not live in ethnic enclaves or large ecological concentrations composed solely or mainly of Indians. Rather, the Indians are dispersed over remarkably great areas, usually in working-class neighborhoods, living among other urban residents of many races and ethnic groups. Typically, the Indians associate very little with their non-Indian neighbors. There are a few exceptions to this pattern of residential dispersion of urban Indians, such as the Mohawk enclave in the North Gowanus section of Brooklyn, or the camps of Sioux on the outskirts of Rapid City, South Dakota.

In Chicago there are no neighborhoods that are predominantly Indian; rather, the Indian residents are scattered throughout the city and its suburbs with, however, the largest number of Indians living in the northern area known as Uptown. In Oklahoma City there is no Indian neighborhood as such, although there are certain sections of the city that are favored by Indians. Indians in Oakland are scattered through a number of typical working-class districts and low-rent housing projects. There are no Indian enclaves in Denver. In Los Angeles, Indians were found to be more widely dispersed than either blacks or Mexican-Americans, although there is a primary concentration of Indians in the low-rental district of central Los Angeles. An additional 28 percent of the Indians live in a "low-class suburban southeastern extension of the city," while the remaining 26 percent are distributed throughout other suburbs and cities of greater Los Angeles (Price, 1968:172). Indians in both Seattle and Albuquerque were found to be more widely dispersed than any other non-white minority. Although there is no ethnic enclave of Indians in Phoenix, Indian residents are for the most part to be found scattered over the southwestern quarter of the city. In Tucson, similarly, Indians are spread out over a south-central sector of the city. It should be noted that the policy of the Bureau of Indian Affairs in assisting migrants in finding housing has been to disperse the Indians over a wide area among the general population, in hope of expediting their assimilation. But, adrift in the anonymity of city life, in many cases separated from family and friends, Indians in the cities often live isolated existences, failing to establish new friendships or to participate in the social life of the community. There is furthermore a high rate of geographical mobility of Indians within the cities, as places of residence are frequently changed.

As mentioned, Indians in the cities have difficulty in getting social services, since the community services provided for them by the federal government on the reservations do not follow them to the cities. The federal government has taken the view that Indians living off the reservations are the responsibility of the communities in which they reside. The urban-based public agencies, however, have maintained the contrary position, regarding the Indians in the cities as still being the responsibility of the several federal agencies that have assisted them on the reservations. Consequently, the urban Indian migrants tend to be left without assistance from either the federal or local welfare agencies. The Employment Assistance Branch of the Bureau of Indian Affairs terminates its services of job placement and counselling for the resettled Indian after he has been in the city for a year. It provides no services for Indians already resident in the city, and none to those Indians who have migrated to urban locales on their own initiative. Various Indian centers in the larger cities attempt to fill the void in providing some social services to urban Indians, but the centers were never intended to function primarily in welfare work,

and limited in funds and facilities, they are able to provide such services on a small scale only.

The Indian centers, of which there are now approximately 30 in the cities where migrants are the most numerous, are somewhat like the settlement houses that have served urban migrants of other ethnic and national proveniences. They provide places where Indians of various tribes may gather for social purposes, and to some extent they assist Indians in finding housing and employment. Certain of the centers provide other welfare and counselling services. The Seattle Indian Center makes available legal services for urban Indians.

Indians in the cities have generally preferred to associate mainly with Indians of their own and other tribes, in both formal and informal social interaction. Although in individual cases friendships with whites and members of other racial and ethnic groups have developed, relations with non-Indians are often superficial and fraught with suspicion and ambivalence. In some of the cities there are various tribal clubs; for instance, there may be a Sioux club, or a Chippewa club, or a Winnebago club, or a Navaho club. But by no means all urban Indians belong to such clubs. Some of the tribal clubs hold monthly powwows, social gatherings which feature singing and dancing of traditional Indian types. Again, many urban Indians do not attend such occasions, nor have they joined any organizations that have predominantly white memberships either. In Phoenix a trend toward Pan-Indianism is apparent in the flourishing Central Plains Indian Club, which has members from such non-Arizona tribes as the Omaha, Cheyenne, Arapaho, Comanche, Pawnee, Osage, Ponca, and Sioux. The club sponsors an All-Indian Days Powwow each spring, which is attended by as many as 1500 Indians.

In New York City organizations of Indians include the American Indian Arts Center, the Thunderbird American Indian Dancers, and the Indian League of the Americas. In Los Angeles there is a variety of Indian social groups, including Indian centers, tribal clubs, Pan-Indian clubs, athletic leagues, and tradition-oriented dance clubs, with which the Indians of the Los Angeles area affiliate to varying degrees, although it has been estimated that only about 20 percent of the Los Angeles Indian residents are active in such organizations.

In Los Angeles, also, are ten Christian churches having predominantly Indian memberships, of which the largest is the Indian Revival Center, affiliated with the Assembly of God. In San Francisco are the American Indian Baptist Church and the Indian Holiness (Pentecostal) Church, as well as the Native American Church. A Presbyterian Church in Brooklyn features sermons in the Mohawk language. Urban Indians are also manifesting a growing interest in the revival and perpetuation of native religions. For instance, in St. Paul, Minnesota, there is an urban chapter of the Chippewa Medicine Lodge religion.

In Seattle in 1968 a new national organization, American Indians United, Inc., was formed with the express objective of aiding urban migrants in their search for employment, housing, recreation, and personal security. In 1969 the executive director of the organization affirmed also that the purpose of the organization was to "strengthen the Indian's identity" and "to obtain for him from both private and federal sources the same services that are now provided for the reservation Indians" (Bureau of Indian Affairs monthly newsletter, *Indian Record,* Oct. 1969, p. 3). In 1972 yet another coalition of urban Indians, known as the National American Indian Council was formed, mainly by representatives of the Indian centers of various cities, with Indians from the Los Angeles and San Francisco Bay areas taking the lead.

Ties to the reservations are persistent among most urban Indians, although some of them, preferring to forget their Indian antecedents, have elected to discard all remnants of "Indianness" in order to disappear into the general urban population. Others, although still recognizable as having some Indian ancestry, have chosen not to associate with Indians or to become affiliated with any Indian organizations, regarding such alliances as disadvantageous to them. But most of the urban Indians keep up an interest in reservation happenings, and they visit on the reservations frequently, particularly if their urban residences are not far from the reservations of their tribal affiliations. Some Indians continue to live on reservations and commute to off-reservation jobs, either daily or weekly, some driving to places of employment many miles from the reservations. Nevertheless, more than half of the enrolled members of some tribes are now living away from their reservations. In the cities the general trend seems to be toward detribalization, of a lessening sense of identity with respect to specific Indian tribes, coupled with the emergence of a more general Indian identity, and with the retention of a strong pride in being Indian.

There has been some friction and mutual distrust, as well as a generation gap, between the urban Indians and the reservation Indians. The migrants to the cities have been predominantly young, with single males disproportionately represented among them. The participants in the relocation program have been virtually all between the ages of 18 and 35 at the time of their resettlement, and on the whole they have been better educated than those who have remained on the reservations, and less traditional in their orientations. As the out-migration has continued, the reservation populations have come to consist disproportionately of the elderly and middle-aged, of children still in school, of the incapacitated, and of those who do not seek employment and thus are not a part of the active labor force.

The youthful urban Indians have demanded better representation on the tribal councils, which many of them regard as dominated by old "Uncle Tomahawks," whom they consider to be tools or pawns for the Bureau of Indian Affairs and other government agencies. Many of the tribes do not grant the same voting and membership privileges to urban Indians as to those still resident on the reservations. The city Indians have little confidence in the ability of the traditionalist reservation leaders to protect the tribal estates against the encroachments of non-Indians. In turn, the reservation Indians have been suspicious of the urban Native Americans, apprehensive that the latter may, in order to claim shares for themselves, scheme to liquidate the tribal resources. For instance, in the 1960s, urban residents of the Colville and Spokane tribes of Washington did indeed demand the liquidation of the tribal holdings and the distribution of the proceeds among registered tribal members. The older Indians still resident on the reservations feel that they have, in a sense, been betrayed by the energetic young migrants, who have chosen to remove their capabilities from the reservation in order to further their personal interests in the cities, with a consequent "brain drain" of potential tribal leaders. The reservation Indians have generally remained aloof from becoming involved in the problems of the urban Native Americans.

Individual Native Americans have varied greatly in the adjustments they have made to urban life. Some have succeeded in various skilled occupations and professions and have progressed financially and in other ways. There is now a growing middle class among the urban Indians, composed of Native Americans who have successfully made the transition from the reservation to urban life. In contrast, the urban experience has disillusioned and defeated other Indians, who, unprepared for the problems confronting them in the city, have given up in despair and returned to the reservation.

In general, the younger Indians, with more education and of mixed blood, are more likely to adjust successfully to the urban environment than are older, less educated, full-blooded Indians, who may have difficulty in finding and holding a job (Martin, 1964).

Although a prime objective of the federal resettlement program has been to foster the assimilation of Indians into the general urban society, life in cities has had the unintended consequence of creating conditions that further Pan-Indian orientations and activities. A neo-Indian identity appears to be emerging, which overrides tribal differences and which promotes the recognition that Indians in cities, regardless of tribal origin, share common problems and interests. The English language has become the *lingua franca* of intertribal organizations in the cities, since the native tongues of the members are exceedingly diverse.

Among the Indians of Los Angeles, it has been reported that:

An awakened pan-Indianism ... often becomes an additional dimension to, and sometimes a substitute for ... tribal affiliation. Although only one-fifth of our respondents are socially active in pan-Indian associations, the great majority of the Indians in the city clearly are ideologically and emotionally affiliated with pan-Indianism. Pan-Indianism thus seems to emerge as a stabilizing element—and perhaps a permanent part of the Indian migrant to metropolitan areas, and a significant facet of the ethnic diversity of the American city (Price, 1968:175).

Most of the activist leaders in the more militant protest movements among Indians in the 1960s and 1970s have come from among the urban Indians. Increasingly vocal and insistent upon Indian rights, the protest groups in what has been called the new Indian nationalism have had their power bases in the cities. Almost exclusively, the participants in these movements have been teen-agers and young adults. The National Indian Youth Council, formed in 1961, has been described as an Indian version of the youth movements of the 1960s (Hertzberg, 1971:292). Most of the members of this organization live away from the reservations. The leaders of the militant American Indian Movement (AIM), too, are mainly urban Indians.

Up to now, because of the conditions of severe economic deprivation on the reservations, most Indians have not really had a free choice between staying on the reservations while making a decent living, or moving to the cities for the sake of employment. In 1960 there were only four factories on Indian reservations, but during the ensuing decade there was an increasing number of small industries established on reservation lands. Despite these new industrial developments, it was estimated in 1969 that only 3 percent of the Indian labor force was employed in industries located on the reservations (Sorkin, 1969:183).

In 1972 the Bureau of Indian Affairs announced a redirection of the Employment Assistance Program to one of developing manpower to complement projected economic developments on the reservations. More on-the-job training funds were to be allocated to the expansion of job development on or near the reservations, at the same time that more resources were to be spent in reservation communities to further the development of the reservation economies. This shift in direction may prove to be effective in providing on-the-reservation Indians with an alternative to migration to the cities, although it is still too early to predict how important a trend the new direction will prove to be.

The growth rate of the American Indian population is now estimated at 2.5 percent a year, as compared with a growth rate of only 1 percent a year for the population of the United States as a whole. Indians, no longer the "vanishing Americans," are now the fastest growing group in the nation, increasing at an annual rate more than double the rate of increase for the population of the entire nation. From all indications, Native Americans are continuing to move into the cities at a rate in excess of the increase of the Indian population on the reservations.

It seems safe to predict that the trend of migration from the reservations to the cities will continue and that it may conceivably increase in volume. Despite the fact that many resettled Indians still feel a strong and persistent attachment to their ancestral homes, the resources on the reservations remain inadequate to support the Indian population explosion, and will continue to be unless far more effective measures are taken to develop industries and other modes of employment than the minor efforts so far made along those lines. Pan-Indianism and the growth of Indian nationalism may also be expected not only to continue, but to be of increasing significance, as the swelling numbers of Native Americans, their ever-progressing sophistication, and their growing unity all compellingly emphasize their insistence that their rights and privileges be fully recognized and respected. Vocal Indian activists in the cities are clamoring for the extension of federal services to all Indians, rather than exclusively to those Indians still resident on the reservations. They will not be put off by evasion or negative responses.

Suggested readings

ABLON, J.
1965 "American Indian Relocation: Problems of Dependency and Management in the City." *Phylon* 26:362–371.
1964 "Relocated American Indians in the San Francisco Bay Area: Social Interaction and Indian Identity." *Human Organization* 23:296–304.

BAHR, H. M.; CHADWICK, B. A.; and DAY, R. C., eds.
1972 *Native Americans Today: Sociological Perspectives.* New York: Harper & Row.

BROPHY, W. A.; and ABERLE, S. D.
1966 *The Indian: America's Unfinished Business.* University of Oklahoma Press.

Bureau of Indian Affairs.
1968 *Answers to Your Questions About American Indians.* Washington: U.S. Government Printing Office.

COLLIER, P.
1970 "The Red Man's Burden." *Ramparts 8* (February 1970): 26–38.

DELORIA, V., JR.
1969 *Custer Died for Your Sins: An Indian Manifesto.* London: McMillan.

DOZIER, E. P.
1966 "Problem Drinking Among American Indians: The Role of Sociocultural Deprivation." *Quarterly Journal of Studies on Alcohol* 27:72–87.

FUCHS, E., and HAVIGHURST, R. J.
1972 *To Live on This Earth.* Garden City, N.Y.: Doubleday.

GRAVES, T. D.
1970 "The Personal Adjustment of Navajo Indian Migrants to Denver, Colorado." *American Anthropologist* 72:35–54.

HERTZBERG, J. W.
1971 *The Search for an American Indian Identity: Modern Pan-Indian Movements.* Syracuse University Press.

HODGE, W. H.
1969 *The Albuquerque Navajos.* Anthropological Papers of the University of Arizona, no. 11.

HURT, W. R.
1961 "The Urbanization of the Yankton Indians." *Human Organization* 20:226–231.

JOSEPHY, A.
1971 *Red Power: The Indians' Fight for Freedom.* New York: American Heritage Press.

KELLY, R. F., and CRAMER, J. O.
1966 *American Indians in Small Cities.* Rehabilitation Monographs no. 1. Northern Arizona University.

KEMNITZER, L. S.
1970 "Familial and Extra-Familial Socialization in Urban Dakota Adolescents." In *The Modern Sioux: Social Systems and Reservation Culture,* ed. E. Nurge, pp. 246–267. The University of Nebraska Press.

LURIE, N. O.
1971 "The Contemporary American Indian Scene." In *North American Indians in Historical Perspective,* ed. E. B. Leacock, and N. O. Lurie, pp. 418–480. Boston: Little, Brown.

MCNICKLE, D.
1973 *Native American Tribalism: Indian Survivals and Renewals.* London, Oxford, and New York: Oxford University Press.

MARTIN, H. W.
1964 "Correlates of Adjustment Among American Indians in an Urban Environment." *Human Organization* 23:290–295.

MERIAM, L.
1928 *The Problem of Indian Administration.* Institute for Government Research, Brookings Institution. Baltimore: The Johns Hopkins Press.

Navajo Yearbook
1958 Window Rock, Arizona.

NEILS, E. M.
1971 *Reservation to City: Indian Migration and Federal Relocation.* The University of Chicago, Department of Geography, Research Paper no. 131.

PAREDES, J. A.
1971 "Toward a Reconceptualization of American Indian Urbanization: A Chippewa Case." *Anthropological Quarterly* 44:256–269.

PRICE, J. A.
1968 "The Migration and Adaptation of American Indians to Los Angeles." *Human Organization* 27:168–175.

SORKIN, A. L.
1971 *American Indians and Federal Aid.* Washington.
1969 "Some Aspects of American Indian Migration." *Social Forces* 48:243–250.

STEINER, S.

1968   *The New Indians.* New York: Dell.

SWETT, D. O.

1963   *Characteristics of the Male Indian Arrest
        Population in San Francisco.* Paper presented at
        the annual meeting of the Southwestern
        Anthropological Association.

TAYLOR, T. W.

1972   *The States and Their Indian Citizens.*
        Washington: Bureau of Indian Affairs.

WADDELL, J. O., and WATSON, O. M., eds.

1973   *American Indian Urbanization.* Lafayette: Purdue,
        Institute for the Study of Social Change,
        Department of Sociology and Anthropology
        Institute Monograph Series no. 4.

1971   *The American Indian in Urban Society.* Boston:
        Little, Brown.

WALKER, D. E., JR.

1972   *The Emergent Native Americans.* Boston: Little,
        Brown.

WEAVER, T. A., and GARTRELL, R. H.

1974   "The Urban Indian: Man of Two Worlds." In
        Indians of Arizona: A Contemporary Perspective,
        ed. T. A. Weaver, pp. 72–96. The University of
        Arizona Press.

List of Some Major North American Indian Tribes

Those tribes in bold-face are described in detail in this book.

Abnaki
Achomawi
Ahtena
Aleut
Algonquin
Alsea
Apache, Eastern
Apache, Western
Arapaho
Arikara
Assiniboine
Atacapa
Atsina (Gros Ventre)
Atsugewi
Aztec (Nahua)

Baffinland Eskimo
Bannock
Beaver
Bella Bella
Bella Coola
Bering Strait Eskimo
Blackfoot
Blood

Caddo
Cáhita
Cahuilla
Caribou Eskimo
Carrier
Cayuga (Iroquois)
Cayuse
Chehalis
Chemehuevi
Cherokee
Cheyenne
Chickasaw
Chilcotin
Chinook
Chipewyan
Chippewa, (Ojibwa)
Chiricahua Apache
Chitimacha
Choctaw
Chontal
Chorotega
Chugach Eskimo
Chumash
Coahuiltec
Cochimi
Cocopa
Coeur d'Alene

Comanche
Comox (Gulf of Georgia Salish)
Concho
Conestoga
Conoy
Coos
Copper Eskimo
Cora
Costanoan
Cowichan (Gulf of Georgia Salish)
Cree
Creek
Crow
Cupeño

Delaware
Diegueño
Dogrib

East Greenland Eskimo
Erie
Eyak

Fox

Gabrielino
Gitskan
Gosiute
Gros Ventre (Atsina)
Gulf of Georgia Salish

Haida
Haisla
Halchidhoma
Han
Hare
Havasupai
Heiltsuk
Hidatsa
Hopi
Huastec
Huichol
Hupa
Huron

Iglulik Eskimo
Illinois
Ingalik
Iowa
Iroquois
　Cayuga
　Mohawk
　Oneida
　Onondaga
　Seneca
　(Tuscarora)

Jicaque
Jicarilla Apache

Kaibab Paiute
Kalapuya
Kalispel
Kansa
Karankawa
Karok
Kaska
Keresan Pueblos, *see* Pueblos, Rio Grande
Kickapoo
Kiowa
Kiowa-Apache
Klallam
Klamath
Klikitat
Koyukon
Kutchin
Kutenai
Kwakiutl

Labrador Eskimo
Lagunero
Lake
Lenca
Lillooet
Lipan Apache
Luiseno
Lummi

Mahican
Maidu
Makah
Malecite
Mandan
Maricopa
Massachusett
Maya
　Lacandon Maya
　Yucatan Maya
Mayo
McKenzie Eskimo
Menomini
Mescalero Apache, *see* Apache, Eastern
Miami
Micmac
Missouri
Miwok
Mixe
Mixtec
Modoc
Mohave
Mohawk (Iroquois)
Molala

Mono
Montagnais
Mosquito
Mountain

Nanticoke
Nabesna
Nahua (Aztec)
Naskapi
Natchez
Navaho
Nespelem
Netsilik Eskimo
Nez Perce
Nicarao
Nicola
Niska
Nootka
North Alaskan Eskimo
Northern Paiute

Ojibwa (Chippewa)
Okanagan
Omaha
Oneida (Iroquois)
Onondaga (Iroquois)
Opatá
Osage
Oto
Otomi
Ottawa

Papago
Patwin
Pawnee
Pennacook
Penobscot
Péricue
Piegan
Pima
Pima Bajo
Plains Cree
Plains Ojibwa
Polar Eskimo
Pomo
Ponca
Potawatomi
Powhatan
Pueblos, Rio Grande
  Keresan
    Acoma
    Cochiti
    Laguna
    Santa Ana
    San Felipe

Pueblos (continued)
    Santo Domingo
    Zia
  Tanoan
    Isleta
    Jemez
    Nambé
    Picuris
    San Ildefonso
    Santa Clara
    Taos
    etc.

Quapaw
Quileute
Quinault

Salinan
San Carlos Apache, *see* Apache, Western
Sanpoil
Sarsi
Sauk
Saulteaux
Sekani
Seneca (Iroquois)
Seri
Serrano
Shasta
Shawnee
Shoshone
Shuswap
Sisseton (Santee Dakota)
Siuslaw
Skagit
Slave
Snuqualmi
South Alaska Eskimo (Chugach)
Southern Paiute
Southhampton Eskimo
Subtiaba
Susequehanna

Tahltan
Tamaulipec
Tanaina
Tanana
Tanoan Pueblos, *see* Pueblos, Rio Grande
Tarahumare
Tarascan
Tenino
Tepecano
Tepehuan
Teton
Thompson
Tillamook

Timucua
Tlingit
Tolowa
Tonkawa
Tonto Apache, *see* Apache, Western
Totonac
Tsetsaut
Tsimshian
Tübatulabal
Tunica
Tuscarora (Iroquois)
Tutchone
Tutelo
Twana

Umatilla
Ute

Waicuri
Walapai
Wappinger
Washo
Wenatchi
West Alaskan Eskimo
West Greenland Eskimo
White Mountain Apache, *see* Apache, Western
Wichita
Wind River Shoshone
Winnebago
Wintun
Wishram
Wiyot

Yakima
Yana
Yankton (Dakota)
Yanktonai (Dakota)
Yaqui
Yavapai
Yellowknives
Yokuts
Yuchi
Yuit
Yuki
Yuma
Yurok

Zacatec
Zapotec
Zoque
Zuni

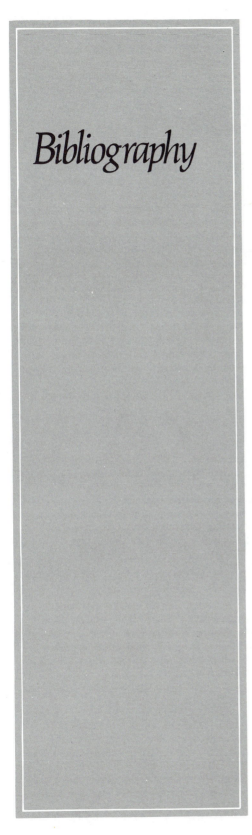

Bibliography

ABERLE, D. F. 1966. *The Peyote Religion Among the Navaho.* Chicago: Aldine.

ABERLE, D. F., AND STEWART, O. C. 1957. *Navaho and Ute Peyotism: A Chronological and Distributional Study.* University of Colorado Studies: Series in Anthropology no. 6.

ABLON, J. 1964. "Relocated American Indians in the San Francisco Bay Area: Social Interaction and Indian Identity." *Human Organization,* 23:296–304.

_____. 1962. "The American Indian Chicago Conference." *Journal of American Indian Education* 2:17–23.

ADAIR, JAMES. 1930. *Adair's History of the American Indians.* Johnson City, Oklahoma: Watauga Press.

ADAIR, JOHN. 1944. *The Navajo and Pueblo Silversmiths.* University of Oklahoma Press.

ADAIR, JOHN, AND VOGT, E. 1949. "Navaho and Zuni Veterans: A Study of Contrasting Modes of Culture Change." *American Anthropologist,* 51:547–561.

ADOVASIO, J. M.; GUNN, J. D.; DONAHUE, J. D.; AND STUCKENRATH, R. 1975. "Excavations at Meadowcroft Rockshelter 1973–1974: A Progress Report." *Pennsylvania Archaeologist,* vol. 44, nos. 3 & 4, to be published by Braun-Brumfield, Inc., Ann Arbor, Michigan.

AIKENS, C. M. 1970. "Hogup Cave." *University of Utah Anthropological Papers,* no. 93.

ALBRECHT, A. C. 1946. "Indian-French Relations at Natchez." *American Anthropologist* 48:321–354.

_____. 1944. "The Location of the Historic Natchez Villages." *Journal of Mississippi History* 6:67–68.

AMSDEN, C. A. 1949. *Navaho Weaving: Its Technic and History.* University of New Mexico Press.

ANASTASIO, A. 1972. "The Southern Plateau: An Ecological Analysis of Group Relations." *Northwest Anthropological Research Notes* 6:109–229.

ANDERSON, D. D. 1970. "Akmak: An Early Archeological Assemblage from Onion Portage, Northwest Alaska." *Acta Arctica* 16. Copenhagen.

_____. 1968. "A Stone Age Campsite at the Gateway to America." *Scientific American* 218:24–33.

ANDERSON, F. G. 1955. "The Pueblo Kachina Cult." *Southwestern Journal of Anthropology* 11:404–419.

ANDREWS, E. W. 1960. "Excavations at Dzibilchaltun, Northwestern Yucatan, Mexico." *Proceedings of the American Philosophical Society* 104:254–265.

AVELEYRA, L. A. DE A. 1955. *El segundo Mamut fosil de Santa Isabel Iztapan, Mexico.* Instituto Nacional de Anthropología e Historia. Mexico, D. F.

BAHR, H. M.; CHADWICK, B. A.; AND DAY, R. C., EDS. 1972. *Native Americans Today: Sociological Perspectives.* New York: Harper & Row.

BAILEY, P. D. 1970. *Ghost Dance Messiah.* Los Angeles: Westernlore Press.

BALDWIN, G. C. 1973. *Indians of the Southwest.* New York: Capricorn Books.

BALIKCI, A. 1970. *The Netsilik Eskimo.* New York: Natural History Press.

BANDELIER, A. F., AND HEWITT, E. F. 1937. *Indians of the Rio Grande Valley*. University of New Mexico Press.

BARKER, M. A. R. 1963–1964. *Klamath Texts; Klamath Dictionary; Klamath Grammar*. University of California Publications in Linguistics, vols. 30, 31, 32.

BARNETT, H. G. 1968. *The Nature and Function of the Potlatch*. University of Oregon, Eugene: Department of Anthropology.

———. 1957. *Indian Shakers*. University of Southern Illinois Press.

———. 1955. *The Coast Salish of British Columbia*. University of Oregon Press.

———. 1939. "Culture Element Distributions IX, Gulf of Georgia Salish." *Anthropological Records* 1:221–295.

———. 1938. "The Nature of the Potlatch." *American Anthropologist* 40:349–358.

———. 1937. "Oregon Coast." *Anthropological Records* 1:155–204.

BARRETT, S. A. 1917. "The Washo Indians." *Bulletin of the Public Museum of the City of Milwaukee* 2:1–52.

———. 1910. "The Material Culture of the Klamath Lake and Modoc Indians of Northeastern California and Southern Oregon." *University of California Publications in American Archaeology and Ethnology* 5:230–292.

BARRETT, S. A., AND GIFFORD, E. W. 1933. "Miwok Material Culture." *Bulletin of the Public Museum of the City of Milwaukee* 2:117–376.

BARTRAM, W. 1958. *The Travels of William Bartram*. New Haven: Yale University Press.

BASSO, K. H. 1971. *The Cibecue Apache*. New York: Holt, Rinehart and Winston.

———, ED. 1971. *Western Apache Raiding and Warfare*. University of Arizona Press.

———. 1969. *Western Apache Witchcraft*. Anthropological Papers of the University of Arizona, 15.

BASSO, K. H., AND OPLER, M. E. 1971. *Apachean Culture History and Ethnology*. Anthropological Papers of the University of Arizona, 21.

BASTIAN, T. 1962. "Some Additional Data on the Beloit College Mound Group (Ro15)." *The Wisconsin Archaeologist* 43:57–64.

BAUMHOFF, M. A. 1958. "California Athabascan Groups." *Anthropological Records* 16:157–237.

BEAGLEHOLE, E. 1935. *Hopi of the Second Mesa*. American Anthropological Association, Memoir 44.

BEAGLEHOLE, E., AND BEAGLEHOLE, P. 1937. "Notes on Hopi Economic Life." *Yale University Publications in Anthropology* 15:1–88.

BEALS, R. L. 1945. *The Contemporary Culture of the Cahita Indians*. Bureau of American Ethnology, Bulletin 142.

———. 1943a. "Northern Mexico and the Southwest." *El Norte de Mexico y el Sur de Estados Unidos*, pp. 191–199. Mexico, D.F.

———. 1943b. "The Aboriginal Culture of the Cahita Indians." *Ibero-Americana* 19.

———. 1933. "Ethnology of the Nisenan."

University of California Publications in American Archaeology and Ethnology 31:335–410.

———. 1932. "The Comparative Ethnology of Northern Mexico." *Ibero-Americana* 2:93–225.

BEARDSLEY, R. 1954. "Temporal and Areal Relationships in Central California Archaeology, Part One." *Reports of the University of California Archaeological Survey*, no. 24.

BEAUCHAMP, W. M. 1905. *History of the Iroquois*. Albany: New York State Museum Bulletin.

BENEDICT. R. 1935. *Zuni Mythology*. Columbia University Contributions to Anthropology, no. 21.

———. 1934. *Patterns of Culture*. New York: Pelican Book Edition.

———. 1923. *The Concept of the Guardian Spirit in North America*. American Anthropological Association, Memoir 29.

———. 1922. "The Vision in Plains Culture." *American Anthropologist* 24:1–23.

BENNETT, J. W. 1946. "The Interpretations of Pueblo Culture: A Question of Values." *Southwestern Journal of Anthropology* 2:361–374.

BENNETT, W. C., AND ZINGG, R. M. 1935. *The Tarahumara, An Inland Tribe of Northern Mexico*. University of Chicago Press.

BENSON, ELIZABETH. P., ED. 1972. *The Cult of the Feline: A Conference on Pre-Columbian Iconography*. Washington: Dumbarton Oaks.

BERLIN, B. 1970. "A Universalist-Evolutionary Approach in Ethnographic Semantics." In *Current Directions in Anthropology*, ed. A. Fischer, vol. 3, no. 3, pt. 2. Washington: American Anthropological Association.

BERREMAN, J. V. 1937. *Tribal Distribution in Oregon*. American Anthropological Association, Memoir 47.

BERNAL, IGNACIO. 1969. *The Olmec World*. University of California Press.

BIRDSELL, J. B. 1951. "The Problem of the Early Peopling of the Americas as Viewed from Asia." *Papers on the Physical Anthropology of the American Indian*, ed. W. S. Laughlin, pp. 1–68. New York: The Viking Fund, Inc.

BIRKET-SMITH, K. 1958. *The Eskimos*. 2d ed. New York: Humanities Press.

———. 1956. *The Chugach Eskimo*. National-museets Skrifter, Ethnografisk Raekke, Bol. 6. Copenhagen: National Museum.

———. 1930. "Contributions to Chipewyan Ethnology." *Fifth Thule Expedition, Report 5*, no. 3, pp. 1–114.

———. 1929. "The Caribou Eskimos." *Fifth Thule Expedition, Report 5*, pp. 1–725.

———. 1924. "Ethnography of the Egedesminde District." *Meddelelser om Gronland* 66:1–484.

BIRKET-SMITH, K., AND DE LAGUNA, F. 1938. *The Eyak Indians of the Copper River Delta*. Copenhagen: National Museum.

BLOOMFIELD, L. 1946. "Algonquian." In *Linguistic Structures*, ed. H. Hoijer. Viking Fund Publications in Anthropology 6:85–129.

BOAS, F. 1966. *Kwakiutl Ethnography*. Edited by H.

Codere, University of Chicago Press.

_____. 1955. *Primitive Art.* New York: Dover.

_____. 1921. *Ethnology of the Kwakiutl.* Annual Report of the Bureau of American Ethnology, 35.

_____. 1916. *Tsimshian Mythology.* Annual Report of the Bureau of American Ethnology, 31.

_____, ED. 1911. *Handbook of American Indian Languages,* vol. I. Bureau of American Ethnology, Bulletin 40.

_____. 1909. "The Kwakiutl of Vancouver Island." *Memoirs of the American Museum of Natural History* 8:307–515.

_____. 1901–1907. *The Eskimo of Baffin Land and Hudson Bay.* Bulletin of the American Museum of Natural History, 15.

_____. 1895. "The Social Organization and the Secret Societies of the Kwakiutl Indians." *Reports of the United States National Museum,* pp. 331–738.

_____. 1888. "The Central Eskimo." *Annual Report of the Bureau of American Ethnology* 6:390–669.

BOGORAZ, V. G. 1929. "Elements of Culture of the Circumpolar Zone." *American Anthropologist* 31:579–601.

BORDEN C. E. 1962. "West Coast Crossties with Alaska." In "Prehistoric Cultural Relations between the Arctic and Temperate Zones of North America," ed. J. M. Campbell, *Arctic Institute of North America Technical Paper,* no. 11, pp. 9–19. Montreal.

BOWERS, A. W. 1950. *Mandan Social and Ceremonial Organization.* University of Chicago Press.

BRAIN, J. P. 1971. "The Natchez 'Paradox'." *Ethnology* 10:215–222.

BRAINERD, G. 1954. *The Maya Civilization.* Los Angeles: Southwest Museum.

BREBEUF, J. DE. 1897. "Relation of the Hurons, 1636." *The Jesuit Relations and Allied Documents* 10:124–317.

BREW, J. O., ED. 1968. *One Hundred Years of Archaeology.* Cambridge: Harvard University Press.

BROPHY, W. A., AND ABERLE, S. D. 1966. *The Indian: America's Unfinished Business.* University of Oklahoma Press.

BROWN, D. 1970. *Bury My Heart at Wounded Knee.* New York: Holt, Rinehart and Winston.

BROWN, J. A. 1968. "The Dimensions of Status in the Burials at Spiro." In *Approaches to the Social Dimensions of Mortuary Practices,* ed. J. A. Brown. Society for American Archaeology, Memoir 25.

BRUNER, E. M. 1955. "Two Processes of Change in Mandan-Hidatsa Kinship Terminology." *American Anthropologist* 57:840–850.

BULLEN, R. P. 1972. "The Orange Period of Peninsular Florida." In *Fiber-Tempered Pottery in Southeastern United States and Northern Colombia: Its Origins, Context, and Significance,* ed. R. P. Bullen and J. P. Stoltman. Florida Anthropological Society Publications, no. 6.

_____. 1965. "Stelae at the Crystal River Site, Florida." *American Antiquity* 31:861–865.

_____. 1961. "Radiocarbon Dates for Southeastern Fiber-Tempered Pottery." *American Antiquity* 27:104–106.

BUNZEL, R. L. 1932a. "An Introduction to Zuni Ceremonialism." *Annual Report of the Bureau of American Ethnology* 47:467–544.

_____. 1932b. "Zuni Katcinas." *Annual Report of the Bureau of American Ethnology* 47:837–1086.

_____. 1929. "The Pueblo Potter." *Columbia University Contributions to Anthropology* 8:1–134.

BURCH, E. S., JR. 1975. *Eskimo Kinsmen.* American Ethnological Society, Monograph 59. St. Paul: West.

_____. 1974. "Eskimo Warfare in Northwest Alaska." *Anthropological Papers of the University of Alaska* 16:1–14.

BUTLER, B. R. 1968. *A Guide to Understanding Idaho Archaeology,* 2d rev. ed. Idaho State University Museum.

_____. 1961. "The Old Cordilleran Culture in the Pacific Northwest." *Occasional Papers of the Idaho State College Museum,* 5.

BYERS, D. D., ED. 1967. *The Prehistory of the Tehuacan Valley. Vol. I, Environment and Subsistence.* University of Texas Press.

CAHN, E. S., ED. 1969. *Our Brother's Keeper: The Indian in White America.* New York: New Community Press.

CALDWELL, J. R. 1958. *Trend and Tradition in the Prehistory of the Eastern United States.* American Anthropological Association, Memoir 88.

CALLEN, E. O. 1967. "Analysis of the Tehuacan Coprolites." In *The Prehistory of the Tehuacan Valley. Volume 1: Environment and Subsistence,* ed. D. S. Byers, pp. 261–289. University of Texas Press.

CALLENDER, C. 1962. *Social Organization of the Central Algonkian Indians.* Milwaukee Public Museum Publications in Anthropology, no. 7.

CAMPBELL, J. M., ED. 1962. "Prehistoric Cultural Relations between the Arctic and Temperate Zones of North America." *Arctic Institute of North America Technical Paper,* no. 11. Montreal.

CAPRON, L. 1953. "The Medicine Bundles of the Florida Seminole and the Green Corn Dance." *Bureau of American Ethnology Bulletin* 111:155–210.

CARDICH, A.; CARDICH, L. A.; AND HAJDUK, A. 1973. "Secuencia Arqueológica y Cronología Radiocarbónica de la Cueva 3 de Los Toldos (Santa Cruz, Argentina)." *Separatas Relaciones,* no. VII. Buenos Aires.

CARTER, G. F. 1945. *Plant Geography and Culture History in the American Southwest.* Viking Fund Publications in Anthropology, vol. 5.

CASO, A. 1960. *Interpretacion de Codice Bodley.* Sociedad Mexicana de Antropología, 2858. Mexico, D.F.

CASTANEDA, C. 1968. *The Teachings of Don Juan: A Yaqui Way of Knowledge.* University of California Press.

CASTETTER, E. F., AND BELL, W. H. 1951. *Yuman Indian Agriculture.* University of New Mexico Press.

_____. 1942. *Pima and Papago Indian Agriculture.* Albuquerque: Inter-American Studies, no. 1.

CAUGHEY, J. W. 1938. *McGillivray of the Creeks.* University of Oklahoma Press.

BIBLIOGRAPHY ■ 545

CHAMBERLAIN, A. F. 1892. "Report on the Kootenay Indians." *Report of the British Association for the Advancement of Science* 62:549–617.

CHARD, C. S. 1961. "Invention versus Diffusion: The Burial Mound Complex of the Eastern United States." *Southwestern Journal of Anthropology* 17:21–25.

———. 1960. "Routes to the Bering Strait." *American Antiquity* 26:283–285.

———. 1959. "New World Origins: a Reappraisal." *American Antiquity* 133:44–49.

CHARLEVOIX, P. F. X. DE. 1722. "Journal d'un Voyage Fait par Ordre du Roi dans L'Amerique Septentrionale." *Histoire et Description Generale de la Nouvelle France*, 6 vols. Paris.

CHIMALPAHIN QUAUHTLEHUNAINITZIN, DOMINGO FRANCISCO DE SAN ANTON MUNON. 1889. *Annales de Domingo Francisco de San Anton Chimalpahin Quauhtlehunainitzin: Sixieme et Septieme Relations (1258–1612).* Paris: Bibliotheque linguistique americaine, vol. 12.

CLINE, W. et al. 1938. *The Sinkaietk or Southern Okanagan of Washington.* General Series in Anthropology, no. 5. Menasha, Wisconsin.

CODERE, H. 1957. "Kwakiutl Society: Rank without Class." *American Anthropologist* 59:473–486.

———. 1956. "The Amiable Side of Kwakiutl Life." *American Anthropologist* 63:334–351.

———. 1950. *Fighting with Property.* Monographs of the American Ethnological Society, 18.

COE, M. D. 1966. *The Maya.* Ancient Peoples and Places series. Praeger paperback P-224.

———. 1962. *Mexico.* Ancient Peoples and Places series. Praeger paperback P-212.

COLDEN, C. 1958. *The History of the Five Nations Depending on the Province of New York.* Ithaca: Cornell University Press. Great Seal Books.

COLE, F., AND DEUEL, T. 1937. *Rediscovering Illinois: Archaeological Explorations in and around Fulton County.* University of Chicago Press.

COLLIER, J. JR. 1947. *Indians of the Americas.* New York: New American Library (Mentor Books).

COLLIER, M., AND COLLIER, J., JR. 1948. "Navaho Farmer." *The Farm Quarterly* 3:17–20, 22–24, 103–106.

COLLINS, H. B., JR. 1964. "The Arctic and Subarctic." In *Prehistoric Man in the New World*, eds. J. D. Jennings and E. Norbeck, pp. 85–114. Rice University Semicentennial Publications. University of Chicago Press.

———. 1960. "'Comments on The Archaeology of Bering Strait,' by J. L. Giddings." *Current Anthropology* 1:131–136.

———. 1951. "The Origin and Antiquity of the Eskimo." *Smithsonian Institution, Annual Report for 1950*, pp. 423–467.

COLLINS, J. 1974. *The Valley of the Spirits.* American Ethnological Society, Monograph 56. University of Washington Press.

COLSON, E. 1953. *The Makah Indians.* University of Minnesota Press.

CONKLIN, H. C. 1968. "Ethnography." *International Encyclopedia of the Social Sciences* 5:172–178.

CONNELLEY, W. E. 1900. *The Wyandots.* Toronto, Report of the Minister of Education.

COOPER, J. M. 1956. *The Gros Ventres of Montana, Part II: Religion and Ritual.* Catholic University of America, Anthropological Series, vol. 16.

———. 1939. "Is the Algonquian Family Hunting Ground System Pre-Columbian?" *American Anthropologist* 41:66–90.

CORKRAN, D. H. 1967. *The Creek Frontier, 1540–1783.* University of Oklahoma Press.

COTTERILL, R. S. 1954. *The Southern Indians: The Story of the Civilized Tribes before Removal.* University of Oklahoma Press.

COVARRUBIAS, M. 1957. *Indian Art of Mexico and Central America.* New York: Augustin.

CRANE, H. R., AND GRIFFIN, J. B. 1958. "University of Michigan Radiocarbon Dates II." *Science* 127:1098–1105.

CRANE, V. W. 1928. *The Southern Frontier, 1670–1732.* Durham: Duke University Press.

CRESSMAN, L. S. 1960. "Cultural Sequences at the Dalles, Oregon: A Contribution to Pacific Northwest Prehistory." *Transactions of the American Philosophical Society* 50:1–108.

———. 1956. "Klamath Prehistory: The Prehistory of the Culture of the Klamath Lake Area, Oregon." *Transactions of the American Philosphical Society*, n.s., vol. 46, pt. 4, pp. 374–513. Philadelphia.

CULIN, S. 1903. *Games of the North American Indians.* Annual Report of the Bureau of American Ethnology, 24.

CURTIS, E. S. 1924–1926. *The North American Indian.* 20 vols. Norwood, Mass.: Plimpton Press.

CUSHING. F. M. 1920. *Zuni Breadstuffs.* Heye Foundation, Indian Notes and Monographs, Museum of the American Indian, vol. 8.

———. 1896. "Outlines of Zuni Creation Myths." *Annual Report of the Bureau of American Ethnology* 6:321-447.

DAIFUKU, H. 1952. "A New Conceptual Scheme for Prehistoric Cultures in the American Southwest." *American Anthropologist* 54:191–200.

DANIELS, W. M. 1953. "Recent Data from Two Paleo-Indian Sites on Medicine Creek, Nebraska." *American Antiquity* 18:380–386.

DARNELL, R., ED. 1970. "Special Issue: Athabascan Studies," *Western Canadian Journal of Anthropology*, vol. 2., no. 1.

DARNELL, R., AND SHERZER, J. 1971. "Areal Linguistic Studies in North America: A Historical Perspective." *International Journal of American Linguistics* 37:20–28.

DAVIS, K. 1941. "Intermarriage in Caste Societies." *American Anthropologist* 43:376–395.

DAVIS, R. T. 1949. *Native Arts of the Pacific Northwest.* Stanford University Press.

DE ANDA, A. A. 1953. "Association of Artifacts with Mammoth in the Valley of Mexico." *American Antiquity* 18:332–338.

DE PESO, C. C. 1956. "The Upper Pima of San Cayetano del Tumacacori." *The Amerind Foundation*, no. 7.

_____. 1953. "The Sobaipuri Indians of the Upper San Pedro Valley, Southeastern Arizona." *The Amerind Foundation*, no. 6.

DEALE, V. B. 1958. "The History of the Potawotamies before 1722." *Ethnohistory* 5:305–360.

DEBO, A. 1961. *The Rise and Fall of the Choctaw Republic.* University of Oklahoma Press.

_____. 1941. *The Road to Disappearance.* University of Oklahoma Press.

_____. 1940. *And Still the Waters Run.* Princeton University Press.

DEEVEY, E. S., JR. 1957. "Limnologic Studies in Middle America." *Transactions of the Connecticut Acadamy of Arts and Sciences* 39:213–328.

DELAND, C. E. 1906–1908. "The Aborigines of South Dakota." *South Dakota Historical Collections* 3:267–586; 4:273–730.

DELORIA, V., JR. 1969. *Custer Died for Your Sins: An Indian Manifesto.* London: McMillan.

DENHARDT, R. M. 1947. *The Horse of the Americas.* University of Oklahoma Press.

DENIG, E. T. 1930. "Indian Tribes of the Upper Missouri." *Annual Report of the Bureau of American Ethnology* 46:375–628.

DENSMORE, F. 1929. *Chippewa Customs.* Bureau of American Ethnology, Bulletin 86.

_____. 1918. *Teton Sioux Music.* Bureau of American Ethnology, Bulletin 41.

DENYS, N. 1908. "The Description and Natural History of the Coasts of North America." *Publications of the Champlain Society* 2:399–452, 572–606.

DEUEL, T. 1957. "The Modoc Shelter." *Illinois State Museum Report of Investigations* 66:106.

DEVEREUX, G. 1961. *Mohave Ethnopsychiatry.* Bureau of American Ethnology, Bulletin 175.

_____. 1951. *Reality and Dream.* New York: International Universities Press.

DIBBLE, C. E. 1942. *Códice en Cruz.* Talleres Linotipigráficos "Numancia." Mexico, D.F.

DIBBLE, D. S., AND LORRAIN, D. 1968. "Bonfire Shelter: A Stratified Bison Kill Site, Val Verde County, Texas." *Miscellaneous Papers*, no. 1. Austin: Texas Memorial Museum.

DIXON, R. B. 1911. "Maidu." *Bureau of American Ethnology, Bulletin* 40:679–734.

_____. 1907. "The Shasta." *Bulletin of the American Museum of Natural History* 17:381–498.

_____. 1905. "The Northern Maidu." *Bulletin of the American Museum of Natural History* 17:119–346.

DIXON. R. B., AND KROEBER, A. L. 1919. "Linguistic Families of California." *University of California Publications in American Archaeology and Ethnology* 11:47–188.

_____. 1913. "New Linguistic Families in California." *American Anthropologist* 15:647–665.

DOBYNS, H. F. 1966. "Estimating Aboriginal American Population, An Appraisal of Techniques with a New Hemispheric Estimate." *Current Anthropology* 7:395–449.

DOBYNS, H. F., AND EULER, R. C. 1970. *Wauba Yuma's People: The Comparative Socio-Political Structure of the Pai Indians of Arizona.* Prescott, Arizona: Prescott College Press.

DONALD, L., AND MERTTON, J. 1975. "Technology on the Northwest Coast: An Analysis of Overall Similarities." *Behavior Science Research* 10:73–100.

DORSEY, J. O. 1882. "Omaha Sociology." *Annual Report of the Bureau of American Ethnology* 3:205–370.

DOWNS, J. F. 1972. *The Navajo.* New York: Holt, Rinehart and Winston.

_____. 1966. *The Two Worlds of the Washo: An Indian Tribe of California and Nevada.* New York: Holt, Rinehart and Winston.

DOZIER, E. P. 1971. "The American Southwest." In *American Indians in Historical Perspective*, E. B. Leacock and N. O. Lurie. ed., New York: Random House.

_____. 1970. *The Pueblo Indians of North America.* New York: Holt, Rinehart and Winston.

_____. 1964. "Pueblo Indians of the Southwest." *Current Anthropology* 5:79–97.

_____. 1958. "Spanish-Catholic Influences on Rio Grande Pueblo Religion." *American Anthropologist* 60:441–448.

_____. 1954. "The Hopi-Tewa of Arizona." *University of California Publications in American Archaeology and Ethnology* 44:259–376.

DRIVER, H. E. 1969. *Indians of North America.* 2d ed. University of Chicago Press.

_____. 1968. "Ethnology." *International Encyclopedia of the Social Sciences* 5:178–186.

_____. 1941. *Girl's Puberty Rites in Western North America.* University of California Anthropological Records 6:2.

_____. 1936. "Wappo Ethnography." *University of California Publications in American Archaeology and Ethnology* 36:179–220.

DRIVER, H. E., AND COFFIN, J. L. 1975. *Classification and Development of North American Indian Cultures: A Statistical Analysis of the Driver-Massey Sample.* Philadelphia: American Philosophical Society, Transactions, vol. 65, pt. 3.

DRIVER, H. E., AND MASSEY, W. C. 1957. *Comparative Studies of North American Indians.* Transactions of the American Philosophical Society, vol. 47.

DRIVER, H. E., et al. 1953. *Indian Tribes of North America.* Indiana University Publications in Anthropology and Linguistics, Memoir 9.

DRUCKER, P. 1965. *Cultures of the North Pacific Coast.* San Francisco: Chandler Publishing Co.

_____. 1958. *The Native Brotherhoods.* Bureau of American Ethnology, Bulletin 168.

_____. 1955. *Indians of the Northwest Coast.* New York: McGraw-Hill.

_____. 1951. *The Northern and Central Nootkan Tribes.* Bureau of American Ethnology, Bulletin 144.

_____. 1950. *Culture Element Distributions: Northwest Coast.* Anthropological Records, vol. 9.

_____. 1941. *Culture Element Distributions: Yuma-Pima.* Anthropological Records, vol. 6.

_____. 1939a. "Rank, Wealth, and Kinship in Northwest Coast Society." *American Anthropologist* 41:55–65.

_____. 1939b. "Contributions to Alsea

Ethnography." *University of California Publications in American Archaeology and Ethnology* 35:81–102.

———. 1936. "The Tolowa and Their Southwest Oregon Kin." *University of California Publications in American Archaeology and Ethnology* 36:221–300.

DRUCKER, P., AND HEIZER, R. F. 1967. *To Make My Name Good: A Reexamination of the Southern Kwakiutl Potlatch.* University of California Press.

DU BOIS, C. 1936. "The Wealth Concept as an Integrative Factor in Tolowa-Tututni Culture." In *Essays in Anthropology Presented to A. L. Kroeber,* pp. 49–65. University of California Press.

———. 1935. "Wintu Ethnography." *University of California Publications in American Archaeology and Ethnology* 36:1–148.

DUMAREST, N. 1919. "Notes on Cochiti." *Memoirs of the American Anthropological Association* 6:137–237.

DUMOND, D. E. 1974. "Archaeology and Prehistory in Alaska." *Warner-Modular Publications in Anthropology.* Andover.

———. 1969. "Toward a Prehistory of the Na-Déné, With a General Comment on Population Movements among Nomadic Hunters." *American Anthropologist* 71:857–863.

EGGAN, F. 1966. *The American Indian, Perspectives for the Study of Social Change.* Chicago: Aldine.

———. 1955. ed. *Social Anthropology of North American Tribes.* 2d ed. University of Chicago Press.

———. 1952. "The Ethnological Cultures and their Archaeological Backgrounds." In *Archaeology of the Eastern United States,* ed. J. B. Griffin, pp. 35–45. University of Chicago Press.

———. 1950. *Social Organization of the Western Pueblos.* University of Chicago Press.

———. 1937a. "The Cheyenne and Arapaho Kinship System." In *Social Anthropology of North American Tribes,* ed. F. Eggan, pp. 35–95. University of Chicago Press.

———. 1937b. "Historical Changes in the Choctaw Kinship System." *American Anthropologist* 36:188–202.

———. 1934. "The Maya Kinship System and Cross-Cousin Marriage." *American Anthropologist* 36:34–52.

EKHOLM, G. F. 1944. "Excavations at Tampico and Panuco in the Huasteca, Mexico." *American Museum of Natural History, Anthropological Papers* 38:321–509.

ELASSER, A. B., AND HEIZER, R. F. 1966. "Excavations of Two Northwestern California Coastal Sites." *Reports of the University of California Archaeological Survey,* no. 67, pp. v–149.

ELLIS, F. H. 1951a. "Pueblo Social Organization and Southwestern Archaeology." *American Anthropologist* 17:148–151.

———. 1951b. "Patterns of Aggression and War Cult in Southwestern Pueblos." *Southwestern Journal of Anthropology* 7:177–201.

EMMONS, G. T. 1911. *The Tahltan Indians.* University of Pennsylvania Monographs in Anthropology, vol. 4.

EWERS, J. C. 1958. *The Blackfeet.* University of Oklahoma Press.

———. 1955. *The Horse in Blackfoot Indian Culture.*

Bureau of American Ethnology, Bulletin 159.

———. 1953. "Of the Crow Nation." *Bureau of American Ethnology,* Bulletin 151:1–74.

———. 1952. "Of the Assiniboine." *Bulletin of the Missouri Historical Society* 8:121–150.

———. 1950. "Of the Arickaras." *Bulletin of the Missouri Historical Society* 6:189–215.

———. 1949. "The Last Bison Drives of the Blackfoot Indians." *Journal of the Washington Academy of Science* 29:355–360.

———. 1939. *Plains Indian Painting.* Stanford University Press.

EZELL, P. H. 1961. *The Hispanic Acculturation of the Gila River Pimas.* American Anthropological Association, Memoir 90.

FAIRBANKS, C. H. 1946. "The Macon Earth Lodge." *American Antiquity* 12:94–108.

FAIRCHILD, H. N. 1928. *The Noble Savage.* New York: Columbia University Press.

FARMER, M. F. 1941. "The Growth of Navaho Culture." *San Diego Museum Bulletin* 6:8–16.

FENNEMAN, N. M. 1931. *Physiography of the Western United States.* New York: McGraw-Hill.

FENTON, W. N., ED. 1968. *Parker on the Iroquois.* Syracuse University Press.

———. 1953. *The Iroquois Eagle Dance.* Bureau of American Ethnology, Bulletin 156.

———. 1940. "Problems Arising from the Historic Northeastern Position of the Iroquois." *Smithsonian Miscellaneous Collections* 100:159–252.

FENTON, W. N. AND GULICK, J., EDS. 1961. *Symposium on Cherokee and Iroquois Culture.* Bureau of American Ethnology, Bulletin 180.

FEY, H. E., AND MCNICKLE, D. 1970. *Indians and Other Americans: Two Ways of Life Meet.* New York: Harper & Row.

———. 1959. *Indians and Other Americans.* New York: Harper & Row.

FISCHER, J. L. 1964. "Solutions for the Natchez Paradox." *Ethnology* 3:53–65.

FITTING, J. E. 1973. *The Development of North American Archaeology.* Garden City, N.Y.: Doubleday (Anchor Books).

FLANNERY, R. 1953. "The Gros Ventres of Montana, Part I: Social Life." *Catholic University of America, Anthropological Series,* vol. 15.

FLETCHER, A. C., AND LA FLESCHE, F. 1906. *The Omaha Tribe.* Annual Report of the Bureau of American Ethnology, 27.

FORD, C. S. 1941. *Smoke from Their Fires.* New Haven: Yale University Press.

FORD, J. A. 1969. *A Comparison of Formative Cultures in the Americas.* Smithsonian Contributions to Anthropology, vol. 11. Washington: Smithsonian Institution Press.

———. 1966. "Early Formative Cultures in Georgia and Florida." *American Antiquity* 31:781–799.

———. 1959. "Eskimo Prehistory in the Vicinity of Point Barrow, Alaska." *American Museum of Natural History, Anthropological Papers,* vol. 47, pt I.

———. 1936. *Analysis of Indian Village Site*

Collections from Louisiana and Mississippi. State of Louisiana, Department of Conservation, Anthropological Study 2.

FORD, J. A., AND WEBB, C. H. 1956. "Poverty Point, a Late Archaic Site in Louisiana." *American Museum of Natural History, Anthropological Papers*, vol. 46, pt I.

FORD, J. A., AND WILLEY, G. R. 1941. "An Interpretation of the Prehistory of the Eastern United States." *American Anthropologist* 43:325–363.

———. 1940. "Crooks Site." *Louisiana Geological Survey, Anthropological Study*, no. 3.

FORDE, C. D. 1931. "Ethnography of the Yuma Indians." *University of California Publications in American Archaeology and Ethnology* 28:83–278.

FOREMAN, G. 1934. *The Five Civilized Tribes.* University of Oklahoma Press.

FOSTER, G. M. 1960. *Culture and Conquest: America's Spanish Heritage.* Viking Fund Publications in Anthropology, no. 27.

———. 1951. "Report on an Ethnological Reconnaissance of Spain." *American Anthropologist* 53:311–325.

———. 1944. "A Summary of Yuki Culture." *Anthropological Records* 5:155–244.

FOWLER, D. D. 1966. "Great Basin Social Organization." In *Current Status of Anthropological Research in the Great Basin: 1964*, ed. W. L. d'Azevedo et al., pp. 57–74. Desert Research Institute, Reno Publications in the Social Sciences and Humanities, no. 1.

FOX, J. R. 1967. *The Keresan Bridge.* London School of Economics Monographs on Social Anthropology, no. 35. The Athlone Press, University of London. New York: Humanities Press.

FRANKLIN, J. 1828. *Narrative of a Second Expedition to the Shores of the Polar Sea.* London.

FRISON, G. C., ED. 1974. *The Casper Site, A Hell Gap Bison Kill on the High Plains.* New York: Academic Press.

GABEL, H. E. 1949. "A Comparative Racial Study of the Papago." *University of New Mexico Publications in Anthropology* 4:1–96.

GAMIO, M. 1945. "Some Considerations of Indianist Policy." In *The Science of Man in the World Crisis*, ed. R. Linton, pp. 399–415. New York: Columbia University Press.

GARBARINO, M. S. 1976. *Native American Heritage.* New York: Little Brown.

GARFIELD, V. E. 1939. "Tsimshian Clan and Society." *University of Washington Publications in Anthropology* 7:167–349.

GARFIELD, V. E. et al. 1951. *The Tsimshian: Their Arts and Music.* Publications of the American Ethnological Society, no. 18.

GARTH, T. R. 1953. "Atsugewi Ethnography." *Anthropological Records* 14:123–212.

GATSCHET, A. S. 1891. "The Karankawa Indians." *Peabody Museum Papers* 1:5–103.

———. 1890. *The Klamath Indians of Southwestern Oregon.* Washington: Contributions to North American Ethnology, Department of the Interior,

United States Geographical and Geological Survey of the Rocky Mountain Region, 2 vols.

GAYTON, A. H. 1948a. "Northern Foothills Yokuts and Western Mono." *Anthropological Records* 10:143–302.

———. 1948b. "Tulare Lake, Southern Valley, and Central Foothills Yokuts." *Anthropological Records* 10:1–140.

———. 1930. "Yokuts-Mono Chiefs and Shamans." *University of California Publications in American Archaeology and Ethnology* 24:361–420.

GEARING, F. 1970. *The Face of the Fox.* Chicago: Aldine.

———. 1962. *Priests and Warriors: Social Structures for Cherokee Politics in the 18th Century.* American Anthropological Association, Memoir 93.

GEARING, F.; NETTING, R. M.; AND PEATTIE, L. R., EDS. 1960. *Documentary History of the Fox Project.* University of Chicago.

GIBSON, A. M. 1971. *The Chickasaws.* University of Oklahoma Press.

GIDDINGS, J. L. 1960. "The Archaeology of Bering Strait." *Current Anthropology* 1:121–138.

———. 1949. "Early Flint Horizons on the North Bering Sea Coast." *Journal of the Washington Academy of Science* 35:85–89.

GIFFORD, E. W. 1955. "Central Miwok Ceremonies." *Anthropological Records* 14:261–318.

———. 1939. "The Coast Yuki." *Anthropos* 34:292–375.

———. 1936. "Northeastern and Western Yavapai." *University of California Publications in American Archaeology and Ethnology* 34: 247–354.

———. 1933. "The Cocopa." *University of California Publications in American Archaeology and Ethnology* 31:257–334.

———. 1932a. "The Northfork Mono." *University of California Publications in American Archaeology and Ethnology* 31:15–65.

———. 1932b. "The Southeastern Yavapai." *University of California Publications in American Archaeology and Ethnology* 29:177–252.

———. 1931. *The Kamia of Imperial Valley.* Bureau of American Ethnology, Bulletin 97.

———. 1916. "Miwok Moieties." *University of California Publications in American Archaeology and Ethnology* 12:139–194.

GILBERT, W. H. 1943. *The Eastern Cherokees.* Bureau of American Ethnology, Bulletin 133.

GILLESPIE, B. C. 1970. "The Yellowknives: Quo Iverunt?" *Proceedings of the 1970 Annual Spring Meeting, American Ethnological Society*, pp. 61–71.

GLADWIN, H. S., AND GLADWIN, W. 1934. "A Method for Designation of Cultures and Their Variations." *Medallion Papers*, no. 15. Gila Pueblo, Globe, Arizona.

GODDARD, P. E. 1931. *Indians of the Southwest.* New York: American Museum of Natural History.

———. 1916. "The Beaver Indians." *Anthropological Papers of the American Museum of Natural History* 10:201–293.

———. 1903. "Life and Culture of the Hupa." *University of California Publications in American Archaeology and Ethnology* 1:1–88.

GOGGIN, J. M., AND STURTEVANT, W. C. 1964. "The Calusa: A Stratified, Nonagricultural Society (With Notes on Sibling Marriage)." In *Explorations in Cultural Anthropology: Essays in Honor of George Peter Murdock,* ed. W. H. Goodenough. New York: McGraw-Hill.

GOLDFRANK, E. S. 1945. "Irrigation Agriculture and Navaho Community Leadership." *American Anthropologist* 47:262–277.

———. 1927. *The Social and Ceremonial Organization of Cochiti.* American Anthropological Association, Memoir 33.

GOLDMAN, I. 1975. *The Mouth of Heaven: An Introduction to Kwakiutl Religious Thought.* New York: Wiley.

———. 1937. "The Zuni of New Mexico." In *Cooperation and Competition among Primitive Peoples,* ed. M. Mead, pp. 313–353. New York: McGraw-Hill.

GOLDSCHMIDT, W. 1951. "Nomlaki Ethnography." *University of California Publications in American Archaeology and Ethnology* 42:303–443.

GOODWIN, G. 1942. *The Social Organization of the Western Apache.* University of Chicago Press.

———. 1938. "White Mountain Apache Religion." *American Anthropologist* 40:24–37.

———. 1935. "The Social Divisions and Economic Life of the Western Apache." *American Anthropologist* 37:55–64.

GOSLIN, R. M. 1952a. "Cultivated and Wild Plant Food from Aboriginal Sites in Ohio." *Ohio Archaeologist* 2:9–29.

———. 1952b. "Mammal and Bird Remains from the Cramer Village Site." *Ohio Archaeologist* 2:20–21.

GRABURN, N. 1969. *Eskimos without Igloos.* Boston: Little, Brown.

GRAVES, T. D. 1970. "The Personal Adjustments of Navaho Indian Migrants to Denver, Colorado." *American Anthropologist* 72:35–54.

GREENBERG, J. H. 1960. "The General Classification of Central and South American Languages." In *Men and Cultures, Selected Papers, 5th International Congress of Anthropological and Ethnological Sciences,* ed. A. F. C. Wallace, pp. 791–794. University of Pennsylvania Press.

GREENBERG, J. H., AND SWADESH, M. 1953. "Jicaque as a Hokan Language." *International Journal of American Linguistics* 19:216–222.

GRIFFIN, J. B. 1967. "Eastern North American Archaeology: A Summary." *Science* 156:175–191.

———. 1964. "The Northeast Woodlands Area." In *Prehistoric Man in the New World,* ed. J. D. Jennings and E. Norbeck, pp. 223–258. Rice University Semicentennial Publications, University of Chicago Press.

———. 1961. "Lake Superior Copper and the Indians." *Anthropological Papers, Museum of Anthropology, University of Michigan,* no. 17.

———. 1960. "Climatic Change: A Contributory Cause of the Growth and Decline of Northern Hopewellian Culture." *Wisconsin Archeologist* 41:21–33.

———, ED. 1952. *Archaeology of Eastern United States.* University of Chicago Press.

———. 1951a. "The Central Mississippi Valley Archaeological Survey, Season 1950." *Journal of the Illinois State Archaeological Society* 1:75–80.

———. 1951b. "Spanish Influence in Southeastern Archaeology." *Eastern States Archaeological Federation, Bulletin* 90:9.

———. 1946. "Cultural Change and Continuity in Eastern United States Archaeology." *Peabody Foundation for Archaeology, Papers* 3:37–95.

———. 1944a. "The Iroquois in American Prehistory." *Papers of the Michigan Academy of Science, Arts and Letters* 29:357–374.

———. 1944b. "The Hasinai Indians of East Texas as Seen by Europeans, 1687–1772." *Philological and Documentary Studies of the Middle American Research Institute* 2:43–165. New Orleans.

GRINNELL, G. B. 1956. *The Fighting Cheyennes.* University of Oklahoma Press.

———. 1923. *The Cheyenne Indians.* New Haven: Yale University Press.

GROSS, H. 1951. "Mastodon, Mammoth, and Man in America." *Bulletin of the Texas Archaeological and Paleontological Society* 22:101–131.

GUNTHER, E. 1927. "Klallam Ethnography." *University of Washington Publications in Anthropology* 1:171–314.

GUTHE, C. E. 1952. "Twenty-five Years of Archaeology in Eastern United States." In *Archaeology of Eastern United States,* ed. J. B. Griffin, pp. 1–12. University of Chicago Press.

HAAG, W. G. 1961. "The Archaic of the Lower Mississippi Valley." *American Antiquity* 26:317–323.

HAAS, M. R. 1959. "Tonkawa and Algonkian." *Anthropological Linguistics* 1:1–6.

———. 1958a. "A New Linguistic Relationship in North America: Algonkian and the Gulf Languages." *Southwestern Journal of Anthropology* 14:231–264.

———. 1958b. "Algonkian-Ritwan: The End of a Controversy." *International Journal of American Linguistics* 24:159–173.

———. 1956. "Natchez and the Muskogean Languages." *Language* 3:61–72.

———. 1954. "The Proto-Hokan-Coahuiltecan Word for 'Water.'" *University of California Publications in Linguistics* 10:1–68.

———. 1952. "The Proto-Gulf word for 'Land.'" *International Journal of American Linguistics* 18:238–240.

———. 1951. "The Proto-Gulf Word for 'Water' (with notes on Siouan-Yuchi)." *International Journal of American Linguistics* 17:71–79.

———. 1941. "The Classification of the Muskogean Languages." In *Language, Culture and Personality,* ed. L. Spier, pp. 41–58. Menasha: George Banta Publishers.

———. 1940. "Creek Inter-Town Relations." *American Anthropologist* 42:479–489.

――――. 1939. "Natchez and Chitimacha Clans and Kinship Terminology." *American Anthropologist* 41:597–610.

HACKENBERG, R. A. 1962. "Economic Alternatives in Arid Lands: A Case of the Pima and Papago Indians." *Ethnology* 1:186–196.

HAEBERLIN, H. K., AND GUNTHER, E. 1930. "The Indians of Puget Sound." *University of Washington Publications in Anthropology* 4:1–83.

HAGAN, W. T. 1958. *The Sac and Fox Indians.* University of Oklahoma Press.

HAILE, B. 1954. "Property Concepts of the Navaho Indians." *Catholic University of America, Anthropological Series,* vol. 17.

――――. 1943. *Origin Legend of the Navaho Flintway.* University of Chicago Press.

――――. 1938. "Navaho Chantways and Ceremonials." *American Anthropologist* 40:639–652.

HALE, K. 1959. "Internal Diversity in Uto-Aztecan II." *International Journal of American Linguistics* 25:114–121.

――――. 1958. "Internal Diversity in Uto-Aztecan I." *International Journal of American Linguistics* 24:101–107.

HALL, E. T., JR. 1944. "Recent Clues to Athapascan Prehistory in the Southwest." *American Anthropologist* 46:98–105.

HALLOWELL, A. I. 1960. "The Beginnings of Anthropology in America." In *Selected Papers from the American Anthropologist, 1888-1920,* ed. F. De Laguna, pp. 1–90. New York: Harper & Row.

――――. 1957a. "The Backwash of the Frontier: The Impact of the Indian on American Culture." In *The Frontier in Perspective,* ed. W. D. Wyman and C. B. Kroeber. University of Wisconsin Press.

――――. 1957b. "The Impact of the American Indian on American Culture." *American Anthropologist* 59:201–217.

――――. 1955. *Culture and Experience.* University of Pennsylvania Press.

――――. 1949. "The Size of Algonkian Hunting Territories, A Function of Ecological Adjustment." *American Anthropologist* 51:35–45.

――――. 1942. *The Role of Conjuring in Saulteaux Society.* University of Pennsylvania Press.

HALPERN, A. M. 1946. "Yuma." In *Linguistic Structures.* ed. H. Hoijer. Viking Fund Publications in Anthropology 6:249–288.

HAMAMSY, L. S. 1957. "The Role of Women in a Changing Navaho Society." *American Anthropologist* 59:101–111.

HAMILTON, H. W. 1952. *The Spiro Mound.* The Missouri Archaeologist, vol. 14.

HARRINGTON, M. R., AND SIMPSON, R. D. 1961. *Tule Springs, Nevada.* Southwest Museum Papers, no. 18.

HARRIS, J. S. 1940. "The White Knife Shoshoni of Nevada." In *Acculturation in Seven American Indian Tribes,* ed. R. Linton, pp. 39–118. Englewood Cliffs, N.J.: Prentice-Hall.

HART, C. W. M. 1943. "A Reconsideration of the Natchez Social Structure." *American Anthropologist* 45:374–386.

HATCHER, E. 1974. *Visual Metaphors: A Formal Analysis of Navaho Art.* American Ethnological Society, Monograph 58. St. Paul: West.

HAURY, E. W. 1967. "First Masters of the American Desert: The Hohokam." *National Geographic Magazine* 131:670–695.

――――. 1962. "The Greater American Southwest." In *Courses Toward Urban Life,* ed. R. J. Braidwood and G. R. Willey, pp. 106–131. Viking Fund Publications in Anthropology, no. 32.

――――. 1953. "Artifacts with Mammoth Remains, Nacto, Arizona." *American Antiquity* 19:1–24.

――――. 1945. "The Problem of Contact between the Southwestern United States and Mexico." *Southwestern Journal of Anthropology* 1:55–74.

――――. 1936. *The Mogollon Culture of Southwestern New Mexico.* Globe, Ariz.: Medallion Papers, no. 20.

――――. 1935a. "Dates from Gila Pueblo." *Tree Ring Bulletin* 2:3–4.

――――. 1935b. "Tree Rings—the Archaeologist's Time Piece." *American Antiquity* 1:98–108.

HAWKES, M. W. 1916. "The Labrador Eskimo." *Memoirs of the Canada Department of Mines, Geological Survey* 91:1–165.

HAWTHORN, A. 1967. *Art of the Kwakiutl Indians and Other Northwest Coast Tribes.* University of Washington Press.

HAYNES, C. V., AND HEMMINGS, E. T. 1968. "Mammoth-Bone Shaft Wrench from Murray Springs, Arizona." *Science,* vol. 159, no. 3811, pp. 186–187.

HECKEWELDER, J. G. E. 1819. "An Account of the History, Manners, and Customs of the Indian Nations, who once Inhabited Pennsylvania and the Neighboring States." *Transactions of the Historical and Literary Committee of the American Philosophical Society* 1:1–340.

HEIZER, R. F. 1964. "The Western Coast of North America." In *Prehistoric Man in the New World,* ed. J. D. Jennings, and E. Norbeck, pp. 117–148. University of Chicago Press.

――――. 1952. "The American Indian: Background and Contributions." In *One America,* ed. F. J. Brown and J. S. Roucek. Englewood Cliffs, N.J.: Prentice-Hall.

HEIZER, R. F. AND WHIPPLE, M. A. 1971. *The California Indians: A Sourcebook.* 2d ed. University of California Press.

HELM, J. 1972. "The Dogrib Indians." In *Hunters and Gatherers Today,* ed. M. G. Bicchieri, pp. 51–83. New York: Holt, Rinehart and Winston.

――――. 1968. "The Nature of the Dogrib Socioterritorial Groups." In *Man the Hunter,* ed. R. B. Lee and I. DeVore, pp. 118–125. Chicago: Aldine.

――――. 1965a. "Bilaterality in the Socio-territorial Organization of the Arctic Drainage Déné." *Ethnology* 4:361–385.

――――. 1965b. Patterns of Allocation among the Arctic Drainage Déné." *Proceedings of the 1965 Annual*

Spring Meeting, American Ethnological Society, pp. 33–45.

———. 1961. *The Lynx Point People: The Dynamics of a Northern Athapaskan Band.* Ottawa: National Museum of Canada, Bulletin 176.

HELM, J., AND LEACOCK, E. B. 1971. "The Hunting Tribes of Subarctic Canada." In *North American Indians in Historical Perspective,* ed. E. B. Leacock and N. O. Lurie, pp. 343–374. New York: Random House.

HELM, J., AND LURIE, N. O. 1961. *The Subsistence Economy of the Dogrib Indians of Lac la Martre in the MacKenzie District of the Northwest Territories.* Ottawa: Northern Coordination and Research Center.

HELM, J. et al. "The Contact History of the Subarctic Athapaskans." Ottawa: National Museum of Man (in press).

HESTER, J. J. 1972. "Blackwater, Locality No. 1." *Publication of the Fort Burgwin Research Center,* no. 8. Dallas: Southern Methodist University.

———. 1960. "Late Pleistocene Extinction and Radiocarbon Dating." *American Antiquity* 26:58–77.

HESTER, T. R. 1973. "Chronological Ordering of Great Basin Prehistory." *Contributions of the University of California Archaeological Research Facility,* no. 17. Berkeley.

HEWETT, E. L., AND DUTTON, B. P. 1945. *The Pueblo Indian World.* University of New Mexico Press.

HEWITT, J. N. B. 1939. "Notes on the Creek Indians." *Bureau of American Ethnology Bulletin* 123:119–160.

———. 1925–1926. *Iroquoian Cosmology.* Annual Report of the Bureau of American Ethnology, 42.

HEWSON, J. 1971. "Beothuk and Algonkin: Evidence Old and New." *International Journal of American Linguistics* 37:85–93.

HICKERSON, H. 1970. *The Chippewa and their Neighbors: A Study in Ethnohistory.* New York: Holt, Rinehart and Winston.

HILGER, M. I. 1952. *Arapaho Child Life and its Cultural Background.* Bureau of American Ethnology, Bulletin 148.

———. 1951. *Chippewa Child Life and its Cultural Background.* Bureau of American Ethnology, Bulletin 146.

HILL, A. T., AND METCALF, G. 1941. "A Site of the Dismal River Aspect in Chase County, Nebraska." *Nebraska History,* vol. 22.

HILL, A. T., AND KIVETT, M. 1940. "Woodland-like Manifestations in Nebraska." *Nebraska History* 21:143–191.

HILL, W. W. 1944. "The Navaho Indians and the Ghost Dance of 1890." *American Anthropologist* 46:523–527.

———. 1940. "Some Navaho Cultural Changes during Two Centuries." *Smithsonian Institution, Miscellaneous Collections* 100:395–415.

———. 1938. *The Agricultural and Hunting Methods of the Navaho Indians.* Yale University Publications in Anthropology, no. 18.

———. 1936. "Navaho Warfare." *Yale University Publications in Anthropology* 5:1–19.

HODGE, F. W. 1937. "History of Hawikuh." *Southwest Museum Papers* 1:1–155.

———. 1907–1910. *Handbook of American Indians North of Mexico.* Bureau of American Ethnology, Bulletin 30, 2 vols.

HODGE, W. H. 1969. *The Albuquerque Navajos.* Anthropological Papers of the University of Arizona, no. 11.

HOEBEL, E. A. 1960. *The Cheyennes: Indians of the Great Plains.* New York: Holt, Rinehart and Winston.

———. 1940. *The Political Organization and Law-Ways of the Comanche Indians.* American Anthropological Association, Memoir 54.

HOEBEL, E. A., AND WALLACE, E. 1952. *The Comanches: Lords of the Southern Plains.* University of Oklahoma Press.

HOFFMAN, W. J. 1893. "The Menomini Indians." *Annual Report of the Bureau of American Ethnology* 14:11–328.

———. 1885–1886. "The Midwewin or Grand Medicine Society of the Ojibwa." *Annual Report of the Bureau of American Ethnology* 7:143–300.

HOIJER, H. 1963. "The Athapaskan Languages." *Studies in the Athapaskan Languages, University of California Publications in Linguistics* 29:1–29.

———. 1956. "Language and Writing." In *Man, Culture, and Society,* ed. H. L. Shapiro. New York: Oxford University Press.

———. 1954. "The Sapir-Whorf Hypothesis." In *Language and Culture, American Anthropological Association,* Memoir 79:92–106.

——— ed. 1946. *Linguistic Structures of Native America.* Viking Fund Publications in Anthropology, no. 6. New York: Wenner-Gren Foundation for Anthropological Research.

———. 1938. "The Southern Athapaskan Languages." *American Anthropologist* 40:75–87.

HOLDEN, W. C. 1936. "Studies of the Yaqui Indians of Sonora." *Texas Technological College Bulletin* 12:1–142.

HOLM, B. 1972. *Crooked Beak of Heaven: Masks and other Ceremonial Art of the Northwest Coast.* University of Washington Press.

HOLM, G. 1911. "Ethnological Sketch of the Angmagsalik Eskimo." *Meddelelser om Grønland* 39:1–147.

HOLMER, N. M. 1954. "The Ojibway on the Walpole Island, Ontario." *Upsala Canadian Studies* 4:1–91.

HOLT, C. 1946. "Shasta Ethnography." *Anthropological Records* 3:299–349.

HONIGMANN, J. J. 1956. "The Attawapiskat Swampy Cree." *Anthropological Papers of the University of Alaska* 5:23–82.

———. 1954. *The Kaska Indians: An Ethnographic Reconstruction.* Yale University Publications in Anthropology, vol. 51.

———. 1949. *Culture and Ethos of Kaska Society.* Yale University Publications in Anthropology, vol. 40.

———. 1946. *Ethnography and Acculturation in the Fort Nelson Slave.* Yale University Publications in Anthropology, vol. 32.

HOOPER, L. 1920. "The Cahuilla Indians." *University of California Publications in American Archaeology and Ethnology* 16:316–380.

HOWLEY, J. P. 1915. *The Beothucks or Red Indians.* Cambridge: Harvard University Press.

HUDDLESTON, L. E. 1967. *Origins of the American Indians: European Concepts, 1492–1729.* Institute of Latin American Studies, Monograph no. 11. University of Texas Press.

HUDSON, C. M. 1970. *The Catawba Nation.* University of Georgia Press.

HULBERT, A. B., AND SCHWARZE, W. W., ED. 1910. "Zeisberger's History of Northern American Indians." *Ohio Archaeological and Historical Quarterly* 19:1–189.

HULSE, F. S. 1963. *The Human Species.* New York: Random House.

HURLEY, W. M. 1975. "An Analysis of Effigy Mound Complexes in Wisconsin." *Anthropological Papers,* no. 59. Museum of Anthropology, University of Michigan, Ann Arbor.

HUSCHER, B. H. 1943. "The Hogan Builders of Colorado." *Southwestern Lore* 9:1–92.

HUSCHER, B. H., AND HUSCHER, H. A. 1942. "Athabaskan Migration via the Intermontane Region." *American Antiquity* 8:80–88.

HYDE, G. E. 1959. *Indians of the High Plains from the Prehistoric Period to the Coming of Europeans.* University of Oklahoma Press.

———. 1951. *Pawnee Indians.* University of Denver Press.

———. 1937. *Red Cloud's Folk.* University of Oklahoma Press.

HYMES, D. H. 1960. "Lexicostatistics So Far." *Current Anthropology* 1:3–44.

———. 1959. "Genetic Classification: Retrospect and Prospect." *Anthropological Linguistics* 1:50–66.

INVERARITY, R. B. 1950. *Art of the Northwest Coast Indians.* University of California Press.

IRVING W. N., AND HARINGTON, C. R. 1968. "Upper Pleistocene Radiocarbon-Dated Artifacts from the Northern Yukon." *Science* 179:335–340.

IRWIN, H. T. 1971. "Developments in Early Man Studies in Western North America, 1960–1970." In *Papers from a Symposium on Early Man in North America, New Developments: 1960–1970,* ed. R. Shutler, Jr. *Arctic Anthropology* 3:42–67.

JABLOW, J. 1951. *The Cheyenne in Plains Indian Trade Relations, 1795–1840.* Monographs of the American Ethnological Society, no. 19.

JACOBS, M. 1959. *The Content and Style of an Oral Literature: Clackamas Chinook Myths and Tales.* Viking Fund Publications in Anthropology, no. 26. New York: Wenner-Gren Foundation.

JARCHO, S. 1959. "Origin of the American Indian as Suggested by Fray de Acosta (1589)." *Isis* 50:430–438.

JELINEK, A. J. 1957. "Pleistocene Faunas and Early Man." *Papers of the Michigan Academy of Science, Arts, and Letters,* vol. 42.

JENKS, A. E. 1898. *The Wild Rice Gatherers.* Annual Report of the Bureau of American Ethnology, 19.

JENNESS, D. 1955. *The Indians of Canada.* Bulletin of the Canadian National Museum, 65. 3d ed. Ottawa: National Museum of Canada.

———. 1946. "Material Culture of the Copper Eskimo." *Report of the Canadian Arctic Expedition* 16:1–148.

———. 1938. "The Sarcee Indians of Alberta." *Bulletin of the Canada Department of Mines, National Museum of Canada* 90:1–98.

———. 1937. "The Sekani Indians of British Columbia." *Bulletin of the Canada Department of Mines, National Museum of Canada* 84:1–82.

———. 1935. "The Ojibwa Indians of Parry Island." *Bulletin of the Canada Department of Mines, National Museum of Canada* 78:1–115.

———. 1922. "The Life of the Copper Eskimos." *Report of the Canadian Arctic Expedition,* vol. 12

JENNINGS, J. D. 1974. *Prehistory of North America.* 2d ed. New York: McGraw-Hill.

———. 1957. *Danger Cave.* Society of American Archaeology, Memoir 23.

———. 1955. "The Archaeology of the Plains: An Assessment (with Special Reference to the Missouri River Basin)." *National Park Service, Memorandum of Agreement No. 14-10-011-287.* Department of Anthropology, University of Utah.

———. 1947. "A Summary of the Culture of the Effigy Mound Builders." *National Park Service.* University of Utah.

JENNINGS, J. D. AND NORBECK, E., EDS. 1964. *Prehistoric Man in the New World.* Rice Semicentennial Publications. University of Chicago Press.

JENNINGS, J. D., AND NORBECK, E. 1955. "Great Basin Prehistory: A Review." *American Antiquity* 21:1–11.

JOHNSON, F. 1951. "Radiocarbon Dating: A Report on the Program to Aid in the Development of a Method of Dating." *Society for American Archaeology, Memoir* 8:58–65.

———. 1946. "Man in Northeastern North America." *Papers of the Robert S. Peabody Foundation for Archaeology,* vol. 3.

JOHNSON, J. B. 1950. *The Opata.* University of New Mexico Publications in Anthropology, vol. 6.

JOHNSTON, B. J. 1955–1956. "The Gabrielino Indians of Southern California." *Masterkey* 29:180–191; 30:6–21, 44–56, 76–89, 125–132, 146–156.

JONES, L. F. 1914. *A Study of the Tlingits of Alaska.* New York: F. H. Revell.

JONES, W. 1939. *Ethnography of the Fox Indians.* Bureau of American Ethnology, Bulletin 125.

JOSEPH, A.; SPICER, R.; AND CHESKY, J. 1949. *The Desert People.* University of Chicago Press.

JOSEPHY, A. M., JR. 1971. *Red Power: The American Indian's Fight for Freedom.* New York: American Heritage Press.

———. 1968. *The Indian Heritage of America.* New York: Knopf.

JOSSELIN DE JONG, J. P. S. 1930. "The Natchez Social Class System." *Proceedings of the 23rd International Congress of Americanists,* pp. 553–561.

KAUT, C. R. 1959. "Notes on Western Apache

Religious and Social Organization." *American Anthropologist* 61:99–102.

———. 1957. *The Western Apache Clan System: Its Origins and Development.* University of New Mexico Press.

KEATING, W. H. 1825. *Narrative of an Expedition to the Source of the St. Peter's River.* London.

KEESING, F. M. 1939. *The Menomini Indians of Wisconsin.* Memoirs of the American Philosophical Society, vol. 10.

KEISER, A. 1933. *The Indian in American Literature.* New York: Oxford University Press.

KELLY, I. T. 1932. "Ethnography of the Surprise Valley Paiute." *University of California Publications in American Archaeology and Ethnology* 31:67–210.

KELLY, W. H. 1954. *Indian Affairs and the Reorganization Act: The Twenty Year Record.* The University of Arizona.

———. 1953. *Indians of the Southwest.* Tucson: Reports of the Bureau of Ethnic Research, no. 1.

KENT, K. P. 1961. "Story of Navaho Weaving." *The Heard Museum,* Phoenix, Arizona.

KIDDER, A. V. 1924. "An Introduction to the Study of Southwestern Archaeology." *Papers of the Southwestern Expedition, No. 1.* Published for the Phillips Academy by the Yale University Press, New Haven.

KING, A. R. 1950. "Cattle Point, A Stratified Site in the Southern Northwest Coast Region." *American Antiquity,* vol. 15, no. 4, Pt. 2. *Memoirs of the Society for American Archaeology,* no. 7. Menasha, Wisconsin.

KINIETZ, W. V. 1946. "Delaware Culture Chronology." *Prehistory Research Series, Indiana Historical Society* 3:1–143.

———. 1940. "The Indian Tribes of the Western Great Lakes." *Occasional Contributions from the Museum of Anthropology of the University of Michigan* 10:161–225.

KIRCHHOFF, P. 1954. "Gatherers and Farmers in the Greater Southwest: A Problem in Classification." *American Anthropologist* 56:529–550.

———. 1952. "Meso-America: Its Geographic Limits, Ethnic Composition and Cultural Characteristics." In *Heritage of Conquest,* ed. S. Tax, pp. 17–30. University of Chicago Press.

———. 1948. *Civilizing the Chichimecs.* Institute of Latin-American Studies, Study no. 5.

KIVETT, M. F. 1949. "A Woodland Pottery Type from Nebraska." *Laboratory of Anthropology, University of Nebraska, Notebook Series* 1:67–69.

KLEIN, R. G. 1973. *Ice-Age Hunters of the Ukraine.* University of Chicago Press.

KLUCKHOHN, C. 1949. "The Philosophy of the Navaho Indians." In *Ideological Differences and World Order,* ed. F. S. C. Northrop, pp. 356–384. New Haven: Yale University Press.

———. 1946. "Personality Formation among the Navaho Indians." *Sociometry* 9:128–132.

———. 1944. "Navaho Witchcraft." *Papers of the Peabody Museum,* no. 22.

KLUCKHOHN, C., AND LEIGHTON, D. C. 1946a. *An Introduction to Navaho Chant Practice.* American Anthropological Association, Memoir 53.

———. 1946b. *The Navaho.* Cambridge: Harvard University Press.

KLUCKHOHN, C.; HILL, W. W.; AND KLUCKHOHN, L. W. 1971. *Navaho Material Culture.* Cambridge: Harvard University Press.

KLUCKHOHN. R., ED. 1962. *Culture and Behavior; Collected Essays of Clyde Kluckhohn.* New York: The Free Press of Glencoe.

KNOROZOV, Y. V. 1958. "The Problem of the Study of Maya Hieroglyphic Writing." *American Antiquity* 23:284–291.

KOPPERT, V. A. 1930. "Contributions to Calyoquot Ethnology." *Catholic University of America, Anthropological Series* 1:1–124.

KRAUSE, A. 1956. *The Tlingit Indians.* American Ethnological Society, Memoir 26. University of Washington Press.

KRIEGER, A. D. 1951. "Radiocarbon Date on the Davis Site in East Texas." *American Antiquity* 17:144–145.

———. 1945. "An Inquiry into Supposed Mexican Influence on a Prehistoric 'Cult' in the Southern United States." *American Anthropologist* 47:483–515.

KROEBER, A. L. 1957. *Style and Civilization.* Ithaca: Cornell University Press.

———. 1955. "Linguistic Time Depth Results So Far and Their Meaning." *International Journal of American Linguistics* 21:91–104.

———. 1952. *The Nature of Culture.* University of Chicago Press.

———. 1948. *Anthropology.* New York: Harcourt Brace Jovanovich.

———. 1943. "Classification of the Yuman Languages." *University of California Publications in Linguistics* 1:21–40.

———. 1939. *Cultural and Natural Areas of Native North America.* University of California Publications in American Archaeology and Ethnology, No. 38.

———. 1937. "Athabascan Kin Term Systems." *American Anthropologist* 39:602–608.

———. 1935. "Walapai Ethnography." *American Anthropological Association,* Memoir 42.

———. 1932. "The Patwin and Their Neighbors." *University of California Publications in American Archaeology and Ethnology* 29:253–364.

———. 1931. "The Seri." *Southwest Museum Papers* 6:1–60.

———. 1928. "Native Culture of the Southwest." *University of California Publications in American Archaeology and Ethnology* 33:375–398.

———. 1925. *Handbook of the Indians of California.* Bureau of American Ethnology, Bulletin 78.

———. 1917. "Zuni Kin and Clan." *American Museum of Natural History, Anthropological Papers,* vol. 28.

———. 1915. "Serian, Tequistlatecan, and Hokan." *University of California Publications in American Archaeology and Ethnology* 11:279–290.

———. 1908. "Ethnography of the Cahuilla Indians." *University of California Publications in American Archaeology and Ethnology* 8:29–68.

———. 1907. "Ethnology of the Gros Ventre." *Anthropological Papers of the American Museum of Natural History* 1:145–281.

———. 1902–1907. "The Arapaho." *Bulletin of the American Museum of Natural History* 18:1–229, 279–454.

———. 1899. "The Eskimo of Smith Sound." *Bulletin of the American Museum of Natural History* 12:265–327.

KRUG, J. A. 1948. *The Navaho, Report of J. A. Krug, Secretary of the Interior.* Washington: Department of the Interior.

KURTZ, D. V. 1974. "Peripheral and Transitional Markets: the Aztec Case." *American Ethnologist* 1:4, 685–706.

LA BARRE, W. 1969. *The Peyote Cult.* New York: Schocken Books.

———. 1960. "Twenty Years of Peyote Studies." *Current Anthropology* 1:45–60.

LAFARGE, O., ED. 1942. *The Changing Indian.* University of Oklahoma Press.

LAGUNA, F. DE. 1960. *The Story of a Tlingit Community.* Bureau of American Ethnology, Bulletin 172.

———. 1947. *The Prehistory of Northern North America as Seen from the Yukon.* Society for American Archaeology, Memoir 12.

LAMB, S. M. 1964. "The Classification of the Uto-Aztecan Languages." *University of California Publications in Linguistics* 34:106–125.

———. 1959. "Some Proposals for Linguistic Taxonomy." *Anthropological Linguistics* 1:33–49.

———. 1958. "Linguistic Prehistory in the Great Basin." *International Journal of American Linguistics* 24:95–100.

LANDES, R. 1970. *The Prairie Potawatomi, Tradition and Ritual in the Twentieth Century.* University of Wisconsin Press.

———. 1968. *Ojibwa Religion and the Midewiwin.* University of Wisconsin Press.

———. 1938. "The Ojibwa Woman." *Columbia University Contributions to Anthropology* 31:1–247.

———. 1937. Ojibwa Sociology." *Columbia University Contributions to Anthropology* 29:1–144.

LANE, K. S. 1952. "The Montagnais Indians, 1600–1640." *Publications of the Kroeber Anthropological Society* 7:1–62. Berkeley.

LANGE, C. H. 1959. *Cochiti.* University of Texas Press.

———. 1958. "The Keresan Component of Southwestern Pueblo Culture." *Southwestern Journal of Anthropology* 14:34–50.

———. 1953. "A Reappraisal of the Evidence of Plains Influences among the Rio Grande Pueblos." *Southwestern Journal of Anthropology* 9:212–230.

LANTIS, M. 1960. *Eskimo Childhood and Interpersonal Relationships.* University of Washington Press.

———. 1955. "Problems of Human Ecology in the American Arctic." *Arctic Research (Special Publication of the Arctic Institute of North America),* pp. 195–208.

———. 1954. "Problems of Human Ecology in the North American Arctic." *Arctic* 7:307–320.

———. 1950. "The Religion of the Eskimos." In *Forgotten Religions,* ed. V. Ferm, pp. 309–339. New York: Philosophical Library.

———. 1946. *The Social Culture of the Nunivak Eskimo.* Transactions, American Philosophical Society, vol. 35.

———. 1938. "The Alaskan Whale Cult and its Affinities." *American Anthropologist* 40:438–464.

LARSEN, H., AND RAINEY, F. G. 1948. *Ipiutak and the Arctic Whale Hunting Culture.* Anthropological Papers, American Museum of Natural History, vol. 42.

LATTA, F. F. 1949. *Handbook of Yokuts Indians.* Oildale, California: Bear State Books.

LAUGHLIN, W. S. 1963a. "The Earliest Aleuts." In "Early Man in the Western American Arctic: A Symposium," ed. F. H. West. *Anthropological Papers of the University of Alaska* 10:73–91.

———. 1963b. "Eskimos and Aleuts: Their Origins and Evolution." *Science* 142:633–645.

———, ed. 1951. *Papers on the Physical Anthropology of the American Indian.* Delivered at the Fourth Viking Fund Summer Seminar in Physical Anthropology held at the Viking Fund, September, 1949. New York: The Viking Fund.

———. 1950. "Blood Groups, Morphology, and Population Size of the Eskimos." *Cold Spring Harbor Symposia on Quantitative Biology* 15:165–173.

LE PAGE DU PRATZ, A. 1758. *Histoire de la Louisiane.* 3 vols. Paris.

LEACOCK, E. 1955. "Matrilocality in a Simple Hunting Economy: Montagnais-Naskapi", *Southwestern Journal of Anthropology* 11:31–47.

———. 1954. *The Montagnais Hunting Territory and Fur Trade.* American Anthropological Association, Memoir 78.

LEACOCK, E. B., AND LURIE, N. O. 1971. *North American Indians in Historical Perspective.* New York: Random House.

LECLERCQ, G. 1910. "New Relations of Gaspesia." *Publications of the Champlain Society* 5:1–452.

LEDUC, T. 1957. "The Work of the Indian Claims Commission under the Act of 1946." *Pacific Historical Review,* February 1957.

LEHMANN, W. 1938. *Die Geschichte der Königreiche von Colhuacan und Mexico.* Quellenwerke zur alten Geschichte Amerikas. Stuttgart: W. Kohlhammer.

LEHMANN, W. P. 1962. *Historical Linguistics: An Introduction.* New York: Holt, Rinehart and Winston.

LEHMER, D. J. 1971. "Introduction to Middle Missouri Archeology." *Anthropological Papers,* 1, National Park Service, Washington.

———. 1954. "The Sedentary Horizon of the Northern Plains." *Southwestern Journal of Anthropology* 10:139–159.

LEIGHTON, D. C., AND ADAIR, J. 1966. *People of the Middle Place: A Study of the Zuni Indians.* New Haven: Human Relations Area Files.

LEIGHTON, A. H., AND LEIGHTON, D. C. 1949.

"Gregorio, the Hand-Trembler." *Peabody Museum Papers* 40:1–177.

———. 1944. *The Navaho Door.* Cambridge: Harvard University Press.

LEIGHTON, D. C., AND KLUCKHOHN, C. 1947. *Children of the People.* Cambridge: Harvard University Press.

LEVIN, N. B. 1964. *The Assiniboine Language.* Publication 32, Indiana University Research Center in Anthropology, Folklore, and Linguistics.

LEVI-STRAUSS, C. 1967. "The Story of Asdiwal." In *The Structural Study of Myth and Totemism,* ed. E. Leach, pp. 1–47. London: Tavistock Publications.

LEVINE, S., AND LURIE, N. O. 1971. *The American Indian Today.* Baltimore: Penguin Books.

LEWIS, T. H. 1907. "The Narrative of the Expedition of Hernando de Soto, by the Gentlemen of Elvas." In *Spanish Explorers in the Southern United States, 1528–1543,* ed. J. F. Jameson. New York: Scribner.

LI, AN-CHE. 1937. "Zuni: Some Observations and Some Queries." *American Anthropologist* 39:62–76.

LIPS, J. E. 1947a. "Notes on Montagnais-Naskapi Economy, Ethos." *Journal de la Société des Americanistes* 12:1–78.

———. 1947b. "Naskapi Law." *Transactions of the American Philosophical Society* 37:379–492.

———. 1939. "Naskapi Trade." *Journal de la Societé des Americanistes* 31:129–195.

LLEWELLYN, K. N., AND HOEBEL, E. A. 1941. *The Cheyenne Way.* University of Oklahoma Press.

LOCKWOOD, F. C. 1938. *The Apache Indians.* New York: Macmillan.

LORAM, C. T., AND MCILWRAITH, T. F. 1943. *The North American Today.* University of Toronto Press.

LOUNSBURY, F. 1964. "A Formal Account of the Crow and Omaha-type Kinship Terminologies." In *Explorations in Cultural Anthropology: Essays in Honor of George Peter Murdock,* ed. W. H. Goodenough, pp. 351–393. New York: McGraw-Hill.

———. 1961. "Iroquois-Cherokee Linguistic Relations." In *Symposium on Cherokee and Iroquois Culture,* ed. W. Fenton and J. Gulick, pp. 11–17. Washington: Bureau of American Ethnology, Bulletin 180.

LOWIE, R. H. 1954. *Indians of the Plains.* New York: McGraw-Hill.

———. 1948. "The Tropical Forests: An Introduction." *Bureau of American Ethnology, Bulletin* 143:1–56.

———. 1939. "Ethnographic Notes on the Washo." *University of California Publications in American Archaeology and Ethnology* 36:301–352.

———. 1935. *The Crow Indians.* New York: Holt, Rinehart and Winston.

———. 1924. "Notes on Shoshonean Ethnography." *Anthropological Papers of the American Museum of Natural History* 20:185–314.

———. 1923. "Culture Connection of California and Plateau Shoshonean Tribes." *University of California Publications in American Archaeology and Ethnology* 20:145–156.

———. 1922. "The Material Culture of the Crow Indians." *Anthropological Papers of the American Museum of Natural History* 21:201–270.

———. 1916. "Plains Indian Age-Societies." *Anthropological Papers of the American Museum of Natural History* 11: 877–992.

———. 1910. "The Assiniboine." *Anthropological Papers of the American Museum of Natural History* 4:1–270.

———. 1908. "The Northern Shoshone." *Anthropological Papers of the American Museum of Natural History* 2:169–306.

LUMHOLTZ, C. 1902. *Unknown Mexico.* New York: Charles Scribner's Sons.

LURIE, N. O. 1961a. "The Voice of the American Indian: Report on the American Indian Chicago Conference." *Current Anthropology* 2:478–500.

———. 1961b. *Mountain Wolf Woman.* University of Michigan Press.

MCALLISTER, J. G., AND NEWCOMB, W. W., JR. 1970. *Daveko, Kiowa-Apache Medicine Man, with a Summary of Kiowa-Apache History and Culture.* Texas Memorial Museum, Bulletin 17.

MACCAULEY, C. 1884. "The Seminole Indians of Florida." *Annual Report of the Bureau of American Ethnology* 5:469–531.

MCCLELLAN, C. 1970. "Introduction." Special Issue: Athabascan Studies, *Western Canadian Journal of Anthropology* 2:vi–xix.

———. 1964. "Culture Contacts in the Early Historic Period in Northwestern North America." *Arctic Anthropology* 2:3–15.

MCCLINTOCK, W. 1910. *The Old North Trail.* London: Constable and Company.

MCCOMBE, L.; VOGT, E. Z.; AND KLUCKHOHN, C. 1951. *Navaho Means People.* Cambridge: Harvard University Press.

MACDONALD, G. F. 1968. "Debert: A Paleo-Indian Site in Central Nova Scotia." *Anthropology Papers,* no. 16. Ottawa: National Museum of Canada.

MCFEAT, T. 1966. *Indians of the North Pacific Coast.* Toronto; McLelland and Stewart.

MCGEE, W. J. 1898. "The Seri Indians." *Annual Report of the Bureau of American Ethnology* 17:9–298.

MACGOWAN, E. S. 1942. "The Arikara Indians." *Minnesota Archaeologist* 8:83–122.

MACGOWAN, K. 1953. *Early Man in the New World.* New York: Macmillan.

MACGOWAN, K., AND HESTER, J. A. JR. 1962. *Early Man in the New World.* New York: Doubleday (Anchor Books).

MCGREGOR, G. 1946. *Warriors without Weapons.* University of Chicago Press.

MCGREGOR, J. C. 1959. "The Middle Woodland Period." *Illinois Archaeological Survey,* Bulletin no. 1.

———. 1952. "The Havana Site." *Illinois State Museum, Scientific Paper,* vol. 5.

———. 1941. *Southwestern Archaeology.* New York: Wiley.

MCILWRAITH, T. F. 1948. *The Bella Coola Indians.* 2 vols. University of Toronto Press.

MCKENNAN, R. A. 1969a. "Athapaskan Groupings

and Social Organization in Central Alaska." *National Museum of Canada, Bulletin* 228:93–115. Ottawa.

———. 1969b. "Athapaskan Groups of Central Alaska at the Time of White Contact." *Ethnohistory* 16:335–343.

———. 1965. *The Chandalar Kutchin.* Montreal: Arctic Institute of North America, Technical Paper no. 17.

———. 1959. *The Upper Tanana Indians.* Yale University Publications in Anthropology, vol. 55.

MCKERN, W. C. 1939. "The Midwestern Taxonomic Method as an Aid to Archaeological Culture Study." *American Antiquity* 4:301–313.

———. 1930. *The Kletzien and Nitschke Mound Groups.* Bulletin of the Public Museum of the City of Milwaukee, vol. 3.

MCLEOD, W. C. 1928. *The American Indian Frontier.* New York: Knopf.

———. 1926. "On Natchez Cultural Origins." *American Anthropologist* 28:409–413.

———. 1924. "Natchez Political Evolution." *American Anthropologist* 26:201–229.

MACNEISH, J. H. 1957. "The Poole-Field Letters." *Anthropologica* 4:47–60.

———. 1956. "Leadership Among the Northeastern Athapascans." *Anthropologica* 2:131–163.

MACNEISH, R. S. 1971. "Speculation about How and Why Food Production and Village Life Developed in the Tehuacan Valley, Mexico." *Archaeology* 24:307–315.

———. 1967. "A Summary of the Subsistence." In *The Prehistory of the Tehuacan Valley. Volume I: Environment and Subsistence,* ed. D. S. Byers, pp. 290–309. University of Texas Press.

———. 1960. "Agricultural Origins in Middle America and Their Diffusion into North America." *Katunob,* vol. 1.

———. 1958. *An Introduction to the Archaeology of Southeast Manitoba.* National Museum of Canada, Bulletin 157.

———. 1957. *The Callison Site in the Light of Archaeological Survey of Southwest Yukon.* National Museum of Canada, Bulletin 162.

———. 1956. *Two Archaeological Sites on Great Bear Lake, Northwest Territories, Canada.* Annual Report of the National Museum for the Fiscal Year 1954–1955. Bulletin no. 136.

———. 1954a. "The Pointed Mountain Site Near Fort Liard, Northwest Territories, Canada." *American Antiquity* 19:234–253.

———. 1954b. "The Development of Agriculture and the Concomitant Development of Civilization in Meso-America, Tamaulipas, Mexico." *American Philosophical Society Yearbook 1954,* pp. 323–327.

———. 1952a. "The Archaeology of the Northeastern United States." In *Archaeology of the Eastern United States,* ed. J. B. Griffin, pp. 46–58. University of Chicago Press.

———. 1952b. "Iroquois Pottery Types." *Bulletin of the National Museum of Canada* 124:1–166.

———. 1950. "A Synopsis of the Archeological Sequence in the Sierra de Tamaulipas." *Revista Méxicana de Estudios Antropológicos* 11:79–96.

———. 1947. "A Preliminary Report on Coastal Tamaulipas, Mexico." *American Antiquity* 18:1–14.

MCNICKLE, D. 1973. *Native American Tribalism: Indian Survivals and Renewals.* London, Oxford, and New York: Oxford University Press.

———. 1949. *They Came Here First.* Philadelphia: Lippincott.

MCQUOWN, N. 1955. "The Indigenous Languages of Latin America." *American Anthropologist* 57:501–570.

MCWILLIAMS, C. 1951. *Brothers under the Skin.* Boston: Little, Brown.

MALAN, V. P. 1958. "The Dakota Indian Family." *South Dakota Agricultural Experiment Station Bulletin* 470:1–71.

MALOUF, C. 1966. "Ethnohistory in the Great Basin." *Desert Research Institute Publications in the Social Sciences and Humanities* 1:1–39.

MANDELBAUM, D. G. 1940. "The Plains Cree." *Anthropological Papers of the American Museum of Natural History* 37:155–316.

MARCUS, J. 1973. "Territorial Organization of the Lowland Classic Maya." *Science* 180:911–916.

MARGRY, P. 1875–1886. "Decouvertes et Etablissements des Français dans l'Ouest et dans le Sud de l'Amérique Septentrionale (1614–1754)." *Memoires et Documents Originaux Recueillis et Publies par Pierre Margry.* Paris.

MARQUINA, I. 1960. *El Templo Mayor de México.* Instituto Nacional de Antropológia e Historia. Mexico, D.F.

MARRIOTT, A. 1948. *Maria, the Potter of San Ildefonso.* University of Oklahoma Press.

MARRIOTT, A., AND RACHLIN, C. K. 1972. *American Indian Mythology.* New York: New American Library (Mentor Books).

MARSH, G., AND SWADESH, M. 1951. "The Eskimo-Aleutian Correspondences." *International Journal of American Linguistics* 17:209–216.

MARTIN, J. F. 1968. "A Reconsideration of Havasupai Land Tenure." *Ethnology* 17:450–460.

MARTIN, P. S. 1973. "The Discovery of America." *Science* 179:969–974.

———. 1952. *Mogollon Cultural Continuity and Change: The Stratigraphic Analysis of Tularosa and Cordova Caves.* Chicago Natural History Museum, Fieldiana, vol. 40.

MARTIN, P. S., AND PLOG, F. 1973. *The Archaeology of Arizona, A Study of the Southwest Region.* Garden City, N.Y.: Doubleday (Natural History Press).

MARTIN, P. S.; QUIMBY, G. L.; AND COLLIER, D. 1947. *Indians before Columbus.* University of Chicago Press.

MARTIN, P. S., AND RINALDO, J. B. 1951. "The Southwestern Co-Tradition." *Southwestern Journal of Anthropology* 7:215–219.

MARTIN, P. S.; RINALDO, J. B.; AND BARTER, E. R. 1957. *Late Mogollon Communities.* Chicago Natural History Museum, Fieldiana, vol. 49.

MARTIN, P. S.; RINALDO, J. B.; BLUHM, E.; CULTER, H. C.; AND GRANGE, R., JR. 1952. "Mogollon Cultural

Continuity and Change." *Fieldiana: Anthropology,* vol. 40. Chicago.

MARTIN, P. S.; SCHOENWETTER, J.; AND ARMS, B. C. 1961. "The Last 10,000 Years." *Geochronology Laboratories, University of Arizona.*

MASON, C. 1964. "Natchez Class Structure." *Ethnohistory* 11:120–133.

MASON, J. A. 1950. *The Language of the Papago of Arizona.* The University Museum, University of Pennsylvania.

———. 1946. "Notes on the Indians of the Great Slave Lake Area." *Yale University Publications in Anthropology* 31:1–46.

———. 1912. "The Ethnology of the Salinan Indians." *University of California Publications in American Archaeology and Ethnology* 10:97–240.

MASON, O. T. 1907. "Environment." *Bureau of American Ethnology, Bulletin* 30:427–430.

MASON, R. J. 1962. "The Paleo-Indian Tradition in Eastern North America." *Current Anthropology* 3:227–278.

MATHIASSEN, T. 1928. "Material Culture of the Iglulik Eskimos." *Report of the Fifth Thule Expedition* 6:1–242.

———. 1927. "Archaeology of the Central Eskimos." *Report of the Fifth Thule Expedition* 4:1–533.

MATTHEWS, W. 1902. "The Night Chant." *American Museum of Natural History, Memoir* 6:1–132.

———. 1901. "Navaho Night Chant." *Journal of American Folklore* 14:12–19.

———. 1897. *Navaho Legends.* American Folklore Society, Memoir 5.

———. 1887. "The Mountain Chant." *Annual Report of the Bureau of American Ethnology* 5:379–467.

———. 1877. "Ethnology and Philology of the Hidatsa Indians." *U.S. Geological and Geographical Survey, Miscellaneous Publications* 7:1–239.

MECHLING, W. H. 1958–1959. "The Malecite Indians with Notes on the Micmacs." *Anthropologica* 7:1–160; 8:161–274.

MEIGHAN, C. W. 1959. "Californian Cultures and the Concept of an Archaic Stage." *American Antiquity* 24:289–318.

MEIGS. P. 1939. "The Kiliwa Indians of Lower California." *Ibero-Americana* 15:1–114.

MEKEEL, S. 1936. "The Economy of a Modern Teton Dakota Community." *Yale University Publications in Anthropology* 6:1–14.

MERIAM, L. 1928. "The Problem of Indian Administration." *Institute for Government Research, Brookings Institution.*

MEYER, W. 1971. *Native Americans: The New Indian Resistance.* New York: International Publishers.

MICHELS, J. W. 1973. *Dating Methods in Archaeology.* Studies in Archeology. New York: Seminar Press.

MILFORT, L. 1959. *Memoirs, or A Quick Glance at My Various Travels and My Sojourn in the Creek Nation.* Atlanta, Ga.: Continental Book Company.

MILLER, G. V., AND PARKINS, A. E. 1934. *Geography of North America.* New York: Wiley.

MILLER, W. R. 1966. "Anthropological Linguistics in the Great Basin." In *The Current Status of Anthropological Research in the Great Basin,* ed. W. L. D'Azevedo et al., pp. 75–112. Reno: Desert Research Institute, Social Sciences and Humanities Publications, no. 1.

MIRSKY, J. 1937. "The Dakota." In *Cooperation and Competition among Primitive Peoples,* ed. M. Mead, pp. 382–427. New York: McGraw-Hill.

MISHKIN, B. 1940. *Rank and Warfare among the Plains Indians.* American Ethnological Society, Memoir 3.

MOMADAY, N. S. 1969. *House Made of Dawn.* New York: Harper & Row.

MONZON, A. 1949. "El Calpulli en la Organización Social de los Tenochca." *Publicaciones del Instituto de Historia,* no. 14. Mexico, D.F.

MOONEY, J. 1928. "The Aboriginal Population of American North of Mexico." *Smithsonian Institution, Miscellaneous Collections,* vol. 80.

———. 1896. *The Ghost Dance Religion.* Annual Report of the Bureau of American Ethnology, 14.

MORGAN, L. H. 1954 (and 1901). *League of the Ho-De-No-Sau-Nee or Iroquois.* New Haven: Yale University Press.

MORGAN, W. 1932. "Navaho Dreams." *American Anthropologist* 34:390–405.

MORICE, A. G. 1895. "Notes Archaeological, Industrial, and Sociological on the Western Denés." *Transactions of the Royal Canadian Institute* 4:1–222.

MORLEY, S. 1956. *The Ancient Maya.* Stanford University Press.

MORRIS, E. H. 1939. "Archaeological Studies in the La Plata District, Southwestern Colorado and Northwestern New Mexico." *Carnegie Institution of Washington Publication,* no. 519. Washington.

MÜLLER, W. 1955. *Weltbild and Kult der Kwakiutl Indianer.* Studien zur Kulturkunde, vol. 15. Wiesbaden.

———. 1954. *Die blaue Hütte.* Studien zur Kulturkunde, vol. 12. Wiesbaden.

MURDOCH, J. 1892. "Ethnological Results of the Point Barrow Expedition." *Annual Report of the Bureau of American Ethnology* 9:3–441.

MURDOCK, G. P. 1975. *Ethnographic Bibliography of North America.* 4th ed. New Haven: Human Relations Area Files.

———. 1949. *Social Structure.* New York: Macmillan.

———. 1936. "Rank and Potlatch among the Haida." *Yale University Publications in Anthropology* 13:1–20.

———. 1934. "Kinship and Social Behavior among the Haida. *American Anthropologist* 36:355–385.

MURPHY, R. F., AND MURPHY, Y. 1960. "Shoshone-Bannock Subsistence and Society." *University of California Anthropological Records* 16:293–338.

MYER, W. E. 1928. "Indian Trails of the Southeast." *Annual Report of the Bureau of American Ethnology* 42:727–857.

MYERHOFF, B. G. 1974. *Peyote Hunt: The Sacred*

Journey of the Huichol Indians. Ithaca: Cornell University Press.

NANSEN, F. 1893. *Eskimo Life.* London: Longmans, Green Company.

National Park Service. 1955. *A Survey of Archaeology and History in the Arkansas-White-Red River Basins.* Washington.

Navajo Yearbook, The. 1961. Compiled by R. W. Young. Window Rock, Arizona: Navajo Agency.

NEIHARDT, J. G. 1932. *Black Elk Speaks.* New York: Morrow.

NEITZEL, R. S. 1965. *Archeology of the Fatherland Site: the Grand Village of the Natchez.* American Museum of Natural History, Anthropological Publications, vol. 51, part 1.

NELSON, E. W. 1899. *The Eskimo about Bering Strait.* Annual Report of the Bureau of American Ethnology, 18.

NELSON, R. K. 1973. *Hunters of the Northern Forest. Designs for Survival among the Alaskan Kutchin.* University of Chicago Press.

———. 1969. *Hunters of the Northern Ice.* University of Chicago Press.

NEUMANN, G. K. 1952. "Archaeology and Race in the American Indian." In *Archaeology of Eastern United States,* ed. J. B. Griffin, pp. 13–34. University of Chicago Press.

NEUMANN, G. K., AND FOWLER, M. L. 1952. *Hopewellian Sites in the Lower Wabash Valley.* Illinois State Museum, Scientific Papers, vol. 5.

NEWCOMB, W. W., JR. 1974. *North American Indians: An Anthropological Perspective.* Palisades, Calif.: Pacific Goodyear Publishing Co., Inc.

———. 1956. "The Culture and Acculturation of the Delaware Indians." *Anthropological Papers of the Museum of Anthropology of the University of Michigan* 10:1–144.

NEWMAN, S. 1954. "American Indian Linguistics in the Southwest." *American Anthropologist* 56:626–634.

NICHOLSON, H. B. 1971. "Religion in Pre-Hispanic Central Mexico." In *Archaeology of Northern Mesoamerica, Part 1, Handbook of Middle American Indians,* ed. R. Wauchope, vol. 10, pp. 395–466. University of Texas Press.

NOMLAND, G. A. 1938. "Bear River Ethnography." *Anthropological Records* 2:91–123.

———. 1935. "Sinkyone Notes." *University of California Publications in American Archaeology and Ethnology* 36:149–178.

NOON, J. A. *Law and Government of the Grand River Iroquois.* Viking Fund Publications in Anthropology, 12.

NOWOTNY, K. A. 1959. *Die Hieroglyphen des Codex Mendoza. (Der Bau einer mittelamerikanischen Wortschrift.)* Amerikanistische Miszellen, Mitteilungen aus den Museum für Völkerkunde und Vorgeschichte Hamburgs, vol. 25.

NUNEZ, T. A., JR. 1958. "Creek Nativism and the Creek War of 1813–1814." *Ethnohistory* 5:1–47, 131–175, 292–301.

OBERG, K. 1973. *The Social Economy of the Tlingit Indians.* American Ethnological Society, Monograph 55. University of Washington Press.

———. 1955. "Types of Social Structure among the Lowland Tribes of South and Central America." *American Anthropologist* 57:472–487.

———. 1934. "Crime and Punishment in Tlingit Society." *American Anthropologist* 36:145–156.

OKLADNIKOV, A. P. 1959. *Ancient Population of Siberia and Its Culture.* Russian Translation Series of the Peabody Museum of Archaeology and Ethnology, Harvard University, vol. 1.

OLSON, R. L. 1940. "The Social Organization of the Haisla." *Anthropological Records* 2:169–200.

———. 1936. *The Quinault Indians.* University of Washington Publications in Anthropology, 6.

———. 1933. "Clan and Moiety in Native America." *University of California Publications in American Archaeology and Ethnology* 33:351–422.

———. 1927. *Adze, Canoe, and House Types of the Northwest Coast.* University of Washington Publications in Anthropology, 2.

OPLER, M. E. 1969. *Apache Odyssey.* New York: Holt, Rinehart and Winston.

———. 1952. "The Creek 'Town' and the Problem of Creek Indian Political Reorganization." In *Human Problems in Technological Change: A Casebook,* ed. E. H. Spicer. New York: Wiley.

———. 1946. "Childhood and Youth in Jicarilla Apache Society." *Publications of the Frederick Webb Hodge Anniversary Publication Fund, Southwest Museum* 5:1–170.

———. 1943. *The Character and Derivation of Jicarilla Holiness Rites.* University of New Mexico Bulletin, Anthropological Series, 4.

———. 1942. *Myths and Tales of the Chiricahua Apache Indians.* American Folk-Lore Society, Memoir 37.

———. 1941. *An Apache Life-Way.* University of Chicago Press.

———. 1940. *Myths and Legends of the Lipan Apache Indians.* American Folk-Lore Society, Memoir 36.

———. 1936. "A Summary of Jicarilla Apache Culture." *American Anthropologist* 38:620–633.

OPLER, M. K. 1971. "The Ute and Paiute Indians of the Great Basin Southern Rim." In *North American Indians in Historical Perspective,* ed. E. B. Leacock and N. O. Lurie, pp. 257–288. New York: Random House.

ORTIZ, A., ED. 1972. *New Perspectives on the Pueblos.* University of New Mexico Press.

———. 1969. *The Tewa World.* University of Chicago Press.

OSGOOD, C. B. 1971. *The Han Indians: A Compilation of Ethnographic and Historical Data on the Alaska-Yukon Boundary Area.* Yale University Publications in Anthropology, no. 74.

———. 1959. *Ingalik Mental Culture.* Yale University Publications in Anthropology, vol. 56.

———. 1958. *Ingalik Social Culture.* Yale University

Publications in Anthropology, vol. 53.

──────. 1940. *Ingalik Material Culture.* Yale University Publications in Anthropology, vol. 22.

──────. 1937. *The Ethnography of the Tanaina.* Yale University Publications in Anthropology, vol. 16.

──────. 1936a. *Contributions to the Ethnography of the Kutchin.* Yale University Publications in Anthropology, vol. 14.

──────. 1936b. "The Distribution of the Northern Athapaskan Indians." *Yale University Publications in Anthropology* 7:1–23.

──────. 1931. "The Ethnography of the Great Bear Lake Indians." *Canadian Department of Mines, Bulletin* 70:31–92.

OSTERMAN, H. 1942. "The Mackenzie Eskimos, after K. Rasmussen's Posthumous Notes." *Report of the Fifth Thule Expedition* 10:1–166.

OWEN, R. C.; DEETZ, J. J. F.; AND FISHER, A. D. 1967. *The North American Indians: A Sourcebook.* New York: Macmillan.

PARK, W. Z. et al. 1938. "Tribal Distribution in the Great Basin." *American Anthropologist* 40:622–638.

PARKER, A. C. 1913. *The Code of Handsome Lake, the Seneca Prophet.* Albany: New York State Museum Bulletin, no. 163.

PARSONS, E. C. 1941. "Notes on the Caddo." *American Anthropological Association, Memoir* 57:1–76.

──────. 1939. *Pueblo Indian Religion.* 2 vols. University of Chicago Press.

──────. 1936. *Taos Pueblo.* General Series in Anthropology, 2. Madison, Wis: G. Banta Co.

──────. 1933. *Hopi and Zuni Ceremonialism.* American Anthropological Association, Memoir 39.

──────. 1930. "Isleta." *Annual Report of the Bureau of American Ethnology* 47:193–466.

──────. 1929. *The Social Organization of the Tewa of New Mexico.* American Anthropological Association, Memoir 36.

──────. 1928. "Notes on the Pima." *American Anthropologist* 30:455–464.

──────. 1925a. *The Pueblo of Jemez.* New Haven: Yale University Press.

──────. 1925b. *A Pueblo Indian Journal.* American Anthropological Association, Memoir 32.

──────. 1917. *Notes on the Zuni.* American Anthropological Association, Memoir 4.

PEARCE, R. H. 1953. *The Savages of America.* Baltimore: Johns Hopkins University Press.

PERROT, N. 1911. "Memoirs on the Manners, Customs, and Religion of the Savages of North America." In E. H. Blair, *The Indian Tribes of the Upper Mississippi Valley,* ed. E. H. Blair, vol. 1, pp. 25–272. Cleveland: Arthur Clark Company.

PETERSON, F. 1962. *Ancient Mexico: An Introduction to the Pre-Hispanic Cultures.* New York: Capricorn Books.

PETITOT, E. 1891. *Autour de Grande Lac des Esclaves.* Paris.

──────. 1876. *Monographie des Esquimaux Tchiglit du Mackenzie et de l'Anderson.* Paris.

PETTIT, G. A. 1950. "The Quileute of La Push, 1775–1945." *Anthropological Records* 14:1–120.

──────. 1946. "Primitive Education in North America." *University of California Publications in American Archaeology and Ethnology* 43:1–182.

PORSILD, M. P. 1915. "Studies on the Material Culture of the Eskimo in West Greenland." *Meddelelser om Grønland* 51:113–250.

PORTER-WEAVER, M. N. 1972. *The Aztecs, Maya, and Their Predecessors: Archaeology of Mesoamerica.* Academic Press.

PORTER-WEAVER, M. N. 1953. *Tlatilco and the Pre-classic Cultures of the New World.* Viking Fund Publications in Anthropology, no. 19.

POWELL, J. W. 1894. "Report of the Director." *Annual Report of the Bureau of American Ethnology* 12:19–48.

──────. 1891. "Indian Linguistic Families of America North of Mexico." *Annual Report of the Bureau of American Ethnology* 7:7–142.

POWERS, W. K. 1973. *Indians of the Northern Plains.* New York: Capricorn Books.

──────. 1972. *Indians of the Southern Plains.* New York: Capricorn Books.

PRICE, J. A. 1968. "The Migration and Adaptation of American Indians to Los Angeles." *Human Organization* 27:168–175.

PROCTOR, E. D. 1893. *The Song of the Ancient People.* Boston.

PROSKOURIAKOFF, T. 1970. *An Album of Maya Architecture.* University of Oklahoma Press.

──────. 1960. "Historical Implications of a Pattern of Dates at Piedras Negras, Guatemala." *American Antiquity* 25:454–475.

PROVINSE, J. H. 1937. "The Underlying Sanctions of Plains Indian Culture." In *Social Anthropology of North American Indian Tribes,* ed. F. Eggan, pp. 341–376. University of Chicago Press.

PRUFER, O. H. 1964. "The Hopewell Cult." *Scientific American* 211:90–102.

QUIMBY, G. I. 1960. *Indian Life in the Upper Great Lakes: 11,000 B. C. to 1800 A.D.* University of Chicago Press.

──────. 1946. "Natchez Social Structure as an Instrument of Assimilation." *American Anthropologist* 48:134–137.

──────. 1942. "The Natchezan Culture Type." *American Antiquity* 7:255–275.

RADIN, P. 1954, 1956. "The Evolution of an American Prose Epic." *Special Publications of the Bollingen Foundation,* vol. 3, no. 5, pp. 1–99, 193–248.

──────. 1950. "Winnebago Culture as Described by Themselves." *Memoirs of the International Journal of American Linguistics (Indiana University Publications in Anthropology and Linguistics)* 3:1–78.

──────. 1945. *The Road of Life and Death.* New York: Pantheon Books.

RADIN, P. et al. 1954. *Der Gottliche Schelm.* Zurich: Rhein Verlag.

──────. 1932. "The Winnebago," In *Social*

Anthropology, pp. 54–65; 262–285. New York: McGraw-Hill.

———. 1916. *The Winnebago Tribe.* Annual Report of the Bureau of American Ethnology, 37.

———. 1919. "The Genetic Relationship of North American Indian Languages." *University of California Publications in American Archaeology and Ethnology* 14:480–502.

RAGIR, S. 1972. "The Early Horizon in Central California Prehistory." *Contributions of the University of California Archaeological Research Facility,* no. 15. Berkeley.

RAPAPORT, R. N. 1954. *Changing Navaho Religious Values.* Papers of the Peabody Museum of American Archaeology and Ethnology, vol. 41.

RASMUSSEN, K. 1932. "Intellectual Culture of the Copper Eskimo." *Report, Canadian Arctic Expedition* 16:1–148.

———. 1931. *The Netsilik Eskimos.* Report of the Fifth Thule Expedition, vol. 8, nos. 1–2.

———. 1930. *Observations on the Intellectual Culture of the Caribou Eskimos.* Report of the Fifth Thule Expedition, vol. 7, no. 2.

———. 1929. *Intellectual Culture of the Iglulik Eskimos.* Report of the Fifth Thule Expedition, vol. 7, no. 1.

———. 1908. *The People of the Polar North.* London: K. Paul, Trench, Trubner & Co.

RAUSCH, R. 1951. "Notes on the Nunamiut Eskimo and Mammals of the Anaktuvuk Pass Region, Brooks Range, Alaska." *Arctic* 4:147–195.

RAY, V. F. 1942. "Cultural Element Distributions: The Plateau." *Anthropological Records* 8:99–257.

———. 1941. "Historic Backgrounds of the Conjuring Complex in the Plateau and the Plains." In *Language, Culture, and Personality,* ed. L. Spier, pp. 204–216. Menasha: George Banta Company.

———. 1939. *Cultural Relations in the Plateau of Northwestern America.* F. W. Hodge Aniversary Fund, Southwest Museum, vol. 3.

———. 1938. "Lower Chinook Ethnographic Notes." *University of Washington Publications in Anthropology* 7:29–165.

———. 1932. *The Sanpoil and Nespelem, Salishan Peoples of Northeastern Washington.* University of Washington Publications in Anthropology, vol. 5.

RAY, V. F. et al. 1938. "Tribal Distribution in Eastern Oregon and Adjacent Regions." *American Anthropologist* 40:384–415.

REDFIELD, R. 1941. *The Folk Culture of Yucatan.* University of Chicago Press.

REED, E. K. 1956a. "Ceremony in the Valley: A Navaho Girl Blossoms into Womanhood." *Arizona Highways* 32:26–29.

———. 1956b. "Types of Village Plan Layouts in the Southwest." In *Prehistoric Settlement Patterns in the New World,* ed. G. R. Willey, pp. 11–17. Viking Fund Publications in Anthropology, 23.

———. 1955a. "Painted Pottery and Zuni History." *Southwestern Journal of Anthropology* 11:178–193.

———. 1955b. "Trends in Southwestern Archaeology." In *New Interpretations of Aboriginal American Culture History,* ed. B. J. Meggers and C. Evans, pp. 46–58. Washington: Anthropological Society of Washington.

———. 1954. "Transition to History in the Pueblo Southwest." *American Anthropologist* 56:592–597.

———. 1950. "East-Central Arizona Archaeology in Relation to the Western Pueblos." *Southwestern Journal of Anthropology* 6:120–138.

———. 1946. "The Distinctive Features and Distribution of the San Juan Anasazi Culture." *Southwestern Journal of Anthropology* 2:295–305.

REICHARD, G. A. 1950. *Navaho Indian Religion: A Study of Symbolism.* 2 vols. New York: Pantheon Books.

———. 1949. "The Navaho and Christianity," *American Anthropologist* 51:66–71.

———. 1944. *Prayer: The Compulsive Word.* Monographs of the American Ethnological Society, 7.

———. 1939. *Dezba, Woman of the Desert.* New York: Augustin.

———. 1936. *Navaho Shepherd and Weaver.* New York: Macmillan.

———. 1934. *Spider Woman.* New York: Macmillan.

———. 1928. *Social Life of the Navaho Indians.* New York: Columbia University Press. Columbia University, Contributions to Anthropology, 7.

REID, H. 1885. "Account of the Indians of Los Angeles County." *Bulletin of the Essex Institute* 17:1–33.

RIGGS, S. R. 1893. "Dakota Grammar, Texts and Ethnography." *Contributions to North American Ethnology, Department of Interior, U.S. Geographical and Geological Survey of the Rocky Mountain Region,* 9:1–232.

RITCHIE, W. A. 1969. *The Archaeology of New York State.* Rev. ed. Garden City, N.Y.: The Natural History Press.

———. 1955. *Recent Discoveries Suggesting an Early Woodland Burial Cult in the Northeast.* New York State Museum and Science Service, Circular 40.

RITZENTHALER, R. E. 1953. "The Potawotami Indians of Wisconsin." *Bulletins of the Public Museum of the City of Milwaukee* 19:99–174.

———. 1950. "The Oneida Indians of Wisconsin." *Bulletins of the Public Museum of the City of Milwaukee* 19:1–52.

———. 1946. "The Osceola Site—An 'Old Copper' Site Near Potosi, Wisconsin." *The Wisconsin Archaeologist* 27:53–70.

RITZENTHALER, R. E., AND RITZENTHALER, P. 1970. *The Woodland Indians of the Western Great Lakes.* Garden City, N.Y.: Natural History Press.

ROBERTS, F. H. H., JR. 1945. "The New World Paleo-Indian." *Smithsonian Annual Report for 1944,* pp. 403–435.

———. 1936. "Additional Information on the Folsom Complex." *Smithsonian Miscellaneous Collections,* vol. 95.

———. 1935. "A Survey of Southwestern Archaeology." *American Anthropologist* 37:1–35.

———. 1932. *The Village of the Great Kivas on the Zuni Reservation.* Bureau of American Ethnology, Bulletin 111.

ROBERTS, J. M. 1956. *Zuni Daily Life.* Notebook of the Laboratory of Anthropology of the University of Nebraska, vol. 3.

ROBERTSON, D. 1959. *Mexican Manuscript Painting of the Early Colonial Period.* New Haven: Yale University Press.

RODNICK, D. 1938. *The Fort Belknap Assinboine of Montana.* New Haven: Yale University Press.

ROE, F. G. 1955. *The Indian and the Horse.* University of Oklahoma Press.

ROGERS, E. S. 1966. *Subsistence Areas of the Cree-Ojibwa of the Eastern Subarctic: A Preliminary Study.* National Museum of Canada, Bulletin 204, pp. 87–118.

———. 1965. "Leadership among the Indians of Eastern Subarctic Canada." *Anthropologica* 7:263–284.

ROHNER, R. P., ED. 1969. *The Ethnography of Franz Boas.* University of Chicago Press.

ROHNER, R. P., AND ROHNER, E. C. 1970. *The Kwakiutl: Indians of British Columbia.* New York: Holt, Rinehart and Winston.

ROSTLUND, E. 1952. *Freshwater Fish and Fishing in Native North America.* University of California Publications in Geography, vol. 9.

ROUSE, I. 1949. "The Southeast and the West Indies." In *Florida Indian and His Neighbors.* ed. J. W. Griffin, pp. 117–137. Winter Park, Florida: Inter-American Center, Rollins College.

RUPPERT, K.; THOMPSON, J. E. S.; AND PROSKOURIAKOFF, T. 1955. *Bonampak, Chiapas, Mexico.* Washington: Carnegie Institution, Publication 602.

RUSSELL, F. 1908. *The Pima Indians.* Annual Report of the Bureau of American Ethnology, 26.

SABLOFF, J. A. 1973. "New Horizons in Mesoamerican Archaeology." Review of article by M. N. Porter, "The Aztecs, the Maya, and Their Predecessors: Archaeology of Mesoamerica." *American Anthropologist* 75:1768–1774.

SAGARD, T. 1939. "The Long Journey to the Country of the Hurons." *Publications of the Champlain Society* 15:1–411.

SAHAGUN, B. DE. 1938. *Historia General de las Cosas de Nueva Espana,* Florentine MSS., Bk. VI, fol. 213V. Mexico, Editorial Pedro Robredo.

SANDERS, W. T., AND MARINO, J. 1970. *New World Prehistory: Archaeology of the American Indian.* Englewood Cliffs, N.J.: Prentice-Hall.

SANDERS, W. T., AND PRICE, B. J. 1968. *Mesoamerica: The Evolution of a Civilization.* New York: Random House.

SANGER, D. 1967. "Prehistory of the Pacific Northwest Plateau as Seen from the Interior of British Columbia." *American Antiquity* 32:186–197.

SAPIR, E. 1929. "Central and North American Languages." *Encyclopaedia Britannica* 5:138–141.

———. 1917. "The Hokan and Coahuiltecan Languages." *International Journal of American Linguistics* 1:280–290.

———. 1916. *Time Perspective in Aboriginal American Culture, a Study in Method.* Museum Bulletin of the Canada Department of Mines, Geological Survey, Anthropological Series, Memoir 90.

———. 1915. "Southern Paiute and Nahuatl: Preliminary Report." *American Anthropologist* 17:534–558.

———. 1913. "Southern Paiute and Nahuatl: A Study in Uto-Aztekan." *Journal de la Société des Americanistes de Paris* 10:379–425.

SAPIR, E., AND SWADESH, M. 1955. *Native Account of Nootka Ethnography.* Publications of the Indiana University Research Center in Anthropology, Folklore, and Linguistics, 1.

———. 1946. "American Indian Grammatical Categories", *Word* 2:103–112.

SAUER, C. O. 1950. "Cultivated Plants of South and Central America." *Bureau of American Ethnology, Bulletin* 143:487–543.

———. 1934. "The Distribution of Aboriginal Tribes and Languages in Northwestern Mexico." *Ibero-Americana* 5:1–90.

SAYCE, R. U. 1933. *Primitive Arts and Crafts.* Cambridge: Cambridge University Press.

SCHMITT, K., AND SCHMITT, I. A. 1952. *Wichita Kinship Past and Present.* University of Oklahoma Press.

SCHNEIDER, D. M., AND ROBERTS, J. M. 1956. *Zuni Kin Terms.* Laboratory of Anthropology, University of Nebraska, Note Book no. 3.

SCHOENWETTER, J. 1962. "The Pollen Analysis of Eighteen Archaeological Sites in Arizona and New Mexico." In *Chapters in the Prehistory of the Indian Tribes of the United States,* P. S. Martin. et al. Philadelphia: Lippincott.

SCHOOLCRAFT, H. R. 1853–1857. *Information Respecting the History, Condition and Prospects of the Indian Tribes of the United States.* Philadelphia: Lippincott.

SCHUYLER, R. L. 1971. "The History of American Archaeology: An Examination of Procedure." *American Antiquity* 36:383–409.

SCHWARTZ, D. W. 1959. "Culture Area and Time Depth: The Four Worlds of the Havasupai." *American Anthropologist* 61:1060–1070.

SEARS, W. H. 1968. "The State and Settlement Patterns in the New World." In *Settlement Archaeology,* ed. K. C. Chang. Palo Alto: National Press Books.

———. 1954. "The Sociopolitical Organization of pre-Columbian Cultures on the Gulf Coastal Plain." *American Anthropologist* 56:339–346.

———. 1952. "Ceramic Developments in the South Appalachia Province." *American Antiquity* 18:101–110.

SELLARDS, E. H. 1954. *Early Man in America.* University of Texas Press.

SELLARDS, E. H.; EVANS, G. L.; AND MEADE, G. E.
1947. "Fossil Bison and Associated Artifacts from
Plainview, Texas." *Bulletin of the Geological Society of
America* 58:927–954.

SELTZER, C. C. 1944. "Racial Prehistory in the
Southwest and the Hawikuh Zuni." *Peabody Museum
Papers* 23:1937.

SERVICE, E. R. 1971. *Primitive Social Organization.*
New York: Random House.

SHEPHARDSON, M. 1963. *Navajo Ways in
Government: A Study in Political Process.* American
Anthropological Association, Memoir 96.

SHEPHARDSON, M., AND HAMMOND, B. 1970. *The
Navajo Mountain Community: Social Organization and
Kinship Terminology.* University of California Press.

SHETRONE, H. C. 1930. *The Mound Builders.*
New York, Appleton-Century Crofts.

SHIMKIN, D. B. 1953. "The Wind River Shoshone Sun
Dance." *Bureau of American Ethnology, Bulletin*
151:397–484.

————. 1947. "Wind River Shoshone
Ethnography." *Anthropological Records* 5:245–288.

SHIPLEY, W. 1957. "Some Yukian-Penutian Lexical
Resemblances." *International Journal of American
Linguistics* 23:269–274.

SHOOK E. M. 1960. "Tikal Stele 29." *Expedition*
2:28–35.

SHUTLER, R., JR., ED. 1971. "Papers from a
Symposium on Early Man in North America, New
Developments: 1960–1970." *Arctic Anthropology* 8:1–91.

SILVERBERG, J. 1957. "The Kickapoo Indians."
Wisconsin Archaeologist 38:61–181.

SIMMONS, L. 1942. *Sun Chief.* New Haven: Yale
University Press.

SIMPSON, G. E., AND YINGER, J. M. 1957. "American
Indians and American Life." *Annals of the American
Academy of Political and Social Science.* vol. 311.

SIMPSON, G. G. 1933. "A Nevada Fauna of
Pleistocene Type and its Probable Association with
Man." *American Museum Novitates* 667:1–10.

SKINNER, A. 1924–1927. *The Mascoutens of Prairie
Potawotami Indians.* Bulletins of the Public Museum of
the City of Milwaukee, 6.

————. 1926. "Ethnology of the Ioway Indians."
Bulletins of the Public Museum of the City of Milwaukee
5:181–354.

————. 1923–1925. *Observations of the Ethnology of
the Sauk Indians.* Bulletins of the Public Museum of
the City of Milwaukee, 5.

————. 1921. *Material Culture of the Menomini.*
Heye Foundation, Indian Notes and Monographs,
Museum of the American Indian, 20.

————. 1913. "Social Life and Ceremonial Bundles
of the Menomini Indians." *Anthropological Papers of
the American Museum of Natural History* 13:1–165.

————. 1911. "Notes on the Eastern Cree and
Northern Saulteaux." *Anthropological Papers of the
American Museum of Natural History* 9:1–116.

SLOBODIN, R. 1962. *Band Organization of the Peel
River Kutchin.* Ottawa: National Museum of Canada,
Bulletin 179.

————. 1960. "Eastern Kutchin Warfare.
Anthropologica new series, 2:76–93.

SLOTKIN, J. S. 1955. "The Menomini Powwow."
*Publications in Anthropology of the Public Museum of
the City of Milwaukee* 4:1–276.

SMITH, C. E., JR. 1967. "Plant Remains." In *The
Prehistory of the Tehuacan Valley, Volume I:
Environment and Subsistence,* ed. D. S. Byers, pp.
220–225. University of Texas Press.

SMITH, E. R. 1952. "The Archeology of Deadman
Cave, Utah: A Revision." *University of Utah
Anthropological Papers,* no. 10.

SMITH, M. W. 1940. *The Puyallup-Nisqually.* Columbia
University Contributions to Anthropology, 32.

SMITH, N. N. 1957. "Notes on the Malecite of
Woodstock, New Brunswick." *Anthropologica* 5:1–40.

SMITH, W., AND ROBERTS, J. M. 1954. *Zuni Law: A Field
of Values.* Papers of the Peabody Museum, vol. 43.

SONNICHSEN, C. L. 1958. *The Mescalero Apaches.*
University of Oklahoma Press.

SORKIN, A. L. 1971. *American Indians and Federal Aid.*
Washington, D.C.: Brookings Institution.

SPARKMAN, P. S. 1908. "The Culture of the Lusieño
Indians." *University of California Publications in
American Archaeology And Ethnology* 8:187–234.

SPECK, F. G. 1949. *Midwinter Rites of the Cayuga
Long House.* University of Pennsylvania Press.

————. 1945. "The Iroquois." *Bulletin of the
Cranbrook Institute of Science* 23:1–94.

————. 1940. *Penobscot Man.* University of
Pennsylvania Museum.

————. 1935. *Naskapi.* University of Oklahoma
Press.

————. 1928. "Chapters on the Ethnology of the
Powhatan Tribes." *Heye Foundation, Indian Notes and
Monographs, Museum of the American Indian* 5:25–83.

————. 1925. "The Rappahannock Indians of
Virginia." *Heye Foundation, Indian Notes and
Monographs, Musuem of the American Indian* 5:25–83.

————. 1924. "The Ethnic Position of the
Southwestern Algonkian." *American Anthropologist*
26:184–200.

————. 1921. *Beothuk and Micmac.* New York:
Heye Foundation, Indian Notes and Monographs, 22.

————. 1915. "The Family Hunting Band as the
Basis of Algonkian Social Organization." *American
Anthropologist* 17:289–305.

————. 1911. "Ceremonial Songs of the Creek and
Yuchi Indians." *University of Pennsylvania Museum,
Anthropology Publications* 1:157–245.

————. 1909. "Ethnology of the Yuchi Indians."
*University of Pennsylvania Museum, Anthropology
Publications* 1:1–154.

————. 1907. "The Creek Indians of Taskigi
Town." *American Anthropologist* 2:99–164.

SPECK, F. G., AND DEXTER, R. W. 1951. "Utilization of
Animals and Plants by the Micmac Indians of New
Brunswick." *Journal of the Washington Academy of
Sciences* 61:250–259.

SPECK, F. G., AND EISELEY, L. C. 1939. "The Significance of the Hunting Territory Systems of the Algonkian in Social Theory." *American Anthropologist* 41:269–280.

SPENCER, K. 1946. *Reflections of Social Life in the Navaho Origin Myth.* University of New Mexico Publications in Anthropology, no. 3.

SPENCER, R. F. 1972. "The Social Composition of the North Alaskan Whaling Crew." In *Alliance in Eskimo Society,* ed. D. L. Guemple. Supplement to 1971 Proceedings, American Ethnological Society. Seattle: University of Washington Press.

———. 1971. Introduction to *Ethnography and Philology of the Hidatsa Indians,* by W. Matthews, pp. v–xxvi. New York: Johnson Reprint Corp.

———. 1967/68. "Die Organization der Ehe unter den Eskimo Nordalaskas." *Wiener Völkerkundliche Mitteilungen* IX/X:13–31.

———. 1959. *The North Alaskan Eskimo: A Study in Ecology and Society.* Bureau of American Ethnology, Bulletin 171.

———. 1958. "Eskimo Polyandry and Social Organization." *Proceedings, 32nd International Congress of Americanists,* pp. 539–544. Copenhagen: Munksgaard.

———. 1956. "Exhortation and the Klamath Ethos." *Proceedings of the American Philosophical Society* 100:77–86.

———. 1952. "Sklaven and Sklavenbesitz unter den Klamath-Indianern." *Zeitschrift fur Ethnologie* 77:1–6.

SPICER, E. H. 1969. *A Short History of the Indians of the United States.* New York: Van Nostrand Reinhold.

———. 1962. *Cycles of Conquest.* University of Arizona Press.

———. 1961. *Perspectives in American Indian Culture Change.* University of Chicago Press.

———. 1954a. *Potam: A Yaqui Village in Sonora.* American Anthropological Association, Memoir 77.

———. 1954b. "Spanish-Indian Acculturation in the Southwest." *American Anthropologist* 56:663–678.

———. 1940. *Pascua: A Yaqui Village in Arizona.* University of Chicago Press.

SPICER, E. H., AND THOMPSON, R. H., EDS. 1972. *Plural Society in the Southwest.* New York: Interbook.

SPIER, L. 1933. *Yuman Tribes of the Gila River.* University of Chicago Press.

———. 1930. *Klamath Ethnography.* University of California Publications in American Archaeology and Ethnology, vol. 30.

———. 1929. "Problems Arising from the Cultural Position of the Havasupai." *American Anthropologist* 21:213–222.

———. 1928. "Havasupai Ethnography." *American Museum of Natural History, Anthropological Papers* 29:81–392.

———. 1923. "Southern Diegueno Customs." *University of California Publications in American Archaeology and Ethnology* 20:297–358.

SPIER, L., AND SAPIR, E. 1930. "Wishram Ethnography." *University of Washington Publications in Anthropology* 3:151–300.

SPINDEN, H. G. 1908. "The Nez Perce Indians." *American Anthropological Association, Memoir* 2:165–274.

SPINDLER, G. D. 1955. *Sociological and Psychological Processes in Menomini Acculturation.* University of California Publications in Culture and Society, 5.

SPOEHR, A. 1947. "Changing Kinship Systems." *Field Museum of Natural History, Anthropology Series* 33:153–235.

———. 1944. "The Florida Seminole Camp." *Field Museum of Natural History, Anthropological Series* 33:117–150.

———. 1942. "Kinship System of the Seminole." *Field Museum of Natural History, Anthropological Series* 33:31–113.

———. 1941. "Creek Inter-town Relations." *American Anthropologist* 43:132–133.

SPRADLEY, J. P., ED. 1969. *Guests Never Leave Hungry: The Autobiography of James Sewid, A Kwakiutl Indian.* New Haven: Yale University Press.

SQUIER, E. G., AND DAVIS, E. H. 1848. "Ancient Monuments of the Mississippi Valley." *Smithsonian Contributions to Knowledge,* vol. 1. Washington.

STANDS-IN-TIMBER, J., AND LIBERTY, M. 1967. *Cheyenne Memories.* New Haven: Yale University Press.

STEEN, C. R. 1955. *Prehistoric Man in the Arkansas-White-Red River Basins.* Washington: National Park Service.

STEENSBY, H. P. 1910. "Contributions to the Ethnology and Anthropogeography of the Polar Eskimos." *Meddelelser om Gronland* 34:253–405.

STEFÁNSSON, V. 1924. *My Life with the Eskimo.* New York: Macmillan.

STEINER, STAN. 1968. *The New Indians.* New York: Harper & Row.

STERN, B. J. 1934. "The Lummi Indians of Northwest Washington." *Columbia University Contributions to Anthropology* 17:1–127.

STERN, T. 1966. *The Klamath Tribe.* American Ethnological Society, Monograph 41. University of Washington Press.

———. 1956. "Some Sources of Variability in Klamath Mythology." *Journal of American Folklore* 69:1–12, 135–146, 377–386.

———. 1952. "Chickahominy." *Proceedings of the American Philosophical Society* 96:157–225.

———. 1948. *The Rubber-Ball Games of the Americas.* American Ethnological Society, Monograph 17. New York: Augustin.

STEVENSON, M. C. 1904. *The Zuni Indians.* Annual Reports of the Bureau of American Ethnology, vol. 23.

STEWARD, J. H. 1955. *Theory of Culture Change: The Methodology of Multilinear Evolution.* University of Illinois Press.

———. 1943. "Culture Element Distributions: Northern and Gosuite Shoshoni." *Anthropological Records* 8:203–392. Berkeley.

———. 1941. "Culture Element Distributions: Nevada Shoshoni". *Anthropological Records*

4:209–360. Berkeley.

———. 1938. *Basin-Plateau Aboriginal Socio-political Groups.* Bureau of American Ethnology, Bulletin 120.

———. 1937. "Ecological Aspects of Southwestern Society." *Anthropos* 32:87–104.

———. 1933. "Ethnography of the Owens Valley Paiute." *University of California Publications in American Archaeology and Ethnology* 33:233–350.

STEWART, K. M. 1947. "Mohave Warfare." *Southwestern Journal of Anthropology* 3:257–278.

———. 1946. "Spirit Possession in Native America." *Southwestern Journal of Anthropology* 2:323–339.

STEWART, O. C. 1966. "Tribal Distributions and Boundaries in the Great Basin." In *The Current Status of Anthropological Research in the Great Basin: 1964,* pp. 167–238. Desert Research Institute, Social Sciences and Humanities Publications, 1. Reno.

———. 1942. "Culture Element Distributions: Ute-Southern Paiute." *Anthropological Records* 6:231–355.

———. 1941. "Northern Paiute." *Anthropological Records* 4:362–446.

STEWART, T. D. 1960. "A Physical Anthropologist's View of the Peopling of the New World." *Southwestern Journal of Anthropology* 15:259–273.

STIGGINS, G. 1831–1844. "A Historical Narrative of the Genealogy Traditions and Downfall of the Ispocaga or Creek Tribe of Indians, Written by One of the Tribe." In "Creek Nativism and the Creek War of 1813–1814," by T. A. Nunez, Jr. *Ethnohistory* 5:1–47, 131–175, 292–301.

STIRLING, M. W. 1942. *Origin Myth of Acoma.* Bureau of American Ethnology, Bulletin 135.

STOLTMAN, J. B. 1972. "The Late Archaic in the Savannah River Region." In *Fiber-Tempered Pottery in Southeastern United States and Northern Colombia: Its Origins, Context, and Significance,* ed. R. P. Bullen and J. B. Stoltman. Florida Anthropological Society Publications, no. 6.

STRONG, W. D. 1929. "Aboriginal Society in Southern California." *University of California Publications in American Archaeology and Ethnology* 26:36–273.

———. 1927. "An Analysis of Southwestern Society." *American Anthropologist* 29:1–61.

STRUEVER, S. 1968. "Woodland Subsistence Settlement Systems in the Lower Illinois Valley." In *New Perspectives in Archeology,* ed. S. R. Binford and L. R. Binford. Chicago: Aldine.

———. 1962. "Apple Creek Archaeological Excavation." *The Carrollton Gazette-Patriot,* September 1962.

STRUEVER, S., AND VICKERY, K. D. 1973. "The Beginnings of Cultivation in the Midwest-Riverine Area of the United States." *American Anthropologist* 75:1197–1220.

STURTEVANT, W. C. 1964. "Studies in Ethnoscience." *American Anthropologist,* 66 (2), *Transcultural Studies in Cognition,* pp. 99–131. Washington: American Anthropological Association.

———. 1960. *The Significance of Ethnological Similarities between Southeastern North America and the Antilles.* Yale University Publications in Anthropology, no. 64.

———. 1958. "Accomplishments and Opportunities in Florida Indian Ethnology." *Florida State University,* 2:15–55.

———. 1954. "The Medicine Bundles and Busks of the Florida Seminole." *Florida Anthropologist* 7:31–72.

SWADESH, M. 1967. "Lexicostatistic Classification." In *Linguistics, Handbook of Middle American Indians,* vol. 5, ed. R. Wauchope, pp. 79–116. University of Texas Press.

———. 1959. "The Mesh Principle in Comparative Linguistics." *Anthropological Linguistics* 1:7–14.

———. 1954. "Time Depths of American Linguistic Groupings." *American Anthropologist* 56:361–377.

———. 1953. "Mosan I–II." *International Journal of American Linguistics* 19:26–44, 233–236.

———. 1946. "South Greenlandic." *Viking Fund Publications in Anthropology* 6:30–54.

SWAN, J. G. 1868. "The Indians of Cape Flattery." *Smithsonian Contributions to Knowledge* 16:1–106.

SWANTON, J. R. 1952. *The Indian Tribes of North America.* Bureau of American Ethnology, Bulletin 145.

———. 1946. *The Indians of the Southeastern United States.* Bureau of American Ethnology, Bulletin 137.

———. 1931. *Source Material for the Social and Ceremonial Life of the Choctaw Indians.* Bureau of American Ethnology, Bulletin 103.

———. 1929. *Myths and Tales of the Southeastern Indians.* Bureau of American Ethnology, Bulletin 88.

———. 1928a. "Aboriginal Culture of the Southeast." *Bureau of American Ethnology, Bulletin* 42:673–726.

———. 1928b. "Religious Beliefs and Medical Practices of the Creek Indians." *Annual Report of the Bureau of American Ethnology* 42:473–672.

———. 1928c. *Social Organization and Social Usages of the Indians of the Creek Confederacy.* Annual Report of the Bureau of American Ethnology, 42.

———. 1928d. "Social and Religious Beliefs and Usages of the Chickasaw Indian." *Annual Report of the Bureau of American Ethnology* 44:169–273.

———. 1928e. "The Interpretation of Aboriginal Mounds by Means of Creek Indian Customs." *Annual Reports, Smithsonian Institution,* pp. 495–506.

———. 1924. "The Muskogean Connection of the Natchez Language." *International Journal of American Linguistics* 3:46–75.

———. 1922. *Early History of the Creek Indians and Their Neighbors.* Bureau of American Ethnology, Bulletin 73.

———. 1911. *Indian Tribes of the Lower Mississippi Valley and Adjacent Coast of the Gulf of Mexico.* Bureau of American Ethnology, Bulletin 43.

———. 1908. "Social Condition, Beliefs and Linguistic Relationship of the Tlingit Indians." *Annual Report of the Bureau of American Ethnology* 26:391–486.

———. 1905. *Contributions to the Ethnology of the Haida.* American Museum of Natural History, Memoir 8.

TANTAQUIDGEON, G. 1942. *A Study of Delaware Indian Medicine Practices and Folk Beliefs.* Pennsylvania Historical Commission.

TAX, S., ED. 1952a. *Heritage of Conquest.* University of Chicago Press.

TAX, S., ED. 1952b. *Indian Tribes of Aboriginal America.* Selected Papers of the XXIXth International Congress of Americanists. University of Chicago Press.

TAYLOR, T. W. 1972. *The States and Their Indian Citizens.* Washington: U.S. Bureau of Indian Affairs.

TEIT, J. A. 1956. "Field Notes on the Tahltan and Ksaka Indians." *Anthropologica* 3:39–171.

———. 1930. "The Salishan Tribes of the Western Plateau." *Annual Report of the Bureau of American Ethnology* 45:295–396.

———. 1928. "The Middle Columbia Salish." *University of Washington Publications in Anthropology* 2:83–128.

———. 1909. "The Shuswap. *American Museum of Natural History, Memoir* 4:447–758.

———. 1906. "The Lillooet Indians." *American Museum of Natural History, Memoir* 4:193–300.

———. 1900. "The Thompson Indians." *American Museum of Natural History, Memoir* 2:163–392.

TERRA, H. DE.; ROMERO, J.; AND STEWART, T. D. 1949. *Tepexpan Man.* Viking Fund Publications in Anthropology, no. 11.

THALBITZER, W. 1917, 1921, 1941. "The Ammasalik Eskimo." *Meddelelser om Gronland* 40:113–564, 569–738; 53:435–481.

———. 1911. "Eskimo." *Bureau of American Ethnology, Bulletin* 40:967–1069.

THOMAS, C. 1894. *Introduction: Report on the Mound Explorations of the Bureau of American Ethnology.* Annual Report of the Bureau of American Ethnology, 12.

THOMPSON, J. E. S. 1973. *The Rise and Fall of Maya Civilization.* University of Oklahoma Press.

———. 1959. "Systems of Hieroglyphic Writing in Middle America and Methods of Deciphering Them." *American Antiquity* 24:349–364.

———. 1954. *The Rise and Fall of Maya Civilization.* University of Oklahoma Press.

THOMPSON, L. 1950. *Culture in Crisis: A Study of the Hopi Indians.* New York: Harper & Row.

———. 1945. "Logico-Aesthetic Integration in Hopi Culture." *American Anthropologist* 47:540–554.

THOMPSON, L., AND JOSEPH, A. 1945. *The Hopi Way.* University of Chicago Press.

THOMPSON, S. 1966. *Tales of the North American Indians.* Indiana University Press.

THORNTON, H. R. 1931. *Among the Eskimos of Wales, Alaska.* Baltimore: Johns Hopkins University Press.

THWAITES, R. G. 1896–1901. *The Jesuit Relations and Allied Documents.* (Travels and Explorations of the Jesuit Missionaries in New France). 73 vols. Cleveland: Burrows Brothers Company.

TITIEV, M. 1944. "Old Oraibi." *Peabody Museum Papers* 22:1–277.

TOLSTOY, P. 1974. "Mesoamerica." In *Prehispanic America,* ed. S. Gorenstein, pp. 29–64. New York: St. Martin's Press.

TOOKER, E. 1964. *An Ethnography of the Huron Indians, 1615–1649.* Bureau of American Ethnology, Bulletin 190.

———. 1963. "Natchez Social Organization: Fact or Anthropological Folklore?" *Ethnohistory* 10:358–372.

TOZZER, A. M. 1941. *Landa's Relacion de las Cosas de Yucatán.* Cambridge.

TRIGGER, B. G. 1969. *The Huron: Farmers of the North.* New York: Holt, Rinehart and Winston.

TROWBRIDGE, C. C. 1939. "Shawnee Traditions." *Occasional Contributions from the Museum of Anthropology of the University of Michigan* 7:1–71.

———. 1938. "Meermeear Traditions." *Occasional Contributions from the Museum of Anthropology of the University of Michigan* 7:1–91.

TURNER, L. M. 1894. "Ethnology of the Ungava District." *Annual Report of the Bureau of American Ethnology* 11:159–267, 267–350.

TURNEY-HIGH, H. H. 1941. *Ethnography of the Kutenai.* American Anthropological Association, Memoir 56.

———. 1937. *The Flathead Indians of Montana.* American Anthropological Association, Memoir 48.

UNDERHILL, R. M. 1965. *Red Man's Religion.* University of Chicago Press.

———. 1956. *The Navahos.* University of Oklahoma Press.

———. 1954. "Intercultural Relations in the Greater Southwest." *American Anthropologist* 56:645–656.

———. 1953. *Red Man's America.* University of Chicago Press.

———. 1948. *Ceremonial Patterns in the Greater Southwest.* Monographs of the American Ethnological Society, 13.

———. 1946a. *First Penthouse Dwellers of America.* Santa Fe: Laboratory of Anthropology.

———. 1946b. *Papago Indian Religion.* Columbia University Contributions to Anthropology, 33.

———. 1941. *The Northern Paiute Indians.* Indian Life and Customs Pamphlets, 1. Washington: U.S. Bureau of Indian Affairs.

———. 1939. *Social Organization of the Papago Indians.* Columbia University Contributions to Anthropology, 30.

———. n.d. *Workaday Life of the Pueblos.* Indian Life and Customs Pamphlets, 4. Phoenix, Arizona: Phoenix Indian School.

U.S. De Soto Expedition Commission 1939. "Final Report of the United States De Soto Expedition Commission." *House Document* 71.

VAILLANT, G. C. 1962. *Aztecs of Mexico: Origin, Rise and Fall of the Aztec Nation.* Revised and annotated by S. B. Vaillant. Garden City, N.Y.: Doubleday.

———. 1941. *The Aztecs of Mexico.* Garden City, N.Y.: Doubleday.

VAN STONE, J. W. 1974. *Athapaskan Adaptations.* Chicago: Aldine.

_____. 1965. _The Changing Culture of the Snowdrift Chipewyan._ Ottawa: National Museum of Canada, Bulletin 209.

_____. 1963. "Changing Patterns of Indian Trapping in the Canadian Subarctic." _Arctic_ 16:159–174.

VETROMILE, E. 1866. _The Abnakis and Their History._ New York.

VICTOR, P. E. 1940. "Contributions à L'Ethnographie des Eskimo d'Angmassalik." _Meddelelser om Grønland_ 125:1213.

VOEGELIN, C. F. 1941. "North American Indian Languages Still Spoken and Their Genetic Relationships." In _Language, Culture, and Personality: Essays in Memory of Edward Sapir,_ ed. L. Spier, pp. 15–40. Menasha: Sapir Memorial Fund.

VOEGELIN, C. F., AND VOEGELIN, F. M. 1964. "Languages of the World: Native America, Fascicle One." _Anthropological Linguistics_ 6:1–149.

_____. 1957. _Hopi Domains: A Lexical Approach to the Problem of Selection._ Indiana University Publications in Anthropology and Linguistics, Memoir 14.

VOEGELIN, C.F., AND VOEGELIN, E. W. 1944. "Map of the North American Indian Languages." _American Ethnological Society,_ Publication 20.

VOEGELIN, E. W. 1955–1956. "The Northern Paiute of Central Oregon." _Ethnohistory_ 2:95–132, 241–272; 3:1–10.

VOGT, E. Z. 1951. _Navaho Veterans._ Peabody Museum Papers, vol. 41.

WADDELL, J. O., AND WATSON O. M., eds. 1973. _American Indian Urbanization._ Lafayette: Purdue, Institute for the Study of Social Change, Department of Sociology and Anthropology Institute Monograph Series, no. 4.

_____, eds. 1971. _The American Indian in Urban Society._ Boston: Little, Brown.

WALKER, D. E., JR. 1972. _The Emergent Native Americans._ Boston: Little, Brown.

WALKER, E. F. 1947. _America's Indian Background._ Southwest Museum Leaflet, no. 18.

_____. 1946. _World Crops Derived from the Indians._ Southwest Museum Leaflet, no. 17.

WALKER, J. R. 1917. "The Sun Dance and Other Ceremonies of the Oglala Division of the Teton Dakota." _American Museum of Natural History, Anthropological Papers_ 16:51–221.

WALLACE, A. F. C. 1970. _Death and Rebirth of the Seneca._ New York: Knopf.

_____. 1951. _The Modal Personality of the Tuscarora Indians._ Bureau of American Ethnology, Bulletin 150.

WALLACE, E., AND HOEBEL, E. A. 1952. _The Comanches._ University of Oklahoma Press.

WALLACE, W. J. 1947. "The Dream in Mohave Life." _Journal of American Folk-Lore_ 60:252–258.

WALLIS, W. D. 1947. _The Canadian Dakota._ American Museum of Natural History, Anthropological Papers, 148.

WALLIS, W. D., AND WALLIS, R. S. 1957. _The Malecite Indians of New Brunswick._ National Museum of Canada, Bulletin 148.

_____. 1955. _The Micmac Indians of Eastern Canada._ Minneapolis: University of Minnesota Press.

WASHBURN, W. E., ED. 1964. _The Indian and the White Man._ Garden City, N.Y.: Doubleday.

WAUCHOPE, R. 1970. _The Indian Background of Latin American History: the Maya, Aztec, Inca, and their Predecessors._ New York: Knopf (Borzoi Books on Latin America).

_____, ED. 1964a. _Handbook of Middle American Indians._ 13 vols. University of Texas Press.

_____. 1964b. "Southern Mesoamerica." In _Prehistoric Man in the New World._ ed. J. D. Jennings and E. Norbeck, pp. 331–388. University of Chicago Press.

_____. 1962. _Lost Tribes and Sunken Continents._ University of Chicago Press.

_____. 1956. _Seminars in Archaeology._ Memoirs of the Society for American Archaeology, no. 11.

_____. 1950. "A Tentative Sequence of pre-Classic Ceramics in Middle America." _Middle American Records, Tulane University_ 1:14, 211–250.

WAX, M. L. 1971. _Indian Americans: Unity and Diversity._ Englewood Cliffs, N.J.: Prentice-Hall.

WEAVER, T., ED. 1974. _Indians of Arizona: A Contemporary Perspective._ University of Arizona Press.

WEAVER, T. A., AND GARTRELL, R. H. 1974. "The Urban Indian: Man of Two Worlds." In _Indians of Arizona: A Contemporary Perspective,_ ed. T. A. Weaver, pp. 72–96. University of Arizona Press.

WEBB, C. H. 1968. "The Extent and Content of Poverty Point Culture." _American Antiquity_ 33:297–321.

WEBB, W. S., AND ELLIOT, J. B. 1942. _The Robbins Mounds._ University of Kentucky Reports in Anthropology and Archaeology, vol. 5.

WEBB, W. S., AND SNOW, C. E. 1945. _The Adena People._ University of Kentucky Reports in Anthropology and Archaeology, vol. 6.

WEDEL, M. M. 1959. "Oneota Sites on the Upper Iowa River." _The Missouri Archaeologist_ 21:1–181.

WEDEL, W. R. 1961a. "Plains Archaeology." _American Antiquity_ 2:24–32.

_____. 1961b. _Prehistoric Man on the Great Plains._ Norman: University of Oklahoma Press.

WELSH, A. 1970. "Community Pattern and Settlement Pattern in the Development of Old Crow Village, Yukon Territory." _Western Canadian Journal of Anthropology_ 2:17–30.

WEST, F. H., ED. 1963. "Early Man in the Western American Arctic: A Symposium." _Anthropological Papers of the University of Alaska,_ vol. 10, no. 2.

WEYER, E. M. 1932. _The Eskimos._ New Haven: Yale University Press.

WHEAT, J. B. 1972. "The Olsen-Chubbuck Site: A Paleo-Indian Bison Kill." _American Antiquity,_ vol. 37, no. 1, pt. 2. (Memoirs of the Society for American Archaeology, no. 26. Washington.)

_____. 1967. "A Paleo-Indian Bison Kill" _Scientific_

American 216:44–52.

———. 1955. *Mogollon Culture Prior to A. D. 1000.* American Anthropological Association, Memoir 82.

———. 1954. "Southwestern Cultural Interrelationships and the Question of Area Co-tradition." *American Anthropologist* 56:576–586.

WHITAKER, T. W.; CUTLER, H. C.; AND MCNEISH, R. S. 1957. "Cucurbit Materials from Three Caves near Ocampo. Tamaulipas." *American Antiquity* 22:352–358.

WHITE, D. R.; MURDOCK, G. P.; AND SCAGLION, R. 1971. "Natchez Class and Rank Reconsidered." *Ethnology* 10:369–388.

WHITE, L. A. 1964. "The World of the Keresan Pueblo Indians." In *Primitive View of the World,* ed. S. Diamond, pp. 83–94. New York: Columbia University Press.

———. 1962. *The Pueblo of Sia, New Mexico.* Bureau of American Ethnology, Bulletin 184.

———. 1943. "New Material from Acoma." *Bulletin of the Bureau of American Ethnology* 136:301–359.

———. 1942. *The Pueblo of Santa Ana.* American Anthropological Association, Memoir 40.

———. 1935. *The Pueblo of Santo Domingo.* American Anthropological Association, Memoir 43.

———. 1932. *The Pueblo of San Felipe.* American Anthropological Association, Memoir 38.

——— _. 1930. "The Acoma Indians." *Annual Reports of the Bureau of American Ethnology* 47:17–192.

WHITEFORD, A. H., AND ZIM, H. S. 1970. *North American Indian Arts.* New York: Golden Press.

WHITING, B. B. 1950. *Paiute Sorcery.* Viking Fund Publications in Anthropology, 15.

WHITMAN, W. 1947. *The Pueblo Indians of San Ildefonso.* Columbia University Contributions to Anthropology, vol. 34.

———. 1937. "The Oto." *Columbia University Contributions to Anthropology* 28:1–32.

WHORF, B. L. 1957. "A Contribution to the Study of the Aztec Language. (Circa 1928)." In *Microfilm Collection on Manuscripts of Middle American Cultural Anthropology, no. 42.*

———. 1956. *Language, Thought and Reality.* New York: Wiley.

———. 1935. "The Comparative Linguistics of Uto-Aztecan." *American Anthropologist* 37:600–608.

WHORF, B. L., AND TRAGER, G. L. 1937. "The Relationships of Uto-Aztecan and Tanoan." *American Anthropologist* 39:609–624.

WILL, G. F. 1924. "Archaeology of the Missouri Valley." *American Museum of Natural History, Anthropological Papers* 22:284–344.

WILL, G. F., AND HECKER, T. C. 1944. "Upper Missouri River Valley Aboriginal Culture in North Dakota." *North Dakota Historical Quarterly,* vol. 11, nos. 1, 2, pp. 5–126.

WILL, G. F., AND SPINDEN, H. J. 1906. *The Mandans: A Study of Their Culture, Archaeology and Language.* Peabody Museum Papers, vol. 3.

WILLEY, G. R. 1971. *An Introduction to American Archaeology: South America,* vol. 2. Englewood Cliffs, N.J.: Prentice-Hall.

———. 1968. "One Hundred Years of Archaeology." In *One Hundred Years of Archaeology,* ed. J. O. Brew, pp. 29–53. Cambridge: Harvard University Press.

———. 1966. *An Introduction to American Archaeology: North and Middle America,* vol. 1. Englewood Cliffs, N.J.: Prentice-Hall.

———. 1958. "Archaeological Perspective on Algonkian-Gulf Linguistic Relationships." *Southwestern Journal of Anthropology* 14:265–272.

———. 1956. "The Structure of Ancient Maya Society." *American Anthropologist* 58:777–782.

———. 1955. "The Prehistoric Civilizations of Nuclear America." *American Anthropologist* 57:571–593.

WILLEY, G. R., AND SABLOFF, J. A. 1974. *A History of American Archeology.* San Francisco: Freeman.

WILLEY, G. R. AND SHIMKIN, D. B. 1971. "The Collapse of Classic Maya Civilization in the Southern Lowlands: A Symposium Summary Statement." *Southwestern Journal of Anthropology* 27:1, 1–18.

WILLIAMS, A. W. 1970. *Navajo Political Process.* Smithsonian Contributions to Anthropology, 9.

WILLIAMS, R. 1643. *A Key into the Language of America.* London.

WILLIS, W. S. 1963. "Patrilineal Institutions in Southeastern North America." *Ethnohistory* 10:250–269.

WILSON, G. L. 1934. "The Hidatsa Earth Lodge." *American Museum of Natural History, Anthropological Papers* 33:320–341.

———. 1917. *Agriculture of the Hidatsa Indians: An Indian Interpretation.* University of Minnesota Studies in the Social Sciences, no. 9.

WINCHELL, N. H. 1911. *The Aborigines of Minnesota.* Minnesota Historical Society.

WINTERS, H. D. 1968. "Value Systems and Trade Cycles of the Late Archaic in the Midwest." In *New Perspectives in Archeology,* ed. S. R. Binford and L. R. Binford. Chicago: Aldine.

WISSLER, C. 1948. *Indians of the United States.* Garden City, N.Y.: Doubleday.

———. 1946. "Our Culture Debt to the Indians." In *When Peoples Meet,* ed. A. Locke and B. H. Stern, pp. 81–85. New York: Hinds, Hayden, and Eldredge.

———. 1944. "The Origin of the American Indian." *Natural History Magazine,* September 1944.

———. 1938 (1917). *The American Indian.* New York: Macmillan.

———. 1937. "Contributions of the American Indian." In *One America, Our Racial and National Minorities,* ed. F. J. Brown and J. S. Roucek. New York: Lippincott.

———. 1927. *North American Indians of the Plains.* New York: American Museum of Natural History, Handbook Series.

———. 1912. *Societies and Ceremonial Associations in the Oglala Division of the Teton-Dakota.* American Museum of Natural History, Anthropological Papers, vol. 11.

———. 1911. "The Social Life of the Blackfoot Indians." *American Museum of Natural History, Anthropological Papers* 7:1–64.

———. 1910. "Material Culture of the Blackfoot Indians." *American Museum of Natural History, Anthropological Papers* 5:1–175.

WITHERSPOON, G. J. 1971. "A New Look at Navaho Social Organization." *American Anthropologist* 72:55–65.

WITHERSPOON, Y. 1961. "A Statistical Device for Comparing Trait Lists." *American Antiquity* 26:433–436.

WITTHOFT, J., AND HUNTER, W. A. 1955. "The Seventeenth-Century Origins of the Shawnee." *Ethnohistory* 2:42–57.

WOOD, W. R. 1967. "An Interpretation of Mandan Culture History." *River Basin Surveys Papers*, no. 39. *Bureau of American Ethnology, Bulletin* no. 198.

WOODBURY, R. 1960. "The Hohokam Canals at Pueblo Grande, Arizona." *American Antiquity* 26:267–270.

WOODWARD, T. S. 1939. *Woodward's Reminiscences of the Creek, or Muscogee Indians*. Tuscaloosa: Alabama Book Store.

WORMINGTON, H. M. 1957. *Ancient Man in North America*. 4th ed. Denver Museum of Natural History, "Popular Series," no. 4.

WRIGHT, H. E. JR., AND FREY, D. G., EDS. 1965. *The Quaternary of the United States*. A Review Volume for the VII Congress of the International Association for Quaternary Research.

WRIGHT, J. V. 1966. *The Ontario Iroquois Tradition*. National Museum of Canada, Bulletin 210.

WYMAN, L. C. 1970. *Blessingway*. University of Arizona Press.

YANOVSKY, E. 1936. "Food Plants of the North American Indians." *U.S. Department of Agriculture, Miscellaneous Publications* 237:1–82.

YARROW, H. C. 1881. "A Further Contribution to the Study of the Mortuary Customs of the North American Indians." *Annual Reports of the Bureau of American Ethnology* 1:89–203.

———. 1880. *Introduction to the Study of Mortuary Customs among the North American Indians*. Washington, D.C.

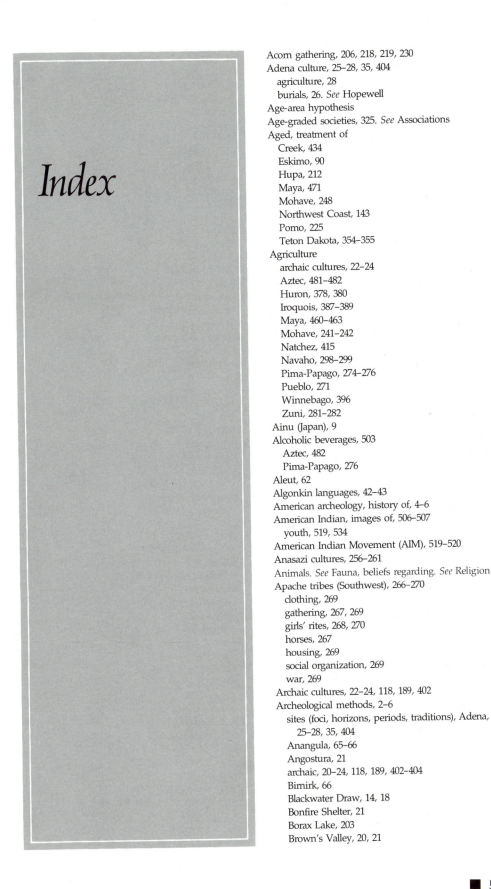

Index

87 88 89 90   20 19 18 17 16 15 14 13 12

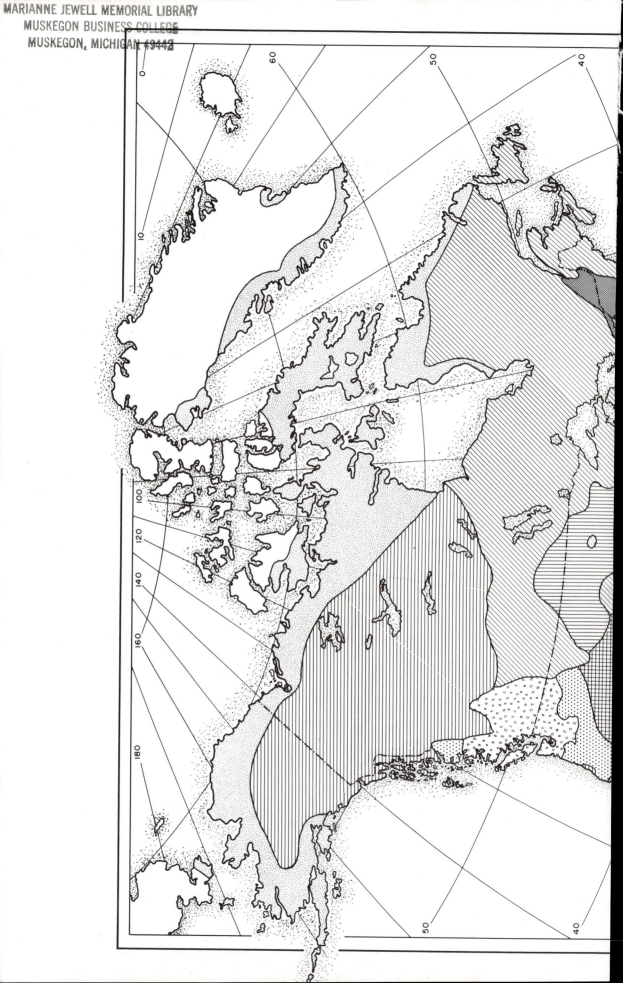